The One-in-a-Million Baby Name Book

The One-in-a-Million Baby Name Book

The BabyNames.com Guide to Choosing the Best Name for Your New Arrival

Jennifer Moss
and BabyNames.com

A PERIGEE BOOK

A PERIGEE BOOK
Published by the Penguin Group
Penguin Group (USA) Inc.
375 Hudson Street, New York, New York 10014, USA

Penguin Group (Canada), 90 Eglinton Avenue East, Suite 700, Toronto, Ontario M4P 2Y3, Canada
(a division of Pearson Penguin Canada Inc.)
Penguin Books Ltd., 80 Strand, London WC2R 0RL, England
Penguin Group Ireland, 25 St. Stephen's Green, Dublin 2, Ireland (a division of Penguin Books Ltd.)
Penguin Group (Australia), 250 Camberwell Road, Camberwell, Victoria 3124, Australia
(a division of Pearson Australia Group Pty. Ltd.)
Penguin Books India Pvt. Ltd., 11 Community Centre, Panchsheel Park, New Delhi—110 017, India
Penguin Group (NZ), 67 Apollo Drive, Rosedale, North Shore 0632, New Zealand
(a division of Pearson New Zealand Ltd.)
Penguin Books (South Africa) (Pty.) Ltd., 24 Sturdee Avenue, Rosebank, Johannesburg 2196, South Africa

Penguin Books Ltd., Registered Offices: 80 Strand, London WC2R 0RL, England

While the author has made every effort to provide accurate telephone numbers and Internet addresses
at the time of publication, neither the publisher nor the author assumes any responsibility for
errors, or for changes that occur after publication. Further, the publisher does not have any control
over and does not assume any responsibility for author or third-party websites or their content.

First edition: July 2008

Library of Congress Cataloging-in-Publication Data

Moss, Jennifer, 1963–
The one-in-a-million baby name book : the BabyNames.com guide to choosing the
best name for your new arrival / Jennifer Moss and BabyNames.com— 1st ed.
      p.   cm.
   "A Perigee Book."
   Includes bibliographical references.
   ISBN 978-0-399-53430-0 (pbk.)
   1. Names, Personal—Dictionaries. I. BabyNames.com (Firm). II. Title.
   CS2377.M67 2008
   929.4'4—dc22   2008009325

PRINTED IN THE UNITED STATES OF AMERICA

10   9   8   7   6   5   4   3   2   1

Most Perigee books are available at special quantity discounts for bulk purchases for sales promotions,
premiums, fund-raising, or educational use. Special books, or book excerpts, can also be created to fit
specific needs. For details, write: Special Markets, Penguin Group (USA) Inc., 375 Hudson Street,
New York, New York 10014.

To *my* baby, Miranda, who is always honest in letting me know what's cool and what's "lame-o!" I love you!

—Mama

No name fits thy nature but thy own!

—William Shakespeare,
Titus Andronicus

Contents

Preface

I AM thrilled to be asked to write a preface to *The One-in-a-Million Baby Name Book* by Jennifer Moss and BabyNames.com. As the founders of the first "baby names" site on the World Wide Web, the Moss family has been in the forefront of the rapid transformation of given names around the world. Parents are choosing more varied names than ever before, as they have ready access to information that lets them choose the perfect "different-but-not-too-different" name almost all of them seem to want. I'm convinced that BabyNames.com

has been instrumental in the huge trend of choosing more unique names—names that are not in the top most popular lists—over the last generation. In 1980, the top ten names given to babies in the United States accounted for 22.7 percent of all boys and 16.0 percent of all girls; in 2005, only 10.1 percent of boys and 8.2 percent of girls received a top ten name. Certainly any expectant parents who post a message on the bulletin boards at BabyNames.com saying they plan to name their child Ethan or Ava because those names are "unique" will quickly learn just how common those names really are—and they will be given scores of suggestions for similar names that are much closer to being unique by the many name aficionados who are regular posters on those boards.

This book is itself unique because it's a collaborative effort, collating information and advice from many site visitors on BabyNames.com, both expectant parents and name enthusiasts, from

around the world. In addition to posts from the United States and Canada, information about popular names and naming customs from England, Scotland, Ireland, Wales, Puerto Rico, France, Spain, Japan, Scandinavia, and other cultures is frequently shared by posters. As someone who has been developing expert knowledge in this field for thirty years, I know I have often learned new things about names and naming from other posters on BabyNames.com, and it's wonderful to have this book to spread more widely the collective wisdom found there.

Of course, even though BabyNames.com attracts posters from around the world, the great majority of them are middle-class women from the majority English-speaking communities in the United States and Canada. As such, parents from other cultural backgrounds will occasionally have to modify some of the advice in this book to fit their own particular circumstances.

But even when such cultural differences are taken into account, this book is a marvelous resource, not only giving good advice to prospective parents but also providing fascinating data on what's going on with names and naming in the United States today. And it once again proves that onomastics—the study of names—is a lot of fun!

So read and enjoy, whether or not you have the task of naming a beloved child in the near future.

CLEVELAND KENT EVANS, PHD
Past President, American Name Society
Associate Professor of Psychology,
Bellevue University

Introduction

ONE of my favorite games as a kid was sitting at the kitchen table and poring through the phonebook for unusual names. When I found one, I would shout, "Hey, Mom, listen to this!" and proceed to announce the interesting names I found. I was always fascinated with names and started collecting a list of them, a hobby that lasted through my adulthood. Because I am a computer programmer, this list eventually made itself into a database, which then became the website BabyNames.com. In 1996, BabyNames.com was the first website to have a database of names and meanings online for the world to share . . . and we had no idea how popular it would become.

Through word of mouth and a little thing called the "search engine," people found out about BabyNames.com and started coming to look up names—by the thousands! As it grew, I knew I couldn't handle running the site on my own so I drafted the smartest women I knew to help me: my sisters and my mother. Luckily, all of our skills complement each other and work with every aspect of the site: I am a technologist, Mallory has a doctorate in nursing, Kate has a master's in education, Sue is a PR/marketing expert, and Mom has been trained in early-childhood development and ran her own infant daycare for many years.

We built a community of name enthusiasts and name-seekers on the BabyNames.com Message Boards, a forum where members could interact and share their own experiences with naming. The boards have since grown to cover many subjects above and beyond just names, including conception, pregnancy, parenting, pets, recipes, entertainment, and more. Many members who join the community have stayed for years—some even dating back to the beginning of the site. Teens, who stopped by to find out the meaning of their name back in the early days, are now getting married and having babies of their own. We feel like proud Internet parents.

BabyNames.com is here to stay, because people will never stop making babies! And once you're pregnant, the most important decision you can make is deciding what to name the child. It's a blessing—a gift that lasts a lifetime, and will affect your child her entire life. We are dedicated to helping everyone with names and naming—whether you are pregnant, thinking about it, writing a school report, or naming your pets.

We've decided to write this book to share with you all the information we've gathered on baby naming during the past decade from the millions of people who visit our site each month. We'll show you how a name is perceived—the characteristics, personality, and how it was rated on a scale of 1 to 5. We will also include stories and quotes from our community members—parents and children—about their names and the naming process. We feel there is nothing better than learning from experience and from those who have been there.

And when you have chosen your perfect name . . . drop us a line. We want to hear your story, too!

Sincerely,
JENNIFER MOSS
Founder of BabyNames.com
jennifer@babynames.com

1

How to Use This Book

CONGRATULATIONS! You are about to make one of the most important decisions you can make for your child: choosing his or her name. Children's names affect how they see themselves and how they are seen by others in this world, and so we are going to help you choose that "one-in-a-million" name by providing you with the Babynames.com One-in-a-Million Formula—a baby-naming approach that covers a number of bases, from family names to celebrities to people you want to honor—to make sure you have considered all your naming options.

Whether you are just beginning to search for names or already have a list in front of you, this book will provide tips, name suggestions, and personality information that go above and beyond the basic name and meaning lists. You will hear stories from our members about the process of choosing names and about living with their own names. This information will help you in determining which names to put on the list, and which to eliminate.

Most important, however, you'll find that our baby-naming formula goes beyond statistics by incorporating all aspects of choosing a name—from personality to characteristics, from perception to sound flow and meaning. We will give you a step-by-step naming guide, along with advice compiled from decades of running a baby-naming community, as well as feedback from that community. Because who better to give you advice than a million parents who have already been through

the baby-naming process? And in the end, we are sure you will pick the perfect name for your perfect little one.

To get started with this book, we recommend you have a "naming notebook" close at hand where you can make notes and keep track of your and your partner's favorite names. If you're just starting your list, we recommend you use a small spiral notebook for notes so you can carry it with you in your pocket, briefcase, or purse. You never know where or when you'll find an interesting name to add to your list.

You can also keep an online list of your favorite names on our website, www.BabyNames.com. The online name list allows you to print the list, email it to friends and family, and even have people vote on your names. It is a valuable tool to help you narrow down your favorite names.

In chapter 2, we will give you seven factors to consider in choosing your favorite baby names. In

2

chapters 3 through 13, we will share with you lists from different categories and sources you may not yet have considered. The rest of the book provides you with a unique alphabetical listing of names, which includes meaning, origin, notes, personality traits, and similar names. You'll notice in this section that each name has a checkbox next to it, so you can check off the names that you like and quickly reference them.

The personality traits listed by each name are compiled from the feedback and impressions of millions of BabyNames.com members. Of course, we're not guaranteeing that if you name your child Jaden he will be intelligent and handsome; however, you will have the advantage of reading the opinions of millions of people on the exact name that you are considering for your child.

Collaborating with Your Partner and Others

Unless you are parenting on your own, choosing a name is a decision between both parents—and like all decisions, it will take good communication and fair compromise. We recommend that you set aside specific times to discuss your baby's name— we will call these "name storming" sessions. These name storming sessions can happen anywhere at anytime—during a car drive, dinnertime, over breakfast, or after the late-late show. To help you with your name storming sessions, we have provided easy tips throughout the book marked with this symbol ✎.

Expecting parents are so excited about their upcoming arrival, it's only natural that you might want to share every little detail with friends and family. But what happens when you tell your mom your name choices and she makes a face? BabyNames.com member Jessica O. of Plymouth, Michigan, says, "It's funny—if you announce the name while pregnant, others just assume that because the child isn't born yet that their comments are welcomed. Yet, if you have the baby in your arms and you tell them the name, it's always, 'Awwwww!'" If you are having trouble finding names, it's great to consult friends and family, but just remember, names are *very personal choices*! Be careful not to make judgments on other people's name suggestions and be aware that others *will* make judgments on yours. You can't let it affect you if you really love a name.

Make sure your name storming sessions are just between you and your partner, because in the end it is *your* decision, not your sister's or mother-in-law's or the neighbor's. And remember, keep this a positive experience and don't be too harsh on your partner's name choices. Baby naming is very personal and your goal is to find the perfect name that you both love!

2

The One-in-a-Million Formula

MANY parents have come to us over the years completely confused, not knowing where to start in finding a name for their baby. Some have several names picked out, but can't agree with their partner. Some just can't find anything that "sounds good" with their last name. And some are so concerned with how the name affects their child—it's an overwhelming burden and responsibility to just decide. It's true that your child's name will affect him throughout his lifetime; however, it doesn't have to be a burden on you! In this chapter, we provide you with the Babynames.com One-in-a-Million Formula to help you narrow down your list and find the perfect name for your baby. The formula incorporates seven key factors that we use regularly in our advice columns and name-consulting service—a winning strategy to finding the perfect name.

☞ Personal History and Traditions
☞ Spelling and Ease of Use
☞ Popularity and Saturation
☞ Jokes, Puns, and Teasing Factors
☞ Pronunciation, Rhythm, and Flow
☞ Gender Identification
☞ The Introduction Test

We believe that if you systematically keep these points in mind, you will be successful in naming your child. Read over the following sections, become familiar with the issues to consider, and decide which factors are important to you and your partner when you're finding the perfect name.

1.
Personal History and Traditions

Many people use their baby's name to honor a family member or friend. Some families and cultures have specific naming traditions, like naming a son after his father or naming after a relative who has recently passed. Some families make their own traditions, by naming all their children with the same first letter or consecutive letters, like Abraham, Benjamin, Caleb, David, and so on.

Are there naming traditions in your family? If so, present them to your partner and both decide whether the tradition is something you want to continue for your child. Don't be pressured into using long-standing naming conventions just because your family has "always done so" and it may be expected of you. Times change and cultures change, and in the end, it's up to you whether you want to follow a family tradition.

If you do want to incorporate a family tradition into your child's name, there are some factors you should consider.

We recommend you do not name your child the same name as any other member in the household. We understand that naming children after parents can be a long-standing tradition, but it can also have a negative effect on your child's individuality. Naming a son after his father may give your child an unspoken message that you want him to be just like his dad—urging him to "fill Dad's shoes." Also, many boys who are named after their fathers are often given diminutive nicknames to differentiate the two in the household. These nicknames can feel demeaning to the boy, because they portray him as smaller or childlike. Nicknames like "Junior" or "Little Tony" may make your boy feel small or perhaps like a "mini-me" replica of his father. Each child should have the opportunity to be an individual in your household and in the world, and that starts with his identity—his name.

A great way to honor your family history is to use a family surname as your child's first or middle name. You may even want to consider using the mother's maiden name as your child's first name, if it is appropriate. Historically in England and the United States, very wealthy families used their family surnames as first names for their child because they wanted to flaunt their important family name. This tradition has now reached the mass public as women wanted their family name or maiden name to be equally represented by their child, and people began using the mother's birth name as a first or middle name for the child. This paved the way for one of the most popular girls' names in recent years: Madison.

Here is a list of some of the more popular surnames that have now been documented as children's given names:

Anderson	Carver	Fisher	Hammer
Bailey	Chase	Flannery	Harper
Barrett	Clinton	Fleming	Harrison
Barrington	Courtland	Fletcher	Jackson
Baxter	Crawford	Forbes	Jordan
Beauchamp	Culver	Forest/Forrest	Kendall
Bingham	Cunningham	Foster	Kennedy
Blake	Curran	Fox	MacKenzie
Blythe	Dana	Franklin	Maddox
Bowie	Delano	Frasier	Madison
Brent	Dempsey	Fulbright	Maxwell
Brynner	Donnelly	Fuller	Morgan
Byrne	Doyle	Gannon	Morse
Byron	Drake	Gardner	Moss
Cagney	Dyson	Gibson	Murphy
Calhoun	Ellison	Gillespie	Newton
Callahan	Emerson	Gilmore	Palmer
Camden	Everett	Grady	Parker
Campbell	Ferguson	Granville	Parry/Perry
Carlin	Ferris	Grayson	Paxton
Carson	Finlay/Finley	Hamilton	Payton/Peyton

Piper	Rylan/Ryland	Temple	Webster
Porter	Sawyer	Tennyson	Wentworth
Preston	Sheridan	Tierney	Winston
Rafferty	Smith	Tudor	Wolfe
Reagan	Tanner	Tyler	Wright
Rhodes	Tate	Tyson	Yancy
Riley	Taylor	Warner	Yates
Roosevelt	Teagan	Warrick	Yeardley

When you are in the process of finding names for your name list, go through the family trees of both parents and write down all the family surnames. Consider people you may want to honor, relatives you were especially close to, or names that you just like.

2.
Spelling and Ease of Use

You and your partner should discuss whether you want to give your child an unusual alternate spelling of a common name. A girl named Gennyphir is destined to have to explain and spell her name for the rest of her life. She will forever be repeating, "No, that's G-E-N-N-Y-P-H-I-R," and then will have to suffer through the reactions of the people who are not used to "creatively spelled" names. According to the BabyNames.com personality surveys that we conducted on our site, people with creatively spelled names are perceived as different or sometimes even strange. For example, people view Zachary as handsome, funny, intelligent, cool, and caring. However, they perceive Xakery as a loser, criminal, untrustworthy, exotic, and unpopular!

Instead of making your child's name extremely unusual, consider being creative in your naming by combining names or changing the beginning letter of a common name, like Timberly (Kimberly with a *T*). Timberly still may have to correct people who ask, "Kimberly?" but it will be a lot easier than spelling Gennyphir! As you'll notice from the user name ratings, Kimberly was rated ★★☆ (2.5 stars),

while the name Timberly received ★★★☆ (3.5 stars out of 5). This goes to show you that people are becoming more accepting of unique names nowadays. Even creating a new name is fine, as long as it's easily spelled and pronounced. You can read more about creating names in chapter 12, Names from the Imagination.

> **People commonly misspell and mispronounce my name, but I've grown used to it and love that I am the only one I know with my name!**
>
> —Tanessa S.,
> Federal Way, Washington

You should also decide if you want alliteration to be a factor. Alliterative names are names where the given (first) name starts with the same letter as your last name. We found that parents either love alliterative names, or don't like them at all! If you think about it, though, it is easier to remember an alliterative name. I chose a triple alliterative name for my child—her initials are MMM—and she adores that! My sister, Mallory Moss, loved her alliterative name—it was easy to say and rolls off the tongue. My college roommate, on the other hand, had the initials VVV and she hated it.

Some famous alliterative names are Bo Bice, Charlie Chaplin, Chevy Chase, David Duchovny, Donald Duck, Fred Flintstone, Harry Hamlin, Jesse Jackson, Marilyn Monroe, Ronald Reagan, and Susan Sarandon.

If you like alliterative names, then you will want to browse baby names by the first letter of your last name. However be careful not to repeat a letter too much; the name Rory Rorshack or Lilly Lulling, for example, may be too much of a tongue twister.

3.
Popularity and Saturation

Over and over we hear from parents that they don't want their child to be one of many in their class with the same name. They say, "I don't want him to be known at school as Jake S. or David #3!" If the name you like is in the top ten this year, this is a likely possibility for your child.

Also consider that names that are extremely popular now may seem dated in twenty years. Take the name Nancy, for example: most people will think of Nancy as a '60s girl. And Tiffany? Definitely an '80s girl! A couple of years ago, I was introduced to a woman who was in her thirties named Taylor. I asked her, "What's your *real* name?" and she was astonished. "How did you know I changed my name?" she asked me. I explained to her that Taylor was rarely used for a girl in the '70s. It turns out her real name was Betty-Jean!

Each year, the U.S. Social Security Administration puts out a list of top names used in the previous year. This is a great resource to see which names are being used most often. It would be wise to also check the BabyNames.com popularity lists, as we rank names that are on our users' top name lists. Because the lists are from expecting parents and hopeful parents, they are more likely to determine *future* name popularity—what names will be popular in the next couple of years.

One advantage to giving your child a popular name is that people will most likely know how to pronounce it and spell it. Everyone wants to see their name on a toothbrush or mug. You know how fun it is to look at those racks of license plates, key fobs, or other personalized items

and look for the names of everyone you know. Of course, you search for your own name first! I could never get anything with Jennifer on it because they were always sold out—the name was too popular!

A drawback to having a common name is that there is always a possibility that someone with that name will become famous (or infamous) and alter the perception of the name. The name Monica, for example, was in the top one hundred most popular during 1995–1997, slowly rising in popularity. This was most likely due to the debut of the popular television show *Friends* in 1994, which featured a character named Monica played by Courteney Cox. Then, in the fall of 1997, a scandal hit the news that made White House aide Monica Lewinski an instant star—but not in a good sense of the word! The name Monica quickly dropped down the charts in the years following the scandal.

If a name has already hit the top twenty, you might want to consider alternatives. The new millennium brought a time of individuality, and more and more people want to be known for being unique and special—being one-in-a-million, not one-of-a-million.

4.
Jokes, Puns, and Teasing Factors

If you are thinking of a name or combination of names that formulate a "funny" phrase or joke, don't do it! You may think you're being clever, but you are guaranteeing a miserable school-life for your child.

Here are some disastrous mistakes parents can make when naming their child:

Creating a funny phrase or pun. Whether your child's name is Beau Hunter, Stormy Weathers, or Crystal Chandel Lear, he or she will most likely be humiliated by it. Rule of thumb: if it makes you laugh, it will make your child's classmates laugh—*at him*! If you think it's cute, it's not. Miss Ima Hogg was born in Texas at the turn of the twentieth century and grew up to be an important stateswoman and philanthropist. Apparently, Miss Hogg's parents didn't realize the error of their ways until after the birth certificate was filed, and they never changed it. Unfortunately she'll always be remembered for her name, rather than her philanthropy!

> **My husband wanted to name our daughter Anita, but I already had the middle name Margherita picked out. So Anita was vetoed, since she would have been well on her way to AA with a name like "I need a margarita."**
>
> —Cindy L.,
> Chicago, Illinois

Initials spell a word. You will also want to check out the initials you create when you choose your child's name. Hannah Avery may sound like a beautiful combination, but if your last name is Garrett, you are giving your daughter the monogram HAG! I've always liked that my name spelled out a word (JAM); however, some kids may not be so forgiving. Avoid initials that spell out opposite sex names like Brenda Oriana Brown (BOB) or Peter Allen Miller (PAM). You also want to definitely avoid letters that are common acronyms like CIA or KKK.

Matching twin names. You wouldn't believe how many parents ask us to come up with "matching" twin names. Our usual philosophy is that you should name your twins as you

would name non-twin siblings. Your twins will have the same looks, room, clothes, school, and maybe friends, but do they have to share a name, too? It is important for their own individuality to have different sounding names.

I will concede, however, that there may be an advantage to matching "twinny-winny" names. I interviewed one teenager named Ashlee who has a twin brother named Ashtyn. She told me she actually loved their matching names because it made them "famous" at school.

"Everyone knows Ashtyn and Ashlee," she said proudly with a big smile on her face.

Schoolyard taunts. Consider the names that kids at school may call your child. In fact, ask one of your kids or friends' kids who is between 8 and 12 what they think of the name you like. You'll be amazed at what teasing they may come up with that you have never considered. For example, did you know a "melvin" is the name of a prank played with a person's underwear? You may not have known that, but your little friend will! Of course, if the kids really want to, they'll come up with a taunt for *any* name, but you can give your child an advantage by starting with a name that doesn't encourage it.

> **Danielle rhymes with smell. You'd think kids would be more creative, but nope, they stuck with that one.**
>
> —Danielle S., Brisbane, Australia

In the end, if you decide you do indeed want an unusual name, so that you can honor your favorite light fixture, sport, or college, be a bit discreet about it. Try to follow the example of the creative couple from Louisiana who named their son Ellis Hugh after their alma mater, Louisiana State University (get it? L-S-U).

5.
Pronunciation, Rhythm, and Flow

> I guess the main reason for not liking my name is that no one can pronounce it correctly. My name is *Lin-KNEE-ah* not *Lin-NAY-ah*. It used to drive me crazy that I would always have to correct people on the pronunciation.
>
> —Linnéa H., Washington, DC

When considering a name for your baby, take into account the name's most common pronunciation. Do you want to use the accepted pronunciation, a different pronunciation, or create one of your own? The name Dana, for example, could be pronounced *DAY-na*, *DAN-na*, or *DON-na* (although the last is very uncommon).

Kelly J. of Owatonna, Minnesota, told us this story about her brother's name: "My brother was given the name Kael Andrew at birth. My parents had chosen the name Kyle, but then my dad's cousin named his baby boy Kyle two months before my brother was born. My parents didn't want to copy the cousin so they spelled my brother's name Kael but still pronounced it *Kyle*. It was a nightmare . . . people assumed that his name was pronounced *Kayle*. My parents would always have to correct people and they said it got really annoying. They legally changed his name to Kyle when he was about one year old."

You'll also want to consider the rhythm or "flow" of a name. Names have a natural sound and rhythm—a way that people hear the syllables in natural musical beats. A name can belong to one of two rhythms: a duplet rhythm where the emphasis is heard on every two syllables, or a triplet rhythm where the emphasis is heard on every third syllable.

• **Famous Duplet Names**
Suri Cruise (**Su**-ri **Cruise**)
Johnny Depp (**John**-ny **Depp**)
Britney Spears (**Brit**-ney **Spears**)
Elvis Presley (**El**-vis **Pres**-ley)
Martin Luther King (**Mar**-tin **Luth**-er **King**)

• **Famous Triplet Names**
Jennifer Garner (**Jenn**-i-fer **Gar**-ner)
Christopher Reeve (**Chris**-to-pher **Reeve**)
Gillian Anderson (**Gill**-i-an **And**-er-son)
Leonardo DiCaprio (Le-on-**ar**-do Di-**cap**-ri-o)
Victoria Beckham (Vic-**tor**-i-a **Beck**-ham)

Once you have narrowed down your list to the top names, conduct a survey among your friends and family: show them the spelling of the name and ask them how they would pronounce it. See if you get different pronunciations or if they have difficulty saying the name. Do they say the name with a natural rhythm that appeals to you and your partner? If it doesn't sound right to you, you may want to reconsider how you spell it or eliminate the name altogether from your list.

6.
Gender Identification

Since the birth of the women's movement in the 1970s, parents started giving their baby girls unisex names or names that have traditionally been used for boys. We believe this is because parents want to put their girls on the same "even playing field" as the boys. Unconsciously, we know that people form opinions about us from our names, as well as our looks and personality. In the past couple of decades it has been increasingly socially acceptable for a girl to have a traditionally male name because it is perceived as strong and powerful. On the other hand, parents will rarely choose a name traditionally used for girls to name their baby boy. Parents—especially fathers—are particularly conscious of choosing boy names that won't get teased on the playground.

Female executive Archie Gottesman said her parents decided she was going to be called Archie even before she was born—whether she was a boy or girl. "When I was born, my parents didn't have a real name picked out yet, so they called me Archie," says Gottesman. "Then when I was about three months old, the pediatrician told my mom that she shouldn't keep calling a baby girl Archie. For some reason, she listened, and they officially named me Margery. But Margery never caught on, so I have always been known as Archie. My driver's license still says Margery, but no one ever calls me that. I probably should have officially changed it to Archie!"

Here is a list of popular "crossover" names that were historically male and are now used as female names, too:

Abby	Cameron/Camryn	Jamie	Quinn
Adrian	Carmen	Jean	Reese
Ainsley	Carson	Jody	Sandy (short for
Alexis	Courtney	Joss	Alexander)
Allison	Daryl	Kelly	Schuyler/Skylar
Ashley	Dion	Laine/Lane	Shelly (short for
Aubrey	Elliot	Lee	Sheldon)
Audrey	Francis/Frances	Lesley/Leslie	Sidney/Sydney
Blair	Greer	Lyn	Valerie
Brittainy	Haley	Mallory	Whitley
Brooke	Hollis	Page/Paige	Whitney

If you are thinking of using "crossover" names consider how it may affect your son or daughter. Don't choose a name for a boy that has primarily been used as a girl's name in recent years. When teen idol Ashley Parker Angel became popular, many people reacted by saying he had a "girl's name." In this case, Angel's gender-ambiguous name has not hurt his career much, and interestingly enough he ended up giving his son one, too: Lyric. But it takes a strong ego for a boy to sport a "girl's" name, and you may not want to put that pressure on your child.

7.
The Introduction Test

The last thing you want to consider is how your child's name sounds out loud. Forget the middle name for this exercise. Go through all the names on your name list and say just the *first* and *last* name out loud. Introduce yourself as your child: "Hello, my name is John Smith." This is how your child will say his or her name most often, and how teachers, coworkers, and friends will say his name.

Which names sound the best to you out loud? Which names sound heavy and awkward? Sometimes a name will look good on paper, but just doesn't sound right when spoken.

The Final Checklist

So, when you have your final name list, run it through these seven factors and see if the names meet your criteria. By the end, you should have one or more names you feel really good about!

The BabyNames.com
One-in-a-Million Formula

❏ **Personal History and Traditions**

Does this name mean something special to you? Have you considered all family names?

❏ **Spelling and Ease of Use**

Is this name easy to spell? Is it easy to pronounce?

❏ **Popularity and Saturation**

What was the rank of this name last year? Where does it appear on the BabyNames.com charts? Are you truly choosing a unique identity or just following the trends?

❏ **Jokes, Puns, and Teasing Factors**

Will your child be teased because of the name or initials? Is it funny to you? Does it rhyme with something teasable?

❏ **Pronunciation, Rhythm, and Flow**

How does the first name sound with your last name? Is it too choppy? Too long? Say it out loud as if you were introducing him or her.

❏ **Gender Identification**

Is the name too frilly? Is it a primarily male or female name? Remember male names work well for girls, but not vice versa.

❏ **The Introduction Test**

Introduce yourself as your child (first and last name only). Does it sound "right" to you?

3

Names with Tradition

In the beginning of the twenty-first century, parents have returned to using old-fashioned names—names that were popular during the first of couple decades of the twentieth century. Why have these traditional names come back into style? Perhaps at the start of the new millennium people are feeling nostalgic for the "good old days." Or, perhaps parents are choosing these names to honor grandparents and ancestors in the family.

The positive side to using a traditional name is that it will be familiar to most people and they will know how to spell it. A possible negative side about using a traditional name is that your child may be perceived as dull or old-fashioned.

> I love my name! Laura is the "little black dress" of names—it's classic and goes with anything.
> —Laura T., Elk Grove, Illinois

Emma is one of the more popular "classic" names now, consistently in the top of the popularity charts. It has been made more popular by teen actress Emma Roberts (Eric Roberts's daughter and Julia Roberts's niece) and Ross and Rachel's baby character on the TV show *Friends*. The ever-classic name Jack, which used to be a nickname for John, is coming into its own as a formal given name. No Emma or Jack will ever have to spell their names over the telephone.

As you can see from the most popular names below, the more traditional boys' names are primarily Biblical, while the girls' names are not. In American culture, Biblical names have always been more popular for boys than girls. Although Mary and Ruth may have been popular in the mid-twentieth century, they have not stayed at the top of the charts. David and Michael, on the other hand, have been on the top of the boys' names chart for the last hundred years.

50 Most Popular Traditional Names—Girls

Ava	Charlotte	Rebecca
Abigail	Eva	Evelyn
Emma	Claire	Genevieve
Isabella	Sadie	Celeste
Olivia	Anna	Kate
Hannah	Sophie	Violet
Grace	Sarah	Eve
Ella	Madeline	Molly
Emily	Victoria	Lillian
Audrey	Julia	Camille
Amelia	Lilly	Stella
Bella	Anastasia	Annabel
Faith	Amanda	Lydia
Elizabeth	Rachel	Carmen
Sophia	Lucy	Maggie
Gabrielle	Hope	Adelaide
Natalie	Caroline	

50 Most Popular Traditional Names—Boys

Ethan	Daniel	Joseph
Caleb	William	Jeremiah
Noah	Luke	Thomas
Jacob	Seth	Charlie
Aaron	Michael	Patrick
Elijah	Samuel	Jonathan
Benjamin	Christopher	Max
Jack	Anthony	Eli
Matthew	Isaiah	John
Owen	Dominic	Levi
Adam	David	Wesley
Zachary	Xavier	Malachi
James	Oliver	Elliot
Nicholas	Jake	Vincent
Lucas	Spencer	Marcus
Isaac	Jared	Jonah
Christian	Micah	

Considering a "classic" name? Peruse these most popular lists from the U.S. Social Security office in the year 1900:

● Top U.S. Girls' Names in 1900

Mary	Alice	Dorothy	Lillie
Helen	Bessie	Martha	Agnes
Anna	Bertha	Hazel	Ella
Margaret	Grace	Ida	Nellie
Ruth	Rose	Irene	Mattie
Elizabeth	Clara	Myrtle	Laura
Florence	Mildred	Eva	Julia
Ethel	Gladys	Catherine	Josephine
Marie	Minnie	Louise	Carrie
Lillian	Gertrude	Edith	Viola
Annie	Pearl	Sarah	Hattie
Edna	Mabel	Elsie	
Emma	Frances	Esther	

● Top U.S. Boys' Names in 1900

John	Willie	Jack	Lawrence
William	Arthur	Earl	Francis
James	Albert	Carl	Alfred
George	Fred	Ernest	Will
Charles	Clarence	Ralph	Daniel
Robert	Paul	David	Eugene
Joseph	Harold	Samuel	Leo
Frank	Roy	Sam	Oscar
Edward	Joe	Howard	Floyd
Henry	Richard	Herbert	Herman
Thomas	Raymond	Andrew	Jesse
Walter	Charlie	Elmer	
Harry	Louis	Lee	

✎ **NAME STORMING:** If you like traditional names, take another look at your family tree and pick out ancestors' names that you like. Did you have a favorite aunt? Does your partner want to honor a particular hero in his or her life? Write down the names of your favorite teachers, mentors, and great-great-grandparents.

4

Names with Character

THERE are many names of characters from books, plays, movies, and television that have become famous in their own right. Every time I meet a woman named Stella, I have to suppress the urge to scream her name like Marlon Brando in *A Streetcar Named Desire*. And who doesn't think of the spoiled Southern belle from *Gone With the Wind* when they hear the name Scarlett?

Here is a list of literary and cinematic characters that are so popular they are identified with their names:

Adrian—Adrian Pennino, *Rocky*

Alice—Alice Nelson, *The Brady Bunch*; Alice Hyatt, *Alice / Alice Doesn't Live Here Anymore*

Alvin—Alvin the Chipmunk, *The Chipmunks*

Annie—Little Orphan Annie, *Annie*; Annie Hall, *Annie Hall*

Arnold—Arnold the Pig, *Green Acres*; Arnold, *Hey Arnold!*

Arthur—Arthur the Aardvark, *Arthur*; Arthur Bach, *Arthur*

Atticus—Atticus Finch, *To Kill a Mockingbird*

Barney—Barney the Dinosaur, *Barney and Friends*; Barney Fife, *The Andy Griffith Show*; Barney Rubble, *The Flintstones*

Betty—Betty Rubble, *The Flintstones*; Betty Boop, *Betty Boop*

Carrie—Carrie White, *Carrie*; Carrie Bradshaw, *Sex and the City*

Cosmo—Cosmo Kramer, *Seinfeld*; Cosmo the Fairy, *The Fairly OddParents*

Chandler—Chandler Bing, *Friends*

Charlotte—Charlotte the Spider, *Charlotte's Web*; Charlotte York, *Sex and the City*

Christine—Christine (car), *Christine*

Chucky—Chucky (ventriloquist doll), *Child's Play*; Chuckie Finster, *Rugrats*

D'Artagnan—D'Artagnan, *The Three Musketeers*

Darrin—Darrin Stevens, *Bewitched*

Dennis—Dennis "The Menace" Mitchell, *Dennis the Menace*

Dora—Dora, *Dora the Explorer*

Dorothy—Dorothy Gale, *The Wizard of Oz*

Ebenezer—Ebenezer Scrooge, *A Christmas Carol*

Eddie—Eddie Haskell, *Leave It to Beaver*; Eddie Munster, *The Munsters*

Names with Character

Eliza—Eliza Doolittle, *Pygmalion / My Fair Lady*

Felicity—Felicity Porter, *Felicity*

Forrest—Forrest Gump, *Forrest Gump*

Freddy—Freddy Krueger, *A Nightmare on Elm Street*

Gilbert—Gilbert Grape, *What's Eating Gilbert Grape*

Hannibal—Hannibal Lecter, *Silence of the Lambs*

Harold—Harold Chasen, *Harold and Maude*; Harold, *Harold and the Purple Crayon*

Harry—Harry Potter, *Harry Potter*

Harvey—Harvey (rabbit), *Harvey*

Hazel—Hazel Burke, *Hazel*

Heathcliff—Heathcliff Cat, cartoon by George Gately; Heathcliff, *Wuthering Heights*

Herman—Herman Munster, *The Munsters*

Holden—Holden Caulfield, *A Catcher in the Rye*

Holly—Holiday "Holly" Golightly, *Breakfast at Tiffany's*

Ichabod—Ichabod Crane, *The Legend of Sleepy Hollow*

Indiana—Indiana Jones, *Raiders of the Lost Ark*

Jeannie—Jeannie Jeannie, *I Dream of Jeannie*

Juliet—Juliet Capulet, *Romeo and Juliet*

Kermit—Kermit the Frog, *Sesame Street*

Leia—Princess Leia, *Star Wars*

Lolita—Lolita Haze, *Lolita*

Luke—Luke Skywalker, *Star Wars*

Mallory—Mallory Keaton, *Family Ties*

Marcia—Marcia Brady, *The Brady Bunch*

Marian—Marian "The Librarian" Paroo, *The Music Man*; Marian Cunningham, *Happy Days*

Mary—Mary Poppins, *Mary Poppins*; Mary Richards, *The Mary Tyler Moore Show*

Napoleon—Napoleon Dynamite; *Napoleon Dynamite*

Neo—Neo, *The Matrix*

Norman—Norman Bates, *Psycho*

Oscar—Oscar the Grouch, *Sesame Street*; Oscar Madison, *The Odd Couple*; Oskar Schindler, *Schindler's List*

Regan—Regan MacNeil, *The Exorcist*

Rhett—Rhett Butler, *Gone With the Wind*

Richie—Richie Cunningham, *Happy Days*; Richie Rich, *Richie Rich*

Robin—Robin Hood, *The Adventures of Robin Hood*; Robin, *Batman*

Romeo—Romeo Montague, *Romeo and Juliet*

Rosemary—Rosemary Woodhouse, *Rosemary's Baby*

Samantha—Samantha Stevens, *Bewitched*; Samantha Jones, *Sex and the City*

Scarlett—Scarlett O'Hara, *Gone With the Wind*

Stanley—Stanley Kowalski, *A Streetcar Named Desire*; Stanley Roper, *Three's Company*

Stella—Stella Kowalski, *A Streetcar Named Desire*

Tony—Tony Soprano, *The Sopranos*

Waldo—Waldo, *Where's Waldo*

Wally—Wally Cleaver, *Leave It to Beaver*

Willy—Willy Wonka, *Willy Wonka and the Chocolate Factory*; Willy, *Free Willy*

Wilma—Wilma Flintstone, *The Flintstones*

Woody—Woody the Cowboy, *Toy Story*; Woody Boyd, *Cheers*

15

> *Gilmore Girls* **definitely made me love the name Lorelai more than I already did. Any name that references a strong female character is all right in my book!**
>
> **—Jessica M.,**
> **Pittsburgh, Pennsylvania**

You may be inspired by a novel or a story but not necessarily use a character name. Longtime BabyNames.com member Melina Raven D. from Lexington, Tennessee, says she got her middle name from the Edgar Allen Poe poem *The Raven*. She has since shared it with her daughter, Matilda Raven.

Disney Characters

Many Disney characters are named from old fairy tales or historical legends and some were just named by the studio itself. If you are interested in giving your child an instantly recognizable and commercially branded name, you may want to consider some of these Disney names:

• Female
Alcmene—*Hercules*
Anastasia—*Anastasia*
Ariel—*The Little Mermaid*
Aurora—*Sleeping Beauty*
Bambi—*Bambi*
Belle—*Beauty and the Beast*
Briar Rose—*Sleeping Beauty*
Calliope—*Hercules*
Cinderella—*Cinderella*
Cruella—*101 Dalmations*
Drizella—*Cinderella*
Fantasia—*Fantasia*
Fauna—*Sleeping Beauty*
Flora—*Sleeping Beauty*
Hera—*Hercules*
Jane—*Tarzan*
Jasmine—*Aladdin*
Lilo—*Lilo and Stitch*
Maleficent—*Sleeping Beauty*
Megara—*Hercules*
Merryweather—*Sleeping Beauty*
Mulan—*Mulan*
Nakoma—*Pocahontas*
Nala—*The Lion King*
Nani—*Lilo and Stitch*

Perdita—*101 Dalmations*
Perla—*Cinderella*
Pocahontas—*Pocahontas*
Sarabi—*The Lion King*
Shanti—*The Jungle Book*
Thalia—*Hercules*
Ursula—*The Little Mermaid*
Wendy—*Peter Pan*
Willow—*Pocahontas*

• Male
Akela—*The Jungle Book*
Aladdin—*Aladdin*
Apollo—*Hercules*
Baloo—*The Jungle Book*
Bartok—*Anastasia*
Charming (Prince)—*Cinderella*
Chip—*Beauty and the Beast*
Demetrius—*Hercules*
Dimitri—*Anastasia*
Eric—*The Little Mermaid*
Gaston—*Beauty and the Beast*
Hercules—*Hercules*
Hubert—*Sleeping Beauty*
Iago—*Aladdin*
Jafar—*Aladdin*
John—*Pocahontas*
Kekata—*Pocahontas*
Kokoum—*Pocahontas*
Louis—*The Little Mermaid*
Lumiere—*Beauty and the Beast*
Maurice—*Beauty and the Beast*
Meeko—*Pocahontas*
Mowgli—*The Jungle Book*
Mufasa—*The Lion King*
Mushu—*Mulan*
Nessus—*Hercules*
Percy—*Pocahontas*
Peter—*Peter Pan*
Philippe—*Beauty and the Beast*
Phillip—*Sleeping Beauty*
Pongo—*101 Dalmations*
Powhatan—*Pocahontas*

Pumbaa—*The Lion King*
Simba—*The Lion King*
Stefan—*Sleeping Beauty*
Tarzan—*Tarzan*
Timon—*The Lion King*
Triton—*The Little Mermaid*
Sebastian—*The Little Mermaid*
Vladimir—*Anastasia*
Yao—*Mulan*

NAME STORMING: Make a list of your favorite children's books, novels, movies, and TV shows. Look up their character names and see if there are any that you would like to add to your name list. A good source for movie and television cast of characters is the Internet Movie Database (www.imdb.com).

17

5

Names That Rock

THE original "MTV generation" is now of childbearing age, and this means that music is affecting our culture and our naming choices more than ever. From Elvis to Seal, we can find interesting and creative names from the music artists we adore. Some parents have even mixed it up by using famous rock 'n' roll surnames as first names—such as Presley or Jagger. Here is a list of unique rock-inspired names for you to consider, some first names, some surnames, and some bands!

Aaliyah—Aaliyah
Abba—Abba
Ace—Ace Frehley, Kiss; Johnny Ace
Aero—Aerosmith
Aerosmith—Aerosmith
Aretha—Aretha Franklin
Avril—Avril Lavigne
Axl—Axl Rose
Beck—Jeff Beck; Beck
Benatar—Pat Benatar
Beyoncé—Beyoncé Knowles
Bon Jovi—Bon Jovi
Bono—Bono Vox, U2
Boss—Bruce "The Boss" Springsteen
Bowie—David Bowie
Boz—Boz Scaggs
Cat—Cat Stevens
Charlotte—Good Charlotte
Chicago—Chicago
Chili—Red Hot Chili Peppers

Cobain—Kurt Cobain, Nirvana
Creed—Creed
Crue—Mötley Crüe
Daltrey—Roger Daltrey, The Who
Derringer—Rick Derringer
Destiny—Destiny's Child
Devo—Devo
Dylan—Bob Dylan
Elton—Elton John
Elvis—Elvis Costello; Elvis Presley
Evanescence—Evanescence
Genesis—Genesis
Gillan—Ian Gillan, The Who
Hagar—Sammy Hagar
Halen—Van Halen
Hendrix—Jimi Hendrix
Huey—Huey Lewis
Hutchence—Michael Hutchence, INXS
Iggy—Iggy Pop
Jagger—Mick Jagger

Jam—The Jam; Pearl Jam
Janick—Janick Gers, Iron Maiden
Janis—Janis Joplin
Jefferson—Jefferson Airplane/Starship
Jett—Joan Jett
Journey—Journey
Korn—Korn
Lennon—John Lennon
Lennox—Annie Lennox
Linkin—Linkin Park
Madonna—Madonna
Marley—Bob Marley
Mercury—Freddy Mercury, Queen
Metallica—Metallica
Mick—Mick Jagger, The Rolling Stones; Mick Box, Uriah Heep; Mick Mars, Mötley Crüe
Moon—Keith Moon, The Who
Morrison—Jim Morrison, The Doors
Morrissey—Morrissey, The Smiths
Nirvana—Nirvana
Ozzy—Ozzy Osbourne
Pepper—Red Hot Chili Peppers
Pink—P!nk, Pink Floyd
Pogue—The Pogues
Presley—Elvis Presley
Prince—Prince; The Fresh Prince (Will Smith)
Ramone—The Ramones
Ringo—Ringo Starr
Rush—Rush
Santana—Carlos Santana, Santana
Seal—Seal
Selena—Selena Quintanilla-Pérez
Shirelle—The Shirelles

Slick—Grace Slick, Jefferson Airplane/Starship
Sly—Sly and the Family Stone
Smokey—Smokey Robinson
Sonic—Sonic Youth
Starr—Ringo Starr
Stevie—Stevie Wonder; Stevie Nicks
Sting—Sting, The Police
Stone—The Rolling Stones; Sly and the Family Stone; Stone Temple Pilots
Styx—Styx
Teena—Teena Marie
Tyler—Steven Tyler, Aerosmith
Uriah—Uriah Heep
Usher—Usher Raymond
Valens—Ritchie Valens
Velvet—The Velvet Underground
Vox—Bono Vox, U2
Wilson—Brian Wilson, The Beach Boys; Ann and Nancy Wilson, Heart
Winter—Edgar Winter
Zappa—Frank Zappa
Zeppelin—Led Zeppelin
Zevon—Warren Zevon

NAME STORMING: Are you a die-hard deadhead or a pop princess? Make a list of your favorite bands and musical artists and see what names inspire you. What was the name of the artist or song that was playing when you and your partner met? When you got married? Consider band names, nicknames, first names, and last names.

6

Names with Fame

APPLE, Suri, Shiloh, and Romeo—the world is abuzz when the latest celebrity announces an unusual moniker for their newborn. Actors and musicians are creative artists by nature; they are stars because they are unique and individualistic and crave the spotlight. So is it really a surprise when they choose a creative, unique name for their offspring? We don't think so. However, if we were to give naming advice to these celebrities, we'd say the same thing we'd say to any other parent: think about how the name will affect your child through life. Would you have wanted to live with the name Fifi-Trixibelle or Pilot Inspektor the rest of your life?

Here is a list of some of the more unusual or *creative* names that celebs have chosen for their offspring over the years:

Indiana August Affleck—Casey Affleck and Summer Phoenix
Summer's brother, the late actor River Phoenix, played young Indiana in *Indiana Jones and the Last Crusade.* As for the middle name, Casey's birthday is in August.

Moses Amadeus Allen—Woody Allen and Mia Farrow

Satchel Seamus Allen—Woody Allen and Mia Farrow

Elijah Blue Allman—Cher and Gregg Allman

> I liked that [Lyric] was an uncommon name 'cause I'm all about being original, and I loved the meaning behind the word since I spend a lot of time songwriting.[1]
> —Ashley Parker Angel

Lyric Angel—Ashley Parker Angel and Tiffany Lynn

Coco Riley Arquette—Courteney Cox and David Arquette
Coco was named after her mother, using the first two letters of her first and last names.

Sosie Ruth Bacon—Kevin Bacon and Kyra Sedgwick

Atticus Baldwin—Isabella Hoffman and Daniel Baldwin
A literary reference to the father character in Harper Lee's novel and movie *To Kill a Mockingbird*.

Ireland Baldwin—Kim Basinger and Alec Baldwin

Jamison Leon Baldwin—Billy Baldwin and Chynna Phillips

Vance Alexander Baldwin—Billy Baldwin and Chynna Phillips

Isadora Barney—Björk and Matthew Barney

Brooklyn Joseph Beckham—David and Victoria Beckham

Cruz David Beckham—David and Victoria Beckham

Romeo James Beckham—David and Victoria Beckham
It is rumored that the Beckhams gave their son this romance name because he was conceived on vacation in Rome.

Seven Sirius Benjamin—André Benjamin and Eryka Badu
Badu has said in interviews that she loves the name Seven because it is a divine number that can't be divided. Seven was also a name referred to on the TV show *Seinfeld*. The character George Costanza loved the name because it was the uniform number of baseball legend Mickey Mantle.

Lyric Benson—Robby Benson and Karla DeVito

> I think that there is so much pressure for celebrities to conform in so many different arenas (weight, dress, movie roles, etc.) that when they have a baby, they know that the decision to name them is theirs alone, and can go about naming a child without the input of producers and agents!
>
> —Brooke C., Denver, Colorado

Zephyr Benson—Robby Benson and Karla DeVito

Chastity Bono—Cher and Sonny Bono
Chastity was a character played by Cher in the movie of the same name. The movie was released in 1969—the same year Chastity was born.

Chianna Maria Bono—Sonny and Mary Bono

Zowie Bowie—David and Angela Bowie
His given name is Duncan Zowie Heywood Jones, as he was given his father's real surname. Zowie Bowie is now also a name of a band that covers Bowie's music.

Mateo Braverly Bratt—Benjamin Bratt and Talisa Soto

Willem Wolf Broad—Billy Idol (William Broad) and Perri Lister

Lucien Buscemi—Steve Buscemi and Jo Andreas

Arpad Flynn Alexander Busson—Elle MacPherson and Arpad Busson

Kal-El Coppola Cage—Nicolas Cage and Alice Kim
Kal-El is comic book superhero Superman's original Kryptonian name. Coppola is Nicolas Cage's real surname.

Sailor Lee Brinkley Cook—Christy Brinkley and Peter Cook

Calico Dashiell Cooper—Alice and Sheryl Cooper

Sonora Rose Cooper—Alice and Sheryl Cooper

Beckett Cypheridge—Melissa Etheridge and Julie Cypher
Mothers Melissa and Julie chose to combine their last names to create a new surname for their children.

Cashel Blake Day-Lewis—Daniel Day-Lewis and Rebecca Miller

Ronan Cal Day-Lewis—Daniel Day-Lewis and Rebecca Miller

Mathilda Plum Doucette—Moon Unit Zappa and Paul Doucette

Carys Zeta Douglas—Catherine Zeta-Jones and Michael Douglas

Francesca Eastwood—Clint Eastwood and Frances Fisher

Kimber Eastwood—Clint Eastwood and Roxanne Tunis

Aurelius Cy Evans—Elle MacPherson and David Evans

Luca Bella Facinelli (f)—Jennie Garth and Peter Facinelli

Raine Finley—Tawny Kitaen and Chuck Finley

Wynter Finley—Tawny Kitaen and Chuck Finley

Aquinnah Kathleen Fox—Michael J. Fox and Tracey Pollen

Fifi-Trixibelle Geldof—Bob Geldof and Paula Yates

Little Pixie Geldof and **Peaches Honeyblossom Geldof**—Bob Geldof and Paula Yates
Geldof and Yates chose three very unusual names for their daughters, names that sound more canine than human. However, we can't help wondering if it was more Yates's decision, since she later had a child with Michael Hutchence named Heavenly Hiraani Tiger Lily.

Homer James Jigme Gere—Richard Gere and Carey Lowell
Named after Richard's father, Homer Gere. Jigme means "fearless" in Tibetan—Gere is a strong supporter of freedom for the Tibetan people.

Poet Sienna Rose Goldberg—Soleil Moon Frye and Jason Goldberg

Greer Grammer (f)—Kelsey Grammer and Barrie Buckner

Mason Olivia Grammer (f)—Kelsey Grammer and Camille Donatucci

Spencer Karen Grammer (f)—Kelsey Grammer and Doreen Alderman

Phoenix Chi Gulzar—Melanie "Scary Spice" Brown and Jimmy Gulzar

Bluebell Madonna Haliwell—Geri "Ginger Spice" Halliwell
Father not disclosed. Geri said in an interview that her daughter is named after the "increasingly rare flower" and the singer, Madonna, whom she admires.

Delilah Belle Hamlin—Harry Hamlin and Lisa Rinna

Levon Green Hawke—Uma Thurman and Ethan Hawke

Grier Hammond Henchy (f)—Brooke Shields and Chris Henchy

Rowan Francis Henchy (f)—Brooke Shields and Chris Henchy

Alcamy Henriksen—Lance and Mary Jane Henriksen
Many sources incorrectly spell this child's name Alchamy, confusing it with the English word *alchemy*.

Sage Ariel Henriksen—Lance Henriksen and Jane Pollack

Elijah Bob Patricus Guggi Q Hewson—Bono Vox (Paul Hewson) and Alison Stewart
This is what happens when you try to appease every family member!

Cash Anthony Hudson—Slash (Saul Hudson) and Perla Hudson

London Emilio Hudson—Slash (Saul Hudson) and Perla Hudson

Heavenly Hiraani Tiger Lily Hutchence—Michael Hutchence and Paula Yates

Paris Michael Katherine Jackson—Michael Jackson and Debbie Rowe

Prince Michael Jackson—Michael Jackson and Debbie Rowe
Going against naming tradition, Michael named his second son Prince Michael Jackson II. Although George Foreman named all of his sons George I, II, III, IV, etc., numerals are supposed to apply to generation—not birth order.

Steveanna Genevieve Jackson—Randy
Jackson and Eliza Shaffe

Alizeh Keshvar Jarrahy—Geena
Davis and Dr. Reza Jarrahy

Kaiis Steven Jarrahy—Geena
Davis and Dr. Reza Jarrahy

Kian William Jarrahy—Geena
Davis and Dr. Reza Jarrahy

Moxie Crimefighter Jillette (f) and **Zolten
Penn Jillette (m)**—Penn and Emily Jillette
Penn said the couple chose their daughter's
middle name for the intimidation factor—
if she's ever pulled over for speeding she
can say, "But officer, we're on the same
side—my middle name is Crimefighter."[2]
The couple subsequently named their
son Zolten, Emily's maiden name.

Atherton Grace Johnson—Don
Johnson and Kelley Phleger

Shiloh Nouvel Jolie-Pitt—Angelina
Jolie and Brad Pitt

Kenya Julia Miambi Sarah Jones—
Quincy Jones and Natassja Kinski

Rashida Jones—Quincy Jones
and Peggy Lipton

Liberty Irene Kasem—Casey and Jean Kasem

Dexter Dean Keaton (f)—Diane Keaton

Cannon Edward King—Larry King
and Shawn Southwick

Chance Armstrong King—Larry
King and Shawn Southwick

Piper Maru Klotz—Gillian
Anderson and Clyde Klotz

Leni Klum—Heidi Klum and Flavio Briatore
Leni is named after Heidi's grandmother.
Heidi gave her daughter her last name,
because by the time she had the baby she
was already separated from father Briatore.

Rafferty Law—Jude Law and Sadie Frost

Amber Rose LeBon—Simon
LeBon and Yasmine

Saffron Sahara LeBon—Simon
LeBon and Yasmine

Tallulah Pine LeBon—Simon
LeBon and Yasmine

Pilot Inspektor Riesgraf Lee—Jason
Lee and Beth Riesgraf
According to Lee's publicist, the
couple just liked the name Pilot and
the name Inspektor came from friend
Danny Masterson's younger brother.

Allegra Sky Leguizamo—John
Leguizamo and Justine Maurer

Ryder Lee Leguizamo—John
Leguizamo and Justine Maurer

Astrella Celeste Leitch—Donovan
Leitch and Linda Lawrence

Ione Skye Leitch—Donovan
Leitch and Enid Karl
Ione grew up to be an actress,
starring in the popular teen flick
Say Anything with John Cusack.

Oriole Nebula Leitch—Donovan
Leitch and Linda Lawrence

Lourdes Maria Ciccone Leon—
Madonna and Carlos Leon
Lourdes is the name of a French town
where millions seek healing each year at
a shrine to the Virgin Mary, or "Madonna."

Alabama Luella—Travis Barker
and Shanna Moakler

Assisi Macmillan—Jade Jagger
and Dan Macmillan

Apple Blythe Alison Martin—Gwyneth
Paltrow and Chris Martin
Gwyneth is a big fan and close friend
of Fiona Apple, and many do not know
that Apple is really Fiona's middle
name. When questioned about the
name, Martin said, "I don't know why
we chose that. It's just a very cool
name."[3] The two middle names were
given in honor of each grandmother.

Speck Wildhorse Mellencamp—John
Mellencamp and Elaine Irwin
Named after John's grandfather, Speck.

Hazel Patricia Moder—Julia
Roberts and Danny Moder

Phinnaeus Walter Moder—Julia
Roberts and Danny Moder
It is unclear why the name Phinnaeus
was chosen; however, Walter is
the name of Julia's father.

Tu Simone Ayer Morrow—Rob
Morrow and Debbon Ayer
TV star Morrow says they named
their daughter Tu Morrow because his
wife's name is also a pun, debonaire.
However, there may be a hidden mean-
ing in it, too—as his wife's last name,
Ayer, means *yesterday* in Spanish.

Zola Ivy Murphy—Eddie Murphy
and Nicole Mitchell

Brawley King Nolte—Nick Nolte
and Rebecca Linger

Alfie Oldman—Gary Oldman
and Lesley Manville

Gulliver Flynn Oldman—Gary
Oldman and Donya Fiorentino

**Poppy Honey Oliver and Daisy Boo
Oliver**—Jamie Oliver and Juliette Norton
It's not a stretch that Jamie Oliver (*The
Naked Chef*) named his first daugh-
ter after two food items. Where he got
Daisy Boo, though, we can't figure out!

Gilliam Chynna Phillips—John
and Michelle Phillips
Chynna chose to take her middle
name to launch her singing career
when she cofounded teen singing group Wilson Phillips. Her siblings' names are Bijou, Mackenzie,
Tamerlane, and Jeffrey.

Condola Phylea Rashad—Phylicia
and Ahmad Rashad

Ryder Russell Robinson—Kate
Hudson and Chris Robinson

Lola Simone Rock—Chris Rock
and Malaak Compton-Rock

Zahra Savannah Rock—Chris Rock
and Malaak Compton-Rock

Enzo Rossi—Patricia Arquette
and Paul Rossi

**Henry Günther Ademola Dashtu
Samuel**—Heidi Klum and Seal
Heidi stated that Henry is named after
his father, whose real name is Sealhenry
Olusegun Olumide Samuel, his two
grandfathers Günther and Ademola,
and a Navy jet—the *Dash Two*.

Eulala Grace Scheel—Marcia Gay
Harden and Thaddeus Scheel

Hudson Harden Scheel—Marcia Gay
Harden and Thaddeus Scheel

Julitta Dee Harden Scheel—Marcia Gay
Harden and Thaddeus Scheel

Shepherd Kellen Seinfeld—Jerry
and Jessica Seinfeld

Willow Camille Reign Smith—Will
Smith and Jada Pinkett

Destry Allyn Spielberg—Stephen
Spielberg and Kate Capshaw

Fuchsia Catherine Sumner—Sting
and Frances Tomelty

Banjo Patrick Taylor—Rachel
Griffiths and Patrick Taylor

Emerson Rose Tenney—Teri
Hatcher and Jon Tenney

Síndri Eldon Thorsson—Björk
and Thor Eldon

Amadeo Turturro—John Turturro
and Katherine Borowitz

Caspar Vaughn—Claudia Schiffer
and Matthew Vaughn

Ocean Alexander Whitaker—Forest
Whitaker and Raye Dowell

Sonnet Noel Whitaker—Forest
Whitaker and Keisha Nash

True Isabella Summer Whitaker—Forest
Whitaker and Keisha Nash

Elettra-Ingrid Wiedemann—Isabella
Rossellini and Jonathan Wiedemann

Rumer Glenn Willis—Bruce
Willis and Demi Moore
Named after British novelist
Rumer Godden.

Scout LaRue Willis—Bruce
Willis and Demi Moore
Named after the child protagonist
in the novel *To Kill a Mockingbird*
by Harper Lee. However, Scout was
the character's nickname—her real
name was Jean Louise Finch.

Tallulah Belle Willis—Bruce
Willis and Demi Moore
Named after dramatic movie
actress Tallulah Bankhead.

Ahmet Rodan Zappa—Frank and Gail Zappa

Diva Muffin Zappa—Frank and Gail Zappa
Supposedly named Diva because
she cried the loudest of all the
babies in the hospital nursery.

**Ian Donald Calvin Euclid "Dweezil"
Zappa**—Frank and Gail Zappa
Many believe Dweezil is Ian's real name,
but that was only the nickname his sisters gave him growing up. He now uses
it as his official stage name, however.

Moon Unit Zappa—Frank and Gail Zappa
Frank Zappa said he knew his children
were going to be unique, so "why not
have a name that goes with it?"[4] Zappa
added that if any of them wanted to
change their names they were free
to do so. So far, they haven't. Moon
Zappa was known for her scathing
imitation of a Valley Girl in her dad's
hit song of the '80s, "Valley Girl."

Roman Zelman—Debra Messing
and Daniel Zelm

Many celebrities have also renamed themselves. Back in the 1930s, no starlet would have
been allowed to keep her own name if it were as
unique as Renée Zellweger. Actors were encouraged to change their names to appeal to the
conservative mainstream Anglo-Saxon society of
middle America, the primary moviegoing public.
The studios wanted names that were easily pro-
nounceable and not too ethnic.

In contrast to the older Hollywood tradition,
today a star may take a unique name in place
of their everyday common one. For example a
singer originally named Dana Owens renamed
herself Queen Latifah as her star persona, and
Brian Warner may have felt his name was a
little too tame for his Marilyn Manson image.
But sometimes the pressure of assimilation still
remains, as demonstrated by celebs like actress
Jennifer Anastassakis, who changed her surname
to Aniston, and TV host Jon Stewart, who dropped
his surname of Leibowitz.

NAME STORMING: If you and your partner are
more creative types, you may want to look into
monikers that are a little out of the ordinary. Are
you a tree enthusiast? Look at tree names. Are you
a Superman collector? Look at superhero names.
You don't need to go as far-out as Kal-El, but you
may want to consider something a little more
mainstream like Clark or Kent. Either way, it's
important to keep in mind that your child's name
shouldn't be unusual just for publicity's sake or to
get attention. Choose a name that your child can
live with the rest of his or her life.

7

Names with Brains

NAMING your child after your favorite physicist may not guarantee that she is going to be as brilliant, but it may make people treat her as if she were. Greek tycoon Aristotle Onassis, for example, was named after the Greek philosopher.

If you want your child to be associated with some of the more famous brains in history, check out this list of famous inventors, mathematicians, philosophers, educators, and scientists. We've listed some first names and some last names—whichever we felt might make good baby names.

Ada—Ada Byron Lovelace, the first computer programmer

Anaxagoras—Greek philosopher, teacher of Socrates

Aristotle—Greek philosopher

Avicenna—Persian philosopher

Banneker—Benjamin Banneker, African-American mathematician, astronomer, clockmaker, and publisher; inventor of the Farmer's Almanac

Bell—Alexander Graham Bell, inventor of the telephone

Benoit—Benoit Mandelbrot, Polish mathematician, first researched mathematical fractal patterns

Blaise—Blaise Pascal, French mathematician and theologist

Boole—George Boole, English mathematician; creator of Boolean algebra

Braille—Louis Braille, inventor of Braille printing for the blind

Carver—George Washington Carver, botanical and agricultural researcher; taught farming techniques to former slaves and mentored African-American children

Copernicus—Nicolaus Copernicus, Polish astronomer

Curie—Marie Curie, biologist; discovered radium and perfected X-ray technology

Darwin—Charles Darwin, English naturalist and creator of the Theory of Evolution

Dewey—John Dewey, American philosopher

Eastman—George Eastman, inventor of photographic film

Einstein—Albert Einstein, theoretical physicist

Fermi—Enrico Fermi, first to split the atom, father of the atomic bomb

Ferris—George Ferris, bridge architect and inventor of the Ferris wheel

Fleming—Alexander Fleming, biologist and inventor of penicillin; Sir Sanford Fleming, creator of Universal Standard Time

Fourier—Joseph Fourier, French physicist

Galileo—Galileo Galilei, Italian physicist, astronomer, philosopher, and astrologer

Goethe—Johann Wolfgang von Goethe, German writer and scientist

Halley—Edmund Halley, English astronomer and mathematician

Hawking—Stephen Hawking, English theoretical physicist

Hertz—Heinrich Hertz, German physicist; his work with electromagnetic radio waves led to the invention of radio

Hubble—Edwin Hubble, American astronomer

Keppler—Johannes Keppler, German astronomer

Lejeune—Johann Peter Gustav Lejeune Dirichlet, German mathematician

Leonardo—Leonardo Da Vinci, inventor, artist, sculptor, and architect; Leonardo Fibonacci, Italian mathematician

Linus—Linus Pauling, quantum chemist; Linus Torvalds, inventor of the Linux Operating System

Locke—John Locke, English philosopher, greatly influenced American democratic ideals

Machiavelli—Niccolo Machiavelli, Italian politician; the term *Machiavellian*, derived from Machiavelli's book *The Prince*, is used to describe a person who manipulates for money or power without concern for others

Marconi—Guglielmo Marconi, inventor of modern radio

Newton—Sir Isaac Newton, English physicist, astronomer, philosopher, and mathematician

Nietzsche—Friedrich Wilhelm Nietzsche, German philosopher

Nobel—Alfred Nobel, Swedish chemist and engineer; invented and patented dynamite; founded the Nobel prizes, awards given in medicine, chemistry, physics, economics, and peace

Pasteur—Louis Pasteur, French microbiologist; discovered that disease was passed by germs; invented pasteurization and the vaccine for rabies

Philo—Philo T. Farnsworth, inventor of the television

Pi—The number 3.14159265 (and so on); represents the ratio of a circle's circumference to its diameter; used extensively in engineering, mathematics, and physics.

Plato—Greek philosopher

Pythagoras—Greek philosopher and theologist; believed that all things could be reduced to numbers

Randice—Randice-Lisa Altschul, inventor of the first disposable cell phone

René—René Descartes, mathematician

Rousseau—Jean Jacques Rousseau, Swiss-French political philosopher

Santorio—Santorio Santorio, Italian physiologist and inventor of the first thermometer

Sartre—Jean Paul Sartre, French philosopher and creator of existentialism

Socrates—Greek philosopher, credited for ideas leading to the foundation of Western philosophy

Tesla—Nikola Tesla, Serbian inventor and physicist; inventor of the X-ray

Tycho—Tycho Brahe, Danish astronomer

Vannevar—Vannevar Bush, created the basics of hypertext, a precursor to HTML, the Internet programming language

Venn—John Venn, English mathematician

Voltaire—Voltaire, French philosopher, historian, and writer

Wren—Christopher Wren, English physician, astronomer, and architect

Wright—Orville and Wilbur Wright, inventors of the airplane

NAME STORMING: Intellectual names can come from many sources—from philosopher's musings to the periodic table of elements. If you are a brainiac, think about the minds that have inspired you throughout the years. It may be as simple as the name of your favorite college professor or the elementary school teacher who first recognized your genius.

Names That Rule

*I*N the past couple of decades, royalty have become celebrity—making headlines with their private and public lives. Many people believe that if they give their child names of famous royalty and rulers that their kid will grow up to be one as well. Royal names are most often traditional and classic names, as these families tend to name their children after the royal ancestors that came before them.

• The Brits

Anne	Edward	Jane
Arabella	Eleanor	John
Arthur	Elizabeth	Mary
Beatrice	Gwenevere	Phillip
Charles	Harry	Richard
Clarence	Henry	Victoria
Diana	James	William

• The Spaniards

Agnes	Felipe	Leonor
Alfonso	Ferdinand	Letizia
Balthazar	Gonzalo	Munia
Berengaria	Helena	Philip
Bermudo	Iñaki	Sancha
Bertha	Iolanda	Sofia / Sophia
Blanche	Isabella	Urraca
Cristina	Joana	Victoria
Digo	Juan Carlos	

• The French

30

Adela / Adelaide	Clemence	Louis
Agnes	Ferdinand	Margaret
Alphonse	Henriette	Marie
Blanche	Henry	Napoleon
Bourbon	Hugh	Philip
Cecile	Isabelle	
Charles	Jeanne	

• The Russians

Alexander	Dimitry	Olga
Alexandra	Elizabeth	Paul
Alexis	Fyodor	Peter
Anna	Ivan	Vasily
Boris	Nicholas	Wilhelmine
Catherine	Nikolai	

• The Americans

Abraham	Grover	Ronald
Andrew	Herbert	Rutherford
Benjamin	James	Theodore/Teddy
Calvin	John	Thomas
Caroline	Lyndon	Ulysses
Chester	Martin	Warren
Dwight	Millard	William
Franklin	Quincy	Woodrow
George	Richard	Zachary
Gerald	Robert	

Abigail	Grace	Mamie
Barbara	Hillary	Martha
Betty	Jacqueline	Mary
Dolley	Lady Bird	Nancy
Edith	Laura	Patricia
Eleanor	Lou Henry	Rosalynn
Elizabeth (Bess)	Lucy	

The Ancients

Agamemnon—Greece
Agrippina—Rome
Ajax—Greece
Alara—Egypt
Antony—Rome
Artemissia—Persia
Aurelius—Greece
Aurelius—Rome
Boudicca—Celtic queen
Cassandra—Troy
Claudius—Rome
Cleopatra—Queen of Egypt
Clytemnestra—Greece
Constantine—Rome
Cyrus—Persia
Darius—Persia
David—Israel
Dido—Carthage
Diocletian—Rome
Elah—Israel

Fabius—Rome
Hadrian—Rome
Hector—Troy
Helen—Troy
Hoshea—Israel
Julius—Rome
Justinian—Rome
Kasaqa—Egypt
Livia—Rome
Lysander—Greece
Marcus—Rome
Meryt—Egypt
Nefertiti—Egypt
Nerva—Rome
Octavian (Augustus)—
  Rome
Omri—Israel
Pertinax—Rome
Priam—Troy
Qalhata—Egypt

Ramses—Egypt
Romulus—Rome
Samsi—Queen of Arabia
Sargon—Assyria
Saul—Israel
Tarquin—Rome
Theodosius—Rome
Timoleon—Greece
Titus—Rome
Tomyris—Queen of
  the Massegetai
Trajan—Rome
Tutankhamen—Egypt
Valens—Rome
Xerxes—Persia
Zenobia—Queen of
  Palmyra (Syria)
Zimri—Israel

Royal Titles

Bantiarna—Irish (Baroness)
Baron
Baroness
Basileus—Greek (King)
Cesar—Latin (King)
Count
Countess/Contessa
Czar/Tsar/Kaiser—
  Russian (King)
Dronning—Nordic (Queen)
Duke—English
Dutchess—English
Earl

Herzog—German (Duke)
King—English
Knyaz—Russian (Prince)
Konge—Nordic (King)
König—German (King)
Königin—German (Queen)
Lady—English
Lord—English
Marquess—French
Marquis—French
Prince—English
Princeps—Latin (Prince)
Princess—English

Principe—Spanish (Prince)
Queen—English
Regina—Latin (Queen)
Reina—Spanish (Queen)
Reine—French (Queen)
Rex—Latin (King)
Rey—Spanish (King)
Ri—Irish (King)
Rigan—Irish (Queen)
Roi—French (King)
Thane—English
Tiarna—Irish (Baron)

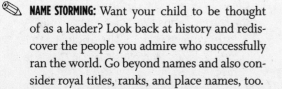 **NAME STORMING:** Want your child to be thought of as a leader? Look back at history and rediscover the people you admire who successfully ran the world. Go beyond names and also consider royal titles, ranks, and place names, too.

9

Names That Score

ATHLETES are a popular source of baby names, especially for boys. But there are just as many great female athlete names out there, too, so you may want to consider an athletic name whether you have a boy or girl.

One woman, who is a die-hard Chicago Cubs fan, named her daughter Wrigley Addison after the famous Cubs stadium, Wrigley Field, which is located on Addison Avenue in Chicago. Now that's a true fan! Another dad insisted that his daughter was named Miami after his favorite football team, the Dolphins. I guess that's better than naming her Dolphin!

New parents Karen and David Hartle of Bloomfield, Missouri, recently named their son ESPN after the television sports channel.[5] They said they saw a special about parents naming their children ESPN and decided that would be a good name. However, the other parents chose to put a vowel between the P and N. The Hartles were purists, though, and decided to use just the letters ESPN.

Maybe you don't want to go that far, but you do want your child's name to be identified with the strength, power, and prowess of an athlete. Take a look at these unique names inspired by both the first and last names of the great sports legends of today and yesteryear.

• Men

Ali—Muhammad Ali, boxing

André—Andre Agassi, tennis

Apolo—Apolo Ohno, speed skating

Bart—Bart Starr, football

Beckham—David "Beck" Beckham, soccer

Blue—Josh Blue, paralympic soccer

Bo—Bo Jackson, football/baseball

Boomer—Norman Julius "Boomer" Esiason, football; Boomer got his nickname while he was still in his mother's womb. The story goes that an old college football pal of his dad's was visiting the family. When Boomer let out a big prenatal kick, the friend said, "Wow! That's quite a little boomer you got!"[6]

Brian—Brian Piccolo, football; Brian Boitano, figure skating

Brooks—Brooks Robinson, baseball

Cal—Cal Ripken Jr., baseball

Cassius—Cassius Clay (aka Muhammad Ali), boxing; Muhammad Ali's original name was Cassius Marcellus Clay Jr. Clay's father

was originally named after a famous abo-
litionist named Cassius Marcellus Clay

Clyde—Clyde Drexler, basketball

Cy—Cy Young, baseball; born Denton
True Young; early in his career, he
was dubbed "The Cyclone," which
eventually got shortened to "Cy"

Daunte—Daunte Culpepper, football

Dempsey—Jack Dempsey, boxing

Derek—Derek Jeter, baseball

Earvin—Earvin "Magic" Johnson, basketball

Emmitt—Emmitt Smith, football

Evander—Evander Holyfield, boxing

Garo—Garo Yepremian, football

Hank/Henry—Hank Aaron, baseball

Heisman—Trophy given to the most
outstanding college football player
of the year; named after college
football coach John Heisman

Honus—Honus Wagner, baseball

Jack—Jack Niklaus, golf

Jenner—Bruce Jenner, decathlon

Jeret—Jeret Peterson, skiing

Jesse—Jesse Owens, track

Jock—The word *jock*, used as a slang
term for athlete, was first documented
by the Harvard student newspaper
Harvard Crimson in 1958. The term
was derived from the athletic support garment, the jock strap. Originally
jock was a euphemism for penis.

Joe—"Joltin'" Joe DiMaggio, baseball, born Giuseppe Paolo DiMaggio
Jr.; also Joe Montana, football

Jordan—Michael Jordan, basketball

Kareem—Kareem Abdul-Jabbar, basketball

Kobe—Kobe Bryant, basketball

Lance—Lance Armstrong, cycling

LeBron—LeBron James, basketball

Lou—Lou Gehrig, baseball

Maddox—Greg Maddox, baseball

Mario—Mario Andretti, auto racing

Mays—Willie Mays, baseball

Nolan—Nolan Ryan, baseball

Oscar—Oscar de la Hoya, boxing

Otto—Otto Graham, football

Payton—Walter Payton, football

Ronaldo—Ronaldo, soccer

Satchel—Satchel Paige, baseball

Sayers—Gale Sayers, football

Shaq/Shaquille—Shaquille
O'Neal, basketball

Thurl—Thurl Bailey, basketball

Tiger—Tiger Woods, golf (real name
Eldrick); Woods is of mixed heri-
tage: African-American, Chinese,
Native American, Thai, and Dutch

Tino—Tino Martinez, baseball

Valentino—Valentino Rossi, auto racing

Walter—Walter Payton, football

Wayne—Wayne Gretzky, hockey

• Women

Althea—Althea Gibson, tennis

Anna— Anna Kournikova, tennis

Annika—Annika Sorenstam, golf

Chamique—Chamique Holdsclaw, basketball

Cynthia—Cynthia Cooper, basketball

Danica—Danica Patrick, auto racing

Dara—Dara Torres, swimming

Delisha—Delisha Milton-Jones, basketball

Dorothy—Dorothy Hamill, figure skating

Evert—Chris Evert, tennis

Evonne—Evonne Goolagon, tennis

Fabiola—Fabiola de Silva, inline skating

Gabrielle—Gabrielle Reece, volleyball

Ila—Ila Borders, baseball

Jia—Jia Perkins, basketball

Joyner—Jackie Joyner Kersee and
Florence Griffith Joyner, track

Katarina—Katarina Witt, figure skating

Kornelia—Kornelia Ender, swimming

Laila—Laila Ali, boxing

Lindsay—Lindsay Davenport, tennis

34

Lokelani—Lokelani McMichael, triathlon
Manon—Manon Rheaume, hockey
Maria—Maria Sharapova, tennis
Marion—Marion Ladewig, bowling
Martina—Martina Navratilova, tennis
Mia—Mia Hamm, soccer
Michelle—Michelle Kwan, figure skating
Misty—Misty Hyman, swimming
Nadia—Nadia Comenici, gymnastics
Nera—Nera White, basketball
Niele—Niele Ivy, basketball
Paulette—Paulette King, basketball
Peggy—Peggy Fleming, ice skating
Picabo—Picabo Street, skiing
Reece—Gabrielle Reece, volleyball
Serena—Serena Williams, tennis
Silken—Silken Laumann, rowing
Steffi—Steffi Graf, tennis
Swin—Swin Cash, basketball
Tara—Tara Nott, weightlifting (first
　　American woman to win an Olympic
　　gold medal in the sport); also,
　　Tara Lipinski, figure skating
Tegla—Tegla Loroupe, marathon running
Tenley—Tenley Albright, figure skating
Venus—Venus Williams, tennis
Wilma—Wilma Rudolph, track

● **Other Sporty Names**
　Adidas—sporting goods company
　Callaway—golf equipment company
　Easton—sporting goods company
　Espn—television sports channel
　Kinnick—Kinnick Stadium, University of Iowa
　Nike—sporting goods company
　Sutton—Eddie Sutton, basketball coach
　　at Oklahoma State University
　Wrigley—Wrigley Field, home
　　of the Chicago Cubs

✎ **NAME STORMING:** If you and your partner are really into sports, you may want to consider names from your favorite teams—or even the team names themselves! Then again, if you don't want to go that far, you may want to just give your child a sporty edge by choosing a strong nickname. Think about it: Would you rather cheer on Dwayne Johnson or "The Rock"? Eldrick Woods or "Tiger"? But remember, no matter how much you may wish your child to be the star quarterback, ultimately your child picks his own destiny in life and you may be cheering on "Bronco," the star poet.

My favorite sports names are usually ones I would never use, but I just love anyway. Tshimanga Biakabutuka (usually pronounced *Tuh-mung-ah Bee-ah-kah-bah-too-kah*) is the most fun name to say out loud. Tshimanga played for the University of Michigan Wolverines football team in the '90s and then went on to play with the Carolina Panthers.

—Julia K., Ann Arbor, Michigan

10

Names That Travel

MANY names, both first and last, were originally derived from the place in which the family lived. So it's not that far-fetched that we like to name children after our favorite places. David and Victoria Beckham reportedly named their sons after the places where they were conceived: Romeo in Rome, Italy, and Brooklyn in Brooklyn, New York. Of course, many places were named after people—so it can go full circle.

We've compiled a list of places that are already used as given names, places from names, and places we think would make interesting baby names.

Abilene, Texas
Acadia, Louisiana
Ada, Idaho
Adair, Iowa/Missouri
Africa, Continent
Aiani, Greece
Alabama, U.S. state
Alameda, California
Albany, New York
Albion, Montana
Algiers, Algeria, Africa
Amberly, Maryland
Amcelle, Maryland
America, Continent
Ancona, Italy
Andria, Italy
Anoka, Minnesota
Antalya, Turkey
Apex, Montana
Araxá, Brazil
Arden, Nevada
Arica, Chile
Asia, Continent
Astoria, Oregon
Atchison, Missouri
Athens, Greece
Attala, Mississippi
Augusta, Maine
Auvergne, France
Avalon, California
Avera, Mississippi
Avignon, France
Avonia, Pennsylvania
Aydin, Turkey
Barcelona, Spain
Barrow, Georgia

36

Barton, Kansas
Baxter, Arkansas
Beira, Mozambique
Belize, Central America
Bethel, Alaska
Biella, Italy
Blaine, Idaho
Bonner, Idaho
Boone, Arkansas
Boone, Illinois
Boston, Massachusetts
Bradley, Arkansas
Bremen, Germany
Brescia, Italy
Cairo, Egypt
Calais, France
Calgary, Alberta, Canada
Calhoun, Alabama
Cambria, Maryland
Candler, Georgia
Cannes, France—Most widely associated
    with its international film festival, and is
    the sister city of Beverly Hills, California;
    it is associated with glamour and wealth
Cantara, New Mexico
Casablanca, Morocco—Most widely known
    for the movie made of the same name
Cason, Louisiana
Catania, Italy
Cayenne, French Guyana
Chaffee, Colorado
Chance, Oklahoma
Charlotte, North Carolina
Charlton, Georgia
Cheyenne, Colorado
Chicago, Illinois
Clay/Clayton, Georgia
Cleveland, Ohio
Colorado, U.S. state
Concord, Massachusetts
Conway, Arkansas
Corinth, Greece
Coventry, England

Dakota, U.S. states (N & S)
Dalian, China
Dalys, Montana
Darraugh, South Carolina
Davao, Philippines
Dayton, Ohio
Delavan, Minnesota
Desha, Arkansas
Deventer, Netherlands
Dixie, Florida—Also a general nick-
    name for the U.S. South
Dodge, Georgia
Dover, England
Drennen, Pennsylvania
Dresden, Germany
Drexel, Missouri
Durango, Mexico
Eden, Minnesota—Also a place
    name in the Bible
Elista, Russia
Ellerslie, Maryland
Ellis, Kansas
Eureka, California
Évora, Portugal
Fallon, Nevada
Fargo, North Dakota
Fayette, Georgia
Fez, Morocco, Africa
Florida, U.S. state
Franklin, Florida
Geneva, Switzerland
Gentry, Missouri
Georgia, U.S. state
Glades, Florida
Grady, Georgia
Greenlee, Arizona
Gwinett, Georgia
Halifax, Nova Scotia, Canada
Hart, Kentucky
Hazen, Maryland/Nevada
Hira, Iraq
Hoxsie, Mississippi
Hyannis (Port), Massachusetts

Ibiza, Spain
Ida, Iowa
Indiana, U.S. state
Inverness, Scotland
Ionia, Michigan
Ixelles, Belgium
Jackman, Nevada
Jamaica
Jambi, Indonesia
Jasper, Iowa
Jenin, Israel
Jet, Oklahoma
Jewell, Ohio
Juneau, Alaska
Kamo, Armenia
Kano, Nigeria
Karo, Louisiana
Kassel, Germany
Katowice, Poland
Kauai, Hawaii
Kendall, Illinois
Kénitra, Morocco
Kenna, New Mexico
Kenya, Africa
Khaniá, Greece
Kielce, Poland
Kienstra, Mississippi
Kiowa, Colorado
Kobe, Japan
Kolomna, Russia
Kyzyl, Russia
Lamar, Georgia
Lanier, Georgia
Laurens, Georgia
Lavery, Pennsylvania
Leonia, New Jersey
Lexington, Kentucky
Lille, France
Logan, Colorado/Kansas
London, England
Londrina, Brazil
Loring, Mississippi
Madera, California

Madison, Wisconsin
Madrid, Spain
Mandalay, Myanmar
Manisa, Turkey
Maracay, Venezuela
Marin, California
Marseilles, France
Mason, Illinois
Maui, Hawaii
McCool, Mississippi
Medary, South Dakota
Mégara, Greece
Mellette, South Dakota
Melrose, New Mexico—Also a trendy
    shopping district of Los Angeles;
    most identified with the '90s tele-
    vision show *Melrose Place*
Mercer, Illinois
Mesa, Colorado
Miera, New Mexico
Milan, Italy
Mohave, Arizona
Montego (Bay), Jamaica
Montreal, Canada
Morelia, Mexico
Nairobi, Kenya, Africa
Nash, North Carolina
Nassau, Florida
Ness, Kansas
Netanya, Israel
Nevada, U.S. state
Neves, Brazil
Nouméa, Oceania
Nowthen, Minnesota
Oceania, Continent
Olinda, Brazil
Olympia, Washington
Ontario, Canada
Orlando, Florida
(New) Orleans, Louisiana
Ouray, Colorado
Oxford, England
Paisley, Scotland

Paris, France
Parran, Nevada
Paulding, Georgia
Paxton, Michigan
Phoenix, Arizona
Polaris, Montana
Pori, Finland
Prague, Czech Republic
Pretoria, South Africa
Providence, Rhode Island
Provo, Utah
Qacentina, Algeria, Africa
Racine, Wisconsin
Raleigh, North Carolina
Ravenna, Italy
Rennes, France
Reno, Nevada
Rio (De Janeiro), Brazil
Rome, Italy
Rosiclare, Illinois
Roswell, New Mexico—Most often identified with UFO sightings; if you are a sci-fi fan and know what SETI stands for, this name may be for you!
Roxie, Mississippi
Samara, Russia
Samoa, Country
Savannah, Georgia
Savona, Italy
Schuyler, New York
Searcy, Arkansas
Seattle, Washington
Selma, Alabama
Seville, Spain
Sheshebee, Minnesota
Shoshone, Idaho
Sitka, Alaska
Somerset, New York
Spalding, Georgia
Story, Iowa
Sullana, Peru
Sumter, Florida
Sundell, Michigan

Surco, Peru
Swann, North Carolina
Sydney, Australia
Tacoma, Washington
Tallinn, Estonia
Tammany, Idaho/Louisiana
Taney, Missouri
Tappen, North Dakota
Taraz, Kazakhstan
Teller, Colorado
Tenafly, New Jersey
Tennessee, U.S. state
Tensas, Louisiana
Terrell, Georgia
Tex, short for Texas, U.S. state
Thayer, Montana
Tilton, New Hampshire
Timon, Brazil
Tioga, New York
Tipton, Indiana
Topanga, California
Torreón, Mexico
Trenton, New Jersey
Trigg, Kentucky
Turin, Italy
Vail, Colorado
Valencia, Spain
Valletta, Europe
Vantaa, Finland
Venice, Italy
Ventura, California
Verona, Italy
Versaille, France
Vienna, Austria
Viersen, Germany
Villard, Minnesota
Vilnius, Lithuania
Virginia, U.S. state
Viron, Greece
Warrick, Indiana
Zaria, Nigeria
Zora, Pennsylvania
Zurich, Switzerland

● Place Names to Avoid

Buga, Colombia
Chihuahua, Mexico
Cumnock, North Carolina
Dickey, North Carolina
Dumfries, Scotland
Frost Bottom, Tennessee
Funkley, Minnesota
Greasy, Oklahoma
Grizzly, Oregon
Hamm, Germany
Ho-Ho-Kus, New Jersey
Horry, South Carolina
Hung-tung, China
Needy, Oregon

Pealiquor (Landing), Maryland
Swett, South Dakota
Thicketty, South Carolina
Tonawanda, New York
Toulouse, France
Trailer Park, Maryland
Worms, Germany

NAME STORMING: Make a list of places that have good memories for you—your hometown, your favorite vacation spot, the town where your grandparents came from—and maybe even where your baby was conceived! If you do like a name, research the place to make sure it won't have any bad history or a bad association for locals.

11

Names Gone Wild

MANY parents prefer to look for their name choices in the natural world—these names have a sense of serenity and quietude. In the 1970s nature names like Sunflower and Meadow became popular among the hippie and New Age crowd. Whereas it's more acceptable for a nature name to be given to a girl, lately there are many boys' names that are also stemming from Mother Earth, so to speak. Actor Rainn Wilson says his name was given to him by his "bohemian parents."[7]

Here is a list of our favorite names from nature:

Acacia—From the acacia tree (English) [tree]

Amaryllis—To sparkle (Greek) [flower]

Amber—Amber (English) [precious stone]

Anemone—Wind (Greek) [flower]

Anise—Anise (English) [herb]

Aster—Star (Greek) [flower]

Autumn—Autumn (English) [season]

Azalea—Dry (Greek) [flower]

Azure—Sky blue (English)

Basil—King (Greek) [herb]

Birch—Birch (English) [tree]

Blaise—Blaze (English)

Blossom—Blossom, flower (English)

Briar—Briar (English) [plant]

Brooke—One who lives near a brook (English)

Calanthe—Beautiful flower (Greek) [flower]

Canyon—Canyon (English)

Carnation—Carnation (English) [flower]

Cascade—To fall (French)

Cassia—Feminine of Cassius (Latin) [tree]

Cedar—Cedar (English) [tree]

Chamomile—Chamomile (English) [plant]

Cloud—Cloud (English)

Clover—Clover (English)

Coral—Coral (English)

Cyprus—Cyprus (English) [tree]

Daisy—Day eye (Old English) [flower]

Dandelion—Dandelion (English) [plant]

Drake—Male duck (English) [bird]

Echo—Sound (Greek)

Fawn—Fawn (English)

Flora—Flower (Latin)

Flower—Flower (English)

Forrest—Forest (English)

Freesia—Freesia (English) [flower]

Gardenia—Gardenia (English) [flower]
Garnet—Hinge (Old English) [precious stone]
Glen/Glenn—Valley (Gaelic)
Gordon—Great hill (Scottish)
Grover—Grove of trees (Old English)
Hallam—At the rocks (English)
Hazel—Hazel (English) [tree]
Heather—Heather (English) [flower]
Heron—Heron (English) [bird]
Holly—Holly (English) [tree]
Hyacinth—Hyacinth (English, Greek) [flower]
Iolanthe—Violet flower (Greek)
Iris—Rainbow (Greek) [flower]
Ivy—Ivy (English) [plant]
Jade—Jade (English) [precious stone]
Jasmine—Jasmine (English) [flower]
Jessamine—Jessamine (English) [flower]
Juniper—Juniper (English) [tree]
Kestrel—Rattle (French) [bird]
Landon—Long hill (Old English)
Lake—Lake (English)
Lark—Lark (English) [bird]
Laurel—Laurel (English) [tree]
Lavender—Lavender (English) [flower]
Leaf—Leaf (English)
Leilani—Heavenly flowers (Hawaiian)
Lilac—Lilac (English) [flower]
Lily—Lily (English) [flower]
Linden—Lime tree (Latin)
Logan—Little hollow (Scottish) [plant]
Lowell—Wolf cub (French)
Magnolia—Magnolia (English) [tree, flower]
Maple—Maple (English) [tree]
Marigold—Marigold (English) [flower]
Maris—From the Sea (Latin)
Mavis—Mavis (Scottish) [bird]
Meadow—Meadow (English)
Morgan—Circle in the sea (Welsh)
Oak—Oak (English) [tree]
Ocean—Ocean (English)
Olive—Olive (English) [tree]
Oneida—Standing rock (English)

Pansy—Thought (French) [flower]
Pearl—Pearl (English)
Penelope—Duck (Greek)
Peony—Peony (English) [flower]
Peregrine—Traveler (Latin) [bird]
Petunia—Petunia (English) [flower]
Phyllis—Foliage (Greek)
Poppy—Poppy (English) [flower]
Prairie—Prairie (English)
Primrose—First Rose (Latin) [flower]
Rain—Rain (English)
Raven—Raven (English)
Reed—Ruddy (Scottish, Old English) [plant]
Ridley—Reed clearing (Old English)
Robin—Robin (English) [bird]
Rose—Rose (English) [flower]
Ruby—Red (Latin) [precious stone]
Sequoia—Sequoia (Native
   American, English) [tree]
Shade—Shade (English)
Sierra—Mountain range (Spanish)
Sky/Skye—Sky (English)
Snow—Snow (English)
Sorrel—Sorrel (English) [plant]
Starling—Little star (English) [bird]
Star/Starr—Star (English)
Stone—Stone (English)
Storm—Storm (English)
Summer—Summer (English)
Sunshine—Light from the sun (English)
Sylvester—Of the forest (Latin)
Tempest—Storm (English)
Terra—Land (Latin)
Tierra—Earth (Spanish)
Tinder—Wood (English)
Todd—Fox (English)
Topaz—Topaz (English) [stone]
Trail—Trail (English)

42

Ursula—Little she-bear (Latin)
Violet—Violet (English) [flower]
Wesley—West Meadow (Old English)
Willow—Willow (English) [tree]
Wren—Wren (English) [bird]
Wolf—Wolf (German, English)
Xylia—From the forest (Greek)
Zephyr—The west wind (Greek)
Zinnia—Zinnia (English) [flower]

✎ **NAME STORMING:** If you and your partner like nature names, make a list of those that mean something to you. What is the state flower or tree where you were born? What is the flower or gemstone associated with your birth month? Maybe there is an animal that you identify with or are particularly fond of—all these can be considered to make a truly unique name.

12

Names from the Imagination

$\mathcal{I}$F you think about it, all names were invented at one point in time. In the past ten years or so, we've noticed that parents are becoming much more creative in their naming choices—for both boys and girls. There are several cultures in the United States in which inventing names has been widely accepted and encouraged for some time: specifically African-Americans and Utah Mormons. It is believed that the naming tradition in both cultures stemmed from the desire to be unique and to shun monikers that were forced upon

them in the past. Therefore, parents intentionally chose to create names rather than using names that were traditionally Anglo or mainstream.

Interestingly, both the Utah Mormons and African-Americans share one tradition of putting the French pronouns "La" or "De" in front of a common name. La and De translate to the word "the"—so using it in a name like DeShawn, for example, is like saying, "The one and only Shawn." It shows pride and individuality. This custom is no different than real estate tycoon Donald Trump calling himself "The Donald."

So how would you go about creating a name? The most common way people invent names is to combine two other more popular names. Here are examples of names from parents who decided to combine two names into one:

Bryson—boy, couldn't decide on
the name Bryan or Jason

Denell—girl, honoring family members
Dennis and Della
Druanna—girl, parents liked the name
Drew and honored Aunt Anna
Jaylene—girl, from parents
Jason and Sharlene
Jezdon—boy, from parents
Brandon and Jessica
Jeslin—girl, from parents Jesse and Lynn
Kaymen—girl, from parents Kayla and Damon
Marlisse—girl, from parents Marty and Lisa
Shreve—girl, from parents Shari and Steve

Another way of inventing a new name is to take a common name and change its first letter. For example, Hayden would be changed to Zaden. There is a drawback, though, in that people are used to the original, common name, so your child may have to spell her new name for people again and again.

Here are examples of actual names submitted

44

by our members where the first letter was changed to create an entirely new name:

Allison—Callison
Beatrix—Leatrix
Bianca—Vianca
Cameron—Tameron
Catherine—Datherine
Celia—Xelia
Darren—Garren
Derrick—Kerrick
Devin—Brevin
Jillian—Dillian
Joseph—Moseph
Kayla—Tayla
Mariah—Jariah, Sariah
Maverick—Laverick
Nathan—Dathan
Olivia—Alivia
Phyllis—Dyllis
Sarah—Karah
Taylor—Kaylor
Vanessa—Janessa

Sometimes a name can be created by accident. For example, one mother said she really liked the name Raison, but because of her dyslexia, she read it as Riason. Since her husband's name was Tyson, she used the *y* instead of an *i* and named her son Ryason.

Jennifer W. of Tifton, Georgia, says, "My best friend's name is Heatherlee, which was due to a big miscommunication on the part of her parents. They were discussing names, and her mom said, 'What about Heather Lee?' And her dad said, 'Oh, I like it—but what should we choose as her middle name?'"

One name that has gained popular momentum in the United States in Nevaeh, which is *heaven* spelled backward. That name in itself has an alternate spelling as many parents have mistakenly spelled it Neveah.

Created Names or Created People?

There are many urban baby-naming legends out there as well. One of the most circulated and well-known legends is the one about the twins named Orangejello and Lemonjello (pronounced *or-AN-gel-o* and *le-MON-gel-o*). We've heard from many, many people who "know someone who went to school" with these famed twins, and one woman on a website has even claimed to have seen their birth certificates! Even author Steven

> My name is Chassidy and I have always had trouble with it. It has been spelled every way you can imagine (from Cassity to Chastity) and pronounced every way you can imagine (from Charity to Charisma). The first day of school every year was a nightmare for me because no teacher could pronounce my name; and when they did say it, a lot of people would laugh and I would get the typical chastity belt comments. Now when I tell people my name, I always have to spell it and I always have to tell them how to pronounce it: like Cassidy but with an "h" in there.
>
> —Chassidy R., Montgomery, Alabama

Levitt included the Orangejello and Lemonjello story in his bestselling book *Freakonomics* as examples of actual naming trends (in the book's endnotes, Levitt states that he heard it from a guy who *swears* he met the boys in a grocery store). And thus, the twins live on in legend-land. Now, there *was* a pitcher for the Houston Astros named Mark Lemongello back in the 1970s—perhaps *he* was the one who started it all!

NAME STORMING: Creating a name is tricky business, but it can be very rewarding and fulfilling if you create a brand-new name for your brand-new child. You don't want to be so inventive that the child will have to spell the name for people the rest of his or her life. You don't want it to be so crazy that the child will be teased throughout his school years. You can create names from anything that inspires you: combining names, using birth dates, changing the first letter of a common name, or favorite books or TV channels, like ESPN. Even if it's just for comic relief, sit down with your partner and have a name-making night. You never know what may come up!

45

13

Names by Meaning

MANY parents want to choose a name that has significant meaning to them, or a meaning that represents characteristics they wish to see in their child. Some people are disappointed when they look up the meaning of their name and see something that is not that flattering like "bent nose" (Cameron) or "ugly head" (Kennedy). However, not every name can mean "beautiful princess."

Authors often choose to use names for their characters that represent the character's personality or role in the story. Take, for example, the main characters of Thomas Harris's *Silence of the Lambs*: the names of the two main characters, Hannibal Lecter and Clarice Starling, are chock-full of meaning. The name Hannibal intentionally rhymes with *cannibal* so the reader constantly associates him with the horrific act. Lecter means "teacher," a role he played in relation to Clarice, teaching her about the criminal mind of a serial killer. Clarice is a diminutive name from Clara, meaning "light, clarity"—something Clarice is seeking throughout the book. Starling means "little star." Clarice is the star of the story, but the diminutive name suggests that she is younger or childlike.

Here is a list of the top twenty-five most-searched meanings on our site, and their associated names:

● **LOVE**

Boys

    Agapito—Beloved (Spanish)
    Amadeus—Love of God (Latin)
    Amando—Worthy of love (Italian)
    Amor—Love (Spanish)
    Balint—Health or love (Hungarian)
    Caradoc—Beloved (Welsh)
    Cariad—Love (Welsh)
    Ceron—Beloved (Welsh)
    Dafydd—Beloved (Welsh)
    David—Beloved (Hebrew)
    Dewey—Beloved (Welsh)
    Dewi—Beloved (Welsh)
    Drury—Love, friendship (English)
    Dulal—Loved one (Sanskrit/East Indian)

Erasmus—Beloved (Greek)

Eros—God of love (Greek)

Filbert—Love bright (English)

Gallagher—Descendant of the lover of foreigners (Celtic/Gaelic)

Habib—Beloved One (Arabic)

Ipo—Sweetheart, lover (Hawaiian)

Jumoke—Everyone loves the child (African)

Keefe—Handsome, beloved (Celtic/Gaelic)

Keefer—Handsome, beloved (Celtic/Gaelic)

Kendi—The loved one (African)

Lolonyo—Love is beautiful (African)

Lolovivi—There's always love (African)

Love—Full of love (English)

Luthando—Love (African)

Moral—Lovely thoughts (American)

Oke—Deer lover (Hawaiian)

Oscar—Deer lover (Celtic/Gaelic)

Penha—Beloved (Swahili)

Phil—Lover of horses (Greek)

Philander—Lover of man (Greek)

Philip—Lover of horses (Greek)

Phillip—Lover of horses (Greek)

Prem—Love, affection (Sanskrit/East Indian)

Pritam—Lover (Sanskrit/East Indian)

Sevilen—Loved (Turkish)

Tene—Love (African)

Thuong—Love tenderly (Vietnamese)

Tivon—Nature lover (Hebrew)

Upendo—Love (African)

Yadid—Beloved (Hebrew)

Zane—Beloved (American)

Girls

Abiba—The beloved one (African)

Adora—Beloved one (Latin)

Agape—Love (Greek)

Ahuva—Beloved (Hebrew)

Ai—Love (Japanese)

Aiko—Little loved one (Japanese)

Aimee—Beloved friend (French)

Aimi—Beautiful love (Japanese)

Amada—Beloved (Spanish)

Amadis—Love of God (Latin)

Amanda—Worthy of love (Latin)

Amor—Love (Spanish)

Amora—Love (Spanish)

Amorina—Love (Spanish)

Amoura—Love (American)

Amy—Beloved (Latin)

Anchoret—Much loved (Welsh)

Angharad—Much loved (Welsh)

Asthore—Loved one (Celtic/Gaelic)

Calantha—Like a lovely blossom (Greek)

Canan—Beloved (Turkish)

Caraf—I love (Welsh)

Caresse—Beloved (American)

Cariad—Love (Welsh)

Carys—To love (Welsh)

Ceri—Love (Welsh)

Cerys—To love (Welsh)

Chaviva—Beloved (Hebrew)

Cheryl—Beloved (French)

Cytheria—Goddess of Love (Greek)

Darla—Dear, loved one (English)

Darlene—Dear, loved one (American)

Dava—Beloved (American)

Davina—Beloved (Celtic/Gaelic)

Didina—Desired, beloved (French)

Drury—Love, friendship (English)

Elon—God loves me (African)

Erasto—Beloved (Italian)

Esme—Loved (French)

Femi—Love me (African)

Filipina—Lover of horses (Polish)

Freja—Norse goddess of love (Scandinavian)

Freya—Goddess of love, fertility, and beauty (Scandinavian)

Frigg—Love (Scandinavian)

Graziella—Lovely and with grace (Italian)

Ife—Lover of art and culture (African)

Juji—Heap of love (African)

Jumoke—Everyone loves the child (African)

Kalila—Beloved (Arabic)

Kayla—Pure and beloved (Celtic/Gaelic)

Kendi—The loved one (African)

48

Lada—Goddess of love and fertility (Slavic)
Lalasa—Love, friendship (Persian)
Lolovivi—There's always love (African)
Love—Full of love (English)
Lovette—Little loved one (English)
Lovey—Loved one (American)
Lovie—Loved one (American)
Mahal—Love (Arabic)
Marianela—Beloved star (Spanish)
Milena—People's love (Russian)
Moral—Lovely thoughts (American)
Neha—Love, affection (Sanskrit/East Indian)
Oke—Deer lover (Hawaiian)
Olathe—Lovely, beautiful (Native American)
Penha—Beloved (Swahili)
Phila—Love (Greek)
Philana—Lover of horses (Greek)
Philantha—Lover of flowers (Greek)
Philena—Lover of mankind (Greek)
Philippa—Lover of horses (Greek)
Phillipa—Lover of horses (Greek)
Philyra—Love of music (Greek)
Pilialoha—Beloved (Hawaiian)
Pippa—Lover of horses (English)
Prema—Love, affection (Sanskrit/East Indian)
Priti—Love (Sanskrit/East Indian)
Priya—Beloved (Sanskrit/East Indian)
Querida—Beloved (Spanish)
Rowa—Lovely vision (Arabic)
Sanam—Beloved, mistress (Arabic)
Sauda—Black, love (Arabic)
Sevda—Passion, love (Turkish)
Sevgi—Love (Turkish)
Sevilen—Loved (Turkish)
Shirina—Love song (American)
Siran—Sweet love (Armenian)
Sirvat—Rose of love (Armenian)
Suki—Beloved (Japanese)
Tanith—Goddess of love (Greek)
Tene—Love (African)
Thandiwe—Beloved (African)
Thisbe—Lover (Greek)
Thuong—Love tenderly (Vietnamese)

Tivona—Nature lover (Hebrew)
Vanida—Wife, beloved woman
    (Sanskrit/East Indian)
Venus—Goddess of love (Greek)
Zane—Beloved (American)
Zuleika—Brilliant and lovely (Arabic)

• BEAUTY/BEAUTIFUL

Boys

Alagan—Handsome (Sanskrit/East Indian)
Bayle—Beautiful (American)
Beale—Handsome (English)
Beau—Beautiful, handsome (French)
Beauchamp—Beautiful field (English)
Beauregard—Beautiful view (English)
Bell—Beautiful (English)
Bello—Beautiful, handsome (Italian)
Calix—Very handsome (Greek)
Daylin—Beautiful day (American)
Hussein—Handsome one (Arabic)
Jamal—Handsome (Arabic)
Jamil—Beautiful, elegant (Arabic)
Japheth—Handsome (Hebrew)
Jun—Handsome (Chinese)
Keefe—Handsome, beloved (Celtic/Gaelic)
Keefer—Handsome, beloved (Celtic/Gaelic)
Ken—Handsome (Celtic/Gaelic)
Kenneth—Handsome (Celtic/Gaelic)
Kenny—Handsome (Celtic/Gaelic)
Kevin—Handsome, beautiful (Celtic/Gaelic)
Kitoko—Beautiful (African)
Lolonyo—Love is beautiful (African)
Memphis—Established and beautiful (Greek)
Menefer—Established and beautiful
    (Egyptian)
Qiao—Pretty, handsome (Chinese)
Quinlan—Descendant of the handsome
    man (Celtic/Gaelic)
Rupin—Handsome (Sanskrit/East Indian)
Shaquille—Handsome (American)
Waseem—Handsome (Arabic)
Yahir—Handsome (Spanish)

Yu jie—Pure, beautiful jade (Chinese)

Yue yan—Happy, beautiful (Chinese)

Zain/Zayn—Handsome (Arabic)

Zene—Beautiful (African)

Girls

Adamma—Beautiful girl (African)

Adin—Beautiful, adorned (Hebrew)

Aimi—Beautiful love (Japanese)

Alpana—Beautiful (Sanskrit/East Indian)

Ani—Very beautiful (Slavic)

Aoife—Beautiful, radiant (Celtic/Gaelic)

Arabela—Beautiful lion (Spanish)

Arabella—Beautiful lion (English)

Ayanna—Beautiful flower (African)

Bayle—Beautiful (American)

Belinda—Beautiful (Spanish)

Belisma—Beautiful (Spanish)

Belita—Beautiful (Spanish)

Bell—Beautiful (English)

Bella—Beautiful (Italian)

Bellini—Little beautiful one (Italian)

Bonita—Pretty, beautiful (Spanish)

Buthainah—Beautiful woman (Arabic)

Cadhla—Beautiful (Celtic/Gaelic)

Calista—Beautiful (Greek)

Calixte—Very beautiful (Greek)

Callia—Beautiful (Greek)

Callie—Beautiful (Greek)

Callista—Most beautiful (Greek)

Caroline—Beautiful woman (Latin)

Clarinda—Beautiful, clear (English)

Damali—Beautiful vision (Arabic)

Daylin—Beautiful day (American)

Donatella—Beautiful gift (Italian)

Eavan—Beautiful radiance (Celtic/Gaelic)

Elu—Beautiful, fair (Native American)

Fayre—Beautiful (English)

Hasana—Beautiful, fair (Arabic)

Hiraani—Beautiful sky (Hawaiian)

Iowa—Beautiful land (Native American)

Jamila—Beautiful, elegant (Arabic)

Jaunie—Pretty, beautiful (Arabic)

Jia li—Good and beautiful (Chinese)

Kalista—Most beautiful one (Greek)

Kalli—Beautiful (American)

Keelia—Beautiful (Celtic/Gaelic)

Keely—Beautiful (Celtic/Gaelic)

Kelis—Beautiful (American)

Kenisha—Beautiful and prosperous (American)

Kenna—Beautiful (Celtic/Gaelic)

Kennice—Beautiful (English)

Kevina—Handsome, beautiful (Celtic/Gaelic)

Kevine—Beautiful (Celtic/Gaelic)

Kitoko—Beautiful (African)

Labonita—Beautiful one (Spanish)

Lewa—Beautiful (African)

Maliha—Attractive, beautiful (Arabic)

Maylin—Beautiful jade (Chinese)

Meiling—Beautiful and delicate (Chinese)

Melinda—Black and beautiful (American)

Memphis—Established and beautiful (Greek)

Menefer—Established and beautiful (Egyptian)

Misa—Beautiful bloom (Japanese)

Misaki—Beautiful bloom (Japanese)

Miu—Beautiful feather (Japanese)

Miyo—Beautiful child (Japanese)

Miyoko—Beautiful child (Japanese)

Naava—Beautiful (Hebrew)

Naomi—Beautiful, gentle (Hebrew)

Nefret—Beautiful (Egyptian)

Noemi—Beautiful, gentle (French)

Olathe—Lovely, beautiful (Native American)

Orabella—Beautiful gold (Italian)

Rupali—Most beautiful (Sanskrit/East Indian)

Salma—Beautiful woman (Arabic)

Shakila—Beautiful (Arabic)

Shakina—Beautiful one (African)

Shayna—God is gracious, beautiful (American)

Suchin—Beautiful thought (Thai)

Sundari—Beautiful (Sanskrit/East Indian)

Tasanee—Beautiful view (Thai)

Vella—Beautiful (American)

Waseemah—Beautiful (Arabic)

Wyanet—Beautiful (Native American)

Xin qian—Happy, beautiful (Chinese)

Xiu—Elegant, beautiful (Chinese)

Yafa—Beautiful, pretty (Hebrew)

Yamilet—Beautiful, elegant (Spanish)

Yu jie—Pure, beautiful jade (Chinese)

Yue yan—Happy, beautiful (Chinese)

Zaina—Beautiful (Arabic)

Zalika—Wondrously beautiful (Arabic)

Zayn—Beautiful (Arabic)

Zaynah—Beautiful (Arabic)

Zeena—Beautiful (African)

Zene—Beautiful (African)

Zi—Graceful, beautiful (Chinese)

Zuri—Beautiful (Swahili)

Zweena—Beautiful (African)

Gavril—God is my strength (Slavic)

Jedrek—Manly, strong (Polish)

Mandla—Strength (African)

Maynard—Brave strength (English)

Ojas—Strong one (Sanskrit/East Indian)

Onan—Strength, power (Hebrew)

Oz—Strength, courage (Hebrew)

Plato—Strong shoulders (Greek)

Tiergan—Strong willed (Celtic/Gaelic)

Trumble—Strong, bold (English)

Uzi—Power, strength (Hebrew)

Valentin—Strength, health (Rumantsch)

Valentine—Strength, health (English)

Valentino—Strength, health (Italian)

Valerian—Strength (English)

Varro—Durable, strong (Latin)

Zeke—God will strengthen (Hebrew)

• STRONG/STRENGTH

Boys

Aaron—Exalted, strong (Hebrew)

Angus—One strength (Celtic/Gaelic)

Arnau—Strong warrior (Spanish)

Az—Strong (Hebrew)

Batzorig—Courageous, strong (Mongolian)

Bernt—Strong, brave bear (German)

Boaz—Strength (Hebrew)

Brogan—Sturdy and strong (Celtic/Gaelic)

Carolos—Strong, manly (Greek)

Cathal—Strong in battle (Celtic/Gaelic)

Denim—Strong cloth (American)

Dhiren—Strong one (Sanskrit/East Indian)

Eitan/Etan—Firm, strong (Hebrew)

Ethan—Firm, strong (Hebrew)

Eyad—Support, might, strength (Arabic)

Eyal—Strength (Hebrew)

Eytan—Firm, strong (Hebrew)

Ezekiel—God will strengthen (Hebrew)

Ezequiel—God will strengthen (Spanish)

Fergie—Strength of man (Celtic/Gaelic)

Fergus—Man strength (Celtic/Gaelic)

Gabriel—God is my strength (Hebrew)

Girls

Arnia—Strong as an eagle (American)

Audra—Noble strength (American)

Audrey—Noble strength (English)

Audria—Noble strength (American)

Brogan—Sturdy and strong (Celtic/Gaelic)

Bryna—Strong one (Celtic/Gaelic)

Bryndis—Of strong armor (Scandinavian)

Denim—Strong cloth (American)

Etana—Dedication, strength (Hebrew)

Fergie—Strength of man (Celtic/Gaelic)

Gavrilla—God is my strength (Russian)

Gertrude—Strong spear (German)

Gesine—Strong spear (German)

Hilliard—War stronghold (English)

Iphigenia—Born strong (Greek)

Keren—Ray, beam or strength, power (Hebrew)

Melisande—Labor, strength (French)

Melissan—Labor, strength (American)

Mildred—Mild strength (English)

Millicent—Mild strength (English)

Passion—Strong desire (American)

Philomena—Strong friend (Greek)

Pilar—Pillar of strength (Spanish)

Shakti—Ability, strength
(Sanskrit/East Indian)
Timber—Wood, strong (American)
Valene—Strong (Latin)
Tillie/Tilly—Battle strength (English)
Truda/Trude/Trudy—Spear strength (Polish)
Valencia—Strength, health (Spanish)
Valentina/Valentine—Strength,
health (Latin/French)
Valeria/Valerie—Strength (Italian/French)

• DARK

Boys

Blake—Pale blond one or dark (English)
Daray—Dark (American)
Darcy—Dark one (Celtic/Gaelic)
Darth—Dark (American)
Delano—Dark (Celtic/Gaelic)
Devin—Descendant of the dark-
haired one (Celtic/Gaelic)
Dolan—Dark haired (Celtic/Gaelic)
Donnelly—Brave, dark man (Celtic/Gaelic)
Dougal—Dark stranger (Celtic/Gaelic)
Douglas—Dark water (Celtic/Gaelic)
Doyle—Dark foreigner (Celtic/Gaelic)
Duff—Dark (Celtic/Gaelic)
Dugan—Dark colored (Celtic/Gaelic)
Duncan—Dark-skinned warrior (Celtic/Gaelic)
Dwayne—Dark, black (English)
Gethin—Dark (Welsh)
Keeran—Little dark one (Celtic/Gaelic)
Keiran—Little and dark (Celtic/Gaelic)
Kern—Dark-haired child (Celtic/Gaelic)
Kerry—Dark princess (Celtic/Gaelic)
Kieran—Little dark one (Celtic/Gaelic)
Mauli—Dark skinned (Hawaiian)
Maurice/Mauricio/Maurizio—Dark
skinned (French/Spanish/Italian)
Mauro—Dark skinned (Italian)
Maurus—Dark skinned (Rumantsch)
Mo/Moe—Dark skinned (American)
Morrie—Dark skinned (American)

Morris—Dark skinned (Latin)
Morse—Dark skinned (English)
Shyam—Dark (Sanskrit/East Indian)
Sullivan—Dark eyed (Celtic/Gaelic)
Tamesis—Dark one (English)
Tynan—Dark (Celtic/Gaelic)

Girls

Adrienne—Dark one (Latin)
Blake—Pale blond one or dark (English)
Daray—Dark (American)
Darcie—Of the dark (English)
Darcy—Dark one (Celtic/Gaelic)
Devin—Descendant of the dark-
haired one (Celtic/Gaelic)
Keaira—Little dark one (Celtic/Gaelic)
Kern—Dark-haired child (Celtic/Gaelic)
Kerri/Kerry—Dark and mysterious
(Celtic/Gaelic)
Kiara—Small, dark (Celtic/Gaelic)
Lamya—Dark complexion (Arabic)
Mahogany—Dark red wood (English)
Morrisa—Dark skinned (American)
Tamal—Dark tree (Sanskrit/East Indian)
Tamesis—Dark one (English)
Tynan—Dark (Celtic/Gaelic)

• FIRE

Boys

Aden/Aidan/Aiden—Little fire (Celtic/Gaelic)
Adish—Fire (Persian)
Atish—Fire, splendor (Persian)
Brant—Firebrand (English)
Dragon—Fire-breathing creature (American)
Ea—Fire (Celtic/Gaelic)
Edan—Little fire (Celtic/Gaelic)
Egan—Little fire (Celtic/Gaelic)
Hotaru—Firefly (Japanese)
Iggy—Firey one (English)
Keahi—Flames, fire (Hawaiian)
Kindle—Set fire (American)
Milintica—He waves fire (Aztec/Nahuatl)

Nuri—My fire (Hebrew)
Paytah—Fire (Native American)
Phyre—Fire (American)
Tyson—Firebrand or son of Denis (English)
Uri—My light, flame, fire (Hebrew)
Xipil—Noble one, of fire (Aztec/Nahuatl)

Girls

Aideen—Little fire (Celtic/Gaelic)
Fiammetta—Firey woman (Italian)
Ildri—Fire and peace (Scandinavian)
Keahi—Flames, fire (Hawaiian)
Kindle—Set fire (American)
Nuri—My fire (Hebrew)
Phyre—Fire (American)
Pyralis—Of fire (Greek)
Safara—Fire (African)
Tanwen—White fire (Welsh)

• LIGHT

Boys

Abner—Father of light (Hebrew)
Artaxiad—Descendant of the joyous light (Armenian)
Awendela—Daylight (Native American)
Barak—Lightning, spark (Hebrew)
Cyan—Light blue-green (American)
Day—Light and hope (American)
Deepak—Light, lamp (Sanskrit/East Indian)
Eron—Peace, enlightened (Hebrew)
Flash—Bright light (American)
Guang—Light (Chinese)
Horus—God of light (Egyptian)
Ilo—Light, joyous, sunshine (African)
Kenzie—Light skinned (Celtic/Gaelic)
Kiran—Ray of light (Sanskrit/East Indian)
Luce—Light (Latin)
Lucian/Lucien—Light (English/French)
Lucifer—Bringer of light (Latin)
Lucio—Light (Italian)
Lucius—Light (Latin)

Manjit—Light of the mind (Sanskrit/East Indian)
Melchior—God is my light (Hebrew)
Mhina—Delightful (African)
Mitsu—Light or honey/nectar (Japanese)
Nuru—Light (Swahili)
Orly—You are my light (Hebrew)
Twila—Twilight (American)
Uri—My light, flame, fire (Hebrew)
Uriah—God is my light (Hebrew)
Uriel—God is my light (Hebrew)
Yair—He will enlighten (Hebrew)
Ye—Light (Chinese)
Ziya—Light (Arabic)
Zohar—Light, brilliance (Hebrew)

Girls

Alaula—Light of dawn (Hawaiian)
Alena—Light (Slavic)
Arin—Enlightened (Hebrew)
Aura—Glowing light (Latin)
Awendela—Daylight (Native American)
Cyan—Light blue-green (American)
Day—Light and hope (American)
Deepnita—Light and happiness (Sanskrit/East Indian)
Delicia—Delightful (Spanish)
Dilana—Of the light (American)
Elaine—Light (English)
Eleora—The Lord is my light (Hebrew)
Eliora—The Lord is my light (Hebrew)
Ellen—Light (Greek)
Flash—Bright light (American)
Helaine—Light (English)
Helen—Light (Greek)
Helena—Light (Greek)
Huda—Enlightenment, guidance (Arabic)
Ilka—Light (Hungarian)
Ilona—Light (Hungarian)
Jyoti/Jyotika—Light (Sanskrit/East Indian)
Kenzie—Light skinned (Celtic/Gaelic)
Kiran—Ray of light (Sanskrit/East Indian)

Konane—Glow like moonlight (Hawaiian)

Lana—Light (Slavic)

Lenci—Light (Hungarian)

Lenka—Light (Slavic)

Lenora/Lenore/Leonor/Leonora—Light
   (Spanish/French/Spanish/Italian)

Leora—Light (Hebrew)

Leyna—Light (American)

Linore—Light (English)

Liora—My light (Hebrew)

Liseli—Light (African)

Lona/Lonna—Light (Hungarian/Slavic)

Lucia/Luciana—Light (Italian)

Lucie/Lucy—Light (French)

Lucille—Light (French)

Lucinda—Light (Spanish)

Lucine—Light (American)

Luz—Light (Spanish)

Lycoris—Twilight (Greek)

Meora—Light, brightness (Hebrew)

Mhina—Delightful (African)

Mitsu—Light or honey/nectar (Japanese)

Mitsuko—Child of light (Japanese)

Naima—Delight, contentedness (Arabic)

Nell/Nellie/Nelly—Light (English)

Neorah—Light (Hebrew)

Nitsa—Light (Greek)

Noga—Splendor, light, Venus (Hebrew)

Noura/Nura—Light (Arabic)

Nuru—Light (Swahili)

Odgerel—Starlight (Mongolian)

Onella—Torch light (Hungarian)

Orli—You are my light (Hebrew)

Orly—You are my light (Hebrew)

Ramya—Pleasing, delightful
   (Sanskrit/East Indian)

Sileny—Moonlight, silence (Slavic)

Sitara—Starlight (Sanskrit/East Indian)

Suruchi—Great delight, happiness
   (Sanskrit/East Indian)

Sveta—Light (Slavic)

Svetlana—Light (Slavic)

Terpsichore—To delight in dance (Latin)

Twila/Twyla—Twilight (American)

Uriela—Light of God (Hebrew)

Urit—Light (Hebrew)

Yitta—Light (Hebrew)

Ziya—Light (Arabic)

• GOD

Boys

Adiel—God's ornament (Hebrew)

Adlai—God is just (Hebrew)

Adonai—God is my Lord (Hebrew)

Adriel—Congregation of God (Hebrew)

Amadeus—Love of God (Latin)

Amiel—My people belong to God (Hebrew)

Ancelin—Little god (French)

Angel/Angelo—Messenger of
   God (Greek/Italian)

Ansel—A god (French)

Ariel—Lion of God (Hebrew)

Artemis—Goddess of the moon
   and hunt (Greek)

Avidan—God is just (Hebrew)

Azriel—God is my aid (Hebrew)

Buenaventura—Good tidings, God
   be with you (Spanish)

Ceres—Goddess of the corn (Greek)

Chael—Who is like God? (Hebrew)

Charan—God's feet (Sanskrit/East Indian)

Chimelu—What God has created (African)

Chinua—God's own blessing (African)

Dane—God is my judge, or from
   Denmark (Scandinavian)

Daniel—God is my judge (Hebrew)

Danil—God is my judge (Slavic)

Danny—God is my judge (English)

Danyl—God is my judge (Hebrew)

Deion—God of wine and revelry (American)

Deo—Godlike (Greek)

Deron—Belongs to God (Armenian)

Deus—God (Latin)

Devanand—Joy of God (Sanskrit/East Indian)

Deven—Like a God (Sanskrit/East Indian)

Devesh—God of gods (Sanskrit/East Indian)

Dion—God of wine and revelry (Greek)

Dionysius/Dionysus—God of wine
and revelry (Greek/Latin)

Dominic/Dominick—Belonging
to God (Latin)

Dominy—Belonging to God (English)

Donar—God of thunder (Scandinavian)

Ean—God is gracious (Celtic/Gaelic)

Elazer—God has helped (Hebrew)

Elchanan—God is gracious (Hebrew)

Eleazar—God has helped (Hebrew)

Elias—The Lord is my God (English)

Elie—The Lord is my God (French)

Elijah—The Lord is my God (Hebrew)

Eliot/Elliot/Elliott—The Lord
is my God (English)

Elisha—God is my salvation (Hebrew)

Elkan—Belonging to God (Hebrew)

Ellis—The Lord is my God (English)

Elya—The Lord is my God (Slavic)

Emanuel/Emmanuael—God
is with us (Hebrew)

Eros—God of love (Greek)

Esai—God is salvation (Spanish)

Esben—God bear (Scandinavian)

Espen—God bear (Scandinavian)

Evan—God is good (Welsh)

Ezekiel/Ezequiel—God will strengthen
(Hebrew/Spanish)

Faunus—God of forests (Latin)

Frey—God of weather (Scandinavian)

Gabriel—God is my strength (Hebrew)

Ganesa—God of intelligence and wisdom
(Sanskrit/East Indian)

Gavril—God is my strength (Slavic)

Gian/Gianni—God is gracious (Italian)

Giovanni—God is gracious (Italian)

Giuseppe—God will add, increase (Italian)

Godfrey—God peace (English)

Gwydion—God of magic (Welsh)

Hannes—God is gracious (Scandinavian)

Hans—God is gracious (Scandinavian)

Hansel—God is gracious (German)

Herne—God of the hunt (Celtic/Gaelic)

Horus—God of light (Egyptian)

Iain—God is gracious (Celtic/Gaelic)

Ian—God is gracious (Celtic/Gaelic)

Illias—The Lord is my God (Greek)

Ilya—The Lord is my God (Russian)

Ion—God is good (Russian)

Isai—God is salvation (American)

Isaiah—God is salvation (Hebrew)

Ishmael/Ismael/Ismail—God
will hear (Hebrew)

Israel—Wrestled with God (Hebrew)

Ivan—God is gracious (Russian)

Jan—God is gracious (Dutch)

Janus—God of beginnings (Latin)

Jean—God is gracious (English)

Jedidiah/Jed—Friend of God (Hebrew)

Jeffery/Jeffrey/Geoffrey—God peace
(English)

Jens—God is gracious (Scandinavian)

Jeremy/Jeremiah—God will uplift (Hebrew)

Joel—God will be willing (Hebrew)

Johann—God is gracious (German)

John—God is gracious (Hebrew)

Jonathan/Jonathon—God
has given (Hebrew)

José—God will increase (Spanish)

Josef/Joseph—God will increase
(German/Hebrew)

Joshua—God is salvation (Hebrew)

Josiah—God will save (Hebrew)

Jovan—God is gracious (Slavic)

Juan—God is gracious (Spanish)

Juno—Goddess of marriage
and childbirth (Latin)

Kadmiel—God is ancient (Hebrew)

Kaniel—God is my reed (Hebrew)

Katriel—God is my crown (Hebrew)

Keon—God is gracious (Hawaiian)

Keoni—God is gracious (Hawaiian)

Kirabo—Gift from God (African)

Lazar—God has helped (Hungarian)

Lazaro/Lazzaro—God has helped (Spanish/Italian)

Lazarus/Lazer—God has helped (Hebrew)

Lemuel—Devoted to God (Hebrew)

Loki—Trickster God (Scandinavian)

Mace—Gift of God (English)

Mahendra—God Indra (Sanskrit/East Indian)

Maik—Who is like God? (English)

Makaio—Gift of God (Hawaiian)

Manolo—God is with us (Spanish)

Manuel—God is with us (Spanish)

Mars—God of war (Greek)

Martin—Servant of Mars, God of war (Latin)

Mateo/Matteo—Gift of God (Spanish/Italian)

Mateusz—Gift of God (Polish)

Mathis—Gift of God (French)

Matias/Mattias/Matthias—Gift of God (Spanish/Hebrew/Greek)

Matteus—Gift of God (American)

Matthew—Gift of God (English)

Mattia—Gift of God (Rumantsch)

McKale—Who is like God? (American)

Melchior—God is my light (Hebrew)

Mercury—God of trade (Latin)

Micah—Who is like God? (Hebrew)

Michael/Michal—Who is like God? (Hebrew)

Michel—Who is like God? (French)

Michon—Who is like God? (French)

Mickey—Who is like God? (American)

Miguel—Who is like God? (Spanish)

Mihaly—Who is like God? (Hungarian)

Mikaili—Who is like God? (African)

Mikhail—Who is like God? (Russian)

Mikko—Who is like God? (Scandinavian)

Mimir—God of prophecy (Scandinavian)

Mischa/Misha—Who is like God? (Russian)

Mitch/Mitchell—Who is like God? (American)

Moeshe—Born of (a god) (Hebrew)

Moriel—God is my teacher (Hebrew)

Morpheus—God of dreams (Greek)

Morrigan—War goddess (Celtic/Gaelic)

Moses—Born of a god (Egyptian)

Moss—Born of a god (English)

Nathaniel—Gift of God (Hebrew)

Nehemiah—God has comforted (Hebrew)

Osborn/Osbourne—God bear (English)

Osgood—God Goth (English)

Osric—God ruler (English)

Oswald—God rule (English)

Oya—Wind warrior goddess (African)

Ozer—God's helper (Hebrew)

Pillan—God of stormy weather (Native American)

Pluto—Roman God of the underworld (Latin)

Priel—Fruit of God (Hebrew)

Rafael/Raphael—God has healed (Spanish/Hebrew)

Raffaello—God has healed (Italian)

Ram—Godlike (Sanskrit/East Indian)

Reda—Favored by God (Arabic)

Reuel—Friend of God (Hebrew)

Samuel—His name is God (Hebrew)

Samuru—His name is God (Japanese)

Saturn—Roman god of Agriculture (Latin)

Sean/Shaun/Shawn—God is gracious (Celtic/Gaelic)

Shane/Shayne—God is gracious (Celtic/Gaelic)

Shmuel—His name is God (Hebrew)

Shoney—Sea God (Celtic/Gaelic)

Tedros—Gift of God (African)

Theophilus—Loving God (Greek)

Theoris—God (Greek)

Thijs—Gift of God (Dutch)

Timothy—To honor God (Greek)

Tobiah/Tobias—God is good (Hebrew)

Toviel—My God is goodness (Hebrew)

Tuvya—God's goodness (Hebrew)

Uriah—God is my light (Hebrew)

Uriel—God is my light (Hebrew)

56

Varun/Varuna—God (Sanskrit/East Indian)

Vashon—God is gracious, merciful (American)

Waldo—God's power (English)

Xannon—Ancient God (American)

Yanni/Yannis—God is gracious (Greek)

Yeriel—God has taught me (Hebrew)

Yeshaya—God is salvation (Hebrew)

Yohance—God's gift (African)

Yosef/Yosefu—God will add (Hebrew)

Zachariah—God has remembered (Hebrew)

Zachary/Zacharee—God has remembered (Hebrew)

Zarek—May God protect the king (Persian)

Zebedeo—Gift of God (Spanish)

Zedekiah—God is righteousness (Hebrew)

Zeke—God will strengthen (Hebrew)

Zeus—God (Greek)

Girls

Adaya—God's jewel (Hebrew)

Adiel/Adriel—God's ornament (Hebrew)

Adonia—God is my Lord (Hebrew)

Aeron—Goddess of war (Welsh)

Aerona—Celtic goddess (Welsh)

Amadis—Love of God (Latin)

Amaris—Promised by God (Hebrew)

Amiel/Amiela—My people belong to God (Hebrew)

Angela/Angie—Messenger of God (English)

Angelica—Messenger of God (Latin)

Angelie/Angelique—Messenger of God (French)

Angelina—Messenger of God (Italian)

Anjelita—Messenger of God (Spanish)

Annona—Goddess of the harvest (Latin)

Aradia—Goddess of witches (Greek)

Ariel/Arielle/Ariella—Lion of God (Hebrew)

Astrid—God's strength (Scandinavian)

Athalia—God is exalted (Hebrew)

Athena—Goddess of wisdom and war (Greek)

Aurora—Goddess of the dawn (Latin)

Avatari—God's incarnation (Sanskrit/East Indian)

Azalia—God has spared (Hebrew)

Azriel—God is my aid (Hebrew)

Babette—My God is my oath (French)

Bellona—Goddess of war (Latin)

Bess/Bessie—God is my oath (English)

Beth—God is my oath (English)

Bethan—God is my oath (Welsh)

Betsy—God is my oath (English)

Bette—God is my oath (American)

Bettina—God is my oath (Italian)

Betty—God is my oath (English)

Beyla—By God! (Slavic)

Buenaventura—Good tidings, God be with you (Spanish)

Cardea—Goddess of protecting the home (Greek)

Carmel—Vineyard of God (Hebrew)

Ceana—God is gracious (Celtic/Gaelic)

Cerelia—Goddess of the harvest (Greek)

Ceres—Goddess of the corn (Greek)

Chaela—Who is like God? (American)

Chaeli—Who is like God? (Celtic/Gaelic)

Chanda—Hindi goddess (Sanskrit/East Indian)

Chinue—God's own blessing (African)

Cytheria—Goddess of love (Greek)

Damara—Fertility goddess (English)

Damia—Goddess of forces of nature (Greek)

Daniela/Daniella—God is my judge (Spanish/Latin)

Danielle—God is my judge (Hebrew)

Danya—Gift of God (Hebrew)

Dea—Goddess (Latin)

Devaki—A god (Sanskrit/East Indian)

Deven—Like a god (Sanskrit/East Indian)

Devi—Goddess of power (Sanskrit/East Indian)

Devica/Devika—Derived from God (Sanskrit/East Indian)

Dianthe—Flower of the gods (Greek)

Diella—Worshipper of God (Latin)

Dina/Dinah—God has judged (Hebrew)

Dion—God of wine and revelry (Greek)

Domenica/Dominica—Belonging to God (Italian/Latin)

Dominique—Of God (French)

Dorika—Gift of God (Hungarian)

Dorotea/Dorothea—Gift of God (Spanish/Greek)

Dorothy—Gift of God (Greek)

Dory—Gift of God (Greek)

Dot/Dotty—Gift of God (Greek)

Duaa—Prayer to God (Arabic)

Elie—The Lord is my God (French)

Elisa—God is my oath (English)

Elisabeth/Elizabeth—God is my oath (Hebrew)

Elisha—God is my salvation (Hebrew)

Eliya—God is my Lord (Hebrew)

Ellis—The Lord is my God (English)

Elon—God loves me (African)

Elya—The Lord is my God (Slavic)

Emanuele—God is with us (Italian)

Epona—French horse goddess (Latin)

Eponine—French horse goddess (English)

Erzsebet—God is my oath (Hungarian)

Evan—God is good (Welsh)

Evana—God is gracious (Latin)

Everlyse—Always consecrated to God (American)

Fabunni—God has given me this (African)

Fauna—Goddess of fertility (Latin)

Faunus—God of forests (Latin)

Fedora—God's gift (Russian)

Freja—Norse goddess of love (Scandinavian)

Freya—Goddess of love, fertility, and beauty (Scandinavian)

Galia/Galya—Wave of God (Hebrew)

Ganesa—God of intelligence and wisdom (Sanskrit/East Indian)

Gavrila—God is my strength (Hungarian)

Gianna—God is gracious (Italian)

Giovanna—God is gracious (Italian)

Grace—Grace of God (Latin)

Gudrun—God's secret (Scandinavian)

Guri—Hindu goddess of plenty (Sanskrit/East Indian)

Gyda—Gods (Scandinavian)

Hedia—Echo of God (Hebrew)

Helsa—Consecrated to God (Scandinavian)

Ianna—God is gracious (American)

Ilithya—Goddess of women in labor (Greek)

Ilse—Consecrated to God (German)

Iokina—God will develop (Hawaiian)

Isabel/Isabella/Isabelle—God is my oath (Spanish/Italian/French)

Isabis—God is my oath (American)

Isi—Consecrated to God (Spanish)

Ismaela—God will hear (Hebrew)

Isoke—Satisfying gift from God (African)

Izzy—God is my oath (Spanish)

Jan—God is gracious (Dutch)

Jana—God is gracious (Slavic)

Janae—God is gracious (American)

Jane/Jayne—God is gracious (English)

Janelle—God is gracious (American)

Janet/Janette—God is gracious (English)

Janice/Janis/Janus—God is gracious (English/English/Latin)

Jayashri—Goddess of victory (Sanskrit/East Indian)

Jean/Jeanne—God is gracious (English/Celtic/Gaelic)

Jeanette—God is gracious (English)

Jeanine—God is gracious (Celtic/Gaelic)

Jeannie—God is gracious (French)

Jessica—God beholds (Hebrew)

Joan—God is gracious (Hebrew)

Joanna/Joanne—God is gracious (English)

Joella/Joelle—God will be willing (Hebrew/French)

Johanna—God is gracious (German)

Josephina/Josephine—God will increase (English/French)

Josie—God will add (American)

Jovanna—God is gracious (Slavic)

58

Juana/Juanita—God is gracious (Spanish)

Juno—Goddess of marriage
and childbirth (Latin)

Katriel—God is my crown (Hebrew)

Kayley—Who is like God? (American)

Keona—God's gracious gift (Hawaiian)

Kirabo—Gift from God (African)

Kwanita—God is gracious (Native American)

Lada—Goddess of love and fertility (Slavic)

Lael—Of God (Hebrew)

Latona—Goddess name (Latin)

Liana—My God has answered (Hebrew)

Libba—God is my oath (American)

Libby—God is my oath (English)

Liesel—God is my oath (German)

Lis/Lise—God is my oath
(Scandinavian/German)

Lisa/Liza—God is my oath (English)

Lisbet/Lizbeth—God is my oath
(German/English)

Lisette/Lizette—God is my oath (French)

Lissa—God is my oath (American)

Liz—God is my oath (English)

Lizeth—God is my oath (American)

Lizina—God is my oath (American)

Loki—Trickster God (Scandinavian)

Lysa—God is my oath (American)

Macayle—Who is like God? (American)

Maceo—Gift of God (Spanish)

Madrona—Mother goddess (Welsh)

Maik/Maika—Who is like God?
(English/French)

Maina—Messenger of God
(Sanskrit/East Indian)

Makaio—Gift of God (Hawaiian)

Makayla—Who is like God? (American)

Malkia—Queen of God (Hebrew)

Manuela—God is with us (Hebrew)

Mars—God of war (Greek)

Martina—Servant of Mars, god of war (Latin)

Mateja—Gift of God (Slavic)

Matia/Matias—Gift of God (Spanish)

Mattea—Gift of God (Latin)

May—Goddess Maia (English)

Mena—Woman, mother-goddess
(Sanskrit/East Indian)

Mercury—God of trade (Latin)

Michaela—Who is like God? (English)

Michele/Michelle—Who is like God? (French)

Micheline—Who is like God? (French)

Michon—Who is like God? (French)

Mickey—Who is like God? (American)

Mikaia—Who is like God? (American)

Mikayla—Who is like God? (American)

Mimir—God of prophecy (Scandinavian)

Mimis—Goddess of harvest (Greek)

Minerva—Goddess of wisdom (Latin)

Mischa/Misha—Who is like God? (Russian)

Moriah—God is my teacher (Hebrew)

Morrigan—War goddess (Celtic/Gaelic)

Nataniela—Gift of God (Hebrew)

Neith—Ancient Egyptian mother
goddess (Egyptian)

Nenet—Goddess of the deep (Egyptian)

Nita—Gift of God (Spanish)

Odelia/Odelya—I will thank God (Hebrew)

Oksana—Praise be to God (Slavic)

Olympia—Mountain of the gods (Greek)

Ontibile—God is watching over me (African)

Oya—Wind warrior goddess (African)

Panthea—All goddesses (Greek)

Pillan—God of stormy weather
(Native American)

Pluto—Roman god of the underworld (Latin)

Raphaela—God has healed (Italian)

Reda—Favored by God (Arabic)

Sabella—Consecrated to God (American)

Sakina—Calm, comfort, presence
of God (Arabic)

Savarna—Like God (East Indian/Sanskrit)

Sean—God is gracious (Celtic/Gaelic)

Seana/Seanna—God is gracious
(Celtic/Gaelic/American)

Selma—God's helmet (English)

Shaina/Shana/Shayna—God is
gracious (American)

Shanae—God is gracious (English)

Shane/Shayne—God is gracious (Celtic/Gaelic)

Shanese—God is gracious (American)

Sharne—God is gracious (American)

Sharvani—Name of the goddess Parvati (Sanskrit/East Indian)

Shauna/Shawna—God is gracious (Celtic/Gaelic)

Sheena—God is gracious (Celtic/Gaelic)

Shoney—Sea god (Celtic/Gaelic)

Shyla—Goddess (Sanskrit/East Indian)

Sian—God's gracious gift (Welsh)

Sine—God is gracious (Celtic/Gaelic)

Sinéad—God is gracious (Celtic/Gaelic)

Siobhan—God is gracious (Celtic/Gaelic)

Tanginika—Lake goddess (American)

Tanith—Goddess of love (Greek)

Tauret—Goddess of pregnant women (Egyptian)

Tea/Thea—Gift of God (Spanish/Greek)

Tekla—Glory of God (Italian)

Tekli—Glory of God (Polish)

Tendai—Be thankful to God (African)

Teofila—House of God (Italian)

Theone—Gift from God (Greek)

Theophania—Appearance of God (Greek)

Theophilia—Friendship of God (Greek)

Thyra—Goddess (Scandinavian)

Tiffany—Appearance of God (English)

Toby—God is good (English)

Tyra—God of battle (Scandinavian)

Umika—Goddess (Sanskrit/East Indian)

Uriela—Light of God (Hebrew)

Venus—Goddess of love (Greek)

Vesta—Goddess of the hearth (Latin)

Waldina—God's power (German)

Xannon—Ancient God (American)

Yanichel—Gift of God (Hebrew)

Yessica—God beholds (Spanish)

Yohance—God's gift (African)

Zabel—God is my oath (Spanish)

Zacharee—God has remembered (Hebrew)

Ziraili—Help of God (African)

Zsoka—God is my oath (Hungarian)

• WATER

Boys

Aquarius—The water bearer (Latin)

Atl—Water (Aztec/Nahuatl)

Calder—From the wild water (Celtic/Gaelic)

Chelan—Deep water (Native American)

Dalit—Draw water (Hebrew)

Douglas—Dark water (Celtic/Gaelic)

Ice—Frozen water (American)

Kuval—Water lily (Sanskrit/East Indian)

Minnesota—Sky-colored water (Native American)

Mississippi—Father of waters (Native American)

Misu—Ripples in the water (Native American)

Mizu—Water (Japanese)

Moshe—Drawn out of the water (Hebrew)

Nahuatl—Four waters (Aztec/Nahuatl)

Nebraska—Flat water (Native American)

Nen—Ancient waters (Egyptian)

Qing yuan—Deep water, clear spring (Chinese)

Shui—Water (Chinese)

Troy—Water or foot soldier (Celtic/Gaelic)

Wisconsin—Gathering of waters (French)

Yaxha—Green water (Spanish)

Girls

Amadahy—Forest water (Native American)

Aqua—Water (Latin)

Aquarius—The water bearer (Latin)

Arethusa—The waterer (Greek)

Atl—Water (Aztec/Nahuatl)

Cascada—Waterfall (Spanish)

Cascata—Waterfall (Italian)

Chelan—Deep water (Native American)

Damla—Drop of water (Turkish)

Kenda—Child of clear, cool water (English)

Kendra—Water baby, magical (English)

60

Kiandra—Water baby, magical (English)

Minnesota—Sky-colored water (Native American)

Mississippi—Father of waters (Native American)

Mist—Particles of water (American)

Misu—Ripples in the water (Native American)

Moesha—Drawn out of the water (American)

Nahuatl—Four waters (Aztec/Nahuatl)

Naida—Water nymph (Arabic)

Nebraska—Flat water (Native American)

Niloufer—Water lily (Persian)

Nixie—Water sprite (German)

Qing yuan—Deep water, clear spring (Chinese)

Sevan—Life-giving sweet water (Armenian)

Shasa—Precious water (African)

Shui—Water (Chinese)

Tallulah/Talulah—Leaping water (Native American)

Thuy—Water (Vietnamese)

Troya—Water or foot soldier (Celtic/Gaelic)

Visola—Longings are waterfalls (African)

Wisconsin—Gathering of waters (French)

Yaxha—Green water (Spanish)

• WARRIOR

Boys

Aloysius—Fame warrior (Latin)

Alvar—Elf warrior (English)

Anakin—Warrior (American)

Arnau—Strong warrior (Spanish)

Arvid—Eagle of the woods, brave warrior (Scandinavian)

Caley—Brave warrior (Celtic/Gaelic)

Calhoun—Warrior (Celtic/Gaelic)

Chad/Chadwick—From the warrior's town (English)

Clovis—Famous warrior (French)

Donagh—Brown warrior (Celtic/Gaelic)

Duncan—Dark-skinned warrior (Celtic/Gaelic)

Findlay/Finlay/Finley—Fair warrior (Celtic/Gaelic)

Flannery—Descendant of the red warrior (Celtic/Gaelic)

Gideon—Great warrior (Hebrew)

Guillermo—Strong-willed warrior (Spanish)

Gunnar—Battle warrior (Scandinavian)

Gwilym—Strong-willed warrior (Welsh)

Harvey—Battle warrior (French)

Hervé—Army warrior (French)

Humphrey—Peaceful warrior (English)

Keith—Warrior descending (Celtic/Gaelic)

Khalon—Strong warrior (American)

Lajos—Famous warrior (Hungarian)

Lewis—Famed warrior (English)

Liam—Strong-willed warrior (Celtic/Gaelic)

Lodovico—Famous warrior (Italian)

Loic—Famed warrior (French)

Lou—Famed warrior (German)

Louie/Louis—Famous warrior (English/German)

Ludovic—Famed warrior (French)

Ludwig—Famous warrior (German)

Luigi—Famous warrior (Italian)

Luis—Famous warrior (Spanish)

Marcel—Young warrior (French)

Marcello/Marcellus—Young warrior (Latin)

Mordechai—Warrior (Hebrew)

Murphy—Sea warrior (Celtic/Gaelic)

Onofre—Peace warrior (Spanish)

Oya—Wind warrior goddess (African)

Rider/Ryder—Knight, mounted warrior (English)

Sloan/Sloane—Warrior (Celtic/Gaelic)

Thane—Warrior or landowner (English)

Tupac—Warrior, messenger (Aztec/Nahuatl)

Umberto—Bright warrior (Italian)

Vila—Strong-willed warrior (Hungarian)

Vilmos—Strong-willed warrior (Hungarian)

Wilhelm—Strong-willed warrior (German)

Will/William—Strong-willed warrior (English)

Willem—Strong-willed warrior (Dutch)

Yaotl—Warrior (Aztec/Nahuatl)

Girls

Arvid—Eagle of the woods, brave warrior (Scandinavian)

Caley—Brave warrior (Celtic/Gaelic)

Flannery—Descendant of the red warrior (Celtic/Gaelic)

Gunda—Female warrior (Scandinavian)

Keitha—Female warrior (Celtic/Gaelic)

Kella—Warrior (Celtic/Gaelic)

Louisa/Louise—Famous warrior (English)

Lula/Lulu—Famous warrior (English)

Marcella—Young warrior (Latin)

Mina—Strong-willed warrior (English)

Minna—Strong-willed warrior (German)

Murphy—Sea warrior (Celtic/Gaelic)

Ouida—Famous warrior (French)

Oya—Wind warrior goddess (African)

Rider/Ryder—Knight, mounted warrior (English)

Sloane—Warrior (Celtic/Gaelic)

Thane—Warrior or landowner (English)

Velma—Strong-willed warrior (Greek)

Wilhelmina—Strong-willed warrior (German)

Yaotl—Warrior (Aztec/Nahuatl)

Zelda—Woman warrior (German)

● PEACE

Boys

Absolom—Father is peace (Hebrew)

An—Peace (Chinese)

Arav—Peaceful (Sanskrit/East Indian)

Axel—My father is peace (Scandinavian)

Bem—Peace (African)

Binh—Peaceful (Vietnamese)

Casimir—Destroys peace (Slavic)

Coilin—Young child; peaceful dove (Celtic/Gaelic)

Damir—To give peace (Slavic)

Dembe—Peace (African)

Dinh—Peace, calm (Vietnamese)

Eron—Peace, enlightened (Hebrew)

Fadri—Peace ruler (Rumantsch)

Federico—Peace ruler (Spanish)

Frederick/Fred—Peace ruler (English)

Fritz—Peace ruler (German)

Geoff/Geoffrey—God peace (English)

Godfrey—God peace (English)

Humphrey—Peaceful warrior (English)

Jeff/Jeffery/Jeffrey—God peace (English)

Jerusalem—Heritage of peace (Hebrew)

Miroslav—Peace and glory (Slavic)

Noach/Noah/Noe—Peace, rest (Hebrew)

On—Peace (Chinese)

Onofre—Peace warrior (Spanish)

Pax/Paz—Peace (Latin/Spanish)

Seifer—Victory peace (German)

Shalom—Peace (Hebrew)

Shlomo—His peace (Hebrew)

Sigfried—Victory, peace (German)

Solomon—Peace (Hebrew)

Wilfred—Will peace (English)

Winfred—Peace friend (English)

Xola—Stay in peace (African)

Yasuo—Peaceful one (Japanese)

Zalman—Peaceful (Hebrew)

Girls

An—Peace (Chinese)

Aquene—Peace (Native American)

Axelle—My father is peace (French)

Bem—Peace (African)

Chamomile—Peace, spice (American)

Chesna—Bringing peace, calm (Slavic)

Chessa—Peaceful (Slavic)

Dembe—Peace (African)

Dove—Bird of peace (American)

Ekanta—Solitude, peaceful (Sanskrit/East Indian)

Farica—Peace ruler (German)

Frederica/Fredrica—Peace ruler (English)

Frida/Frieda—Peace (German)

Fritzi—Peace ruler (German)

Gzifa—Peaceful one (African)

Ildri—Fire and peace (Scandinavian)

Iren—Peace (Slavic)

Irene—Peace (Greek)
Irina—Peace (Russian)
Jereni—Peaceful (Slavic)
Jerusalem—Heritage of peace (Hebrew)
Malia—Calm and peaceful (Hawaiian)
Mircea—Peace (Slavic)
Noe—Rest, peace (French)
Orya—Peace (Russian)
Pax/Paz—Peace (Latin/Spanish)
Phalen—Peaceful (Latin)
Salama—Peace, security (Arabic)
Salome—Welcome, peace (Hebrew)
Selam—Peace (African)
Selima—Brings comfort, peace (Hebrew)
Serenity—Peaceful disposition (English)
Shalom—Peace (Hebrew)
Shanti—Peace, calm (Sanskrit/East Indian)
Sheehan—Descendant of the peaceful
    one (Celtic/Gaelic)
Sorina—Peaceful, serene (American)
Winifred—Peace friend (English)
Xola—Stay in peace (African)
Zulema—Peace (Hebrew)

● FLOWER

Boys

Fiorello—Little flower (Italian)
Florian—Flowering (Latin)
Flurin—Flowering (Rumantsch)
Lavender—A purple flowering
    plant (English)
Lotem—Bush of golden flowers (Hebrew)
Nalin—Lotus flower (Sanskrit/East Indian)
Poppy—From the flower (Latin)
Talasi—Cornflower (Native American)

Girls

Aiyana—Flower blossom (African)
Altantsetseg—Golden flower (Mongolian)
Amaranta/Amarante—Flower
    that never fades (Latin)

Anthea—Flowery (Greek)
Aoi—Hollyhock flower (Japanese)
Ardice—Flowering field (Hebrew)
Ayanna—Beautiful flower (African)
Blodwyn—Fair flower (Welsh)
Blossom—Flower, bloom (English)
Bluma—Flower, bloom (Hebrew)
Chameli—Flower (Sanskrit/East Indian)
Cleantha—Famous flower (Greek)
Clover—Meadow flower (English)
Coaxoch—Serpent flower (Aztec/Nahuatl)
Daffodil—Yellow flower (English)
Dahlia—Flower named for
    botanist A. Dahl (Greek)
Daisy—Daisy flower (American)
Diantha/Dianthe—Divine flower (Greek)
Eolande—Violet flower (American)
Fiorella—Little flower (Italian)
Fiorenza—Flower (Italian)
Firenze—Flower, blossom (Hungarian)
Fjola—Flower (Scandinavian)
Fleur—Flower (French)
Flora—Flowering (Latin)
Floramaria—Flower of Mary (Spanish)
Florence—Prosperous, flowering (Latin)
Floria/Floriane—Flowering (Latin)
Florida—Feast of flowers (Spanish)
Flower—Flower (English)
Gardenia—Gardenia flower (English)
Geranium—Geranium flower (English)
Ginata—Flower (Italian)
Hue—Lily flower (Vietnamese)
Huong—Scent of the flower (Vietnamese)
Hyacinth—The flower (Greek)
Iantha/Ianthe—Violet-colored flower (Greek)
Iolanthe—Violet flower (Greek)
Jasmin—Jasmine flower (Persian)
Jessamine—Jasmine flower (French)
Jessenia—Flower (Arabic)
Jola/Jolanda—Violet flower (Slavic)
Jui—Flower (Sanskrit/East Indian)
Kamilia—Camellia flower (Polish)

Keeya—Garden flower (African)
Ketaki—Flower (Sanskrit/East Indian)
Kohana—Little flower (Japanese)
Lavender—A purple flowering plant (English)
Lei—Flower bud (Chinese)
Leiko—Little flower (Hawaiian)
Leilani—Heavenly flower (Hawaiian)
Lily/Lilly/Lillian—Lily flower (English)
Lotus—The flower (Greek)
Lynnea—Flower (Scandinavian)
Magnolia—Flower name (French)
Marigold—Yellow flower (English)
Miki—Flower stalk (Japanese)
Mliss—Flower (Cambodian)
Napua—The flowers (Hawaiian)
Nitza—Bud from a flower (Hebrew)
Nizana—Flower bud (Hebrew)
Ornella—Flowering ash tree (Italian)
Ozanka—Wall germander flower (Slavic)
Palesa—Flower (African)
Pansy—Violet flower (American)
Peony—Flower (Greek)
Petunia—Flower (English)
Philantha—Lover of flowers (Greek)
Poppy—From the flower (Latin)
Posy—Small flower (English)
Quetzalxochitl—Precious flower, queen (Aztec/Nahuatl)
Quynh—Night blooming flower (Vietnamese)
Rose/Rosie—Rose flower (English)
Saffron—Yellow flower (English)
Sen—Lotus flower (Vietnamese)
Sumana—Flower (Sanskrit/East Indian)
Talasi—Cornflower (Native American)
Tansy—Flower (Native American)
Violet—Purple or blue flower (French)
Xochitl—Flower (Aztec/Nahuatl)
Yamka—Budding flower (Native American)
Yoland/Yolanda—Violet flower (French/Spanish)
Zagiri—Flower (Armenian)
Zahara—Flower, most exquisite (Arabic)

Zahrah—Flower, blossom (Arabic)
Zinna/Zinnia—Rayed flower (Latin)
Zubaida/Zubeda—Essence, flower (Arabic)
Zytka—Rose flower (Polish)

● HOPE

Boys

Amil—Hopeful (Arabic)
Day—Light and hope (American)
Themba—Trust, hope, and faith (African)
Umed—Hope (Sanskrit/East Indian)
Umut—Hope (Turkish)
Xi-wang—Hope (Chinese)

Girls

Amal—Hope, expectation (Arabic)
Arrayah—A ray of hope (American)
Asha—Hope or wish (Sanskrit/East Indian)
Day—Light and hope (American)
Elpida—Hope (Greek)
Esperanza—Hope (Spanish)
Hope—Hope (English)
Nadia/Nadie—Hope (Slavic/English)
Nadine—Hope (French)
Nozomi—Hope (Japanese)
Speranza—Hope (Italian)
Themba—Trust, hope, and faith (African)
Umay—Hope (Turkish)
Umut—Hope (Turkish)
Xi-wang—Hope (Chinese)

● PRINCE/PRINCESS

Boys

Amir/Amiri—Prince, rich, cultivated (Arabic)
Brend—Prince (Celtic/Gaelic)
Brendan/Brendon/Brennan—Prince (Celtic/Gaelic)
Kerry—Dark princess (Celtic/Gaelic)
Mael—Chief, prince (French)
Manelin—Prince of princes (Persian)

64

Taifa—Nation, tribe, princedom (Arabic)
Vlad—Prince (Slavic)

Girls

Amira—Princess, rich, cultivated (Arabic)
Armelle—Princess (French)
Begum—Princess (Turkish)
Brenna—Princess (Celtic/Gaelic)
Damita—Baby princess (Spanish)
Farsiris—Princess (Persian)
Gimbya—Princess (African)
Jahzara—Princess (African)
Kerry—Dark princess (Celtic/Gaelic)
Nimeesha—Princess (African)
Panchali—Princess (Sanskrit/East Indian)
Parmida—Princess (Persian)
Sadie—Princess (English)
Sara/Sarah—Princess (Hebrew)
Sarai—My princess (Hebrew)
Sarane—Gracious princess (American)
Sari—Princess (Hebrew)
Sariah—Princess (American)
Sarina—Princess, one who laughs (Hebrew)
Tazanna—Princess (Native American)
Yepa—Winter princess (Native American)
Zara—Princess (English)
Zaria—Princess (American)
Zarita—Princess (Spanish)

• GIFT

Boys

Diara—Gift (Latin)
Donato—A gift (Italian)
Jesse—Gift (Hebrew)
Kirabo—Gift from God (African)
Mace—Gift of God (English)
Makaio—Gift of God (Hawaiian)
Mateo/Matteo—Gift of God (Spanish/
     Italian)
Mateusz—Gift of God (Polish)
Mathis—Gift of God (French)

Matias/Mattias—Gift of God
     (Spanish/Hebrew)
Matt/Matthew—Gift of God (English)
Matteus—Gift of God (American)
Matthias—Gift of God (Greek)
Mattia—Gift of God (Rumantsch)
Nathaniel—Gift of God (Hebrew)
Shiloah—His gift (American)
Shiloh—His gift (Hebrew)
Tedros—Gift of God (African)
Teo—Divine gift (Italian)
Theo/Theodore—Divine gift (Greek)
Thijs—Gift of God (Dutch)
Treat—Special snack or gift (American)
Varen—Gifts (Sanskrit/East Indian)
Yohance—God's gift (African)
Zavad—Gift (Hebrew)
Zebedeo—Gift of God (Spanish)
Zenas—Gift of Zeus (Greek)

Girls

Adia—Gift (Swahili)
Danya—Gift of God (Hebrew)
Diara—Gift (Latin)
Donatella—Beautiful gift (Italian)
Dora/Dore—Gift (Greek)
Doreen—Gift (Celtic/Gaelic)
Dori—Gift (Greek)
Dorielle—Small gift (French)
Dorika—Gift of God (Hungarian)
Dorotea—Gift of God (Spanish)
Dorothy/Dorothea—Gift of God (Greek)
Dory—Gift of God (Greek)
Dot/Dotty—Gift of God (Greek)
Eudora—Excellent gift (Greek)
Eydie—Rich gift (English)
Fedora—God's gift (Russian)
Heba—Gift (Arabic)
Isadora—Gift of Isis (Greek)
Isoke—Satisfying gift from God (African)
Jesse—Gift (Hebrew)
Keona—God's gracious gift (Hawaiian)

Kirabo—Gift from God (African)
Maceo—Gift of God (Spanish)
Makaio—Gift of God (Hawaiian)
Makana—Gift (Hawaiian)
Matana—Gift (Hebrew)
Matat—Gift (Hebrew)
Mateja—Gift of God (Slavic)
Matia/Matias—Gift of God (Spanish)
Mattea—Gift of God (Latin)
Nataniela—Gift of God (Hebrew)
Nita—Gift of God (Spanish)
Pandora—All gifts (Greek)
Shiloh—His gift (Hebrew)
Sian—God's gracious gift (Welsh)
Synnove—Sun gift (Scandinavian)
Tea/Thea—Gift of God (Spanish/Greek)
Theodora—Divine gift (Greek)
Theone—Gift from God (Greek)
Treat—Special snack or gift (American)
Truma—Offering, gift (Hebrew)
Yanichel—Gift of God (Hebrew)
Yohance—God's gift (African)
Zenas—Gift of Zeus (Greek)

• STAR

Boys

Astin—Starlike (French)
Astro—Of the stars (Greek)
Hoshi—Star (Japanese)
Sirius—Dog star (Greek)
Star—Star (American)
Sterling—Starling (English)
Taariq—Morning star (Arabic)
Tarachand—Star (Sanskrit/East Indian)
Tariq—Morning star (Sanskrit/East Indian)
Xing—Star (Chinese)
Xing xing—Twin stars (Chinese)

Girls

Asta—Bright as a star (Latin)
Aster—Star (English)

Astin—Starlike (French)
Astra—From the stars (Greek)
Citlali—Star (Native American)
Danica/Danika—Morning star (Hebrew)
Daw—Stars (Thai)
Estee—Star (French)
Estela/Estella/Estelle—Star
  (Spanish/Spanish/Latin)
Ester/Esther—Star or myrtle
  leaf (Hebrew/Persian)
Estralita—Little star (Spanish)
Estrella—Star (Spanish)
Étoile—Star (French)
Hesper—Evening star (Greek)
Hester—Star (Greek)
Hoshi—Star (Japanese)
Hoshiko—Star (Japanese)
Kochava—Star (Hebrew)
Marianela—Beloved star (Spanish)
Odgerel—Starlight (Mongolian)
Seren—Star (Welsh)
Sidra—Star born (Latin)
Sitara—Starlight (Sanskrit/East Indian)
Star—Star (American)
Stella—Star (Latin)
Tarachand—Star (Sanskrit/East Indian)
Tarika—Star (Sanskrit/East Indian)
Thuraya—Stars and the planets (Arabic)
Trella—Star (Spanish)
Uttara—Royal daughter, star
  (Sanskrit/East Indian)
Xing—Star (Chinese)
Xing xing—Twin stars (Chinese)

• MOON

Boys

Artemis—Goddess of the moon
  and hunt (Greek)
Jericho—Moon city (Greek)
Mahak—Waning of the moon (Arabic)
Meztli—Moon (Aztec/Nahuatl)

65

66

Ming yue—Bright moon (Chinese)

Moon—From the moon (American)

Moon-unit—One that orbits
the moon (American)

Qamar—Moon (Arabic)

Sahar—Moon (Hebrew)

Yamir—Moon (Sanskrit/East Indian)

Yue—Moon (Chinese)

Girls

Artemis—Goddess of the moon
and hunt (Greek)

Aysel—Moon flood (Turkish)

Chandra—Moon (Sanskrit/East Indian)

Channary—Full moon (Cambodian)

Chantrea—Moon (Cambodian)

Crescentia—Crescent-shaped,
moon (German)

Hang—Moon (Vietnamese)

Ilandere—Moon woman (American)

Jocasta—Shining moon (Greek)

Kamaria—Moon (Persian)

Konane—Glow like moonlight (Hawaiian)

Levana—Moon or white (Hebrew)

Luna—The moon (Italian)

Mahdis—Moon-like (Persian)

Mahina—Moon (Hawaiian)

Mahsa—Like the moon (Persian)

Meztli—Moon (Aztec/Nahuatl)

Ming yue—Bright moon (Chinese)

Moon—From the moon (American)

Moon-unit—One that orbits
the moon (American)

Nguyet—Moon (Vietnamese)

Parvani—Full moon (Sanskrit/East Indian)

Qamra—Moon (Greek)

Selena—Moon (Spanish)

Selene—Moon (Greek)

Selina—Moon (English)

Sileny—Moonlight, silence (Slavic)

Sohalia—Moon glow (Sanskrit/East Indian)

Somatra—Greater than the moon
(Sanskrit/East Indian)

Taini—Returning moon (Native
American)

Varali—Moon (Sanskrit/East Indian)

Yue—Moon (Chinese)

• BRAVE

Boys

Alp—Hero, brave (Turkish)

Arvid—Eagle of the woods, brave
warrior (Scandinavian)

Arwan—Brave, courageous (Persian)

Barnard—Brave bear (English)

Benard—Brave bear (French)

Bern—Brave (French)

Bernt—Strong, brave bear (German)

Caley—Brave warrior (Celtic/Gaelic)

Devlin—Brave, fierce (Celtic/Gaelic)

Donnelly—Brave, dark man (Celtic/
Gaelic)

Ellard—Noble and brave (English)

Gellert—Brave with spear (Hungarian)

Gerard—Brave with spear (English)

Gerardo—Spear brave (Spanish)

Hertz—Brave, bold (German)

Howard—Heart brave (English)

Hudd—Brave ruler (English)

Jarah—Boldness, bravery (Arabic)

Jarrett—Spear brave (English)

Jerod—Spear brave (English)

Kabili—Honest, brave (Swahili)

Leonard/Leonardo—Lion brave
(English/Italian)

Lon—Lion brave (English)

Maynard—Brave strength (English)

Nardo—Bear brave (Spanish)

Nuhad—Brave (Arabic)

Prewitt—Brave, valorous (English)

Reynard—Counsel brave (French)

Ricardo—Brave ruler (Spanish)

Richard—Brave ruler (English)

Rico—Brave ruler (Spanish)

Saddam—Brave (Arabic)

Valiant—Brave (English)
Virendra—Brave, noble person
(Sanskrit/East Indian)
Willard—Will brave (English)

Girls

Arvid—Eagle of the woods, brave
warrior (Scandinavian)
Bern—Brave (French)
Bernadette—Brave as a bear (French)
Caley—Brave warrior (Celtic/Gaelic)
Hero—Brave one of the people (Greek)
Jarah—Boldness, bravery (Arabic)
Keena—Brave (Celtic/Gaelic)
Kinga—Bravery in war (Hungarian)
Nuhad—Brave (Arabic)
Sarama—Harshness, bravery (Arabic)
Terrwyn—Fair and brave (Welsh)
Valiant—Brave (English)
Valora—Bravery (American)
Virendra—Brave, noble person
(Sanskrit/East Indian)
Virika—Brave one (Sanskrit/East Indian)

• ANGEL

Boys

Angelito—Little angel (Spanish)
Michelangelo—Archangel Michael (Italian)

Girls

Angeni—Angel (Native American)
Arella—Angel (Hebrew)
Erela—Angel, messenger (Hebrew)
Malaika—Angel (African)
Mariangely—Maria of the
angels (American)
Melangell—Dear angel (Welsh)
Serafina—Seraphim, angel (Latin)
Seraphim—Angel (Latin)
Tangia—The angel (American)
Tevy—Angel (Cambodian)
Tuyen—Angel (Vietnamese)

• SMART

Boys

Aldan—Old, wise (English)
Alvis—Elf wise (English)
Channer—Wise (English)
Clever—Smart one (American)
Cong—Intelligent, clever (Chinese)
Elvis—All wise (Scandinavian)
Hassan—Pious, wise (Arabic)
Kavi—Wise poet (Sanskrit/East Indian)
Lukman—Wise, intelligent (Arabic)
Yi min—Smart (Chinese)
Zeroun—Respected, wise (Armenian)

Girls

Alima—Learned, wise (Arabic)
Channery—Wise (American)
Clever—Smart one (American)
Kavi—Wise poet (Sanskrit/East Indian)
Narissara—Smart woman (Thai)
Prudence—Cautious, intelligent (English)
Ramira—Wise, famous (Spanish)
Savvy—Smart (American)
Tomoko/Tomoyo—Intelligent (Japanese)
Trang—Serious, intelligent (Vietnamese)
Veta—Intelligent (Spanish)
Yi min—Smart (Chinese)
Zahina—Intelligent (Arabic)

• SUN

Boys

Ciro—Of the sun (Italian)
Cyrus—Of the sun (Persian)
Dayton—Bright and sunny town (English)
Diata—Short form of Sundiata (African)
Dinesh—Son of the sun
(Sanskrit/East Indian)
Divakar—Sun (Sanskrit/East Indian)
Divyesh—Sun (Sanskrit/East Indian)
Gandhi—Sun (Sanskrit/East Indian)
Gisli—Ray of sunshine (Scandinavian)

Grian—Sun (Celtic/Gaelic)

Gunesh—The sun (Turkish)

Ilo—Light, joyous, sunshine (African)

Kirit—Shining like the sun
 (Sanskrit/East Indian)

Misae—White sun (Native American)

Naranbaatar—Sun hero (Mongolian)

Ravi—Sun (Sanskrit/East Indian)

Samson—Sun or service (Hebrew)

Shadow—Shade from sun (English)

Sol—Sun (Spanish)

Solaris—Of the sun (Latin)

Stash—Sun's rays (American)

Sunday—Born on Sunday (American)

Suvan—The sun (Sanskrit/East Indian)

Tai yang—Sun (Chinese)

Girls

Alba—Dawn, sunrise (Latin)

Dawn—Sunrise (English)

Donoma—Sight of the sun (Native
 American)

Dysis—Sunset (Greek)

Gayora—Valley of sun (Hebrew)

Gisli—Ray of sunshine (Scandinavian)

Gunesh—The sun (Turkish)

Ha—Sunshine and warmth (Vietnamese)

Helia—Sun (Greek)

Heulwen—Sun blessed, fair (Welsh)

Kalinda—The sun (Sanskrit/East Indian)

Kianga—Sunshine (African)

Kirit—Shining like the sun
 (Sanskrit/East Indian)

Kosuke—Rising sun (Japanese)

Lumina—Sunshine (Slavic)

Marisol—Combination of Maria
 and sol or "sun" (Spanish)

Misae—White sun (Native American)

Nolcha—Sun (Native American)

Nomasonto—Daughter born or conceived
 on Sunday (African)

Shadow—Shade from sun (English)

Sol—Sun (Spanish)

Solaris—Of the sun (Latin)

Soleil—Sun (French)

Sulwyn—Sun blessed, fair (Welsh)

Sunday—Born on Sunday (American)

Sunny—Sunny (English)

Sunshine—Sunshine (English)

Synnove—Sun gift (Scandinavian)

Syrita—Sun (American)

Xia—Glow of the sunrise (Chinese)

Yuuna—Sun plant (Japanese)

• PURE

Boys

Apu—Pure, virtuous, divine
 (Sanskrit/East Indian)

Asho—Pure of heart (Persian)

Azra—Pure (Hebrew)

Cary—Pure (English)

Casta—Pure (Spanish)

Dhaval—White, pure (Sanskrit/East Indian)

Galahad—Pure, noble, and selfless (English)

Jie—Pure (Chinese)

Kasen—Pure (Scandinavian)

Kendis—Pure (American)

Sachet—Pure existence, thought
 (Sanskrit/East Indian)

Yu jie—Pure, beautiful jade (Chinese)

Zaccheus—Pure, clear, bright (Hebrew)

Zakiya—Pure, clear, bright (Hebrew)

Girls

Agnes—Pure (Greek)

Annice—Pure (English)

Annis—Pure (English)

Azra—Pure (Hebrew)

Bimala—Pure (Sanskrit/East Indian)

Cadee—Pure (American)

Cady—Pure (American)

Cailyn/Kaelin—Pure (American)

Caitir—Pure (Celtic/Gaelic)

Caitlin/Caitlyn—Pure (Celtic/
  Gaelic/American)
Carey—Pure (Celtic/Gaelic)
Cary—Pure (English)
Catalin/Catalina—Pure (Spanish)
Catherine—Pure (Greek)
Cathleen—Pure (Celtic/Gaelic)
Catrin—Pure (Welsh)
Glennis—Pure, holy (American)
Glenys—Pure, holy (Celtic/Gaelic)
Glynis—Pure, holy, or valley (Welsh)
Inez—Pure, holy (Spanish)
Jie—Pure (Chinese)
Kaelin—Pure (Celtic/Gaelic)
Kaethe—Pure (German)
Kaia—Pure (Scandinavian)
Kaitlin—Pure (Celtic/Gaelic)
Kaitlyn—Pure (Celtic/Gaelic)
Karen/Karena—Pure (Scandinavian)
Kari—Pure (Scandinavian)
Karida—Pure, loyal (Arabic)
Karin/Karina—Pure (Scandinavian)
Kasen—Pure (Scandinavian)
Kasia—Pure (Polish)
Kat—Pure (English)
Katalin—Pure (Hungarian)
Katarina—Pure (Italian)
Kate—Pure (English)
Katelin/Katelyn—Pure (American)
Katen—Pure (Dutch)
Katerina—Pure (Slavic)
Katharine/Katherine/Kathryn—Pure (Greek)
Kathleen—Pure (Celtic/Gaelic)
Katia—Pure (Slavic)
Katina—Pure (Italian)
Katoka—Pure (Hungarian)
Katrina—Pure (German)
Kaya—Pure (Scandinavian)
Kayla—Pure and beloved (Celtic/Gaelic)
Kayleen—Pure lass (American)
Kendis—Pure (American)
Kera—Pure (Celtic/Gaelic)

Kerryn—Dusky and pure (American)
Kitty—Pure (English)
Nakia—Pure, faithful (Egyptian)
Niesha—Pure (American)
Sachet—Pure existence, thought
  (Sanskrit/East Indian)
Sada—Pure one (Japanese)
Safa—Pure (Arabic)
Sareh—Pure (Persian)
Tahirah—Pure (Arabic)
Trinh—Pure (Vietnamese)
Virginia—Virginal, pure (Latin)
Yu jie—Pure, beautiful jade (Chinese)

• POWER

Boys

Arnaldo—Eagle power (Spanish)
Arnaud—Eagle power (French)
Arnold/Arnoldo—Eagle power
  (German/Spanish)
Kana—Powerful (Japanese)
Kellan/Kellen—Powerful (Celtic/Gaelic)
Li—Pretty, powerful (Chinese)
Medwin—Powerful friend (German)
Montgomery—From the hill of the
  powerful man (English)
Nero—Powerful (Latin)
Onan—Strength, power (Hebrew)
Tiger—Powerful cat, tiger (American)
Ull—Wolf power (German)
Uzi—Power, strength (Hebrew)
Virote—Power (Thai)
Waldo—God's power (English)

Girls

Amandla—Power (African)
Charisma—Personal power, attraction (Greek)
Devi—Goddess of power
  (Sanskrit/East Indian)
Kana—Powerful (Japanese)
Katima—Powerful daughter (American)

Kellyn—Powerful (Celtic/Gaelic)
Keren—Ray, beam or strength, power (Hebrew)
Li—Pretty, powerful (Chinese)
Qadr—Power, fate (Arabic)
Senalda—Victory power (Spanish)
Tiger—Powerful cat, tiger (American)
Ull—Wolf power (German)
Wakanda—Possesses magical powers
    (Native American)
Waldina—God's power (German)
Zaila—Might, power (Arabic)

• BLACK

Boys

Ciaran—Black (Celtic/Gaelic)
Donovan—Brown black (Celtic/Gaelic)
Dwayne—Dark, black (English)
Ferrari—Blacksmith (Italian)
Jett—Jet black (English)
Keir—Black (Celtic/Gaelic)
Kishan—Black (Sanskrit/East Indian)
Kistna—Black (Sanskrit/East Indian)
Krishna—Black (Sanskrit/East Indian)
Melanion—Black (Greek)
Merle—Blackbird (English)
Montenegro—Black mountain (Spanish)
Raven—Blackbird (English)
Siyavash—Black bull (Persian)
Smith—Blacksmith (English)
Temujin—Of iron, blacksmith (Mongolian)

Girls

Braith—Black and white (Welsh)
Ceara/Ciara—Black (Celtic/Gaelic)
Ferrari—Blacksmith (Italian)
Guadalupe—River of black stones (Spanish)
Huyen—Jet black (Vietnamese)
Keir—Black (Celtic/Gaelic)
Keira—Black haired (Celtic/Gaelic)
Kira—Black (Celtic/Gaelic)
Krishna—Black (Sanskrit/East Indian)

Layla/Leila/Leyla—Night, black (Arabic)
Melania/Melanie—Black (Greek)
Melinda—Black and beautiful (American)
Merle—Blackbird (English)
Montsho—Black (African)
Mora—Blackberry (Spanish)
Raven—Blackbird (English)
Sauda—Black, love (Arabic)

• HAPPY/HAPPINESS/JOY

Boys

Asher—Blessed, happy (Hebrew)
Corliss—Happy, free from care (English)
Felix—Happy and prosperous (Latin)
Fisseha—Happiness, joy (African)
Gad—Happiness, luck, fortune (Hebrew)
Gainell—Happy, shiny (American)
Gil, Gilon—Joy (Hebrew)
Hani—Cheerful and happy (Arabic)
Happy—Joyful (American)
Ilo—Light, joyous, sunshine (African)
Jabulani—Be happy (African)
Kaemon—Joyful (Japanese)
Kamin—Joyful (Japanese)
Le—Joy (Chinese)
Leslie—Joy (English)
Lok—Joy (Chinese)
Macario—Happy (Spanish)
Marnin—Causing joy (Hebrew)
Omanand—Joy of Om (Sanskrit/East Indian)
Sanyu—Happiness (Japanese)
Sasson—Joy (Hebrew)
Seeley—Very happy (English)
Simcha—Joy, festivity (Hebrew)
Vidor—Happy (Hungarian)
Yue yan—Happy, beautiful (Chinese)
Zorion—Happy (Portuguese)

Girls

Abbie/Abby—Joy of the father (English)
Abigail—Joy of the father (Hebrew)

Ada—Noble, happy (German)

Adrina—Happiness (Italian)

Agalia—Bright joy (Greek)

Aida—Happy (Italian)

Alegria—Happiness (Spanish)

Aliza—Joyful (Hebrew)

Alize—Joyful (Hebrew)

Allegra—Joy (Latin)

Ananda—Bliss and joy (Sanskrit/East Indian)

Ayoka—One who causes joy (African)

Bayarmaa—Mother of joy (Mongolian)

Beata/Beate—Happy (Latin/German)

Beatrice—Bringer of joy (French)

Beatrix/Beatriz—Bringer of joy (English/Latin)

Betrys—Bringer of joy (Welsh)

Bliss—Perfect joy (English)

Blissany—Full of grace and joy (American)

Blithe/Blythe—Happy (English)

Bly—Gentle, happy (English)

Content—Satisfied, happy (American)

Corliss—Happy, free from care (English)

Deepnita—Light and happiness (Sanskrit/East Indian)

Diza—Joyous (Hebrew)

Dreama—Joyous music (American)

Elata—Happy (Latin)

Eowyn—Horse of joy (English)

Euphrosyne—Full of joy (Greek)

Farah—Joy (Arabic)

Felice—Fortunate, happy (Latin)

Felicia/Felicity—Happiness (Latin)

Felician—Happiness (Hungarian)

Frieda—Peace, joy (German)

Gail/Gayle—Joy of the father (English)

Gay—Merry, happy (English)

Gaynell—Happy, shiny (American)

Gili—My joy, rejoice (Hebrew)

Gioia—Happiness (Italian)

Hanh—Apricot tree, happiness (Vietnamese)

Harsha—Happiness (Sanskrit/East Indian)

Hedva—Joy (Hebrew)

Joie—Joy (French)

Jovia—Happy (Latin)

Jovianne—Happy (French)

Jovie—Joyful (American)

Jovita—Happy (Latin)

Joy—Happiness (Latin)

Joylyn—Combination of Joy and Lynn (American)

Jubilee—Joy, celebration (Hebrew)

Kioko—Meets world with happiness (Japanese)

Latisha—Joy (American)

Le—Joy (Chinese)

Lesley/Leslie—Joy (English)

Leticia/Letitia—Joy (Spanish/Latin)

Licia—Happy (Spanish)

Luana—Enjoyment (Hawaiian)

Lutisha—Joy (American)

Macaria—Happy (Greek)

Marnina—Causing joy (Hebrew)

Merridy—Happy song (American)

Merry—Cheerful, happy (English)

Nanda—Full of joy, achiever (Sanskrit/East Indian)

Rena—Joy (Hebrew)

Ronli—Joy is mine (Hebrew)

Rowena—Fame joy (English)

Sanyu—Happiness (Japanese)

Saran—Joy (African)

Sasson—Joy (Hebrew)

Seeley—Very happy (English)

Shawdi—Joy (Persian)

Simcha—Joy, festivity (Hebrew)

Suruchi—Great delight, happiness (Sanskrit/East Indian)

Tisha—Joy (American)

Trixie—Bringer of joy (English)

Xin qian—Happy, beautiful (Chinese)

Yi—Happy (Chinese)

Yi ze—Happy, shiny as a pearl (Chinese)

Yue yan—Happy, beautiful (Chinese)

• WOLF

Boys

Adolf/Adolph—Noble wolf (German)

Adolfo—Noble wolf (Italian)

Conan—Hound, wolf (Celtic/Gaelic)

Errol—Boar wolf (English)

Faolan—Wolf (Celtic/Gaelic)

Leavitt—Wolf cub (English)

Lobo—Wolf (Spanish)

Lowell—Little wolf (English)

Mingan—Grey wolf (Native American)

Rafe—Wolf counsel (English)

Ralph—Wolf counsel (English)

Randall—Shield wolf (English)

Randolph—Shield wolf (English)

Raúl—Wolf counsel (Spanish)

Redell—Wolf counsel (American)

Rolf—Famous wolf (Scandinavian)

Rollin—Wolf counsel (English)

Rollo—Famous wolf (English)

Rudolph—Famous wolf (English)

Rudy—Famous wolf (American)

Seath—Wolfish (Celtic/Gaelic)

Syaoran—Little wolf (Chinese)

Torolf—Thor's wolf (Scandinavian)

Ulf—Wolf (German)

Ull—Wolf power (German)

Ulmer—Famous wolf (English)

Ulric—Wolf ruler (English)

Velvel—Wolf (Hebrew)

Wolfe—The wolf (English)

Wolfgang—Wolf way (English)

Zev—Wolf (Hebrew)

Zevi—My wolf (Hebrew)

Girls

Lupe—From the river of the wolf (Spanish)

Lupita—From the river of the wolf (Spanish)

Redell—Wolf counsel (American)

Rollin—Wolf counsel (English)

Seath—Wolfish (Celtic/Gaelic)

Tala—Wolf (Native American)

Ulf—Wolf (German)

Ull—Wolf power (German)

NAME STORMING: When you do your name research, make sure you use an accurate source like BabyNames.com. Many other baby name books and websites contain incorrect information that has been perpetuated by replicating other bad sources. Many people submit their own names to websites with wishful meanings like "gorgeous one" or "brave warrior," so choose a source that you know is historically accurate. For a list of accurate sources we recommend, see chapter 16.

14

Alphabetical Listing of Names

Here is an alphabetical list of names for you to browse and consider, with special information collected from our website users. Aside from the name, sex, meaning, and origin, you will also see an average rating, characteristics, and "also likes"—other favorite names by people who liked that particular name. The ratings are calculated on a scale from 1 to 5; ★ = Not My Style at All, ★★ = Don't Like It, ★★★ = It's OK, ★★★★ = Like It, and ★★★★★ = Love It. The characteristics listed by each name indicate the top five traits that people identify with the name, in order. Some characteristics may conflict with each other, which is normal since people identify different traits with the same name, depending on their life experiences and people they have met.

Aadi *(French)* ♀   RATING: ★★
Beginning
  People think of Aadi as exotic, creative, pretty, funny, cool
  People who like the name Aadi also like Aaralyn, Aaliyah, Ada, Adia, Adeline, Abbie, Adie, Adalia, Abeni, Abrianna

Aaliyah *(Arabic)* ♀   RATING: ★★★★
High, sublime—Also spelled Aliyah; Aaliyah, singer
  People think of Aaliyah as pretty, popular, intelligent, sexy, funny
  People who like the name Aaliyah also like Adriana, Abigail, Abrianna, Aaralyn, Arianna, Alyssa, Ava, Alexia, Destiny, Faith

Aaralyn *(American)* ♀   RATING: ★★★
Combination of Aaron and Lyn
  People think of Aaralyn as pretty, creative, intelligent, elegant, exotic

People who like the name Aaralyn also like Abrianna, Aaliyah, Adriana, Abigail, Ashlyn, Arianna, Ava, Aeryn, Cailyn, Kaelyn

Aaron *(Hebrew)* ♂   RATING: ★★★
Exalted, strong—In the Bible, the brother of Moses; also spelled Arron; Aaron Carter, singer
  People think of Aaron as handsome, funny, intelligent, cool, caring
  People who like the name Aaron also like Adam, Aiden, Ethan, Andrew, Alexander, Caleb, Benjamin, Jacob, Anthony, Nathan

Aba *(Turkish)* ♂   RATING: ★★☆
Father
  People think of Aba as aggressive, loser, weird, lazy, big
  People who like the name Aba also like Aaron, Abel, Abba, Abdullah, Abdukrahman, Abe, Abdulrahman, Abbott, Abner, Abdulkareem

Abarne *(Spanish)* ♀   RATING: ★★
Branches—Basque origin
> People think of Abarne as aggressive, exotic, funny, pretty, popular
> People who like the name Abarne also like Aaralyn, Adalira, Aadi, Abrienda, Adalia, Abeni, Aaliyah, Abbie, Acacia, Abril

Abba *(Hebrew)* ♂   RATING: ★☆
Father—Also a '70s music group
> People think of Abba as creative, weird, criminal, nerdy, religious
> People who like the name Abba also like Aaron, Abie, Abbott, Abner, Abel, Adam, Abe, Abdullah, Abraham, Aden

Abbey *(English)* ♀   RATING: ★★★☆
Nunnery—Short for Abigail
> People think of Abbey as stuck-up, criminal, loser, lazy, slow
> People who like the name Abbey also like Emma, Lily, Grace, Hannah, Elizabeth, Ava, Olivia, Isabella, Abigail, Abbie

Abbie *(English)* ♀♂   RATING: ★★★☆
Joy of the father—Short for Abraham or Abigail; Abbie Hoffman, political activist
> People think of Abbie as pretty, funny, caring, popular, young
> People who like the name Abbie also like Abigail, Ava, Emma, Amber, Aaliyah, Adriana, Aimee, Hannah, Alexa, Chloe

Abbott *(English)* ♂   RATING: ★★★
Abbot—Bud Abbott, part of comedy duo Abbott and Costello; George Abbott, Broadway producer
> People think of Abbott as intelligent, handsome, caring, sexy, funny
> People who like the name Abbott also like Aiden, Aaron, Adam, Aden, Abel, Asher, Adrian, Andrew, Alexander, Adair

Abby *(English)* ♀♂   RATING: ★★★☆
Joy of the father—Short for Abigail or Abraham
> People think of Abby as pretty, funny, caring, young, creative
> People who like the name Abby also like Bailey, Addison, Alexis, Madison, Brooke, Avery, Ashley, Aidan, Ally, Aubrey

Abdukrahman *(Arabic)* ♂   RATING: ★★★
Servant of the most gracious God—Variation of Abdulrahman
> People think of Abdukrahman as loser, weird, nerdy, aggressive, lazy
> People who like the name Abdukrahman also like Abdulkareem, Abdullah, Abdulrahman, Abraham, Aaron, Abel, Abbott, Abner, Aden, Abe

Abdulkareem *(Arabic)* ♂   RATING: ★☆
Servant of the most generous God—Abdul Kareem Jabbar, basketball player
> People think of Abdulkareem as aggressive, leader, religious, powerful, intelligent

> People who like the name Abdulkareem also like Abdukrahman, Abdulrahman, Abdullah, Abbott, Aaron, Abel, Abraham, Ace, Abe, Abram

Abdullah *(Arabic)* ♂   RATING: ★★★
Servant of Allah
> People think of Abdullah as religious, powerful, handsome, intelligent, popular
> People who like the name Abdullah also like Abdukrahman, Abdulrahman, Abdulkareem, Abel, Aaron, Abe, Abbott, Adam, Abraham, Abner

Abdulrahman *(Arabic)* ♂   RATING: ★★★
Servant of the most gracious God
> People think of Abdulrahman as exotic, aggressive, powerful, popular, leader
> People who like the name Abdulrahman also like Abdukrahman, Abdulkareem, Abdullah, Abel, Abraham, Aaron, Abe, Abbott, Abram, Abner

Abe *(English)* ♂   RATING: ★★★
Father of nations—Short for Abraham; Abe Vigoda, actor; "Honest Abe" Abraham Lincoln, U.S. president
> People think of Abe as intelligent, caring, trustworthy, funny, old-fashioned
> People who like the name Abe also like Aaron, Aden, Adam, Ace, Abel, Abraham, Aiden, Abram, Abbott, Andrew

Abel *(Hebrew)* ♂   RATING: ★★★☆
A breath—In the Bible, the brother of Cain
> People think of Abel as cool, intelligent, handsome, funny, caring
> People who like the name Abel also like Aaron, Adam, Aden, Aiden, Adrian, Isaac, Alexander, Gabriel, Abraham, Caleb

Abeni *(African)* ♀   RATING: ★★★
Girl prayed for—Yoruba origin
> People think of Abeni as pretty, exotic, funny, creative, caring
> People who like the name Abeni also like Aaralyn, Aaliyah, Abrianna, Adalia, Adia, Abigail, Adara, Adamma, Abbie, Aadi

Abhay *(Sanskrit/East Indian)* ♂   RATING: ★★☆
Fearless
> People think of Abhay as sexy, creative, popular, powerful, aggressive
> People who like the name Abhay also like Aden, Adarsh, Abel, Ajay, Adit, Aaron, Adish, Adair, Abner, Adam

Abia *(Arabic)* ♀   RATING: ★★
Great
> People think of Abia as pretty, intelligent, exotic, caring, funny
> People who like the name Abia also like Aaliyah, Adia, Adara, Abeni, Aaralyn, Aadi, Adalia, Abbie, Abigail, Ada

Abiba *(African)* ♀   RATING: ★★☆
The beloved one—North African origin
> People think of Abiba as sexy, pretty, lazy, intelligent, quiet

People who like the name Abiba also like Abeni, Adamma, Abia, Adalia, Aaliyah, Adila, Abigail, Aadi, Ada, Adia

Abie (*English*) ♂   RATING: ★★★
Father of a nation—Variation of Abraham
People think of Abie as boy next door, big, cool, popular, winner
People who like the name Abie also like Aaron, Adam, Aden, Abe, Ace, Abel, Abram, Aiden, Alexander, Abraham

Abigail (*Hebrew*) ♀   RATING: ★★★☆
Joy of the Father—Abigail Adams, first lady; Abigail Breslin, actress; Abigail Van Buren, columnist
People think of Abigail as pretty, funny, intelligent, caring, creative
People who like the name Abigail also like Hannah, Emma, Ava, Isabella, Olivia, Grace, Chloe, Amelia, Gabrielle, Audrey

Abner (*Hebrew*) ♂   RATING: ★★★
Father of light
People think of Abner as trustworthy, intelligent, handsome, leader, powerful
People who like the name Abner also like Aaron, Aden, Abel, Abbott, Ace, Adam, Aiden, Abraham, Abe, Abram

Abra (*Hebrew*) ♀   RATING: ★★
Mother of nations—Feminine form of Abraham
People think of Abra as intelligent, caring, funny, pretty, trustworthy
People who like the name Abra also like Abigail, Abrianna, Adara, Abbie, Aaliyah, Aaralyn, Adamina, Abeni, Ada, Adin

Abraham (*Hebrew*) ♂   RATING: ★★
Father of nations—Abraham Lincoln, U.S. president
People think of Abraham as intelligent, handsome, caring, funny, cool
People who like the name Abraham also like Adam, Aaron, Alexander, Gabriel, Andrew, Benjamin, Elijah, Abel, Isaac, Jacob

Abram (*Hebrew*) ♂   RATING: ★★
High Father—Short for Abiyram
People think of Abram as handsome, intelligent, leader, powerful, caring
People who like the name Abram also like Aden, Aaron, Aiden, Adam, Abel, Abraham, Noah, Gabriel, Caleb, Alexander

Abrianna (*American*) ♀   RATING: ★★★★
Combination of Abbie and Brianna, or Abra and Anna
People think of Abrianna as pretty, creative, intelligent, popular, funny
People who like the name Abrianna also like Adriana, Abigail, Aaralyn, Aaliyah, Arianna, Aubrianna, Ariana, Isabella, Alana, Alexa

Abrienda (*Spanish*) ♀   RATING: ★★★
Opening
People think of Abrienda as pretty, creative, intelligent, exotic, funny
People who like the name Abrienda also like Abrianna, Aaralyn, Abigail, Adriana, Adalia, Adalira, Aaliyah, Adeline, Abril, Aceline

Abril (*Latin*) ♀   RATING: ★★★
April
People think of Abril as pretty, cool, creative, popular, caring
People who like the name Abril also like Abigail, Abrianna, Aaliyah, Abbie, Adriana, Adalia, Aaralyn, Adora, Ada, Adeline

Absolom (*Hebrew*) ♂   RATING: ★★★
Father is peace
People think of Absolom as religious, handsome, nerdy, leader, cool
People who like the name Absolom also like Abner, Aaron, Adam, Adair, Aden, Abraham, Abe, Ace, Abram, Adonis

Abu (*African*) ♂   RATING: ★☆
Nobility—Western African origin
People think of Abu as funny, handsome, creative, popular, intelligent
People who like the name Abu also like Abel, Ace, Abner, Adam, Aden, Aaron, Abraham, Adair, Abram, Acton

Acacia (*Greek*) ♀   RATING: ★★☆
Thorny tree—Also a fraternity name and plant name
People think of Acacia as pretty, creative, intelligent, caring, exotic
People who like the name Acacia also like Aaralyn, Abigail, Accalia, Aaliyah, Aurora, Adalia, Adriana, Abrianna, Adrienne, Ava

Accalia (*Greek*) ♀   RATING: ★★★☆
In Greek mythology, the foster mother of Romulus and Remus, founders of Rome
People think of Accalia as exotic, sexy, pretty, powerful, artsy
People who like the name Accalia also like Acacia, Aaralyn, Adalia, Abrianna, Aaliyah, Aceline, Adalira, Adara, Adelaide, Aeryn

Ace (*Latin*) ♂   RATING: ★★★☆
One, ace—*Ace Ventura*, movie and character played by Jim Carrey; Ace Young, singer
People think of Ace as cool, handsome, popular, intelligent, funny
People who like the name Ace also like Aiden, Adam, Aaron, Aden, Adrian, Alexander, Andrew, Anthony, Caleb, Chase

Aceline (*French*) ♀   RATING: ★★★☆
Noble at birth
People think of Aceline as elegant, pretty, intelligent, exotic, artsy

75

People who like the name Aceline also like Adeline, Abrianna, Adalia, Aaralyn, Adalira, Adriana, Adelaide, Aaliyah, Accalia, Aislin

Acton *(English)* ♂ RATING: ★★★
From the oak tree settlement
People think of Acton as creative, powerful, trendy, intelligent, sexy
People who like the name Acton also like Aiden, Aden, Adam, Adair, Ace, Aaron, Adrian, Abbott, Anson, Alexander

Ada *(German)* ♀ RATING: ★★★
Noble, happy—Ada Byron, first computer programmer
People think of Ada as pretty, intelligent, caring, funny, creative
People who like the name Ada also like Ava, Abigail, Audrey, Amelia, Eva, Ella, Adelaide, Adia, Bella, Adalia

Adah *(Hebrew)* ♀ RATING: ★★★
Adornment
People think of Adah as pretty, intelligent, creative, trustworthy, caring
People who like the name Adah also like Ada, Abigail, Adalia, Ava, Adara, Aaliyah, Adia, Adela, Aida, Aaralyn

Adahy *(Native American)* ♂ RATING: ★★★
Timber/woods—Cherokee origin; variation of Adohi
People think of Adahy as pretty, caring, artsy, creative, energetic
People who like the name Adahy also like Abbott, Abie, Baxter, Jett, Nicholas, Agostino, Abel, Bastien, Jiro, Noah

Adair *(English)* ♂ RATING: ★★★☆
Noble spear—Scottish variation of Edgar
People think of Adair as intelligent, caring, artsy, funny, elegant
People who like the name Adair also like Aiden, Aden, Alexander, Adrian, Adam, Asher, Aaron, Ace, Alastair, Alden

Adalia *(German)* ♀ RATING: ★★★★
Noble
People think of Adalia as pretty, elegant, exotic, caring, intelligent
People who like the name Adalia also like Abigail, Adriana, Abrianna, Aaralyn, Aaliyah, Adeline, Adela, Adelaide, Ada, Alaina

Adalira *(Spanish)* ♀ RATING: ★★★★
Noble—Variation of Adela
People think of Adalira as pretty, exotic, intelligent, girl next door, elegant
People who like the name Adalira also like Adalia, Aaralyn, Aceline, Abrianna, Aeryn, Adara, Adriana, Aderyn, Adora, Adeline

Adam *(Hebrew)* ♂ RATING: ★★★
Of the Earth—In the Bible, the first created man; Adam Ant, musician; Adam Brody, actor; Adam Sandler, actor; Adam West, actor
People think of Adam as handsome, funny, intelligent, caring, cool

People who like the name Adam also like Aaron, Andrew, Ethan, Benjamin, Aiden, Alexander, Jacob, Caleb, Matthew, Anthony

Adamina *(Hebrew)* ♀ RATING: ★★
Of the Earth—Feminine form of Adam
People think of Adamina as pretty, intelligent, exotic, elegant, popular
People who like the name Adamina also like Abrianna, Adara, Adalia, Aaliyah, Aaralyn, Adina, Adalira, Abigail, Adriana, Aceline

Adamma *(African)* ♀ RATING: ★★★
Beautiful girl—Ibo origin
People think of Adamma as pretty, sexy, popular, elegant, caring
People who like the name Adamma also like Adora, Abeni, Adara, Adia, Adalia, Aaralyn, Abrianna, Aaliyah, Adrina, Adina

Adara *(Hebrew)* ♀ RATING: ★★★
Exalted, praised
People think of Adara as pretty, exotic, intelligent, elegant, creative
People who like the name Adara also like Adalia, Abigail, Aaralyn, Adriana, Abrianna, Adora, Adeline, Adele, Aaliyah, Aurora

Adarsh *(Sanskrit/East Indian)* ♂ RATING: ★★★
An ideal
People think of Adarsh as trustworthy, intelligent, wealthy, untrustworthy, aggressive
People who like the name Adarsh also like Adit, Ajay, Adish, Ashwin, Amish, Abhay, Aaron, Adair, Adam, Alagan

Addison *(English)* ♀♂ RATING: ★★★★
Child of Adam
People think of Addison as intelligent, pretty, popular, caring, funny
People who like the name Addison also like Avery, Caden, Aidan, Madison, Bailey, Hayden, Riley, Logan, Cadence, Brayden

Addo *(African)* ♀ RATING: ★★★
King of the road—Ghanaian origin
People think of Addo as ethnic, exotic, poor, aggressive, lazy
People who like the name Addo also like Adalia, Adelle, Adia, Adara, Adamma, Abeni, Adeline, Abigail, Adie, Accalia

Ade *(African)* ♂ RATING: ★★
Crown, royal—Also an English nickname for Adrian
People think of Ade as cool, funny, handsome, energetic, intelligent
People who like the name Ade also like Aden, Ace, Adam, Aaron, Aiden, Abel, Adair, Abe, Adem, Adli

Adel *(German)* ♀ RATING: ★★★☆
Noble, kind—Variation of Adele; also Hebrew name meaning God is eternal
People think of Adel as caring, creative, trustworthy, cool, intelligent

People who like the name Adel also like Abigail, Ada, Adela, Adeline, Adalia, Abbie, Adelle, Adele, Adelaide, Alana

Adela *(German)* ♀   RATING: ★★☆
Noble—Short for Adelaide
People think of Adela as pretty, caring, intelligent, young, funny
People who like the name Adela also like Adalia, Abigail, Adeline, Adele, Adelaide, Ada, Alana, Adriana, Adelle, Ava

Adelaide *(German)* ♀   RATING: ★★★★
Of a noble kin—Also a city in Australia
People think of Adelaide as pretty, intelligent, elegant, creative, caring
People who like the name Adelaide also like Abigail, Adeline, Amelia, Ava, Audrey, Adele, Adrienne, Aurora, Adriana, Adalia

Adele *(German)* ♀   RATING: ★★★★
Noble, kind
People think of Adele as pretty, caring, intelligent, creative, funny
People who like the name Adele also like Abigail, Adelaide, Ava, Amelia, Adeline, Chloe, Audrey, Adelle, Adela, Alana

Adelheid *(German)* ♀   RATING: ★★☆
Of noble kin—Variation of Adelaide
People think of Adelheid as sexy
People who like the name Adelheid also like Crystal, Aurora, Arielle, Arabella, Adele, Siobhan, Tess, Freja, Iona, Isla

Adelie *(French)* ♀   RATING: ★★★☆
Noble
People think of Adelie as pretty, elegant, intelligent, caring, creative
People who like the name Adelie also like Adeline, Adalia, Adelaide, Aaralyn, Abigail, Adelle, Adele, Abbie, Abrianna, Adela

Adelina *(Spanish)* ♀   RATING: ★★★☆
Noble
People think of Adelina as pretty, caring, funny, cool, creative
People who like the name Adelina also like Adeline, Aaliyah, Adriana, Abigail, Adalia, Amelia, Adrianna, Adela, Adrina, Aliana

Adeline *(English)* ♀   RATING: ★★★★
Noble
People think of Adeline as pretty, intelligent, creative, elegant, caring
People who like the name Adeline also like Abigail, Adelaide, Ava, Amelia, Audrey, Adrienne, Adriana, Abrianna, Bella, Annabelle

Adelio *(Spanish)* ♂   RATING: ★★★
Noble
People think of Adelio as ethnic, intelligent, powerful, leader, handsome

People who like the name Adelio also like Ace, Aden, Adrian, Adair, Aaron, Abel, Alejandro, Adriano, Adonis, Adam

Adelle *(German)* ♀   RATING: ★★★★
Noble, kind
People think of Adelle as pretty, caring, elegant, funny, creative
People who like the name Adelle also like Abigail, Adeline, Adelaide, Adele, Ava, Audrey, Adalia, Amelia, Adrienne, Ada

Adelphie *(Greek)* ♀   RATING: ★★★
Dearest sister
People think of Adelphie as exotic, pretty, trustworthy, elegant, creative
People who like the name Adelphie also like Abigail, Adelaide, Adia, Adara, Adelina, Adina, Aceline, Adalia, Aderes, Aderyn

Adem *(American)* ♂   RATING: ★★★☆
Of the Earth—Variation of Adam
People think of Adem as cool, energetic, handsome, aggressive, leader
People who like the name Adem also like Aden, Adam, Aiden, Adrian, Aaron, Adair, Abel, Ace, Alexander, Acton

Aden *(Celtic/Gaelic)* ♂   RATING: ★★★★
Little fire—Variation of Aidan; also a region in Southern Yemen
People think of Aden as handsome, intelligent, popular, creative, energetic
People who like the name Aden also like Aiden, Ethan, Caleb, Kaden, Braden, Aaron, Adam, Alexander, Adrian, Ian

Adena *(Hebrew)* ♀   RATING: ★★★
Variation of Adina
People think of Adena as intelligent, pretty, caring, creative, popular
People who like the name Adena also like Abigail, Adina, Adeline, Adara, Aaliyah, Aaralyn, Adalia, Adel, Alaina, Adrienne

Adeola *(African)* ♀   RATING: ★★
Crown has honor—Nigerian origin
People think of Adeola as intelligent, popular, funny, pretty, caring
People who like the name Adeola also like Adalia, Aderes, Aaralyn, Adara, Adila, Adalira, Aderyn, Abeni, Aceline, Adamma

Aderes *(Hebrew)* ♀   RATING: ★★★☆
Protector
People think of Aderes as powerful, pretty, intelligent, exotic, trustworthy
People who like the name Aderes also like Aderyn, Adara, Adalia, Aaralyn, Abrianna, Adia, Aceline, Adina, Acacia, Accalia

78

Aderyn *(Welsh)* ♀   RATING: ★★★☆
Bird
  People think of Aderyn as pretty, creative, intelligent,
  elegant, energetic
  People who like the name Aderyn also like Aeryn,
  Aaralyn, Aelwen, Adara, Adriana, Adalia, Adeline,
  Abigail, Adelaide, Aislin

Adia *(Swahili)* ♀   RATING: ★★★★
Gift—Also a song by Sarah McLachlan
  People think of Adia as pretty, creative, intelligent, car-
  ing, artsy
  People who like the name Adia also like Ava, Abigail,
  Ada, Adriana, Aria, Amaya, Audrey, Aaralyn, Adalia,
  Anya

Adie *(English)* ♀   RATING: ★★★★
Noble—Short for Ada or Adele
  People think of Adie as pretty, funny, intelligent, popu-
  lar, young
  People who like the name Adie also like Ava, Abbie,
  Abigail, Adeline, Adia, Ady, Ada, Alexa, Audrey, Adriana

Adiel *(Hebrew)* ♀♂   RATING: ★★★
God's ornament
  People think of Adiel as intelligent, creative, religious,
  leader, cool
  People who like the name Adiel also like Adriel,
  Addison, Ariel, Aidan, Azriel, Amiel, Abby, Aindrea,
  Adria, Afton

Adila *(Arabic)* ♀   RATING: ★★★☆
Just, fair
  People think of Adila as pretty, leader, creative, funny,
  young
  People who like the name Adila also like Adalia, Adia,
  Abeni, Aaliyah, Aaralyn, Adeline, Adina, Adela, Adara,
  Ada

Adin *(Hebrew)* ♀   RATING: ★★★★
Beautiful, adorned—Feminine form of Aden
  People think of Adin as creative, cool, trustworthy,
  leader, energetic
  People who like the name Adin also like Abigail, Ava,
  Adia, Aaralyn, Adriana, Abrianna, Adina, Aaliyah, Ada,
  Abbie

Adina *(Hebrew)* ♀   RATING: ★★★★
Noble, delicate
  People think of Adina as pretty, intelligent, funny, cre-
  ative, cool
  People who like the name Adina also like Abigail,
  Adriana, Aaliyah, Adalia, Alana, Alaina, Adia, Abrianna,
  Adrina, Aaralyn

Adish *(Persian)* ♂   RATING: ★★
Fire
  People think of Adish as handsome, popular, young,
  sexy, leader
  People who like the name Adish also like Aden, Aiden,
  Aaron, Abel, Adam, Adarsh, Adit, Adelio, Adonis, Ace

Adit *(Sanskrit/East Indian)* ♂   RATING: ★★★
From the beginning
  People think of Adit as intelligent, energetic, cool,
  aggressive, popular
  People who like the name Adit also like Adarsh, Ashwin,
  Adish, Amish, Arav, Arnav, Ajay, Aaron, Atish, Ade

Adita *(Sanskrit/East Indian)* ♀   RATING: ★★★
From the beginning—Feminine form of Adit
  People think of Adita as pretty, sexy, funny, young, artsy
  People who like the name Adita also like Adina, Adeline,
  Adila, Adalia, Adara, Anaya, Adelaide, Adela, Adah, Ada

Adlai *(Hebrew)* ♂   RATING: ★★
God is just—Variation of Adaliah; Adlai Stevenson,
politician
  People think of Adlai as leader, intelligent, handsome,
  energetic, quiet
  People who like the name Adlai also like Aden, Abel,
  Adair, Aaron, Adli, Admon, Abram, Adam, Adonai, Adish

Adli *(Arabic)* ♂   RATING: ★★
Honest—Short for Adlai
  People think of Adli as intelligent, funny, caring, leader,
  trustworthy
  People who like the name Adli also like Aden, Adlai,
  Adam, Adair, Aaron, Abram, Abraham, Ade, Abner,
  Admon

Admon *(Hebrew)* ♂   RATING: ★★☆
Red
  People think of Admon as weird, intelligent, unpopular,
  exotic, religious
  People who like the name Admon also like Aden, Aaron,
  Aiden, Adam, Adair, Adonis, Abner, Abel, Ace, Adlai

Adohi *(Native American)* ♂   RATING: ★★☆
From the woods—Cherokee origin
  People think of Adohi as powerful, young, energetic
  People who like the name Adohi also like Adolfo, Adolf,
  Adolph, Aaron, Yaholo, Casper, Barny, Oleg, Zan, Viho

Adolf *(German)* ♂   RATING: ★★★
Noble wolf—Adolf Cluss, architect; Adolf Count Graf
von Nassau, German king; Adolf von Menzel, artist;
Adolf Hitler, Nazi dictator
  People think of Adolf as aggressive, criminal, powerful,
  leader, untrustworthy
  People who like the name Adolf also like Aden, Aaron,
  Ace, Adolph, Adolfo, Adam, Aiden, Abel, Abraham,
  Adonis

Adolfo *(Italian)* ♂   RATING: ★★★
Noble wolf
  People think of Adolfo as aggressive, caring, artsy, cool,
  big
  People who like the name Adolfo also like Adam,
  Aaron, Adrian, Adolph, Alfonso, Ace, Adelio, Agostino,
  Abraham, Abner

Adolph (German) ♂　　　RATING: ★★
Noble wolf—Adolphe Menjou, actor
  People think of Adolph as aggressive, criminal, untrustworthy, powerful, leader
  People who like the name Adolph also like Adolfo, Aaron, Adam, Ace, Aden, Adolf, Abner, Abel, Albert, Abraham

Adonai (Hebrew) ♂　　　RATING: ★★
God is my Lord
  People think of Adonai as trustworthy, funny, religious, powerful, caring
  People who like the name Adonai also like Aaron, Aiden, Aden, Alexander, Adonis, Alijah, Adair, Adrian, Adam, Abraham

Adoncia (Spanish) ♀　　　RATING: ★★★
Sweet
  People think of Adoncia as pretty, sexy, powerful, aggressive, intelligent
  People who like the name Adoncia also like Adonica, Adriana, Amorina, Abrienda, Abarne, Adalira, Adelphie, Adina, Aaliyah, Aletta

Adonia (Hebrew) ♀　　　RATING: ★★
God is my Lord
  People think of Adonia as pretty, intelligent, caring, exotic, sexy
  People who like the name Adonia also like Abrianna, Abigail, Adriana, Adrina, Adora, Aaralyn, Adara, Adalia, Adina, Aaliyah

Adonica (American) ♀　　　RATING: ★★★
Combination of Adam and Monica
  People think of Adonica as pretty, leader, intelligent, trustworthy, funny
  People who like the name Adonica also like Abrianna, Aaliyah, Adriana, Aaralyn, Adalia, Adrienne, Adora, Adonia, Alecia, Adina

Adonis (Greek) ♂　　　RATING: ★★
Lord—Greek god of everlasting youth and beauty
  People think of Adonis as handsome, sexy, powerful, leader, popular
  People who like the name Adonis also like Aiden, Adrian, Alexander, Aden, Aaron, Ace, Adam, Adair, Andrew, Anthony

Adora (Latin) ♀　　　RATING: ★★☆
Beloved one
  People think of Adora as pretty, caring, quiet, intelligent, creative
  People who like the name Adora also like Aurora, Adriana, Abigail, Adalia, Adrina, Ava, Bella, Adara, Abrianna, Amora

Adorjan (Hungarian) ♂　　　RATING: ★★☆
Person from Hadria (Northern Italy)—Variation of Adrian
  People think of Adorjan as weird, intelligent, creative, ethnic, funny

People who like the name Adorjan also like Adair, Aiden, Adish, Admon, Adolfo, Adonis, Adrian, Aimon, Adli, Acton

Adria (Greek) ♀♂　　　RATING: ★★★★
Person from Hadria (Northern Italy)—Also a Catalan (Spanish) male name
  People think of Adria as pretty, creative, intelligent, trustworthy, funny
  People who like the name Adria also like Addison, Aidan, Alexis, Avery, Caden, Aubrey, Adriel, Bailey, Brayden, Andrea

Adrian (Latin) ♂　　　RATING: ★★★
Person from Hadria (Northern Italy)—Also spelled Adrien; Adrian Grenier, actor
  People think of Adrian as handsome, funny, intelligent, cool, caring
  People who like the name Adrian also like Aiden, Alexander, Aaron, Ethan, Andrew, Adam, Gabriel, Caleb, Aden, Anthony

Adriana (Spanish) ♀　　　RATING: ★★★★
Person from Hadria (Northern Italy)—Feminine form of Adrian
  People think of Adriana as pretty, funny, intelligent, caring, sexy
  People who like the name Adriana also like Arianna, Ariana, Abigail, Adrienne, Isabella, Ava, Abrianna, Alexa, Aaliyah, Audrey

Adrianna (Latin) ♀　　　RATING: ★★★★☆
Person from Hadria (Northern Italy)—Feminine form of Adrian
  People think of Adrianna as pretty, funny, intelligent, caring, creative
  People who like the name Adrianna also like Arianna, Abigail, Aaliyah, Abrianna, Adriana, Isabella, Ava, Brianna, Adrienne, Gabriella

Adriano (Spanish) ♂　　　RATING: ★★★
Person from Hadria (Northern Italy)
  People think of Adriano as handsome, exotic, intelligent, popular, sexy
  People who like the name Adriano also like Adrian, Alejandro, Aaron, Adam, Antonio, Adelio, Aiden, Ace, Abel, Angelo

Adriel (Hebrew) ♀♂　　　RATING: ★★★★
Congregation of God
  People think of Adriel as intelligent, handsome, caring, funny, creative
  People who like the name Adriel also like Aidan, Addison, Ariel, Azriel, Adria, Avery, Aubrey, Alexis, Ainsley, Jaden

Adrienne (Latin) ♀　　　RATING: ★★
Person from Hadria (Northern Italy)—Adrienne Rich, poet
  People think of Adrienne as pretty, intelligent, creative, funny, caring

People who like the name Adrienne also like Adriana, Abigail, Ava, Audrey, Arianna, Alexandra, Chloe, Alexandria, Amelia, Isabella

Adrina *(Italian)* ♀ RATING: ★★★★
Happiness
People think of Adrina as pretty, popular, exotic, intelligent, elegant
People who like the name Adrina also like Adriana, Abrianna, Adrienne, Ariana, Angelina, Alana, Aaralyn, Isabella, Abigail, Arianna

Adsila *(Native American)* ♀ RATING: ★☆
Blossom—Cherokee origin
People think of Adsila as pretty, leader, exotic, trustworthy, powerful
People who like the name Adsila also like Adrina, Aaralyn, Adora, Abrianna, Aeryn, Adrienne, Aiko, Adalia, Alora, Adila

Ady *(American)* ♀ RATING: ★★★☆
Noble—Short for Adele
People think of Ady as pretty, funny, creative, young, caring
People who like the name Ady also like Adie, Ava, Abbie, Abigail, Adriana, Alexa, Audrey, Bella, Ada, Adeline

Adymn *(American)* ♂ RATING: ★★★★
Created name—Combination of Adam and the word *hymn*
People think of Adymn as poor, boy next door, religious, leader, trendy
People who like the name Adymn also like Aden, Aiden, Adrian, Aaron, Adam, Anakin, Abram, Abraham, Alastair, Adair

Aelwen *(Welsh)* ♀ RATING: ★★★★
Fair brow
People think of Aelwen as pretty, elegant, creative, exotic, quiet
People who like the name Aelwen also like Arwen, Aeryn, Aderyn, Aerona, Aaralyn, Aislin, Abigail, Adalia, Aurora, Amelia

Aerith *(American)* ♀ RATING: ★★★
Character in the video game "Final Fantasy VII"
People think of Aerith as caring, intelligent, elegant, pretty, artsy
People who like the name Aerith also like Amelia, Sora, Aelwen, Faye, Aerona, Alice, Tatiana, Terra, Aria, Lilac

Aeron *(Welsh)* ♀ RATING: ★★★☆
Goddess of war—From Agrona, the Celtic goddess of war and battle
People think of Aeron as funny, powerful, cool, sporty, intelligent
People who like the name Aeron also like Aeryn, Adrianna, Arwen, Aaralyn, Aderyn, Amber, Alexandra, Aelwen, Adriana, Aerona

Aerona *(Welsh)* ♀ RATING: ★★★☆
Goddess of war—From Agrona, the Celtic goddess of war and battle
People think of Aerona as exotic, creative, intelligent, elegant, cool
People who like the name Aerona also like Aelwen, Aeryn, Adriana, Aaralyn, Adalia, Aderyn, Abrianna, Abigail, Aurora, Adrienne

Aeryn *(American)* ♀ RATING: ★★★☆
Ireland—Variation of Erin
People think of Aeryn as pretty, intelligent, creative, energetic, funny
People who like the name Aeryn also like Kaelyn, Aaralyn, Arwen, Ava, Alana, Abigail, Adrienne, Aislin, Adriana, Caelan

Affleck *(Celtic/Gaelic)* ♂ RATING: ★★☆
From Auchinleck, Scotland—Variation of Auchinleck; pronounced *Affleck*
People think of Affleck as loser, weird, slow, nerdy, untrustworthy
People who like the name Affleck also like Aiden, Alexander, Arthur, Adrian, Aimon, Alan, Ace, Anderson, Allen, Adam

Afia *(Swahili)* ♀ RATING: ★☆
Health
People think of Afia as pretty, exotic, creative, intelligent, trustworthy
People who like the name Afia also like Acacia, Afya, Adalia, Adora, Adia, Adrina, Adara, Adamma, Adrienne, Aiko

Afon *(Welsh)* ♀ ♂ RATING: ★☆
River
People think of Afon as poor, cool, lazy, nerdy, old-fashioned
People who like the name Afon also like Adria, Aquarius, Aiken, Aidan, Azure, Alpine, Arion, Avalon, Afton, Austin

Afra *(Hebrew)* ♀ RATING: ★★★
Young deer
People think of Afra as pretty, intelligent, creative, caring, funny
People who like the name Afra also like Aaliyah, Aizza, Adriana, Adamina, Adara, Aerona, Adora, Aeryn, Adin, Aelwen

Afric *(Celtic/Gaelic)* ♀ RATING: ★☆
Person from Africa
People think of Afric as pretty, funny, old, ethnic, cool
People who like the name Afric also like Aideen, Aeryn, Aileen, Adriana, Aine, Ailis, Adora, Allene, Alana, Ailish

Africa *(English)* ♀ ♂ RATING: ★★★
Person from Africa
People think of Africa as exotic, creative, aggressive, weird, powerful
People who like the name Africa also like Alexis, Aidan, Arizona, Abby, Addison, Afton, Ashanti, Angel, Adriel, Alex

Afrodille *(French)* ♀ RATING: ★★☆
Daffodil
> People think of Afrodille as wild, weird, exotic, nerdy, artsy
> People who like the name Afrodille also like Adsila, Adrina, Aaralyn, Abrianna, Adrienne, Aelwen, Aerona, Aeryn, Aimee, Adalia

Afton *(English)* ♀ ♂ RATING: ★★★★
From Affa's settlement—Also a Scottish river; "Flow Gently, Sweet Afton," traditional Scottish song
> People think of Afton as pretty, funny, caring, intelligent, creative
> People who like the name Afton also like Addison, Aidan, Avery, Ainsley, Ashton, Bailey, Caden, Hayden, Aspen, Brayden

Afya *(Russian)* ♀ RATING: ★★☆
Variation of the Latin name Agrippina; also short for Agrafena
> People think of Afya as exotic, pretty, wild, winner, trendy
> People who like the name Afya also like Acacia, Afia, Adara, Aeryn, Adrina, Adriana, Ada, Aaralyn, Adsila, Aelwen

Agalia *(Greek)* ♀ RATING: ★★★
Bright joy
> People think of Agalia as weird, exotic, creative, aggressive, old-fashioned
> People who like the name Agalia also like Adalia, Adora, Adrina, Adia, Alana, Aaralyn, Abigail, Aeryn, Aiko, Amara

Agamemnon *(Greek)* ♂ RATING: ★★
Very resolute
> People think of Agamemnon as exotic, powerful, aggressive, leader, intelligent
> People who like the name Agamemnon also like Adonis, Aiden, Ajax, Adair, Aden, Alexander, Apollo, Alastair, Adam, Adrian

Agape *(Greek)* ♀ RATING: ★★☆
Love
> People think of Agape as powerful, exotic, caring, creative, religious
> People who like the name Agape also like Afia, Adsila, Ariana, Anna, Abeni, Adriana, Esther, Keely, Kamea, Agnes

Agapito *(Spanish)* ♂ RATING: ★★
Beloved little one
> People think of Agapito as loser, funny, poor, old, old-fashioned
> People who like the name Agapito also like Aron, Anson, Alban, Aloysius, Alejandro, Amadeus, Anton, Chico, Carlos, Adriano

Agata *(Polish)* ♀ RATING: ★★★☆
Virtuous, good—Variation of Agatha
> People think of Agata as pretty, funny, intelligent, creative, sexy
> People who like the name Agata also like Adrina, Ada, Adelaide, Alicia, Adalia, Adrienne, Aceline, Agnes, Afya, Alice

Agatha *(Greek)* ♀ RATING: ★★★
Virtuous, good—Agatha Christie, mystery writer
> People think of Agatha as intelligent, old-fashioned, pretty, creative, trustworthy
> People who like the name Agatha also like Abigail, Audrey, Alice, Amelia, Adriana, Ava, Adrienne, Agnes, Ada, Adelaide

Aggie *(English)* ♀ RATING: ★★★
Virtuous, good—Short for Agatha or Agnes
> People think of Aggie as funny, caring, pretty, intelligent, trustworthy
> People who like the name Aggie also like Abbie, Abigail, Alexa, Ava, Amelia, Agatha, Aimee, Adora, Audrey, Adeline

Aglaia *(Greek)* ♀ RATING: ★★★
Brilliance—One of the three graces
> People think of Aglaia as intelligent, exotic, energetic, ethnic, weird
> People who like the name Aglaia also like Aerona, Adalia, Agalia, Adrina, Adia, Aeryn, Aelwen, Aaralyn, Adrienne, Aceline

Agnes *(Greek)* ♀ RATING: ★☆
Pure—Agnes Moorhead, actress
> People think of Agnes as intelligent, caring, pretty, creative, funny
> People who like the name Agnes also like Abigail, Agatha, Alice, Ava, Amelia, Audrey, Adelaide, Adeline, Adrina, Adrienne

Agostino *(Italian)* ♂ RATING: ★★★
Great
> People think of Agostino as cool, exotic, aggressive, intelligent, leader
> People who like the name Agostino also like Alfonso, Amando, Angelo, Aiden, Adolfo, Alejandro, Adonis, Ace, Adelio, Aaron

Agrata *(Sanskrit/East Indian)* ♀ RATING: ★☆
Going in front, or taking the lead
> People think of Agrata as leader, aggressive, cool, intelligent, powerful
> People who like the name Agrata also like Alpana, Agnes, Amithi, Adita, Aiko, Adora, Anila, Avani, Adrina, Aisha

Agu *(African)* ♂ RATING: ★★★
Leopard—Western African origin
> People think of Agu as funny, unpopular, big, lazy, religious
> People who like the name Agu also like Ajani, Ajax, Abner, Aden, Abel, Adish, Aiden, Adonis, Agostino, Adymn

82

Ahanu (*Native American*) ♂ RATING: ★★★
He laughs—Algonquin origin
> People think of Ahanu as exotic, intelligent, creative, powerful, ethnic
> People who like the name Ahanu also like Akando, Aiden, Ajani, Akamu, Adam, Aimon, Ace, Adymn, Adair, Abel

Ahava (*Hebrew*) ♀ RATING: ★★★☆
Friendship—Also a Biblical river
> People think of Ahava as pretty, exotic, creative, intelligent, artsy
> People who like the name Ahava also like Aiko, Adalia, Amaris, Adina, Aaralyn, Amara, Ailani, Aizza, Aderes, Aaliyah

Ahmad (*Arabic*) ♂ RATING: ★★★☆
Most praised
> People think of Ahmad as handsome, funny, popular, leader, cool
> People who like the name Ahmad also like Ahmed, Ajani, Aden, Aiden, Amir, Adrian, Adam, Adonis, Alexander, Aaron

Ahmed (*Arabic*) ♂ RATING: ★★★☆
Most praised—Variation of Mohammad; according to ancient beliefs, a home with an Ahmed or Mohammad will be blessed
> People think of Ahmed as intelligent, funny, cool, caring, handsome
> People who like the name Ahmed also like Ahmad, Aaron, Aiden, Abraham, Adam, Alexander, Adair, Aden, Abram, Abner

Ahuva (*Hebrew*) ♀ RATING: ★★☆
Beloved
> People think of Ahuva as sexy, caring, trustworthy, pretty, creative
> People who like the name Ahuva also like Abigail, Agata, Adamma, Anne, Aliana, Annalise, Ailish, Aceline, Aila, Ailis

Ai (*Japanese*) ♀ RATING: ★★★
Love—Same meaning in (old) Vietnamese
> People think of Ai as pretty, exotic, young, creative, caring
> People who like the name Ai also like Aiko, Amaya, Aneko, Ayame, Amarante, Aira, Emiko, Aimee, Ailani, Adriana

Aida (*Italian*) ♀ RATING: ★★☆
Happy; *Aida*, opera by Verdi
> People think of Aida as pretty, intelligent, creative, caring, funny
> People who like the name Aida also like Ava, Ada, Adriana, Amelia, Abigail, Adia, Alana, Adrienne, Alexandra, Adrina

Aidan (*Celtic/Gaelic*) ♀♂ RATING: ★★★☆
Little fire—Also spelled Ayden, Aiden, or Aden; Aidan Quinn, actor
> People think of Aidan as handsome, intelligent, energetic, funny, caring

> People who like the name Aidan also like Addison, Caden, Avery, Hayden, Connor, Logan, Bailey, Dylan, Riley, Madison

Aideen (*Celtic/Gaelic*) ♀ RATING: ★★★★
Little fire—Feminine form of Aidan
> People think of Aideen as pretty, intelligent, caring, creative, funny
> People who like the name Aideen also like Alana, Aeryn, Aislin, Aileen, Aaralyn, Adrienne, Adriana, Aislinn, Abigail, Abrianna

Aiden (*Celtic/Gaelic*) ♂ RATING: ★★★★
Little fire—Variation of Aidan
> People think of Aiden as handsome, intelligent, energetic, funny, caring
> People who like the name Aiden also like Ethan, Caleb, Aden, Kaden, Braden, Tristan, Noah, Jayden, Gavin, Landon

Aiken (*English*) ♀♂ RATING: ★★★☆
Little Adam—Scottish variation of Atkin
> People think of Aiken as creative, energetic, leader, funny, caring
> People who like the name Aiken also like Aidan, Addison, Caden, Avery, Ainsley, Bailey, Ashton, Aubrey, Alec, Aspen

Aiko (*Japanese*) ♀ RATING: ★★★★
Little loved one
> People think of Aiko as pretty, caring, creative, intelligent, artsy
> People who like the name Aiko also like Amaya, Ai, Aneko, Emiko, Ayame, Aeryn, Amarante, Amber, Aisha, Aira

Aila (*American*) ♀ RATING: ★★★★
Variation of Ayla or Isla
> People think of Aila as pretty, creative, intelligent, exotic, caring
> People who like the name Aila also like Ava, Aeryn, Aaralyn, Alana, Adia, Aislin, Aideen, Ayla, Aira, Ada

Ailani (*Hawaiian*) ♀ RATING: ★★★★☆
High chief
> People think of Ailani as pretty, exotic, popular, intelligent, creative
> People who like the name Ailani also like Adriana, Aaliyah, Amaya, Leilani, Abrianna, Alana, Kailani, Alayna, Aaralyn, Alaina

Aileen (*Celtic/Gaelic*) ♀ RATING: ★★★☆
Variation of Evelyn (Aevelyn); often mistaken for a form of Helen
> People think of Aileen as pretty, funny, caring, intelligent, creative
> People who like the name Aileen also like Abigail, Alana, Aideen, Aeryn, Aimee, Adriana, Amber, Audrey, Eileen, Alanna

Ailis *(Celtic/Gaelic)* ♀   RATING: ★★☆
Of a noble kin—Variation of Alice; pronounced *Eye-lish*
> People think of Ailis as pretty, intelligent, creative, wild, caring
> People who like the name Ailis also like Aislin, Aeryn, Alana, Aideen, Ailish, Aileen, Aislinn, Aine, Ailsa, Aila

Ailish *(Celtic/Gaelic)* ♀   RATING: ★★
Of a noble kin—Variation of Ailis or Alice
> People think of Ailish as pretty, funny, intelligent, creative, popular
> People who like the name Ailish also like Alana, Ailsa, Aeryn, Aislinn, Ailis, Aileen, Aislin, Aine, Aideen, Aisling

Ailsa *(Celtic/Gaelic)* ♀   RATING: ★★★☆
A Scottish island—Also short for a Norse name meaning elf victory
> People think of Ailsa as pretty, funny, intelligent, creative, caring
> People who like the name Ailsa also like Alana, Aeryn, Ailish, Aislin, Ailis, Abigail, Aileen, Adriana, Alanna, Aine

Aim *(American)* ♀ ♂   RATING: ★★★☆
Direct toward target
> People think of Aim as nerdy, loser, weird, quiet, aggressive
> People who like the name Aim also like Aiken, Aidan, Afton, Aindrea, Abby, Ainsley, Aldis, Ainslie, Addison, Africa

Aimee *(French)* ♀   RATING: ★★★
Beloved friend—Aimee Mann, singer
> People think of Aimee as pretty, funny, caring, creative, intelligent
> People who like the name Aimee also like Abigail, Amber, Emma, Abbie, Chloe, Ava, Amelia, Alexandra, Adriana, Hannah

Aimi *(Japanese)* ♀   RATING: ★★★☆
Beautiful love
> People think of Aimi as cool, energetic, artsy, intelligent, caring
> People who like the name Aimi also like Amaya, Ai, Aiko, Jin, Amarante, Anastasia, Hana, Aaliyah, Ayame, Kaida

Aimon *(French)* ♂   RATING: ★★★☆
House, home—Variation of Eamonn or Edmund
> People think of Aimon as cool, energetic, handsome, intelligent, elegant
> People who like the name Aimon also like Aiden, Aden, Aaron, Alaric, Adrian, Alexander, Adam, Adair, Alden, Ace

Aindrea *(Celtic/Gaelic)* ♀ ♂   RATING: ★★★
Man—Variation of Andrew
> People think of Aindrea as pretty, intelligent, cool, caring, sexy
> People who like the name Aindrea also like Aidan, Alexis, Ainsley, Andrea, Addison, Afton, Abby, Alex, Ainslie, Adriel

Aine *(Celtic/Gaelic)* ♀   RATING: ★★★☆
Radiance—In Celtic mythology, the Queen of the Elves; pronounced *AWN-ya*
> People think of Aine as pretty, intelligent, funny, creative, caring
> People who like the name Aine also like Aislin, Aeryn, Alana, Aislinn, Ailis, Aileen, Aideen, Ailish, Ailsa, Aisling

Ainsley *(English)* ♀ ♂   RATING: ★★☆
Person from Annesley or Ansley, England
> People think of Ainsley as pretty, intelligent, creative, funny, popular
> People who like the name Ainsley also like Addison, Avery, Aidan, Bailey, Aubrey, Hayden, Caden, Madison, Riley, Logan

Ainslie *(English)* ♀ ♂   RATING: ★★★★
Person from Annesley or Ansley, England
> People think of Ainslie as pretty, energetic, funny, creative, intelligent
> People who like the name Ainslie also like Ainsley, Addison, Aidan, Avery, Bailey, Aubrey, Ashton, Alexis, Caden, Cadence

Aira *(American)* ♀   RATING: ★★★★
Of the wind
> People think of Aira as pretty, creative, cool, intelligent, caring
> People who like the name Aira also like Aria, Amaya, Amara, Aurora, Aaralyn, Aiko, Ava, Aeryn, Aura, Aila

Airell *(Celtic/Gaelic)* ♂   RATING: ★★★☆
Nobleman
> People think of Airell as cool, handsome, intelligent, sexy, popular
> People who like the name Airell also like Aiden, Adrian, Aden, Alexander, Aaron, Alan, Alaric, Aimon, Alistair, Arthur

Airlia *(American)* ♀   RATING: ★★
Feminine form of Airlie; probably a variation of Earley, meaning eagle wood
> People think of Airlia as creative, leader, caring, pretty, exotic
> People who like the name Airlia also like Adara, Adalia, Adalira, Aira, Adriana, Aeryn, Ailani, Aria, Anastasia, Aurora

Aisha *(Arabic)* ♀   RATING: ★★☆
Prosperous—Wife of the Prophet Muhammad
> People think of Aisha as pretty, funny, caring, intelligent, creative
> People who like the name Aisha also like Aaliyah, Adriana, Alana, Amaya, Abigail, Amber, Ava, Alexia, Aysha, Abrianna

Aislin *(Celtic/Gaelic)* ♀   RATING: ★★★★
Vision, dream
> People think of Aislin as pretty, intelligent, creative, caring, artsy
> People who like the name Aislin also like Aeryn, Aislinn, Ava, Alana, Ashlyn, Aaralyn, Caelan, Aisling, Kaelyn, Aideen

84

Aisling (*Celtic/Gaelic*) ♀   RATING: ★★★★
Vision, dream—Pronounced *ASH-ling*
> People think of Aisling as pretty, intelligent, creative, caring, funny
> People who like the name Aisling also like Aislinn, Aislin, Aeryn, Alana, Ava, Aideen, Abigail, Ailish, Aileen, Ailis

Aitana (*Portuguese*) ♀   RATING: ★★★★
Glory—Basque origin
> People think of Aitana as exotic, pretty, intelligent, creative, funny
> People who like the name Aitana also like Abrianna, Aaralyn, Ailani, Adriana, Amara, Adalia, Alaina, Aaliyah, Alana, Aislin

Aithley (*English*) ♀   RATING: ★★★
Born in a garden
> People think of Aithley as pretty, girl next door, lazy, young, energetic
> People who like the name Aithley also like Aeryn, Aceline, Aelwen, Aislin, Alana, Aderyn, Alecia, Adalira, Aislinn, Abrianna

Aiyana (*African*) ♀   RATING: ★★★★
Flower blossom—Ethiopian origin
> People think of Aiyana as pretty, caring, intelligent, creative, popular
> People who like the name Aiyana also like Aaliyah, Arianna, Anaya, Anya, Amaya, Aliana, Alana, Ava, Ariana, Alexandria

Aizza (*Arabic*) ♀   RATING: ★★★☆
Saffron; crocus
> People think of Aizza as pretty, exotic, creative, winner, funny
> People who like the name Aizza also like Aisha, Aaliyah, Aiko, Alessa, Adrina, Ailani, Alana, Ahava, Alaina, Adalia

Aja (*Sanskrit/East Indian*) ♀ ♂   RATING: ★★
To drive, propel—Also a variation of Asia
> People think of Aja as pretty, funny, intelligent, creative, popular
> People who like the name Aja also like Aidan, Alexis, Avery, Ariel, Akia, Addison, Ari, Alex, Ameya, Aiken

Ajani (*African*) ♂   RATING: ★★★★
He who wins the struggle
> People think of Ajani as creative, intelligent, handsome, powerful, energetic
> People who like the name Ajani also like Aiden, Alijah, Aden, Amir, Aaron, Ajax, Ajay, Adonis, Ahmad, Alexander

Ajax (*Greek*) ♂   RATING: ★★★
Of the Earth
> People think of Ajax as powerful, aggressive, leader, wild, energetic
> People who like the name Ajax also like Aiden, Ace, Aden, Axel, Ajay, Adonis, Adrian, Adam, Alexander, Ajani

Ajay (*Sanskrit/East Indian*) ♂   RATING: ★★☆
Unconquerable—Also an American name from the initials A.J.
> People think of Ajay as popular, intelligent, funny, caring, cool
> People who like the name Ajay also like Aiden, Aden, Aaron, Adam, Ace, Alexander, Andrew, Adrian, Anthony, Caleb

Akamu (*Hawaiian*) ♂   RATING: ★★★
Of the Earth—Variation of Adam
> People think of Akamu as exotic, ethnic, handsome, cool, creative
> People who like the name Akamu also like Aiden, Adonis, Ahanu, Akando, Aden, Abel, Adish, Alaric, Ajani

Akando (*Native American*) ♂   RATING: ★★★
Ambush
> People think of Akando as aggressive, powerful, energetic, criminal, intelligent
> People who like the name Akando also like Ahanu, Akamu, Aiden, Alaric, Alastair, Ambrose, Ajani, Alexander, Alagan, Anakin

Akantha (*Greek*) ♀   RATING: ★★
Thorn
> People think of Akantha as big, exotic, weird, loser, caring
> People who like the name Akantha also like Akilah, Amara, Abrienda, Ania, Alia, Aaralyn, Aquene, Aeron, Azura, Adara

Akeelah (*American*) ♀   RATING: ★★★☆
Eagle—Variation of Aquila
> People think of Akeelah as pretty, intelligent, creative, funny, caring
> People who like the name Akilah also like Aaliyah, Adriana, Adrienne, Abrianna, Ailani, Amaya, Alaina, Anaya, Alanna, Adrina

Aki (*Japanese*) ♂   RATING: ★★★
Sky
> People think of Aki as intelligent, powerful, elegant, creative, young
> People who like the name Aki also like Akio, Botan, Haru, Luke, Anthony, Keiji, Adrian, Diego, Christopher, Hotaru

Akia (*African*) ♀ ♂   RATING: ★★★★
First born—Ugandan origin
> People think of Akia as pretty, intelligent, sexy, creative, caring
> People who like the name Akia also like Aidan, Alexis, Addison, Ashanti, Aiken, Ameya, Alex, Aubrey, Aja, Caden

Akili (*African*) ♀   RATING: ★★
Wisdom—Western African origin
> People think of Akili as caring, creative, sexy, young, exotic

People who like the name Akili also like Amani, Amaya, Amara, Aiko, Aisha, Aaliyah, Ailani, Anastasia, Adalia, Aaralyn

Akio *(Japanese)* ♂ RATING: ★★
Bright boy
People think of Akio as creative, intelligent, handsome, cool, caring
People who like the name Akio also like Aiden, Aden, Aaron, Ryu, Haruki, Ace, Hiroshi, Anakin, Adrian, Alexander

Akiva *(Hebrew)* ♂ RATING: ★★★★
To hold by the heel—Variation of Jacob
People think of Akiva as trustworthy, leader, creative, funny, popular
People who like the name Akiva also like Aiden, Aaron, Asher, Aden, Adrian, Aleron, Adam, Alexander, Akio, Abie

Akuji *(American)* ♂ RATING: ★★★☆
Dead and awake—Character in the video game "Akuji: The Heartless"
People think of Akuji as exotic, intelligent, aggressive, sexy, quiet
People who like the name Akuji also like Ajani, Aiden, Adish, Aden, Anoki, Axel, Agu, Ajax, Astro, Ambrose

Al *(English)* ♂ RATING: ★★
Short for names beginning with Al—Al Gore, politician; Al Hirt, musician; "Weird Al" Yankovic, satirist songwriter
People think of Al as intelligent, funny, sexy, weird, cool
People who like the name Al also like Alan, Adam, Allen, Alexander, Albert, Alfred, Aaron, Anthony, Allan, Andrew

Alabama *(Native American)* ♀♂ RATING: ★★★☆
Thicket clearing—U.S. state
People think of Alabama as pretty, creative, poor, wild, loser
People who like the name Alabama also like Addison, Aidan, Austin, Bailey, Ainsley, Arizona, Avery, Caden, Brooklyn, Angel

Alagan *(Sanskrit/East Indian)* ♂ RATING: ★★★
Handsome
People think of Alagan as handsome, lazy, leader, untrustworthy, powerful
People who like the name Alagan also like Ajay, Amish, Aiden, Aden, Alain, Ashwin, Adonis, Ajani, Adair, Adarsh

Alain *(French)* ♂ RATING: ★★★☆
Little rock—Variation of Alan
People think of Alain as funny, intelligent, cool, handsome, caring
People who like the name Alain also like Aiden, Aden, Alexander, André, Alastair, Aaron, Adam, Andrew, Adrian, Adair

Alaina *(French)* ♀ RATING: ★★★
Little rock—Feminine form of Alain; also a variation of Elena
People think of Alaina as pretty, funny, intelligent, creative, caring
People who like the name Alaina also like Alana, Alayna, Abigail, Adriana, Ava, Alanna, Arianna, Ariana, Abrianna, Alexa

Alair *(English)* ♂ RATING: ★★★
Cheerful, merry
People think of Alair as creative, cool, intelligent, popular, energetic
People who like the name Alair also like Aiden, Alastair, Adair, Alden, Alexander, Alain, Alaric, Aaron, André, Aimon

Alake *(African)* ♀ RATING: ★★★
One to be honored—Nigerian origin
People think of Alake as exotic, creative, weird, popular, cool
People who like the name Alake also like Adalia, Abigail, Alana, Adara, Abeni, Amber, Akili, Adora, Adeline, Alexia

Alamea *(Hawaiian)* ♀ RATING: ★★
Precious, whole
People think of Alamea as exotic, pretty, intelligent, creative, funny
People who like the name Alamea also like Ailani, Alaula, Alohilani, Adonia, Alana, Aiko, Amaya, Alika, Abrianna, Adriana

Alameda *(Spanish)* ♀ RATING: ★★★
From the poplar tree
People think of Alameda as exotic, ethnic, pretty, loser, lazy
People who like the name Alameda also like Adriana, Abrienda, Alegria, Adrina, Adalia, Adrienne, Acacia, Ailani, Aletta, Aleda

Alan *(English)* ♂ RATING: ★★★☆
Little rock—Alan Alda, actor; Alan Rickman, actor
People think of Alan as handsome, funny, intelligent, caring, trustworthy
People who like the name Alan also like Aaron, Adam, Aiden, Andrew, Alexander, Anthony, Adrian, Allen, Ethan, Aden

Alana *(Celtic/Gaelic)* ♀ RATING: ★★★☆
Little rock—Feminine form of Alan
People think of Alana as pretty, funny, intelligent, caring, creative
People who like the name Alana also like Ava, Adriana, Abigail, Alaina, Ariana, Alanna, Alexa, Alayna, Alyssa, Amber

Alanna *(Celtic/Gaelic)* ♀ RATING: ★★★
Little child—Feminine form of Alan
People think of Alanna as pretty, funny, intelligent, creative, caring
People who like the name Alanna also like Alana, Abigail, Adriana, Arianna, Ava, Alaina, Alayna, Alyssa, Alexa, Aaliyah

Alannis (*Greek*) ♀   RATING: ★★★☆
From Atlantis—Alanis Morissette, singer
> People think of Alannis as pretty, powerful, energetic, intelligent, sexy
> People who like the name Alannis also like Alanna, Abigail, Alaina, Alana, Ava, Anastasia, Adriana, Amber, Alexia, Alexandra

Alaqua (*Native American*) ♀   RATING: ★★★
Sweet gum tree
> People think of Alaqua as exotic, pretty, elegant, quiet, sexy
> People who like the name Alaqua also like Aleshanee, Adalia, Aaliyah, Aerona, Aaralyn, Adsila, Abrianna, Amaya, Adriana, Ailani

Alaric (*German*) ♂   RATING: ★★★★
Noble ruler, elf ruler—Last king of the Goths who overthrew Rome
> People think of Alaric as handsome, intelligent, leader, powerful, caring
> People who like the name Alaric also like Aiden, Alastair, Alexander, Alistair, Braeden, Adair, Aden, Adrian, Alexavier, Alan

Alarice (*German*) ♀   RATING: ★★★☆
Noble ruler—Feminine form of Alaric
> People think of Alarice as trustworthy, leader, caring, sexy, wild
> People who like the name Alarice also like Adalia, Abrianna, Aaralyn, Aurora, Ailani, Anastasia, Adeline, Aeryn, Alaina, Analiese

Alary (*German*) ♀♂   RATING: ★★★
Elf ruler—Possibly short for Alaric
> People think of Alary as pretty, intelligent, exotic, trendy, sporty
> People who like the name Alary also like Ari, Blaze, Arya, Baden, Aidan, Brody, Ashton, Arden, Briar, Afton

Alaska (*Native American*) ♀   RATING: ★★★☆
Great land—U.S. state
> People think of Alaska as creative, pretty, intelligent, artsy, funny
> People who like the name Alaska also like Abigail, Amber, Autumn, Adriana, Aaliyah, Anastasia, Aurora, Adrienne, Asia, Ava

Alastair (*English*) ♂   RATING: ★★★★
Defender of men—Scottish variation of Alexander
> People think of Alastair as handsome, intelligent, trustworthy, leader, powerful
> People who like the name Alastair also like Alexander, Aiden, Alistair, Adrian, Aaron, Adam, Benjamin, Asher, Ethan, Caleb

Alaula (*Hawaiian*) ♀   RATING: ★★★☆
Light of dawn
> People think of Alaula as pretty, exotic, young, cool, elegant
> People who like the name Alaula also like Ailani, Alamea, Alohilani, Aiko, Amaya, Aurora, Alora, Aira, Aeryn, Alanna

Alaura (*American*) ♀   RATING: ★★☆
Laurel—Variation of Laura; also a combination of Al and Laura
> People think of Alaura as pretty, creative, intelligent, caring, funny
> People who like the name Alaura also like Aurora, Ava, Abigail, Alanna, Alana, Alayna, Alena, Aeryn, Abrianna, Alora

Alawi (*Arabic*) ♂   RATING: ★★☆
Descendant of Hazrat Ali
> People think of Alawi as exotic, poor, ethnic, wild, weird
> People who like the name Alawi also like Alagan, Adair, Alair, Arif, Aimon, Ayman, Aaron, Adli, Ahmed, Alejandro

Alayna (*American*) ♀   RATING: ★★★☆
Feminine form of Alain; also a variation of Elaina or Alaina
> People think of Alayna as pretty, funny, intelligent, creative, energetic
> People who like the name Alayna also like Alaina, Alana, Adriana, Alanna, Ava, Arianna, Abigail, Abrianna, Ariana, Aaliyah

Alba (*Latin*) ♀   RATING: ★★★☆
Dawn, sunrise—Latin name for Scotland
> People think of Alba as pretty, intelligent, caring, young, elegant
> People who like the name Alba also like Ava, Adrina, Alma, Aria, Abrianna, Adrienne, Adriana, Alena, Alana, Amber

Alban (*Latin*) ♂   RATING: ★☆
From Alba
> People think of Alban as sexy, funny, intelligent, handsome, ethnic
> People who like the name Alban also like Ace, Aden, Anton, Alan, Adair, Anthony, Asher, Alastair, Alaric, Anderson

Albany (*Latin*) ♀♂   RATING: ★★★☆
From Albany, Scotland—Also capital city of New York
> People think of Albany as pretty, funny, powerful, big, criminal
> People who like the name Albany also like Bailey, Addison, Aidan, Avery, Aubrey, Alexis, Ainsley, Ashton, Aspen, Austin

Albert (*English*) ♂   RATING: ★★
Noble and bright
> People think of Albert as handsome, intelligent, funny, caring, cool
> People who like the name Albert also like Adam, Aaron, Alexander, Andrew, Alfred, Arthur, Alan, Adrian, Anthony, Aiden

Alberta (*English*) ♀   RATING: ★★★
Noble and bright—Also a Canadian province
> People think of Alberta as pretty, trustworthy, caring, funny, leader

People who like the name Alberta also like Amber, Adriana, Alice, Alexa, Alicia, Adeline, Amanda, Abbie, Abigail, Alecia

Alberto *(Spanish)* ♂   RATING: ★★★☆
Noble and bright—Variation of Albert
People think of Alberto as funny, handsome, cool, energetic, caring
People who like the name Alberto also like Antonio, Adam, Adrian, Alejandro, Alexander, Aaron, Andrés, Alfonso, Albert, Alan

Albin *(Latin)* ♂   RATING: ★☆
Fair
People think of Albin as creative, funny, caring, young, leader
People who like the name Albin also like Aiden, Alan, Alaric, Aldon, Aden, Alden, Anton, Allen, Alvin, Alexander

Albina *(Latin)* ♀   RATING: ★★★
Fair
People think of Albina as funny, intelligent, pretty, exotic, young
People who like the name Albina also like Adrina, Abrianna, Alda, Alba, Angelina, Adriana, Adeline, Alecia, Adela, Alicia

Alda *(Italian)* ♀   RATING: ★★★☆
Old—Alan Alda, actor
People think of Alda as pretty, intelligent, cool, old, trustworthy
People who like the name Alda also like Adrina, Ambra, Aria, Albina, Alba, Alana, Aida, Abrianna, Angelina, Ada

Aldan *(English)* ♂   RATING: ★★☆
Old, wise
People think of Aldan as handsome, popular, old, intelligent, old-fashioned
People who like the name Aldan also like Alden, Aiden, Aden, Aaron, Adrian, Aldon, Adam, Alexander, Braden, Alton

Alden *(English)* ♂   RATING: ★★★☆
Half Danish—Variation of the surname Haldane
People think of Alden as intelligent, cool, funny, handsome, caring
People who like the name Alden also like Aiden, Aden, Braden, Alexander, Ethan, Aaron, Caleb, Adrian, Holden, Andrew

Aldis *(English)* ♀♂   RATING: ★★
From the old house
People think of Aldis as intelligent, cool, young, popular, pretty
People who like the name Aldis also like Aidan, Ainsley, Avery, Afton, Alexis, Arden, Aiken, Astin, Aim, Adriel

Aldon *(English)* ♂   RATING: ★★
From Aldon, England
People think of Aldon as handsome, caring, intelligent, cool, sexy

People who like the name Aldon also like Aiden, Alden, Aden, Aldan, Aaron, Alton, Asher, Adrian, Andrew, Adam

Aldona *(American)* ♀   RATING: ★★★☆
From Aldon, England—Feminine form of Aldon
People think of Aldona as caring, exotic, creative, trustworthy, sexy
People who like the name Aldona also like Adalia, Alena, Alecia, Adriana, Adela, Adrina, Adeline, Alicia, Abrianna, Alaura

Aldonza *(Spanish)* ♀   RATING: ★★☆
Good-natured
People think of Aldonza as leader, pretty, intelligent, exotic, powerful
People who like the name Aldonza also like Adelina, Alegria, Adalira, Aletta, Abril, Abrienda, Abarne, Anastacia, Emiko, Olivia

Aleah *(American)* ♀   RATING: ★★★☆
High, sublime—Variation of Aaliyah
People think of Aleah as pretty, funny, caring, young, creative
People who like the name Aleah also like Aaliyah, Ava, Arianna, Abigail, Adriana, Adrianna, Amber, Alaina, Alyssa, Alana

Alec *(English)* ♀♂   RATING: ★★★
Defender of men—Short for Alex; Alec Baldwin, actor; Sir Alec Guinness, actor
People think of Alec as handsome, funny, intelligent, cool, popular
People who like the name Alec also like Aidan, Addison, Alex, Bailey, Caden, Ashton, Blake, Austin, Avery, Hayden

Alecia *(English)* ♀   RATING: ★★★★
Of a noble kin—Variation of Alicia
People think of Alecia as pretty, funny, caring, intelligent, trustworthy
People who like the name Alecia also like Alicia, Abigail, Adriana, Alana, Alexia, Alexa, Amber, Aaliyah, Alexandra, Alaina

Aleda *(Latin)* ♀   RATING: ★★★★
Small and winged
People think of Aleda as pretty, funny, caring, creative, energetic
People who like the name Aleda also like Amaya, Alena, Aiko, Alana, Adalia, Alida, Aira, Adalira, Adela, Aelwen

Alegria *(Spanish)* ♀   RATING: ★★
Happiness
People think of Alegria as pretty, energetic, young, creative, funny
People who like the name Alegria also like Allegra, Adriana, Abrianna, Alana, Abigail, Anastasia, Alayna, Adalia, Alena, Alexia

88

Alejandro *(Spanish)* ♂   RATING: ★★★★
Defender of men—Variation of Alexander
> People think of Alejandro as handsome, intelligent, funny, sexy, cool
> People who like the name Alejandro also like Adrian, Alexander, Antonio, Aiden, Andrés, Anthony, Gabriel, Andrew, Alexavier, Adam

Alem *(Arabic)* ♂   RATING: ★★★☆
World leader
> People think of Alem as caring, leader, nerdy, popular, creative
> People who like the name Alem also like Aden, Aaron, Aiden, Alain, Alastair, Alden, Akio, Alexander, Adymn, Alejandro

Alena *(Slavic)* ♀   RATING: ★★★
Light—Variation of Helen
> People think of Alena as pretty, intelligent, funny, creative, caring
> People who like the name Alena also like Alana, Ava, Alaina, Alanna, Alayna, Adriana, Abigail, Alexa, Amelia, Adrienne

Aleron *(Latin)* ♂   RATING: ★★★☆
Eagle
> People think of Aleron as handsome, powerful, intelligent, cool, trustworthy
> People who like the name Aleron also like Aiden, Alaric, Aden, Alastair, Adam, Alden, Alexavier, Adrian, Axel, Alexander

Aleshanee *(Native American)* ♀   RATING: ★★★☆
She always plays—Coos origin
> People think of Aleshanee as pretty, funny, energetic, intelligent, sexy
> People who like the name Aleshanee also like Aaliyah, Amaya, Aaralyn, Abrianna, Ayasha, Ailani, Alora, Adriana, Alanna, Aeryn

Alessa *(Italian)* ♀   RATING: ★★★★
Defender of men—Short for Alessandra
> People think of Alessa as pretty, intelligent, creative, young, sexy
> People who like the name Alessa also like Alyssa, Alissa, Abigail, Alexa, Adriana, Aaliyah, Arianna, Alexia, Alanna, Abrianna

Aleta *(Portuguese)* ♀   RATING: ★★
Truth
> People think of Aleta as creative, intelligent, caring, pretty, funny
> People who like the name Aleta also like Alena, Amara, Alana, Alessa, Aida, Ava, Alaina, Adalia, Adia, Aimee

Aletha *(American)* ♀   RATING: ★★★☆
Truth—Variation of Alethea
> People think of Aletha as trustworthy, caring, intelligent, quiet, creative
> People who like the name Aletha also like Alethea, Adeline, Abrianna, Abigail, Aleta, Alana, Amanda, Adalia, Amelia, Amber

Alethea *(Greek)* ♀   RATING: ★★★☆
Truth
> People think of Alethea as pretty, intelligent, creative, funny, trustworthy
> People who like the name Alethea also like Anastasia, Althea, Abigail, Amara, Abrianna, Alecia, Adalia, Alessa, Alana, Athena

Aletta *(Spanish)* ♀   RATING: ★★★★
Winged one
> People think of Aletta as intelligent, pretty, creative, caring, elegant
> People who like the name Aletta also like Adriana, Aira, Ava, Alena, Alana, Adrienne, Adeline, Aurora, Amber, Alaina

Alex *(English)* ♀ ♂   RATING: ★★★☆
Defender of men—Short for Alexander or Alexandra
> People think of Alex as funny, cool, intelligent, caring, handsome
> People who like the name Alex also like Alexis, Bailey, Aidan, Austin, Cameron, Ryan, Ashley, Blake, Ashton, Addison

Alexa *(American)* ♀   RATING: ★★★☆
Defender
> People think of Alexa as pretty, funny, intelligent, creative, caring
> People who like the name Alexa also like Alexia, Ava, Abigail, Alexandra, Adriana, Emma, Chloe, Alyssa, Alexandria, Amber

Alexander *(Greek)* ♂   RATING: ★★★☆
Defender of men—Alexander Hamilton, U.S. statesman
> People think of Alexander as handsome, intelligent, funny, caring, leader
> People who like the name Alexander also like Andrew, Ethan, Benjamin, Aiden, Aaron, Nicholas, Jacob, Caleb, Zachary, Adam

Alexandra *(Greek)* ♀   RATING: ★★★☆
Defender of men—Also spelled Alejandra or Alessandra
> People think of Alexandra as pretty, funny, intelligent, caring, creative
> People who like the name Alexandra also like Alexandria, Abigail, Alexa, Ava, Isabella, Adriana, Alexia, Emma, Olivia, Hannah

Alexandria *(Greek)* ♀   RATING: ★★★☆
From Alexandria, Egypt
> People think of Alexandria as pretty, intelligent, funny, creative, caring
> People who like the name Alexandria also like Alexandra, Abigail, Alexia, Adriana, Alexa, Isabella, Anastasia, Arianna, Ava, Hannah

Alexavier *(American)* ♂   RATING: ★★★☆
Combination of Alex and Xavier
> People think of Alexavier as powerful, handsome, popular, intelligent, leader

People who like the name Alexavier also like Alexander, Aiden, Xavier, Adrian, Aden, Anthony, Adam, Caleb, Andrew, Aaron

Alexei (*Russian*) ♂   RATING: ★★★★
Defender—Variation of the Greek name Alexios
> People think of Alexei as handsome, intelligent, creative, caring, funny
> People who like the name Alexei also like Aiden, Alexander, Adrian, Alexavier, Aden, Aaron, Andrew, Adam, Gabriel, Anthony

Alexia (*American*) ♀   RATING: ★★★★
Defender of men—Feminine form of Alexander, Alexis, or Alexei
> People think of Alexia as pretty, intelligent, funny, popular, creative
> People who like the name Alexia also like Alexa, Alexandria, Alexandra, Adriana, Abigail, Ava, Aaliyah, Alyssa, Arianna, Amber

Alexis (*Russian*) ♀ ♂   RATING: ★★★★
Defender of men—Short for Alexander; Alexis Carrington, character on *Dynasty*, played by Joan Collins
> People think of Alexis as pretty, funny, intelligent, creative, caring
> People who like the name Alexis also like Bailey, Madison, Addison, Riley, Brooke, Mackenzie, Aidan, Cameron, Taylor, Caden

Aleydis (*Dutch*) ♀   RATING: ★★☆
Of noble kin
> People think of Aleydis as quiet, pretty, intelligent, caring, elegant
> People who like the name Aleydis also like Aliana, Alena, Adara, Aadi, Amara, Aceline, Aria, Anya, Adalia, Alexia

Alfonso (*Italian*) ♂   RATING: ★☆
Noble and ready
> People think of Alfonso as funny, handsome, cool, caring, intelligent
> People who like the name Alfonso also like Alexander, Aaron, Antonio, Adam, Adrian, Andrew, Anthony, Amando, Alejandro, Alan

Alfred (*English*) ♂   RATING: ★★★☆
Counselor—Alfred Hitchcock, director; Alfred P. Sloan, philanthropist/former CEO of General Motors
> People think of Alfred as intelligent, handsome, funny, caring, cool
> People who like the name Alfred also like Albert, Adam, Alexander, Aaron, Alan, Andrew, Arthur, Adrian, Aiden, Anthony

Algernon (*English*) ♂   RATING: ★★★
With a moustache—Variation of a medieval Norman nickname
> People think of Algernon as handsome, intelligent, weird, energetic, funny
> People who like the name Algernon also like Alastair, Ambrose, Alistair, Adam, Aiden, Alfred, Archibald, Alexander, Alden, Atticus

Ali (*Arabic*) ♀ ♂   RATING: ★★★
Noble, sublime—Variation of Aly; also short for Allison; Ali Larter, actress; Ali MacGraw, actress
> People think of Ali as funny, popular, cool, intelligent, caring
> People who like the name Ali also like Alexis, Bailey, Alex, Ally, Addison, Abby, Aubrey, Aidan, Ashley, Allie

Alia (*Arabic*) ♀   RATING: ★★★
Noble, sublime—Variation of Alyia or Aaliyah
> People think of Alia as pretty, intelligent, creative, funny, caring
> People who like the name Alia also like Aaliyah, Ava, Aliya, Aliana, Adriana, Alexia, Amaya, Alessa, Alana, Alexa

Aliana (*Latin*) ♀   RATING: ★★★★☆
Noble, gracious—Combination of Alia and Anne
> People think of Aliana as pretty, intelligent, elegant, exotic, sexy
> People who like the name Aliana also like Adriana, Arianna, Ariana, Alana, Ava, Abrianna, Abigail, Aaliyah, Alaina, Alayna

Aliane (*French*) ♀   RATING: ★★★☆
Noble, gracious—Combination of Alia and Anne
> People think of Aliane as pretty, funny, artsy, intelligent, young
> People who like the name Aliane also like Aliana, Alaina, Alicia, Adrina, Alayna, Adalia, Adriana, Alia, Aceline, Annabel

Alice (*English*) ♀   RATING: ★★★☆
Of a noble kin—From the same origin as Adelaide; Alice Walker, author; *Alice in Wonderland*, book and film character
> People think of Alice as pretty, intelligent, creative, caring, funny
> People who like the name Alice also like Amelia, Abigail, Audrey, Ava, Charlotte, Amber, Grace, Anna, Alicia, Olivia

Alicia (*English*) ♀   RATING: ★★★
Of noble kin—Alicia Keys, singer; Alicia Silverstone, actress
> People think of Alicia as pretty, funny, caring, intelligent, creative
> People who like the name Alicia also like Amber, Alyssa, Abigail, Amelia, Alexa, Adriana, Alissa, Amanda, Aaliyah, Alexandra

Alick (*English*) ♀ ♂   RATING: ★★★☆
Defender of men—Short for Alexander
> People think of Alick as leader, handsome, funny, intelligent, popular
> People who like the name Alick also like Alec, Addison, Aidan, Avery, Alex, Austin, Bailey, Ashton, Caden, Alexis

Alida (*Latin*) ♀   RATING: ★★☆
Small, winged
> People think of Alida as pretty, intelligent, caring, creative, elegant

People who like the name Alida also like Aurora, Ava, Alana, Adalia, Amaya, Aleda, Adriana, Alicia, Amelia, Alena

Alijah *(American)* ♂ RATING: ★★☆
The Lord is my God—Variation of Elijah
People think of Alijah as intelligent, handsome, popular, caring, funny
People who like the name Alijah also like Elijah, Aiden, Caleb, Aden, Isaiah, Aaron, Ethan, Alexander, Kaden, Adrian

Alika *(Hawaiian)* ♀ RATING: ★★★★
Of a noble kin—Variation of Alice
People think of Alika as pretty, exotic, energetic, funny, intelligent
People who like the name Alika also like Ailani, Amaya, Alohilani, Alana, Aaliyah, Aaralyn, Amara, Alayna, Alamea, Aiko

Alima *(Arabic)* ♀ RATING: ★★
Learned, wise
People think of Alima as energetic, young, trustworthy, pretty, cool
People who like the name Alima also like Amina, Aisha, Amal, Aiko, Anisa, Alana, Almira, Alina, Amara, Amena

Alina *(Slavic)* ♀ RATING: ★★★
Noble, kind—Variation of Adeline
People think of Alina as pretty, funny, intelligent, creative, caring
People who like the name Alina also like Alena, Alana, Alaina, Ava, Amaya, Aliana, Abigail, Alissa, Alia, Adriana

Alisa *(English)* ♀ RATING: ★★★
Of a noble kin—Variation of Alicia or Elisa
People think of Alisa as pretty, funny, caring, intelligent, creative
People who like the name Alisa also like Alissa, Alyssa, Alicia, Alexia, Abigail, Amber, Alana, Alisha, Arianna, Adriana

Alisha *(American)* ♀ RATING: ★★★
Of noble kin—Variation of Alicia
People think of Alisha as pretty, funny, caring, intelligent, creative
People who like the name Alisha also like Alicia, Alissa, Alyssa, Amber, Abigail, Alana, Adriana, Aaliyah, Alexa, Alexandra

Alison *(English)* ♀ RATING: ★★★☆
Little Alice—Variation of Alice
People think of Alison as funny, pretty, caring, intelligent, creative
People who like the name Alison also like Abigail, Allison, Amber, Alissa, Amanda, Emily, Allyson, Alexandra, Audrey, Ava

Alissa *(English)* ♀ RATING: ★★★☆
Of a noble kin—Variation of Alice or Alicia
People think of Alissa as pretty, funny, intelligent, caring, creative

People who like the name Alissa also like Alyssa, Abigail, Amber, Alicia, Alexa, Adriana, Arianna, Hailey, Alana, Alexia

Alistair *(Celtic/Gaelic)* ♂ RATING: ★★★★
Defender of men—Also the Scottish variation of Alexander
People think of Alistair as intelligent, handsome, creative, leader, caring
People who like the name Alistair also like Aiden, Alastair, Alexander, Liam, Aden, Tristan, Adam, Adrian, Aaron, Owen

Aliya *(Arabic)* ♀ RATING: ★★★★☆
Sublime, eminent
People think of Aliya as pretty, intelligent, popular, caring, funny
People who like the name Aliya also like Aaliyah, Alia, Ava, Amaya, Adriana, Abigail, Ariana, Alyssa, Alissa, Alexia

Aliza *(Hebrew)* ♀ RATING: ★★★☆
Joyful
People think of Aliza as pretty, funny, creative, cool, intelligent
People who like the name Aliza also like Abigail, Alissa, Aaliyah, Ava, Amelia, Alana, Alyssa, Alize, Aliya, Alexa

Alize *(Hebrew)* ♀ RATING: ★★☆
Joyful
People think of Alize as pretty, sexy, popular, exotic, funny
People who like the name Alize also like Aliza, Aaliyah, Alessa, Aaralyn, Abigail, Alana, Adriana, Adalia, Alanna, Amara

Alka *(Sanskrit/East Indian)* ♀ RATING: ★★★
Young
People think of Alka as young, funny, popular, ethnic, intelligent
People who like the name Alka also like Alpana, Amara, Avani, Anila, Agrata, Anaya, Asha, Amithi, Amma, Adita

Allan *(English)* ♂ RATING: ★★★☆
Little rock
People think of Allan as handsome, caring, funny, intelligent, trustworthy
People who like the name Allan also like Alan, Allen, Alexander, Andrew, Aaron, Adam, Aiden, Anthony, Adrian, Aden

Allard *(English)* ♀♂ RATING: ★★★
Noble, bold
People think of Allard as old, weird, loser, nerdy, powerful
People who like the name Allard also like Aubrey, Aidan, Aldis, Artemis, Arden, Alex, Avery, Afton, Ainsley, Astin

Allayna *(American)* ♀ RATING: ★★★★☆
Little rock—Feminine form of Alain; also a variation of Elena
People think of Allayna as pretty, creative, trustworthy, caring, funny

People who like the name Allayna also like Alayna, Alaina, Alana, Adriana, Aaliyah, Aaralyn, Alanna, Abigail, Abrianna, Arianna

Allegra *(Latin)* ♀　　　RATING: ★★★★
Joy
People think of Allegra as pretty, intelligent, creative, energetic, funny
People who like the name Allegra also like Ava, Aurora, Abigail, Amelia, Alexandra, Audrey, Isabella, Bella, Adriana, Alexa

Allen *(English)* ♂　　　RATING: ★★☆
Little rock
People think of Allen as handsome, intelligent, funny, caring, cool
People who like the name Allen also like Aaron, Adam, Andrew, Alexander, Aiden, Alan, Anthony, Allan, Benjamin, Adrian

Allene *(American)* ♀　　　RATING: ★★★★
Little rock—Feminine form of Allen; also possibly a variation of Eileen
People think of Allene as funny, caring, pretty, sexy, energetic
People who like the name Allene also like Alana, Aeryn, Aislin, Aideen, Aislinn, Aileen, Aine, Adeline, Alena, Ailis

Allete *(French)* ♀　　　RATING: ★★★☆
Winged
People think of Allete as pretty, creative, leader, intelligent, elegant
People who like the name Allete also like Angelique, Aimee, Adeline, Aceline, Adrienne, Aeryn, Alanna, Amaya, Alora, Alana

Allie *(English)* ♀♂　　　RATING: ★★★☆
Short for names starting with Al—*Kate and Allie*, TV show
People think of Allie as pretty, funny, intelligent, popular, caring
People who like the name Allie also like Bailey, Alexis, Addison, Ally, Avery, Aubrey, Brooke, Madison, Caden, Aidan

Allison *(German)* ♀　　　RATING: ★★★
Little Alice
People think of Allison as pretty, funny, intelligent, caring, creative
People who like the name Allison also like Abigail, Hannah, Emily, Emma, Ava, Grace, Hailey, Alyssa, Audrey, Natalie

Ally *(English)* ♀♂　　　RATING: ★★★★
Friend, partner—Short for names starting with Al; *Ally McBeal*, TV show
People think of Ally as pretty, funny, popular, creative, cool
People who like the name Ally also like Abby, Alexis, Bailey, Allie, Brooke, Alex, Ashley, Addison, Madison, Ashton

Allyson *(English)* ♀　　　RATING: ★★★★
Little Alice—June Allyson, actress
People think of Allyson as pretty, funny, caring, intelligent, creative
People who like the name Allyson also like Abigail, Allison, Alyssa, Ashlyn, Alison, Ava, Hailey, Audrey, Alexandra, Emma

Alma *(Latin)* ♀　　　RATING: ★★
Nourishing—Also Spanish for soul; first used following the Battle of Alma in the Crimean War
People think of Alma as pretty, caring, funny, intelligent, cool
People who like the name Alma also like Ava, Amelia, Adriana, Alana, Abigail, Adela, Amanda, Alena, Amalia, Alexandra

Almira *(Spanish)* ♀　　　RATING: ★★★☆
Noble fame
People think of Almira as pretty, elegant, exotic, intelligent, cool
People who like the name Almira also like Amara, Adriana, Alana, Aliana, Aaliyah, Amalia, Amelia, Aisha, Ariana, Adara

Alodia *(Latin)* ♀　　　RATING: ★★☆
Riches
People think of Alodia as pretty, sexy, creative, powerful, funny
People who like the name Alodia also like Carminda, Adalira, Benecia, Brisa, Belicia, Arwen, Carlota, Belisma, Cadelaria, Candelaria

Alodie *(French)* ♀　　　RATING: ★★★
Wealthy
People think of Alodie as pretty, intelligent, creative, trendy, old-fashioned
People who like the name Alodie also like Amelie, Audrey, Aceline, Aaralyn, Aerona, Aurora, Aelwen, Alicia, Ava, Adalia

Aloha *(Hawaiian)* ♀　　　RATING: ★★
Greetings
People think of Aloha as exotic, pretty, funny, popular, caring
People who like the name Aloha also like Alohilani, Angelina, Amber, Adriana, Alexa, Ailani, Abrianna, Amanda, Amaya, Abigail

Alohilani *(Hawaiian)* ♀　　　RATING: ★★★☆
Bright sky
People think of Alohilani as exotic, pretty, cool, creative, funny
People who like the name Alohilani also like Ailani, Aolani, Aloha, Aulani, Alika, Aaliyah, Amaya, Aaralyn, Alamea, Angelina

Alonsa *(Portuguese)* ♀　　　RATING: ★★
Noble, ready
People think of Alonsa as criminal, exotic, old-fashioned, old, unpopular

People who like the name Alonsa also like Aleta, Adalia, Alexa, Alena, Alecia, Alannis, Alaina, Aitana, Alicia, Alegria

Alonzo (*Spanish*) ♂   RATING: ★★★
Noble, ready
> People think of Alonzo as handsome, popular, cool, funny, caring
> People who like the name Alonzo also like Antonio, Adrian, Alfonso, Alejandro, Abel, Alexander, Andrew, Anthony, Adam, Aaron

Alora (*American*) ♀   RATING: ★★★★☆
Combination of Alice and Laura
> People think of Alora as pretty, creative, intelligent, funny, caring
> People who like the name Alora also like Aurora, Ava, Amara, Alana, Abigail, Adriana, Amaya, Adalia, Alexa, Alanna

Aloysius (*Latin*) ♂   RATING: ★☆
Fame warrior—From the same origin as Louis
> People think of Aloysius as intelligent, handsome, creative, funny, powerful
> People who like the name Aloysius also like Aiden, Alastair, Ambrose, Alistair, Amadeus, Adam, Aden, Axel, Alaric, Alan

Alp (*Turkish*) ♂   RATING: ★★☆
Hero, brave
> People think of Alp as handsome, weird, leader, trustworthy, energetic
> People who like the name Alp also like Alphonse, Aden, Abu, Adohi, Abner, Donnel, Lance, Lancelot, Loman, Dax

Alpana (*Sanskrit/East Indian*) ♀   RATING: ★★★
Beautiful
> People think of Alpana as exotic, elegant, funny, powerful, caring
> People who like the name Alpana also like Avani, Amithi, Anaya, Alka, Anila, Amara, Agrata, Asha, Aiko, Armelle

Alperen (*Turkish*) ♂   RATING: ★★
Heroic mystic
> People think of Alperen as aggressive, ethnic, cool
> People who like the name Alperen also like Yadid, Adonis, Adohi, Yair, Adit, Adarsh, Adair, Yamir, Adolph, Adolfo

Alpha (*Greek*) ♀   RATING: ★☆
The Greek letter Alpha—First letter of Greek alphabet, identified with the "first" or "strongest"
> People think of Alpha as powerful, exotic, funny, creative, intelligent
> People who like the name Alpha also like Amber, Alexa, Alexandra, Alice, Aimee, Andra, Adara, Allegra, Alexandria, Adriana

Alphonse (*French*) ♂   RATING: ★★★★
Noble, ready
> People think of Alphonse as intelligent, caring, trustworthy, creative, handsome
> People who like the name Alphonse also like Aiden, Axel, Alastair, Alistair, Adrian, Arthur, Aloysius, Alain, Alexander, Atticus

Alpine (*American*) ♀♂   RATING: ★★☆
From the Alps mountains in Europe
> People think of Alpine as leader, sporty, energetic, funny, poor
> People who like the name Alpine also like Cricket, Aspen, Bailey, Ashton, Aquarius, Ceres, Aries, Ashanti, Avalon, Austin

Alsatia (*French*) ♀   RATING: ★★★
From the Alsace-Loraine area of France
> People think of Alsatia as pretty, trustworthy, intelligent, elegant, creative
> People who like the name Alsatia also like Aceline, Adalia, Adeline, Adrienne, Alaina, Aerona, Adelaide, Aaralyn, Armelle, Anastasia

Alta (*Latin*) ♀♂   RATING: ★★★☆
Tall, lofty
> People think of Alta as pretty, intelligent, funny, caring, creative
> People who like the name Alta also like Aidan, Alva, Asa, Afton, Ari, Arden, Alexis, Alex, Akia, Ameya

Altan (*Turkish*) ♂   RATING: ★★★☆
Red dawn—Altan Erbulak, author
> People think of Altan as powerful, leader, caring, funny, popular
> People who like the name Altan also like Aden, Aiden, Alden, Adrian, Alton, Asher, Alexander, Aaron, Alaric, Alan

Altantsetseg (*Mongolian*) ♀   RATING: ★★☆
Golden flower
> People think of Altantsetseg as weird, nerdy, exotic, quiet, pretty
> People who like the name Altantsetseg also like Angeni, Anthea, Alohilani, Alethea, Alberta, Anastacia, Adin, Faylinn, Aglaia, Amanda

Altessa (*American*) ♀   RATING: ★★★
Combination of Alice and Tessa; also a brand name
> People think of Altessa as pretty, trendy, young, leader, wild
> People who like the name Altessa also like Adriana, Aurora, Adalia, Abrianna, Amaya, Aaralyn, Audrey, Adeline, Alayna, Amber

Althea (*Greek*) ♀   RATING: ★★
Marshmallow—Althea Gibson, tennis player
> People think of Althea as intelligent, trustworthy, funny, caring, creative
> People who like the name Althea also like Aurora, Amaya, Athena, Anastasia, Abigail, Amelia, Amara, Arwen, Amber, Alethea

Altin *(Turkish)* ♀   RATING: ★★☆
Gold
- People think of Altin as popular, old-fashioned, stuck-up, nerdy, artsy
- People who like the name Altin also like Darla, Aaliyah, Arlanna, Aimee, Arianne, Daphne, Audrey, Ailis, Phila, Amberlin

Alton *(English)* ♂   RATING: ★★★☆
Old town
- People think of Alton as handsome, trustworthy, intelligent, funny, cool
- People who like the name Alton also like Aiden, Alden, Aden, Aaron, Adam, Andrew, Caleb, Alexander, Adrian, Ethan

Altsoba *(Native American)* ♀   RATING: ★★☆
All war—Navajo origin
- People think of Altsoba as aggressive, weird, leader, sexy, religious
- People who like the name Altsoba also like Aleshanee, Anevay, Alaqua, Amadahy, Adsila, Ankti, Angeni, Allete, Aletta, Alora

Alucia *(Spanish)* ♀   RATING: ★★★
Combination of Anna and Lucia
- People think of Alucia as energetic, pretty, religious, ethnic, winner
- People who like the name Alucia also like Alegria, Amorina, Adriana, Almira, Aracely, Aletta, Carlota, Belita, Belicia, California

Alva *(Latin)* ♀♂   RATING: ★★
Fair complected
- People think of Alva as intelligent, funny, caring, creative, pretty
- People who like the name Alva also like Aidan, Alexis, Alta, Avery, Astin, Arden, Alex, Ariel, Addison, Aldis

Alvar *(English)* ♂   RATING: ★★★
Elf warrior
- People think of Alvar as intelligent, handsome, powerful, creative, elegant
- People who like the name Alvar also like Aiden, Alvis, Albert, Alfred, Aden, Alexander, Aston, Atticus, Balin, Alastair

Alvaro *(Spanish)* ♂   RATING: ★☆
Guardian
- People think of Alvaro as handsome, caring, intelligent, funny, cool
- People who like the name Alvaro also like Alejandro, Antonio, Alexander, Alfonso, Adrian, Alberto, Andrés, Angelito, Anthony, Amando

Alvin *(American)* ♂   RATING: ★★★
Noble friend—Alvin Ailey, dancer and choreographer; *Alvin and the Chipmunks*, TV show
- People think of Alvin as funny, caring, intelligent, cool, handsome
- People who like the name Alvin also like Adam, Alan, Aaron, Alexander, Allen, Aiden, Andrew, Adrian, Ace, Albert

Alvis *(English)* ♂   RATING: ★★☆
Elf wise—Variation of Elvis
- People think of Alvis as weird, funny, handsome, intelligent, ethnic
- People who like the name Alvis also like Alvin, Alan, Aiden, Alfred, Aden, Alastair, Alden, Alexander, Abie, Aldon

Alyce *(American)* ♀   RATING: ★★★☆
Of noble kin—Variation of Alice
- People think of Alyce as pretty, caring, funny, trustworthy, intelligent
- People who like the name Alyce also like Ava, Alice, Amelia, Alicia, Angela, Alexa, Audrey, Abbie, Annabel, Allison

Alyn *(American)* ♀   RATING: ★★☆
Little rock—Feminine form of Alan
- People think of Alyn as funny, creative, caring, leader, pretty
- People who like the name Alyn also like Aaralyn, Ashlyn, Ava, Aeryn, Adriana, Alana, Alexa, Amber, Adeline, Ariana

Alyson *(English)* ♀   RATING: ★★★★
Little Alice—Variation of Allison
- People think of Alyson as pretty, funny, caring, intelligent, creative
- People who like the name Alyson also like Alyssa, Allison, Allyson, Abigail, Amber, Alison, Ava, Audrey, Alexandra, Alissa

Alyssa *(Greek)* ♀   RATING: ★★★☆
Rational—Alyssa Milano, actress
- People think of Alyssa as pretty, funny, caring, creative, intelligent
- People who like the name Alyssa also like Abigail, Ava, Alissa, Emma, Hannah, Hailey, Amber, Adriana, Alexa, Isabella

Amable *(Latin)* ♀   RATING: ★☆
Lovable
- People think of Amable as weird, caring, artsy, girl next door, pretty
- People who like the name Amable also like Amorina, Amora, Adora, Amanda, Alana, Adrina, Amaranta, Amadis, Alegria, Amity

Amada *(Spanish)* ♀   RATING: ★★★
Beloved
- People think of Amada as caring, funny, pretty, trustworthy, intelligent
- People who like the name Amada also like Ariana, Adrianna, Aaliyah, Aimee, Adriana, Anisa, Amorina, Adelina, Aracely, Amanda

Amadahy *(Native American)* ♀   RATING: ★★★★
Forest water—Cherokee origin
- People think of Amadahy as pretty, caring, exotic, ethnic, intelligent
- People who like the name Amadahy also like Amaya, Angeni, Alora, Aleshanee, Anevay, Adsila, Aradia, Ailani, Amayeta, Aelwen

94

Amadeus *(Latin)* ♂   RATING: ★★
Love of God—Wolfgang Amadeus Mozart, composer; *Amadeus*, film and Broadway musical
> People think of Amadeus as intelligent, handsome, creative, powerful, elegant
> People who like the name Amadeus also like Alexander, Adrian, Aiden, Alastair, Aaron, Adonis, Atticus, Andrew, Anakin, Aden

Amadis *(Latin)* ♀   RATING: ★★★☆
Love of God—Variation of Amadeus
> People think of Amadis as creative, religious, artsy, pretty, quiet
> People who like the name Amadis also like Amaris, Adalia, Amara, Amani, Amaya, Anaya, Adora, Amalia, Adalira, Amalie

Amal *(Arabic)* ♀   RATING: ★★
Hope, expectation
> People think of Amal as funny, intelligent, pretty, creative, young
> People who like the name Amal also like Amani, Aaliyah, Aisha, Alima, Adrina, Aida, Amara, Adara, Ailani, Aiko

Amalia *(Latin)* ♀   RATING: ★★★☆
Hardworking—Variation of Amelia; often used in South America
> People think of Amalia as pretty, intelligent, funny, creative, caring
> People who like the name Amalia also like Amelia, Ava, Amalie, Abigail, Amaya, Adriana, Amara, Bella, Annabella, Aaliyah

Amalie *(Latin)* ♀   RATING: ★★★★
Hard worker—Widely used in Germany
> People think of Amalie as pretty, intelligent, creative, artsy, caring
> People who like the name Amalie also like Amelie, Ava, Amelia, Amalia, Abigail, Audrey, Bella, Adriana, Autumn, Amaya

Aman *(Arabic)* ♂   RATING: ★★★☆
Trust, safety—Also Hindi for peace
> People think of Aman as intelligent, handsome, funny, popular, cool
> People who like the name Aman also like Amir, Aden, Andrew, Ajani, Amin, Angelo, Amando, Alexander, Aaron, Amil

Amanda *(Latin)* ♀   RATING: ★★★
Worthy of love—Amanda Bynes, actress; Amanda Plummer, actress
> People think of Amanda as pretty, funny, caring, intelligent, creative
> People who like the name Amanda also like Amber, Abigail, Alyssa, Alexandra, Amy, Emma, Emily, Hannah, Samantha, Allison

Amandla *(African)* ♀   RATING: ★★
Power
> People think of Amandla as wild, powerful, unpopular, artsy, sneaky

> People who like the name Amandla also like Amani, Amanda, Amber, Angelina, Alexandria, Abeni, Amadis, Alanna, Amaya, Aaralyn

Amando *(Italian)* ♂   RATING: ★★★
Worthy of love
> People think of Amando as handsome, sexy, wealthy, intelligent, sporty
> People who like the name Amando also like Alfonso, Angelo, Aaron, Alexander, Antonio, Aden, Alejandro, Anthony, Alexavier, Aiden

Amani *(Persian)* ♀   RATING: ★★★★
Security, trust
> People think of Amani as pretty, funny, intelligent, trustworthy, young
> People who like the name Amani also like Amaya, Amara, Anaya, Ayanna, Aaliyah, Ailani, Adriana, Ariana, Amaris, Aaralyn

Amantha *(American)* ♀   RATING: ★★★
Combination of Amanda and Samantha
> People think of Amantha as weird, young, funny, trustworthy, poor
> People who like the name Amantha also like Annabella, Adrianna, Isabella, Alexandra, Alecia, Abrianna, Abigail, Arabella, Allegra, Aaralyn

Amara *(Sanskrit/East Indian)* ♀   RATING: ★★★★☆
Eternal
> People think of Amara as pretty, intelligent, creative, caring, funny
> People who like the name Amara also like Amaya, Ava, Alana, Adriana, Ariana, Abigail, Amani, Anaya, Alexa, Amelia

Amaranta *(Latin)* ♀   RATING: ★★
Flower that never fades
> People think of Amaranta as pretty, exotic, trustworthy, sexy, powerful
> People who like the name Amaranta also like Aurora, Amaya, Amarante, Amara, Adrienne, Ava, Autumn, Aaralyn, Adora, Abrianna

Amarante *(Japanese)* ♀   RATING: ★★★★
Flower that never fades
> People think of Amarante as pretty, exotic, intelligent, elegant, creative
> People who like the name Amarante also like Amaya, Aiko, Aneko, Ayame, Ai, Amaranta, Aradia, Emiko, Sakura, Arwen

Amaris *(Hebrew)* ♀   RATING: ★★★☆
Promised by God
> People think of Amaris as pretty, creative, intelligent, caring, funny
> People who like the name Amaris also like Amara, Abigail, Amaya, Adalia, Anaya, Alana, Arielle, Alayna, Arianna, Annalise

Amaryllis *(Greek)* ♀   RATING: ★★★☆
Sparkling—Also a type of flower
People think of Amaryllis as pretty, creative, exotic, intelligent, elegant
People who like the name Amaryllis also like Anastasia, Aurora, Adriana, Adelaide, Amber, Amaya, Ava, Amelia, Alexandria, Abigail

Amaya *(Japanese)* ♀   RATING: ★★★★☆
Night rain
People think of Amaya as pretty, intelligent, creative, caring, funny
People who like the name Amaya also like Ava, Amara, Anaya, Adriana, Aaliyah, Alana, Ayanna, Ariana, Abigail, Maya

Amayeta *(Native American)* ♀   RATING: ★★★
Big berries—Miwok origin
People think of Amayeta as exotic, ethnic, sexy, trustworthy, young
People who like the name Amayeta also like Amadahy, Aleshanee, Angeni, Alora, Adalia, Alaqua, Adsila, Amaya, Ayasha, Amelia

Amber *(English)* ♀   RATING: ★★★
Precious stone—Amber Valletta, model/actress
People think of Amber as pretty, funny, caring, creative, intelligent
People who like the name Amber also like Abigail, Amanda, Alyssa, Chloe, Hailey, Paige, Ava, Faith, Audrey, Alexa

Amberlin *(American)* ♀   RATING: ★★★☆
Combination of Amber and Lin
People think of Amberlin as pretty, popular, quiet, girl next door, trendy
People who like the name Amberlin also like Ashlyn, Abigail, Adrianna, Alaina, Amelia, Abbie, Audriana, Aubrianna, Adrienne, Arianna

Amberly *(American)* ♀   RATING: ★★★★
Combination of Amber and Kimberly
People think of Amberly as pretty, funny, caring, popular, creative
People who like the name Amberly also like Abigail, Amber, Ashlyn, Ava, Abrianna, Amelia, Anastasia, Alexa, Angelina, Audrey

Ambra *(Italian)* ♀   RATING: ★★★★
Amber colored
People think of Ambra as pretty, intelligent, creative, energetic, sexy
People who like the name Ambra also like Angelina, Adrina, Amber, Abrianna, Ariana, Adriana, Ava, Aria, Alana, Alexa

Ambrea *(American)* ♀   RATING: ★★★
Combination of Amber and Andrea
People think of Ambrea as pretty, intelligent, caring, energetic, funny
People who like the name Ambrea also like Abrianna, Andralyn, Ashlyn, Aubrianna, Angelina, Aria, Amberly, Amelia, Amber, Aaliyah

Ambrose *(Greek)* ♂   RATING: ★★★☆
Immortal—Ambrose Bierce, essayist and author
People think of Ambrose as intelligent, handsome, caring, trustworthy, creative
People who like the name Ambrose also like Aiden, Alexander, Alastair, Asher, Adam, Aden, Adrian, Aaron, Anthony, Andrew

Ambrosia *(Greek)* ♀   RATING: ★★★
Immortal
People think of Ambrosia as intelligent, pretty, exotic, creative, funny
People who like the name Ambrosia also like Aurora, Chloe, Aaliyah, Anastasia, Aria, Adriana, Sabrina, Annabelle, Amara, Celeste

Ambrosine *(Greek)* ♀   RATING: ★★★
Immortal—Feminine form of Ambrose
People think of Ambrosine as pretty, exotic, intelligent, powerful, elegant
People who like the name Ambrosine also like Anastasia, Aurora, Adrienne, Amber, Amaya, Athena, Amaryllis, Aiko, Adalira, Adriana

Amelia *(Latin)* ♀   RATING: ★★★★
To strive, excel, rival—Originally a variation of Aemilia; Amelia Bedelia, children's book character; Amelia Earhart, aviator
People think of Amelia as pretty, intelligent, funny, creative, caring
People who like the name Amelia also like Ava, Abigail, Olivia, Isabella, Emma, Ella, Grace, Audrey, Hannah, Chloe

Amelie *(French)* ♀   RATING: ★★★★☆
Hardworking—*Amelie*, movie title
People think of Amelie as pretty, creative, intelligent, artsy, elegant
People who like the name Amelie also like Amelia, Ava, Audrey, Chloe, Abigail, Ella, Isabella, Olivia, Charlotte, Isabelle

Amena *(Arabic)* ♀   RATING: ★★★★
Trustworthy, honest—Variation of Amina
People think of Amena as pretty, exotic, trustworthy, caring, funny
People who like the name Amena also like Amaya, Amina, Amara, Anaya, Aisha, Amani, Amelia, Adriana, Aaralyn, Aaliyah

Amergin *(Celtic/Gaelic)* ♂   RATING: ★★★
Born of song—Pronounced *Av-ir-in*
People think of Amergin as creative, powerful, young, energetic, sneaky
People who like the name Amergin also like Aiden, Alistair, Alaric, Alastair, Aden, Angus, Artan, Arlen, Arthur, Atticus

America *(German)* ♀ ♂   RATING: ★★★☆
Home ruler—From the same origin as Emery and Aimery; America Ferrera, actress
People think of America as intelligent, funny, pretty, creative, leader

People who like the name America also like Angel, Alexis, Ariel, Addison, Aidan, Americus, Andrea, Ashton, Avery, Aubrey

Americus *(German)* ♀♂ RATING: ★★★☆
Home ruler—Feminine form of America, now accepted for both sexes
People think of Americus as pretty, funny, creative, popular, leader
People who like the name Americus also like Alexis, Aidan, Addison, Ashton, Avery, Aubrey, Ariel, Angel, America, Andrea

Amerigo *(Italian)* ♂ RATING: ★★★
Home ruler—Amerigo Vespucci, Italian explorer
People think of Amerigo as leader, weird, powerful, slow, intelligent
People who like the name Amerigo also like Alfonso, Agostino, Amando, Alexander, Amadeus, Adam, Andrew, Ajax, Alejandro, Alexavier

Amery *(American)* ♀ RATING: ★★★☆
Home ruler—Short for America
People think of Amery as caring, pretty, intelligent, popular, artsy
People who like the name Amery also like Audrey, Abrianna, Maylin, Hope, Amory, Faith, Grace, Ava, Brielle, Aurora

Ames *(French)* ♀♂ RATING: ★★★☆
Friend
People think of Ames as creative, trustworthy, intelligent, cool, elegant
People who like the name Ames also like Aidan, Avery, Astin, Arden, Austin, Alexis, Aure, Alex, Angel, Aren

Ameya *(Sanskrit/East Indian)* ♀♂ RATING: ★★☆
Boundless
People think of Ameya as creative, energetic, pretty, intelligent, cool
People who like the name Ameya also like Aidan, Akia, Alexis, Ashton, Caden, Avery, Ari, Arden, Aubrey, Azriel

Ami *(French)* ♀ RATING: ★★★
Friend
People think of Ami as funny, creative, caring, intelligent, cool
People who like the name Ami also like Aimee, Amber, Amy, Ava, Abigail, Amelia, Alicia, Annabel, Alana, Alexia

Amie *(French)* ♀ RATING: ★★★★☆
Friend
People think of Amie as pretty, caring, funny, creative, intelligent
People who like the name Amie also like Aimee, Amy, Abbie, Ami, Amber, Adriana, Amelia, Ava, Abigail, Anna

Amiel *(Hebrew)* ♀♂ RATING: ★★★★
My people belong to God
People think of Amiel as caring, intelligent, handsome, cool, funny
People who like the name Amiel also like Ariel, Azriel, Aidan, Ari, Adriel, Arien, Addison, Arion, Angel, Alexis

Amil *(Arabic)* ♂ RATING: ★★★
Hopeful
People think of Amil as intelligent, leader, popular, funny, powerful
People who like the name Amil also like Amir, Aden, Amin, Alijah, Amish, Ambrose, Alexander, Amiri, Adam, Alain

Amin *(Arabic)* ♂ RATING: ★★★☆
Trustworthy, honest
People think of Amin as intelligent, handsome, trustworthy, funny, caring
People who like the name Amin also like Amir, Amil, Aden, Alijah, Allen, Ambrose, Alastair, Aiden, Aimon, Alaric

Amina *(Arabic)* ♀ RATING: ★★☆
Trustworthy, honest
People think of Amina as pretty, intelligent, caring, funny, trustworthy
People who like the name Amina also like Amaya, Amara, Amelia, Ava, Amena, Aurora, Adina, Alana, Aaliyah, Adriana

Aminia *(American)* ♀ RATING: ★★★☆
Trustworthy, honest—Variation of Amina
People think of Aminia as quiet, pretty, intelligent, creative, young
People who like the name Aminia also like Anaya, Amina, Anisa, Ayanna, Abrianna, Aysha, Alayna, Alana, Amani, Amaya

Amir *(Arabic)* ♂ RATING: ★★★☆
Prince, rich, cultivated—Many Arabic names can be translated into English as Amir
People think of Amir as handsome, intelligent, funny, cool, leader
People who like the name Amir also like Aden, Amiri, Aiden, Aaron, Ajani, Amil, Alijah, André, Adrian, Alexander

Amira *(Arabic)* ♀ RATING: ★★★★
Princess, rich, cultivated—Feminine form of Amir
People think of Amira as pretty, wealthy, leader, intelligent, elegant
People who like the name Amira also like Ava, Olivia, Amaya, Amara, Audrey, Lydia, Mira, Ella, Mia, Amelia

Amiri *(Arabic)* ♂ RATING: ★★★☆
Princely—Amiri Baraka, poet/playwright
People think of Amiri as intelligent, funny, exotic, sexy, handsome
People who like the name Amiri also like Amir, Alijah, Aden, Aiden, Alaric, Azizi, Ajani, Ace, Amil, André

Amish *(Sanskrit/East Indian)* ♂ RATING: ★★★
Free of deceit—Pronounced *Ah-MEESH* in India; also a sect of Mennonites in the United States, pronounced *AH-mish*
People think of Amish as funny, aggressive, sexy, old-fashioned, intelligent
People who like the name Amish also like Ashwin, Arav, Alagan, Atish, Amrit, Adarsh, Arnav, Ajay, Adit, Adish

Amita *(Sanskrit/East Indian)* ♀   RATING: ★★★
Limitless
> People think of Amita as trustworthy, pretty, cool, caring, exotic
> People who like the name Amita also like Anaya, Avani, Adita, Amithi, Alka, Anila, Amrita, Amma, Amara, Agrata

Amithi *(Sanskrit/East Indian)* ♀   RATING: ★★★
Boundlessness
> People think of Amithi as exotic, ethnic, intelligent, elegant, sexy
> People who like the name Amithi also like Avani, Alpana, Agrata, Anila, Anaya, Anjali, Amaya, Amara, Aisha, Anika

Amitola *(Native American)* ♀   RATING: ★★★
Rainbow
> People think of Amitola as pretty, exotic, elegant, creative, caring
> People who like the name Amitola also like Aponi, Aleshanee, Alora, Amorina, Angeni, Adsila, Aolani, Abrianna, Amaya, Aaliyah

Amity *(English)* ♀   RATING: ★★
Friendship
> People think of Amity as pretty, caring, intelligent, creative, funny
> People who like the name Amity also like Amelia, Ava, Abigail, Amber, Autumn, Audrey, Anastasia, Aurora, Annabelle, Alexa

Amma *(Sanskrit/East Indian)* ♀   RATING: ★★
Mother
> People think of Amma as caring, intelligent, pretty, trustworthy, funny
> People who like the name Amma also like Anaya, Ava, Alanna, Amaya, Anastasia, Amara, Anila, Ani, Aimee, Alexandria

Amor *(Spanish)* ♀♂   RATING: ★★★★
Love—Also a term of endearment
> People think of Amor as pretty, sexy, exotic, popular, creative
> People who like the name Amor also like Angel, Alex, Alexis, Ariel, Aidan, Aubrey, Andrea, Ari, Artemis, Arien

Amora *(Spanish)* ♀   RATING: ★★★★☆
Love
> People think of Amora as pretty, exotic, caring, elegant, sexy
> People who like the name Amora also like Aurora, Amorina, Adriana, Amara, Amaya, Adora, Anastasia, Abrianna, Angelina, Alana

Amorina *(Spanish)* ♀   RATING: ★★
Love
> People think of Amorina as pretty, caring, young, intelligent, sexy
> People who like the name Amorina also like Amora, Adriana, Adora, Angelina, Anastasia, Aurora, Alana, Amelia, Abrianna, Aaliyah

Amory *(English)* ♀   RATING: ★★★★☆
Home ruler—Variation of Amery
> People think of Amory as intelligent, cool, elegant, pretty, creative
> People who like the name Amory also like Ava, Aurora, Aaralyn, Alexa, Ashlyn, Alana, Autumn, Abrianna, Amber, Audrey

Amos *(Hebrew)* ♂   RATING: ★★★☆
Burdened, laden—Tori Amos, singer; *Amos 'n' Andy*, radio show
> People think of Amos as intelligent, handsome, funny, popular, cool
> People who like the name Amos also like Alexander, Adam, Andrew, Aaron, Adrian, Aiden, Asher, Angus, Alastair, Ambrose

Amrit *(Sanskrit/East Indian)* ♂   RATING: ★★★☆
Nectar
> People think of Amrit as intelligent, funny, religious, creative, artsy
> People who like the name Amrit also like Amish, Ashwin, Arav, Adarsh, Alagan, Ajay, Adit, Ansel, Arnav, Atish

Amrita *(Sanskrit/East Indian)* ♀   RATING: ★★★☆
Nectar
> People think of Amrita as pretty, exotic, intelligent, popular, funny
> People who like the name Amrita also like Amara, Anaya, Alpana, Anjali, Amma, Amithi, Anila, Amorina, Alka, Avatari

Amser *(Welsh)* ♀   RATING: ★★★
Time
> People think of Amser as pretty, energetic, weird, elegant, girl next door
> People who like the name Amser also like Arwen, Aderyn, Aeryn, Aelwen, Aideen, Alana, Amaya, Aerona, Aradia, Awen

Amy *(Latin)* ♀   RATING: ★★★
Beloved—Amy Grant, singer; Amy Irving, actress; Amy Smart, actress; Amy Winehouse, singer
> People think of Amy as pretty, funny, caring, intelligent, creative
> People who like the name Amy also like Amber, Abigail, Amanda, Anna, Emily, Emma, Hannah, Ava, Amelia, Allison

An *(Chinese)* ♀♂   RATING: ★★
Peace
> People think of An as intelligent, quiet, funny, cool, popular
> People who like the name An also like Angel, Aidan, Alex, Andrea, Ari, Alexis, Asa, Arizona, Arden, Aubrey

Ana *(Spanish)* ♀   RATING: ★★★
Gracious, merciful—Variation of Anne
> People think of Ana as pretty, funny, caring, intelligent, creative

People who like the name Ana also like Ava, Anna, Adriana, Amelia, Abigail, Emma, Alexa, Alexandra, Amy, Audrey

Anah *(Hebrew)* ♀   RATING: ★★★
Answer
People think of Anah as pretty, intelligent, elegant, creative, girl next door
People who like the name Anah also like Ava, Hannah, Ana, Adara, Amalia, Amaris, Julia, Keziah, Juliana, Anastasia

Anahid *(Armenian)* ♀   RATING: ★★★☆
Stainless, immaculate—Pahlavi origin; Armenian goddess of the moon, associated with the Roman goddess Diana
People think of Anahid as intelligent, exotic, funny, sexy, cool
People who like the name Anahid also like Amadahy, Amber, Amaris, Ailani, Amara, Anastasia, Abigail, Adalia, Anielka, Amaya

Anaïs *(French)* ♀   RATING: ★★★★☆
Name of a perfume—Anaïs Nin, writer
People think of Anaïs as pretty, creative, intelligent, caring, exotic
People who like the name Anaïs also like Ava, Anaya, Amaya, Amelie, Amelia, Amaris, Chloe, Alana, Aurora, Anya

Anakin *(American)* ♂   RATING: ★★★★☆
Warrior—Anakin Skywalker, created by George Lucas for the *Star Wars* character
People think of Anakin as powerful, leader, handsome, intelligent, aggressive
People who like the name Anakin also like Aiden, Alexander, Aden, Aaron, Andrew, Caleb, Adam, Adrian, Ethan, Kaden

Analiese *(German)* ♀   RATING: ★★★
Combination of Anna and Elise
People think of Analiese as pretty, intelligent, caring, funny, creative
People who like the name Analiese also like Annalise, Abigail, Ava, Analise, Annabelle, Amelia, Anastasia, Ashlyn, Arianna, Isabella

Analise *(German)* ♀   RATING: ★★★★☆
Combination of Anna and Elise
People think of Analise as pretty, elegant, intelligent, caring, funny
People who like the name Analise also like Annalise, Analiese, Ava, Abigail, Amelia, Annabelle, Adriana, Arianna, Audrey, Anastasia

Analu *(Hawaiian)* ♂   RATING: ★★
Manly—Variation of Andrew
People think of Analu as exotic, weird, creative, pretty, quiet
People who like the name Analu also like Aiden, Ace, Alejandro, Alastair, Aden, Alain, Alair, Alexander, Adrian, Anton

Anana *(African)* ♀   RATING: ★★★☆
Fourth born
People think of Anana as exotic, pretty, quiet, intelligent, trustworthy
People who like the name Anana also like Anisa, Amara, Amber, Amaya, Anaya, Amani, Abrianna, Ayanna, Alana, Ania

Ananda *(Sanskrit/East Indian)* ♀ ♂   RATING: ★★★★
Bliss, joy—Ananda Lewis, actress/TV host
People think of Ananda as creative, intelligent, pretty, caring, funny
People who like the name Ananda also like Aidan, Alexis, Ameya, Ashanti, Angel, Aubrey, Ashton, Ariel, Ainsley, Arizona

Anando *(Sanskrit/East Indian)* ♂   RATING: ★★
Bliss
People think of Anando as lazy, funny, exotic, aggressive, nerdy
People who like the name Anando also like Angelo, Alexavier, Andrew, Aaron, Anwar, Aden, Antonio, Anton, Amando, Alejandro

Anastacia *(Spanish)* ♀   RATING: ★★★
Resurrection
People think of Anastacia as pretty, popular, intelligent, creative, sexy
People who like the name Anastacia also like Anastasia, Adriana, Abigail, Angelina, Aurora, Ava, Amelia, Alexandria, Amber, Alexandra

Anastasia *(Greek)* ♀   RATING: ★★★★
Resurrection—Daughter of Russia's Czar Nicholas
People think of Anastasia as pretty, intelligent, elegant, creative, funny
People who like the name Anastasia also like Abigail, Isabella, Alexandria, Ava, Alexandra, Aurora, Amelia, Adriana, Arianna, Angelina

Anatola *(Greek)* ♀   RATING: ★★★
From Anatolia
People think of Anatola as exotic, creative, old-fashioned, weird, energetic
People who like the name Anatola also like Anastasia, Annabelle, Adalia, Ava, Alexia, Alexandria, Adriana, Amara, Adara, Angelina

Anatole *(French)* ♂   RATING: ★★★
From Anatolia
People think of Anatole as handsome, intelligent, old-fashioned, powerful, caring
People who like the name Anatole also like Ancelin, Alexander, Aaron, Adair, Angelo, Anton, Ansel, Anakin, Adam, Alden

Anaya *(Sanskrit/East Indian)* ♀   RATING: ★★★★☆
Completely free
People think of Anaya as pretty, intelligent, caring, creative, funny
People who like the name Anaya also like Amaya, Ayanna, Aaliyah, Amara, Anya, Ava, Ariana, Amani, Adriana, Arianna

Ancelin (French) ♂   RATING: ★★★
Little God
- People think of Ancelin as energetic, cool, intelligent, religious, young
- People who like the name Ancelin also like Aiden, Aden, Ansel, Alain, Adair, Asher, Alastair, Alistair, Anakin, Anatole

Anchoret (Welsh) ♀   RATING: ★★★
Much loved—Medieval variation of Angharad
- People think of Anchoret as pretty, nerdy, old-fashioned, poor, trendy
- People who like the name Anchoret also like Aelwen, Arwen, Aderyn, Aradia, Aria, Adalia, Aerona, Alora, Aurora, Aeryn

Ande (African) ♂   RATING: ★★★
Pillar
- People think of Ande as intelligent, funny, creative, sporty, leader
- People who like the name Ande also like Andrew, Alexander, Adrian, Adam, Aden, Alan, Anthony, Aaron, Aiden, Anderson

Andeana (American) ♀   RATING: ★★★
Combination of Andi and Anna
- People think of Andeana as pretty, intelligent, funny, creative, young
- People who like the name Andeana also like Adriana, Abrianna, Anastasia, Alayna, Alaina, Alecia, Ailani, Alanna, Abigail, Adrienne

Anders (English) ♂   RATING: ★★★★
Son of Andrew
- People think of Anders as handsome, intelligent, funny, popular, cool
- People who like the name Anders also like Asher, Anderson, Aiden, Alexander, Andrew, Aaron, Adam, Anson, Archer, Axel

Anderson (English) ♂   RATING: ★★★
Son of Andrew—Anderson Cooper, newscaster
- People think of Anderson as intelligent, handsome, leader, powerful, popular
- People who like the name Anderson also like Aiden, Alexander, Andrew, Jackson, Braden, Aaron, Benjamin, Emerson, Adam, Aden

Andie (English) ♀♂   RATING: ★★★★
Manly—Feminine form of Andy or Andrew; Andie MacDowell, actress
- People think of Andie as funny, pretty, creative, energetic, cool
- People who like the name Andie also like Bailey, Addison, Aidan, Avery, Allie, Alexis, Alex, Caden, Ashton, Andrea

Andra (American) ♀   RATING: ★★★★
Manly—Feminine form of Andrew
- People think of Andra as pretty, creative, intelligent, funny, popular
- People who like the name Andra also like Alexa, Adriana, Amber, Audrey, Ava, Alexia, Amanda, Abigail, Amelia, Alexandria

Andralyn (American) ♀   RATING: ★★★☆
Combination of Andra and Lynn
- People think of Andralyn as leader, creative, pretty, popular, wild
- People who like the name Andralyn also like Aaralyn, Ashlyn, Abrianna, Adriana, Abigail, Analiese, Cailyn, Audriana, Aeryn, Annalise

André (French) ♂   RATING: ★★☆
Manly—Variation of Andrew; André Agassi, tennis player; André Braugher, actor; André Benjamin (aka Andre 3★★★), actor/musician
- People think of André as handsome, cool, funny, intelligent, sexy
- People who like the name André also like Anthony, Adrian, Aiden, Alexander, Andrew, Aaron, Adam, Aden, Caleb, Antonio

Andrea (Italian) ♀♂   RATING: ★★★☆
Manly—Feminine form of Andrew; pronounced ANN-dree-a or Ahn-DRAY-a; Andrea Bocelli, tenor
- People think of Andrea as pretty, funny, caring, intelligent, creative
- People who like the name Andrea also like Alexis, Aubrey, Bailey, Ashley, Brooke, Austin, Alex, Madison, Addison, Cameron

Andreas (Greek) ♂   RATING: ★★★★
Manly
- People think of Andreas as intelligent, handsome, sexy, cool, funny
- People who like the name Andreas also like Alexander, Adrian, Andrew, Aaron, André, Aiden, Adam, Anthony, Aden, Anton

Andren (Scandinavian) ♀♂   RATING: ★★☆
Manly—Variation of Andrew
- People think of Andren as handsome, cool, young, funny, boy next door
- People who like the name Andren also like Alexis, Arden, Aidan, Avery, Aubrey, Addison, Austin, Ashton, Caden, Blaine

Andrés (Spanish) ♂   RATING: ★★★★
Manly—Variation of Andrew; Andrés Segovia, classical guitarist
- People think of Andrés as handsome, funny, cool, intelligent, sexy
- People who like the name Andrés also like Adrian, Antonio, Alejandro, Andrew, Alexander, Anthony, Aiden, Armando, Adam, André

Andrew (Greek) ♂   RATING: ★★★☆
Manly—First apostle of Christ; Andrew Jackson, U.S. president; Andrew Johnson, U.S. president; Andrew Wyeth, artist
- People think of Andrew as handsome, funny, intelligent, caring, cool

People who like the name Andrew also like Alexander, Ethan, Benjamin, Aaron, Adam, Matthew, Aiden, Jacob, Anthony, Caleb

Andrin *(Rumantsch)* ♂ RATING: ★★★
Ruler of the home—Variation of Henry
People think of Andrin as creative, cool, sporty, popular, intelligent
People who like the name Andrin also like Aden, Ansel, Ethan, Adrian, Andrew, Braden, Aaron, Aiden, Kaden, Adam

Andrina *(American)* ♀ RATING: ★★★
Combination of Andrea and Tina
People think of Andrina as pretty, caring, cool, creative, funny
People who like the name Andrina also like Adrianna, April, Abrianna, Arianna, Alana, Alexandria, Audrina, Adriana, Audriana, Alaina

Andromeda *(Greek)* ♀ RATING: ★★★★
Ruler of men—In Greek mythology, the daughter of Cassiopeia
People think of Andromeda as exotic, powerful, pretty, intelligent, elegant
People who like the name Andromeda also like Aurora, Anastasia, Athena, Arwen, Adriana, Ava, Amara, Amber, Aeryn, Aphrodite

Andy *(English)* ♀♂ RATING: ★★☆
Manly—Short for Andrew; Andy Garcia, actor; Andy Griffith, actor; Andy Warhol, artist
People think of Andy as funny, handsome, intelligent, cool, caring
People who like the name Andy also like Alex, Austin, Alexis, Bailey, Angel, Ashley, Ashton, Alec, Blake, Avery

Aneko *(Japanese)* ♀ RATING: ★★☆
Older sister
People think of Aneko as pretty, intelligent, caring, creative, popular
People who like the name Aneko also like Aiko, Amaya, Ayame, Amarante, Emiko, Ai, Anastasia, Aeryn, Aurora, Adriana

Anemone *(Greek)* ♀ RATING: ★☆
Breath—Pronounced *Ah-NEH-mo-nee*
People think of Anemone as powerful, exotic, pretty, intelligent, elegant
People who like the name Anemone also like Aurora, Anastasia, Aeryn, Aneko, Armelle, Aiko, Amaya, Andromeda, Arwen, Ava

Anevay *(Native American)* ♀ RATING: ★★★
Superior
People think of Anevay as pretty, powerful, funny, leader, popular
People who like the name Anevay also like Angeni, Anaya, Aaralyn, Ayasha, Amaya, Aleshanee, Amadahy, Ava, Alora, Ailani

Angel *(Greek)* ♀♂ RATING: ★★★☆
Messenger of God—Pronounced *An-HEL* in Spanish
People think of Angel as caring, pretty, funny, cool, intelligent
People who like the name Angel also like Alexis, Bailey, Alex, Ariel, Ashley, Ashton, Brooke, Dakota, Jade, Aidan

Angela *(English)* ♀ RATING: ★★★
Messenger of God—From the Greek *angelos*; Angela Bassett, actress; Angela Lansbury, actress
People think of Angela as pretty, funny, caring, intelligent, trustworthy
People who like the name Angela also like Angelina, Abigail, Amber, Amanda, Adriana, Alicia, Alyssa, Angelica, Audrey, Alexandra

Angelica *(Latin)* ♀ RATING: ★★★
Messenger of God—Also a spice; Anjelica Huston, actress; Angelica Pickles, from *Rugrats* cartoon
People think of Angelica as pretty, funny, intelligent, caring, creative
People who like the name Angelica also like Angelina, Abigail, Amelia, Anastasia, Amber, Adriana, Angela, Angelique, Amanda, Alexandra

Angelie *(French)* ♀ RATING: ★★★☆
Messenger of God
People think of Angelie as pretty, caring, funny, intelligent, creative
People who like the name Angelie also like Angelique, Angelina, Angelica, Ava, Angela, Adriana, Aliana, Abigail, Alaina, Arianna

Angelina *(Italian)* ♀ RATING: ★★★★
Messenger of God—Angelina Jolie, actress
People think of Angelina as pretty, sexy, intelligent, caring, funny
People who like the name Angelina also like Isabella, Adriana, Abigail, Ava, Arianna, Anastasia, Alyssa, Alexandria, Amber, Amelia

Angelique *(French)* ♀ RATING: ★★★
Messenger of God
People think of Angelique as pretty, caring, intelligent, funny, creative
People who like the name Angelique also like Angelina, Angelica, Arianna, Adriana, Anastasia, Aaliyah, Alexandria, Abigail, Alexandra, Annabelle

Angelito *(Spanish)* ♂ RATING: ★★
Little angel
People think of Angelito as handsome, cool, caring, trustworthy, young
People who like the name Angelito also like Antonio, Angelo, Alejandro, Aiden, Andrés, Alexander, Alberto, Anthony, Armando, Andrew

Angelo *(Italian)* ♂ RATING: ★★★☆
Messenger of God
People think of Angelo as handsome, popular, funny, caring, intelligent

People who like the name Angelo also like Anthony, Antonio, Aiden, Alexander, Adrian, Aaron, Gabriel, Andrew, Adam, André

Angeni *(Native American)* ♀   RATING: ★★★★
Angel—Potawatomi origin; based on the English word angel
People think of Angeni as exotic, pretty, caring, creative, intelligent
People who like the name Angeni also like Ayasha, Alora, Angelique, Angelina, Amaya, Aleshanee, Aaralyn, Aiko, Amara, Anastasia

Angharad *(Welsh)* ♀   RATING: ★★★
Much loved—Variation of Anchoret
People think of Angharad as pretty, leader, trendy, trustworthy, wild
People who like the name Angharad also like Arwen, Briallen, Rhiannon, Kiara, Aeryn, Hermione, Faye, Isabel, Keira, Silvia

Angie *(English)* ♀   RATING: ★★★☆
Messenger of God—Short for Angela; "Angie," song by Rod Stewart; Angie Dickinson, actress
People think of Angie as pretty, funny, caring, creative, intelligent
People who like the name Angie also like Angelina, Amanda, Angela, Amy, Amber, Abigail, Audrey, Angelica, Adriana, April

Angus *(Celtic/Gaelic)* ♂   RATING: ★★★☆
One strength—Scottish origin; also type of cow or beef; Angus Young, musician
People think of Angus as handsome, intelligent, funny, powerful, creative
People who like the name Angus also like Aiden, Alistair, Arthur, Alexander, Aaron, Adam, Benjamin, Alastair, Andrew, Atticus

Ani *(Slavic)* ♀   RATING: ★★☆
Very beautiful
People think of Ani as pretty, creative, intelligent, funny, artsy
People who like the name Ani also like Ava, Aria, Ania, Ana, Amara, Alana, Anaya, Ariana, Adia, Anya

Ania *(Slavic)* ♀   RATING: ★★★★☆
Gracious, merciful—Variation of Anne
People think of Ania as pretty, creative, intelligent, exotic, caring
People who like the name Ania also like Anya, Amaya, Anaya, Anika, Ani, Ava, Alana, Ariana, Aria, Amara

Aniela *(Hebrew)* ♀   RATING: ★★★
Gracious, merciful
People think of Aniela as pretty, caring, creative, energetic, artsy
People who like the name Aniela also like Abigail, Adara, Annabelle, Dalia, Bella, Dahlia, Aurelia, Amara, Ariana, Ava

Anielka *(Polish)* ♀   RATING: ★★
Gracious, merciful
People think of Anielka as pretty, sexy, intelligent, creative, caring
People who like the name Anielka also like Aaralyn, Anika, Abrianna, Adalia, Armelle, Alanna, Amaya, Anastasia, Alayna, Alana

Anik *(Sanskrit/East Indian)* ♂   RATING: ★★☆
Soldier—Bengali origin
People think of Anik as handsome, intelligent, funny, creative, cool
People who like the name Anik also like Ashwin, Arav, Arnav, Kami, Rushil, Savir, Nikkos, Xanto, Kanoa, Ekram

Anika *(Scandinavian)* ♀   RATING: ★★★★
Gracious, merciful—Variation of Anne
People think of Anika as pretty, intelligent, funny, creative, caring
People who like the name Anika also like Ava, Anya, Abigail, Amelia, Ariana, Alana, Arianna, Audrey, Anastasia, Chloe

Anila *(Sanskrit/East Indian)* ♀   RATING: ★★★★
Child of the wind—Anil, Hindu god of the wind
People think of Anila as sexy, pretty, intelligent, funny, cool
People who like the name Anila also like Anaya, Amaya, Amara, Avani, Asha, Anisa, Aira, Alena, Aurora, Aiko

Anisa *(Arabic)* ♀   RATING: ★★★★
Companion, faithful friend
People think of Anisa as pretty, intelligent, funny, caring, creative
People who like the name Anisa also like Anaya, Amaya, Ariana, Alana, Ayanna, Ava, Adriana, Aaliyah, Abigail, Alyssa

Anise *(English)* ♀   RATING: ★★★★
Spice—Main ingredient in licorice; fabled to be an aphrodisiac
People think of Anise as pretty, creative, intelligent, funny, caring
People who like the name Anise also like Amber, Ashlyn, Ava, Aurora, Alexa, Anisa, Abigail, Audrey, Annalise, Amelia

Anita *(Hebrew)* ♀   RATING: ★★★☆
Gracious, merciful—Variation of Ann; Anita Bryant, singer/spokesperson; character in *West Side Story*
People think of Anita as pretty, intelligent, caring, funny, trustworthy
People who like the name Anita also like Abigail, Audrey, Amber, Amy, Amanda, Alice, Alana, Amelia, Alicia, Annabella

Anitra *(American)* ♀   RATING: ★★★
Gracious, merciful—Variation of Ann
People think of Anitra as pretty, caring, trustworthy, funny, creative
People who like the name Anitra also like Anika, Aaralyn, Alayna, Amara, Alora, Adriana, Aira, Abrianna, Abigail, Alana

Anja *(Russian)* ♀ RATING: ★★★★
Gracious, merciful—Variation of Ann or Hannah
People think of Anja as pretty, intelligent, creative, funny, caring
People who like the name Anja also like Anya, Ava, Anika, Anaya, Amaya, Adalia, Alana, Anastasia, Arwen, Ariana

Anjali *(Sanskrit/East Indian)* ♀ RATING: ★★★★
Tribute
People think of Anjali as pretty, intelligent, creative, caring, funny
People who like the name Anjali also like Anaya, Avani, Amara, Anya, Amaya, Aaliyah, Asha, Ailani, Amithi, Alpana

Anjelita *(Spanish)* ♀ RATING: ★★☆
Messenger of God
People think of Anjelita as pretty, young, leader, cool, energetic
People who like the name Anjelita also like Angelina, Adriana, Aaliyah, Amorina, Angelique, Annalise, Abrianna, Amora, Ariana, Angelica

Ankti *(Native American)* ♀ RATING: ★☆
Repeat the dance—Hopi origin
People think of Ankti as pretty, popular, energetic, caring, exotic
People who like the name Ankti also like Amaya, Anevay, Amadahy, Ayasha, Aiko, Aradia, Angeni, Ayita, Aneko, Alora

Ann *(Hebrew)* ♀ RATING: ★★★☆
Gracious, merciful—Originally a variation of Hannah; Ann-Margret, singer/actress; Raggedy Ann, children's doll
People think of Ann as caring, pretty, funny, intelligent, trustworthy
People who like the name Ann also like Anna, Abigail, Anne, Amber, Amy, Amanda, Annabel, Alexa, Allison, Amelia

Anna *(Hebrew)* ♀ RATING: ★★★
Gracious, merciful—Originally a variation of Hannah; Anna Paquin, actress; Anna Nicole Smith, model/spokesperson
People think of Anna as pretty, funny, caring, intelligent, creative
People who like the name Anna also like Ava, Emma, Abigail, Hannah, Grace, Ella, Emily, Olivia, Elizabeth, Amelia

Annabel *(English)* ♀ RATING: ★★★
Combination of Anna and Bella
People think of Annabel as pretty, intelligent, caring, funny, creative
People who like the name Annabel also like Abigail, Annabelle, Annabella, Ava, Amelia, Isabella, Bella, Anna, Annalise, Audrey

Annabella *(English)* ♀ RATING: ★★★
Combination of Anna and Bella—Also spelled Anabella; Anabella Sciorra, actress
People think of Annabella as pretty, intelligent, caring, creative, elegant
People who like the name Annabella also like Isabella, Annabelle, Abigail, Bella, Ava, Arabella, Annabel, Adriana, Amelia, Angelina

Annabelle *(English)* ♀ RATING: ★★★★
Combination of Anna and Bella
People think of Annabelle as pretty, intelligent, elegant, caring, funny
People who like the name Annabelle also like Abigail, Isabelle, Isabella, Annabella, Ava, Emma, Amelia, Audrey, Bella, Chloe

Annalise *(German)* ♀ RATING: ★★★★
Combination of Anna and Elise, or Anna and Lisa
People think of Annalise as pretty, intelligent, creative, funny, elegant
People who like the name Annalise also like Abigail, Annabelle, Analiese, Ava, Amelia, Analise, Arianna, Isabella, Annabella, Adriana

Anne *(Hebrew)* ♀ RATING: ★★★
Gracious, merciful—Originally a variation of Hannah; Anne Archer, actress; Anne Frank, author; Anne Hathaway, actress; Anne Heche, actress
People think of Anne as pretty, intelligent, caring, funny, creative
People who like the name Anne also like Anna, Abigail, Emma, Elizabeth, Ava, Grace, Amelia, Audrey, Alexandra, Claire

Anneke *(Scandinavian)* ♀ RATING: ★★★★
Little Ann—Variation of Ann
People think of Anneke as pretty, creative, intelligent, trustworthy, caring
People who like the name Anneke also like Anika, Analiese, Abigail, Amelie, Ava, Anastasia, Aeryn, Adeline, Annalise, Amber

Anneliese *(German)* ♀ RATING: ★★★★☆
Combination of Anne and Elise
People think of Anneliese as pretty, intelligent, elegant, creative, caring
People who like the name Anneliese also like Annalise, Analiese, Ava, Abigail, Annelise, Annabelle, Anastasia, Amelia, Isabella, Chloe

Annelise *(German)* ♀ RATING: ★★★★
Combination of Anne and Lisa
People think of Annelise as pretty, intelligent, elegant, creative, funny
People who like the name Annelise also like Annalise, Anneliese, Analiese, Abigail, Analise, Ava, Amelia, Annabelle, Arianna, Amber

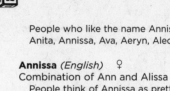
Annette *(French)* ♀ RATING: ★★☆
Gracious, merciful—Variation of Anne; Annette Bening, actress; Annette Funicello, singer/actress
> People think of Annette as pretty, caring, funny, intelligent, trustworthy
> People who like the name Annette also like Abigail, Annabelle, Amber, Amanda, Amelia, Audrey, Angelina, Annabel, Annalise, Alexandra

Annica *(American)* ♀ RATING: ★★★★
Variation of Annika
> People think of Annica as pretty, popular, trustworthy, intelligent, creative
> People who like the name Annica also like Ava, Anika, Abrianna, Aurora, Alexa, Arianna, Abigail, Annalise, Amelia, Adriana

Annice *(English)* ♀ RATING: ★★★☆
Pure—From the medieval English pronunciation of Agnes, *Annis*
> People think of Annice as pretty, creative, intelligent, caring, religious
> People who like the name Annice also like Alexandra, Ashlyn, Annalise, Alicia, Abigail, Amber, Audrey, Annica, Annabel, Ashtyn

Annick *(French)* ♀ RATING: ★★★★
Gracious, merciful—Variation of Ann
> People think of Annick as pretty, funny, intelligent, creative, trustworthy
> People who like the name Annick also like Ava, Antoinette, Aurora, Alexandra, Annabelle, Anya, Annabella, Analiese, Audrey, Angelique

Annie *(English)* ♀ RATING: ★★☆
Gracious, merciful—Short for Ann, Anne, or Anna
> People think of Annie as pretty, funny, caring, intelligent, creative
> People who like the name Annie also like Ava, Anna, Abigail, Amelia, Emma, Amy, Anne, Grace, Annabelle, Annabel

Annika *(German)* ♀ RATING: ★★★★
Gracious, merciful
> People think of Annika as pretty, creative, intelligent, caring, energetic
> People who like the name Annika also like Ava, Abigail, Anika, Olivia, Anna, Emma, Amelia, Lauren, Hannah, Isabella

Annily *(American)* ♀ RATING: ★★★
Combination of Ann and Emily
> People think of Annily as pretty, exotic, popular, trustworthy, artsy
> People who like the name Annily also like Ashlyn, Ava, Hannah, Olivia, Hailey, Abbie, Abigail, Claire, Sienna, Felicity

Annis *(English)* ♀ RATING: ★★★☆
Pure—Variation of Agnes
> People think of Annis as intelligent, caring, funny, leader, creative

People who like the name Annis also like Annice, Anise, Anita, Annissa, Ava, Aeryn, Alecia, Audrey, Alicia, Alice

Annissa *(English)* ♀ RATING: ★★★★
Combination of Ann and Alissa
> People think of Annissa as pretty, creative, cool, trustworthy, funny
> People who like the name Annissa also like Alyssa, Abigail, Annalise, Arianna, Anisa, Ashlyn, Arissa, Annabelle, Alicia, Ava

Annona *(Latin)* ♀ RATING: ★★★
Goddess of the harvest
> People think of Annona as pretty, trendy, quiet, artsy, intelligent
> People who like the name Annona also like Aradia, Aurora, Amara, Amaya, Annora, Aleda, Anastasia, Asta, Annabella, Althea

Annora *(English)* ♀ RATING: ★★★★
Honor—Medieval variation of Honora
> People think of Annora as intelligent, pretty, caring, creative, trustworthy
> People who like the name Annora also like Aurora, Anastasia, Amara, Ava, Amelia, Abigail, Anya, Amaya, Annalise, Arwen

Annot *(English)* ♀ RATING: ★★☆
Gracious, merciful—Medieval variation of Ann or Anne
> People think of Annot as weird, artsy, creative, big, quiet
> People who like the name Annot also like Amora, Alana, Annabella, Alena, Apple, Atara, Anise, Andra, Aizza, Angie

Anouk *(Native American)* ♀ RATING: ★★★
Favor, grace—Inuit origin
> People think of Anouk as pretty, intelligent, creative, artsy, energetic
> People who like the name Anouk also like Simone, Anaïs, Chloe, Arwen, Aitana, Amelie, Abigail, Bianca, Olivia, Naomi

Anoush *(Armenian)* ♀ RATING: ★★★☆
Sweet—Also Pahlavi for immortal
> People think of Anoush as pretty, quiet, caring, funny, creative
> People who like the name Anoush also like Ava, Aiko, Anya, Anaïs, Amaya, Amani, Anaya, Aisha, Amara, Aliana

Ansel *(French)* ♂ RATING: ★★
A god—Ansel Adams, photographer
> People think of Ansel as creative, handsome, intelligent, artsy, cool
> People who like the name Ansel also like Aiden, Asher, Aden, Anson, Axel, Anton, Aaron, Alden, André, Ace

Anson *(English)* ♂ RATING: ★★★★
Son of Ann—Anson Williams, actor/director
> People think of Anson as handsome, intelligent, funny, popular, leader

People who like the name Anson also like Aiden, Asher, Aden, Braden, Alden, Anderson, Aaron, Ethan, Adrian, Owen

Anstice *(Greek)* ♀♂   RATING: ★★★
Resurrection—Medieval variation of Anastasia
People think of Anstice as aggressive, creative, powerful, intelligent, sexy
People who like the name Anstice also like Aidan, Arden, Avery, Aiken, Avalon, Aquarius, Angel, Astin, Azriel, Ashton

Anthea *(Greek)* ♀   RATING: ★★★★
Flowery
People think of Anthea as pretty, intelligent, trustworthy, sexy, caring
People who like the name Anthea also like Athena, Althea, Aurora, Ariana, Anastasia, Abigail, Alana, Alexandria, Adriana, Arabella

Anthony *(Latin)* ♂   RATING: ★★★
Unknown meaning—From a Roman surname; Anthony Hopkins, actor; Anthony LaPaglia, actor; Anthony Michael Hall, actor
People think of Anthony as handsome, funny, cool, intelligent, caring
People who like the name Anthony also like Andrew, Alexander, Aaron, Adam, Benjamin, Aiden, Ethan, Matthew, Adrian, Jacob

Antoine *(French)* ♂   RATING: ★★★☆
Unknown meaning—Variation of Antony or Anthony
People think of Antoine as handsome, funny, intelligent, popular, sexy
People who like the name Antoine also like Anthony, Antonio, Alexander, Adrian, André, Caleb, Christopher, Anton, Aaron, Andrew

Antoinette *(French)* ♀   RATING: ★★★★
Feminine form of Antoine; Marie Antoinette, queen of France
People think of Antoinette as pretty, intelligent, funny, caring, creative
People who like the name Antoinette also like Anastasia, Abigail, Aurora, Angelique, Alexandria, Adriana, Belle, Amber, Annabelle, Ava

Anton *(French)* ♂   RATING: ★★★★
Unknown meaning—French or old Latin form of Anthony
People think of Anton as handsome, intelligent, funny, cool, popular
People who like the name Anton also like Aiden, Aaron, Alexander, Adam, Aden, Andrew, Anthony, Adrian, André, Asher

Antonella *(Italian)* ♀   RATING: ★★★☆
Daughter of Anthony
People think of Antonella as pretty, sexy, intelligent, exotic, caring
People who like the name Antonella also like Alexa, Annabella, Alexia, Angelina, Samantha, Arabella, Isabella, Alissa, Bianca, Sophia

Antonia *(English)* ♀   RATING: ★★★★
Unknown meaning—From the Roman surname Antony
People think of Antonia as pretty, intelligent, caring, creative, funny
People who like the name Antonia also like Ava, Adriana, Amelia, Alexandra, Audrey, Abigail, Aurora, Alexa, Arianna, Anastasia

Antonie *(English)* ♀   RATING: ★★★☆
Unknown meaning
People think of Antonie as aggressive, powerful, intelligent, energetic, criminal
People who like the name Antonie also like Abrianna, Antonia, Arabella, Annabel, Alanna, Alexandra, Antoinette, Annalise, Anna, Analiese

Antonio *(Spanish)* ♂   RATING: ★★★☆
Unknown meaning—Variation of Anthony; Antonio Banderas, actor; Antonio Sabato Jr., actor
People think of Antonio as handsome, funny, cool, sexy, popular
People who like the name Antonio also like Anthony, Alexander, Adrian, Aaron, Andrew, Alejandro, Adam, Angelo, Aiden, Antony

Antony *(Latin)* ♂   RATING: ★★☆
Unknown meaning—Mark Antony, ancient Roman leader
People think of Antony as popular, handsome, funny, intelligent, sexy
People who like the name Antony also like Anthony, Andrew, Alexander, Antonio, Aaron, Adam, Adrian, Aiden, Anton, Benjamin

Antranig *(Armenian)* ♂   RATING: ★★☆
First son
People think of Antranig as powerful, slow, quiet, weird, popular
People who like the name Antranig also like Ambrose, Aiden, Amadeus, Anwar, Alistair, Alagan, Arkadiy, Atticus, Asher, Apollo

Antwan *(American)* ♂   RATING: ★★★
Variation of Antoine
People think of Antwan as popular, funny, handsome, sexy, energetic
People who like the name Antwan also like Anthony, Antonio, Aaron, Alexander, Adrian, Antoine, Andrew, Aiden, Adam, André

Anunciacion *(Spanish)* ♀   RATING: ★★
Announces
People think of Anunciacion as poor, weird, ethnic, stuck-up, creative
People who like the name Anunciacion also like Cyrah, Cianna, Calla, Annis, Alba, Arva, Aleta, Brianne, Breanna, Blossom

Anwar *(Arabic)* ♂   RATING: ★★★☆
More luminous—Anwar Sadat, former president of Egypt
People think of Anwar as handsome, intelligent, cool, sexy, caring

People who like the name Anwar also like Aiden, Adam, Aaron, Aden, Anton, Asher, Alastair, Ansel, Anakin, Alden

Anya *(Russian)* ♀ RATING: ★★☆
Gracious, merciful—Variation of Anne or Hannah
People think of Anya as pretty, creative, intelligent, funny, caring
People who like the name Anya also like Ava, Amelia, Anastasia, Abigail, Amaya, Aurora, Ella, Chloe, Alana, Emma

Aoi *(Japanese)* ♀ RATING: ★★☆
Hollyhock flower
People think of Aoi as nerdy, poor
People who like the name Aoi also like Aimi, Ai, Chika, Naomi, Aoko, Ayame, Adel, Mardi, Alaina, Qi

Aoife *(Celtic/Gaelic)* ♀ RATING: ★★★☆
Beautiful, radiant—Pronounced *EEfa*
People think of Aoife as pretty, funny, intelligent, caring, popular
People who like the name Aoife also like Aeryn, Ava, Aislin, Alana, Aislinn, Arwen, Aine, Aisling, Aurora, Aideen

Aoko *(Japanese)* ♀ RATING: ★★★
Unknown meaning
People think of Aoko as exotic, creative, young, intelligent, cool
People who like the name Aoko also like Aiko, Amaya, Aneko, Amani, Ayame, Aisha, Anya, Ailani, Asha, Aelwen

Aolani *(Hawaiian)* ♀ RATING: ★★★★
Cloud from heaven
People think of Aolani as pretty, exotic, trustworthy, caring, young
People who like the name Aolani also like Ailani, Alohilani, Amaya, Aulani, Kailani, Aurora, Adriana, Leilani, Alayna, Aria

Aphrodite *(Greek)* ♀ RATING: ★★
Born from sea foam—Greek goddess of love, born with strong powers of attraction; origin of the word *aphrodisiac*
People think of Aphrodite as pretty, sexy, exotic, powerful, elegant
People who like the name Aphrodite also like Aurora, Athena, Anastasia, Amber, Alexandria, Arabella, Alexandra, Angelina, Arianna, Adriana

Apiatan *(Native American)* ♂ RATING: ★★☆
Lance made with wood—Kiowa origin
People think of Apiatan as weird, powerful, energetic, young, trustworthy
People who like the name Apiatan also like Anoki, Ahanu, Alagan, Akando, Adair, Arif, Alastair, Atalo, Archer, Aquila

Apollo *(Greek)* ♂ RATING: ★★
Destroyer—Greek god of the sun; Apolo Anton Ohno, speed skater
People think of Apollo as intelligent, handsome, powerful, leader, cool
People who like the name Apollo also like Alexander, Aiden, Aaron, Ace, Adrian, Adam, Andrew, Axel, Atticus, Adonis

Apollonia *(Greek)* ♀ RATING: ★★★
Feminine form of Apollo; Apollonia Kotero, singer
People think of Apollonia as exotic, pretty, elegant, cool, funny
People who like the name Apollonia also like Audrey, Anastasia, Abigail, Aurelia, Calista, Bianca, Callista, Bella, Colette, Jasmine

Aponi *(Native American)* ♀ RATING: ★★★☆
Butterfly—Sioux origin
People think of Aponi as caring, intelligent, artsy, pretty, quiet
People who like the name Aponi also like Alora, Amber, Angeni, Amitola, Amaya, Aurora, Aimee, Arwen, Ayasha, Anastasia

Apostolos *(Greek)* ♂ RATING: ★★☆
Of the Apostles
People think of Apostolos as intelligent, creative, handsome, caring, exotic
People who like the name Apostolos also like Amadeus, Aloysius, Aaron, Apollo, Aristotle, Alfonso, Adam, Alan, Arnaldo, Anderson

Apple *(English)* ♀ RATING: ★★★
From the fruit apple—Apple Martin, daughter of Gwyneth Paltrow and Chris Martin
People think of Apple as weird, pretty, loser, nerdy, girl next door
People who like the name Apple also like Ava, Amber, April, Autumn, Audrey, Amelia, Abigail, Alana, Aurora, Anastasia

Apria *(American)* ♀ RATING: ★★★
From the fruit apricot
People think of Apria as pretty, intelligent, quiet, creative, elegant
People who like the name Apria also like Aurora, Abrianna, Ava, Adriana, Amaya, Autumn, Aeryn, Alena, Alana, Aaralyn

April *(Latin)* ♀ RATING: ★★★
Opening—The month April was originally called Aprilis in Latin, possibly after the god Apollo
People think of April as pretty, funny, caring, creative, intelligent
People who like the name April also like Amber, Abigail, Autumn, Audrey, Ava, Faith, Chloe, Alexandra, Emma, Amanda

Apu *(Sanskrit/East Indian)* ♂ RATING: ★☆
Pure, virtuous, divine
People think of Apu as exotic, weird, nerdy, loser, intelligent

People who like the name Apu also like Ashwin, Angus, Apollo, Alexander, Ajay, Antonio, Axel, Adam, Aiden, Anakin

Aqua *(Latin)* ♀   RATING: ★★★☆
Water
> People think of Aqua as pretty, creative, cool, popular, caring
> People who like the name Aqua also like April, Amber, Anastasia, Aurora, Alexa, Alexandra, Autumn, Angelina, Alexandria, Alana

Aquarius *(Latin)* ♀ ♂   RATING: ★★★
The water bearer—Used for children born under this astrological sign
> People think of Aquarius as creative, intelligent, caring, exotic, cool
> People who like the name Aquarius also like Angel, Aidan, Aries, Artemis, Alexis, Alex, Avery, Ashanti, Addison, Ash

Aquene *(Native American)* ♀   RATING: ★★★☆
Peace—Sioux origin
> People think of Aquene as pretty, elegant, exotic, artsy, young
> People who like the name Aquene also like Angeni, Alana, Ayasha, Arwen, Alora, Aurora, Adrina, Adalia, Aleshanee, Angelina

Aquila *(Latin)* ♂   RATING: ★★
Eagle
> People think of Aquila as intelligent, caring, cool, creative, sexy
> People who like the name Aquila also like Aiden, Alejandro, Axel, Alexander, Alexavier, Adam, Angelito, Aaron, Apollo, Alastair

Ara *(American)* ♀   RATING: ★★★☆
Lion—Feminine form of Ari
> People think of Ara as pretty, intelligent, creative, trustworthy, quiet
> People who like the name Ara also like Ava, Aurora, Anna, Charlotte, Bianca, Ada, Alaina, Audrey, Arabella, Arianna

Arabela *(Spanish)* ♀   RATING: ★★★
Beautiful lion
> People think of Arabela as pretty, exotic, elegant, creative, powerful
> People who like the name Arabela also like Arabella, Adriana, Ava, Annabella, Isabella, Abrianna, Ariana, Angelina, Arianna, Abigail

Arabella *(English)* ♀   RATING: ★★★★
Beautiful lion—Combination of Ara and Bella
> People think of Arabella as pretty, elegant, intelligent, creative, caring
> People who like the name Arabella also like Isabella, Bella, Ava, Annabella, Abigail, Arianna, Annabelle, Amelia, Anastasia, Aurora

Arabia *(English)* ♀ ♂   RATING: ★★☆
Person from the Arabic region
> People think of Arabia as intelligent, young, pretty, powerful, leader
> People who like the name Arabia also like Chandler, Avery, Briar, Albany, Britain, Camden, Brazil, Aubrey, Africa, Brooklyn

Aracely *(Spanish)* ♀   RATING: ★★
Heavenly altar
> People think of Aracely as pretty, caring, funny, intelligent, sexy
> People who like the name Aracely also like Abigail, Ariana, Arianna, Angelina, Adriana, Aaliyah, Arabella, Abrianna, Arcelia, Angelica

Aradia *(Greek)* ♀   RATING: ★★★
Goddess of witches—Daughter of the goddess Diana
> People think of Aradia as exotic, powerful, intelligent, elegant, pretty
> People who like the name Aradia also like Aurora, Arwen, Amaya, Athena, Aeryn, Adrienne, Anastasia, Amara, Adriana, Ava

Aragorn *(English)* ♂   RATING: ★★★☆
Created by J.R.R. Tolkien for the *Lord of the Rings* character
> People think of Aragorn as leader, powerful, handsome, intelligent, trustworthy
> People who like the name Aragorn also like Aden, Andrew, Anakin, Aiden, Boden, Aaron, Xavier, Chase, Axel, Callum

Aram *(Armenian)* ♂   RATING: ★☆
Royal highness
> People think of Aram as handsome, intelligent, powerful, creative, trustworthy
> People who like the name Aram also like Aiden, Aden, Asher, Adam, Aaron, Andrew, Alastair, Anton, Alexander, Adrian

Arama *(Spanish)* ♀   RATING: ★★☆
Of the Virgin Mary
> People think of Arama as girl next door, exotic, pretty, ethnic, religious
> People who like the name Arama also like Ariana, Abrianna, Adalia, Armelle, Arella, Atira, Alegria, Aracely, Aria, Aimee

Aran *(Thai)* ♂   RATING: ★★★★
Forest
> People think of Aran as handsome, energetic, caring, funny, intelligent
> People who like the name Aran also like Aiden, Aden, Asher, Adam, Aaron, Alexander, Artan, Akio, Alaric, Alan

Arash *(Persian)* ♂   RATING: ★★★★
Hero
> People think of Arash as intelligent, handsome, popular, funny, sexy
> People who like the name Arash also like Aiden, Aaron, Aran, Alagan, Asho, Artan, Alain, Adair, Arav, Anakin

Arav (Sanskrit/East Indian) ♂　RATING: ★☆
Peaceful
> People think of Arav as handsome, intelligent, cool, creative, winner
> People who like the name Arav also like Arnav, Amish, Ashwin, Atish, Adit, Amrit, Alagan, Aran, Adarsh, Arash

Arawn (Welsh) ♀♂　RATING: ★★★☆
King of the otherworld
> People think of Arawn as intelligent, powerful, creative, leader, aggressive
> People who like the name Arawn also like Aidan, Arien, Arden, Artemis, Aren, Astin, Avery, Aiken, Aspen, Angel

Arcelia (Spanish) ♀　RATING: ★★
Treasure
> People think of Arcelia as pretty, funny, creative, popular, caring
> People who like the name Arcelia also like Adriana, Aracely, Aaralyn, Adrina, Ariana, Anastasia, Aurelia, Armelle, Alana, Alexia

Arch (English) ♂　RATING: ★★★
Short for Archer or Archibald
> People think of Arch as nerdy, loser, weird, poor, caring
> People who like the name Arch also like Axel, Albert, Arne, August, Arthur, Archer, Asher, Alan, Aiden, Andrew

Archana (Sanskrit/East Indian) ♀　RATING: ★★★☆
Worshiping one
> People think of Archana as religious, caring, intelligent, pretty, young
> People who like the name Archana also like Alpana, Anila, Asha, Amithi, Anjali, Avatari, Avani, Armande, Arlet, Amara

Archer (English) ♂　RATING: ★★
Bowman
> People think of Archer as handsome, intelligent, leader, energetic, powerful
> People who like the name Archer also like Asher, Aiden, Alexander, Aden, Alastair, Ace, Caleb, Adrian, Adam, Andrew

Archibald (English) ♂　RATING: ★★★
Truly bold—Archibald Leach (aka Cary Grant), actor; Archibald MacLeish, writer/actor
> People think of Archibald as powerful, funny, intelligent, leader, old-fashioned
> People who like the name Archibald also like Alexander, Albert, Archie, Adam, Arthur, Axel, Anthony, Arnold, Atticus, Alastair

Archie (German) ♂　RATING: ★★★☆
Short for Archibald; Archie Andrews, comic character; Archie Panjabi, actress; Archie Shepp, jazz musician
> People think of Archie as funny, caring, popular, intelligent, handsome
> People who like the name Archie also like Aaron, Adam, Ace, Alexander, Angus, Arthur, Aiden, Andrew, Alfred, Albert

Archwood (English) ♂　RATING: ★★
Trees forming arches
> People think of Archwood as weird, exotic
> People who like the name Archwood also like Axel, Alan, Adam, Anderson, Aaron, Arthur, Alexavier, Anton, Aron, Alonzo

Ardara (Celtic/Gaelic) ♀　RATING: ★★★
Fort on the hill
> People think of Ardara as sexy, pretty, quiet, intelligent, artsy
> People who like the name Ardara also like Aeryn, Alana, Aislin, Ailis, Aislinn, Aideen, Ailsa, Aileen, Aine, Aila

Ardelis (Latin) ♀　RATING: ★★★
Warm
> People think of Ardelis as creative, pretty, slow, intelligent, elegant
> People who like the name Ardelis also like Aradia, Aurelia, Adalia, Aaralyn, Amaryllis, Alaina, Amalie, Anastasia, Aurora, Adalira

Ardelle (Latin) ♀　RATING: ★★★☆
Warm
> People think of Ardelle as creative, intelligent, leader, caring, funny
> People who like the name Ardelle also like Ava, Aurelia, Audrey, Aria, Aurora, Amelia, Adelle, Alena, Aimee, Alana

Arden (English) ♀♂　RATING: ★★☆
From the eagle valley—Arden Myrin, actress/comedian
> People think of Arden as creative, pretty, intelligent, popular, energetic
> People who like the name Arden also like Avery, Aidan, Addison, Caden, Aubrey, Ashton, Bailey, Hayden, Ainsley, Blake

Ardice (Hebrew) ♀　RATING: ★★
Flowering field
> People think of Ardice as trustworthy, weird, quiet, pretty, artsy
> People who like the name Ardice also like Amaris, Adina, Aliza, Arielle, Ardith, Abigail, Atara, Ariella, Ayala, Arella

Ardith (American) ♀　RATING: ★★★☆
Combination of Ara and Judith
> People think of Ardith as old-fashioned, weird, creative, unpopular, old
> People who like the name Ardith also like Abigail, Anne, Arella, Ardice, Anna, Anaïs, Abbie, Ariella, Alessa, Aliza

Arella (Hebrew) ♀　RATING: ★★☆
Angel
> People think of Arella as pretty, elegant, intelligent, quiet, creative
> People who like the name Arella also like Ariella, Arabella, Abigail, Aurora, Arielle, Ava, Ayanna, Aria, Amaya, Ariana

Aren *(Scandinavian)* ♀ ♂   RATING: ★★★★☆
Eagle ruler
> People think of Aren as cool, intelligent, creative, popular, funny
> People who like the name Aren also like Aidan, Avery, Arden, Caden, Addison, Arien, Ashton, Aubrey, Ari, Ariel

Aretha *(American)* ♀   RATING: ★★★☆
Excellence—Possibly from the Greek word *arete*; Aretha Franklin, singer
> People think of Aretha as pretty, creative, caring, funny, popular
> People who like the name Aretha also like Aurora, Amber, Alana, April, Amanda, Arianna, Anastasia, Alicia, Alice, Angelina

Arethusa *(Greek)* ♀   RATING: ★★☆
The waterer
> People think of Arethusa as weird, funny, old-fashioned, artsy, uptight
> People who like the name Arethusa also like Aradia, Aurora, Anastasia, Aideen, Aira, Aaralyn, Amara, Alena, Athena, Angeni

Arezo *(Persian)* ♀   RATING: ★★★
Wish
> People think of Arezo as pretty, young, religious, trendy, exotic
> People who like the name Arezo also like Aiko, Amani, Ariana, Aadi, Arwen, Anoush, Asha, Adrina, Aizza, Aaliyah

Argus *(Greek)* ♂   RATING: ★★☆
Bright—Various characters in Greek mythology
> People think of Argus as intelligent, nerdy, loser, big, powerful
> People who like the name Argus also like Aiden, Atticus, Ansel, Ambrose, Angus, Axel, Augustus, Alexander, Asher, Alaric

Argyle *(English)* ♂   RATING: ★★★
From Argyll, Scotland—Also a pattern of plaid
> People think of Argyle as creative, cool, exotic, artsy, trustworthy
> People who like the name Argyle also like Atticus, Anson, Alastair, Arthur, Aiden, Angus, Archer, Ambrose, Adair, Alexander

Ari *(Hebrew)* ♀ ♂   RATING: ★★★☆
Lion—Also short for the Greek name Aristotle
> People think of Ari as intelligent, creative, cool, energetic, powerful
> People who like the name Ari also like Avery, Aidan, Ariel, Addison, Caden, Aubrey, Bailey, Arien, Alexis, Alec

Aria *(Italian)* ♀   RATING: ★★★★
Solo melody; air—A solo song in an opera; a nymph in mythology; the Eastern province of the ancient Persian empire
> People think of Aria as pretty, creative, intelligent, artsy, elegant

> People who like the name Aria also like Ava, Ariana, Aurora, Arianna, Amaya, Anya, Isabella, Adriana, Angelina, Amara

Ariabod *(Persian)* ♂   RATING: ★☆
Tribe leader
> People think of Ariabod as exotic, elegant, intelligent, wealthy, ethnic
> People who like the name Ariabod also like Aric, Ambrose, Atticus, Aiden, Alexander, Arthur, Amadeus, Axel, Argyle, Amando

Ariadne *(Greek)* ♀   RATING: ★★★☆
Very holy
> People think of Ariadne as pretty, intelligent, exotic, creative, elegant
> People who like the name Ariadne also like Aurora, Ariana, Ava, Adrienne, Arianna, Adelaide, Anastasia, Abigail, Alexandra, Chloe

Ariana *(Italian)* ♀   RATING: ★★★☆
Very holy—Variation of Ariadne
> People think of Ariana as pretty, funny, intelligent, caring, creative
> People who like the name Ariana also like Adriana, Arianna, Ava, Alana, Abigail, Isabella, Alyssa, Audrey, Angelina, Alexa

Ariane *(French)* ♀   RATING: ★★★
Very holy—Variation of Ariadne
> People think of Ariane as pretty, intelligent, funny, caring, creative
> People who like the name Ariane also like Ariana, Arianna, Arianne, Alana, Adriana, Ava, Adrienne, Aurora, Alaina, Amelie

Arianna *(Italian)* ♀   RATING: ★★★☆
Very holy—Variation of Ariadne
> People think of Arianna as pretty, intelligent, funny, creative, caring
> People who like the name Arianna also like Adriana, Abigail, Ava, Isabella, Brianna, Ariana, Alyssa, Abrianna, Gabriella, Hailey

Arianne *(French)* ♀   RATING: ★★★☆
Very holy—Variation of Ariana
> People think of Arianne as pretty, intelligent, funny, creative, caring
> People who like the name Arianne also like Arianna, Ariana, Adrienne, Adriana, Ariane, Ava, Abigail, Audrey, Alana, Alaina

Aric *(Hebrew)* ♂   RATING: ★★★★☆
Variation of Ari or Ariel
> People think of Aric as handsome, intelligent, funny, caring, leader
> People who like the name Aric also like Aiden, Alexander, Aden, Adrian, Aaron, Anthony, Andrew, Adam, Asher, Alexavier

Arich (*Thai*) ♀ ♂   RATING: ★★★
Unknown meaning—Pronounced *Are-ish*
> People think of Arich as exotic, aggressive, artsy, pretty, trustworthy
> People who like the name Arich also like Aidan, Ari, Avery, Amiel, Arden, Aiken, Azra, Ashton, Ariel, Arion

Aricin (*All Nationalities*) ♂   RATING: ★★★☆
Unknown meaning
> People think of Aricin as intelligent, handsome, cool, powerful, ethnic
> People who like the name Aricin also like Aiden, Alaric, Alastair, Ambrose, Aden, Anton, Adair, Alair, Arlen, Alton

Ariel (*Hebrew*) ♀ ♂   RATING: ★★★
Lion of God—Character in Disney's *The Little Mermaid*
> People think of Ariel as pretty, funny, intelligent, creative, caring
> People who like the name Ariel also like Alexis, Aidan, Bailey, Addison, Aubrey, Avery, Brooke, Angel, Ashton, Caden

Ariella (*Hebrew*) ♀   RATING: ★★★★☆
Lion of God—Variation of Ariel
> People think of Ariella as pretty, creative, intelligent, caring, popular
> People who like the name Ariella also like Arianna, Arielle, Arabella, Ariana, Adriana, Ava, Abigail, Bella, Isabella, Aurora

Arielle (*Hebrew*) ♀   RATING: ★★★★
Lion of God—Variation of Ariel
> People think of Arielle as pretty, intelligent, creative, funny, caring
> People who like the name Arielle also like Arianna, Ariella, Abigail, Ava, Gabrielle, Chloe, Ariana, Aurora, Amelia, Isabella

Arien (*Hebrew*) ♀ ♂   RATING: ★★★★
Enchanted
> People think of Arien as pretty, cool, intelligent, young, popular
> People who like the name Arien also like Aidan, Ariel, Avery, Caden, Ari, Addison, Arion, Aubrey, Arden, Ashton

Aries (*Latin*) ♀ ♂   RATING: ★★★★
The ram—Used for children born under this astrological sign; Aries Spears, actor/comedian
> People think of Aries as powerful, creative, intelligent, aggressive, leader
> People who like the name Aries also like Ariel, Alexis, Caden, Addison, Aidan, Avery, Aubrey, Bailey, Austin, Artemis

Arif (*Arabic*) ♂   RATING: ★★★☆
Knowledgeable
> People think of Arif as intelligent, leader, popular, caring, funny
> People who like the name Arif also like Amir, Adam, Ambrose, Adair, Asho, André, Asher, Alagan, Anoki, Argus

Arin (*Hebrew*) ♀   RATING: ★★★★
Enlightened
> People think of Arin as intelligent, energetic, funny, pretty, creative
> People who like the name Arin also like Ava, Abigail, Aeryn, Ariana, Aurora, Adin, Alexa, Arielle, Amber, Audrey

Arion (*Hebrew*) ♀ ♂   RATING: ★★★★
With melody
> People think of Arion as intelligent, powerful, caring, handsome, funny
> People who like the name Arion also like Arien, Aidan, Ari, Ariel, Avery, Ashton, Caden, Alexis, Azriel, Arden

Arissa (*American*) ♀   RATING: ★★★★☆
Best—Variation of Arista
> People think of Arissa as pretty, funny, caring, energetic, intelligent
> People who like the name Arissa also like Arianna, Alyssa, Ariana, Adriana, Alana, Alissa, Alexia, Abrianna, Alaina, Alexa

Arista (*Greek*) ♀   RATING: ★★★★
Best—Also a music recording label
> People think of Arista as intelligent, trustworthy, pretty, creative, energetic
> People who like the name Arista also like Aurora, Anastasia, Arissa, Audrey, Autumn, Ava, Bianca, Aria, Arianna, Alexia

Aristotle (*Greek*) ♂   RATING: ★☆
Best—Aristotle, Greek philosopher; Aristotle Onassis, tycoon
> People think of Aristotle as intelligent, creative, powerful, old-fashioned, leader
> People who like the name Aristotle also like Apollo, Alexander, Aiden, Ambrose, Andrew, Anakin, Atticus, Alastair, Anthony, Angus

Arizona (*Spanish*) ♀ ♂   RATING: ★★★★
Good oak—U.S. state; often mistaken as Native American origin; from the Basque words *aritz ona* meaning good oak
> People think of Arizona as exotic, cool, girl next door, funny, intelligent
> People who like the name Arizona also like Dakota, Ariel, Austin, Aidan, Bailey, Ashton, Addison, Aspen, Caden, Avery

Arkadiy (*Russian*) ♂   RATING: ★☆
Bold—Variation of Archibald
> People think of Arkadiy as intelligent, handsome, exotic, aggressive, old-fashioned
> People who like the name Arkadiy also like Anakin, Atticus, Asher, Aiden, Argus, Amadeus, Aristotle, Aden, Alexander, Alagan

Arkansas (*French*) ♀ ♂   RATING: ★★★☆
South wind—U.S. state; from *Arkansaes*, a French name for the Quapaw tribe who lived in that region
> People think of Arkansas as weird, lazy, loser, unpopular, poor

People who like the name Arkansas also like Arizona, Alabama, Austin, Angel, Aidan, Ashanti, Ali, Ashton, Aquarius, Arden

Arlais *(Welsh)* ♀　　　　　　RATING: ★★
From the temple
　People think of Arlais as quiet, pretty, intelligent, old, artsy
　People who like the name Arlais also like Aelwen, Aderyn, Aislin, Arwen, Aeryn, Aerona, Alana, Aaralyn, Ava, Ailani

Arlanna *(American)* ♀　　　RATING: ★★☆
Combination of Arlene and Anna
　People think of Arlanna as pretty, caring, sexy, elegant, popular
　People who like the name Arlanna also like Arabella, Anya, Anthea, Adrianna, Abrianna, April, Aubrianna, Angela, Ami, Abigail

Arlen *(Celtic/Gaelic)* ♂　　RATING: ★★☆
Pledge
　People think of Arlen as intelligent, handsome, leader, creative, trustworthy
　People who like the name Arlen also like Aiden, Aden, Alden, Alaric, Alan, Arthur, Anson, Artan, Atticus, Ace

Arlene *(Celtic/Gaelic)* ♀　　RATING: ★★★
Pledge—Arlene Francis, TV personality
　People think of Arlene as caring, pretty, funny, intelligent, creative
　People who like the name Arlene also like Aileen, Alana, Aeryn, Aideen, Amber, Arianna, Audrey, Amanda, Alyssa, Aislinn

Arlet *(Sanskrit/East Indian)* ♀　RATING: ★★★☆
East Indian spice
　People think of Arlet as exotic, pretty, caring, quiet, intelligent
　People who like the name Arlet also like Avani, Amara, Anaya, Asha, Adara, Adalia, Anila, Amma, Alessa, Amithi

Arlette *(French)* ♀　　　　RATING: ★★★☆
Eagle
　People think of Arlette as pretty, creative, funny, intelligent, caring
　People who like the name Arlette also like Audrey, Ariana, Antoinette, Belle, Angelique, Ava, Autumn, Aurora, Annette, Austine

Arline *(French)* ♀　　　　RATING: ★★★☆
Eagle
　People think of Arline as pretty, popular, funny, caring, intelligent
　People who like the name Arline also like Angelina, Aimee, Annalise, Adalia, Annabel, Alena, Amber, Angie, Alice, Adrina

Arlo *(German)* ♂　　　　RATING: ★★
Hill—Also short for Arlen or Carlo; Arlo Guthrie, musician
　People think of Arlo as creative, funny, cool, caring, intelligent

People who like the name Arlo also like Aiden, Axel, Ansel, Asher, Archer, August, Arlen, Ace, Angelo, Atticus

Armand *(French)* ♂　　　RATING: ★★
Army man—From the same origin as Herman; Armand Assante, actor
　People think of Armand as handsome, intelligent, powerful, trustworthy, sexy
　People who like the name Armand also like Aiden, Alexander, Anthony, Adrian, Aaron, Andrew, Amadeus, Adam, André, Antonio

Armande *(French)* ♀　　　RATING: ★★
Army man—Variation of Armand
　People think of Armande as weird, exotic, quiet, criminal, aggressive
　People who like the name Armande also like Antoinette, Aimee, Amani, Armelle, Adalia, Angelique, Amelie, Aceline, Allete, Aurorette

Armando *(Spanish)* ♂　　RATING: ★★★☆
Army man—Variation of Armand
　People think of Armando as handsome, funny, cool, sexy, popular
　People who like the name Armando also like Antonio, Alejandro, Adrian, Alexander, Andrés, Anthony, Angelo, Adam, Andrew, Aaron

Armani *(African)* ♀♂　　　RATING: ★★★★
From the House of Armand—Giorgio Armani, fashion designer
　People think of Armani as intelligent, creative, caring, pretty, funny
　People who like the name Armani also like Alexis, Ashanti, Ariel, Aidan, Jaden, Ashton, Bailey, Avery, Brooklyn, Angel

Armelle *(French)* ♀　　　RATING: ★★★☆
Princess
　People think of Armelle as pretty, elegant, caring, intelligent, popular
　People who like the name Armelle also like Aurora, Alanna, Alaina, Abrianna, Amber, Arianna, Arabella, Angelina, Anastasia, Alana

Armen *(Armenian)* ♂　　RATING: ★★
Armenian
　People think of Armen as handsome, caring, creative, powerful, cool
　People who like the name Armen also like Aiden, Anton, Andrew, Adrian, André, Altan, Adam, Armand, Aimon, Aden

Armina *(Latin)* ♀　　　　RATING: ★★☆
Noble
　People think of Armina as intelligent, exotic, funny, elegant, creative
　People who like the name Armina also like Aliana, Aria, Aurora, Alana, Amorina, Amara, Amelia, Adrina, Ania, Ariana

Armon *(German)* ♂   RATING: ★★☆
Army man—Variation of Armand
> People think of Armon as funny, handsome, winner, intelligent, trustworthy
> People who like the name Armon also like Aiden, André, Anton, Aric, Archer, Axel, Aden, Alexander, Alexei, Alastair

Arnaldo *(Spanish)* ♂   RATING: ★★★
Eagle power—Variation of Arnold
> People think of Arnaldo as nerdy, popular, intelligent, handsome, sexy
> People who like the name Arnaldo also like Antonio, Andrés, Angelito, Alvaro, Alberto, Alejandro, Amadeus, Alfonso, Anthony, Apollo

Arnau *(Spanish)* ♂   RATING: ★★☆
Strong warrior
> People think of Arnau as exotic, aggressive, powerful, leader, handsome
> People who like the name Arnau also like Amando, Azizi, Amergin, Ansel, Artan, Alexei, Atticus, Avel, Aiden, Asher

Arnaud *(French)* ♂   RATING: ★★★
Eagle power—Variation of Arnold
> People think of Arnaud as weird, loser, intelligent, nerdy, popular
> People who like the name Arnaud also like André, Alain, Ansel, Aiden, Alaric, Arne, Avent, Axel, Alistair, Alexei

Arnav *(Sanskrit/East Indian)* ♂   RATING: ★★★
Ocean
> People think of Arnav as cool, intelligent, handsome, energetic, young
> People who like the name Arnav also like Arav, Ashwin, Amish, Adit, Atish, Adarsh, Alagan, Amrit, Amil, Asho

Arne *(German)* ♂   RATING: ★★★
Eagle—Variation of Arnold
> People think of Arne as handsome, sporty, leader, intelligent, trustworthy
> People who like the name Arne also like Axel, Albert, Arch, Aiden, Angus, Alain, Arnold, Alvin, August, André

Arnia *(American)* ♀   RATING: ★★★☆
Strong as an eagle—Feminine form of Arnold or Arnie
> People think of Arnia as powerful, intelligent, winner, wild, girl next door
> People who like the name Arnia also like Aira, Audrey, Anastasia, Alana, Aura, Aria, Aurora, Astra, Avari, Ava

Arnie *(English)* ♂   RATING: ★★★☆
Eagle power—Short for Arnold
> People think of Arnie as intelligent, caring, nerdy, young, funny
> People who like the name Arnie also like Alfred, Archie, Ace, Anton, Alton, Alan, Anderson, Angus, Allen, Adam

Arnold *(German)* ♂   RATING: ★★★
Eagle power—Arnold Palmer, golfer; Arnold Schwarzenegger, actor/politician
> People think of Arnold as funny, handsome, cool, intelligent, sexy
> People who like the name Arnold also like Arthur, Andrew, Aaron, Albert, Alan, Anthony, Alexander, Alfred, Adam, Adrian

Arnoldo *(Spanish)* ♂   RATING: ★★☆
Eagle power—Variation of Arnold
> People think of Arnoldo as creative, young, trustworthy, intelligent, cool
> People who like the name Arnoldo also like Antonio, Alejandro, Alvaro, Andrés, Alberto, Arnaldo, Angelito, Armando, Aquila, Axel

Arnon *(Hebrew)* ♀♂   RATING: ★★★
Roaring stream
> People think of Arnon as funny, young, aggressive, weird, big
> People who like the name Arnon also like Aidan, Arion, Aubrey, Arden, Ariel, Ari, Aren, Astin, Artemis, Alex

Aron *(Hebrew)* ♂   RATING: ★★
Teaching; singing
> People think of Aron as handsome, funny, intelligent, caring, creative
> People who like the name Aron also like Aaron, Aiden, Aden, Adam, Alexander, Andrew, Anthony, Caleb, Adrian, Asher

Arrian *(Latin)* ♀♂   RATING: ★★★★
Holy
> People think of Arrian as intelligent, exotic, creative, caring, sexy
> People who like the name Arrian also like Avery, Aidan, Arien, Ashton, Addison, Ariel, Aubrey, Caden, Alexis, Arden

Arsenio *(Spanish)* ♂   RATING: ★★☆
Virile—Arsenio Hall, actor/TV host
> People think of Arsenio as leader, funny, handsome, young, caring
> People who like the name Arsenio also like Deshawn, Antonio, Ramiro, Jabulani, Angelito, Danniell, Kaemon, Mateusz, Darius, Carmine

Art *(English)* ♂   RATING: ★★
Bear—Short for Arthur; Art Carney, actor/comedian
> People think of Art as creative, funny, cool, handsome, intelligent
> People who like the name Art also like Adam, Ace, Aaron, Aiden, Alan, Andrew, Adrian, Arthur, Anthony, Alfred

Artan *(Celtic/Gaelic)* ♂   RATING: ★★★☆
Little bear
> People think of Artan as intelligent, handsome, caring, creative, funny
> People who like the name Artan also like Aiden, Alistair, Alaric, Arlen, Arthur, Aden, Bowen, Alastair, Axel, Braeden

Artaxiad (*Armenian*) ♂   RATING: ★☆
Descendant of the joyous light—Also an Armenian line of kings
> People think of Artaxiad as powerful, weird, exotic, leader, aggressive
> People who like the name Artaxiad also like Alaric, Amadeus, Aloysius, Alastair, Amando, Adair, Aiden, Alexavier, Arif, Adonis

Artemas (*Greek*) ♂   RATING: ★★
Of Artemis
> People think of Artemas as handsome, powerful, leader, intelligent, weird
> People who like the name Artemas also like Aiden, Andrew, Alexander, Anthony, Atticus, Apollo, Ambrose, Amadeus, Alastair, Alden

Artemis (*Greek*) ♀♂   RATING: ★★
Goddess of the moon and hunt—In Greek mythology, the daughter of Leto and Zeus, and the twin of Apollo; Artemis Gordon, from TV show and movie *Wild Wild West*
> People think of Artemis as intelligent, powerful, leader, creative, elegant
> People who like the name Artemis also like Aidan, Ariel, Avery, Alexis, Ash, Arden, Aubrey, Addison, Caden, Azure

Artemus (*Greek*) ♀♂   RATING: ★★★☆
Of Artemis
> People think of Artemus as intelligent, artsy, aggressive, exotic, wealthy
> People who like the name Artemus also like Artemis, Aidan, Astin, Arien, Angel, Arden, Ari, Avery, Aubrey, Addison

Arthur (*Celtic/Gaelic*) ♂   RATING: ★★
Bear—Arthur, children's cartoon; Arthur Miller, playwright
> People think of Arthur as intelligent, handsome, funny, caring, cool
> People who like the name Arthur also like Alexander, Aiden, Benjamin, Aaron, Andrew, Adam, Anthony, Aden, Alan, Adrian

Artie (*American*) ♂   RATING: ★☆
Bear—Short for Arthur
> People think of Artie as funny, intelligent, popular, cool, handsome
> People who like the name Artie also like Arthur, Aiden, Albert, Alexander, Alfred, Alan, Adam, Art, Aaron, Archie

Artois (*French*) ♀♂   RATING: ★★
From Artois, Netherlands
> People think of Artois as aggressive, uptight, weird, criminal, big
> People who like the name Artois also like Astin, Artemis, Afton, Aure, Aidan, Andren, Arawn, Azure, Aldis, Ames

Arty (*American*) ♂   RATING: ★★☆
Bear—Short for Arthur
> People think of Arty as caring, cool, funny, energetic, powerful
> People who like the name Arty also like Artie, Arthur, Adam, Allan, Alan, Alexander, Alfred, Allen, Axel, Al

Arva (*Latin*) ♀   RATING: ★★
Fertile
> People think of Arva as exotic, old, funny, creative, girl next door
> People who like the name Arva also like Ava, Ave, Aurora, Amelia, Aracely, Amorina, Aislin, Aradia, Aideen, Aria

Arvid (*Scandinavian*) ♀♂   RATING: ★☆
Eagle of the woods; brave warrior—In Hebrew, means wandering
> People think of Arvid as intelligent, trustworthy, artsy, aggressive, funny
> People who like the name Arvid also like Aidan, Ashton, Avery, Alex, Ashley, Aiken, Ash, Arden, Astin, Artemis

Arvin (*German*) ♂   RATING: ★★★☆
Friend to all
> People think of Arvin as handsome, intelligent, caring, creative, funny
> People who like the name Arvin also like Alvin, Aaron, Axel, Ansel, Aiden, Aden, Arthur, Andrew, Alan, Ambrose

Arwan (*Persian*) ♂   RATING: ★★★
Brave, courageous
> People think of Arwan as pretty, young, intelligent, quiet, powerful
> People who like the name Arwan also like Adam, Aiden, Aden, Aaron, Alastair, Alain, Asher, Allen, Artan, Anton

Arwen (*Welsh*) ♀   RATING: ★★★★☆
Muse—Created by J.R.R. Tolkien for the *Lord of the Rings* character
> People think of Arwen as pretty, elegant, intelligent, creative, caring
> People who like the name Arwen also like Aurora, Ava, Aeryn, Chloe, Audrey, Aelwen, Amelia, Abigail, Emma, Anastasia

Arya (*Persian*) ♀♂   RATING: ★★★★
Friend; faithful
> People think of Arya as intelligent, pretty, exotic, elegant, powerful
> People who like the name Arya also like Aidan, Caden, Avery, Aubrey, Arden, Ariel, Ari, Azra, Addison, Cadence

Asa (*Japanese*) ♀♂   RATING: ★★★☆
Born at dawn—Also Hebrew meaning physician; Asa Buchanan, character on *One Life to Live*
> People think of Asa as intelligent, handsome, funny, cool, caring
> People who like the name Asa also like Aidan, Avery, Aubrey, Addison, Ari, Austin, Ariel, Caden, Bailey, Ashton

Asabi *(African)* ♀   RATING: ★☆
One of select birth—Nigerian origin
> People think of Asabi as pretty, exotic, intelligent, creative, powerful
> People who like the name Asabi also like Ava, Anaya, Aimee, Amber, Ayoka, Aurora, Alana, Amani, Aiko, Amaya

Asasia *(Greek)* ♀   RATING: ★★
Form of Acacia
> People think of Asasia as pretty, wealthy, funny, exotic, energetic
> People who like the name Asasia also like Anastasia, Asia, Aaralyn, Ailani, Aurora, Ava, Alanna, Analiese, Amaya, Acacia

Ash *(English)* ♀ ♂   RATING: ★★★☆
From the ash tree—Short for Ashley or Ashton
> People think of Ash as cool, caring, creative, funny, intelligent
> People who like the name Ash also like Aidan, Ashton, Austin, Bailey, Addison, Caden, Alex, Avery, Alec, Blake

Asha *(Sanskrit/East Indian)* ♀   RATING: ★★★★
Hope, wish
> People think of Asha as pretty, intelligent, creative, funny, caring
> People who like the name Asha also like Ava, Amara, Aisha, Anya, Anaya, Amber, Amelia, Amaya, Aaliyah, Aurora

Ashanti *(African)* ♀ ♂   RATING: ★★★★
African tribe name—Ghanaian origin; Ashanti, singer
> People think of Ashanti as pretty, popular, sexy, intelligent, funny
> People who like the name Ashanti also like Angel, Alexis, Bailey, Ashton, Ariel, Ashley, Andrea, Aubrey, Austin, Alex

Ashby *(English)* ♀ ♂   RATING: ★★
Farm by the ash tree
> People think of Ashby as intelligent, caring, trustworthy, quiet, pretty
> People who like the name Ashby also like Avery, Ashton, Addison, Bailey, Aubrey, Ainsley, Caden, Aidan, Alexis, Austin

Asher *(Hebrew)* ♂   RATING: ★★★☆
Blessed, happy
> People think of Asher as handsome, intelligent, creative, caring, leader
> People who like the name Asher also like Aiden, Caleb, Ethan, Noah, Aden, Elijah, Alexander, Gabriel, Isaac, Benjamin

Ashlee *(American)* ♀   RATING: ★★★★
From the ash tree field—Variation of Ashley; Ashlee Simpson, singer
> People think of Ashlee as pretty, funny, popular, creative, caring
> People who like the name Ashlee also like Abigail, Alyssa, Amber, Ashleigh, Ashlyn, Chloe, Aimee, Audrey, Hailey, Hannah

Ashleigh *(English)* ♀   RATING: ★★★☆
From the ash tree field
> People think of Ashleigh as pretty, funny, caring, intelligent, creative
> People who like the name Ashleigh also like Abigail, Ashlyn, Amber, Hannah, Chloe, Audrey, Ava, Alyssa, Caitlyn, Hailey

Ashley *(English)* ♀ ♂   RATING: ★★★
From the ash tree field—Ashley Judd, actress; Ashley Wilkes, from *Gone With the Wind*
> People think of Ashley as pretty, funny, caring, cool, creative
> People who like the name Ashley also like Alexis, Madison, Brooke, Bailey, Taylor, Austin, Ryan, Ashton, Dylan, Alex

Ashling *(Celtic/Gaelic)* ♀ ♂   RATING: ★★★☆
Dream, vision
> People think of Ashling as pretty, young, funny, caring, intelligent
> People who like the name Ashling also like Aidan, Avery, Ainsley, Bailey, Aubrey, Astin, Alexis, Ashton, Addison, Ash

Ashlyn *(English)* ♀   RATING: ★★★☆
Combination of Ashley and Lynn
> People think of Ashlyn as pretty, funny, creative, caring, intelligent
> People who like the name Ashlyn also like Ava, Abigail, Hailey, Cailyn, Emma, Hannah, Kaelyn, Ashtyn, Alyssa, Isabella

Asho *(Persian)* ♂   RATING: ★☆
Pure of heart
> People think of Asho as young, intelligent, weird, creative, trustworthy
> People who like the name Asho also like Alagan, Ambrose, Arash, Aron, Anoki, Amadeus, Aden, Arif, Adonis, Alaric

Ashton *(English)* ♀ ♂   RATING: ★★★
Ash tree town—Ashton Kutcher, actor
> People think of Ashton as funny, caring, popular, intelligent, cool
> People who like the name Ashton also like Addison, Caden, Bailey, Austin, Aidan, Hayden, Avery, Blake, Madison, Logan

Ashtyn *(English)* ♀   RATING: ★★★
Ash tree town—Variation of Ashton
> People think of Ashtyn as pretty, caring, funny, popular, intelligent
> People who like the name Ashtyn also like Ashlyn, Ava, Jadyn, Abigail, Audrey, Alexa, Hailey, Arianna, Cailyn, Alyssa

Ashwin *(Sanskrit/East Indian)* ♂   RATING: ★★★☆
Seventh Hindu month
> People think of Ashwin as intelligent, handsome, funny, trustworthy, young

People who like the name Ashwin also like Amish, Aaron, Aiden, Aden, Ajay, Asher, Adit, Arnav, Alastair, Adarsh

Asia *(Greek)* ♀　　　RATING: ★★★★☆
Resurrection—Also a continent
People think of Asia as pretty, funny, popular, intelligent, creative
People who like the name Asia also like Ava, Aaliyah, Anastasia, Adriana, Autumn, Amber, Audrey, Ariana, Amaya, Aurora

Asis *(Hebrew)* ♀　　　RATING: ★★★
New wine—Pronounced *Ah-sees*
People think of Asis as sexy, exotic, religious, ethnic, loser
People who like the name Asis also like Aurora, Armelle, Amaris, Amara, Ava, Abigail, Alana, Aria, Asia, Aspasia

Aspasia *(Greek)* ♀　　　RATING: ★★★☆
Welcome
People think of Aspasia as pretty, creative, exotic, intelligent, old-fashioned
People who like the name Aspasia also like Aurora, Anastasia, Armelle, Aster, Amara, Aceline, Asta, Aeryn, Alana, Althea

Aspen *(American)* ♀♂　　　RATING: ★★★★
The Aspen tree—Also a city in Colorado
People think of Aspen as pretty, intelligent, popular, funny, creative
People who like the name Aspen also like Avery, Caden, Addison, Aidan, Bailey, Ashton, Hayden, Aubrey, Cadence, Austin

Asta *(Latin)* ♀　　　RATING: ★★★☆
Bright as a star
People think of Asta as intelligent, pretty, trustworthy, creative, caring
People who like the name Asta also like Aurora, Ava, Aiko, Aria, Anastasia, Astra, Aida, Aster, Aura, Amara

Aster *(English)* ♀　　　RATING: ★★
Star
People think of Aster as cool, young, creative, artsy, elegant
People who like the name Aster also like Ava, Astrid, Aurora, Audrey, Arwen, Abigail, Astra, Amber, Amelia, Adelaide

Astin *(French)* ♀♂　　　RATING: ★★★★
Starlike
People think of Astin as creative, intelligent, funny, caring, trustworthy
People who like the name Astin also like Addison, Aidan, Avery, Caden, Ashton, Austin, Arden, Ainsley, Aubrey, Bailey

Aston *(English)* ♂　　　RATING: ★★★☆
Noble stone—Variation of Athelstan
People think of Aston as handsome, intelligent, cool, funny, popular

People who like the name Aston also like Aiden, Aden, Braden, Asher, Alexander, Ethan, Braeden, Andrew, Anson, Caleb

Astra *(Greek)* ♀　　　RATING: ★★
From the stars
People think of Astra as creative, exotic, pretty, artsy, weird
People who like the name Astra also like Aurora, Ava, Astrid, Arwen, Athena, Aria, Anastasia, Aster, Alana, Amber

Astrid *(Scandinavian)* ♀　　　RATING: ★★★☆
God's strength
People think of Astrid as creative, pretty, intelligent, cool, artsy
People who like the name Astrid also like Ava, Aurora, Audrey, Chloe, Amelia, Arwen, Abigail, Anastasia, Bella, Charlotte

Astro *(Greek)* ♂　　　RATING: ★☆
Of the stars—Astro, character on *The Jetsons*
People think of Astro as intelligent, funny, handsome, nerdy, leader
People who like the name Astro also like Apollo, Andrew, Aiden, Axel, Adam, Aden, Asher, Anton, Ace, Ajax

Atalanta *(Greek)* ♀　　　RATING: ★★
Unswaying—In Greek mythology, a woman who refused to marry anyone who couldn't beat her in a footrace
People think of Atalanta as powerful, exotic, artsy, leader, energetic
People who like the name Atalanta also like Aurora, Anastasia, Athena, Arwen, Adriana, Adeline, Asia, Amber, Alexandra, Amara

Atalaya *(Arabic)* ♀　　　RATING: ★★★☆
Watchtower
People think of Atalaya as pretty, intelligent, powerful, energetic, sexy
People who like the name Atalaya also like Aaliyah, Amaya, Anaya, Autumn, Abrianna, Alana, Arianna, Ava, Ariana, Aaralyn

Atalo *(Greek)* ♂　　　RATING: ★☆
Youthful
People think of Atalo as winner, young, ethnic, artsy, weird
People who like the name Atalo also like Aiden, Alair, Aimon, Apollo, Axel, Ambrose, Alexander, Atticus, André, Asher

Atara *(Hebrew)* ♀　　　RATING: ★★★★
Crown, blessed
People think of Atara as pretty, young, elegant, cool, powerful
People who like the name Atara also like Atira, Amara, Ayanna, Arella, Amaris, Aurora, Abigail, Amaya, Ariella, Aria

Ataret *(Hebrew)* ♀ RATING: ★★☆
Crown, blessed
> People think of Ataret as pretty, ethnic, religious, elegant, quiet
> People who like the name Ataret also like Atara, Atira, Arella, Athalia, Amara, Alessa, Alia, Anaïs, Arielle, Ariella

Athalia *(Hebrew)* ♀ RATING: ★★★★
God is exalted
> People think of Athalia as pretty, exotic, intelligent, leader, religious
> People who like the name Athalia also like Adalia, Abigail, Aurora, Amaris, Ariella, Arianna, Abrianna, Azalia, Arella, Ariana

Athena *(Greek)* ♀ RATING: ★★★★☆
Goddess of wisdom and war—Athens, Greece, was named after the goddess Athena
> People think of Athena as pretty, intelligent, creative, elegant, powerful
> People who like the name Athena also like Aurora, Anastasia, Ava, Abigail, Amelia, Alexandra, Adriana, Audrey, Angelina, Bella

Atira *(Hebrew)* ♀ RATING: ★★★☆
Prayer
> People think of Atira as creative, sexy, ethnic, elegant, religious
> People who like the name Atira also like Atara, Amaris, Arella, Amara, Athalia, Aria, Amaya, Aurora, Abigail, Adalia

Atish *(Persian)* ♂ RATING: ★★★
Fire, splendor—Lord Ganpati, an East Indian god
> People think of Atish as intelligent, energetic, young, powerful, leader
> People who like the name Atish also like Amish, Ashwin, Arav, Arnav, Adit, Adish, Adarsh, Alagan, Aiden, Amil

Atticus *(English)* ♂ RATING: ★★★☆
Fatherlike—Atticus Finch, character in *To Kill a Mockingbird* by Harper Lee
> People think of Atticus as intelligent, handsome, trustworthy, leader, caring
> People who like the name Atticus also like Aiden, Asher, Alexander, Noah, Elijah, Jack, Caleb, Oliver, Liam, Ethan

Auberon *(German)* ♀ RATING: ★★☆
Noble bear
> People think of Auberon as popular, powerful, quiet, creative, elegant
> People who like the name Auberon also like Adalia, Aileen, Aimee, Aurora, Ailis, Beyla, Adriana, Alexa, Aideen, Candra

Auberta *(French)* ♀ RATING: ★★★☆
Noble, bright
> People think of Auberta as old, unpopular, poor, intelligent, lazy
> People who like the name Auberta also like Autumn, Austine, Aubrianna, Aileen, Augusta, Amanda, Alaska, Armelle, Aimee, Axelle

Aubrey *(English)* ♀ ♂ RATING: ★★★★
Noble ruler
> People think of Aubrey as pretty, funny, intelligent, creative, popular
> People who like the name Aubrey also like Avery, Addison, Bailey, Caden, Hayden, Madison, Aidan, Riley, Alexis, Logan

Aubrianna *(American)* ♀ RATING: ★★★★☆
Combination of Aubrey and Anna
> People think of Aubrianna as pretty, creative, intelligent, popular, funny
> People who like the name Aubrianna also like Abrianna, Arianna, Adriana, Audriana, Audrey, Ashlyn, Ava, Abigail, Ariana, Brianna

Auburn *(American)* ♀ ♂ RATING: ★★★☆
Reddish brown
> People think of Auburn as trendy, funny, popular, winner, trustworthy
> People who like the name Auburn also like Bailey, Aidan, Avery, Aubrey, Alex, Angel, Alexis, Addison, Andy, Brooklyn

Audi *(German)* ♀ ♂ RATING: ★★★★
Car manufacturer
> People think of Audi as creative, elegant, nerdy, pretty, sexy
> People who like the name Audi also like Aubrey, Aidan, Avery, Ashton, Bailey, Aspen, Addison, Austin, Ariel, Alexis

Audra *(American)* ♀ RATING: ★★☆
Noble strength—Audra Lindley, actress
> People think of Audra as pretty, funny, intelligent, caring, creative
> People who like the name Audra also like Audrey, Ava, Abigail, Ashlyn, Alana, Adrienne, Amelia, Alexa, Aurora, Adriana

Audrey *(English)* ♀ RATING: ★★★☆
Noble strength—Audrey Hepburn, actress; Audrey Tautou, actress
> People think of Audrey as pretty, intelligent, creative, elegant, funny
> People who like the name Audrey also like Ava, Abigail, Emma, Olivia, Grace, Chloe, Amelia, Ella, Hannah, Claire

Audria *(American)* ♀ RATING: ★★★
Noble strength—Variation of Audrey
> People think of Audria as leader, intelligent, young, funny, creative
> People who like the name Audria also like Audrey, Ava, Audriana, Adrianna, Arianna, Aubrianna, Ariana, Alexandria, Alexa, Audra

Audriana *(American)* ♀ RATING: ★★★★☆
Combination of Audrey and Anna
> People think of Audriana as pretty, funny, caring, young, cool
> People who like the name Audriana also like Audrey, Adriana, Arianna, Aubrianna, Ava, Abrianna, Ariana, Abigail, Alexandria, Ashlyn

Audrina *(English)* ♀   RATING: ★★★★
Noble strength—Variation of Audrey
People think of Audrina as pretty, popular, sexy, creative, intelligent
People who like the name Audrina also like Audrey, Ava, Adriana, Audriana, Aubrianna, Arianna, Adrina, Bella, Alexandria, Abrianna

August *(English)* ♂   RATING: ★★☆
Great—Variation of Augustus; used for children born in this month
People think of August as intelligent, leader, handsome, powerful, creative
People who like the name August also like Aiden, Alexander, Adrian, Adam, Aaron, Andrew, Aden, Atticus, Asher, Benjamin

Augusta *(English)* ♀   RATING: ★★★☆
Great—Feminine form of Augustin or August; also the capital of Maine
People think of Augusta as intelligent, pretty, creative, funny, trustworthy
People who like the name Augusta also like Audrey, Aurora, Ava, Autumn, Alexandra, Abigail, Annabel, Amelia, Anastasia, Aurelia

Augustin *(French)* ♂   RATING: ★★
Great
People think of Augustin as intelligent, handsome, sexy, funny, powerful
People who like the name Augustin also like Alexander, August, Andrew, Anthony, Aiden, Anton, Adrian, Augustus, André, Alastair

Augustus *(Latin)* ♂   RATING: ★★★☆
Great—Augustus Gloop, character in *Charlie and the Chocolate Factory* by Roald Dahl
People think of Augustus as powerful, leader, intelligent, handsome, old-fashioned
People who like the name Augustus also like Alexander, Andrew, Adam, Aiden, August, Atticus, Aaron, Arthur, Anthony, Angus

Aulani *(Hawaiian)* ♀   RATING: ★★★☆
King's messenger
People think of Aulani as exotic, energetic, funny, pretty, caring
People who like the name Aulani also like Ailani, Aolani, Alohilani, Amaya, Aurora, Kailani, Ava, Amara, Leilani, Amani

Aulii *(Hawaiian)* ♀♂   RATING: ★★★
Delicious
People think of Aulii as popular, exotic, pretty, intelligent, caring
People who like the name Aulii also like Azriel, Azra, Azure, Arden, Ashanti, Asa, Aidan, Azize, Avery, Ari

Aura *(Latin)* ♀   RATING: ★★★☆
Glowing light
People think of Aura as pretty, intelligent, caring, creative, elegant
People who like the name Aura also like Aurora, Ava, Aria, Amara, Autumn, Amaya, Aira, Aurelia, Amber, Abigail

Aure *(French)* ♀♂   RATING: ★★★☆
Soft air, breeze
People think of Aure as exotic, creative, intelligent, pretty, elegant
People who like the name Aure also like Astin, Aidan, Avery, Aren, Ariel, Arden, Ash, Ames, Ari, Alexis

Aurelia *(Latin)* ♀   RATING: ★★★★☆
Golden—Feminine form of Aurleius
People think of Aurelia as pretty, intelligent, elegant, creative, caring
People who like the name Aurelia also like Aurora, Ava, Amelia, Audrey, Arianna, Adriana, Arabella, Anastasia, Amelie, Ariana

Aurelio *(Spanish)* ♂   RATING: ★★★
Golden
People think of Aurelio as handsome, cool, intelligent, sexy, funny
People who like the name Aurelio also like Adrian, Braden, Benjamin, Ace, Aaron, Armand, Brent, Basil, Liam, Miles

Aurelius *(Latin)* ♂   RATING: ★★★☆
Golden—Marcus Aurelius, Roman emperor
People think of Aurelius as handsome, intelligent, powerful, creative, popular
People who like the name Aurelius also like Aiden, Alexander, Atticus, Ambrose, Augustus, Arthur, Alexavier, Asher, Alastair, Amadeus

Aurora *(Latin)* ♀   RATING: ★★★
Goddess of the dawn—Aurora borealis, aka the northern lights
People think of Aurora as pretty, intelligent, elegant, creative, caring
People who like the name Aurora also like Ava, Audrey, Anastasia, Abigail, Chloe, Autumn, Amelia, Bella, Arianna, Isabella

Aurorette *(French)* ♀   RATING: ★★☆
Variation of Aurora
People think of Aurorette as nerdy, old, loser, weird, pretty
People who like the name Aurorette also like Aurora, Angelique, Antoinette, Anastasia, Armelle, Aradia, Belle, Adrienne, Alaina, Alana

Auryon *(American)* ♀   RATING: ★★☆
Hunter—Feminine form of Orion
People think of Auryon as sexy, powerful, exotic, cool, intelligent
People who like the name Auryon also like Aurora, Aaralyn, Ava, Avari, Arabella, Aradia, Arwen, Adeline, Alyn, Aeryn

Austin *(English)* ♀♂   RATING: ★★★
Great—Short for Augustine; a city in Texas; Austin
Powers, movie character
  People think of Austin as handsome, funny, cool, intel-
  ligent, popular
  People who like the name Austin also like Bailey,
  Dylan, Logan, Ashton, Blake, Addison, Madison, Caden,
  Cameron, Hayden

Austine *(French)* ♀   RATING: ★★
Great—Variation of Augustine
  People think of Austine as caring, intelligent, pretty,
  cool, young
  People who like the name Austine also like Autumn,
  Aurora, Ava, Audrey, Ashlyn, April, Alaina, Amelia,
  Ashtyn, Arabella

Autumn *(Latin)* ♀   RATING: ★★★★
Fall season
  People think of Autumn as pretty, creative, funny, intel-
  ligent, caring
  People who like the name Autumn also like Ava, Audrey,
  Abigail, Chloe, Amber, Hannah, Aurora, Faith, Emma,
  Hailey

Ava *(Latin)* ♀   RATING: ★★★★
Like a bird—Originally short for Avis; Ava Gardner,
actress
  People think of Ava as pretty, elegant, intelligent, popu-
  lar, creative
  People who like the name Ava also like Ella, Emma,
  Olivia, Isabella, Eva, Grace, Chloe, Abigail, Audrey, Bella

Avak *(Armenian)* ♂   RATING: ★★☆
Great
  People think of Avak as intelligent, funny, powerful,
  leader, handsome
  People who like the name Avak also like Adam, Atticus,
  Ansel, Anoki, Alastair, Axel, Ambrose, Andrew, Aston,
  Avel

Avalbane *(Celtic/Gaelic)* ♀   RATING: ★☆
White orchard
  People think of Avalbane as intelligent, weird, old-
  fashioned, religious, stuck-up
  People who like the name Avalbane also like Aeryn,
  Aislin, Alana, Aideen, Aisling, Aislinn, Ailis, Aileen,
  Ardara, Arwen

Avalon *(Celtic/Gaelic)* ♀♂   RATING: ★★☆
Apple Island, where King Arthur went after death
  People think of Avalon as pretty, creative, intelligent,
  elegant, cool
  People who like the name Avalon also like Avery, Aidan,
  Bailey, Addison, Ariel, Aspen, Ashton, Ainsley, Cadence,
  Alexis

Avani *(Sanskrit/East Indian)* ♀   RATING: ★★★★☆
Earth
  People think of Avani as exotic, pretty, intelligent, cre-
  ative, powerful

People who like the name Avani also like Amara,
Amaya, Ava, Anaya, Amani, Avari, Ayanna, Aurora, Aria,
Ailani

Avari *(American)* ♀   RATING: ★★☆
Of the heavens, from the sky
  People think of Avari as pretty, intelligent, creative,
  elegant, energetic
  People who like the name Avari also like Ava, Avani,
  Amaya, Aria, Ashlyn, Audrey, Ayanna, Aira, Aeryn,
  Aurora

Avariella *(American)* ♀   RATING: ★★★☆
Combination of Ava and Ariel
  People think of Avariella as young, popular, pretty,
  powerful, winner
  People who like the name Avariella also like Avarielle,
  Arabella, Adriana, Ava, Abrianna, Aaralyn, Ariella,
  Annabella, Audriana, Annabelle

Avarielle *(American)* ♀   RATING: ★★★★
Combination of Ava and Ariel
  People think of Avarielle as pretty, intelligent, powerful,
  cool, leader
  People who like the name Avarielle also like Avariella,
  Aaralyn, Ava, Anastasia, Abrianna, Abigail, Aurora,
  Arwen, Adriana, Arabella

Avatari *(Sanskrit/East Indian)* ♀   RATING: ★★☆
God's incarnation
  People think of Avatari as funny, sexy, cool, aggressive,
  pretty
  People who like the name Avatari also like Avani,
  Amara, Asha, Alpana, Anaya, Anila, Amber, Aiko, Amma,
  Aurora

Ave *(Latin)* ♀   RATING: ★★★★
Hail, all bow to—Short for Ave Maria, or Hail Mary;
pronounced *Ah-vay*
  People think of Ave as intelligent, elegant, pretty, trust-
  worthy, powerful
  People who like the name Ave also like Ava, Autumn,
  Amelia, Aurora, Abigail, Audrey, Annabella, Amanda,
  Alice, Aideen

Avedis *(Armenian)* ♂   RATING: ★★
Glad tidings
  People think of Avedis as intelligent, creative, trust-
  worthy, handsome, caring
  People who like the name Avedis also like Avel, Aiden,
  Azizi, Axel, Alaric, Anakin, Atticus, Alexavier, Asher,
  Amadeus

Avel *(Greek)* ♂   RATING: ★★
Breath
  People think of Avel as handsome, powerful, pretty,
  leader, intelligent
  People who like the name Avel also like Aiden, Axel,
  Aden, Abel, Ansel, Andrew, Atticus, Ambrose, Adair,
  Aron

Aveline *(French)* ♀   RATING: ★★★★
Medieval English variation of Evelyn
> People think of Aveline as pretty, elegant, intelligent, caring, artsy
> People who like the name Aveline also like Ava, Adeline, Aurora, Audrey, Amelia, Amelie, Adelaide, Aeryn, Adrienne, Arwen

Avent *(French)* ♂   RATING: ★★☆
Born during Advent
> People think of Avent as religious, big, quiet, exotic, caring
> People who like the name Avent also like Aiden, Ansel, Alain, André, Arnaud, Aston, Archer, Alastair, Axel, Aden

Avery *(English)* ♀ ♂   RATING: ★★★★
Elf ruler—Variation of Aubrey; Avery Schreiber, comedian; James Avery, actor
> People think of Avery as pretty, intelligent, creative, funny, popular
> People who like the name Avery also like Addison, Aidan, Hayden, Bailey, Aubrey, Caden, Riley, Logan, Cameron, Parker

Avi *(Hebrew)* ♀ ♂   RATING: ★★★★
Father—Also means sun in Eastern Indian languages
> People think of Avi as intelligent, funny, popular, creative, cool
> People who like the name Avi also like Ari, Avery, Aidan, Aubrey, Ariel, Alexis, Addison, Alex, Arden, Asa

Avian *(French)* ♀   RATING: ★★☆
Birdlike
> People think of Avian as intelligent, artsy, powerful, funny, leader
> People who like the name Avian also like Ava, Aurora, Aria, Amaya, Alaina, Avril, Arianna, Autumn, Alena, Aimee

Avidan *(Hebrew)* ♂   RATING: ★★★☆
God is just
> People think of Avidan as intelligent, handsome, quiet, weird, exotic
> People who like the name Avidan also like Aiden, Aaron, Asher, Aden, Alijah, Adam, Alexander, Adrian, Gabriel, Atticus

Avinoam *(Hebrew)* ♀ ♂   RATING: ★☆
Blessed father
> People think of Avinoam as exotic, ethnic, artsy, weird, creative
> People who like the name Avinoam also like Amiel, Arion, Arien, Azra, Ariel, Azriel, Ari, Aure, Azize, Avi

Avis *(English)* ♀ ♂   RATING: ★★
Variation of Avice—Not connected to Latin word *avis* meaning bird
> People think of Avis as creative, energetic, caring, intelligent, cool
> People who like the name Avis also like Avery, Arden, Azure, Avon, Aidan, Artemis, Aubrey, Ash, Angel, Azra

Avital *(Hebrew)* ♀   RATING: ★★★★☆
Father of dew
> People think of Avital as intelligent, pretty, exotic, artsy, funny
> People who like the name Avital also like Aviva, Alake, Archana, Amani, Arella, Ariella, Atira, Abigail, Armande, Aderes

Aviv *(Hebrew)* ♂   RATING: ★★★☆
Spring, renewal
> People think of Aviv as caring, pretty, intelligent, young, exotic
> People who like the name Aviv also like Aden, Aaron, Asher, Adam, Aiden, Axel, Alexander, Az, Amos, Abram

Aviva *(Hebrew)* ♀   RATING: ★★★★
Spring, renewal—Feminine form of Aviv
> People think of Aviva as pretty, intelligent, creative, energetic, cool
> People who like the name Aviva also like Ava, Aurora, Abigail, Amara, Aria, Ayla, Adina, Ariella, Adara, Amaya

Avon *(Welsh)* ♀ ♂   RATING: ★★
River—Also an English river
> People think of Avon as funny, caring, young, cool, intelligent
> People who like the name Avon also like Aidan, Ariel, Avery, Aubrey, Austin, Artemis, Azure, Astin, Arden, Addison

Avonaco *(Native American)* ♂   RATING: ★★☆
Lean bear—Cheyenne origin
> People think of Avonaco as weird, nerdy, aggressive, uptight, old-fashioned
> People who like the name Avonaco also like Akando, Anoki, Ahanu, Aiden, Artan, Aleron, Akiva, Ancelin, Akio, Anakin

Avongara *(African)* ♀   RATING: ★★☆
To tie—Zande clan origin
> People think of Avongara as handsome, exotic, criminal, loser, lazy
> People who like the name Avongara also like Azura, Adara, Anastasia, Abiba, Abeni, Aaralyn, Alberta, Amandla, Aideen, Ayoka

Avril *(French)* ♀   RATING: ★★★☆
The month of April—Avril Lavigne, singer
> People think of Avril as cool, pretty, popular, funny, creative
> People who like the name Avril also like Autumn, Amber, April, Ava, Audrey, Abigail, Anastasia, Amelia, Aimee, Aurora

Avye *(Arabic)* ♀   RATING: ★★★
Keeper of the gate
> People think of Avye as artsy, exotic, quiet, pretty, girl next door
> People who like the name Avye also like Amaya, Ava, Amara, Aiko, Aideen, Anaya, Aradia, Aurora, Abia, Aeryn

Awen *(Welsh)* ♀   RATING: ★★★☆
Muse
> People think of Awen as creative, pretty, intelligent, trustworthy, artsy
> People who like the name Awen also like Arwen, Aurora, Ava, Awena, Aislin, Anya, Aelwen, Autumn, Aria, Alana

Awena *(Welsh)* ♀   RATING: ★★★
Muse
> People think of Awena as sexy, funny, girl next door, weird, artsy
> People who like the name Awena also like Arwen, Awen, Aurora, Aelwen, Autumn, Alana, Aradia, Aislin, Aderyn, Athena

Awendela *(Native American)* ♀ ♂   RATING: ★★★
Daylight—Penobscot origin
> People think of Awendela as intelligent, artsy, pretty, creative, powerful
> People who like the name Awendela also like Azure, Aidan, Arizona, Artemis, Avery, Arien, Alexis, Astin, Ariel, Ash

Awentia *(Native American)* ♀   RATING: ★★☆
Fawn—Variation of Awenita
> People think of Awentia as ethnic, quiet, artsy, untrustworthy, pretty
> People who like the name Awentia also like Amadahy, Aquene, Arwen, Ayasha, Aponi, Adsila, Amayeta, Angeni, Anevay, Armelle

Axel *(Scandinavian)* ♂   RATING: ★★
My father is peace—Variation of Absalom
> People think of Axel as handsome, cool, powerful, intelligent, energetic
> People who like the name Axel also like Aiden, Ace, Alexander, Adam, Adrian, Aaron, Andrew, Anthony, Aden, Asher

Axelle *(French)* ♀   RATING: ★★
My father is peace—Feminine form of Axel
> People think of Axelle as pretty, intelligent, caring, creative, artsy
> People who like the name Axelle also like Armelle, Aurora, Alaina, Adrienne, Alexia, Amber, Alexa, Asia, Alana, Audrey

Axl *(American)* ♂   RATING: ★★
Variation of Axel; Axl Rose, musician
> People think of Axl as handsome, aggressive, wild, leader, creative
> People who like the name Axl also like Axel, Aiden, Ace, Aden, Anakin, August, Alexavier, Andrew, Alastair, Adam

Aya *(Hebrew)* ♀   RATING: ★★☆
Bird—Also an Israeli bird of prey
> People think of Aya as pretty, intelligent, creative, elegant, exotic
> People who like the name Aya also like Ava, Amaya, Ayla, Anya, Aria, Aurora, Ayanna, Anaïs, Aaliyah, Amara

Ayala *(Hebrew)* ♀   RATING: ★★★★
A female deer, doe
> People think of Ayala as pretty, intelligent, leader, exotic, creative
> People who like the name Ayala also like Amaya, Ayanna, Ava, Ayla, Aaliyah, Ariella, Adriana, Abigail, Amara, Ayame

Ayame *(Japanese)* ♀   RATING: ★★★★
Iris
> People think of Ayame as pretty, intelligent, creative, elegant, energetic
> People who like the name Ayame also like Amaya, Aiko, Aneko, Emiko, Sakura, Amarante, Ai, Arwen, Aurora, Kaida

Ayanna *(African)* ♀   RATING: ★★★★☆
Beautiful flower
> People think of Ayanna as pretty, intelligent, caring, funny, creative
> People who like the name Ayanna also like Amaya, Anaya, Arianna, Adriana, Ariana, Aaliyah, Alayna, Amani, Alanna, Ava

Ayasha *(Native American)* ♀   RATING: ★★☆
Little one—Cheyenne origin
> People think of Ayasha as pretty, funny, exotic, caring, trustworthy
> People who like the name Ayasha also like Ayanna, Amaya, Aaliyah, Aleshanee, Amara, Aisha, Angeni, Ayita, Aysha, Abrianna

Ayita *(African)* ♀   RATING: ★★
Dance
> People think of Ayita as energetic, creative, intelligent, pretty, artsy
> People who like the name Ayita also like Ayasha, Amaya, Ayanna, Aiko, Alora, Amber, Aradia, Alena, Alanna, Anaya

Ayla *(Hebrew)* ♀   RATING: ★★★
Oak tree—Also Turkish meaning moon glow; character in the *Clan of the Cave Bear* novels by Jean Auel
> People think of Ayla as pretty, intelligent, creative, funny, caring
> People who like the name Ayla also like Ava, Abigail, Emma, Ashlyn, Ella, Amelia, Anya, Amaya, Chloe, Aria

Ayman *(Arabic)* ♂   RATING: ★★
Holy; right-handed worker
> People think of Ayman as intelligent, trustworthy, caring, handsome, sporty
> People who like the name Ayman also like Aiden, Aimon, Alain, Altan, Aden, Ahmad, Alair, Adrian, Avidan, Aaron

Ayoka *(African)* ♀   RATING: ★★★
One who causes joy—Nigerian origin
> People think of Ayoka as caring, ethnic, pretty, funny, lazy
> People who like the name Ayoka also like Aiko, Anisa, Ayanna, Ani, Anaya, Amani, Aysha, Abeni, Amaya, Asabi

Aysel *(Turkish)* ♀   RATING: ★★★★
Moon flood
> People think of Aysel as pretty, elegant, intelligent, exotic, funny
> People who like the name Aysel also like Amaya, Aiko, Alena, Aislin, Aeryn, Arwen, Aaralyn, Amara, Aradia, Aster

Aysha *(Arabic)* ♀   RATING: ★★★★
Prosperous—Variation of Aisha
> People think of Aysha as pretty, intelligent, creative, caring, sexy
> People who like the name Aysha also like Aisha, Aaliyah, Ayanna, Amaya, Anaya, Ayasha, Ava, Arianna, Asha, Alayna

Az *(Hebrew)* ♂   RATING: ★★★
Strong
> People think of Az as intelligent, weird, funny, young, unpopular
> People who like the name Az also like Asher, Axel, Aden, Aaron, Atticus, Azizi, Alijah, Ajax, Anoki, Ace

Azalia *(Hebrew)* ♀   RATING: ★★★★
God has spared
> People think of Azalia as pretty, intelligent, creative, exotic, caring
> People who like the name Azalia also like Amaya, Abigail, Adalia, Aaliyah, Ava, Anaya, Athalia, Amaris, Aaralyn, Ayanna

Azana *(Arabic)* ♀   RATING: ★★★
Announcement; call to prayer
> People think of Azana as pretty, exotic, religious, creative, ethnic
> People who like the name Azana also like Ayanna, Aaliyah, Aysha, Amaya, Azalia, Anaya, Azura, Avani, Amani, Aaralyn

Azhar *(Arabic)* ♂   RATING: ★☆
Shining, bright
> People think of Azhar as handsome, intelligent, caring, cool, powerful
> People who like the name Azhar also like Aiden, Amir, Axel, Allan, Ambrose, Alair, Azizi, Alain, Alijah, Aaron

Azia *(American)* ♀ ♂   RATING: ★★★☆
From the East—Variation of Asia
> People think of Azia as funny, lazy, pretty, powerful, young
> People who like the name Azia also like Azra, Avery, Azure, Azriel, Alexis, Aspen, Akia, Arya, Aubrey, Ariel

Aziza *(Arabic)* ♀   RATING: ★★★★
Highly esteemed
> People think of Aziza as funny, caring, creative, exotic, cool
> People who like the name Aziza also like Ailani, Aria, Aurora, Azura, Ayanna, Aaliyah, Adalia, Aaralyn, Aysha, Amaya

Azize *(Arabic)* ♀ ♂   RATING: ★☆
Highly esteemed
> People think of Azize as big, energetic, exotic, popular, aggressive
> People who like the name Azize also like Azriel, Azra, Azure, Amiel, Aidan, Aja, Aulii, Arion, Ashanti, Ariel

Azizi *(Arabic)* ♂   RATING: ★★★
Highly esteemed
> People think of Azizi as ethnic, big, handsome, young, weird
> People who like the name Azizi also like Amiri, Ajani, Aiden, Alain, Axel, Aaron, Alaric, Az, Anakin, Alejandro

Azra *(Hebrew)* ♀ ♂   RATING: ★★★★
Pure—Possible variation of Ezra or Azriel
> People think of Azra as pretty, exotic, intelligent, creative, funny
> People who like the name Azra also like Azriel, Aidan, Avery, Ari, Azure, Ariel, Aubrey, Arya, Addison, Arden

Azriel *(Hebrew)* ♀ ♂   RATING: ★★★★
God is my aid—Character on *The Smurfs*
> People think of Azriel as powerful, trustworthy, intelligent, creative, religious
> People who like the name Azriel also like Ariel, Aidan, Azra, Adriel, Avery, Jaden, Addison, Caden, Alexis, Aubrey

Azuka *(African)* ♀   RATING: ★★☆
Support is paramount—West African origin
> People think of Azuka as stuck-up, winner, unpopular, weird, nerdy
> People who like the name Azuka also like Azura, Ayanna, Aneko, Arwen, Aadi, Abeni, Amaya, Aziza, Aster, Atira

Azul *(Spanish)* ♀ ♂   RATING: ★★★
The color blue
> People think of Azul as creative, pretty, exotic, sexy, energetic
> People who like the name Azul also like Azure, Azra, Ariel, Angel, Azriel, Addison, Ari, Alexis, Artemis, Ash

Azura *(Spanish)* ♀   RATING: ★★
Sky blue
> People think of Azura as exotic, pretty, elegant, caring, creative
> People who like the name Azura also like Aurora, Adriana, Ava, Autumn, Amora, Amber, Aaliyah, Amaya, Adrienne, Aria

Azure *(Latin)* ♀ ♂   RATING: ★★★☆
Bluish color
> People think of Azure as exotic, creative, intelligent, pretty, caring
> People who like the name Azure also like Avery, Aidan, Alexis, Caden, Bailey, Ariel, Ashton, Aubrey, Addison, Angel

Baba *(Sanskrit/East Indian)* ♀   RATING: ★★★
Father
People think of Baba as weird, caring, funny, big, lazy
People who like the name Baba also like Abeni, Abbie, Babette, Amanda, Adamma, Belle, Abigail, Bella, Annabelle, Alexandra

Baback *(Persian)* ♂   RATING: ★★★
Little father
People think of Baback as loser, unpopular, popular, intelligent, energetic
People who like the name Baback also like Amish, Ajay, Ambrose, Alain, Atticus, Anton, Aiden, Ajax, Asher, Adli

Babette *(French)* ♀   RATING: ★☆
My God is my oath—Variation of Elizabeth
People think of Babette as pretty, sexy, exotic, caring, creative
People who like the name Babette also like Belle, Abigail, Bianca, Bella, Anastasia, Aurora, Bernadette, Chloe, Beatrice, Antoinette

Baby *(English)* ♀♂   RATING: ★★☆
Infant—Character from the movie *Dirty Dancing*
People think of Baby as young, sexy, funny, pretty, cool
People who like the name Baby also like Bailey, Angel, Caden, Billie, Alexis, Blair, Brooklyn, Brooke, Blake, Abby

Bach Yen *(Vietnamese)* ♀   RATING: ★★★☆
White
People think of Bach Yen as weird, stuck-up, aggressive, intelligent, lazy
People who like the name Bach Yen also like Baka, Bambi, Ballari, Baina, Abeni, Baba, Amma, Aceline, Belle, Da-xia

Bade *(Arabic)* ♂   RATING: ★★
Incomparable—Also spelled Badi
People think of Bade as cool, young, handsome, funny, powerful
People who like the name Bade also like Aiden, Aden, Blade, Braeden, Braden, Bastien, Brice, Balin, Asher, Caleb

Baden *(German)* ♀♂   RATING: ★★★☆
Bather—Also spelled Badan, Badin, Badon, or Badyn; Baden Cook, bicyclist; Sir Robert Baden-Powell, Boy Scouts founder
People think of Baden as intelligent, popular, caring, energetic, sporty
People who like the name Baden also like Caden, Bailey, Addison, Blaine, Brayden, Aidan, Hayden, Cade, Jaden, Blake

Badu *(African)* ♀   RATING: ★★☆
Tenth-born child—From the Ashanti people of Ghana
People think of Badu as poor, unpopular, ethnic, powerful, intelligent

People who like the name Badu also like Baba, Abeni, Baka, Bela, Akili, Aira, Aceline, Adia, Abrianna, Aisha

Baeddan *(Welsh)* ♂   RATING: ★★★
Boar
People think of Baeddan as popular, exotic, lazy, loser, cool
People who like the name Baeddan also like Braeden, Braden, Aiden, Balin, Aden, Boden, Belden, Brennan, Asher, Brice

Bahari *(African)* ♂   RATING: ★★★☆
One who sails—Egyptian origin
People think of Bahari as leader, exotic, big, wild, religious
People who like the name Bahari also like Aiden, Bade, Ajani, Balin, Beau, Ambrose, Aden, Anoki, Barak, Bairn

Bailey *(English)* ♀♂   RATING: ★★★☆
Bailiff, steward
People think of Bailey as funny, pretty, popular, creative, intelligent
People who like the name Bailey also like Riley, Madison, Caden, Addison, Hayden, Blake, Logan, Taylor, Mackenzie, Brooke

Baina *(Arabic)* ♀   RATING: ★★★★
Clear
People think of Baina as weird, exotic, creative, artsy, caring
People who like the name Baina also like Bianca, Cailyn, Ayanna, Bella, Amaya, Abrianna, Brea, Belle, Basanti, Aurora

Baird *(Celtic/Gaelic)* ♂   RATING: ★★
Minstrel, poet
People think of Baird as creative, caring, nerdy, intelligent, handsome
People who like the name Baird also like Aiden, Bairn, Braeden, Bowen, Arthur, Brennan, Braden, Balin, Broderick, Branden

Bairn *(Celtic/Gaelic)* ♂   RATING: ★★
Child, born
People think of Bairn as funny, handsome, weird, popular, energetic
People who like the name Bairn also like Baird, Bevan, Bowen, Balin, Braeden, Aiden, Aden, Bade, Branden, Braden

Baka *(Sanskrit/East Indian)* ♀   RATING: ★☆
An Indian sage—Possibly meaning crane
People think of Baka as poor, unpopular, untrustworthy, lazy, weird
People who like the name Baka also like Adalia, Ballari, Baina, Aurora, Astra, Basanti, Amrita, Anila, Aira, Abrianna

Baldasarre *(Italian)* ♂   RATING: ★★★☆
Baal protect the king—Variation of Balthasar
People think of Baldasarre as aggressive, weird, powerful, loser, sneaky

People who like the name Baldasarre also like Biagio, Balin, Bello, Benito, Cirocco, Bade, Agostino, Balthasar, Aiden, Baxter

Balin *(English)* ♂   RATING: ★★★★
A knight of the Round Table
> People think of Balin as leader, handsome, caring, intelligent, creative
> People who like the name Balin also like Braden, Braeden, Aiden, Aden, Caleb, Brice, Benjamin, Kaden, Conner, Cole

Balint *(Hungarian)* ♂   RATING: ★★☆
Health; love—Variation of Valentine
> People think of Balint as powerful, wealthy, funny, trustworthy, intelligent
> People who like the name Balint also like Balin, Ballard, Bardia, Bendek, Banyan, Bade, Beale, Baron, Baxter, Arash

Ballard *(English)* ♂   RATING: ★★★
Bald-headed man—Originally a surname
> People think of Ballard as sexy, old, loser, nerdy, funny
> People who like the name Ballard also like Balin, Brice, Bowen, Barnard, Baron, Caleb, Baird, Bastien, Baxter, Dalton

Ballari *(Sanskrit/East Indian)* ♀   RATING: ★★★
Walking quietly
> People think of Ballari as weird, creative, quiet, cool, exotic
> People who like the name Ballari also like Basanti, Brielle, Aaralyn, Baina, Bella, Bianca, Benecia, Belle, Aurora, Adalia

Balthasar *(English)* ♂   RATING: ★★★☆
Baal protect the king
> People think of Balthasar as powerful, aggressive, handsome, leader, intelligent
> People who like the name Balthasar also like Aiden, Alexander, Benjamin, Bastien, Alastair, Baxter, Basil, Balin, Atticus, Braeden

Bambi *(Italian)* ♀   RATING: ★☆
Child—Deer character from the movie *Bambi*
> People think of Bambi as pretty, caring, funny, creative, young
> People who like the name Bambi also like Bella, Belle, Amber, Bianca, Abigail, Aurora, Bambina, Angelina, Becca, Faith

Bambina *(Italian)* ♀   RATING: ★★★☆
Baby girl
> People think of Bambina as pretty, exotic, young, sexy, caring
> People who like the name Bambina also like Bambi, Bella, Angelina, Bianca, Adrina, Bellini, Abrianna, Aria, Anastasia, Camilla

Ban *(Vietnamese)* ♂   RATING: ★★★
Unknown meaning
> People think of Ban as weird, poor, nerdy, loser, old

People who like the name Ban also like Bade, Basil, August, Bairn, Axel, Adam, Balin, Bao, Bernard, Beau

Banagher *(Celtic/Gaelic)* ♂   RATING: ★★☆
Pointed hill
> People think of Banagher as weird, big, aggressive, poor, unpopular
> People who like the name Banagher also like Braeden, Aiden, Bowen, Baird, Bairn, Cargan, Bevan, Alaric, Amergin, Artan

Bandana *(Spanish)* ♀♂   RATING: ★★
Head wrap
> People think of Bandana as popular, cool, pretty, poor, intelligent
> People who like the name Bandana also like Bailey, Beckett, Belen, Banner, Baden, Barras, Blake, Blair, Barrett, Banji

Bandele *(African)* ♂   RATING: ★☆
Follow me home—West African origin
> People think of Bandele as caring, trustworthy, powerful, intelligent, creative
> People who like the name Bandele also like Basil, Aiden, Balin, Bahari, Aden, Brock, Braima, Braeden, Aaron, Anakin

Banji *(African)* ♀♂   RATING: ★★★☆
Second-born of twins
> People think of Banji as funny, weird, young, exotic, aggressive
> People who like the name Banji also like Bailey, Abby, Baby, Baylee, Baden, Barrett, Bem, Aidan, Blake, Riley

Banks *(English)* ♀♂   RATING: ★★★
Edge of the river—Originally a surname
> People think of Banks as handsome, intelligent, cool, powerful, popular
> People who like the name Banks also like Bailey, Brody, Caden, Addison, Cade, Blaine, Bennett, Brady, Cooper, Carter

Banner *(American)* ♀♂   RATING: ★★★★
Flag
> People think of Banner as weird, cool, trustworthy, intelligent, handsome
> People who like the name Banner also like Bailey, Caden, Blaine, Blake, Baden, Blair, Addison, Bennett, Beckett, Cade

Banyan *(English)* ♂   RATING: ★★★
The banyan tree
> People think of Banyan as intelligent, creative, handsome, wild, exotic
> People who like the name Banyan also like Balin, Braden, Bastien, Bowen, Baron, Brock, Baxter, Booker, Braeden, Basil

Bao *(Vietnamese)* ♂   RATING: ★★★
To order, bid
> People think of Bao as funny, intelligent, cool, trustworthy, artsy

People who like the name Bao also like Baeddan, Beau, Ban, Bahari, Bazyli, Bedros, Bash, Barak, Balin, Basil

Baqer *(Arabic)* ♂   RATING: ★★☆
Man of knowledge
People think of Baqer as cool, weird, ethnic, religious, boy next door
People who like the name Baqer also like Bastien, Bijan, Barak, Bairn, Benjamin, Cadmus, Boden, Bardia, Barid, Baxter

Barak *(Hebrew)* ♂   RATING: ★★★★
Lightning, spark—Also spelled Barack; Barack Obama, politician
People think of Barak as aggressive, powerful, intelligent, energetic, leader
People who like the name Barak also like Aiden, Braden, Braeden, Benjamin, Bastien, Asher, Caleb, Aden, Blade, Bade

Barb *(Latin)* ♀   RATING: ★★★
Stranger—Short for Barbara
People think of Barb as old-fashioned, old, funny, lazy, big
People who like the name Barb also like Amelia, Amy, Amanda, Ana, Bridget, Bethany, Alicia, Becca, Ava, Angelina

Barbara *(Greek)* ♀   RATING: ★★
Stranger—Barbara Walters, TV journalist; Barbara Bach, actress; Barbara Billingsley, actress
People think of Barbara as caring, intelligent, creative, funny, pretty
People who like the name Barbara also like Abigail, Amanda, Elizabeth, Bethany, Amber, Bianca, Audrey, Alexandra, Cassandra, April

Barbie *(American)* ♀   RATING: ★★★
Stranger—Short for Barbara; Barbie, doll by Mattel
People think of Barbie as popular, pretty, stuck-up, sexy, girl next door
People who like the name Barbie also like Bella, Belle, Amber, Faith, Abigail, Anastasia, Annabella, Ava, Elle, Bethany

Barbod *(Persian)* ♂   RATING: ★★☆
Guitar
People think of Barbod as weird, winner, sexy, loser, elegant
People who like the name Barbod also like Aiden, Bardia, Bade, Arlen, Bijan, Baldasarre, Ambrose, Azhar, Bastien, Boden

Barbra *(American)* ♀   RATING: ★★★☆
Stranger—Variation of Barbara; Barbra Streisand, singer
People think of Barbra as caring, trustworthy, creative, funny, intelligent
People who like the name Barbra also like Alexa, Audrey, Beth, Bridget, Amber, Alissa, Alexandra, Alison, Becca, Amanda

Barclay *(English)* ♂   RATING: ★★★☆
Birch wood—Originally a surname
People think of Barclay as intelligent, cool, funny, weird, leader
People who like the name Barclay also like Benjamin, Baxter, Caleb, Braden, Braeden, Balin, Byron, Bowen, Benson, Bradley

Bardia *(Persian)* ♂   RATING: ★☆
Exalted, lofty
People think of Bardia as cool, sexy, intelligent, creative, popular
People who like the name Bardia also like Barbod, Bijan, Bastien, Barak, Axel, Balin, Bendek, Baqer, Baxter, Adish

Barid *(Persian)* ♂   RATING: ★★
Messenger
People think of Barid as slow, big, trustworthy, sneaky, funny
People who like the name Barid also like Barak, Braden, Balin, Baird, Benson, Banyan, Ajay, Barclay, Braeden, Basil

Barke *(African)* ♂   RATING: ★☆
Blessings
People think of Barke as big, exotic, caring, girl next door, young
People who like the name Barke also like Axel, Aiden, Basil, Bendek, Aram, Blade, Bade, Beau, Barak, Beale

Barnabas *(Greek)* ♂   RATING: ★★★
Son of consolation—From the Hebrew; Barnabas Collins, character from *Dark Shadows*
People think of Barnabas as nerdy, big, handsome, old-fashioned, aggressive
People who like the name Barnabas also like Benjamin, Basil, Alastair, Alexander, Atticus, Baxter, Benedict, Bastien, Ambrose, Arthur

Barnard *(English)* ♂   RATING: ★★★
Brave bear—Variation of Bernard; also a surname
People think of Barnard as nerdy, intelligent, caring, leader, old-fashioned
People who like the name Barnard also like Adam, Benjamin, Ballard, Baron, Albert, Alexander, Basil, Balin, Alastair, Archibald

Barney *(English)* ♂   RATING: ★★★
Short for Barnaby or Barnard; Barney, children's TV dinosaur character; Barney Fife, *Andy Griffith Show* character; Barney Rubble, *The Flintstones* character
People think of Barney as nerdy, loser, lazy, weird, big
People who like the name Barney also like Jack, Archie, Jacob, Benjamin, Bradley, Harry, Byron, Noah, Adam, Isaac

Barny *(German)* ♂   RATING: ★☆
Short for Barnaby or Barnard
People think of Barny as loser, weird, nerdy, unpopular, old-fashioned
People who like the name Barny also like Archie, Berg, Alvin, Arnold, Albert, Arne, Alfred, Adam, Barney, Aden

Baron *(English)* ♂ RATING: ★★
Noble man
> People think of Baron as intelligent, handsome, powerful, leader, wealthy
> People who like the name Baron also like Braden, Aiden, Caleb, Ethan, Byron, Benjamin, Aaron, Noah, Gabriel, Brice

Barr *(English)* ♀♂ RATING: ★☆
Barrier, gate; maker of bars
> People think of Barr as weird, popular, powerful, exotic, slow
> People who like the name Barr also like Avery, Barrett, Baden, Aubrey, Addison, Bern, Bailey, Beckett, Barras, Banner

Barras *(English)* ♀♂ RATING: ★★
Tradesman—Originally a surname
> People think of Barras as intelligent, unpopular, weird, wild, loser
> People who like the name Barras also like Beagan, Beckett, Barr, Barrett, Blair, Avery, Brayden, Bern, Bennett, Brynn

Barrett *(English)* ♀♂ RATING: ★★★★
Trader—Originally a surname
> People think of Barrett as handsome, intelligent, leader, funny, energetic
> People who like the name Barrett also like Bennett, Bailey, Addison, Caden, Blake, Avery, Hayden, Parker, Brayden, Aidan

Barrington *(English)* ♂ RATING: ★★★
From Barentin, France, or Barrington, England—Originally a surname
> People think of Barrington as handsome, wealthy, intelligent, old-fashioned, creative
> People who like the name Barrington also like Baxter, Braden, Alastair, Brighton, Broderick, Benson, Braeden, Braxton, Aiden, Anderson

Barry *(Celtic/Gaelic)* ♂ RATING: ★★★☆
Fair headed—Short for Finbar; Barry Bostwick, actor; Barry Manilow, singer/songwriter; Barry White, singer
> People think of Barry as intelligent, handsome, funny, caring, trustworthy
> People who like the name Barry also like Aaron, Brian, Aiden, Adam, Alan, Brandon, Andrew, Bradley, Anthony, Braeden

Bart *(Hebrew)* ♂ RATING: ★☆
Short for Bartholomew—Bartholomew, apostle; Bart Simpson, cartoon character from *The Simpsons*; Bart Starr, football quarterback
> People think of Bart as funny, popular, cool, intelligent, handsome
> People who like the name Bart also like Adam, Aaron, Alexander, Benjamin, Anthony, Bradley, Andrew, Caleb, Brad, Ben

Barth *(Hebrew)* ♂ RATING: ★★☆
Short for Bartholomew
> People think of Barth as nerdy, weird, lazy, wealthy, old-fashioned
> People who like the name Barth also like Benson, Baxter, Basil, Bart, Aden, Bradley, Bade, Benjamin, Bevan, Abraham

Bartholemew *(Hebrew)* ♂ RATING: ★★★
Son of Tolmai
> People think of Bartholemew as intelligent, big, sexy, nerdy, funny
> People who like the name Bartholemew also like Benjamin, Alexander, Benedict, Adam, Elijah, Aaron, Bradley, Ben, Anthony, Basil

Bartholomew *(Hebrew)* ♂ RATING: ★★★
Son of Tolmai
> People think of Bartholomew as intelligent, creative, nerdy, energetic, funny
> People who like the name Bartholomew also like Benjamin, Alexander, Caleb, Aaron, Adam, Brandon, Edward, Aiden, Andrew, Bartholemew

Barto *(Spanish)* ♂ RATING: ★★☆
Bright—Also short for Bartholomew
> People think of Barto as handsome, weird, loser, boy next door, poor
> People who like the name Barto also like Barak, Biagio, Adelio, Bedros, Basil, Antonio, Boden, Angelito, Axel, Bernardo

Barton *(English)* ♂ RATING: ★☆
From Barr's town—Originally a surname
> People think of Barton as intelligent, funny, nerdy, handsome, weird
> People who like the name Barton also like Braden, Aiden, Baron, Braeden, Benjamin, Braxton, Byron, Brennan, Brock, Brice

Baruch *(Hebrew)* ♂ RATING: ★★★
Blessed
> People think of Baruch as religious, exotic, intelligent, old-fashioned, unpopular
> People who like the name Baruch also like Benjamin, Basil, Asher, Barak, Caleb, Abram, Bartholemew, Adam, Aden, Abel

Bary *(Celtic/Gaelic)* ♂ RATING: ★★
Fair headed—Short for Finbar; also a variation of Barry
> People think of Bary as handsome, funny, cool, young, caring
> People who like the name Bary also like Arthur, Barry, Bairn, Baird, Bowen, Brian, Angus, Aiden, Boyd, Allen

Basanti *(Sanskrit/East Indian)* ♀ RATING: ★☆
Spring
> People think of Basanti as exotic, funny, big, young, weird
> People who like the name Basanti also like Ballari, Anastasia, Baina, Aaliyah, Belicia, Belle, Bianca, Chandra, Bellona, Amaya

Base (English) ♂ RATING: ★★☆
The short one
People think of Base as weird, funny, young, handsome, cool
People who like the name Base also like Blade, Berke, Bash, Braden, Baron, Baxter, Aiden, Caleb, Brice, Bade

Bash (Turkish) ♂ RATING: ★★★
Chief, commander
People think of Bash as leader, funny, powerful, cool, popular
People who like the name Bash also like Blade, Aiden, Axel, Base, Bade, Bowen, Basil, Asher, Brant, Ace

Basil (English) ♂ RATING: ★★★☆
King—From the Greek name Basilios; also a spice; Basil Rathbone, actor
People think of Basil as intelligent, handsome, cool, creative, caring
People who like the name Basil also like Aiden, Caleb, Adam, Benjamin, Braden, Aden, Alexander, Asher, August, Bastien

Bast (Persian) ♂ RATING: ★★☆
Place of shelter
People think of Bast as big, weird, aggressive, criminal, exotic
People who like the name Bast also like Bade, Basil, Ashwin, Anton, Aiden, Baxter, Bastien, Base, Bash, Asher

Bastien (French) ♂ RATING: ★★★★
Venerable, revered
People think of Bastien as intelligent, creative, powerful, leader, handsome
People who like the name Bastien also like Aiden, Sebastian, Caleb, Braden, Ethan, Gabriel, Braeden, Tristan, Benjamin, Elijah

Bat (English) ♂ RATING: ★★☆
Son of Tolmai—Short for Bartholomew; Bat Masterson, Old West law officer
People think of Bat as weird, leader, wild, unpopular, winner
People who like the name Bat also like Baxter, Berke, Bade, Bradley, Basil, Byron, Bash, Buzz, Ben, Base

Bathsheba (Hebrew) ♀ RATING: ★★★
Daughter of an oath—In the Bible, the mother of Solomon
People think of Bathsheba as weird, exotic, pretty, intelligent, creative
People who like the name Bathsheba also like Bianca, Bella, Belle, Aurora, Beatrice, Abigail, Babette, Anastasia, Aisha, Delilah

Batu (Mongolian) ♀♂ RATING: ★★☆
Loyal
People think of Batu as young, quiet, trustworthy, powerful, leader
People who like the name Batu also like Brayden, Blaze, Mika, Blair, Brynn, Oya, Barras, Lave, Nuri, Baylee

Batzorig (Mongolian) ♂ RATING: ★★★☆
Courageous, strong
People think of Batzorig as loser, unpopular, lazy, weird, aggressive
People who like the name Batzorig also like Calix, Caine, Balthasar, Fearghus, Agamemnon, Cavan, Fabrizio, Ignatius, Arif, Barrington

Baxter (English) ♂ RATING: ★★
A baker—Originally a surname for bakers
People think of Baxter as handsome, intelligent, funny, cool, popular
People who like the name Baxter also like Caleb, Braden, Benjamin, Aiden, Braxton, Byron, Jackson, Ethan, Dexter, Alexander

Bayan (Arabic) ♀ RATING: ★★★
Clear in meaning
People think of Bayan as intelligent, popular, funny, trustworthy, caring
People who like the name Bayan also like Bree, Aliana, Caelan, Aderyn, Brie, Brielle, Ashlyn, Bethany, Brea, Grace

Bayard (French) ♂ RATING: ★☆
With red-brown hair—Originally an English surname
People think of Bayard as poor, loser, weird, slow, unpopular
People who like the name Bayard also like Bastien, Beau, Belden, Ansel, Beale, Alain, Balin, Aiden, André, Basil

Bayarmaa (Mongolian) ♀ RATING: ★★☆
Mother of joy
People think of Bayarmaa as exotic, caring, weird, funny, religious
People who like the name Bayarmaa also like Alexandra, Gabby, Chaela, Caelan, Alisha, Bach Yen, Rosaline, Bathsheba, Bree, Badu

Bayle (American) ♀♂ RATING: ★★☆
Beautiful—Variation of Beau
People think of Bayle as intelligent, elegant, popular, girl next door, powerful
People who like the name Bayle also like Bailey, Caden, Baylee, Brayden, Blake, Jaden, Cadence, Blaine, Madison, Aidan

Baylee (English) ♀♂ RATING: ★★★
Bailiff
People think of Baylee as funny, pretty, popular, creative, young
People who like the name Baylee also like Bailey, Caden, Addison, Brayden, Madison, Hayden, Blake, Cadence, Jaden, Riley

Bazyli (Polish) ♂ RATING: ★★★
King—Variation of Basilios
People think of Bazyli as exotic, funny, wild, popular, leader
People who like the name Bazyli also like Bade, Basil, Balin, Baeddan, Balthasar, Aiden, Bastien, Bahari, Aden, Belden

Bea (American) ♀ RATING: ★★
Blessed—Short for Beatrice; Bea Arthur, actress
People think of Bea as creative, pretty, caring, funny, intelligent
People who like the name Bea also like Belle, Ava, Bella, Beatrice, Grace, Bianca, Aurora, Chloe, Hope, Charlotte

Beacher (English) ♂ RATING: ★★
From the beech tree
People think of Beacher as handsome, cool, weird, trustworthy, big
People who like the name Beacher also like Balin, Beck, Braden, Berke, Booker, Bastien, Aiden, Brice, Barrington, Brighton

Beagan (Celtic/Gaelic) ♀♂ RATING: ★★★
Small
People think of Beagan as handsome, caring, old, trendy, intelligent
People who like the name Beagan also like Brogan, Blair, Caden, Aidan, Brody, Brayden, Bailey, Breckin, Blaine, Brady

Beale (English) ♂ RATING: ★★★
Handsome—Originally a surname
People think of Beale as trustworthy, lazy, stuck-up, criminal, powerful
People who like the name Beale also like Beau, Belden, Bastien, Alain, Aston, Aiden, Boden, Cole, Alastair, Bade

Beata (Latin) ♀ RATING: ★★★★
Happy
People think of Beata as pretty, intelligent, funny, sexy, creative
People who like the name Beata also like Beatrice, Bianca, Bella, Bela, Bethany, Bea, Bridget, Ava, Bertha, Beonica

Beate (German) ♀ RATING: ★★★
Happy
People think of Beate as pretty, creative, funny, elegant, trustworthy
People who like the name Beate also like Bella, Annabella, Blossom, Belle, Beatriz, Bellona, Benita, Alba, Amalie, Beatrix

Beatrice (French) ♀ RATING: ★★
Bringer of joy
People think of Beatrice as pretty, funny, intelligent, caring, creative
People who like the name Beatrice also like Abigail, Charlotte, Amelia, Audrey, Ava, Bianca, Olivia, Alice, Eleanor, Emma

Beatrix (English) ♀ RATING: ★★★★
Bringer of joy—Beatrix, queen of the Netherlands; Beatrix Potter, author
People think of Beatrix as intelligent, creative, artsy, pretty, cool
People who like the name Beatrix also like Beatrice, Ava, Abigail, Charlotte, Audrey, Bianca, Amelia, Fiona, Aurora, Chloe

Beatriz (Latin) ♀ RATING: ★★
Bringer of joy—Variation of Beatrice or Beatrix
People think of Beatriz as pretty, funny, intelligent, caring, cool
People who like the name Beatriz also like Beatrice, Bianca, Beatrix, Bella, Isabella, Celeste, Cassandra, Adriana, Angelica, Daniela

Beau (French) ♂ RATING: ★★★★
Beautiful, handsome—Beau Bridges, actor
People think of Beau as handsome, popular, funny, cool, intelligent
People who like the name Beau also like Aiden, Caleb, Ethan, Noah, Cole, Braden, Benjamin, Chase, Elijah, Jackson

Beauchamp (English) ♂ RATING: ★★★
Beautiful field—Originally a surname, from the French; pronounced BEE-cham
People think of Beauchamp as funny, creative, caring, uptight, artsy
People who like the name Beauchamp also like Beauregard, Barclay, Belden, Alain, Beau, Bastien, Brock, Bradley, Alastair, Bowen

Beauregard (English) ♂ RATING: ★★★☆
Beautiful view—Pronounced BO-regard, from the French
People think of Beauregard as powerful, old-fashioned, elegant, wealthy, handsome
People who like the name Beauregard also like Aiden, Beau, Alastair, Bastien, Benjamin, Benedict, Caleb, Archer, Atticus, Baxter

Bebe (French) ♀ RATING: ★★★
Baby—Bebe Moore Campbell, author; Bebe Neuwirth, actress
People think of Bebe as sexy, pretty, cool, popular, intelligent
People who like the name Bebe also like Bella, Belle, Beatrice, Bianca, Becca, Ava, Bambi, Brielle, Blossom, Aurora

Becca (English) ♀ RATING: ★★★
Short for Rebecca
People think of Becca as pretty, funny, energetic, creative, cool
People who like the name Becca also like Abigail, Bethany, Amber, Hailey, Bella, Ava, Faith, Hannah, Emma, Chloe

Beck (English) ♂ RATING: ★★★★
From the brook—Originally a surname; Beck Hansen, musician
People think of Beck as creative, intelligent, cool, funny, artsy
People who like the name Beck also like Aiden, Braden, Caleb, Cole, Ethan, Aden, Asher, Jack, Finn, Brice

Becka (English) ♀ RATING: ★★★☆
Short for Rebecca
People think of Becka as pretty, funny, creative, trustworthy, caring

People who like the name Becka also like Becca, Bethany, Bella, Abigail, Amber, Becky, Alexa, Alexandra, Audrey, Callie

Beckett *(English)* ♀ ♂   RATING: ★★★★
From Beckett—Originally a surname; Samuel Beckett, playwright
People think of Beckett as intelligent, cool, handsome, creative, leader
People who like the name Beckett also like Bennett, Addison, Avery, Bailey, Barrett, Caden, Aidan, Blake, Logan, Parker

Becky *(English)* ♀   RATING: ★★★☆
Short for Rebecca—Becky Thatcher, character from *The Adventures of Tom Sawyer* by Mark Twain
People think of Becky as funny, pretty, caring, intelligent, creative
People who like the name Becky also like Bethany, Amber, Becca, Abigail, Amanda, Bella, Emily, Amy, Beth, Emma

Bede *(English)* ♀ ♂   RATING: ★★★
Saint of scholars
People think of Bede as intelligent, weird, trustworthy, funny, creative
People who like the name Bede also like Brook, Bennett, Beverly, Caden, Brayden, Blake, Blaine, Cade, Blaise, Bron

Bedros *(Greek)* ♂   RATING: ★★
Stone—Variation of Peter
People think of Bedros as criminal, ethnic, poor, sneaky, aggressive
People who like the name Bedros also like Boden, Ambrose, Barak, Brant, Cadmus, Braeden, Baeddan, Benedict, Bash, Alaric

Begum *(Turkish)* ♀   RATING: ★★☆
Princess—In old Turkish, empire of India
People think of Begum as popular, leader, trustworthy, boy next door, ethnic
People who like the name Begum also like Ranjana, Samira, Jahzara, Aceline, Priyanka, Freja, Farsiris, Saleema, Tatum, Aaliyah

Bel *(Sanskrit/East Indian)* ♀ ♂   RATING: ★★★☆
Sacred wood
People think of Bel as sexy, creative, cool, young, exotic
People who like the name Bel also like Bell, Bailey, Caden, Casey, Blair, Cassidy, Brody, Addison, Angel, Cade

Bela *(Slavic)* ♀ ♂   RATING: ★★★
Fair skinned
People think of Bela as pretty, intelligent, artsy, creative, elegant
People who like the name Bela also like Bella, Ava, Belle, Ella, Abigail, Chloe, Isabella, Eva, Emma, Bianca

Belay *(African)* ♂   RATING: ★★
Above, superior
People think of Belay as cool, leader, weird, creative, powerful
People who like the name Belay also like Benedict, Barke, Beale, Ajani, Ande, Alem, Anwar, Andrew, Adem, Brand

Belden *(English)* ♂   RATING: ★★
From Beldon hill—Originally a surname
People think of Belden as old, old-fashioned, poor, wild, powerful
People who like the name Belden also like Braeden, Braden, Balin, Aiden, Alden, Bastien, Boden, Benson, Bowen, Aden

Belen *(Spanish)* ♀ ♂   RATING: ★★★☆
Bethlehem—Also a flower
People think of Belen as pretty, funny, intelligent, caring, creative
People who like the name Belen also like Bennett, Aubrey, Bailey, Avery, Caden, Cameron, Blair, Baden, Addison, Brogan

Belicia *(Spanish)* ♀   RATING: ★★
Combination of Bella and Alicia—South American origin
People think of Belicia as pretty, sexy, caring, girl next door, exotic
People who like the name Belicia also like Belinda, Bianca, Adalia, Adriana, Benecia, Belita, Belle, Abigail, Bella, Breanna

Belinda *(Spanish)* ♀   RATING: ★★
Beautiful—Belinda Carlisle, singer
People think of Belinda as pretty, caring, funny, intelligent, creative
People who like the name Belinda also like Bianca, Abigail, Bella, Charlotte, Cassandra, Isabella, Bethany, Bridget, Amelia, Brianna

Belisma *(Spanish)* ♀   RATING: ★★★☆
Beautiful—Short for Bellisima
People think of Belisma as funny, pretty, powerful, popular, cool
People who like the name Belisma also like Bella, Bianca, Amaya, Aradia, Celeste, Adalira, Belicia, Aurora, Adriana, Brielle

Belita *(Spanish)* ♀   RATING: ★☆
Beautiful
People think of Belita as pretty, sexy, funny, exotic, creative
People who like the name Belita also like Belinda, Belicia, Bianca, Bella, Adriana, Bonita, Anjelita, Belle, Cailyn

Bell *(English)* ♀ ♂   RATING: ★★★☆
Beautiful—Probably short for Isabel
People think of Bell as pretty, caring, young, trustworthy, creative
People who like the name Bell also like Bailey, Angel, Brooke, Alexis, Blake, Blair, Ariel, Dakota, Caden, Jade

Bella *(Italian)* ♀   RATING: ★★★
Beautiful—Short for Isabella
People think of Bella as pretty, elegant, caring, intelligent, popular
People who like the name Bella also like Isabella, Ava, Ella, Emma, Belle, Grace, Chloe, Abigail, Olivia, Faith

Belle *(French)* ♀   RATING: ★★★
Beauty—Also a woman from the U.S. South; character from Disney's *Beauty and the Beast*
People think of Belle as pretty, elegant, caring, intelligent, creative
People who like the name Belle also like Bella, Ava, Isabelle, Chloe, Isabella, Annabelle, Abigail, Emma, Ella, Grace

Bellini *(Italian)* ♀   RATING: ★★★
Little beautiful one—Originally a surname
People think of Bellini as pretty, sexy, funny, creative, caring
People who like the name Bellini also like Bella, Adrina, Bambina, Bianca, Isabella, Angelina, Aria, Belle, Chloe, Gianna

Bello *(Italian)* ♂   RATING: ★★★☆
Beautiful, handsome—Maria Bello, actress
People think of Bello as handsome, funny, exotic, cool, intelligent
People who like the name Bello also like Benito, Beau, Baldasarre, Angelo, Benigno, Amando, Basil, Adam, Biagio, Blade

Bellona *(Latin)* ♀   RATING: ★★★
Goddess of war
People think of Bellona as exotic, elegant, aggressive, leader, powerful
People who like the name Bellona also like Aurora, Bella, Belle, Adrienne, Celeste, Adriana, Aradia, Bianca, Brielle, Breena

Belva *(American)* ♀   RATING: ★★☆
Combination of Bella and Alva—Belva Plain, author
People think of Belva as caring, intelligent, old-fashioned, trustworthy, old
People who like the name Belva also like Benita, Bellona, Beryl, Blossom, Belle, Bella, Bianca, Breena, Bonita, Beyla

Bem *(African)* ♀♂   RATING: ★★★
Peace
People think of Bem as intelligent, unpopular, poor, popular, religious
People who like the name Bem also like Banji, Bern, Berne, Briar, Baby, Blake, Blaise, Blair, Beverly, Breckin

Ben *(Hebrew)* ♂   RATING: ★★★
Short for Benjamin or Benedict—Ben Stiller, actor/director; "Big Ben" clock tower in London
People think of Ben as funny, handsome, cool, intelligent, popular
People who like the name Ben also like Benjamin, Adam, Jack, Aaron, Ethan, Caleb, Jake, Luke, Jacob, Noah

Bena *(Native American)* ♀   RATING: ★★
Pheasant
People think of Bena as pretty, caring, nerdy, exotic, weird
People who like the name Bena also like Bly, Chickoa, Bella, Bethany, Chumani, Aleshanee, Breena, Beyla, Kaya, Cholena

Benard *(French)* ♂   RATING: ★★★
Brave bear—Variation of Bernard
People think of Benard as caring, intelligent, leader, cool, old
People who like the name Benard also like Bernard, Benjamin, Braden, Adam, Brian, Bastien, André, Bradley, Burke, Belden

Bendek *(Polish)* ♂   RATING: ★★☆
Blessed—Variation of Benedict
People think of Bendek as weird, funny, loser, handsome, aggressive
People who like the name Bendek also like Baxter, Bastien, Balin, Belden, Barak, Benjamin, Bairn, Brant, Barclay, Aiden

Benecia *(Spanish)* ♀   RATING: ★★★
Benevolent one—Feminine form of Benicio
People think of Benecia as pretty, creative, funny, intelligent, caring
People who like the name Benecia also like Belicia, Bianca, Bella, Brielle, Ava, Abrianna, Belle, Alana, Benita, Ariana

Benedetta *(Italian)* ♀   RATING: ★★☆
Blessed—Variation of Benedicta
People think of Benedetta as sexy, exotic, young, pretty, intelligent
People who like the name Benedetta also like Adrina, Babette, Belicia, Elisabeth, Ariana, Bambi, Carmelita, Carlotta, Angelique, Bernadette

Benedict *(Latin)* ♂   RATING: ★★★☆
Blessed—Benedict Arnold, U.S. traitor
People think of Benedict as intelligent, handsome, caring, powerful, religious
People who like the name Benedict also like Benjamin, Dominic, Gabriel, Aaron, Elijah, Andrew, Alexander, Caleb, Ethan, Isaac

Benevuto *(Italian)* ♂   RATING: ★★☆
Welcomed birth
People think of Benevuto as weird, unpopular, loser
People who like the name Benevuto also like Angelito, Darshan, Archibald, Ambrose, Alexander, Aric, Artemas, Jevonte, Aram, Archer

Benicio *(Spanish)* ♂   RATING: ★★
Benevolent one—Benicio del Toro, actor
People think of Benicio as handsome, sexy, intelligent, creative, exotic
People who like the name Benicio also like Benito, Gabriel, Aden, Antonio, Bastien, Benjamin, Diego, Braeden, Angelo, Elijah

Benigno (Italian) ♂   RATING: ★★★
Friendly, kind
> People think of Benigno as caring, leader, creative, intelligent, funny
> People who like the name Benigno also like Benito, Bello, Biagio, Benjamin, Baldasarre, Amadeus, Alfonso, Aiden, Basil, Benedict

Benita (Italian) ♀   RATING: ★★
Blessed—Feminine form of Benito
> People think of Benita as pretty, funny, creative, caring, intelligent
> People who like the name Benita also like Bella, Bianca, Belle, Bonita, Benecia, Angelina, Blossom, Bethany, Belita, Ashlyn

Benito (Italian) ♂   RATING: ★☆
Short for Benedict
> People think of Benito as popular, cool, creative, handsome, funny
> People who like the name Benito also like Aaron, Aiden, Angelo, Alejandro, Anthony, Antonio, Benjamin, Andrew, Benigno, Adam

Benjamin (English) ♂   RATING: ★★★
Son of my right hand—From the Hebrew; Benjamin Bratt, actor; Benjamin Franklin, inventor/U.S. statesman
> People think of Benjamin as handsome, intelligent, funny, caring, cool
> People who like the name Benjamin also like Ethan, Jacob, Andrew, Caleb, Alexander, Noah, Matthew, Joshua, Nicholas, Gabriel

Benjy (Hebrew) ♂   RATING: ★★
Short for Benjamin—Benji, movie dog
> People think of Benjy as nerdy, funny, creative, handsome, energetic
> People who like the name Benjy also like Benjamin, Aaron, Braden, Caleb, Bradley, Adam, Adrian, Ben, Beau, Benny

Bennett (Latin) ♀♂   RATING: ★★★★
Little blessed one—Bennett Cerf, author/punster; Constance and Joan Bennett, actress sisters
> People think of Bennett as handsome, intelligent, funny, caring, trustworthy
> People who like the name Bennett also like Addison, Bailey, Avery, Caden, Carter, Blake, Barrett, Hayden, Aidan, Beckett

Benny (Hebrew) ♂   RATING: ★★★☆
Son of my right hand—Short for Benjamin; Benny Hill, comedian
> People think of Benny as funny, handsome, intelligent, caring, sporty
> People who like the name Benny also like Benjamin, Benjy, Adam, Ben, Andrew, Aaron, Brian, Anthony, Jack, Bradley

Beno (Hebrew) ♂   RATING: ★★☆
Son
> People think of Beno as funny, handsome, cool, weird, intelligent
> People who like the name Beno also like Benjy, Aron, Basil, Ben, Barak, Bedros, Boden, Abel, Abe, Aiden

Benoit (French) ♂   RATING: ★★★
Blessed
> People think of Benoit as caring, intelligent, popular, handsome, leader
> People who like the name Benoit also like Bastien, Aiden, Beau, Benjamin, Alain, Burke, Berke, Belden, Benson, Bijan

Benson (English) ♂   RATING: ★★☆
Son of Benedict
> People think of Benson as handsome, funny, cool, popular, caring
> People who like the name Benson also like Braden, Benjamin, Aiden, Ethan, Caleb, Braeden, Emerson, Bradley, Dawson, Cole

Beonica (American) ♀   RATING: ★★★☆
Combination of Bea and Monica
> People think of Beonica as weird, funny, popular, pretty, exotic
> People who like the name Beonica also like Bianca, Aaliyah, Bethany, Abigail, Bella, Abrianna, Cailyn, Breanna, Belle, Beyoncé

Berdine (German) ♀   RATING: ★★★
Short for Bernardine
> People think of Berdine as quiet, old-fashioned, nerdy, old, caring
> People who like the name Berdine also like Bernadette, Berenice, Benita, Becca, Beatrice, Beryl, Bernice, Ballari, Baina, Beatrix

Berenice (English) ♀   RATING: ★☆
Victorious
> People think of Berenice as pretty, funny, intelligent, caring, sexy
> People who like the name Berenice also like Beatrice, Bianca, Alicia, Bernadette, Bethany, Bernice, Belle, Adeline, Becca, Belinda

Berg (German) ♂   RATING: ★☆
Mountain
> People think of Berg as intelligent, big, nerdy, weird, loser
> People who like the name Berg also like Axel, Adam, Arnold, Caleb, Bade, Brant, Balin, Beck, Albert, Ballard

Berit (Scandinavian) ♀   RATING: ★★★☆
Exalted, lofty—Variation of Bridget
> People think of Berit as funny, energetic, intelligent, pretty, creative
> People who like the name Berit also like Bella, Blythe, Amory, Bianca, Becca, Ava, Bree, Audrey, Brea, Breanna

129

Berke (English) ♂ RATING: ★★☆
Birch tree
People think of Berke as unpopular, nerdy, loser, untrustworthy, sneaky
People who like the name Berke also like Braden, Burke, Aiden, Brock, Brice, Gavin, Ethan, Braeden, Caleb, Benjamin

Bern (French) ♀♂ RATING: ★☆
Brave—Short for Bernard
People think of Bern as big, powerful, leader, intelligent, old-fashioned
People who like the name Bern also like Bennett, Blaise, Berne, Astin, Blair, Caden, Barrett, Cade, Aidan, Blake

Bernadette (French) ♀ RATING: ★★
Brave as a bear
People think of Bernadette as pretty, caring, funny, intelligent, trustworthy
People who like the name Bernadette also like Charlotte, Bianca, Beatrice, Abigail, Bridget, Anastasia, Belle, Chloe, Genevieve, Ava

Bernadine (French) ♀ RATING: ★★★
Bold as a bear—Feminine form of Bernard
People think of Bernadine as caring, funny, creative, popular, trustworthy
People who like the name Bernadine also like Bernadette, Bernice, Beatrice, Bethany, Bianca, Belle, Antoinette, Giselle, Brielle, Claudette

Bernard (French) ♂ RATING: ★★
Bold as a bear
People think of Bernard as funny, intelligent, handsome, caring, trustworthy
People who like the name Bernard also like Benjamin, Andrew, Caleb, Adam, Brian, Charles, Aaron, Alexander, Anthony, Arthur

Bernardo (Spanish) ♂ RATING: ★★★☆
Bold as a bear—Variation of Bernard
People think of Bernardo as handsome, funny, aggressive, intelligent, criminal
People who like the name Bernardo also like Antonio, Alejandro, Andrew, Andrés, Benjamin, Armando, Angelo, Carlos, Bernard, Adam

Berne (French) ♀♂ RATING: ★★☆
Bold as a bear—Short for Bernard
People think of Berne as big, weird, girl next door, loser, leader
People who like the name Berne also like Bern, Blaise, Blake, Briar, Billie, Bailey, Astin, Baden, Ash, Aidan

Bernice (French) ♀ RATING: ★★★☆
Brings victory
People think of Bernice as caring, intelligent, pretty, trustworthy, funny
People who like the name Bernice also like Beatrice, Bernadette, Bianca, Bridget, Belinda, Belle, Abigail, Charlotte, Berenice, Breanna

Bernie (French) ♂ RATING: ★☆
Bold as a bear—Short for Bernard
People think of Bernie as intelligent, handsome, big, funny, cool
People who like the name Bernie also like Bart, Bernard, Beau, Benjy, Ben, Archie, Aden, André, Barth, Alain

Bernt (German) ♂ RATING: ★★
Strong, brave bear
People think of Bernt as intelligent, leader, funny, handsome, nerdy
People who like the name Bernt also like Aiden, Beau, Asher, Arne, Berg, Brant, Brandon, Axel, Aden, Brand

Berny (French) ♂ RATING: ★★☆
Bold as a bear—Short for Bernard
People think of Berny as big, old, funny, elegant, loser
People who like the name Berny also like Bernard, Bernie, Beau, Alfred, Anton, Boone, Belden, Barnard, Abel, Bayard

Bert (German) ♂ RATING: ★★★
Bright—Short for Bertram or Bertrand; Bert Lahr, actor; *Sesame Street* character
People think of Bert as intelligent, handsome, cool, caring, funny
People who like the name Bert also like Albert, Adam, Archibald, August, Anthony, Benjamin, Arnold, Aiden, Axel, Arvin

Bertha (German) ♀ RATING: ★★★
Bright
People think of Bertha as big, old-fashioned, unpopular, weird, old
People who like the name Bertha also like Beatrice, Bridget, Blossom, Bella, Bethany, Bianca, Becca, Belle, Beth, Bernice

Bertille (French) ♀ RATING: ★☆
Bright
People think of Bertille as big, artsy, uptight, stuck-up, trendy
People who like the name Bertille also like Belle, Brielle, Bella, Beatrice, Alaina, Adelie, Adeline, Beatrix, Becca, Bebe

Beryl (English) ♀ RATING: ★☆
Semiprecious stone
People think of Beryl as intelligent, creative, caring, trustworthy, energetic
People who like the name Beryl also like Ava, Blythe, Bella, Aurora, Bethany, Becca, Breena, Bianca, Arwen, Autumn

Bess (English) ♀ RATING: ★★★☆
God is my oath—Short for Elizabeth
People think of Bess as caring, pretty, elegant, creative, old-fashioned
People who like the name Bess also like Bella, Ava, Belle, Abigail, Beth, Audrey, Bianca, Bethany, Grace, Amber

Bessie *(English)* ♀ RATING: ★☆
God is my oath—Short for Elizabeth; Bessie Smith, singer
  People think of Bessie as funny, caring, trustworthy, creative, pretty
  People who like the name Bessie also like Bella, Belle, Abigail, Becca, Ava, Blossom, Betsy, Amelia, Abbie, Chloe

Betelgeuse *(German)* ♀♂ RATING: ★★★
Hand of the central one—Also a star; Arabic origin
  People think of Betelgeuse as weird, unpopular, exotic, nerdy, criminal
  People who like the name Betelgeuse also like Caden, Calypso, Bailey, Bricen, Billie, Addison, Brooklyn, Brody, Blake, Ainsley

Beth *(English)* ♀ RATING: ★★☆
God is my oath—Short for Elizabeth
  People think of Beth as pretty, funny, caring, intelligent, creative
  People who like the name Beth also like Bethany, Grace, Hannah, Bella, Faith, Abigail, Elizabeth, Ava, Emma, Amber

Betha *(Celtic/Gaelic)* ♀ RATING: ★★★
Life
  People think of Betha as caring, intelligent, creative, pretty, trustworthy
  People who like the name Betha also like Breanna, Brea, Breena, Aeryn, Bella, Bree, Alana, Aislin, Caitlyn, Bridget

Bethan *(Welsh)* ♀ RATING: ★★★☆
God is my oath—Short for Elizabeth
  People think of Bethan as funny, pretty, intelligent, caring, creative
  People who like the name Bethan also like Bethany, Bella, Beth, Hannah, Abigail, Chloe, Grace, Abbie, Ava, Emma

Bethany *(English)* ♀ RATING: ★★☆
Place of figs—Also a town near Jerusalem; a Biblical place name
  People think of Bethany as pretty, caring, funny, intelligent, creative
  People who like the name Bethany also like Abigail, Hannah, Faith, Chloe, Emily, Hailey, Emma, Grace, Brianna, Paige

Bethesda *(Hebrew)* ♀ RATING: ★★☆
House of mercy—Also a city in Maryland
  People think of Bethesda as weird, exotic, uptight, sporty, old-fashioned
  People who like the name Bethesda also like Belicia, Becca, Bethany, Adalia, Brielle, Beyla, Belle, Beatrice, Charlotte, Bianca

Bethwyn *(Welsh)* ♀ RATING: ★★☆
Combination of Beth and Gwyn
  People think of Bethwyn as young, funny, creative, weird, pretty

People who like the name Bethwyn also like Braewyn, Bronwyn, Arwen, Aeryn, Elwyn, Belle, Aelwen, Briallen, Gwyneth, Blythe

Betrys *(Welsh)* ♀ RATING: ★☆
Bringer of joy—Variation of Beatrice
  People think of Betrys as creative, nerdy, quiet, wild, loser
  People who like the name Betrys also like Briallen, Carys, Blodwen, Beatrix, Aderyn, Aelwen, Brighid, Arwen, Bronwyn, Beatrice

Betsy *(English)* ♀ RATING: ★★★☆
God is my oath—Short for Elizabeth; Betsy Ross, seamstress of the first U.S. flag
  People think of Betsy as funny, pretty, caring, creative, intelligent
  People who like the name Betsy also like Abigail, Ava, Amelia, Audrey, Bella, Charlotte, Grace, Betty, Beatrice, Bethany

Bette *(American)* ♀ RATING: ★★★☆
God is my oath—Short for Elizabeth; Bette Davis, actress; Bette Midler, actress/singer
  People think of Bette as sexy, creative, cool, leader, intelligent
  People who like the name Bette also like Belle, Bella, Audrey, Betsy, Charlotte, Bianca, Ava, Abigail, Emma, Betty

Bettina *(Italian)* ♀ RATING: ★★★★
God is my oath—Short for Elizabeth
  People think of Bettina as pretty, intelligent, funny, trustworthy, caring
  People who like the name Bettina also like Bianca, Bella, Chloe, Beatrice, Belle, Bethany, Abigail, Aurora, Charlotte, Angelina

Betty *(English)* ♀ RATING: ★★★☆
God is my oath—Short for Elizabeth; Betty Crocker, food brand; Betty Ford, U.S. first lady; Betty Page, model
  People think of Betty as pretty, caring, funny, intelligent, creative
  People who like the name Betty also like Abigail, Betsy, Bethany, Elizabeth, Bridget, Amanda, Alice, Belle, Bella, Beth

Beulah *(Hebrew)* ♀ RATING: ★☆
Married—*The Beulah Show*, the first radio and TV show to star an African American; Beulah Bondi, actress
  People think of Beulah as creative, old-fashioned, trustworthy, caring, pretty
  People who like the name Beulah also like Belle, Bella, Bianca, Becca, Ava, Blossom, Aurora, Bethany, Beyla, Benita

Bevan *(Celtic/Gaelic)* ♂ RATING: ★★
Son of Evan
  People think of Bevan as funny, sexy, caring, popular, handsome

People who like the name Bevan also like Aiden, Braden, Braeden, Conner, Caleb, Aden, Bowen, Brennan, Branden, Brendan

Beverly (*English*) ♀ ♂   RATING: ★★★☆
From the beaver stream—Beverly Cleary, author; Beverly Sills, opera singer
> People think of Beverly as pretty, caring, creative, trustworthy, funny
> People who like the name Beverly also like Bailey, Brooke, Blake, Blair, Dakota, Cameron, Brooklyn, Aubrey, Alexis, Ashley

Bevis (*English*) ♂   RATING: ★★★
Dear son
> People think of Bevis as loser, unpopular, weird, lazy, slow
> People who like the name Bevis also like Baxter, Balin, Aden, Brant, Bono, Aiden, Brock, Benjamin, Blade, Angus

Beyla (*Slavic*) ♀   RATING: ★★★☆
By God—Variation of Isabella
> People think of Beyla as artsy, caring, pretty, religious, elegant
> People who like the name Beyla also like Bella, Belle, Brea, Bianca, Bela, Brielle, Ava, Chloe, Cailyn, Blythe

Beyoncé (*American*) ♀   RATING: ★★★☆
From the Creole surname Beyince—Beyoncé Knowles, singer/actress
> People think of Beyoncé as sexy, pretty, popular, cool, powerful
> People who like the name Beyoncé also like Aaliyah, Bianca, Amber, Belle, Amanda, Ciara, Bethany, Bella, Adriana, Brianna

Bhavna (*Sanskrit/East Indian*) ♀   RATING: ★★★
Good feelings
> People think of Bhavna as pretty, intelligent, exotic, caring, funny
> People who like the name Bhavna also like Basanti, Amithi, Brinda, Avani, Bianca, Bian, Alpana, Anjali, Ballari, Breena

Biagio (*Italian*) ♂   RATING: ★★★
Limping—Variation of Blaise
> People think of Biagio as handsome, quiet, lazy, funny, slow
> People who like the name Biagio also like Baldasarre, Agostino, Benito, Benigno, Angelo, Alfonso, Barto, Bello, Bazyli, Cirocco

Bian (*Vietnamese*) ♀   RATING: ★★★
Secretive
> People think of Bian as exotic, sexy, powerful, leader, intelligent
> People who like the name Bian also like Bly, Biana, Aiko, Bhavna, Breena, Ceri, Bice, Bela, Beatrix, Bree

Biana (*American*) ♀   RATING: ★★★☆
Fair skinned—Short for Bianca
> People think of Biana as pretty, cool, young, sexy, intelligent
> People who like the name Biana also like Bianca, Abrianna, Bella, Briana, Ariana, Cailyn, Callie, Belle, Calista, Adriana

Bianca (*Italian*) ♀   RATING: ★★★
White—Bianca Jagger, model
> People think of Bianca as pretty, funny, intelligent, popular, caring
> People who like the name Bianca also like Isabella, Ava, Chloe, Olivia, Bella, Abigail, Brianna, Adriana, Faith, Emma

Bibiana (*Italian*) ♀   RATING: ★★★☆
Alive—Variation of Vivian
> People think of Bibiana as pretty, intelligent, creative, caring, sexy
> People who like the name Bibiana also like Bianca, Aaliyah, Bethany, Bibiane, Breanna, Benita, Bella, Brielle, Bambi, Bellini

Bibiane (*French*) ♀   RATING: ★★★
Alive—Variation of Vivian
> People think of Bibiane as intelligent, winner, energetic, funny, powerful
> People who like the name Bibiane also like Bianca, Bibiana, Bernadette, Beatrice, Belle, Bernice, Bebe, Cerise, Bella, Beatrix

Bice (*Italian*) ♀   RATING: ★★☆
Short for Beatrice—Pronounced *BEE-chay*
> People think of Bice as pretty, old-fashioned, weird, caring, aggressive
> People who like the name Bice also like Bambina, Bambi, Bianca, Brielle, Cira, Abigail, Blossom, Bella, Bly, Cascata

Bidelia (*Celtic/Gaelic*) ♀   RATING: ★★☆
Exalted, lofty—Probably a variation of Bridget
> People think of Bidelia as trustworthy, energetic, old-fashioned, exotic, unpopular
> People who like the name Bidelia also like Aislinn, Aeryn, Betha, Breena, Bridget, Ailsa, Alana, Aislin, Breanna, Brea

Bien (*Vietnamese*) ♂   RATING: ★★☆
Ocean, sea—Also Spanish for good or fine
> People think of Bien as ethnic, big, exotic, criminal, wild
> People who like the name Bien also like Bade, Aden, Brandon, Asher, Boden, Beau, Brock, Aiden, Ajax, Berke

Bijan (*Persian*) ♂   RATING: ★★★☆
Hero—Bijan Pakzad, designer
> People think of Bijan as handsome, intelligent, funny, caring, cool
> People who like the name Bijan also like Aiden, Asher, Braeden, Benjamin, Beau, Alexander, Boden, Björn, Balin, Aden

Bikita *(American)* ♀   RATING: ★★
Combination of Bea and Nikita
  People think of Bikita as caring, young, unpopular, weird, ethnic
  People who like the name Bikita also like Baina, Breanna, Belita, Brea, Bianca, Ayanna, Aaliyah, Calista, Bibiana, Anaya

Bill *(English)* ♂   RATING: ★★
Short for William; William "Bill" Clinton, U.S. President; Bill Cosby, actor/comedian; Bill Gates, founder of Microsoft; Bill Nye "The Science Guy," TV host
  People think of Bill as intelligent, funny, caring, handsome, creative
  People who like the name Bill also like Adam, Brian, Andrew, Aaron, Brad, Anthony, Benjamin, Bradley, Chad, Alexander

Billie *(German)* ♀♂   RATING: ★★
Short for Wilhelmina—Billie Holiday, jazz singer; Billie Jean King, tennis player
  People think of Billie as funny, caring, creative, pretty, intelligent
  People who like the name Billie also like Bailey, Brooke, Dakota, Blake, Charlie, Blair, Alexis, Madison, Caden, Billy

Billy *(English)* ♀♂   RATING: ★★
Short for William—Billy Baldwin, actor; Billy the Kid, U.S. outlaw
  People think of Billy as funny, handsome, cool, popular, intelligent
  People who like the name Billy also like Bailey, Blake, Charlie, Alex, Billie, Cameron, Alexis, Bobby, James, Ashley

Bimala *(Sanskrit/East Indian)* ♀   RATING: ★★☆
Pure
  People think of Bimala as ethnic, weird, popular, old-fashioned, creative
  People who like the name Bimala also like Breanna, Ballari, Basanti, Bella, Adia, Bhavna, Amithi, Anaya, Asha, Baina

Bin *(English)* ♂   RATING: ★★☆
Short for Bingham
  People think of Bin as poor, quiet, slow, old-fashioned, boy next door
  People who like the name Bin also like Brad, Bill, Balin, Aiden, Beck, Bernard, Adam, Barney, Beacher, Brian

Bina *(Italian)* ♀   RATING: ★★★☆
Short for names ending with –bina
  People think of Bina as pretty, sexy, funny, caring, intelligent
  People who like the name Bina also like Belle, Bly, Bibiana, Bella, Breanna, Betha, Bena, Bea, Bela, Beyla

Bindi *(Sanskrit/East Indian)* ♀   RATING: ★★★★☆
A drop—Also a forehead decoration in India; Bindi Irwin, TV host/daughter of Steve Irwin
  People think of Bindi as pretty, energetic, intelligent, caring, creative
  People who like the name Bindi also like Chloe, Ava, Chandra, Olivia, Bella, Bianca, Belle, Grace, Layla, Emma

Bing *(English)* ♂   RATING: ★★★☆
Short for Bingham; Bing Crosby, singer/actor
  People think of Bing as caring, cool, handsome, intelligent, creative
  People who like the name Bing also like Braden, Bishop, Axel, Booker, Bond, Blade, Boden, Baron, Barrington, Barnabas

Bingham *(English)* ♂   RATING: ★★★
From the farm of Binna's people
  People think of Bingham as weird, slow, nerdy, loser, old-fashioned
  People who like the name Bingham also like Braeden, Braden, Brice, Bradford, Benjamin, Bradley, Anderson, Bowen, Booker, Baxter

Binh *(Vietnamese)* ♂   RATING: ★★★
Peaceful
  People think of Binh as intelligent, weird, young, trustworthy, cool
  People who like the name Binh also like Aden, Brad, Bijan, Berke, Brant, Ansel, Amadeus, Adam, Beno, Aiden

Birch *(English)* ♂   RATING: ★★★
Birch tree
  People think of Birch as creative, handsome, funny, young, intelligent
  People who like the name Birch also like Braden, Berke, Aiden, Blade, Basil, Adam, Burke, Boone, Ansel, Baxter

Bishop *(English)* ♂   RATING: ★★★☆
Bishop
  People think of Bishop as handsome, intelligent, powerful, leader, caring
  People who like the name Bishop also like Benjamin, Blade, Aiden, Braden, Brice, Alexander, Alastair, Asher, Caleb, Archer

Biton *(Greek)* ♂   RATING: ★★☆
Unknown meaning
  People think of Biton as loser, aggressive, old-fashioned, old, energetic
  People who like the name Biton also like Boden, Bairn, Baron, Bond, Blade, Bowen, Belden, Barak, Brand, Bastien

Björk *(Scandinavian)* ♀   RATING: ★★★
Birch tree—Pronounced *ByORK*; Björk, singer
  People think of Björk as weird, exotic, creative, artsy, pretty
  People who like the name Björk also like Bela, Bella, Becca, Beatrix, Ava, Bree, Bambi, Breanna, Belle, Beyoncé

Björn *(Scandinavian)* ♂   RATING: ★★★
Bear—Björn Borg, tennis player; BabyBjörn, brand
  People think of Björn as intelligent, caring, handsome, cool, funny

B

People who like the name Björn also like Benjamin, Braeden, Aiden, Alexander, Caleb, Ethan, Gabriel, Brice, Adrian, Bastien

Blade *(English)* ♂   RATING: ★★★★
Knife, sword
People think of Blade as powerful, cool, handsome, aggressive, leader
People who like the name Blade also like Aiden, Braden, Chase, Drake, Kaden, Braeden, Brice, Chance, Ace, Cole

Blaine *(Celtic/Gaelic)* ♀♂   RATING: ★★★★
Yellow
People think of Blaine as funny, intelligent, handsome, cool, caring
People who like the name Blaine also like Blake, Bailey, Caden, Blair, Addison, Brayden, Hayden, Aidan, Logan, Cadence

Blair *(Celtic/Gaelic)* ♀♂   RATING: ★★★★
Field, plain—Also a Scottish surname; Tony Blair, former prime minister of the United Kingdom
People think of Blair as pretty, popular, funny, intelligent, cool
People who like the name Blair also like Bailey, Blake, Blaine, Caden, Brooke, Addison, Hayden, Riley, Cameron, Aidan

Blaise *(French)* ♀♂   RATING: ★★☆
Limping
People think of Blaise as handsome, intelligent, cool, creative, funny
People who like the name Blaise also like Blaine, Bailey, Blake, Blair, Caden, Blaze, Addison, Brayden, Aidan, Avery

Blake *(English)* ♀♂   RATING: ★★★
Pale blond one; dark—Opposite meanings, but both are acceptable; Blake Edwards, filmmaker
People think of Blake as handsome, funny, intelligent, cool, popular
People who like the name Blake also like Bailey, Caden, Logan, Hayden, Blaine, Dylan, Austin, Cameron, Addison, Madison

Blanca *(Spanish)* ♀   RATING: ★★★☆
White
People think of Blanca as pretty, funny, caring, cool, young
People who like the name Blanca also like Bianca, Adriana, Aurora, Belinda, Ava, Anastasia, Angelina, Belle, Isabel, Aaliyah

Blanche *(French)* ♀   RATING: ★★
White—Blanche Dubois, character in *A Streetcar Named Desire* by Tenessee Williams
People think of Blanche as funny, pretty, caring, elegant, old-fashioned
People who like the name Blanche also like Belle, Bianca, Bridget, Celeste, Ava, Amelia, April, Bella, Beatrice, Audrey

Blaze *(English)* ♀♂   RATING: ★★★
Flame
People think of Blaze as wild, energetic, powerful, cool, handsome
People who like the name Blaze also like Blake, Caden, Blaine, Bailey, Blair, Dakota, Brayden, Aidan, Blaise, Addison

Blenda *(Latin)* ♀   RATING: ★★☆
Dazzling bright
People think of Blenda as funny, intelligent, pretty, girl next door, popular
People who like the name Blenda also like Bianca, Blossom, Bella, Bethany, Beyoncé, Celeste, Cassandra, Breanna, Amber, Bonnie

Bliss *(English)* ♀♂   RATING: ★★★★
Perfect joy
People think of Bliss as pretty, creative, caring, elegant, funny
People who like the name Bliss also like Bailey, Caden, Blair, Addison, Alexis, Blake, Blaine, Cadence, Dakota, Avery

Blissany *(American)* ♀   RATING: ★★★
Full of grace and joy—Combination of Bliss and Bethany
People think of Blissany as pretty, intelligent, creative, trustworthy, caring
People who like the name Blissany also like Belle, Bella, Bianca, Bridget, Bethany, Basanti, Brandice, Abigail, Blondelle, Carissa

Blithe *(English)* ♀   RATING: ★★★
Happy—*Blithe Spirit*, play by Noel Coward
People think of Blithe as pretty, funny, popular, artsy, elegant
People who like the name Blithe also like Blythe, Ava, Chloe, Bella, Charlotte, Belle, Grace, Audrey, Amelia, Claire

Blodwyn *(Welsh)* ♀   RATING: ★★★
Fair flower—Variation of Blodwen
People think of Blodwyn as creative, weird, energetic, pretty, intelligent
People who like the name Blodwyn also like Arwen, Bronwyn, Aelwen, Bronwen, Aeryn, Aderyn, Briallen, Breena, Aaralyn, Brielle

Blondelle *(American)* ♀   RATING: ★★★
Little blond one
People think of Blondelle as stuck-up, lazy, weird, pretty, slow
People who like the name Blondelle also like Belle, Blossom, Bella, Bianca, Bethany, Calista, Cassandra, Bonnie, Hannah, Blythe

Blossom *(English)* ♀   RATING: ★★★☆
Flower, bloom—*Blossom*, TV show
People think of Blossom as pretty, creative, caring, artsy, elegant

People who like the name Blossom also like Belle, Amber, Bethany, Faith, Aurora, Bella, Daisy, Abigail, Chloe, Bianca

Blue *(American)* ♀ ♂   RATING: ★★
The color—Character on *Blue's Clues*
People think of Blue as cool, creative, funny, intelligent, caring
People who like the name Blue also like Bailey, Addison, Avery, Blake, Caden, Blaine, Blaze, Aidan, Brody, Brooklyn

Bluma *(Hebrew)* ♀   RATING: ★☆
Flower, bloom
People think of Bluma as funny, intelligent, exotic, artsy, elegant
People who like the name Bluma also like Breena, Blossom, Cayla, Bly, Beulah, Chava, Belle, Bianca, Becca, Bhavna

Bly *(English)* ♀   RATING: ★★
Gentle, happy—Originally a surname
People think of Bly as creative, quiet, caring, young, old-fashioned
People who like the name Bly also like Bella, Belle, Blythe, Blossom, Bena, Breena, Ava, Brie, Cailyn, Kaya

Blythe *(English)* ♀   RATING: ★★★☆
Happy—Blythe Danner, actress
People think of Blythe as pretty, intelligent, caring, popular, funny
People who like the name Blythe also like Ava, Bella, Blithe, Chloe, Audrey, Abigail, Grace, Charlotte, Amelia, Belle

Bo *(Slavic)* ♂   RATING: ★★★☆
Living—Bo Bice, singer; Bo Jackson, athlete
People think of Bo as handsome, popular, cool, funny, caring
People who like the name Bo also like Beau, Caleb, Cole, Benjamin, Aden, Aiden, Chase, Noah, Ethan, Braden

Boaz *(Hebrew)* ♂   RATING: ★☆
Strength
People think of Boaz as handsome, leader, powerful, caring, trustworthy
People who like the name Boaz also like Caleb, Benjamin, Ezekiel, Asher, Aiden, Aaron, Beau, Abel, Bo, Braden

Bob *(English)* ♂   RATING: ★★★
Short for Robert—Also to move up and down; Bob Marley, musician; Bob Newhart, actor/comedian
People think of Bob as loser, funny, weird, nerdy, lazy
People who like the name Bob also like Jack, Brad, Bill, Brian, Andrew, Benjamin, Bradley, Anthony, Aaron, Brandon

Bobby *(American)* ♀ ♂   RATING: ★★★☆
Short for Robert—Bobby Brown, singer
People think of Bobby as funny, cool, handsome, caring, intelligent

People who like the name Bobby also like Bailey, Blake, Brooke, Billy, Cameron, Alex, Alexis, Billie, Blair, Ashley

Boden *(Scandinavian)* ♂   RATING: ★★★★
Sheltered
People think of Boden as handsome, intelligent, sporty, cool, trustworthy
People who like the name Boden also like Braden, Aiden, Braeden, Kaden, Asher, Caleb, Ethan, Benjamin, Holden, Cole

Bohdan *(Slavic)* ♂   RATING: ★★★★
Proud ruler—Variation of Bohden
People think of Bohdan as intelligent, handsome, cool, funny, exotic
People who like the name Bohdan also like Boden, Braeden, Braden, Aiden, Bowen, Kaden, Balin, Tristan, Brennan, Coen

Bolormaa *(Mongolian)* ♀   RATING: ★★
Crystal mother
People think of Bolormaa as old-fashioned, elegant, weird, ethnic, sexy
People who like the name Bolormaa also like Rosaline, Callista, Alessa, Aisling, Quintessa, Elisabeth, Gazelle, Awena, Allete, Querida

Bona *(Italian)* ♀   RATING: ★★★
Good
People think of Bona as creative, slow, funny, leader, weird
People who like the name Bona also like Camilla, Bice, Carlotta, Bambi, Angelina, Bambina, Camila, Cira, Bellini, Aria

Bonaventure *(English)* ♂   RATING: ★★★
Good luck—Also a surname from the French
People think of Bonaventure as weird, exotic, intelligent, criminal, funny
People who like the name Bonaventure also like Alastair, Braeden, Benedict, Braden, Broderick, Benjamin, Byron, Banyan, Cassius, Aiden

Bond *(English)* ♂   RATING: ★★
Husbandman, farmer—James Bond, movie character created by Ian Fleming; Ward Bond, actor
People think of Bond as intelligent, aggressive, powerful, popular, leader
People who like the name Bond also like Braden, Blade, Brant, Brock, Bishop, Booker, Aiden, Balin, Axel, Berke

Bonfilia *(Italian)* ♀   RATING: ★★☆
Good daughter
People think of Bonfilia as big, old-fashioned, exotic, girl next door, religious
People who like the name Bonfilia also like Adrina, Bina, Cascata, Aceline, Bianca, Carlina, Cosima, Ambra, Charlot, Chiara

Boniface *(English)* ♂   RATING: ★★★
Well-doer
People think of Boniface as loser, stuck-up, old-fashioned, unpopular, lazy

People who like the name Boniface also like Benedict, Benjamin, Braden, Bonaventure, Ambrose, Beauregard, Alastair, Boden, Basil, Bradford

Bonifacy *(Polish)* ♂   RATING: ★★
Well-doer
People think of Bonifacy as exotic, nerdy, lazy, slow, artsy
People who like the name Bonifacy also like Benedict, Bendek, Abdulrahman, Apollo, Broderick, Boyce, Abdulkareem, Anando, Benjamin, Basil

Bonita *(Spanish)* ♀   RATING: ★★★☆
Pretty, beautiful
People think of Bonita as pretty, sexy, funny, caring, cool
People who like the name Bonita also like Bella, Belle, Bianca, Cassandra, Bethany, Blossom, Celeste, Catalina, Breanna, Belita

Bonner *(English)* ♂   RATING: ★★★
Gentle, courteous—Originally a surname
People think of Bonner as popular, weird, wild, sporty, loser
People who like the name Bonner also like Braden, Brice, Brock, Aiden, Baxter, Boone, Barclay, Booker, Bishop, Bowen

Bonnie *(English)* ♀   RATING: ★★★☆
Pretty girl—Bonnie Bedelia, actress; Bonnie Raitt, singer
People think of Bonnie as pretty, funny, caring, intelligent, creative
People who like the name Bonnie also like Bella, Bridget, Bree, Ava, Amelia, Amber, Bethany, Emma, Audrey, Faith

Bono *(English)* ♂   RATING: ★★★
Short for names beginning with Bon; Bono Vox, singer/philanthropist
People think of Bono as intelligent, cool, leader, caring, powerful
People who like the name Bono also like Brock, Beck, Bo, Adam, Aiden, Brad, Beau, Alton, Cole, Braxton

Booker *(English)* ♂   RATING: ★★★☆
Bleacher—Booker T. Washington, civil rights activist/teacher
People think of Booker as funny, handsome, sporty, sexy, sneaky
People who like the name Booker also like Braden, Aiden, Brock, Baxter, Jackson, Dawson, Cole, Chase, Benjamin, Brice

Boone *(English)* ♂   RATING: ★☆
From Bohon, France—Originally a surname
People think of Boone as handsome, cool, sporty, popular, intelligent
People who like the name Boone also like Cole, Aiden, Beau, Braden, Ethan, Caleb, Brock, Benjamin, Aaron, Asher

Booth *(English)* ♂   RATING: ★★☆
Bothy (a herdsman's hut)
People think of Booth as funny, cool, popular, artsy, handsome
People who like the name Booth also like Booker, Chase, Baxter, Aiden, Colton, Blade, Braden, Beau, Bowen, Boone

Boris *(Slavic)* ♂   RATING: ★☆
Small—Boris Becker, tennis player; Boris Karloff, actor
People think of Boris as intelligent, cool, funny, caring, handsome
People who like the name Boris also like Adam, Benjamin, Aiden, Basil, Alexander, Caleb, Byron, Bradley, Felix, Braden

Borka *(Slavic)* ♂   RATING: ★★★
Fighter
People think of Borka as weird, lazy, criminal, aggressive, sneaky
People who like the name Borka also like Brac, Boris, Bastien, Barak, Bade, Braden, Bohdan, Balin, Bowen, Berg

Borna *(Armenian)* ♂   RATING: ★★★
Youthful
People think of Borna as cool, young, pretty, energetic, leader
People who like the name Borna also like Basil, Bash, Brac, Bastien, Brand, Bijan, Benjamin, Amadeus, Brennan, Boyd

Botan *(Japanese)* ♂   RATING: ★★★
Peony
People think of Botan as creative, weird, young, pretty, funny
People who like the name Botan also like Akio, Haru, Haruki, Hiroshi, Ryu, Keitaro, Kaemon, Keiji, Makoto, Jiro

Bowen *(Welsh)* ♂   RATING: ★★★★
Son of Owen
People think of Bowen as handsome, intelligent, creative, caring, sporty
People who like the name Bowen also like Aiden, Braeden, Cole, Owen, Braden, Conner, Caleb, Tristan, Liam, Colin

Bowie *(Celtic/Gaelic)* ♂   RATING: ★★
Yellow haired—David Bowie, musician
People think of Bowie as artsy, handsome, cool, funny, creative
People who like the name Bowie also like Bowen, Aiden, Aden, Braden, Braeden, Conner, Owen, Branden, Benjamin, Beck

Boyce *(English)* ♂   RATING: ★★★☆
From the woods—Also a surname from the French word *bois*
People think of Boyce as trustworthy, young, handsome, quiet, caring
People who like the name Boyce also like Braden, Brice, Braeden, Brock, Bowen, Benson, Balin, Boyd, Braxton, Bastien

Boyd *(Celtic/Gaelic)* ♂   RATING: ★★
Blond
> People think of Boyd as handsome, intelligent, caring, funny, cool
> People who like the name Boyd also like Braden, Conner, Aiden, Caleb, Braeden, Ethan, Brock, Brice, Benjamin, Beau

Bozica *(Slavic)* ♀   RATING: ★☆
Born at Christmas
> People think of Bozica as ethnic, pretty, nerdy, poor, old
> People who like the name Bozica also like Chumani, Calixte, Basanti, Breena, Bonita, Bellona, Braith, Blenda, Chenoa, Bracha

Brac *(Welsh)* ♂   RATING: ★★
Free
> People think of Brac as aggressive, weird, big, loser, criminal
> People who like the name Brac also like Braden, Braeden, Aiden, Boden, Aden, Cole, Brock, Asher, Benson, Blade

Bracha *(Hebrew)* ♀   RATING: ★★★
A blessing
> People think of Bracha as funny, creative, girl next door, religious, pretty
> People who like the name Bracha also like Breanna, Breena, Brielle, Ariella, Abigail, Beyla, Arella, Ceana, Cassara, Candra

Brad *(English)* ♂   RATING: ★★★
From the broad meadow—Originally short for Bradley or Bradshaw; Brad Garrett, actor/comedian; Brad Pitt, actor
> People think of Brad as handsome, funny, intelligent, cool, popular
> People who like the name Brad also like Aaron, Bradley, Brandon, Benjamin, Chad, Brian, Braden, Adam, Andrew, Ethan

Bradan *(Celtic/Gaelic)* ♂   RATING: ★★★☆
Salmon
> People think of Bradan as handsome, powerful, intelligent, leader, funny
> People who like the name Bradan also like Braden, Aiden, Aden, Braeden, Brennan, Tristan, Ethan, Keagan, Benjamin, Kaden

Braden *(English)* ♂   RATING: ★★★★
From the wide valley
> People think of Braden as handsome, funny, popular, cool, intelligent
> People who like the name Braden also like Aiden, Ethan, Caleb, Kaden, Braeden, Landon, Gavin, Jayden, Jackson, Jacob

Bradford *(English)* ♂   RATING: ★★★☆
From the broad ford—Originally a surname
> People think of Bradford as handsome, intelligent, funny, caring, creative
> People who like the name Bradford also like Bradley, Benjamin, Braden, Aiden, Alexander, Brock, Caleb, Jackson, Andrew, Ethan

Bradley *(English)* ♂   RATING: ★★★
From the broad meadow—Originally a surname; Bradley Whitford, actor
> People think of Bradley as handsome, funny, caring, intelligent, cool
> People who like the name Bradley also like Benjamin, Ethan, Jacob, Brandon, Braden, Caleb, Andrew, Alexander, Aiden, Aaron

Bradshaw *(English)* ♂   RATING: ★★★
From the broad field, forest—Originally a surname
> People think of Bradshaw as leader, aggressive, intelligent, popular, sporty
> People who like the name Bradshaw also like Braden, Bradford, Bradley, Broderick, Aiden, Braxton, Byron, Alexander, Brice, Burke

Brady *(Celtic/Gaelic)* ♀♂   RATING: ★★★★
Descendant of Bradach—*The Brady Bunch*, TV show; Wayne Brady, actor/comedian
> People think of Brady as handsome, funny, sporty, popular, intelligent
> People who like the name Brady also like Brody, Bailey, Logan, Blake, Caden, Hayden, Riley, Addison, Brayden, Carter

Braeden *(English)* ♂   RATING: ★★★
Son of Bradan
> People think of Braeden as handsome, intelligent, energetic, funny, popular
> People who like the name Braeden also like Aiden, Braden, Kaden, Caleb, Ethan, Cole, Landon, Tristan, Jayden, Conner

Braewyn *(English)* ♀   RATING: ★★★☆
Combination of Braeden and Bronwyn
> People think of Braewyn as exotic, creative, quiet, caring, pretty
> People who like the name Braewyn also like Aeryn, Bronwyn, Kaelyn, Brea, Arwen, Caelan, Aaralyn, Aislin, Aelwen, Erin

Braima *(African)* ♂   RATING: ★★☆
Father of multitudes—Variation of Abraham
> People think of Braima as exotic, quiet, cool, creative, funny
> People who like the name Braima also like Bandele, Amiri, Broderick, Brant, Bahari, Ciaran, Branden, Braeden, Biton, Caleb

Braith *(Welsh)* ♀   RATING: ★★★☆
Black and white
> People think of Braith as elegant, energetic, pretty, creative, popular
> People who like the name Braith also like Bronwyn, Arwen, Aderyn, Carys, Bella, Briallen, Bronwen, Aelwen, Bridget, Ava

138

Bram *(English)* ♂   RATING: ★★★☆
Father of a multitude—Short for Abraham; Bram
Stoker, author
  People think of Bram as handsome, intelligent, creative,
  funny, caring
  People who like the name Bram also like Aiden, Braden,
  Finn, Alexander, Caleb, Brandon, Conner, Braeden, Liam,
  Elijah

Bran *(Celtic/Gaelic)* ♂   RATING: ★★★☆
Raven—Origin of many old Gaelic place names and
two rivers in Scotland; also a magical hound in Irish
mythology; also a Celtic god in the Welsh Mabinogion
  People think of Bran as powerful, leader, aggressive,
  weird, trustworthy
  People who like the name Bran also like Aiden, Caleb,
  Brice, Brant, Liam, Brian, Brandon, Aden, Brent, Asher

Brand *(English)* ♂   RATING: ★★★☆
Sword—Short for Brandon; also a symbol of
ownership
  People think of Brand as aggressive, handsome, cool,
  powerful, popular
  People who like the name Brand also like Brant, Braden,
  Brock, Caleb, Brandon, Blade, Braeden, Aiden, Brent,
  Branden

Branden *(Celtic/Gaelic)* ♂   RATING: ★★★
Little raven
  People think of Branden as funny, handsome, cool, car-
  ing, creative
  People who like the name Branden also like Brandon,
  Aiden, Braden, Brendan, Benjamin, Braeden, Ethan,
  Caleb, Jacob, Bradley

Brandi *(American)* ♀   RATING: ★★★★
Warm, comforting
  People think of Brandi as pretty, caring, funny, creative,
  trustworthy
  People who like the name Brandi also like Amber,
  Brianna, Faith, Breanna, Hailey, Destiny, Bethany,
  Cassandra, Adriana, Chloe

Brandice *(American)* ♀   RATING: ★★
Combination of Brandi and Candice
  People think of Brandice as pretty, intelligent, caring,
  funny, sexy
  People who like the name Brandice also like Abrianna,
  Bianca, Bella, Aaralyn, Belle, Carissa, Alexandria, Brielle,
  Carleigh, Cailyn

Brandie *(American)* ♀   RATING: ★★★★
Variation of Brandy or Brandi
  People think of Brandie as pretty, funny, caring, trust-
  worthy, cool
  People who like the name Brandie also like Brandi,
  Brandy, Abigail, Cassandra, Breanna, Bella, Brandee,
  Chloe, Bethany, Emily

Brando *(Italian)* ♂   RATING: ★★☆
Sword—Short for Aldobrando and Luitprando; Marlon
Brando, actor
  People think of Brando as popular, big, weird, leader,
  powerful
  People who like the name Brando also like Gabriel,
  Branson, Beau, Brandon, Axel, Conner, Branden,
  Cadmus, Fabian, Antoine

Brandon *(Celtic/Gaelic)* ♂   RATING: ★★★☆
Little raven
  People think of Brandon as handsome, funny, cool,
  intelligent, caring
  People who like the name Brandon also like Ethan,
  Benjamin, Aiden, Jacob, Andrew, Caleb, Aaron, Nathan,
  Justin, Alexander

Brandy *(American)* ♀   RATING: ★★★
Brandy—Brandy Johnson, gymnast; Brandy Norwood,
actress/singer
  People think of Brandy as pretty, funny, caring, creative,
  intelligent
  People who like the name Brandy also like Amber,
  Hailey, Bethany, Emily, Brianna, Cassandra, Bridget,
  Abigail, Faith, Bianca

Branson *(English)* ♂   RATING: ★★★★
Son of Brand
  People think of Branson as handsome, intelligent, car-
  ing, popular, funny
  People who like the name Branson also like Braden,
  Aiden, Braeden, Bryson, Braxton, Ethan, Kaden,
  Brennan, Conner, Cole

Brant *(English)* ♂   RATING: ★★★★
Firebrand
  People think of Brant as handsome, funny, intelligent,
  cool, caring
  People who like the name Brant also like Braden, Caleb,
  Aiden, Ethan, Brice, Conner, Aden, Braeden, Brent, Cole

Branwen *(Welsh)* ♀   RATING: ★★★
White crow
  People think of Branwen as pretty, intelligent, energetic,
  elegant, creative
  People who like the name Branwen also like Kiara,
  Aeron, Hermione, Zoe, Belle, Chloe, Iris, Arwen, Abigail,
  Ivy

Branxton *(English)* ♀♂   RATING: ★★
Unknown meaning
  People think of Branxton as cool, popular, creative, car-
  ing, leader
  People who like the name Branxton also like Bailey,
  Caden, Brayden, Blaine, Addison, Brooklyn, Hayden,
  Blake, Carter, Carson

Brasen *(American)* ♀♂   RATING: ★★★★
Bold
  People think of Brasen as handsome, leader, popular,
  powerful, intelligent

People who like the name Brasen also like Caden, Brayden, Jaden, Addison, Bailey, Bricen, Blaine, Hayden, Brody, Blake

Brasilia *(Spanish)* ♀   RATING: ★★☆
From Brazil
People think of Brasilia as stuck-up, intelligent
People who like the name Brasilia also like Daniela, Marisa, Angelique, Tristana, Catalina, Brienda, Adriana, Selena, Nadalia, Danielle

Braun *(German)* ♂   RATING: ★★★☆
Brown—Also a surname and a brand
People think of Braun as aggressive, lazy, loser, weird, boy next door
People who like the name Braun also like Brock, Brice, Aiden, Beau, Axel, Brant, Baron, Booker, Bowen, Brac

Braxton *(English)* ♂   RATING: ★★★★
Brock's town—Toni Braxton, singer
People think of Braxton as handsome, popular, intelligent, sporty, cool
People who like the name Braxton also like Braden, Aiden, Jackson, Ethan, Landon, Caleb, Kaden, Gavin, Jayden, Bryson

Bray *(English)* ♂   RATING: ★★★☆
Bricklayer
People think of Bray as handsome, leader, caring, intelligent, energetic
People who like the name Bray also like Aiden, Benjamin, Brock, Adrian, Beau, Brice, Braden, Brayton, Chase, Cody

Brayden *(Celtic/Gaelic)* ♀♂   RATING: ★★★★
Son of Bradan—Also a surname
People think of Brayden as handsome, intelligent, popular, funny, energetic
People who like the name Brayden also like Caden, Hayden, Bailey, Addison, Riley, Aidan, Logan, Jaden, Connor, Madison

Braylin *(American)* ♀   RATING: ★★★☆
Combination of Bray and Lin
People think of Braylin as funny, popular, pretty, creative, intelligent
People who like the name Braylin also like Ava, Cailyn, Ashlyn, Olivia, Bella, Paige, Kaelyn, Jadyn, Abigail, Aaralyn

Brayton *(English)* ♂   RATING: ★★★☆
From Bray's town
People think of Brayton as handsome, intelligent, funny, popular, cool
People who like the name Brayton also like Braden, Braxton, Braeden, Aiden, Bryson, Kaden, Caleb, Ethan, Brice, Aden

Brazil *(Celtic/Gaelic)* ♀♂   RATING: ★★★☆
Strife—Also a country in South America
People think of Brazil as exotic, sexy, pretty, popular, intelligent

People who like the name Brazil also like Brooklyn, Brayden, Aidan, Bailey, Blair, Brady, Brody, Avery, Blake, Brogan

Brea *(American)* ♀   RATING: ★★★★☆
Beauty beyond sight
People think of Brea as pretty, intelligent, funny, popular, creative
People who like the name Brea also like Breanna, Bree, Ava, Bella, Kaelyn, Chloe, Brenna, Abigail, Brianna, Belle

Breanna *(Celtic/Gaelic)* ♀   RATING: ★★★★
Exalted, lofty—Feminine form of Brian
People think of Breanna as pretty, funny, creative, caring, intelligent
People who like the name Breanna also like Brianna, Abigail, Hailey, Caitlyn, Hannah, Briana, Emma, Isabella, Arianna, Bianca

Breck *(Celtic/Gaelic)* ♂   RATING: ★★★★
Freckled
People think of Breck as intelligent, funny, powerful, handsome, leader
People who like the name Breck also like Aiden, Braeden, Braden, Cole, Conner, Brock, Caleb, Bowen, Brennan, Tristan

Breckin *(Celtic/Gaelic)* ♀♂   RATING: ★★★★
Freckled
People think of Breckin as intelligent, energetic, creative, funny, popular
People who like the name Breckin also like Aidan, Brayden, Brody, Caden, Hayden, Avery, Addison, Bailey, Parker, Brynn

Brede *(Celtic/Gaelic)* ♀♂   RATING: ★★★
Exalted, lofty—Variation of Bridget
People think of Brede as intelligent, pretty, cool, winner, lazy
People who like the name Brede also like Blaine, Blair, Brogan, Brynn, Breckin, Briar, Brayden, Caden, Bron, Blaise

Bree *(Celtic/Gaelic)* ♀   RATING: ★★★★
Variation of Brie; also short for names starting with Bri
People think of Bree as pretty, funny, creative, caring, intelligent
People who like the name Bree also like Ava, Bella, Brea, Breanna, Chloe, Brianna, Emma, Audrey, Faith, Abigail

Breeda *(Celtic/Gaelic)* ♀   RATING: ★★★
Exalted
People think of Breeda as pretty, trustworthy, funny, young, cool
People who like the name Breeda also like Cayla, Bianca, Adrina, Alaina, Breanna, Breena, Aila, Ayla, Aria, Alba

Breena *(Celtic/Gaelic)* ♀   RATING: ★★★
Fairy land
People think of Breena as pretty, creative, intelligent, young, artsy

People who like the name Breena also like Breanna, Bree, Brea, Brenna, Bella, Brianna, Alana, Bianca, Aeryn, Briana

Breindel (*Hebrew*) ♀♂   RATING: ★★★☆
Blessing
People think of Breindel as creative, leader, popular, energetic, intelligent
People who like the name Breindel also like Brayden, Caden, Jaden, Breckin, Blaine, Azriel, Adriel, Ariel, Cadence, Brasen

Brencis (*Slavic*) ♀♂   RATING: ★★
Crowned with laurel
People think of Brencis as energetic, pretty, slow, trendy, old-fashioned
People who like the name Brencis also like Blaise, Breindel, Brede, Breckin, Bem, Bern, Blake, Blair, Bennett, Blaine

Brend (*Celtic/Gaelic*) ♂   RATING: ★★
Prince—Short for Brendan
People think of Brend as young, sexy, funny, handsome, powerful
People who like the name Brend also like Bowen, Breck, Conner, Brennan, Brendan, Conley, Brendon, Baird, Brian, Brandon

Brenda (*Scandinavian*) ♀   RATING: ★★★☆
Sword—Feminine form of Brand
People think of Brenda as caring, pretty, funny, intelligent, trustworthy
People who like the name Brenda also like Amanda, Amber, Bethany, Abigail, Brianna, Bridget, Breanna, Angela, Caitlyn, Bianca

Brendan (*Celtic/Gaelic*) ♂   RATING: ★★★☆
Prince—Brendan Behan, author; Brendan Fraiser, actor
People think of Brendan as handsome, intelligent, funny, cool, energetic
People who like the name Brendan also like Brandon, Aiden, Braden, Ethan, Brennan, Caleb, Benjamin, Braeden, Gavin, Alexander

Brendon (*Celtic/Gaelic*) ♂   RATING: ★★★★
Prince
People think of Brendon as handsome, funny, cool, sexy, popular
People who like the name Brendon also like Brandon, Aiden, Braden, Brendan, Ethan, Andrew, Caleb, Alexander, Bradley, Branden

Brendy (*American*) ♀   RATING: ★★★
Sword—Short for Brenda
People think of Brendy as funny, popular, pretty, trendy, creative
People who like the name Brendy also like Breena, Bianca, Breanna, Brielle, Becca, Beyoncé, Alicia, Bree, Belle, Bethany

Brenna (*Celtic/Gaelic*) ♀   RATING: ★★★★☆
Princess—Feminine form of Brendan or Brennan
People think of Brenna as pretty, funny, intelligent, caring, creative
People who like the name Brenna also like Ava, Emma, Brianna, Bella, Breanna, Abigail, Ella, Hannah, Ashlyn, Chloe

Brennan (*Celtic/Gaelic*) ♂   RATING: ★★★☆
Tear, sorrow—From the Irish word *braon*
People think of Brennan as handsome, intelligent, funny, caring, popular
People who like the name Brennan also like Aiden, Braden, Brendan, Ethan, Braeden, Caleb, Tristan, Gavin, Noah, Conner

Brent (*English*) ♂   RATING: ★★★☆
Hill—Brent Musberger, sportscaster
People think of Brent as handsome, caring, funny, intelligent, cool
People who like the name Brent also like Braden, Ethan, Bradley, Caleb, Benjamin, Brandon, Aaron, Aiden, Brice, Andrew

Brett (*Celtic/Gaelic*) ♀♂   RATING: ★★★☆
Breton—Brett Favre, football player
People think of Brett as funny, handsome, intelligent, cool, caring
People who like the name Brett also like Blake, Bailey, Brooke, Cameron, Caden, Carter, Connor, Logan, Evan, Riley

Brevyn (*American*) ♀♂   RATING: ★★★
Created name, probably derived from Kevin
People think of Brevyn as handsome, aggressive, sporty, popular, leader
People who like the name Brevyn also like Aidan, Brody, Kade, Hayden, Devin, Keegan, Bricen, Brett, Bailey, Addison

Brewster (*English*) ♂   RATING: ★☆
Brewer—Originally a surname
People think of Brewster as young, aggressive, old-fashioned, funny, nerdy
People who like the name Brewster also like Braden, Baxter, Braeden, Aiden, Broderick, Brock, Ethan, Baron, Brandon, Benjamin

Breyon (*American*) ♂   RATING: ★★★☆
Variation of Brian
People think of Breyon as cool, popular, intelligent, handsome, young
People who like the name Breyon also like Braden, Braeden, Bryson, Braxton, Aden, Brayton, Caleb, Aiden, Kaden, Branden

Briallen (*Celtic/Gaelic*) ♀   RATING: ★★★☆
Primrose—Cornish origin
People think of Briallen as pretty, intelligent, elegant, quiet, funny
People who like the name Briallen also like Brielle, Breanna, Breena, Bronwyn, Brianna, Kaelyn, Brea, Caelan, Arwen, Brenna

Brian *(Celtic/Gaelic)* ♂   RATING: ★★★
High, noble—Brian Cox, actor; Brian Dennehy, actor; Brian De Palma, movie director
  People think of Brian as handsome, funny, intelligent, cool, caring
  People who like the name Brian also like Benjamin, Andrew, Brandon, Adam, Aaron, Ethan, Alexander, Daniel, Anthony, Caleb

Briana *(Celtic/Gaelic)* ♀   RATING: ★★★
High, noble—Feminine form of Brian
  People think of Briana as pretty, funny, intelligent, caring, cool
  People who like the name Briana also like Brianna, Breanna, Brianne, Adriana, Hailey, Bianca, Abigail, Hannah, Chloe, Ava

Brianna *(Celtic/Gaelic)* ♀   RATING: ★★★☆
High, noble—Feminine form of Brian
  People think of Brianna as pretty, funny, caring, creative, intelligent
  People who like the name Brianna also like Breanna, Abigail, Hailey, Isabella, Hannah, Arianna, Emma, Caitlyn, Ava, Adriana

Brianne *(Celtic/Gaelic)* ♀   RATING: ★★★
High, noble
  People think of Brianne as pretty, funny, intelligent, caring, creative
  People who like the name Brianne also like Brianna, Breanna, Briana, Hailey, Abigail, Hannah, Caitlyn, Bethany, Faith, Chloe

Briar *(English)* ♀♂   RATING: ★★★★
Shrub, small tree
  People think of Briar as intelligent, pretty, creative, cool, funny
  People who like the name Briar also like Bailey, Blair, Caden, Avery, Blaine, Addison, Blake, Aidan, Brayden, Logan

Brice *(English)* ♂   RATING: ★★★
Speckled
  People think of Brice as handsome, intelligent, caring, funny, cool
  People who like the name Brice also like Braden, Ethan, Aiden, Caleb, Cole, Kaden, Chase, Gavin, Aden, Conner

Bricen *(Welsh)* ♀♂   RATING: ★★★★
Son of Brice—Variation of Bryson
  People think of Bricen as handsome, cool, popular, funny, intelligent
  People who like the name Bricen also like Caden, Brayden, Bailey, Blaine, Addison, Bryce, Hayden, Cadence, Jaden, Blake

Brick *(English)* ♂   RATING: ★★★
From the bridge—Also a block of concrete; character in *Cat on a Hot Tin Roof* by Tennessee Williams
  People think of Brick as aggressive, powerful, weird, handsome, funny

People who like the name Brick also like Brice, Braden, Beau, Aiden, Blade, Booker, Brant, Dawson, Caleb, Brinley

Bridget *(Celtic/Gaelic)* ♀   RATING: ★★★★
Exalted, lofty
  People think of Bridget as pretty, funny, caring, intelligent, popular
  People who like the name Bridget also like Abigail, Audrey, Chloe, Ava, Emma, Charlotte, Hannah, Grace, Claire, Bianca

Bridgit *(Celtic/Gaelic)* ♀   RATING: ★★☆
Exalted, lofty
  People think of Bridgit as pretty, energetic, caring, funny, creative
  People who like the name Bridgit also like Abigail, Bridget, Bella, Breanna, Bethany, Fiona, Chloe, Faith, Bianca, Brianna

Bridie *(Celtic/Gaelic)* ♀   RATING: ★★★★
Exalted, lofty—Short for Bridget
  People think of Bridie as pretty, caring, funny, young, intelligent
  People who like the name Bridie also like Bella, Amelia, Bridget, Breanna, Abigail, Ava, Brianna, Caitlyn, Bree, Genevieve

Brie *(French)* ♀   RATING: ★★★★
From region of France—Also a type of cheese
  People think of Brie as pretty, funny, intelligent, caring, popular
  People who like the name Brie also like Ava, Bree, Bella, Belle, Chloe, Emma, Brielle, Audrey, Paige, Abigail

Brielle *(French)* ♀   RATING: ★★★★
Short for Gabrielle
  People think of Brielle as pretty, funny, popular, creative, caring
  People who like the name Brielle also like Ava, Bella, Chloe, Isabella, Gabrielle, Brianna, Bianca, Emma, Ella, Belle

Brienda *(Spanish)* ♀   RATING: ★★★
Open—Short for Abrienda
  People think of Brienda as creative, pretty, artsy, trustworthy, caring
  People who like the name Brienda also like Belinda, Belicia, Catalina, Bianca, Adriana, Breanna, Brianna, Brielle, Abrienda, Abrianna

Brier *(English)* ♂   RATING: ★★★☆
Shrub, tree—Variation of Briar
  People think of Brier as popular, intelligent, pretty, aggressive, handsome
  People who like the name Brier also like Braden, Braeden, Asher, Aiden, Caleb, Brighton, Ethan, Braxton, Cole, Coen

Brigette *(French)* ♀   RATING: ★★★★
Exalted, lofty
  People think of Brigette as pretty, funny, intelligent, caring, popular

People who like the name Brigette also like Bridget, Abigail, Charlotte, Hailey, Belle, Bianca, Ava, Isabella, Chloe, Audrey

Brigham (English) ♂   RATING: ★★★★
From the bridge settlement—Also a surname; Brigham Young, Mormon leader
People think of Brigham as leader, handsome, intelligent, powerful, religious
People who like the name Brigham also like Brighton, Braden, Caleb, Cole, Brock, Braxton, Bradford, Aiden, Broderick, Brinley

Brighid (Celtic/Gaelic) ♀   RATING: ★★★☆
Exalted, lofty—Pronounced *Breed*; also the Celtic Triple Goddess; also the first female saint to study in the Christian monasteries in Old Ireland
People think of Brighid as pretty, popular, intelligent, girl next door, young
People who like the name Brighid also like Aeryn, Brigid, Bridget, Brea, Breena, Breanna, Alana, Bridgit, Aislin, Bree

Brighton (English) ♂   RATING: ★★★★
From the bright town
People think of Brighton as handsome, intelligent, energetic, popular, creative
People who like the name Brighton also like Braden, Aiden, Braeden, Caleb, Ethan, Jackson, Landon, Braxton, Gavin, Bryson

Brigid (Celtic/Gaelic) ♀   RATING: ★★
Exalted, lofty—Pronounced *Breed* in Ireland
People think of Brigid as intelligent, pretty, caring, creative, funny
People who like the name Brigid also like Bridget, Fiona, Brighid, Breanna, Deirdre, Aeryn, Bridgit, Genevieve, Brea, Ava

Brigit (Scandinavian) ♀   RATING: ★★★☆
Exalted, lofty
People think of Brigit as funny, creative, pretty, intelligent, elegant
People who like the name Brigit also like Bridget, Daphne, Bella, Abigail, Brigette, Amelia, Brigitte, Callie, Aeryn, Celeste

Brigitte (French) ♀   RATING: ★★★
Exalted, lofty—Brigitte Bardot, actress
People think of Brigitte as pretty, intelligent, creative, caring, funny
People who like the name Brigitte also like Belle, Isabella, Charlotte, Audrey, Isabelle, Bridget, Chloe, Bella, Abigail, Gabrielle

Brilane (English) ♀ ♂   RATING: ★★
From Brigham Lane
People think of Brilane as pretty, exotic, uptight, loser, lazy
People who like the name Brilane also like Caden, Brayden, Bailey, Addison, Brooklyn, Blaine, Brynn, Cadence, Brinly, Hayden

Brilliant (American) ♀ ♂   RATING: ★★☆
To sparkle
People think of Brilliant as stuck-up, loser, slow, unpopular, uptight
People who like the name Brilliant also like Bliss, Bailey, Blake, Blair, Brooklyn, Blaine, Baby, Blaise, Brooke, Britain

Brina (American) ♀   RATING: ★★★☆
Short for Sabrina
People think of Brina as pretty, intelligent, creative, caring, funny
People who like the name Brina also like Breena, Bella, Chloe, Brielle, Bianca, Cailyn, Bethany, Cara, Ashlyn, Breanna

Brinda (Sanskrit/East Indian) ♀   RATING: ★★★
Of the basil plant
People think of Brinda as intelligent, caring, cool, energetic, funny
People who like the name Brinda also like Bhavna, Chandra, Amithi, Bethany, Chahna, Breanna, Brianna, Bella, Denali, Bianca

Brinkley (English) ♀ ♂   RATING: ★★★
From Brinca's field—Christie Brinkley, fashion model; David Brinkley, newscaster; a city in Arkansas
People think of Brinkley as creative, leader, funny, trustworthy, ethnic
People who like the name Brinkley also like Brooklyn, Addison, Hadley, Avery, Delaney, Brady, Caden, Kenley, Barrett, Camdyn

Brinley (English) ♂   RATING: ★★★★
Burnt meadow
People think of Brinley as pretty, popular, creative, intelligent, girl next door
People who like the name Brinley also like Braden, Aiden, Braeden, Grayson, Ethan, Noah, Braxton, Brennan, Landon, Caleb

Brinly (English) ♀ ♂   RATING: ★★★★
Burnt meadow
People think of Brinly as pretty, girl next door, creative, caring, funny
People who like the name Brinly also like Bailey, Addison, Caden, Avery, Brayden, Brynn, Ainsley, Brooklyn, Aubrey, Hayden

Briony (American) ♀   RATING: ★★★
Poisonous climbing vine—Variation of Bryony
People think of Briony as pretty, sexy, intelligent, winner, sneaky
People who like the name Briony also like Chloe, Ava, Emily, Brianna, Grace, Sophie, Bronwyn, Ella, Libby, Hannah

Brisa (Spanish) ♀   RATING: ★★★★
Breeze, small wind
People think of Brisa as pretty, creative, caring, energetic, funny

People who like the name Brisa also like Brea, Belicia, Bianca, Brielle, Breanna, Chloe, Brianna, Cailyn, Breena, Ava

Briseis *(Greek)* ♀   RATING: ★★★☆
Daughter of Bris—Also a type of moth
People think of Briseis as pretty, exotic, intelligent, sexy, elegant
People who like the name Briseis also like Isolde, Ava, Adrienne, Giselle, Arabella, Sienna, Gwyneth, Carys, Aurora, Felicity

Brit *(English)* ♀♂   RATING: ★★★☆
Exalted, lofty—Variation of Bridget
People think of Brit as funny, pretty, popular, cool, sporty
People who like the name Brit also like Britt, Bailey, Blake, Brooke, Ashton, Alexis, Brooklyn, Brody, Brynn, Aubrey

Brita *(English)* ♀   RATING: ★★★☆
Exalted, lofty—Variation of Bridget
People think of Brita as pretty, intelligent, funny, trustworthy, creative
People who like the name Brita also like Bree, Bridget, Bella, Chloe, Audrey, Breanna, Aurora, Bethany, Bianca, Ashlyn

Britain *(English)* ♀♂   RATING: ★★★☆
From Great Britain
People think of Britain as intelligent, cool, sexy, funny, popular
People who like the name Britain also like Brooklyn, Bailey, Avery, Caden, Addison, Hayden, Blake, Blaine, Cameron, London

Britannia *(English)* ♀   RATING: ★★☆
From Great Britain
People think of Britannia as popular, sexy, powerful, creative, winner
People who like the name Britannia also like Bridget, Brianna, Bella, Bianca, Bethany, Britany, Anastasia, Aurora, Destiny, Brielle

Britany *(English)* ♀   RATING: ★★☆
From Great Britain
People think of Britany as pretty, funny, popular, caring, cool
People who like the name Britany also like Bridget, Britney, Brianna, Amber, Brittany, Bethany, Caitlyn, Breanna, Abigail, Hailey

Britney *(English)* ♀   RATING: ★★★
From Great Britain—Britney Spears, singer
People think of Britney as pretty, popular, funny, sexy, young
People who like the name Britney also like Brianna, Amber, Hailey, Bethany, Jessica, Bridget, Amanda, Abigail, Chloe, Emma

Britt *(Scandinavian)* ♀♂   RATING: ★★★★
Exalted, lofty—Variation of Bridget; also short for Brittany
People think of Britt as intelligent, funny, pretty, creative, trustworthy
People who like the name Britt also like Blake, Brooke, Bailey, Caden, Brady, Addison, Brody, Brynn, Blaine, Brit

Britta *(Scandinavian)* ♀   RATING: ★★★☆
Exalted, lofty—Variation of Bridget
People think of Britta as pretty, intelligent, creative, funny, caring
People who like the name Britta also like Bianca, Ava, Bella, Chloe, Bridget, Aurora, Anika, Eva, Astrid, Ella

Brittania *(English)* ♀   RATING: ★★★☆
From Britain
People think of Brittania as pretty, intelligent, funny, creative, cool
People who like the name Brittania also like Brianna, Britannia, Bethany, Brielle, Chelsea, Breanna, Belle, Bianca, Audrey, Ashlyn

Brittany *(English)* ♀   RATING: ★★☆
From Britain—Also spelled Britney, Britnee, Brittainy, or Britany
People think of Brittany as funny, pretty, caring, creative, intelligent
People who like the name Brittany also like Bethany, Amber, Brianna, Abigail, Emma, Hannah, Bridget, Amanda, Hailey, Emily

Brittnee *(English)* ♀   RATING: ★★
From Britain—Variation of Brittany
People think of Brittnee as pretty, popular, caring, funny, creative
People who like the name Brittnee also like Brittany, Britney, Britany, Brittney, Ashleigh, Abigail, Bridget, Brianna, Caitlyn, Ashlyn

Brittney *(English)* ♀   RATING: ★★★★
From Britain—Variation of Brittany
People think of Brittney as pretty, funny, caring, cool, popular
People who like the name Brittney also like Brittany, Amber, Abigail, Hailey, Allison, Brianna, Alyssa, Ashleigh, Britney, Chelsea

Brock *(English)* ♂   RATING: ★★★
Badger—Originally a surname
People think of Brock as handsome, funny, sporty, intelligent, popular
People who like the name Brock also like Braden, Caleb, Brice, Aiden, Ethan, Cole, Chase, Conner, Kaden, Benjamin

Broden *(American)* ♂   RATING: ★★★
Brother—Variation of Brody
People think of Broden as handsome, leader, funny, caring, popular
People who like the name Broden also like Braden, Aiden, Ethan, Braeden, Kaden, Gavin, Brock, Bryson, Cody, Brennan

Broderick (Welsh) ♂ RATING: ★★
Son of Rhydderch—Also an English surname;
Broderick Crawford, actor; Matthew Broderick, actor
People think of Broderick as intelligent, handsome, leader, powerful, sporty
People who like the name Broderick also like Aiden, Braeden, Braden, Caleb, Conner, Benjamin, Brock, Ethan, Brice, Tristan

Brody (Celtic/Gaelic) ♀♂ RATING: ★★★★
Brother—Also short for Broderick; also spelled Brodie; Brody Jenner, TV personality/model; Adam Brody, actor
People think of Brody as handsome, popular, cool, funny, intelligent
People who like the name Brody also like Brady, Bailey, Caden, Logan, Hayden, Brayden, Riley, Addison, Avery, Blake

Brogan (Celtic/Gaelic) ♀♂ RATING: ★★★★
Sturdy, strong
People think of Brogan as intelligent, funny, popular, leader, trustworthy
People who like the name Brogan also like Brody, Caden, Brayden, Logan, Addison, Aidan, Bailey, Hayden, Brady, Connor

Bron (English) ♀♂ RATING: ★★★
Short for Bronwen or Auberon
People think of Bron as funny, handsome, intelligent, lazy, powerful
People who like the name Bron also like Brogan, Briar, Brede, Brayden, Brody, Blaine, Blaise, Brook, Breckin

Brone (English) ♂ RATING: ★★☆
Brown
People think of Brone as funny, big, wild, uptight, boy next door
People who like the name Brone also like Brock, Brinley, Berke, Belden, Barclay, Braeden, Blade, Braden, Brice, Byrne

Bronson (English) ♂ RATING: ★★☆
Variation of Branson—Also a surname; Bronson Pinchot, actor; Charles Bronson, actor
People think of Bronson as handsome, cool, intelligent, popular, funny
People who like the name Bronson also like Braden, Bryson, Caleb, Brock, Aiden, Bradley, Braxton, Ethan, Byron, Jackson

Bronwen (Welsh) ♀ RATING: ★★
Fair breast
People think of Bronwen as pretty, creative, intelligent, artsy, caring
People who like the name Bronwen also like Bronwyn, Arwen, Chloe, Bella, Ava, Claire, Amelia, Bianca, Eva, Gwendolyn

Bronwyn (Welsh) ♀ RATING: ★★★★
Fair breast
People think of Bronwyn as pretty, intelligent, creative, funny, energetic
People who like the name Bronwyn also like Ava, Arwen, Bronwen, Abigail, Chloe, Aurora, Faith, Hannah, Bella, Amelia

Brook (English) ♀♂ RATING: ★★★
Small stream
People think of Brook as pretty, funny, popular, caring, trustworthy
People who like the name Brook also like Bailey, Brooke, Blake, Madison, Alexis, Brooklyn, Caden, Blair, Hayden, Austin

Brooke (English) ♀♂ RATING: ★★★☆
Small stream—Brooke Adams, actress/producer; Brooke Shields, model/actress
People think of Brooke as pretty, funny, popular, caring, creative
People who like the name Brooke also like Bailey, Madison, Blake, Taylor, Riley, Alexis, Brooklyn, Hayden, Addison, Dylan

Brooklee (American) ♀♂ RATING: ★★★
Combination of Brook and Lee; also a variation of Brooklyn
People think of Brooklee as trendy, pretty, religious, girl next door, lazy
People who like the name Brooklee also like Brooklyn, Baylee, Caden, Jade, Payton, Aubrey, Bailey, Jaden, Brook, Keegan

Brooklyn (American) ♀♂ RATING: ★★★☆
New York borough—From the Dutch town Breukelen; Anglicized to Brookland and then Brooklyn
People think of Brooklyn as pretty, popular, funny, intelligent, cool
People who like the name Brooklyn also like Bailey, Madison, Brooke, Caden, Hayden, Addison, Dakota, Riley, Blake, Avery

Brooks (English) ♂ RATING: ★★★
From the brook—Also a surname; Mel Brooks, screenwriter/comedian; Garth Brooks, singer
People think of Brooks as handsome, intelligent, popular, funny, leader
People who like the name Brooks also like Braden, Aiden, Jackson, Caleb, Chase, Brock, Landon, Cole, Dawson, Brice

Broox (American) ♂ RATING: ★★☆
Created name—Variation of Brooks
People think of Broox as funny, artsy, cool, young, energetic
People who like the name Broox also like Braxton, Lucas, Dawson, Brooks, Brock, Garrison, Richard, Kaden, Fisher, Dalton

Brosh (Hebrew) ♂   RATING: ★★☆
Cypress
People think of Brosh as weird, loser, nerdy, aggressive, unpopular
People who like the name Brosh also like Balin, Ansel, Brock, Adish, Beau, Byram, Bahari, Bade, Barclay, Basil

Bruce (English) ♂   RATING: ★★★
From the town of Bruis—Bruce Hornsby, musician; Bruce Springsteen, musician; Bruce Willis, actor
People think of Bruce as handsome, intelligent, funny, powerful, caring
People who like the name Bruce also like Brian, Benjamin, Andrew, David, Alexander, Ethan, Bradley, Christopher, Aaron, Caleb

Bruis (Celtic/Gaelic) ♂   RATING: ★☆
From the town of Bruis—Variation of Bruce
People think of Bruis as aggressive, big, poor, sexy, handsome
People who like the name Bruis also like Aiden, Bowen, Brian, Callum, Brandon, Brennan, Cavan, Bairn, Baird, Arlen

Bruno (German) ♂   RATING: ★★★
Brown one
People think of Bruno as big, handsome, powerful, aggressive, intelligent
People who like the name Bruno also like Benjamin, Adam, Axel, Brandon, Aaron, Andrew, Adrian, Anthony, Caleb, Ethan

Bryan (English) ♂   RATING: ★★★
High, noble—Variation of Brian
People think of Bryan as handsome, funny, intelligent, caring, cool
People who like the name Bryan also like Brian, Brandon, Caleb, Andrew, Benjamin, Aiden, Aaron, Ethan, Alexander, Adam

Bryanne (American) ♀   RATING: ★★★☆
High, noble—Feminine form of Brian
People think of Bryanne as pretty, caring, funny, intelligent, popular
People who like the name Bryanne also like Breanna, Brianna, Brianne, Cailyn, Briana, Caitlyn, Hailey, Hannah, Bethany, Ashlyn

Bryant (Celtic/Gaelic) ♂   RATING: ★★★
Son of Brian—Bryant Gumbel, TV personality
People think of Bryant as funny, handsome, intelligent, cool, caring
People who like the name Bryant also like Aiden, Caleb, Ethan, Braden, Conner, Ian, Aden, Garrett, Braeden, Chase

Bryce (English) ♀♂   RATING: ★★★☆
Speckled—Saint Brice
People think of Bryce as handsome, funny, intelligent, energetic, popular
People who like the name Bryce also like Blake, Caden, Bailey, Brayden, Hayden, Addison, Logan, Avery, Dylan, Connor

Brye (American) ♀   RATING: ★★★
Combination of Bree and Skye
People think of Brye as wild, creative, young, intelligent, exotic
People who like the name Brye also like Brea, Bree, Cailyn, Bryanne, Bella, Jadyn, Ava, Isabella, Faith, Chloe

Brygida (Polish) ♀   RATING: ★★★
Exalted, lofty—Variation of Bridget
People think of Brygida as exotic, pretty, trustworthy, intelligent, wealthy
People who like the name Brygida also like Abrianna, Aaralyn, Abigail, Aeryn, Brighid, Cianna, Amaya, Brielle, Bryanne, Buthainah

Bryna (Celtic/Gaelic) ♀   RATING: ★★★★
Strong one—Feminine form of Bryan
People think of Bryna as pretty, funny, intelligent, creative, caring
People who like the name Bryna also like Brea, Breanna, Ava, Cailyn, Brielle, Brianna, Brenna, Keely, Keira, Breena

Bryndis (Scandinavian) ♀   RATING: ★★
Of strong armor
People think of Bryndis as intelligent, leader, trustworthy, powerful, energetic
People who like the name Bryndis also like Brynja, Aaralyn, Brielle, Ceri, Caia, Briallen, Cerise, Aeryn, Bronwen, Charisma

Brynja (Scandinavian) ♀   RATING: ★★★
Armor
People think of Brynja as caring, energetic, creative, funny, pretty
People who like the name Brynja also like Bryndis, Adalia, Alida, Bian, Anika, Catori, Cyrah, Ciara, Ceri, Chumani

Brynn (Celtic/Gaelic) ♀♂   RATING: ★★★
Hill
People think of Brynn as pretty, intelligent, funny, creative, energetic
People who like the name Brynn also like Bailey, Caden, Avery, Addison, Aidan, Aubrey, Brayden, Hayden, Brooke, Logan

Brynner (Celtic/Gaelic) ♂   RATING: ★★★
Hill—Yul Brynner, actor
People think of Brynner as popular, handsome, weird, religious, intelligent
People who like the name Brynner also like Aden, Asher, Aiden, Brennan, Conlan, Tristan, Grayson, Braden, Keiran, Crevan

Bryony (English) ♀   RATING: ★★★☆
Poisonous climbing vine
People think of Bryony as funny, pretty, intelligent, trustworthy, creative
People who like the name Bryony also like Chloe, Abigail, Bronwyn, Bethany, Bianca, Ava, Emma, Charlotte, Breanna, Bella

145

Bryson *(American)* ♂ RATING: ★★★★☆
Son of Brice—Originally an English surname
People think of Bryson as handsome, funny, intelligent, caring, popular
People who like the name Bryson also like Braden, Aiden, Kaden, Ethan, Brice, Jayden, Caleb, Landon, Grayson, Braeden

Bubba *(American)* ♂ RATING: ★★★
Brother—Also an American nickname
People think of Bubba as big, lazy, loser, slow, cool
People who like the name Bubba also like Braden, Caleb, Beau, Chase, Brice, Cody, Aiden, Clay, Buddy, Andrew

Buck *(American)* ♂ RATING: ★★☆
Deer; cowboy
People think of Buck as handsome, wild, sporty, funny, cool
People who like the name Buck also like Beau, Chase, Andrew, Blade, Caleb, Cody, Adam, Colton, Benjamin, Braden

Bud *(American)* ♂ RATING: ★★★☆
Messenger, friend—Bud Abbott, comedian/actor
People think of Bud as slow, caring, big, aggressive, trustworthy
People who like the name Bud also like Buddy, Brad, Buck, Braden, Andrew, Aiden, Beau, Adam, Brian, Brant

Buddy *(American)* ♂ RATING: ★★★☆
Friend—Buddy Rich, musician
People think of Buddy as funny, cool, handsome, caring, intelligent
People who like the name Buddy also like Bradley, Brad, Benjamin, Caleb, Andrew, Brock, Brandon, Aaron, Braden, Aiden

Buffy *(American)* ♀ RATING: ★★★☆
Possibly from Elizabeth—*Buffy the Vampire Slayer*, TV show
People think of Buffy as pretty, sexy, leader, energetic, powerful
People who like the name Buffy also like Bella, Faith, Belle, Anastasia, Chloe, Anya, April, Ava, Amber, Cassandra

Bunny *(American)* ♀ RATING: ★★★
Little rabbit
People think of Bunny as funny, pretty, sexy, energetic, popular
People who like the name Bunny also like Bella, Cinnamon, Candy, Butterfly, Blossom, Buffy, Bianca, Belle, Coco, Bonnie

Burgess *(English)* ♂ RATING: ★★★
Town citizen—Also a surname; Burgess Meredith, actor
People think of Burgess as big, funny, loser, handsome, lazy
People who like the name Burgess also like Baron, Axel, Braden, Bowen, Burke, Brewster, Archie, Aston, Archibald, Barnard

Burian *(Slavic)* ♂ RATING: ★★☆
Near the woods
People think of Burian as quiet, intelligent, loser, trustworthy, big
People who like the name Burian also like Braden, Balin, Bevan, Aiden, Bryson, Caleb, Burton, Bowen, Brant, Brac

Burke *(French)* ♂ RATING: ★★★★
From the fortress
People think of Burke as handsome, intelligent, powerful, popular, funny
People who like the name Burke also like Braden, Ethan, Cole, Aiden, Caleb, Brice, Holden, Conner, Owen, Landon

Burt *(English)* ♂ RATING: ★☆
Short for names beginning with Burt or ending in -bert; Burt Reynolds, actor
People think of Burt as old-fashioned, lazy, nerdy, old, loser
People who like the name Burt also like Brock, Bradley, Braden, Chad, Adam, Blade, Benjamin, Bradford, Byron, Brad

Burton *(English)* ♂ RATING: ★★★☆
Town of the fortress—Richard Burton, actor
People think of Burton as handsome, funny, creative, intelligent, powerful
People who like the name Burton also like Dalton, Braden, Brice, Chase, Bradley, Caleb, Cole, Byron, Aiden, Dawson

Butch *(American)* ♀ ♂ RATING: ★☆
Manly—Originally a nickname for Butcher
People think of Butch as aggressive, big, criminal, powerful, weird
People who like the name Butch also like Bobby, Bailey, Blake, Bennett, Blaine, Bryce, Brooke, Beckett, Briar, Brooklyn

Buthainah *(Arabic)* ♀ RATING: ★★★
Beautiful woman
People think of Buthainah as pretty, elegant, funny, ethnic, young
People who like the name Buthainah also like Brielle, Chavi, Chantel, Cianna, Cytheria, Callia, Aelwen, Bambi, Basanti, Calandra

Butterfly *(American)* ♀ RATING: ★☆
A butterfly—Butterfly McQueen, actress
People think of Butterfly as pretty, exotic, young, elegant, weird
People who like the name Butterfly also like Blossom, Belle, Faith, Autumn, Abigail, Daisy, Chloe, Amber, Alexa, Destiny

Buzz *(Celtic/Gaelic)* ♂ RATING: ★☆
Village in the woods—Short for Busby; also an American nickname; Buzz Aldrin, astronaut
People think of Buzz as aggressive, weird, wild, big, intelligent

People who like the name Buzz also like Brock, Arthur, Aiden, Brandon, Blade, Breck, Angus, Cole, Alistair, Arlen

Byram *(English)* ♂   RATING: ★★☆
From the barns—Also a surname; variation of Byron
People think of Byram as big, nerdy, sporty, caring, powerful
People who like the name Byram also like Byron, Caleb, Braden, Brice, Brant, Brock, Barclay, Balin, Baxter, Braeden

Byrd *(English)* ♂   RATING: ★★★
Like a bird—Lynda Byrd (Johnson) Robb, daughter of U.S. President Lyndon Johnson
People think of Byrd as funny, weird, intelligent, old, creative
People who like the name Byrd also like Aiden, August, Braeden, Griffin, Cole, Cody, Colt, Brant, Braxton, Brandon

Byrne *(English)* ♂   RATING: ★★★
Son of Brian—Originally an Irish surname
People think of Byrne as intelligent, creative, energetic, cool, funny
People who like the name Byrne also like Byron, Braden, Braeden, Balin, Brice, Bradley, Caleb, Aiden, Brian, Berke

Byron *(English)* ♂   RATING: ★★☆
From the barns—Ada Byron, first computer programmer; Lord Byron, poet
People think of Byron as handsome, intelligent, funny, caring, trustworthy
People who like the name Byron also like Caleb, Aiden, Braden, Ethan, Benjamin, Jacob, Kaden, Aaron, Brice, Alexander

Cable *(American)* ♀♂   RATING: ★★★
Rope
People think of Cable as loser, weird, nerdy, poor, unpopular
People who like the name Cable also like Caden, Cade, Bailey, Blaine, Camden, Carter, Cameron, Blake, Cael, Carson

Cache *(American)* ♀♂   RATING: ★★
Storage place
People think of Cache as cool, funny, exotic, powerful, popular
People who like the name Cache also like Caden, Cade, Bailey, Camden, Cadence, Jaden, Addison, Carter, Avery, Blaine

Cactus *(American)* ♀♂   RATING: ★★★
From the cactus plant
People think of Cactus as weird, loser, unpopular, nerdy, lazy

People who like the name Cactus also like Caden, Bailey, Cade, Calypso, Cameron, Cricket, Blaine, Carter, Capricorn, Cadence

Cade *(English)* ♀♂   RATING: ★★★★
Stout, sturdy—Originally a surname
People think of Cade as handsome, intelligent, funny, popular, cool
People who like the name Cade also like Caden, Hayden, Bailey, Addison, Cadence, Blake, Carter, Jaden, Avery, Aidan

Cadee *(American)* ♀   RATING: ★★★★
Pure—Short for Catherine or Cadence
People think of Cadee as pretty, young, intelligent, popular, funny
People who like the name Cadee also like Cailyn, Cady, Caitlyn, Callie, Chloe, Ava, Bella, Carleigh, Belle, Faith

Cadelaria *(Spanish)* ♀   RATING: ★★☆
Born at Candlemas, the Feast of the Presentation of Christ in the Temple
People think of Cadelaria as exotic, poor, pretty, popular, loser
People who like the name Cadelaria also like Calandra, Catalina, Camelia, Calista, Adalira, Cytheria, Celeste, Calida, Cailyn, Celestyn

Caden *(American)* ♀♂   RATING: ★★★★
Fighter—Also spelled Cayden, Caiden, Kaden, or Cadyn
People think of Caden as handsome, intelligent, energetic, funny, popular
People who like the name Caden also like Hayden, Jaden, Cadence, Addison, Bailey, Brayden, Aidan, Cade, Logan, Madison

Cadence *(Latin)* ♀♂   RATING: ★★★★
Rhythm—Musical term; also spelled Kadence
People think of Cadence as pretty, creative, intelligent, energetic, funny
People who like the name Cadence also like Caden, Addison, Bailey, Hayden, Madison, Jaden, Riley, Cameron, Aidan, Mackenzie

Cadhla *(Celtic/Gaelic)* ♀   RATING: ★★★
Beautiful
People think of Cadhla as exotic, pretty, elegant, unpopular, creative
People who like the name Cadhla also like Aislin, Caia, Caitlin, Cailyn, Cadelaria, Aoife, Carla, Callie, Carina, Aislinn

Cadmus *(Greek)* ♂   RATING: ★★★☆
From the East
People think of Cadmus as intelligent, old-fashioned, ethnic, powerful, leader
People who like the name Cadmus also like Calix, Aiden, Drake, Bade, Caleb, Calder, Ambrose, Braeden, Ciaran, Damien

148

Cady *(American)* ♀ RATING: ★★☆
Pure—Short for Catherine or Cadence
People think of Cady as pretty, funny, popular, caring, cool
People who like the name Cady also like Cailyn, Cadee, Callie, Chloe, Caitlyn, Bella, Grace, Ava, Emma, Hailey

Cael *(Celtic/Gaelic)* ♀♂ RATING: ★★★★☆
Slender
People think of Cael as intelligent, handsome, creative, energetic, powerful
People who like the name Cael also like Caden, Cade, Aidan, Addison, Jaden, Avery, Cadence, Hayden, Connor, Bailey

Caelan *(Celtic/Gaelic)* ♀ RATING: ★★★★☆
Slender lad
People think of Caelan as creative, intelligent, pretty, energetic, funny
People who like the name Caelan also like Cailyn, Kaelyn, Chloe, Ava, Ashlyn, Aeryn, Caitlyn, Jadyn, Paige, Isabella

Caesar *(Latin)* ♂ RATING: ★★
Thick head of hair—Roman Emperors; Gaius Julius Caesar, Roman political leader
People think of Caesar as powerful, leader, handsome, intelligent, cool
People who like the name Caesar also like Adrian, Caleb, Aiden, Aaron, Benjamin, Brandon, Christopher, Elijah, Alexander, Cyrus

Cagney *(Celtic/Gaelic)* ♀♂ RATING: ★★
Unknown meaning—James Cagney, actor
People think of Cagney as intelligent, aggressive, creative, lazy, funny
People who like the name Cagney also like Caden, Bailey, Cadence, Camden, Cassidy, Brayden, Brody, Avery, Delaney, Carter

Cai *(Welsh)* ♀♂ RATING: ★★☆
Rejoice—Short for Caius
People think of Cai as cool, intelligent, caring, creative, funny
People who like the name Cai also like Caden, Kai, Cade, Cael, Cadence, Aidan, Bailey, Jaden, Hayden, Connor

Caia *(Latin)* ♀ RATING: ★★★★☆
To rejoice—Feminine form of Caius
People think of Caia as pretty, exotic, elegant, energetic, popular
People who like the name Caia also like Kaia, Cailyn, Ava, Bella, Caelan, Chloe, Ella, Amaya, Cara, Ciara

Cailean *(Celtic/Gaelic)* ♀♂ RATING: ★★★☆
Whelp
People think of Cailean as pretty, intelligent, caring, funny, popular
People who like the name Cailean also like Caden, Aidan, Cadence, Brayden, Connor, Cael, Caley, Addison, Hayden, Cameron

Cailyn *(American)* ♀ RATING: ★★★★
Pure—Variation of Caitlyn
People think of Cailyn as pretty, funny, creative, caring, intelligent
People who like the name Cailyn also like Kaelyn, Caitlyn, Hailey, Chloe, Ashlyn, Emma, Abigail, Caelan, Ava, Jadyn

Cain *(Hebrew)* ♀♂ RATING: ★★★☆
Craftsman—Also a surname
People think of Cain as handsome, intelligent, aggressive, powerful, cool
People who like the name Cain also like Caden, Cade, Bailey, Jaden, Connor, Blake, Blaine, Carter, Carson, Logan

Caine *(Celtic/Gaelic)* ♂ RATING: ★★★★☆
Son of the fighter
People think of Caine as aggressive, handsome, leader, intelligent, powerful
People who like the name Caine also like Caleb, Aiden, Cole, Aden, Kane, Chase, Gavin, Kaden, Braden, Ethan

Cairbre *(Celtic/Gaelic)* ♂ RATING: ★★★☆
Unknown meaning
People think of Cairbre as handsome, intelligent, trustworthy, creative, popular
People who like the name Cairbre also like Braeden, Ciaran, Callahan, Callum, Aiden, Broderick, Cargan, Cavan, Brennan, Alaric

Cairo *(Arabic)* ♀♂ RATING: ★★★★☆
City in Egypt
People think of Cairo as exotic, creative, powerful, cool, trustworthy
People who like the name Cairo also like Caden, Bailey, Cadence, Brooklyn, Dakota, Cameron, Aidan, Cade, Blake, Camden

Cais *(Vietnamese)* ♀♂ RATING: ★★
Rejoicer—Variation of Caius
People think of Cais as aggressive, big, exotic, slow, lazy
People who like the name Cais also like Caden, Cadence, Cai, Cael, Cade, Cain, Christian, Cailean, Casey, Caley

Caitir *(Celtic/Gaelic)* ♀ RATING: ★★★
Pure—Scottish form of Catherine; pronounced *kotcher*
People think of Caitir as intelligent, creative, old-fashioned, pretty, exotic
People who like the name Caitir also like Caelan, Ceana, Caitlin, Aeryn, Ciara, Caitlyn, Cecelia, Alana, Ailsa, Catriona

Caitlin *(Celtic/Gaelic)* ♀ RATING: ★★★☆
Pure—Irish form of Catherine; pronounced *Cotch-LEEN* in Irish or *KATE-lin* in English
People think of Caitlin as pretty, funny, intelligent, caring, creative
People who like the name Caitlin also like Caitlyn, Kaitlyn, Abigail, Chloe, Hannah, Emily, Grace, Emma, Hailey, Cailyn

Caitlyn *(American)* ♀   RATING: ★★★
Pure—Variation of the Irish name Caitlin
People think of Caitlyn as pretty, funny, caring, intelligent, creative
People who like the name Caitlyn also like Kaitlyn, Cailyn, Abigail, Hailey, Hannah, Chloe, Brianna, Caitlin, Emma, Isabella

Cal *(English)* ♀ ♂   RATING: ★★☆
Short form of names beginning with Cal
People think of Cal as handsome, cool, intelligent, caring, funny
People who like the name Cal also like Caden, Carter, Carson, Cade, Cameron, Bailey, Cooper, Blake, Casey, Cael

Cala *(Sanskrit/East Indian)* ♀   RATING: ★★★☆
Craft, skill—Sometimes pronounced *KAY-la*
People think of Cala as pretty, funny, energetic, creative, caring
People who like the name Cala also like Calla, Cara, Bella, Cailyn, Callie, Chloe, Ava, Ciara, Calista, Caia

Calais *(Greek)* ♀ ♂   RATING: ★★★★
Of changeful hue—Also a city in France
People think of Calais as creative, caring, intelligent, exotic, trustworthy
People who like the name Calais also like Caden, Cadence, Cade, Cael, Blair, Cailean, Calypso, Aidan, Camdyn, Blaine

Calandra *(Greek)* ♀   RATING: ★★☆
Singing bird
People think of Calandra as pretty, caring, intelligent, creative, energetic
People who like the name Calandra also like Calista, Aurora, Cassandra, Chloe, Callista, Calantha, Celeste, Cailyn, Abigail, Carissa

Calantha *(Greek)* ♀   RATING: ★★★★
Like a lovely blossom
People think of Calantha as pretty, exotic, intelligent, elegant, quiet
People who like the name Calantha also like Calandra, Calista, Callista, Callia, Cailyn, Calla, Celestyn, Carina, Calliope, Cassandra

Calder *(Celtic/Gaelic)* ♂   RATING: ★★
From the wild water—Originally an English surname
People think of Calder as handsome, intelligent, funny, creative, caring
People who like the name Calder also like Aiden, Cole, Caleb, Tristan, Cullen, Conner, Callum, Braeden, Asher, Colin

Caldwell *(English)* ♀ ♂   RATING: ★★★☆
From the cold stream—Originally a surname
People think of Caldwell as intelligent, quiet, popular, creative, sporty
People who like the name Caldwell also like Camden, Carter, Caden, Cadence, Carrington, Christian, Carson, Chandler, Corbin, Ainsley

Cale *(American)* ♂   RATING: ★★☆
Rage like a dog—Short for Caleb
People think of Cale as intelligent, handsome, cool, funny, popular
People who like the name Cale also like Caleb, Cole, Aiden, Ethan, Chase, Braden, Kaden, Conner, Gavin, Ian

Caleb *(Hebrew)* ♂   RATING: ★★★☆
Rage like a dog—Also spelled Kaleb
People think of Caleb as handsome, intelligent, funny, caring, cool
People who like the name Caleb also like Ethan, Jacob, Aiden, Noah, Elijah, Benjamin, Cole, Gabriel, Isaac, Kaden

Caley *(Celtic/Gaelic)* ♀ ♂   RATING: ★★★☆
Brave warrior
People think of Caley as pretty, funny, creative, caring, intelligent
People who like the name Caley also like Caden, Bailey, Cadence, Cassidy, Jaden, Madison, Riley, Aidan, Brayden, Casey

Calhoun *(Celtic/Gaelic)* ♂   RATING: ★★★☆
Warrior—Will Calhoun, musician
People think of Calhoun as powerful, intelligent, weird, aggressive, leader
People who like the name Calhoun also like Callahan, Aiden, Callum, Conan, Caleb, Liam, Conner, Ciaran, Braeden, Calder

Calida *(Spanish)* ♀   RATING: ★★★☆
Warm
People think of Calida as caring, pretty, intelligent, girl next door, ethnic
People who like the name Calida also like Calista, Calandra, Callia, Cailyn, Cadee, Adalia, Carminda, Caelan, Carissa, Camelia

California *(Spanish)* ♀   RATING: ★★★
Name of a mythical land—U.S. state
People think of California as pretty, sexy, cool, popular, exotic
People who like the name California also like Hailey, Hannah, Autumn, Candace, Paige, Amber, Charlotte, April, Ava, Cady

Calista *(Greek)* ♀   RATING: ★★★★
Beautiful—Calista Flockhart, actress
People think of Calista as pretty, creative, intelligent, popular, funny
People who like the name Calista also like Chloe, Callista, Celeste, Ava, Cailyn, Kalista, Isabella, Abigail, Bella, Bianca

Calix *(Greek)* ♂   RATING: ★★★★☆
Very handsome
People think of Calix as handsome, intelligent, cool, leader, trustworthy
People who like the name Calix also like Aiden, Caleb, Aden, Tristan, Kaden, Damien, Cole, Cale, Braden, Braeden

150

Calixte *(Greek)* ♀ RATING: ★★★★
Very beautiful—Variation of Callista
People think of Calixte as exotic, pretty, intelligent, funny, popular
People who like the name Calixte also like Calista, Callista, Calliope, Caelan, Callia, Callie, Cailyn, Calla, Calandra, Cytheria

Calla *(Greek)* ♀ RATING: ★★★★
Beauty—Short for Callista
People think of Calla as pretty, creative, caring, intelligent, funny
People who like the name Calla also like Callie, Ava, Ella, Callia, Bella, Chloe, Grace, Cailyn, Calista, Cora

Callahan *(Celtic/Gaelic)* ♂ RATING: ★★★★
Little cell
People think of Callahan as sporty, leader, popular, handsome, cool
People who like the name Callahan also like Aiden, Caleb, Aden, Callum, Calder, Cole, Calhoun, Keagan, Cullen, Liam

Callia *(Greek)* ♀ RATING: ★★★★☆
Beautiful—Variation of Callista
People think of Callia as pretty, caring, intelligent, creative, elegant
People who like the name Callia also like Cailyn, Callie, Calista, Chloe, Calla, Ava, Bella, Ella, Caelan, Emma

Callie *(Greek)* ♀ RATING: ★★★
Beautiful—Short for Calista
People think of Callie as pretty, funny, creative, caring, intelligent
People who like the name Callie also like Chloe, Ava, Hailey, Emma, Hannah, Cailyn, Abigail, Bella, Grace, Isabella

Calliope *(Greek)* ♀ RATING: ★★★☆
Fair face—Also a musical instrument on a merry-go-round
People think of Calliope as pretty, creative, funny, intelligent, elegant
People who like the name Calliope also like Chloe, Cassandra, Calista, Aurora, Penelope, Callista, Camille, Arwen, Charlotte, Daphne

Callista *(Greek)* ♀ RATING: ★★★★☆
Most beautiful—Also spelled Calista; Calista Flockhart, actress
People think of Callista as pretty, elegant, intelligent, creative, popular
People who like the name Callista also like Calista, Chloe, Abigail, Cailyn, Isabella, Ava, Aurora, Faith, Kalista, Hailey

Callum *(Celtic/Gaelic)* ♂ RATING: ★★★★
Dove—Callum Keith Rennie, actor
People think of Callum as handsome, funny, intelligent, cool, caring
People who like the name Callum also like Caleb, Liam, Aiden, Ethan, Owen, Jack, Noah, Joshua, Aaron, Conner

Calum *(Celtic/Gaelic)* ♂ RATING: ★★★★
Dove
People think of Calum as handsome, cool, intelligent, funny, caring
People who like the name Calum also like Caleb, Callum, Aiden, Liam, Conner, Ethan, Cole, Braeden, Jack, Kaden

Calvin *(Latin)* ♂ RATING: ★★☆
Bald—Calvin Klein, fashion designer
People think of Calvin as intelligent, funny, handsome, caring, cool
People who like the name Calvin also like Caleb, Ethan, Gavin, Jacob, Nathan, Cody, Cole, Alexander, Benjamin, Isaac

Calvine *(Latin)* ♀ RATING: ★★☆
Bald—Feminine form of Calvin
People think of Calvine as weird, big, loser, girl next door, wealthy
People who like the name Calvine also like Calista, Callista, Caitlyn, Calixte, Carolina, Camelia, Cailyn, Charity, Caia, Cambree

Calypso *(Greek)* ♀♂ RATING: ★★★★
Hidden—Also a form of music/dance
People think of Calypso as exotic, pretty, creative, sexy, intelligent
People who like the name Calypso also like Caden, Cadence, Cassidy, Bailey, Azure, Blaine, Ceres, Aidan, Blake, Artemis

Cam *(Celtic/Gaelic)* ♀♂ RATING: ★★★☆
Short for names beginning with Cam
People think of Cam as cool, handsome, funny, intelligent, popular
People who like the name Cam also like Cameron, Caden, Camden, Cade, Brody, Carter, Camryn, Bailey, Connor, Cadence

Cambree *(American)* ♀ RATING: ★★★★☆
From Wales—Variation of the name Cambria
People think of Cambree as pretty, popular, energetic, creative, trendy
People who like the name Cambree also like Cambria, Bella, Chloe, Ashlyn, Cailyn, Faith, Emma, Carleigh, Ava, Callie

Cambria *(Latin)* ♀ RATING: ★★★★
From Wales
People think of Cambria as pretty, creative, funny, caring, popular
People who like the name Cambria also like Cambree, Chloe, Ava, Bianca, Cailyn, Bella, Caelan, Aurora, Isabella, Celeste

Camden *(English)* ♀♂ RATING: ★★★★
From the valley of the camps
People think of Camden as intelligent, handsome, funny, popular, energetic
People who like the name Camden also like Caden, Cameron, Hayden, Addison, Carson, Cadence, Carter, Bailey, Jaden, Avery

Camdyn *(English)* ♀♂ RATING: ★★★★☆
From the valley of the camps
> People think of Camdyn as popular, energetic, pretty, creative, cool
> People who like the name Camdyn also like Caden, Cadence, Camden, Bailey, Hayden, Brayden, Addison, Camryn, Cameron, Avery

Camelia *(Latin)* ♀ RATING: ★★★★
Young, virginal
> People think of Camelia as pretty, creative, funny, intelligent, sexy
> People who like the name Camelia also like Amelia, Camille, Camilla, Cailyn, Abigail, Chloe, Celeste, Cassandra, Ava, Bella

Cameo *(Greek)* ♀♂ RATING: ★★★★
Shadow portrait
> People think of Cameo as exotic, pretty, creative, artsy, caring
> People who like the name Cameo also like Cameron, Caden, Cassidy, Cade, Cadence, Calypso, Bailey, Casey, Blake, Artemis

Cameron *(Celtic/Gaelic)* ♀♂ RATING: ★★★☆
Bent nose—Cameron Crowe, director; Cameron Diaz, actress; James Cameron, director; Kirk Cameron, actor
> People think of Cameron as funny, handsome, intelligent, cool, caring
> People who like the name Cameron also like Madison, Caden, Connor, Logan, Bailey, Hayden, Dylan, Riley, Taylor, Addison

Camila *(Italian)* ♀ RATING: ★★☆
Perfect—Variation of Camilla
> People think of Camila as pretty, intelligent, funny, creative, cool
> People who like the name Camila also like Camilla, Isabella, Camille, Camelia, Cassandra, Arianna, Callie, Emma, Amelia, Charlotte

Camilla *(Italian)* ♀ RATING: ★★☆
Perfect—Camilla Mountbatten-Windsor, the Duchess of Cornwall
> People think of Camilla as pretty, intelligent, caring, funny, creative
> People who like the name Camilla also like Camille, Isabella, Ava, Bella, Chloe, Amelia, Bianca, Charlotte, Gabriella, Emma

Camille *(French)* ♀ RATING: ★★★☆
Perfect
> People think of Camille as pretty, funny, intelligent, creative, caring
> People who like the name Camille also like Chloe, Ava, Olivia, Claire, Abigail, Amelia, Charlotte, Isabella, Camilla, Hannah

Camisha *(American)* ♀ RATING: ★★★☆
Combination of Camilla and Alisha
> People think of Camisha as pretty, funny, caring, cool, popular

People who like the name Camisha also like Camille, Aaliyah, Calista, Cailyn, Camelia, Canika, Cassandra, Ciara, Carissa, Callista

Campbell *(Celtic/Gaelic)* ♀♂ RATING: ★★★☆
Crooked mouth—Campbell Scott, actor; Glen Campbell, singer
> People think of Campbell as intelligent, funny, cool, creative, energetic
> People who like the name Campbell also like Addison, Cameron, Bailey, Avery, Carter, Carson, Caden, Cooper, Camden, Riley

Camryn *(American)* ♀♂ RATING: ★★★★
Bent nose—Variation of Cameron; Camryn Manheim, actress
> People think of Camryn as pretty, funny, popular, creative, energetic
> People who like the name Camryn also like Cameron, Caden, Bailey, Addison, Hayden, Cadence, Madison, Avery, Camdyn, Logan

Can *(Turkish)* ♂ RATING: ★★★☆
Life, soul
> People think of Can as exotic, sexy, young, weird, creative
> People who like the name Can also like Cale, Caleb, Conner, Carlos, Callum, Caradoc, Calum, Brant, Cavan, Colt

Canan *(Turkish)* ♀ RATING: ★★★☆
Beloved
> People think of Canan as pretty, sexy, aggressive, powerful, cool
> People who like the name Canan also like Caelan, Cailyn, Calla, Celeste, Callie, Ava, Cadee, Carys, Bella, Chloe

Candace *(English)* ♀ RATING: ★★★☆
Queen of Ethiopia—Variation of Candice; Candace Cameron, actress
> People think of Candace as pretty, funny, caring, intelligent, trustworthy
> People who like the name Candace also like Chloe, Faith, Caitlyn, Hailey, Hannah, Cassandra, Abigail, Grace, Candice, Brianna

Candelaria *(Spanish)* ♀ RATING: ★★☆
Candle
> People think of Candelaria as intelligent, pretty, funny, trustworthy, creative
> People who like the name Candelaria also like Cadelaria, Calandra, Calla, Carminda, Carlota, Calida, Celerina, Callista, Calista, Cassandra

Candice *(Greek)* ♀ RATING: ★★☆
Queen of Ethiopia—Variation of Candace; Candice Bergen, actress
> People think of Candice as pretty, funny, caring, creative, intelligent
> People who like the name Candice also like Faith, Hailey, Chloe, Abigail, Candace, Caitlyn, Amber, Bianca, Cassandra, Isabella

Candid (*American*) ♀♂   RATING: ★★☆
White or hidden—Short for Candide
> People think of Candid as caring, artsy, pretty, cool, exotic
> People who like the name Candid also like Caden, Casey, Cadence, Cassidy, Carter, Camdyn, Cade, Chandler, Camryn, Cameron

Candida (*Latin*) ♀   RATING: ★★★☆
White
> People think of Candida as trustworthy, pretty, aggressive, funny, caring
> People who like the name Candida also like Cambria, Camilla, Clarissa, Chloe, Celeste, Cara, Claudia, Carla, Cassandra, Bianca

Candide (*French*) ♀♂   RATING: ★★★
White—Opera by Leonard Bernstein, based on a novel by Voltaire; originally a male name, used more frequently in modern times for females
> People think of Candide as funny, weird, creative, artsy, cool
> People who like the name Candide also like Carmen, Cadence, Cassidy, Carey, Carter, Carlin, Caley, Caden, Courtney, Casey

Candie (*American*) ♀   RATING: ★★★☆
Bright, sweet—Short for Candace or Candice; "Candies" brand shoes
> People think of Candie as pretty, funny, popular, trendy, cool
> People who like the name Candie also like Cassandra, Callie, Candy, Cailyn, Amber, Belle, Chloe, Carrie, Cassie, Bella

Candra (*Greek*) ♀   RATING: ★★★★
Combination of Candice and Sandra—Also variation of Candace
> People think of Candra as pretty, funny, sexy, intelligent, leader
> People who like the name Candra also like Cailyn, Carissa, Candace, Calista, Cassandra, Cambree, Calandra, Chloe, Celeste, Caressa

Candy (*American*) ♀   RATING: ★★
Bright, sweet—Short for Candace or Candice
> People think of Candy as pretty, funny, sexy, popular, cool
> People who like the name Candy also like Amber, Faith, Candace, Hailey, Cassandra, Chelsea, April, Amanda, Chloe, Caitlyn

Canika (*American*) ♀   RATING: ★★★
Combination of Candice and Annika
> People think of Canika as exotic, sexy, ethnic, pretty, poor
> People who like the name Canika also like Cailyn, Camisha, Cara, Calista, Cayla, Caelan, Chloe, Carissa, Cadee, Carina

Canon (*English*) ♂   RATING: ★★★★
Clergyman—Also a musical round; also an electronics manufacturer
> People think of Canon as handsome, powerful, energetic, intelligent, sporty
> People who like the name Canon also like Kaden, Braden, Aiden, Conner, Colton, Caleb, Colin, Cole, Chase, Ethan

Canta (*Latin*) ♀   RATING: ★★☆
Song
> People think of Canta as pretty, elegant, artsy, weird, creative
> People who like the name Canta also like Celeste, Camelia, Ceana, Cara, Catrin, Celina, Celestyn, Caroline, Cailyn, Ceri

Cantara (*Latin*) ♀   RATING: ★★☆
Small bridge
> People think of Cantara as exotic, pretty, artsy, caring, girl next door
> People who like the name Cantara also like Cadee, Catalina, Chloe, Ceana, Cailyn, Celeste, Cassandra, Cassara, Calandra, Carina

Canute (*Scandinavian*) ♂   RATING: ★★☆
Knot—Variation of Knute
> People think of Canute as big, quiet, ethnic, loser, unpopular
> People who like the name Canute also like Caleb, Cale, Aiden, Calder, Beau, Crevan, Cassius, Brennan, Caine, Carver

Caolan (*Celtic/Gaelic*) ♂   RATING: ★★
Slender lad—Variation of Caelan
> People think of Caolan as handsome, intelligent, caring, cool, funny
> People who like the name Caolan also like Callum, Calder, Cole, Cavan, Aiden, Cian, Braeden, Cargan, Caine, Cullen

Caprice (*French*) ♀   RATING: ★★
Impulsive, whimsical—Caprice, model
> People think of Caprice as pretty, creative, sexy, caring, funny
> People who like the name Caprice also like Chloe, Celeste, Calista, Aurora, Ava, Charlotte, Bianca, Belle, Claire, Bella

Capricorn (*Latin*) ♀♂   RATING: ★☆
The goat—Used for children born under this astrological sign
> People think of Capricorn as intelligent, powerful, aggressive, exotic, weird
> People who like the name Capricorn also like Bailey, Caden, Brooke, Aquarius, Calypso, Casey, Cameron, Carson, Cassidy, Blake

Capucine (*French*) ♀   RATING: ★★☆
Hood
> People think of Capucine as elegant, pretty, exotic, weird, creative

People who like the name Capucine also like Caprice, Cayenne, Candace, Camille, Cosette, Cerise, Brielle, Cecile, Celine, Cassara

Cara *(Italian)* ♀   RATING: ★★★☆
Dear
People think of Cara as pretty, funny, caring, creative, intelligent
People who like the name Cara also like Chloe, Ava, Claire, Emma, Cailyn, Grace, Hannah, Bella, Isabella, Kara

Caradoc *(Welsh)* ♂   RATING: ★★★
Beloved
People think of Caradoc as handsome, intelligent, powerful, leader, elegant
People who like the name Caradoc also like Calix, Cale, Callum, Caleb, Braden, Calder, Aiden, Braeden, Bairn, Cadmus

Caraf *(Welsh)* ♀   RATING: ★☆
I love
People think of Caraf as caring, energetic, quiet, old-fashioned, funny
People who like the name Caraf also like Ceri, Carys, Calixte, Cambria, Caelan, Caron, Calista, Ciel, Ceridwen, Crwys

Cardea *(Greek)* ♀   RATING: ★★★
Goddess of protecting the home
People think of Cardea as pretty, ethnic, old-fashioned, wealthy, trendy
People who like the name Cardea also like Calista, Chandra, Cytheria, Cailyn, Calandra, Calantha, Ciara, Carina, Calixte, Caia

Caressa *(American)* ♀   RATING: ★★☆
Loving touch
People think of Caressa as pretty, caring, creative, funny, sexy
People who like the name Caressa also like Carissa, Cailyn, Bella, Faith, Belle, Calista, Charissa, Clarissa, Hailey, Chloe

Caresse *(American)* ♀   RATING: ★★★★
Beloved—From the French word *caress*
People think of Caresse as caring, pretty, sexy, cool, elegant
People who like the name Caresse also like Caressa, Cailyn, Belle, Calista, Carissa, Charity, Aurora, Cassandra, Chloe, Callista

Carey *(Celtic/Gaelic)* ♀♂   RATING: ★★★☆
Pure—MacDonald Carey, actor
People think of Carey as caring, intelligent, funny, trustworthy, creative
People who like the name Carey also like Casey, Bailey, Caley, Caden, Cassidy, Cameron, Brooke, Blair, Connor, Carson

Cargan *(Celtic/Gaelic)* ♂   RATING: ★★★
Little rock
People think of Cargan as intelligent, sexy, trendy, wealthy, creative
People who like the name Cargan also like Braeden, Aden, Caleb, Aiden, Cavan, Conlan, Keagan, Conley, Ciaran, Calder

Cariad *(Welsh)* ♀♂   RATING: ★★★
Love
People think of Cariad as handsome, exotic, caring, cool, ethnic
People who like the name Cariad also like Carman, Cache, Camden, Carey, Cain, Casey, Caley, Alec, Camryn, Caldwell

Carina *(Greek)* ♀   RATING: ★★★★
Dear one—Variation of Cara
People think of Carina as pretty, caring, funny, intelligent, creative
People who like the name Carina also like Carissa, Cailyn, Isabella, Chloe, Bianca, Cassandra, Cara, Ava, Hannah, Bella

Carissa *(American)* ♀   RATING: ★★★
Combination of Carrie and Alissa
People think of Carissa as pretty, funny, caring, creative, intelligent
People who like the name Carissa also like Caitlyn, Cailyn, Chloe, Clarissa, Hailey, Alyssa, Hannah, Cassandra, Isabella, Abigail

Carl *(German)* ♂   RATING: ★★
Manly—Carl Lewis, athlete
People think of Carl as funny, handsome, intelligent, caring, cool
People who like the name Carl also like Chad, Adam, Aaron, Caleb, Daniel, Charles, Christopher, Anthony, Ethan, Brian

Carla *(Italian)* ♀   RATING: ★★★★
Free—Feminine form of Charles; Carla Gugino, actress
People think of Carla as pretty, caring, funny, intelligent, creative
People who like the name Carla also like Caitlyn, Chloe, Cara, Carly, Claire, Bianca, Emma, Cassandra, Chelsea, Cailyn

Carleigh *(English)* ♀   RATING: ★★★★
Feminine form of Charles
People think of Carleigh as pretty, energetic, funny, creative, popular
People who like the name Carleigh also like Cailyn, Chloe, Hailey, Caitlyn, Abigail, Ashlyn, Paige, Ava, Carly, Faith

Carlen *(Celtic/Gaelic)* ♀♂   RATING: ★★★☆
From Carlin-Champion
People think of Carlen as funny, pretty, creative, popular, caring
People who like the name Carlen also like Caden, Carlin, Cameron, Cadence, Carter, Camdyn, Carson, Brayden, Aidan, Camden

Carlin (*Celtic/Gaelic*) ♀♂   RATING: ★★★★☆

Little champion—George Carlin, comedian

People think of Carlin as funny, creative, caring, trust-worthy, intelligent

People who like the name Carlin also like Caden, Cadence, Cameron, Connor, Caley, Carson, Cassidy, Bailey, Carter, Camdyn

Carlina (*Italian*) ♀   RATING: ★★★

Free—Variation of Carla

People think of Carlina as pretty, caring, funny, creative, cool

People who like the name Carlina also like Carla, Cara, Isabella, Bianca, Cailyn, Angelina, Carina, Cassandra, Gabriella, Cassara

Carlos (*Spanish*) ♂   RATING: ★★★☆

Free man—Variation of Charles; Carlos Santana, musician

People think of Carlos as handsome, cool, funny, intel-ligent, caring

People who like the name Carlos also like Anthony, Antonio, Adrian, Caleb, Diego, Benjamin, Gabriel, Andrew, Alejandro, David

Carlota (*Spanish*) ♀   RATING: ★★

Free—Feminine form of Charles

People think of Carlota as exotic, old, loser, aggressive, cool

People who like the name Carlota also like Carolina, Celeste, Carmelita, Gabriella, Caroline, Camille, Carminda, Isabella, Carla, Calista

Carlotta (*Italian*) ♀   RATING: ★★

Free—Feminine form of Charles

People think of Carlotta as pretty, energetic, sexy, exotic, creative

People who like the name Carlotta also like Camilla, Isabella, Arabella, Angelina, Charlotte, Cassandra, Aurora, Bianca, Bella, Anastasia

Carlow (*Celtic/Gaelic*) ♂   RATING: ★★

Quadruple lake—Irish place name

People think of Carlow as leader, intelligent, cool, quiet, creative

People who like the name Carlow also like Aiden, Callum, Cavan, Calix, Bowie, Braeden, Caleb, Calder, Cole, Conley

Carlton (*English*) ♂   RATING: ★★★☆

From the town of the Free Men

People think of Carlton as intelligent, handsome, cool, caring, trustworthy

People who like the name Carlton also like Caleb, Cole, Conner, Bradley, Chase, Clayton, Chad, Dalton, Cody, Benjamin

Carly (*American*) ♀   RATING: ★★★

Short for Carlotta—Also spelled Carley; Carly Simon, singer/songwriter

People think of Carly as pretty, funny, caring, creative, energetic

People who like the name Carly also like Emma, Chloe, Ava, Emily, Hailey, Hannah, Claire, Paige, Callie, Cailyn

Carlyn (*Greek*) ♀   RATING: ★★★★

Variation of Caroline

People think of Carlyn as pretty, funny, caring, popular, cool

People who like the name Carlyn also like Cailyn, Chloe, Carleigh, Carly, Callie, Caitlyn, Ava, Faith, Ashlyn, Grace

Carlynda (*American*) ♀   RATING: ★★★

Combination of Carla and Linda

People think of Carlynda as elegant, old, artsy, loser, girl next door

People who like the name Carlynda also like Cailyn, Carissa, Carleigh, Cassara, Cara, Carly, Calista, Caitlyn, Celeste, Candace

Carman (*English*) ♀♂   RATING: ★★★☆

Man—Originally a surname

People think of Carman as funny, creative, sexy, cool, popular

People who like the name Carman also like Cameron, Carmen, Caden, Bailey, Cadence, Camryn, Casey, Camden, Carson, Jaden

Carmel (*Hebrew*) ♀   RATING: ★★★

Vineyard of God

People think of Carmel as pretty, funny, caring, creative, popular

People who like the name Carmel also like Carmela, Isabella, Amber, Carissa, Cassie, Cassandra, Carmelita, Aaliyah, Cadee, Mia

Carmela (*Hebrew*) ♀   RATING: ★★★☆

Garden

People think of Carmela as pretty, caring, intelligent, creative, funny

People who like the name Carmela also like Camille, Bianca, Cassandra, Ava, Camilla, Chloe, Isabella, Celeste, Carissa, Carina

Carmelita (*Spanish*) ♀   RATING: ★★★☆

Little poem—Diminutive form of Carmen

People think of Carmelita as pretty, caring, funny, young, cool

People who like the name Carmelita also like Catalina, Camelia, Calista, Carmela, Cailyn, Camille, Callista, Celeste, Carissa, Camilla

Carmen (*Latin*) ♀♂   RATING: ★★★★☆

Poem—*Carmen*, opera by Bizet; Carmen Miranda, singer/actress; Carmen Rasmusen, singer

People think of Carmen as pretty, funny, caring, cre-ative, intelligent

People who like the name Carmen also like Cameron, Bailey, Cadence, Caden, Brooke, Dakota, Hayden, Madison, Carter, Carson

Carminda (*Spanish*) ♀   RATING: ★★★☆

Combination of Carmen and Linda

People think of Carminda as pretty, popular, creative, cool, funny

People who like the name Carminda also like Celeste, Carmelita, Catalina, Calida, Belita, Chandra, Bella, Cassara, Carina, Adrienne

Carmine *(Italian)* ♂ RATING: ★★☆
Song
People think of Carmine as handsome, intelligent, sexy, popular, powerful
People who like the name Carmine also like Caleb, Aiden, Jayden, Chase, Anthony, Gabriel, Dominic, Tristan, Giovanni, Nicholas

Carnig *(Armenian)* ♂ RATING: ★☆
Small lamb
People think of Carnig as weird, quiet, popular, young, sporty
People who like the name Carnig also like Cavan, Caleb, Cale, Callum, Casimir, Calix, Calum, Conley, Brone, Conlan

Carol *(English)* ♀♂ RATING: ★★☆
Variation of Charles—Also a song; also spelled Carole; Carol Burnett, comedian; Carole Lombard, actress
People think of Carol as caring, funny, intelligent, trustworthy, pretty
People who like the name Carol also like Ashley, Cameron, Cassidy, Casey, Brooke, Courtney, Bailey, Caden, Carson, Blair

Carolena *(American)* ♀ RATING: ★★★★
Feminine form of Charles
People think of Carolena as creative, caring, intelligent, pretty, funny
People who like the name Carolena also like Isabella, Angelina, Camilla, Gabriella, Cianna, Adriana, Charlotte, Cassandra, Abigail, Carina

Carolina *(German)* ♀ RATING: ★★☆
Feminine form of Charles
People think of Carolina as pretty, funny, caring, intelligent, cool
People who like the name Carolina also like Caroline, Isabella, Ava, Hannah, Bella, Abigail, Amelia, Charlotte, Olivia, Chloe

Caroline *(Latin)* ♀ RATING: ★★★
Beautiful woman—Feminine form of Charles; Caroline Kennedy, daughter of U.S. President John F. Kennedy
People think of Caroline as pretty, funny, caring, intelligent, creative
People who like the name Caroline also like Charlotte, Abigail, Ava, Emma, Claire, Grace, Olivia, Hannah, Elizabeth, Audrey

Carolos *(Greek)* ♂ RATING: ★☆
Strong, manly
People think of Carolos as handsome, creative, trustworthy, popular, funny
People who like the name Carolos also like Cole, Calix, Caleb, Cody, Brandon, Aden, Adrian, Chance, Anthony, Charles

Carolyn *(English)* ♀ RATING: ★★★☆
Little womanly one
People think of Carolyn as caring, pretty, intelligent, funny, creative
People who like the name Carolyn also like Caroline, Claire, Grace, Hannah, Abigail, Chloe, Charlotte, Emma, Caitlyn, Emily

Caron *(Welsh)* ♀ RATING: ★★★★
Loving, kind—Leslie Caron, actress
People think of Caron as caring, trustworthy, intelligent, pretty, quiet
People who like the name Caron also like Ceana, Carys, Caelan, Cara, Celeste, Chloe, Ceri, Catrin, Cambria, Calista

Caroun *(Armenian)* ♀ RATING: ★★☆
Spring
People think of Caroun as leader, powerful, wealthy, young, popular
People who like the name Caroun also like Cascata, Creda, Celestyn, Carys, Calista, Cassara, Chava, Cleo, Celia, Camelia

Carr *(Celtic/Gaelic)* ♂ RATING: ★★☆
Marshland
People think of Carr as energetic, popular, weird, creative, intelligent
People who like the name Carr also like Cole, Conner, Cavan, Caleb, Callum, Ciaran, Braeden, Calder, Brandon, Aiden

Carrie *(American)* ♀ RATING: ★★☆
Short for names beginning with Car—Carrie Underwood, singer; Carrie Fisher, actress/writer; *Carrie*, novel and movie by Steven King
People think of Carrie as caring, pretty, funny, creative, intelligent
People who like the name Carrie also like Emma, Chloe, Emily, Caitlyn, Hannah, Hailey, Amber, Carly, Callie, Cassie

Carrington *(English)* ♀♂ RATING: ★★★★
Town of the Marsh—Family on the TV show *Dynasty*
People think of Carrington as intelligent, pretty, caring, popular, funny
People who like the name Carrington also like Caden, Carter, Addison, Hayden, Bailey, Carson, Cadence, Avery, Cameron, Chandler

Carson *(American)* ♀♂ RATING: ★★★★
Christian—A surname probably from Karsten; Carson Daly, TV host
People think of Carson as funny, handsome, popular, intelligent, cool
People who like the name Carson also like Carter, Caden, Cameron, Addison, Bailey, Hayden, Connor, Parker, Logan, Mason

Carsten *(German)* ♂ RATING: ★★★★
Christian
People think of Carsten as intelligent, handsome, creative, cool, caring

People who like the name Carsten also like Braden, Kaden, Caleb, Ethan, Jackson, Aiden, Conner, Dawson, Tristan, Colton

Carsyn (*American*) ♀ ♂   RATING: ★★★★
Variation of Carson
People think of Carsyn as funny, popular, pretty, intelligent, sporty
People who like the name Carsyn also like Caden, Carson, Carter, Addison, Camdyn, Bailey, Camryn, Brayden, Hayden, Cadence

Carter (*English*) ♀ ♂   RATING: ★★★☆
Driver of a cart—Jimmy Carter, U.S. president; Aaron and Nick Carter, singers
People think of Carter as handsome, intelligent, funny, popular, leader
People who like the name Carter also like Carson, Caden, Parker, Hayden, Connor, Bailey, Cameron, Addison, Logan, Avery

Carver (*English*) ♂   RATING: ★★☆
Wood carver—George Washington Carver, scientist
People think of Carver as handsome, popular, intelligent, cool, caring
People who like the name Carver also like Caleb, Conner, Chase, Braden, Cole, Aiden, Dawson, Kaden, Clayton, Chance

Cary (*English*) ♀ ♂   RATING: ★★★☆
Pure—Variation of Carey; Cary Grant, actor
People think of Cary as intelligent, caring, funny, handsome, cool
People who like the name Cary also like Casey, Carey, Caden, Carter, Connor, Caley, Cassidy, Cameron, Carson, Camden

Carys (*Welsh*) ♀   RATING: ★★★☆
To love
People think of Carys as pretty, intelligent, creative, caring, funny
People who like the name Carys also like Ava, Olivia, Charlotte, Chloe, Ella, Grace, Emma, Amelia, Bella, Claire

Cascada (*Spanish*) ♀   RATING: ★★★☆
Waterfall
People think of Cascada as exotic, pretty, cool, elegant, sexy
People who like the name Cascada also like Cassandra, Bianca, Calista, Celeste, Cassia, Belle, Charisma, Catalina, Candace, Ceana

Cascata (*Italian*) ♀   RATING: ★☆
Waterfall
People think of Cascata as exotic, elegant, intelligent, creative, powerful
People who like the name Cascata also like Calista, Camilla, Cianna, Celeste, Cira, Catalina, Carlotta, Aria, Arabella, Candace

Casey (*Celtic/Gaelic*) ♀ ♂   RATING: ★★★★
Vigilant in war—Also an Irish surname; also spelled Kasey; "Casey at the Bat," famous poem; Casey Kasim, voiceover personality
People think of Casey as funny, caring, intelligent, cool, pretty
People who like the name Casey also like Bailey, Caden, Cameron, Riley, Connor, Dylan, Logan, Cassidy, Hayden, Brooke

Cashlin (*English*) ♀   RATING: ★★★☆
Vain—Combination of Cash and Linda
People think of Cashlin as trendy, popular, pretty, poor, sexy
People who like the name Cashlin also like Carleigh, Ashlyn, Cailyn, Cambree, Chloe, Cadee, Jadyn, Celeste, Emma, Bella

Casimir (*Slavic*) ♂   RATING: ★★★★
Destroys peace
People think of Casimir as intelligent, handsome, sexy, cool, exotic
People who like the name Casimir also like Caleb, Calix, Aiden, Braeden, Calder, Cassius, Cedric, Elijah, Brennan, Braden

Caspar (*German*) ♂   RATING: ★★
Treasurer—From the same origin as Jasper
People think of Caspar as quiet, intelligent, funny, caring, handsome
People who like the name Caspar also like Caleb, Casper, Benjamin, Chad, Cole, Jacob, Alexander, Chance, Isaac, Noah

Casper (*German*) ♂   RATING: ★★
Treasurer—From the same origin as Jasper; *Casper the Friendly Ghost*, cartoon; Casper Weinberger, former U.S. secretary of defense
People think of Casper as intelligent, handsome, caring, young, creative
People who like the name Casper also like Caleb, Jasper, Chase, Benjamin, Sebastian, Ethan, Aiden, Cole, Oliver, Alexander

Caspian (*English*) ♂   RATING: ★★★
Of the Caspy People—From the Caspian Sea; *Prince Caspian*, novel by C. S. Lewis
People think of Caspian as powerful, leader, intelligent, trustworthy, handsome
People who like the name Caspian also like Tristan, Adrian, Caleb, Silas, Alexander, Sebastian, Cedric, Gabriel, Calix, Alastair

Cassandra (*Greek*) ♀   RATING: ★★★
She who entangles men—Shakespeare character in *Troilus and Cressida*
People think of Cassandra as pretty, funny, intelligent, caring, creative
People who like the name Cassandra also like Abigail, Isabella, Chloe, Hannah, Alexandra, Emma, Brianna, Gabrielle, Hailey, Caitlyn

Cassara (*American*) ♀   RATING: ★★☆
Combination of Cass and Ara
> People think of Cassara as pretty, intelligent, elegant, exotic, caring
> People who like the name Cassara also like Cailyn, Carissa, Cassandra, Cara, Chloe, Bella, Cianna, Celeste, Chailyn, Abrianna

Cassia (*Greek*) ♀   RATING: ★★★★☆
Cinnamon
> People think of Cassia as creative, pretty, intelligent, elegant, caring
> People who like the name Cassia also like Cassandra, Ava, Chloe, Cailyn, Callie, Celeste, Alexia, Aurora, Bella, Calista

Cassidy (*Celtic/Gaelic*) ♀ ♂   RATING: ★★★
Curly haired—Cassidy, MTV VJ; David Cassidy, singer/actor
> People think of Cassidy as pretty, funny, intelligent, creative, popular
> People who like the name Cassidy also like Bailey, Cadence, Caden, Cameron, Madison, Addison, Mackenzie, Hayden, Avery, Connor

Cassie (*English*) ♀   RATING: ★★★☆
Short for Cassandra
> People think of Cassie as pretty, funny, caring, creative, intelligent
> People who like the name Cassie also like Callie, Hailey, Cassandra, Chloe, Emma, Hannah, Caitlyn, Abigail, Faith, Claire

Cassius (*Latin*) ♂   RATING: ★★★☆
Vain—Cassius Clay (aka Muhammad Ali), boxer
> People think of Cassius as powerful, intelligent, handsome, popular, aggressive
> People who like the name Cassius also like Caleb, Gabriel, Aiden, Alexander, Sebastian, Gavin, Braeden, Cyrus, Atticus, Cole

Casta (*Spanish*) ♂   RATING: ★★
Pure—Variation of Catherine; also short for Jocasta, meaning shining moon
> People think of Casta as artsy, pretty, sexy, exotic, caring
> People who like the name Casta also like Caleb, Calix, Cale, Callum, Alejandro, Cassius, Ceallach, Casper, Barto, Braeden

Castel (*Spanish*) ♀ ♂   RATING: ★★
To the castle
> People think of Castel as handsome, intelligent, funny, caring, winner
> People who like the name Castel also like Caden, Cadence, Cade, Carrington, Cassidy, Cairo, Carman, Camden, Aubrey, Brooklyn

Catalin (*Spanish*) ♀   RATING: ★★★
Pure—Variation of Catherine
> People think of Catalin as pretty, popular, young, girl next door, funny
> People who like the name Catalin also like Cailyn, Caitlyn, Chloe, Celeste, Catalina, Cassandra, Isabella, Caitlin, Candace, Faith

Catalina (*Spanish*) ♀   RATING: ★★★★
Pure—Island off the shore of Los Angeles
> People think of Catalina as pretty, creative, caring, funny, intelligent
> People who like the name Catalina also like Isabella, Cassandra, Adriana, Bianca, Angelina, Chloe, Gabriella, Celeste, Calista, Cailyn

Cate (*English*) ♀   RATING: ★★★★
Short for Catherine—Cate Blanchett, actress
> People think of Cate as creative, funny, intelligent, pretty, caring
> People who like the name Cate also like Ava, Kate, Chloe, Claire, Ella, Grace, Catherine, Charlotte, Bella, Olivia

Cathal (*Celtic/Gaelic*) ♂   RATING: ★☆
Strong in battle—Pronounced *Ko-HAL* in Irish
> People think of Cathal as leader, powerful, trustworthy, energetic, handsome
> People who like the name Cathal also like Callum, Aiden, Cian, Crevan, Faolan, Ciaran, Calhoun, Cormac, Calder, Cavan

Catherine (*Greek*) ♀   RATING: ★★★
Pure—Also spelled Katherine; Catherine the Great, Russian empress; Catherine Keener, actress; Catherine Zeta-Jones, actress
> People think of Catherine as pretty, funny, intelligent, caring, creative
> People who like the name Catherine also like Elizabeth, Emma, Abigail, Grace, Charlotte, Hannah, Claire, Caroline, Emily, Isabella

Cathleen (*Celtic/Gaelic*) ♀   RATING: ★★★☆
Pure—Variation of Kathleen
> People think of Cathleen as pretty, funny, intelligent, caring, trustworthy
> People who like the name Cathleen also like Catherine, Caitlyn, Hannah, Cassandra, Caitlin, Faith, Chloe, Chelsea, Caroline, Grace

Cathy (*Greek*) ♀   RATING: ★★★☆
Pure—Short for Catherine
> People think of Cathy as caring, pretty, funny, trustworthy, intelligent
> People who like the name Cathy also like Catherine, Chelsea, Cassandra, Amanda, Amber, Caroline, Christina, Carrie, Caitlin, Carissa

Cato (*Latin*) ♀ ♂   RATING: ★★★☆
Good judgment
> People think of Cato as intelligent, powerful, leader, young, energetic
> People who like the name Cato also like Caden, Cadence, Bailey, Cain, Cai, Coby, Cade, Cassidy, Carey, Casey

Caton (French) ♀　　　RATING: ★★★☆
Pure—Variation of Catherine
　People think of Caton as intelligent, funny, popular, wild, cool
　People who like the name Caton also like Cailyn, Caelan, Cashlin, Chloe, Carly, Kaydence, Cadee, Cara, Calista, Cate

Catori (Native American) ♀　　　RATING: ★★
Spirit—Hopi origin
　People think of Catori as pretty, exotic, quiet, funny, religious
　People who like the name Catori also like Calista, Chenoa, Chloe, Abrianna, Chickoa, Chumani, Callista, Celeste, Cassandra, Cailyn

Catrin (Welsh) ♀　　　RATING: ★★☆
Pure—Variation of Catherine
　People think of Catrin as pretty, intelligent, funny, caring, girl next door
　People who like the name Catrin also like Cailyn, Carys, Caitlyn, Caitlin, Callie, Calista, Claire, Arwen, Catriona, Carissa

Catriona (Celtic/Gaelic) ♀　　　RATING: ★★★★
Variation of Catherine
　People think of Catriona as pretty, creative, caring, intelligent, cool
　People who like the name Catriona also like Fiona, Ciara, Alana, Caitlin, Ceana, Brianna, Caitlyn, Cassandra, Genevieve, Aeryn

Cavan (Celtic/Gaelic) ♂　　　RATING: ★★☆
Irish place name
　People think of Cavan as handsome, caring, popular, creative, cool
　People who like the name Cavan also like Caleb, Conner, Cullen, Cole, Aiden, Braeden, Kaden, Coen, Colin, Chase

Cayenne (French) ♀　　　RATING: ★★★★
Hot spice
　People think of Cayenne as sexy, pretty, popular, energetic, exotic
　People who like the name Cayenne also like Ciara, Caitlyn, Celeste, Cailyn, Cheyenne, Chloe, Caprice, Cassandra, Calista, Carleigh

Cayla (Hebrew) ♀　　　RATING: ★★★★
Crown of laurel—Variation of Kayla
　People think of Cayla as pretty, funny, caring, intelligent, creative
　People who like the name Cayla also like Cailyn, Kayla, Caitlyn, Chloe, Hannah, Hailey, Emma, Cara, Callie, Carly

Ceallach (Celtic/Gaelic) ♂　　　RATING: ★★★
Bright-headed—Pronounced KAY-lock
　People think of Ceallach as creative, weird, artsy, loser, intelligent
　People who like the name Ceallach also like Callum, Cairbre, Callahan, Ciaran, Caolan, Cavan, Cargan, Braeden, Cian, Calder

Ceana (Celtic/Gaelic) ♀　　　RATING: ★★★★☆
God is gracious—Variation of Seana; also short for Oceana, meaning ocean
　People think of Ceana as pretty, intelligent, creative, sexy, trustworthy
　People who like the name Ceana also like Cianna, Cailyn, Chloe, Ciara, Kaelyn, Caelan, Breanna, Seanna, Arianna, Emma

Ceara (Celtic/Gaelic) ♀　　　RATING: ★★★
Black—Variation of Ciara
　People think of Ceara as pretty, energetic, caring, wild, lazy
　People who like the name Ceara also like Callie, Emma, Ciara, Kayla, Keira, Ceana, Cheyenne, Catriona, Chloe, Ava

Cece (Celtic/Gaelic) ♀　　　RATING: ★★☆
Blind of self-beauty—Short for Cecile or Cecilia
　People think of Cece as pretty, creative, sexy, funny, intelligent
　People who like the name Cece also like Bree, Cecelia, Celeste, Ciara, Bridget, Ava, Celia, Cecily, Chanel, Bella

Cecelia (Celtic/Gaelic) ♀　　　RATING: ★★★☆
Blind of self-beauty—Variation of Cecilia
　People think of Cecelia as pretty, intelligent, funny, caring, creative
　People who like the name Cecelia also like Charlotte, Amelia, Ava, Abigail, Isabella, Chloe, Claire, Audrey, Olivia, Fiona

Cecil (English) ♂　　　RATING: ★★★
Blind of self-beauty—Cecil Beaton, movie set designer and photographer
　People think of Cecil as intelligent, funny, quiet, caring, creative
　People who like the name Cecil also like Caleb, Cedric, Charles, Cole, Calvin, Aaron, Aiden, Chad, Adam, Cody

Cecile (French) ♀　　　RATING: ★★★☆
Blind of self-beauty—Feminine form of Cecil
　People think of Cecile as pretty, creative, intelligent, caring, cool
　People who like the name Cecile also like Camille, Chloe, Cecilia, Celeste, Abigail, Charlotte, Ava, Claire, Audrey, Belle

Cecilia (Latin) ♀　　　RATING: ★★★★
Blind of self-beauty—Feminine form of Cecil
　People think of Cecilia as pretty, funny, intelligent, creative, caring
　People who like the name Cecilia also like Isabella, Olivia, Amelia, Abigail, Chloe, Ava, Hannah, Charlotte, Emma, Claire

Cecily (Celtic/Gaelic) ♀　　　RATING: ★★★★
Blind of self-beauty—Feminine form of Cecil
　People think of Cecily as pretty, intelligent, caring, creative, funny
　People who like the name Cecily also like Ava, Chloe, Charlotte, Audrey, Claire, Cecelia, Olivia, Bianca, Isabella, Celeste

Cedar *(American)* ♀♂   RATING: ★★★
Type of tree
> People think of Cedar as creative, intelligent, energetic, powerful, cool
> People who like the name Cedar also like Caden, Dakota, Avery, Sage, Cameron, Aspen, Cade, Bailey, Ryder, Camden

Cedric *(English)* ♂   RATING: ★★★☆
Character created by Sir Walter Scott in *Ivanhoe*; Cedric the Entertainer, comedian; Sir Cedric Hardwick, actor
> People think of Cedric as handsome, cool, intelligent, popular, funny
> People who like the name Cedric also like Caleb, Aiden, Ethan, Alexander, Chase, Cole, Adrian, Gabriel, Conner, Isaac

Cele *(French)* ♀   RATING: ★★☆
Short for Cecile
> People think of Cele as sporty, elegant, uptight, cool, energetic
> People who like the name Cele also like Carlyn, Cadee, Caitlyn, Cardea, Candra, Carleigh, Cece, Ceana, Cerise, Catherine

Celerina *(Spanish)* ♀   RATING: ★★★
Quick
> People think of Celerina as pretty, sexy, popular, artsy, creative
> People who like the name Celerina also like Catalina, Caressa, Charity, Carissa, Calista, Chandra, Celeste, Candace, Ceana, Carminda

Celeste *(Latin)* ♀   RATING: ★★★
Heavenly—Celeste Holm, actress
> People think of Celeste as pretty, creative, intelligent, caring, funny
> People who like the name Celeste also like Chloe, Faith, Isabella, Ava, Bianca, Cassandra, Hannah, Charlotte, Abigail, Bella

Celestine *(Latin)* ♂   RATING: ★★★☆
Heavenly
> People think of Celestine as pretty, intelligent, caring, creative, energetic
> People who like the name Celestine also like Caleb, Aiden, Gabriel, Aaron, Alexander, Calix, Constantine, Clayton, Benjamin, Asher

Celestyn *(Polish)* ♀   RATING: ★★★★
Heavenly
> People think of Celestyn as pretty, exotic, caring, intelligent, weird
> People who like the name Celestyn also like Celeste, Cailyn, Calista, Caressa, Brielle, Belle, Carleigh, Celine, Cadee, Isabella

Celia *(Latin)* ♀   RATING: ★★★
Heaven
> People think of Celia as pretty, intelligent, caring, funny, creative

> People who like the name Celia also like Ava, Amelia, Olivia, Ella, Claire, Audrey, Cecilia, Chloe, Grace, Emma

Celina *(Latin)* ♀   RATING: ★★★★
Heaven
> People think of Celina as pretty, funny, caring, creative, intelligent
> People who like the name Celina also like Celine, Celeste, Angelina, Ciara, Chloe, Faith, Cassandra, Hailey, Amelia, Bianca

Celine *(French)* ♀   RATING: ★★★
Heaven—Celine Dion, singer
> People think of Celine as pretty, intelligent, creative, funny, caring
> People who like the name Celine also like Celeste, Celina, Chloe, Claire, Hailey, Emily, Bianca, Belle, Charlotte, Cassandra

Cenedra *(All Nationalities)* ♀   RATING: ★★★
Fantasy name—Originally spelled Ce'Nedra; character from The Belgariad and The Malloreon fantasy series by David Eddings
> People think of Cenedra as exotic, sexy, popular, wild, funny
> People who like the name Cenedra also like Catori, Canta, Calista, Ceana, Cailyn, Canika, Adara, Celerina, Ceyla, Carissa

Cenobia *(Spanish)* ♀   RATING: ★★☆
From Zeus—From the Greek name Zenobia
> People think of Cenobia as sexy, intelligent, creative, pretty, wild
> People who like the name Cenobia also like Cambria, Celeste, Callia, California, Ceridwen, Calista, Calla, Carminda, Calixte, Catriona

Cerelia *(Greek)* ♀   RATING: ★★★
Goddess of the harvest
> People think of Cerelia as exotic, artsy, pretty, powerful, creative
> People who like the name Cerelia also like Cassia, Ava, Aelwen, Calista, Arwen, Chloe, Aeryn, Charlotte, Caia, Aurora

Ceres *(Greek)* ♀♂   RATING: ★★
Goddess of the corn
> People think of Ceres as pretty, intelligent, elegant, exotic, young
> People who like the name Ceres also like Caden, Calypso, Cade, Avery, Cadence, Dante, Aidan, Camdyn, Cael, Bailey

Ceri *(Welsh)* ♀   RATING: ★★☆
Love—Pronounced *Kerry*
> People think of Ceri as caring, intelligent, funny, pretty, creative
> People who like the name Ceri also like Chloe, Cailyn, Callie, Ciara, Calista, Arwen, Cora, Carys, Ava, Celeste

159

Ceridwen *(Welsh)* ♀   RATING: ★★★★
Fair poetry—Pronounced *ke-RID-wen*
> People think of Ceridwen as creative, intelligent, caring, pretty, elegant
> People who like the name Ceridwen also like Aeryn, Arwen, Aelwen, Genevieve, Ciara, Celeste, Braewyn, Bronwen, Brea, Caelan

Cerise *(French)* ♀   RATING: ★★☆
Cherry
> People think of Cerise as pretty, sexy, creative, trustworthy, exotic
> People who like the name Cerise also like Celeste, Charisse, Celine, Chloe, Caprice, Claire, Ciara, Camille, Carina, Charlize

Ceron *(Welsh)* ♂   RATING: ★★★☆
Beloved
> People think of Ceron as young, cool, trustworthy, handsome, caring
> People who like the name Ceron also like Caleb, Ethan, Cian, Calix, Coen, Asher, Aiden, Conner, Gabriel, Cale

Cesar *(Spanish)* ♂   RATING: ★★
Thick head of hair—Also a title for Roman emperors
> People think of Cesar as handsome, funny, cool, intelligent, caring
> People who like the name Cesar also like Carlos, Caleb, Caesar, Adam, Calvin, Diego, Victor, Aden, Adrian, Anthony

Ceteria *(Latin)* ♀   RATING: ★★☆
The other ones
> People think of Ceteria as pretty, funny, intelligent, sexy, ethnic
> People who like the name Ceteria also like Celeste, Cambria, Celina, Celia, Cecilia, Cerelia, Ceri, Cilicia, Canta, Claudia

Ceyla *(American)* ♀   RATING: ★★★★
Variation of Kayla or Sela
> People think of Ceyla as pretty, funny, young, caring, creative
> People who like the name Ceyla also like Cailyn, Chloe, Ceana, Cayla, Celeste, Ceri, Callia, Calista, Ciara, Cianna

Chad *(English)* ♂   RATING: ★★☆
From the warrior's town—Also short for Chadwick; also a country in Africa; Chad Michael Murray, actor
> People think of Chad as handsome, funny, cool, caring, intelligent
> People who like the name Chad also like Caleb, Cody, Ethan, Cole, Chase, Benjamin, Aaron, Braden, Bradley, Nathan

Chael *(Hebrew)* ♂   RATING: ★★
Who is like God?—Short for Michael
> People think of Chael as intelligent, creative, boy next door, trustworthy, caring
> People who like the name Chael also like Aiden, Caleb, Cale, Kael, Cole, Elijah, Asher, Aden, Kaden, Conner

Chaela *(Celtic/Gaelic)* ♀   RATING: ★★★★☆
Who is like God?—Short for Michaela
> People think of Chaela as pretty, caring, popular, funny, powerful
> People who like the name Chaela also like Chaeli, Kaelyn, Ceana, Caelan, Chloe, Ciara, Cailyn, Breanna, Kayla, Chailyn

Chaeli *(Celtic/Gaelic)* ♀   RATING: ★★★
Who is like God?—Short for Michaela
> People think of Chaeli as pretty, creative, intelligent, energetic, caring
> People who like the name Chaeli also like Chaela, Kaelyn, Cailyn, Chailyn, Caelan, Ceana, Alana, Ciara, Chloe, Kaylee

Chahna *(Sanskrit/East Indian)* ♀   RATING: ★★★☆
Renowned, famous
> People think of Chahna as pretty, energetic, exotic, caring, cool
> People who like the name Chahna also like Chailyn, Chandra, Celeste, Channah, Bianca, Chantel, Charlize, Cailyn, Ciara, Carleigh

Chailyn *(American)* ♀   RATING: ★★★★
Combination of Chai and Lynn
> People think of Chailyn as pretty, creative, cool, energetic, funny
> People who like the name Chailyn also like Cailyn, Jadyn, Kaelyn, Chloe, Carleigh, Hailey, Kailey, Ava, Ashlyn, Chaeli

Chaim *(Hebrew)* ♂   RATING: ★★★★
Life—"L'Chaim" is a Hebrew toast to life
> People think of Chaim as creative, intelligent, religious, caring, quiet
> People who like the name Chaim also like Caleb, Asher, Cale, Benjamin, Chael, Aden, Elijah, Gabriel, Calix, Aaron

Chaka *(Arabic)* ♀   RATING: ★★★
Chakra, energy center—Chaka Khan, singer
> People think of Chaka as leader, aggressive, sexy, creative, intelligent
> People who like the name Chaka also like Catalina, Chakra, Ciara, Chantel, Cala, Chandra, Cassandra, Calista, Chanel, Camilla

Chakotay *(American)* ♂   RATING: ★★☆
Character created for *Star Trek: Voyager*
> People think of Chakotay as weird, religious, untrustworthy, poor, slow
> People who like the name Chakotay also like Chill, Chase

Chakra *(Sanskrit/East Indian)* ♀   RATING: ★★★
Circle, wheel; energy center of the body—In Hinduism, there are seven chakras in the body, corresponding with the seven colors of the rainbow
> People think of Chakra as exotic, energetic, intelligent, sneaky, powerful
> People who like the name Chakra also like Celeste, Calista, Adara, Chelsea, Chandra, Charisma, Chaka, Caprice, Calandra, Aurora

Chalondra *(American)* ♀　　RATING: ★★☆
Combination of Charlotte and Alondra
　People think of Chalondra as pretty, leader, powerful, poor, quiet
　People who like the name Chalondra also like Chandra, Cassandra, Calandra, Ayanna, Chloe, Aaralyn, Caprice, Camisha, Celina, Carissa

Chalsie *(American)* ♀　　RATING: ★★☆
Port for chalk or limestone—Variation of Chelsea
　People think of Chalsie as pretty, weird, nerdy, intelligent, stuck-up
　People who like the name Chalsie also like Carly, Cailyn, Chloe, Charlize, Caitlyn, Chailyn, Cayla, Charity, Claire, Chanel

Chaman *(Sanskrit/East Indian)* ♂　　RATING: ★★
Garden
　People think of Chaman as exotic, sexy, weird, slow, creative
　People who like the name Chaman also like Adarsh, Chatura, Chayton, Ajay, Caleb, Boden, Cale, Barid, Cole, Charan

Chameli *(Sanskrit/East Indian)* ♀　　RATING: ★★★☆
Flower
　People think of Chameli as pretty, exotic, sexy, wild, trendy
　People who like the name Chameli also like Chandra, Chloe, Celeste, Cassandra, Charissa, Charisma, Chahna, Avani, Channah, Chaeli

Chamomile *(American)* ♀　　RATING: ★★☆
Peace; spice
　People think of Chamomile as pretty, caring, girl next door, weird, wild
　People who like the name Chamomile also like Autumn, Clover, Abigail, Calista, Charity, Adeline, Cinnamon, Charisma, Emma, Cara

Chan *(Chinese)* ♀　　RATING: ★★★☆
Snow
　People think of Chan as funny, caring, cool, trustworthy, young
　People who like the name Chan also like Celeste, Bela, Aneko, Breena, Belle, Blossom, Jia Li, Cecelia, Jolie, Astrid

Chana *(Hebrew)* ♀　　RATING: ★★☆
Gracious—Variation of Hannah
　People think of Chana as pretty, intelligent, caring, funny, creative
　People who like the name Chana also like Channah, Cayla, Ciara, Cailyn, Chloe, Chanel, Chantel, Carissa, Cianna, Calista

Chance *(English)* ♂　　RATING: ★★★☆
Fortune, luck
　People think of Chance as handsome, funny, cool, popular, intelligent
　People who like the name Chance also like Chase, Caleb, Cole, Aiden, Ethan, Conner, Braden, Kaden, Gavin, Cody

Chancellor *(English)* ♂　　RATING: ★★☆
Keeper of records
　People think of Chancellor as powerful, intelligent, aggressive, handsome, cool
　People who like the name Chancellor also like Chance, Caleb, Chase, Benjamin, Chauncey, Colton, Dawson, Conner, Cody, Bradley

Chanda *(Sanskrit/East Indian)* ♀　　RATING: ★★★☆
Hindi goddess
　People think of Chanda as pretty, funny, intelligent, caring, creative
　People who like the name Chanda also like Chandra, Bianca, Basanti, Avani, Charissa, Chameli, Celeste, Chahna, Chakra, Asha

Chandler *(English)* ♀♂　　RATING: ★★★
Candlemaker—Chandler Bing, character on TV show *Friends*; Raymond Chandler, novelist
　People think of Chandler as funny, popular, caring, intelligent, cool
　People who like the name Chandler also like Caden, Carter, Bailey, Carson, Addison, Hayden, Connor, Cameron, Avery, Blake

Chandra *(Sanskrit/East Indian)* ♀　　RATING: ★★☆
Moon
　People think of Chandra as pretty, intelligent, creative, funny, trustworthy
　People who like the name Chandra also like Celeste, Cassandra, Aurora, Ciara, Chloe, Calista, Cailyn, Bella, Faith, Adriana

Chanel *(French)* ♀　　RATING: ★★★★
Channel—Coco Chanel, designer, maker of the Chanel brand
　People think of Chanel as pretty, popular, funny, sexy, creative
　People who like the name Chanel also like Chloe, Ava, Giselle, Chantel, Isabella, Bella, Faith, Paige, Claire, Bianca

Channah *(Hebrew)* ♀　　RATING: ★★★★
Gracious—Variation of Hannah
　People think of Channah as elegant, pretty, exotic, artsy, intelligent
　People who like the name Channah also like Hannah, Celeste, Chandra, Cailyn, Cassara, Ceana, Chana, Chailyn, Chloe, Cianna

Channary *(Cambodian)* ♀　　RATING: ★★★☆
Full moon
　People think of Channary as exotic, sexy, creative, pretty, weird
　People who like the name Channary also like Cassara, Chantrea, Brielle, Abrianna, Chloe, Chandra, Chailyn, Cianna, Channah, Arwen

Channer *(English)* ♀♂　　RATING: ★★★
Wise—Variation of Channing
　People think of Channer as intelligent, cool, weird, exotic, aggressive

161

People who like the name Channer also like Caden, Carter, Cadence, Channing, Cade, Chandler, Avery, Camdyn, Connor, Camden

Channery *(American)* ♀   RATING: ★★★★☆
Wise—Variation of Channing
People think of Channery as pretty, creative, exotic, trendy, caring
People who like the name Channery also like Caelan, Caressa, Chloe, Cailyn, Bella, Charleigh, Cambree, Belle, Calliope, Channah

Channing *(English)* ♀ ♂   RATING: ★★★★
From the place of Cana's people
People think of Channing as sexy, popular, handsome, cool, caring
People who like the name Channing also like Caden, Hayden, Carter, Avery, Addison, Chandler, Bailey, Cadence, Carson, Cameron

Channon *(English)* ♀ ♂   RATING: ★★★☆
Clergyman—Originally a surname
People think of Channon as intelligent, caring, funny, trustworthy, old-fashioned
People who like the name Channon also like Caden, Carter, Channing, Cameron, Camden, Camryn, Cadence, Casey, Camdyn, Cade

Chantal *(French)* ♀   RATING: ★★★★
A French place name—St. Jeanne-Francoise de Chantal
People think of Chantal as pretty, funny, caring, intelligent, creative
People who like the name Chantal also like Chantel, Chloe, Faith, Bianca, Celeste, Cassandra, Hailey, Chanel, Charlotte, Emma

Chantel *(French)* ♀   RATING: ★★★★
Variation of Chantal
People think of Chantel as pretty, funny, caring, intelligent, popular
People who like the name Chantel also like Chloe, Chanel, Chantal, Caitlyn, Hailey, Bianca, Abigail, Faith, Aaliyah, Cassandra

Chanton *(French)* ♀   RATING: ★★☆
We sing
People think of Chanton as weird, wild, young, lazy, wealthy
People who like the name Chanton also like Celine, Chanel, Camille, Cerise, Chantal, Claire, Clemence, Caprice, Ciel, Aceline

Chantoya *(American)* ♀   RATING: ★★★
Praised woman, singer
People think of Chantoya as unpopular, lazy, weird, elegant, religious
People who like the name Chantoya also like Chassidy, Clarissa, Ciara, Beyoncé, Charity, Camisha, Aaliyah, Caressa, Calandra, Cady

Chantrea *(Cambodian)* ♀   RATING: ★★★☆
Moon
People think of Chantrea as pretty, exotic, sexy, ethnic, girl next door
People who like the name Chantrea also like Calista, Chloe, Ciara, Chandra, Charisse, Channary, Chantel, Cassandra, Amaya, Amara

Chantry *(English)* ♀ ♂   RATING: ★★★
Singing of the Mass—Originally a surname
People think of Chantry as popular, handsome, intelligent, pretty, energetic
People who like the name Chantry also like Avery, Caden, Carmen, Aubrey, Addison, Cheyne, Blaze, Cade, Cassidy, Carrington

Chao *(Chinese)* ♀ ♂   RATING: ★☆
Surpassing
People think of Chao as funny, weird, artsy, aggressive, unpopular
People who like the name Chao also like Caden, Blair, Cai, Casey, Cameo, Camdyn, Bailey, Coriander, Coby, Blaise

Chapa *(Native American)* ♀   RATING: ★★☆
Beaver—Lakota origin
People think of Chapa as old-fashioned, ethnic, leader, religious, loser
People who like the name Chapa also like Catori, Cocheta, Chickoa, Chenoa, Chumani, Anevay, Bena, Kaya, Cholena, Bly

Charan *(Sanskrit/East Indian)* ♂   RATING: ★★★
God's feet
People think of Charan as intelligent, caring, funny, trustworthy, popular
People who like the name Charan also like Ajay, Chatura, Chetan, Calix, Caleb, Adarsh, Crevan, Adit, Ciaran, Cullen

Charis *(Greek)* ♀ ♂   RATING: ★★☆
Grace
People think of Charis as pretty, caring, intelligent, trustworthy, creative
People who like the name Charis also like Caden, Cadence, Aidan, Hayden, Cade, Cameron, Cassidy, Christian, Avery, Bailey

Charisma *(Greek)* ♀   RATING: ★★
Personal power, attraction
People think of Charisma as pretty, popular, intelligent, caring, creative
People who like the name Charisma also like Chloe, Faith, Cassandra, Bianca, Celeste, Cordelia, Destiny, Adriana, Charity, Ava

Charissa *(Greek)* ♀   RATING: ★★★★
Grace
People think of Charissa as pretty, intelligent, funny, trustworthy, caring
People who like the name Charissa also like Carissa, Chloe, Cassandra, Cailyn, Clarissa, Claire, Charisse, Caressa, Caitlyn, Faith

Charisse *(French)* ♀   RATING: ★★★★☆
Grace, beauty, kindness—Cyd Charisse, dancer/actress
People think of Charisse as pretty, caring, funny, intelligent, creative
People who like the name Charisse also like Chloe, Charissa, Carissa, Charlize, Cailyn, Camille, Claire, Belle, Grace, Caressa

Charity *(English)* ♀   RATING: ★★☆
Giving, kindness
People think of Charity as caring, pretty, intelligent, trustworthy, funny
People who like the name Charity also like Faith, Chloe, Grace, Hailey, Destiny, Abigail, Hannah, Isabella, Hope, Belle

Charla *(American)* ♀   RATING: ★★★★
Feminine form of Charles
People think of Charla as pretty, funny, intelligent, caring, trustworthy
People who like the name Charla also like Charlotte, Chloe, Chelsea, Charlee, Chantel, Cara, Charlize, Bianca, Caitlyn, Ava

Charlee *(American)* ♀   RATING: ★★☆
Feminine form of Charlie or Charles
People think of Charlee as pretty, funny, intelligent, popular, energetic
People who like the name Charlee also like Chloe, Ava, Charlotte, Charleigh, Charlize, Claire, Bella, Ashlyn, Carleigh, Cailyn

Charleen *(English)* ♀   RATING: ★★★☆
Feminine form of Charles
People think of Charleen as pretty, caring, funny, creative, young
People who like the name Charleen also like Claire, Charlene, Charlize, Chloe, Cassandra, Chelsea, Chantel, Abigail, Belle, Desiree

Charleigh *(American)* ♀   RATING: ★★★★☆
Feminine form of Charles or Charly
People think of Charleigh as pretty, funny, popular, intelligent, energetic
People who like the name Charleigh also like Carleigh, Charlee, Chloe, Ava, Gabrielle, Cailyn, Hailey, Elle, Abigail, Claire

Charlene *(English)* ♀   RATING: ★★
Free—Variation of Caroline; also feminine form of Charles
People think of Charlene as pretty, funny, caring, trustworthy, intelligent
People who like the name Charlene also like Charlotte, Chelsea, Chloe, Audrey, Hailey, Caitlyn, Charity, Grace, Cassandra, Callie

Charles *(German)* ♂   RATING: ★★☆
Free man—Charles, Prince of Wales; Charles Barkley, athlete; Charles Bronson, actor
People think of Charles as handsome, intelligent, funny, caring, cool

People who like the name Charles also like Benjamin, Andrew, Alexander, William, Ethan, Nicholas, Jack, Gabriel, Christopher, Matthew

Charlie *(English)* ♀ ♂   RATING: ★★★
Free man—Short for Charles; Charlie Chaplin, actor/director; Charlie Sheen, actor
People think of Charlie as funny, cool, popular, intelligent, caring
People who like the name Charlie also like Bailey, Dylan, Ryan, Riley, Cameron, Connor, Hayden, Logan, James, Carter

Charlize *(French)* ♀   RATING: ★★★★
Feminine form of Charles—Charlize Theron, actress
People think of Charlize as pretty, sexy, elegant, intelligent, popular
People who like the name Charlize also like Chloe, Charlotte, Isabella, Ava, Bella, Scarlett, Claire, Grace, Giselle, Hailey

Charlotte *(English)* ♀   RATING: ★★☆
Free—Feminine form of Charles
People think of Charlotte as pretty, intelligent, funny, caring, creative
People who like the name Charlotte also like Olivia, Ava, Chloe, Grace, Abigail, Claire, Emma, Amelia, Isabella, Hannah

Charlton *(English)* ♂   RATING: ★★★☆
From the town of the free men
People think of Charlton as intelligent, caring, handsome, trustworthy, cool
People who like the name Charlton also like Caleb, Clayton, Chase, Byron, Carver, Carlton, Chad, Cole, Dawson, Aaron

Charmaine *(English)* ♀   RATING: ★★★☆
Charm
People think of Charmaine as pretty, caring, trustworthy, intelligent, funny
People who like the name Charmaine also like Chloe, Charlotte, Charlize, Charity, Cassandra, Chelsea, Charisse, Belle, Camille, Chantel

Charo *(Spanish)* ♀   RATING: ★★★
Rosary—Variation of Rosario; Charo, singer/actress/guitarist
People think of Charo as exotic, sexy, funny, aggressive, creative
People who like the name Charo also like Ciara, Cytheria, Calista, Cleopatra, Callia, Cinnamon, Chumani, Cascata, Cira, Bree

Chars *(English)* ♂   RATING: ★★
Free man—Short for Charles
People think of Chars as exotic, old-fashioned, ethnic, sexy, stuck-up
People who like the name Chars also like Caleb, Chauncey, Chayton, Callum, Colton, Creighton, Byron, Clay, Calder, Conner

164

Chas *(English)* ♀♂ RATING: ★★★☆
Free man—Short for Charles
People think of Chas as caring, young, intelligent, cool, handsome
People who like the name Chas also like Caden, Cadence, Cade, Casey, Hayden, Cooper, Camden, Christian, Carter, Connor

Chase *(English)* ♂ RATING: ★★★★
Hunter—Also short for Chauncey
People think of Chase as handsome, funny, popular, intelligent, cool
People who like the name Chase also like Cole, Caleb, Ethan, Aiden, Chance, Gavin, Landon, Braden, Cody, Conner

Chassidy *(American)* ♀ RATING: ★★★☆
Combination of Chastity and Cassidy
People think of Chassidy as pretty, funny, cool, young, popular
People who like the name Chassidy also like Chastity, Hailey, Destiny, Faith, Charity, Chloe, Audrey, Cailyn, Hannah, Bella

Chastity *(English)* ♀ RATING: ★★★☆
Purity—Chastity Bono, daughter of singers Sonny Bono and Cher
People think of Chastity as pretty, caring, funny, popular, cool
People who like the name Chastity also like Charity, Hailey, Chloe, Faith, Destiny, Bianca, Chassidy, Isabella, Cailyn, Celeste

Chatura *(Sanskrit/East Indian)* ♂ RATING: ★☆
Four
People think of Chatura as intelligent, handsome, sexy, weird, funny
People who like the name Chatura also like Ajay, Charan, Adarsh, Amish, Chaman, Ashwin, Arnav, Cyrus, Bairn, Ceallach

Chauncey *(English)* ♂ RATING: ★★★☆
Chancellor
People think of Chauncey as handsome, intelligent, popular, funny, powerful
People who like the name Chauncey also like Chance, Caleb, Aiden, Chase, Conner, Cole, Cody, Tristan, Aden, Brice

Chava *(Hebrew)* ♀ RATING: ★★★☆
Life
People think of Chava as pretty, intelligent, trustworthy, religious, quiet
People who like the name Chava also like Chaviva, Amaya, Channah, Cayla, Cara, Chavi, Charlotte, Celeste, Chumani, Camille

Chavez *(Spanish)* ♂ RATING: ★★
Keys—Also a surname
People think of Chavez as handsome, popular, sexy, funny, young

People who like the name Chavez also like Diego, Aiden, Chase, Caleb, Carlos, Cruz, Jayden, Alexander, Chance, Bradley

Chavi *(Hebrew)* ♀ RATING: ★★
Life
People think of Chavi as young, intelligent, popular, pretty, winner
People who like the name Chavi also like Channah, Chava, Avari, Chandra, Chenoa, Chailyn, Cassara, Cyrah, Bly, Catori

Chaviva *(Hebrew)* ♀ RATING: ★☆
Beloved
People think of Chaviva as sexy, funny, energetic, aggressive, pretty
People who like the name Chaviva also like Chava, Channah, Claral, Aviva, Celeste, Cara, Callia, Chavi, Chumani, Cassara

Chay *(English)* ♀♂ RATING: ★★★★☆
Diminutive form of Charles—Chay Blyth, sailor
People think of Chay as intelligent, funny, cool, popular, caring
People who like the name Chay also like Caden, Brayden, Cael, Cade, Aidan, Shay, Bailey, Connor, Cadence, Blair

Chaya *(Hebrew)* ♀ RATING: ★★★☆
Life
People think of Chaya as intelligent, pretty, caring, creative, wealthy
People who like the name Chaya also like Candy, Angelina, Hannah, Desiree, Alayna, Arielle, Eloise, Jasmine, Kristine, Latisha

Chayan *(Hebrew)* ♂ RATING: ★★★
Life
People think of Chayan as intelligent, leader, handsome, caring, cool
People who like the name Chayan also like Braden, Conner, Chase, Colton, Brendan, Braeden, Caleb, Byron, Cody, Gabriel

Chaylse *(English)* ♀ RATING: ★★☆
Port for chalk or limestone—Variation of Chelsea
People think of Chaylse as pretty, intelligent, energetic, funny, lazy
People who like the name Chaylse also like Chloe, Charlize, Chelsea, Carleigh, Cailyn, Caelan, Ava, Claudia, Hannah, Ciara

Chayton *(Native American)* ♂ RATING: ★★★★
Falcon—Sioux
People think of Chayton as intelligent, handsome, energetic, caring, powerful
People who like the name Chayton also like Aiden, Caleb, Ethan, Kaden, Chase, Clayton, Colton, Landon, Braden, Cody

Chaz (English) ♂   RATING: ★★★☆
Free man—Short for Charles
People think of Chaz as handsome, funny, cool, popular, sexy
People who like the name Chaz also like Chase, Caleb, Cole, Chad, Chance, Cody, Conner, Aiden, Kaden, Gavin

Chazz (American) ♂   RATING: ★★☆
Free man—Short for Charles; Chazz Palminteri, actor
People think of Chazz as cool, handsome, aggressive, popular, weird
People who like the name Chazz also like Chaz, Chase, Chance, Caleb, Cody, Colton, Kaden, Calvin, Chad, Conner

Cheche (Spanish) ♀♂   RATING: ★☆
Small thing
People think of Cheche as funny, creative, sexy, powerful, young
People who like the name Cheche also like Caden, Blair, Chay, Cadence, Clayne, Cain, Cato, Cyan, Brede, Camdyn

Chelle (French) ♀   RATING: ★★★☆
Short for Michelle
People think of Chelle as pretty, cool, sexy, creative, funny
People who like the name Chelle also like Ciara, Chelsea, Charisse, Chanel, Desiree, Celine, Chantal, Belle, Alaina, Chloe

Chelsa (English) ♀   RATING: ★★★☆
Port for chalk or limestone—Variation of Chelsea
People think of Chelsa as pretty, caring, intelligent, creative, popular
People who like the name Chelsa also like Chelsea, Ava, Becca, Carly, Bethany, Chloe, Felicity, Cailyn, Arianna, Christa

Chelsea (English) ♀   RATING: ★★★★
Port for chalk or limestone—Chelsea Clinton, first daughter; Chelsea Handler, comedian
People think of Chelsea as funny, pretty, caring, creative, intelligent
People who like the name Chelsea also like Chloe, Hannah, Hailey, Abigail, Emma, Paige, Caitlyn, Ava, Emily, Claire

Chelsey (English) ♀♂   RATING: ★★★★
Port for chalk or limestone—Variation of Chelsea
People think of Chelsey as pretty, funny, caring, cool, creative
People who like the name Chelsey also like Bailey, Brooke, Alexis, Madison, Cameron, Caden, Ashley, Courtney, Kelsey, Cassidy

Chelsi (American) ♀   RATING: ★★★★
Port for chalk or limestone
People think of Chelsi as pretty, funny, caring, young, cool
People who like the name Chelsi also like Chelsea, Chloe, Callie, Destiny, Faith, Cailyn, Caitlyn, Hailey, Carly, Breanna

Chelsia (American) ♀   RATING: ★★☆
Port for chalk or limestone—Variation of Chelsea
People think of Chelsia as popular, pretty, girl next door, funny, intelligent
People who like the name Chelsia also like Chelsea, Chelsi, Carleigh, Carly, Destiny, Celina, Bridget, Cassie, Christa, Breanna

Chen (Chinese) ♀♂   RATING: ★★★☆
Dawn
People think of Chen as trustworthy, cool, energetic, funny, intelligent
People who like the name Chen also like Cameron, Caden, Corey, Cade, Cassidy, Blake, Carmen, Casey, Courtney, Cong

Cheng (Chinese) ♂   RATING: ★☆
Accomplished
People think of Cheng as cool, intelligent, ethnic, young, nerdy
People who like the name Cheng also like Cale, Brooks, Aden, Carmine, Colin, Aiden, Angelo, Claude, Balthasar, Benito

Chenille (American) ♀   RATING: ★★★
Soft, nubby fabric
People think of Chenille as handsome, wealthy, poor, young, energetic
People who like the name Chenille also like Chantel, Adia, Arianna, Desiree, Arlene, Becca, Jeneva, Enya, Antonia, Marina

Chenoa (Native American) ♀   RATING: ★★
From Chenoa, Illinois—Possibly named after a town in Kentucky, hometown of the Illinois town's founder
People think of Chenoa as creative, intelligent, caring, pretty, funny
People who like the name Chenoa also like Kaya, Catori, Ciara, Chickoa, Chumani, Ayasha, Cassandra, Cholena, Cocheta, Aleshanee

Cher (French) ♀♂   RATING: ★★★☆
Dear one—Cher, singer/actress
People think of Cher as pretty, funny, popular, caring, cool
People who like the name Cher also like Carson, Casey, Carey, Bailey, Blair, Demi, Christian, Chris, Bell, Cassidy

Cheree (French) ♀   RATING: ★★★
Dear one—A classic Cajun name
People think of Cheree as intelligent, caring, pretty, trustworthy, sexy
People who like the name Cheree also like Desiree, Claire, Belle, Caprice, Cheri, Aimee, Bethany, Chantel, Chantal, Colette

Cheri (French) ♀   RATING: ★★★☆
Dear
People think of Cheri as caring, pretty, funny, trustworthy, creative
People who like the name Cheri also like Chloe, Cherie, Callie, Belle, Chelsea, Aimee, Charlize, Chanel, Charisse, Crystal

Cherie *(French)* ♀   RATING: ★★
Dear
> People think of Cherie as pretty, caring, creative, funny, intelligent
> People who like the name Cherie also like Belle, Claire, Charisse, Callie, Chloe, Cailyn, Camille, Clara, Bianca, Chantel

Cherlin *(American)* ♀   RATING: ★★
Combination of Cher and Lin
> People think of Cherlin as pretty, old-fashioned, young, girl next door, elegant
> People who like the name Cherlin also like Cordelia, Chelsea, Chelsi, Cashlin, Chailyn, Charity, Celia, Charlotte, Carlyn, Constance

Cherry *(American)* ♀   RATING: ★★★
Cherry fruit—Also short for Cheryl
> People think of Cherry as pretty, funny, creative, sexy, caring
> People who like the name Cherry also like Chloe, Chelsea, Amber, Cassandra, Charlotte, Crystal, Cinnamon, Blossom, Bethany, Carly

Cheryl *(French)* ♀   RATING: ★★★☆
Beloved—Cheryl Ladd, actress ; Cheryl Tiegs, actress/model
> People think of Cheryl as caring, pretty, funny, intelligent, trustworthy
> People who like the name Cheryl also like Chelsea, Chloe, Amber, Claire, Charlotte, Bethany, Faith, Caroline, Catherine, Clarissa

Chesmu *(Native American)* ♂   RATING: ★★
Gritty
> People think of Chesmu as weird, slow, old-fashioned, religious, ethnic
> People who like the name Chesmu also like Chayton, Akando, Anoki, Chogan, Ahanu, Bedros, Chatura, Apiatan, Ciaran, Asher

Chesna *(Slavic)* ♀   RATING: ★★★☆
Bringing peace, calm
> People think of Chesna as pretty, creative, quiet, funny, religious
> People who like the name Chesna also like Chenoa, Cianna, Callista, Ceana, Cayla, Claudia, Cocheta, Cady, Chessa, Charisma

Chess *(American)* ♀   RATING: ★★☆
Free—Short for Francesca
> People think of Chess as intelligent, weird, unpopular, nerdy, quiet
> People who like the name Chess also like Breanna, Brenna, Cara, Charissa, Chessa, Brianna, Claudia, Calista, Caelan, Anne

Chessa *(Slavic)* ♀   RATING: ★★★★
Peaceful
> People think of Chessa as intelligent, creative, caring, funny, pretty

> People who like the name Chessa also like Chloe, Cailyn, Caelan, Carissa, Calista, Ciara, Celeste, Callista, Caroline, Claire

Chester *(English)* ♂   RATING: ★★★☆
A fortress, camp—Short for Rochester; Chester Gould, creator of comic *Dick Tracy*
> People think of Chester as handsome, funny, intelligent, trustworthy, cool
> People who like the name Chester also like Caleb, Adam, Aaron, Chad, Chase, Christopher, Benjamin, Bradley, Clayton, Clark

Chet *(English)* ♂   RATING: ★★★☆
Short for Chester—Chet Atkins, singer; Chet Baker, musician; Chet Huntley, newscaster
> People think of Chet as handsome, funny, sexy, cool, intelligent
> People who like the name Chet also like Caleb, Chase, Cole, Clayton, Cody, Chad, Conner, Ethan, Aiden, Colton

Chetan *(Sanskrit/East Indian)* ♂   RATING: ★★★
Life
> People think of Chetan as intelligent, caring, cool, young, energetic
> People who like the name Chetan also like Charan, Adarsh, Chatura, Ajay, Kishan, Chaman, Alagan, Chase, Amish, Ketan

Cheyenne *(Native American)* ♀   RATING: ★★★★
Unintelligible speakers—Sioux origin; also spelled Cheyanne
> People think of Cheyenne as pretty, funny, creative, caring, young
> People who like the name Cheyenne also like Chloe, Savannah, Hailey, Faith, Paige, Isabella, Emma, Abigail, Hannah, Ava

Cheyne *(English)* ♀ ♂   RATING: ★★★★☆
From the oak grove
> People think of Cheyne as funny, intelligent, creative, caring, handsome
> People who like the name Cheyne also like Caden, Connor, Brayden, Bailey, Cassidy, Dakota, Aidan, Cameron, Camryn, Caley

Chezarina *(Italian)* ♀   RATING: ★★☆
Feminine form of Cesar
> People think of Chezarina as pretty, artsy, exotic, funny, elegant
> People who like the name Chezarina also like Bellini, Cassara, Donatella, Aceline, Cynzia, Ciara, Chiara, Catalina, Bianca, Cascata

Chi *(Chinese)* ♂   RATING: ★★★☆
Younger energy—Rare as a Chinese name; more often Cantonese
> People think of Chi as exotic, young, funny, intelligent, pretty
> People who like the name Chi also like Chance, Caleb, Chase, Cian, Cole, Aden, Blade, Conner, Chaz, Gabriel

Chiara *(Italian)* ♀ RATING: ★★★★
Illustrious—Pronounced *key-AH-ra*
People think of Chiara as pretty, intelligent, creative, elegant, funny
People who like the name Chiara also like Ava, Isabella, Ciara, Chloe, Bianca, Gianna, Cara, Ella, Mia, Amelia

Chick *(English)* ♀♂ RATING: ★★★
Short for Charles—Baby bird; also slang for girl/female; Chick Hearn, announcer/actor
People think of Chick as sexy, pretty, trendy, girl next door, sneaky
People who like the name Chick also like Christmas, Casey, Brook, Cristy, Brooke, Cassidy, Cooper, Clever, Blake, Blaine

Chickoa *(Native American)* ♀ RATING: ★★★
Daybreak
People think of Chickoa as pretty, cool, wild, weird, poor
People who like the name Chickoa also like Chumani, Catori, Chenoa, Cholena, Cocheta, Bena, Kaya, Chapa, Angeni, Ceana

Chico *(Spanish)* ♂ RATING: ★★★☆
Short for Francisco—Spanish for boy; *Chico and the Man*, TV series
People think of Chico as funny, handsome, popular, cool, exotic
People who like the name Chico also like Chance, Adrian, Caleb, Cosmo, Carlos, Cody, Adam, Chase, Ace, Anthony

Chika *(Japanese)* ♀ RATING: ★☆
Near
People think of Chika as pretty, funny, sexy, exotic, creative
People who like the name Chika also like Aneko, Aiko, Amaya, Ai, Amarante, Emiko, Ayame, Sakura, Gin, Suki

Chill *(English)* ♂ RATING: ★☆
Short for Chilton—Slang for relax; Chill Wills, actor/composer
People think of Chill as loser, lazy, unpopular, weird, funny
People who like the name Chill also like Cedric, Blade, Cole, Chase, Bade, Chip, Beck, Basil, Chance, André

Chilton *(English)* ♂ RATING: ★★★
A town by the river
People think of Chilton as wealthy, loser, intelligent, nerdy, handsome
People who like the name Chilton also like Caleb, Cole, Brighton, Clayton, Chad, Colton, Braxton, Carver, Brant, Cedric

Chilli/Chilly *(American)* ♀♂ RATING: ★★★
Cold
People think of Chilly as nerdy, weird, cool, exotic, unpopular
People who like the name Chilli also like Christian, Cooper, Brooklyn, Cade, Carmen, Carter, Cameron, Carson, Charlie, Bailey

Chimelu *(African)* ♂ RATING: ★★☆
What God has created—Igbo origin
People think of Chimelu as powerful, intelligent, leader, creative, nerdy
People who like the name Chimelu also like Charles, Calix, Aaron, Chayton, Cyrus, Cyril, Kazi, Cody, Anando, Azizi

China *(English)* ♀ RATING: ★★★☆
From China
People think of China as pretty, funny, intelligent, exotic, sexy
People who like the name China also like Asia, Chloe, Charlotte, Bianca, Charlize, Charity, Cinnamon, Cheyenne, Clara, Chanel

Chinara *(Persian)* ♀ RATING: ★★★☆
Oriental plane tree
People think of Chinara as pretty, young, elegant, quiet, leader
People who like the name Chinara also like Cyrah, Charisse, Calandra, Ciara, Chenoa, Chantrea, Calista, Cynara, Ceana, Ayanna

Chinua *(African)* ♂ RATING: ★★
God's own blessing—Nigerian origin; Chinua Achebe, author
People think of Chinua as intelligent, handsome, exotic, caring, creative
People who like the name Chinua also like Ciaran, Liam, Zeke, Chimelu, Chetan, Crevan, Micheal, Callum, Taye, Tristan

Chinue *(African)* ♀ RATING: ★★★
God's own blessing—Feminine form of Chinua
People think of Chinue as intelligent, trustworthy, cool, girl next door, pretty
People who like the name Chinue also like Chipo, Ceana, Callia, Chinara, Ciel, Cleo, Calixte, Chaviva, Chione, Bronwyn

Chione *(Greek)* ♀ RATING: ★★★★
Snow queen—Pronounced *key-OH-nee*
People think of Chione as pretty, intelligent, exotic, sexy, elegant
People who like the name Chione also like Chloe, Calliope, Cassandra, Breena, Isis, Calista, Amaya, Aradia, Cleo, Chumani

Chip *(English)* ♂ RATING: ★★
Short for Charles—Chip and Dale, cartoon characters
People think of Chip as handsome, funny, intelligent, caring, powerful
People who like the name Chip also like Cody, Caleb, Chad, Cole, Ace, Chance, Chase, Clay, Adam, Andrew

Chipo *(African)* ♀ RATING: ★★★
A gift—Shona origin
People think of Chipo as weird, exotic, old-fashioned, aggressive, unpopular
People who like the name Chipo also like Chinue, Chaviva, Caresse, Channery, Colleen, Ciel, Chavi, Ayanna, Chava, Cleo

Chiquita *(Spanish)* ♀   RATING: ★★★☆
Little girl—Term of endearment
> People think of Chiquita as pretty, popular, trustworthy, intelligent, funny
> People who like the name Chiquita also like Calista, Celeste, Catalina, Cassandra, Cinnamon, Bella, Chloe, Aaliyah, Camelia, Aurora

Chita *(Spanish)* ♀   RATING: ★★
Conception—Short for Conchita or Concepcion; Chita Rivera, dancer/actress
> People think of Chita as sexy, young, exotic, caring, ethnic
> People who like the name Chita also like Daniella, Celina, Belita, Joy, Nina, Cecilia, Juanita, Pia, Julia, Dorinda

Chitt *(Sanskrit/East Indian)* ♂   RATING: ★★☆
Mind—Often used by Sikhs
> People think of Chitt as weird, funny, slow, popular, poor
> People who like the name Chitt also like Amish, Clyde, Colton, Ajay, Chael, Alagan, Chatura, Benito, Colt, Conner

Chloë *(Greek)* ♀   RATING: ★★★★
Verdant, blooming—Chloë Sevigny, actress
> People think of Chloe as pretty, funny, creative, intelligent, popular
> People who like the name Chloe also like Ava, Emma, Olivia, Hannah, Abigail, Isabella, Grace, Paige, Claire, Ella

Chloris *(Greek)* ♀   RATING: ★☆
Greenish—Chloris Leachman, actress
> People think of Chloris as funny, aggressive, weird, pretty, energetic
> People who like the name Chloris also like Calandra, Chloe, Calliope, Cleo, Charissa, Cordelia, Carissa, Clover, Charisma, Cleopatra

Chogan *(American)* ♂   RATING: ★★★
Unknown meaning—The word "chógan" was recorded as a Narragansett word meaning black bird in 1643; however, there is no such word in the Narragansett language
> People think of Chogan as weird, leader, handsome, energetic, aggressive
> People who like the name Chogan also like Caleb, Chayton, Calix, Cian, Braeden, Caine, Calder, Cole, Crevan, Ciaran

Chole *(American)* ♀   RATING: ★★★☆
Victory of the people—Short for Nichole
> People think of Chole as pretty, popular, funny, caring, energetic
> People who like the name Chole also like Emma, Olivia, Hannah, Isabelle, Paige, Sophie, Hailey, Charlotte, Faith, Natalie

Cholena *(Native American)* ♀   RATING: ★★★
Bird
> People think of Cholena as pretty, sexy, powerful, old-fashioned, leader

People who like the name Cholena also like Chenoa, Chickoa, Catori, Chumani, Cocheta, Kaya, Bena, Ayasha, Chloe, Adsila

Chrina *(American)* ♀   RATING: ★★★
Short for Christina
> People think of Chrina as funny, pretty, caring, wild, sexy
> People who like the name Chrina also like Ciara, Christiana, Caprice, Chastity, Cora, Cianna, Cinnamon, Corina, Candice, Chailyn

Chris *(Greek)* ♀ ♂   RATING: ★★★
Short for names beginning with Chris—Chris O'Donnell, actor; Chris Rock, comedian/actor; Chris Tucker, actor
> People think of Chris as funny, handsome, cool, sexy, caring
> People who like the name Chris also like Christian, Cameron, Blake, Casey, Ryan, Alex, Bailey, James, Brooke, Carter

Chrissy *(English)* ♀   RATING: ★★★☆
Short for Christina—Chrissy Hynde, singer
> People think of Chrissy as pretty, funny, creative, caring, cool
> People who like the name Chrissy also like Chloe, Cassandra, Caitlyn, Amber, Carly, Hailey, Chelsea, Carissa, Claire, Christine

Christa *(English)* ♀   RATING: ★★★★
Feminine form of Christopher—Christa McAuliffe, teacher aboard *The Challenger* space shuttle; Christa Miller, actress
> People think of Christa as pretty, caring, creative, funny, trustworthy
> People who like the name Christa also like Chloe, Hannah, Faith, Emma, Chelsea, Christine, Christina, Isabella, Hailey, Cassandra

Christian *(English)* ♀ ♂   RATING: ★★★☆
Follower of Christ—Christian Bale, actor; Christian Slater, actor
> People think of Christian as handsome, funny, intelligent, cool, popular
> People who like the name Christian also like Cameron, Caden, Connor, Hayden, Dylan, Bailey, Madison, Carter, Logan, Evan

Christiana *(English)* ♀   RATING: ★★★★
Follower of Christ
> People think of Christiana as pretty, intelligent, funny, caring, creative
> People who like the name Christiana also like Isabella, Ava, Emma, Cassandra, Arianna, Christina, Bella, Faith, Hannah, Alexandria

Christiane *(French)* ♀   RATING: ★★★
Christ-bearer
> People think of Christiane as trustworthy, intelligent, creative, elegant, energetic

People who like the name Christiane also like Adriana, Ariana, Jennifer, Chandra, Charissa, Chailyn, Jacqueline, Carla, Charlee, Corinne

Christina (English) ♀ RATING: ★★★
Follower of Christ—Christina Aguilera, singer; Christina Applegate, actress; Christina Ricci, actress
 People think of Christina as pretty, funny, caring, intelligent, creative
 People who like the name Christina also like Hannah, Emma, Emily, Elizabeth, Chloe, Cassandra, Christine, Danielle, Isabella, Abigail

Christine (English) ♀ RATING: ★★★★
Follower of Christ—Christine Boskoff, mountaineer; Christine Lahti, actress; car from the Stephen King novel and movie *Christine*
 People think of Christine as pretty, funny, caring, intelligent, creative
 People who like the name Christine also like Christina, Claire, Elizabeth, Emma, Chloe, Hannah, Gabrielle, Grace, Faith, Charlotte

Christmas (English) ♀ ♂ RATING: ★★★
Christ-feast
 People think of Christmas as religious, funny, pretty, caring, creative
 People who like the name Christmas also like Christian, Cassidy, Bailey, Christy, Casey, Charlie, Colby, Carmen, Chelsey, Cameron

Christoffer (Scandinavian) ♂ RATING: ★★☆
Christ-bearer—Variation of Christopher
 People think of Christoffer as funny, caring, trustworthy, popular, cool
 People who like the name Christoffer also like Christopher, Caleb, Alexander, Benjamin, Aaron, Matthew, Jacob, Aiden, Conner, Ethan

Christopher (Greek) ♂ RATING: ★★★☆
Christ-bearer—Christopher Lowell, interior designer; Christopher Reeve, actor/writer; Christopher Walken, actor
 People think of Christopher as handsome, funny, intelligent, caring, cool
 People who like the name Christopher also like Benjamin, Alexander, Matthew, Nicholas, Andrew, Jacob, Ethan, Caleb, Michael, Joshua

Christos (Greek) ♂ RATING: ★★★☆
Short for Christopher
 People think of Christos as handsome, funny, intelligent, cool, creative
 People who like the name Christos also like Alexander, Christopher, Aiden, Caleb, Gabriel, Constantine, Andrew, Anthony, André, Benjamin

Christy (English) ♀ ♂ RATING: ★★☆
Follower of Christ—Short for Christine; also spelled Christie
 People think of Christy as pretty, funny, caring, intelligent, trustworthy

People who like the name Christy also like Courtney, Brooke, Ashley, Bailey, Casey, Christian, Cassidy, Alexis, Brooklyn, Madison

Chroma (Greek) ♀ RATING: ★★☆
Color
 People think of Chroma as ethnic, artsy, creative, weird, exotic
 People who like the name Chroma also like Calandra, Chloris, Cambria, Cordelia, Cinnamon, Cyrah, Chloe, Carleigh, Calliope, Cassara

Chuck (American) ♂ RATING: ★★
Short for Charles—Chuck Berry, musician; Chuck Jones, animator; Chuck Norris, actor
 People think of Chuck as funny, handsome, caring, cool, big
 People who like the name Chuck also like Chad, Clay, Caleb, Chester, Adam, Alexander, Eddie, Charles, Clint, Aiden

Chumani (Native American) ♀ RATING: ★☆
Dewdrop—Sioux origin
 People think of Chumani as creative, funny, popular, winner, young
 People who like the name Chumani also like Chickoa, Catori, Cocheta, Chenoa, Cholena, Cora, Kaya, Hateya, Calista, Bena

Chung (Vietnamese) ♂ RATING: ★★★
Common
 People think of Chung as intelligent, nerdy, ethnic, loser, exotic
 People who like the name Chung also like Calvin, Brooks, Cleveland, Carlos, Cole, Cheng, Alexander, Colt, Andrew, Brock

Chuong (Vietnamese) ♂ RATING: ★★☆
Chapter
 People think of Chuong as exotic, ethnic, popular, criminal, young
 People who like the name Chuong also like Coen, Conley, Cody, Clark, Cicero, Chauncey, Allan, Atalo, Armando, Argus

Chyna (English) ♀ RATING: ★★☆
From China
 People think of Chyna as pretty, funny, intelligent, caring, young
 People who like the name Chyna also like Chloe, China, Cheyenne, Brianna, Aaliyah, Bianca, Chelsea, Destiny, Charity, Ciara

Chynna (American) ♀ RATING: ★★☆
Variation of China—Chynna Phillips, singer
 People think of Chynna as funny, pretty, creative, caring, popular
 People who like the name Chynna also like Chloe, Aaliyah, Ciara, Destiny, Cheyenne, Charlize, Brianna, Jasmine, Chyna, Bella

Cian (Celtic/Gaelic) ♂   RATING: ★★☆
Ancient
  People think of Cian as handsome, intelligent, powerful,
  young, creative
  People who like the name Cian also like Aiden, Ciaran,
  Liam, Braeden, Cole, Colin, Callum, Keiran, Kael, Caleb

Cianna (American) ♀   RATING: ★★★
Ancient—Feminine form of Cian
  People think of Cianna as pretty, intelligent, funny,
  popular, caring
  People who like the name Cianna also like Ciara,
  Isabella, Gianna, Cailyn, Ceana, Sienna, Chloe, Abrianna,
  Arianna, Ariana

Ciara (Celtic/Gaelic) ♀   RATING: ★★★★
Black
  People think of Ciara as pretty, funny, creative, popular,
  caring
  People who like the name Ciara also like Chloe, Hailey,
  Kiara, Faith, Aaliyah, Ava, Emma, Brianna, Keira,
  Breanna

Ciaran (Celtic/Gaelic) ♂   RATING: ★★☆
Black—Pronounced KEE-ran
  People think of Ciaran as intelligent, handsome, funny,
  popular, creative
  People who like the name Ciaran also like Keiran, Aiden,
  Tristan, Liam, Braeden, Callum, Caleb, Conner, Declan,
  Cian

Cicada (Greek) ♀   RATING: ★★☆
Loud insect of the night—Pronounced chic-KAY-da
  People think of Cicada as weird, exotic, cool, lazy,
  caring
  People who like the name Cicada also like Ciara,
  Chloe, Chailyn, Acacia, Ceana, Aurora, Cascata, Brielle,
  Cambria, Calista

Cicely (English) ♀   RATING: ★★★★
Blind of self-beauty—Variation of Cecilia; Cicely Tyson,
actress
  People think of Cicely as pretty, funny, intelligent, car-
  ing, energetic
  People who like the name Cicely also like Charlotte,
  Cicily, Cecily, Ava, Bella, Chloe, Celeste, Claire, Cecelia,
  Audrey

Cicero (Latin) ♂   RATING: ★★
Chickpea—Roman author and historian
  People think of Cicero as handsome, intelligent, weird,
  energetic, trustworthy
  People who like the name Cicero also like Aiden, Calix,
  Constantine, Caleb, Asher, Chance, Apollo, Conner,
  Tristan, Christos

Cicily (English) ♀   RATING: ★★★☆
Blind of self-beauty—Variation of Cecilia
  People think of Cicily as pretty, intelligent, leader, funny,
  caring
  People who like the name Cicily also like Chloe, Cicely,
  Isabella, Claire, Charlotte, Audrey, Cecily, Bella, Ava,
  Cambria

Cid (Spanish) ♂   RATING: ★★★☆
Lord—El Cid, Spanish hero
  People think of Cid as popular, sporty, funny, intelligent,
  weird
  People who like the name Cid also like Conner, Calix,
  Aden, Colin, Cullen, Cole, Chase, Anthony, Braeden,
  Caleb

Ciel (French) ♀   RATING: ★★★★
From Heaven; heavenly—Sometimes pronounced seel
or shell
  People think of Ciel as pretty, exotic, creative, intel-
  ligent, elegant
  People who like the name Ciel also like Celeste, Chloe,
  Caia, Ciara, Carina, Celestyn, Cara, Ava, Celine, Celia

Cili (Hungarian) ♀   RATING: ★★☆
Short for Cecilia
  People think of Cili as sneaky, poor, quiet, old-fashioned,
  old
  People who like the name Cili also like Chloe, Celeste,
  Clover, Cicily, Ciara, Camille, Cassara, Cianna, Claire,
  Channah

Cilicia (Latin) ♀   RATING: ★★★
Ancient province of Asia
  People think of Cilicia as pretty, exotic, creative, popu-
  lar, funny
  People who like the name Cilicia also like Faith, Cianna,
  Cecilia, Clarissa, Ciara, Celeste, Charissa, Breanna, Bella,
  Chloe

Cillian (Celtic/Gaelic) ♂   RATING: ★★★★
Little cell
  People think of Cillian as handsome, intelligent, sexy,
  elegant, caring
  People who like the name Cillian also like Aiden, Tristan,
  Ciaran, Caleb, Braeden, Liam, Cole, Cullen, Colin, Ethan

Cinco (Spanish) ♂   RATING: ★★☆
Five, fifth-born
  People think of Cinco as loser, young, handsome, nerdy,
  poor
  People who like the name Cinco also like Chico, Aiden,
  Cole, Alexavier, Colt, Curran, Alexander, Boaz, Conor,
  Colin

Cinderella (English) ♀   RATING: ★☆
Girl by the cinders—Cinderella, children's storybook
character
  People think of Cinderella as pretty, elegant, caring,
  intelligent, young
  People who like the name Cinderella also like Belle,
  Anastasia, Cassandra, Destiny, Amber, Bella, Clarissa,
  Chloe, Faith, Ciara

Cindy (Greek) ♀   RATING: ★★☆
Short for Cynthia or Lucinda—Also spelled Cindi;
Cindy Crawford, model; Cyndi Lauper, singer
  People think of Cindy as pretty, funny, caring, intel-
  ligent, cool

People who like the name Cindy also like Emily, Cassandra, Cynthia, Daisy, Chloe, Faith, Amber, Claire, Christina, Crystal

Cinnamon *(American)* ♀　　　　RATING: ★★
The spice
People think of Cinnamon as pretty, sexy, funny, intelligent, creative
People who like the name Cinnamon also like Chloe, Clover, Amber, Chelsea, Autumn, Coco, Blossom, Cassandra, Isabella, Crystal

Cinzia *(Italian)* ♀　　　　RATING: ★★★
From Kinthos—Variation of Cynthia; pronounced *Chin-ZEE-ah*
People think of Cinzia as creative, sexy, pretty, funny, elegant
People who like the name Cinzia also like Cira, Cynzia, Cascata, Caprice, Celeste, Camilla, Gemma, Aria, Arianna, Cianna

Ciqala *(Native American)* ♀ ♂　　　RATING: ★☆
Little one—Dakota origin
People think of Ciqala as exotic, pretty, quiet, caring, wild
People who like the name Ciqala also like Cadence, Caden, Cree, Cade, Brynn, Cain, Cailean, Cael, Charis, Cassidy

Cira *(Italian)* ♀　　　　RATING: ★★★★
Of the sun—Feminine form of Ciro
People think of Cira as creative, pretty, intelligent, funny, popular
People who like the name Cira also like Ciara, Cianna, Cara, Isabella, Chloe, Ava, Aria, Bella, Angelina, Cailyn

Cirila *(Greek)* ♀　　　　RATING: ★★★
Lordly—From Cyril
People think of Cirila as pretty, trustworthy, caring, popular, young
People who like the name Cirila also like Cira, Cleopatra, Chloris, Charissa, Chloe, Cytheria, Claral, Callia, Cholena, Calixte

Ciro *(Italian)* ♂　　　　RATING: ★★★☆
Of the sun—Variation of Cyrus
People think of Ciro as handsome, energetic, intelligent, funny, cool
People who like the name Ciro also like Calix, Cicero, Aiden, Atticus, Cian, Mateo, Damien, Cyrus, Cody, Chase

Cirocco *(Italian)* ♂　　　　RATING: ★★★
Ancient Egyptian wind
People think of Cirocco as energetic, exotic, creative, funny, young
People who like the name Cirocco also like Baldasarre, Aiden, Calix, Cruz, Biagio, Cassius, Ciro, Caleb, Angelo, Cicero

Cissy *(English)* ♀　　　　RATING: ★☆
Short for Cecilia
People think of Cissy as pretty, girl next door, loser, young, popular

People who like the name Cissy also like Clarissa, Carleigh, Celeste, Carly, Chrissy, Carissa, Cailyn, Chelsea, Chloe, Caitlyn

Claire *(French)* ♀　　　　RATING: ★★★
Illustrious—Also spelled Clare or Clair; Claire Danes, actress; Claire Forlani, actress
People think of Claire as pretty, intelligent, caring, funny, creative
People who like the name Claire also like Chloe, Grace, Ava, Emma, Olivia, Hannah, Abigail, Paige, Charlotte, Ella

Clara *(Latin)* ♀　　　　RATING: ★★☆
Illustrious—Clara Bow, actress
People think of Clara as pretty, intelligent, caring, creative, funny
People who like the name Clara also like Claire, Emma, Ava, Charlotte, Ella, Chloe, Grace, Olivia, Amelia, Abigail

Claral *(French)* ♀　　　　RATING: ★★
Clear, bright
People think of Claral as weird, cool, pretty, trendy, sneaky
People who like the name Claral also like Celine, Ciel, Charisse, Cadee, Caressa, Charissa, Chantel, Cosette, Caprice, Cailyn

Clare *(English)* ♀　　　　RATING: ★★★
Illustrious
People think of Clare as pretty, caring, intelligent, funny, creative
People who like the name Clare also like Claire, Grace, Emma, Chloe, Hannah, Ava, Clara, Isabella, Faith, Emily

Clarence *(English)* ♂　　　　RATING: ★★★
British title—Clarence Thomas, Supreme Court justice; Clarence Williams III, actor
People think of Clarence as handsome, intelligent, funny, cool, sexy
People who like the name Clarence also like Alexander, Caleb, Charles, Christopher, Benjamin, Aiden, Adrian, Anthony, Chad, Clayton

Clarice *(English)* ♀　　　　RATING: ★★★★
Illustrious—Clarice Starling, character in novel and movie *Silence of the Lambs* by Thomas Harris
People think of Clarice as pretty, intelligent, caring, funny, creative
People who like the name Clarice also like Claire, Clarissa, Chloe, Charlotte, Clara, Calista, Cassandra, Camille, Abigail, Cailyn

Clarimonde *(German)* ♀　　　　RATING: ★★
Illustrious protector
People think of Clarimonde as pretty, intelligent, elegant, creative, trustworthy
People who like the name Clarimonde also like Calandra, Brielle, Aerona, Celestyn, Calixte, Charisma, Carleigh, Claudette, Chantel, Aurora

Clarissa (Latin) ♀ RATING: ★★☆
Illustrious—Variation of Clarice; *Clarissa Explains It All*, TV show
People think of Clarissa as pretty, caring, funny, intelligent, creative
People who like the name Clarissa also like Cassandra, Carissa, Chloe, Abigail, Isabella, Claire, Faith, Hailey, Caitlyn, Hannah

Clark (English) ♂ RATING: ★★☆
Clerk—Also a surname; Clark Gable, actor; Clark Kent, Superman's alter ego; Dick Clark, TV/radio host; Petula Clark, singer
People think of Clark as handsome, intelligent, caring, trustworthy, funny
People who like the name Clark also like Cole, Ethan, Caleb, Benjamin, Chase, Conner, Cody, Jack, Andrew, Clay

Clarke (English) ♂ RATING: ★★★★
Clerk
People think of Clarke as intelligent, handsome, cool, trustworthy, funny
People who like the name Clarke also like Ethan, Caleb, Cole, Aiden, Jackson, Clayton, Chase, Benjamin, Bradley, Dawson

Claude (Latin) ♂ RATING: ★★☆
Lame—Claude Raines, actor; Jean-Claude Van Damme, actor
People think of Claude as cool, funny, handsome, intelligent, caring
People who like the name Claude also like Cody, Caleb, Cole, Chad, Clark, Clarence, Cedric, Chance, Colin, Oliver

Claudette (French) ♀ RATING: ★★★☆
Lame—Feminine form of Claude; Claudette Colbert, actress
People think of Claudette as pretty, caring, intelligent, creative, funny
People who like the name Claudette also like Charlotte, Claudia, Claire, Chloe, Camille, Bianca, Celeste, Belle, Clarissa, Chelsea

Claudia (Latin) ♀ RATING: ★★☆
Lame—Feminine form of Claude
People think of Claudia as pretty, funny, intelligent, caring, creative
People who like the name Claudia also like Charlotte, Chloe, Claire, Ava, Olivia, Bianca, Isabella, Emma, Grace, Gabrielle

Claudio (Latin) ♂ RATING: ★★★☆
Lame—Variation of Claude
People think of Claudio as handsome, intelligent, creative, sexy, caring
People who like the name Claudio also like Carlos, Alejandro, Adrian, Caleb, Conner, Cody, Diego, Damien, Clayton, Clay

Clay (English) ♂ RATING: ★★☆
Mortal—Clay Aiken, singer
People think of Clay as handsome, funny, intelligent, cool, caring
People who like the name Clay also like Cole, Caleb, Chase, Ethan, Conner, Cody, Clayton, Jacob, Braden, Ian

Clayland (English) ♂ RATING: ★★☆
From Clayton (town of Clay)
People think of Clayland as handsome, cool, creative, trustworthy, caring
People who like the name Clayland also like Clayton, Clarke, Beck, Cordell, Calhoun, Culver, Carver, Aiden, Barrington, Lawson

Clayne (English) ♀ ♂ RATING: ★★☆
Town near clay land—May be short for Clayton
People think of Clayne as nerdy, stuck-up, big, weird, untrustworthy
People who like the name Clayne also like Caden, Carson, Camdyn, Cade, Chandler, Blake, Blaine, Carter, Camden, Coby

Clayton (English) ♂ RATING: ★★★★
From the town on clay land
People think of Clayton as handsome, intelligent, funny, caring, cool
People who like the name Clayton also like Caleb, Ethan, Aiden, Braden, Cole, Conner, Jackson, Gavin, Kaden, Landon

Clea (Greek) ♀ RATING: ★★☆
Variation of Cleo or Cleantha; Clea Duvall, actress
People think of Clea as pretty, creative, exotic, elegant, caring
People who like the name Clea also like Cleo, Chloe, Amelia, Ella, Clara, Calista, Eva, Ava, Cora, Caelan

Cleantha (Greek) ♀ RATING: ★★☆
Famous flower
People think of Cleantha as big, old-fashioned, girl next door, exotic, cool
People who like the name Cleantha also like Calantha, Cora, Charissa, Calista, Chloe, Cianna, Callista, Cassandra, Callia, Brielle

Cleatus (Greek) ♂ RATING: ★☆
Illustrious
People think of Cleatus as poor, lazy, intelligent, weird, unpopular
People who like the name Cleatus also like Caleb, Chester, Calix, Clayton, Coen, Cole, Clark, Cody, Crispin, Benjamin

Cleavant (English) ♂ RATING: ★★
A steep bank
People think of Cleavant as nerdy, loser, old, slow, boy next door
People who like the name Cleavant also like Craig, Cid, Clyde, Cole, Cavan, Cody, Cruz, Crevan, Cleavon, Alaric

Cleave *(English)* ♂   RATING: ★★☆
Variation of Cleavon
People think of Cleave as handsome, energetic, leader, boy next door, popular
People who like the name Cleave also like Cruz, Cutler, Callum, Clyde, Chase, Ace, Colton, Clay, Cort, Colman

Cleavon *(English)* ♂   RATING: ★★☆
A steep bank—Cleavon Little, actor
People think of Cleavon as handsome, quiet, caring, ethnic, intelligent
People who like the name Cleavon also like Cordell, Cutler, Byron, Conner, Byrne, Cody, Colton, Cedric, Braeden, Collier

Clem *(English)* ♂   RATING: ★☆
Short for Clement
People think of Clem as handsome, caring, intelligent, popular, weird
People who like the name Clem also like Conner, Clint, Clayton, Clinton, Chad, Clay, Colt, Beck, Braeden, Braden

Clemance *(French)* ♀   RATING: ★★☆
Mercy
People think of Clemance as intelligent, girl next door, wild, uptight, trustworthy
People who like the name Clemance also like Clemence, Cosette, Celine, Charisse, Clementine, Calista, Claire, Caressa, Colleen, Caprice

Clemence *(French)* ♀   RATING: ★★★★
Mercy
People think of Clemence as pretty, caring, intelligent, creative, funny
People who like the name Clemence also like Corina, Chloe, Clemance, Camille, Cosette, Cecile, Belle, Celine, Cayenne, Claire

Clemency *(English)* ♀♂   RATING: ★★★
Mercy
People think of Clemency as weird, pretty, trustworthy, funny, caring
People who like the name Clemency also like Bailey, Caden, Carrington, Brook, Blake, Carson, Blaine, Cade, Cassidy, Briar

Clemens *(Latin)* ♂   RATING: ★☆
Mercy—Samuel Clemens, aka Mark Twain, author
People think of Clemens as handsome, caring, intelligent, aggressive, wild
People who like the name Clemens also like Cole, Crispin, Aiden, Byron, Colton, Brice, Adair, Chase, Bastien, Bradley

Clement *(English)* ♂   RATING: ★★★☆
Gentle, merciful
People think of Clement as intelligent, handsome, creative, trustworthy, leader
People who like the name Clement also like Aiden, Caleb, Benjamin, Christopher, Cole, Ethan, Brian, Alexander, Constantine, Cody

Clementine *(English)* ♀   RATING: ★★★★
Gentle, merciful—"My Darling Clementine," American folk song
People think of Clementine as pretty, intelligent, creative, artsy, elegant
People who like the name Clementine also like Charlotte, Amelia, Chloe, Claire, Ava, Clara, Olivia, Abigail, Aurora, Scarlett

Cleo *(Greek)* ♀   RATING: ★★★☆
To praise, acclaim—Short for Cleopatra
People think of Cleo as pretty, funny, intelligent, creative, caring
People who like the name Cleo also like Chloe, Ava, Claire, Amelia, Bella, Abigail, Paige, Charlotte, Grace, Emma

Cleopatra *(Greek)* ♀   RATING: ★★
Glory of the father—Cleopatra, ancient queen of Egypt
People think of Cleopatra as pretty, exotic, powerful, intelligent, elegant
People who like the name Cleopatra also like Cassandra, Cleo, Anastasia, Chloe, Aurora, Amber, Charlotte, Athena, Charisma, Bianca

Cleta *(American)* ♀   RATING: ★★★
Feminine form of Cletus
People think of Cleta as pretty, caring, funny, trustworthy, loser
People who like the name Cleta also like Cleo, Clea, Cleopatra, Clio, Cassia, Charissa, Cira, Charisma, Cara, Cloris

Cleveland *(English)* ♂   RATING: ★★★☆
From the hilly land—Also a city in Ohio; Cleveland Amory, animal activist/author; Cleveland Kent Evans, name expert/professor; Grover Cleveland, U.S. president
People think of Cleveland as handsome, intelligent, caring, funny, cool
People who like the name Cleveland also like Clayton, Aiden, Alexander, Cole, Clint, Brent, Brock, Bradford, Brice, Caleb

Clever *(American)* ♀♂   RATING: ★★☆
Smart one
People think of Clever as intelligent, leader, powerful, creative, handsome
People who like the name Clever also like Caden, Blaine, Carter, Carson, Bliss, Cooper, Blake, Blair, Bryce, Beckett

Cliff *(English)* ♂   RATING: ★★
Short for Clifford or Heathcliff
People think of Cliff as handsome, funny, intelligent, cool, caring
People who like the name Cliff also like Clay, Chad, Caleb, Cole, Clayton, Clark, Chase, Clint, Benjamin, Brent

174

Clifford (*English*) ♂   RATING: ★☆
From the cliff ford—Big dog character in children's book series
> People think of Clifford as caring, handsome, funny, intelligent, cool
> People who like the name Clifford also like Caleb, Jacob, Clayton, Ethan, Anthony, Benjamin, Clinton, Isaac, Charles, Alexander

Clifton (*English*) ♂   RATING: ★★★☆
From a town near a cliff
> People think of Clifton as funny, handsome, intelligent, caring, cool
> People who like the name Clifton also like Clayton, Caleb, Cole, Colin, Dalton, Colton, Clinton, Ethan, Braden, Dawson

Clint (*English*) ♂   RATING: ★★
Short for Clinton—Clint Black, singer; Clint Eastwood, actor
> People think of Clint as handsome, funny, intelligent, cool, caring
> People who like the name Clint also like Cole, Ethan, Caleb, Conner, Cody, Colin, Chase, Chad, Adam, Andrew

Clinton (*English*) ♂   RATING: ★★★☆
Town on a hill—George Clinton, musician; William Clinton, U.S. president
> People think of Clinton as handsome, funny, caring, intelligent, cool
> People who like the name Clinton also like Clayton, Caleb, Cole, Ethan, Braden, Aiden, Jackson, Colin, Cody, Colton

Clio (*Greek*) ♀   RATING: ★★★★
Proclaimer—Also awards given to the advertising and design industry
> People think of Clio as pretty, funny, intelligent, creative, artsy
> People who like the name Clio also like Cleo, Chloe, Charlotte, Cora, Belle, Bella, Ciara, Ella, Amelia, Clea

Clive (*English*) ♂   RATING: ★★★☆
Cliff dweller—Clive Barker, actor/director; Clive Davis, music producer
> People think of Clive as intelligent, leader, handsome, trustworthy, weird
> People who like the name Clive also like Cole, Caleb, Chase, Ethan, Aiden, Colin, Oliver, Jacob, Ian, Benjamin

Clodia (*Latin*) ♀   RATING: ★★★
Unknown meaning
> People think of Clodia as pretty, intelligent, trendy, slow, wealthy
> People who like the name Clodia also like Chloe, Carleigh, Charisma, Christina, Ceana, Claudia, Chantel, Ciara, Charlize, Clara

Cloris (*Greek*) ♀   RATING: ★★☆
Variation of Chloris; Cloris Leachman, actress
> People think of Cloris as weird, old-fashioned, nerdy, loser, exotic

> People who like the name Cloris also like Cerelia, Cora, Becca, Cleo, Blossom, Cleopatra, Clarissa, Claire, Calista, Charissa

Clove (*German*) ♀♂   RATING: ★★☆
Nail; spice
> People think of Clove as weird, loser, pretty, unpopular, old
> People who like the name Clove also like Caden, Bailey, Colby, Cameron, Camdyn, Carson, Carter, Corbin, Cadence, Cade

Clover (*English*) ♀   RATING: ★★
Meadow flower
> People think of Clover as creative, pretty, artsy, caring, young
> People who like the name Clover also like Chloe, Claire, Ava, Aurora, Daisy, Faith, Autumn, Amber, Bella, Cassandra

Clovis (*French*) ♂   RATING: ★★★
Famous warrior—Variation of Louis
> People think of Clovis as powerful, sexy, trustworthy, creative, old-fashioned
> People who like the name Clovis also like Barclay, Aiden, Balin, Ansel, Anton, Archer, Axel, Avidan, Aston, Belden

Clyde (*Celtic/Gaelic*) ♂   RATING: ★★★☆
Scottish river
> People think of Clyde as handsome, funny, intelligent, trustworthy, caring
> People who like the name Clyde also like Cole, Aiden, Clayton, Caleb, Chase, Cody, Colin, Ethan, Calvin, Ian

Coby (*Hebrew*) ♀♂   RATING: ★★★★
Supplanter—Short for Jacob
> People think of Coby as handsome, funny, caring, cool, energetic
> People who like the name Coby also like Colby, Caden, Bailey, Carter, Cameron, Carson, Blake, Hayden, Brody, Logan

Cocheta (*Native American*) ♀   RATING: ★★★
That you cannot imagine
> People think of Cocheta as creative, weird, intelligent, exotic, quiet
> People who like the name Cocheta also like Catori, Chumani, Chenoa, Kaya, Chickoa, Kachina, Ayasha, Cholena, Cora, Hateya

Coco (*American*) ♀   RATING: ★★★
Chocolate bean—Coco Arquette, daughter of Courteney Cox and David Arquette; Coco Chanel, designer
> People think of Coco as pretty, cool, popular, sexy, funny
> People who like the name Coco also like Chloe, Bella, Ava, Olivia, Ella, Isabella, Lola, Claire, Elle, Chanel

Cocoa (American) ♀♂   RATING: ★★★
Powdered chocolate
> People think of Cocoa as exotic, creative, energetic, funny, sexy
> People who like the name Cocoa also like Brooklyn, Capricorn, Cassidy, Carson, Hayden, Cactus, Albany, Cricket, Calypso, Blue

Cody (English) ♂   RATING: ★★★
Descendant of Oda—Also an Irish surname
> People think of Cody as funny, handsome, cool, popular, intelligent
> People who like the name Cody also like Caleb, Cole, Ethan, Chase, Aiden, Conner, Jacob, Braden, Noah, Nathan

Coe (English) ♀♂   RATING: ★★★
Jackdaw—Also a surname
> People think of Coe as creative, handsome, weird, sexy, wild
> People who like the name Coe also like Cade, Chay, Cameron, Cooper, Coby, Caley, Caden, Corbin, Cassidy, Corey

Coen (German) ♂   RATING: ★★★★☆
Variation of Conrad
> People think of Coen as handsome, intelligent, funny, cool, caring
> People who like the name Coen also like Aiden, Caleb, Cole, Kaden, Ethan, Braden, Conner, Gavin, Aden, Koen

Coilin (Celtic/Gaelic) ♂   RATING: ★★★
Young child; peaceful dove
> People think of Coilin as funny, handsome, caring, intelligent, creative
> People who like the name Coilin also like Caleb, Conner, Cole, Ethan, Aiden, Colin, Cody, Kaden, Benjamin, Braden

Colandra (American) ♀   RATING: ★★
Swarthy, manly—Combination of Cole and Andra
> People think of Colandra as loser, nerdy, weird, poor, slow
> People who like the name Colandra also like Carmelita, Avril, Colleen, Cara, Caitlin, Chamomile, Chassidy, Cheyenne, Cadhla, Corinna

Colby (English) ♀♂   RATING: ★★★☆
From Koli's farm—Also a type of cheese
> People think of Colby as funny, handsome, intelligent, popular, cool
> People who like the name Colby also like Caden, Bailey, Connor, Hayden, Carter, Logan, Coby, Cameron, Blake, Addison

Cole (English) ♂   RATING: ★★★★
Victory of the people—Originally short for Nicholas; Nat King Cole, singer; Natalie Cole, singer
> People think of Cole as handsome, cool, funny, intelligent, popular
> People who like the name Cole also like Caleb, Ethan, Aiden, Chase, Conner, Noah, Gavin, Cody, Colin, Jacob

Coleman (English) ♂   RATING: ★★★★
Dove; charcoal burner—Also a surname; Coleman Hawkins, jazz musician
> People think of Coleman as handsome, funny, intelligent, caring, cool
> People who like the name Coleman also like Cole, Conner, Caleb, Colton, Clayton, Jackson, Braden, Ethan, Chase, Landon

Colette (French) ♀   RATING: ★★★★
Variation of Nicole—Also spelled Collette
> People think of Colette as pretty, creative, intelligent, caring, funny
> People who like the name Colette also like Chloe, Charlotte, Claire, Cosette, Ava, Celeste, Isabelle, Camille, Bianca, Isabella

Coligny (French) ♀♂   RATING: ★☆
From Coligny, France
> People think of Coligny as stuck-up, weird, untrustworthy, sneaky, exotic
> People who like the name Coligny also like Blaise, Coty, Aure, Astin, Candide, Corin, Bern, Carlin, Ciqala, Ames

Colin (English) ♂   RATING: ★★★★
Short for Nicholas
> People think of Colin as handsome, funny, intelligent, caring, cool
> People who like the name Colin also like Ethan, Aiden, Caleb, Cole, Conner, Ian, Gavin, Owen, Braden, Noah

Colista (Greek) ♀   RATING: ★★★☆
Combination of Colette and Calista
> People think of Colista as caring, artsy, pretty, creative, girl next door
> People who like the name Colista also like Calista, Callista, Kalista, Cailyn, Chloe, Celeste, Colette, Cianna, Callie, Isabella

Colleen (American) ♀   RATING: ★★★☆
Girl—From the Irish word for girl
> People think of Colleen as pretty, funny, caring, intelligent, creative
> People who like the name Colleen also like Claire, Abigail, Charlotte, Chloe, Audrey, Grace, Hannah, Faith, Emily, Hailey

Collice (Celtic/Gaelic) ♀   RATING: ★★★
Variation of Colleen
> People think of Collice as old-fashioned, weird, lazy, creative, quiet
> People who like the name Collice also like Colleen, Ciara, Breena, Bree, Cecelia, Erin, Cambria, Ceana, Bridget, Eileen

Collier (English) ♂   RATING: ★★★★☆
Coal miner
> People think of Collier as leader, handsome, intelligent, caring, winner
> People who like the name Collier also like Caleb, Chase, Aiden, Conner, Cole, Ethan, Chance, Collin, Jackson, Dawson

Collin (*English*) ♂   RATING: ★★★
Variation of Colin
> People think of Collin as handsome, funny, intelligent, cool, caring
> People who like the name Collin also like Caleb, Ethan, Aiden, Conner, Cole, Colin, Gavin, Chase, Ian, Braden

Colm (*Celtic/Gaelic*) ♂   RATING: ★★
Dove
> People think of Colm as intelligent, handsome, cool, caring, popular
> People who like the name Colm also like Callum, Liam, Cullen, Cole, Caleb, Declan, Conner, Ciaran, Cillian, Braeden

Colman (*English*) ♂   RATING: ★★☆
Little dove
> People think of Colman as intelligent, caring, funny, handsome, trustworthy
> People who like the name Colman also like Cole, Colton, Coleman, Caleb, Braeden, Chase, Clayton, Colin, Conner, Conley

Colorado (*Spanish*) ♀♂   RATING: ★★★☆
(Red) Colored—U.S. state
> People think of Colorado as loser, weird, intelligent, wild, cool
> People who like the name Colorado also like Caden, Bailey, Carter, Dakota, Arizona, Cameron, Cadence, Cade, Cassidy, Colby

Colt (*American*) ♂   RATING: ★★★★
Young horse
> People think of Colt as handsome, intelligent, cool, young, sporty
> People who like the name Colt also like Cole, Colton, Caleb, Chase, Conner, Cody, Aiden, Ethan, Braden, Kaden

Colton (*English*) ♂   RATING: ★★★☆
Cole's town
> People think of Colton as handsome, funny, cool, sporty, intelligent
> People who like the name Colton also like Cole, Caleb, Ethan, Aiden, Conner, Landon, Braden, Kaden, Chase, Gavin

Colum (*Celtic/Gaelic*) ♂   RATING: ★★☆
Dove
> People think of Colum as handsome, intelligent, cool, trustworthy, funny
> People who like the name Colum also like Callum, Cullen, Conner, Liam, Aiden, Ciaran, Colin, Caleb, Conlan, Cavan

Columbia (*Latin*) ♀   RATING: ★★★☆
Dove
> People think of Columbia as aggressive, leader, caring, sexy, powerful
> People who like the name Columbia also like Blossom, Crystal, Celeste, Colleen, Chelsea, Claudia, Cinnamon, Autumn, Catherine, Cheyenne

Columbo (*Italian*) ♂   RATING: ★★
Dove—*Columbo*, TV show
> People think of Columbo as poor, exotic, energetic, aggressive, lazy
> People who like the name Columbo also like Dario, Agostino, Demario, Biagio, Dino, Donato, Brando

Columbus (*Latin*) ♂   RATING: ★★
Dove—Christopher Columbus, discoverer of America
> People think of Columbus as creative, old-fashioned, leader, intelligent, old
> People who like the name Columbus also like Charles, Alexander, Dalton, Clarence, Carver, Denton, Christopher, Emmett, David, Deacon

Colwyn (*Welsh*) ♀♂   RATING: ★★★
Welsh river
> People think of Colwyn as intelligent, uptight, leader, quiet, powerful
> People who like the name Colwyn also like Caden, Blaine, Camdyn, Aidan, Camden, Avery, Cade, Corbin, Hayden, Connor

Comfort (*English*) ♀   RATING: ★☆
Comfort—Early American Puritan origin
> People think of Comfort as pretty, caring, weird, funny, lazy
> People who like the name Comfort also like Chelsea, Blossom, Cinnamon, Constance, Faith, Ciara, Cecelia, Caitlyn, Caitlin, Calista

Conan (*Celtic/Gaelic*) ♂   RATING: ★★★☆
Hound, wolf—Conan O'Brien, writer/TV host; *Conan the Barbarian*, movie
> People think of Conan as intelligent, funny, handsome, wild, leader
> People who like the name Conan also like Aiden, Cole, Conner, Caleb, Cody, Colin, Liam, Ethan, Chase, Conley

Conary (*Celtic/Gaelic*) ♀♂   RATING: ★★
Variation of Connery
> People think of Conary as intelligent, pretty, creative, caring, cool
> People who like the name Conary also like Camden, Caden, Blair, Connor, Cassidy, Aidan, Cael, Hayden, Brayden, Avery

Concepción (*Spanish*) ♀   RATING: ★★☆
Conception
> People think of Concepción as caring, leader, ethnic, trustworthy, exotic
> People who like the name Concepción also like Isis, Charisma, Arianna, Brielle, Anastacia, Harmony, Consuelo, Ashlyn, Kaia, Ariella

Concetta (*Italian*) ♀   RATING: ★★★
Conception
> People think of Concetta as pretty, funny, caring, cool, sexy
> People who like the name Concetta also like Brianna, Abigail, Cleo, Bianca, Amaryllis, Beyoncé, Coral, Bella, Amelie, Aura

Cong *(Chinese)* ♀♂　　RATING: ★★☆
Intelligent, clever
> People think of Cong as intelligent, criminal, weird, nerdy, ethnic
> People who like the name Cong also like Chen, Chao, Carmen, Cai, Camdyn, Calypso, Brooke, Caden, Ciqala, Blaze

Conlan *(Celtic/Gaelic)* ♂　　RATING: ★★☆
Hero
> People think of Conlan as handsome, leader, intelligent, caring, cool
> People who like the name Conlan also like Conner, Aiden, Conley, Cole, Liam, Colin, Cullen, Declan, Braeden, Caleb

Conley *(Celtic/Gaelic)* ♂　　RATING: ★★★★
Great chief
> People think of Conley as leader, funny, intelligent, energetic, sporty
> People who like the name Conley also like Conner, Cole, Aiden, Caleb, Conlan, Colin, Braeden, Ethan, Cullen, Braden

Connecticut *(Native American)* ♀♂　　RATING: ★★☆
Beside the long river—From Quinnehtukqut, meaning beside the long tidal river; also a U.S. state
> People think of Connecticut as loser, old-fashioned, unpopular, quiet, cool
> People who like the name Connecticut also like Brooklyn, Cooper, Arizona, Colorado, Bailey, Colby, Camden, Connor, Caden, Cadence

Conner *(Celtic/Gaelic)* ♂　　RATING: ★★★☆
High desire
> People think of Conner as handsome, funny, intelligent, caring, cool
> People who like the name Conner also like Aiden, Ethan, Caleb, Cole, Braden, Colin, Jacob, Gavin, Noah, Kaden

Connie *(English)* ♀♂　　RATING: ★★
Short for Constance; Connie Chung, newscaster; Connie Francis, singer
> People think of Connie as caring, funny, pretty, intelligent, creative
> People who like the name Connie also like Ashley, Cameron, Courtney, Carter, Casey, Corey, Brooke, Charlie, Bailey, Caden

Connley *(Celtic/Gaelic)* ♂　　RATING: ★★★
Great chief
> People think of Connley as handsome, funny, powerful, intelligent, sporty
> People who like the name Connley also like Conner, Cole, Conley, Aiden, Caleb, Braeden, Cullen, Clayton, Colton, Braden

Connor *(Celtic/Gaelic)* ♀♂　　RATING: ★★★☆
High desire—From the Irish name Concohobar
> People think of Connor as handsome, funny, intelligent, cool, popular
> People who like the name Connor also like Logan, Caden, Cameron, Dylan, Madison, Riley, Aidan, Bailey, Hayden, Carter

Conor *(Celtic/Gaelic)* ♂　　RATING: ★★★★
High desire
> People think of Conor as handsome, funny, intelligent, cool, popular
> People who like the name Conor also like Aiden, Conner, Caleb, Cole, Ethan, Colin, Tristan, Aden, Liam, Benjamin

Conrad *(English)* ♂　　RATING: ★★★☆
Bold counsel—Joseph Conrad, author; William Conrad, actor
> People think of Conrad as handsome, intelligent, leader, powerful, trustworthy
> People who like the name Conrad also like Caleb, Cole, Ethan, Aiden, Conner, Gavin, Benjamin, Drake, Colin, Chase

Conroy *(English)* ♂　　RATING: ★★
Detachment of troops—Originally a surname
> People think of Conroy as intelligent, leader, old-fashioned, wealthy, uptight
> People who like the name Conroy also like Conrad, Conner, Aiden, Caleb, Cole, Cody, Conlan, Braeden, Colin, Chase

Constance *(English)* ♀　　RATING: ★★☆
Constant—Constance Bennett, actress
> People think of Constance as pretty, trustworthy, caring, funny, intelligent
> People who like the name Constance also like Faith, Chloe, Grace, Abigail, Hannah, Charlotte, Isabella, Bianca, Audrey, Charity

Constantine *(Latin)* ♂　　RATING: ★★★★
Constant—Constantine Maroulis, singer; Michael Constantine, actor
> People think of Constantine as intelligent, handsome, powerful, cool, funny
> People who like the name Constantine also like Alexander, Aiden, Caleb, Gabriel, Dominic, Ethan, Drake, Cole, Xavier, Damien

Consuelo *(Spanish)* ♀　　RATING: ★★
Consolation
> People think of Consuelo as caring, pretty, creative, exotic, funny
> People who like the name Consuelo also like Claudia, Catalina, Ciara, Cayla, Calista, Charlize, Constance, Chelsea, Catriona, Colette

Content *(American)* ♀　　RATING: ★★☆
Satisfied, happy
> People think of Content as handsome, energetic, trendy, powerful, intelligent
> People who like the name Content also like Cassara, Carrie, Comfort, Charisma, Cashlin, Cordelia, Carleigh, Cady, Chastity, Clover

178

Conway (Celtic/Gaelic) ♂ RATING: ★★★☆
Hound of Meath—Also a Welsh surname, from Conway, Wales; Tim Conway, comedian
> People think of Conway as intelligent, funny, trustworthy, handsome, caring
> People who like the name Conway also like Conner, Caleb, Braeden, Conrad, Aiden, Cole, Conley, Conlan, Ewan, Cullen

Conyers (American) ♂ RATING: ★★
From Coignieres, France—Also an English surname; also a city in Georgia; John Conyers, U.S. Congressman
> People think of Conyers as intelligent, funny, powerful, winner, popular
> People who like the name Conyers also like Conley, Bryson, Colton, Clayton, Bradley, Anson, Anthony, Boyd, Archer, Alaric

Cooper (English) ♀♂ RATING: ★★★☆
Barrel maker—Alice Cooper, singer; Gary Cooper, actor; Jackie Cooper, actor
> People think of Cooper as handsome, sporty, funny, cool, popular
> People who like the name Cooper also like Carter, Connor, Parker, Caden, Bailey, Hayden, Addison, Logan, Carson, Riley

Cora (Greek) ♀ RATING: ★★☆
Heart, maiden
> People think of Cora as pretty, caring, creative, intelligent, funny
> People who like the name Cora also like Ava, Chloe, Ella, Emma, Claire, Hannah, Clara, Olivia, Eva, Grace

Coral (English) ♀ RATING: ★★★☆
Reef formation; pinkish/orange color—Also a form of sea life
> People think of Coral as pretty, creative, caring, funny, intelligent
> People who like the name Coral also like Chloe, Abigail, Charlotte, Caitlyn, Jasmine, Amber, Celeste, Claire, Hailey, Bella

Coralia (Greek) ♀ RATING: ★★★☆
Like coral
> People think of Coralia as creative, pretty, intelligent, exotic, caring
> People who like the name Coralia also like Cora, Coralie, Chloe, Corinna, Cordelia, Ciara, Camille, Charity, Aurora, Cailyn

Coralie (French) ♀ RATING: ★★☆
Little maiden
> People think of Coralie as pretty, intelligent, funny, caring, creative
> People who like the name Coralie also like Camille, Chloe, Cora, Aurora, Cailyn, Claire, Ava, Brielle, Hannah, Paige

Corazon (Spanish) ♀ RATING: ★★★☆
Heart
> People think of Corazon as pretty, exotic, funny, trustworthy, intelligent
> People who like the name Corazon also like Catalina, Celeste, Ciara, Destiny, Belita, Claudia, Ava, Gabriella, Isabel, Carina

Corbeau (French) ♀♂ RATING: ★★☆
Crow, raven
> People think of Corbeau as creative, quiet, popular, artsy, sporty
> People who like the name Corbeau also like Coty, Cael, Blair, Blaine, Corbin, Aure, Astin, Dior, Calypso, Cade

Corbett (English) ♂ RATING: ★★
Raven—Originally a surname
> People think of Corbett as intelligent, funny, trustworthy, artsy, caring
> People who like the name Corbett also like Caleb, Braden, Aiden, Cole, Chase, Ethan, Colton, Landon, Braeden, Gavin

Corbin (English) ♀♂ RATING: ★★☆
Raven—Also a surname; Corbin Bernsen, actor
> People think of Corbin as handsome, funny, intelligent, cool, energetic
> People who like the name Corbin also like Caden, Connor, Carson, Hayden, Logan, Carter, Addison, Avery, Cadence, Bailey

Corby (English) ♀♂ RATING: ★★★☆
From Corc's farm—Also a surname; also short for Corbin
> People think of Corby as funny, caring, creative, cool, popular
> People who like the name Corby also like Colby, Coby, Bailey, Caden, Corbin, Carter, Chandler, Blake, Blaine, Cameron

Cordelia (English) ♀ RATING: ★★★★
Unknown meaning—Character in King Lear by William Shakespeare
> People think of Cordelia as elegant, intelligent, pretty, creative, popular
> People who like the name Cordelia also like Amelia, Bianca, Chloe, Abigail, Charlotte, Aurora, Olivia, Emma, Audrey, Fiona

Cordell (English) ♂ RATING: ★★★★
Rope maker
> People think of Cordell as handsome, intelligent, funny, caring, powerful
> People who like the name Cordell also like Cole, Caleb, Conner, Chase, Clay, Collin, Chance, Clayton, Colin, Dawson

Cordero (Spanish) ♂ RATING: ★★★★
Little lamb
> People think of Cordero as caring, young, handsome, intelligent, powerful

People who like the name Cordero also like Antonio, Cole, Chase, Chance, Colin, Beau, Cordell, Carlos, Cody, Armando

Corentine *(Celtic/Gaelic)* ♀♂   RATING: ★☆
Name of a Breton bishop
People think of Corentine as trustworthy, nerdy, quiet, intelligent, loser
People who like the name Corentine also like Carlen, Brooklyn, Cyan, Caden, Carlin, Ciqala, Camdyn, Cadence, Aidan, Crescent

Coretta *(American)* ♀   RATING: ★★★
Little heart—Coretta Scott King, wife of Dr. Martin Luther King Jr.
People think of Coretta as intelligent, pretty, caring, leader, funny
People who like the name Coretta also like Elise, Aurora, Corinne, Denise, Corina, Camille, Brielle, Cordelia, Cora, Caelan

Corey *(Celtic/Gaelic)* ♀♂   RATING: ★★★
Hollow—Corey Feldman, actor; Corey Haim, actor
People think of Corey as funny, cool, handsome, caring, intelligent
People who like the name Corey also like Bailey, Cameron, Connor, Caden, Casey, Dylan, Blake, Logan, Madison, Jordan

Coriander *(Greek)* ♀♂   RATING: ★★★☆
Romance; spice
People think of Coriander as creative, intelligent, exotic, caring, quiet
People who like the name Coriander also like Cadence, Connor, Cassidy, Crescent, Ember, Cameo, Colby, Camdyn, Cailean, Addison

Corin *(English)* ♀♂   RATING: ★★☆
Spear
People think of Corin as creative, intelligent, caring, funny, popular
People who like the name Corin also like Caden, Addison, Aidan, Connor, Jaden, Carter, Cameron, Corbin, Camryn, Carson

Corina *(French)* ♀   RATING: ★★★☆
Maiden
People think of Corina as pretty, funny, caring, intelligent, creative
People who like the name Corina also like Carina, Chloe, Isabella, Cora, Cassandra, Ava, Hailey, Claire, Breanna, Faith

Corine *(American)* ♀   RATING: ★★★★
Maiden
People think of Corine as weird, pretty, aggressive, stuck-up, intelligent
People who like the name Corine also like Corinne, Claire, Camille, Chloe, Isabella, Corina, Hailey, Ava, Grace, Emma

Corinna *(Greek)* ♀   RATING: ★★☆
Maiden
People think of Corinna as pretty, caring, funny, trustworthy, creative
People who like the name Corinna also like Corinne, Arianna, Chloe, Isabella, Brianna, Bella, Cassandra, Carina, Eva, Faith

Corinne *(French)* ♀   RATING: ★★★★
Maiden—Variation of Cora
People think of Corinne as pretty, intelligent, caring, creative, funny
People who like the name Corinne also like Claire, Ava, Chloe, Olivia, Charlotte, Grace, Camille, Hannah, Isabella, Emma

Corinthia *(Greek)* ♀   RATING: ★★★
From Corinth, a city in ancient Greece
People think of Corinthia as pretty, creative, funny, intelligent, sexy
People who like the name Corinthia also like Chloe, Cassandra, Clara, Corinne, Abigail, Calandra, Carissa, Cianna, Charlotte, Cleopatra

Corliss *(English)* ♀♂   RATING: ★★
Happy, free from care—Originally a surname
People think of Corliss as creative, pretty, intelligent, leader, caring
People who like the name Corliss also like Caden, Coye, Corbin, Cato, Coy, Addison, Cadence, Colby, Cade, Bailey

Cormac *(Celtic/Gaelic)* ♂   RATING: ★★★☆
Destroying son
People think of Cormac as handsome, intelligent, funny, leader, energetic
People who like the name Cormac also like Aiden, Declan, Liam, Cole, Callum, Braeden, Caleb, Cullen, Callahan, Calder

Cornelia *(Latin)* ♀   RATING: ★★★☆
Horn—Feminine form of Cornelius
People think of Cornelia as pretty, intelligent, caring, trustworthy, funny
People who like the name Cornelia also like Cordelia, Charlotte, Bianca, Claudia, Chloe, Celia, Amelia, Cassandra, Chelsea, Bridget

Cornelius *(Latin)* ♂   RATING: ★★
Horn
People think of Cornelius as intelligent, handsome, funny, caring, powerful
People who like the name Cornelius also like Benjamin, Felix, Oliver, Aiden, Adam, Clarence, Sebastian, Caleb, Curtis, Isaac

Cornell *(English)* ♂   RATING: ★★★☆
From Cornhill or Cornwell—Originally a surname; also a variation of Cornelius
People think of Cornell as intelligent, handsome, sexy, popular, funny

People who like the name Cornell also like Caleb, Colin, Aiden, Cole, Conley, Brian, Cedric, Cordell, Conner, Conan

Cort (English) ♂   RATING: ★★★☆
Bold or short—Bud Cort, actor
People think of Cort as funny, cool, sporty, handsome, energetic
People who like the name Cort also like Cole, Chase, Colton, Colin, Caleb, Aiden, Conner, Ethan, Braden, Chance

Cory (Celtic/Gaelic) ♀♂   RATING: ★★★
Hollow—Cory Dangerfield, actor
People think of Cory as funny, caring, intelligent, handsome, cool
People who like the name Cory also like Bailey, Cameron, Caden, Connor, Dylan, Blake, Corey, Ryan, Riley, Austin

Corydon (Greek) ♂   RATING: ★★☆
Lark—From Greek *korudos* meaning lark; also spelled Coridan
People think of Corydon as funny, sneaky, loser, weird, old-fashioned
People who like the name Corydon also like Chase, Aiden, Cargan, Colton, Cale, Brant, Brinley, Cullen, Conner, Courtland

Cosette (French) ♀   RATING: ★★
Victorious people
People think of Cosette as pretty, elegant, caring, young, intelligent
People who like the name Cosette also like Colette, Charlotte, Claire, Chloe, Genevieve, Ava, Camille, Giselle, Audrey, Belle

Cosima (Italian) ♀   RATING: ★★
Order—Feminine form of Cosmo
People think of Cosima as exotic, pretty, creative, wild, sexy
People who like the name Cosima also like Bianca, Ciara, Charlotte, Desdemona, Celeste, Cassia, Cara, Claire, Cira, Cosette

Cosma (Italian) ♀   RATING: ★★☆
Heavens, cosmos
People think of Cosma as exotic, nerdy, funny, powerful, young
People who like the name Cosma also like Celina, Nalanie, Davina, Celia, Bianca, Maya, Ciel, Celestyn, Bambi, Danika

Cosmo (English) ♂   RATING: ★★
Order—First name of *Seinfeld* character Kramer
People think of Cosmo as funny, creative, energetic, intelligent, weird
People who like the name Cosmo also like Chance, Cody, Cole, Axel, Caleb, Chase, Jasper, Oliver, Conan, Ace

Costa (Spanish) ♀♂   RATING: ★★☆
From the coast
People think of Costa as funny, handsome, religious, popular, cool
People who like the name Costa also like Britain, Belen, Caden, Devin, Ainslie, Brooklyn, Ivory, Morgan, Dharma, Dayton

Coty (French) ♀♂   RATING: ★★★☆
Small slope, hillside
People think of Coty as funny, caring, cool, weird, trustworthy
People who like the name Coty also like Caden, Coby, Colby, Corey, Bailey, Cameron, Connor, Dakota, Brody, Casey

Courtland (English) ♂   RATING: ★★★★
Land of the court
People think of Courtland as handsome, intelligent, popular, caring, funny
People who like the name Courtland also like Braden, Ethan, Cole, Caleb, Jackson, Aiden, Brighton, Holden, Emerson, Chase

Courtney (English) ♀♂   RATING: ★★★
From Courtenay, France—Also spelled Courteney; Courtney Love, actress/singer; Courtney Thorne-Smith, actress; Courtney Vance, actor; Courteney Cox, actress
People think of Courtney as pretty, funny, caring, intelligent, creative
People who like the name Courtney also like Brooke, Bailey, Madison, Cameron, Ashley, Taylor, Connor, Alexis, Ryan, Dylan

Coy (English) ♀♂   RATING: ★★★☆
Quiet, still—Also means shy
People think of Coy as caring, funny, intelligent, handsome, energetic
People who like the name Coy also like Cade, Caden, Corbin, Carter, Blaine, Cooper, Bailey, Carson, Parker, Chandler

Coye (English) ♀♂   RATING: ★★
Quiet, still
People think of Coye as caring, quiet, funny, trustworthy, intelligent
People who like the name Coye also like Caden, Cade, Blake, Blaine, Carson, Colby, Coy, Cameron, Brasen, Corey

Coyne (French) ♂   RATING: ★☆
Modest
People think of Coyne as weird, artsy, loser, trustworthy, funny
People who like the name Coyne also like Caleb, Cavan, Cole, Calix, Alain, Cale, Colin, Cullen, Avent, Ansel

Craig (Celtic/Gaelic) ♂   RATING: ★★☆
From the crag—Craig Kilborn, talk show host; Jenny Craig, diet maven
People think of Craig as funny, handsome, intelligent, caring, cool

People who like the name Craig also like Caleb, Ethan, Conner, Benjamin, Aiden, Aaron, Adam, Brandon, Cole, Cody

Crane *(English)* ♀♂　　　　RATING: ★★☆
Long-necked bird—Originally a surname
People think of Crane as pretty, trendy, lazy, intelligent, trustworthy
People who like the name Crane also like Coby, Bailey, Corbin, Caden, Cade, Blair, Aubrey, Corey, Cameron, Cory

Crawford *(Celtic/Gaelic)* ♂　　　　RATING: ★★★
Crossing of blood—Originally a surname
People think of Crawford as intelligent, winner, caring, cool, wild
People who like the name Crawford also like Carver, Clark, Caine, Alastair, Lachlan, Benjamin, Isaac, Caleb, Oscar, Aiden

Crayton *(American)* ♂　　　　RATING: ★★
Town near rocks—Variation of Creighton
People think of Crayton as sporty, powerful, funny, trustworthy, caring
People who like the name Crayton also like Aiden, Creighton, Cale, Grayson, Cullen, Kyson, Ketan, Colton, Kynton, Beck

Creda *(English)* ♀　　　　RATING: ★★☆
Faith
People think of Creda as quiet, old-fashioned, pretty, weird, unpopular
People who like the name Creda also like Ciel, Chumani, Celeste, Calixte, Ceana, Cleo, Chastity, Cora, Celia, Celestyn

Cree *(Native American)* ♀♂　　　　RATING: ★★★★
Tribe name—From the French word *Kristineaux*, used for the First Nations people; shortened to Kri or Cree in English; Cree Summer, actress/voiceover artist
People think of Cree as pretty, funny, cool, young, intelligent
People who like the name Cree also like Caden, Cadence, Dakota, Cade, Cassidy, Avery, Bailey, Cai, Blaine, Cameron

Creighton *(English)* ♂　　　　RATING: ★★
Town near rocks
People think of Creighton as intelligent, handsome, funny, creative, popular
People who like the name Creighton also like Cole, Caleb, Aiden, Conner, Ethan, Clayton, Colin, Braden, Grayson, Colton

Creola *(American)* ♀♂　　　　RATING: ★☆
Native to the land; Creole
People think of Creola as weird, ethnic, old-fashioned, funny, exotic
People who like the name Creola also like Ceres, Caden, Clayne, Camden, Carrington, Cyan, Camdyn, Cain, Brasen, Cheche

Crescent *(English)* ♀♂　　　　RATING: ★★★
Crescent—Also the shape of an incomplete moon; also French bakery item (croissant)
People think of Crescent as creative, intelligent, exotic, artsy, girl next door
People who like the name Crescent also like Cadence, Cade, Caden, Blaine, Blair, Colby, Christian, Cameron, Camdyn, Cassidy

Crescentia *(German)* ♀　　　　RATING: ★★★
Crescent-shaped, moon
People think of Crescentia as creative, young, exotic, funny, intelligent
People who like the name Crescentia also like Cleopatra, Anastasia, Acacia, Celeste, Chloe, Claudette, Oceana, Charity, Arwen, Astra

Crete *(Latin)* ♀　　　　RATING: ★★
Short for Lucretia—Also an island off of Greece
People think of Crete as exotic, ethnic, loser, poor, wealthy
People who like the name Crete also like Crystal, Ciara, Celeste, Cosima, Bellona, Chione, Clover, Catriona, Ceri, Cayenne

Crevan *(Celtic/Gaelic)* ♂　　　　RATING: ★★
Fox
People think of Crevan as sneaky, handsome, intelligent, creative, cool
People who like the name Crevan also like Aiden, Conner, Braeden, Cavan, Ciaran, Tristan, Devlin, Faolan, Bowen, Cole

Cricket *(American)* ♀♂　　　　RATING: ★★★☆
Loud insect of the night
People think of Cricket as pretty, funny, energetic, popular, creative
People who like the name Cricket also like Caden, Bailey, Piper, Corbin, Cassidy, Cameron, Cadence, Brooklyn, Chandler, Blake

Crispin *(Latin)* ♂　　　　RATING: ★★★☆
Curly haired—Crispin Glover, actor
People think of Crispin as intelligent, quiet, handsome, funny, creative
People who like the name Crispin also like Caleb, Aiden, Chase, Gabriel, Cole, Ethan, Braden, Ian, Elijah, Landon

Crista *(English)* ♀　　　　RATING: ★★★★
Feminine form of beginning names with Christ—Also spelled Christa or Krista
People think of Crista as pretty, funny, creative, intelligent, cool
People who like the name Crista also like Faith, Caitlyn, Christa, Cailyn, Hailey, Cassandra, Brianna, Carissa, Ashlyn, Clarissa

Cristina *(Spanish)* ♀　　　　RATING: ★★★★
Christ bearer—Cristina Saralegui, TV host
People think of Cristina as pretty, funny, intelligent, caring, creative

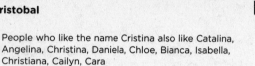
People who like the name Cristina also like Catalina, Angelina, Christina, Daniela, Chloe, Bianca, Isabella, Christiana, Cailyn, Cara

Cristobal *(Spanish)* ♀ RATING: ★★★
Christ bearer—Spanish variation of Christopher
People think of Cristobal as funny, intelligent, young, cool, creative
People who like the name Cristobal also like Consuelo, Catalina, Crista, Ciara, Cianna, Candra, Calista, Aine, Chelsea, Amalia

Cristy *(English)* ♀♂ RATING: ★★★☆
Short for Cristina
People think of Cristy as caring, intelligent, funny, creative, trustworthy
People who like the name Cristy also like Christy, Casey, Caley, Courtney, Cassidy, Brooke, Caden, Alexis, Christian, Cadence

Cruella *(American)* ♀ RATING: ★★☆
Evil, cruel—Created for character in Disney's *101 Dalmations*
People think of Cruella as aggressive, criminal, untrustworthy, stuck-up, sneaky
People who like the name Cruella also like Cassandra, Constance, Calista, Colleen, Claudia, Carly, Cailyn, Crystal, Cynthia, Caitlyn

Cruz *(Spanish)* ♂ RATING: ★★★★
The cross bearer
People think of Cruz as cool, handsome, popular, funny, leader
People who like the name Cruz also like Cole, Caleb, Chase, Ethan, Aiden, Elijah, Gavin, Dominic, Conner, Xavier

Cruzita *(Spanish)* ♀ RATING: ★★☆
Little cross—Feminine form of Cruz
People think of Cruzita as exotic, pretty, creative, funny, trustworthy
People who like the name Cruzita also like Carlota, Chelsea, Catalin, Cristobal, Aileen, Elysia, Cilicia, Alaina, Catalina, Ailani

Crwys *(Welsh)* ♀ RATING: ★★★
Cross
People think of Crwys as weird, loser, unpopular, nerdy, criminal
People who like the name Crwys also like Cambria, Caelan, Carys, Braith, Cambree, Chloe, Bronwyn, Caraf, Ceri, Arwen

Crystal *(Latin)* ♀ RATING: ★★★
Earth mineral or brilliant glass—Crystal Gayle, singer; Billy Crystal, actor
People think of Crystal as pretty, funny, caring, creative, trustworthy
People who like the name Crystal also like Amber, Faith, Chloe, Abigail, Destiny, Jasmine, Caitlyn, Chelsea, Emily, Cassandra

Csilla *(Hungarian)* ♀ RATING: ★★
Protection
People think of Csilla as intelligent, sexy, caring, elegant, pretty
People who like the name Csilla also like Carys, Cynzia, Cassara, Cora, Camille, Channah, Camilla, Cocheta, Cwen, Chantrea

Csongor *(Hungarian)* ♂ RATING: ★★☆
Hunting bird
People think of Csongor as handsome, sexy, exotic, weird, intelligent
People who like the name Csongor also like Cyrus, Bade, Adrian, Ace, Cicero, Chase, Cassius, Ban, August, Caradoc

Cullen *(Celtic/Gaelic)* ♂ RATING: ★★★★
From Cullen, Scotland—Also a Scottish surname
People think of Cullen as handsome, intelligent, funny, energetic, popular
People who like the name Cullen also like Aiden, Cole, Colin, Caleb, Conner, Ethan, Owen, Chase, Liam, Tristan

Culver *(English)* ♂ RATING: ★★★
Dove
People think of Culver as lazy, energetic, funny, weird, creative
People who like the name Culver also like Caleb, Cole, Cullen, Conner, Chase, Chance, Clayton, Braden, Carver, Cody

Cunningham *(Celtic/Gaelic)* ♂ RATING: ★★★
Village of milk
People think of Cunningham as intelligent, creative, funny, caring, powerful
People who like the name Cunningham also like Callahan, Charles, Caleb, Curran, Calhoun, Clifton, Clayton, Carver, Cole, Colton

Curran *(Celtic/Gaelic)* ♂ RATING: ★★★★
Hero
People think of Curran as handsome, intelligent, caring, leader, trustworthy
People who like the name Curran also like Cullen, Cole, Aiden, Conner, Braeden, Owen, Cavan, Conley, Ethan, Conlan

Curry *(Celtic/Gaelic)* ♂ RATING: ★★★☆
A marsh or an herb—Tim Curry, actor
People think of Curry as creative, aggressive, funny, young, sexy
People who like the name Curry also like Clay, Cullen, Conner, Craig, Cole, Barry, Brian, Conley, Callum, Brennan

Curt *(Latin)* ♂ RATING: ★★★☆
Short for Curtis—Curt Cobain, musician
People think of Curt as funny, cool, handsome, intelligent, sexy
People who like the name Curt also like Conner, Caleb, Cole, Chad, Cody, Ethan, Clay, Curtis, Craig, Joshua

Curtis (*Latin*) ♂   RATING: ★★☆
Courteous—Jamie Lee Curtis, actress
People think of Curtis as handsome, funny, caring, cool, intelligent
People who like the name Curtis also like Caleb, Ethan, Benjamin, Cody, Jacob, Cole, Adam, Christopher, Conner, Alexander

Cuthbert (*English*) ♂   RATING: ★★★
Brilliant—Elisha Cuthbert, actress
People think of Cuthbert as intelligent, caring, handsome, leader, funny
People who like the name Cuthbert also like Cordell, Chester, Cole, Colton, Beck, Clinton, Constantine, Caleb, Coleman, Clark

Cutler (*English*) ♂   RATING: ★★★
Knife maker
People think of Cutler as aggressive, powerful, sneaky, intelligent, sexy
People who like the name Cutler also like Caleb, Braden, Carver, Cullen, Chase, Colton, Cutter, Clayton, Conner, Cody

Cutter (*English*) ♂   RATING: ★★
Gem cutter
People think of Cutter as aggressive, funny, weird, popular, criminal
People who like the name Cutter also like Conner, Colton, Caleb, Clayton, Colin, Aiden, Cole, Gage, Braden, Cullen

Cuyler (*Celtic/Gaelic*) ♂   RATING: ★★★★
Chapel, shelter—Pronounced *KY-ler*
People think of Cuyler as handsome, caring, energetic, intelligent, boy next door
People who like the name Cuyler also like Aiden, Caleb, Cullen, Conner, Cole, Kaden, Keagan, Conley, Cavan, Braden

Cwen (*English*) ♀   RATING: ★★
Queen
People think of Cwen as weird, elegant, creative, powerful, leader
People who like the name Cwen also like Chloe, Cytheria, Bella, Carys, Calixte, Blythe, Caelan, Ciara, Caitlyn, Charlotte

Cy (*Greek*) ♂   RATING: ★★★☆
Short for Cyril—Cy Young, baseball player
People think of Cy as intelligent, handsome, cool, popular, winner
People who like the name Cy also like Cole, Caleb, Conner, Kaden, Cale, Cody, Eli, Beau, Coen, Cyrus

Cyan (*American*) ♀♂   RATING: ★★★☆
Light blue-green
People think of Cyan as creative, artsy, cool, energetic, pretty
People who like the name Cyan also like Caden, Bailey, Carson, Aidan, Cade, Blake, Cadence, Hayden, Dakota, Dylan

Cyanne (*English*) ♀   RATING: ★★★★☆
Graceful, fordly—Combination of Cyril and Anne
People think of Cyanne as pretty, intelligent, trustworthy, caring, leader
People who like the name Cyanne also like Cailyn, Cianna, Ciara, Chloe, Kaelyn, Ava, Cora, Arianna, Keira, Caelan

Cybele (*English*) ♀   RATING: ★★★☆
She of the hair—From the Greek
People think of Cybele as intelligent, pretty, exotic, creative, artsy
People who like the name Cybele also like Brielle, Candace, Claudette, Claudia, Calista, Clarimonde, Cora, Cianna, Celeste, Carleigh

Cybil (*Greek*) ♀   RATING: ★★★☆
Soothsayer
People think of Cybil as intelligent, funny, caring, elegant, cool
People who like the name Cybil also like Chloe, Charlotte, Cassandra, Claire, Abigail, Hannah, Bethany, Cora, Caitlyn, Clara

Cybill (*Greek*) ♀   RATING: ★★
Soothsayer—Cybill Shepherd, actress
People think of Cybill as pretty, weird, funny, intelligent, cool
People who like the name Cybill also like Bianca, Camille, Eve, Catherine, Abigail, Chloe, Carissa, Celeste, Bridget, Arianna

Cybille (*French*) ♀   RATING: ★★☆
Soothsayer
People think of Cybille as old, funny, old-fashioned, weird, exotic
People who like the name Cybille also like Camille, Chloe, Claire, Cecile, Belle, Antoinette, Charlotte, Charisma, Faith, Felicity

Cyd (*Greek*) ♀♂   RATING: ★★★☆
A public hill—Cyd Charisse, actress/dancer
People think of Cyd as creative, funny, caring, energetic, pretty
People who like the name Cyd also like Casey, Cade, Cooper, Blair, Cain, Corey, Cameron, Corbin, Cassidy, Caden

Cyma (*Greek*) ♀   RATING: ★☆
Flourish
People think of Cyma as pretty, exotic, caring, sexy, elegant
People who like the name Cyma also like Cora, Calixte, Cyrah, Cleantha, Cytheria, Catherine, Catori, Cynzia, Channah, Celina

Cynara (*Greek*) ♀   RATING: ★★☆
From the island of Zinara
People think of Cynara as pretty, intelligent, creative, caring, funny
People who like the name Cynara also like Amara, Cianna, Cassara, Celeste, Amaya, Samara, Cytheria, Cyrah, Inara, Damara

Cyndi *(Greek)* ♀   RATING: ★★★☆
Short for Cynthia or Lucinda; Cyndi Lauper, singer/actress
> People think of Cyndi as pretty, caring, funny, creative, popular
> People who like the name Cyndi also like Clarissa, Cynthia, Chloe, Carissa, Cassandra, Cindy, Bridget, Faith, Emily, Claire

Cynna *(American)* ♀   RATING: ★★☆
Short for Cynthia; Cynna Kydd, athlete
> People think of Cynna as pretty, caring, artsy, creative, cool
> People who like the name Cynna also like Cyrah, Cianna, Ceana, Charity, Chassidy, Cheyenne, Cambree, Candra, Channah, Colette

Cynthia *(Greek)* ♀   RATING: ★★★☆
From Kinthos—Also the moon goddess; Cynthia Nixon, actress
> People think of Cynthia as pretty, caring, funny, intelligent, creative
> People who like the name Cynthia also like Cassandra, Isabella, Faith, Hailey, Chloe, Bethany, Hannah, Charlotte, Emily, Claire

Cynzia *(Italian)* ♀   RATING: ★★★☆
From Kynthos—Variation of Cynthia
> People think of Cynzia as exotic, weird, artsy, ethnic, trendy
> People who like the name Cynzia also like Aria, Camilla, Cira, Cytheria, Cianna, Cascata, Abrianna, Adrina, Gianna, Cinzia

Cyrah *(African)* ♀   RATING: ★★★★
Enthroned
> People think of Cyrah as pretty, creative, caring, powerful, intelligent
> People who like the name Cyrah also like Cianna, Ciara, Cailyn, Constance, Cyanne, Caelan, Charisma, Adia, Chloe, Jadyn

Cyril *(Greek)* ♂   RATING: ★★★☆
Lordly
> People think of Cyril as intelligent, handsome, funny, trustworthy, cool
> People who like the name Cyril also like Cyrus, Gabriel, Caleb, Benjamin, Colin, Dominic, Aiden, Conner, Cedric, Elijah

Cyrus *(Persian)* ♂   RATING: ★★★
Of the sun—Cyrus Vance, former U.S. secretary of state; Billy Ray Cyrus, singer; Miley Cyrus, actress/singer
> People think of Cyrus as intelligent, handsome, powerful, cool, leader
> People who like the name Cyrus also like Caleb, Gabriel, Ethan, Cole, Chase, Aiden, Elijah, Drake, Noah, Kaden

Cytheria *(Greek)* ♀   RATING: ★★★☆
Goddess of love—From the island of Cythera
> People think of Cytheria as sexy, exotic, pretty, elegant, wild
> People who like the name Cytheria also like Cassandra, Calista, Aurora, Cailyn, Celeste, Cleopatra, Bianca, Cynthia, Calixte, Isis

Czar *(Russian)* ♂   RATING: ★★☆
Ruler
> People think of Czar as energetic, handsome, caring, quiet, leader
> People who like the name Czar also like Cyrus, Ciro, Patrick, Boden, Cyril, Creighton, Chase, Cordero, Cornell, Chance

Czarina *(Russian)* ♀   RATING: ★★★
Female ruler
> People think of Czarina as pretty, elegant, creative, popular, leader
> People who like the name Czarina also like Ivy, Cady, Evita, Tiana, Beatrix, Jazzelle, Delilah, Faye, Toyah, Cinnamon

— 🄳 —

Da-xia *(Chinese)* ♀   RATING: ★☆
Big hero
> People think of Da-xia as exotic, pretty, funny, nerdy, poor
> People who like the name Da-xia also like Amaya, Kaida, Danika, Emiko, Aneko, Kaori, Destiny, Danica, Daisy, Jia Li

Dacey *(English)* ♀♂   RATING: ★★★☆
Unknown meaning
> People think of Dacey as pretty, funny, creative, girl next door, popular
> People who like the name Dacey also like Caden, Bailey, Jacey, Addison, Darcy, Delaney, Jaden, Blair, Dakota, Hayden

Dacia *(Latin)* ♀   RATING: ★★★☆
From the city of Dacia, near Rome
> People think of Dacia as pretty, energetic, intelligent, funny, caring
> People who like the name Dacia also like Gabriella, Paige, Dahlia, Hailey, Bianca, Faith, Ashlyn, Gabrielle, Ava, Aurora

Dacian *(Latin)* ♂   RATING: ★★★
From the city of Dacia, near Rome
> People think of Dacian as handsome, caring, intelligent, trustworthy, energetic
> People who like the name Dacian also like Darian, Daemyn, Drake, Gabriel, Aiden, Damien, Damian, Kaden, Dawson, Jayden

Daemyn *(American)* ♂   RATING: ★★★★
Constant, loyal—Variation of Damon
> People think of Daemyn as handsome, powerful, cool, leader, sexy
> People who like the name Daemyn also like Damian, Kaden, Damien, Aiden, Jayden, Caleb, Dominic, Damon, Darian, Aden

Daffodil (*English*) ♀   RATING: ★★★
Yellow flower
> People think of Daffodil as pretty, artsy, cool, elegant, creative
> People who like the name Daffodil also like Daisy, Blossom, Belle, Dahlia, Daphne, Aurora, Clover, Hannah, Jasmine, Abigail

Dafydd (*Welsh*) ♂   RATING: ★★★☆
Beloved—Variation of David; pronounced *DAV-ith*
> People think of Dafydd as intelligent, handsome, caring, cool, sexy
> People who like the name Dafydd also like Oliver, Daniel, Cody, Aiden, Rhys, David, Kael, Alexander, Aaron, Dominic

Dagan (*Hebrew*) ♀♂   RATING: ★★★★
Grain of corn
> People think of Dagan as handsome, intelligent, funny, creative, powerful
> People who like the name Dagan also like Caden, Jaden, Hayden, Addison, Dakota, Mason, Bailey, Brayden, Logan, Aidan

Dagmar (*Scandinavian*) ♀   RATING: ★★★☆
Dear, famous
> People think of Dagmar as intelligent, pretty, funny, elegant, creative
> People who like the name Dagmar also like Damaris, Damara, Astrid, Ava, Adrienne, Damita, Fiona, Anika, Adelaide, Danica

Dahlia (*Greek*) ♀   RATING: ★★☆
Flower named for botanist A. Dahl—Black Dahlia, infamous 1940s murder case in Los Angeles
> People think of Dahlia as pretty, exotic, intelligent, elegant, creative
> People who like the name Dahlia also like Daphne, Chloe, Ava, Bianca, Isabella, Faith, Amelia, Delilah, Bella, Abigail

Daiki (*Japanese*) ♂   RATING: ★★★
Big, shining
> People think of Daiki as exotic, leader, trendy, funny, pretty
> People who like the name Daiki also like Kaemon, Ryu, Damian, Itachi, Keitaro, Hiroshi, Riku, Haru, Haruki, Grayson

Daire (*Celtic/Gaelic*) ♂   RATING: ★★
Fruitful, fertile—Pronounced *DAIR-ry*
> People think of Daire as intelligent, artsy, funny, creative, exotic
> People who like the name Daire also like Aiden, Declan, Braeden, Devlin, Kael, Ciaran, Edan, Tristan, Cole, Liam

Daisuke (*Japanese*) ♂   RATING: ★★★
Lionhearted
> People think of Daisuke as intelligent, trustworthy, artsy, caring, young
> People who like the name Daisuke also like Ryu, Hotaru, Mizu, Hiroshi, Haru, Haruki, Kamin, Zain, Itachi, Khalon

Daisy (*American*) ♀   RATING: ★★☆
Daisy flower—Originally meant the day's eye; Daisy Fuentes, actress; *Princess Daisy* by Judith Krantz
> People think of Daisy as pretty, funny, caring, young, intelligent
> People who like the name Daisy also like Grace, Faith, Emma, Chloe, Bella, Isabella, Hannah, Lily, Emily, Ella

Dajuan (*American*) ♂   RATING: ★★★☆
Combination of Da and Juan
> People think of Dajuan as handsome, caring, young, popular, funny
> People who like the name Dajuan also like Dayshaun, Deshawn, Daemyn, Jayden, Demario, Elijah, Damir, Damon, Darius, Dominic

Dakota (*Native American*) ♀♂   RATING: ★★★
The allies—Sioux origin
> People think of Dakota as funny, caring, intelligent, cool, young
> People who like the name Dakota also like Bailey, Madison, Caden, Hayden, Dylan, Mackenzie, Riley, Jaden, Logan, Addison

Dale (*German*) ♀♂   RATING: ★★☆
Valley—Dale Carnegie, inspirational/motivational writer; Dale Earnhart, race car driver; Dale Evans, wife of Roy Rogers/actress
> People think of Dale as funny, intelligent, handsome, caring, trustworthy
> People who like the name Dale also like Dylan, Bailey, Dakota, Drew, Cameron, Kyle, Blake, Hayden, James, Dallas

Dalia (*Hebrew*) ♀   RATING: ★★★★
A branch, bough
> People think of Dalia as pretty, creative, caring, funny, intelligent
> People who like the name Dalia also like Dahlia, Delia, Isabella, Ava, Daphne, Eva, Emma, Faith, Daria, Ella

Dalila (*Arabic*) ♀   RATING: ★★★★☆
Guide, model
> People think of Dalila as pretty, intelligent, caring, young, sexy
> People who like the name Dalila also like Dahlia, Delilah, Layla, Destiny, Isabella, Bianca, Daphne, Adriana, Faith, Aurora

Dalit (*Hebrew*) ♂   RATING: ★★★
Draw water—Pronounced *dah-LEET*
> People think of Dalit as caring, pretty, intelligent, cool, trustworthy
> People who like the name Dalit also like Tamas, Dash, Mahak, Alijah, Ephraim, Lajos, Hades, Mateo, Landis, Adish

Dallan (*Celtic/Gaelic*) ♂   RATING: ★★★☆
From the dale
> People think of Dallan as sporty, handsome, intelligent, funny, caring

People who like the name Dallan also like Dalton, Ethan, Kaden, Jace, Braden, Landon, Drake, Dallin, Caleb, Aiden

Dallas *(Celtic/Gaelic)* ♀ ♂   RATING: ★★★☆
Dweller at the house in the dale—Also a city in Texas; TV series; Dallas Green, baseball coach
People think of Dallas as funny, cool, energetic, handsome, intelligent
People who like the name Dallas also like Dakota, Caden, Bailey, Hayden, Austin, Madison, Dylan, Logan, Jaden, Blake

Dallin *(Celtic/Gaelic)* ♂   RATING: ★★☆
From the dale
People think of Dallin as funny, handsome, intelligent, caring, cool
People who like the name Dallin also like Aiden, Ethan, Jackson, Braden, Landon, Aden, Keagan, Dallan, Gavin, Owen

Dallon *(English)* ♀ ♂   RATING: ★★★☆
Variation of Dallin
People think of Dallon as trustworthy, caring, intelligent, handsome, cool
People who like the name Dallon also like Caden, Dakota, Jaden, Brayden, Addison, Dallas, Hayden, Camdyn, Cadence, Carter

Dalton *(English)* ♂   RATING: ★★★★
From the valley town—Dalton Trumbo, screenwriter; Timothy Dalton, actor
People think of Dalton as handsome, funny, cool, intelligent, sporty
People who like the name Dalton also like Ethan, Dawson, Aiden, Landon, Caleb, Braden, Kaden, Gavin, Jackson, Cole

Damali *(Arabic)* ♀   RATING: ★★
Beautiful vision
People think of Damali as pretty, intelligent, exotic, funny, caring
People who like the name Damali also like Damita, Damaris, Damara, Desiree, Destiny, Inara, Danika, Danica, Denali, Amaya

Damalis *(Greek)* ♀   RATING: ★★☆
Calf
People think of Damalis as trustworthy, ethnic, funny, sexy, cool
People who like the name Damalis also like Thisbe, Daphne, Dysis, Hesper, Palila, Camila, Tahlia, Corinna, Iwalani, Bebe

Damani *(American)* ♀ ♂   RATING: ★★★★
Tomorrow—South American origin
People think of Damani as handsome, funny, young, intelligent, leader
People who like the name Damani also like Jaden, Dante, Domani, Dakota, Daylin, Caden, Cadence, Kalani, Aidan, Dorian

Damara *(English)* ♀   RATING: ★★★★
Fertility goddess
People think of Damara as pretty, creative, young, energetic, exotic
People who like the name Damara also like Damaris, Dahlia, Amara, Ciara, Samara, Aurora, Destiny, Amaya, Danae, Faith

Damaris *(Greek)* ♀   RATING: ★★★★☆
Calf
People think of Damaris as pretty, intelligent, caring, funny, creative
People who like the name Damaris also like Damara, Destiny, Amaris, Daphne, Dahlia, Diana, Danika, Damali, Danica, Desiree

Damek *(Slavic)* ♂   RATING: ★★★
Earth—Variation of Adam
People think of Damek as quiet, handsome, energetic, boy next door, sporty
People who like the name Damek also like Caleb, Damir, Aiden, Daemyn, Damien, Kaden, Damon, Ethan, Aden, Elijah

Damia *(Greek)* ♀   RATING: ★★
Goddess of forces of nature
People think of Damia as pretty, intelligent, caring, creative, funny
People who like the name Damia also like Daria, Dahlia, Aurora, Danae, Dea, Amara, Damita, Amaya, Danica, Celeste

Damian *(Greek)* ♂   RATING: ★★★★
To tame, subdue
People think of Damian as handsome, intelligent, funny, cool, powerful
People who like the name Damian also like Damien, Ethan, Damon, Aiden, Dominic, Caleb, Gabriel, Kaden, Adrian, Jayden

Damien *(Greek)* ♂   RATING: ★★★★
To tame, subdue—Character in *The Omen* film series
People think of Damien as handsome, intelligent, powerful, funny, aggressive
People who like the name Damien also like Aiden, Gabriel, Ethan, Dominic, Caleb, Damian, Adrian, Damon, Kaden, Gavin

Damir *(Slavic)* ♂   RATING: ★★★★☆
To give peace
People think of Damir as intelligent, handsome, cool, funny, caring
People who like the name Damir also like Damien, Darius, Amir, Dajuan, Elijah, Darian, Dayshaun, Daemyn, Kaden, Zamir

Damita *(Spanish)* ♀   RATING: ★★★★
Baby princess—Lili Damita, actress
People think of Damita as pretty, exotic, ethnic, aggressive, caring
People who like the name Damita also like Danya, Gabriella, Destiny, Danae, Damara, Danika, Danica, Damali, Damia, Dea

Damon *(Greek)* ♂   RATING: ★★★★
To tame, subdue—Damon Wayans, actor/comedian;
Matt Damon, actor
  People think of Damon as handsome, intelligent, funny,
  cool, sexy
  People who like the name Damon also like Damien,
  Ethan, Damian, Aiden, Caleb, Gavin, Kaden, Dominic,
  Cole, Braden

Dan *(English)* ♂   RATING: ★★☆
Short for Daniel—Dan Aykroyd, actor; Dan
Castellaneta, voice of Homer Simpson
  People think of Dan as funny, cool, handsome, caring,
  intelligent
  People who like the name Dan also like Daniel, Jack,
  Jake, Adam, David, Ethan, Aaron, Eric, Jacob, Justin

Dana *(American)* ♀♂   RATING: ★★☆
Danish, from Denmark—Also a surname; Dana
Delaney, actress
  People think of Dana as funny, pretty, caring, creative,
  intelligent
  People who like the name Dana also like Brooke, Bailey,
  Madison, Dylan, Dakota, Ryan, Ashley, Caden, Taylor,
  Connor

Danae *(Greek)* ♀   RATING: ★★★★
She who judges
  People think of Danae as pretty, intelligent, caring,
  funny, creative
  People who like the name Danae also like Danica,
  Hailey, Chloe, Dominique, Desiree, Faith, Hannah, Jadyn,
  Isabella, Janae

Dane *(Scandinavian)* ♂   RATING: ★★☆
God is my judge; from Denmark—Also a dog breed,
Great Dane; Dane Cook, comedian/actor
  People think of Dane as handsome, funny, intelligent,
  cool, creative
  People who like the name Dane also like Ethan, Cole,
  Gavin, Aiden, Noah, Kaden, Caleb, Owen, Jackson,
  Landon

Daneil *(American)* ♂   RATING: ★★★☆
The champion—Variation of Neil
  People think of Daneil as handsome, funny, cool, intel-
  ligent, caring
  People who like the name Daneil also like Nicholas,
  Aaron, David, Daniel, Andrew, Alexander, Benjamin,
  Christopher, Jacob, Gabriel

Danelea *(Celtic/Gaelic)* ♀   RATING: ★★★☆
Danish meadow
  People think of Danelea as pretty, funny, popular, cool,
  leader
  People who like the name Danelea also like Kaelyn,
  Danelle, Isabella, Genevieve, Gabriella, Erin, Eva, Danica,
  Destiny, Keaira

Danelle *(American)* ♀   RATING: ★★★☆
Feminine form of Daniel
  People think of Danelle as pretty, funny, caring, intel-
  ligent, creative

People who like the name Danelle also like Danielle,
Hannah, Hailey, Isabella, Gabrielle, Abigail, Faith, Caitlyn,
Gabriella, Emily

Dani *(English)* ♀   RATING: ★★☆
God is my judge—Short for Danielle or Daniela
  People think of Dani as pretty, funny, creative, cool,
  caring
  People who like the name Dani also like Emma, Faith,
  Paige, Danielle, Hailey, Hannah, Emily, Chloe, Isabella,
  Eva

Danica *(Hebrew)* ♀   RATING: ★★☆
Morning Star—Also spelled Danika; Danica McKellar,
actress; Danica Patrick, race car driver
  People think of Danica as pretty, creative, intelligent,
  funny, caring
  People who like the name Danica also like Danika,
  Isabella, Abigail, Hailey, Ava, Hannah, Gabrielle, Chloe,
  Emma, Olivia

Daniel *(Hebrew)* ♂   RATING: ★★★
God is my judge—Daniel Day-Lewis, actor
  People think of Daniel as handsome, funny, intelligent,
  caring, cool
  People who like the name Daniel also like Ethan,
  Benjamin, Matthew, Jacob, Joshua, David, Andrew,
  Caleb, Nathan, Gabriel

Daniela *(Spanish)* ♀   RATING: ★★★☆
God is my judge
  People think of Daniela as pretty, funny, intelligent, cool,
  caring
  People who like the name Daniela also like Isabella,
  Danielle, Adriana, Gabriella, Gabriela, Hannah, Emma,
  Ava, Faith, Abigail

Daniella *(Latin)* ♀   RATING: ★★★★
God is my judge—Feminine form of Daniel
  People think of Daniella as pretty, funny, intelligent,
  cool, popular
  People who like the name Daniella also like Isabella,
  Gabriella, Danielle, Ella, Abigail, Hannah, Ava, Hailey,
  Emily, Emma

Danielle *(Hebrew)* ♀   RATING: ★★★
God is my judge—Feminine form of Daniel
  People think of Danielle as pretty, funny, caring, intel-
  ligent, creative
  People who like the name Danielle also like Hannah,
  Gabrielle, Abigail, Hailey, Emma, Isabella, Chloe, Faith,
  Emily, Samantha

Danil *(Slavic)* ♂   RATING: ★★★
God is my judge
  People think of Danil as lazy, popular, cool, powerful,
  nerdy
  People who like the name Danil also like Daniel, Darren,
  Daneil, Darius, Darrion, Alexander, Danniell, Dawson,
  Damon, Cyrus

Danniell *(French)* ♂　　　　RATING: ★★☆
God is my judge
> People think of Danniell as funny, intelligent, trustworthy, popular, creative
> People who like the name Danniell also like Gabriel, Daniel, Damian, Christopher, Benjamin, Jayden, Jeremiah, Nathan, Darren, Damien

Dannon *(American)* ♂　　　　RATING: ★★☆
Variation of Danson—Also a brand of yogurt
> People think of Dannon as intelligent, funny, handsome, caring, cool
> People who like the name Dannon also like Dawson, Kaden, Braden, Damon, Ethan, Conner, Caleb, Denton, Dalton, Jayden

Danny *(English)* ♀♂　　　　RATING: ★★☆
God is my judge—Short for Daniel, Danielle, or Daniela
> People think of Danny as funny, handsome, cool, caring, intelligent
> People who like the name Danny also like Dylan, Cameron, Charlie, Bailey, Ryan, Alex, James, Hayden, Casey, Caden

Dante *(Latin)* ♀♂　　　　RATING: ★★★★☆
Everlasting
> People think of Dante as handsome, intelligent, cool, powerful, sexy
> People who like the name Dante also like Dakota, Caden, Jaden, Bailey, Dylan, Hayden, Aidan, Cadence, Connor, Jade

Danton *(English)* ♂　　　　RATING: ★★★☆
Everlasting—Variation of Dante
> People think of Danton as boy next door, funny, sporty, handsome, wild
> People who like the name Danton also like Dalton, Denton, Dawson, Kaden, Braden, Ethan, Deacon, Caleb, Tristan, Aiden

Danya *(Hebrew)* ♀　　　　RATING: ★★★★
Gift of God
> People think of Danya as pretty, creative, intelligent, caring, funny
> People who like the name Danya also like Danica, Hannah, Dara, Danika, Liana, Anya, Danae, Jadyn, Chloe, Damita

Danyl *(Hebrew)* ♂　　　　RATING: ★★★
God is my judge
> People think of Danyl as funny, creative, leader, cool, intelligent
> People who like the name Danyl also like Daniel, Caleb, Damir, Aaron, Alijah, Dawson, Aden, Cole, Damien, Jeremy

Daphne *(Greek)* ♀　　　　RATING: ★★★★
Laurel tree—Greek water nymph; Daphne Du Maurier, author; characters on *Scooby Doo* and *Frasier*
> People think of Daphne as pretty, intelligent, creative, caring, funny

> People who like the name Daphne also like Chloe, Abigail, Hannah, Faith, Emma, Olivia, Bianca, Isabella, Claire, Eva

Dara *(Hebrew)* ♀　　　　RATING: ★★☆
Compassionate
> People think of Dara as pretty, caring, intelligent, funny, trustworthy
> People who like the name Dara also like Daria, Faith, Ava, Chloe, Eva, Emma, Bella, Grace, Hannah, Emily

Daray *(American)* ♀♂　　　　RATING: ★★★★
Dark
> People think of Daray as intelligent, wild, popular, creative, cool
> People who like the name Daray also like Dante, Caden, Darcy, Jaden, Aidan, Daylin, Devan, Darby, Blake, Dallas

Darby *(Celtic/Gaelic)* ♀♂　　　　RATING: ★★
From the deer park farm—Also a translation of the Irish name Diarmuid
> People think of Darby as pretty, funny, creative, intelligent, energetic
> People who like the name Darby also like Darcy, Bailey, Caden, Avery, Aidan, Addison, Delaney, Hayden, Connor, Logan

Darcie *(English)* ♀　　　　RATING: ★★☆
Dark one
> People think of Darcie as pretty, funny, intelligent, caring, creative
> People who like the name Darcie also like Grace, Paige, Emma, Ella, Isabella, Faith, Gabrielle, Daphne, Sadie, Ava

Darcy *(Celtic/Gaelic)* ♀♂　　　　RATING: ★★★★
Dark one
> People think of Darcy as intelligent, funny, caring, creative, pretty
> People who like the name Darcy also like Bailey, Dylan, Logan, Riley, Madison, Aidan, Cameron, Dakota, Connor, Hayden

Dard *(Greek)* ♂　　　　RATING: ★★★
Son of Zeus
> People think of Dard as boy next door, weird, handsome, nerdy, loser
> People who like the name Dard also like Deiter, Euclid, Aden, David, Dash, Declan, Demetrius, Aiden, Dax, Davis

Dareh *(Persian)* ♂　　　　RATING: ★★
Circle
> People think of Dareh as young, handsome, trustworthy, ethnic, weird
> People who like the name Dareh also like Aiden, Damian, Drake, Darin, Darian, Conner, Dacian, Darius, Draco, Darren

Darena *(American)* ♀　　　　RATING: ★★★
Feminine form of Darren
> People think of Darena as caring, pretty, trendy, weird, creative

People who like the name Darena also like Delia, Davina, Daria, Danika, Dara, Danica, Darla, Diana, Destiny, Dulcinea

Daria (*Greek*) ♀   RATING: ★★★☆
Upholder of the good
People think of Daria as pretty, intelligent, funny, creative, cool
People who like the name Daria also like Dahlia, Amelia, Emma, Chloe, Dara, Ava, Daphne, Bianca, Eva, Abigail

Darian (*English*) ♂   RATING: ★★★★
Upholder of the good
People think of Darian as funny, intelligent, caring, creative, popular
People who like the name Darian also like Ethan, Aiden, Damien, Tristan, Kaden, Damian, Adrian, Caleb, Gavin, Jayden

Darice (*Persian*) ♀   RATING: ★★★☆
Queenly—Feminine form of Darius
People think of Darice as pretty, trustworthy, caring, intelligent, funny
People who like the name Darice also like Daphne, Destiny, Danae, Hannah, Delilah, Danica, Daisy, Helena, Dara, Olivia

Darin (*Celtic/Gaelic*) ♂   RATING: ★★☆
Small; great—Variation of Darren
People think of Darin as handsome, funny, caring, intelligent, cool
People who like the name Darin also like Aiden, Ethan, Ian, Darren, Conner, Dillon, Aden, Kaden, Caleb, Jayden

Dario (*Italian*) ♂   RATING: ★★
Upholder of the good—Variation of Darius
People think of Dario as handsome, intelligent, cool, sexy, popular
People who like the name Dario also like Dominic, Gabriel, Sebastian, Darian, Adrian, Damian, Diego, Fabian, Darius, Alexander

Darion (*American*) ♂   RATING: ★★★
Combination of Darius and Marion
People think of Darion as funny, intelligent, cool, aggressive, sexy
People who like the name Darion also like Darius, Jayden, Darian, Damon, Tristan, Kaden, Damian, Aaron, Daemyn, Damien

Darius (*Persian*) ♂   RATING: ★★★★
Upholder of the good—Darius the Great, Persian king
People think of Darius as handsome, intelligent, funny, cool, popular
People who like the name Darius also like Darian, Damien, Dominic, Damian, Aiden, Caleb, Damon, Alexander, Elijah, Ethan

Dark (*American*) ♀   RATING: ★★★
Little or no light
People think of Dark as sneaky, sexy, aggressive, powerful, wild

People who like the name Dark also like Kyra, Heather, Brandi, Ciara, Belle, Dominique, Sabrina, Blossom, Roxy, Cassie

Darla (*English*) ♀   RATING: ★★
Dear, loved one—Darla Hood, "Our Gang/Little Rascals" cast member
People think of Darla as funny, creative, caring, pretty, intelligent
People who like the name Darla also like Faith, Daphne, Emma, Bella, Hailey, Chloe, Daisy, Amber, Grace, Darlene

Darlene (*American*) ♀   RATING: ★★★☆
Dear, loved one
People think of Darlene as pretty, caring, funny, intelligent, trustworthy
People who like the name Darlene also like Darla, Daphne, Emma, Desiree, Hannah, Faith, Danielle, Hailey, Abigail, Diana

Darnell (*English*) ♂   RATING: ★★
Plant—Also a surname; Linda Darnell, actress
People think of Darnell as handsome, popular, funny, sexy, cool
People who like the name Darnell also like Damien, Darius, Dominic, Damian, Darian, Darren, Daniel, Anthony, Deshawn, Bradley

Darra (*Celtic/Gaelic*) ♀♂   RATING: ★★★☆
Fruitful, fertile—Feminine form of Darren
People think of Darra as pretty, creative, exotic, funny, caring
People who like the name Darra also like Darcy, Caden, Aidan, Daylin, Brynn, Connor, Delaney, Skye, Taryn, Skylar

Darrell (*English*) ♀♂   RATING: ★★☆
From Airelle, France—Also a surname; female character in a series of stories by Enid Blyton
People think of Darrell as funny, handsome, intelligent, popular, caring
People who like the name Darrell also like Dylan, Dakota, Caden, Hayden, Jordan, Blake, Dante, Jaden, Bailey, Cameron

Darren (*American*) ♂   RATING: ★★☆
People think of Darren as handsome, funny, intelligent, caring, cool
People who like the name Darren also like Ethan, Caleb, Aaron, Daniel, Aiden, Nathan, Ian, Justin, Gavin, David

Darrion (*Celtic/Gaelic*) ♂   RATING: ★★★
Upholder of the good
People think of Darrion as handsome, intelligent, funny, cool, powerful
People who like the name Darrion also like Aiden, Darian, Devlin, Darren, Darius, Damien, Darin, Braden, Tristan, Caleb

Darrius (*Persian*) ♂   RATING: ★★★☆
Upholder of the good—Grandson of Cyrus the Great
People think of Darrius as handsome, intelligent, trustworthy, cool, funny

People who like the name Darrius also like Darius, Gabriel, Damien, Darian, Darrion, Ethan, Caleb, Dominic, Jayden, Donovan

Darshan (*Sanskrit/East Indian*) ♂   RATING: ★★
Sight, view
People think of Darshan as funny, intelligent, handsome, exotic, lazy
People who like the name Darshan also like Dayshaun, Darius, Deshawn, Darian, Dasan, Darrius, Demario, Dajuan, Darren, Damian

Darth (*American*) ♂   RATING: ★★☆
Dark—Darth Vader, created by George Lucas for the *Star Wars* character
People think of Darth as aggressive, powerful, criminal, weird, untrustworthy
People who like the name Darth also like Anakin, Dash, Damien, Luke, Deacon, Ace, Caleb, Dominic, Donovan, Isaiah

Daru (*Sanskrit/East Indian*) ♀   RATING: ★★☆
Of the cedar tree
People think of Daru as quiet, ethnic, cool, loser, leader
People who like the name Daru also like Dhyana, Devi, Danika, Denali, Dara, Deepnita, Devaki, Devika, Divya, Diandra

Daruka (*Sanskrit/East Indian*) ♀♂   RATING: ★★☆
Tree
People think of Daruka as exotic, young, artsy, wild, quiet
People who like the name Daruka also like Deva, Deven, Dharma, Tarachand, Kavi, Dante, Keeran, Ari, Devin, Delaney

Darva (*Slavic*) ♀   RATING: ★★☆
Honeybee—Variation of Debra; Darva Conger, reality TV star
People think of Darva as pretty, popular, creative, loser, old
People who like the name Darva also like Dysis, Dava, Damita, Darya, Dasha, Diandra, Davina, Danya, Dora, Damara

Darwin (*English*) ♂   RATING: ★★
Dear friend—Charles Darwin, scientist/evolutionist
People think of Darwin as intelligent, weird, nerdy, loser, creative
People who like the name Darwin also like Ethan, Gabriel, Dawson, Dalton, Drake, Gavin, Noah, Daniel, Felix, Elijah

Darya (*Russian*) ♀   RATING: ★★★★
Upholder of the good
People think of Darya as creative, funny, pretty, intelligent, trustworthy
People who like the name Darya also like Dara, Danika, Dasha, Dahlia, Chloe, Danica, Dysis, Danae, Danya, Gwendolyn

Daryl (*English*) ♀♂   RATING: ★★★☆
People think of Daryl as funny, caring, intelligent, handsome, creative
People who like the name Daryl also like Dylan, Dakota, Devon, Bailey, Taylor, Hayden, Delaney, Connor, Devan, Casey

Dasan (*Native American*) ♂   RATING: ★★
Chief
People think of Dasan as intelligent, caring, creative, winner, handsome
People who like the name Dasan also like Kaden, Darin, Damon, Braden, Damien, Damian, Elijah, Dominic, Dyami, Deron

Dash (*English*) ♂   RATING: ★★★☆
From the ash—Also short for Dashiell
People think of Dash as handsome, cool, sporty, energetic, funny
People who like the name Dash also like Drake, Chase, Dawson, Gage, Braden, Dax, Chance, Deacon, Cole, Aiden

Dasha (*Russian*) ♀   RATING: ★★★★
Short for names beginning with Da
People think of Dasha as pretty, intelligent, caring, funny, cool
People who like the name Dasha also like Destiny, Danica, Danya, Daphne, Danae, Calista, Danika, Danielle, Ava, Dahlia

Dashiell (*French*) ♂   RATING: ★★
Page boy—From the French surname De Chiel; also spelled Dashel, Dashell; Dashiell Hammett, author
People think of Dashiell as handsome, intelligent, creative, energetic, popular
People who like the name Dashiell also like Gabriel, Tristan, Elijah, Dominic, Cole, Isaac, Darian, Liam, Gavin, Oliver

Dason (*American*) ♂   RATING: ★★★
Combination of David and Jason
People think of Dason as handsome, popular, energetic, cool, intelligent
People who like the name Dason also like Kaden, Dathan, Braden, Aiden, Caleb, Keagan, Dane, Gavin, Caine, Chance

Dathan (*American*) ♂   RATING: ★★★
Combination of David and Nathan
People think of Dathan as intelligent, handsome, cool, caring, creative
People who like the name Dathan also like Ethan, Dason, Alexander, Landon, Kaden, Dalton, Tristan, Seth, Ian, Grayson

Datherine (*American*) ♀   RATING: ★☆
Combination of David and Catherine
People think of Datherine as creative, intelligent, exotic, nerdy, powerful
People who like the name Datherine also like Daphne, Dreama, Diandra, Destiny, Dawn, Darlene, Emberlynn, Fiona, Davina, Darla

Dava *(American)* ♀   RATING: ★★★★
Beloved—Feminine form of David
> People think of Dava as caring, pretty, intelligent, creative, funny
> People who like the name Dava also like Dara, Destiny, Ava, Delilah, Davina, Danya, Eva, Daphne, Dawn, Drea

Davan *(English)* ♀   RATING: ★★★★☆
Combination of David and Alan
> People think of Davan as intelligent, creative, funny, caring, powerful
> People who like the name Davan also like Jadyn, Grace, Kaelyn, Cailyn, Emma, Bella, Ava, Caelan, Gabrielle, Hannah

Dave *(English)* ♂   RATING: ★★★★
Short for David—Dave Brubeck, musician; Dave Foley, actor
> People think of Dave as funny, handsome, intelligent, cool, trustworthy
> People who like the name Dave also like David, Aaron, Daniel, Adam, Brian, Chad, Cody, Nathan, Jacob, Aiden

Daveigh *(American)* ♀♂   RATING: ★★★★
Short for David—Feminine form of Davey or David; pronounced *Davey* or *dah-VAY*
> People think of Daveigh as funny, pretty, trendy, caring, artsy
> People who like the name Daveigh also like Hayden, Dakota, Bailey, Addison, Cadence, Dylan, Caden, Logan, Brayden, Devin

David *(Hebrew)* ♂   RATING: ★★★
Beloved—David Mamet, playwright; David Morse, actor; David Letterman, talk show host; David Schwimmer, actor
> People think of David as handsome, funny, intelligent, caring, cool
> People who like the name David also like Daniel, Matthew, Benjamin, Aaron, Jacob, Andrew, Ethan, Michael, Joshua, Caleb

Davida *(Hebrew)* ♀   RATING: ★★★☆
Beloved—Feminine form of David
> People think of Davida as pretty, caring, cool, intelligent, trustworthy
> People who like the name Davida also like Davina, Dara, Dea, Desiree, Destiny, Dava, Danica, Dahlia, Danika, Deandra

Davin *(Scandinavian)* ♀♂   RATING: ★★★★
Finnish person
> People think of Davin as handsome, funny, intelligent, trustworthy, caring
> People who like the name Davin also like Caden, Dylan, Hayden, Jaden, Logan, Devin, Brody, Addison, Riley, Evan

Davina *(Celtic/Gaelic)* ♀   RATING: ★★★★
Beloved
> People think of Davina as pretty, intelligent, caring, creative, sexy
> People who like the name Davina also like Fiona, Kaelyn, Faith, Ciara, Danica, Alana, Hazel, Chloe, Jadyn, Kara

Davis *(English)* ♂   RATING: ★★★★
Son of David—Bette Davis, actress; Sammy Davis Jr., actor/singer
> People think of Davis as funny, handsome, intelligent, popular, leader
> People who like the name Davis also like Jackson, Ethan, Dawson, Gavin, David, Aiden, Jacob, Emerson, Braden, Caleb

Davu *(African)* ♂   RATING: ★☆
The beginning—Somali origin
> People think of Davu as artsy, creative, weird, cool, funny
> People who like the name Davu also like Dumi, Ajani, Chimelu, Darin, Delano, Diallo, Derron, Gazali, Dasan, Darren

Daw *(Thai)* ♀   RATING: ★★★
Stars
> People think of Daw as quiet, exotic, creative, young, weird
> People who like the name Daw also like Dea, Dysis, Dawn, Danika, Demeter, Darya, Dhyana, Da-xia, Drucilla, Diane

Dawn *(English)* ♀   RATING: ★★☆
Sunrise—Dawn Wells, actress
> People think of Dawn as pretty, caring, funny, creative, intelligent
> People who like the name Dawn also like Faith, Grace, Hailey, Hannah, Amber, Emma, Chloe, Claire, Destiny, Paige

Dawson *(English)* ♂   RATING: ★★★
Son of Ralph—Rhymes with Raw, from Rawf, the medieval pronunciation of Ralph; Richard Dawson, actor; *Dawson's Creek*, TV show
> People think of Dawson as handsome, intelligent, caring, funny, energetic
> People who like the name Dawson also like Ethan, Aiden, Landon, Dalton, Jackson, Braden, Gavin, Caleb, Kaden, Cole

Dax *(French)* ♂   RATING: ★★★★
Leader—Dax Shepard, actor
> People think of Dax as handsome, cool, intelligent, leader, funny
> People who like the name Dax also like Drake, Maddox, Chase, Ethan, Gage, Aiden, Deacon, Cole, Dominic, Noah

Day *(American)* ♀♂   RATING: ★★★★
Light, hope
> People think of Day as intelligent, exotic, pretty, creative, funny
> People who like the name Day also like Dakota, Bailey, Blaze, Dallas, Angel, Dylan, Blaine, Demi, Dayton, Cassidy

Daylann (*American*) ♀ RATING: ★★★
Combination of Dale and Ann
People think of Daylann as popular, cool, young, nerdy, loser
People who like the name Daylann also like Cailyn, Ashlyn, Aaralyn, Emberlynn, Alexandra, Alexa, Jadyn, Caitlyn, Audrey, Danica

Daylin (*American*) ♀ ♂ RATING: ★★★★☆
Beautiful day
People think of Daylin as intelligent, caring, pretty, creative, funny
People who like the name Daylin also like Caden, Jaden, Hayden, Dakota, Brayden, Aidan, Rylan, Bailey, Cadence, Dylan

Dayshaun (*American*) ♂ RATING: ★★★★
Combination of Day and Shaun
People think of Dayshaun as handsome, funny, intelligent, popular, young
People who like the name Dayshaun also like Deshawn, Jayden, Dajuan, Darius, Dominic, Damian, Damien, Demetrius, Kaden, Dominick

Dayton (*English*) ♀ ♂ RATING: ★★★
Bright, sunny town—City in Ohio
People think of Dayton as handsome, funny, popular, intelligent, energetic
People who like the name Dayton also like Dakota, Caden, Hayden, Bailey, Jaden, Dylan, Parker, Addison, Madison, Payton

Dea (*Latin*) ♀ RATING: ★★
Goddess
People think of Dea as pretty, intelligent, caring, creative, cool
People who like the name Dea also like Chloe, Drea, Aurora, Iris, Ava, Danica, Danae, Damia, Cora, Genevieve

Deacon (*English*) ♂ RATING: ★★☆
Pastor
People think of Deacon as handsome, intelligent, funny, popular, leader
People who like the name Deacon also like Ethan, Aiden, Jackson, Noah, Landon, Elijah, Caleb, Braden, Gavin, Kaden

Dean (*English*) ♂ RATING: ★★★★
From the valley—Dean Cain, actor; Dean Martin, actor; Jan & Dean, singing group
People think of Dean as handsome, funny, cool, intelligent, caring
People who like the name Dean also like Ethan, Cole, Caleb, Aiden, Ian, Jacob, Owen, Nathan, Daniel, Benjamin

Deana (*American*) ♀ RATING: ★★☆
From the valley—Feminine form of Dean
People think of Deana as funny, caring, trustworthy, pretty, creative
People who like the name Deana also like Danielle, Deanna, Faith, Bianca, Hailey, Emma, Eva, Caitlyn, Hannah, Grace

Deance (*American*) ♂ RATING: ★★
Combination of Deanne and Lance—Deance Wyatt, actor
People think of Deance as sexy, popular, trendy, trustworthy, unpopular
People who like the name Deance also like Cyrus, Chilton, Kesler, Calder, Archie, Sherwood, Adelio, Brend, Bradley, Bart

Deandra (*American*) ♀ RATING: ★★
Combination of Dee and Andra
People think of Deandra as pretty, funny, sexy, intelligent, popular
People who like the name Deandra also like Diandra, Gabriella, Destiny, Isabella, Danica, Faith, Hannah, Deanna, Ariana, Desiree

Deanna (*Latin*) ♀ RATING: ★★☆
Variation of Diana
People think of Deanna as pretty, funny, caring, intelligent, creative
People who like the name Deanna also like Hannah, Hailey, Breanna, Faith, Brianna, Desiree, Grace, Amber, Danielle, Arianna

Deanne (*American*) ♀ RATING: ★★★★
Variation of Diane
People think of Deanne as pretty, caring, creative, funny, trustworthy
People who like the name Deanne also like Deanna, Faith, Emma, Caitlyn, Hailey, Danielle, Grace, Amanda, Emily, Gabrielle

Debbie (*English*) ♀ RATING: ★★
Short for Deborah—Debbie Reynolds, singer/actress
People think of Debbie as funny, caring, pretty, trustworthy, intelligent
People who like the name Debbie also like Deborah, Faith, Debra, Amanda, Emma, Eva, Abigail, Emily, Daisy, Amber

Debby (*English*) ♀ RATING: ★★★☆
Short for Deborah
People think of Debby as pretty, caring, funny, intelligent, creative
People who like the name Debby also like Debbie, Deborah, Daisy, Deena, Diana, Daphne, Dawn, Kacy, Darlene, Danielle

Deborah (*Hebrew*) ♀ RATING: ★★★☆
Bee
People think of Deborah as caring, funny, intelligent, pretty, creative
People who like the name Deborah also like Abigail, Elizabeth, Hannah, Rebecca, Grace, Danielle, Samantha, Sarah, Emma, Rachel

Debra (*English*) ♀ RATING: ★★★☆
Bee—Debra Messing, actress; Debra Winger, actress
People think of Debra as caring, intelligent, trustworthy, funny, pretty

People who like the name Debra also like Deborah, Debbie, Faith, Becky, Cassandra, Danielle, Emma, Diana, Bethany, Denise

December *(English)* ♀ ♂   RATING: ★★★☆
Born in December—Means tenth month on the ancient Roman calendar
People think of December as pretty, creative, intelligent, artsy, caring
People who like the name December also like Dakota, Jade, Caden, Cadence, Madison, Dallas, Hayden, Jaden, Brooklyn, Bailey

Decima *(Latin)* ♀   RATING: ★★☆
The tenth
People think of Decima as pretty, young, funny, popular, caring
People who like the name Decima also like Deidra, Dea, Deirdre, Deanna, Dava, Delicia, Dulcina, Deirdra, Dysis, Delia

Decker *(English)* ♂   RATING: ★★★☆
Digger of ditches—Originally a surname
People think of Decker as creative, handsome, popular, powerful, weird
People who like the name Decker also like Dawson, Ethan, Aiden, Drake, Jackson, Jacob, Conner, Dalton, Deacon, Braden

Declan *(Celtic/Gaelic)* ♂   RATING: ★★★☆
Unknown meaning
People think of Declan as handsome, intelligent, cool, popular, funny
People who like the name Declan also like Aiden, Ethan, Liam, Tristan, Noah, Caleb, Owen, Lachlan, Cole, Jacob

Dee *(American)* ♀   RATING: ★★★☆
Short for names beginning with D
People think of Dee as funny, intelligent, pretty, caring, popular
People who like the name Dee also like Destiny, Dawn, Faith, Daisy, Bridget, Paige, Diana, Hailey, Bella, Bethany

Deena *(English)* ♀   RATING: ★★★☆
From the valley—Feminine form of Dean
People think of Deena as funny, pretty, energetic, caring, intelligent
People who like the name Deena also like Deanna, Deana, Faith, Darla, Hailey, Isabella, Dawn, Desiree, Bethany, Emma

Deepak *(Sanskrit/East Indian)* ♂   RATING: ★☆
Light, lamp—Deepak Chopra, author/philosopher
People think of Deepak as cool, caring, intelligent, handsome, powerful
People who like the name Deepak also like Ashwin, Gautam, Gaurav, Manjit, Ajay, Kishan, Darshan, Charan, Dinesh, Adit

Deepnita *(Sanskrit/East Indian)* ♀   RATING: ★★☆
Light, happiness
People think of Deepnita as handsome, cool, girl next door, young, exotic

People who like the name Deepnita also like Denali, Devaki, Devica, Avani, Dhyana, Divya, Amithi, Devika, Daru, Eshana

Deianira *(Greek)* ♀   RATING: ★★★
Troublemaker—In Greek mythology, the wife of Herakles
People think of Deianira as popular, pretty, exotic, powerful, sexy
People who like the name Deianira also like Danika, Deandra, Dysis, Deirdra, Deidra, Danica, Dimaia, Diandra, Dasha, Danya

Deidra *(Celtic/Gaelic)* ♀   RATING: ★★★☆
She who chatters
People think of Deidra as pretty, funny, intelligent, caring, creative
People who like the name Deidra also like Fiona, Ciara, Genevieve, Deirdre, Deirdra, Desiree, Keira, Faith, Bianca, Hailey

Deion *(American)* ♂   RATING: ★★★☆
Form of Dionysius; Deion Sanders, athlete
People think of Deion as handsome, intelligent, energetic, cool, popular
People who like the name Deion also like Damien, Damon, Damian, Demetrius, Caleb, Darian, Darius, Jayden, Braden, Darrion

Deiondre *(American)* ♀ ♂   RATING: ★★★☆
Valley
People think of Deiondre as popular, leader, caring, creative, cool
People who like the name Deiondre also like Dante, Jaden, Caden, Dorian, Devon, Dakota, Dallas, Devan, Cameron, Delaine

Deirdra *(Celtic/Gaelic)* ♀   RATING: ★★★★
She who chatters
People think of Deirdra as pretty, intelligent, creative, caring, sexy
People who like the name Deirdra also like Deirdre, Deidra, Genevieve, Kaelyn, Chloe, Gwendolyn, Dierdra, Isabella, Cassandra, Kiara

Deirdre *(Celtic/Gaelic)* ♀   RATING: ★★☆
She who chatters—Deirdre Lovejoy, actress
People think of Deirdre as pretty, funny, intelligent, caring, creative
People who like the name Deirdre also like Fiona, Genevieve, Deirdra, Audrey, Deidra, Keira, Aurora, Chloe, Alana, Bianca

Deiter *(German)* ♂   RATING: ★★★☆
Army of the people
People think of Deiter as cool, caring, artsy, intelligent, weird
People who like the name Deiter also like Aiden, Dawson, Caleb, Derek, Landon, Dalton, Ethan, Deacon, Cole, Coen

194

Dejanae (*American*) ♀ RATING: ★★★
From Dijon, France—Variation of the French word
Dijonnaise
  People think of Dejanae as funny, pretty, sexy, energetic, intelligent
  People who like the name Dejanae also like Aaliyah, Destiny, Desiree, Danae, Eternity, Essence, Aliana, Leila, Janae, Jenaya

Deka (*African*) ♀ ♂ RATING: ★★
Pleasing—Somali origin
  People think of Deka as cool, pretty, lazy, weird, powerful
  People who like the name Deka also like Dante, Devon, Dorian, Dakota, Dior, Demi, Delaney, Denver, Des, Devin

Dekel (*Hebrew*) ♂ RATING: ★★☆
Palm tree
  People think of Dekel as sexy, cool, loser, energetic, nerdy
  People who like the name Dekel also like Derron, Chael, Derex, Dawson, Desmond, Darin, Darian, Denzel, Dasan, Devlin

Del (*English*) ♀ ♂ RATING: ★★
Short for names beginning with Del
  People think of Del as intelligent, weird, energetic, cool, funny
  People who like the name Del also like Dylan, Delaney, Delaine, Drew, Dallas, Darby, Duff, Derby, Dorsey, Denver

Delaine (*French*) ♀ ♂ RATING: ★★☆
From Laine, France—Also a Huguenot surname
  People think of Delaine as pretty, intelligent, funny, energetic, popular
  People who like the name Delaine also like Delaney, Caden, Avery, Bailey, Brayden, Dakota, Cadence, Hayden, Blair, Dylan

Delaney (*English*) ♀ ♂ RATING: ★★★★
From the alder grove—Also a surname; Dana Delaney, actress; Kim Delaney, actress
  People think of Delaney as pretty, funny, intelligent, energetic, creative
  People who like the name Delaney also like Addison, Avery, Caden, Hayden, Madison, Bailey, Logan, Mackenzie, Aidan, Riley

Delano (*Celtic/Gaelic*) ♂ RATING: ★★★☆
Dark—Franklin Delano Roosevelt, U.S. president
  People think of Delano as handsome, cool, funny, powerful, caring
  People who like the name Delano also like Devlin, Aiden, Donovan, Tristan, Dolan, Conner, Faolan, Liam, Darrion, Keagan

Delaware (*German*) ♀ ♂ RATING: ★★☆
U.S. state, named for Baron De La Ware
  People think of Delaware as pretty, funny, caring, wild, energetic
  People who like the name Delaware also like Dakota, Delaney, Dylan, Delaine, Dayton, Denver, Devon, Dorian, Devin, Dallas

Delbert (*English*) ♂ RATING: ★☆
Noble, bright
  People think of Delbert as caring, funny, creative, trustworthy, old-fashioned
  People who like the name Delbert also like Darren, Benjamin, Denton, Derek, Dawson, Daniel, Dexter, Drake, Dean, Derrick

Delfina (*Italian*) ♀ RATING: ★★★★
Woman from Delphi
  People think of Delfina as intelligent, creative, pretty, cool, exotic
  People who like the name Delfina also like Davina, Danica, Delphina, Delphine, Donatella, Destiny, Dara, Daphne, Bianca, Delilah

Delia (*Greek*) ♀ RATING: ★★☆
From Delos—Also short for Cordelia
  People think of Delia as pretty, intelligent, funny, creative, trustworthy
  People who like the name Delia also like Ava, Chloe, Emma, Isabella, Ella, Olivia, Amelia, Daphne, Hannah, Dahlia

Delicia (*Spanish*) ♀ RATING: ★★★★
Delightful
  People think of Delicia as pretty, funny, caring, intelligent, sexy
  People who like the name Delicia also like Destiny, Damita, Daniela, Danika, Delilah, Danica, Dahlia, Delia, Desiree, Dasha

Delila (*Hebrew*) ♀ RATING: ★★☆
One who weakened
  People think of Delila as pretty, popular, exotic, cool, creative
  People who like the name Delila also like Delilah, Chloe, Isabella, Ava, Dalila, Daphne, Isabelle, Abigail, Gabriella, Eva

Delilah (*Hebrew*) ♀ RATING: ★★☆
One who weakened
  People think of Delilah as pretty, intelligent, creative, caring, funny
  People who like the name Delilah also like Chloe, Ava, Faith, Isabella, Emma, Aurora, Abigail, Charlotte, Bianca, Grace

Deliz (*American*) ♀ RATING: ★★☆
Short form of Delizia
  People think of Deliz as creative, pretty, caring, popular, weird
  People who like the name Deliz also like Drea, Dea, Desiree, Diza, Destiny, Danya, Dysis, Danae, Della, Damita

Della (*English*) ♀ RATING: ★★★★
Of the nobility
  People think of Della as pretty, popular, funny, intelligent, trustworthy
  People who like the name Della also like Bella, Ella, Ava, Stella, Delia, Chloe, Isabella, Belle, Daisy, Eva

Delling (*Scandinavian*) ♀♂   RATING: ★★☆
Fascinating
> People think of Delling as weird, nerdy, loser, creative, young
> People who like the name Delling also like Devan, Dylan, Davin, Darby, Delaney, Dorian, Dyre, Dayton, Drew, Denim

Delma (*Celtic/Gaelic*) ♀   RATING: ★★☆
Forever good
> People think of Delma as caring, intelligent, trustworthy, creative, old-fashioned
> People who like the name Delma also like Amal, Eadoin, Fareeda, Davina, Betha, Farsiris, Siran, Deidra, Luella, Farah

Delora (*American*) ♀   RATING: ★★★
Variation of Dolores
> People think of Delora as creative, aggressive, trustworthy, unpopular, sexy
> People who like the name Delora also like Destiny, Daisy, Dara, Dawn, Desiree, Danika, Diana, Darla, Deborah, Helena

Delores (*Spanish*) ♀   RATING: ★★★
Variation of Dolores
> People think of Delores as trustworthy, leader, creative, caring, intelligent
> People who like the name Delores also like Daisy, Dolores, Dominique, Darla, Claudia, Bella, Danelle, Diane, Destiny, Faith

Delphina (*Greek*) ♀   RATING: ★★★☆
Woman from Delphi
> People think of Delphina as pretty, exotic, funny, cool, elegant
> People who like the name Delphina also like Daphne, Delilah, Delphine, Daria, Belle, Dahlia, Diandra, Adriana, Faith, Destiny

Delphine (*French*) ♀   RATING: ★★★★
Woman from Delphi
> People think of Delphine as pretty, intelligent, elegant, creative, artsy
> People who like the name Delphine also like Daphne, Chloe, Gabrielle, Delphina, Giselle, Jasmine, Genevieve, Josephine, Violet, Scarlett

Delta (*Greek*) ♀   RATING: ★★☆
Mouth of a river—Also a letter in the Greek alphabet; Delta Burke, actress/designer
> People think of Delta as pretty, creative, intelligent, popular, caring
> People who like the name Delta also like Destiny, Grace, Faith, Chloe, Jasmine, Daisy, Isabella, Daphne, Eva, Gabriella

Delu (*African*) ♀   RATING: ★☆
The only girl—Hausa origin
> People think of Delu as young, creative, energetic, unpopular, winner

> People who like the name Delu also like Dea, Destiny, Damita, Dysis, Donatella, Didina, Dava, Diza, Darva, Delphina

Demario (*Italian*) ♂   RATING: ★★★★
Son of Mario
> People think of Demario as handsome, sexy, funny, cool, popular
> People who like the name Demario also like Dayshaun, Dajuan, Darian, Darius, Demetrius, Deshawn, Darnell, Damian, Daemyn, Elijah

Dembe (*African*) ♀♂   RATING: ★★★
Peace—Ugandan origin
> People think of Dembe as big, ethnic, intelligent, exotic, religious
> People who like the name Dembe also like Dakota, Ezra, Jumoke, Kendi, Banji, Diara, Halyn, Ciqala, Ashanti, Daylin

Demeter (*Greek*) ♀   RATING: ★★★☆
Barley mother—Greek goddess of the earth
> People think of Demeter as exotic, pretty, intelligent, trustworthy, powerful
> People who like the name Demeter also like Demetria, Demetra, Dawn, Destiny, Desdemona, Damaris, Dahlia, Diana, Daphne, Celeste

Demetra (*Greek*) ♀   RATING: ★★★☆
Devotee of Demeter
> People think of Demetra as intelligent, pretty, creative, popular, elegant
> People who like the name Demetra also like Demetria, Cassandra, Aurora, Demeter, Damara, Alexandria, Daphne, Calista, Isis, Desiree

Demetria (*Greek*) ♀   RATING: ★★★☆
Devotee of Demeter
> People think of Demetria as pretty, caring, funny, sexy, intelligent
> People who like the name Demetria also like Demetra, Aurora, Genevieve, Delilah, Anastasia, Destiny, Adriana, Bella, Daphne, Audrey

Demetrius (*Greek*) ♂   RATING: ★★★★
Devotee of Demeter
> People think of Demetrius as handsome, funny, intelligent, cool, popular
> People who like the name Demetrius also like Demitrius, Damien, Darius, Gabriel, Damian, Sebastian, Elijah, Dominic, Xavier, Drake

Demi (*French*) ♀♂   RATING: ★★★☆
Half, small—Also short for Demetria; Demi Moore, actress
> People think of Demi as pretty, funny, popular, young, cool
> People who like the name Demi also like Dakota, Bailey, Brooke, Drew, Jade, Dylan, Caden, Madison, Hayden, Alexis

196

Demitrius *(Greek)* ♂ RATING: ★★★☆
Devotee of Demeter
> People think of Demitrius as handsome, intelligent, creative, caring, trustworthy
> People who like the name Demitrius also like Demetrius, Dmitri, Drake, Damien, Darius, Aiden, Dominic, Xavier, Gabriel, Damian

Dempsey *(Celtic/Gaelic)* ♂ RATING: ★★★★
Descendant of the proud one—Also a surname; Jack Dempsey, boxer
> People think of Dempsey as funny, handsome, cool, intelligent, sexy
> People who like the name Dempsey also like Aiden, Dawson, Tristan, Conner, Finley, Dalton, Jackson, Owen, Donovan, Holden

Dempster *(English)* ♂ RATING: ★★☆
Judge
> People think of Dempster as weird, loser, unpopular, poor, stuck-up
> People who like the name Dempster also like Dawson, Deiter, Dempsey, Dermot, Denton, Darius, Abbott, Demetrius, Danton, Deacon

Dena *(Hebrew)* ♀ RATING: ★★★☆
Judgment—Variation of Dinah
> People think of Dena as caring, pretty, funny, creative, intelligent
> People who like the name Dena also like Dara, Chloe, Deena, Danielle, Faith, Danica, Dina, Diana, Mia, Dea

Denali *(Sanskrit/East Indian)* ♀ RATING: ★★★★
Great one
> People think of Denali as creative, pretty, exotic, intelligent, funny
> People who like the name Denali also like Desiree, Dahlia, Destiny, Eva, Dhyana, Danica, Avani, Chandra, Damali, Danae

Denham *(English)* ♂ RATING: ★★★☆
From the valley farm
> People think of Denham as caring, trustworthy, young, trendy, lazy
> People who like the name Denham also like Dawson, Darwin, Drake, Dempsey, Dominic, Devlin, Dalton, Broderick, Jacob, Dane

Denholm *(English)* ♂ RATING: ★★☆
Dweller by the holly in the valley—Denholm Elliot, actor
> People think of Denholm as weird, powerful, handsome, old-fashioned, intelligent
> People who like the name Denholm also like Devlin, Declan, Dempsey, Callahan, Ewan, Dawson, Brennan, Calhoun, Desmond, Fynn

Denim *(American)* ♀♂ RATING: ★★★☆
Strong cloth
> People think of Denim as popular, cool, handsome, sexy, intelligent

People who like the name Denim also like Dakota, Caden, Dayton, Dylan, Cameron, Drew, Denver, Dallas, Jade, Hayden

Denis *(French)* ♂ RATING: ★★★☆
Devotee of Dionysus—Variation of Dennis
> People think of Denis as handsome, intelligent, funny, cool, caring
> People who like the name Denis also like David, Alexander, Gabriel, Daniel, Daneil, Anthony, Dean, Adam, Caleb, Dennis

Denise *(French)* ♀ RATING: ★★★☆
Devotee of Dionysus—Feminine form of Dennis; Denise Richards, actress
> People think of Denise as caring, pretty, funny, intelligent, creative
> People who like the name Denise also like Desiree, Hailey, Hannah, Danielle, Destiny, Nicole, Elizabeth, Faith, Bianca, Cassandra

Deniz *(Turkish)* ♀♂ RATING: ★★★
Sea
> People think of Deniz as funny, elegant, intelligent, pretty, creative
> People who like the name Deniz also like Dior, Desi, Demi, Sabriel, Akia, Domani, Sol, Damani

Denna *(Hebrew)* ♀ RATING: ★★
Glen, valley
> People think of Denna as pretty, intelligent, creative, caring, quiet
> People who like the name Denna also like Isabella, Deena, Delilah, Danielle, Diana, Abigail, Daphne, Isabelle, Jasmine, Desiree

Dennis *(English)* ♂ RATING: ★★
Devotee of Dionysus—Originally from the Greek name Dionysus; Dennis Quaid, actor; Dennis the Menace, cartoon character
> People think of Dennis as funny, handsome, intelligent, cool, caring
> People who like the name Dennis also like David, Daniel, Ethan, Jacob, Benjamin, Joshua, Justin, Christopher, Jason, Derek

Denton *(English)* ♂ RATING: ★★★☆
From the town in the valley
> People think of Denton as handsome, caring, cool, popular, intelligent
> People who like the name Denton also like Dalton, Dawson, Kaden, Ethan, Braden, Caleb, Dominic, Danton, Drake, Dillon

Denver *(American)* ♀♂ RATING: ★★☆
From the passage of the Danes—City in Colorado; John Denver, singer
> People think of Denver as handsome, funny, energetic, caring, cool
> People who like the name Denver also like Dakota, Dallas, Caden, Hayden, Dylan, Bailey, Hunter, Parker, Brooklyn, Madison

Denzel *(English)* ♂   RATING: ★★★☆
From Denzell, England—Denzel Washington, actor
People think of Denzel as handsome, intelligent, funny, popular, cool
People who like the name Denzel also like Dominic, Ethan, Gabriel, Damien, Damian, Jayden, Elijah, Daniel, Tristan, Jacob

Deo *(Greek)* ♂   RATING: ★☆
Godlike
People think of Deo as popular, leader, energetic, powerful, boy next door
People who like the name Deo also like Cyrus, Diego, Dax, Drake, Damien, Calix, Draco, Adonis, Elijah, Noah

Deon *(American)* ♀♂   RATING: ★★★★
Devotee of Dionysus
People think of Deon as cool, funny, handsome, sexy, intelligent
People who like the name Deon also like Devon, Dante, Dion, Dakota, Dylan, Dorian, Jordan, Jaden, Bailey, Jade

Derby *(English)* ♀♂   RATING: ★★
From the deer park farm—Also a hat; also the Kentucky Derby horse race; pronounced *darby* by Brits
People think of Derby as energetic, creative, young, funny, sporty
People who like the name Derby also like Darby, Delaney, Dallas, Bailey, Colby, Caden, Dylan, Brody, Darcy, Carter

Derek *(English)* ♂   RATING: ★★★
People ruler—Derek Jeter, baseball player
People think of Derek as handsome, funny, intelligent, cool, popular
People who like the name Derek also like Ethan, Jacob, Caleb, Jared, Nathan, Nicholas, Aiden, Andrew, Ian, Benjamin

Derenik *(Armenian)* ♂   RATING: ★★★
Monk
People think of Derenik as funny, caring, creative, intelligent, trustworthy
People who like the name Derenik also like Benjamin, Darian, Daneil, Darius, Kael, Ethan, Keenan, Damien, Jaegar, Garrett

Derex *(American)* ♂   RATING: ★★★
People ruler—Variation of Derek
People think of Derex as handsome, energetic, popular, cool, caring
People who like the name Derex also like Dawson, Dominic, Christopher, Dalton, Damien, Alexander, Alexavier, Darius, Derek, Drake

Derica *(American)* ♀   RATING: ★★
People ruler
People think of Derica as pretty, popular, leader, cool, young
People who like the name Derica also like Danica, Desiree, Dara, Destiny, Dominique, Faith, Chloe, Dericia, Danika, Deandra

Dericia *(American)* ♀   RATING: ★★★
Combination of Derek and Alicia
People think of Dericia as ethnic, exotic, aggressive, young, winner
People who like the name Dericia also like Derica, Dominique, Destiny, Daphne, Dawn, Diandra, Desiree, Diana, Dominica, Davina

Derion *(American)* ♂   RATING: ★★☆
Upholder of the good—Variation of Darian
People think of Derion as big, criminal, young, pretty, stuck-up
People who like the name Derion also like Darius, Darion, Kaden, Demetrius, Demario, Dyson, Damien, Donovan, Darian, Deron

Dermot *(Celtic/Gaelic)* ♂   RATING: ★★★☆
Variation of Diarmuid—Dermot Mulroney, actor
People think of Dermot as handsome, sexy, intelligent, funny, caring
People who like the name Dermot also like Declan, Aiden, Finn, Owen, Keiran, Colin, Cole, Liam, Ethan, Tristan

Deron *(Armenian)* ♂   RATING: ★★★★☆
Belongs to God
People think of Deron as intelligent, handsome, funny, leader, caring
People who like the name Deron also like Dominic, Elijah, Derron, Gabriel, Ethan, Jayden, Caleb, Aiden, Darin, Ian

Derora *(Hebrew)* ♀   RATING: ★★
Running streams
People think of Derora as cool, uptight, exotic, wild, creative
People who like the name Derora also like Dara, Desiree, Delilah, Darlene, Dysis, Destiny, Danica, Dorothea, Deandra, Derica

Derrick *(English)* ♂   RATING: ★★★★
People ruler—Variation of Derek
People think of Derrick as handsome, funny, intelligent, caring, cool
People who like the name Derrick also like Ethan, Derek, Jacob, Andrew, Aiden, Nathan, Daniel, Caleb, Ian, Benjamin

Derring *(English)* ♀♂   RATING: ★★
Bold
People think of Derring as weird, unpopular, lazy, nerdy, uptight
People who like the name Derring also like Devon, Delaney, Dakota, Landen, Devan, Camdyn, Caden, Hayden, Devin, Dacey

Derron *(English)* ♂   RATING: ★★☆
Great
People think of Derron as creative, popular, leader, caring, young
People who like the name Derron also like Deron, Dillon, Dawson, Darren, Caleb, Kaden, Ethan, Aiden, Damon, Damien

198

Derry *(Celtic/Gaelic)* ♀♂　　RATING: ★★
County in Ireland—Fictional town in many Stephen King novels
> People think of Derry as intelligent, funny, creative, leader, popular
> People who like the name Derry also like Devan, Hadley, Casey, Darcy, Rylie, Dorsey, Delaney, Reilly, Dallas, Darby

Des *(English)* ♀♂　　RATING: ★★★☆
Short for Desi, Desiderio, or Desmond
> People think of Des as funny, pretty, caring, lazy, trustworthy
> People who like the name Des also like Dante, Desi, Dorian, Cade, Darcy, Devin, Drew, Dylan, Jaden, Demi

Desdemona *(Greek)* ♀　　RATING: ★★★☆
Misery—Character in *Othello* by Shakespeare
> People think of Desdemona as exotic, sexy, intelligent, elegant, pretty
> People who like the name Desdemona also like Aurora, Daphne, Anastasia, Chloe, Cassandra, Dahlia, Bianca, Ophelia, Celeste, Destiny

Deshawn *(American)* ♂　　RATING: ★★★★
Combination of De and Shawn—Variation of Sean or John
> People think of Deshawn as handsome, sexy, cool, funny, popular
> People who like the name Deshawn also like Dayshaun, Jayden, Dajuan, Isaiah, Dominic, Darius, Damian, Damien, Elijah, Darian

Desi *(Spanish)* ♀♂　　RATING: ★★☆
Desired—Short for Desiderio; Desi Arnaz, actor/producer/singer
> People think of Desi as creative, funny, pretty, young, caring
> People who like the name Desi also like Dakota, Dante, Caden, Bailey, Jaden, Demi, Cadence, Dylan, Hayden, Devan

Desiderio *(Spanish)* ♂　　RATING: ★☆
Desired
> People think of Desiderio as funny, handsome, popular, creative, boy next door
> People who like the name Desiderio also like Alejandro, Demetrius, Dominic, Dominick, Alexander, Xavier, Angelito, Daemyn, Enrique, Dionysius

Desiree *(French)* ♀　　RATING: ★★☆
Desired
> People think of Desiree as pretty, funny, sexy, caring, intelligent
> People who like the name Desiree also like Destiny, Faith, Hailey, Chloe, Aaliyah, Jasmine, Hannah, Gabrielle, Bianca, Paige

Desma *(Greek)* ♀　　RATING: ★★
Pledge, bond
> People think of Desma as intelligent, caring, leader, girl next door, funny

> People who like the name Desma also like Diana, Dessa, Despina, Dara, Delia, Davina, Dysis, Daria, Damia, Desdemona

Desmond *(Celtic/Gaelic)* ♂　　RATING: ★★★☆
Man from Desmond—Desmond Tutu, South African bishop
> People think of Desmond as handsome, funny, intelligent, cool, sexy
> People who like the name Desmond also like Dominic, Tristan, Donovan, Ian, Dawson, Caleb, Damon, Ethan, Damien, Damian

Despina *(Greek)* ♀　　RATING: ★★★☆
Lady
> People think of Despina as pretty, sexy, caring, exotic, intelligent
> People who like the name Despina also like Desma, Delphina, Diana, Dysis, Destiny, Dara, Daria, Delphine, Calista, Callista

Dessa *(Russian)* ♀　　RATING: ★★☆
Variation of Odessa—Also a Russian city
> People think of Dessa as funny, pretty, creative, intelligent, caring
> People who like the name Dessa also like Daphne, Ava, Della, Bianca, Drea, Desiree, Ella, Bella, Callie, Keira

Destino *(Spanish)* ♂　　RATING: ★★☆
Destiny
> People think of Destino as cool, handsome, sexy, popular, funny
> People who like the name Destino also like Desiderio, Eduardo, Angelito, Darius, Adriano, Jacques, Micah, Fabiano, Derek, Arsenio

Destiny *(American)* ♀　　RATING: ★★★★
Fate
> People think of Destiny as pretty, funny, caring, popular, creative
> People who like the name Destiny also like Faith, Desiree, Aaliyah, Hailey, Trinity, Jasmine, Hannah, Chloe, Brianna, Isabella

Deunoro *(Spanish)* ♂　　RATING: ★★
Saint
> People think of Deunoro as handsome, exotic, popular, young, energetic
> People who like the name Deunoro also like Desiderio, Armando, Damien, Damian, Cody, Daneil, Alvaro, Alexander, Darius, Adolf

Deva *(Sanskrit/East Indian)* ♀♂　　RATING: ★★★★☆
Divinity
> People think of Deva as exotic, artsy, creative, intelligent, elegant
> People who like the name Deva also like Dakota, Devan, Deven, Dante, Caden, Dayton, Connor, Diara, Dharma, Dylan

Devaki *(Sanskrit/East Indian)* ♀　　RATING: ★★☆
A god
> People think of Devaki as leader, intelligent, ethnic, pretty, untrustworthy
> People who like the name Devaki also like Denali, Devika, Divya, Deepnita, Devi, Devica, Dhyana, Daru, Danika, Deandra

Devan *(Celtic/Gaelic)* ♀♂　　RATING: ★★★★
Poet
> People think of Devan as intelligent, funny, caring, creative, cool
> People who like the name Devan also like Dylan, Caden, Evan, Aidan, Logan, Jaden, Hayden, Connor, Devin, Devon

Devanand *(Sanskrit/East Indian)* ♂　　RATING: ★★☆
Joy of god
> People think of Devanand as leader, religious, handsome, creative, powerful
> People who like the name Devanand also like Devesh, Dhaval, Deepak, Dulal, Diedrick, Dhiren, Divyesh, Darshan, Chaman, Diallo

Deven *(Sanskrit/East Indian)* ♀♂　　RATING: ★★★☆
Like a god
> People think of Deven as intelligent, handsome, funny, cool, popular
> People who like the name Deven also like Devin, Devan, Jaden, Caden, Dylan, Devon, Dakota, Logan, Bailey, Evan

Deverell *(English)* ♂　　RATING: ★★☆
From the river of the fertile upland region
> People think of Deverell as untrustworthy, stuck-up, wild, cool, criminal
> People who like the name Deverell also like Elliot, Chilton, Dominy, Declan, Cole, Deshawn, Deion, Dragan, Derron, Barclay

Devesh *(Sanskrit/East Indian)* ♂　　RATING: ★★☆
God of gods
> People think of Devesh as wild, lazy, sneaky, funny, big
> People who like the name Devesh also like Dhaval, Divyesh, Adit, Devanand, Adarsh, Chetan, Jagat, Geet, Lokesh, Dhiren

Devi *(Sanskrit/East Indian)* ♀　　RATING: ★★★★
Goddess of power
> People think of Devi as exotic, intelligent, pretty, sexy, trustworthy
> People who like the name Devi also like Kali, Chandra, Dea, Dawn, Fiona, Hazel, Damia, Ava, Freya, Aurora

Devica *(Sanskrit/East Indian)* ♀　　RATING: ★★☆
Derived from God—Variation of Devika
> People think of Devica as exotic, pretty, old-fashioned, young, ethnic
> People who like the name Devica also like Divya, Devi, Dhyana, Denali, Devika, Devaki, Deepnita, Deandra, Diana, Dominique

Devika *(Sanskrit/East Indian)* ♀　　RATING: ★★★☆
Derived from God—Mother of Krishna
> People think of Devika as pretty, caring, funny, intelligent, creative
> People who like the name Devika also like Danika, Denali, Devi, Divya, Devaki, Dhyana, Devica, Danica, Delia, Davina

Devin *(Celtic/Gaelic)* ♀♂　　RATING: ★★★★
Descendant of the dark-haired one
> People think of Devin as funny, intelligent, cool, caring, handsome
> People who like the name Devin also like Dylan, Caden, Evan, Logan, Hayden, Riley, Bailey, Aidan, Madison, Connor

Devlin *(Celtic/Gaelic)* ♂　　RATING: ★★★★
Brave; fierce
> People think of Devlin as handsome, intelligent, leader, cool, powerful
> People who like the name Devlin also like Aiden, Declan, Tristan, Ethan, Donovan, Liam, Keagan, Conner, Kaden, Gavin

Devon *(English)* ♀♂　　RATING: ★★★★
From the tribe of Dumnonii—Also a county in England
> People think of Devon as funny, intelligent, caring, cool, creative
> People who like the name Devon also like Dylan, Hayden, Bailey, Logan, Caden, Evan, Cameron, Aidan, Riley, Dakota

Devona *(English)* ♀　　RATING: ★★
From the tribe of Dumnonii—Feminine form of Devon
> People think of Devona as pretty, trustworthy, intelligent, funny, caring
> People who like the name Devona also like Drea, Davina, Fiona, Bella, Faith, Danica, Hailey, Diana, Damara, Denise

Devonee *(American)* ♀　　RATING: ★★★
Feminine form of Devon
> People think of Devonee as pretty, energetic, funny, girl next door, caring
> People who like the name Devonee also like Desiree, Callie, Belle, Aaliyah, Jadyn, Bianca, Ebony, Janae, Angelina, Aimee

Devorah *(Hebrew)* ♀　　RATING: ★★★☆
Honeybee
> People think of Devorah as pretty, caring, intelligent, powerful, creative
> People who like the name Devorah also like Daphne, Delilah, Eva, Dara, Desiree, Deborah, Dava, Eve, Dysis, Dawn

Devorit *(Hebrew)* ♀　　RATING: ★★
Variation of Devorah—Pronounced *Devoris*
> People think of Devorit as weird, nerdy, unpopular, loser, lazy
> People who like the name Devorit also like Dena, Delilah, Devorah, Deena, Denna, Donnica, Davida, Debra, Deborah, Dolores

200

Dewayne (*American*) ♂ RATING: ★☆
Wagon maker—Variation of Dwayne
People think of Dewayne as intelligent, caring, handsome, funny, cool
People who like the name Dewayne also like Ethan, Aaron, Christopher, Damian, Dwayne, Brandon, Dustin, Anthony, Ian, Cody

Dewei (*Chinese*) ♂ RATING: ★☆
Of great principle
People think of Dewei as wild, weird, ethnic, aggressive, exotic
People who like the name Dewei also like Hiroshi, Akio, Guang, Botan, Aran, Charan, Fai, Jiro, Haru, Haruki

Dewey (*Welsh*) ♂ RATING: ★★★★
Beloved—Originally from the Welsh name Dewi; also a variation of David; Dewey decimal system, invented by Melvil Dewey
People think of Dewey as intelligent, funny, caring, creative, handsome
People who like the name Dewey also like Ethan, Caleb, Dempsey, Jacob, Gavin, Duncan, Felix, David, Darwin, Dominic

Dewitt (*German*) ♂ RATING: ★★★
Blond—DeWitt Clinton, former governor of New York
People think of Dewitt as intelligent, weird, powerful, quiet, aggressive
People who like the name Dewitt also like Drake, David, Emery, Ian, Dawson, Derek, Fletcher, Fabian, Dave, Dirk

Dex (*English*) ♀ RATING: ★★
Short for Dexter or Dextra
People think of Dex as creative, popular, intelligent, nerdy, winner
People who like the name Dex also like Zoe, Zoey, Dea, Aurora, Dawn, Scarlett, Davan, Daisy, Faith, Ella

Dexter (*English*) ♂ RATING: ★★
Dyer of clothes—Originally an occupational surname; also Latin meaning main-handed, dexterous; *Dexter*, TV show; *Dexter's Laboratory*, cartoon
People think of Dexter as handsome, intelligent, funny, cool, sexy
People who like the name Dexter also like Drake, Caleb, Oliver, Isaac, Ethan, Baxter, Jack, Alexander, Ian, Jacob

Dextra (*American*) ♀ RATING: ★☆
Dyer of clothes—Feminine form of Dexter
People think of Dextra as funny, intelligent, powerful, exotic, creative
People who like the name Dextra also like Drucilla, Dysis, Deirdra, Donatella, Dreama, Desiree, Decima, Dulcina, Derora, Diantha

Dezi (*Spanish*) ♂ RATING: ★★★
Desired—Variation of Desi or Desiderio
People think of Dezi as creative, popular, intelligent, young, powerful
People who like the name Dezi also like Joaquin, Fox, Michael, Ben, Jack, Malcolm, Marcelino, Rex, Santo, Diedrick

Dezso (*Hungarian*) ♂ RATING: ★★☆
Desired—Variation of Desiderius
People think of Dezso as nerdy, sexy, old-fashioned, poor, leader
People who like the name Dezso also like Azizi, Dexter, Deo, Gideon, Angelo, Frederick, Davu, Kael, Diedrick, Damon

Dharma (*Sanskrit/East Indian*) ♀ ♂ RATING: ★★★☆
Ultimate law of all things—*Dharma & Greg*, TV show
People think of Dharma as creative, funny, artsy, exotic, intelligent
People who like the name Dharma also like Avery, Dakota, Dylan, Hayden, Aidan, Bailey, Cadence, Darcy, Madison, Addison

Dhaval (*Sanskrit/East Indian*) ♂ RATING: ★★☆
White, pure
People think of Dhaval as handsome, cool, intelligent, leader, caring
People who like the name Dhaval also like Devesh, Dhiren, Ravi, Devanand, Dulal, Kuval, Divyesh, Deepak, Manas, Nalin

Dhiren (*Sanskrit/East Indian*) ♂ RATING: ★★★
Strong one
People think of Dhiren as energetic, powerful, winner, intelligent, sporty
People who like the name Dhiren also like Dhaval, Dulal, Devesh, Elijah, Divyesh, Dyami, Ravi, Gagan, Chetan, Gideon

Dhyana (*Sanskrit/East Indian*) ♀ RATING: ★★★
Meditation
People think of Dhyana as artsy, creative, funny, powerful, cool
People who like the name Dhyana also like Denali, Danika, Dysis, Destiny, Danica, Drea, Dahlia, Dara, Divya, Daru

Diallo (*African*) ♂ RATING: ★☆
Bold
People think of Diallo as intelligent, handsome, sexy, cool, powerful
People who like the name Diallo also like Dragan, Delano, Faolan, Drake, Darius, Diego, Dasan, Anando, Haben, Damien

Diamond (*English*) ♀ ♂ RATING: ★★★☆
Brilliant gem
People think of Diamond as pretty, popular, sexy, funny, young
People who like the name Diamond also like Dakota, Jade, Angel, Alexis, Bailey, Jordan, Brooklyn, Brooke, Madison, Ashanti

Dian (*American*) ♀ ♂ RATING: ★★★☆
Variation of Dion or Diane
People think of Dian as intelligent, creative, funny, pretty, energetic
People who like the name Dian also like Caden, Darcy, Dion, Dorian, Devon, Dylan, Deon, Jade, Aidan, Blair

Diana *(Greek)* ♀   RATING: ★★☆
Divine—Originally short for Diviana; also the Greek goddess of the hunt; Princess Diana, princess of Wales/humanitarian; Diana Ross, singer
- People think of Diana as pretty, caring, intelligent, funny, creative
- People who like the name Diana also like Emma, Hannah, Elizabeth, Isabella, Abigail, Grace, Olivia, Chloe, Claire, Emily

Diandra *(American)* ♀   RATING: ★★★★☆
Combination of Diana and Sandra
- People think of Diandra as pretty, intelligent, funny, popular, creative
- People who like the name Diandra also like Deandra, Destiny, Danielle, Ariana, Danica, Isabella, Dominique, Cailyn, Adriana, Desiree

Diane *(French)* ♀   RATING: ★★★☆
Divine—Variation of Diana; Diane Keaton, actress; Diane Lane, actress; Diane Sawyer, TV host
- People think of Diane as caring, funny, pretty, intelligent, trustworthy
- People who like the name Diane also like Diana, Faith, Emily, Emma, Elizabeth, Danielle, Hannah, Hailey, Grace, Daisy

Dianne *(American)* ♀   RATING: ★★
Divine—Variation of Diane
- People think of Dianne as funny, caring, trustworthy, intelligent, pretty
- People who like the name Dianne also like Diana, Hailey, Danielle, Emma, Elizabeth, Emily, Abigail, Victoria, Hannah, Daisy

Diantha *(Greek)* ♀   RATING: ★★★
Divine flower
- People think of Diantha as trustworthy, intelligent, creative, unpopular, quiet
- People who like the name Diantha also like Dianthe, Diandra, Delphina, Davina, Destiny, Gianna, Diana, Delilah, Dara, Dustine

Dianthe *(Greek)* ♀   RATING: ★★★
Flower of the gods
- People think of Dianthe as pretty, elegant, intelligent, cool, religious
- People who like the name Dianthe also like Diantha, Delphina, Diandra, Dea, Damia, Delphine, Diana, Daffodil, Damaris, Desiree

Diara *(Latin)* ♀♂   RATING: ★★
Gift
- People think of Diara as pretty, funny, intelligent, popular, caring
- People who like the name Diara also like Dante, Caden, Dylan, Daylin, Jaden, Aidan, Dakota, Jade, Dior, Devan

Diata *(African)* ♂   RATING: ★★★
Short for Sundiata—One of the first kings of Mali
- People think of Diata as young, caring, old-fashioned, old, energetic

People who like the name Diata also like Dumi, Lehana, Penda, Bandele, Gavivi, Darian, Nyack, Kynan, Roman, Anakin

Dick *(English)* ♂   RATING: ★☆
Short for Richard—Dick Cheney, U.S. vice president; Dick Tracy, comic character; Dick Van Dyke, actor; Dick Van Patten, actor
- People think of Dick as sexy, loser, big, stuck-up, weird
- People who like the name Dick also like Daniel, Dean, Dillon, Derek, Ethan, David, Benjamin, Edward, George, Dominic

Didier *(French)* ♂   RATING: ★★★☆
Desire—Pronounced *did-YAY*
- People think of Didier as handsome, creative, intelligent, caring, funny
- People who like the name Didier also like Dominic, Brandon, Gabriel, Drake, Dax, Damian, Beau, Daniel, Jacques, Aiden

Didina *(French)* ♀   RATING: ★☆
Desired; beloved
- People think of Didina as exotic, funny, girl next door, big, lazy
- People who like the name Didina also like Desiree, Darlene, Dava, Decima, Dominique, Dena, Dea, Dixie, Diandra, Dolly

Didrika *(German)* ♀   RATING: ★★☆
People ruler—Feminine form of Derek
- People think of Didrika as criminal, aggressive, weird, nerdy, ethnic
- People who like the name Didrika also like Diandra, Drucilla, Danika, Derica, Dasha, Dorinda, Deidra, Dara, Della, Donatella

Diedrick *(German)* ♂   RATING: ★★★
People ruler—Variation of Derek
- People think of Diedrick as intelligent, handsome, energetic, creative, leader
- People who like the name Diedrick also like Drake, Damien, Derek, Deacon, Damian, Dillon, Dominic, Dawson, Dalton, Darian

Diego *(Spanish)* ♂   RATING: ★★★★
Short for San Diego—San Diego is St. James of Santiago; Diego Rivera, artist
- People think of Diego as handsome, intelligent, funny, cool, sexy
- People who like the name Diego also like Gabriel, Dominic, Ethan, Jacob, Elijah, Adrian, Lucas, Antonio, Noah, Isaac

Diella *(Latin)* ♀   RATING: ★★★☆
Worshipper of God
- People think of Diella as pretty, elegant, religious, popular, caring
- People who like the name Diella also like Danya, Isabella, Grace, Ceana, Jadyn, Danielle, Faith, Bella, Gianna, Dominica

Diem (*Latin*) ♀ ♂   RATING: ★★
Day—Also a Vietnamese name meaning pretty
People think of Diem as pretty, exotic, caring, sexy, popular
People who like the name Diem also like Caden, Bailey, Addison, Dakota, Avery, Demi, Delaney, Aubrey, Parker, Logan

Diep (*Vietnamese*) ♀   RATING: ★★☆
Unknown meaning
People think of Diep as weird, ethnic, pretty, poor, intelligent
People who like the name Diep also like Didina, Devorit, Deliz, Deanne, Daria, Dorie, Dulcea, Darlita, Deana, Deirdre

Dierdra (*American*) ♀   RATING: ★★★
Variation of Deirdre
People think of Dierdra as caring, intelligent, leader, pretty, funny
People who like the name Dierdra also like Deirdra, Deidra, Deirdre, Daphne, Keira, Chloe, Danica, Fiona, Brianna, Kaelyn

Dieter (*German*) ♂   RATING: ★★★☆
Army of the people
People think of Dieter as funny, intelligent, handsome, energetic, powerful
People who like the name Dieter also like Aiden, Gabriel, Dawson, Braden, Deacon, Landon, Ethan, Deiter, Aden, Noah

Dilana (*American*) ♀   RATING: ★★★☆
Of the light—Variation of Lana or Svetlana
People think of Dilana as pretty, powerful, exotic, artsy, leader
People who like the name Dilana also like Abigail, Danica, Ava, Danielle, Chloe, Ayanna, Tatiana, Anastacia, Jazzelle, Destiny

Dillan (*Celtic/Gaelic*) ♂   RATING: ★★★☆
Born from the ocean—Variation of Dylan
People think of Dillan as handsome, cool, funny, sexy, energetic
People who like the name Dillan also like Dillon, Ethan, Aiden, Conner, Caleb, Braden, Ian, Cole, Jayden, Kaden

Dillian (*American*) ♀ ♂   RATING: ★★★☆
Combination of Dillon and Gillian
People think of Dillian as funny, intelligent, young, sexy, quiet
People who like the name Dillian also like Dakota, Dylan, Caden, Bailey, Jaden, Connor, Ashton, Blake, Brooke, Cameron

Dillon (*Welsh*) ♂   RATING: ★★★★
Born from the ocean—Also an English surname; variation of Dylan
People think of Dillon as funny, handsome, cool, intelligent, caring
People who like the name Dillon also like Ethan, Caleb, Aiden, Ian, Jacob, Cole, Gavin, Braden, Kaden, Conner

Dima (*Russian*) ♂   RATING: ★★
Devotee of Demeter—Short for Dimitri
People think of Dima as intelligent, sexy, handsome, funny, cool
People who like the name Dima also like Draco, Damien, Dmitri, Felix, Cody, Dragan, Chase, Dillon, Devlin, Drago

Dimaia (*American*) ♀   RATING: ★★★
Daughter of Maia
People think of Dimaia as pretty, trendy, powerful, popular, leader
People who like the name Dimaia also like Dominique, Diandra, Damia, Deianira, Dysis, Olivia, Desdemona, Danya, Deandra, Destiny

Dina (*Hebrew*) ♀   RATING: ★★
God has judged
People think of Dina as pretty, intelligent, funny, caring, trustworthy
People who like the name Dina also like Dinah, Diana, Daphne, Danielle, Isabella, Isabelle, Hailey, Hannah, Emily, Emma

Dinah (*Hebrew*) ♀   RATING: ★★☆
God has judged—Dinah Shore, entertainer
People think of Dinah as pretty, funny, caring, intelligent, trustworthy
People who like the name Dinah also like Abigail, Hannah, Ava, Eva, Claire, Gabrielle, Charlotte, Faith, Grace, Chloe

Dinesh (*Sanskrit/East Indian*) ♂   RATING: ★★★☆
Son of the sun
People think of Dinesh as energetic, handsome, intelligent, sexy, powerful
People who like the name Dinesh also like Deepak, Naresh, Gyan, Ashwin, Manjit, Ekram, Gagan, Kuval, Gautam, Devesh

Dinh (*Vietnamese*) ♂   RATING: ★★★
Peace, calm
People think of Dinh as handsome, powerful, energetic, weird, religious
People who like the name Dinh also like Dax, Donovan, Gabriel, Gideon, Brandon, Binh, Dacian, Bien, Felix, Isaac

Dino (*Italian*) ♂   RATING: ★☆
Short for names ending with Dino—Character on *The Flintstones*
People think of Dino as intelligent, handsome, funny, cool, leader
People who like the name Dino also like Draco, Dominic, Gino, Felix, Leo, Allen, Cole, Diego, Dario, Caleb

Dinos (*Greek*) ♂   RATING: ★★☆
Short for Constantine
People think of Dinos as funny, cool, handsome, caring, exotic
People who like the name Dinos also like Damien, Damian, Declan, Clark, Dasan, Darius, Deo, Cole, Dillon, Cody

Diogo *(Portuguese)* ♂ RATING: ★★★
Variation of Diego
> People think of Diogo as cool, creative, funny, young, intelligent
> People who like the name Diogo also like Dominic, Paulo, Dmitri, Sancho, Valentin, Nicholas, Nathaniel, Bradan, Zachary, Kaipo

Dion *(Greek)* ♀♂ RATING: ★★★★
God of wine and revelry—Dion, singer; Celine Dion, singer
> People think of Dion as funny, cool, popular, intelligent, sexy
> People who like the name Dion also like Dylan, Jade, Deon, Connor, Jordan, Drew, Jaden, Blake, Dakota, Alexis

Dionna *(American)* ♀ RATING: ★★★
Divine lady—Combination of Dionne and Donna
> People think of Dionna as pretty, funny, creative, intelligent, popular
> People who like the name Dionna also like Colleen, Farah, Desiree, Eve, Dea, Genevieve, Faith, Cleo, Charity, Felicia

Dionne *(French)* ♀ RATING: ★★★☆
Divine—Variation of Diana
> People think of Dionne as pretty, funny, intelligent, creative, popular
> People who like the name Dionne also like Desiree, Dixie, Brielle, Giselle, Dawn, Adrienne, Celine, Deanna, Ciara, Chloe

Dionysius *(Greek)* ♂ RATING: ★☆
God of wine and revelry
> People think of Dionysius as trustworthy, weird, loser, old-fashioned, funny
> People who like the name Dionysius also like Demetrius, Darius, Demitrius, Dionysus, Dmitri, Dashiell, Drake, Erasmus, Sirius, Alexander

Dionysus *(Latin)* ♂ RATING: ★★★
God of wine and revelry
> People think of Dionysus as intelligent, weird, sexy, aggressive, energetic
> People who like the name Dionysus also like Dionysius, Dmitri, Damien, Alexavier, Damian, Lorenzo, Caesar, Morpheus, David, Alastair

Dior *(French)* ♀♂ RATING: ★★
Present—Christian Dior, fashion designer
> People think of Dior as sexy, pretty, trendy, elegant, popular
> People who like the name Dior also like Bailey, Hayden, Dakota, Brooklyn, Caden, Dylan, Dante, Jaden, Dallas, Blair

Dirk *(German)* ♂ RATING: ★★★☆
Famous ruler—Originally short for Derek
> People think of Dirk as funny, handsome, intelligent, sexy, cool
> People who like the name Dirk also like Ethan, Caleb, Drake, Ian, Dustin, Aiden, Braden, Cole, Isaac, Jacob

Divakar *(Sanskrit/East Indian)* ♂ RATING: ★★☆
Sun
> People think of Divakar as exotic, unpopular, sexy, religious, elegant
> People who like the name Divakar also like Divyesh, Chetan, Charan, Devesh, Deepak, Chatura, Gagan, Kaushal, Kishan, Gautam

Divya *(Sanskrit/East Indian)* ♀ RATING: ★★★★
Divine brilliance
> People think of Divya as pretty, intelligent, caring, creative, young
> People who like the name Divya also like Devika, Devica, Dhyana, Devaki, Diandra, Denali, Devi, Chandra, Deepnita, Dena

Divyesh *(Sanskrit/East Indian)* ♂ RATING: ★★☆
Sun
> People think of Divyesh as aggressive, powerful, caring, ethnic, energetic
> People who like the name Divyesh also like Devesh, Divakar, Deepak, Adarsh, Chetan, Dinesh, Geet, Chatura, Gaurav, Dhiren

Dixie *(French)* ♀ RATING: ★★★★
From the U.S. South—Louisiana issued a $10 bill called the *dix* (the French word for ten), which were nicknamed "dixies"; the South then became known as "Dixieland" or Dixie
> People think of Dixie as pretty, funny, energetic, intelligent, wild
> People who like the name Dixie also like Daisy, Faith, Bella, Belle, Grace, Destiny, Desiree, Emma, Abigail, Claire

Dixon *(English)* ♂ RATING: ★★★★
Son of Richard
> People think of Dixon as handsome, sexy, intelligent, cool, funny
> People who like the name Dixon also like Dawson, Ethan, Conner, Dalton, Jackson, Drake, Chase, Braden, Kaden, Gavin

Diza *(Hebrew)* ♀ RATING: ★★★
Joyous
> People think of Diza as funny, leader, intelligent, pretty, trendy
> People who like the name Diza also like Dava, Danya, Dysis, Dasha, Dena, Devorah, Dara, Dolly, Destiny, Delilah

Dmitri *(Slavic)* ♂ RATING: ★★★★☆
Devotee of Demeter—Variation of Demitrius or Demeter; also spelled Dimitri, Dmitry, or Dimitry
> People think of Dmitri as handsome, intelligent, creative, caring, funny
> People who like the name Dmitri also like Dominic, Aiden, Damien, Caleb, Demitrius, Drake, Ethan, Adrian, Gavin, Tristan

Doane *(English)* ♂   RATING: ★★☆
Variation of Dwayne
> People think of Doane as intelligent, weird, loser, cool, leader
> People who like the name Doane also like Drake, Ethan, Fynn, Emerson, Heath, Finn, Isaac, Langston, Deron, Waldron

Dobry *(Polish)* ♂   RATING: ★☆
Good
> People think of Dobry as funny, unpopular, intelligent, nerdy, poor
> People who like the name Dobry also like Emerson, Braeden, Braden, Dallan, Dolan, Keagan, Gannon, Heath, Gage, Brice

Doctor *(English)* ♂   RATING: ★★★
The seventh son of the seventh son
> People think of Doctor as powerful, weird, intelligent, handsome, unpopular
> People who like the name Doctor also like Daniel, Dalton, Dawson, Andrew, Aiden, Duke, Deacon, Dean, Christopher, Maddox

Dolan *(Celtic/Gaelic)* ♂   RATING: ★★★★
Dark haired
> People think of Dolan as funny, intelligent, popular, creative, leader
> People who like the name Dolan also like Aiden, Dillon, Donovan, Aden, Ethan, Edan, Braden, Dawson, Gavin, Ian

Dolly *(American)* ♀   RATING: ★★★
Cute child—Short for Dorothy or Dolores; Dolly Madison, U.S. first lady; Dolly Parton, singer/actress
> People think of Dolly as pretty, intelligent, popular, caring, sexy
> People who like the name Dolly also like Daisy, Destiny, Faith, Dixie, Bella, Grace, Daphne, Dawn, Bridget, Desiree

Dolores *(Spanish)* ♀   RATING: ★★★☆
Sorrows—From Maria de los Dolores (Mary of the Sorrows), another name for the Virgin Mary
> People think of Dolores as caring, pretty, intelligent, creative, trustworthy
> People who like the name Dolores also like Felicity, Eleanor, Genevieve, Celeste, Daphne, Deirdre, Diana, Fiona, Delilah, Dorothy

Dolph *(German)* ♂   RATING: ★☆
Short for Randolph or Adolph—Dolph Lundgren, actor
> People think of Dolph as pretty, big, intelligent, artsy, quiet
> People who like the name Dolph also like Ethan, Drake, Draco, Dax, Gabriel, Dash, Dirk, Duncan, Henry, Edgar

Dom *(Latin)* ♂   RATING: ★★★☆
Short for Dominic—Dom DeLuise, actor
> People think of Dom as handsome, intelligent, sexy, cool, popular

> People who like the name Dom also like Dominic, Aden, Aiden, Adrian, Maddox, Damian, Duncan, Daniel, Dawson, Damien

Domani *(Italian)* ♀ ♂   RATING: ★★★☆
Tomorrow
> People think of Domani as handsome, exotic, intelligent, sexy, cool
> People who like the name Domani also like Damani, Dakota, Dante, Dylan, Jaden, Devan, Caden, Demi, Aidan, Dorian

Domenica *(Italian)* ♀   RATING: ★★★★
Belonging to God—Variation of Dominica
> People think of Domenica as pretty, intelligent, creative, caring, cool
> People who like the name Domenica also like Gianna, Donatella, Dominica, Dominique, Giovanna, Angelina, Isabella, Arianna, Gabriella, Bianca

Dominic *(Latin)* ♂   RATING: ★★★
Belonging to God
> People think of Dominic as handsome, funny, intelligent, cool, caring
> People who like the name Dominic also like Ethan, Gabriel, Elijah, Caleb, Aiden, Damien, Gavin, Jacob, Benjamin, Isaac

Dominica *(Latin)* ♀   RATING: ★★
Belonging to God
> People think of Dominica as pretty, creative, caring, intelligent, sexy
> People who like the name Dominica also like Dominique, Gabriella, Bella, Isabella, Domenica, Destiny, Bianca, Danielle, Danica, Faith

Dominick *(Latin)* ♂   RATING: ★★★
Belonging to God—Dominick Dunne, writer
> People think of Dominick as handsome, intelligent, funny, caring, cool
> People who like the name Dominick also like Ethan, Gabriel, Dominic, Caleb, Elijah, Jacob, Alexander, Aiden, Damien, Benjamin

Dominique *(French)* ♀   RATING: ★★★☆
Belonging to God—Feminine form of Dominic
> People think of Dominique as funny, pretty, intelligent, sexy, creative
> People who like the name Dominique also like Isabella, Gabrielle, Chloe, Faith, Gabriella, Bianca, Olivia, Hannah, Adriana, Destiny

Dominy *(English)* ♂   RATING: ★★★
Belonging to God—Variation of Dominick
> People think of Dominy as funny, loser, wealthy, trustworthy, wild
> People who like the name Dominy also like Nathaniel, Aiden, Dominick, Damian, Jayden, Gabriel, Deion, Deron, Tobias, Braden

204

Domitilla *(Italian)* ♀　　　　RATING: ★★☆
Tamed
　People think of Domitilla as sexy, old-fashioned, power-
　ful, religious, exotic
　People who like the name Domitilla also like Donatella,
　Domenica, Angelina, Camilla, Cianna, Aria, Delila,
　Delfina, Bellini, Carlotta

Don *(English)* ♀ ♂　　　　RATING: ★★
World leader; man—Short for Donald; Don Ameche,
actor; Don Johnson, actor
　People think of Don as intelligent, funny, caring, hand-
　some, trustworthy
　People who like the name Don also like Danny, Austin,
　Connor, Dakota, James, Darcy, Ryan, Aidan, Cassidy,
　Dylan

Donae *(American)* ♀　　　　RATING: ★★☆
Woman, lady—Variation of Donna or Dona
　People think of Donae as intelligent, pretty, quiet, ele-
　gant, trustworthy
　People who like the name Donae also like Jadyn,
　Braylin, Jazlynn, Nevaeh, Arianna, Desiree, Cassandra,
　Iliana, Liana, Samantha

Donagh *(Celtic/Gaelic)* ♂　　　　RATING: ★★☆
Brown warrior—From the same origin as Duncan
　People think of Donagh as weird, big, aggressive,
　powerful, wild
　People who like the name Donagh also like Duncan,
　Ciaran, Callum, Dermot, Braeden, Donovan, Declan,
　Donnan, Darin, Brennan

Donal *(Celtic/Gaelic)* ♂　　　　RATING: ★★★☆
World leader
　People think of Donal as intelligent, funny, caring, trust-
　worthy, leader
　People who like the name Donal also like Liam,
　Donovan, Declan, Ian, Brendan, Finn, Tristan, Dermot,
　Conan, Duncan

Donald *(Celtic/Gaelic)* ♂　　　　RATING: ★★
World leader—Donald Duck, cartoon character;
Donald Rumsfeld, U.S. secretary of defense; Donald
Trump, real estate tycoon
　People think of Donald as funny, intelligent, handsome,
　caring, trustworthy
　People who like the name Donald also like David,
　Daniel, Benjamin, Douglas, Michael, Andrew, Edward,
　Christopher, Jacob, Alexander

Donar *(Scandinavian)* ♂　　　　RATING: ★★★
God of thunder
　People think of Donar as aggressive, nerdy, uptight, big,
　powerful
　People who like the name Donar also like Drake, Soren,
　Darwin, Dawson, Bedros, Reidar, Dean, Dane, Björn,
　Dominic

Donat *(Slavic)* ♂　　　　RATING: ★☆
Given
　People think of Donat as weird, handsome, sexy, win-
　ner, big

People who like the name Donat also like Daneil, Derek,
Colin, Deo, Daniel, Denis, Dominick, Leonardo, Dermot,
Darren

Donata *(Latin)* ♀　　　　RATING: ★★☆
The giving one
　People think of Donata as ethnic, pretty, exotic, wild,
　sexy
　People who like the name Donata also like Donatella,
　Dulcina, Damita, Deirdra, Dara, Dextra, Delu, Diana,
　Dysis, Destiny

Donatella *(Italian)* ♀　　　　RATING: ★★★☆
Beautiful gift—Donatella Versace, designer
　People think of Donatella as exotic, intelligent, elegant,
　caring, wealthy
　People who like the name Donatella also like Isabella,
　Desiree, Bella, Bianca, Gabriella, Angelina, Gianna,
　Giselle, Chloe, Arabella

Donato *(Italian)* ♂　　　　RATING: ★★★
A gift
　People think of Donato as handsome, caring, intelligent,
　funny, creative
　People who like the name Donato also like Draco,
　Gabriel, Dominic, Caleb, Elijah, Giovanni, Damian, Ethan,
　Xander, Dario

Donelle *(Celtic/Gaelic)* ♀　　　　RATING: ★★★★
World leader
　People think of Donelle as caring, intelligent, funny,
　trustworthy, creative
　People who like the name Donelle also like Deidra,
　Davina, Desiree, Danelea, Kaelyn, Keira, Destiny, Alana,
　Erin, Bridget

Dong *(Vietnamese)* ♂　　　　RATING: ★★★
Winter
　People think of Dong as nerdy, loser, intelligent, weird,
　funny
　People who like the name Dong also like Ethan, Isaac,
　Dung, Eliot, Dean, Aaron, Dawson, Conner, Daniel, Ian

Donna *(Latin)* ♀　　　　RATING: ★★★☆
Lady, woman—Donna Karan, designer; Donna Mills,
actress
　People think of Donna as caring, pretty, funny, intel-
　ligent, trustworthy
　People who like the name Donna also like Faith, Daisy,
　Hannah, Jessica, Eva, Amanda, Emily, Grace, Bianca,
　Fiona

Donnan *(Celtic/Gaelic)* ♂　　　　RATING: ★★☆
Brown
　People think of Donnan as nerdy, weird, trustworthy,
　old-fashioned, lazy
　People who like the name Donnan also like Dolan,
　Dallin, Aiden, Brennan, Conner, Edan, Conlan, Grady,
　Keagan, Dermot

206

Donnel *(Celtic/Gaelic)* ♂ RATING: ★★★
World leader—Variation of Donald
> People think of Donnel as handsome, intelligent, funny, trustworthy, caring
> People who like the name Donnel also like Donovan, Darian, Ethan, Conner, Dominic, Aden, Brennan, Dillan, Dolan, Damien

Donnelly *(Celtic/Gaelic)* ♂ RATING: ★★★☆
Brave, dark man
> People think of Donnelly as intelligent, leader, caring, aggressive, powerful
> People who like the name Donnelly also like Donovan, Conner, Aiden, Dawson, Liam, Dempsey, Conley, Devlin, Everett, Dalton

Donnica *(Latin)* ♀ RATING: ★★★
Lady
> People think of Donnica as pretty, cool, popular, caring, intelligent
> People who like the name Donnica also like Danica, Danika, Donatella, Bianca, Davina, Dominique, Dominica, Drucilla, Drea, Kyla

Donny *(English)* ♂ RATING: ★★★☆
Short for Donald—Donny Most, actor; Donny Osmond, singer
> People think of Donny as sexy, funny, intelligent, handsome, cool
> People who like the name Donny also like Daniel, Cody, Dillon, Dominic, Dustin, Brandon, Brian, Donovan, Drake, David

Donoma *(Native American)* ♀ RATING: ★★★
Sight of the sun—Omaha origin
> People think of Donoma as weird, slow, unpopular, untrustworthy, uptight
> People who like the name Donoma also like Kaya, Kachina, Kaliska, Dyani, Hateya, Desiree, Kiona, Donatella, Kimama, Cholena

Donovan *(Celtic/Gaelic)* ♂ RATING: ★★★★
Brown black—Donovan, singer; Donovan Bailey, Olympic runner
> People think of Donovan as handsome, intelligent, funny, creative, caring
> People who like the name Donovan also like Aiden, Dominic, Ethan, Tristan, Gavin, Caleb, Elijah, Gabriel, Ian, Conner

Dooley *(Celtic/Gaelic)* ♂ RATING: ★☆
Brown hero
> People think of Dooley as funny, big, sporty, popular, intelligent
> People who like the name Dooley also like Dempsey, Bowie, Duncan, Doyle, Dugan, Donovan, Calhoun, Finley, Devlin, Conner

Dora *(Greek)* ♀ RATING: ★★★☆
Gift—Short for Theodora or Eudora; *Dora the Explorer*, cartoon
> People think of Dora as funny, caring, pretty, creative, intelligent

> People who like the name Dora also like Daphne, Iris, Eva, Cora, Ava, Faith, Daisy, Grace, Hannah, Dara

Dorcas *(Greek)* ♀ RATING: ★★★
A gazelle
> People think of Dorcas as nerdy, loser, unpopular, weird, old-fashioned
> People who like the name Dorcas also like Davina, Desiree, Daphne, Darcie, Dawn, Darlene, Deirdre, Delta, Danika, Delphine

Dore *(Greek)* ♀ RATING: ★★☆
A gift
> People think of Dore as pretty, weird, trustworthy, nerdy, funny
> People who like the name Dore also like Drea, Dysis, Dori, Deirdre, Deirdra, Despina, Diana, Deidra, Diane, Debra

Doreen *(Celtic/Gaelic)* ♀ RATING: ★★★☆
Gift
> People think of Doreen as caring, funny, intelligent, trustworthy, pretty
> People who like the name Doreen also like Eileen, Erin, Donna, Deborah, Darlene, Colleen, Cathleen, Ciara, Daisy, Aileen

Dori *(Greek)* ♀ RATING: ★★★☆
Gift—Short for Dora; Dori Prevan, poet/songwriter
> People think of Dori as creative, funny, pretty, caring, sexy
> People who like the name Dori also like Chloe, Hannah, Faith, Dara, Eva, Ava, Abigail, Isabella, Isabelle, Grace

Doria *(Greek)* ♀ RATING: ★★
From the sea—Variation of Dorian
> People think of Doria as intelligent, creative, caring, funny, artsy
> People who like the name Doria also like Daria, Daphne, Dahlia, Hanna, Dawn, Erica, Drea, Dora, Elisabeth, Cassia

Dorian *(Greek)* ♀♂ RATING: ★★★★
From the sea
> People think of Dorian as intelligent, creative, handsome, cool, sexy
> People who like the name Dorian also like Dylan, Hayden, Caden, Julian, Aidan, Logan, Jaden, Addison, Dante, Bailey

Dorie *(American)* ♀ RATING: ★★★★
The sea—Short for Doris
> People think of Dorie as funny, creative, pretty, intelligent, caring
> People who like the name Dorie also like Dori, Dory, Daisy, Desiree, Doris, Hannah, Dawn, Erin, Dora, Doreen

Dorielle *(French)* ♀ RATING: ★★★
Small gift
> People think of Dorielle as trendy, cool
> People who like the name Dorielle also like Elaina, Elaine, Elise, Donelle, Darlita, Cherie, Amaryllis, Dulcina, Kyra, Camila

Dorika *(Hungarian)* ♀   RATING: ★★☆
Gift of God—Short for Dorothy
  People think of Dorika as aggressive, loser, exotic,
  weird, nerdy
  People who like the name Dorika also like Adia,
  Donatella, Danya, Kyra, Lia, Yanichel, Jitka, Hiraani,
  Raquel, Vivian

Dorinda *(Spanish)* ♀   RATING: ★★★☆
Talented
  People think of Dorinda as pretty, creative, funny, intel-
  ligent, caring
  People who like the name Dorinda also like Felicity,
  Faith, Bella, Hazel, Desiree, Deborah, Fiona, Dawn,
  Donatella, Daria

Doris *(Greek)* ♀   RATING: ★★★☆
Sea—Doris Day, actress
  People think of Doris as pretty, intelligent, funny, caring,
  creative
  People who like the name Doris also like Dora, Faith,
  Daphne, Fiona, Daisy, Dolores, Darla, Deborah, Iris, Dolly

Dorit *(Greek)* ♀   RATING: ★★☆
Variation of Dorothy—Also spelled Dorrit; *Little Dorrit*
by Charles Dickens
  People think of Dorit as intelligent, pretty, quiet, popu-
  lar, powerful
  People who like the name Dorit also like Dena, Devorah,
  Dara, Dysis, Daphne, Derica, Dorie, Delphine, Darlene,
  Dolly

Dorothea *(Greek)* ♀   RATING: ★★★
Gift of God—Also spelled Dorotea
  People think of Dorothea as pretty, intelligent, creative,
  funny, caring
  People who like the name Dorothea also like Daphne,
  Dawn, Dorothy, Charlotte, Danelle, Destiny, Desiree,
  Delilah, Drucilla, Aurora

Dorothy *(Greek)* ♀   RATING: ★★
Gift of God—Dorothy Gale, character in *The Wizard
of Oz*; Dorothy Dandridge, actress; Dorothy Lamour,
actress
  People think of Dorothy as caring, pretty, intelligent,
  trustworthy, funny
  People who like the name Dorothy also like Abigail,
  Charlotte, Faith, Daphne, Grace, Fiona, Hannah, Audrey,
  Claire, Emily

Dorsey *(Celtic/Gaelic)* ♀ ♂   RATING: ★★★
From Dorset—Tommy Dorsey, musician
  People think of Dorsey as funny, trustworthy, nerdy,
  intelligent, sporty
  People who like the name Dorsey also like Delaney,
  Darby, Brody, Brayden, Bailey, Blair, Dylan, Brady, Darcy,
  Logan

Dory *(Greek)* ♀   RATING: ★★
Gift of God—Short for Dorothy
  People think of Dory as funny, intelligent, pretty, young,
  creative

People who like the name Dory also like Dori, Hannah,
Jadyn, Chloe, Grace, Destiny, Bella, Dorie, Isabel, Hope

Dot *(Greek)* ♀   RATING: ★☆
Gift of God—Short for Dorothy
  People think of Dot as artsy, old, caring, funny,
  trustworthy
  People who like the name Dot also like Dawn, Lily, Drea,
  Becca, Dixie, Charlotte, Isabelle, Bonnie, Grace, Hazel

Dotty *(Greek)* ♀   RATING: ★★★
Gift of God—Short for Dorothy
  People think of Dotty as old-fashioned, funny, ener-
  getic, trustworthy, pretty
  People who like the name Dotty also like Daisy, Dolly,
  Ella, Elle, Claire, Dorothy, Daphne, Belle, Bella, Elisabeth

Doug *(English)* ♂   RATING: ★★★
Dark warrior—Short for Douglas
  People think of Doug as funny, cool, handsome, caring,
  sexy
  People who like the name Doug also like Ethan, Chad,
  Jack, David, Ian, Jacob, Anthony, Jake, Derek, Brandon

Dougal *(Celtic/Gaelic)* ♂   RATING: ★★★
Dark stranger—Variation of Douglas
  People think of Dougal as lazy, old, intelligent, quiet,
  cool
  People who like the name Dougal also like Devlin,
  Donovan, Dugan, Dermot, Douglas, Tristan, Dolan,
  Delano, Liam, Dominic

Douglas/Douglass *(Celtic/Gaelic)* ♂   RATING: ★★★☆
Dark water—Also a Scottish surname; Douglas
Fairbanks Jr., actor; Kirk and Michael Douglas, actors
  People think of Douglas as handsome, intelligent, funny,
  caring, cool
  People who like the name Douglas also like Benjamin,
  Ethan, Nicholas, Daniel, Andrew, David, Jacob,
  Alexander, Gabriel, Matthew

Dov *(Hebrew)* ♂   RATING: ★★★
Bear—Variation of David; also Yiddish for bear
  People think of Dov as quiet, artsy, weird, caring,
  intelligent
  People who like the name Dov also like Caleb, Jonah,
  Asher, Nathaniel, Eli, Benjamin, Elijah, Alijah, Isaac,
  Aaron

Dove *(American)* ♀   RATING: ★★★☆
Bird of peace
  People think of Dove as caring, pretty, intelligent,
  elegant, young
  People who like the name Dove also like Destiny, Dawn,
  Faith, Daisy, Daphne, Belle, Hope, Grace, Aurora, Eva

Doyle *(Celtic/Gaelic)* ♂   RATING: ★★★☆
Dark foreigner—Sir Arthur Conan Doyle, author; David
Doyle, actor
  People think of Doyle as handsome, funny, intelligent,
  leader, caring

People who like the name Doyle also like Cole, Duncan, Tristan, Ethan, Drake, Donovan, Braeden, Conner, Ian, Noah

Dracen *(English)* ♀♂　　RATING: ★★★
Dragon
People think of Dracen as intelligent, powerful, leader, handsome, creative
People who like the name Dracen also like Caden, Cade, Jaden, Addison, Camden, Brayden, Bailey, Dylan, Drew, Logan

Draco *(Italian)* ♂　　RATING: ★★★☆
Dragon
People think of Draco as powerful, handsome, sexy, wealthy, leader
People who like the name Draco also like Drake, Aiden, Damien, Dominic, Gabriel, Drago, Elijah, Ian, Damon, Tristan

Dragan *(Slavic)* ♂　　RATING: ★★★★
Dear
People think of Dragan as intelligent, sexy, powerful, cool, handsome
People who like the name Dragan also like Drake, Draco, Braeden, Tristan, Gavin, Xander, Damien, Gabriel, Darian, Aiden

Drago *(Italian)* ♂　　RATING: ★☆
Dragon
People think of Drago as powerful, aggressive, handsome, sexy, intelligent
People who like the name Drago also like Draco, Drake, Aiden, Damien, Damian, Blade, Darius, Diego, Dragan, Tristan

Dragon *(American)* ♂　　RATING: ★★★
Fire-breathing creature
People think of Dragon as aggressive, powerful, wild, weird, exotic
People who like the name Dragon also like Drake, Draco, Blade, Aiden, Damian, Fox, Kaden, Dragan, Damon, Dominic

Drake *(English)* ♂　　RATING: ★★☆
Dragon—Drake Bell, actor/singer
People think of Drake as handsome, cool, popular, intelligent, funny
People who like the name Drake also like Ethan, Aiden, Gavin, Caleb, Chase, Cole, Ian, Braden, Dawson, Gabriel

Drea *(Greek)* ♀　　RATING: ★★★★☆
Courageous—Pronounced *DRAY-uh*; short for Andrea; Drea De Matteo, actress
People think of Drea as pretty, sexy, intelligent, funny, creative
People who like the name Drea also like Ava, Bella, Chloe, Eva, Grace, Isabella, Brea, Faith, Paige, Emma

Dreama *(American)* ♀　　RATING: ★★★★
Joyous music
People think of Dreama as creative, caring, artsy, pretty, intelligent

People who like the name Dreama also like Destiny, Faith, Dove, Harmony, Grace, Hannah, Daphne, Dawn, Belle, Delilah

Drew *(English)* ♀♂　　RATING: ★★★
Manly—Short for Andrew; Drew Barrymore, actress/producer; Drew Pearson, radio commentator
People think of Drew as funny, handsome, intelligent, cool, caring
People who like the name Drew also like Dylan, Logan, Hayden, Evan, Caden, Bailey, Blake, Riley, Cameron, Ryan

Dru *(American)* ♀♂　　RATING: ★★☆
Variation of Drew or short for Drucilla—Dru Hill, musician
People think of Dru as intelligent, creative, caring, popular, pretty
People who like the name Dru also like Drew, Caden, Dylan, Dakota, Bailey, Hayden, Jaden, Blake, Logan, Avery

Druce *(English)* ♂　　RATING: ★★★
From Dreux, France—Also a surname
People think of Druce as cool, trustworthy, intelligent, creative, weird
People who like the name Druce also like Aiden, Edan, Daire, Donovan, Devlin, Conner, Gavin, Owen, Drake, Everett

Drucilla *(Latin)* ♀　　RATING: ★☆
Mighty
People think of Drucilla as pretty, sexy, elegant, powerful, weird
People who like the name Drucilla also like Faith, Fiona, Cordelia, Aurora, Cassandra, Charlotte, Felicity, Daphne, Dawn, Darla

Drury *(English)* ♀♂　　RATING: ★★★
Love, friendship—Also a surname from Norman French; Drury Lane, London's theater district
People think of Drury as trustworthy, funny, leader, popular, pretty
People who like the name Drury also like Dorian, Drew, Arden, Darby, Caden, Dylan, Dusty, Dayton, Aidan, Keegan

Dryden *(English)* ♂　　RATING: ★★★★
Dry town, valley
People think of Dryden as funny, cool, caring, handsome, creative
People who like the name Dryden also like Kaden, Drake, Dawson, Braden, Aiden, Dalton, Ethan, Braeden, Gavin, Aden

Duaa *(Arabic)* ♀　　RATING: ★☆
Prayer to God
People think of Duaa as intelligent, caring, aggressive, elegant, popular
People who like the name Duaa also like Damali, Dawn, Inara, Demetra, Dysis, Danya, Devorah, Diana, Dara, Dea

Duane *(Celtic/Gaelic)* ♂ RATING: ★★★☆
Wagon maker
People think of Duane as intelligent, handsome, caring, funny, cool
People who like the name Duane also like Dwayne, Owen, Tristan, Caleb, Jayden, Conner, Aiden, Cody, Drake, Chad

Duante *(American)* ♂ RATING: ★★☆
Combination of Duane and Dante
People think of Duante as intelligent, aggressive, sporty, weird, young
People who like the name Duante also like Aiden, Darian, Deshawn, Dustin, Elijah, Jayden, Donovan, Drake, Caleb, Dominic

Duard *(English)* ♂ RATING: ★★
Wealthy guardian—Variation of Eduard or Edward
People think of Duard as trustworthy, funny, sexy, cool, loser
People who like the name Duard also like Darian, Enrico, Darwin, Elmer, Eamon, Denton, Kaden, Kian, Raphael, Deshawn

Dubois *(French)* ♂ RATING: ★★☆
Woodcutter—Literally from wood or from the woods, but also used as a surname to indicate a person's profession
People think of Dubois as sexy, weird, creative, artsy, intelligent
People who like the name Dubois also like Demario, Dyson, Daiki, Cordell, Denton, Dayshaun, Derrick, Dajuan, Dermot, Demetrius

Duc *(Vietnamese)* ♂ RATING: ★★★
Moral, good
People think of Duc as handsome, intelligent, trustworthy, powerful, weird
People who like the name Duc also like Declan, Duke, Dixon, Aden, Jayden, Coen, Dalton, Beau, Kail, Kael

Dude *(American)* ♂ RATING: ★★★
Man, cowboy—Originally used for cowboys; now used as a familiar term for a man
People think of Dude as weird, cool, lazy, loser, powerful
People who like the name Dude also like Earl, Deiter, Cornelius, Ford, Aiden, Arlo, David, Angelito, Dawson, Ethan

Dudley *(English)* ♂ RATING: ★★★
From Dudda's meadow—Dudley Moore, actor
People think of Dudley as nerdy, weird, lazy, loser, unpopular
People who like the name Dudley also like Drake, Cole, Aiden, Dawson, Gavin, Caleb, Braden, Dustin, Nathan, Dalton

Duena *(Spanish)* ♀ RATING: ★★☆
Protect the companion
People think of Duena as pretty, ethnic, intelligent, funny, caring

People who like the name Duena also like Dorinda, Damita, Dolores, Dora, Debby, Dysis, Delfina, Duaa, Diana, Danya

Duer *(Celtic/Gaelic)* ♂ RATING: ★☆
Heroic
People think of Duer as caring, nerdy, trustworthy, old-fashioned, loser
People who like the name Duer also like Crevan, Ciaran, Dermot, Cairbre, Cathal, Calum, Darin, Braeden, Callum, Breck

Duff *(Celtic/Gaelic)* ♀♂ RATING: ★☆
Dark—Hilary Duff, singer/actress
People think of Duff as funny, sexy, handsome, exotic, poor
People who like the name Duff also like Darcy, Dylan, Connor, Devin, Devan, Darby, Cassidy, Drew, Kieran, Dorsey

Dugan *(Celtic/Gaelic)* ♂ RATING: ★★★☆
Dark colored
People think of Dugan as handsome, funny, caring, intelligent, creative
People who like the name Dugan also like Duncan, Drake, Aiden, Caleb, Keagan, Dawson, Cullen, Donovan, Dalton, Ethan

Duka *(African)* ♂ RATING: ★★
All
People think of Duka as boy next door, powerful, aggressive, intelligent, weird
People who like the name Duka also like Colin, Decker, Bono, Ace, Kasim, Felix, Dalton, Abu, Donovan, Jaron

Duke *(English)* ♂ RATING: ★★★☆
Title of nobility—Patty Duke, actress
People think of Duke as handsome, sporty, powerful, leader, popular
People who like the name Duke also like Drake, Ethan, Cole, Chase, Aiden, Caleb, Jack, Braden, Cody, Derek

Dulal *(Sanskrit/East Indian)* ♂ RATING: ★★
Loved one
People think of Dulal as weird, powerful, nerdy, caring, criminal
People who like the name Dulal also like Kami, Gyan, Dhiren, Deepak, Gagan, Naresh, Chatura, Ajay, Sanjay, Kuval

Dulce *(Spanish)* ♀ RATING: ★★★★
Sweet
People think of Dulce as pretty, funny, intelligent, caring, young
People who like the name Dulce also like Bianca, Chloe, Bella, Daisy, Giselle, Isabella, Daniela, Isabel, Desiree, Destiny

Dulcea *(Spanish)* ♀ RATING: ★★★
Sweet
People think of Dulcea as pretty, intelligent, elegant, caring, powerful

People who like the name Dulcea also like Damita, Dulcina, Dulcinea, Dysis, Desiree, Darla, Delicia, Dolly, Deirdre, Dulce

Dulcina *(Latin)* ♀   RATING: ★★☆
Sweet
People think of Dulcina as pretty, exotic, intelligent, creative, trustworthy
People who like the name Dulcina also like Dulcinea, Donatella, Delilah, Dysis, Faith, Felicity, Delphina, Desiree, Flora, Davina

Dulcinea *(Latin)* ♀   RATING: ★★★★
Sweet—Character in *Don Quixote* and *Man of La Mancha*
People think of Dulcinea as pretty, elegant, exotic, intelligent, ethnic
People who like the name Dulcinea also like Dulcina, Isabella, Delia, Davina, Delilah, Dahlia, Delphine, Drea, Darena, Danica

Dumi *(African)* ♂   RATING: ★★★
The inspirer—South African origin
People think of Dumi as slow, unpopular, big, weird, intelligent
People who like the name Dumi also like Diata, Davu, Jabari, Daemyn, Dragan, Alem, Dmitri, Ian, Darian, Aden

Duncan *(Celtic/Gaelic)* ♂   RATING: ★★☆
Dark-skinned warrior
People think of Duncan as handsome, intelligent, funny, popular, caring
People who like the name Duncan also like Ethan, Aiden, Caleb, Conner, Ian, Colin, Gabriel, Cole, Benjamin, Drake

Dung *(Vietnamese)* ♂   RATING: ★★★
Bravery
People think of Dung as weird, loser, unpopular, nerdy, lazy
People who like the name Dung also like Colton, Dong, Dawson, Caleb, Daniel, Bubba, Boyd, Mario, Rico, Ajax

Dunixi *(Greek)* ♀♂   RATING: ★☆
Variation of Dionysius
People think of Dunixi as weird, ethnic, powerful, leader, exotic
People who like the name Dunixi also like Dorian, Dion, Ember, Devon, Devan, Devin, Demi, Deon, Echo, Dian

Dunn *(English)* ♂   RATING: ★★★
Brown
People think of Dunn as weird, slow, loser, poor, unpopular
People who like the name Dunn also like Harris, Duke, Drake, Gabe, Dean, Emery, Holden, Faris, Finley, Finn

Dunne *(English)* ♀♂   RATING: ★★★
Brown
People think of Dunne as weird, handsome, caring, popular, funny

People who like the name Dunne also like Connor, Dylan, Delaney, Darby, Dorian, Drew, Flynn, Carson, Ellis, Delaine

Durand *(French)* ♂   RATING: ★★☆
Stong, enduring
People think of Durand as intelligent, funny, trustworthy, handsome, cool
People who like the name Durand also like Marshall, Bryson, Deo, Dominic, Montego, Dominy, Magnus, Donovan, Nicholas, Darwin

Durin *(German)* ♂   RATING: ★★★☆
Mythical dwarf
People think of Durin as young, sneaky, aggressive, handsome, lazy
People who like the name Durin also like Aiden, Dryden, Dustin, Braeden, Gavan, Edan, Keagan, Drake, Koen, Isaac

Durriyah *(Arabic)* ♀   RATING: ★★☆
Brightly shine
People think of Durriyah as intelligent, pretty, leader, elegant, energetic
People who like the name Durriyah also like Destiny, Desiree, Katarina, Damali, Devorah, Deandra, Duaa, Darlita, Damaris, Dionne

Dusan *(Slavic)* ♂   RATING: ★☆
Divine spirit—Pronounced *DOO-shan*
People think of Dusan as creative, intelligent, cool, caring, funny
People who like the name Dusan also like Casimir, Conner, Elijah, Daniel, Dawson, Darian, Damian, Lankston, Amir, Daemyn

Duscha *(Slavic)* ♀♂   RATING: ★☆
Divine spirit
People think of Duscha as old-fashioned, unpopular, ethnic, young, quiet
People who like the name Duscha also like Darby, Devon, Dorian, Dylan, Jaden, Pascha, Daray, Daylin, Dana, Devin

Dustin *(English)* ♂   RATING: ★★☆
Thor's stone—Also a surname from Thorsteinn
People think of Dustin as handsome, funny, intelligent, caring, cool
People who like the name Dustin also like Ethan, Justin, Caleb, Cody, Jacob, Chase, Braden, Gavin, Aiden, Nathan

Dustine *(American)* ♀   RATING: ★★★☆
Feminine form of Dustin
People think of Dustine as pretty, caring, intelligent, creative, trustworthy
People who like the name Dustine also like Destiny, Desiree, Chloe, Daphne, Emberlynn, Elle, Emma, Danae, Audrey, Cassandra

Dusty (*English*) ♀♂   RATING: ★★
Short for Dustin—Dusty Springfield, singer
> People think of Dusty as funny, intelligent, wild, creative, energetic
> People who like the name Dusty also like Dakota, Bailey, Caden, Hayden, Dylan, Dallas, Madison, Blake, Logan, Taylor

Dutch (*English*) ♂   RATING: ★★
From the Netherlands—Dutch Schultz, gangster; nickname of Ronald Reagan, U.S. president
> People think of Dutch as intelligent, handsome, funny, popular, leader
> People who like the name Dutch also like Finn, Aiden, Drake, Gunnar, Garrett, Chase, Deacon, Jacob, Gage, Miles

Duval (*French*) ♂   RATING: ★★★☆
From the valley—James Duval, actor
> People think of Duval as intelligent, artsy, handsome, energetic, creative
> People who like the name Duval also like Dawson, Devlin, Drake, Everett, Darius, Dalton, Conner, Colton, Dominic, Lucien

Duy (*Vietnamese*) ♂   RATING: ★★★★☆
Save
> People think of Duy as weird, intelligent, quiet, ethnic, cool
> People who like the name Duy also like Denis, Darwin, Damon, Cornell, Conrad, Clint, Amir, Burton, Brian, Braden

Duyen (*Vietnamese*) ♀   RATING: ★★★
Charm, grace
> People think of Duyen as caring, pretty, funny, intelligent, young
> People who like the name Duyen also like Desiree, Dara, Dahlia, Della, Dustine, Drea, Dysis, Davan, Danika, Dori

Dwayne (*English*) ♂   RATING: ★★★☆
Dark, black
> People think of Dwayne as handsome, funny, intelligent, caring, cool
> People who like the name Dwayne also like Ethan, Dwight, Bradley, Justin, Elijah, Jacob, Cody, Dean, Caleb, Damien

Dwight (*English*) ♂   RATING: ★★★
Devotee of Dionysus—Also a surname from Diot, a medieval form of Denis; Dwight D. Eisenhower, U.S. president
> People think of Dwight as funny, handsome, caring, intelligent, leader
> People who like the name Dwight also like Dwayne, David, Ethan, Caleb, Dustin, Dean, Dawson, Jacob, Elijah, Conner

Dwyn (*Welsh*) ♀♂   RATING: ★★★
To steal—Short for Dwynwyn
> People think of Dwyn as cool, caring, creative, energetic, intelligent

> People who like the name Dwyn also like Aidan, Shae, Ali, Tayten, Talon, Rylan, Sage, Halyn, Lakota, Devin

Dyami (*Native American*) ♂   RATING: ★★★★
Eagle—Keresan origin; also a word for north
> People think of Dyami as intelligent, handsome, cool, ethnic, popular
> People who like the name Dyami also like Dasan, Aiden, Aden, Mikasi, Cody, Damien, Braeden, Tristan, Daemyn, Kele

Dyan (*American*) ♀   RATING: ★★★☆
Divine—Variation of Diane; Dyan Cannon, actress
> People think of Dyan as funny, pretty, trustworthy, intelligent, caring
> People who like the name Dyan also like Daphne, Emma, Dara, Deanne, Emily, Dawn, Diane, Emilia, Deanna, Chloe

Dyani (*Native American*) ♀   RATING: ★★
Deer
> People think of Dyani as pretty, funny, creative, intelligent, energetic
> People who like the name Dyani also like Kaya, Leilani, Kailani, Destiny, Kiona, Ayasha, Soraya, Ailani, Keani, Hateya

Dyanne (*American*) ♀   RATING: ★★★☆
Variation of Diane
> People think of Dyanne as funny, old-fashioned, caring, popular, young
> People who like the name Dyanne also like Diane, Dyan, Drea, Deanne, Deanna, Davina, Shaylee, Deidra, Bridget, Donna

Dylan (*Welsh*) ♀♂   RATING: ★★★☆
Born from the ocean; son of the sea—Dylan Thomas, poet; Bob Dylan, singer/songwriter
> People think of Dylan as funny, handsome, cool, intelligent, popular
> People who like the name Dylan also like Logan, Hayden, Riley, Madison, Ryan, Connor, Bailey, Caden, Tyler, Evan

Dyllis (*American*) ♀   RATING: ★★
Genuine—Variation of the Welsh name Dilys
> People think of Dyllis as unpopular, nerdy, loser, quiet, powerful
> People who like the name Dyllis also like Decima, Dympna, Delora, Della, Delilah, Deirdre, Drucilla, Hazel, Donelle, Darlene

Dympna (*Celtic/Gaelic*) ♀   RATING: ★☆
Little fawn
> People think of Dympna as caring, popular, trustworthy, pretty, funny
> People who like the name Dympna also like Aeryn, Genevieve, Deidra, Deirdre, Deirdra, Davina, Breena, Kiora, Hazel, Keaira

211

Dyre *(Scandinavian)* ♀♂   RATING: ★★★☆
Dear heart
> People think of Dyre as creative, weird, intelligent, popular, quiet
> People who like the name Dyre also like Caden, Dante, Daylin, Dakota, Blake, Cade, Jaden, Blair, Ember, Cadence

Dysis *(Greek)* ♀   RATING: ★★
Sunset
> People think of Dysis as pretty, elegant, exotic, powerful, cool
> People who like the name Dysis also like Isis, Aurora, Iris, Dahlia, Chloe, Hazel, Drea, Dea, Daphne, Donatella

Dyson *(English)* ♂   RATING: ★★★
Son of Denise—From Dy, a medieval short form of Dionisia (Denise)
People think of Dyson as leader, handsome, intelligent, popular, cool
People who like the name Dyson also like Aiden, Braden, Dalton, Dawson, Kaden, Tyson, Drake, Jackson, Bryson, Braxton

Ea *(Celtic/Gaelic)* ♂   RATING: ★☆
Fire—Variation of Hugh
> People think of Ea as exotic, weird, cool, loser, wild
> People who like the name Ea also like Edan, Kael, Ciaran, Liam, Eamon, Ewan, Tristan, Faolan, Daire, Aiden

Eadoin *(Celtic/Gaelic)* ♀   RATING: ★★★☆
Jealousy
> People think of Eadoin as weird, exotic, wild, intelligent, ethnic
> People who like the name Eadoin also like Eavan, Aeryn, Aelwen, Keaira, Fiona, Ceridwen, Caelan, Arwen, Fallon, Maeve

Eamon *(Celtic/Gaelic)* ♂   RATING: ★★★★
Rich protector—Variation of Edmund
> People think of Eamon as handsome, intelligent, caring, trustworthy, funny
> People who like the name Eamon also like Liam, Ethan, Aiden, Declan, Tristan, Gabriel, Ian, Owen, Elijah, Keiran

Ean *(Celtic/Gaelic)* ♂   RATING: ★★★★
God is gracious—Manx variation of John; also variation of Ian
> People think of Ean as handsome, intelligent, caring, creative, energetic
> People who like the name Ean also like Ian, Ethan, Aiden, Elijah, Aden, Kaden, Gabriel, Liam, Gavin, Edan

Eara *(Celtic/Gaelic)* ♀   RATING: ★★★☆
From the East
> People think of Eara as pretty, exotic, artsy, creative, intelligent

> People who like the name Eara also like Aeryn, Eavan, Edana, Keaira, Keira, Genevieve, Fiona, Erin, Kaelyn, Enya

Earl *(English)* ♂   RATING: ★★★★
Pledge, nobleman—Also a surname; Earl Campbell, football player; *My Name Is Earl*, TV show
> People think of Earl as funny, intelligent, handsome, caring, trustworthy
> People who like the name Earl also like Ethan, Isaac, Ian, Jack, Jacob, David, Caleb, Thomas, Edgar, Charles

Earlene *(English)* ♀   RATING: ★☆
Pledge, nobleman—Feminine form of Earl
> People think of Earlene as old-fashioned, weird, poor, quiet, caring
> People who like the name Earlene also like Edalene, Eavan, Breanna, Fenella, Alana, Fallon, Eara, Genevieve, Aeryn, Eileen

Early *(American)* ♀   RATING: ★★★
Before due time or date—Old English or Puritan origin
> People think of Early as popular, weird, cool, pretty, quiet
> People who like the name Early also like Elle, Faith, Chloe, Ella, Bianca, Grace, Aurora, Daphne, Butterfly, Honey

Earnest *(English)* ♂   RATING: ★★★☆
Earnest
> People think of Earnest as intelligent, handsome, nerdy, funny, caring
> People who like the name Earnest also like Ethan, Ernest, Edgar, Elijah, Caleb, Gabriel, Edmund, Marcus, Earl, Isaac

Easter *(English)* ♀   RATING: ★☆
Festival of Austron, goddess of fertility and sunrise
> People think of Easter as cool, funny, popular, caring, intelligent
> People who like the name Easter also like Faith, Elle, Bethany, Gabrielle, Destiny, Emma, Hannah, Ella, Emily, Felicity

Eavan *(Celtic/Gaelic)* ♀   RATING: ★★☆
Beautiful radiance
> People think of Eavan as pretty, intelligent, creative, elegant, exotic
> People who like the name Eavan also like Aeryn, Kaelyn, Fiona, Caelan, Fallon, Erin, Ava, Eva, Keaira, Keira

Eben *(Hebrew)* ♂   RATING: ★★★★
Stone of help—Short for Ebenezer
> People think of Eben as intelligent, handsome, caring, funny, trustworthy
> People who like the name Eben also like Ethan, Elijah, Gabriel, Caleb, Isaac, Holden, Aden, Edan, Asher, Kaden

Ebenezer *(Hebrew)* ♂   RATING: ★★★
Stone of help—Ebenezer Scrooge, character in *A Christmas Carol* by Charles Dickens
> People think of Ebenezer as slow, old-fashioned, unpopular, loser, uptight

People who like the name Ebenezer also like Gavin, Dalton, Brac, Isaiah, Duka, Edwin, Bade, Klaus, Johnavan, Lucas

Ebony *(English)* ♀   RATING: ★★★★
Ebony—Also a fashion magazine
  People think of Ebony as pretty, funny, intelligent, caring, popular
  People who like the name Ebony also like Faith, Amber, Hailey, Destiny, Jasmine, Chloe, Ella, Eva, Ava, Grace

Echo *(Greek)* ♀♂   RATING: ★★★☆
Reverberating sound—Also a nymph who sorrowed from unrequited love until the only thing that remained was her voice in Greek mythology
  People think of Echo as creative, pretty, intelligent, caring, cool
  People who like the name Echo also like Dakota, Bailey, Caden, Hayden, Ember, Jade, Cadence, Eden, Jaden, Phoenix

Ed *(English)* ♂   RATING: ★★
Short for names beginning with Ed; Ed Asner, actor; Ed Wynn, actor
  People think of Ed as cool, funny, intelligent, caring, creative
  People who like the name Ed also like Edward, Eric, Felix, Edmund, Elijah, Frederick, Finn, Albert, Eliot, Henry

Edalene *(English)* ♀   RATING: ★★
Noble
  People think of Edalene as old-fashioned, intelligent, slow, creative, leader
  People who like the name Edalene also like Edaline, Eilis, Adeline, Hazel, Breanna, Erin, Edana, Alana, Genevieve, Fiona

Edaline *(English)* ♀   RATING: ★★★
Noble
  People think of Edaline as elegant, old-fashioned, creative, pretty, artsy
  People who like the name Edaline also like Edeline, Edalene, Adeline, Eva, Isabella, Ava, Hailey, Emma, Bella, Kaelyn

Edan *(Celtic/Gaelic)* ♂   RATING: ★★★★☆
Little fire—Variation of Aidan
  People think of Edan as handsome, intelligent, funny, caring, creative
  People who like the name Edan also like Ethan, Aiden, Aden, Tristan, Kaden, Ian, Cole, Elijah, Conner, Keagan

Edana *(Celtic/Gaelic)* ♀   RATING: ★★
Tiny flame
  People think of Edana as pretty, exotic, creative, artsy, energetic
  People who like the name Edana also like Eavan, Aeryn, Alana, Enya, Genevieve, Eara, Eithne, Kaelyn, Erin, Chaela

Edda *(German)* ♀   RATING: ★★
With clear goals
  People think of Edda as intelligent, elegant, caring, powerful, pretty
  People who like the name Edda also like Lorelei, Elle, Aurora, Fiona, Gwyneth, Elsie, Becca, Emily, Hazel, Aurelia

Eddie *(English)* ♂   RATING: ★★☆
Short for names beginning with Ed—Eddie Haskel, punky character on *Leave it to Beaver*; Eddie Munster, character on *The Munsters*; Eddie Van Halen, musician
  People think of Eddie as funny, cool, handsome, caring, intelligent
  People who like the name Eddie also like Jacob, Ethan, Adam, Anthony, Daniel, Aaron, David, Andrew, Eric, Justin

Eddy *(English)* ♂   RATING: ★★★☆
Short for names beginning with Ed
  People think of Eddy as funny, cool, popular, handsome, intelligent
  People who like the name Eddy also like Jacob, Adam, Eddie, Ethan, Gabriel, Daniel, Dawson, Isaac, David, Jack

Edeline *(English)* ♀   RATING: ★★★☆
Noble
  People think of Edeline as pretty, intelligent, trustworthy, elegant, funny
  People who like the name Edeline also like Edaline, Adeline, Isabella, Charlotte, Madeline, Abigail, Helena, Elise, Hannah, Cailyn

Eden *(Hebrew)* ♀♂   RATING: ★★★
Paradise
  People think of Eden as pretty, creative, intelligent, caring, funny
  People who like the name Eden also like Hayden, Caden, Addison, Aidan, Evan, Avery, Jaden, Riley, Bailey, Cadence

Edena *(English)* ♀   RATING: ★★★
Variation of Edna; also a feminine form of Edward; also short for Edwina
  People think of Edena as pretty, caring, winner, young, sexy
  People who like the name Edena also like Elana, Hannah, Emily, Kaelyn, Emma, Gracie, Evana, Elena, Felicia, Cailyn

Edgar *(English)* ♂   RATING: ★★★☆
Rich spear—Edgar Allen Poe, playwright/author; Edgar Winter, musician
  People think of Edgar as funny, handsome, intelligent, cool, caring
  People who like the name Edgar also like Ethan, Edward, Alexander, Benjamin, Gabriel, Christopher, Victor, Daniel, Elijah, Adam

Edge *(American)* ♀♂   RATING: ★★☆
Border, end of a surface
  People think of Edge as loser, weird, unpopular, aggressive, nerdy

People who like the name Edge also like Dallas, Harley, Blair, Gemini, Payton, Ryan, Diamond, Mason, Madison, Addison

Edie (*English*) ♀ 　　　　　　RATING: ★★★★
Short for Edith or Edwina
People think of Edie as pretty, funny, creative, intelligent, artsy
People who like the name Edie also like Ava, Ella, Eva, Emma, Evie, Chloe, Elle, Bella, Sadie, Grace

Edison (*English*) ♂ 　　　　　　RATING: ★★☆
Son of Edward—Thomas Edison, inventor
People think of Edison as handsome, intelligent, popular, cool, caring
People who like the name Edison also like Ethan, Emerson, Elijah, Caleb, Gabriel, Isaac, Harrison, Jackson, Aiden, Grayson

Edita (*Spanish*) ♀ 　　　　　　RATING: ★★★☆
Rich war—Variation of Edith
People think of Edita as pretty, cool, caring, quiet, elegant
People who like the name Edita also like Eldora, Evita, Ella, Elana, Adriana, Esperanza, Amelie, Gabriela, Elle, Eva

Edith (*English*) ♀ 　　　　　　RATING: ★★★☆
Rich war—Edith Wharton, author
People think of Edith as pretty, caring, intelligent, creative, funny
People who like the name Edith also like Faith, Audrey, Grace, Eva, Eleanor, Iris, Hannah, Charlotte, Daisy, Emma

Edmund (*English*) ♂ 　　　　　　RATING: ★★★☆
Rich protector—Edmund Gwenn, actor
People think of Edmund as intelligent, handsome, powerful, caring, funny
People who like the name Edmund also like Gabriel, Ethan, Edward, Elijah, Aiden, William, Caleb, Jacob, Benjamin, Charles

Edna (*Hebrew*) ♀ 　　　　　　RATING: ★☆
Delicacy, tenderness—Edna St. Vincent Millay, poet/playwright
People think of Edna as pretty, intelligent, funny, caring, sexy
People who like the name Edna also like Olivia, Eva, Esther, Charlotte, Abigail, Eve, Eliza, Hannah, Gabrielle, Beatrice

Edolie (*English*) ♀ 　　　　　　RATING: ★★
Noble, good
People think of Edolie as creative, pretty, young, trustworthy, slow
People who like the name Edolie also like Fern, Ava, Elise, Amelie, Felicity, Chloe, Fawn, Genevieve, Lana, Effie

Edric (*English*) ♂ 　　　　　　RATING: ★★★★
Prosperous ruler
People think of Edric as intelligent, handsome, creative, caring, trustworthy

People who like the name Edric also like Ian, Ethan, Edan, Gabriel, Aiden, Elijah, Kaden, Aden, Elden, Derek

Eduardo (*Spanish*) ♂ 　　　　　　RATING: ★★★☆
Variation of Edward
People think of Eduardo as handsome, funny, intelligent, cool, sexy
People who like the name Eduardo also like Gabriel, Diego, Enrique, Fernando, Alejandro, Esteban, Adrian, Jacob, Carlos, Andrés

Edward (*English*) ♂ 　　　　　　RATING: ★★☆
wealthy guardian
People think of Edward as intelligent, handsome, caring, funny, trustworthy
People who like the name Edward also like William, Alexander, Ethan, Benjamin, Daniel, Nicholas, Matthew, David, Jacob, Andrew

Edwin (*English*) ♂ 　　　　　　RATING: ★★★☆
Prosperous friend
People think of Edwin as funny, intelligent, handsome, caring, cool
People who like the name Edwin also like Ethan, Jacob, Owen, Gabriel, Nathan, Edward, Elijah, Matthew, Cole, Ian

Edwina (*English*) ♀ 　　　　　　RATING: ★★★
Feminine form of Edwin
People think of Edwina as intelligent, caring, creative, trustworthy, pretty
People who like the name Edwina also like Erin, Erica, Elaina, Edith, Fern, Eleanor, Enya, Elana, Eva, Bianca

Edythe (*English*) ♀ 　　　　　　RATING: ★★☆
Rich war—Variation of Edith
People think of Edythe as old-fashioned, slow, nerdy, unpopular, quiet
People who like the name Edythe also like Felicity, Edith, Adora, Ella, Hailey, Emberlynn, Elysia, Olivia, Adeline, Audrey

Effie (*English*) ♀ 　　　　　　RATING: ★★★☆
Short for Euphemia
People think of Effie as pretty, creative, funny, caring, intelligent
People who like the name Effie also like Eva, Ella, Ava, Emma, Ellie, Genevieve, Belle, Evie, Bella, Fiona

Efrat (*Hebrew*) ♀ 　　　　　　RATING: ★★☆
Israeli place name
People think of Efrat as intelligent, nerdy, unpopular, sexy, weird
People who like the name Efrat also like Daphne, Gzifa, Cinnamon, Ina, Kabibe, Kaida, Inara, Izzy, Ariella, Adara

Efrem (*Hebrew*) ♂ 　　　　　　RATING: ★★
Very fruitful—Variation of Ephraim
People think of Efrem as handsome, caring, intelligent, funny, creative
People who like the name Efrem also like Ephraim, Elijah, Ethan, Aden, Liam, Caleb, Benjamin, Gabriel, Eli, Noah

Egan *(Celtic/Gaelic)* ♂   RATING: ★★★☆
Little fire
> People think of Egan as handsome, energetic, caring, intelligent, creative
> People who like the name Egan also like Aiden, Ethan, Keagan, Edan, Kaden, Liam, Owen, Tristan, Ian, Conner

Egil *(Scandinavian)* ♂   RATING: ★★★
Pledge
> People think of Egil as weird, aggressive, loser, intelligent, unpopular
> People who like the name Egil also like Ulric, Edan, Ea, Brock, Colin, Noah, William, Emil, Silas, Brian

Ehren *(German)* ♂   RATING: ★★☆
Honorable—Variation of Aaron or Ehron; Ehren Kruger, screenwriter
> People think of Ehren as caring, funny, handsome, trustworthy, sexy
> People who like the name Ehren also like Aiden, Ethan, Gabriel, Elijah, Ian, Jacob, Landon, Tristan, Gavin, Jayden

Eileen *(Celtic/Gaelic)* ♀   RATING: ★★☆
Variation of Evelyn—Eileen Farrell, opera singer; Eileen Heckert, actress
> People think of Eileen as pretty, funny, intelligent, caring, creative
> People who like the name Eileen also like Aileen, Elizabeth, Erin, Claire, Faith, Fiona, Emily, Emma, Abigail, Hannah

Eilis *(Celtic/Gaelic)* ♀   RATING: ★★★★
Of a noble kin
> People think of Eilis as intelligent, creative, pretty, caring, funny
> People who like the name Eilis also like Erin, Eva, Ailis, Ella, Aislin, Genevieve, Elise, Eavan, Ava, Ciara

Eira *(Welsh)* ♀   RATING: ★★★☆
Snow
> People think of Eira as pretty, intelligent, creative, quiet, elegant
> People who like the name Eira also like Hannah, Eva, Eirwyn, Audrey, Faith, Caitlin, Elise, Abigail, Aira, Iliana

Eirny *(Scandinavian)* ♀   RATING: ★★★
New healing
> People think of Eirny as nerdy, pretty, intelligent, creative, caring
> People who like the name Eirny also like Aradia, Elin, Aurora, Arwen, Fallon, Anika, Chloe, Jadyn, Adalia, Galena

Eirwyn *(Welsh)* ♀   RATING: ★★★☆
White as snow
> People think of Eirwyn as elegant, exotic, intelligent, pretty, creative
> People who like the name Eirwyn also like Arwen, Rhiannon, Bronwyn, Gwendolyn, Erin, Aelwen, Isabella, Rosalyn, Hermione, Gabrielle

Eitan *(Hebrew)* ♂   RATING: ★★★★
Firm, strong—Variation of Ethan
> People think of Eitan as intelligent, popular, energetic, handsome, winner
> People who like the name Eitan also like Ethan, Gabriel, Aiden, Aden, Noah, Kaden, Joshua, Elijah, Eytan, Jacob

Eithne *(Celtic/Gaelic)* ♀   RATING: ★★★★
Unknown meaning—Actual name of the singer Enya; pronounced *Enya*
> People think of Eithne as pretty, intelligent, elegant, artsy, exotic
> People who like the name Eithne also like Aeryn, Genevieve, Enya, Edana, Keaira, Ceridwen, Fallon, Erin, Eilis, Eavan

Ekanta *(Sanskrit/East Indian)* ♀   RATING: ★★☆
Solitude, peaceful
> People think of Ekanta as exotic, trustworthy, sexy, popular, girl next door
> People who like the name Ekanta also like Ishana, Eshana, Ebony, Asha, Damita, Destiny, Laksha, Sitara, Evana, Electra

Ekram *(Sanskrit/East Indian)* ♂   RATING: ★★☆
Honor
> People think of Ekram as ethnic, religious, funny, intelligent, energetic
> People who like the name Ekram also like Elias, Ashwin, Chatura, Ajay, Gabriel, Rohan, Edan, Kami, Dinesh, Eric

Eladio *(Spanish)* ♂   RATING: ★★☆
Man from Greece
> People think of Eladio as caring, pretty, leader, intelligent, elegant
> People who like the name Eladio also like Julio, Adriano, Carlos, Eduardo, Aiden, Enzo, Agapito, Avel, Alejandro, Arsenio

Elaina *(Greek)* ♀   RATING: ★★★★
Variation of Helen
> People think of Elaina as pretty, intelligent, creative, caring, funny
> People who like the name Elaina also like Emma, Ava, Isabella, Ella, Alaina, Hannah, Faith, Eva, Hailey, Abigail

Elaine *(English)* ♀   RATING: ★★★☆
Light—French form of Helen
> People think of Elaine as pretty, caring, funny, intelligent, creative
> People who like the name Elaine also like Emma, Claire, Faith, Isabelle, Elaina, Hannah, Emily, Elizabeth, Isabella, Gabrielle

Elam *(Arabic)* ♀♂   RATING: ★★★☆
Highland—Also one of the oldest recorded civilizations in what is now known as Iran
> People think of Elam as caring, intelligent, creative, handsome, trustworthy
> People who like the name Elam also like Jaden, Blake, Blaine, Bailey, Avery, Devin, Connor, Evan, Ezra, Carter

Elan *(Hebrew)* ♀♂   RATING: ★★
Tree
> People think of Elan as intelligent, creative, caring, funny, handsome
> People who like the name Elan also like Hayden, Eden, Jaden, Caden, Jordan, Connor, Reese, Cade, Ezra, Avery

Elana *(Spanish)* ♀   RATING: ★★★★
Variation of Helen
> People think of Elana as pretty, funny, caring, intelligent, creative
> People who like the name Elana also like Emma, Ella, Elaina, Eva, Alana, Ava, Elena, Hailey, Isabella, Olivia

Eland *(English)* ♂   RATING: ★★☆
From the meadowland
> People think of Eland as intelligent, creative, cool, sexy, handsome
> People who like the name Eland also like Giles, Josh, Ben, Nathan, Max, Edmund, Elijah, Matthew, Jarrett, Luke

Elani *(American)* ♀   RATING: ★★★★
Variation of Helen or Eleanor
> People think of Elani as pretty, funny, leader, elegant, creative
> People who like the name Elani also like Elana, Eva, Elena, Ella, Emma, Elaina, Faith, Leilani, Olivia, Ava

Elata *(Latin)* ♀   RATING: ★★☆
Happy
> People think of Elata as exotic, energetic, pretty, funny, sneaky
> People who like the name Elata also like Celeste, Ella, Belle, Bella, Hazel, Ceridwen, Edana, Elana, Emiko, Electra

Elchanan *(Hebrew)* ♂   RATING: ★★☆
God is gracious—Variation of John
> People think of Elchanan as weird, intelligent, nerdy, quiet, funny
> People who like the name Elchanan also like Ephraim, Eleazar, Michael, Fletcher, Ezekiel, Emanuel, Micah, Efrem, Joel, Jedidiah

Elda *(English)* ♀   RATING: ★★★☆
Old
> People think of Elda as caring, intelligent, slow, old-fashioned, weird
> People who like the name Elda also like Hazel, Dawn, Emilia, Esperanza, Ella, Elia, Gwen, Emma, Garnet, Estelle

Elden *(English)* ♂   RATING: ★★★★
The old servant—Originally a surname
> People think of Elden as handsome, caring, intelligent, powerful, young
> People who like the name Elden also like Ethan, Aiden, Kaden, Holden, Grayson, Drake, Gabriel, Alden, Gavin, Cole

Eldon *(English)* ♂   RATING: ★★★☆
The old servant—Originally a surname
> People think of Eldon as trustworthy, intelligent, old-fashioned, handsome, caring
> People who like the name Eldon also like Ethan, Elden, Gavin, Isaac, Drake, Kaden, Caleb, Jayden, Dawson, Everett

Eldora *(American)* ♀   RATING: ★☆
Combination of Ella and Dora
> People think of Eldora as sexy, exotic, quiet, old-fashioned, ethnic
> People who like the name Eldora also like Ella, Elle, Scarlett, Bella, Adora, Eleanor, Olivia, Blossom, Emberlynn, Ebony

Eleanor *(French)* ♀   RATING: ★★
Uncertain meaning—Eleanor Roosevelt, U.S. first lady/political activist
> People think of Eleanor as intelligent, pretty, elegant, caring, funny
> People who like the name Eleanor also like Charlotte, Abigail, Grace, Olivia, Amelia, Ella, Emma, Hannah, Claire, Elizabeth

Eleazar *(Hebrew)* ♂   RATING: ★★★★
God has helped
> People think of Eleazar as caring, funny, intelligent, cool, trustworthy
> People who like the name Eleazar also like Ezekiel, Elijah, Gabriel, Isaac, Isaiah, Caleb, Benjamin, Jeremiah, Eitan, Adonai

Electra *(Greek)* ♀   RATING: ★★★★
Amber—Play by Sophocles
> People think of Electra as exotic, sexy, pretty, intelligent, powerful
> People who like the name Electra also like Faith, Destiny, Cassandra, Ebony, Aurora, Ella, Celeste, Hailey, Eva, Giselle

Elena *(Greek)* ♀   RATING: ★★★
Variation of Helen or Elaina; Elena Verdugo, actress
> People think of Elena as pretty, intelligent, funny, creative, elegant
> People who like the name Elena also like Ella, Olivia, Emma, Eva, Isabella, Ava, Hannah, Grace, Abigail, Chloe

Eleora *(Hebrew)* ♀   RATING: ★★★☆
The Lord is my light
> People think of Eleora as elegant, intelligent, pretty, caring, religious
> People who like the name Eleora also like Eliora, Emilia, Elysia, Eva, Makayla, Abigail, Hannah, Elise, Ebony, Felicity

Elettra *(Italian)* ♀   RATING: ★★★
Shining bright
> People think of Elettra as pretty, exotic, sexy, elegant, trendy
> People who like the name Elettra also like Bianca, Oriana, Cassandra, Camilla, Hermione, Celina, Emberlynn, Aderyn, Bice, Lia

Elgin (*English*) ♂   RATING: ★★★☆
Noble
> People think of Elgin as intelligent, caring, handsome, funny, winner
> People who like the name Elgin also like Ethan, Gavin, Darian, Elijah, Holden, Landon, Drake, Egan, Caleb, Emerson

Eli (*Hebrew*) ♂   RATING: ★★★★☆
Height—Also short for Elijah; Eli Whitney, inventor
> People think of Eli as handsome, intelligent, funny, popular, cool
> People who like the name Eli also like Elijah, Ethan, Noah, Caleb, Ian, Isaac, Gabriel, Aiden, Jacob, Gavin

Elia (*Italian*) ♀   RATING: ★★★★
Variation of Elijah
> People think of Elia as pretty, creative, intelligent, caring, funny
> People who like the name Elia also like Ella, Eva, Ava, Elle, Isabella, Elise, Amelia, Elyse, Gabriella, Faith

Elias (*English*) ♂   RATING: ★★☆
The Lord is my God—Variation of Elijah
> People think of Elias as intelligent, handsome, caring, cool, funny
> People who like the name Elias also like Elijah, Ethan, Noah, Gabriel, Isaac, Caleb, Isaiah, Aiden, Eli, Benjamin

Elie (*French*) ♀♂   RATING: ★★★★
The Lord is my God—Short for Elijah (male) or Eleanor (female)
> People think of Elie as funny, pretty, caring, intelligent, sexy
> People who like the name Elie also like Madison, Caden, Bailey, Hayden, Avery, Addison, Logan, Jaden, Evan, Aubrey

Elijah (*Hebrew*) ♂   RATING: ★★★
The Lord is my God—Elijah Wood, actor
> People think of Elijah as handsome, intelligent, caring, funny, creative
> People who like the name Elijah also like Ethan, Noah, Isaiah, Caleb, Gabriel, Isaac, Jacob, Aiden, Benjamin, Ian

Elin (*Scandinavian*) ♀   RATING: ★★★★☆
Variation of Helen—Also Swedish variation of Ellen; also a Welsh name
> People think of Elin as pretty, intelligent, funny, caring, energetic
> People who like the name Elin also like Ella, Erin, Ava, Grace, Elle, Elise, Eve, Olivia, Emma, Callie

Elinor (*English*) ♀   RATING: ★★★★
Variation of Eleanor—Elinor Dashwood, character in *Sense and Sensibility* by Jane Austen
> People think of Elinor as intelligent, pretty, funny, caring, trustworthy
> People who like the name Elinor also like Eleanor, Ava, Emma, Bella, Caroline, Faith, Charlotte, Felicity, Grace, Abigail

Eliora (*Hebrew*) ♀   RATING: ★★★★
The Lord is my light—Variation of Eleora
> People think of Eliora as pretty, caring, elegant, trustworthy, quiet
> People who like the name Eliora also like Eleora, Eva, Abigail, Elyse, Elia, Eleanor, Ella, Athalia, Giselle, Ophelia

Eliot (*English*) ♂   RATING: ★★☆
The Lord is my God—Short for Elijah
> People think of Eliot as intelligent, funny, handsome, cool, young
> People who like the name Eliot also like Ethan, Elijah, Caleb, Jacob, Isaac, Noah, Jack, Ian, Owen, Gabriel

Elisa (*English*) ♀   RATING: ★★★★☆
God is my oath—Variation of Elizabeth
> People think of Elisa as pretty, caring, intelligent, funny, creative
> People who like the name Elisa also like Elise, Emma, Ella, Isabella, Hannah, Grace, Eva, Faith, Emily, Olivia

Elisabeth (*Hebrew*) ♀   RATING: ★★★☆
God is my oath
> People think of Elisabeth as pretty, intelligent, caring, funny, creative
> People who like the name Elisabeth also like Elizabeth, Isabella, Emma, Hannah, Abigail, Emily, Grace, Faith, Isabelle, Olivia

Elise (*French*) ♀   RATING: ★★★
Variation of Elisa—Also short for Elizabeth; Elise Harmon, actress
> People think of Elise as pretty, intelligent, creative, funny, caring
> People who like the name Elise also like Ella, Emma, Ava, Grace, Claire, Hannah, Olivia, Abigail, Isabella, Chloe

Elisha (*Hebrew*) ♀♂   RATING: ★★★★
God is my salvation
> People think of Elisha as funny, trustworthy, pretty, caring, creative
> People who like the name Elisha also like Jaden, Evan, Bailey, Dakota, Dylan, Caden, Hayden, Madison, Jordan, Riley

Elita (*Latin*) ♀   RATING: ★★
The chosen one
> People think of Elita as funny, intelligent, pretty, creative, exotic
> People who like the name Elita also like Ella, Enya, Emily, Bella, Elana, Olivia, Celeste, Isabella, Eva, Aurora

Elitia (*American*) ♀   RATING: ★★★
Elite one—Pronounced *Alicia* or *E-LI-ta*
> People think of Elitia as elegant, pretty, exotic, caring, ethnic
> People who like the name Elitia also like Olivia, Elise, Elita, Elysia, Enya, Grace, Felicity, Eliora, Estelle, Emberlynn

Eliza *(English)* ♀   RATING: ★★★★
Short for Elizabeth—Eliza Doolittle, character in
Pygmalion and *My Fair Lady*
> People think of Eliza as pretty, intelligent, funny, creative, caring
> People who like the name Eliza also like Ava, Ella, Olivia, Emma, Eva, Charlotte, Isabella, Elizabeth, Grace, Abigail

Elizabeth *(Hebrew)* ♀   RATING: ★★★☆
God is my oath—Queens Elizabeth I and II of England;
Elizabeth Hurley, actress; Elizabeth Taylor, actress
> People think of Elizabeth as pretty, intelligent, funny, caring, creative
> People who like the name Elizabeth also like Emma, Hannah, Grace, Emily, Abigail, Isabella, Olivia, Faith, Ava, Isabelle

Eljah *(American)* ♂   RATING: ★★★★
Variation of Elijah
> People think of Eljah as handsome, funny, intelligent, caring, young
> People who like the name Eljah also like Elijah, Ethan, Gabriel, Jacob, Isaiah, Caleb, Alexander, Isaac, Jackson, Benjamin

Elkan *(Hebrew)* ♂   RATING: ★★★
Belonging to God
> People think of Elkan as trustworthy, leader, powerful, intelligent, religious
> People who like the name Elkan also like Ethan, Elijah, Gabriel, Isaac, Edan, Aden, Isaiah, Elden, Caleb, Elias

Elke *(Dutch)* ♀   RATING: ★☆
Noble, kind—Variation of Adelaide; Elke Sommer, actress
> People think of Elke as pretty, intelligent, creative, caring, funny
> People who like the name Elke also like Elsa, Eva, Bianca, Claire, Ivy, Arwen, Emma, Ava, Liesel, Keira

Ella *(Spanish)* ♀   RATING: ★★★
Young girl—Also short for Eleanor; Ella Fitzgerald, jazz singer
> People think of Ella as pretty, caring, intelligent, elegant, funny
> People who like the name Ella also like Ava, Emma, Isabella, Olivia, Grace, Eva, Elle, Chloe, Hannah, Bella

Ellard *(English)* ♂   RATING: ★★☆
Noble, brave
> People think of Ellard as old-fashioned, lazy, loser, funny, unpopular
> People who like the name Ellard also like Ethan, Charles, Thatcher, Conrad, Barrington, Emmett, Emerson, Edric, Diedrick, Boyce

Ellasyn *(American)* ♀   RATING: ★★★
Son or daughter of Ellis—Variation of Ellison
> People think of Ellasyn as elegant, intelligent, popular, girl next door, pretty
> People who like the name Ellasyn also like Ella, Ashlyn, Kaelyn, Olivia, Emberlynn, Ava, Cailyn, Jadyn, Claire, Chloe

Elle *(French)* ♀   RATING: ★★★★
Short for names beginning with El; Elle MacPherson, fashion model; also a fashion magazine
> People think of Elle as pretty, popular, elegant, intelligent, funny
> People who like the name Elle also like Ella, Ava, Emma, Eva, Chloe, Isabella, Grace, Bella, Olivia, Isabelle

Ellema *(African)* ♀   RATING: ★★★
Milking a cow
> People think of Ellema as intelligent, energetic, exotic, caring, ethnic
> People who like the name Ellema also like Estelle, Elitia, Ella, Hazina, Felicity, Eternity, Elita, Fayola, Bethany, Eliza

Ellen *(Greek)* ♀   RATING: ★★☆
Light—Variation of Helen; Ellen Burstyn, actress; Ellen DeGeneres, actress/comedian/talk show host; Ellen Pompeo, actress
> People think of Ellen as pretty, funny, intelligent, caring, creative
> People who like the name Ellen also like Ella, Emma, Eva, Grace, Olivia, Emily, Erin, Elizabeth, Eleanor, Claire

Ellery *(English)* ♀ ♂   RATING: ★★★★
Variation of Hilary; also a surname; Ellery Queen, fictional detective
> People think of Ellery as pretty, intelligent, creative, popular, caring
> People who like the name Ellery also like Avery, Hayden, Addison, Ainsley, Hadley, Aubrey, Caden, Cadence, Parker, Blake

Ellette *(English)* ♀   RATING: ★★★★
Short for names beginning with El
> People think of Ellette as pretty, funny, sexy, leader, elegant
> People who like the name Ellette also like Ella, Elle, Emma, Aurora, Estelle, Ava, Olivia, Felicity, Eva, Scarlett

Ellie *(Greek)* ♀   RATING: ★★★
Short for names beginning with El, especially Eleanor and Ellen
> People think of Ellie as pretty, funny, caring, intelligent, energetic
> People who like the name Ellie also like Ella, Emma, Ava, Grace, Olivia, Elle, Chloe, Eva, Emily, Hannah

Elliot *(English)* ♂   RATING: ★★★★
The Lord is my God—Originally from Elijah; Elliot Gould, actor
> People think of Elliot as intelligent, funny, handsome, caring, cool
> People who like the name Elliot also like Ethan, Elijah, Noah, Oliver, Jacob, Owen, Isaac, Benjamin, Nathan, Caleb

Elliott *(English)* ♂   RATING: ★★★★
The Lord is my God—Originally from Elijah
> People think of Elliott as intelligent, handsome, funny, caring, cool

People who like the name Elliott also like Ethan, Elijah, Noah, Jacob, Benjamin, Isaac, Caleb, Gabriel, Oliver, Ian

Ellis *(English)* ♀♂   RATING: ★★☆
The Lord is my God—Variation of Elijah or Alice
People think of Ellis as intelligent, funny, handsome, creative, cool
People who like the name Ellis also like Avery, Evan, Addison, Hayden, Riley, Eden, Bailey, Parker, Quinn, Carter

Ellison *(English)* ♂   RATING: ★★★★
Son of Elias
People think of Ellison as intelligent, creative, pretty, popular, caring
People who like the name Ellison also like Emerson, Ethan, Jackson, Grayson, Harrison, Dawson, Edison, Everett, Caleb, Holden

Elmer *(English)* ♂   RATING: ★★★☆
Noble, famous—Elmer Fudd, Looney Tunes character
People think of Elmer as funny, intelligent, handsome, caring, trustworthy
People who like the name Elmer also like Ethan, Edgar, Isaac, Earl, Benjamin, Emerson, David, Gordon, George, Joshua

Elmo *(English)* ♂   RATING: ★☆
Protector—Variation of Elmer; Elmo, character on *Sesame Street*
People think of Elmo as weird, funny, cool, loser, nerdy
People who like the name Elmo also like Jack, Elijah, Jasper, Jacob, Jared, Ethan, Gabriel, Felix, Kaden, Joshua

Elod *(Hungarian)* ♂   RATING: ★★
Ancestor
People think of Elod as boy next door, lazy, cool, funny, unpopular
People who like the name Elod also like Eamon, Adair, Dugan, Caolan, Cyrus, Boyd, Gavin, Orestes, Giancarlo, Byram

Eloise *(French)* ♀   RATING: ★★
Variation of Louise—Title character in *Eloise* by Kay Thompson
People think of Eloise as pretty, funny, intelligent, elegant, creative
People who like the name Eloise also like Charlotte, Ella, Ava, Eva, Olivia, Eleanor, Elise, Emma, Chloe, Amelia

Elon *(African)* ♀   RATING: ★★★★☆
God loves me
People think of Elon as caring, pretty, funny, intelligent, creative
People who like the name Elon also like Grace, Ayanna, Evana, Gianna, Liana, Anaya, Athalia, Chloe, Emily, Jahzara

Elpida *(Greek)* ♀   RATING: ★★★☆
Hope
People think of Elpida as exotic, pretty, funny, quiet, elegant

People who like the name Elpida also like Calliope, Cassandra, Erimentha, Aurora, Idola, Dysis, Electra, Esperanza, Lydia, Esme

Elroy *(French)* ♂   RATING: ★★★☆
The king—Elroy Jetson, character on *The Jetsons*
People think of Elroy as intelligent, handsome, funny, weird, leader
People who like the name Elroy also like Ethan, Elliot, Leroy, Edgar, Elijah, Oliver, Isaac, Byron, Gabriel, Jake

Elsa *(Scandinavian)* ♀   RATING: ★★★★
Short for Elizabeth—Elsa Lanchester, actress
People think of Elsa as pretty, creative, intelligent, funny, caring
People who like the name Elsa also like Ella, Ava, Elsie, Eva, Emma, Grace, Olivia, Mia, Faith, Elise

Elsie *(German)* ♀   RATING: ★★★☆
Short for Elizabeth
People think of Elsie as pretty, caring, funny, trustworthy, intelligent
People who like the name Elsie also like Emma, Ella, Ava, Eva, Ellie, Grace, Elle, Elise, Olivia, Elsa

Elspeth *(Celtic/Gaelic)* ♀   RATING: ★★★★
Scottish variation of Elizabeth
People think of Elspeth as creative, intelligent, elegant, pretty, trustworthy
People who like the name Elspeth also like Scarlett, Genevieve, Ava, Elisabeth, Fiona, Elyse, Olivia, Tabitha, Eva, Isabella

Elsu *(Native American)* ♂   RATING: ★★★
Flying falcon
People think of Elsu as cool, wild, weird, exotic, powerful
People who like the name Elsu also like Chayton, Dyami, Tokala, Ezhno, Hakan, Edan, Ahanu, Gavan, Ohanzee, Gavin

Elton *(English)* ♂   RATING: ★★★☆
The old town—Elton John, musician
People think of Elton as intelligent, popular, cool, handsome, funny
People who like the name Elton also like Ethan, Jackson, Dawson, Elliot, Dalton, Emerson, Ian, Benjamin, Gavin, Braden

Elu *(Native American)* ♀   RATING: ★★★
Beautiful, fair
People think of Elu as creative, pretty, quiet, exotic, intelligent
People who like the name Elu also like Hateya, Kaya, Adsila, Chumani, Dysis, Cocheta, Fala, Istas, Bly, Ayasha

Elvin *(English)* ♂   RATING: ★☆
Elf friend—Originally a surname
People think of Elvin as cool, funny, intelligent, handsome, popular
People who like the name Elvin also like Aiden, Edan, Tristan, Gavin, Ethan, Faolan, Ewan, Devlin, Cole, Owen

Elvina (*English*) ♀   RATING: ★★★☆
Feminine form of Elvin
> People think of Elvina as funny, intelligent, caring, pretty, creative
> People who like the name Elvina also like Genevieve, Estelle, Emily, Gwendolyn, Enya, Keely, Eshana, Eva, Adrienne, Aurora

Elvira (*Spanish*) ♀   RATING: ★☆
Foreign; true—Elvira, Queen of the Dark, TV character
> People think of Elvira as pretty, intelligent, creative, caring, funny
> People who like the name Elvira also like Ella, Bianca, Samara, Layla, Anastasia, Cassandra, Fiona, Aurora, Elle, Adriana

Elvis (*Scandinavian*) ♂   RATING: ★★
All wise—Elvis Costello, musician; Elvis Presley, singer/actor; Elvis Stojko, figure skater
> People think of Elvis as cool, handsome, popular, funny, sexy
> People who like the name Elvis also like Gavin, Ethan, Gabriel, Aaron, Jacob, Felix, David, Adam, Benjamin, Jack

Elwyn (*English*) ♀   RATING: ★★★★
Elf friend—Originally a surname
> People think of Elwyn as creative, trustworthy, intelligent, pretty, artsy
> People who like the name Elwyn also like Arwen, Aelwen, Gwendolyn, Bronwyn, Aeryn, Kaelyn, Ella, Eva, Genevieve, Ava

Ely (*English*) ♂   RATING: ★★★★
Height—Variation of Eli
> People think of Ely as funny, intelligent, handsome, exotic, young
> People who like the name Ely also like Ethan, Eli, Elijah, Caleb, Isaac, Gabriel, Aiden, Braden, Zachary, Noah

Elyse (*American*) ♀   RATING: ★★★★
Variation of Elise or Elizabeth; Elyse Knox, actress
> People think of Elyse as pretty, funny, intelligent, caring, creative
> People who like the name Elyse also like Elise, Ella, Ava, Emma, Hannah, Eva, Chloe, Isabella, Grace, Olivia

Elysia (*Latin*) ♀   RATING: ★★★★
Heaven
> People think of Elysia as pretty, creative, intelligent, funny, caring
> People who like the name Elysia also like Elyse, Hailey, Isabella, Emma, Elise, Chloe, Ella, Alyssa, Faith, Ava

Eman (*Arabic*) ♀   RATING: ★★★☆
Faith
> People think of Eman as young, intelligent, leader, powerful, pretty
> People who like the name Eman also like Layla, Farah, Inara, Asha, Iman, Kya, Kayla, Esperanza, Hannah, Jadyn

Emanuel (*Hebrew*) ♂   RATING: ★★★★
God is with us
> People think of Emanuel as handsome, intelligent, cool, funny, creative
> People who like the name Emanuel also like Elijah, Gabriel, Ethan, Isaiah, Isaac, Samuel, Benjamin, Caleb, Joshua, Jacob

Emanuele (*Italian*) ♀   RATING: ★★
God is with us—Feminine form of Emanuel
> People think of Emanuele as elegant, exotic, religious, caring, intelligent
> People who like the name Emanuele also like Isabella, Gabriella, Isabelle, Eva, Evangeline, Emma, Faith, Gabrielle, Bianca, Giselle

Ember (*English*) ♀ ♂   RATING: ★★★★☆
Spark, burning low
> People think of Ember as creative, pretty, intelligent, artsy, exotic
> People who like the name Ember also like Caden, Eden, Hayden, Dakota, Cadence, Jade, Jaden, Bailey, Avery, Riley

Emberlynn (*American*) ♀   RATING: ★★☆
Combination of Ember and Lynn
> People think of Emberlynn as pretty, intelligent, creative, artsy, elegant
> People who like the name Emberlynn also like Faith, Isabella, Aaralyn, Emma, Kaelyn, Jadyn, Cailyn, Chloe, Gabrielle, Hailey

Emelda (*Spanish*) ♀   RATING: ★★★☆
Entire battle—Variation of Imelda
> People think of Emelda as caring, trustworthy, intelligent, funny, leader
> People who like the name Emelda also like Cassandra, Felicity, Hailey, Evangeline, Aurora, Fiona, Iris, Emilia, Hazel, Ava

Emele (*French*) ♀   RATING: ★★☆
Industrious, admiring
> People think of Emele as cool, pretty, sexy, intelligent, elegant
> People who like the name Emele also like Emma, Ella, Emily, Isabella, Elle, Amelie, Eva, Isabelle, Ellie, Elisabeth

Emelyn (*American*) ♀   RATING: ★★★☆
Combination of Emily and Lyn
> People think of Emelyn as elegant, pretty, caring, creative, sexy
> People who like the name Emelyn also like Destiny, Carleigh, Olivia, Emily, Emma, Isabelle, Ashlyn, Jadyn, Kalista, Maylin

Emera (*German*) ♀   RATING: ★★★☆
Industrious leader—Feminine form of Emery
> People think of Emera as pretty, intelligent, elegant, creative, caring
> People who like the name Emera also like Eva, Ella, Ava, Amara, Emma, Keira, Cora, Hailey, Gabrielle, Lorelei

Emerald *(English)* ♀   RATING: ★★☆
Green gemstone
> People think of Emerald as pretty, creative, intelligent, elegant, artsy
> People who like the name Emerald also like Faith, Isabella, Destiny, Sapphire, Emma, Chloe, Scarlett, Felicity, Amber, Bianca

Emerson *(English)* ♂   RATING: ★★★★
Son of Emery—Originally a surname
> People think of Emerson as intelligent, handsome, leader, creative, popular
> People who like the name Emerson also like Ethan, Jackson, Landon, Aiden, Noah, Elijah, Owen, Emery, Grayson, Gavin

Emery *(English)* ♂   RATING: ★★★★
Work ruler—Originally a surname
> People think of Emery as intelligent, creative, popular, trustworthy, pretty
> People who like the name Emery also like Emerson, Ethan, Aiden, Elijah, Noah, Landon, Kaden, Gavin, Braden, Jackson

Emiko *(Japanese)* ♀   RATING: ★★★★☆
Smiling child
> People think of Emiko as pretty, intelligent, creative, caring, funny
> People who like the name Emiko also like Aiko, Amaya, Ayame, Aneko, Sakura, Keiko, Kaida, Inari, Hitomi, Hana

Emil *(German)* ♂   RATING: ★★★
To strive, excel, rival—Emil Jennings, actor
> People think of Emil as handsome, intelligent, funny, cool, caring
> People who like the name Emil also like Ethan, Ian, Samuel, Gabriel, Liam, Benjamin, Elijah, Isaac, Owen, Caleb

Emile *(French)* ♂   RATING: ★★★☆
To strive, excel, rival—Emile Zola, writer
> People think of Emile as quiet, stuck-up, caring, girl next door, lazy
> People who like the name Emile also like Ethan, Aiden, Holden, Daniel, Etienne, Tristan, Elias, Adrian, Damien, Gabriel

Emilia *(Latin)* ♀   RATING: ★★★★
To strive, excel, rival
> People think of Emilia as pretty, intelligent, creative, caring, funny
> People who like the name Emilia also like Amelia, Emma, Isabella, Ella, Emily, Ava, Olivia, Grace, Abigail, Eva

Emiliana *(Spanish)* ♀   RATING: ★★★☆
To strive, excel, rival
> People think of Emiliana as pretty, creative, cool, exotic, intelligent
> People who like the name Emiliana also like Ella, Emilia, Emily, Gabriela, Catalina, Sofia, Elana, Bianca, Daniela, Lola

Emilie *(French)* ♀   RATING: ★★★
To strive, excel, rival
> People think of Emilie as pretty, funny, creative, intelligent, caring
> People who like the name Emilie also like Emma, Emily, Isabella, Hannah, Ella, Grace, Isabelle, Hailey, Chloe, Faith

Emilio *(Italian)* ♂   RATING: ★★
To strive, excel, rival—Emilio Estevez, actor/director
> People think of Emilio as handsome, funny, intelligent, cool, caring
> People who like the name Emilio also like Gabriel, Antonio, Elijah, Ethan, Isaac, Angelo, Dominic, Anthony, Giovanni, Sebastian

Emily *(English)* ♀   RATING: ★★★☆
To strive, excel, rival—Variation of Amelia or the Latin name Aemilia; Emily Dickinson, poet; Emily Procter, actress
> People think of Emily as pretty, funny, intelligent, caring, creative
> People who like the name Emily also like Emma, Hannah, Grace, Olivia, Abigail, Elizabeth, Hailey, Isabella, Chloe, Natalie

Emlyn *(Welsh)* ♀♂   RATING: ★★☆
To strive, excel, rival—Also an American combination of Emma and Lyn
> People think of Emlyn as intelligent, pretty, caring, elegant, energetic
> People who like the name Emlyn also like Caden, Avery, Aidan, Jaden, Hayden, Bailey, Evelyn, Madison, Cadence, Ember

Emma *(Latin)* ♀   RATING: ★★★☆
Entire—Emma ("Baby Spice") Bunton, singer; Emma Lazarus, poet; Emma Roberts, actress
> People think of Emma as pretty, funny, caring, intelligent, creative
> People who like the name Emma also like Ava, Ella, Hannah, Emily, Grace, Olivia, Isabella, Abigail, Chloe, Hailey

Emmanuel *(Hebrew)* ♂   RATING: ★★★★
God is with us
> People think of Emmanuel as handsome, caring, intelligent, funny, cool
> People who like the name Emmanuel also like Elijah, Gabriel, Emanuel, Ethan, Isaiah, Isaac, Daniel, Jeremiah, Benjamin, Joshua

Emmet *(English)* ♂   RATING: ★★★★
Entire—Also a surname; also a variation of Emma
> People think of Emmet as handsome, intelligent, sporty, cool, caring
> People who like the name Emmet also like Ethan, Elijah, Caleb, Gavin, Isaac, Owen, Everett, Eli, Elliot, Jacob

Emmett *(English)* ♂   RATING: ★★☆
Entire—Also a surname; also a variation of Emma
> People think of Emmett as handsome, intelligent, funny, caring, creative

222

People who like the name Emmett also like Ethan, Owen, Everett, Emerson, Noah, Caleb, Elijah, Aiden, Gabriel, Benjamin

Emmly *(American)* ♀   RATING: ★★☆
To strive, excel, rival—Also a variation of Emily
People think of Emmly as funny, pretty, girl next door, creative, slow
People who like the name Emmly also like Emma, Emily, Emilie, Emmy, Faith, Erica, Elizabeth, Hailey, Jadyn, Gabrielle

Emmy *(English)* ♀   RATING: ★★★
Short for Emily—Also the awards given for TV programming
People think of Emmy as pretty, caring, funny, creative, young
People who like the name Emmy also like Emma, Emily, Ella, Elle, Ava, Ellie, Eva, Bella, Olivia, Chloe

Emory *(English)* ♂   RATING: ★★★★
Variation of Amery—Also a surname
People think of Emory as intelligent, funny, leader, caring, popular
People who like the name Emory also like Emery, Ethan, Emerson, Elijah, Noah, Aiden, Landon, Kaden, Cole, Jackson

Emsley *(English)* ♀♂   RATING: ★★★★
From the elm wood
People think of Emsley as creative, pretty, intelligent, caring, funny
People who like the name Emsley also like Ainsley, Caden, Hadley, Hayden, Riley, Keaton, Addison, Parker, Kinsey, Landen

Ena *(Celtic/Gaelic)* ♀   RATING: ★★★★☆
Variation of Eithne
People think of Ena as pretty, intelligent, creative, caring, funny
People who like the name Ena also like Enya, Ava, Ella, Eva, Fiona, Emma, Erin, Edana, Maeve, Ciara

Enan *(Celtic/Gaelic)* ♂   RATING: ★★★
Unknown meaning—Also an Irish saint
People think of Enan as intelligent, cool, handsome, nerdy, caring
People who like the name Enan also like Edan, Ean, Eamon, Liam, Ethan, Darian, Aiden, Owen, Conner, Elijah

Enapay *(Native American)* ♂   RATING: ★★☆
Courageous appearance—Sioux origin
People think of Enapay as elegant, pretty, intelligent, powerful, old-fashioned
People who like the name Enapay also like Kele, Elsu, Ahanu, Ezhno, Dyami, Pallaton, Tokala, Tuari, Orsen, Enoch

Encarna *(Spanish)* ♀   RATING: ★★
Encarnation
People think of Encarna as exotic, lazy, weird, pretty, old-fashioned

People who like the name Encarna also like Devorah, Calista, Arianna, Angelique, Sadah, Katelyn, Cyrah, Manoush, Nichole, Corinne

Eneco *(Spanish)* ♂   RATING: ★★☆
Fiery one—Variation of Ignatius
People think of Eneco as ethnic, powerful, sporty, religious, boy next door
People who like the name Eneco also like Ace, Lucius, Brando, Dalton, Malachi, Buzz, Mateo, Jaegar, Cosmo, Benny

Enid *(Welsh)* ♀   RATING: ★★★
Soul
People think of Enid as intelligent, pretty, caring, funny, creative
People who like the name Enid also like Genevieve, Emma, Arwen, Eleanor, Fiona, Gwendolyn, Maeve, Chloe, Audrey, Charlotte

Eniko *(Hungarian)* ♀   RATING: ★★★
Dear
People think of Eniko as sexy, caring, old-fashioned, trustworthy, leader
People who like the name Eniko also like Janae, Demetria, Cailyn, Emiko, Jesimae, Corinne, Emberlynn, Danya, Elaina, Cassandra

Ennis *(Celtic/Gaelic)* ♀♂   RATING: ★☆
Island—Also a surname
People think of Ennis as creative, intelligent, exotic, quiet, caring
People who like the name Ennis also like Aidan, Connor, Brody, Teagan, Cameron, Quinn, Flynn, Dylan, Darby, Hadley

Enoch *(Hebrew)* ♂   RATING: ★★★☆
Dedicated
People think of Enoch as intelligent, handsome, caring, trustworthy, leader
People who like the name Enoch also like Elijah, Gabriel, Ethan, Caleb, Isaac, Ezekiel, Isaiah, Gideon, Noah, Seth

Enola *(American)* ♀   RATING: ★★★
The word *alone* spelled backward—*Enola Gay*, WWII plane that dropped the atomic bomb on Hiroshima
People think of Enola as pretty, caring, old-fashioned, creative, powerful
People who like the name Enola also like Amelia, Layla, Ellie, Alora, Erin, Ava, Daphne, Kaya, Eleanor, Emilia

Enrico *(Italian)* ♂   RATING: ★★★★
Home ruler—Variation of Henry; Enrico Caruso, Italian tenor
People think of Enrico as handsome, funny, caring, intelligent, energetic
People who like the name Enrico also like Emilio, Lorenzo, Enrique, Fabian, Elijah, Tristan, Giovanni, Antonio, Leonardo, Diego

Enrique *(Spanish)* ♂   RATING: ★★
Home ruler—Variation of Henry
> People think of Enrique as handsome, funny, intelligent, cool, sexy
>
> People who like the name Enrique also like Diego, Antonio, Elijah, Gabriel, Carlos, Alejandro, Adrian, Esteban, Ethan, Fabian

Enya *(Celtic/Gaelic)* ♀   RATING: ★★☆
Variation of Eithne, the actual name of the singer Enya, created so that people could pronounce her name correctly
> People think of Enya as pretty, elegant, intelligent, creative, exotic
>
> People who like the name Enya also like Fiona, Erin, Chloe, Emma, Ella, Aurora, Faith, Eva, Kaelyn, Genevieve

Enye *(Celtic/Gaelic)* ♀   RATING: ★★★
Grace—Variation of Enya, Eithne, or Anna
> People think of Enye as exotic, elegant, pretty, young, caring
>
> People who like the name Enye also like Enya, Elyse, Eva, Faith, Grace, Brianna, Eve, Amaya, Emma, Aeryn

Enzo *(Italian)* ♂   RATING: ★★★★
Short for Lorenzo
> People think of Enzo as handsome, cool, intelligent, popular, energetic
>
> People who like the name Enzo also like Leo, Ethan, Gabriel, Felix, Ian, Oliver, Alexander, Jacob, Rocco, Vincent

Eoin *(Celtic/Gaelic)* ♂   RATING: ★★★
Desire born—Irish variation of Owen; Eoin Collins, tennis player; Eoin Jess, soccer player; Eoin MacNeill, scholar/revolutionary
> People think of Eoin as quiet, intelligent, trustworthy, caring
>
> People who like the name Eoin also like George, Declan, Alan, Gannon, Ravi, Teague, Silas, Ciaran, Dermot, Asher

Eolande *(American)* ♀   RATING: ★☆
Violet flower—Variation of Yolanda
> People think of Eolande as weird, exotic, creative, pretty, criminal
>
> People who like the name Eolande also like Aeryn, Deirdre, Eavan, Hazel, Enya, Eilis, Maeve, Fiona, Arwen, Daphne

Ephraim *(Hebrew)* ♂   RATING: ★★★★
Very fruitful—In the Bible, the son of Joseph
> People think of Ephraim as intelligent, handsome, creative, leader, caring
>
> People who like the name Ephraim also like Ethan, Elijah, Caleb, Gabriel, Noah, Isaac, Gavin, Isaiah, Owen, Liam

Epifanio *(Italian)* ♂   RATING: ★☆
Manifestation—From the Greek
> People think of Epifanio as handsome, ethnic, intelligent, powerful, exotic

> People who like the name Epifanio also like Erasmus, Eros, Daire, Algernon, Atalo, Fiachra, Amadeus, Damien, Euclid, Fidelio

Epona *(Latin)* ♀   RATING: ★★★
French horse goddess
> People think of Epona as weird, unpopular, elegant, intelligent, trustworthy
>
> People who like the name Epona also like Eve, Jolene, Queenie, Sarah, Zoe, Verena, Delia, Juliet, Rachel, Hailey

Eponine *(English)* ♀   RATING: ★★★☆
French horse goddess—Variation of Epona; character in *Les Misérables* by Victor Hugo
> People think of Eponine as quiet, leader, powerful, sneaky, trustworthy
>
> People who like the name Eponine also like Cosette, Ophelia, Sofia, Rosalyn, Liesel, Chloe, Alyssa, Isabella, Isabelle, Penelope

Erasmus *(Greek)* ♂   RATING: ★★★☆
Beloved
> People think of Erasmus as intelligent, handsome, creative, leader, elegant
>
> People who like the name Erasmus also like Gabriel, Elijah, Cadmus, Calix, Galen, Drake, Lysander, Felix, Faustus, Damon

Erasto *(Italian)* ♀   RATING: ★★☆
Beloved
> People think of Erasto as handsome, popular, intelligent, ethnic, funny
>
> People who like the name Erasto also like Johari, Julisha, Elon, Juji, Gimbya, Roma, Orella, Tarana, Delfina, Isabella

Erelah *(Hebrew)* ♀   RATING: ★★
Holy messenger
> People think of Erelah as intelligent, elegant, exotic, ethnic, creative
>
> People who like the name Erelah also like Delilah, Elysia, Samara, Jadyn, Eliora, Sephora, Ella, Arella, Danica, Eva

Eric *(Scandinavian)* ♂   RATING: ★★★
Always ruler—Originally short for Frederick; variation: Erick; Eric the Red, explorer; Eric Roberts, actor
> People think of Eric as funny, handsome, intelligent, cool, caring
>
> People who like the name Eric also like Ethan, Aaron, Andrew, Benjamin, Jacob, Matthew, Nathan, Christopher, David, Adam

Erica *(English)* ♀   RATING: ★★★
Always ruler—Feminine form of Eric; also Latin for Heather
> People think of Erica as pretty, funny, caring, intelligent, creative
>
> People who like the name Erica also like Emily, Emma, Elizabeth, Hannah, Hailey, Faith, Erin, Paige, Grace, Olivia

223

224

Erik (*Scandinavian*) ♂   RATING: ★★★☆
Always ruler—Variation of Eric; also short for Frederick
> People think of Erik as handsome, intelligent, funny, caring, cool
> People who like the name Erik also like Ethan, Ian, Aiden, Nathan, Caleb, Aaron, Nicholas, Jacob, Alexander, Matthew

Erika (*Scandinavian*) ♀   RATING: ★★★
Always ruler—Feminine form of Erik
> People think of Erika as pretty, funny, caring, intelligent, creative
> People who like the name Erika also like Emma, Emily, Erica, Faith, Hailey, Hannah, Erin, Chloe, Isabella, Grace

Erimentha (*Greek*) ♀   RATING: ★☆
Collector of thoughts; determined protector
> People think of Erimentha as intelligent, quiet, elegant, pretty, trustworthy
> People who like the name Erimentha also like Desdemona, Hypatia, Giselle, Iris, Dysis, Cassandra, Phaedra, Ophelia, Evangeline, Hesper

Erin (*Celtic/Gaelic*) ♀   RATING: ★★★
Ireland
> People think of Erin as pretty, funny, caring, intelligent, creative
> People who like the name Erin also like Emma, Emily, Hannah, Grace, Paige, Faith, Hailey, Elizabeth, Chloe, Ava

Eris (*Greek*) ♀   RATING: ★★
Strife—Greek goddess
> People think of Eris as exotic, sexy, pretty, powerful, elegant
> People who like the name Eris also like Iris, Ava, Aurora, Emma, Faith, Isis, Helena, Erin, Fiona, Ivy

Erix (*American*) ♂   RATING: ★★☆
Always ruler—Variation of Eric or Eryx
> People think of Erix as trendy, lazy, popular, cool, powerful
> People who like the name Erix also like Ethan, Darian, Aaron, Dane, Dustin, Efrem, Elijah, Eben, Aron, Elton

Erla (*Scandinavian*) ♀   RATING: ★★☆
Wagtail bird—Short for Maríuerla
> People think of Erla as sexy, pretty, powerful, funny, weird
> People who like the name Erla also like Elsa, Kelda, Elin, Emily, Eris, Dea, Krista, Becca, Evana, Celina

Erling (*Scandinavian*) ♀ ♂   RATING: ★★★
Descendant
> People think of Erling as trustworthy, intelligent, creative, slow, nerdy
> People who like the name Erling also like Delling, Carrington, Darby, Dyre, Chay, Hayden, Hadley, Ellery, Brogan, Flynn

Erma (*Greek*) ♀   RATING: ★☆
Universal, whole—Originally from Hermione; Erma Bombeck, writer
> People think of Erma as intelligent, pretty, caring, creative, popular
> People who like the name Erma also like Ella, Estelle, Emma, Chantal, Eva, Felicity, Ava, Bianca, Giselle, Delilah

Ermen (*German*) ♂   RATING: ★★
Universal, whole
> People think of Ermen as aggressive, criminal, big
> People who like the name Ermen also like Rico, Iago, Arlo, Stefan, Xavier, Coen, Finn, Ehren, Gunther, Harmon

Ermengarde (*German*) ♀   RATING: ★★☆
Whole, universal
> People think of Ermengarde as pretty, old-fashioned, intelligent, unpopular, artsy
> People who like the name Ermengarde also like Annabella, Delta, Bianca, Lida, Crystal, Baina, Mahogany, Carla, Dorothy, Beatrix

Ermin (*Greek*) ♂   RATING: ★☆
Universal, whole—Originally from Hermione
> People think of Ermin as nerdy, cool, funny, loser, powerful
> People who like the name Ermin also like Barnabas, Calix, Favian, Leander, Matthias, Cadmus, Constantine, Christopher, Lysander, Damien

Erna (*English*) ♀   RATING: ★★★☆
Earnest—Short for Ernesta
> People think of Erna as caring, trustworthy, intelligent, pretty, old-fashioned
> People who like the name Erna also like Delila, Elin, Evangeline, Eshana, Deanna, Evangelia, Destiny, Dominique, Emerald, Flower

Ernest (*English*) ♂   RATING: ★★★☆
Earnest—Ernest Borgnine, actor; Ernest Hemingway, author
> People think of Ernest as handsome, intelligent, funny, cool, caring
> People who like the name Ernest also like Ethan, Eric, Benjamin, Jacob, Elijah, Daniel, Charles, Gabriel, Edgar, Earnest

Ernie (*English*) ♂   RATING: ★☆
Short for Ernest
> People think of Ernie as funny, handsome, cool, caring, energetic
> People who like the name Ernie also like Felix, Jacob, Ernest, Frank, Earl, Isaac, Eddie, Erik, Edgar, Ethan

Erno (*Hungarian*) ♂   RATING: ★☆
Variation of Ernest
> People think of Erno as nerdy, loser, lazy, poor, handsome
> People who like the name Erno also like Edgar, Enzo, Edric, Amos, Faris, Ignatius, Ambrose, Hank, Eben, Boris

Eron *(Hebrew)* ♂   RATING: ★★★☆
Peace, enlightened—Variation of Aaron
> People think of Eron as young, creative, sexy, caring, handsome
> People who like the name Eron also like Ethan, Aaron, Elijah, Gabriel, Noah, Aden, Caleb, Kaden, Edan, Aiden

Eros *(Greek)* ♂   RATING: ★★★★
God of love
> People think of Eros as handsome, popular, sexy, weird, aggressive
> People who like the name Eros also like Elijah, Chase, Gavin, Xander, Calix, Aiden, Ethan, Damien, Damian, Felix

Errigal *(Celtic/Gaelic)* ♀♂   RATING: ★★☆
Irish mountain
> People think of Errigal as nerdy, weird, intelligent, old-fashioned, religious
> People who like the name Errigal also like Ennis, Teagan, Devan, Carey, Gemini, Gael, Oran, Casey, Daray, Brayden

Errin *(Celtic/Gaelic)* ♀   RATING: ★★★★
Ireland—Variation of Erin
> People think of Errin as pretty, creative, funny, energetic, caring
> People who like the name Errin also like Erin, Caitlyn, Brianna, Kayla, Kaitlyn, Emma, Kaelyn, Bree, Lana, Caitlin

Errol *(English)* ♂   RATING: ★★☆
Boar wolf—Errol Flynn, swashbuckling actor
> People think of Errol as handsome, intelligent, leader, funny, old-fashioned
> People who like the name Errol also like Ethan, Liam, Everett, Emerson, Oliver, Noah, Emery, Heath, Felix, Fletcher

Erscilia *(Spanish)* ♀   RATING: ★★
Delicate
> People think of Erscilia as nerdy, weird, poor, untrustworthy, loser
> People who like the name Erscilia also like Gabriela, Esperanza, Abigail, Juandalynn, Constance, Eva, Gabrielle, Graciela, Mercedes, Ava

Erv *(English)* ♂   RATING: ★★
Short for Ervin
> People think of Erv as loser, nerdy, slow, unpopular, old-fashioned
> People who like the name Erv also like Emmet, Henrik, Abbott, Harold, Demetrius, Clint, Deacon, Gaston, Abner, Bowie

Ervin *(English)* ♂   RATING: ★☆
From Irvine, Scotland
> People think of Ervin as caring, intelligent, handsome, funny, creative
> People who like the name Ervin also like Elvin, Ian, Daire, Gavin, Ethan, Cedric, Gabriel, Dustin, Jayden, Elden

Erwin *(English)* ♂   RATING: ★★★☆
Variation of Ervin
> People think of Erwin as funny, intelligent, handsome, caring, trustworthy
> People who like the name Erwin also like Ethan, Elvin, Edan, Gordon, Justin, Tristan, Fabian, Fynn, Cole, Conner

Eryx *(Greek)* ♂   RATING: ★★☆
Boxer—In Greek mythology, a boxer
> People think of Eryx as artsy, weird, quiet, aggressive, powerful
> People who like the name Eryx also like Cullen, Cody, Ethan, Sid, Zachary, Orrin, Xander

Erzsebet *(Hungarian)* ♀   RATING: ★☆
God is my oath—Variation of Elizabeth
> People think of Erzsebet as powerful, untrustworthy, loser, weird, lazy
> People who like the name Erzsebet also like Fiona, Aurora, Violet, Felicity, Keira, Gabrielle, Eva, Jasmine, Esperanza, Iris

Esben *(Scandinavian)* ♂   RATING: ★★★
God bear
> People think of Esben as caring, funny, creative, wild, cool
> People who like the name Esben also like Emerson, Elijah, Faolan, Fynn, Finn, Gabe, Gabriel, Eben, Braden, Emmet

Eshana *(Sanskrit/East Indian)* ♀   RATING: ★★★★
Wish, desire
> People think of Eshana as pretty, exotic, sexy, ethnic, intelligent
> People who like the name Eshana also like Ishana, Eva, Felicity, Felicia, Jasmine, Inara, Chandra, Emberlynn, Camisha, Ebony

Eshe *(African)* ♀   RATING: ★★★☆
Life—West African origin
> People think of Eshe as exotic, pretty, intelligent, sexy, creative
> People who like the name Eshe also like Iris, Ava, Kya, Gabrielle, Chloe, Dawn, Fiona, Eve, Jolie, Esme

Esma *(Spanish)* ♀   RATING: ★★
Emerald—Short for Esmeralda
> People think of Esma as pretty, funny, popular, sexy, powerful
> People who like the name Esma also like Ella, Emma, Aurora, Esme, Alaina, Layla, Electra, Kiara, Aeryn, Lara

Esme *(French)* ♀   RATING: ★★★★
Loved
> People think of Esme as pretty, intelligent, elegant, creative, artsy
> People who like the name Esme also like Ava, Chloe, Ella, Iris, Olivia, Eva, Charlotte, Fiona, Grace, Isabella

Esmeralda (*Greek*) ♀   RATING: ★★★★
Emerald
  People think of Esmeralda as pretty, funny, intelligent, caring, creative
  People who like the name Esmeralda also like Isabella, Hannah, Gabriella, Cassandra, Anastasia, Faith, Fiona, Emily, Bianca, Emma

Esmerelda (*Spanish*) ♀   RATING: ★★★☆
Emerald
  People think of Esmerelda as pretty, exotic, caring, cool, elegant
  People who like the name Esmerelda also like Gabriella, Jasmine, Isabella, Esperanza, Bianca, Faith, Anastasia, Cassandra, Elizabeth, Bella

Espen (*Scandinavian*) ♂   RATING: ★★★☆
God bear—Also an American name from the TV sports network ESPN
  People think of Espen as handsome, sporty, popular, intelligent, exotic
  People who like the name Espen also like Ethan, Landon, Caleb, Isaac, Kaden, Holden, Aiden, Jayden, Maddox, Conner

Esperanza (*Spanish*) ♀   RATING: ★★
Hope
  People think of Esperanza as pretty, intelligent, funny, young, exotic
  People who like the name Esperanza also like Isabella, Esmerelda, Gabriella, Eva, Isabel, Adriana, Faith, Aurora, Estrella, Ella

Espn (*American*) ♀♂   RATING: ★★☆
TV network ESPN—Originally an acronym for Entertainment and Sports Programming Network
  People think of Espn as weird, sporty, loser, aggressive, funny
  People who like the name Espn also like Jade, Alexis, Alec, Aidan, Phoenix, Mackenzie, Cameron, Addison, Haley, Madison

Essence (*American*) ♀   RATING: ★★★☆
Aura, nature
  People think of Essence as pretty, funny, creative, cool, sexy
  People who like the name Essence also like Destiny, Amaya, Felicity, Chloe, Aaliyah, Hailey, Isabella, Jasmine, Faith, Trinity

Essien (*African*) ♂   RATING: ★★★
Sixth-born son—Ghanaian origin
  People think of Essien as handsome, nerdy, ethnic, caring, leader
  People who like the name Essien also like Landon, Elijah, Edan, Etan, Damien, Ethan, Dacian, Gabriel, Caleb, Darian

Esteban (*Spanish*) ♂   RATING: ★★★★
Crown—Variation of Steven
  People think of Esteban as handsome, funny, cool, intelligent, leader

People who like the name Esteban also like Enrique, Sebastian, Diego, Eduardo, Fabian, Ethan, Gabriel, Dominic, Antonio, Xavier

Estelle (*Latin*) ♀   RATING: ★★★★
Star
  People think of Estelle as pretty, elegant, intelligent, caring, creative
  People who like the name Estelle also like Ella, Ava, Eva, Isabella, Faith, Elle, Grace, Isabelle, Charlotte, Stella

Ester (*Hebrew*) ♀   RATING: ★★★
Star; myrtle leaf
  People think of Ester as old-fashioned, slow, intelligent, religious, quiet
  People who like the name Ester also like Esther, Eva, Abigail, Hannah, Emma, Grace, Emily, Eve, Isabella, Faith

Esther (*Persian*) ♀   RATING: ★★★☆
Star; myrtle leaf—Esther Williams, swimmer/actress
  People think of Esther as pretty, intelligent, caring, creative, funny
  People who like the name Esther also like Eva, Grace, Hannah, Emma, Olivia, Abigail, Ella, Elizabeth, Charlotte, Felicity

Estralita (*Spanish*) ♀   RATING: ★★★
Little star
  People think of Estralita as pretty, exotic, trustworthy, energetic, intelligent
  People who like the name Estralita also like Estrella, Estelle, Evangeline, Eternity, Esperanza, Carmelita, Esmerelda, Gabriella, Evita, Blossom

Estrella (*Spanish*) ♀   RATING: ★★
Star
  People think of Estrella as pretty, funny, popular, cool, caring
  People who like the name Estrella also like Esperanza, Isabella, Estelle, Gabriella, Eva, Aurora, Ella, Celeste, Esmerelda, Adriana

Etan (*Hebrew*) ♂   RATING: ★★★
Firm, strong
  People think of Etan as intelligent, powerful, caring, handsome, funny
  People who like the name Etan also like Ethan, Edan, Kaden, Caleb, Eitan, Aden, Gabriel, Elijah, Aiden, Jackson

Etana (*Hebrew*) ♀   RATING: ★★
Dedication, strength—Feminine form of Ethan
  People think of Etana as intelligent, energetic, creative, pretty, trustworthy
  People who like the name Etana also like Eva, Samara, Eliora, Adina, Elia, Abigail, Jadyn, Ella, Felicity, Liana

Etenia (*Native American*) ♀   RATING: ★★
Wealthy
  People think of Etenia as wealthy, weird, pretty, uptight, winner
  People who like the name Etenia also like Ayasha, Kaya, Catori, Kachina, Ella, Chenoa, Eva, Eve, Sora, Soraya

Eternity (American) ♀　　RATING: ★★★☆
Everlasting
　People think of Eternity as pretty, intelligent, popular, powerful, trustworthy
　People who like the name Eternity also like Faith, Destiny, Harmony, Hailey, Serenity, Trinity, Felicity, Ebony, Grace, Jasmine

Ethan (Hebrew) ♂　　RATING: ★★★
Firm, strong
　People think of Ethan as handsome, intelligent, funny, caring, energetic
　People who like the name Ethan also like Aiden, Caleb, Noah, Jacob, Nathan, Elijah, Gavin, Ian, Owen, Benjamin

Ethanael (American) ♂　　RATING: ★★★★
Combination of Ethan and Nathaniel
　People think of Ethanael as powerful, leader, intelligent, sexy, handsome
　People who like the name Ethanael also like Ethan, Nathaniel, Elijah, Jayden, Gabriel, Isaiah, Kaden, Aiden, Ian, Isaac

Ethel (English) ♀　　RATING: ★★★
Noble—Ethel Barrymore, actress; Ethel Merman, singer/actress; Ethel Waters, singer
　People think of Ethel as old-fashioned, pretty, intelligent, caring, funny
　People who like the name Ethel also like Emma, Audrey, Grace, Emily, Felicity, Amber, Estelle, Eva, Ivy, Gabrielle

Ethelda (English) ♀　　RATING: ★★
Combination of Ethel and Zelda
　People think of Ethelda as quiet, slow, sexy, caring, intelligent
　People who like the name Ethelda also like Hope, Hazelle, Estrella, Garnet, Blossom, Ginger, Ginny, Faylinn, Jane, Leanna

Ethelred (English) ♀♂　　RATING: ★★☆
Noble counsel—Originally Æthelred, King of England
　People think of Ethelred as old-fashioned, poor, slow, unpopular, weird
　People who like the name Ethelred also like Ezra, Evelyn, Emlyn, Sequoia, Harley, Bryce, Hayden, Hunter, Montana, Devin

Etienne (French) ♂　　RATING: ★★★★☆
Crown—Variation of Stephen or Steven
　People think of Etienne as handsome, creative, intelligent, trustworthy, cool
　People who like the name Etienne also like Ethan, Gabriel, Tristan, Noah, Elijah, Alexander, Lucien, Caleb, Adrian, Owen

Étoile (French) ♀　　RATING: ★☆
Star
　People think of Étoile as pretty, artsy, popular, intelligent, elegant
　People who like the name Étoile also like Elle, Ella, Giselle, Belle, Eva, Adeline, Faith, Eloise, Fleur, Brielle

Etta (English) ♀　　RATING: ★★★☆
Ruler of the home—Short for Henrietta; Etta James, singer
　People think of Etta as intelligent, funny, elegant, creative, energetic
　People who like the name Etta also like Ella, Eva, Ava, Emma, Bella, Grace, Elle, Stella, Isabella, Ada

Etty (English) ♀　　RATING: ★★★
Short for Henrietta
　People think of Etty as old-fashioned, weird, girl next door, funny, sporty
　People who like the name Etty also like Evie, Eva, Ellie, Ava, Elisabeth, Ella, Etta, Elle, Bethany, Lilly

Euclid (Greek) ♂　　RATING: ★★★☆
Very glorious
　People think of Euclid as quiet, handsome, religious, creative, intelligent
　People who like the name Euclid also like Basil, Calix, Blade, Kaden, Erasmus, Edan, Aden, Galen, Felix, Elijah

Eudora (Greek) ♀　　RATING: ★★★☆
Excellent gift—Eudora Welty, author
　People think of Eudora as intelligent, trustworthy, creative, girl next door, funny
　People who like the name Eudora also like Isadora, Esmeralda, Iris, Aurora, Faith, Calliope, Adora, Helena, Iliana, Calista

Eugene (English) ♂　　RATING: ★☆
Well born—From the Greek
　People think of Eugene as intelligent, funny, handsome, nerdy, cool
　People who like the name Eugene also like Ethan, Caleb, Nicholas, Nathan, Benjamin, Owen, Elijah, Brandon, Aiden, Nathaniel

Eugenia (Greek) ♀　　RATING: ★★★☆
Well born—Feminine form of Eugene
　People think of Eugenia as pretty, intelligent, caring, funny, creative
　People who like the name Eugenia also like Evangeline, Genevieve, Beatrice, Emma, Charlotte, Eunice, Eva, Georgia, Catherine, Esmeralda

Eulalia (Greek) ♀　　RATING: ★★★★
Well spoken
　People think of Eulalia as pretty, caring, creative, elegant, cool
　People who like the name Eulalia also like Cleo, Iris, Aurora, Cassandra, Eva, Daphne, Abigail, Bianca, Jacinda, Calista

Eulalie (Greek) ♀　　RATING: ★★★☆
Well spoken
　People think of Eulalie as intelligent, elegant, exotic, pretty, funny
　People who like the name Eulalie also like Evangeline, Fiona, Grace, Dahlia, Layla, Elysia, Ophelia, Isabelle, Celia, Caroline

Eunice *(Greek)* ♀   RATING: ★★★☆
Good victory—Eunice Shriver, creator of the Special Olympics
> People think of Eunice as pretty, caring, intelligent, funny, trustworthy
> People who like the name Eunice also like Chloe, Elena, Iris, Hazel, Eugenia, Cassandra, Naomi, Felicia, Eve, Gwyneth

Euphemia *(Greek)* ♀   RATING: ★☆
Well spoken
> People think of Euphemia as caring, pretty, trustworthy, elegant, funny
> People who like the name Euphemia also like Calliope, Genevieve, Dysis, Celeste, Electra, Desdemona, Anemone, Eurydice, Drucilla, Calandra

Euphrosyne *(Greek)* ♀   RATING: ★★☆
Full of joy
> People think of Euphrosyne as exotic, powerful, intelligent, wealthy, quiet
> People who like the name Euphrosyne also like Desiree, Celeste, Erimentha, Xanthe, Cecelia, Thais, Glain, Aura, Desdemona, Cassandra

Euridice *(Greek)* ♀   RATING: ★☆
Wide justice
> People think of Euridice as pretty, exotic, cool, old-fashioned, wealthy
> People who like the name Euridice also like Eurydice, Charisma, Cassandra, Ophelia, Penelope, Delphine, Gabrielle, Felicity, Giselle, Denali

Eurydice *(Greek)* ♀   RATING: ★★☆
Wide justice
> People think of Eurydice as pretty, exotic, sexy, caring, creative
> People who like the name Eurydice also like Ophelia, Isis, Delilah, Ivy, Fiona, Isolde, Aurora, Aurelia, Daphne, Iris

Eustace *(Greek)* ♀♂   RATING: ★★★
Fruitful
> People think of Eustace as old-fashioned, artsy, creative, boy next door, intelligent
> People who like the name Eustace also like Drew, Logan, Addison, Greer, Darby, Hunter, Blake, Dylan, Gemini, Gryphon

Eustacia *(Greek)* ♀   RATING: ★★★
Fruitful—Eustacia Vye, character in *Return of the Native* by Thomas Hardy
> People think of Eustacia as old-fashioned, exotic, nerdy, ethnic, uptight
> People who like the name Eustacia also like Anastasia, Iris, Charisma, Kalista, Abigail, Lydia, Adalia, Eva, Genevieve, Aurora

Eva *(Hebrew)* ♀   RATING: ★★★☆
Giver of life—Eva Gabor, actress; Eva Pigford, model
> People think of Eva as pretty, intelligent, creative, caring, funny

> People who like the name Eva also like Ava, Emma, Ella, Isabella, Grace, Olivia, Hannah, Eve, Chloe, Faith

Evadne *(Greek)* ♀   RATING: ★★
Greek mythological figure
> People think of Evadne as elegant, artsy, exotic, intelligent, cool
> People who like the name Evadne also like Dysis, Lydia, Garnet, Maris, Hypatia, Phaedra, Erimentha, Evanthe, Eris, Desdemona

Evan *(Welsh)* ♀♂   RATING: ★★★☆
God is good—Variation of John; Evan Hunter, author
> People think of Evan as handsome, intelligent, funny, cool, caring
> People who like the name Evan also like Logan, Dylan, Hayden, Ryan, Connor, Caden, Riley, Aidan, Cameron, Avery

Evana *(Latin)* ♀   RATING: ★★★★
God is gracious—Variation of John
> People think of Evana as pretty, elegant, exotic, intelligent, creative
> People who like the name Evana also like Eva, Ava, Isabella, Elana, Ella, Emma, Olivia, Hannah, Faith, Bella

Evangelia *(Greek)* ♀   RATING: ★★★★
Bringer of good news
> People think of Evangelia as pretty, intelligent, elegant, creative, exotic
> People who like the name Evangelia also like Evangeline, Eva, Isabella, Ella, Ava, Angelina, Abigail, Felicity, Sabrina, Emma

Evangeline *(English)* ♀   RATING: ★★★★
Messenger of good news—Evangeline Lilly, actress
> People think of Evangeline as pretty, elegant, intelligent, caring, creative
> People who like the name Evangeline also like Ava, Eva, Isabella, Olivia, Emma, Charlotte, Grace, Genevieve, Chloe, Faith

Evania *(Greek)* ♀   RATING: ★★★★
Tranquil
> People think of Evania as elegant, caring, creative, funny, pretty
> People who like the name Evania also like Eva, Ella, Evana, Kaelyn, Gianna, Eve, Emilia, Genevieve, Felicity, Gabrielle

Evanthe *(Greek)* ♀   RATING: ★★★
Blooming
> People think of Evanthe as pretty, exotic, sexy, weird, trustworthy
> People who like the name Evanthe also like Evania, Genevieve, Evangeline, Celeste, Iolanthe, Emberlynn, Calliope, Electra, Eve, Calista

Eve *(Hebrew)* ♀   RATING: ★★★
Life—In the Bible, the first woman; Eve Arden, actress; Eve Arnold, photographer
> People think of Eve as pretty, creative, intelligent, funny, caring

People who like the name Eve also like Eva, Ava, Faith, Grace, Ella, Emma, Olivia, Isabella, Hannah, Chloe

Evelia (Spanish) ♀ RATING: ★★★☆
Combination of Eva and Cecilia
People think of Evelia as intelligent, pretty, caring, trustworthy, elegant
People who like the name Evelia also like Eva, Ava, Ella, Evelina, Giselle, Lorelei, Emily, Isabella, Olivia, Eve

Evelien (Dutch) ♀ RATING: ★★☆
Variation of Evelyn
People think of Evelien as caring, pretty, funny, young, intelligent
People who like the name Evelien also like Emilie, Eve, Gabrielle, Eva, Evelina, Emilia, Isabella, Elle, Emma, Isabelle

Evelina (Slavic) ♀ RATING: ★★★★☆
Variation of Evelyn
People think of Evelina as pretty, intelligent, caring, funny, trustworthy
People who like the name Evelina also like Isabella, Eva, Eve, Evangeline, Ava, Emma, Gabriella, Bianca, Ella, Emily

Evelyn (English) ♀♂ RATING: ★★☆
Originally a form of Ava—Evelyn Ashford, track star; Evelyn Waugh, novelist
People think of Evelyn as pretty, intelligent, caring, elegant, funny
People who like the name Evelyn also like Hayden, Evan, Avery, Jocelyn, Madison, Caden, Cadence, Dylan, Logan, Riley

Ever (American) ♀♂ RATING: ★★★
Always—Ever Carradine, actress
People think of Ever as cool, popular, funny, intelligent, powerful
People who like the name Ever also like Evan, Addison, Dylan, River, Ember, Logan, Kai, Sawyer, Ryan, Reese

Everett (English) ♂ RATING: ★★☆
Wild boar herd—Also a surname; Rupert Everett, actor; Tom Everett Scott, actor
People think of Everett as handsome, intelligent, trustworthy, cool, powerful
People who like the name Everett also like Ethan, Emerson, Owen, Gavin, Jackson, Aiden, Noah, Caleb, Gabriel, Elijah

Everley (English) ♂ RATING: ★★★
From the boar meadow
People think of Everley as pretty, creative, trendy, trustworthy, intelligent
People who like the name Everley also like Everett, Jackson, Grayson, Emerson, Finley, Holden, Ethan, Landon, Maddox, Tristan

Everly (English) ♂ RATING: ★★☆
From the boar meadow—Variation of Everley
People think of Everly as pretty, funny, popular, leader, intelligent

People who like the name Everly also like Everett, Jackson, Holden, Emerson, Keagan, Emery, Finley, Owen, Landon, Deacon

Everlyse (American) ♀ RATING: ★★★
Always consecrated to God—Combination of Ever and Lisa
People think of Everlyse as quiet, caring, elegant, cool, funny
People who like the name Everlyse also like Evangeline, Emberlynn, Serenity, Elyse, Hailey, Bianca, Evangelia, Cailyn, Audra, Ashlyn

Evers (English) ♂ RATING: ★★
Wild boar
People think of Evers as unpopular, loser, lazy, intelligent, slow
People who like the name Evers also like Everett, Emerson, Finn, Brighton, Griffin, Chase, Landon, Liam, Holden, Wade

Evette (American) ♀ RATING: ★★★★
Yew—Variation of Yvette
People think of Evette as sexy, caring, funny, intelligent, energetic
People who like the name Evette also like Eva, Eve, Giselle, Ella, Claire, Gabrielle, Chloe, Faith, Elise, Fiona

Evia (Greek) ♀ RATING: ★★★
Greek island—From the island Euboea in the Aegean Sea
People think of Evia as pretty, exotic, popular, ethnic, elegant
People who like the name Evia also like Elle, Livia, Amaranta, Elise, Alika, Mea, Emmy, Adita, Ellie, Jillian

Evie (English) ♀ RATING: ★★★
Short for Eve
People think of Evie as pretty, creative, funny, intelligent, caring
People who like the name Evie also like Eva, Ava, Ella, Eve, Emma, Grace, Ellie, Olivia, Isabella, Bella

Evita (Spanish) ♀ RATING: ★★★☆
Short for Eva—Evita Perón, politician
People think of Evita as pretty, intelligent, funny, creative, powerful
People who like the name Evita also like Eva, Ella, Emma, Bianca, Eve, Ava, Isabella, Fiona, Bella, Giselle

Evonne (American) ♀ RATING: ★★★☆
Yew—Variation of Yvonne
People think of Evonne as pretty, trustworthy, funny, sexy, caring
People who like the name Evonne also like Eve, Evette, Isabella, Emma, Faith, Destiny, Eva, Ella, Ebony, Genevieve

Ewa (Polish) ♀ RATING: ★★★☆
Variation of Eva
People think of Ewa as pretty, intelligent, creative, caring, elegant

People who like the name Ewa also like Eva, Kassia, Olesia, Magda, Roza, Celeste, Cara, Grace, Jania, Zofia

Ewan *(Celtic/Gaelic)* ♂   RATING: ★★☆
Born of yew—Ewan McGregor, actor
People think of Ewan as handsome, intelligent, funny, creative, caring
People who like the name Ewan also like Ethan, Liam, Aiden, Owen, Tristan, Ian, Noah, Elijah, Gavin, Benjamin

Eyad *(Arabic)* ♂   RATING: ★★★
Support, might, strength
People think of Eyad as intelligent, caring, handsome, powerful, aggressive
People who like the name Eyad also like Faris, Jihan, Jaser, Eben, Ethan, Gabriel, Eyal, Elijah, Baqer, Ayman

Eyal *(Hebrew)* ♂   RATING: ★★★☆
Strength
People think of Eyal as intelligent, sexy, trustworthy, funny, powerful
People who like the name Eyal also like Gabriel, Eitan, Amir, Ezekiel, Edan, Niran, Haben, Gideon, Caleb, Aden

Eydie *(English)* ♀   RATING: ★★
Rich gift—Eydie Gorme, singer
People think of Eydie as pretty, trustworthy, religious, sporty, popular
People who like the name Eydie also like Edie, Chloe, Evie, Ella, Eva, Amelia, Emilia, Daphne, Emma, Grace

Eytan *(Hebrew)* ♂   RATING: ★★★
Firm, strong—Variation of Ethan
People think of Eytan as intelligent, handsome, trendy, young, popular
People who like the name Eytan also like Ethan, Eitan, Kaden, Etan, Aden, Edan, Elijah, Gabriel, Isaac, Galen

Ezekiel *(Hebrew)* ♂   RATING: ★★
God will strengthen
People think of Ezekiel as intelligent, handsome, caring, powerful, funny
People who like the name Ezekiel also like Elijah, Isaiah, Gabriel, Isaac, Ethan, Caleb, Noah, Jeremiah, Nathaniel, Aiden

Ezell *(American)* ♂   RATING: ★★☆
Noble—Also a surname; probably a variation of Adel
People think of Ezell as cool, sexy, popular, handsome, intelligent
People who like the name Ezell also like Elijah, Ezekiel, Axel, Daemyn, Colt, Amir, Avel, Balin, Calix, Caine

Ezhno *(Native American)* ♂   RATING: ★☆
He walks alone
People think of Ezhno as wild, exotic, intelligent, powerful, creative
People who like the name Ezhno also like Dasan, Mikasi, Chayton, Cian, Ahanu, Dyami, Adish, Tuari, Kele, Bade

Ezra *(Hebrew)* ♀♂   RATING: ★★★★
Help—Primarily male, but also used as a Persian girl's name; Ezra Jack Keats, author; Ezra Pound, poet/critic
People think of Ezra as intelligent, creative, handsome, funny, caring
People who like the name Ezra also like Evan, Eden, Caden, Hayden, Avery, Addison, Bailey, Jaden, Riley, Logan

---

F

Fabian *(Italian)* ♂   RATING: ★★★☆
Bean grower—Fabian, singer
People think of Fabian as handsome, funny, cool, intelligent, caring
People who like the name Fabian also like Gabriel, Jacob, Adrian, Ethan, Elijah, Damien, Isaac, Damian, Ian, Sebastian

Fabiana *(Italian)* ♀   RATING: ★★★☆
Bean grower—Feminine form of Fabian
People think of Fabiana as pretty, exotic, sexy, intelligent, popular
People who like the name Fabiana also like Isabella, Gabriella, Gianna, Natalia, Faith, Bianca, Hannah, Hailey, Bella, Abrianna

Fabiano *(Italian)* ♂   RATING: ★☆
Bean grower
People think of Fabiano as sexy, handsome, cool, ethnic, lazy
People who like the name Fabiano also like Fabian, Gabriel, Nathan, Damian, Angelo, Leo, Ethan, Fabrizio, Emanuel, Draco

Fabienne *(French)* ♀   RATING: ★★★☆
Bean grower
People think of Fabienne as funny, pretty, sexy, caring, popular
People who like the name Fabienne also like Faith, Felicity, Gabrielle, Dominique, Giselle, Belle, Fabiana, Genevieve, Isabella, Hannah

Fabio *(Italian)* ♂   RATING: ★☆
Bean grower—Fabio, romance novel cover model
People think of Fabio as handsome, sexy, popular, cool, exotic
People who like the name Fabio also like Fabian, Jacob, Caleb, Ethan, Gabriel, Felix, Ian, David, Daniel, Zachary

Fabiola *(Italian)* ♀   RATING: ★☆
Bean grower
People think of Fabiola as funny, pretty, intelligent, caring, cool
People who like the name Fabiola also like Fabiana, Isabella, Bianca, Gianna, Cassandra, Hannah, Natalia, Faith, Giovanna, Sabrina

Fabrizio *(Italian)* ♂   RATING: ★★★☆
Craftsman
> People think of Fabrizio as handsome, intelligent, sexy, creative, cool
> People who like the name Fabrizio also like Fabian, Ian, Ethan, Giovanni, Elijah, Jacob, Gabriel, Sebastian, Fabio, Aiden

Fabunni *(African)* ♀   RATING: ★☆
God has given me this
> People think of Fabunni as weird, artsy, exotic, funny, girl next door
> People who like the name Fabunni also like Jahzara, Hazina, Kya, Fayola, Damita, Evangeline, Halima, Hawa, Kia, Malaika

Fadey *(Slavic)* ♂   RATING: ★★
Praise—Variation of Thaddeus
> People think of Fadey as nerdy, handsome, exotic, caring, creative
> People who like the name Fadey also like Faris, Gabe, Felton, Finn, Aden, Maddox, Gideon, Caleb, Ethan, Fynn

Fadri *(Rumantsch)* ♂   RATING: ★★☆
Peace ruler—Variation of Frederick
> People think of Fadri as exotic, powerful, wild, young, old-fashioned
> People who like the name Fadri also like Galen, Matteo, Xavier, Yorick, Erasmus, Bade, Halden, Koen, Yered, Adair

Fai *(Chinese)* ♂   RATING: ★★★☆
Beginning—Cantonese origin
> People think of Fai as intelligent, handsome, funny, cool, caring
> People who like the name Fai also like Kaden, Damien, Gage, Aden, Ethan, Faolan, Kael, Caleb, Damian, Dalton

Fairfax *(English)* ♂   RATING: ★★☆
Fair haired—Originally a surname
> People think of Fairfax as stuck-up, weird, unpopular, intelligent, nerdy
> People who like the name Fairfax also like Harrison, Finley, Everett, Gabriel, Emerson, Fletcher, Lysander, Drake, Fox, Maddox

Fairly *(English)* ♀♂   RATING: ★★★
From the clearing overgrown with ferns—Originally a surname
> People think of Fairly as weird, creative, unpopular, pretty, quiet
> People who like the name Fairly also like Madison, Bailey, Mackenzie, Harper, Caden, Dakota, Halyn, Parker, Skylar, Reagan

Faith *(English)* ♀   RATING: ★★☆
Belief with no proof
> People think of Faith as pretty, caring, funny, intelligent, creative
> People who like the name Faith also like Grace, Hope, Hannah, Hailey, Paige, Emma, Isabella, Abigail, Chloe, Olivia

Fala *(Native American)* ♀   RATING: ★★
A crow—Choctaw origin
> People think of Fala as exotic, creative, pretty, ethnic, leader
> People who like the name Fala also like Kaya, Tala, Freya, Faith, Faye, Luna, Gabrielle, Ebony, Kiara, Chloe

Falala *(African)* ♀   RATING: ★★★
Born in abundance
> People think of Falala as weird, unpopular, loser, pretty, funny
> People who like the name Falala also like Faylinn, Felicity, Daisy, Dahlia, Fay, Faye, Fayola, Fiona, Baba, Eldora

Falk *(German)* ♂   RATING: ★★☆
Hawk—Yiddish origin
> People think of Falk as leader, weird, wild, powerful, aggressive
> People who like the name Falk also like Frye, Fisher, Elias, Ethan, Jared, Chase, Duke, Coen, Cadmus, Forrest

Fallon *(Celtic/Gaelic)* ♀   RATING: ★★☆
Of a ruling family
> People think of Fallon as pretty, funny, intelligent, creative, popular
> People who like the name Fallon also like Faith, Ava, Grace, Chloe, Fiona, Paige, Isabella, Hailey, Hannah, Olivia

Fanchon *(French)* ♀   RATING: ★☆
Free, whimsical
> People think of Fanchon as funny, caring, pretty, intelligent, trustworthy
> People who like the name Fanchon also like Giselle, Caprice, Eloise, Nicole, Faylinn, Selene, Fleur, Fawn, Breena, Fay

Fancy *(English)* ♀   RATING: ★★★
Decorated
> People think of Fancy as pretty, sexy, funny, girl next door, popular
> People who like the name Fancy also like Faith, Grace, Hailey, Belle, Abigail, Isabella, Hope, Gabriella, Macy, Amber

Fanny *(American)* ♀   RATING: ★★★
Free—Short for Frances; also slang for buttocks
> People think of Fanny as old-fashioned, weird, slow, lazy, poor
> People who like the name Fanny also like Elizabeth, Adrianna, Christine, Jennifer, Matilda, Molly, Rebecca, Daniella, Chloe, Danielle

Fantasia *(Spanish)* ♀   RATING: ★★★☆
Fantasy—Pronounced *Fan-TAY-zha* in English or *Fahn-tah-SEE-ah* in Spanish; Fantasia Barrino, singer; *Fantasia*, film
> People think of Fantasia as pretty, intelligent, creative, funny, caring
> People who like the name Fantasia also like Jasmine, Aaliyah, Faith, Elizabeth, Angelica, Isabella, Isabelle, Adriana, Destiny, Hailey

Faolan (Celtic/Gaelic) ♂ RATING: ★★★
Wolf
People think of Faolan as intelligent, handsome, power-ful, caring, wild
People who like the name Faolan also like Aiden, Kael, Braeden, Tristan, Liam, Keagan, Devlin, Edan, Ciaran, Crevan

Farah (Arabic) ♀ RATING: ★★☆
Joy
People think of Farah as pretty, funny, popular, caring, creative
People who like the name Farah also like Faith, Grace, Hannah, Emma, Chloe, Eva, Fiona, Hailey, Layla, Felicity

Fareeda (Arabic) ♀ RATING: ★★★☆
Unique
People think of Fareeda as intelligent, elegant, creative, pretty, young
People who like the name Fareeda also like Farah, Jamila, Fatima, Asha, Breena, Francesca, Felicia, Cassandra, Damali, Faylinn

Farica (German) ♀ RATING: ★☆
Peace ruler—Feminine form of Frederick
People think of Farica as nerdy, pretty, lazy, untrust-worthy, loser
People who like the name Farica also like Felicity, Gabrielle, Emilie, Angelina, Rhiannon, Delphine, Aurora, Faylinn, Dahlia, Daphne

Faris (Arabic) ♂ RATING: ★★★★
Horseman, knight
People think of Faris as intelligent, creative, cool, hand-some, leader
People who like the name Faris also like Ethan, Caleb, Kaden, Ferris, Elijah, Gabriel, Finn, Felix, Finley, Faolan

Farley (English) ♀♂ RATING: ★★★☆
From the fern-covered clearing
People think of Farley as funny, energetic, creative, cool, intelligent
People who like the name Farley also like Bailey, Hayden, Parker, Brody, Hadley, Flynn, Caden, Riley, Logan, Harley

Farrah (English) ♀♂ RATING: ★★☆
Ironsmith—Originally a surname; also from the Arabic Farah, meaning joy; Farrah Fawcett, actress
People think of Farrah as pretty, intelligent, sexy, funny, caring
People who like the name Farrah also like Hayden, Dakota, Madison, Cadence, Bailey, Jade, Jaden, Parker, Taylor, Brooklyn

Farrell (Celtic/Gaelic) ♂ RATING: ★★★★
Descendant of the man of valor
People think of Farrell as intelligent, handsome, leader, cool, energetic
People who like the name Farrell also like Ethan, Finley, Ian, Fabian, Dillon, Liam, Gavin, Aiden, Gabriel, Devlin

Farren (English) ♀♂ RATING: ★★★★
Iron-gray—Also short for Ferdinand
People think of Farren as intelligent, creative, pretty, funny, popular
People who like the name Farren also like Caden, Hayden, Jaden, Aidan, Bailey, Cadence, Landen, Parker, Logan, Addison

Farsiris (Persian) ♀ RATING: ★★★☆
Princess—Daughter of a Persian king
People think of Farsiris as powerful, pretty, exotic, sexy, elegant
People who like the name Farsiris also like Farah, Faith, Faylinn, Dysis, Calista, Aurora, Ilandere, Felicity, Ailani, Faye

Fathi (Arabic) ♂ RATING: ★★☆
Victory
People think of Fathi as lazy, loser, nerdy, intelligent, slow
People who like the name Fathi also like Fox, Faris, Fai, Favian, Caleb, Feo, Darren, Darius, Emery, Dalton

Fathia (Arabic) ♀ RATING: ★★★
Victory
People think of Fathia as intelligent, pretty, winner, exotic, sneaky
People who like the name Fathia also like Farah, Felicia, Fatima, Faith, Inara, Baina, Heba, Aisha, Damara, Feryal

Fatima (Arabic) ♀ RATING: ★★
Daughter of the prophet
People think of Fatima as pretty, intelligent, funny, car-ing, trustworthy
People who like the name Fatima also like Bianca, Isabella, Eva, Anastasia, Faith, Felicia, Felicity, Destiny, Francesca, Gabrielle

Fauna (Latin) ♀ RATING: ★★
Goddess of fertility
People think of Fauna as pretty, exotic, creative, ele-gant, powerful
People who like the name Fauna also like Aurora, Fiona, Faith, Daphne, Chloe, Hazel, Ivy, Bella, Gabrielle, Felicity

Faunia (Latin) ♀ RATING: ★★☆
Young deer
People think of Faunia as quiet, pretty, young, weird, artsy
People who like the name Faunia also like Estelle, Celeste, Bella, Caitlin, Clarissa, Florence, Aura, Hailey, Felicity, Katarina

Faunus (Latin) ♀♂ RATING: ★★☆
God of forests
People think of Faunus as weird, unpopular, handsome, old-fashioned, quiet
People who like the name Faunus also like Echo, Devin, Jocelyn, Cameo, Gryphon, Dorsey, Flynn, Briar, Dharma, Calypso

Fausta (*Italian*) ♀   RATING: ★★★
Lucky
> People think of Fausta as exotic, weird, creative, artsy, aggressive
> People who like the name Fausta also like Fiorella, Faustine, Fabiana, Fiorenza, Cascata, Aria, Carlotta, Italia, Adrina, Camila

Faustine (*French*) ♀   RATING: ★★★
Lucky
> People think of Faustine as funny, cool, creative, pretty, caring
> People who like the name Faustine also like Felicity, Gemma, Gianna, Bianca, Fausta, Adrina, Camilla, Danika, Fiorella, Angelina

Fausto (*Spanish*) ♂   RATING: ★★★☆
Lucky
> People think of Fausto as handsome, funny, cool, sexy, caring
> People who like the name Fausto also like Federico, Faustus, Joaquin, Felix, Alejandro, Fabian, Fernando, Adam, Gabriel, Diego

Faustus (*Latin*) ♂   RATING: ★☆
Lucky
> People think of Faustus as criminal, cool, handsome, unpopular, intelligent
> People who like the name Faustus also like Drake, Erasmus, Fausto, Aiden, Ambrose, Liam, Fox, Ian, Fynn, Gabriel

Fauve (*French*) ♀   RATING: ★★★☆
Wild, uninhibited—From the Fauvists, a group of artists who used exceptionally vibrant colors
> People think of Fauve as wild, exotic, artsy, pretty, elegant
> People who like the name Fauve also like Faye, Fleur, Genevieve, Fawn, Fay, Gabrielle, Dahlia, Elle, Selene, Étoile

Favian (*English*) ♂   RATING: ★★
Variation of Fabian
> People think of Favian as funny, handsome, intelligent, exotic, powerful
> People who like the name Favian also like Fabian, Gabriel, Kaden, Ethan, Jayden, Giovanni, Elias, Adrian, Damien, Drake

Fawn (*English*) ♀   RATING: ★★★☆
Young deer
> People think of Fawn as pretty, caring, creative, trustworthy, quiet
> People who like the name Fawn also like Faith, Dawn, Hailey, Fiona, Ebony, Felicity, Gabriella, Faye, Hope, Erin

Fawzi (*Arabic*) ♂   RATING: ★★☆
Victorious
> People think of Fawzi as funny, cool, big, exotic, creative
> People who like the name Fawzi also like Fabrizio, Fathi, Adam, Eyad, Glen, Fausto, Ajax, Dominic, Faris, Fox

Fawzia (*Arabic*) ♀   RATING: ★★★
Victorious
> People think of Fawzia as exotic, weird, energetic, intelligent, funny
> People who like the name Fawzia also like Farah, Feryal, Dasha, Fathia, Fareeda, Velvet, Adamina, Tahirah, Eman, Willamena

Faxon (*Latin*) ♂   RATING: ★☆
Thick haired
> People think of Faxon as loser, uptight, wealthy, untrustworthy, leader
> People who like the name Faxon also like Finley, Kael, Drake, Ian, Felix, Maddox, Dryden, Holden, Chase, Gavin

Fay (*French*) ♀   RATING: ★★★☆
Fairy, elf
> People think of Fay as pretty, intelligent, caring, funny, creative
> People who like the name Fay also like Faith, Faye, Emma, Grace, Chloe, Hailey, Felicity, Paige, Isabella, Fiona

Faye (*French*) ♀   RATING: ★★★★
Fairy, elf
> People think of Faye as pretty, intelligent, caring, creative, funny
> People who like the name Faye also like Faith, Chloe, Hannah, Ava, Emma, Hailey, Paige, Grace, Isabella, Ella

Faylinn (*Celtic/Gaelic*) ♀   RATING: ★★
A graceful woman—From the Irish Failenn
> People think of Faylinn as pretty, intelligent, artsy, young, elegant
> People who like the name Faylinn also like Kaelyn, Faith, Faye, Fallon, Cailyn, Aurora, Hailey, Emma, Jadyn, Fiona

Fayola (*African*) ♀   RATING: ★★★
Good fortune walks with honor
> People think of Fayola as pretty, intelligent, funny, weird, leader
> People who like the name Fayola also like Hazina, Estelle, Faith, Faylinn, Felicity, Blossom, Ayanna, Destiny, Abrianna, Evangeline

Fayre (*English*) ♀   RATING: ★★★★
Beautiful—Old English name meaning fair one
> People think of Fayre as pretty, exotic, elegant, sexy, intelligent
> People who like the name Fayre also like Faylinn, Faye, Faith, Fallon, Farah, Femi, Fern, Bella, Brea, Calliope

Fearghus (*Celtic/Gaelic*) ♂   RATING: ★★★
Strong man
> People think of Fearghus as weird, nerdy, old-fashioned, aggressive, funny
> People who like the name Fearghus also like Braeden, Faolan, Callum, Duncan, Ewan, Ciaran, Liam, Devlin, Callahan, Calhoun

234

February (*American*) ♀♂   RATING: ★★★
Born in February
> People think of February as weird, funny, unpopular, pretty, loser
> People who like the name February also like December, Jade, Bailey, Forest, Storm, Cadence, Freedom, Caden, Chandler, Winter

Fedele (*Spanish*) ♂   RATING: ★★☆
Faithful
> People think of Fedele as old-fashioned, intelligent, trustworthy, boy next door, artsy
> People who like the name Fedele also like David, Mario, Alfred, Francisco, John, Joseph, Federico, Finn, Adolf, Roderick

Fedella (*Spanish*) ♀   RATING: ★★☆
Faithful—Variation of Fedelia or Fidel
> People think of Fedella as religious, exotic, intelligent, unpopular, elegant
> People who like the name Fedella also like Felicity, Fiona, Felice, Francesca, Estelle, Faith, Bryanne, Laurel, Blossom, Larissa

Federico (*Spanish*) ♂   RATING: ★★★★
Peace ruler
> People think of Federico as intelligent, cool, handsome, funny, leader
> People who like the name Federico also like Fernando, Antonio, Gabriel, Enrique, Carlos, Diego, Alejandro, Andrés, Francisco, Fabian

Fedora (*Russian*) ♀   RATING: ★★★
God's gift—Variation of Theodora; also Italian for hat
> People think of Fedora as exotic, intelligent, sexy, creative, cool
> People who like the name Fedora also like Fiona, Chloe, Ophelia, Calandra, Faylinn, Celeste, Alexandria, Charisma, Faith, Kiara

Feivel (*Hebrew*) ♂   RATING: ★★
Bright one—Yiddish origin
> People think of Feivel as intelligent, caring, trustworthy, unpopular, sneaky
> People who like the name Feivel also like Gabriel, Felix, Benjamin, Elijah, Jeremiah, Gideon, Joel, Jayden, Nathaniel, Isaac

Feleti (*All nationalities*) ♂   RATING: ★☆
Tonga origin; Feleti Sevele, prime minister of Tonga
> People think of Feleti as old-fashioned, weird, slow, exotic, trendy
> People who like the name Feleti also like Elden, Enrico, Fox, Faris, Felix, Ezekiel, Gerard, Fabian, Gareth, Adolfo

Felice (*Latin*) ♀   RATING: ★★☆
Fortunate, happy
> People think of Felice as pretty, funny, caring, intelligent, creative
> People who like the name Felice also like Felicity, Felicia, Faith, Hailey, Grace, Olivia, Gabrielle, Hannah, Fiona, Isabella

Felicia (*Latin*) ♀   RATING: ★★☆
Happiness
> People think of Felicia as pretty, funny, caring, intelligent, creative
> People who like the name Felicia also like Faith, Felicity, Hailey, Isabella, Hannah, Gabriella, Eva, Abigail, Jasmine, Bianca

Felician (*Hungarian*) ♀   RATING: ★★☆
Happiness
> People think of Felician as intelligent, pretty, caring, energetic, young
> People who like the name Felician also like Aceline, Alyssa, Lyra, Adel, Aleshanee, Anja, Aneko, Hyacinth, Zahara, Lilika

Felicity (*Latin*) ♀   RATING: ★★
Happiness—Felicity Huffman, actress; *Felicity*, TV show
> People think of Felicity as pretty, creative, intelligent, caring, funny
> People who like the name Felicity also like Faith, Grace, Emma, Isabella, Hannah, Chloe, Abigail, Hailey, Gabrielle, Paige

Felix (*Latin*) ♂   RATING: ★★
Happy, prosperous—Felix the Cat, cartoon character; Felix Unger, main character of Neil Simon play, movie, and TV show *The Odd Couple*
> People think of Felix as funny, handsome, intelligent, cool, popular
> People who like the name Felix also like Oliver, Ethan, Isaac, Gabriel, Jacob, Elijah, Lucas, Sebastian, Ian, Noah

Fell (*English*) ♂   RATING: ★☆
Dweller on the mountain—Originally a surname
> People think of Fell as nerdy, big, loser, weird, leader
> People who like the name Fell also like Griffin, Fox, Felton, Fletcher, Fraley, Knox, Field, Graham, Tristan, Harlow

Felton (*English*) ♂   RATING: ★★
From the town by the field
> People think of Felton as intelligent, handsome, sexy, winner, caring
> People who like the name Felton also like Dalton, Everett, Holden, Braden, Lawson, Jackson, Ethan, Gabriel, Weston, Aden

Femi (*African*) ♀   RATING: ★★★★☆
Love me—Nigerian origin
> People think of Femi as pretty, exotic, funny, caring, sexy
> People who like the name Femi also like Chloe, Iris, Faith, Isis, Faye, Kaya, Gemma, Enya, Aiko, Emiko

Femke (*Dutch*) ♀   RATING: ★★★☆
Girl—From the northern part of the Netherlands, of Friesian origin
> People think of Femke as intelligent, caring, funny, pretty, girl next door

People who like the name Femke also like Celeste, Keira, Bella, Chloe, Isabella, Femi, Caia, Maya, Helena, Hannah

Fenella (*Celtic/Gaelic*) ♀ RATING: ★★★☆
Fair shouldered
People think of Fenella as pretty, funny, creative, caring, intelligent
People who like the name Fenella also like Fiona, Genevieve, Fallon, Breena, Breanna, Erin, Caitlin, Serena, Ianna, Alana

Feng (*Chinese*) ♀ RATING: ★☆
Maple; phoenix
People think of Feng as ethnic, criminal, sneaky, lazy, weird
People who like the name Feng also like Da-xia, Amaya, Jia Li, Li Mei, Kaida, Aiko, Kaori, Emiko, Isis, Gin

Fennella (*Celtic/Gaelic*) ♀ RATING: ★☆
Fair shouldered
People think of Fennella as elegant, creative, funny, energetic, intelligent
People who like the name Fennella also like Fiona, Breena, Brea, Ceana, Fenella, Breanna, Alana, Genevieve, Bianca, Bryanne

Feo (*Italian*) ♂ RATING: ★☆
Short for Maffeo or Feodoro—Also Spanish for ugly
People think of Feo as unpopular, loser, untrustworthy, nerdy, weird
People who like the name Feo also like Felix, Fox, Ace, Aiden, Cyrus, Max, Enrique, Seth, Caleb, Sirius

Feoras (*Celtic/Gaelic*) ♂ RATING: ★☆
Rock—Variation of Peter
People think of Feoras as handsome, sexy, quiet, caring, trustworthy
People who like the name Feoras also like Faolan, Devlin, Galvin, Fearghus, Ewan, Ciaran, Aiden, Calhoun, Braeden, Cian

Ferdinand (*German*) ♂ RATING: ★★★☆
To be courageous
People think of Ferdinand as handsome, caring, cool, intelligent, powerful
People who like the name Ferdinand also like Frederick, Jack, Oliver, Gabriel, Felix, Jacob, Benjamin, Ethan, Victor, Alexander

Fergal (*Celtic/Gaelic*) ♂ RATING: ★★★
Valorous
People think of Fergal as sporty, energetic, intelligent, handsome, caring
People who like the name Fergal also like Ewan, Eamon, Fearghus, Callum, Fergus, Ciaran, Guthrie, Finley, Devlin, Finn

Fergie (*Celtic/Gaelic*) ♀♂ RATING: ★★★
Strength of man—Short for the surname Ferguson; nickname of Lady Sarah Ferguson and singer Stacy Ferguson
People think of Fergie as popular, pretty, sexy, wealthy, cool
People who like the name Fergie also like Cooper, Addison, Dakota, Bailey, Brady, Freedom, Caden, Hayden, Jade, Poppy

Fergus (*Celtic/Gaelic*) ♂ RATING: ★★★☆
Man strength
People think of Fergus as handsome, cool, leader, intelligent, funny
People who like the name Fergus also like Angus, Isaac, Ethan, Felix, Finn, Jack, Ian, Alastair, Jacob, Oscar

Ferguson (*Celtic/Gaelic*) ♂ RATING: ★★★☆
Son of Fergus—Originally a surname
People think of Ferguson as old-fashioned, weird, wealthy, intelligent, slow
People who like the name Ferguson also like Ethan, Fletcher, Oliver, Aiden, Elijah, Aaron, Finley, Sebastian, Emerson, Liam

Fern (*English*) ♀ RATING: ★★
Fern
People think of Fern as pretty, funny, creative, caring, intelligent
People who like the name Fern also like Fiona, Felicity, Ivy, Faith, Chloe, Grace, Freya, Eva, Violet, Hazel

Fernando (*Spanish*) ♂ RATING: ★★
Daring, adventurous—Fernando Lamas, actor
People think of Fernando as funny, handsome, cool, intelligent, caring
People who like the name Fernando also like Gabriel, Fabian, Adrian, Diego, Enrique, Antonio, Jacob, Eduardo, Carlos, Ethan

Ferrari (*Italian*) ♀♂ RATING: ★★★
Blacksmith—Italian car brand
People think of Ferrari as exotic, aggressive, handsome, cool, popular
People who like the name Ferrari also like Cadence, Cheyne, Dallas, Lavender, Jade, Austin, Luca, Domani, Montana, Kai

Ferris (*English*) ♂ RATING: ★★★★
From Ferrieres, France—Also a surname; Ferris Bueller, movie character in *Ferris Bueller's Day Off*; Ferris wheel, amusement ride
People think of Ferris as handsome, cool, creative, sneaky, nerdy
People who like the name Ferris also like Gavin, Liam, Ethan, Holden, Oliver, Finn, Cole, Gabriel, Noah, Tristan

Ferrol (*Spanish*) ♂ RATING: ★★
Spanish place name
People think of Ferrol as exotic, caring, intelligent, trustworthy, wild

People who like the name Ferrol also like Jett, Felton, Jackson, Holt, Fletcher, Finn, Maxwell, Drake, Emery, Fox

Feryal *(Arabic)* ♀   RATING: ★★★☆
Decoration, ornamentation
   People think of Feryal as intelligent, pretty, popular, exotic, trustworthy
   People who like the name Feryal also like Farah, Giselle, Emilia, Breanna, Heba, Evania, Eman, Layla, Faylinn, Brea

Fews *(Celtic/Gaelic)* ♀♂   RATING: ★★☆
Woods
   People think of Fews as weird, nerdy, loser, unpopular, lazy
   People who like the name Fews also like Cael, Daray, Carlin, Brody, Ennis, Devan, Brayden, Delaine, Greer, Caley

Fia *(Latin)* ♀   RATING: ★★
Short for Fiametta, Fiorella, and Sofia
   People think of Fia as pretty, creative, elegant, caring, intelligent
   People who like the name Fia also like Fiona, Eva, Evie, Ava, Faye, Eve, Mia, Lana, Fiana, Dea

Fiachra *(Celtic/Gaelic)* ♂   RATING: ★★★
Raven
   People think of Fiachra as exotic, elegant, creative, intelligent, quiet
   People who like the name Fiachra also like Ciaran, Faolan, Daire, Edan, Cian, Aiden, Alistair, Keiran, Liam, Egan

Fiammetta *(Italian)* ♀   RATING: ★★☆
Little flame
   People think of Fiammetta as exotic, intelligent, elegant, pretty, wild
   People who like the name Fiammetta also like Fausta, Lia, Natalia, Katarina, Fina, Fabiola, Fabiana, Faye, Imelda, Fiorenza

Fiana *(Celtic/Gaelic)* ♀   RATING: ★★★★
Vine—Fiana Toibin, actress
   People think of Fiana as pretty, caring, creative, sexy, funny
   People who like the name Fiana also like Fiona, Faith, Kaelyn, Bianca, Felicity, Iliana, Keira, Felicia, Kara, Brianna

Fico *(Italian)* ♂   RATING: ★★☆
Short for Federico
   People think of Fico as funny, nerdy, sporty, religious, winner
   People who like the name Fico also like Elroy, Ethan, Biagio, Enzo, Gino, Fordon, Bono, Euclid, Fabian, Flint

Fidel *(Latin)* ♂   RATING: ★★★☆
Faithful—Fidel Castro, Cuban leader
   People think of Fidel as leader, powerful, intelligent, caring, cool

People who like the name Fidel also like Gabriel, Jacob, Felix, Adam, Fabian, Ethan, Jack, Joshua, Isaac, Adrian

Fidelia *(Spanish)* ♀   RATING: ★☆
Faithful
   People think of Fidelia as cool, old-fashioned, funny, pretty, slow
   People who like the name Fidelia also like Gabriella, Catalina, Giselle, Ella, Cecelia, Fiona, Clara, Cassandra, Dahlia, Hazel

Fidelina *(Spanish)* ♀   RATING: ★★★
Little faithful one
   People think of Fidelina as pretty, religious, funny, quiet, caring
   People who like the name Fidelina also like Catalina, Janice, Isabella, Felicia, Felicity, Belle, Mariana, Esperanza, Fidelia, Fiorella

Fidelio *(Italian)* ♂   RATING: ★★★☆
Faithful—*Fidelio*, opera by Ludwig van Beethoven
   People think of Fidelio as exotic, weird, young, quiet, cool
   People who like the name Fidelio also like Emilio, Benito, Dario, Fabian, Amando, Fabiano, Draco, Leonardo, Alexander, Raffaello

Fidella *(Latin)* ♀   RATING: ★☆
Faithful
   People think of Fidella as religious, pretty, trustworthy, young, intelligent
   People who like the name Fidella also like Faith, Felicity, Farah, Hazel, Felice, Felicia, Brea, Breena, Betha, Hailey

Field *(English)* ♂   RATING: ★☆
A field, clearing
   People think of Field as handsome, aggressive, weird, slow, energetic
   People who like the name Field also like Drake, Maddox, Finley, Jonas, Grayson, Landon, Fletcher, Lucas, Miles, Graham

Fielding *(English)* ♂   RATING: ★★☆
From the field
   People think of Fielding as energetic, wealthy, powerful, trendy, funny
   People who like the name Fielding also like Harlow, Clark, Chase, Tucker, Hart, Ogden, Harris, Orson, Deacon, Alden

Fifi *(French)* ♀   RATING: ★☆
Short for Josephine
   People think of Fifi as pretty, young, energetic, funny, sexy
   People who like the name Fifi also like Belle, Gigi, Felicity, Faith, Emma, Chanel, Fleur, Destiny, Daphne, Claire

Filbert *(English)* ♂   RATING: ★★★
Love bright—Also a type of nut
   People think of Filbert as intelligent, nerdy, funny, loser, sexy

People who like the name Filbert also like Fox, Fletcher, Felix, Fulbright, Ethan, Frederick, Ferris, Felton, Hanley, Geoffrey

Filia *(Greek)* ♀   RATING: ★★★
Friendship
People think of Filia as pretty, exotic, intelligent, weird, artsy
People who like the name Filia also like Faith, Helia, Electra, Iris, Hazel, Femi, Candice, Estrella, Iola, Charissa

Filipina *(Polish)* ♀   RATING: ★★★☆
Lover of horses
People think of Filipina as exotic, pretty, artsy, creative, intelligent
People who like the name Filipina also like Felicity, Felicia, Eternity, Faith, Destiny, Evangeline, Harmony, Dawn, Erica, Cleo

Fina *(Italian)* ♀   RATING: ★★★
Short for Serafina
People think of Fina as intelligent, pretty, creative, cool, young
People who like the name Fina also like Fausta, Aria, Mina, Sabella, Anya, Fabiana, Fabiola, Gina, Aida, Fiorenza

Findlay *(Celtic/Gaelic)* ♂   RATING: ★★★☆
Fair warrior
People think of Findlay as intelligent, creative, powerful, handsome, quiet
People who like the name Findlay also like Finley, Finlay, Finn, Liam, Tristan, Fynn, Emerson, Jack, Jackson, Ethan

Fineen *(Celtic/Gaelic)* ♂   RATING: ★★
Little fair one
People think of Fineen as energetic, caring, trustworthy, sporty, funny
People who like the name Fineen also like Finley, Finn, Liam, Callahan, Ewan, Tristan, Fionan, Calhoun, Darian, Brennan

Fini *(French)* ♀   RATING: ★★★
Short for Josephine
People think of Fini as exotic, loser, weird, pretty, trustworthy
People who like the name Fini also like Fern, Fiona, Emily, Emma, Gwen, Ivy, Bela, Flo, Garnet, Fay

Finlay *(Celtic/Gaelic)* ♂   RATING: ★★★★
Fair warrior
People think of Finlay as intelligent, handsome, cool, creative, caring
People who like the name Finlay also like Finley, Ethan, Finn, Noah, Jacob, Jack, Callum, Liam, Aiden, Oliver

Finley *(Celtic/Gaelic)* ♂   RATING: ★★★★☆
Fair warrior
People think of Finley as intelligent, funny, cool, popular, caring
People who like the name Finley also like Finn, Owen, Noah, Ethan, Jackson, Liam, Emerson, Aiden, Landon, Holden

Finn *(Celtic/Gaelic)* ♂   RATING: ★★
Fair—Also a Nordic name meaning man from Finland
People think of Finn as handsome, intelligent, cool, creative, funny
People who like the name Finn also like Fynn, Liam, Ethan, Finley, Jack, Noah, Owen, Oliver, Caleb, Jackson

Finna *(Celtic/Gaelic)* ♀   RATING: ★★★
Fair
People think of Finna as pretty, young, loser, funny, girl next door
People who like the name Finna also like Fiona, Fallon, Aislinn, Caelan, Maeve, Brea, Erin, Finnea, Aislin, Brenna

Finnea *(American)* ♀   RATING: ★★
Feminine form of Finn or Finnian
People think of Finnea as girl next door, quiet, popular, pretty, exotic
People who like the name Finnea also like Fiona, Genevieve, Aeryn, Fallon, Ryann, Hazel, Gillian, Eavan, Kaelyn, Sabrina

Finola *(Celtic/Gaelic)* ♀   RATING: ★★★
Fair shouldered—Finola Hughes, actress/TV host
People think of Finola as pretty, intelligent, caring, funny, elegant
People who like the name Finola also like Fiona, Isabella, Genevieve, Gwyneth, Chloe, Charlotte, Maeve, Gillian, Blythe, Faith

Fiona *(Celtic/Gaelic)* ♀   RATING: ★★☆
White, fair—Fiona Apple, singer
People think of Fiona as pretty, intelligent, funny, creative, caring
People who like the name Fiona also like Ava, Olivia, Chloe, Emma, Faith, Genevieve, Isabella, Hannah, Abigail, Grace

Fionan *(Celtic/Gaelic)* ♂   RATING: ★★
Fair
People think of Fionan as intelligent, popular, cool, sporty, sexy
People who like the name Fionan also like Faolan, Finn, Braeden, Fynn, Owen, Brennan, Eamon, Fionn, Ciaran, Cillian

Fionn *(Celtic/Gaelic)* ♂   RATING: ★★★☆
Fair haired—Pronounced *FEE-un*
People think of Fionn as handsome, intelligent, funny, popular, pretty
People who like the name Fionn also like Finn, Liam, Owen, Ciaran, Declan, Fynn, Keiran, Callum, Tristan, Ewan

Fionnuala *(Celtic/Gaelic)* ♀   RATING: ★☆
Fair shouldered
People think of Fionnuala as pretty, caring, intelligent, popular, funny
People who like the name Fionnuala also like Fiona, Maeve, Saoirse, Deirdre, Aoife, Erin, Genevieve, Colleen, Caitlin, Finola

Fionnula (Celtic/Gaelic) ♀   RATING: ★★★
White, fair—Variation of Fiona
> People think of Fionnula as exotic, pretty, powerful, intelligent, elegant
> People who like the name Fionnula also like Brianne, Fionnuala, Deirdre, Finna, Deidra, Brianna, Glenda, Maisie, Betha, Aislinn

Fiorella (Italian) ♀   RATING: ★★★★
Little flower
> People think of Fiorella as pretty, intelligent, creative, caring, cool
> People who like the name Fiorella also like Isabella, Fiorenza, Camilla, Bianca, Francesca, Gianna, Aria, Gemma, Giovanna, Belle

Fiorello (Italian) ♂   RATING: ★☆
Little flower—Fiorello LaGuardia, politician
> People think of Fiorello as weird, exotic, popular, cool, funny
> People who like the name Fiorello also like Fabian, Giovanni, Giuseppe, Fidelio, Maurizio, Gaetano, Michelangelo, Giancarlo, Giacomo, Giorgio

Fiorenza (Italian) ♀   RATING: ★★★
Flower
> People think of Fiorenza as pretty, elegant, artsy, caring, creative
> People who like the name Fiorenza also like Fiorella, Isabella, Graziella, Aria, Gianna, Donatella, Giovanna, Domenica, Gemma, Angelina

Firenze (Hungarian) ♀   RATING: ★★☆
Flower, blossom—Variation of Florence
> People think of Firenze as aggressive, powerful, weird, exotic, creative
> People who like the name Firenze also like Magnolia, Ophelia, Lotus, Annalise, Miette, Olive, Avril, Clementine, Catherine, Fauve

Fisher (English) ♂   RATING: ★★★☆
Fisherman—Fisher Stevens (aka Steven Fisher), actor
> People think of Fisher as handsome, funny, intelligent, sporty, boy next door
> People who like the name Fisher also like Ethan, Jackson, Cole, Tucker, Gavin, Ian, Isaac, Fletcher, Holden, Owen

Fisk (English) ♂   RATING: ★★★
A fish
> People think of Fisk as funny, trustworthy, weird, sexy, nerdy
> People who like the name Fisk also like Fisher, Keagan, Foster, Griffin, Fletcher, Flint, Finn, Fynn, Grayson, Harrison

Fisseha (African) ♂   RATING: ★★☆
Happiness, joy—Ethiopian origin; Fisseha Adugna, Ethiopian ambassador
> People think of Fisseha as ethnic, funny, young, old-fashioned, unpopular

People who like the name Fisseha also like Ilo, Ilori, Dumi, Mikaili, Gamada, Diata, Casimir, Kafele, Kanelo, Kasim

Fitzwilliam (English) ♂   RATING: ★★★★
Son of William—Fitzwilliam Darcy, character in *Pride and Prejudice* by Jane Austen
> People think of Fitzwilliam as handsome, intelligent, powerful, wealthy, trustworthy
> People who like the name Fitzwilliam also like Cole, Owen, Tristan, Ian, Finley, Dermot, Finn, Aiden, Darian, Conner

Fjola (Scandinavian) ♀   RATING: ★★★☆
Flower—Variation of Violet
> People think of Fjola as pretty, young, exotic, old-fashioned, creative
> People who like the name Fjola also like Freja, Anika, Astrid, Elsa, Fiona, Synnove, Thora, Gretel, Freya, Felicia

Flan (Celtic/Gaelic) ♂   RATING: ★☆
Red—Also a sweet custard dessert
> People think of Flan as big, nerdy, loser, weird, lazy
> People who like the name Flan also like Dermot, Callahan, Bowen, Fionan, Gallagher, Gilmore, Glenn, Donovan, Farrell, Daire

Flann (Celtic/Gaelic) ♀ ♂   RATING: ★☆
Red
> People think of Flann as big, poor, intelligent, lazy, unpopular
> People who like the name Flann also like Flynn, Gael, Taryn, Cael, Aidan, Duff, Flannery, Greer, Breckin, Darcy

Flannery (Celtic/Gaelic) ♀ ♂   RATING: ★★★★
Descendant of the red warrior
> People think of Flannery as intelligent, creative, leader, powerful, artsy
> People who like the name Flannery also like Flynn, Hadley, Reagan, Parker, Brady, Brody, Quinn, Keegan, Teagan, Bailey

Flash (American) ♀ ♂   RATING: ★★★☆
Bright light—Flash Gordon, comic character
> People think of Flash as energetic, powerful, wild, popular, cool
> People who like the name Flash also like Dylan, Forest, Hayden, Blaze, Hunter, Blaine, Bailey, Caden, Parker, Ember

Flavian (Greek) ♂   RATING: ★★★
Yellow, blond
> People think of Flavian as funny, powerful, intelligent, young, sexy
> People who like the name Flavian also like Calix, Cicero, Erasmus, Keiran, Damian, Gabriel, Tristan, Nikkos, Christos, Fabian

Flavio (Spanish) ♂   RATING: ★★★
Yellow haired
> People think of Flavio as funny, intelligent, young, leader, weird

People who like the name Flavio also like Gabriel, Valentino, Ramiro, Valentin, Johnathan, Ferdinand, Giuseppe, Diego, Fabian, Joshua

Fleming *(French)* ♂   RATING: ★★
From Flanders
> People think of Fleming as weird, nerdy, intelligent, loser, funny
> People who like the name Fleming also like Wyatt, Ian, Matthew, Bronson, Ethan, Kane, Max, Teige, Francisco, David

Fleta *(English)* ♀   RATING: ★★☆
Swift
> People think of Fleta as exotic, intelligent, artsy, young, pretty
> People who like the name Fleta also like Ginger, Freya, Jetta, Genevieve, Bianca, Briallen, Miette, Gillian, Faylinn, Fiona

Fletcher *(English)* ♂   RATING: ★★★☆
Arrow maker—Originally a surname
> People think of Fletcher as handsome, funny, intelligent, cool, popular
> People who like the name Fletcher also like Ethan, Jackson, Owen, Oliver, Isaac, Caleb, Harrison, Holden, Cole, Benjamin

Fleur *(French)* ♀   RATING: ★★★★
Flower
> People think of Fleur as pretty, elegant, popular, artsy, intelligent
> People who like the name Fleur also like Faith, Genevieve, Chloe, Fiona, Giselle, Charlotte, Elle, Jasmine, Belle, Grace

Flint *(English)* ♂   RATING: ★★
Flint rock
> People think of Flint as intelligent, energetic, handsome, leader, trustworthy
> People who like the name Flint also like Drake, Fletcher, Chase, Jack, Ian, Fynn, Caleb, Ethan, Cole, Kaden

Flo *(English)* ♀   RATING: ★★★
Short for Florence
> People think of Flo as funny, pretty, caring, popular, energetic
> People who like the name Flo also like Faith, Felicity, Ivy, Lana, Daisy, Emily, Elizabeth, Gwen, Flora, Dawn

Flora *(Latin)* ♀   RATING: ★★★☆
Flowering
> People think of Flora as pretty, caring, trustworthy, creative, elegant
> People who like the name Flora also like Fiona, Faith, Grace, Ava, Isabella, Eva, Charlotte, Iris, Bella, Olivia

Floramaria *(Spanish)* ♀   RATING: ★★☆
Flower of Mary
> People think of Floramaria as creative, exotic, pretty, intelligent, artsy

People who like the name Floramaria also like Bianca, Evita, Gabriella, Estrella, Blossom, Felicity, Anastasia, Magdalena, Isadora, Emberlynn

Florence *(Latin)* ♀   RATING: ★★
Prosperous, flowering—Florence Henderson, singer/actress; Florence Nightingale, nurse from the Crimean War
> People think of Florence as pretty, creative, intelligent, caring, funny
> People who like the name Florence also like Olivia, Violet, Victoria, Charlotte, Emily, Beatrice, Faith, Gabrielle, Grace, Scarlett

Floria *(Latin)* ♀   RATING: ★★★
Flowering
> People think of Floria as pretty, girl next door, quiet, exotic, young
> People who like the name Floria also like Flora, Fiona, Olivia, Bella, Ivy, Sabrina, Victoria, Isabella, Keira, Gracie

Florian *(Latin)* ♂   RATING: ★★★☆
Flowering
> People think of Florian as intelligent, handsome, caring, sexy, funny
> People who like the name Florian also like Ethan, Felix, Thomas, Fabian, Conrad, Dominic, Ferdinand, Elijah, Jonah, Nelson

Floriane *(Latin)* ♀   RATING: ★★★
Flowering
> People think of Floriane as pretty, slow, nerdy, old-fashioned, artsy
> People who like the name Floriane also like Floria, Bella, Felicity, Delilah, Ivy, Farah, Gazelle, Caroline, Celeste, Blythe

Florida *(Spanish)* ♀   RATING: ★★★
Feast of flowers—U.S. state
> People think of Florida as popular, sexy, young, funny, creative
> People who like the name Florida also like Faith, Hope, Bethany, Samantha, Olivia, Scarlett, Fiona, Jasmine, Grace, Isabel

Florrie *(English)* ♀   RATING: ★★★
Short for Florence
> People think of Florrie as pretty, trustworthy, creative, young, funny
> People who like the name Florrie also like Felicity, Alana, Felicia, Grace, Francesca, Elise, Emilia, Jasmine, Evana, Felice

Flower *(English)* ♀   RATING: ★★★★
Flower
> People think of Flower as pretty, creative, artsy, caring, intelligent
> People who like the name Flower also like Faith, Blossom, Jasmine, Grace, Paige, Felicity, Hope, Chloe, Emma, Heather

240

Floyd (English) ♂   RATING: ★★☆
Gray—Also a Welsh surname
> People think of Floyd as intelligent, caring, handsome, funny, cool
> People who like the name Floyd also like Isaac, Jacob, Drake, Jack, Felix, Aiden, Owen, David, Finn, Ethan

Flurin (Rumantsch) ♂   RATING: ★★☆
Flowering—Variation of Florian
> People think of Flurin as creative, intelligent, boy next door, quiet, cool
> People who like the name Flurin also like Joel, Alexander, Oliver, Koen, Ezekiel, Jedidiah, Jason, Rafael, Eleazar, Yannis

Flynn (Celtic/Gaelic) ♀♂   RATING: ★★★★
Descendant of the red-haired man—Originally a surname
> People think of Flynn as funny, intelligent, creative, handsome, cool
> People who like the name Flynn also like Hayden, Quinn, Logan, Dylan, Aidan, Bailey, Connor, Avery, Caden, Riley

Fola (African) ♀   RATING: ★★★
Honor
> People think of Fola as intelligent, creative, pretty, caring, energetic
> People who like the name Fola also like Isabis, Hawa, Kya, Kia, Hazina, Keeya, Isoke, Femi, Lily, Kamea

Fonda (Spanish) ♀♂   RATING: ★☆
Foundation—Henry Fonda, actor; Jane Fonda, actress; Peter Fonda, actor
> People think of Fonda as caring, intelligent, funny, leader, pretty
> People who like the name Fonda also like Lindsey, Keanu, Pat, Jersey, Starbuck, Kyle, Hilary, Jade, Tracy, Cameron

Forbes (English) ♂   RATING: ★☆
Prosperous—Also a person from Forbes, Scotland
> People think of Forbes as handsome, popular, leader, caring, cool
> People who like the name Forbes also like Duncan, Dawson, Fletcher, Ethan, Liam, Ewan, Drake, Findlay, Gabe, Fisher

Ford (English) ♂   RATING: ★★
River crossing—Gerald R. Ford, U.S. president; Henry Ford, automobile maker
> People think of Ford as handsome, intelligent, popular, funny, cool
> People who like the name Ford also like Ethan, Jackson, Chase, Cole, Jack, Holden, Jacob, Caleb, Braden, Ian

Fordon (English) ♂   RATING: ★★★
From the ridge way
> People think of Fordon as weird, big, criminal, wild, loser
> People who like the name Fordon also like Drake, Darian, Braden, Fynn, Galen, Heath, Blade, Jett, Grayson, Cole

Forest (English) ♀♂   RATING: ★★★☆
From the woods—Forest Whitaker, actor/producer/director
> People think of Forest as funny, caring, creative, intelligent, cool
> People who like the name Forest also like Hunter, Hayden, Bailey, Dakota, Madison, Caden, Blake, Parker, Avery, Ember

Forever (American) ♀   RATING: ★★
Never ending
> People think of Forever as pretty, intelligent, young, weird, energetic
> People who like the name Forever also like Faith, Destiny, Eternity, Hope, Heaven, Harmony, Honey, Chloe, Blossom, Felicity

Forrest (English) ♂   RATING: ★★★☆
Of the woods, forest—Forrest Gump, movie character
> People think of Forrest as caring, intelligent, handsome, trustworthy, cool
> People who like the name Forrest also like Jackson, Ethan, Caleb, Landon, Jacob, Cole, Gabriel, Noah, Drake, Ian

Forrester (English) ♂   RATING: ★★★
Of the forest
> People think of Forrester as handsome, intelligent, popular, weird, cool
> People who like the name Forrester also like Fletcher, Drake, Holden, Ethan, Jackson, Everett, Harrison, Gabriel, Braden, Dawson

Forster (English) ♂   RATING: ★★☆
Variation of Forester; originally a surname
> People think of Forster as nerdy, weird, quiet, powerful, loser
> People who like the name Forster also like Forrester, Finn, Slade, Fox, Tyson, Caleb, Garrett, Harrison, Owen, Forrest

Fortune (English) ♂   RATING: ★★
Luck, fate
> People think of Fortune as cool, creative, powerful, funny, caring
> People who like the name Fortune also like Drake, Elijah, Gavin, Fai, Ethan, Chance, Isaiah, Blade, Cody, Braden

Foster (English) ♂   RATING: ★★☆
Variation of Forester; originally a surname; Foster Brooks, comedian
> People think of Foster as intelligent, funny, trustworthy, creative, handsome
> People who like the name Foster also like Jackson, Noah, Holden, Landon, Ethan, Cole, Owen, Dawson, Emerson, Gabriel

Fountain (English) ♀♂   RATING: ★★☆
A spring
> People think of Fountain as cool, sexy, intelligent, artsy, powerful

241

People who like the name Fountain also like Forest, Freedom, Ember, Delaney, Liberty, Storm, Bailey, Angel, Denver, Diamond

Fox *(English)* ♂   RATING: ★★★☆
Foxlike—Also a surname; Fox Mulder, character on *The X-Files*; TV network
People think of Fox as intelligent, handsome, sneaky, cool, sexy
People who like the name Fox also like Ethan, Jack, Benjamin, Aiden, Gabriel, Drake, Finn, Maddox, Noah, Elijah

Foy *(French)* ♂   RATING: ★★★
Faith—Originally an English surname
People think of Foy as intelligent, lazy, sexy, girl next door, leader
People who like the name Foy also like Ewan, Fynn, Finley, Ian, Fox, Harvey, Grant, Gage, Mace, Darian

Fraley *(English)* ♂   RATING: ★☆
Friar
People think of Fraley as slow, unpopular, exotic, uptight, ethnic
People who like the name Fraley also like Holden, Gage, Keagan, Jackson, Kaden, Finley, Fletcher, Garrison, Everett, Edan

Fran *(English)* ♀♂   RATING: ★★★
Free—Short for Francis or Frances; Fran Drescher, actress
People think of Fran as funny, creative, caring, intelligent, pretty
People who like the name Fran also like Drew, Dylan, Flynn, Darcy, Cassidy, Dakota, Bailey, Blair, Blaine, Holly

Frances *(Latin)* ♀   RATING: ★★
Free—Frances McDormand, actress
People think of Frances as funny, intelligent, caring, pretty, creative
People who like the name Frances also like Ava, Elizabeth, Grace, Audrey, Hannah, Eva, Olivia, Charlotte, Faith, Amelia

Francesca *(Latin)* ♀   RATING: ★★★★
Free
People think of Francesca as pretty, intelligent, funny, creative, caring
People who like the name Francesca also like Isabella, Olivia, Grace, Ava, Charlotte, Gabriella, Emma, Bianca, Gabrielle, Amelia

Franchesca *(American)* ♀   RATING: ★★★☆
Free—Variation of Francesca
People think of Franchesca as pretty, funny, popular, sexy, cool
People who like the name Franchesca also like Isabella, Faith, Abigail, Gabriella, Hannah, Chloe, Grace, Gabrielle, Bianca, Francesca

Francine *(French)* ♀   RATING: ★★★☆
Free—Variation of Frances
People think of Francine as pretty, funny, caring, intelligent, trustworthy
People who like the name Francine also like Fiona, Francesca, Charlotte, Frances, Olivia, Emily, Felicity, Giselle, Abigail, Eva

Francis *(Latin)* ♂   RATING: ★★★☆
Free—Francis Ford Coppola, filmmaker
People think of Francis as intelligent, caring, funny, handsome, cool
People who like the name Francis also like Gabriel, Alexander, Nathan, Ethan, Jacob, Elijah, David, Daniel, Nicholas, Isaac

Francisco *(Spanish)* ♂   RATING: ★★★★
Free—Francisco Franco, Spanish head of state (1939-1975)
People think of Francisco as funny, cool, handsome, caring, intelligent
People who like the name Francisco also like Diego, Gabriel, Antonio, Fernando, Ethan, Alexander, Pablo, Jacob, David, Ricardo

Franco *(Italian)* ♂   RATING: ★★★☆
Free
People think of Franco as handsome, funny, intelligent, cool, energetic
People who like the name Franco also like Lorenzo, Gabriel, Marco, Jacob, Giovanni, Lucas, Diego, Matteo, Fabian, Angelo

François *(French)* ♂   RATING: ★★★☆
Free—François Truffaut, filmmaker
People think of François as handsome, funny, intelligent, caring, creative
People who like the name François also like Ethan, Frederick, Jacques, André, Felix, Pierre, Gabriel, Etienne, Patrick, Aiden

Frank *(English)* ♂   RATING: ★★
Free, truthful—Short for Francis; Frank Sinatra, singer/actor; Frank Lloyd Wright, architect
People think of Frank as funny, handsome, intelligent, caring, cool
People who like the name Frank also like Jack, David, Ethan, Matthew, Daniel, Jacob, Charles, Edward, Nicholas, Andrew

Franklin *(English)* ♂   RATING: ★★★☆
Free man—Franklin D. Roosevelt, U.S. president
People think of Franklin as caring, handsome, intelligent, funny, cool
People who like the name Franklin also like Alexander, Nicholas, Benjamin, Ethan, Jacob, Daniel, Matthew, Samuel, Adam, William

Franz *(German)* ♂   RATING: ★★★☆
Free—Franz Liszt, composer
People think of Franz as handsome, intelligent, trustworthy, creative, cool

People who like the name Franz also like Oliver, Fritz, Isaac, Noah, Jack, Axel, Fynn, Ian, Liam, Finn

Frasier *(English)* ♂   RATING: ★★
Strawberry—*Frasier*, TV show
People think of Frasier as funny, popular, handsome, intelligent, wild
People who like the name Frasier also like Ethan, Jacob, Fletcher, Benjamin, Jackson, Gavin, Aiden, Ian, Isaac, Duncan

Frayne *(English)* ♂   RATING: ★★☆
Dweller by an ash tree—Originally a surname
People think of Frayne as intelligent, creative, leader, artsy, caring
People who like the name Frayne also like Faolan, Fynn, Gabriel, Devlin, Isaac, Jayden, Gage, Galen, Edan, Kaden

Frazier *(English)* ♂   RATING: ★★★
Strawberry—Originally a surname
People think of Frazier as funny, popular, cool, intelligent, aggressive
People who like the name Frazier also like Grayson, Gavin, Ethan, Colton, Gabriel, Ivan, Elijah, Hudson, Xavier, Brendan

Fred *(English)* ♀ ♂   RATING: ★★
Peace ruler—Short for Frederick; Fred Flintstone, TV cartoon character; Fred MacMurray, actor
People think of Fred as funny, handsome, cool, intelligent, caring
People who like the name Fred also like James, Drew, Joe, Christian, Charlie, Sam, Evan, Darcy, Austin, Toby

Freddy *(English)* ♀ ♂   RATING: ★★★★
Peace ruler—Short for Frederick; Freddy Mercury, singer; Freddy Krueger, horror movie character; Freddy Prinze, actor/comedian
People think of Freddy as funny, cool, popular, handsome, caring
People who like the name Freddy also like Charlie, Bailey, Danny, Taylor, Connor, Cameron, Alex, Ryan, James, Dylan

Frederica *(English)* ♀   RATING: ★★
Peace ruler—Feminine form of Frederick
People think of Frederica as intelligent, exotic, caring, creative, pretty
People who like the name Frederica also like Charlotte, Amelia, Audrey, Francesca, Faith, Fiona, Abigail, Cecily, Fay, Bella

Frederick *(English)* ♂   RATING: ★★★☆
Peace ruler
People think of Frederick as intelligent, handsome, funny, caring, trustworthy
People who like the name Frederick also like Ethan, Alexander, Edward, Gabriel, Jacob, Benjamin, Nicholas, William, Daniel, Isaac

Fredrica *(English)* ♀   RATING: ★☆
Peace ruler—Feminine form of Frederick
People think of Fredrica as funny, pretty, cool, intelligent, trustworthy
People who like the name Fredrica also like Isabelle, Genevieve, Scarlett, Cassandra, Faith, Gwen, Isabella, Aurora, Bianca, Richelle

Fredricka *(English)* ♀   RATING: ★★★
Peace ruler—Feminine form of Frederick
People think of Fredricka as funny, pretty, sexy, intelligent, caring
People who like the name Fredricka also like Charlotte, Estelle, Gracie, Isabel, Dawn, Lauren, Lillian, Flora, Georgia, Isabella

Freed *(English)* ♂   RATING: ★☆
Wood, woodland—Originally a surname
People think of Freed as lazy, quiet, artsy, energetic, poor
People who like the name Freed also like Holden, Maddox, Jackson, Langston, Isaiah, Edan, Hampton, Dawson, Gage, Hanley

Freedom *(American)* ♀ ♂   RATING: ★★★☆
Not in captivity
People think of Freedom as funny, intelligent, leader, creative, energetic
People who like the name Freedom also like Justice, Liberty, Dakota, Bailey, Jade, Forest, Brooke, Hayden, Ember, Angel

Freeman *(English)* ♂   RATING: ★★★☆
Free man—Freeman Gisden, actor/writer; Morgan Freeman, actor
People think of Freeman as funny, intelligent, trustworthy, sexy, winner
People who like the name Freeman also like Fynn, Foster, Fuller, Benjamin, Drake, Ethan, Gabriel, Dalton, Jackson, Dawson

Freida *(German)* ♀   RATING: ★★★☆
Pease—Short for names ending with –fried
People think of Freida as pretty, cool, caring, funny, sexy
People who like the name Freida also like Fiona, Felicity, Grace, Giselle, Eva, Penelope, Anya, Hannah, Freya, Frieda

Freira *(Spanish)* ♀   RATING: ★★☆
Sister
People think of Freira as weird, exotic, stuck-up, nerdy, quiet
People who like the name Freira also like Freya, Freja, Calista, Ella, Felicity, Laurel, Cora, Femi, Freida, Anika

Freja *(Scandinavian)* ♀   RATING: ★★★★
Norse goddess of love
People think of Freja as pretty, intelligent, creative, caring, powerful
People who like the name Freja also like Freya, Genevieve, Astrid, Celeste, Giselle, Hazel, Aurora, Layla, Isis, Thora

Fremont *(English)* ♂   RATING: ★★☆
Freedom mountain
> People think of Fremont as loser, nerdy, old-fashioned, trustworthy, leader
> People who like the name Fremont also like Foster, Langston, Drake, Gage, Fletcher, Holden, Frey, Emerson, Dane, Galen

French *(American)* ♀♂   RATING: ★☆
From France—French Stewart, actor
> People think of French as popular, handsome, exotic, funny, wild
> People who like the name French also like Flash, Forest, Ember, Cassidy, Carrington, Evan, Blake, Blair, Eden, Evelyn

Frey *(Scandinavian)* ♂   RATING: ★★
God of weather
> People think of Frey as creative, weird, intelligent, popular, winner
> People who like the name Frey also like Cole, Finn, Gabriel, Edan, Fynn, Ethan, Finley, Conley, Fuller, Drake

Freya *(Scandinavian)* ♀   RATING: ★★★☆
Goddess of love, fertility, and beauty
> People think of Freya as pretty, creative, intelligent, funny, caring
> People who like the name Freya also like Grace, Ava, Olivia, Eva, Amelia, Ella, Mia, Faith, Charlotte, Chloe

Frick *(English)* ♂   RATING: ★★☆
Brisk, vigorous—Originally a surname
> People think of Frick as aggressive, funny, caring, unpopular, trustworthy
> People who like the name Frick also like Felix, Felton, Filbert, Dermot, Crispin, Arlo, Huckleberry, Albert, Ford, Frye

Frida *(German)* ♀   RATING: ★★★☆
Peace—Frida Kahlo, artist
> People think of Frida as pretty, intelligent, cool, caring, leader
> People who like the name Frida also like Fiona, Penelope, Josephine, Mariana, Iris, Faith, Freida, Savannah, Imani, Fleur

Frieda *(German)* ♀   RATING: ★☆
Peace, joy
> People think of Frieda as caring, intelligent, pretty, creative, trustworthy
> People who like the name Frieda also like Ava, Farah, Freida, Fiona, Grace, Felicity, Freya, Francesca, Giselle, Faith

Frigg *(Scandinavian)* ♀   RATING: ★★★
Love—In Norse mythology, wife to Oainn; related to the verb *ao frja* meaning to love
> People think of Frigg as unpopular, nerdy, weird, funny, loser
> People who like the name Frigg also like Dysis, Calliope, Hailey, Blythe, Erin, Hazel, Femi, Darva, Camelia, Layla

Fritz *(German)* ♂   RATING: ★★★☆
Peace ruler—Originally short for Frederick
> People think of Fritz as intelligent, funny, handsome, energetic, young
> People who like the name Fritz also like Ethan, Felix, Oliver, Isaac, Fabian, Finn, Miles, Caleb, Gabe, Ian

Fritzi *(German)* ♀   RATING: ★☆
Peace ruler—Variation of Freida
> People think of Fritzi as wild, weird, old-fashioned, energetic, creative
> People who like the name Fritzi also like Fiona, Penelope, Genevieve, Chanel, Dixie, Giselle, Chloe, Abrianna, Belle, Emma

Fruma *(Hebrew)* ♀   RATING: ★★
Pious woman
> People think of Fruma as old-fashioned, aggressive, nerdy, religious, loser
> People who like the name Fruma also like Femke, Elpida, Hateya, Camelia, Cayla, Eshana, Calista, Chava, Cocheta, Farsiris

Frye *(English)* ♂   RATING: ★☆
Free—Originally a surname
> People think of Frye as exotic, sexy, trustworthy, young, funny
> People who like the name Frye also like Fynn, Felix, Galen, Faris, Felton, Fuller, Blade, Gage, Elden, Finn

Fulbright *(English)* ♂   RATING: ★★☆
Very bright
> People think of Fulbright as weird, nerdy, lazy, unpopular, poor
> People who like the name Fulbright also like Filbert, Fletcher, Flint, Forrester, Ephraim, Foster, Harlow, Fuller, Deiter, Graham

Fuller *(English)* ♂   RATING: ★★
Cloth bleacher—Originally a surname
> People think of Fuller as cool, intelligent, energetic, trustworthy, leader
> People who like the name Fuller also like Holden, Jackson, Ethan, Emerson, Fisher, Braden, Dalton, Ian, Grayson, Dawson

Fynn *(Celtic/Gaelic)* ♂   RATING: ★★★★
Fair—Variation of Finn
> People think of Fynn as cool, funny, handsome, intelligent, leader
> People who like the name Fynn also like Finn, Ethan, Noah, Owen, Finley, Liam, Oliver, Jackson, Jacob, Ian

Gabby *(English)* ♀   RATING: ★★★★
God is my strength—Short for Gabriela or Gabrielle
> People think of Gabby as funny, pretty, cool, young, popular

244

People who like the name Gabby also like Hailey, Gabrielle, Gabriella, Emma, Grace, Faith, Hannah, Isabella, Abigail, Emily

Gabe (*English*) ♂ RATING: ★★★
God is my strength—Short for Gabriel
People think of Gabe as handsome, cool, popular, intelligent, funny
People who like the name Gabe also like Gabriel, Ethan, Gavin, Caleb, Gage, Jacob, Ian, Aiden, Kaden, Cole

Gabi/Gaby (*French*) ♀ RATING: ★★★☆
God is my strength—Short for Gabriela or Gabrielle
People think of Gabi as pretty, funny, cool, creative, caring
People who like the name Gabi also like Gabby, Gabriella, Gabrielle, Emma, Gabriela, Isabella, Faith, Grace, Bella, Isabelle

Gabriel (*Hebrew*) ♂ RATING: ★★★★
God is my strength
People think of Gabriel as handsome, intelligent, caring, funny, trustworthy
People who like the name Gabriel also like Ethan, Elijah, Noah, Caleb, Jacob, Gavin, Isaac, Benjamin, Aiden, Ian

Gabriela (*Spanish*) ♀ RATING: ★★★★
God is my strength
People think of Gabriela as pretty, funny, intelligent, caring, creative
People who like the name Gabriela also like Isabella, Gabrielle, Gabriella, Abigail, Adriana, Faith, Grace, Emma, Hailey, Isabelle

Gabriella (*Italian*) ♀ RATING: ★★★★
God is my strength
People think of Gabriella as pretty, intelligent, funny, popular, creative
People who like the name Gabriella also like Isabella, Gabrielle, Hannah, Olivia, Abigail, Ava, Emma, Grace, Hailey, Ella

Gabrielle (*French*) ♀ RATING: ★★★☆
God is my strength
People think of Gabrielle as pretty, funny, intelligent, creative, caring
People who like the name Gabrielle also like Abigail, Hannah, Grace, Isabella, Isabelle, Olivia, Hailey, Emma, Gabriella, Ava

Gad (*Hebrew*) ♂ RATING: ★☆
Happiness, luck, fortune
People think of Gad as weird, big, winner, lazy, wild
People who like the name Gad also like Gabriel, Aden, Ethan, Jack, Kaden, David, Earl, Ivan, Isaac, Ian

Gada (*Hebrew*) ♀ RATING: ★☆
Feminine form of Gad; also the bank of a river
People think of Gada as religious, ethnic, slow, old-fashioned, young
People who like the name Gada also like Aaralyn, Galya, Atara, Gianna, Athalia, Ballari, Avariella, Eliora, Gaia, Edana

Gael (*Celtic/Gaelic*) ♀ ♂ RATING: ★★
A Gael—Irish/Scottish person; also a variation of Gail
People think of Gael as intelligent, creative, handsome, sexy, cool
People who like the name Gael also like Aidan, Cael, Connor, Flynn, Jaden, Caden, Riley, Jade, Kaelin, Cadence

Gaenor (*Welsh*) ♀ RATING: ★★★
White ghost, phantom—Late medieval form of Guinevere
People think of Gaenor as creative, funny, pretty, exotic, sexy
People who like the name Gaenor also like Gwendolyn, Deirdre, Arwen, Briallen, Gwyneth, Enid, Rhiannon, Aderyn, Faylinn, Gwen

Gaerwn (*Welsh*) ♂ RATING: ★☆
White fort—Variation of Caerwyn
People think of Gaerwn as loser, intelligent, exotic, creative, old-fashioned
People who like the name Gaerwn also like Gavin, Garren, Gideon, Ancelin, Tristan, Gareth, Galen, Gabriel, Faolan, Gavan

Gaetan (*French*) ♂ RATING: ★★
From Gaeta, Italy—Also a term of endearment
People think of Gaetan as caring, loser, nerdy, quiet, lazy
People who like the name Gaetan also like Galen, Cole, Kaden, Ethan, Gabriel, Edan, Caleb, Gavin, Elijah, Jayden

Gaetana (*Italian*) ♀ RATING: ★★★
From Gaeta, Italy—Feminine form of Gaetano
People think of Gaetana as big, stuck-up, untrustworthy, poor, trendy
People who like the name Gaetana also like Gianna, Giovanna, Isabella, Angelina, Fiorella, Gemma, Camilla, Cira, Carlotta, Fausta

Gaetane (*French*) ♀ RATING: ★☆
From Gaeta, Italy—Feminine form of Gaetan
People think of Gaetane as funny, quiet, weird, sexy, exotic
People who like the name Gaetane also like Gaetana, Giulia, Graziella, Faustine, Bambi, Giovanna, Fabiola, Carlotta, Fiorenza, Cascata

Gaetano (*Italian*) ♂ RATING: ★★★
From Gaeta; Italy
People think of Gaetano as intelligent, handsome, trustworthy, powerful, cool
People who like the name Gaetano also like Giovanni, Gabriel, Anthony, Gustavo, Gavin, Giancarlo, Giorgio, Oliver, Ethan, Carmine

Gafna (*Hebrew*) ♀ RATING: ★★
Vine
People think of Gafna as ethnic, sexy, exotic, winner, nerdy
People who like the name Gafna also like Danica, Aolani, Gabby, Gaenor, Gail, Apria, Dena, Ide, Daffodil, Gada

Gagan *(Sanskrit/East Indian)* ♂   RATING: ★★★
Heavenly sky
> People think of Gagan as intelligent, religious, sexy, pretty, funny
> People who like the name Gagan also like Gage, Gyan, Ashwin, Galen, Grayson, Alagan, Aiden, Nalin, Calix, Egan

Gage *(English)* ♂   RATING: ★★☆
Measurer—Originally a surname
> People think of Gage as handsome, intelligent, funny, popular, cool
> People who like the name Gage also like Gavin, Ethan, Kaden, Aiden, Gabriel, Caleb, Landon, Chase, Jackson, Cole

Gaia *(Latin)* ♀   RATING: ★★★☆
Earth
> People think of Gaia as creative, pretty, intelligent, powerful, caring
> People who like the name Gaia also like Kaia, Grace, Ava, Arwen, Eva, Fiona, Aurora, Faith, Iris, Giselle

Gail *(English)* ♀   RATING: ★★★☆
Joy of the father—Short for Abigail
> People think of Gail as intelligent, caring, funny, pretty, creative
> People who like the name Gail also like Faith, Hannah, Grace, Abigail, Hailey, Emily, Gabrielle, Paige, Gabby, Fiona

Gainell *(American)* ♂   RATING: ★★☆
Happy, shiny—Also a surname of unknown origin
> People think of Gainell as intelligent, big, creative, quiet, caring
> People who like the name Gainell also like Jace, Dalton, Eitan, Fai, Fox, Darren, Jadon, Jason, Joel, Daemyn

Gaius *(Latin)* ♂   RATING: ★★★★
Person of Earth—Gaius Julius Caesar, Roman emperor
> People think of Gaius as leader, intelligent, powerful, handsome, winner
> People who like the name Gaius also like Gareth, Galen, Gabriel, Aiden, Gavin, Gideon, Felix, Alexander, Blade, Grant

Gala *(Scandinavian)* ♀   RATING: ★★★☆
Singer—Also Old French for festivity or party
> People think of Gala as pretty, artsy, elegant, intelligent, creative
> People who like the name Gala also like Faith, Gaia, Eva, Ava, Gabriella, Giselle, Kala, Grace, Genevieve, Eve

Galahad *(English)* ♂   RATING: ★★
Pure, noble, selfless—Sir Galahad, the noblest and most virtuous of the knights in King Arthur's Round Table
> People think of Galahad as leader, handsome, powerful, trustworthy, caring
> People who like the name Galahad also like Tristan, Gabriel, Gideon, Gavin, Arthur, Lysander, Jasper, Edan, Aiden, Gage

Galatea *(Greek)* ♀   RATING: ★★★
Milk white—In Greek mythology, an ivory statue of a maiden brought to life by Pygmalion's prayer
> People think of Galatea as pretty, intelligent, elegant, powerful, caring
> People who like the name Galatea also like Genevieve, Galena, Chloe, Aurora, Calandra, Electra, Desdemona, Iris, Fiona, Kaida

Gale *(English)* ♀ ♂   RATING: ★★
Pleasant, merry—Also a surname; variation of Gail; short for Abigail
> People think of Gale as trustworthy, intelligent, caring, energetic, funny
> People who like the name Gale also like Jaden, Hayden, Connor, Evan, Caden, Logan, Riley, Jade, Blake, Aidan

Galen *(Greek)* ♂   RATING: ★★★☆
Calm
> People think of Galen as intelligent, funny, caring, creative, handsome
> People who like the name Galen also like Gavin, Gabriel, Ethan, Aiden, Kaden, Tristan, Caleb, Braden, Ian, Landon

Galena *(Greek)* ♀   RATING: ★★
Calm
> People think of Galena as pretty, young, intelligent, popular, artsy
> People who like the name Galena also like Gabrielle, Isabella, Helena, Genevieve, Gabriella, Emma, Aurora, Chloe, Cassandra, Felicia

Galeno *(Spanish)* ♂   RATING: ★★
Calm
> People think of Galeno as ethnic, sexy, criminal, poor, creative
> People who like the name Galeno also like Fernando, Federico, Macario, Dominic, Fausto, Gabriel, Caleb, Adelio, Rafael, Draco

Gali *(Hebrew)* ♀   RATING: ★★★
My wave
> People think of Gali as pretty, funny, elegant, caring, quiet
> People who like the name Gali also like Kali, Kaelyn, Izzy, Gili, Julia, Callie, Jena, Faye, Aya, Kaia

Galia *(Hebrew)* ♀   RATING: ★★
Wave of God
> People think of Galia as pretty, creative, elegant, intelligent, cool
> People who like the name Galia also like Galya, Gabrielle, Grace, Gianna, Giselle, Ella, Faith, Isabel, Samara, Hannah

Galiena *(German)* ♀   RATING: ★★★
High one
> People think of Galiena as exotic, pretty, young, trendy, criminal
> People who like the name Galiena also like Lorelei, Giselle, Gaia, Ava, Eva, Grace, Gabriella, Emma, Jadyn, Faith

246

Gallagher *(Celtic/Gaelic)* ♂   RATING: ★★★☆
Descendant of the lover of foreigners—Also a surname; Gallagher, comedian
> People think of Gallagher as intelligent, caring, creative, funny, popular
> People who like the name Gallagher also like Liam, Gabriel, Finn, Gavin, Aiden, Owen, Tristan, Ethan, Jackson, Jack

Gallia *(Latin)* ♀   RATING: ★★
From Gaul, France
> People think of Gallia as exotic, powerful, ethnic, pretty, sexy
> People who like the name Gallia also like Genevieve, Gillian, Maeve, Ianna, Kaelyn, Maisie, Breena, Ryann, Caitlin, Alana

Galvin *(Celtic/Gaelic)* ♂   RATING: ★★★☆
Sparrow
> People think of Galvin as intelligent, funny, caring, boy next door, trustworthy
> People who like the name Galvin also like Gavin, Kaden, Gabriel, Aiden, Keagan, Ethan, Conner, Tristan, Drake, Ian

Galya *(Hebrew)* ♀   RATING: ★★☆
Wave of God
> People think of Galya as pretty, weird, artsy, intelligent, powerful
> People who like the name Galya also like Galia, Jadyn, Gabrielle, Faith, Isabella, Giselle, Gianna, Samara, Elisa, Felicia

Gamada *(African)* ♂   RATING: ★☆
Glad, pleased—Possibly of Indonesian origin
> People think of Gamada as old-fashioned, ethnic, slow, aggressive, quiet
> People who like the name Gamada also like Fisseha, Gavivi, Davu, Abu, Jafari, Jabulani, Jimmy, Ethanael, Abba, Iggy

Gambhiri *(Sanskrit/East Indian)* ♀   RATING: ★★☆
Noble
> People think of Gambhiri as exotic, intelligent, ethnic, untrustworthy, poor
> People who like the name Gambhiri also like Lajita, Laksha, Gaura, Kapila, Kavindra, Garima, Bhavna, Avani, Basanti, Kirtana

Gamma *(Greek)* ♀   RATING: ★★☆
Third letter of Greek alphabet
> People think of Gamma as slow, nerdy, weird, sexy, popular
> People who like the name Gamma also like Electra, Faith, Gemma, Iris, Effie, Giselle, Fay, Helena, Iola, Gabriella

Ganesa *(Sanskrit/East Indian)* ♀♂   RATING: ★★
God of intelligence and wisdom
> People think of Ganesa as pretty, sexy, exotic, elegant, popular

> People who like the name Ganesa also like Genesis, Cadence, Dharma, Kyan, Blair, Deva, Hayden, Skylar, Haley, Jocelyn

Ganit *(Hebrew)* ♀   RATING: ★☆
Garden
> People think of Ganit as religious, pretty, old-fashioned, loser, unpopular
> People who like the name Ganit also like Izzy, Abbie, Efrat, Aadi, Damali, Nicole, Chava, Gzifa, Caitir, Kamea

Gannon *(Celtic/Gaelic)* ♂   RATING: ★★★☆
Fair complected
> People think of Gannon as handsome, powerful, intelligent, funny, cool
> People who like the name Gannon also like Gavin, Gage, Aiden, Grayson, Kaden, Gabriel, Owen, Braeden, Grady, Griffin

Ganya *(Hebrew)* ♀   RATING: ★☆
Garden of the Lord
> People think of Ganya as lazy, poor, intelligent, weird, cool
> People who like the name Ganya also like Galya, Gala, Naomi, Samara, Elise, Hope, Iris, Gada, Hana, Emilia

Garan *(Welsh)* ♀♂   RATING: ★★★
Stork
> People think of Garan as powerful, energetic, intelligent, handsome, exotic
> People who like the name Garan also like Caden, Hayden, Jaden, Cade, Evan, Logan, Riley, Addison, Camdyn, Arden

Gardenia *(English)* ♀   RATING: ★★
Gardenia flower
> People think of Gardenia as artsy, pretty, elegant, creative, leader
> People who like the name Gardenia also like Gabriella, Giselle, Faith, Belle, Felicity, Genevieve, Bianca, Fiona, Jasmine, Cassandra

Gardner *(English)* ♂   RATING: ★★
Gardener—Originally a surname
> People think of Gardner as creative, weird, trustworthy, caring, old-fashioned
> People who like the name Gardner also like Graham, Gage, Ethan, Garrett, Harrison, Gavin, Grayson, Aiden, Kaden, Jack

Gareth *(Welsh)* ♂   RATING: ★★★★
Spear rule—Variation of Garrett
> People think of Gareth as handsome, caring, funny, intelligent, trustworthy
> People who like the name Gareth also like Ethan, Gavin, Gabriel, Tristan, Aiden, Liam, Caleb, Ian, Noah, Isaac

Garfield *(English)* ♂   RATING: ★★★
From the triangular field—Garfield, cartoon cat; James Garfield, U.S. president; John Garfield, film actor
> People think of Garfield as funny, handsome, cool, lazy, caring

People who like the name Garfield also like Gilbert, Fletcher, David, Gabe, Eric, Earl, Dawson, Deacon, Alexander, Gerard

Gari *(American)* ♀   RATING: ★★☆

Spear rule—Feminine form of Gary

People think of Gari as aggressive, cool, handsome, intelligent, sexy

People who like the name Gari also like Julia, Karis, Kori, Mea, Gala, Agnes, Elia, Gypsy, Kia, Odette

Garima *(Sanskrit/East Indian)* ♀   RATING: ★★★

Warmth

People think of Garima as funny, pretty, popular, creative, exotic

People who like the name Garima also like Avani, Eshana, Brinda, Chahna, Jaya, Kalinda, Ishana, Bhavna, Kamana, Alpana

Garin *(Armenian)* ♂   RATING: ★★★☆

Ancient city in Armenia

People think of Garin as handsome, intelligent, funny, caring, sporty

People who like the name Garin also like Garren, Gavin, Aiden, Ethan, Kaden, Grayson, Galen, Gage, Gabriel, Gavan

Garland *(English)* ♀   RATING: ★★★☆

Maker of Garlands—Also a surname; Judy Garland, actress/singer

People think of Garland as caring, funny, handsome, intelligent, popular

People who like the name Garland also like Giselle, Isabelle, Belle, Felicity, Grace, Gabrielle, Gemma, Dawn, Bethany, Aurora

Garnet *(English)* ♀   RATING: ★★★☆

A red semiprecious gem—Also a surname meaning little warren; also spelled Garnett, Garnetta, or Garnette

People think of Garnet as intelligent, creative, cool, leader, energetic

People who like the name Garnet also like Faith, Grace, Giselle, Hazel, Scarlett, Gabrielle, Iris, Fiona, Ivy, Genevieve

Garran *(American)* ♂   RATING: ★★★★☆

Combination of Gareth and Darren; also spelled Garren

People think of Garren as handsome, intelligent, funny, cool, popular

People who like the name Garren also like Gavin, Kaden, Aiden, Ethan, Gabriel, Keagan, Noah, Grayson, Jayden, Garin

Garrett *(English)* ♂   RATING: ★★★

Spear rule—Also a surname; variation of Gerald or Gerard; also spelled Garett; Garrett Morris, comedian

People think of Garrett as handsome, funny, intelligent, cool, popular

People who like the name Garrett also like Gavin, Ethan, Aiden, Caleb, Landon, Ian, Jackson, Jacob, Cole, Noah

Garrick *(English)* ♂   RATING: ★★★★

From a place covered by oaks—Also a surname from a French place name

People think of Garrick as handsome, caring, intelligent, funny, sexy

People who like the name Garrick also like Garrett, Kaden, Gavin, Jackson, Braden, Gabriel, Ethan, Grayson, Ian, Garrison

Garrison *(English)* ♂   RATING: ★★★☆

Son of Gerard—Originally a surname; Garrison Keillor, author/humorist

People think of Garrison as handsome, funny, trustworthy, intelligent, sporty

People who like the name Garrison also like Grayson, Jackson, Gavin, Harrison, Garrett, Ethan, Landon, Braden, Griffin, Kaden

Garron *(English)* ♂   RATING: ★★★☆

Form of Garren

People think of Garron as popular, intelligent, leader, cool, trustworthy

People who like the name Garron also like Gavin, Garren, Kaden, Garrick, Ethan, Gage, Grayson, Gabriel, Conner, Drake

Garry *(English)* ♂   RATING: ★★★☆

Short for Garrett or Gareth

People think of Garry as funny, handsome, lazy, trustworthy, caring

People who like the name Garry also like Jack, Gabriel, Aaron, Luke, Justin, Matthew, Elliot, Ethan, Jason, Gavin

Garson *(English)* ♂   RATING: ★★☆

Valet

People think of Garson as nerdy, weird, sexy, slow, boy next door

People who like the name Garson also like Gavin, Holden, Graham, Grayson, Griffin, Caleb, Jayden, Jackson, Fletcher, Garren

Garth *(English)* ♂   RATING: ★★

Garden keeper—Originally a surname

People think of Garth as handsome, intelligent, caring, trustworthy, funny

People who like the name Garth also like Jacob, Gavin, Ethan, Cole, Jared, Lance, Nicholas, Joshua, Benjamin, Gabriel

Garvey *(Celtic/Gaelic)* ♂   RATING: ★★

Rough

People think of Garvey as handsome, intelligent, energetic, cool, caring

People who like the name Garvey also like Grady, Donovan, Grant, Gannon, Finn, Gabriel, Gideon, Dillon, Grayson, Liam

Gary *(English)* ♂   RATING: ★★

Spear rule—Originally short for Garrett or Gareth

People think of Gary as funny, handsome, intelligent, caring, sexy

People who like the name Gary also like Nathan, Ethan, Aaron, David, Ian, Joshua, Jason, Jack, Caleb, Jared

Gasha (Russian) ♀   RATING: ★★☆
Good—Variation of Agatha
People think of Gasha as exotic, pretty, ethnic, aggressive, quiet
People who like the name Gasha also like Hazel, Gaia, Layla, Isabella, Katia, Harmony, Hailey, Jadyn, Destiny, Fern

Gaston (French) ♂   RATING: ★★★☆
From Gascony, France
People think of Gaston as handsome, popular, sexy, intelligent, energetic
People who like the name Gaston also like Gavin, Ethan, Gage, Braden, Garrett, Gabriel, Kaden, Nicholas, Grayson, Jacob

Gates (English) ♂   RATING: ★★★☆
Dweller by the gates—Also a surname; Bill Gates, founder of Microsoft
People think of Gates as weird, intelligent, wealthy, stuck-up, nerdy
People who like the name Gates also like Gage, Jackson, Grayson, Garrett, Chase, Gavin, Kaden, Ethan, Holden, Landon

Gaura (Sanskrit/East Indian) ♀   RATING: ★★☆
Fair skinned
People think of Gaura as artsy, pretty, exotic, religious, funny
People who like the name Gaura also like Chandra, Indira, Laksha, Gauri, Kirtana, Kali, Amara, Keaira, Sitara, Ishana

Gaurav (Sanskrit/East Indian) ♂   RATING: ★★★
Pride
People think of Gaurav as intelligent, weird, unpopular, ethnic, caring
People who like the name Gaurav also like Adarsh, Gautam, Deepak, Gyan, Ashwin, Jatin, Manjit, Adit, Ajay, Chatura

Gauri (Sanskrit/East Indian) ♀   RATING: ★★★
Fair, white—Also spelled Gowri or Gori
People think of Gauri as pretty, caring, religious, funny, trustworthy
People who like the name Gauri also like Chandra, Leela, Gaura, Opal, Jaya, Janya, Shanti, Kalinda, Laksha, Devi

Gautam (Sanskrit/East Indian) ♂   RATING: ★★★
Clan name of Buddha
People think of Gautam as sexy, intelligent, caring, handsome, cool
People who like the name Gautam also like Gaurav, Ashwin, Deepak, Gyan, Ajay, Jatin, Adarsh, Sanjiv, Chatura, Jagat

Gautier (French) ♂   RATING: ★★★
Army rule
People think of Gautier as stuck-up, uptight, loser, unpopular, weird

People who like the name Gautier also like Alain, Ansel, Gerard, Gaston, Dashiell, Lucien, Beau, Erasmus, Feleti, Felix

Gavan (Celtic/Gaelic) ♂   RATING: ★★★
Unknown meaning—Also an Irish surname
People think of Gavan as handsome, funny, intelligent, cool, powerful
People who like the name Gavan also like Gavin, Aiden, Ethan, Kaden, Ian, Gabriel, Keagan, Tristan, Aden, Caleb

Gavin (English) ♂   RATING: ★★★
White hawk—Variation of Gawain
People think of Gavin as handsome, intelligent, funny, cool, creative
People who like the name Gavin also like Ethan, Aiden, Caleb, Noah, Landon, Gabriel, Ian, Owen, Kaden, Jacob

Gavino (Italian) ♂   RATING: ★★☆
From the city of Gabium
People think of Gavino as funny, big, handsome, young, cool
People who like the name Gavino also like Gabriel, Damian, Javier, Aiden, Fabian, Ruben, Valentino, Giancarlo, Nathan, Dario

Gavivi (African) ♂   RATING: ★★☆
Money is sweet—Western African origin
People think of Gavivi as exotic, ethnic, aggressive, pretty, wild
People who like the name Gavivi also like Lehana, Iniko, Diata, Roman, Garin, Haben, Deacon, Mikaili, Gabe, Idris

Gavril (Slavic) ♂   RATING: ★★★
God is my strength—Variation of Gabriel
People think of Gavril as creative, young, intelligent, popular, weird
People who like the name Gavril also like Gabriel, Aiden, Elijah, Jayden, Gideon, Kael, Ethan, Caleb, Jeremiah, Gavin

Gavrila (Hungarian) ♀   RATING: ★★☆
God is my strength—Feminine form of Gavril
People think of Gavrila as big, aggressive, loser, slow, religious
People who like the name Gavrila also like Gianna, Moriah, Liana, Grace, Gabriella, Gabrielle, Giovanna, Samara, Galya, Isabella

Gavrilla (Russian) ♀   RATING: ★★☆
God is my strength—Feminine form of Gavril or Gabriel
People think of Gavrilla as wealthy, loser, quiet, popular, weird
People who like the name Gavrilla also like Gabrielle, Gabriella, Eva, Donatella, Gwendolyn, Gypsy, Lydia, Genevieve, Giselle, Gavrila

Gavyn (American) ♀♂   RATING: ★★★☆
Variation of Gavin
People think of Gavyn as handsome, creative, intelligent, cool, funny

People who like the name Gavyn also like Caden, Addison, Hayden, Avery, Jaden, Cadence, Bailey, Payton, Brayden, Landen

Gay/Gaye *(English)* ♀   RATING: ★☆
Merry, happy
People think of Gay as loser, weird, nerdy, unpopular, sexy
People who like the name Gay also like Katelyn, Colleen, Leighanna, Joyce, Bella, Heather, Georgianna, Linda, Hailey, Ginger

Gayle *(English)* ♀   RATING: ★★★☆
Joy of the father—Variation of Gail; short for Abigail
People think of Gayle as caring, pretty, intelligent, creative, funny
People who like the name Gayle also like Grace, Paige, Faith, Hannah, Bethany, Heather, Hailey, Abigail, Gail, Fiona

Gaylord *(English)* ♂   RATING: ★★★
Lively, brisk—Originally a surname from the French Gaillard
People think of Gaylord as loser, nerdy, weird, unpopular, sexy
People who like the name Gaylord also like Jacob, Ethan, Oliver, Jack, Grant, Benjamin, Zachary, Gabriel, Jackson, Elijah

Gaynell *(American)* ♀   RATING: ★★☆
Happy, shiny—Combination of Gay and Nell
People think of Gaynell as caring, unpopular, old-fashioned, funny, pretty
People who like the name Gaynell also like Giselle, Layla, Leala, Lara, Katima, Helena, Kiara, Esma, Lark, Lulu

Gayora *(Hebrew)* ♀   RATING: ★★
Valley of sun—Combination of Gay and Yora
People think of Gayora as nerdy, unpopular, weird, loser, poor
People who like the name Gayora also like Calista, Larissa, Nora, Isis, Carissa, Jessamine, Fiona, Deandra, Cherry, Eldora

Gazali *(Arabic)* ♂   RATING: ★☆
Native of Ghazal, Iran—Correctly transliterated Ghazali
People think of Gazali as ethnic, powerful, popular, cool, religious
People who like the name Gazali also like Gabriel, Davu, Noah, Jayden, Galvin, Kael, Giovanni, Ajani, Jeremiah, Asher

Gazelle *(Latin)* ♀   RATING: ★★
Graceful deer
People think of Gazelle as pretty, exotic, energetic, elegant, cool
People who like the name Gazelle also like Giselle, Faith, Gabriella, Gabrielle, Genevieve, Bianca, Grace, Jazzelle, Iris, Fiona

Gazit *(Hebrew)* ♀   RATING: ★★
Hewn stone
People think of Gazit as intelligent, loser, criminal, weird, old-fashioned
People who like the name Gazit also like Mary, Mystery, Liesel, Bluma, Ginny, Delilah, Dinah, Devorit, Dena, Anaïs

Geet *(Sanskrit/East Indian)* ♂   RATING: ★★
Song
People think of Geet as weird, unpopular, funny, loser, trustworthy
People who like the name Geet also like Dinesh, Gagan, Devesh, Divyesh, Jatin, Divakar, Charan, Deepak, Adarsh, Chetan

Gefen *(Hebrew)* ♀   RATING: ★★☆
Vine—Also spelled Geffen
People think of Gefen as weird, nerdy, creative, religious, ethnic
People who like the name Gefen also like Gwen, Fiona, Grace, Dawn, Fallon, Georgia, Gwyneth, Abigail, Deana, Carmela

Gefjun *(Scandinavian)* ♀   RATING: ★★
One who endows wealth
People think of Gefjun as criminal, aggressive, old-fashioned, intelligent, unpopular
People who like the name Gefjun also like Elsa, Brynja, Bryndis, Inga, Helsa, Britta, Metta, Gefen, Mariuerla, Thora

Geir *(Scandinavian)* ♂   RATING: ★★☆
Spear
People think of Geir as handsome, sporty, exotic, caring, funny
People who like the name Geir also like Garrick, Finn, Boden, Gunnar, Gareth, Fynn, Garron, Gideon, Grayson, Liam

Gelilah *(Hebrew)* ♀   RATING: ★★★
Rolling hills
People think of Gelilah as pretty, energetic, caring, elegant, funny
People who like the name Gelilah also like Daphne, Gianna, Jane, Delilah, Hazel, Selina, Chantel, Jazlynn, Isabella, Blossom

Gella *(Hebrew)* ♀   RATING: ★★★
One with golden hair
People think of Gella as pretty, stuck-up, intelligent, trendy, artsy
People who like the name Gella also like Gabrielle, Gwendolyn, Cassandra, Brielle, Chloe, Jasmine, Eva, Evangeline, Claire, Bella

Gellert *(Hungarian)* ♂   RATING: ★★☆
Brave with spear—Variation of Gerard
People think of Gellert as nerdy, loser, big, exotic, energetic
People who like the name Gellert also like Gabriel, Zander, Dacian, Braden, Bo, Gage, Isaac, Braxton, Daneil, Darren

249

Gelsey (*English*) ♀   RATING: ★★★☆
Jasmine
  People think of Gelsey as creative, pretty, wild, old-fashioned, trustworthy
  People who like the name Gelsey also like Ivy, Gemma, Isabel, Hailey, Grace, Felicity, Gabby, Ginny, Giselle, Maisie

Gemala (*American*) ♀   RATING: ★★☆
Precious oak tree—Combination of Gem and Ayla
  People think of Gemala as weird, aggressive, sexy, artsy, exotic
  People who like the name Gemala also like Giselle, Gezana, Gerianne, Gigi, Ormanda, Deirdra, Gianna, Hanne, Gelsey, Keaira

Gemini (*Latin*) ♀ ♂   RATING: ★★★☆
The twins—Used for children born under this astrological sign
  People think of Gemini as funny, creative, intelligent, pretty, powerful
  People who like the name Gemini also like Dakota, Bailey, Caden, Jade, Ember, Hayden, Madison, Genesis, Jaden, Taylor

Gemma (*Italian*) ♀   RATING: ★★★★
Precious stone
  People think of Gemma as pretty, funny, caring, intelligent, creative
  People who like the name Gemma also like Emma, Isabella, Hannah, Grace, Chloe, Ava, Charlotte, Bella, Olivia, Ella

Gen (*Japanese*) ♀   RATING: ★★★☆
Spring—Also spelled Genn, Jen, or Jenn
  People think of Gen as pretty, wild, funny, leader, popular
  People who like the name Gen also like Emiko, Gin, Amaya, Hana, Haruko, Inari, Ayame, Jin, Kaida, Aneko

Gene (*English*) ♀ ♂   RATING: ★★★☆
Well born—Originally short for Eugene; also a basic biological sequence; Gene Kelly, actor/dancer; Gene Tierney, actress; Gene Wilder, actor
  People think of Gene as caring, cool, funny, handsome, intelligent
  People who like the name Gene also like Hayden, Dylan, James, Evan, Evelyn, Bailey, Madison, Taylor, Parker, Sean

Genera (*Latin*) ♀   RATING: ★★☆
General, generic
  People think of Genera as caring, intelligent, pretty, trustworthy, funny
  People who like the name Genera also like Georgina, Sara, Kendra, Tamara, Gillian, Kennice, Kera, Amelia, Skyla, Lavinia

Genero (*Latin*) ♂   RATING: ★☆
General, generic
  People think of Genero as cool, quiet, creative, pretty, caring

People who like the name Genero also like Dustin, Fox, Felix, Giona, Cyrus, Brad, Dillon, Fabian, Favian, Marcello

Genesis (*Greek*) ♀ ♂   RATING: ★★★★☆
Beginning
  People think of Genesis as pretty, intelligent, caring, funny, creative
  People who like the name Genesis also like Jaden, Hayden, Caden, Jade, Dakota, Cadence, Jocelyn, Jordan, Bailey, Alexis

Genet (*African*) ♀   RATING: ★★★☆
Heaven—Ethiopian origin; also spelled Genat
  People think of Genet as pretty, intelligent, elegant, wealthy, trustworthy
  People who like the name Genet also like Bella, Gimbya, Johari, Amani, Faith, Bree, Ife, Gabrielle, Giselle, Gianna

Geneva (*French*) ♀   RATING: ★★☆
Juniper berry—City in Switzerland
  People think of Geneva as pretty, intelligent, creative, caring, funny
  People who like the name Geneva also like Genevieve, Giselle, Olivia, Gabrielle, Isabella, Aurora, Gianna, Emma, Scarlett, Ava

Genevieve (*French*) ♀   RATING: ★★★
Woman of the people—Genevieve Bujold, actress
  People think of Genevieve as pretty, intelligent, creative, elegant, caring
  People who like the name Genevieve also like Isabella, Gabrielle, Olivia, Charlotte, Ava, Grace, Hannah, Gwendolyn, Abigail, Emma

Genica (*American*) ♀   RATING: ★★★☆
Combination of Genevieve and Jessica
  People think of Genica as creative, pretty, intelligent, trustworthy, young
  People who like the name Genica also like Genevieve, Jadyn, Faith, Gianna, Bianca, Danica, Hailey, Gabriella, Gabrielle, Isabella

Genna (*American*) ♀   RATING: ★★★☆
Fair phantom—Variation of Jenna
  People think of Genna as pretty, funny, popular, caring, energetic
  People who like the name Genna also like Grace, Jenna, Genevieve, Alana, Kara, Emma, Ella, Isabella, Gabriella, Gabrielle

Genoveva (*Spanish*) ♀   RATING: ★★★
White phantom—Variation of Genevieve
  People think of Genoveva as caring, intelligent, pretty, funny, creative
  People who like the name Genoveva also like Gabriella, Isabella, Cecilia, Gianna, Alyson, Arianna, Genevieve, Graciela, Giovanna, Bridget

Gent (*English*) ♂   RATING: ★★☆
Gentleman
  People think of Gent as intelligent, funny, trustworthy, old-fashioned, slow

People who like the name Gent also like Gage, Grant, Grayson, Drake, Gavin, Ethan, Kent, Chase, Leo, Fletcher

Gentry *(English)* ♀ ♂   RATING: ★★★★
Nobility of birth—Originally a surname
People think of Gentry as intelligent, energetic, popular, funny, caring
People who like the name Gentry also like Hayden, Caden, Avery, Addison, Parker, Cadence, Logan, Hunter, Bailey, Carson

Geoff *(English)* ♂   RATING: ★★
God peace—Short for Geoffrey
People think of Geoff as funny, caring, cool, handsome, trustworthy
People who like the name Geoff also like Geoffrey, Gavin, Ethan, Benjamin, Gabriel, David, Eric, Ian, Aaron, Caleb

Geoffrey *(English)* ♂   RATING: ★★★☆
God peace
People think of Geoffrey as handsome, funny, intelligent, caring, trustworthy
People who like the name Geoffrey also like Gabriel, Jacob, Ethan, Joshua, Benjamin, Ian, Gavin, Nicholas, Aaron, Isaac

Geona *(Italian)* ♂   RATING: ★★★
A dove—Variation of Jonah
People think of Geona as pretty, popular, powerful, aggressive, trustworthy
People who like the name Geona also like Gabriel, Giona, Ethan, Jayden, Garren, Kaden, Timothy, Darren, Chance, Jason

Geordi *(English)* ♂   RATING: ★★★
Short for George or Jordan
People think of Geordi as caring, intelligent, creative, funny, sporty
People who like the name Geordi also like Jacob, Ethan, Grayson, Gabriel, Isaac, Gideon, Jack, Jared, Braden, Joshua

George *(Greek)* ♂   RATING: ★★
Farmer—George Clooney, actor; George Lopez, actor/comedian; George Washington, U.S. president
People think of George as handsome, funny, intelligent, caring, cool
People who like the name George also like Jack, Henry, Jacob, Benjamin, Oliver, William, Daniel, Alexander, Isaac, Nicholas

Georgette *(French)* ♀   RATING: ★★
Feminine form of George
People think of Georgette as pretty, funny, intelligent, trustworthy, creative
People who like the name Georgette also like Georgia, Isabella, Genevieve, Gabriella, Gwendolyn, Elizabeth, Charlotte, Gabrielle, Giselle, Georgianna

Georgia *(English)* ♀   RATING: ★★★
Farmer—Feminine form of George; also a U.S. state
People think of Georgia as pretty, funny, intelligent, caring, creative
People who like the name Georgia also like Ava, Grace, Olivia, Ella, Charlotte, Isabella, Chloe, Hannah, Emma, Amelia

Georgianna *(English)* ♀   RATING: ★★★★
Combination of Georgia and Anna
People think of Georgianna as pretty, intelligent, caring, funny, elegant
People who like the name Georgianna also like Isabella, Genevieve, Grace, Georgia, Abigail, Gabriella, Ella, Elizabeth, Charlotte, Hailey

Georgianne *(English)* ♀   RATING: ★★★☆
Combination of Georgia and Anne
People think of Georgianne as intelligent, caring, creative, popular, funny
People who like the name Georgianne also like Georgianna, Grace, Abigail, Georgia, Amelia, Victoria, Isabella, Olivia, Jasmine, Georgina

Georgina *(English)* ♀   RATING: ★★
Feminine form of George—Also short for Georgia
People think of Georgina as pretty, funny, caring, intelligent, creative
People who like the name Georgina also like Grace, Georgia, Amelia, Hannah, Isabella, Abigail, Charlotte, Faith, Olivia, Emily

Gerald *(English)* ♂   RATING: ★★
Spear rule—Gerald Ford, U.S. president
People think of Gerald as intelligent, handsome, funny, caring, cool
People who like the name Gerald also like Gabriel, George, David, Andrew, Jacob, Daniel, Ethan, Isaac, Justin, Charles

Geraldine *(English)* ♀   RATING: ★☆
Spear rule—Feminine form of Gerald; also spelled Geraldene
People think of Geraldine as caring, intelligent, funny, pretty, creative
People who like the name Geraldine also like Gabrielle, Giselle, Jacqueline, Cassandra, Gwyneth, Hailey, Fiona, Faith, Grace, Iris

Geraldo *(Spanish)* ♂   RATING: ★☆
Spear rule—Variation of Gerald; pronounced *her-AHL-doe*
People think of Geraldo as funny, handsome, cool, intelligent, energetic
People who like the name Geraldo also like Fernando, Diego, Ruben, Joaquin, Julio, Eduardo, Alejandro, Luis, Francisco, Jason

Geranium *(English)* ♀   RATING: ★★
Geranium flower
People think of Geranium as weird, slow, funny, wild, elegant

People who like the name Geranium also like Blossom, Hope, Ivy, Fiona, Gazelle, Audrey, Constance, Butterfly, Emma, Estelle

People who like the name Germain also like Belle, Emilie, Ella, Elle, Dominique, Giselle, Bella, Jacqueline, Estelle, Genevieve

Gerard (*English*) ♂   RATING: ★★
Brave with spear—Gerard Way, singer
People think of Gerard as handsome, sexy, creative, cool, intelligent
People who like the name Gerard also like Ethan, Aiden, Gabriel, Jack, Joshua, Caleb, Nathan, Justin, Daniel, Adam

Germaine (*French*) ♀   RATING: ★★
Brother
People think of Germaine as intelligent, funny, pretty, young, sexy
People who like the name Germaine also like Giselle, Hailey, Genevieve, Desiree, Elle, Gabrielle, Claudette, Chloe, Fiona, Adrienne

Gerardo (*Spanish*) ♂   RATING: ★★★
Spear brave—Variation of Gerard
People think of Gerardo as handsome, funny, cool, intelligent, caring
People who like the name Gerardo also like Gabriel, Fernando, Fabian, Leonardo, Angelo, Giovanni, Ramiro, Adam, David, Giancarlo

Gerodi (*Italian*) ♂   RATING: ★☆
Hero or hill
People think of Gerodi as weird, loser, pretty, powerful, unpopular
People who like the name Gerodi also like Gaetan, Tristan, Braeden, Edan, Declan, Cole, Maddox, Trey, Danton, Leonardo

Gerd (*Scandinavian*) ♀   RATING: ★★☆
Garden
People think of Gerd as nerdy, old-fashioned, weird, handsome, trustworthy
People who like the name Gerd also like Elin, Gudrun, Keely, Lis, Erla, Chantal, Metta, Savea, Malin, Mariuerla

Geronimo (*Italian*) ♂   RATING: ★★☆
Holy name—Variation of Jerome
People think of Geronimo as intelligent, funny, handsome, sexy, creative
People who like the name Geronimo also like Michael, Rafael, Sebastian, Fabian, Joshua, Timothy, Maximilian, Gabriel, Damian, Mateo

Gerda (*Scandinavian*) ♀   RATING: ★★★☆
Garden
People think of Gerda as caring, energetic, pretty, wild, creative
People who like the name Gerda also like Lana, Genevieve, Iris, Hazel, Ingrid, Gersemi, Larissa, Isabelle, Daphne, Lark

Gerry (*German*) ♀♂   RATING: ★★★☆
Short for Gerald
People think of Gerry as intelligent, lazy, trustworthy, funny, caring
People who like the name Gerry also like Jerry, Fred, Jesse, Evan, Addison, Jamie, Gene, Brooke, Jordan, Joe

Geri (*English*) ♀   RATING: ★★★☆
Short for Geraldine; Geri Halliwell, singer
People think of Geri as funny, caring, intelligent, creative, popular
People who like the name Geri also like Faith, Emma, Fiona, Gwen, Hailey, Daphne, Paige, Georgia, Grace, Gracie

Gersemi (*Scandinavian*) ♀   RATING: ★★★
Jewel
People think of Gersemi as pretty, creative, weird, artsy, exotic
People who like the name Gersemi also like Emberlynn, Bella, Faylinn, Femi, Emma, Eliora, Dara, Jeanette, Eldora, Elsa

Gerianne (*American*) ♀   RATING: ★☆
Combination of Geraldine and Anne
People think of Gerianne as pretty, caring, creative, funny, leader
People who like the name Gerianne also like Gianna, Gabrielle, Giselle, Ginger, Gabriella, Jenna, Hailey, Geraldine, Heather, Margaux

Gershom (*Hebrew*) ♂   RATING: ★☆
Stranger
People think of Gershom as handsome, intelligent, trustworthy, caring, lazy
People who like the name Gershom also like Gabriel, Gideon, Griffith, Gyan, Garrick, Elijah, Gibson, Ethan, Gary, Gordon

Gerik (*Polish*) ♂   RATING: ★★★☆
Spear ruler
People think of Gerik as loser, nerdy, girl next door, old-fashioned, big
People who like the name Gerik also like Gavin, Gabriel, Aiden, Nathan, Gage, Kaden, Aden, Braden, Caleb, Galen

Gertrude (*German*) ♀   RATING: ★★★
Strong spear—Gertrude Stein, writer
People think of Gertrude as old-fashioned, slow, nerdy, unpopular, loser
People who like the name Gertrude also like Charlotte, Gretchen, Gwendolyn, Margaret, Beatrice, Ava, Olivia, Fiona, Eleanor, Hannah

Germain (*French*) ♀   RATING: ★★
A German
People think of Germain as cool, wealthy, popular, weird, exotic

Gesine (*German*) ♀   RATING: ★★★
Strong spear—Short for Gertrude
People think of Gesine as creative, intelligent, exotic, artsy, elegant

People who like the name Gesine also like Rhian, Ophelia, Maura, Selene, Zelda, Stasia, Dhyana, Aeryn, Keaira, Malise

Gezana (*Spanish*) ♀　　　　　　RATING: ★★☆
Reference to the incarnation
People think of Gezana as exotic, old-fashioned, artsy, energetic, loser
People who like the name Gezana also like Gabriella, Giselle, Gaia, Adriana, Isabella, Gisela, Sofia, Gianna, Grazia, Ginger

Ghada (*Arabic*) ♀　　　　　　RATING: ★★☆
Young girl
People think of Ghada as cool, sexy, young, intelligent, pretty
People who like the name Ghada also like Layla, Gemma, Iris, Keira, Ella, Kayla, Heba, Electra, Hazel, Larissa

Ghazi (*Arabic*) ♂　　　　　　RATING: ★★★
Hero, commander
People think of Ghazi as trustworthy, leader, handsome, powerful, energetic
People who like the name Ghazi also like Jaser, Faris, Gideon, Baqer, Jericho, Imaran, Jabari, Jabilo, Irem, Adish

Ghita (*Greek*) ♀　　　　　　RATING: ★★★
Pearl—Short for Margherita
People think of Ghita as pretty, religious, funny, elegant, intelligent
People who like the name Ghita also like Giselle, Olivia, Layla, Gita, Adia, Calista, Jasmine, Helena, Flora, Dahlia

Gia (*Italian*) ♀　　　　　　RATING: ★★★★
Short for Gianna—Gia Carangi, fashion model
People think of Gia as pretty, exotic, sexy, creative, intelligent
People who like the name Gia also like Gianna, Isabella, Mia, Ava, Grace, Chloe, Emma, Eva, Bianca, Gabriella

Giacomo (*Italian*) ♂　　　　　　RATING: ★☆
Supplanter—Variation of Jacob or James
People think of Giacomo as handsome, ethnic, intelligent, wealthy, funny
People who like the name Giacomo also like Gabriel, Giovanni, Giancarlo, Matteo, Leonardo, Jack, Giorgio, Ethan, Nicholas, Nico

Giada (*Italian*) ♀　　　　　　RATING: ★★★★
Jade
People think of Giada as pretty, exotic, elegant, creative, intelligent
People who like the name Giada also like Gianna, Gabriella, Ava, Isabella, Bianca, Genevieve, Gia, Lucia, Sienna, Ella

Gian (*Italian*) ♂　　　　　　RATING: ★★★☆
God is gracious—Variation of John
People think of Gian as big, nerdy, aggressive, caring, criminal

People who like the name Gian also like Dominic, Sebastian, Rohan, Taran, Desmond, Ace, Gavin, Travis, Dean, Brendan

Giancarlo (*Italian*) ♂　　　　　　RATING: ★★
Combination of Gian and Carlo
People think of Giancarlo as handsome, funny, intelligent, cool, sexy
People who like the name Giancarlo also like Giovanni, Gabriel, Anthony, Ethan, Fabian, Aiden, Alexander, Xavier, Dominic, Matteo

Gianna (*Italian*) ♀　　　　　　RATING: ★★★★
God is gracious—Feminine form of John
People think of Gianna as pretty, funny, intelligent, popular, creative
People who like the name Gianna also like Isabella, Ava, Gabriella, Olivia, Giovanna, Arianna, Emma, Ella, Hannah, Natalia

Gianni (*Italian*) ♂　　　　　　RATING: ★★★★
God is gracious—Variation of Johnny
People think of Gianni as handsome, sexy, cool, popular, funny
People who like the name Gianni also like Giovanni, Gabriel, Aiden, Angelo, Elijah, Anthony, Dominic, Jayden, Fabian, Gavin

Gibson (*English*) ♂　　　　　　RATING: ★★★★
Son of Gilbert—Also a guitar manufacturer
People think of Gibson as handsome, intelligent, cool, creative, funny
People who like the name Gibson also like Jackson, Gavin, Grayson, Emerson, Gabriel, Gage, Dawson, Griffin, Drake, Braden

Gideon (*Hebrew*) ♂　　　　　　RATING: ★★☆
Great warrior
People think of Gideon as intelligent, handsome, powerful, trustworthy, leader
People who like the name Gideon also like Gabriel, Ethan, Elijah, Caleb, Gavin, Noah, Isaac, Benjamin, Aiden, Isaiah

Gigi (*French*) ♀　　　　　　RATING: ★★
Originally short for names starting with G, like Georgette, or with "gi" in them, like Virginia; *Gigi*, film starring Leslie Caron
People think of Gigi as pretty, funny, intelligent, cool, energetic
People who like the name Gigi also like Ava, Isabella, Giselle, Genevieve, Grace, Daisy, Gianna, Eva, Bella, Faith

Gil (*Hebrew*) ♀ ♂　　　　　　RATING: ★★
Joy
People think of Gil as handsome, intelligent, cool, energetic, sexy
People who like the name Gil also like Evan, Jaden, Ezra, Caden, Logan, Blake, Eden, Gael, Coby, Gene

Gilad *(Hebrew)* ♂   RATING: ★★★
Hill of testimony, monument
> People think of Gilad as nerdy, weird, intelligent, ethnic, exotic
> People who like the name Gilad also like Garrick, Gilead, Ethan, Benjamin, Gabriel, Gideon, Ephraim, Heath, Elijah, Garrison

Gilbert *(English)* ♂   RATING: ★★★
Bright pledge—Gilbert Gottfried, comedian/actor
> People think of Gilbert as handsome, intelligent, funny, caring, cool
> People who like the name Gilbert also like Gabriel, Gregory, Ethan, Nicholas, Andrew, Benjamin, Garrett, Jacob, Matthew; Jack

Gilda *(English)* ♀   RATING: ★★★☆
Golden—Gilda Radner, comedian/actress
> People think of Gilda as funny, intelligent, creative, powerful, caring
> People who like the name Gilda also like Bianca, Felicity, Iris, Bella, Cassandra, Eva, Ophelia, Faith, Ava, Gabriella

Gilead *(Hebrew)* ♂   RATING: ★★☆
Biblical place name; variation of Gilad
> People think of Gilead as religious, powerful, winner, intelligent, nerdy
> People who like the name Gilead also like Gabriel, Gideon, Gavin, Ephraim, Gilad, Ethan, Braeden, Isaac, Jeremiah, Jonah

Giles *(English)* ♂   RATING: ★★
Pledge; young goat—From the Latin *aegidius* meaning goat kid; or from the German *gisel* meaning pledge; St. Giles
> People think of Giles as intelligent, handsome, caring, funny, trustworthy
> People who like the name Giles also like Ethan, Ian, Gabriel, Jackson, Graham, Jacob, Caleb, Aiden, Gideon, Landon

Gili *(Hebrew)* ♀   RATING: ★★
My joy, rejoice
> People think of Gili as pretty, funny, caring, quiet, energetic
> People who like the name Gili also like Ellie, Gigi, Isabella, Layla, Gemma, Giselle, Genevieve, Kaelyn, Carly, Eve

Gilles *(French)* ♂   RATING: ★★★☆
Variation of Giles
> People think of Gilles as intelligent, funny, sexy, trustworthy, handsome
> People who like the name Gilles also like Bradley, Wade, Tristan, Ansel, Silvain, Drake, Brandon, Felix, Miles, Etienne

Gillespie *(Celtic/Gaelic)* ♂   RATING: ★☆
Servant of the bishop—Dizzy Gillespie, jazz musician
> People think of Gillespie as aggressive, slow, intelligent, old-fashioned, caring

People who like the name Gillespie also like Gilmore, Garrett, Gallagher, Galvin, Bowen, Liam, Edan, Braeden, Callum, Callahan

Gillian *(English)* ♀   RATING: ★★★★☆
Downy—Originally a feminine form of Julian; Gillian Anderson, actress
> People think of Gillian as pretty, funny, intelligent, creative, caring
> People who like the name Gillian also like Jillian, Olivia, Hannah, Abigail, Grace, Faith, Genevieve, Paige, Emma, Hailey

Gilmore *(Celtic/Gaelic)* ♂   RATING: ★★★
Servant of Mary
> People think of Gilmore as funny, leader, intelligent, wild, cool
> People who like the name Gilmore also like Gabriel, Finley, Garrett, Fynn, Gallagher, Liam, Dermot, Gillespie, Grady, Galvin

Gilon *(Hebrew)* ♂   RATING: ★☆
Joy
> People think of Gilon as weird, leader, intelligent, poor, handsome
> People who like the name Gilon also like Ethan, Ely, Gabe, Kyson, Dolan, Darian, Esben, Etan, Aden, Edric

Gimbya *(African)* ♀   RATING: ★☆
Princess
> People think of Gimbya as exotic, aggressive, intelligent, slow, poor
> People who like the name Gimbya also like Jahzara, Hazina, Ayanna, Johari, Nala, Malaika, Nimeesha, Kamili, Juji, Lewa

Gin *(Japanese)* ♀   RATING: ★★★☆
Silver—Also short for Virginia
> People think of Gin as energetic, pretty, intelligent, powerful, quiet
> People who like the name Gin also like Emiko, Amaya, Jin, Ayame, Hitomi, Kaori, Gen, Kaida, Hana, Kagami

Gina *(Italian)* ♀   RATING: ★★☆
Queen—Short for Regina
> People think of Gina as funny, pretty, caring, intelligent, creative
> People who like the name Gina also like Grace, Isabella, Hailey, Angelina, Faith, Hannah, Gabrielle, Emma, Gabriella, Paige

Ginata *(Italian)* ♀   RATING: ★★☆
Flower
> People think of Ginata as exotic, weird, ethnic, pretty, artsy
> People who like the name Ginata also like Gianna, Isabella, Angelina, Gemma, Giovanna, Bellini, Natalia, Camilla, Ariana, Bianca

Ginerva *(Italian)* ♀   RATING: ★★★☆
Variation of Guinevere—Also spelled Ginevra
> People think of Ginerva as pretty, intelligent, young, caring, energetic

People who like the name Ginerva also like Gabriella, Genevieve, Kara, Gianna, Kayla, Clarissa, Isabella, Iris, Jane, Enya

Ginevra *(Italian)* ♀   RATING: ★★★☆
Fair one—Variation of Genevieve
People think of Ginevra as pretty, intelligent, caring, funny, popular
People who like the name Ginevra also like Charlotte, Hermione, Arianna, Scarlett, Emma, Evangeline, Veronica, Bianca, Aurora, Lily

Ginger *(English)* ♀   RATING: ★★
Reddish orange color—Also a spice
People think of Ginger as pretty, funny, creative, caring, energetic
People who like the name Ginger also like Faith, Grace, Hailey, Hannah, Chloe, Isabella, Paige, Gabrielle, Hazel, Emma

Ginnifer *(American)* ♀   RATING: ★★★
Variation of Jennifer
People think of Ginnifer as stuck-up, weird, creative, caring, trendy
People who like the name Ginnifer also like Gabrielle, Gabriella, Felicity, Gwendolyn, Giselle, Bella, Genevieve, Katarina, Cassandra, Elizabeth

Ginny *(English)* ♀   RATING: ★★
Short for Virginia
People think of Ginny as pretty, caring, funny, creative, intelligent
People who like the name Ginny also like Emma, Faith, Grace, Hailey, Isabella, Hannah, Genevieve, Abigail, Lily, Gabrielle

Gino *(Italian)* ♂   RATING: ★★
Farmer—Originally short for Georgino
People think of Gino as handsome, cool, sexy, intelligent, creative
People who like the name Gino also like Giovanni, Gavin, Gabriel, Leo, Carmine, Nico, Jacob, Angelo, Enzo, Dominic

Gioia *(Italian)* ♀   RATING: ★★★
Happiness—Pronounced JOY-a
People think of Gioia as intelligent, pretty, trustworthy, elegant, creative
People who like the name Gioia also like Gabriella, Katarina, Malia, Giada, Jana, Giovanna, Giuliana, Gabrielle, Cara, Gaetana

Giolla *(Celtic/Gaelic)* ♂   RATING: ★☆
Servant
People think of Giolla as poor, slow, old-fashioned, untrustworthy, slow
People who like the name Giolla also like Dane, Wyatt, Damien, Giona, Joel, Marco, Elden, Ethan, Weston, Tyrell

Giona *(Italian)* ♂   RATING: ★★
A dove—Variation of Jonah
People think of Giona as intelligent, pretty, elegant, creative, young

People who like the name Giona also like Giovanni, Jayden, Gabriel, Brock, Maddox, Gavin, Geona, Brennan, Gideon, Fabian

Giorgio *(Italian)* ♂   RATING: ★★
Farmer—Giorgio Armani, fashion designer
People think of Giorgio as handsome, intelligent, cool, sexy, funny
People who like the name Giorgio also like Giovanni, Gabriel, Giancarlo, Nicholas, Sebastian, Emilio, Gino, Giacomo, Grant, Massimo

Giovanna *(Italian)* ♀   RATING: ★★★★
God is gracious
People think of Giovanna as pretty, intelligent, funny, caring, sexy
People who like the name Giovanna also like Gianna, Isabella, Gabriella, Natalia, Genevieve, Ava, Gabrielle, Emma, Olivia, Giselle

Giovanni *(Italian)* ♂   RATING: ★★★★
God is gracious—Giovanni Ribisi, actor
People think of Giovanni as handsome, cool, sexy, intelligent, funny
People who like the name Giovanni also like Gabriel, Ethan, Dominic, Jayden, Gavin, Anthony, Aiden, Isaiah, Jacob, Elijah

Gisela *(German)* ♀   RATING: ★★☆
Pledge
People think of Gisela as pretty, intelligent, sexy, caring, trustworthy
People who like the name Gisela also like Giselle, Isabella, Gianna, Gabriella, Ava, Grace, Genevieve, Eva, Ella, Gabriela

Giselle *(French)* ♀   RATING: ★★☆
Pledge
People think of Giselle as pretty, exotic, sexy, elegant, intelligent
People who like the name Giselle also like Gabrielle, Isabella, Ava, Isabelle, Grace, Genevieve, Chloe, Eva, Olivia, Emma

Gisli *(Scandinavian)* ♀♂   RATING: ★★★
Ray of sunshine
People think of Gisli as pretty, energetic, trustworthy, trendy, ethnic
People who like the name Gisli also like Jada, Jaden, Kenley, Caden, Skylar, Blake, Blaine, Lyric, Jocelyn, Eden

Gita *(Sanskrit/East Indian)* ♀   RATING: ★★★☆
Song
People think of Gita as pretty, caring, intelligent, creative, trustworthy
People who like the name Gita also like Giselle, Ghita, Ava, Layla, Chandra, Gwendolyn, Chloe, Devi, Asha, Gwen

Gitano *(Italian)* ♂   RATING: ★★☆
Gypsy
People think of Gitano as artsy, handsome, boy next door, caring, cool

G

People who like the name Gitano also like Giovanni, Giancarlo, Feleti, Gustavo, Gaetano, Aiden, Giorgio, Gabriel, Devlin, Declan

Gitel *(Hebrew)* ♀   RATING: ★☆
Good
People think of Gitel as funny, elegant, intelligent, pretty, artsy
People who like the name Gitel also like Gemma, Faith, Giselle, Gita, Gwennan, Felicia, Larissa, Larisa, Gittel, Erin

Gittel *(Hebrew)* ♀   RATING: ★☆
Good
People think of Gittel as pretty, elegant, intelligent, caring, old-fashioned
People who like the name Gittel also like Gwennan, Larisa, Gemma, Felicia, Giselle, Lovette, Francesca, Eulalie, Katelyn, Emberlynn

Giulia *(Italian)* ♀   RATING: ★★★★
Downy—Variation of Julia
People think of Giulia as pretty, creative, funny, intelligent, sexy
People who like the name Giulia also like Gianna, Isabella, Gemma, Natalia, Bianca, Angelina, Mia, Sophia, Giovanna, Camilla

Giuliana *(Italian)* ♀   RATING: ★★★☆
Downy—Variation of Juliana; Giuliana DePandi, TV host
People think of Giuliana as pretty, intelligent, caring, exotic, funny
People who like the name Giuliana also like Isabella, Gianna, Arianna, Gabriella, Bianca, Natalia, Angelina, Julianna, Giovanna, Olivia

Giulio *(Italian)* ♂   RATING: ★★★
Downy
People think of Giulio as powerful, handsome, winner, popular, exotic
People who like the name Giulio also like Gitano, Draco, Enzo, Carmine, Giona, Gino, Giacomo, Giancarlo, Giovanni, Gabriel

Giuseppe *(Italian)* ♂   RATING: ★★★★
God will increase—Variation of Joseph
People think of Giuseppe as handsome, funny, sexy, cool, intelligent
People who like the name Giuseppe also like Giovanni, Isaiah, Ethan, Sebastian, Gabriel, Angelo, Elijah, Carmine, Vincent, Gustavo

Giustina *(Italian)* ♀   RATING: ★★☆
Fair, just—Variation of Justine
People think of Giustina as weird, old-fashioned, religious, pretty, young
People who like the name Giustina also like Desiree, Sapphire, Giuliana, Savannah, Gabby, Gaetana, Giada, Gaia, Gabriella, Bianca

Giverny *(French)* ♀   RATING: ★☆
From Giverny, France
People think of Giverny as pretty, intelligent, popular, artsy, caring
People who like the name Giverny also like Genevieve, Isolde, Giselle, Imogene, Isis, Iria, Coralie, Bryndis, Caprice, Savannah

Giza *(Arabic)* ♀   RATING: ★☆
Hewn stone
People think of Giza as pretty, ethnic, intelligent, quiet, creative
People who like the name Giza also like Delilah, Chloe, Delila, Cassia, Carmela, Enye, Silvana, Cara, Elisabeth, Danica

Gizela *(Polish)* ♀   RATING: ★★★
Pledge
People think of Gizela as pretty, sexy, cool, girl next door, big
People who like the name Gizela also like Giselle, Gisela, Gabriella, Isabella, Gianna, Genevieve, Hazel, Mia, Ava, Juliana

Gizi *(Hungarian)* ♀   RATING: ★☆
Pledge
People think of Gizi as creative, wild, cool, weird, exotic
People who like the name Gizi also like Gizela, Kalli, Kawena, Kasia, Gen, Gyda, Ivie, Iona, Juji, Dixie

Gladys *(Welsh)* ♀   RATING: ★★★☆
Country—Gladys Knight, singer
People think of Gladys as pretty, intelligent, funny, caring, cool
People who like the name Gladys also like Gloria, Priscilla, Isolde, Emily, Giselle, Gwendolyn, Fiona, Audrey, Faith, Gwyneth

Glain *(Welsh)* ♀   RATING: ★★
Jewel
People think of Glain as old-fashioned, slow, quiet, poor, loser
People who like the name Glain also like Mabyn, Mairwen, Gwennan, Bronwen, Bronwyn, Carys, Gwyneth, Olwen, Blodwyn, Aeryn

Glen *(Celtic/Gaelic)* ♂   RATING: ★★
A secluded, woody valley
People think of Glen as handsome, funny, caring, intelligent, trustworthy
People who like the name Glen also like Ethan, Grant, Owen, Cole, Glenn, Ian, Justin, Colin, Aiden, Brian

Glenda *(Celtic/Gaelic)* ♀   RATING: ★★★☆
Holy, good
People think of Glenda as funny, intelligent, pretty, caring, trustworthy
People who like the name Glenda also like Genevieve, Fiona, Faith, Erin, Felicia, Alana, Hazel, Bianca, Ivy, Ciara

Glenn *(Celtic/Gaelic)* ♂   RATING: ★★
From the glen
> People think of Glenn as funny, handsome, intelligent, caring, trustworthy
> People who like the name Glenn also like Ethan, Daniel, Gabriel, Ian, Jacob, Jason, Joshua, Nathan, Aaron, Glen

Glenna *(American)* ♀   RATING: ★★★★
From the glen—Feminine form of Glen
> People think of Glenna as pretty, funny, caring, intelligent, popular
> People who like the name Glenna also like Grace, Erin, Genevieve, Gillian, Bella, Isabella, Felicity, Gabrielle, Gwen, Evangeline

Glennis *(American)* ♀   RATING: ★☆
Pure, holy—Variation of Glenys or Glynis
> People think of Glennis as intelligent, caring, creative, pretty, funny
> People who like the name Glennis also like Glenys, Giselle, Genevieve, Glynis, Aurora, Skyla, Maeve, Margot, Odessa, Laurel

Glenys *(Celtic/Gaelic)* ♀   RATING: ★★★
Pure, holy
> People think of Glenys as pretty, trustworthy, caring, funny, intelligent
> People who like the name Glenys also like Ryann, Keely, Glynis, Meara, Ceana, Aeryn, Maeve, Bella, Kaelyn, Alana

Glora *(Latin)* ♀   RATING: ★★★
Glory—Variation of Gloria
> People think of Glora as pretty, intelligent, funny, popular, caring
> People who like the name Glora also like Flora, Faith, Emily, Gloria, Estelle, Isabelle, Cassandra, Isabel, Emma, Felicia

Gloria *(Latin)* ♀   RATING: ★★☆
Glory—Gloria Estefan, singer; Gloria Vanderbilt, fashion designer; "Gloria," song by Van Morrison
> People think of Gloria as caring, pretty, funny, intelligent, creative
> People who like the name Gloria also like Grace, Faith, Hannah, Gabrielle, Gabriella, Hailey, Olivia, Elizabeth, Emma, Natalie

Gloriann *(American)* ♀   RATING: ★★★
Combination of Gloria and Ann
> People think of Gloriann as funny, creative, trustworthy, intelligent, old-fashioned
> People who like the name Gloriann also like Gabriella, Gabrielle, Isabella, Gloria, Grace, Gianna, Glory, Veronica, Isabelle, Emberlynn

Glory *(English)* ♀   RATING: ★★★☆
Glory
> People think of Glory as pretty, caring, trustworthy, intelligent, funny
> People who like the name Glory also like Faith, Grace, Hope, Harmony, Autumn, Hailey, Destiny, Jasmine, Gracie, Chloe

Glyn *(Welsh)* ♀♂   RATING: ★★
Valley
> People think of Glyn as funny, caring, handsome, weird, cool
> People who like the name Glyn also like Flynn, Glynn, Hayden, Dylan, Brynn, Halyn, Emlyn, Shea, Blair, Hunter

Glynis *(Welsh)* ♀   RATING: ★☆
Pure, holy; valley
> People think of Glynis as pretty, intelligent, funny, creative, caring
> People who like the name Glynis also like Glenys, Bree, Fiona, Rhiannon, Moira, Arwen, Genevieve, Glynnis, Aeryn, Shayla

Glynn *(Welsh)* ♀♂   RATING: ★★★☆
Valley, vale—Originally only for males, but now acceptable for both sexes
> People think of Glynn as intelligent, creative, leader, cool, trustworthy
> People who like the name Glynn also like Glyn, Hayden, Morgan, Riley, Hadley, Corbin, Flynn, Jaden, Hunter, Carey

Glynnis *(American)* ♀   RATING: ★★★
Pure, holy
> People think of Glynnis as creative, intelligent, cool, pretty, caring
> People who like the name Glynnis also like Glynis, Gillian, Fiona, Breanna, Erin, Genevieve, Brenna, Bella, Glenys, Ryann

Godana *(African)* ♂   RATING: ★★
Male child
> People think of Godana as religious, handsome, exotic, caring, wild
> People who like the name Godana also like Davu, Bryson, Dekel, Diallo, Gagan, Gyan, Guban, Dragan, Abu, Darren

Godfrey *(English)* ♂   RATING: ★★★
God peace
> People think of Godfrey as intelligent, caring, religious, cool, wealthy
> People who like the name Godfrey also like Joshua, Gabriel, Jeremiah, Elijah, Geoffrey, Gideon, Giovanni, Jacob, Gerard, Fletcher

Golda *(English)* ♀   RATING: ★★★☆
Made of gold
> People think of Golda as sexy, pretty, caring, powerful, elegant
> People who like the name Golda also like Fiona, Grace, Scarlett, Bella, Gwyneth, Goldie, Laurel, Juliette, Bianca, Hope

Goldie *(English)* ♀   RATING: ★★★
Made of gold—Short for Golda; Goldie Hawn, actress
> People think of Goldie as funny, pretty, caring, popular, trustworthy
> People who like the name Goldie also like Gracie, Hope, Gabriella, Claire, Emily, Ivy, Ginger, Bella, Daphne, Gigi

Goldy *(English)* ♀   RATING: ★★☆
Made of gold—Short for Golda
People think of Goldy as funny, popular, intelligent, energetic, young
People who like the name Goldy also like Ivy, Hope, Goldie, Georgianna, Jemma, Marissa, Charity, Ethel, Bella, Victoria

Gomer *(Hebrew)* ♂   RATING: ★☆
To complete—*Gomer Pyle*, TV show
People think of Gomer as loser, poor, unpopular, weird, slow
People who like the name Gomer also like Griffin, Drake, Elroy, Felix, Gage, Flint, Finn, Dawson, Brock, Beau

Gordon *(English)* ♂   RATING: ★★
From Gordon, Scotland—Gordon Ramsay, chef/TV host/author
People think of Gordon as funny, intelligent, handsome, cool, caring
People who like the name Gordon also like Gavin, Ethan, Ian, Isaac, Caleb, Jacob, Gabriel, Aaron, Nicholas, Benjamin

Gordy *(English)* ♂   RATING: ★★★
From Gordon, Scotland—Short for Gordon
People think of Gordy as funny, nerdy, trustworthy, handsome, weird
People who like the name Gordy also like Gordon, Gabriel, Grayson, Cody, Jason, Gabe, Garrick, Holden, Jayden, Griffin

Gore *(English)* ♂   RATING: ★★☆
Triangular-shaped land—Gore Vidal, author; Al Gore, politician
People think of Gore as sneaky, lazy, aggressive, untrustworthy, big
People who like the name Gore also like Maddox, Grayson, Jackson, Ace, Brock, Heath, Griffin, Gram, Hampton, Tony

Goro *(Japanese)* ♂   RATING: ★☆
Fifth
People think of Goro as big, nerdy, ethnic, poor, lazy
People who like the name Goro also like Hiroshi, Haru, Haruki, Akio, Keitaro, Kaemon, Keiji, Makoto, Jiro, Ryu

Govind *(Sanskrit/East Indian)* ♂   RATING: ★★☆
Rescuer of the Earth
People think of Govind as powerful, exotic, intelligent, handsome, trustworthy
People who like the name Govind also like Gagan, Gautam, Gyan, Chatura, Devesh, Karan, Divyesh, Ketan, Kaushal, Jag

Grace *(Latin)* ♀   RATING: ★★★★
Grace of God—Grace Jones, singer/model; Grace Kelly, actress/princess of Monaco
People think of Grace as pretty, caring, intelligent, funny, elegant
People who like the name Grace also like Emma, Ava, Hannah, Faith, Olivia, Isabella, Ella, Abigail, Chloe, Emily

Graceland *(American)* ♀♂   RATING: ★★★
Land of Grace—Estate of Elvis Presley
People think of Graceland as pretty, elegant, exotic, funny, caring
People who like the name Graceland also like Cassidy, Bailey, Hayden, Brooklyn, Dakota, Madison, Addison, Kendall, Parker, Brady

Gracie *(English)* ♀   RATING: ★★★★
Grace of God—Short for Grace
People think of Gracie as pretty, caring, funny, intelligent, creative
People who like the name Gracie also like Grace, Emma, Olivia, Hannah, Faith, Ava, Isabella, Ella, Hailey, Chloe

Graciela *(Spanish)* ♀   RATING: ★★★★
Grace
People think of Graciela as pretty, creative, caring, intelligent, funny
People who like the name Graciela also like Grace, Isabella, Gabriella, Gabriela, Gracie, Gianna, Gabrielle, Ava, Giselle, Olivia

Gradin *(American)* ♂   RATING: ★★★☆
Of high rank—Variation of Grady
People think of Gradin as handsome, boy next door, cool, leader, intelligent
People who like the name Gradin also like Grayson, Gavin, Ethan, Aiden, Kaden, Braden, Gage, Landon, Grady, Grant

Grady *(Celtic/Gaelic)* ♂   RATING: ★★★★
Of high rank
People think of Grady as handsome, caring, popular, intelligent, funny
People who like the name Grady also like Gavin, Ethan, Grant, Grayson, Aiden, Jackson, Noah, Caleb, Conner, Ian

Graham *(English)* ♂   RATING: ★★☆
From Grantham, England
People think of Graham as handsome, intelligent, funny, caring, trustworthy
People who like the name Graham also like Ethan, Grant, Gavin, Owen, Jackson, Ian, Gabriel, Noah, Landon, Aiden

Gram *(English)* ♂   RATING: ★★★
Variation of Graham
People think of Gram as handsome, intelligent, young, nerdy, caring
People who like the name Gram also like Ethan, Graham, Kaden, Grayson, Jack, Grant, Jackson, Gage, Gavin, Dalton

Granger *(English)* ♂   RATING: ★★★
Farmer
People think of Granger as trustworthy, handsome, intelligent, cool, caring
People who like the name Granger also like Jackson, Gage, Grady, Grayson, Holden, Gavin, Garrison, Graham, Colton, Griffin

Grant *(Celtic/Gaelic)* ♂   RATING: ★★★
Great—Grant Wood, artist
> People think of Grant as handsome, intelligent, funny, cool, popular
> People who like the name Grant also like Ethan, Gavin, Owen, Ian, Cole, Gabriel, Caleb, Jackson, Aiden, Graham

Granville *(French)* ♂   RATING: ★☆
Large village
> People think of Granville as caring, cool, funny, intelligent, trustworthy
> People who like the name Granville also like Gaston, Dashiell, Gordon, Garrick, Percival, Garrison, Gaylord, Griffin, André, Galahad

Gratia *(Italian)* ♀   RATING: ★★
Grace
> People think of Gratia as pretty, exotic, energetic, elegant, powerful
> People who like the name Gratia also like Gratiana, Gianna, Isabella, Aria, Giovanna, Hazel, Bella, Grace, Fiorenza, Ariana

Gratiana *(Italian)* ♀   RATING: ★★
Grace
> People think of Gratiana as pretty, leader, sexy, elegant, creative
> People who like the name Gratiana also like Gianna, Isabella, Giovanna, Gratia, Luciana, Natalia, Adriana, Arianna, Grace, Ariana

Gray *(English)* ♂   RATING: ★★★☆
Color—Originally one with gray hair
> People think of Gray as intelligent, creative, handsome, cool, leader
> People who like the name Gray also like Grayson, Jackson, Gavin, Ethan, Gabriel, Owen, Graham, Luke, Jack, Grady

Grayson *(English)* ♂   RATING: ★★★★
Son of the gray-haired one
> People think of Grayson as handsome, intelligent, popular, leader, trustworthy
> People who like the name Grayson also like Ethan, Gavin, Jackson, Landon, Noah, Braden, Aiden, Kaden, Caleb, Holden

Grazia *(Italian)* ♀   RATING: ★★★
Grace
> People think of Grazia as exotic, leader, pretty, trendy, elegant
> People who like the name Grazia also like Natalia, Gabriella, Isabella, Olivia, Gemma, Gianna, Gratia, Mariana, Giovanna, Ella

Graziella *(Italian)* ♀   RATING: ★★★★
Lovely, with grace—Also spelled Graciela
> People think of Graziella as pretty, sexy, intelligent, exotic, trustworthy
> People who like the name Graziella also like Isabella, Gianna, Giovanna, Bianca, Graciela, Gabriella, Camilla, Natalia, Angelina, Adriana

Greco *(Italian)* ♂   RATING: ★★☆
From Greece—Also a surname; El Greco, artist
> People think of Greco as handsome, exotic, powerful, intelligent, popular
> People who like the name Greco also like Andrew, Leo, Canon, Brian, Giovanni, Brandon, Gabe, Benjamin, Jarrett, Draco

Greer *(Celtic/Gaelic)* ♀♂   RATING: ★★★☆
Watchful, guardian
> People think of Greer as intelligent, creative, pretty, funny, leader
> People who like the name Greer also like Parker, Avery, Logan, Addison, Hayden, Reagan, Riley, Aidan, Quinn, Reese

Greg *(Greek)* ♂   RATING: ★★☆
Vigilant, watchful—Short for Gregory; Greg Kinnear, actor; Greg Oden, athlete
> People think of Greg as funny, cool, handsome, caring, intelligent
> People who like the name Greg also like Ethan, Nathan, Jack, Ian, Jared, Adam, David, Luke, Jason, Aaron

Gregg *(Greek)* ♂   RATING: ★★★☆
Vigilant, watchful—Short for Gregory
> People think of Gregg as funny, handsome, intelligent, cool, caring
> People who like the name Gregg also like Aaron, Gregory, Ethan, Isaac, Jacob, Jason, Anthony, Noah, Adam, Chad

Gregory *(Greek)* ♂   RATING: ★★☆
Vigilant, watchful
> People think of Gregory as handsome, intelligent, funny, caring, trustworthy
> People who like the name Gregory also like Matthew, Benjamin, Ethan, Nicholas, Jacob, Alexander, Andrew, Zachary, Gabriel, Daniel

Grenier *(French)* ♂   RATING: ★★
Grainery keeper—Adrian Grenier, actor
> People think of Grenier as poor, quiet, unpopular, weird, loser
> People who like the name Grenier also like Waylon, Dermot, Demetrius, Deiter, Davis, Titus, Dalton, Constantine, Draco, Cleavant

Greta *(German)* ♀   RATING: ★★★★
A pearl—Short for Margaret
> People think of Greta as pretty, intelligent, creative, funny, caring
> People who like the name Greta also like Grace, Ava, Ella, Isabella, Gretchen, Olivia, Hannah, Eva, Audrey, Claire

Gretchen *(German)* ♀   RATING: ★★
A pearl—Variation of Margaret
> People think of Gretchen as pretty, intelligent, funny, creative, caring
> People who like the name Gretchen also like Grace, Olivia, Hannah, Emma, Isabella, Abigail, Gabrielle, Faith, Paige, Claire

Gretel *(German)* ♀ RATING: ★★★☆
A pearl—Variation of Margaret; *Hansel and Gretel*, fairy tale
> People think of Gretel as pretty, intelligent, caring, creative, funny
> People who like the name Gretel also like Greta, Ava, Gabrielle, Gretchen, Isabella, Grace, Giselle, Liesel, Layla, Hannah

Grietje *(Dutch)* ♀ RATING: ★★★☆
A pearl—Variation of Margriet or Margaret
> People think of Grietje as caring, old-fashioned, quiet, popular, weird
> People who like the name Grietje also like Genevieve, Esme, Arwen, Eliora, Grace, Gracie, Nixie, Gianna, Giovanna, Della

Griffin *(Welsh)* ♂ RATING: ★★★★
From gryphon, a fabled monster—Griffin Dunne, actor; Merv Griffin, TV producer
> People think of Griffin as handsome, intelligent, cool, leader, popular
> People who like the name Griffin also like Ethan, Gavin, Owen, Jackson, Grayson, Noah, Landon, Aiden, Caleb, Gabriel

Griffith *(Welsh)* ♂ RATING: ★★★☆
Griffin lord—Andy Griffith, actor
> People think of Griffith as powerful, aggressive, funny, leader, intelligent
> People who like the name Griffith also like Griffin, Gavin, Gabriel, Ethan, Owen, Jacob, Graham, Tristan, Grayson, Garrett

Griselda *(German)* ♀ RATING: ★☆
Gray battle
> People think of Griselda as intelligent, pretty, caring, funny, creative
> People who like the name Griselda also like Priscilla, Larissa, Cassandra, Grizelda, Mara, Daphne, Iris, Cordelia, Greta, Cecilia

Grizelda *(German)* ♀ RATING: ★★☆
Variation of Griselda; the medieval morality tale "Patient Grissel" (or "Patient Griselda")
> People think of Grizelda as pretty, weird, popular, intelligent, aggressive
> People who like the name Grizelda also like Giselle, Griselda, Isis, Harmony, Faith, Daphne, Bianca, Chantal, Helena, Jennelle

Grover *(English)* ♂ RATING: ★★
From the grove—Grover Cleveland Alexander, baseball player; Grover Cleveland, U.S. president; Grover, character on *Sesame Street*
> People think of Grover as aggressive, old-fashioned, powerful, big, funny
> People who like the name Grover also like Graham, Griffin, Fletcher, Holden, Jack, Jackson, Ethan, Miles, Gavin, Brooks

Gryphon *(Greek)* ♀ ♂ RATING: ★★★☆
Mythological beast—Variation of Griffin
> People think of Gryphon as aggressive, powerful, wild, intelligent, handsome
> People who like the name Gryphon also like Hayden, Phoenix, Dylan, Orion, Quinn, Caden, Aidan, Cadence, Ryder, Rowan

Gryta *(Polish)* ♀ RATING: ★★
A pearl—Variation of Margaret
> People think of Gryta as weird, intelligent, religious, energetic, funny
> People who like the name Gryta also like Greta, Giselle, Iola, Gretel, Ghita, Helena, Candace, Gretchen, Enya, Electra

Guadalupe *(Spanish)* ♀ RATING: ★★★★
River of black stones—From the title of the Virgin Mary; also spelled Guadelupe
> People think of Guadalupe as pretty, caring, funny, intelligent, trustworthy
> People who like the name Guadalupe also like Mercedes, Adriana, Destiny, Bella, Ginger, Grace, Bianca, Jasmine, Marisol, Isabella

Gualtier *(Italian)* ♂ RATING: ★☆
Army ruler—Variation of Walter
> People think of Gualtier as loser, nerdy, lazy, exotic, uptight
> People who like the name Gualtier also like Giancarlo, Giacomo, Gideon, Giovanni, Gabriel, Gitano, Gaetano, Giulio, Benito, Drake

Guang *(Chinese)* ♂ RATING: ★★★
Light
> People think of Guang as quiet, nerdy, intelligent, weird, elegant
> People who like the name Guang also like Grady, Gradin, Galvin, Garth, Goro, Fadey, Feleti, Faris, Felix, Gavan

Guban *(African)* ♂ RATING: ★★
Burnt—Somali origin
> People think of Guban as weird, nerdy, funny, wild, handsome
> People who like the name Guban also like Gazali, Haben, Davu, Edgar, Farrell, Gareth, Hajari, Ilo, Bahari, Kimoni

Gudrun *(Scandinavian)* ♀ RATING: ★★★
God's secret
> People think of Gudrun as big, aggressive, lazy, slow, intelligent
> People who like the name Gudrun also like Gersemi, Isolde, Mahala, Ingrid, Elisabeth, Enye, Ailis, Ginger, Gunda, Iris

Guenevere *(Welsh)* ♀ RATING: ★★★★☆
White ghost, phantom
> People think of Guenevere as elegant, pretty, creative, intelligent, artsy

People who like the name Guenevere also like Genevieve, Gwendolyn, Isabella, Gwyneth, Guinevere, Gabrielle, Aurora, Fiona, Abigail, Emma

Guido *(Italian)* ♂   RATING: ★★★☆
Forest guide
People think of Guido as intelligent, funny, handsome, lazy, caring
People who like the name Guido also like Giovanni, Ethan, Basil, Felix, Dominic, Jack, Bruno, Edward, Glen, Maxwell

Guiliaine *(French)* ♀   RATING: ★★★
Hostage—Variation of Ghislaine
People think of Guiliaine as weird, wealthy, young, religious, intelligent
People who like the name Guiliaine also like Gianna, Genevieve, Charlotte, Guenevere, Bianca, Grace, Gigi, Felicia, Giovanna, Daphne

Guillermina *(Spanish)* ♀   RATING: ★☆
Strong-willed warrior—Feminine form of Guillermo
People think of Guillermina as funny, caring, trustworthy, creative, pretty
People who like the name Guillermina also like Gabriella, Janet, Carmelita, Ginger, Fern, Gypsy, Garnet, Freira, Georgianna, Floramaria

Guillermo *(Spanish)* ♂   RATING: ★★★☆
Strong-willed warrior—Variation of William; pronounced *gee-YEHR-mo* with a hard *G*
People think of Guillermo as funny, handsome, intelligent, caring, sexy
People who like the name Guillermo also like Fernando, Gabriel, Fabian, Esteban, Enrique, Antonio, Carlos, Federico, Felix, Marco

Guinevere *(Welsh)* ♀   RATING: ★★★★
White ghost, phantom—Also spelled Guinivere
People think of Guinevere as pretty, elegant, intelligent, artsy, creative
People who like the name Guinevere also like Genevieve, Gwendolyn, Gwyneth, Isabella, Olivia, Aurora, Giselle, Fiona, Grace, Hannah

Gunda *(Scandinavian)* ♀   RATING: ★★☆
Female warrior
People think of Gunda as aggressive, powerful, big, weird, criminal
People who like the name Gunda also like Brynja, Gretel, Sonja, Bryndis, Zelda, Brenda, Fjola, Synnove, Inga, Ingrid

Gunesh *(Turkish)* ♀♂   RATING: ★★
The sun
People think of Gunesh as popular, funny, young
People who like the name Gunesh also like Cain, Nyoka, Brody, Blake, Connor, Barrett, Coby, Nyako, Channing

Gunnar *(Scandinavian)* ♂   RATING: ★★★★
Battle warrior
People think of Gunnar as handsome, powerful, leader, aggressive, intelligent

People who like the name Gunnar also like Gavin, Gage, Kaden, Gabriel, Owen, Ethan, Jackson, Braden, Caleb, Grayson

Gunther *(German)* ♂   RATING: ★★
War army
People think of Gunther as handsome, powerful, leader, cool, aggressive
People who like the name Gunther also like Ethan, Gunnar, Aiden, Gavin, Tristan, Dawson, Gabriel, Gage, Jacob, Luke

Gur *(Hebrew)* ♂   RATING: ★★★
Baby lion
People think of Gur as weird, aggressive, criminal, unpopular, loser
People who like the name Gur also like Lev, Joel, Alijah, Ewan, Iram, Casper, Caleb, Aden, Fynn, Kaleb

Guri *(Sanskrit/East Indian)* ♀   RATING: ★★☆
Hindu goddess of plenty
People think of Guri as ethnic, exotic, old-fashioned, young, funny
People who like the name Guri also like Kali, Chandra, Devi, Jaya, Jui, Leela, Amara, Medea, Isis, Hina

Gurit *(Hebrew)* ♀   RATING: ★★
Young lion
People think of Gurit as weird, pretty, exotic, criminal, young
People who like the name Gurit also like Guri, Ceri, Cecilia, Freya, Magdalene, Sema, Elvina, Erica, Guadalupe, Jamila

Gurnam *(Sanskrit/East Indian)* ♂   RATING: ★★☆
Name of the guru
People think of Gurnam as loser, nerdy, old-fashioned, powerful, weird
People who like the name Gurnam also like Charan, Divyesh, Deepak, Kaushal, Dinesh, Gaurav, Hajari, Divakar, Gagan, Gautam

Gus *(English)* ♂   RATING: ★★★☆
Short for Gustav, Angus, or August
People think of Gus as funny, handsome, caring, big, cool
People who like the name Gus also like Oliver, Oscar, Jack, Gabe, Noah, Isaac, Ethan, Henry, Eli, Jacob

Gustav *(German)* ♂   RATING: ★☆
Staff of the Goths
People think of Gustav as intelligent, trustworthy, cool, funny, handsome
People who like the name Gustav also like Gabriel, Ethan, Felix, Aiden, Isaac, Jacob, Caleb, Oliver, Tristan, Alexander

Gustave *(French)* ♂   RATING: ★★★
Staff of the Goths
People think of Gustave as powerful, big, leader, artsy, old-fashioned

People who like the name Gustave also like Gustav, Aiden, Charles, Ivan, Jacob, Frederick, Vincent, Gabriel, Hamlet, Frank

Gustavo *(Italian)* ♂ RATING: ★☆
Staff of the Goths
People think of Gustavo as handsome, funny, intelligent, cool, sexy
People who like the name Gustavo also like Gabriel, Fabian, Giovanni, Adrian, Adam, Jacob, Isaac, Enrique, Benjamin, Fernando

Gusty *(American)* ♀ ♂ RATING: ★★☆
Revered, windy—Short for Augusta or August
People think of Gusty as energetic, trustworthy, young, creative, loser
People who like the name Gusty also like Ember, Casey, Hadley, Echo, Cameron, Lyric, Lavender, Cadence, Dacey, Madison

Guthrie *(Celtic/Gaelic)* ♂ RATING: ★☆
From the windy place—Woody Guthrie, singer/songwriter
People think of Guthrie as intelligent, creative, handsome, caring, aggressive
People who like the name Guthrie also like Liam, Griffin, Ewan, Finley, Garrison, Sullivan, Grady, Desmond, Owen, Donovan

Guy *(German/French)* ♂ RATING: ★★★☆
Unknown meaning—Also a familiar word for a male person
People think of Guy as intelligent, handsome, funny, cool, sexy
People who like the name Guy also like Jacob, Aiden, Ethan, Ian, Oliver, Gabriel, Jack, Elijah, Cole, Isaac

Guzman *(Spanish)* ♂ RATING: ★★
Good man—Luis Guzman, actor
People think of Guzman as funny, cool, sexy, criminal, popular
People who like the name Guzman also like Raymond, Victor, Mauricio, Ricardo, Edgar, David, Diego, Rufus, Damien, Daneil

Gwen *(Welsh)* ♀ RATING: ★★★★
Blessed ring—Short for Gwendolyn; Gwen Stefani, singer
People think of Gwen as pretty, funny, creative, intelligent, caring
People who like the name Gwen also like Grace, Emma, Ava, Faith, Hannah, Gwyneth, Ella, Eva, Olivia, Hailey

Gwendolyn *(Welsh)* ♀ RATING: ★★☆
Blessed ring
People think of Gwendolyn as pretty, intelligent, creative, caring, funny
People who like the name Gwendolyn also like Genevieve, Gwyneth, Grace, Isabella, Gabrielle, Abigail, Olivia, Emma, Hannah, Charlotte

Gwenifer *(Welsh)* ♀ RATING: ★★★
White ghost, phantom
People think of Gwenifer as pretty, elegant, sexy, stuck-up, weird
People who like the name Gwenifer also like Gwendolyn, Genevieve, Guenevere, Gabrielle, Giselle, Gwen, Gwyneth, Isabella, Cassandra, Faith

Gwenllian *(Welsh)* ♀ RATING: ★★★
White flood
People think of Gwenllian as pretty, quiet, elegant, slow, intelligent
People who like the name Gwenllian also like Gwendolyn, Genevieve, Gwyneth, Gwennan, Gwenifer, Emma, Guenevere, Caelan, Jillian, Grace

Gwennan *(Welsh)* ♀ RATING: ★★★☆
Blessed
People think of Gwennan as pretty, funny, intelligent, creative, elegant
People who like the name Gwennan also like Gwyneth, Gwendolyn, Grace, Genevieve, Emma, Arwen, Gillian, Olivia, Caelan, Cailyn

Gwilym *(Welsh)* ♂ RATING: ★★★
Strong-willed warrior—Variation of William
People think of Gwilym as intelligent, handsome, aggressive, sexy, trustworthy
People who like the name Gwilym also like Gwydion, Faris, Gavan, Broderick, Byram, Fletcher, Gaius, Guthrie, Bowie, Dewey

Gwydion *(Welsh)* ♂ RATING: ★★★★
God of magic
People think of Gwydion as intelligent, powerful, leader, handsome, artsy
People who like the name Gwydion also like Gareth, Gideon, Gavin, Gavan, Gabriel, Drake, Galahad, Aiden, Edan, Elijah

Gwylan *(Welsh)* ♀ RATING: ★★★
Seagull
People think of Gwylan as unpopular, old-fashioned, lazy, nerdy, elegant
People who like the name Gwylan also like Gwyneth, Gwendolyn, Gwen, Rhiannon, Elwyn, Gwennan, Caelan, Ciara, Genevieve, Morwen

Gwyn *(Welsh)* ♂ RATING: ★★☆
Fair, white, blessed
People think of Gwyn as pretty, creative, caring, intelligent, funny
People who like the name Gwyn also like Gavin, Ethan, Ian, Owen, Kaden, Cole, Aiden, Landon, Jayden, Liam

Gwyneth *(Welsh)* ♀ RATING: ★★☆
Fortunate, blessed—Gwyneth Paltrow, actress
People think of Gwyneth as pretty, elegant, intelligent, creative, artsy
People who like the name Gwyneth also like Grace, Gwendolyn, Genevieve, Emma, Hannah, Ava, Abigail, Isabella, Olivia, Gabrielle

Gyala *(Hungarian)* ♂ RATING: ★★
Downy—Variation of Julius
People think of Gyala as nerdy, artsy, popular, trendy, old-fashioned
People who like the name Gyala also like Damian, Gabe, Ethan, Gabriel, Grayson, Maddock, Abraham, Hagan, Asher, Dashiell

Gyan *(Sanskrit/East Indian)* ♂ RATING: ★★★☆
Knowledge
People think of Gyan as intelligent, handsome, cool, leader, creative
People who like the name Gyan also like Grant, Grayson, Ethan, Gabriel, Gideon, Liam, Gagan, Gage, Edan, Gaurav

Gyda *(Scandinavian)* ♀ RATING: ★★★
Gods
People think of Gyda as old-fashioned, exotic, nerdy, slow, weird
People who like the name Gyda also like Jana, Florence, Inga, Ingrid, Isabella, Maegan, Gabrielle, Corinne, Giselle, Jordana

Gypsy *(English)* ♀ RATING: ★★
A bohemian traveler—Gypsy Rose Lee, dancer
People think of Gypsy as pretty, exotic, creative, wild, artsy
People who like the name Gypsy also like Faith, Grace, Harmony, Aurora, Jasmine, Bella, Scarlett, Ava, Ivy, Celeste

Gyula *(Hungarian)* ♂ RATING: ★★☆
Downy—Variation of Julius
People think of Gyula as intelligent, sexy, uptight, girl next door, loser
People who like the name Gyula also like Elijah, Gershom, Filbert, Gaylord, Darnell, Gwydion, Buzz, Gyan, Galahad, Giovanni

Gzifa *(African)* ♀ RATING: ★★★
Peaceful one—Ghanaian origin
People think of Gzifa as trustworthy, pretty, poor, unpopular, loser
People who like the name Gzifa also like Dysis, Femi, Nysa, Seanna, Gaia, Gemma, Mahal, Ina, Jia Li, Kya

Ha *(Vietnamese)* ♀ RATING: ★☆
Sunshine, warmth
People think of Ha as intelligent, pretty, funny, caring, aggressive
People who like the name Ha also like Dysis, Enya, Hazel, Lana, Katrina, Electra, Hannah, Halo, Calista, Helga

Haben *(African)* ♂ RATING: ★★★☆
Pride
People think of Haben as caring, powerful, cool, handsome, funny

People who like the name Haben also like Ethan, Aden, Ian, Owen, Nathan, Holden, Isaac, Wade, Kaden, Drake

Habib *(Arabic)* ♂ RATING: ★★★
Beloved one
People think of Habib as cool, handsome, intelligent, exotic, sexy
People who like the name Habib also like David, Jabir, Faris, Fabian, Elijah, Isaac, Jamal, Holden, Hashim, Emanuel

Hachi *(Japanese)* ♀ ♂ RATING: ★☆
Eight
People think of Hachi as energetic, caring, trendy, trustworthy, funny
People who like the name Hachi also like Hoshi, Kishi, Cade, Misu, Sanyu, Hiroko, Kai, Helki, Dakota, Mika

Hada *(African)* ♀ RATING: ★★
Salty place
People think of Hada as stuck-up, quiet, trustworthy, young, leader
People who like the name Hada also like Grace, Faith, Heaven, Ayanna, Aurora, Gwyneth, Hailey, Harmony, Fayola, Eternity

Hadar *(Hebrew)* ♀ ♂ RATING: ★★★
Splendor, glory
People think of Hadar as pretty, leader, creative, winner, energetic
People who like the name Hadar also like Eden, Hayden, Camden, Ezra, Jade, Raven, Kiran, Nolan, Sasha, Gael

Hadassah *(Hebrew)* ♀ RATING: ★★★☆
Myrtle tree
People think of Hadassah as religious, pretty, intelligent, trustworthy, caring
People who like the name Hadassah also like Hannah, Gabrielle, Emma, Elizabeth, Chloe, Ella, Esther, Isabella, Abigail, Gwendolyn

Hades *(Greek)* ♂ RATING: ★★★
Sightless—Also a name for Hell
People think of Hades as aggressive, powerful, sexy, criminal, wild
People who like the name Hades also like Drake, Damien, Gabriel, Blade, Kaden, Sirius, Kael, Chase, Aiden, Felix

Hadley *(English)* ♀ ♂ RATING: ★★★
From Hadda's Field—Also a surname; Tony Hadley, singer
People think of Hadley as pretty, intelligent, popular, creative, funny
People who like the name Hadley also like Hayden, Addison, Avery, Bailey, Caden, Parker, Riley, Logan, Cadence, Madison

Hadria *(Greek)* ♀ RATING: ★★★
Town in Northern Italy—Old spelling of the modern city Adria, Italy
People think of Hadria as funny, cool, wild, sporty, young

People who like the name Hadria also like Gabriella, Cambria, Adrina, Audrey, Ophelia, Luna, Iris, Bronwyn, Nixie, Magnolia

Hafwen *(Welsh)* ♀　　　RATING: ★★★☆
Summer blessed
> People think of Hafwen as pretty, unpopular, ethnic, aggressive, quiet
> People who like the name Hafwen also like Aislin, Bronwyn, Arwen, Isolde, Elle, Bronwen, Gwyneth, Aelwen, Telyn, Grace

Hagan *(English)* ♂　　　RATING: ★★★★
Protector—Originally a surname
> People think of Hagan as handsome, popular, intelligent, cool, young
> People who like the name Hagan also like Kaden, Hagen, Holden, Keagan, Gavin, Aiden, Ian, Gage, Landon, Jayden

Hagen *(English)* ♂　　　RATING: ★★
Variation of Hagan
> People think of Hagen as handsome, intelligent, young, creative, trustworthy
> People who like the name Hagen also like Hagan, Kaden, Aiden, Holden, Ethan, Braden, Owen, Walker, Landon, Gavin

Hagop *(Armenian)* ♂　　　RATING: ★★★
Supplanter—Variation of Jacob
> People think of Hagop as sexy, handsome, weird, energetic, intelligent
> People who like the name Hagop also like Fabio, Qabil, Santo, Daire, Faris, Ea, Jaser, Damien, Yahto, Darren

Haig *(English)* ♂　　　RATING: ★★★
Enclosure—Also a surname; also an Armenian name meaning giant
> People think of Haig as weird, loser, winner, wild, nerdy
> People who like the name Haig also like Hagen, Emerson, Jebediah, Fai, Isaac, Ethan, Everett, Jonah, Noah, Hampton

Haile *(English)* ♀　　　RATING: ★★★
From the hay clearing
> People think of Haile as pretty, popular, funny, cool, young
> People who like the name Haile also like Hailey, Hannah, Jadyn, Faith, Isabella, Hallie, Kailey, Paige, Emma, Ava

Hailey *(English)* ♀　　　RATING: ★★★☆
From the hay clearing
> People think of Hailey as pretty, funny, caring, creative, intelligent
> People who like the name Hailey also like Hannah, Emma, Paige, Faith, Isabella, Abigail, Chloe, Grace, Emily, Olivia

Haines *(English)* ♂　　　RATING: ★★★★
Dweller by the enclosure
> People think of Haines as intelligent, funny, young, artsy, quiet

People who like the name Haines also like Holden, Landon, Hanley, Dalton, Grayson, Jackson, Lawson, Harrison, Emerson, Jamison

Hajar *(Arabic)* ♀　　　RATING: ★★★★
Very hot afternoon
> People think of Hajar as pretty, intelligent, creative, cool, religious
> People who like the name Hajar also like Femi, Farah, Ha, Fareeda, Hala, Cala, Haracha, Candy, Callia, Felice

Hajari *(Sanskrit/East Indian)* ♂　　　RATING: ★★★
Commander of more than one thousand soldiers
> People think of Hajari as powerful, cool, ethnic, winner, unpopular
> People who like the name Hajari also like Ajani, Isaiah, Jabari, Dyami, Darshan, Jamar, Kimoni, Jatin, Hashim, Zachariah

Hakan *(Scandinavian)* ♂　　　RATING: ★★★★
From the high dynasty—Variation of Haakon
> People think of Hakan as handsome, powerful, sexy, popular, aggressive
> People who like the name Hakan also like Kael, Kaden, Keagan, Galen, Gavin, Tyson, Aiden, Dasan, Blade, Ian

Hal *(English)* ♂　　　RATING: ★★★☆
Army ruler—Short for Harold; Hal Holden, actor; Hal Linden, actor
> People think of Hal as funny, caring, handsome, intelligent, popular
> People who like the name Hal also like Ian, Jacob, Jack, Chase, Colin, Cole, Caleb, Conner, Owen, Luke

Hala *(Arabic)* ♀　　　RATING: ★★★☆
Halo, ring, glory
> People think of Hala as pretty, caring, intelligent, funny, trustworthy
> People who like the name Hala also like Hana, Inara, Eva, Isabella, Faith, Grace, Hazel, Kiara, Cala, Natalie

Halden *(Scandinavian)* ♂　　　RATING: ★★
Half-Danish
> People think of Halden as aggressive, winner, wild, sexy, wealthy
> People who like the name Halden also like Holden, Braden, Kaden, Aiden, Alden, Jackson, Maddox, Harrison, Jayden, Grayson

Haldis *(Scandinavian)* ♀♂　　　RATING: ★★★
Stone spirit
> People think of Haldis as powerful, trustworthy, leader, intelligent, wild
> People who like the name Haldis also like Hadley, Dante, Halyn, Morgan, Sawyer, Arya, Nida, London, Parker, James

Halen *(English)* ♀♂　　　RATING: ★★★★
From the hay land
> People think of Halen as popular, intelligent, creative, handsome, cool

People who like the name Halen also like Hayden, Caden, Jaden, Halyn, Hadley, Landen, Cadence, Addison, Haley, Haven

Haley (*English*)　♀♂　　　RATING: ★★★☆
From the hay clearing—Haley Joel Osment, actor
People think of Haley as pretty, funny, creative, caring, intelligent
People who like the name Haley also like Madison, Hayden, Bailey, Riley, Taylor, Jaden, Logan, Jordan, Dylan, Ryan

Hali (*Greek*)　♀　　　RATING: ★★★
Sea
People think of Hali as pretty, funny, creative, intelligent, energetic
People who like the name Hali also like Hailey, Faith, Isabella, Chloe, Emma, Ava, Grace, Jadyn, Hannah, Paige

Halia (*Hawaiian*)　♀　　　RATING: ★★★★
Memorial
People think of Halia as pretty, cool, elegant, caring, exotic
People who like the name Halia also like Hannah, Malia, Isabelle, Hailey, Leilani, Gabriella, Hope, Kailani, Iliana, Chloe

Halima (*Arabic*)　♀　　　RATING: ★★★☆
Patient, tolerant
People think of Halima as pretty, intelligent, caring, leader, creative
People who like the name Halima also like Jahzara, Harmony, Hannah, Hazel, Hermione, Hasana, Ophelia, Adia, Helena, Iliana

Hall (*English*)　♂　　　RATING: ★★☆
From the manor
People think of Hall as popular, intelligent, funny, creative, sexy
People who like the name Hall also like Jackson, Nathan, Ethan, Jack, Maddox, Henry, Finley, Finn, Everett, Fox

Hallam (*English*)　♀♂　　　RATING: ★★☆
Dweller at the rocks
People think of Hallam as big, cool, old-fashioned, exotic, creative
People who like the name Hallam also like Caden, Halyn, Aidan, Willow, Connor, Haley, Jade, Charlie, Hadley, Hayden

Hallan (*English*)　♂　　　RATING: ★★★
Dweller at the rocks—Variation of Hallam
People think of Hallan as slow, intelligent, poor, old-fashioned, unpopular
People who like the name Hallan also like Holden, Cole, Hagan, Kael, Halden, Grayson, Kaden, Hagen, Jace, Maddox

Halle (*Scandinavian*)　♀　　　RATING: ★★★☆
Heroine—Halle Berry, actress
People think of Halle as pretty, intelligent, funny, popular, caring

People who like the name Halle also like Hailey, Grace, Hannah, Emma, Ava, Isabella, Paige, Faith, Ella, Olivia

Hallie (*English*)　♀　　　RATING: ★★★★
Praise the Lord; hallelujah
People think of Hallie as pretty, funny, creative, intelligent, caring
People who like the name Hallie also like Hailey, Hannah, Emma, Faith, Isabella, Grace, Paige, Chloe, Olivia, Callie

Hallmar (*Scandinavian*)　♂　　　RATING: ★★☆
Famous stone
People think of Hallmar as big, weird, ethnic, old-fashioned, handsome
People who like the name Hallmar also like Casimir, Faxon, Malachi, Soren, Mikhail, Miles, Dalton, Brice, Nathaniel, Vasilis

Halo (*Greek*)　♀　　　RATING: ★★★☆
Divine aura—Circle of light, usually depicted above the head of a holy person or angel
People think of Halo as cool, creative, trustworthy, exotic, caring
People who like the name Halo also like Harmony, Faith, Heaven, Hazel, Aurora, Genevieve, Hailey, Isis, Hope, Serenity

Halona (*Native American*)　♀　　　RATING: ★★★☆
Fortunate
People think of Halona as pretty, exotic, caring, intelligent, creative
People who like the name Halona also like Kaya, Hateya, Kachina, Kiona, Imala, Topanga, Hannah, Ayasha, Angeni, Chenoa

Halyn (*American*)　♀♂　　　RATING: ★★★★☆
Unique, special, unlike another—Possibly a combination of Haley and Lynn
People think of Halyn as pretty, creative, funny, cool, popular
People who like the name Halyn also like Hayden, Caden, Jaden, Cadence, Bailey, Aidan, Riley, Dylan, Jade, Madison

Ham (*Hebrew*)　♂　　　RATING: ★★★
Hot
People think of Ham as weird, loser, poor, sexy, nerdy
People who like the name Ham also like Aaron, Fox, Herbert, Feivel, David, Adam, Eli, Hans, Aden, Dan

Hamal (*Arabic*)　♂　　　RATING: ★★
Lamb
People think of Hamal as exotic, caring, ethnic, poor, intelligent
People who like the name Hamal also like Jamal, Faris, Amir, Hashim, Jamil, Habib, Tariq, Ghazi, Jaser, Jabir

Hamilton (*English*)　♀♂　　　RATING: ★★★☆
From Hamela's settlement
People think of Hamilton as intelligent, handsome, leader, sporty, powerful

People who like the name Hamilton also like Hayden, Hunter, Parker, Preston, Evan, Addison, Bailey, Carter, Madison, Harper

Hamish *(Celtic/Gaelic)* ♂   RATING: ★☆
Supplanter—Variation of James
People think of Hamish as intelligent, funny, handsome, caring, popular
People who like the name Hamish also like Lachlan, Isaac, Angus, Jack, Tristan, Oliver, Ewan, Declan, Jacob, Caleb

Hamlet *(English)* ♂   RATING: ★★★
Home—Short for Hamo; *Hamlet* by William Shakespeare
People think of Hamlet as old-fashioned, intelligent, handsome, leader, creative
People who like the name Hamlet also like Henry, Jacob, Noah, Alexander, Ethan, Benjamin, Gabriel, Jack, Isaac, Daniel

Hamlin *(English)* ♂   RATING: ★★
Home—Short for Hamo; also a surname; Harry Hamlin, actor
People think of Hamlin as nerdy, slow, loser, big, old-fashioned
People who like the name Hamlin also like Hampton, Harrison, Holden, Emerson, Ethan, Nathan, Gavin, Braden, Ian, Cole

Hammer *(English)* ♂   RATING: ★★★
Maker of hammers—Also means dweller in the village
People think of Hammer as aggressive, big, criminal, leader, loser
People who like the name Hammer also like Kaden, Tyson, Blade, Ethan, Nathan, Gage, Ian, Gunnar, Keagan, Tristan

Hampton *(English)* ♂   RATING: ★★★☆
From the village by the town—Originally a surname
People think of Hampton as leader, funny, intelligent, trendy, creative
People who like the name Hampton also like Holden, Jackson, Landon, Ethan, Dawson, Everett, Emerson, Harrison, Maddox, Heath

Hana *(Japanese)* ♀   RATING: ★★★
Bud, blossom
People think of Hana as pretty, caring, intelligent, creative, funny
People who like the name Hana also like Hannah, Hailey, Hanna, Grace, Emma, Amaya, Faith, Isabella, Kaiya, Ella

Hang *(Vietnamese)* ♀   RATING: ★★★
Moon
People think of Hang as funny, caring, cool, creative, popular
People who like the name Hang also like Lana, Larisa, Hedy, Lola, Hazelle, Lark, Marietta, Natara, Hallie, Satinka

Hanh *(Vietnamese)* ♀   RATING: ★★
Apricot tree; happiness
People think of Hanh as creative, pretty, intelligent, elegant, leader
People who like the name Hanh also like Joie, Anya, Aiko, Antoinette, Althea, Ai, Calista, Alpana, Keiko, Anika

Hani *(Arabic)* ♂   RATING: ★★★★
Cheerful, happy
People think of Hani as popular, intelligent, funny, caring, cool
People who like the name Hani also like Faris, Aiden, Gabriel, Gavin, Ian, Felix, Galen, Liam, Lucas, Crispin

Hank *(American)* ♂   RATING: ★★
Ruler of the home—Short for Henry; Hank Aaron, baseball player; Hank Williams Jr., singer/songwriter
People think of Hank as handsome, intelligent, cool, leader, funny
People who like the name Hank also like Henry, Jack, Ethan, Oliver, Luke, Daniel, Tucker, Ian, Isaac, Jacob

Hanley *(English)* ♂   RATING: ★★☆
From the high field
People think of Hanley as funny, creative, trustworthy, intelligent, sporty
People who like the name Hanley also like Holden, Braden, Ethan, Jackson, Grayson, Kaden, Radley, Dalton, Cole, Landon

Hanna *(Hebrew)* ♀   RATING: ★★★☆
Grace
People think of Hanna as pretty, funny, caring, intelligent, creative
People who like the name Hanna also like Hannah, Hailey, Emma, Isabella, Grace, Abigail, Paige, Ava, Faith, Isabelle

Hannah *(Hebrew)* ♀   RATING: ★★★★
Grace—*Hannah Montana*, TV show
People think of Hannah as pretty, funny, caring, creative, intelligent
People who like the name Hannah also like Emma, Hailey, Abigail, Grace, Olivia, Isabella, Chloe, Emily, Ava, Paige

Hannan *(Arabic)* ♀   RATING: ★★★☆
Most compassionate
People think of Hannan as pretty, caring, funny, creative, popular
People who like the name Hannan also like Hannah, Hailey, Emma, Paige, Faith, Grace, Audrey, Gianna, Abigail, Ava

Hanne *(Scandinavian)* ♀   RATING: ★★★★
Grace
People think of Hanne as creative, funny, pretty, caring, young
People who like the name Hanne also like Hannah, Halle, Iris, Jadyn, Isabel, Elisabeth, Olivia, Hanna, Ella, Felicia

Hannelore *(German)* ♀   RATING: ★★★☆
Combination of Hannah and Lora
> People think of Hannelore as pretty, creative, intelligent, young, caring
> People who like the name Hannelore also like Belle, Helena, Josephine, Fiona, Faye, Larissa, Hazel, Lorelei, Hannah, Anastasia

Hannes *(Scandinavian)* ♂   RATING: ★★★
God is gracious—Variation of Johannes (John)
> People think of Hannes as intelligent, quiet, creative, handsome, cool
> People who like the name Hannes also like Hans, Heath, Mattox, Dane, Hansel, Braden, Jaxon, Jayden, Sebastian, Hayes

Hannibal *(Hebrew)* ♂   RATING: ★☆
One who Baal has favored—Phoenician/Carthaginian variation of Hananbaal; Hannibal Barka, Carthaginian general; Hannibal Lecter, character in *Silence of the Lambs* by Thomas Harris
> People think of Hannibal as aggressive, criminal, intelligent, powerful, weird
> People who like the name Hannibal also like Ian, Jacob, Gabriel, Jackson, Wade, Henry, Lucas, Damien, Booker, Felix

Hans *(Scandinavian)* ♂   RATING: ★★
God is gracious—Variation of John
> People think of Hans as intelligent, handsome, creative, caring, powerful
> People who like the name Hans also like Ian, Hansel, Gabriel, Daniel, Isaac, Ethan, Jacob, Jeremiah, Henry, Liam

Hansel *(German)* ♂   RATING: ★★★☆
God is gracious—Variation of John; *Hansel and Gretel*, fairy tale
> People think of Hansel as handsome, sexy, young, intelligent, popular
> People who like the name Hansel also like Hans, Caleb, Elijah, Oliver, Gabriel, Benjamin, Isaac, Ethan, Hector, Alexander

Hanzila *(African)* ♀♂   RATING: ★☆
Road, path
> People think of Hanzila as big, weird, funny, exotic, wild
> People who like the name Hanzila also like Katriel, Cheche, Diara, Deka, Ashanti, Harley, Haven, Bell, Jocelyn, Daylin

Hao *(Vietnamese)* ♀♂   RATING: ★★★☆
Good, perfect
> People think of Hao as sexy, handsome, powerful, intelligent, young
> People who like the name Hao also like Keanu, Kyan, Kione, Forest, Porsche, Bliss, Kiyoshi, Kizzy, Kyrie, Bennett

Happy *(American)* ♀♂   RATING: ★☆
Joyful
> People think of Happy as funny, weird, loser, cool, energetic
> People who like the name Happy also like Madison, Love, Lucky, Holly, Forest, Freedom, Casey, Angel, Haven, Justice

Haracha *(African)* ♀   RATING: ★★★
Frog
> People think of Haracha as exotic, funny, weird, loser, quiet
> People who like the name Haracha also like Hazina, Hada, Kya, Izefia, Eshe, Halima, Hova, Kimmy, Camisha, Ifama

Hardy *(English)* ♂   RATING: ★★
Courageous, strong—Also a surname; Thomas Hardy, author
> People think of Hardy as leader, handsome, aggressive, trustworthy, intelligent
> People who like the name Hardy also like Keagan, Cole, Ethan, Caleb, Gage, Harrison, Holden, Hanley, Dawson, Chase

Harlan *(English)* ♀♂   RATING: ★★★★
Dweller by the boundary wood—Also a surname; Harlan Coben, author
> People think of Harlan as handsome, intelligent, funny, leader, cool
> People who like the name Harlan also like Hayden, Jaden, Evan, Caden, Addison, Hunter, Harley, Hadley, Parker, Landen

Harley *(English)* ♀♂   RATING: ★★★★
From the hares' wood—Harley-Davidson, motorcycle manufacturer
> People think of Harley as funny, cool, popular, energetic, wild
> People who like the name Harley also like Hayden, Bailey, Riley, Madison, Dakota, Logan, Hunter, Caden, Jaden, Dylan

Harlow *(English)* ♂   RATING: ★★★☆
From the mound of the people—Gene Harlow, actress; Shalom Harlow, fashion model
> People think of Harlow as pretty, exotic, creative, sexy, caring
> People who like the name Harlow also like Holden, Gavin, Jackson, Harrison, Oliver, Maddox, Landon, Asher, Emerson, Noah

Harmon *(German)* ♂   RATING: ★★★★
Soldier—Variation of Herman
> People think of Harmon as handsome, leader, intelligent, caring, funny
> People who like the name Harmon also like Kaden, Ethan, Gabriel, Braden, Harrison, Holden, Jacob, Caleb, Grayson, Emerson

Harmony *(English)* ♀   RATING: ★★★
Musical combination of chords
> People think of Harmony as pretty, caring, creative, intelligent, funny
> People who like the name Harmony also like Faith, Hope, Hailey, Hannah, Melody, Grace, Destiny, Chloe, Isabella, Paige

Harold (*Scandinavian*) ♂   RATING: ★☆
Army ruler—Harold Lloyd, actor; Harold Pinter, play-wright; Harold Washington, politician
> People think of Harold as funny, handsome, intelligent, caring, cool
> People who like the name Harold also like Henry, Jack, Daniel, Gabriel, Jacob, Matthew, Charles, Harry, Nathan, Ethan

Haroun (*Arabic*) ♂   RATING: ★★☆
Teaching, singing—Variation of Aaron
> People think of Haroun as handsome, young, sneaky, intelligent, popular
> People who like the name Haroun also like Gabriel, Hugh, Josiah, Hassan, Mattias, Harmon, Landers, Jamal, Noah, Lachlan

Harper (*English*) ♀♂   RATING: ★★★★
Harp player—Harper Lee, author
> People think of Harper as intelligent, creative, artsy, pretty, funny
> People who like the name Harper also like Hayden, Parker, Addison, Avery, Logan, Carter, Hadley, Hunter, Bailey, Riley

Harriet (*English*) ♀   RATING: ★★★☆
Home ruler—Feminine form of Harry or Henry; Harriet Tubman, leader of the U.S. underground railroad
> People think of Harriet as pretty, intelligent, funny, caring, creative
> People who like the name Harriet also like Charlotte, Hannah, Grace, Lucy, Olivia, Emily, Faith, Isabelle, Ella, Felicity

Harris (*English*) ♂   RATING: ★★★☆
Son of Harry
> People think of Harris as funny, handsome, intelligent, leader, energetic
> People who like the name Harris also like Harrison, Jackson, Holden, Ethan, Jack, Cole, Landon, Oliver, Nicholas, Jacob

Harrison (*English*) ♂   RATING: ★★★★
Son of Harry—Harrison Ford, actor
> People think of Harrison as handsome, intelligent, funny, cool, popular
> People who like the name Harrison also like Jackson, Ethan, Jack, Noah, Jacob, Benjamin, Holden, Aiden, Gavin, Owen

Harry (*English*) ♂   RATING: ★★
Army ruler—Originally short for Harold or Henry; Prince Harry of England; Harry Hamlin, actor
> People think of Harry as handsome, funny, intelligent, cool, popular
> People who like the name Harry also like Jack, Henry, Oliver, William, Ethan, Jacob, Noah, Daniel, Thomas, Matthew

Harsha (*Sanskrit/East Indian*) ♀   RATING: ★★★☆
Happiness
> People think of Harsha as intelligent, popular, exotic, caring, young

> People who like the name Harsha also like Ishana, Hetal, Harmony, Divya, Hanna, Ella, Jaya, Jui, Kavindra, Jyotika

Hart (*English*) ♂   RATING: ★★
Deer or stag
> People think of Hart as caring, popular, trustworthy, intelligent, handsome
> People who like the name Hart also like Holden, Ethan, Landon, Gabriel, Owen, Heath, Jack, Liam, Jackson, Kaden

Hartmann (*German*) ♂   RATING: ★★
Hardy man
> People think of Hartmann as intelligent, funny, cool, creative, trustworthy
> People who like the name Hartmann also like Hans, Hansel, Josiah, Carsten, Harmon, Jaron, Heinrich, Christopher, Jadon, Waylon

Hartwell (*English*) ♂   RATING: ★★☆
Stag's spring
> People think of Hartwell as weird, wealthy, old-fashioned, trustworthy, nerdy
> People who like the name Hartwell also like Harris, Everett, Holden, Harvey, Dawson, Jackson, Fletcher, Harrison, Nicholas, Landon

Haru (*Japanese*) ♂   RATING: ★★★★
Born in the spring
> People think of Haru as intelligent, cool, handsome, caring, energetic
> People who like the name Haru also like Haruki, Ryu, Hiroshi, Akio, Botan, Keitaro, Keiji, Jiro, Suoh, Makoto

Haruki (*Japanese*) ♂   RATING: ★★★☆
Shining brightly
> People think of Haruki as intelligent, artsy, funny, handsome, trustworthy
> People who like the name Haruki also like Haru, Hiroshi, Ryu, Akio, Keitaro, Makoto, Botan, Kaemon, Jiro, Keiji

Haruko (*Japanese*) ♀   RATING: ★★★☆
Spring born
> People think of Haruko as cool, young, energetic, creative, exotic
> People who like the name Haruko also like Emiko, Aiko, Sakura, Hitomi, Ayame, Hana, Kaori, Hoshiko, Amaya, Kaiyo

Haruni (*Arabic*) ♂   RATING: ★☆
Messengership
> People think of Haruni as exotic, funny, leader, intelligent, weird
> People who like the name Haruni also like Iggy, Kasim, Kimoni, Haben, Kame, Ilo, Hajari, Kayonga, Kazi, Kanelo

Harva (*American*) ♀   RATING: ★☆
Feminine form of Harvey
> People think of Harva as young, funny, wild, leader, weird
> People who like the name Harva also like Leighanna, Mahogany, Keena, Lara, Malvina, Hope, Hazel, Jennelle, Jetta, Kyra

Harvey *(French)* ♂   RATING: ★★
Battle warrior—Breton origin; Harvey Firestone, founder of Firestone Tire & Rubber Co.; Harvey Keitel, actor; Harvey Wallbanger, alcoholic drink
> People think of Harvey as handsome, funny, intelligent, caring, popular
> People who like the name Harvey also like Ethan, Harrison, Jack, Oliver, Jacob, Isaac, Bradley, Cody, Nathan, Justin

Hasad *(Turkish)* ♂   RATING: ★☆
Harvest
> People think of Hasad as ethnic, weird, slow, handsome, cool
> People who like the name Hasad also like Isaac, Mario, Elijah, Hans, Malik, Jamal, Jared, Marco, Tomas, Marcus

Hasana *(Arabic)* ♀   RATING: ★★★☆
Beautiful, fair
> People think of Hasana as exotic, pretty, sexy, trustworthy, intelligent
> People who like the name Hasana also like Hazel, Genevieve, Layla, Jahzara, Giselle, Hailey, Hazina, Celeste, Iliana

Hashim *(Arabic)* ♂   RATING: ★☆
Destroyer; breaker of bread
> People think of Hashim as handsome, intelligent, powerful, aggressive, cool
> People who like the name Hashim also like Jamal, Faris, Abdullah, Hajari, Jabir, Habib, Kadeem, Amir, Hassan, Jamil

Hassan *(Arabic)* ♂   RATING: ★★★☆
Pious, wise—Not to be confused with Hasan meaning handsome
> People think of Hassan as handsome, intelligent, funny, caring, cool
> People who like the name Hassan also like Isaiah, Gabriel, Isaac, Jared, Jamal, Amir, Elijah, Jayden, Xavier, Cyrus

Hastin *(Sanskrit/East Indian)* ♂   RATING: ★★★
Elephant
> People think of Hastin as handsome, cool, energetic, intelligent, young
> People who like the name Hastin also like Holden, Halden, Aden, Kaden, Haben, Jayden, Korbin, Gabriel, Heaton, Noah

Hateya *(Native American)* ♀   RATING: ★★★★
To make a footprint
> People think of Hateya as pretty, creative, energetic, girl next door, trustworthy
> People who like the name Hateya also like Kaya, Halona, Chumani, Kachina, Ayasha, Kiona, Cocheta, Dysis, Miakoda, Hannah

Havard *(Scandinavian)* ♂   RATING: ★★☆
High guardian
> People think of Havard as intelligent, untrustworthy, wealthy, popular, creative
> People who like the name Havard also like Landon, Kaden, Keith, Tristan, Drake, Nathan, Deacon, Elijah, Darren, Joel

Haven *(English)* ♀ ♂   RATING: ★★★★☆
Safe place—Also spelled Havyn
> People think of Haven as pretty, intelligent, caring, creative, funny
> People who like the name Haven also like Hayden, Caden, Jaden, Bailey, Hunter, Madison, Cadence, Logan, Eden, Addison

Havily *(American)* ♀   RATING: ★★
Combination of Haven and Emily
> People think of Havily as creative, weird, intelligent, cool, elegant
> People who like the name Havily also like Hannah, Hailey, Grace, Isabella, Jadyn, Harmony, Chloe, Makayla, Gabrielle, Ashlyn

Hawa *(Arabic)* ♀   RATING: ★★★
Variation of Eve
> People think of Hawa as intelligent, religious, ethnic, funny, creative
> People who like the name Hawa also like Hazina, Fola, Myeisha, Hidi, Isabis, Kia, Layla, Hija, Kumani, Harmony

Hawaii *(Hawaiian)* ♀ ♂   RATING: ★★★
Home of the Polynesians—U.S. state
> People think of Hawaii as exotic, pretty, winner, funny, popular
> People who like the name Hawaii also like Angel, Dakota, Hayden, Kaili, Jacey, Ireland, Madison, Caden, Casey, Taylor

Hayden *(English)* ♀ ♂   RATING: ★★★★☆
From the hay downs—Hayden Christensen, actor; Hayden Panettiere, actress
> People think of Hayden as handsome, intelligent, funny, popular, cool
> People who like the name Hayden also like Caden, Logan, Riley, Madison, Addison, Bailey, Jaden, Dylan, Aidan, Parker

Hayes *(English)* ♂   RATING: ★★★★
Lives by the forest, brush—Also a surname; Helen Hayes, actress; Isaac Hayes, actor
> People think of Hayes as intelligent, handsome, funny, cool, leader
> People who like the name Hayes also like Holden, Jackson, Landon, Grayson, Maddox, Kaden, Grant, Ethan, Cole, Elijah

Hayley *(English)* ♀ ♂   RATING: ★★★☆
From the hay clearing—Also spelled Haylie
> People think of Hayley as pretty, funny, caring, intelligent, creative
> People who like the name Hayley also like Hayden, Madison, Bailey, Riley, Taylor, Haley, Mackenzie, Dylan, Jordan, Logan

Hayward (*English*) ♂ RATING: ★☆
From the hedge enclosure
   People think of Hayward as nerdy, poor, weird, loser, powerful
   People who like the name Hayward also like Harrison, Garrison, Holden, Dawson, Hampton, Finley, Jackson, Grayson, Fletcher, Ethan

Hazel (*Celtic/Gaelic*) ♀ RATING: ★★☆
The hazel tree
   People think of Hazel as pretty, intelligent, funny, caring, creative
   People who like the name Hazel also like Ava, Hailey, Faith, Hannah, Isabella, Emma, Grace, Chloe, Ella, Paige

Hazelle (*English*) ♀ RATING: ★★★☆
The tazel tree
   People think of Hazelle as pretty, artsy, creative, caring, criminal
   People who like the name Hazelle also like Hazel, Hailey, Felicity, Isabella, Faith, Hannah, Emma, Bella, Charlotte, Belle

Hazina (*African*) ♀ RATING: ★★
Good—Possibly from the Arabic Hasina meaning beautiful
   People think of Hazina as ethnic, intelligent, energetic, exotic, weird
   People who like the name Hazina also like Jahzara, Fayola, Ayanna, Hannah, Hazel, Johari, Malaika, Mandisa, Heaven, Gimbya

Heath (*English*) ♂ RATING: ★★☆
Heathland—Originally short for Heathcliff; Heath Ledger, actor
   People think of Heath as handsome, caring, funny, cool, popular
   People who like the name Heath also like Ethan, Gavin, Jacob, Seth, Caleb, Landon, Ian, Aiden, Noah, Tristan

Heather (*English*) ♀ RATING: ★★★
Heather plant—Heather Graham, actress; Heather Locklear, actress
   People think of Heather as pretty, funny, caring, creative, intelligent
   People who like the name Heather also like Hannah, Hailey, Faith, Grace, Samantha, Emily, Emma, Jessica, Lauren, Elizabeth

Heaton (*English*) ♂ RATING: ★★★
From the high town
   People think of Heaton as handsome, quiet, funny, leader, intelligent
   People who like the name Heaton also like Holden, Heath, Kaden, Ethan, Tristan, Jayden, Landon, Gage, Maddox, Drake

Heaven (*English*) ♀ RATING: ★★☆
Heaven—Also spelled Heavynne; sometimes spelled backward as Nevaeh
   People think of Heaven as pretty, caring, creative, trustworthy, intelligent

People who like the name Heaven also like Faith, Harmony, Hope, Destiny, Hailey, Grace, Hannah, Trinity, Isabella, Emma

Heba (*Arabic*) ♀ RATING: ★★★☆
Gift
   People think of Heba as pretty, funny, cool, intelligent, creative
   People who like the name Heba also like Inara, Layla, Fareeda, Feryal, Hanna, Eman, Hannah, Iris, Hazina, Farah

Hector (*Greek*) ♂ RATING: ★★
Anchor, steadfast—Hector Elizondo, actor
   People think of Hector as handsome, funny, cool, intelligent, caring
   People who like the name Hector also like Gabriel, Isaac, Jacob, Adam, Ian, Henry, Ethan, Jack, Benjamin, Felix

Hedda (*German*) ♀ RATING: ★★☆
Battle war—Short for Hedwig; Hedda Hopper, gossip columnist
   People think of Hedda as old-fashioned, slow, funny, weird, loser
   People who like the name Hedda also like Hannah, Emma, Nerissa, Iris, Bronwyn, Beatrix, Claire, Leah, Maeve, Sophie

Hedia (*Hebrew*) ♀ RATING: ★★★
Echo of God
   People think of Hedia as religious, big, loser, wealthy, unpopular
   People who like the name Hedia also like Hannah, Liana, Helsa, Samara, Harmony, Mabel, Jadyn, Madeleine, Seanna, Isabella

Hedva (*Hebrew*) ♀ RATING: ★★
Joy
   People think of Hedva as poor, ethnic, intelligent, lazy, artsy
   People who like the name Hedva also like Dysis, Helia, Devorah, Hosanna, Deirdre, Dolly, Helena, Dulcinea, Delia, Diana

Hedwig (*German*) ♀ RATING: ★☆
Battle war
   People think of Hedwig as powerful, pretty, wild, intelligent, elegant
   People who like the name Hedwig also like Hermione, Fiona, Lorelei, Daphne, Isis, Jezebel, Ingrid, Cambria, Mia, Celine

Hedy (*English*) ♀ RATING: ★★
Battle war—Short for Hedwig; Hedy Lamarr, actress
   People think of Hedy as pretty, funny, creative, leader, trustworthy
   People who like the name Hedy also like Sophie, Genevieve, Ava, Lana, Nysa, Ivy, Fern, Justine, Delilah, Mia

Hedya *(Hebrew)* ♀   RATING: ★★
Variation of Hedia
  People think of Hedya as weird, funny, exotic, poor, old-fashioned
  People who like the name Hedya also like Giselle, Meara, Athalia, Daphne, Hazina, Hestia, Belle, Hermia, Celeste, Keira

Heidi *(German)* ♀   RATING: ★★★★
Of noble kin—Short for Adelheid or Adelaide; Heidi Klum, fashion model/TV host
  People think of Heidi as pretty, funny, caring, intelligent, creative
  People who like the name Heidi also like Hannah, Hailey, Emma, Faith, Grace, Chloe, Ava, Olivia, Isabella, Abigail

Heinrich *(German)* ♂   RATING: ★★★
Ruler of the home
  People think of Heinrich as intelligent, handsome, sexy, leader, powerful
  People who like the name Heinrich also like Henrik, Gabriel, Hans, Alaric, Isaac, Wendell, Wyatt, Napoleon, Wilhelm, Eric

Heinz *(German)* ♂   RATING: ★★★☆
Ruler of the home—Short for Heinrich
  People think of Heinz as slow, big, funny, caring, criminal
  People who like the name Heinz also like Kaden, Felix, Daniel, Gabriel, Holden, Henry, Glen, Huck, Herbert, Homer

Helaine *(English)* ♀   RATING: ★★★☆
Light—Variation of Helen
  People think of Helaine as caring, intelligent, girl next door, quiet, weird
  People who like the name Helaine also like Helena, Iris, Daphne, Harmony, Hannah, Olivia, Isabelle, Hailey, Heidi, Gabrielle

Helen *(Greek)* ♀   RATING: ★★
Light—Helen Hayes, actress; Helen Hunt, actress; Helen Keller, author/teacher
  People think of Helen as pretty, intelligent, caring, funny, creative
  People who like the name Helen also like Hannah, Grace, Emily, Claire, Elizabeth, Charlotte, Helena, Isabelle, Emma, Faith

Helena *(Greek)* ♀   RATING: ★★☆
Light—Mother of Constantine the Great; Helena Bonham Carter, actress; Helena Rubenstein, cosmetic designer.
  People think of Helena as pretty, intelligent, elegant, creative, funny
  People who like the name Helena also like Isabella, Hannah, Olivia, Ava, Grace, Isabelle, Emma, Eva, Sophia, Faith

Helene *(French)* ♀   RATING: ★★★☆
Variation of Helen
  People think of Helene as pretty, intelligent, creative, caring, funny

People who like the name Helene also like Helena, Hannah, Emma, Gabrielle, Grace, Isabella, Eva, Claire, Olivia, Isabelle

Helga *(Scandinavian)* ♀   RATING: ★☆
Holy
  People think of Helga as big, aggressive, powerful, loser, energetic
  People who like the name Helga also like Helena, Hannah, Ingrid, Fiona, Hilda, Heidi, Helen, Erica, Emma, Isabella

Helia *(Greek)* ♀   RATING: ★★★★
Sun
  People think of Helia as pretty, leader, elegant, old-fashioned, young
  People who like the name Helia also like Helena, Iliana, Calista, Iris, Dawn, Chloe, Elena, Bethany, Isabella, Hailey

Helki *(Native American)* ♀♂   RATING: ★★☆
Touch—Miwok origin
  People think of Helki as ethnic, weird, funny, intelligent, unpopular
  People who like the name Helki also like Kishi, Mika, Halyn, Misae, Nida, Misu, Niabi, Talasi, Taregan, Dakota

Heller *(English)* ♂   RATING: ★★☆
Dweller on the hill—Also a surname; Joseph Heller, author
  People think of Heller as sexy, cool, aggressive, powerful, leader
  People who like the name Heller also like Holden, Mattox, Walker, Olin, Miles, Foster, Emery, Landon, Espen, Halden

Heloise *(French)* ♀   RATING: ★☆
Famous fighter—Heloise, advice columnist
  People think of Heloise as intelligent, elegant, pretty, leader, artsy
  People who like the name Heloise also like Eloise, Genevieve, Isabelle, Beatrice, Giselle, Daphne, Eleanor, Belle, Isabella, Harriet

Helsa *(Scandinavian)* ♀   RATING: ★★☆
Consecrated to God
  People think of Helsa as caring, intelligent, pretty, religious, trustworthy
  People who like the name Helsa also like Heidi, Hedia, Harmony, Hannah, Lesa, Halle, Inga, Tegan, Isabel, Lucinda

Heman *(Hebrew)* ♂   RATING: ★★☆
Faithful
  People think of Heman as intelligent, handsome, religious, aggressive, trustworthy
  People who like the name Heman also like Gabriel, Ethan, Isaac, Aden, Hanley, Matthew, Gideon, Isaiah, Jeremy, Damien

Henri *(French)* ♂   RATING: ★★★☆
Ruler of the home—Variation of Henry
  People think of Henri as intelligent, handsome, funny, creative, cool

271

People who like the name Henri also like Henry, Gabriel, Isaac, Harrison, Jack, Oliver, Jacob, Ethan, Felix, Harry

Henrietta (*English*) ♀   RATING: ★☆
Ruler of the home—Feminine form of Henry
People think of Henrietta as pretty, intelligent, caring, powerful, funny
People who like the name Henrietta also like Isabella, Charlotte, Isabelle, Faith, Harriet, Grace, Constance, Hannah, Fiona, Gabriella

Henriette (*French*) ♀   RATING: ★★★☆
Ruler of the home—Feminine form of Henry
People think of Henriette as caring, old-fashioned, pretty, intelligent, elegant
People who like the name Henriette also like Harriet, Heather, Olivia, Isabelle, Henrietta, Florence, Felicity, Catherine, Isabella, Daphne

Henrik (*Scandinavian*) ♂   RATING: ★★★★
Ruler of the home—Variation of Henry
People think of Henrik as handsome, intelligent, cool, funny, creative
People who like the name Henrik also like Liam, Oliver, Gabriel, Noah, Elias, Isaac, Lucas, Henry, Hugh, Maddox

Henrike (*German*) ♀   RATING: ★★☆
Ruler of the home—Feminine form of Henrik
People think of Henrike as intelligent, big, creative, funny, aggressive
People who like the name Henrike also like Miyo, Hermione, Sora, Brenna, Karla, Hedia, Kaya, Emma, Hermia, Nariko

Henry (*German*) ♂   RATING: ★★☆
Ruler of the home—Henry David Thoreau, author/ poet; Henry Rollins, musician
People think of Henry as handsome, intelligent, funny, caring, cool
People who like the name Henry also like Jack, Benjamin, Oliver, William, Noah, Isaac, Jacob, Owen, Ethan, Gabriel

Hera (*Greek*) ♀   RATING: ★★★
Protectress—In Roman mythology, Juno
People think of Hera as pretty, intelligent, powerful, energetic, aggressive
People who like the name Hera also like Aurora, Chloe, Ivy, Isis, Hannah, Cassandra, Genevieve, Kiara, Anastasia, Arwen

Herb (*English*) ♂   RATING: ★☆
Army bright—Short for Herbert; also a plant, spice
People think of Herb as lazy, weird, aggressive, funny, old-fashioned
People who like the name Herb also like Glenn, Howie, Ethan, Homer, Herbert, Daniel, Hank, Houston, Cody, Chad

Herbert (*English*) ♂   RATING: ★☆
Army bright
People think of Herbert as funny, caring, intelligent, handsome, cool

People who like the name Herbert also like Henry, Ethan, Isaac, Jacob, Gabriel, Harold, Justin, Geoffrey, Edgar, Nathan

Herbst (*German*) ♂   RATING: ★★☆
Autumn
People think of Herbst as winner, sexy, artsy, funny, trustworthy
People who like the name Herbst also like Lamont, Miguel, Hector, Marlon, Manuel, Drake, Llewellyn, Drago, Lorenzo, Moses

Hercules (*Latin*) ♂   RATING: ★★★☆
Glory of Hera—In Greek mythology, Herakles; associated with strength and power
People think of Hercules as powerful, big, handsome, leader, funny
People who like the name Hercules also like Jacob, Gabriel, Jason, Benjamin, Ethan, David, Joshua, Oliver, Noah, Thomas

Heremon (*Celtic/Gaelic*) ♂   RATING: ★☆
Variation of Irving
People think of Heremon as nerdy, aggressive, loser, ethnic, weird
People who like the name Heremon also like Braeden, Callum, Daire, Iain, Edan, Gillespie, Faolan, Ciaran, Cairbre, Callahan

Heriberto (*Spanish*) ♂   RATING: ★★★☆
Army bright—Variation of Herbert
People think of Heriberto as funny, handsome, cool, aggressive, caring
People who like the name Heriberto also like Fernando, Marco, Gabriel, Hernando, Joaquin, Salvador, Rafael, Anthony, Carlos, Alberto

Herman (*German*) ♂   RATING: ★★★
Army man
People think of Herman as intelligent, handsome, old-fashioned, funny, trustworthy
People who like the name Herman also like Hector, Harold, Hank, Harvey, Samuel, Isaac, Henry, Herbert, Dominic, Eli

Hermia (*Greek*) ♀   RATING: ★★★☆
Messenger
People think of Hermia as pretty, intelligent, elegant, creative, leader
People who like the name Hermia also like Helena, Cassandra, Aurora, Hazel, Charlotte, Ava, Cora, Delilah, Isis, Daphne

Hermione (*Greek*) ♀   RATING: ★★★★
Pillar queen—Hermione Gingold, actress
People think of Hermione as intelligent, pretty, caring, leader, trustworthy
People who like the name Hermione also like Faith, Isabella, Hannah, Charlotte, Hailey, Emma, Chloe, Isabelle, Grace, Olivia

Hernando *(Spanish)* ♂   RATING: ★★☆
To be courageous—Variation of Ferdinand
> People think of Hernando as exotic, nerdy, weird, handsome, old-fashioned
> People who like the name Hernando also like Diego, Ivan, Eduardo, Fernando, Anthony, Isaac, Juan, Federico, Pablo, Carlos

Herne *(Celtic/Gaelic)* ♂   RATING: ★★☆
God of the hunt
> People think of Herne as weird, unpopular, criminal, loser, poor
> People who like the name Herne also like Faolan, Braeden, Conner, Bowen, Kael, Ewan, Edan, Darren, Devlin, Ciaran

Hero *(Greek)* ♀   RATING: ★☆
Brave one of the people
> People think of Hero as intelligent, powerful, leader, young, creative
> People who like the name Hero also like Hope, Faith, Grace, Hazel, Hermione, Aurora, Bianca, Persephone, Ophelia, Harmony

Herschel *(Hebrew)* ♂   RATING: ★★★
Deer—Herschel Bernardi, actor; Sir William Herschel, astronomer
> People think of Herschel as intelligent, exotic, winner, handsome, caring
> People who like the name Herschel also like Gabriel, Isaac, Ethan, Daniel, Benjamin, Emanuel, Oliver, Owen, Michael, Sebastian

Hertz *(German)* ♂   RATING: ★★
Brave, bold
> People think of Hertz as weird, lazy, old-fashioned, loser, leader
> People who like the name Hertz also like Henri, Elliot, Curtis, Frey, Buddy, Hansel, Glenn, Edison, Forrest, Hal

Hervé *(French)* ♂   RATING: ★☆
Army warrior—Variation of Harvey; Hervé Villechaize, actor
> People think of Hervé as funny, caring, intelligent, creative, handsome
> People who like the name Hervé also like Henri, Bayard, Elroy, Gautier, Lionel, Sinclair, Hector, Royce, Heinz, Coyne

Hesper *(Greek)* ♀   RATING: ★★★
Evening star
> People think of Hesper as pretty, old-fashioned, artsy, wild, intelligent
> People who like the name Hesper also like Iris, Hazel, Cassandra, Isis, Hypatia, Celeste, Fiona, Ivy, Ava, Helena

Hessa *(Arabic)* ♀   RATING: ★★★
Destiny
> People think of Hessa as creative, pretty, loser, leader, intelligent
> People who like the name Hessa also like Jamila, Kassandra, Gracie, Natalie, Cassandra, Isabella, Adara, Catalina, Malia, Bianca

Hester *(Greek)* ♀   RATING: ★☆
Star
> People think of Hester as pretty, intelligent, creative, artsy, caring
> People who like the name Hester also like Hazel, Chloe, Ava, Gabrielle, Phoebe, Imogene, Faye, Daphne, Iris, Helena

Hestia *(Greek)* ♀   RATING: ★★
Hearth
> People think of Hestia as elegant, trustworthy, ethnic, exotic, pretty
> People who like the name Hestia also like Maeve, Helena, Hazel, Aurora, Iris, Medea, Isis, Hermione, Celeste, Freya

Hetal *(Sanskrit/East Indian)* ♀   RATING: ★☆
Friendly
> People think of Hetal as nerdy, cool, caring, trustworthy, lazy
> People who like the name Hetal also like Avani, Harsha, Himani, Kanika, Bhavna, Hazel, Ishana, Jyotika, Jyoti, Gauri

Heulwen *(Welsh)* ♀   RATING: ★★★
Sun blessed, fair
> People think of Heulwen as caring, intelligent, popular, weird, artsy
> People who like the name Heulwen also like Gwyneth, Bronwen, Morwen, Blodwyn, Bronwyn, Sulwyn, Olwen, Hafwen, Rhoswen, Bethwyn

Hewitt *(English)* ♂   RATING: ★★★☆
From the cutting
> People think of Hewitt as intelligent, creative, wild, funny, powerful
> People who like the name Hewitt also like Ethan, Holden, Owen, Ian, Grayson, Gavin, Fletcher, Everett, Dawson, Heath

Hidalgo *(Spanish)* ♂   RATING: ★★★
Noble one
> People think of Hidalgo as handsome, trustworthy, powerful, intelligent, caring
> People who like the name Hidalgo also like Julio, Gabriel, Alejandro, Javier, Gideon, Jacob, Isaiah, Lucas, Maddox, Enrique

Hide *(Japanese)* ♀   RATING: ★★★
Excellent—Pronounced *HEE-day*
> People think of Hide as creative, weird, funny, cool, ethnic
> People who like the name Hide also like Emiko, Ai, Gin, Kaori, Jin, Sakura, Hitomi, Hana, Aiko, Hoshiko

Hidi *(African)* ♀   RATING: ★★★☆
Root
> People think of Hidi as ethnic, funny, quiet, weird, old-fashioned
> People who like the name Hidi also like Jasmine, Emily, Lexi, Harmony, Heidi, Hope, Faith, Ivy, Bella, Felicity

274

Hien *(Vietnamese)* ♀♂   RATING: ★★★
Meek, gentle
People think of Hien as intelligent, caring, energetic, cool, creative
People who like the name Hien also like Hayden, Kaelin, Ember, Landen, Jaden, Kyler, Keaton, Ellery, Lane, Ezra

Hiero *(Greek)* ♂   RATING: ★★★
Holy
People think of Hiero as powerful, ethnic, exotic, artsy, intelligent
People who like the name Hiero also like Damien, Gabriel, Micah, Jayden, Caleb, Kael, Seth, Faris, Damon, Gideon

Hieu *(Vietnamese)* ♂   RATING: ★★★
Pious, understanding
People think of Hieu as caring, funny, creative, intelligent, energetic
People who like the name Hieu also like Chance, Darren, Benjamin, Fai, Bradley, Cole, Aden, Abel, Isaiah, Brad

Hija *(Spanish)* ♀   RATING: ★☆
Daughter
People think of Hija as exotic, ethnic, pretty, wild, young
People who like the name Hija also like Hazina, Kissa, Iris, Leah, Johari, Abeni, Hoshiko, Kaiya, Dysis, Ayanna

Hila *(Hebrew)* ♀   RATING: ★★★★
Halo, crown
People think of Hila as intelligent, pretty, caring, creative, popular
People who like the name Hila also like Hannah, Emilia, Emma, Ava, Heaven, Estelle, Hope, Amelia, Helena, Emilie

Hilaire *(French)* ♀♂   RATING: ★★★
Cheerful—Variation of Hilary
People think of Hilaire as pretty, popular, elegant, intelligent, creative
People who like the name Hilaire also like Hilary, Brooke, Hayden, Blair, Haley, Madison, Jaden, Mackenzie, Alexis, Morgan

Hilary *(Greek)* ♀♂   RATING: ★★★★
Cheerful—Hilary Duff, actress
People think of Hilary as pretty, funny, intelligent, caring, creative
People who like the name Hilary also like Brooke, Madison, Hayden, Holly, Bailey, Mackenzie, Dakota, Cameron, Morgan, Dylan

Hilda *(English)* ♀   RATING: ★☆
Battle
People think of Hilda as intelligent, caring, trustworthy, sexy, pretty
People who like the name Hilda also like Helena, Helga, Fiona, Heidi, Isabella, Emma, Olivia, Grace, Charlotte, Heather

Hilde *(French)* ♀   RATING: ★★★☆
Battle
People think of Hilde as intelligent, creative, cool, old-fashioned, funny
People who like the name Hilde also like Olivia, Hailey, Justine, Ivy, Sophie, Thora, Eleanor, Felicity, Hallie, Louisa

Hillary *(Greek)* ♀♂   RATING: ★★☆
Cheerful—Hillary Rodham Clinton, politician; Sir Edmund Hillary, first person to climb Mt. Everest
People think of Hillary as pretty, funny, caring, creative, intelligent
People who like the name Hillary also like Hayden, Madison, Brooke, Bailey, Mackenzie, Logan, Hilary, Taylor, Caden, Morgan

Hilliard *(English)* ♀♂   RATING: ★★★
War stronghold—Originally a surname
People think of Hilliard as slow, aggressive, sexy, unpopular, uptight
People who like the name Hilliard also like Logan, Hayden, Darby, Harper, Carrington, Briar, Paris, Flynn, Manning, Parker

Himani *(Sanskrit/East Indian)* ♀   RATING: ★★★
Snow
People think of Himani as pretty, intelligent, creative, trustworthy, cool
People who like the name Himani also like Eshana, Avani, Niyati, Hetal, Gianna, Kimaya, Leilani, Deepnita, Kerani, Liana

Hina *(Sanskrit/East Indian)* ♀   RATING: ★★★★
Henna
People think of Hina as intelligent, pretty, funny, caring, cool
People who like the name Hina also like Kali, Chandra, Leilani, Devi, Layla, Isis, Jaya, Lanica, Iris, Kamea

Hinda *(Hebrew)* ♀   RATING: ★★☆
Female deer
People think of Hinda as pretty, funny, creative, exotic, sexy
People who like the name Hinda also like Ratana, Reyna, Kyla, Taya, Shirina, Saniya, Erin, Olivia, Tana, Lola

Hinto *(Native American)* ♂   RATING: ★☆
Blue haired—Dakota origin
People think of Hinto as powerful, sexy, wild, boy next door, young
People who like the name Hinto also like Minowa, Avonaco, Mingan, Quana, Mikasi, Indra, Kael, Huslu, Tocho, Dasan

Hiraani *(Hawaiian)* ♀   RATING: ★★★
Beautiful sky
People think of Hiraani as exotic, leader, funny, intelligent, elegant
People who like the name Hiraani also like Aoife, Seren, Makelina, Sitara, Tallulah, Mythri, Lara, Davina, Mahina, Ailish

Hiram (*Hebrew*) ♂   RATING: ★★★☆
Exalted brother
> People think of Hiram as intelligent, handsome, funny, caring, leader
> People who like the name Hiram also like Jonah, Ethan, Isaac, Caleb, Gideon, Gabriel, Elijah, Joseph, Daniel, Isaiah

Hiroko (*Japanese*) ♀ ♂   RATING: ★★★☆
Magnanimous, generous child
> People think of Hiroko as pretty, funny, young, cool, creative
> People who like the name Hiroko also like Kiyoshi, Hoshi, Kana, Seiko, Sanyu, Kumi, Rin, Yuki, Natsu, Ren

Hiroshi (*Japanese*) ♂   RATING: ★★★☆
Generous
> People think of Hiroshi as cool, handsome, intelligent, caring, quiet
> People who like the name Hiroshi also like Haruki, Ryu, Akio, Haru, Keitaro, Makoto, Kaemon, Keiji, Suoh, Shino

Hirsi (*Arabic*) ♂   RATING: ★★
Amulet
> People think of Hirsi as exotic, unpopular, caring, cool, ethnic
> People who like the name Hirsi also like Haben, Ilom, Kayonga, Kazi, Bahari, Belay, Kasim, Dumi, Ilo, Chimelu

Hisano (*Japanese*) ♀   RATING: ★☆
Open plain
> People think of Hisano as unpopular, loser, nerdy, weird, funny
> People who like the name Hisano also like Hoshiko, Inari, Emiko, Haruko, Hitomi, Kagami, Gin, Amaya, Kaiyo, Kaori

Hita (*Arabic*) ♀   RATING: ★★☆
Prudence, caution
> People think of Hita as exotic, ethnic, pretty, weird, religious
> People who like the name Hita also like Vinita, Kalila, Kalinda, Lula, Rayya, Hetal, Saniya, Heba, Tevy, Kaliska

Hitomi (*Japanese*) ♀   RATING: ★★★★
Blue eyes
> People think of Hitomi as pretty, creative, intelligent, exotic, elegant
> People who like the name Hitomi also like Kaida, Amaya, Sakura, Aiko, Emiko, Hoshiko, Kaori, Ayame, Haruko, Hana

Hoai (*Vietnamese*) ♂   RATING: ★☆
Always, eternal
> People think of Hoai as young, quiet, lazy, trustworthy, popular
> People who like the name Hoai also like Fai, Fox, Declan, Ea, Ja, Egan, Esben, Haruki, Cyrus, Devlin

Hoang (*Vietnamese*) ♂   RATING: ★★★
Phoenix
> People think of Hoang as intelligent, trustworthy, sexy, caring, energetic
> People who like the name Hoang also like Fox, Adish, Ea, Fortune, Damien, Ace, Darren, Beau, Ryu, Merric

Hogan (*Celtic/Gaelic*) ♂   RATING: ★★★☆
Youth
> People think of Hogan as funny, cool, popular, intelligent, caring
> People who like the name Hogan also like Holden, Ethan, Gavin, Ian, Keagan, Maddox, Landon, Kaden, Jackson, Gage

Holbrook (*English*) ♂   RATING: ★★★
Dweller by the brook in a hollow—Also a surname; Hal Holbrook, actor
> People think of Holbrook as weird, nerdy, intelligent, unpopular, stuck-up
> People who like the name Holbrook also like Holden, Harrison, Fletcher, Finley, Emerson, Finn, Grayson, Holt, Gannon, Gage

Holden (*English*) ♂   RATING: ★★★☆
From the hollow in the valley—Holden Caulfield, character in *The Catcher in the Rye* by J. D. Salinger
> People think of Holden as handsome, intelligent, cool, creative, funny
> People who like the name Holden also like Ethan, Landon, Aiden, Noah, Gavin, Jackson, Caleb, Kaden, Tristan, Braden

Holiday (*English*) ♀   RATING: ★★★
Born on a holy day—Also a surname; Billie Holiday, jazz singer; Judy Holliday, singer/actress
> People think of Holiday as creative, young, pretty, energetic, intelligent
> People who like the name Holiday also like Faith, Chloe, Hope, Honey, Bianca, Grace, Destiny, Lola, Autumn, Mystery

Hollace (*English*) ♀ ♂   RATING: ★★★
Near the holly—Originally a surname
> People think of Hollace as pretty, artsy, intelligent, sporty, creative
> People who like the name Hollace also like Hollis, Hayden, Parker, Greer, Harper, Evelyn, London, Halyn, Payton, Holly

Holland (*American*) ♀ ♂   RATING: ★★★★☆
From Holland—Holland Taylor, actress
> People think of Holland as pretty, intelligent, creative, funny, popular
> People who like the name Holland also like Hayden, Addison, Parker, Madison, Dakota, Carter, Riley, Harper, Hadley, Aidan

Hollis (*English*) ♀ ♂   RATING: ★★
Near the holly
> People think of Hollis as intelligent, caring, funny, trustworthy, leader
> People who like the name Hollis also like Hayden, Avery, Harper, Hadley, Parker, Madison, Mason, Brooke, Morgan, Kendall

Holly *(English)* ♀♂   RATING: ★★★★
Plant with red berries—Also spelled Holli, Hollie,
Hollye; Holly Hunter, actress
  People think of Holly as pretty, funny, caring, creative,
  intelligent
  People who like the name Holly also like Madison,
  Brooke, Bailey, Hayden, Riley, Dylan, James, Jordan,
  Jade, Taylor

Holt *(English)* ♂   RATING: ★★★☆
Wood
  People think of Holt as intelligent, powerful, trustwor-
  thy, handsome, funny
  People who like the name Holt also like Holden, Cole,
  Jackson, Jack, Braden, Kaden, Chase, Ian, Gage, Gavin

Homer *(Greek)* ♂   RATING: ★★★
Hostage—Homer, philosopher/author; Homer Hadley
Hickam, writer; Homer Simpson, cartoon character
  People think of Homer as weird, lazy, loser, unpopular,
  funny
  People who like the name Homer also like Isaac, Ethan,
  Jacob, Henry, Harvey, Benjamin, Bradley, Joshua, Heath,
  Holden

Honey *(American)* ♀   RATING: ★★★☆
Sweet as honey—Also short for Honora; also a term of
endearment
  People think of Honey as pretty, sexy, popular, caring,
  creative
  People who like the name Honey also like Hope, Faith,
  Jasmine, Harmony, Hailey, Hannah, Daisy, Isabella,
  Grace, Chloe

Hong *(Vietnamese)* ♀   RATING: ★★★★
Pink, rosy
  People think of Hong as caring, cool, intelligent, funny,
  pretty
  People who like the name Hong also like Elle, Felice,
  Farah, Keiko, Ciara, Laraine, Brea, Hailey, Justine,
  Blossom

Honora *(Latin)* ♀   RATING: ★★★☆
Honor
  People think of Honora as intelligent, elegant, creative,
  pretty, leader
  People who like the name Honora also like Grace,
  Felicity, Faith, Aurora, Ava, Hannah, Eva, Olivia, Bianca,
  Cassandra

Honoria *(Latin)* ♀   RATING: ★★★
Honor
  People think of Honoria as trustworthy, pretty, ener-
  getic, intelligent, old-fashioned
  People who like the name Honoria also like Honora,
  Felicity, Genevieve, Faith, Cordelia, Aurora, Hailey,
  Charity, Sophia, Ivy

Hop *(Vietnamese)* ♀   RATING: ★★★
Consistant
  People think of Hop as wild, big, energetic, lazy,
  unpopular

People who like the name Hop also like Dolly, Hailey,
Tiana, Latisha, Jia Li, Carissa, Victoria, Latifah, Femi,
Jenaya

Hope *(English)* ♀   RATING: ★★★☆
Desire; faith
  People think of Hope as pretty, caring, funny, trust-
  worthy, intelligent
  People who like the name Hope also like Faith, Grace,
  Hannah, Hailey, Isabella, Paige, Emma, Chloe, Olivia, Ava

Horace *(Latin)* ♂   RATING: ★★★
Unknown meaning—Horace (Horatius), Roman poet
  People think of Horace as intelligent, trustworthy,
  aggressive, funny, old-fashioned
  People who like the name Horace also like Henry, Isaac,
  Felix, Herbert, Earl, Hank, Jackson, Jacob, Hector,
  Charles

Horatio *(Latin)* ♂   RATING: ★★★
Unknown meaning—Character in *Hamlet* by William
Shakespeare
  People think of Horatio as intelligent, leader, old-
  fashioned, caring, trustworthy
  People who like the name Horatio also like Edgar,
  Sebastian, Harrison, Victor, Matthew, Vincent, Erik,
  Vladimir, Atticus, Pablo

Horizon *(American)* ♀♂   RATING: ★★★
Apparent edge of land
  People think of Horizon as creative, pretty, cool, ele-
  gant, popular
  People who like the name Horizon also like Hayden,
  Madison, Raine, Imagine, Shadow, Caden, Presley, Echo,
  Dakota, Logan

Horst *(German)* ♂   RATING: ★★☆
Man from the woods
  People think of Horst as handsome, big, intelligent,
  weird, aggressive
  People who like the name Horst also like Henrik,
  Ambrose, Elton, Deiter, Dalton, Ford, Darwin, Felix,
  Ephraim, Henry

Horus *(Egyptian)* ♂   RATING: ★★★☆
God of light
  People think of Horus as leader, religious, powerful,
  trustworthy, creative
  People who like the name Horus also like Galen, Cyrus,
  Jacob, Gavin, Jake, Jeremiah, Basil, Alexander, Hector,
  Fox

Hosanna *(Greek)* ♀   RATING: ★★
Praise
  People think of Hosanna as intelligent, creative, reli-
  gious, energetic, young
  People who like the name Hosanna also like Hannah,
  Isabella, Harmony, Grace, Hailey, Hope, Heaven, Hazel,
  Evangeline, Destiny

Hosea *(Hebrew)* ♂ RATING: ★★★☆
Salvation
> People think of Hosea as handsome, caring, religious, leader, trustworthy
> People who like the name Hosea also like Isaiah, Elijah, Isaac, Jeremiah, Caleb, Gabriel, Josiah, Jonah, Micah, Ezekiel

Hoshi *(Japanese)* ♀♂ RATING: ★★★☆
Star
> People think of Hoshi as pretty, weird, intelligent, energetic, artsy
> People who like the name Hoshi also like Kiyoshi, Seiko, Hiroko, Mitsu, Kana, Maemi, Rin, Sanyu, Natsu, Asa

Hoshiko *(Japanese)* ♀ RATING: ★★★☆
Star
> People think of Hoshiko as exotic, aggressive, weird, elegant, young
> People who like the name Hoshiko also like Emiko, Aiko, Hitomi, Kaida, Sakura, Amaya, Keiko, Haruko, Inari, Kaori

Hotah *(Native American)* ♂ RATING: ★☆
Gray; brown—Sioux origin
> People think of Hotah as weird, intelligent
> People who like the name Hotah also like Casimir, Adohi, Zorion, Xanti, Hinto, Inigo, Mingan, Dusan, Ohanzee, Dasan

Hotaru *(Japanese)* ♂ RATING: ★★★
Firefly
> People think of Hotaru as young, exotic, powerful, intelligent, elegant
> People who like the name Hotaru also like Hiroshi, Haru, Haruki, Daisuke, Christopher, Makoto, Riku, Diego, Luke, Daiki

Houston *(English)* ♂ RATING: ★★★☆
From Hugh's town—Originally a surname; also a city in Texas
> People think of Houston as funny, handsome, cool, energetic, sporty
> People who like the name Houston also like Jackson, Ethan, Gavin, Kaden, Aiden, Jacob, Braden, Dawson, Cole, Conner

Hova *(Armenian)* ♀ RATING: ★☆
Wind
> People think of Hova as leader, cool, religious, elegant, trustworthy
> People who like the name Hova also like Helena, Hazina, Fayola, Kiden, Heidi, Cosette, Isis, Ivy, Jezebel, Pandora

Hovan *(Armenian)* ♂ RATING: ★★☆
Variation of John
> People think of Hovan as weird, aggressive, nerdy, energetic, loser
> People who like the name Hovan also like Jayden, Gabriel, Maddox, Braden, Holden, Isaac, Jacob, Tyson, Elijah, Deron

Howard *(English)* ♂ RATING: ★★
Heart brave—Howard Cosell, sportscaster; Howard Hawks, filmmaker; Howard Hughes, tycoon/filmmaker; Howard Stern, radio host
> People think of Howard as intelligent, handsome, caring, funny, trustworthy
> People who like the name Howard also like Nicholas, Isaac, Ethan, Henry, William, Jacob, Edward, Oliver, Daniel, Matthew

Howe *(English)* ♂ RATING: ★☆
From the hill or ridge—Originally a surname
> People think of Howe as cool, popular, funny, trustworthy, aggressive
> People who like the name Howe also like Holt, Heath, Ian, Hart, Harvey, Waite, Slade, Nash, Gabe, Gage

Howell *(Welsh)* ♂ RATING: ★★★☆
Seeing clearly—Variation of Hywel, an English surname
> People think of Howell as handsome, intelligent, funny, caring, creative
> People who like the name Howell also like Dawson, Fletcher, Wade, Finley, Heath, Gabriel, Nathan, Emerson, Russell, Tristan

Howie *(English)* ♂ RATING: ★★★☆
Heart brave—Short for Howard or Howell; Howie Mandel, actor/TV host
> People think of Howie as intelligent, popular, funny, handsome, sexy
> People who like the name Howie also like Harvey, Ethan, Owen, Gavin, Harrison, Jack, Jackson, Jacob, Elijah, Hank

Hubert *(English)* ♂ RATING: ★☆
Mind bright
> People think of Hubert as intelligent, handsome, funny, leader, trustworthy
> People who like the name Hubert also like Isaac, Jacob, Ethan, Earl, Henry, Hector, Edmund, Sebastian, Caleb, Herbert

Huck *(American)* ♂ RATING: ★★★☆
Short for Huckleberry
> People think of Huck as funny, handsome, boy next door, energetic, old-fashioned
> People who like the name Huck also like Finn, Oliver, Jack, Ian, Gavin, Cole, Maddox, Holden, Chase, Landon

Huckleberry *(American)* ♂ RATING: ★★★
Sweet berry—Huckleberry "Huck" Finn, literary character
> People think of Huckleberry as old-fashioned, weird, funny, lazy, creative
> People who like the name Huckleberry also like Jack, Huck, Henry, Daniel, Elijah, Caleb, Benjamin, Samuel, Owen, Harry

Huda *(Arabic)* ♀ RATING: ★★★☆
Enlightenment, guidance
> People think of Huda as pretty, funny, trustworthy, intelligent, popular

278

People who like the name Huda also like Eman, Asha, Damali, Heba, Feryal, Eva, Gasha, Fareeda, Inara, Jamila

Hudson (*English*) ♂　　　　　　RATING: ★★★☆
Son of Hudd—Hudd is short for Richard, Hugh, or the Old English name Hudde
　People think of Hudson as handsome, intelligent, popular, cool, leader
　People who like the name Hudson also like Harrison, Jackson, Emerson, Holden, Landon, Ethan, Gavin, Aiden, Grayson, Dawson

Hue (*Vietnamese*) ♀　　　　　　RATING: ★★★
Lily flower
　People think of Hue as caring, pretty, artsy, cool, intelligent
　People who like the name Hue also like Hope, Faith, Harmony, Blossom, Olivia, Isis, Hailey, Hana, Jasmine, Lily

Huela (*Spanish*) ♀　　　　　　RATING: ★★
Feminine form of Hugh; also short for Consuela
　People think of Huela as funny, pretty, trustworthy, energetic, exotic
　People who like the name Huela also like Hope, Victoria, Heidi, Chloe, Daphne, Hazel, Nora, Nyla, Iris, Bethany

Huey (*German*) ♂　　　　　　RATING: ★★
Bright in mind and spirit—Short for Hugh or Hubert; Huey Lewis, singer/songwriter
　People think of Huey as funny, handsome, intelligent, creative, cool
　People who like the name Huey also like Isaac, Felix, Hugh, Henry, Luke, Jack, Ethan, Ian, Jacob, Daniel

Hugh (*German*) ♂　　　　　　RATING: ★★
Bright in mind and spirit—Hugh Beaumont, actor; Hugh Grant, actor
　People think of Hugh as intelligent, handsome, caring, funny, cool
　People who like the name Hugh also like Ethan, Ian, Jack, Liam, Isaac, Oliver, Noah, Henry, Caleb, Jacob

Hugo (*German*) ♂　　　　　　RATING: ★★
Bright in mind and spirit—Variation of Hugh
　People think of Hugo as handsome, intelligent, funny, caring, cool
　People who like the name Hugo also like Hugh, Oliver, Oscar, Felix, Gabriel, Isaac, Sebastian, Henry, Jack, Noah

Humberto (*Spanish*) ♂　　　　　　RATING: ★★★
Bright
　People think of Humberto as handsome, funny, intelligent, sexy, caring
　People who like the name Humberto also like Nicholas, Justin, Derek, Edgar, Maximilian, Samuel, Branden, Demetrius, Eduardo, Jason

Hume (*English*) ♂　　　　　　RATING: ★☆
From the river island—Hume Cronyn, actor
　People think of Hume as trustworthy, powerful, slow, wealthy, big

People who like the name Hume also like Griffin, Fox, Declan, Felix, Holden, Nathan, Elliot, Finn, Harlow, Fairfax

Hummer (*American*) ♀♂　　　　　　RATING: ★★
Short for Humvee, a military vehicle; also a car brand
　People think of Hummer as loser, aggressive, weird, big, criminal
　People who like the name Hummer also like Humvee, Harley, Hayden, Caden, Cadence, Dylan, Harlan, Dorian, Jade, Casey

Humphrey (*English*) ♂　　　　　　RATING: ★☆
Peaceful warrior
　People think of Humphrey as nerdy, old-fashioned, weird, slow, wealthy
　People who like the name Humphrey also like Jacob, Geoffrey, Gabriel, Charles, Henry, Caleb, Alexander, Joshua, Elijah, Francis

Humvee (*American*) ♀♂　　　　　　RATING: ★☆
Acronym for High-Mobility Multipurpose Wheeled Vehicle
　People think of Humvee as aggressive, loser, big, criminal, lazy
　People who like the name Humvee also like Hummer, Avery, Taylor, Hunter, Reilly, Hayden, Forest, Reese, Kyle, Darcy

Hung (*Vietnamese*) ♂　　　　　　RATING: ★★★☆
Hero
　People think of Hung as cool, handsome, intelligent, weird, funny
　People who like the name Hung also like Nimrod, Caleb, Gordon, Conner, Gabe, Everett, Cole, Ford, Gage, Ean

Hunter (*English*) ♀♂　　　　　　RATING: ★★★☆
One who hunts—Hunter Tylo, actress; Holly Hunter, actress
　People think of Hunter as handsome, funny, intelligent, popular, energetic
　People who like the name Hunter also like Hayden, Logan, Madison, Riley, Parker, Dylan, Caden, Bailey, Connor, Taylor

Huong (*Vietnamese*) ♀　　　　　　RATING: ★★★☆
Scent of the flower
　People think of Huong as intelligent, pretty, caring, funny, cool
　People who like the name Huong also like Keiko, Felicity, Electra, Helena, Fleur, Hazel, Eshana, Chastity, Ginger, Blossom

Huslu (*Native American*) ♂　　　　　　RATING: ★★★☆
Hairy bear
　People think of Huslu as weird, exotic, ethnic, big, aggressive
　People who like the name Huslu also like Chayton, Anoki, Ahanu, Ezhno, Faris, Hakan, Edan, Elsu, Fabio, Apiatan

Hussein *(Arabic)* ♂   RATING: ★☆
Handsome one—Saddam Hussein, former Iraqi leader
> People think of Hussein as handsome, aggressive, criminal, intelligent, untrustworthy
>
> People who like the name Hussein also like Adam, Orlando, Heath, Hassan, Kale, Darren, Caesar, Jacob, Tristan, Andrew

Huy *(Vietnamese)* ♂   RATING: ★☆
Glorious
> People think of Huy as intelligent, handsome, funny, powerful, cool
>
> People who like the name Huy also like Dustin, Jasper, Kurt, José, Howard, Jonas, Gabe, Kaden, Byron, Carmine

Huyen *(Vietnamese)* ♀   RATING: ★★★
Jet black
> People think of Huyen as pretty, energetic, funny, weird, slow
>
> People who like the name Huyen also like Kiara, Keaira, Ebony, Eshana, Jillian, Juniper, Keiko, Feng, Keira, Dysis

Hy *(English)* ♂   RATING: ★★☆
Life—Short for Hyman
> People think of Hy as loser, nerdy, unpopular, criminal, weird
>
> People who like the name Hy also like Caleb, Seth, Vince, Roberto, Graham, Nathan, Fairfax, Ruben, Heath, Samuel

Hyacinth *(Greek)* ♀   RATING: ★★★☆
The flower
> People think of Hyacinth as intelligent, pretty, caring, quiet, funny
>
> People who like the name Hyacinth also like Genevieve, Hazel, Aurora, Harmony, Chloe, Iris, Cassandra, Hannah, Fiona, Hermione

Hyman *(Hebrew)* ♂   RATING: ★☆
Life
> People think of Hyman as creative, trendy, sexy, weird, loser
>
> People who like the name Hyman also like Ethan, David, Elijah, Bradley, Avidan, Jebediah, Hugh, Manuel, Cyrus, Blade

Hypatia *(Greek)* ♀   RATING: ★★★★
High, supreme
> People think of Hypatia as intelligent, pretty, powerful, wealthy, aggressive
>
> People who like the name Hypatia also like Aurora, Hermione, Isis, Lorelei, Desdemona, Ophelia, Erimentha, Helena, Calliope, Fiona

Hyroniemus *(Latin)* ♂   RATING: ★★★
Sacred name—Also spelled Hieronymus; Hieronymus Bosch, painter
> People think of Hyroniemus as exotic, poor, old-fashioned, intelligent, unpopular
>
> People who like the name Hyroniemus also like Latimer, Huckleberry, Cyrus, Alastair, Faris, Humphrey, Langston, Felix, Ignatius, Lamont

— I —

Iago *(Spanish)* ♂   RATING: ★★★☆
Supplanter—Variation of Jacob; character in *Othello* by William Shakespeare
> People think of Iago as criminal, untrustworthy, intelligent, sexy, exotic
>
> People who like the name Iago also like Fabian, Finn, Maddox, Bradley, Kaden, Edan, Oliver, Ethan, Ian, Jacob

Iain *(Celtic/Gaelic)* ♂   RATING: ★★★☆
God is gracious—Variation of John
> People think of Iain as handsome, intelligent, funny, trustworthy, caring
>
> People who like the name Iain also like Aiden, Ethan, Ian, Liam, Gabriel, Jacob, Ewan, Tristan, Conner, Isaac

Ian *(Celtic/Gaelic)* ♂   RATING: ★★★
God is gracious—Variation of John; pronounced *EE-an* or *EYE-an*; Ian Ziering, actor
> People think of Ian as handsome, intelligent, funny, caring, cool
>
> People who like the name Ian also like Ethan, Aiden, Isaac, Noah, Caleb, Gavin, Jacob, Owen, Gabriel, Nathan

Ianna *(American)* ♀   RATING: ★★★☆
God is gracious—Feminine form of Ian
> People think of Ianna as pretty, funny, creative, caring, cool
>
> People who like the name Ianna also like Isabella, Iliana, Kaelyn, Hailey, Genevieve, Ilana, Jadyn, Ava, Gabriella, Abrianna

Iantha *(Greek)* ♀   RATING: ★★☆
Violet-colored flower
> People think of Iantha as leader, wealthy, popular, weird, religious
>
> People who like the name Iantha also like Aelwen, Adora, Ebony, Rhiannon, Janelle, Ivette, Zabel, Cassandra, Neci, Florence

Ianthe *(Greek)* ♀   RATING: ★★
Violet-colored flower
> People think of Ianthe as exotic, pretty, intelligent, artsy, elegant
>
> People who like the name Ianthe also like Iolanthe, Iris, Cassandra, Xanthe, Aurora, Daphne, Isis, Calliope, Isabella, Dysis

Ibtesam *(Arabic)* ♀   RATING: ★★★
Smiling
> People think of Ibtesam as caring, funny, cool, powerful, old-fashioned
>
> People who like the name Ibtesam also like Inara, Damali, Heba, Ida, Eavan, Bela, Ha, Imani, Calliope, Adia

Ice *(American)* ♂   RATING: ★★★
Frozen water—Nickname made popular by rappers Ice Cube, Ice Tea, and Vanilla Ice
> People think of Ice as cool, sneaky, loser, nerdy, weird

People who like the name Ice also like Ace, Jayden, Nathan, Titus, Lucas, Simon, Tristan, Eric, Cole, Gareth

Ichabod *(Hebrew)* ♂   RATING: ★★☆
Departed glory—Ichabod Crane, character in *The Legend of Sleepy Hollow* by Washington Irving
People think of Ichabod as intelligent, trustworthy, old-fashioned, quiet, weird
People who like the name Ichabod also like Jacob, Isaac, Caleb, Elijah, Ethan, Gabriel, Oliver, Jack, Jonah, Felix

Ichigo *(Japanese)* ♀   RATING: ★★★★
Strawberry
People think of Ichigo as caring, leader, pretty, energetic, young
People who like the name Ichigo also like Inari, Haruko, Kaida, Sakura, Gin, Hoshiko, Mai, Kagami, Jin, Hitomi

Ida *(German)* ♀   RATING: ★★★☆
Hardworking—Ida Lupino, actress/singer/dancer
People think of Ida as funny, pretty, intelligent, caring, creative
People who like the name Ida also like Ava, Ada, Isabella, Eva, Grace, Faith, Ivy, Iris, Charlotte, Isabelle

Idalee *(American)* ♀   RATING: ★★★
Combination of Ida and Lee
People think of Idalee as funny, intelligent, pretty, cool, energetic
People who like the name Idalee also like Idalia, Kaelyn, Cailyn, Hannah, Jaclyn, Hailey, Ianna, Lana, Isabella, Jadyn

Idalia *(Spanish)* ♀   RATING: ★★★☆
Combination of Ida and Lia
People think of Idalia as intelligent, funny, caring, pretty, leader
People who like the name Idalia also like Isabella, Iliana, Isabelle, Adalia, Hailey, Gabriella, Layla, Hannah, Ianna, Nadia

Idalis *(Spanish)* ♀   RATING: ★★★
Combination if Ida and Elissa—Idalis deLeon, VJ/actress
People think of Idalis as pretty, creative, intelligent, exotic, quiet
People who like the name Idalis also like Idalia, Bianca, Isabella, Dahlia, Isabel, Jacqueline, Ilyssa, Nicole, Cassandra, Ariana

Idana *(American)* ♀   RATING: ★★
Combination of Ida and Anna
People think of Idana as old-fashioned, trendy, unpopular, weird, artsy
People who like the name Idana also like Ianna, Idalia, Iliana, Alana, Idania, Hailey, Hannah, Ilyssa, Isabella, Isabelle

Idania *(Slavic)* ♀   RATING: ★★
Hardworking
People think of Idania as pretty, intelligent, sexy, creative, caring

People who like the name Idania also like Iliana, Idalia, Ianna, Isabella, Ilana, Hailey, Isabel, Faith, Rianna, Hannah

Ide *(Celtic/Gaelic)* ♀   RATING: ★★★
Thirst—Pronounced *EE-duh*
People think of Ide as nerdy, loser, weird, unpopular, old-fashioned
People who like the name Ide also like Ianna, Enya, Isla, Genevieve, Brea, Aeryn, Iris, Breanna, Allene, Edana

Iden *(English)* ♀♂   RATING: ★★
From the marsh land pasture—Originally a surname
People think of Iden as young, cool, pretty, caring, intelligent
People who like the name Iden also like Caden, Jaden, Hayden, Aidan, Eden, Landen, Parker, Jordan, Halyn, Cadence

Idola *(Greek)* ♀   RATING: ★★☆
Vision
People think of Idola as caring, elegant, nerdy, energetic, pretty
People who like the name Idola also like Iris, Iliana, Iola, Cassandra, Inara, Calista, Ianna, Dysis, Electra, Esmeralda

Idra *(Hebrew)* ♀   RATING: ★★
Fig tree
People think of Idra as pretty, quiet, slow, lazy, old-fashioned
People who like the name Idra also like Idalia, Iliana, Isadora, Iren, Idana, Ivy, Dysis, Ilana, Hazel, Chloe

Idris *(Arabic)* ♂   RATING: ★★★☆
Righteous—Also Welsh meaning running lord; Idris Elba, actor
People think of Idris as handsome, intelligent, sexy, exotic, cool
People who like the name Idris also like Ian, Gideon, Kaden, Isaac, Maddox, Aiden, Drake, Ethan, Liam, Cyrus

Iduia *(Spanish)* ♀   RATING: ★☆
Civilization—Basque origin
People think of Iduia as nerdy, weird, poor, big, exotic
People who like the name Iduia also like Cadee, Brandee, Patricia, Isabella, Blanca, Charity, Bonita, Ita, Peggy, Jessica

Ifama *(African)* ♀   RATING: ★★☆
All is well—Nigerian origin
People think of Ifama as ethnic, aggressive, exotic, slow, untrustworthy
People who like the name Ifama also like Kayin, Keeya, Iren, Iliana, Idra, Kumani, Eavan, Inari, Kissa, Kainda

Ife *(African)* ♀   RATING: ★★★
Lover of art and culture—Western African origin
People think of Ife as caring, exotic, funny, pretty, creative
People who like the name Ife also like Kamili, Kabibe, Hazina, Gimbya, Ifama, Kissa, Baba, Jahzara, Genet, Karimah

Ige *(African)* ♂   RATING: ★☆
Born by breech—Nigerian origin
> People think of Ige as weird, big, criminal, aggressive, unpopular
> People who like the name Ige also like Adem, Azizi, Ilo, Jengo, Kayonga, Alvin, Guban, Kazi, Elliot, Jafari

Iggi *(African)* ♂   RATING: ★★★☆
Only son—Eritrean origin
> People think of Iggi as weird, big, energetic, loser, girl next door
> People who like the name Iggi also like Iggy, Fynn, Dexter, Casper, Maddox, Ollie, Damien, Ethan, Ingo, Ian

Iggy *(English)* ♂   RATING: ★☆
Firey one—Short for Ignatius; Iggy Pop, musician
> People think of Iggy as weird, funny, creative, cool, sexy
> People who like the name Iggy also like Ian, Felix, Ethan, Jack, Isaac, Jacob, Caleb, Maddox, Gabriel, Max

Ignatius *(Latin)* ♂   RATING: ★★★★
Fiery one
> People think of Ignatius as powerful, intelligent, handsome, leader, creative
> People who like the name Ignatius also like Gabriel, Isaac, Elijah, Felix, Ian, Oliver, Caleb, Cyrus, Ethan, Jonah

Ijlal *(Arabic)* ♀   RATING: ★★☆
Honor, respect
> People think of Ijlal as exotic, young, cool, aggressive, elegant
> People who like the name Ijlal also like Farah, Damali, Bayan, Fareeda, Samara, Heba, Inara, Ibtesam, Inaya, Abia

Ike *(American)* ♂   RATING: ★★
He will laugh—Short for Isaac or Dwight; "I Like Ike" was the presidential campaign slogan for Dwight D. Eisenhower; Ike Barinholtz, actor/comedian; Ike Turner, musician
> People think of Ike as powerful, handsome, intelligent, caring, funny
> People who like the name Ike also like Isaac, Ian, Ethan, Caleb, Jace, Jacob, Jake, Oliver, Cole, Lance

Ikia *(Greek)* ♀   RATING: ★★★☆
Unknown meaning
> People think of Ikia as pretty, exotic, intelligent, creative, caring
> People who like the name Ikia also like Jadyn, Hannah, Isabella, Ilana, Ilona, Hailey, Iliana, Makaila, Faith, Alanna

Ilana *(Hebrew)* ♀   RATING: ★★★
Tree
> People think of Ilana as pretty, intelligent, creative, caring, popular
> People who like the name Ilana also like Iliana, Isabella, Alana, Eva, Hannah, Hailey, Ianna, Faith, Isabelle, Ella

Ilandere *(American)* ♀   RATING: ★★★☆
Moon woman—Combination of the Basque words Ila (moon) and Andere (woman)
> People think of Ilandere as weird, exotic, artsy, elegant, young
> People who like the name Ilandere also like Kamaria, Isis, Faylinn, Amaya, Farsiris, Aysel, Chandra, Faye, Keaira, Aiko

Ilar *(Welsh)* ♀ ♂   RATING: ★★☆
Cheerful—Variation of Hilary
> People think of Ilar as girl next door, boy next door, creative, aggressive, funny
> People who like the name Ilar also like Oberon, Dante, Cadence, Skye, Echo, Iden, Garan, Blaze, Hadley, Raven

Ilaria *(Italian)* ♀   RATING: ★★★☆
Cheerful
> People think of Ilaria as pretty, elegant, exotic, popular, caring
> People who like the name Ilaria also like Arianna, Aria, Kaelyn, Kaydence, Gianna, Kaylee, Adrina, Cara, Kara, Melina

Ilario *(Italian)* ♂   RATING: ★★★☆
Cheerful
> People think of Ilario as ethnic, sexy, funny, young, exotic
> People who like the name Ilario also like Gabriel, Kaden, Giovanni, Darian, Antonio, Felix, Angelo, Fabian, Ethan, Lorenzo

Ildri *(Scandinavian)* ♀   RATING: ★★★★
Fire; peace
> People think of Ildri as pretty, sexy, quiet, powerful, intelligent
> People who like the name Ildri also like Maren, Hannah, Aideen, Adrienne, Hailey, Freja, Sonja, Arwen, Cordelia, Keaira

Iliana *(Greek)* ♀   RATING: ★★★
Bright
> People think of Iliana as pretty, intelligent, caring, funny, creative
> People who like the name Iliana also like Isabella, Ilana, Isabelle, Adriana, Kaelyn, Arianna, Hailey, Hannah, Chloe, Olivia

Ilithya *(Greek)* ♀   RATING: ★★★
Goddess of women in labor
> People think of Ilithya as exotic, elegant, funny, intelligent, creative
> People who like the name Ilithya also like Isis, Aurora, Celeste, Kaira, Iris, Kaiya, Iliana, Hypatia, Electra, Hazel

Ilka *(Hungarian)* ♀   RATING: ★★☆
Light—Short for Ilona
> People think of Ilka as intelligent, quiet, trustworthy, creative, pretty
> People who like the name Ilka also like Jadyn, Jalie, Hailey, Cashlin, Bridget, Gabriella, Isanne, Joyce, Keira, Vonda

Illeana (*Italian*) ♀ RATING: ★★★★
Bright—Variation of Helen; Illeana Douglas, actress
People think of Illeana as pretty, artsy, creative, elegant, intelligent
People who like the name Illeana also like Isabella, Isolde, Elise, Olivia, Annabelle, Bella, Emma, Serena, Celia, Amy

Illias (*Greek*) ♂ RATING: ★★
The Lord is my God—Variation of Elias
People think of Illias as trustworthy, intelligent, handsome, powerful, elegant
People who like the name Illias also like Isaiah, Ian, Elijah, Isaac, Jayden, Elias, Noah, Jeremiah, Gabriel, Gavin

Illinois (*Native American*) ♀♂ RATING: ★★★
Superior tribe—Algonquin origin; U.S. state
People think of Illinois as weird, young, caring, pretty, powerful
People who like the name Illinois also like Dakota, Indiana, Ireland, Infinity, Kansas, Ivory, Texas, Jade, Nebraska, Colorado

Ilo (*African*) ♂ RATING: ★★★☆
Light, joyous, sunshine—Nigerian origin
People think of Ilo as intelligent, energetic, caring, young, artsy
People who like the name Ilo also like Ian, Elijah, Noah, Iniko, Tucker, Lucas, Oliver, Chimelu, Ipo, Haben

Ilom (*African*) ♂ RATING: ★★☆
My enemies are many—Ibo origin; short for Ilomerika
People think of Ilom as exotic, quiet, funny, weird, sexy
People who like the name Ilom also like Jabari, Hirsi, Belay, Diata, Peter, Ilo, Jack, Kasim, Chimelu, Jafari

Ilona (*Hungarian*) ♀ RATING: ★★★★
Light—Variation of Helen
People think of Ilona as intelligent, pretty, creative, elegant, funny
People who like the name Ilona also like Iliana, Isabella, Hannah, Faith, Ilana, Ianna, Lana, Kyla, Ilyssa, Helena

Ilori (*African*) ♂ RATING: ★★
Special treasure—Nigerian origin
People think of Ilori as exotic, trustworthy, creative, intelligent, young
People who like the name Ilori also like Jayden, Isaac, Inoke, Isaiah, Bandele, Gabriel, Ian, Jason, Iniko, Jace

Ilse (*German*) ♀ RATING: ★★
Consecrated to God—Short for Elisabeth
People think of Ilse as creative, caring, intelligent, pretty, funny
People who like the name Ilse also like Isabelle, Isabella, Liesel, Abigail, Lorelei, Ilyssa, Ivy, Hannah, Isolde, Fiona

Ilya (*Russian*) ♂ RATING: ★★★★
The Lord is my God—Variation of Elijah
People think of Ilya as handsome, intelligent, cool, sexy, creative

People who like the name Ilya also like Elijah, Gabriel, Liam, Ian, Isaac, Gavin, Alexander, Landon, Tristan, Holden

Ilyssa (*American*) ♀ RATING: ★★★★
Rational—Variation of Alyssa
People think of Ilyssa as pretty, funny, artsy, popular, intelligent
People who like the name Ilyssa also like Isabella, Hailey, Faith, Alyssa, Gabrielle, Isabelle, Hannah, Jadyn, Alissa, Jasmine

Imagine (*American*) ♀♂ RATING: ★★★
To think, believe—Song by John Lennon
People think of Imagine as creative, artsy, weird, pretty, exotic
People who like the name Imagine also like Infinity, Dakota, Journey, Justice, Skye, Jade, Hunter, Hayden, Jocelyn, Addison

Imala (*Native American*) ♀ RATING: ★★☆
Disciplinarian
People think of Imala as popular, trustworthy, exotic, slow, creative
People who like the name Imala also like Halona, Kaya, Hateya, Ianna, Ella, Ayasha, Isabella, Kayla, Istas, Violet

Iman (*Arabic*) ♀ RATING: ★★
Faith—Iman, fashion model
People think of Iman as funny, pretty, intelligent, caring, creative
People who like the name Iman also like Imani, Amani, Faith, Ayanna, Jahzara, Layla, Samara, Eman, Hannah, Iliana

Imani (*Arabic*) ♀ RATING: ★★★★☆
Faith
People think of Imani as pretty, intelligent, popular, funny, caring
People who like the name Imani also like Aaliyah, Ayanna, Amani, Faith, Anaya, Jasmine, Isabella, Jadyn, Dominique, Iliana

Imaran (*Arabic*) ♂ RATING: ★★★
Prosperity—Variation of Imran
People think of Imaran as intelligent, funny, cool, energetic, handsome
People who like the name Imaran also like Isaiah, Kaden, Jayden, Aiden, Caleb, Isaac, Tristan, Ajani, Alijah, Ethan

Imelda (*Italian*) ♀ RATING: ★★★☆
Entire battle—Imelda Marcos, politician/former first lady of the Philippines
People think of Imelda as intelligent, pretty, funny, creative, caring
People who like the name Imelda also like Isabella, Angelina, Gianna, Cassandra, Donatella, Camilla, Bianca, Calista, Lucia, Ivette

Imogen (English) ♀   RATING: ★★★★
Innocent, girl—Created by William Shakespeare from Innogen; Imogen Heap, singer/songwriter
People think of Imogen as pretty, intelligent, creative, artsy, elegant
People who like the name Imogen also like Olivia, Grace, Ava, Isabella, Charlotte, Chloe, Ella, Amelia, Abigail, Isabelle

Imogene (Latin) ♀   RATING: ★★★★
Image, likeness—Imogene Coca, comedian
People think of Imogene as creative, pretty, intelligent, artsy, caring
People who like the name Imogene also like Olivia, Faith, Isabelle, Ava, Charlotte, Felicity, Paige, Genevieve, Hannah, Isabella

Imran (Arabic) ♂   RATING: ★★★
Prosperity
People think of Imran as untrustworthy, wealthy, religious
People who like the name Imran also like Cy, Ince, Clayton, Leander, Liam, Lysander, Alain, Marcel, Marius, Alistair

Ina (English) ♀   RATING: ★★★★
Short for names ending in -ina—Also a variation of Eithne or Enya
People think of Ina as pretty, intelligent, caring, creative, elegant
People who like the name Ina also like Iris, Eva, Ava, Isabella, Gabrielle, Isabelle, Sofia, Chloe, Grace, Bella

Inara (Arabic) ♀   RATING: ★★★★★
Illuminating, shining—Inara, character on *Firefly*
People think of Inara as exotic, pretty, elegant, sexy, creative
People who like the name Inara also like Inari, Isabella, Iliana, Chloe, Hannah, Gabrielle, Isis, Jasmine, Aurora, Leila

Inari (Japanese) ♀   RATING: ★★
Successful one—Place name in Japan and Finland
People think of Inari as pretty, creative, exotic, quiet, elegant
People who like the name Inari also like Amaya, Emiko, Sakura, Kaori, Kaida, Inara, Kaiya, Suki, Ayame, Kagami

Inaya (Arabic) ♀   RATING: ★★★
Solitude; kindness; grace
People think of Inaya as intelligent, caring, creative, pretty, energetic
People who like the name Inaya also like Inara, Inari, Imani, Aaliyah, Amaya, Amina, Farah, Anaya, Maya, Olivia

Ince (Hungarian) ♂   RATING: ★★☆
Innocent
People think of Ince as poor, nerdy, quiet, ethnic, creative
People who like the name Ince also like Isaiah, Haben, Drake, Jayden, Ethan, Jeremiah, Kaden, Dillan, Elvin, Juan

Inci (Turkish) ♀   RATING: ★★☆
Pearl
People think of Inci as nerdy, weird, poor, slow, lazy
People who like the name Inci also like Edana, Isha, Halima, Cocheta, Nascha, Shanti, Ide, Imani, Nakia, Veata

Independence (American) ♀   RATING: ★★★
Freedom
People think of Independence as exotic, pretty, cool, leader, intelligent
People who like the name Independence also like Harmony, Faith, Destiny, Isabella, Isabelle, Chloe, Eternity, Hope, Jasmine, Trinity

India (English) ♀   RATING: ★★★
From India—Character in *Gone With the Wind* by Margaret Mitchell
People think of India as pretty, intelligent, funny, exotic, creative
People who like the name India also like Ava, Isabella, Grace, Emma, Olivia, Jasmine, Chloe, Faith, Hannah, Eva

Indiana (American) ♀♂   RATING: ★★★★
Land of Indians—U.S. state; Indiana Jones, character created by George Lucas
People think of Indiana as intelligent, energetic, popular, creative, young
People who like the name Indiana also like Dakota, Hayden, Dylan, Hunter, Madison, Jade, Logan, Riley, Brooklyn, Bailey

Indira (Sanskrit/East Indian) ♀   RATING: ★★★★
Bestower of wealth—Epithet of the Goddess Lakshmi; Indira Ghandi, prime minister of India
People think of Indira as pretty, intelligent, sexy, exotic, funny
People who like the name Indira also like Isabella, Fiona, Eva, Isis, Isabelle, Isadora, Inara, India, Ciara, Samara

Indivar (Sanskrit/East Indian) ♂   RATING: ★☆
Blue lotus
People think of Indivar as ethnic, exotic, intelligent, elegant, leader
People who like the name Indivar also like Deepak, Manjit, Dinesh, Isaiah, Gautam, Ajay, Imaran, Gaurav, Ashwin, Jatin

Indiya (American) ♀   RATING: ★★★☆
Variation of India
People think of Indiya as exotic, sexy, pretty, sporty, girl next door
People who like the name Indiya also like Isabella, India, Indira, Ava, Giselle, Genevieve, Mia, Isabelle, Jenaya, Amaya

Indra (Sanskrit/East Indian) ♂   RATING: ★★★☆
Controls the rain
People think of Indra as intelligent, pretty, exotic, leader, powerful
People who like the name Indra also like Gabriel, Caleb, Maddox, Sebastian, Gideon, Jayden, Aiden, Oliver, Iniko, Isaiah

284

Inez (*Spanish*) ♀   RATING: ★★★☆
Pure, holy—Variation of Agnes
> People think of Inez as intelligent, pretty, creative, trustworthy, cool
>
> People who like the name Inez also like Isabel, Ava, Isabella, Iris, Eva, Layla, Ivy, Isabelle, Imogene, Jacqueline

Infinity (*American*) ♀ ♂   RATING: ★★★☆
Endless
> People think of Infinity as intelligent, creative, young, leader, artsy
>
> People who like the name Infinity also like Jade, Dakota, Ivory, Justice, Bailey, Hayden, Jaden, Madison, Liberty, Taylor

Inga (*Scandinavian*) ♀   RATING: ★★★☆
Belonging to Ing, a Nordic deity
> People think of Inga as pretty, intelligent, caring, creative, funny
>
> People who like the name Inga also like Ingrid, Isabella, Iris, Ilse, Fiona, Irene, Ava, Abigail, Astrid, Eva

Inge (*Scandinavian*) ♀   RATING: ★★★☆
Belonging to Ing, a Nordic deity
> People think of Inge as intelligent, caring, trustworthy, pretty, creative
>
> People who like the name Inge also like Ingrid, Iris, Inga, Isabel, Ilse, Isabelle, Ivy, Magnolia, Nora, Scarlett

Ingeborg (*German*) ♀   RATING: ★★☆
Ing's protection
> People think of Ingeborg as old-fashioned, nerdy, funny, ethnic, intelligent
>
> People who like the name Ingeborg also like Eleanor, Eliza, Ida, Jeanne, Minerva, Sarah, Frances, Kanika, Ina, Leah

Ingo (*Scandinavian*) ♂   RATING: ★☆
Belonging to Ing, a Nordic deity
> People think of Ingo as intelligent, handsome, leader, caring, cool
>
> People who like the name Ingo also like Ian, Ike, Lance, Jayden, Iago, Chase, Maddox, Gabe, Cyrus, Jack

Ingrid (*Scandinavian*) ♀   RATING: ★★★★
Ing's beauty
> People think of Ingrid as pretty, intelligent, funny, creative, caring
>
> People who like the name Ingrid also like Olivia, Grace, Fiona, Ava, Isabella, Iris, Eva, Astrid, Isabelle, Hannah

Inigo (*Portuguese*) ♂   RATING: ★★
Fiery—Variation of Ignatius; Inigo Jones, architect
> People think of Inigo as intelligent, powerful, handsome, cool, energetic
>
> People who like the name Inigo also like Gabriel, Caleb, Kael, Aiden, Felix, Diego, Xavier, Damien, Lysander, Sebastian

Iniko (*African*) ♂   RATING: ★★★
Born during troubled times—Nigerian origin
> People think of Iniko as funny, aggressive, intelligent, popular, cool
>
> People who like the name Iniko also like Gabriel, Ian, Inoke, Benjamin, Indra, Damien, Ethan, Joshua, Jacob, Lehana

Inocencia (*Spanish*) ♀   RATING: ★★★
Innocence
> People think of Inocencia as trustworthy, exotic, caring, pretty, weird
>
> People who like the name Inocencia also like Abrianna, Isabella, Adriana, Harmony, Gabriella, Anastasia, Aurora, Bianca, Hope, Magdalena

Inoke (*Hawaiian*) ♂   RATING: ★★★
Devoted—Fijian origin; Inoke Luveni, Fijian politician
> People think of Inoke as exotic, funny, ethnic, religious, sneaky
>
> People who like the name Inoke also like Ilori, Iniko, Gideon, Damon, Ian, Ewan, Kale, Ipo, Ethan, Gabriel

Integra (*Latin*) ♀   RATING: ★★★☆
Important
> People think of Integra as exotic, aggressive, powerful, leader, energetic
>
> People who like the name Integra also like Isabella, Isabelle, Inocencia, Ivy, Amelia, Flora, Aurora, Destiny, Bianca, Iris

Iokina (*Hawaiian*) ♀   RATING: ★★
God will develop
> People think of Iokina as exotic, ethnic, cool, pretty, caring
>
> People who like the name Iokina also like Iolana, Iolani, Iwalani, Kamea, Miliani, Kailani, Leilani, Iris, Isabella, Aolani

Iola (*Greek*) ♀   RATING: ★★
Violet
> People think of Iola as pretty, trustworthy, young, cool, caring
>
> People who like the name Iola also like Layla, Iris, Iona, Iliana, Ivy, Isis, Kaia, Giselle, Kara, Genevieve

Iolana (*Hawaiian*) ♀   RATING: ★★★☆
Soar like an eagle
> People think of Iolana as pretty, exotic, caring, intelligent, powerful
>
> People who like the name Iolana also like Iolani, Kailani, Iliana, Isabella, Iola, Aolani, Leilani, Kaya, Malia, Iokina

Iolani (*Hawaiian*) ♀   RATING: ★★★
To fly like a hawk
> People think of Iolani as exotic, intelligent, creative, pretty, powerful
>
> People who like the name Iolani also like Leilani, Iolana, Kailani, Ilana, Faith, Iliana, Harmony, Isis, Hannah, Aolani

Iolanthe *(Greek)* ♀   RATING: ★★★
Violet flower
People think of Iolanthe as exotic, elegant, creative, unpopular, pretty
People who like the name Iolanthe also like Ianthe, Iris, Giselle, Desdemona, Hermione, Isabelle, Iola, Evanthe, Isis, Helena

Ion *(Russian)* ♂   RATING: ★★
God is good—Variation of John
People think of Ion as aggressive, handsome, sexy, powerful, wild
People who like the name Ion also like Ian, Aiden, Ean, Kael, Jayden, Ethan, Gabriel, Kaden, Isaac, Cole

Iona *(Celtic/Gaelic)* ♀   RATING: ★★★★
From Iona, Scotland
People think of Iona as pretty, caring, intelligent, creative, funny
People who like the name Iona also like Olivia, Ava, Chloe, Isabella, Ella, Amelia, Genevieve, Keira, Fiona, Iris

Ione *(Greek)* ♀   RATING: ★★★★
From Ionia
People think of Ione as pretty, creative, artsy, intelligent, energetic
People who like the name Ione also like Fiona, Genevieve, Grace, Alana, Erin, Aeryn, Keira, Isla, Maeve, Emma

Iorwen *(Welsh)* ♀   RATING: ★★★☆
Fair, blessed lady
People think of Iorwen as elegant, creative, pretty, caring, intelligent
People who like the name Iorwen also like Elwyn, Aelwen, Arwen, Fiona, Gwyneth, Iris, Isolde, Isabelle, Dahlia, Gwendolyn

Iowa *(Native American)* ♀   RATING: ★★★
Beautiful land—U.S. state
People think of Iowa as pretty, wild, cool, powerful, weird
People who like the name Iowa also like Iris, Shania, Independence, Istas, Bly, Kaya, Calista, Pepper, Jewel, Alyssa

Iphigenia *(Greek)* ♀   RATING: ★★★
Born strong
People think of Iphigenia as weird, exotic, intelligent, powerful, pretty
People who like the name Iphigenia also like Penelope, Isaura, Iolanthe, Desdemona, Helena, Hypatia, Erimentha, Ianthe, Iola, Cleo

Iphigenie *(French)* ♀   RATING: ★☆
Variation of Iphigenia
People think of Iphigenie as exotic, sexy, funny, pretty, slow
People who like the name Iphigenie also like Giselle, Isis, Persephone, Demeter, Ilandere, Hypatia, Aurora, Indira, Isolde, Lysandra

Ipo *(Hawaiian)* ♂   RATING: ★☆
Sweetheart, lover
People think of Ipo as ethnic, big, energetic, wild, sneaky
People who like the name Ipo also like Inoke, Iniko, Ian, Ilo, Bo, Isaac, Kael, Anoki, Felix, Indra

Ira *(Hebrew)* ♀♂   RATING: ★★★★
Watchful—In Polynesian mythology, a sky goddess
People think of Ira as intelligent, caring, funny, trustworthy, handsome
People who like the name Ira also like Ezra, Blake, Logan, Hayden, Evan, Hunter, Dylan, Avery, Jada, Caden

Iram *(Hebrew)* ♂   RATING: ★★★
City of the nation
People think of Iram as intelligent, funny, trustworthy, creative, energetic
People who like the name Iram also like Gabriel, Isaiah, Ethan, Isaac, Ian, Noah, Jonah, Elijah, Gavin, Micah

Irela *(Celtic/Gaelic)* ♀   RATING: ★★☆
From Ireland
People think of Irela as artsy, pretty, lazy, big, intelligent
People who like the name Irela also like Naomi, Ilana, Nadia, Kayla, Isabel, Lena, Brianna, Selena, Caelan, Briana

Ireland *(American)* ♀♂   RATING: ★★★☆
Homage to Ireland—Ireland Baldwin, daughter of Kim Basinger and Alec Baldwin
People think of Ireland as pretty, creative, popular, intelligent, caring
People who like the name Ireland also like Hayden, Brooklyn, Dakota, Bailey, Logan, Avery, Parker, London, Aidan, Jaden

Irem *(Turkish)* ♂   RATING: ★★★
Garden in heaven
People think of Irem as caring, funny, intelligent, popular, pretty
People who like the name Irem also like Isaiah, Isaac, Jamal, Faris, Jaser, Jaron, Aaron, Keiran, Josiah, Gabriel

Iren *(Slavic)* ♀   RATING: ★★★☆
Peace
People think of Iren as elegant, pretty, energetic, sexy, intelligent
People who like the name Iren also like Irene, Iris, Jadyn, Ivy, Ophelia, Emily, Emma, Eva, Iliana, Scarlett

Irene *(Greek)* ♀   RATING: ★★★☆
Peace
People think of Irene as pretty, intelligent, caring, funny, creative
People who like the name Irene also like Isabella, Isabelle, Hannah, Faith, Abigail, Iris, Olivia, Fiona, Emma, Audrey

Iria *(American)* ♀   RATING: ★★
Colorful, rainbow—From the Greek name Iris
People think of Iria as pretty, weird, young, wild, energetic

People who like the name Iria also like Iris, Isis, Elia, Cailyn, Nora, Dawn, Gwendolyn, Kiara, Inari, Ivy

Irina *(Russian)* ♀   RATING: ★★★☆
Peace
People think of Irina as pretty, intelligent, funny, sexy, creative
People who like the name Irina also like Isabella, Nadia, Faith, Isabelle, Hannah, Fiona, Grace, Eva, Olivia, Isabel

Iris *(Greek)* ♀   RATING: ★★★★
Colorful, rainbow—Ancient symbol of power, which was dedicated to the god Juno
People think of Iris as pretty, intelligent, creative, caring, funny
People who like the name Iris also like Violet, Ava, Ivy, Grace, Chloe, Faith, Isabella, Olivia, Hannah, Emma

Irisa *(English)* ♀   RATING: ★★★
Iris
People think of Irisa as pretty, intelligent, trendy, popular, weird
People who like the name Irisa also like Isabella, Iris, Faith, Hannah, Olivia, Ilyssa, Bianca, Isabelle, Emma, Hailey

Irish *(American)* ♀ ♂   RATING: ★★☆
From Ireland
People think of Irish as intelligent, leader, caring, pretty, young
People who like the name Irish also like Ireland, Bailey, Hayden, Jaden, Madison, Connor, Jade, London, Mason, Logan

Irma *(German)* ♀   RATING: ★☆
Whole, entire
People think of Irma as funny, pretty, intelligent, trustworthy, caring
People who like the name Irma also like Iris, Isabella, Ingrid, Isabelle, Violet, Irene, Olivia, Hazel, Inga, Sabrina

Irving *(English)* ♂   RATING: ★★
From Irving, Scotland—Irving Berlin, composer
People think of Irving as intelligent, funny, handsome, caring, cool
People who like the name Irving also like Isaac, Owen, Oliver, Liam, Vincent, Victor, Xavier, Felix, Ivan, Tristan

Irwin *(American)* ♂   RATING: ★★★
From Irvine, Scotland—"Crocodile Hunter" Steve Irwin, conservationist/TV host
People think of Irwin as weird, old-fashioned, stuck-up, exotic, cool
People who like the name Irwin also like Galen, Oscar, Sloan, Maxton, Garvey, Owen, Spence, Olson, Holden, Cavan

Isaac *(Hebrew)* ♂   RATING: ★★★☆
He will laugh—Also spelled Issac; Isaac Asimov, author; Isaac Hayes, actor
People think of Isaac as intelligent, handsome, funny, caring, energetic

People who like the name Isaac also like Isaiah, Ethan, Jacob, Noah, Elijah, Caleb, Ian, Gabriel, Zachary, Benjamin

Isabel *(Spanish)* ♀   RATING: ★★★☆
God is my oath
People think of Isabel as pretty, intelligent, funny, caring, creative
People who like the name Isabel also like Isabella, Emma, Isabelle, Olivia, Hannah, Grace, Ava, Abigail, Faith, Ella

Isabella *(Italian)* ♀   RATING: ★★★☆
God is my oath—Isabella Rossellini, actress
People think of Isabella as pretty, elegant, intelligent, popular, caring
People who like the name Isabella also like Ava, Olivia, Emma, Isabelle, Gabriella, Ella, Abigail, Grace, Hannah, Bella

Isabelle *(French)* ♀   RATING: ★★★★☆
God is my oath
People think of Isabelle as pretty, intelligent, elegant, caring, funny
People who like the name Isabelle also like Isabella, Abigail, Grace, Olivia, Emma, Hannah, Gabrielle, Ava, Chloe, Hailey

Isabis *(American)* ♀   RATING: ★★★
God is my oath
People think of Isabis as loser, poor, weird, nerdy, religious
People who like the name Isabis also like Isabella, Isabelle, Gabrielle, Iris, Abigail, Giselle, Isabel, Hazina, Isoke, Isadora

Isadora *(Greek)* ♀   RATING: ★★☆
Gift of Isis—Isadora Duncan, dancer
People think of Isadora as pretty, exotic, intelligent, elegant, creative
People who like the name Isadora also like Isabella, Genevieve, Isabelle, Olivia, Aurora, Hannah, Gabrielle, Ava, Bella, Amelia

Isaiah *(Hebrew)* ♂   RATING: ★★★★
God is salvation—Jewish prophet
People think of Isaiah as handsome, intelligent, funny, caring, energetic
People who like the name Isaiah also like Isaac, Elijah, Noah, Ethan, Gabriel, Caleb, Jeremiah, Jacob, Ian, Aiden

Isandro *(Spanish)* ♀   RATING: ★★
One who is freed—Variation of Lysander
People think of Isandro as lazy, funny, criminal, weird, big
People who like the name Isandro also like Savanna, Lola, Sofia, Juliana, Alegria, Estrella, Daniella, Adelina, Kaelyn, Caitlin

Isanne *(American)* ♀   RATING: ★★★
Combination of Isabel and Anne
People think of Isanne as pretty, quiet, elegant, old-fashioned, funny

People who like the name Isanne also like Idalia, Isabella, Isabel, Ianna, Isolde, Irene, Iliana, Isabelle, Inari, Isis

Isaura *(Spanish)* ♀ RATING: ★★★☆
From Isauria, an ancient land that is now part of Turkey
People think of Isaura as pretty, exotic, funny, weird, intelligent
People who like the name Isaura also like Isabella, Isis, Isadora, Isabelle, Giselle, Amaya, Iris, Isabel, Genevieve, Ophelia

Isha *(Sanskrit/East Indian)* ♀ RATING: ★★★★
One who protects
People think of Isha as intelligent, pretty, caring, creative, cool
People who like the name Isha also like Ishana, Isis, Isabella, Amara, Isadora, Eva, Hailey, Iliana, Inari, Jadyn

Ishana *(Sanskrit/East Indian)* ♀ RATING: ★★★
Prosperous
People think of Ishana as pretty, ethnic, powerful, intelligent, popular
People who like the name Ishana also like Isabella, Eshana, Iliana, Isha, Ianna, Inara, Isabel, Indira, Adriana, Anaya

Ishmael *(Hebrew)* ♂ RATING: ★★★☆
God will hear
People think of Ishmael as funny, intelligent, powerful, sexy, popular
People who like the name Ishmael also like Isaiah, Isaac, Elijah, Gabriel, Jeremiah, Ethan, Caleb, Samuel, Noah, Ezekiel

Isi *(Spanish)* ♀ RATING: ★★★
Consecrated to God—Short for Isabelle
People think of Isi as exotic, pretty, intelligent, cool, powerful
People who like the name Isi also like Isabel, Isis, Isabella, Olivia, Izzy, Ivy, Bella, Annalise, Isabelle, Eve

Isis *(Egyptian)* ♀ RATING: ★★★★☆
Throne—Goddess, wife of Osiris and mother of Horus
People think of Isis as pretty, intelligent, exotic, powerful, sexy
People who like the name Isis also like Iris, Aurora, Ivy, Isabella, Ava, Fiona, Chloe, Jasmine, Eva, Bella

Isla *(Celtic/Gaelic)* ♀ RATING: ★★
Island—Isla Fisher, actress
People think of Isla as pretty, creative, intelligent, caring, exotic
People who like the name Isla also like Ava, Eva, Chloe, Grace, Ella, Isabella, Mia, Layla, Genevieve, Lily

Isleen *(Celtic/Gaelic)* ♀ RATING: ★★★
Variation of Eileen
People think of Isleen as powerful, exotic, artsy, creative, caring

People who like the name Isleen also like Isla, Ianna, Shayla, Isabelle, Erin, Keaira, Sabrina, Breanna, Eileen, Seanna

Ismael *(Hebrew)* ♂ RATING: ★★★★
God will hear
People think of Ismael as handsome, funny, caring, intelligent, cool
People who like the name Ismael also like Isaac, Isaiah, Ishmael, Gabriel, Elijah, Joshua, Jeremiah, Adrian, Daniel, Samuel

Ismaela *(Hebrew)* ♀ RATING: ★★
God will hear—Feminine form of Ismael
People think of Ismaela as exotic, elegant, pretty, artsy, ethnic
People who like the name Ismaela also like Isabella, Isabelle, Isadora, Annalise, Isabel, Naomi, Iliana, Liana, Samara, Moriah

Ismail *(Arabic)* ♂ RATING: ★★
God will hear
People think of Ismail as religious, intelligent, ethnic, weird, nerdy
People who like the name Ismail also like Isaiah, Ishmael, Ismael, Ethan, Isaac, Gabriel, Joel, Jadon, Micah, Jayden

Ismet *(Turkish)* ♂ RATING: ★☆
Honor
People think of Ismet as weird, ethnic, exotic, religious, nerdy
People who like the name Ismet also like Isaac, Ingo, Flint, Isaiah, Niran, Tristan, Gabriel, Gideon, Ishmael, Pedro

Isoke *(African)* ♀ RATING: ★★★
Satisfying gift from God
People think of Isoke as exotic, sexy, ethnic, pretty, leader
People who like the name Isoke also like Isabis, Isis, Imani, Jahzara, Malaika, Isabella, Isabelle, Isolde, Hazina, Anaya

Isolde *(Celtic/Gaelic)* ♀ RATING: ★★★★☆
She who is gazed upon—*Tristan und Isolde*, opera by Richard Wagner, based on the ancient fable of Tristan and Iseult
People think of Isolde as pretty, elegant, intelligent, exotic, caring
People who like the name Isolde also like Genevieve, Isabella, Ava, Fiona, Gwendolyn, Arwen, Aurora, Olivia, Isabelle, Grace

Isondo *(African)* ♀ RATING: ★★☆
The wheel—Nguni origin
People think of Isondo as big, nerdy, loser, winner, lazy
People who like the name Isondo also like Cyrah, Ana, Hester, Kerri, Maire, Fayola, Eithne

Isra *(Arabic)* ♀♂　　　RATING: ★★★☆
Riches
>People think of Isra as pretty, intelligent, cool, young, elegant
>People who like the name Isra also like Ezra, Kai, Jade, Dante, Flynn, Rowan, Hayden, Hunter, London, Zephyr

Israel *(Hebrew)* ♂　　　RATING: ★★★★☆
Wrestled with God
>People think of Israel as handsome, intelligent, funny, cool, creative
>People who like the name Israel also like Isaiah, Isaac, Elijah, Gabriel, Jeremiah, Caleb, Noah, Ethan, Ian, Jacob

Issay *(African)* ♂　　　RATING: ★★
Hairy—South African origin
>People think of Issay as weird, loser, nerdy, exotic, unpopular
>People who like the name Issay also like Isaac, Isaiah, Analu, Kimoni, Barak, Ilori, Gabriel, Upendo, Inoke, Makalo

Istas *(Native American)* ♀　　　RATING: ★★
Snow
>People think of Istas as exotic, creative, powerful, artsy, energetic
>People who like the name Istas also like Kaya, Chumani, Amadahy, Halona, Hateya, Catori, Isaura, Ayasha, Cocheta, Dysis

Istvan *(Hungarian)* ♂　　　RATING: ★★☆
Crown
>People think of Istvan as sexy, wealthy, funny, elegant, creative
>People who like the name Istvan also like Ethan, Eugene, Ewan, Etienne, Ethanael, Essien, Eytan

Ita *(Spanish)* ♀　　　RATING: ★★★
Short for names ending in Ita
>People think of Ita as pretty, trustworthy, girl next door, intelligent, religious
>People who like the name Ita also like Isabella, Italia, Itala, Lina, Gemma, Stella, Leola, Orella, Melita, Gina

Itachi *(Japanese)* ♂　　　RATING: ★★★☆
Weasel—In Japanese mythology, weasels are an ill omen, signifying bad luck and death
>People think of Itachi as criminal, powerful, intelligent, handsome, sneaky
>People who like the name Itachi also like Haru, Daiki, Donovan, Dominic, Gabriel, Eric, Leland, Mikhail, Simon, Warren

Itala *(Italian)* ♀　　　RATING: ★★★
From Italy
>People think of Itala as ethnic, pretty, exotic, elegant, poor
>People who like the name Itala also like Isabella, Natalia, Gianna, Italia, Bianca, Gemma, Chloe, Giovanna, Bella, Donatella

Italia *(Italian)* ♀　　　RATING: ★★☆
Italy
>People think of Italia as pretty, trendy, exotic, creative, funny
>People who like the name Italia also like Isabella, Gianna, Natalia, Bella, Gabriella, Angelina, Ava, Olivia, Giovanna, Bianca

Ithaca *(Greek)* ♀♂　　　RATING: ★★☆
Home of Ulysses—Also a Greek island in the Ionian Sea; also a town and university in New York
>People think of Ithaca as exotic, trendy, artsy, trustworthy, weird
>People who like the name Ithaca also like Logan, Keeran, Porter, Ash, Bailey, Dante, Avery, Aiken, Jordan, Blaise

Ivan *(Russian)* ♂　　　RATING: ★★☆
God is gracious—Variation of John
>People think of Ivan as handsome, intelligent, funny, cool, caring
>People who like the name Ivan also like Ian, Isaac, Ethan, Gabriel, Gavin, Isaiah, Noah, Elijah, Nathan, Caleb

Ivana *(Russian)* ♀　　　RATING: ★★★☆
Feminine form of Ivan—Ivana Trump, Olympic athlete/model/ex-wife of tycoon Donald Trump
>People think of Ivana as intelligent, pretty, funny, sexy, caring
>People who like the name Ivana also like Isabella, Hannah, Ivy, Hailey, Bianca, Gabriella, Gianna, Olivia, Abigail, Isabelle

Ives *(English)* ♀♂　　　RATING: ★★☆
Land of heroes—Originally a surname meaning from St. Ives, England
>People think of Ives as exotic, old-fashioned, slow, untrustworthy, lazy
>People who like the name Ives also like Delaney, Hayden, Camden, Dorian, Zeal, Chandler, Kelsea, Normandie, Dylan, Logan

Ivette *(French)* ♀　　　RATING: ★★★☆
Yew—Variation of Yvette
>People think of Ivette as pretty, funny, intelligent, cool, caring
>People who like the name Ivette also like Isabelle, Isabella, Isabel, Jacqueline, Iris, Faith, Hailey, Giselle, Evette, Desiree

Ivi *(English)* ♀　　　RATING: ★★★☆
Ivy plant—Variation of Ivy
>People think of Ivi as pretty, exotic, elegant, aggressive, energetic
>People who like the name Ivi also like Ivy, Iris, Hailey, Ivie, Olivia, Isabella, Kali, Isabelle, Ava, Jewel

Ivie *(English)* ♀　　　RATING: ★★☆
Ivy plant—Variation of Ivy
>People think of Ivie as pretty, creative, funny, intelligent, cool
>People who like the name Ivie also like Ivy, Isabella, Ava, Isabel, Paige, Faith, Eva, Iris, Isabelle, Hannah

Ivo (English) ♂ RATING: ★☆
Yew
> People think of Ivo as handsome, intelligent, creative, funny, powerful
> People who like the name Ivo also like Ivan, Ian, Adam, Isaac, Gabriel, Mikhail, Milo, Galen, Lysander, Kaden

Ivory (English) ♀♂ RATING: ★★☆
White as elephant tusks
> People think of Ivory as pretty, caring, funny, creative, intelligent
> People who like the name Ivory also like Jade, Dakota, Hayden, Bailey, Jaden, Jordan, Madison, Taylor, Brooke, Riley

Ivria (Hebrew) ♀ RATING: ★★★
A Hebrew woman
> People think of Ivria as pretty, exotic, caring, trendy, sexy
> People who like the name Ivria also like Ivy, Ivi, Ivana, India, Ishana, Dysis, Isha, Isis, Idalia, Iria

Ivrit (Hebrew) ♂ RATING: ★☆
The Hebrew language
> People think of Ivrit as pretty, funny, religious, wild, cool
> People who like the name Ivrit also like Drake, Bo, Isaac, Gabriel, Gavin, Caleb, Dalton, Eytan, Josiah, Jacob

Ivy (English) ♀ RATING: ★★☆
Climbing vine plant
> People think of Ivy as pretty, intelligent, creative, funny, artsy
> People who like the name Ivy also like Ava, Olivia, Faith, Iris, Chloe, Isabella, Grace, Fiona, Paige, Emma

Iwalani (Hawaiian) ♀ RATING: ★★★
Heavenly seagull
> People think of Iwalani as exotic, creative, weird, pretty, intelligent
> People who like the name Iwalani also like Kailani, Keani, Iolani, Iokina, Miliani, Noelani, Malia, Leilani, Kamea, Iolana

Izefia (African) ♀ RATING: ★☆
I have no child
> People think of Izefia as unpopular, exotic, old-fashioned, quiet, lazy
> People who like the name Izefia also like Imelda, Ivana, Iola, Isabis, Isadora, Ishana, Ivy, Indira, Ivette, Jahzara

Izzy (Spanish) ♀ RATING: ★★
God is my oath—Short for Isabel
> People think of Izzy as funny, pretty, creative, energetic, cool
> People who like the name Izzy also like Isabella, Ivy, Grace, Isabelle, Ava, Faith, Eva, Paige, Olivia, Ella

— J —

Jabari (Arabic) ♂ RATING: ★★★☆
Fearless—Swahili origin
> People think of Jabari as handsome, funny, popular, cool, energetic
> People who like the name Jabari also like Jayden, Jeremiah, Kaden, Jamar, Isaiah, Jadon, Jevonte, Jamal, Jamil, Jason

Jabilo (African) ♂ RATING: ★☆
Medicine man
> People think of Jabilo as weird, big, lazy, intelligent, nerdy
> People who like the name Jabilo also like Jabari, Ja, Jadon, Jabir, Jabulani, Jack, Jacob, Jafari, Jamal, Jengo

Jabir (Arabic) ♂ RATING: ★★★
Comforter
> People think of Jabir as handsome, caring, funny, popular, intelligent
> People who like the name Jabir also like Jamal, Jabari, Jamil, Jaser, Jamar, Ja, Jadon, Jacob, Jay, Jackson

Jabulani (African) ♂ RATING: ★★★☆
Be happy
> People think of Jabulani as poor, handsome, aggressive, intelligent, trustworthy
> People who like the name Jabulani also like Jabari, Jayden, Joshua, Ja, Jamon, Jafari, Asher, Jabilo, Jabir, Jafaru

Jace (American) ♂ RATING: ★★★
Short for Jason or the initials J.C.
> People think of Jace as handsome, funny, popular, cool, energetic
> People who like the name Jace also like Jayden, Kaden, Aiden, Jackson, Ethan, Chase, Braden, Jacob, Gavin, Landon

Jacey (American) ♀♂ RATING: ★★★★
From the initials J.C.—Also spelled Jacie; short for Jacinda
> People think of Jacey as pretty, funny, creative, popular, energetic
> People who like the name Jacey also like Jaden, Caden, Bailey, Madison, Hayden, Jade, Addison, Riley, Jordan, Mackenzie

Jachai (Hebrew) ♂ RATING: ★★★☆
Supplanter
> People think of Jachai as handsome, cool, exotic, popular, trustworthy
> People who like the name Jachai also like Jeremiah, Josiah, Jadon, Jayden, Jace, Malachi, Jaron, Jabari, Aden, Jamon

Jacinda (English) ♀ RATING: ★★★☆
Hyacinth
> People think of Jacinda as pretty, intelligent, caring, creative, funny

People who like the name Jacinda also like Chloe, Jadyn, Isabella, Ava, Grace, Abigail, Jasmine, Gabriella, Olivia, Gabrielle

Jacinta *(Spanish)* ♀ RATING: ★★
Hyacinth
People think of Jacinta as pretty, funny, creative, intelligent, caring
People who like the name Jacinta also like Jacinda, Isabella, Jasmine, Hannah, Bianca, Jaclyn, Charlotte, Jadyn, Isabelle, Chloe

Jack *(English)* ♂ RATING: ★★★
Supplanter—Short for John or Jackson
People think of Jack as handsome, funny, cool, intelligent, popular
People who like the name Jack also like Jacob, Ethan, Jake, Benjamin, Noah, Jackson, Luke, Owen, Aiden, Matthew

Jackie *(English)* ♀ RATING: ★★★☆
Supplanter—Short for Jacqueline; also spelled Jacqui
People think of Jackie as funny, pretty, caring, cool, creative
People who like the name Jackie also like Jacqueline, Hailey, Jaclyn, Faith, Jessica, Lauren, Isabella, Hannah, Emma, Jasmine

Jackson *(English)* ♂ RATING: ★★★
Son of Jack
People think of Jackson as handsome, popular, intelligent, funny, cool
People who like the name Jackson also like Ethan, Jacob, Noah, Aiden, Landon, Caleb, Jack, Gavin, Owen, Braden

Jaclyn *(American)* ♀ RATING: ★★★
Supplanter—Variation of Jacqueline
People think of Jaclyn as pretty, funny, intelligent, caring, creative
People who like the name Jaclyn also like Jacqueline, Jadyn, Hailey, Isabella, Hannah, Faith, Paige, Emma, Abigail, Grace

Jacob *(Hebrew)* ♂ RATING: ★★★☆
Supplanter
People think of Jacob as handsome, funny, intelligent, cool, caring
People who like the name Jacob also like Ethan, Caleb, Joshua, Noah, Benjamin, Isaac, Zachary, Nathan, Matthew, Jackson

Jacoba *(Hebrew)* ♀ RATING: ★★★☆
Supplanter—Feminine form of Jacob
People think of Jacoba as pretty, intelligent, trustworthy, aggressive, girl next door
People who like the name Jacoba also like Jadyn, Jaclyn, Johanna, Jenaya, Janeeva, Jacinda, Jazlynn, Jacquelle, Jasmine, Janelle

Jacqueline *(French)* ♀ RATING: ★★★
Supplanter—Feminine form of Jacques
People think of Jacqueline as pretty, funny, intelligent, caring, creative
People who like the name Jacqueline also like Isabella, Hannah, Gabrielle, Abigail, Grace, Isabelle, Hailey, Olivia, Faith, Samantha

Jacquelle *(French)* ♀ RATING: ★★★☆
Supplanter—Feminine form of Jacques
People think of Jacquelle as pretty, intelligent, funny, caring, cool
People who like the name Jacquelle also like Jacqueline, Jadyn, Jasmine, Jaclyn, Janelle, Isabella, Isabelle, Gabrielle, Jazlynn, Abigail

Jacques *(French)* ♂ RATING: ★★★☆
Supplanter—Variation of Jacob; Jacques Cousteau, ecologist/filmmaker
People think of Jacques as intelligent, handsome, popular, creative, cool
People who like the name Jacques also like Jacob, Jackson, Jack, Aiden, Alexander, Justin, Jared, Jeremiah, André, Jason

Jada *(American)* ♀♂ RATING: ★★★☆
Variation of Jade—Also a Hebrew male name in the Old Testament; Jada Pinkett Smith, actress/musician
People think of Jada as pretty, funny, intelligent, popular, creative
People who like the name Jada also like Jaden, Jade, Jordan, Madison, Caden, Hayden, Bailey, Jalen, Cadence, Jocelyn

Jade *(English)* ♀♂ RATING: ★★★★
Green gemstone
People think of Jade as pretty, funny, creative, caring, intelligent
People who like the name Jade also like Jaden, Madison, Jada, Jordan, Hayden, Bailey, Caden, Dakota, Riley, Logan

Jaden *(American)* ♀♂ RATING: ★★★★
Combination of Jay and Aiden—Also spelled Jaiden
People think of Jaden as intelligent, handsome, funny, popular, creative
People who like the name Jaden also like Caden, Hayden, Jade, Madison, Jordan, Bailey, Logan, Riley, Aidan, Cadence

Jadon *(American)* ♂ RATING: ★★★★
Variation of Jaden—Also the Hebrew male name Yadon, meaning "he will judge," could be rendered as Jadon in English
People think of Jadon as handsome, funny, intelligent, popular, energetic
People who like the name Jadon also like Jayden, Kaden, Aiden, Ethan, Jacob, Caleb, Jace, Braden, Jared, Aden

Jadyn *(American)* ♀　　　RATING: ★★★☆
Variation of Jaden
> People think of Jadyn as pretty, funny, intelligent, energetic, creative
> People who like the name Jadyn also like Kaelyn, Hailey, Isabella, Hannah, Cailyn, Paige, Ava, Emma, Faith, Ashlyn

Jadzia *(Polish)* ♀　　　RATING: ★★★★
War battle—Short for Jadwiga
> People think of Jadzia as pretty, funny, creative, leader, intelligent
> People who like the name Jadzia also like Jahzara, Jadyn, Jazlynn, Jazzelle, Jalena, Jalia, Janelle, Jacinda, Jamila, Jelena

Jaegar *(German)* ♂　　　RATING: ★★
Hunter—Also a surname
> People think of Jaegar as handsome, powerful, aggressive, wild, sexy
> People who like the name Jaegar also like Jaeger, Jagger, Jacob, Jack, Tristan, Aiden, Alexander, Jayden, Kaden, Keagan

Jaeger *(German)* ♂　　　RATING: ★★
Hunter
> People think of Jaeger as handsome, intelligent, popular, sporty, exotic
> People who like the name Jaeger also like Jackson, Jacob, Jaegar, Ethan, Jaxon, Jace, Gavin, Jayden, Landon, Jack

Jael *(Hebrew)* ♀　　　RATING: ★★★★
Wild mountain goat
> People think of Jael as intelligent, pretty, creative, funny, caring
> People who like the name Jael also like Jadyn, Kaelyn, Jolie, Jazlynn, Abigail, Jalena, Jaide, Hannah, Gabrielle, Aaliyah

Jaela *(American)* ♀　　　RATING: ★★★☆
Wild mountain goat—Variation of Jael; also spelled Jaella
> People think of Jaela as pretty, funny, creative, intelligent, caring
> People who like the name Jaela also like Jadyn, Jenaya, Jaelyn, Jazlynn, Jahzara, Kayla, Jaide, Ava, Eva, Janae

Jaelyn *(American)* ♀　　　RATING: ★★★☆
Supplanter—Short for Jacqueline
> People think of Jaelyn as pretty, intelligent, funny, creative, energetic
> People who like the name Jaelyn also like Jadyn, Kaelyn, Hailey, Ashlyn, Jazlynn, Emma, Cailyn, Jasmine, Kailey, Jeslyn

Jaetyn *(American)* ♀♂　　　RATING: ★★☆
Created name—Variation of Jaden
> People think of Jaetyn as artsy, pretty, religious, winner, poor
> People who like the name Jaetyn also like Jacey, Jaden, Payton, Jade, Kaycee, Logan, Taylor, Keaton, Mason, Cadence

Jafari *(Arabic)* ♂　　　RATING: ★★★
Rivulet, stream—Swahili origin
> People think of Jafari as intelligent, ethnic, exotic, popular, weird
> People who like the name Jafari also like Jabari, Ja, Johnathan, Joshua, Jamar, Jamal, Jacques, Jason, Jamil, Ethan

Jafaru *(African)* ♂　　　RATING: ★★☆
Rivulet, stream—Variation of Jafari
> People think of Jafaru as exotic, young, trustworthy, powerful, intelligent
> People who like the name Jafaru also like Ja, Jafari, Jabulani, Kasim, William, Jerome, Lawrence, Andrew, Jay, Kenyi

Jag *(Sanskrit/East Indian)* ♂　　　RATING: ★★★☆
The universe—Also short for Jaguar
> People think of Jag as aggressive, leader, powerful, handsome, cool
> People who like the name Jag also like Jace, Jagger, Jackson, Jett, Jack, Jacob, Jared, Jayden, Maddox, Jaxon

Jagannath *(Sanskrit/East Indian)* ♂　　　RATING: ★★★
World lord—Same origin as juggernaut, from the festival for the god Jagannath
> People think of Jagannath as aggressive, weird, untrustworthy, sneaky, powerful
> People who like the name Jagannath also like Jagat, Janardan, Jag, Jatin, Chetan, Indra, Adarsh, Ashwin, Ajay, Charan

Jagat *(Sanskrit/East Indian)* ♂　　　RATING: ★★☆
World
> People think of Jagat as untrustworthy, lazy, weird, sneaky, wealthy
> People who like the name Jagat also like Jag, Jatin, Janardan, Jagannath, Jack, Jacob, Adit, Adarsh, Ja, Jabir

Jagger *(English)* ♂　　　RATING: ★★
Carter, peddlar—Mick Jagger, singer/songwriter
> People think of Jagger as cool, handsome, wild, popular, creative
> People who like the name Jagger also like Jackson, Landon, Kaden, Maddox, Gavin, Ethan, Jace, Tristan, Noah, Gage

Jaguar *(English)* ♂　　　RATING: ★★★☆
Large spotted feline—Also an automobile brand name
> People think of Jaguar as exotic, powerful, aggressive, wild, energetic
> People who like the name Jaguar also like Jett, Jayden, Jacob, Jagger, Blade, Jackson, Justin, Leo, Jasper, Alexander

Jahzara *(African)* ♀　　　RATING: ★★★★☆
Princess—Ethiopian origin
> People think of Jahzara as pretty, exotic, popular, intelligent, creative

People who like the name Jahzara also like Jadyn, Jadzia, Jamila, Ayanna, Johari, Jazzelle, Jazlynn, Jenaya, Aaliyah, Janelle

Jaide *(American)* ♀ RATING: ★★★★
Variation of Jade
People think of Jaide as pretty, popular, funny, caring, creative
People who like the name Jaide also like Jadyn, Jasmine, Hailey, Kaelyn, Isabella, Chloe, Ava, Hannah, Faith, Jaclyn

Jaime *(Spanish)* ♀♂ RATING: ★★★★
Supplanter—Variation of James; pronounced *JAY-mee* or *HI-may*
People think of Jaime as funny, caring, intelligent, creative, cool
People who like the name Jaime also like James, Jade, Jaden, Jordan, Madison, Jamie, Bailey, Taylor, Ryan, Hayden

Jaimin *(American)* ♀♂ RATING: ★★★★
Supplanter—Variation of Jaimie
People think of Jaimin as handsome, funny, caring, cool, popular
People who like the name Jaimin also like Jaden, Jordan, Jalen, Jada, Jade, Hayden, Caden, Jacey, Jesse, Jamie

Jairdan *(American)* ♀♂ RATING: ★★★☆
Combination of Jair and Jordan
People think of Jairdan as handsome, exotic, popular, trendy, young
People who like the name Jairdan also like Jaden, Jalen, Caden, Aidan, Jordan, Addison, Hayden, Jacey, Jada, Cadence

Jake *(Hebrew)* ♂ RATING: ★★★☆
Supplanter—Short for Jacob; Jake LaMotta, boxer
People think of Jake as handsome, funny, cool, popular, intelligent
People who like the name Jake also like Jacob, Jack, Ethan, Luke, Joshua, Jackson, Matthew, Nathan, Noah, Caleb

Jalen *(American)* ♀♂ RATING: ★★★★
Combination of Jay and Allen—Also spelled Jaylen
People think of Jalen as funny, handsome, popular, intelligent, caring
People who like the name Jalen also like Jaden, Caden, Hayden, Jade, Jordan, Madison, Bailey, Jada, Logan, Riley

Jalena *(Slavic)* ♀ RATING: ★★★★
Bright—Variation of Jelena or Helen
People think of Jalena as pretty, sexy, intelligent, funny, creative
People who like the name Jalena also like Jadyn, Jazlynn, Jelena, Jalia, Janelle, Jeslyn, Kaelyn, Isabella, Jacinda, Jalene

Jalene *(American)* ♀ RATING: ★★★★
Feminine form of Jalen
People think of Jalene as pretty, caring, funny, trustworthy, intelligent
People who like the name Jalene also like Jadyn, Jalena, Jazlynn, Hailey, Janelle, Jaclyn, Kailey, Jolene, Faith, Jalia

Jalia *(Arabic)* ♀ RATING: ★★★★
Clear, manifest
People think of Jalia as pretty, funny, caring, intelligent, cool
People who like the name Jalia also like Jadyn, Jalena, Jaya, Jalila, Jenaya, Jazlynn, Janae, Janelle, Jania, Jazzelle

Jalie *(American)* ♀ RATING: ★★★☆
Combination of Jay and Lee
People think of Jalie as pretty, funny, popular, intelligent, creative
People who like the name Jalie also like Jadyn, Jolie, Jalia, Hailey, Janae, Jazlynn, Cailyn, Gracie, Ella, Jeslyn

Jalil *(Arabic)* ♂ RATING: ★★★☆
Great, revered
People think of Jalil as funny, cool, intelligent, powerful, handsome
People who like the name Jalil also like Jamil, Jamal, Jabari, Jayden, Kadin, Jace, Khalil, Kalil, Javana, Jamar

Jalila *(Arabic)* ♀ RATING: ★★
Great, revered
People think of Jalila as pretty, intelligent, creative, cool, sexy
People who like the name Jalila also like Jalia, Jadyn, Jalena, Jamila, Jazlynn, Jahzara, Jasmine, Jaya, Jazzelle, Jeslyn

Jam *(American)* ♀♂ RATING: ★★★
A sweet condiment; musical get-together
People think of Jam as weird, artsy, funny, energetic, creative
People who like the name Jam also like Jada, Jade, Jersey, Jazz, Justice, Jacey, Jude, Jie, Jamie, Jamaica

Jamaica *(American)* ♀♂ RATING: ★★★☆
From Jamaica—Island in the Caribbean
People think of Jamaica as pretty, exotic, funny, intelligent, creative
People who like the name Jamaica also like Jade, Jaden, Jada, Jamie, James, Jordan, Jacey, Dakota, Madison, Jalen

Jamal *(Arabic)* ♂ RATING: ★★☆
Handsome
People think of Jamal as handsome, funny, popular, sexy, cool
People who like the name Jamal also like Jamar, Jayden, Justin, Jeremiah, Jared, Isaiah, Jamil, Jacob, Jeremy, Jason

Jamar *(Arabic)* ♂ RATING: ★★★★
Sparks
People think of Jamar as handsome, funny, caring, cool, sexy
People who like the name Jamar also like Jamal, Jayden, Jamil, Jabari, Jeremiah, Jadon, Jared, Justin, Elijah, Joshua

Jame *(Hebrew)* ♀♂ RATING: ★★★☆
Supplanter—Short for James
People think of Jame as sexy, funny, caring, creative, energetic
People who like the name Jame also like Jaden, James, Jade, Jamie, Jada, Jordan, Jaime, Jesse, Jude, Jersey

James *(Hebrew)* ♀♂ RATING: ★★★
Supplanter—Originally an English variation of Jacob; James Gandolfini, actor; James Earl Jones, actor; James Taylor, musician
People think of James as handsome, funny, intelligent, caring, cool
People who like the name James also like Ryan, Dylan, Jordan, Evan, Hayden, Logan, Jaden, Madison, Cameron, Riley

Jamese *(English)* ♀♂ RATING: ★★★☆
Variation of James
People think of Jamese as cool, sexy, creative, caring, lazy
People who like the name Jamese also like Jade, Jaden, Jada, Jamie, Jaime, Jalen, Jacey, Jameson, Jersey, Jude

Jameson *(English)* ♀♂ RATING: ★★★★
Son of James
People think of Jameson as intelligent, handsome, popular, energetic, funny
People who like the name Jameson also like Hayden, Addison, Jaden, Parker, Mason, Bailey, Madison, Caden, Logan, Riley

Jamie *(English)* ♀♂ RATING: ★★★☆
Supplanter—Also spelled Jaimie; Jamie Lee Curtis, actress; Jamie Kennedy, comedian/actor
People think of Jamie as funny, caring, pretty, intelligent, cool
People who like the name Jamie also like James, Ryan, Jordan, Dylan, Madison, Bailey, Taylor, Riley, Brooke, Tyler

Jamil *(Arabic)* ♂ RATING: ★★
Beautiful, elegant
People think of Jamil as handsome, intelligent, funny, sexy, popular
People who like the name Jamil also like Jamar, Jamal, Jabari, Jayden, Jadon, Jacob, Isaiah, Joshua, Jeremiah, Jared

Jamila *(Arabic)* ♀ RATING: ★★★☆
Beautiful, elegant
People think of Jamila as pretty, intelligent, funny, caring, creative

People who like the name Jamila also like Jadyn, Jahzara, Janelle, Jasmine, Jenaya, Jasmin, Jacinda, Jalena, Jazzelle, Isabella

Jamison *(English)* ♂ RATING: ★★★
Son of James
People think of Jamison as handsome, intelligent, creative, caring, trustworthy
People who like the name Jamison also like Jackson, Jacob, Aiden, Jayden, Landon, Noah, Gavin, Ethan, Elijah, Tristan

Jamon *(Hebrew)* ♂ RATING: ★★★★
Right hand of favor—Also means ham in Spanish
People think of Jamon as handsome, funny, cool, caring, intelligent
People who like the name Jamon also like Jayden, Jadon, Jaron, Jace, Jacob, Isaiah, Jared, Jeremiah, Caleb, Jonah

Jamuna *(Sanskrit/East Indian)* ♀ RATING: ★★★
Holy river
People think of Jamuna as creative, pretty, weird, powerful, funny
People who like the name Jamuna also like Janika, Jaya, Jyotika, Jana, Jahzara, Jamila, Jadzia, Jacinta, Janine, Jui

Jan *(Dutch)* ♀♂ RATING: ★★★
God is gracious—Pronounced *Yahn* in Dutch (male), a variation of John; pronounced *Jan* in English (female), short for Janet or Janice
People think of Jan as funny, caring, intelligent, creative, young
People who like the name Jan also like Jesse, Jordan, Jamie, Jade, Jess, James, Jaden, Jaime, Jocelyn, Jayme

Jana *(Slavic)* ♀ RATING: ★★★☆
God is gracious
People think of Jana as pretty, intelligent, funny, caring, creative
People who like the name Jana also like Jadyn, Hannah, Isabella, Jenna, Chloe, Emma, Grace, Abigail, Janelle, Ava

Janae *(American)* ♀ RATING: ★★★★
God is gracious—Variation of Jana
People think of Janae as pretty, funny, intelligent, popular, creative
People who like the name Janae also like Jadyn, Janelle, Danae, Jasmine, Jazlynn, Aaliyah, Jenaya, Hailey, Chloe, Isabella

Janardan *(Sanskrit/East Indian)* ♂ RATING: ★★☆
Lord Vishnu
People think of Janardan as weird, powerful, sexy, young, wild
People who like the name Janardan also like Jagat, Jag, Jatin, Jagannath, Jadon, Jayden, Jamon, Jace, Justis, Jeffery

293

294

Jane (English) ♀   RATING: ★★☆
God is gracious—Jane Austen, author; Jane Fonda, actress; Jane Seymour, actress
> People think of Jane as pretty, intelligent, caring, funny, creative
> People who like the name Jane also like Emma, Grace, Claire, Hannah, Elizabeth, Olivia, Ella, Ava, Audrey, Charlotte

Janeeva (American) ♀   RATING: ★★★☆
Juniper berry—Variation of Geneva
> People think of Janeeva as pretty, powerful, exotic, funny, popular
> People who like the name Janeeva also like Jazlynn, Jenaya, Jalena, Janelle, Jania, Jaya, Jazzelle, Isabella, Jacinda, Jasmine

Janelle (American) ♀   RATING: ★★☆
God is gracious—Short for of Jane; also popular in Australia
> People think of Janelle as pretty, funny, intelligent, caring, creative
> People who like the name Janelle also like Isabella, Jadyn, Jasmine, Hailey, Gabrielle, Hannah, Jacqueline, Jazzelle, Faith, Jillian

Janessa (American) ♀   RATING: ★★★★
Combination of Jan and Vanessa
> People think of Janessa as pretty, funny, energetic, creative, caring
> People who like the name Janessa also like Jadyn, Aaliyah, Isabella, Abigail, Janelle, Larissa, Jasmine, Faith, Gabrielle, Bianca

Janet (English) ♀   RATING: ★★★★
God is gracious—Feminine form of John; Janet Jackson, singer; Janet Leigh, actress
> People think of Janet as funny, intelligent, pretty, caring, creative
> People who like the name Janet also like Jessica, Jacqueline, Jennifer, Jasmine, Hannah, Faith, Jane, Isabel, Jeanette, Elizabeth

Janeth (American) ♀   RATING: ★★★☆
Combination of Janet and Elizabeth
> People think of Janeth as pretty, funny, intelligent, trustworthy, young
> People who like the name Janeth also like Janelle, Jadyn, Janet, Janice, Jazzelle, Janette, Janna, Jahzara, Jacqueline, Jana

Janette (English) ♀   RATING: ★★★★
God is gracious—Variation of Jeanette
> People think of Janette as pretty, funny, intelligent, caring, trustworthy
> People who like the name Janette also like Janelle, Jacqueline, Jasmine, Jeanette, Janet, Isabella, Jessica, Isabelle, Jennifer, Jaclyn

Jania (Polish) ♀   RATING: ★★★★
Feminine form of John—Variation of Jane
> People think of Jania as pretty, young, creative, popular, funny

People who like the name Jania also like Jadyn, Janelle, Janya, Jalia, Janae, Jenaya, Jazzelle, Janika, Jana, Janna

Janice (English) ♀   RATING: ★★★☆
God is gracious—Variation of Jane; Janice Dickinson, model
> People think of Janice as caring, pretty, funny, intelligent, creative
> People who like the name Janice also like Jasmine, Janelle, Jessica, Janet, Hannah, Jacqueline, Jennifer, Jadyn, Hailey, Lauren

Janika (Slavic) ♀   RATING: ★★★★
Feminine form of John—Variation of Jane
> People think of Janika as pretty, sexy, funny, intelligent, creative
> People who like the name Janika also like Jadyn, Janelle, Kaelyn, Jamila, Hannah, Danika, Jania, Jazlynn, Danica, Jahzara

Janina (Polish) ♀   RATING: ★★★★
Short for Jana
> People think of Janina as pretty, funny, intelligent, caring, creative
> People who like the name Janina also like Jania, Janika, Jadyn, Janice, Jamila, Janelle, Jazlynn, Janine, Jalena, Janeeva

Janine (English) ♀   RATING: ★★☆
Short for Jane
> People think of Janine as funny, pretty, caring, intelligent, creative
> People who like the name Janine also like Janelle, Jessica, Jacqueline, Jenna, Julia, Jasmine, Jillian, Paige, Emma, Justine

Janis (English) ♀   RATING: ★★★☆
God is gracious—Variation of Janice; Janis Joplin, singer/songwriter
> People think of Janis as creative, caring, intelligent, funny, trustworthy
> People who like the name Janis also like Janice, Jane, Jasmine, Janet, Jaclyn, Jacqueline, Janelle, Julia, Janette, Janine

Janna (English) ♀   RATING: ★★☆
Variation of Jane
> People think of Janna as pretty, creative, funny, caring, intelligent
> People who like the name Janna also like Hannah, Jenna, Jadyn, Hailey, Jana, Jillian, Paige, Abigail, Chloe, Olivia

Jannik (Dutch) ♂   RATING: ★★☆
Short for Jan
> People think of Jannik as intelligent, cool, sporty, old-fashioned, sexy
> People who like the name Jannik also like Jayden, Damien, Jace, Jacob, Samuel, Heath, Keagan, Asher, Sebastian, Joachim

Janny *(American)* ♀   RATING: ★★
Short for Janna—Also can be short for Janet, Janis, or Jane
- People think of Janny as funny, intelligent, pretty, cool, young
- People who like the name Janny also like Janna, Jazlynn, Jaclyn, Jadyn, Jenibelle, Jemma, Jacqueline, Jenaya, Janice, Janine

January *(American)* ♀   RATING: ★★
Born in January
- People think of January as creative, pretty, intelligent, funny, caring
- People who like the name January also like Faith, Jasmine, Juliet, Isabelle, Charlotte, Scarlett, Emma, Isabel, Ava, Isabella

Janus *(Latin)* ♀♂   RATING: ★★★☆
God of beginnings
- People think of Janus as intelligent, funny, popular, cool, exotic
- People who like the name Janus also like Jaden, Jada, Jade, James, Jordan, Jude, Jaime, Jayme, Jean, Jocelyn

Janya *(American)* ♀   RATING: ★★★★☆
Combination of Jane and Anya
- People think of Janya as pretty, funny, creative, popular, intelligent
- People who like the name Janya also like Jadyn, Jaya, Jania, Jahzara, Jeslyn, Jana, Jalia, Jenaya, Jazzelle, Janae

Japheth *(Hebrew)* ♂   RATING: ★★★
Handsome
- People think of Japheth as handsome, exotic, intelligent, caring, cool
- People who like the name Japheth also like Jebediah, Asher, Judah, Josiah, Jaron, Joshua, Isaac, Jethro, Jonah, Alijah

Jara *(Spanish)* ♀   RATING: ★★★★
Rockrose
- People think of Jara as pretty, intelligent, exotic, caring, creative
- People who like the name Jara also like Jadyn, Jalia, Jana, Jaya, Jazlynn, Chloe, Amara, Jeslyn, Jasmine, Kara

Jarah *(Arabic)* ♀♂   RATING: ★★★★☆
Boldness, bravery
- People think of Jarah as pretty, energetic, sexy, creative, caring
- People who like the name Jarah also like Jaden, Jada, Jariah, Jalen, Jade, Jacey, Jesse, Jorryn, Jordan, Caden

Jared *(Hebrew)* ♂   RATING: ★★★
Descendent—Jared Leto, actor/singer
- People think of Jared as handsome, funny, intelligent, cool, caring
- People who like the name Jared also like Jacob, Ethan, Caleb, Joshua, Nathan, Justin, Noah, Aiden, Jayden, Zachary

Jariah *(American)* ♀♂   RATING: ★★★★☆
Combination of Jane and Mariah
- People think of Jariah as pretty, popular, intelligent, leader, caring
- People who like the name Jariah also like Jaden, Jade, Jalen, Jada, Jarah, Jairdan, Caden, Jacey, Jordan, Journey

Jariath *(American)* ♂   RATING: ★★
Created name
- People think of Jariath as handsome, powerful, intelligent, weird, aggressive
- People who like the name Jariath also like Caleb, Josiah, Jayden, Gabriel, Jaron, Japheth, Jeremiah, Joel, Jadon, Jedidiah

Jaron *(Hebrew)* ♂   RATING: ★★★★
Singing
- People think of Jaron as funny, handsome, intelligent, cool, caring
- People who like the name Jaron also like Jayden, Kaden, Jared, Ethan, Caleb, Jacob, Jadon, Braden, Jace, Aiden

Jarrett *(English)* ♂   RATING: ★★☆
Spear brave—Variation of Gerard; also a surname
- People think of Jarrett as handsome, intelligent, funny, caring, popular
- People who like the name Jarrett also like Jared, Jackson, Ethan, Jayden, Jacob, Garrett, Noah, Gavin, Braden, Caleb

Jarvis *(English)* ♂   RATING: ★★★★
Spear man—Originally a surname from medieval first name Gervase; Jarvis Cocker, singer/songwriter
- People think of Jarvis as handsome, funny, cool, caring, sexy
- People who like the name Jarvis also like Jayden, Jacob, Jeremiah, Jasper, Jason, Jadon, Caleb, Jackson, Justin, Elijah

Jase *(American)* ♂   RATING: ★★★★
Healer—Short for Jason
- People think of Jase as handsome, cool, popular, leader, funny
- People who like the name Jase also like Jace, Jayden, Kaden, Aiden, Chase, Caleb, Braden, Gavin, Ethan, Landon

Jaser *(Arabic)* ♂   RATING: ★★★☆
Fearless—Usually pronounced *JAH-sser*
- People think of Jaser as aggressive, handsome, energetic, powerful, lazy
- People who like the name Jaser also like Jayden, Jace, Kaden, Jasper, Jacob, Aden, Aiden, Jack, Jeremiah, Jamal

Jasmin *(Persian)* ♀   RATING: ★★★
Jasmine flower
- People think of Jasmin as pretty, funny, caring, cool, creative

People who like the name Jasmin also like Jasmine, Faith, Hailey, Jadyn, Isabella, Hannah, Olivia, Grace, Chloe, Paige

Jasmine (*Persian*) ♀ RATING: ★★★
Jasmine flower
People think of Jasmine as pretty, funny, intelligent, caring, cool
People who like the name Jasmine also like Isabella, Faith, Hannah, Hailey, Chloe, Olivia, Grace, Gabrielle, Isabelle, Paige

Jasna (*Slavic*) ♀ RATING: ★★★
Clarity
People think of Jasna as intelligent, pretty, exotic, creative, energetic
People who like the name Jasna also like Bianca, Abigail, Gabriela, Jadyn, Marisol, Gabriella, Jadzia, Eva, Lada, Jovanna

Jason (*Greek*) ♂ RATING: ★★★
Healer—Jason Bateman, actor; Jason Ritter, actor
People think of Jason as handsome, funny, intelligent, caring, cool
People who like the name Jason also like Justin, Jacob, Ethan, Matthew, Joshua, Nathan, Nicholas, Andrew, Aaron, Jared

Jasper (*English*) ♂ RATING: ★★★★
Treasurer—Variation of Casper; also a semiprecious stone; one of the three Magi
People think of Jasper as intelligent, handsome, cool, funny, caring
People who like the name Jasper also like Jackson, Noah, Ethan, Jacob, Jack, Caleb, Oliver, Jayden, Isaac, Elijah

Jatin (*Sanskrit/East Indian*) ♂ RATING: ★★★
Having matted hair
People think of Jatin as sexy, creative, intelligent, cool, handsome
People who like the name Jatin also like Jayden, Jace, Jadon, Jaron, Javen, Javan, Jase, Aiden, Kaden, Jag

Jaunie (*Arabic*) ♀ RATING: ★★★
Pretty, beautiful
People think of Jaunie as pretty, young, exotic, creative, caring
People who like the name Jaunie also like Jahzara, Jaya, Jadzia, Jazlynn, Joelle, Jamila, Janelle, Jacinda, Joie, Jereni

Java (*Arabic*) ♀♂ RATING: ★★★
Island in Indonesia—Also a computer programming language; also a nickname for coffee
People think of Java as exotic, sexy, funny, powerful, young
People who like the name Java also like Jada, Jade, Jaden, Dakota, Jude, Jacey, Echo, Jax, Azure, Justice

Javan (*Arabic*) ♂ RATING: ★★★★
Youth
People think of Javan as handsome, intelligent, energetic, funny, young
People who like the name Javan also like Jayden, Kaden, Jaron, Jadon, Javen, Isaac, Aiden, Isaiah, Jace, Elijah

Javana (*Sanskrit/East Indian*) ♂ RATING: ★★★☆
Young man
People think of Javana as pretty, popular, caring, trustworthy, funny
People who like the name Javana also like Jayden, Javen, Jace, Maddox, Javan, Jadon, Kaden, Jackson, Jaxon, Isaac

Javen (*Arabic*) ♂ RATING: ★★☆
Youth
People think of Javen as funny, handsome, popular, intelligent, sexy
People who like the name Javen also like Jayden, Kaden, Jace, Jeremiah, Jadon, Jaron, Jackson, Javan, Gavin, Ethan

Javier (*Spanish*) ♂ RATING: ★★☆
New house—Variation of Xavier; pronounced *Hah-vee-EYR*
People think of Javier as handsome, funny, cool, intelligent, sexy
People who like the name Javier also like Xavier, Jayden, Gabriel, Elijah, Antonio, Jacob, Adrian, Alejandro, Isaiah, Jeremiah

Javon (*American*) ♂ RATING: ★★★★
Combination of James and Von
People think of Javon as handsome, cool, funny, sexy, intelligent
People who like the name Javon also like Jayden, Jadon, Kaden, Jabari, Jace, Jamal, Jevonte, Jason, Javan, Jacob

Jax (*American*) ♀♂ RATING: ★★★☆
Son of Jack—Variation of Jackson
People think of Jax as handsome, cool, intelligent, popular, funny
People who like the name Jax also like Caden, Jaden, Jade, Logan, Riley, Ryder, James, Jordan, Mason, Quinn

Jaxith (*Hungarian*) ♂ RATING: ★★★
Kind-hearted
People think of Jaxith as funny, energetic, cool, caring, old-fashioned
People who like the name Jaxith also like Jarvis, Jedidiah, Jason, Jasper, Jayden, Jack, Ezekiel, Jared, Aiden, Jaxon

Jaxon (*American*) ♂ RATING: ★★★★☆
Son of Jack—Variation of Jackson
People think of Jaxon as handsome, intelligent, sporty, popular, energetic
People who like the name Jaxon also like Jackson, Kaden, Jayden, Aiden, Ethan, Gavin, Jace, Landon, Maddox, Noah

Jay *(Latin)* ♂   RATING: ★★★
A bird in the crow family—Also short for James or
John; Jay Gatsby, character in *The Great Gatsby* by
F. Scott Fitzgerald; Jay Leno, comedian/TV host
> People think of Jay as funny, handsome, intelligent,
> cool, caring
> People who like the name Jay also like Jack, Jake,
> Jason, Jayden, Joshua, Jacob, Jackson, Aaron, Justin,
> Ethan

Jaya *(Sanskrit/East Indian)* ♀   RATING: ★★★★
Victory
> People think of Jaya as pretty, intelligent, energetic,
> funny, caring
> People who like the name Jaya also like Jadyn, Jeslyn,
> Jenaya, Jazlynn, Jalia, Ava, Jasmine, Janya, Jahzara,
> Grace

Jayashri *(Sanskrit/East Indian)* ♀   RATING: ★★★
Goddess of victory
> People think of Jayashri as exotic, cool, pretty, ethnic,
> creative
> People who like the name Jayashri also like Jaya,
> Jahzara, Jamuna, Amara, Avani, Jadzia, Anjali, Kerani,
> Devica, Kamala

Jaycee *(American)* ♀♂   RATING: ★★★☆
From the initials J.C.—Also an acronym for Jesus
Christ
> People think of Jaycee as pretty, young, trendy, wealthy,
> funny
> People who like the name Jaycee also like Jacey, Jaden,
> Riley, Addison, Caden, Hayden, Jade, Bailey, Alexis,
> Taylor

Jayden *(American)* ♂   RATING: ★★★★☆
Variation of Jaden
> People think of Jayden as handsome, funny, popular,
> energetic, intelligent
> People who like the name Jayden also like Aiden,
> Kaden, Ethan, Caleb, Landon, Jacob, Braden, Noah,
> Tristan, Jackson

Jayme *(English)* ♀♂   RATING: ★★★
Variation of James
> People think of Jayme as funny, pretty, caring, trust-
> worthy, intelligent
> People who like the name Jayme also like Jaden, Jamie,
> Jaime, Jordan, Jade, James, Hayden, Jalen, Jacey, Jesse

Jayne *(American)* ♀   RATING: ★★★☆
God is gracious—Variation of Jane; Jayne Mansfield,
actress
> People think of Jayne as funny, pretty, caring, popular,
> cool
> People who like the name Jayne also like Emma, Grace,
> Hannah, Natalie, Olivia, Isabella, Amelia, Chloe, Abigail,
> Elizabeth

Jazlynn *(American)* ♀   RATING: ★★★★★
Combination of Jasmine and Lynn
> People think of Jazlynn as pretty, sexy, popular, funny,
> creative

> People who like the name Jazlynn also like Jadyn,
> Jeslyn, Jasmine, Gabriella, Jazzelle, Kaelyn, Jaclyn,
> Isabella, Destiny, Faith

Jazz *(American)* ♀♂   RATING: ★★★☆
Style of music
> People think of Jazz as creative, cool, artsy, funny,
> popular
> People who like the name Jazz also like Jade, Jaden,
> Hunter, Jordan, Phoenix, Dakota, Jesse, Jacey, Jude,
> Taylor

Jazzelle *(American)* ♀   RATING: ★★★
Variation of Giselle or Jazz
> People think of Jazzelle as pretty, exotic, sexy, intel-
> ligent, creative
> People who like the name Jazzelle also like Janelle,
> Jazlynn, Giselle, Jadyn, Jasmine, Isabella, Jeslyn,
> Gabriella, Gabrielle, Jahzara

Jazziell *(American)* ♀   RATING: ★★★
Variation of Jazzelle
> People think of Jazziell as pretty, creative, sexy, power-
> ful, elegant
> People who like the name Jazziell also like Jazzelle,
> Jazlynn, Jahzara, Jalena, Janelle, Giselle, Jadzia, Jaya,
> Jasmine, Alexia

Jean *(English)* ♀♂   RATING: ★★★☆
God is gracious—French male name; English female
name; Jean Patou, fragrance mogul; Jean Smart,
actress; Jean Stapleton, actress
> People think of Jean as caring, intelligent, funny, pretty,
> trustworthy
> People who like the name Jean also like Jade, James,
> Jaden, Jordan, Jada, Brooke, Mackenzie, Jocelyn,
> Hayden, Jamie

Jean-Baptiste *(French)* ♂   RATING: ★☆
St. John the Baptist—Also spelled Jeanbaptiste
> People think of Jean-Baptiste as religious, weird, loser,
> popular, wealthy
> People who like the name Jean-Baptiste also like
> Jacques, Justin, Jayden, Jack, Ethan, Jeremiah, Jared,
> Jefferson, Jonah, Javier

Jeana *(American)* ♀   RATING: ★★★★
Variation of Gina
> People think of Jeana as caring, creative, funny, pretty,
> energetic
> People who like the name Jeana also like Jenna,
> Jasmine, Jessica, Jadyn, Janelle, Jena, Jana, Jaclyn,
> Jewel, Jazzelle

Jeanette *(English)* ♀   RATING: ★★
God is gracious—Variation of Jean; Jeanette
MacDonald, singer/actress
> People think of Jeanette as caring, pretty, funny, intel-
> ligent, trustworthy
> People who like the name Jeanette also like Jacqueline,
> Janelle, Isabella, Hailey, Jessica, Jasmine, Jennifer, Faith,
> Janet, Olivia

298

Jeanine *(Celtic/Gaelic)* ♀   RATING: ★★☆
God is gracious
People think of Jeanine as funny, pretty, caring, intelligent, creative
People who like the name Jeanine also like Jeanette, Jessica, Janelle, Hannah, Jillian, Jennifer, Janine, Emma, Isabella, Jacqueline

Jeanne *(Celtic/Gaelic)* ♀   RATING: ★★☆
God is gracious—Variation of Jane; Jeanne Crain, actress
People think of Jeanne as intelligent, pretty, trustworthy, funny, caring
People who like the name Jeanne also like Jeanette, Jennifer, Jasmine, Hailey, Hannah, Jessica, Elizabeth, Jacqueline, Fiona, Jillian

Jeannie *(French)* ♀   RATING: ★★★☆
God is gracious—Variation of Jean; *I Dream of Jeannie*, TV show
People think of Jeannie as funny, pretty, intelligent, caring, creative
People who like the name Jeannie also like Jacqueline, Josephine, Claire, Chelsea, Hannah, Jessica, Janet, Isabella, Charlotte, Fiona

Jeb *(American)* ♂   RATING: ★★★☆
Short for James or Joseph
People think of Jeb as intelligent, trustworthy, caring, handsome, funny
People who like the name Jeb also like Jacob, Jed, Jace, Noah, Jebediah, Jonah, Isaiah, Jedidiah, Gabriel, Isaac

Jebediah *(Hebrew)* ♂   RATING: ★★★☆
Combination of Jeb and Jedediah
People think of Jebediah as religious, intelligent, leader, old-fashioned, caring
People who like the name Jebediah also like Jedidiah, Elijah, Gabriel, Jeremiah, Isaac, Isaiah, Jacob, Jonah, Josiah, Zachariah

Jed *(American)* ♂   RATING: ★★★
Friend of God—Short for Jedidiah
People think of Jed as handsome, intelligent, caring, cool, funny
People who like the name Jed also like Jack, Jacob, Joel, Jake, Ethan, Isaac, Noah, Jackson, Jett, Justin

Jedidiah *(Hebrew)* ♂   RATING: ★★★★
Friend of God
People think of Jedidiah as handsome, intelligent, trustworthy, religious, caring
People who like the name Jedidiah also like Jeremiah, Elijah, Josiah, Isaiah, Jebediah, Caleb, Jacob, Joshua, Gabriel, Benjamin

Jedrek *(Polish)* ♂   RATING: ★★★☆
Manly, strong—Short for Andrew
People think of Jedrek as intelligent, handsome, energetic, powerful, leader

People who like the name Jedrek also like Jayden, Aiden, Kaden, Ethan, Caleb, Jacob, Jared, Jadon, Jaron, Aden

Jeff *(English)* ♂   RATING: ★★☆
God peace—Short for Jeffrey; Jeff Bridges, actor
People think of Jeff as handsome, funny, intelligent, cool, caring
People who like the name Jeff also like Jack, Justin, Jake, Jason, Jacob, Jared, Scott, Nathan, Matthew, Joshua

Jefferson *(English)* ♂   RATING: ★★
Son of Jeffrey—Jefferson Davis, president of the Confederacy during the U.S. Civil War; Thomas Jefferson, U.S. president
People think of Jefferson as intelligent, cool, funny, handsome, trustworthy
People who like the name Jefferson also like Jackson, Jacob, Jack, Harrison, Ethan, Jake, Joshua, Emerson, Alexander, Justin

Jeffery *(English)* ♂   RATING: ★★★★
God peace—Variation of Jeffrey
People think of Jeffery as funny, handsome, caring, intelligent, cool
People who like the name Jeffery also like Jacob, Joshua, Andrew, Justin, Jeremy, Jason, Benjamin, Matthew, Jared, Alexander

Jeffrey *(English)* ♂   RATING: ★★☆
God peace—Jeffrey Dahmer, serial killer
People think of Jeffrey as handsome, funny, intelligent, caring, trustworthy
People who like the name Jeffrey also like Jacob, Jason, Joshua, Jeremy, Andrew, Benjamin, Matthew, Justin, Nicholas, Jared

Jela *(African)* ♀♂   RATING: ★★★
Father suffered during birth—Swahili origin, meaning jail
People think of Jela as young, weird, wild, poor, exotic
People who like the name Jela also like Jaden, Jalen, Jada, Jade, Jordan, Jarah, Jumoke, Jacey, Jiva, Jariah

Jelena *(Slavic)* ♀   RATING: ★★★★☆
Bright—Variation of Helen
People think of Jelena as pretty, intelligent, creative, funny, elegant
People who like the name Jelena also like Jalena, Jazlynn, Janelle, Jeslyn, Jadyn, Jenaya, Jazzelle, Jacqueline, Isabella, Jasmine

Jem *(English)* ♀♂   RATING: ★★★★
Short for James or Jemima; also a variation of Gem
People think of Jem as intelligent, creative, caring, cool, trustworthy
People who like the name Jem also like Jade, Jada, Jocelyn, Jaden, Jesse, Jordan, James, Jude, Alexis, Jalen

Jemima *(Hebrew)* ♀   RATING: ★★★★
Dove—Aunt Jemima, brand of breakfast foods;
Jemima Puddleduck, children's book character
   People think of Jemima as pretty, caring, trustworthy,
   intelligent, elegant
   People who like the name Jemima also like Jasmine,
   Isabella, Ava, Grace, Eva, Charlotte, Olivia, Amelia, Lucy,
   Abigail

Jemma *(English)* ♀   RATING: ★★☆
Precious stone—Variation of Gemma or Jemima
   People think of Jemma as pretty, funny, caring, popular,
   intelligent
   People who like the name Jemma also like Gemma,
   Isabella, Hannah, Jenna, Grace, Emma, Chloe, Olivia,
   Paige, Jasmine

Jen *(English)* ♀   RATING: ★★★
Fair phantom—Short for Jennifer; also spelled Jenn
   People think of Jen as funny, pretty, caring, intelligent,
   trustworthy
   People who like the name Jen also like Jenna, Jennifer,
   Jessica, Emma, Isabella, Hailey, Faith, Hannah, Jasmine,
   Emily

Jena *(American)* ♀   RATING: ★★★☆
Variation of Gina
   People think of Jena as pretty, funny, caring, intelligent,
   creative
   People who like the name Jena also like Jenna, Hailey,
   Emma, Grace, Olivia, Hannah, Ava, Isabella, Jadyn, Faith

Jenaya *(American)* ♀   RATING: ★★★★☆
Variation of Jenny
   People think of Jenaya as pretty, trendy, funny, sexy,
   intelligent
   People who like the name Jenaya also like Jadyn,
   Jazlynn, Jennaya, Amaya, Janae, Janelle, Jaya, Jeslyn,
   Jazzelle, Jahzara

Jendayi *(African)* ♀   RATING: ★★★☆
Thankful—Zimbabwe origin
   People think of Jendayi as pretty, exotic, creative, funny,
   ethnic
   People who like the name Jendayi also like Jahzara,
   Jenaya, Jadyn, Jadzia, Jazzelle, Jamila, Jia Li, Jeslyn,
   Jaya, Janae

Jeneil *(American)* ♀   RATING: ★★★
Variation of Chenille
   People think of Jeneil as aggressive, artsy, pretty, funny,
   caring
   People who like the name Jeneil also like Jazzelle,
   Janelle, Jeslyn, Jadyn, Jenaya, Jazlynn, Jaclyn, Jalena,
   Jennelle, Jalia

Jeneva *(American)* ♀   RATING: ★★★★
Juniper berry; fair phantom—Variation of Geneva or
Jennifer, or a combination of those two names
   People think of Jeneva as pretty, sexy, funny, creative,
   intelligent

People who like the name Jeneva also like Jenna,
Genevieve, Jadyn, Janeeva, Juliana, Jenibelle, Jaya,
Jeslyn, Kiara, Janelle

Jengo *(African)* ♂   RATING: ★★☆
Building—Swahili origin; also means one with reddish
complexion
   People think of Jengo as exotic, sexy, sporty, aggres-
   sive, weird
   People who like the name Jengo also like Landon,
   Jasper, Jett, Jag, Ja, Jabari, Jabilo, Jaxon, Iggy, Jabir

Jenibelle *(American)* ♀   RATING: ★★★★
Combination of Jenny and Belle
   People think of Jenibelle as pretty, creative, elegant,
   caring, quiet
   People who like the name Jenibelle also like Isabella,
   Hannah, Annabelle, Isabelle, Jasmine, Jadyn, Gabrielle,
   Jazlynn, Belle, Abigail

Jenis *(American)* ♀   RATING: ★★
Variation of Janis
   People think of Jenis as sexy, exotic, pretty, young,
   intelligent
   People who like the name Jenis also like Jadyn, Jenna,
   Jaclyn, Jennis, Julia, Jillian, Janeeva, Jasmin, Janelle,
   Jennessa

Jenna *(English)* ♀   RATING: ★★★
Fair phantom—Short for Jennifer; Jenna Fischer,
actress
   People think of Jenna as pretty, funny, caring, intel-
   ligent, creative
   People who like the name Jenna also like Emma,
   Hannah, Ava, Grace, Olivia, Hailey, Paige, Emily, Ella,
   Isabella

Jennaya *(American)* ♀   RATING: ★★★★☆
Variation of Jenny
   People think of Jennaya as funny, pretty, intelligent,
   creative, popular
   People who like the name Jennaya also like Jadyn,
   Jenaya, Jennessa, Jazlynn, Jenna, Jazzelle, Jeslyn,
   Hannah, Kaelyn, Anaya

Jennelle *(English)* ♀   RATING: ★★★★
Short for Jennifer
   People think of Jennelle as pretty, funny, trustworthy,
   intelligent, caring
   People who like the name Jennelle also like Janelle,
   Jennessa, Hailey, Jasmine, Jadyn, Jenna, Jessica,
   Isabella, Jennifer, Jeslyn

Jennessa *(American)* ♀   RATING: ★★★★
Combination of Jennifer and Vanessa
   People think of Jennessa as pretty, energetic, creative,
   popular, funny
   People who like the name Jennessa also like Isabella,
   Hailey, Jadyn, Faith, Jazlynn, Gabriella, Jasmine, Janelle,
   Jennelle, Jessica

300

Jennica *(English)* ♀　　RATING: ★★★★
Combination of Jennifer and Jessica—Also spelled Jenica
People think of Jennica as pretty, funny, creative, popular, cool
People who like the name Jennica also like Jadyn, Jeslyn, Isabelle, Jessica, Arianna, Danica, Hailey, Jazlynn, Isabella, Hannah

Jennie *(English)* ♀　　RATING: ★★★★
Short for Jennifer
People think of Jennie as pretty, funny, caring, intelligent, trustworthy
People who like the name Jennie also like Jennifer, Jenny, Jenna, Julie, Jessica, Julia, Josie, Mandy, Emily, Jasmine

Jennifer *(English)* ♀　　RATING: ★★★☆
Fair phantom; white wave—Cornish form of the Welsh name Gwynhwyfar also spelled Jenifer, Gennyphir, Gennifer, or Ginnifer; Jennifer Aniston, actress; Jennifer Hudson, singer/actress; Jennifer Lopez, singer/actress
People think of Jennifer as pretty, funny, caring, intelligent, creative
People who like the name Jennifer also like Jessica, Elizabeth, Emily, Hannah, Hailey, Emma, Rebecca, Samantha, Faith, Rachel

Jennis *(American)* ♀　　RATING: ★★★
Variation of Janis
People think of Jennis as wild, pretty, caring, leader, trustworthy
People who like the name Jennis also like Jenis, Jillian, Jennifer, Jazlynn, Jeslyn, Jennica, Jennyl, Jenibelle, Jadyn, Jera

Jenny *(English)* ♀　　RATING: ★★★
Short for Jennifer
People think of Jenny as pretty, funny, caring, intelligent, creative
People who like the name Jenny also like Jennifer, Jessica, Hannah, Elizabeth, Emily, Isabella, Emma, Hailey, Claire, Daisy

Jennyl *(American)* ♀　　RATING: ★★★
Combination of Jennifer and Beryl
People think of Jennyl as pretty, sexy, energetic, unpopular, poor
People who like the name Jennyl also like Jazlynn, Jeslyn, Jadyn, Janelle, Jasmine, Joylyn, Jennelle, Jennica, Jaclyn, Jahzara

Jens *(Scandinavian)* ♂　　RATING: ★★★☆
God is gracious—Variation of John
People think of Jens as intelligent, handsome, funny, cool, creative
People who like the name Jens also like Jacob, Joel, Jeremiah, Jared, Jack, Aaron, Jeremy, Jayden, Jake, Josh

Jensen *(Scandinavian)* ♀♂　　RATING: ★★★★
Son of Jens
People think of Jensen as handsome, intelligent, funny, sexy, popular
People who like the name Jensen also like Hayden, Jaden, Logan, Caden, Addison, Riley, Parker, Bailey, Jordan, Madison

Jenski *(English)* ♀♂　　RATING: ★☆
Coming home
People think of Jenski as energetic, ethnic, loser, creative, weird
People who like the name Jenski also like Jensen, Jordan, Jersey, Jaime, Jayme, Jamie, Jermaine, James, Jairdan, Jameson

Jera *(American)* ♀　　RATING: ★★★★
Feminine form of Gerald or Gerard
People think of Jera as intelligent, pretty, caring, trustworthy, creative
People who like the name Jera also like Jadyn, Jalena, Jazlynn, Jeslyn, Jaya, Jalia, Jillian, Jahzara, Janelle, Jara

Jered *(Hebrew)* ♂　　RATING: ★★☆
Variation of Jared
People think of Jered as handsome, funny, cool, popular, energetic
People who like the name Jered also like Jared, Jacob, Jayden, Justin, Jeremiah, Joshua, Jeremy, Ethan, Jackson, Aaron

Jeremiah *(Hebrew)* ♂　　RATING: ★★★
God will uplift
People think of Jeremiah as handsome, intelligent, caring, funny, trustworthy
People who like the name Jeremiah also like Elijah, Isaiah, Joshua, Caleb, Gabriel, Isaac, Jacob, Noah, Ethan, Jeremy

Jeremy *(Hebrew)* ♂　　RATING: ★★★★
God will uplift—Variation of Jeremiah; Jeremy Irons, actor; Jeremy Piven, actor
People think of Jeremy as handsome, funny, intelligent, caring, cool
People who like the name Jeremy also like Jacob, Joshua, Ethan, Justin, Nathan, Matthew, Jason, Zachary, Jeremiah, Caleb

Jeren *(American)* ♀♂　　RATING: ★★★
Spear rule; holy name—Variation of Jerome, Jerry, Geraldine, or Gerald
People think of Jeren as intelligent, exotic, popular, pretty, wild
People who like the name Jeren also like Jaden, Hayden, Caden, Addison, Logan, Mason, Cameron, James, Kyler, Dylan

Jereni *(Slavic)* ♀　　RATING: ★★
Peaceful
People think of Jereni as exotic, pretty, cool, girl next door, old-fashioned

People who like the name Jereni also like Jadyn, Jazzelle, Janelle, Jahzara, Jera, Jazlynn, Jamila, Jewel, Jana, Jenibelle

Jeri *(English)* ♀   RATING: ★★★★
Short for Geraldine
People think of Jeri as pretty, funny, caring, trustworthy, intelligent
People who like the name Jeri also like Julia, Jaclyn, Jacqueline, Jenna, Jolie, Jadyn, Julianna, Julie, Juliet, Isabella

Jericho *(Greek)* ♂   RATING: ★★★★
Moon city—In the Bible, a city conquered by Joshua
People think of Jericho as handsome, intelligent, funny, cool, trustworthy
People who like the name Jericho also like Jeremiah, Isaiah, Isaac, Ethan, Jayden, Gabriel, Noah, Jacob, Elijah, Jackson

Jermaine *(French)* ♀♂   RATING: ★★★☆
From Germany
People think of Jermaine as handsome, sexy, cool, funny, intelligent
People who like the name Jermaine also like Jaden, Jordan, James, Jada, Jade, Madison, Julian, Jacey, Jalen, Cameron

Jerod *(English)* ♂   RATING: ★★☆
Spear brave—Variation of Gerard; also a surname
People think of Jerod as intelligent, handsome, caring, trustworthy, funny
People who like the name Jerod also like Jared, Jayden, Jacob, Jeremiah, Justin, Ethan, Jeremy, Caleb, Jadon, Ian

Jeroen *(Dutch)* ♂   RATING: ★★★☆
Holy name—Variation of Jerome
People think of Jeroen as intelligent, handsome, funny, caring, popular
People who like the name Jeroen also like Jayden, Javan, Jerod, Jihan, Jadon, Jerrick, Joshua, Josiah, Kaden, Jeremiah

Jerold *(English)* ♂   RATING: ★★★
Spear rule—Variation of Gerald
People think of Jerold as cool, funny, popular, loser, sporty
People who like the name Jerold also like Johnathan, Justin, Jayden, Jack, Jeremy, Jerrick, Jacob, Jared, Jason, Jerome

Jerom *(American)* ♂   RATING: ★★
Holy name
People think of Jerom as funny, handsome, winner, leader, sexy
People who like the name Jerom also like Justin, Jerome, Jason, Jayden, Joshua, Jonathan, Jerod, Jerrick, Jaron, Jeremy

Jerome *(Latin)* ♂   RATING: ★★★☆
Holy name—From the Greek name Hieronymos; Jerome Kern, composer; Jerome Robbins, choreographer
People think of Jerome as handsome, funny, intelligent, cool, energetic
People who like the name Jerome also like Jacob, Jeremiah, Joshua, Jeremy, Isaac, Jared, Justin, Xavier, Jayden, Jason

Jerrell *(English)* ♂   RATING: ★★☆
Spear rule—Variation of Gerald; also a surname
People think of Jerrell as handsome, cool, funny, caring, sexy
People who like the name Jerrell also like Jayden, Jamal, Jeremy, Jabari, Justin, Jerome, Jared, Joshua, Jaron, Deshawn

Jerrica *(American)* ♀   RATING: ★★★★
Combination of Jeri and Jessica—Also spelled Jerica
People think of Jerrica as pretty, funny, caring, intelligent, creative
People who like the name Jerrica also like Jadyn, Jazlynn, Jasmine, Isabella, Jeslyn, Jazzelle, Jasmin, Justine, Jacinda, Hailey

Jerrick *(American)* ♂   RATING: ★★
Combination of Gerald and Derek
People think of Jerrick as handsome, intelligent, popular, powerful, aggressive
People who like the name Jerrick also like Jayden, Jaron, Jackson, Jarrett, Kaden, Jared, Aiden, Justin, Caleb, Jeremiah

Jerrin *(American)* ♂   RATING: ★★★
Combination of Jerod and Derrin
People think of Jerrin as nerdy, artsy, powerful, winner, girl next door
People who like the name Jerrin also like Duane, Cody, Adair, Beau, Franklin, Isaiah, Josiah, Nicholas, Theodore, Woodrow

Jerrod *(English)* ♂   RATING: ★★★☆
Variation of Gerard—Originally a surname
People think of Jerrod as handsome, funny, caring, sexy, intelligent
People who like the name Jerrod also like Jared, Jacob, Jeremy, Jarrett, Justin, Jayden, Jerod, Jered, Joshua, Braden

Jerry *(English)* ♀♂   RATING: ★★★★
Short for names beginning with Jer or Ger
People think of Jerry as funny, cool, intelligent, handsome, caring
People who like the name Jerry also like James, Jesse, Jamie, Jordan, Jaden, Cameron, Bailey, Austin, Evan, Joey

302

Jersey (*English*) ♀♂   RATING: ★★★★☆
Grassy island—One of the Channel Islands off the coast of the UK; another word for sweater; New Jersey, U.S. state
> People think of Jersey as popular, cool, sexy, pretty, sporty
> People who like the name Jersey also like Jaden, Jade, Jordan, Dakota, Hayden, Brooklyn, Madison, Harley, Bailey, Jacey

Jerusha (*Hebrew*) ♀   RATING: ★☆
Inheritance
> People think of Jerusha as pretty, intelligent, energetic, creative, funny
> People who like the name Jerusha also like Jorah, Jillian, Jadyn, Jezebel, Johnna, Julia, Joella, Joelle, Johanna, Jael

Jesimae (*American*) ♀   RATING: ★★☆
Combination of Jessie and Mae
> People think of Jesimae as old-fashioned, poor, pretty, girl next door, young
> People who like the name Jesimae also like Jazlynn, Jeslyn, Jadyn, Jazzelle, Janae, Jasmine, Jadzia, Janelle, Jamila, Jezebel

Jeslyn (*American*) ♀   RATING: ★★★☆
Combination of Jessie and Lynn
> People think of Jeslyn as pretty, intelligent, funny, popular, creative
> People who like the name Jeslyn also like Jadyn, Kaelyn, Jazlynn, Cailyn, Ashlyn, Isabella, Kailey, Hailey, Jaclyn, Aaralyn

Jess (*English*) ♀♂   RATING: ★★★
Short for Jesse or Jessica
> People think of Jess as funny, intelligent, caring, pretty, cool
> People who like the name Jess also like Jesse, Jade, Jordan, Ryan, James, Jamie, Jaden, Madison, Hayden, Brooke

Jessamine (*French*) ♀   RATING: ★★★★☆
Jasmine flower
> People think of Jessamine as pretty, creative, exotic, artsy, young
> People who like the name Jessamine also like Jasmine, Jazlynn, Isabella, Jeslyn, Isabelle, Josephine, Jacqueline, Jadyn, Giselle, Justine

Jesse (*Hebrew*) ♀♂   RATING: ★★★★
Gift—Jesse Jackson, politician; Jesse McCartney, singer
> People think of Jesse as funny, handsome, cool, caring, intelligent
> People who like the name Jesse also like Jordan, Jaden, Ryan, James, Riley, Dylan, Logan, Hayden, Tyler, Taylor

Jessen (*German*) ♂   RATING: ★★★
From Jessen, Germany
> People think of Jessen as handsome, boy next door, sporty, intelligent, trustworthy
> People who like the name Jessen also like Jayden, Jackson, Aiden, Sebastian, Landon, Slade, Brennan, Charles, Andrew, Elliot

Jessenia (*Arabic*) ♀   RATING: ★★
Flower—Also spelled Yesenia in South America
> People think of Jessenia as pretty, funny, caring, creative, sexy
> People who like the name Jessenia also like Jasmine, Jessica, Jeslyn, Jennessa, Janelle, Jasmin, Isabella, Layla, Jacqueline, Jacinda

Jessica (*Hebrew*) ♀   RATING: ★★★
God beholds—Created by William Shakespeare for a character in *The Merchant of Venice*; probably derived from Jesca (Yiska), a minor Biblical character; Jessica Biel, actress; Jessica Simpson, singer; Jessica Tandy, actress
> People think of Jessica as pretty, funny, caring, intelligent, creative
> People who like the name Jessica also like Hannah, Emily, Emma, Samantha, Grace, Abigail, Isabella, Elizabeth, Hailey, Jennifer

Jessie (*English*) ♀   RATING: ★★★☆
Short for Jessica or Jean—In Scotland, short for Jean or Jane
> People think of Jessie as funny, pretty, caring, intelligent, creative
> People who like the name Jessie also like Jessica, Hailey, Hannah, Jasmine, Jennifer, Chloe, Emily, Faith, Jenna, Isabella

Jesus (*Spanish*) ♂   RATING: ★★
Variation of Joshua—Greek form of the Hebrew name that gives us the modern name Joshua; it is most common in Spanish-speaking countries where it is pronounced *Hay-zoos*
> People think of Jesus as religious, powerful, caring, leader, intelligent
> People who like the name Jesus also like Javier, Juan, Julio, José, Alejandro, Joseph, Antonio, John, Jack, Johnathan

Jethro (*Hebrew*) ♂   RATING: ★★★★
Abundance
> People think of Jethro as intelligent, handsome, creative, leader, trustworthy
> People who like the name Jethro also like Jacob, Jeremiah, Jeremy, Jonah, Elijah, Jonas, Ethan, Justin, Jayden, Caleb

Jett (*English*) ♂   RATING: ★★★★
Jet black—Also a stone, or an airplane
> People think of Jett as handsome, cool, energetic, popular, intelligent
> People who like the name Jett also like Jackson, Jack, Noah, Ethan, Aiden, Cole, Jacob, Jace, Maddox, Chase

Jetta *(Scandinavian)* ♀ RATING: ★★★☆
Short for Henrietta or Marietta—Model of Volkswagen car
  People think of Jetta as pretty, funny, creative, exotic, powerful
  People who like the name Jetta also like Jadyn, Aurora, Emma, Juliet, Ivy, Layla, Bella, Jasmine, Jaya, Audrey

Jevin *(American)* ♂ RATING: ★★★☆
Combination of Jay and Kevin
  People think of Jevin as funny, creative, handsome, cool, intelligent
  People who like the name Jevin also like Kaden, Jace, Jayden, Jaron, Justin, Aden, Jaxon, Jase, Gavin, Jeremiah

Jevonte *(American)* ♂ RATING: ★★★☆
Combination of Javan and Dante
  People think of Jevonte as handsome, funny, popular, sexy, young
  People who like the name Jevonte also like Jayden, Jabari, Jeremiah, Jamal, Kaden, Jamar, Javan, Isaiah, Jadon, Javon

Jewel *(English)* ♀ RATING: ★★☆
Precious stone—Also spelled Jewell; Jewel, singer/songwriter
  People think of Jewel as pretty, creative, caring, intelligent, popular
  People who like the name Jewel also like Faith, Jasmine, Grace, Hannah, Isabella, Hailey, Ava, Jadyn, Paige, Chloe

Jezebel *(Hebrew)* ♀ RATING: ★★★
Unexalted—In the Bible, queen in Israel; because of the movie *Jezebel* starring Bette Davis, the name is often associated with a seductress
  People think of Jezebel as sexy, exotic, pretty, powerful, popular
  People who like the name Jezebel also like Isabella, Faith, Isabel, Jasmine, Isabelle, Chloe, Hailey, Gabrielle, Giselle, Jadyn

Jia Li *(Chinese)* ♀ RATING: ★★★★
Good, beautiful
  People think of Jia Li as pretty, exotic, intelligent, elegant, ethnic
  People who like the name Jia Li also like Jadyn, Jeslyn, Jadzia, Amaya, Jahzara, Janelle, Jazlynn, Jolie, Jewel, Jaya

Jiang *(Chinese)* ♀♂ RATING: ★★☆
River
  People think of Jiang as pretty, quiet, young, powerful, elegant
  People who like the name Jiang also like Brooklyn, Arien, Azure, Carey, Devon, Cassidy, Mason, Christian, Bliss, Sarki

Jie *(Chinese)* ♀♂ RATING: ★★★★
Pure—Mandarin origin
  People think of Jie as intelligent, caring, energetic, funny, trustworthy

People who like the name Jie also like Jaden, Jorryn, Kai, Jade, Jax, Jazz, Jariah, Jarah, Jesse, Jumoke

Jihan *(Arabic)* ♂ RATING: ★★★
The universe
  People think of Jihan as pretty, intelligent, creative, trustworthy, caring
  People who like the name Jihan also like Jayden, Aden, Jabari, Josiah, Julius, Jared, Javan, Elijah, Jamil, Jaron

Jiles *(American)* ♀♂ RATING: ★★★
Variation of Giles
  People think of Jiles as handsome, elegant, wealthy, cool, artsy
  People who like the name Jiles also like Jaden, Jada, Jules, Jorryn, Jameson, Jax, Jensen, Jude, Julian, Jayme

Jill *(English)* ♀ RATING: ★★☆
Short for Jillian—Jill Scott, singer; Jill St. John, actress
  People think of Jill as pretty, funny, intelligent, caring, trustworthy
  People who like the name Jill also like Jillian, Claire, Hannah, Emma, Grace, Emily, Jessica, Jane, Sarah, Paige

Jillian *(English)* ♀ RATING: ★★★
Youthful—Medieval variation of Julian
  People think of Jillian as pretty, funny, intelligent, creative, caring
  People who like the name Jillian also like Ava, Olivia, Hannah, Isabella, Grace, Emma, Hailey, Julia, Chloe, Lauren

Jim *(English)* ♂ RATING: ★★★☆
Short for James—Jim Belushi, actor; Jim Morrison, singer
  People think of Jim as funny, handsome, intelligent, caring, trustworthy
  People who like the name Jim also like Jack, Jake, Joshua, Johnathan, Benjamin, Jared, Jeremy, Josh, Jackson, Jacob

Jimbo *(American)* ♂ RATING: ★★★
Short for James
  People think of Jimbo as loser, lazy, aggressive, poor, weird
  People who like the name Jimbo also like Jacob, Jake, Jett, Jason, Jasper, Jimmy, Jack, Angus, Jeremy, Jethro

Jimmy *(English)* ♂ RATING: ★★
Short for James—Jimmy Smits, actor
  People think of Jimmy as funny, handsome, cool, sexy, intelligent
  People who like the name Jimmy also like Jack, Justin, Jake, Jason, Jacob, Jeremy, Joshua, Jackson, Johnathan, Matthew

Jin *(Japanese)* ♀ RATING: ★★★☆
Tenderness—Also means gold in Chinese
  People think of Jin as intelligent, trustworthy, caring, creative, cool
  People who like the name Jin also like Kaida, Keiko, Kimi, Emiko, Mai, Kaori, Aiko, Gin, Amaya, Sakura

Jinan *(Arabic)* ♀   RATING: ★★★
Paradise gardens
People think of Jinan as elegant, funny, pretty, caring, intelligent
People who like the name Jinan also like Jamila, Jalia, Jana, Rowa, Jena, Rayya, Daphne, Jui, Jalila, Jesimae

Jinelle *(English)* ♀   RATING: ★★☆
Variation of Janelle
People think of Jinelle as funny, pretty, creative, cool, energetic
People who like the name Jinelle also like Janelle, Jillian, Jadyn, Jeslyn, Jennelle, Jazlynn, Jazzelle, Isabella, Jasmine, Ashlyn

Jira *(African)* ♀   RATING: ★★★
Related by blood
People think of Jira as weird, pretty, slow, energetic, trustworthy
People who like the name Jira also like Jia Li, Jahzara, Jaya, Jadyn, Jeslyn, Jara, Johari, Jora, Jazlynn, Jera

Jirair *(Armenian)* ♂   RATING: ★★☆
Agile
People think of Jirair as aggressive, exotic, creative, wild, intelligent
People who like the name Jirair also like Javier, Jedrek, Jerrick, Javan, Jayden, Jeremiah, Jerod, Jeroen, Kaden, Jaron

Jiro *(Japanese)* ♂   RATING: ★★★☆
The second male
People think of Jiro as handsome, funny, cool, caring, boy next door
People who like the name Jiro also like Ryu, Haruki, Hiroshi, Haru, Akio, Kaemon, Keitaro, Makoto, Ringo, Suoh

Jitka *(Slavic)* ♀   RATING: ★★☆
From Judaea—Short for Judita or Judith
People think of Jitka as intelligent, pretty, exotic, wild, young
People who like the name Jitka also like Hazel, Vonda, Darva, Gretchen, Halo, Charlotte, Vesna, Laquinta, Harmony, Latika

Jiva *(Sanskrit/East Indian)* ♀♂   RATING: ★★★
Living, existing
People think of Jiva as exotic, weird, ethnic, creative, caring
People who like the name Jiva also like Jada, Jaden, Jalen, Jade, Jordan, Kiran, Jarah, Jorryn, Jory, Jacey

Jo *(Hebrew)* ♀♂   RATING: ★★☆
Short for names beginning with Jo, such as Joseph, Joanne, and Josiah
People think of Jo as funny, caring, intelligent, pretty, trustworthy
People who like the name Jo also like Jade, Jordan, Jesse, Jaden, Jamie, Madison, Riley, Ryan, Jude, Jocelyn

Joachim *(Hebrew)* ♂   RATING: ★★★☆
Raised by Yahweh—Pronounced *Wah-KEEM*
People think of Joachim as intelligent, handsome, creative, trustworthy, cool
People who like the name Joachim also like Isaac, Jacob, Gabriel, Joaquin, Jeremiah, Elijah, Ethan, Joshua, Josiah, Joel

Joan *(Hebrew)* ♀   RATING: ★★
God is gracious
People think of Joan as intelligent, caring, funny, pretty, creative
People who like the name Joan also like Hannah, Joanna, Grace, Jessica, Jane, Faith, Elizabeth, Emma, Julia, Jennifer

Joann *(English)* ♀   RATING: ★★★☆
Variation of Joanne
People think of Joann as funny, pretty, caring, creative, intelligent
People who like the name Joann also like Joanna, Jessica, Joanne, Hailey, Jennifer, Joan, Emily, Jasmine, Joyce, Jillian

Joanna *(English)* ♀   RATING: ★★★☆
God is gracious—Joanna Cassidy, actress
People think of Joanna as pretty, funny, caring, intelligent, creative
People who like the name Joanna also like Hannah, Emma, Isabella, Jessica, Abigail, Grace, Jacqueline, Natalie, Faith, Sarah

Joanne *(English)* ♀   RATING: ★★★☆
God is gracious
People think of Joanne as caring, funny, pretty, intelligent, trustworthy
People who like the name Joanne also like Hannah, Joanna, Jessica, Emily, Abigail, Samantha, Jennifer, Isabella, Jasmine, Faith

Joaquin *(Spanish)* ♂   RATING: ★★★★☆
Raised by Yahweh—Pronounced *Wa-KEEN*; Joaquin Phoenix, actor
People think of Joaquin as handsome, intelligent, creative, sexy, cool
People who like the name Joaquin also like Ethan, Elijah, Jackson, Aiden, Gabriel, Noah, Gavin, Jacob, Tristan, Isaac

Job *(Hebrew)* ♂   RATING: ★★★
Persecuted
People think of Job as religious, intelligent, handsome, popular, trustworthy
People who like the name Job also like Jacob, Gabriel, Jayden, Isaac, Jonah, Isaiah, Caleb, Noah, Joshua, Ethan

Jobeth *(American)* ♀   RATING: ★★★
Combination of Jo and Beth—Jobeth Williams, actress
People think of Jobeth as caring, creative, funny, weird, leader
People who like the name Jobeth also like Jillian, Jaclyn, Jasmine, Jessica, Joylyn, Macy, Mallory, Jordane, Jeslyn, Jolene

Jocasta *(Greek)* ♀   RATING: ★★★★
Shining moon—In Greek mythology, the queen of Thebes who married her own son, Oedipus
> People think of Jocasta as elegant, pretty, exotic, intelligent, sexy
> People who like the name Jocasta also like Jezebel, Jeslyn, Layla, Jillian, Jemma, Jazlynn, Gwendolyn, Jana, Grace, Jenna

Jocelin *(French)* ♀ ♂   RATING: ★★★
Little Goth
> People think of Jocelin as pretty, creative, young, trustworthy, intelligent
> People who like the name Jocelin also like Jocelyn, Jaden, Jade, Madison, Caden, Jordan, Jacey, Aidan, Hayden, Mackenzie

Jocelyn *(English)* ♀ ♂   RATING: ★★★★
Little Goth
> People think of Jocelyn as pretty, funny, caring, intelligent, creative
> People who like the name Jocelyn also like Jaden, Hayden, Madison, Jordan, Riley, Bailey, Logan, Caden, Cadence, Addison

Jock *(English)* ♂   RATING: ★★★
Short for John—Also slang for athlete, from the athletic supporter jock strap; Jock Whitney, newspaper publisher/philanthropist/diplomat
> People think of Jock as handsome, sporty, popular, cool, funny
> People who like the name Jock also like Jack, Jacob, Jayden, Brock, Cole, Marshall, Jace, Jett, Jasper, Nathan

Jody *(English)* ♀ ♂   RATING: ★★★
Short for names beginning with J—Also spelled Jodi or Jodie; Jodie Foster, actress
> People think of Jody as funny, caring, trustworthy, creative, intelligent
> People who like the name Jody also like Jaden, Jade, Jordan, Bailey, Brooke, Cameron, James, Madison, Jesse, Riley

Joe *(English)* ♀ ♂   RATING: ★★★☆
Short for Joseph—Also a nickname for coffee; Joe DiMaggio, baseball player; Joe Montana, football player; Joe Pesci, actor; Joe Spano, actor
> People think of Joe as funny, handsome, sexy, cool, intelligent
> People who like the name Joe also like James, Jesse, Jordan, Charlie, Joey, Sam, Ryan, Taylor, Alex, Jamie

Joel *(Hebrew)* ♂   RATING: ★★★
God will be willing—Joel Grey, actor
> People think of Joel as handsome, funny, intelligent, caring, cool
> People who like the name Joel also like Jacob, Ethan, Noah, Isaac, Joshua, Caleb, Gabriel, Nathan, Elijah, Benjamin

Joella *(Hebrew)* ♀   RATING: ★★☆
God will be willing
> People think of Joella as caring, creative, intelligent, pretty, trustworthy
> People who like the name Joella also like Joelle, Isabella, Jolie, Jolene, Johanna, Chloe, Jillian, Ava, Gabriella, Abigail

Joelle *(French)* ♀   RATING: ★★☆
God will be willing
> People think of Joelle as pretty, intelligent, funny, caring, creative
> People who like the name Joelle also like Hannah, Gabrielle, Ava, Jadyn, Olivia, Jolie, Janelle, Isabella, Isabelle, Paige

Joey *(English)* ♀ ♂   RATING: ★★★
Short for Joseph, Josiah, or Josephine—Joey Bishop, actor/comedian; Joey Fatone, singer; Joey McIntyre, singer
> People think of Joey as funny, cool, handsome, caring, young
> People who like the name Joey also like Ryan, Jordan, Riley, Jade, Jaden, Bailey, James, Jesse, Taylor, Logan

Johann *(German)* ♂   RATING: ★★★☆
God is gracious—Variation of John; pronounced *YO-han*; Johann Sebastian Bach, composer
> People think of Johann as handsome, intelligent, cool, creative, leader
> People who like the name Johann also like Joshua, Jayden, Ethan, Jonathan, Jovan, Joseph, Matthew, Johnathan, Justin, Jack

Johanna *(German)* ♀   RATING: ★★★☆
God is gracious—Feminine form of John
> People think of Johanna as pretty, funny, caring, intelligent, creative
> People who like the name Johanna also like Hannah, Isabella, Abigail, Emma, Hailey, Jadyn, Grace, Paige, Faith, Elizabeth

Johari *(African)* ♀   RATING: ★★
Jewel—Swahili origin
> People think of Johari as exotic, caring, popular, pretty, creative
> People who like the name Johari also like Jahzara, Amaya, Jenaya, Jazlynn, Jamila, Jadyn, Amani, Jasmine, Johanna, Jia Li

John *(Hebrew)* ♂   RATING: ★★
God is gracious—John Glenn, astronaut; John F. Kennedy, U.S. president; John Travolta, actor
> People think of John as handsome, funny, intelligent, caring, cool
> People who like the name John also like Jack, Matthew, Jacob, Michael, Andrew, William, David, Joseph, Daniel, Benjamin

Johnathan *(Hebrew)* ♂   RATING: ★★★
Variation of Jonathan; also combination of John and Nathan
> People think of Johnathan as handsome, funny, intelligent, cool, caring
> People who like the name Johnathan also like Joshua, Jacob, Matthew, Ethan, Jonathan, Benjamin, Nathan, Justin, Nicholas, Joseph

Johnavan *(American)* ♂   RATING: ★★★
Combination of John and Avon
> People think of Johnavan as weird, creative, nerdy, unpopular, cool
> People who like the name Johnavan also like Johnathan, Jayden, Jadon, Jacob, Kaden, Jared, Johnavon, Jackson, Gavin, Aiden

Johnavon *(American)* ♂   RATING: ★★★
Combination of John and Avon
> People think of Johnavon as funny, energetic, creative, wealthy, uptight
> People who like the name Johnavon also like Jayden, Jadon, Johnavan, Nathaniel, Johnathan, Jeremiah, Jacob, Aiden, Kaden, Jackson

Johnda *(American)* ♀   RATING: ★☆
Combination of John and Glenda or Brenda
> People think of Johnda as funny, young, trustworthy, cool, popular
> People who like the name Johnda also like Johnna, Johanna, Jadyn, Joella, Jeanette, Joelle, Janelle, Jania, Janice, Janika

Johnna *(American)* ♀   RATING: ★★☆
Feminine form of John
> People think of Johnna as intelligent, pretty, trustworthy, funny, creative
> People who like the name Johnna also like Jadyn, Johanna, Jillian, Eva, Abigail, Jolie, Chloe, Joelle, Grace, Hannah

Johnny *(Hebrew)* ♂   RATING: ★★★
Short for John—Johnny Carson, TV host; Johnny Cash, singer/songwriter; Johnny Depp, actor
> People think of Johnny as handsome, funny, cool, sexy, caring
> People who like the name Johnny also like Jack, Jacob, Justin, Jake, Johnathan, Joseph, Jason, Joshua, John, Adam

Johnson *(English)* ♂   RATING: ★★★☆
Son of John—Also a surname
> People think of Johnson as funny, energetic, cool, trustworthy, intelligent
> People who like the name Johnson also like Jackson, Jacob, Joshua, Jared, Justin, Jack, Johnathan, Emerson, Jayden, Jamison

Joie *(French)* ♀   RATING: ★★★
Joy—Joie Lee, actress/sister of Spike Lee
> People think of Joie as pretty, creative, artsy, popular, funny

> People who like the name Joie also like Jolie, Jadyn, Joy, Joelle, Ava, Chloe, Faith, Emma, Hope, Grace

Jojo *(American)* ♀   RATING: ★★★☆
Short for names beginning with Jo—Jojo, singer
> People think of Jojo as sexy, cool, girl next door, leader, funny
> People who like the name Jojo also like Hope, Isabella, Faith, Charlotte, Abigail, Emma, Alana, Cady, Gabriella, Pearl

Jokull *(Scandinavian)* ♂   RATING: ★★★
Glacier of ice
> People think of Jokull as powerful, big, weird, aggressive, unpopular
> People who like the name Jokull also like Aiden, Jace, Jayden, Hakan, Jaegar, Leif, Lance, Johnavon, Ryker, Jedrek

Jola *(Slavic)* ♀   RATING: ★★★★
Violet flower—Short for Jolanda or Yolanda
> People think of Jola as pretty, caring, religious, intelligent, leader
> People who like the name Jola also like Jolie, Jadyn, Jaya, Jeslyn, Joella, Jana, Jalia, Layla, Jolene, Jorja

Jolanda *(Slavic)* ♀   RATING: ★★★
Violet flower—Variation of Yolanda
> People think of Jolanda as aggressive, uptight, girl next door, winner, lazy
> People who like the name Jolanda also like Arianna, Jamila, Aaliyah, Carmelita, Cytheria, Amora, Aurora, Adonica, Jovita, Camisha

Jolene *(American)* ♀   RATING: ★★☆
Combination of Jo and Eileen
> People think of Jolene as pretty, funny, intelligent, caring, creative
> People who like the name Jolene also like Hailey, Jolie, Jillian, Isabella, Hannah, Jasmine, Emma, Jaclyn, Grace, Joelle

Jolie *(French)* ♀   RATING: ★★★★
Pretty—Angelina Jolie, actress
> People think of Jolie as pretty, sexy, intelligent, creative, funny
> People who like the name Jolie also like Ava, Chloe, Isabella, Olivia, Grace, Sadie, Hannah, Paige, Ella, Hailey

Jolisa *(American)* ♀   RATING: ★★★
Combination of Joe and Lisa
> People think of Jolisa as funny, pretty, caring, energetic, creative
> People who like the name Jolisa also like Jolene, Jessica, Jadyn, Janelle, Jazlynn, Joanna, Jolie, Mariana, Jazzelle, Katarina

Jolyon *(English)* ♂   RATING: ★★
Downy—Variation of Julian; character in *The Forsyte Saga* by John Galsworthy
> People think of Jolyon as poor, intelligent, old-fashioned, creative, young

People who like the name Jolyon also like Jayden, Aden, Jacob, Jared, Jovan, Asher, Jadon, Johnathan, Kyson, Jaron

Jon (*English*) ♂　　　RATING: ★★★
Variation of John—Also short for Jonathan; Jon Lovitz, actor/comedian
People think of Jon as funny, handsome, intelligent, caring, cool
People who like the name Jon also like Jonathan, Jacob, Jack, John, Jake, Josh, Joshua, Johnathan, Jason, Aaron

Jonah (*Hebrew*) ♂　　　RATING: ★★★
A dove
People think of Jonah as intelligent, handsome, caring, creative, funny
People who like the name Jonah also like Noah, Elijah, Ethan, Jacob, Jonas, Caleb, Isaac, Gabriel, Isaiah, Joshua

Jonas (*Hebrew*) ♂　　　RATING: ★★☆
A dove—Jonas Brothers, musicians
People think of Jonas as intelligent, handsome, caring, funny, creative
People who like the name Jonas also like Jonah, Noah, Elijah, Ethan, Caleb, Jacob, Gabriel, Isaac, Joshua, Isaiah

Jonathan (*Hebrew*) ♂　　　RATING: ★★★
God has given—Jonathan Frakes, actor; Jonathan Price, actor; Jonathan Rhys-Meyers, actor; Jonathan Winters, comedian
People think of Jonathan as handsome, intelligent, funny, caring, cool
People who like the name Jonathan also like Joshua, Matthew, Jacob, Ethan, Nathan, Nicholas, Benjamin, Andrew, Daniel, Gabriel

Jonathon (*Hebrew*) ♂　　　RATING: ★★★
God has given
People think of Jonathon as handsome, funny, caring, intelligent, energetic
People who like the name Jonathon also like Joshua, Johnathan, Jacob, Benjamin, Matthew, Jonathan, Nicholas, Ethan, Jeremy, Justin

Jonco (*American*) ♂　　　RATING: ★★☆
Short for John or Jonathan
People think of Jonco as loser, weird, aggressive, exotic, slow
People who like the name Jonco also like Jengo, Jack, Jasper, Jacob, Jett, Josef, Joshua, Jedidiah, Jarvis, Jackson

Jonell (*American*) ♀　　　RATING: ★★★
Feminine form of Jon
People think of Jonell as slow, energetic, funny, cool, ethnic
People who like the name Jonell also like Sheryl, Janika, Danielle, Julia, Janya, Kristina, Sybil, Sheela, Mariah, Svara

Jones (*Welsh*) ♂　　　RATING: ★★★☆
Son of John—Also a surname
People think of Jones as funny, cool, sexy, popular, creative
People who like the name Jones also like Jack, Jackson, Joshua, Jason, Jace, Cole, Jefferson, John, Jacob, Jonathan

Joni (*American*) ♀　　　RATING: ★★★★
Short for Joan; Joni Mitchell, singer/songwriter
People think of Joni as pretty, caring, funny, creative, trustworthy
People who like the name Joni also like Kyla, Chloe, Jaide, Jadyn, Natalie, Lauren, Jeri, Emma, Mia, Jessica

Jonila (*American*) ♀　　　RATING: ★★☆
Combination of Jon and Nila
People think of Jonila as pretty, intelligent, exotic, elegant, young
People who like the name Jonila also like Joella, Jadyn, Jolene, Janelle, Jovanna, Johanna, Jeslyn, Jania, Johnna, Jennaya

Jonny (*English*) ♂　　　RATING: ★★★☆
Short for John or Jonathan
People think of Jonny as handsome, funny, cool, sexy, popular
People who like the name Jonny also like Jack, Josh, Jake, Justin, Jacob, Jonathan, Jimmy, Johnny, Johnathan, Jackson

Jora (*American*) ♀　　　RATING: ★★★★
Farmer—Feminine form of Jory
People think of Jora as intelligent, cool, aggressive, creative, criminal
People who like the name Jora also like Jorah, Jadyn, Joie, Jeslyn, Jaya, Jezebel, Jolie, Jazlynn, Genevieve, Jillian

Jorah (*American*) ♀　　　RATING: ★★★★
Feminine form of Jory
People think of Jorah as intelligent, caring, funny, pretty, creative
People who like the name Jorah also like Jora, Jadyn, Jeslyn, Jolie, Jaide, Jillian, Jael, Leah, Jordana, Jenna

Jordan (*Hebrew*) ♀♂　　　RATING: ★★★★
To flow down—Also a country in the Middle East; a river name; also spelled Jordyn; Michael Jordan, basketball player
People think of Jordan as funny, cool, intelligent, caring, popular
People who like the name Jordan also like Jaden, Madison, Logan, Taylor, Riley, Hayden, Dylan, Bailey, Cameron, Ryan

Jordana (*Hebrew*) ♀　　　RATING: ★★★★
To flow down—Jordana Brewster, actress
People think of Jordana as pretty, intelligent, creative, trustworthy, funny
People who like the name Jordana also like Isabella, Jadyn, Ava, Paige, Hailey, Abigail, Kaelyn, Gabriella, Adriana, Grace

Jordane (French) ♀   RATING: ★★☆
Feminine form of Jordan
  People think of Jordane as popular, intelligent, creative, pretty, sexy
  People who like the name Jordane also like Jadyn, Jaclyn, Jeslyn, Isabella, Jazlynn, Jasmine, Paige, Emma, Hannah, Jillian

Jorge (Spanish) ♂   RATING: ★★
Farmer—Variation of George; pronounced HOR-hay
  People think of Jorge as funny, handsome, cool, caring, intelligent
  People who like the name Jorge also like Justin, Jayden, Javier, Johnathan, Jonathan, Jack, Jacob, Jeremy, Andrew, Jason

Jorja (American) ♀   RATING: ★★★★
Variation of Georgia; Jorja Fox, actress
  People think of Jorja as pretty, funny, intelligent, creative, cool
  People who like the name Jorja also like Olivia, Georgia, Grace, Isabella, Ava, Jillian, Chloe, Jadyn, Abigail, Charlotte

Jorjanna (American) ♀   RATING: ★★★
Variation of Georgianna
  People think of Jorjanna as lazy, exotic, old-fashioned, popular, weird
  People who like the name Jorjanna also like Jorja, Jolene, Jacqueline, Jazzelle, Jenibelle, Janelle, Jazlynn, Jordana, Jana, Jasmine

Jorn (Scandinavian) ♂   RATING: ★★
Farmer—Variation of George; pronounced Yurn
  People think of Jorn as intelligent, handsome, powerful, funny, lazy
  People who like the name Jorn also like Jaron, Jaeger, Kael, Jadon, Aiden, Asher, Jonas, Jace, Jayden, Jake

Jorryn (American) ♀♂   RATING: ★★★★☆
Combination of Jory and Torin
  People think of Jorryn as intelligent, funny, pretty, creative, handsome
  People who like the name Jorryn also like Jaden, Hayden, Jordan, Caden, Jalen, Jocelyn, Jacey, Jensen, Jade, Addison

Jory (English) ♀♂   RATING: ★★★★
Farmer—Cornish variation of George
  People think of Jory as creative, funny, cool, intelligent, caring
  People who like the name Jory also like Jaden, Jordan, Caden, Logan, Jacey, Riley, Reese, Hayden, Parker, Rory

José (Spanish) ♂   RATING: ★★★☆
God will increase—Variation of Joseph; pronounced Ho-ZAY; José Conseco; baseball player
  People think of José as funny, handsome, cool, caring, intelligent
  People who like the name José also like Juan, Joshua, Jacob, Justin, Gabriel, Diego, Joseph, Julio, Miguel, Carlos

Josef (German) ♂   RATING: ★★★
God will increase—Variation of Joseph
  People think of Josef as intelligent, handsome, funny, caring, trustworthy
  People who like the name Josef also like Jacob, Joseph, Joshua, Jared, Noah, Joel, Gabriel, Jake, Jonah, Johnathan

Joseph (Hebrew) ♂   RATING: ★★★★
God will increase—Joseph Cotton, actor; Joseph Fiennes, actor
  People think of Joseph as handsome, funny, intelligent, caring, cool
  People who like the name Joseph also like Jacob, Joshua, Ethan, Benjamin, Matthew, Andrew, Nicholas, Michael, Daniel, Samuel

Josephina (English) ♀   RATING: ★★★☆
God will increase—Feminine form of Joseph
  People think of Josephina as pretty, caring, funny, trustworthy, creative
  People who like the name Josephina also like Josephine, Isabella, Jacqueline, Julianna, Julia, Natalie, Juliet, Gabriella, Sabrina, Jasmine

Josephine (French) ♀   RATING: ★★★★
God will increase—Feminine form of Joseph
  People think of Josephine as pretty, intelligent, creative, caring, funny
  People who like the name Josephine also like Isabella, Abigail, Charlotte, Isabelle, Hannah, Olivia, Sophia, Jacqueline, Ava, Emma

Josh (English) ♂   RATING: ★★★☆
Short for Joshua—Josh Hartnett, actor; Josh Holloway, actor
  People think of Josh as funny, cool, handsome, sexy, popular
  People who like the name Josh also like Joshua, Jake, Jacob, Ethan, Justin, Jack, Jason, Aaron, Luke, Jared

Joshlynn (American) ♀   RATING: ★★★☆
Combination of Joshua and Lynn
  People think of Joshlynn as pretty, funny, creative, intelligent, caring
  People who like the name Joshlynn also like Jadyn, Josephine, Jeslyn, Jacqueline, Kaelyn, Isabella, Jazlynn, Faith, Jasmine, Johanna

Joshua (Hebrew) ♂   RATING: ★★★☆
God is salvation
  People think of Joshua as handsome, funny, intelligent, caring, cool
  People who like the name Joshua also like Jacob, Ethan, Matthew, Noah, Benjamin, Zachary, Caleb, Nathan, Nicholas, Daniel

Joshwa (American) ♂   RATING: ★★★☆
Variation of Joshua
  People think of Joshwa as young, sexy, funny, loser, intelligent

People who like the name Joshwa also like Joshua, Jacob, Jeremiah, Jayden, Justin, Josh, Jared, Nathan, Ethan, Joseph

Josiah *(Hebrew)* ♂   RATING: ★★☆
God will save
People think of Josiah as handsome, intelligent, caring, leader, religious
People who like the name Josiah also like Isaiah, Elijah, Jeremiah, Noah, Isaac, Jonah, Joshua, Caleb, Gabriel, Micah

Josie *(American)* ♀   RATING: ★★★
God will add—Short for Josephine or Joanne; *Josie and the Pussycats*, cartoon
People think of Josie as pretty, funny, caring, intelligent, creative
People who like the name Josie also like Hannah, Grace, Sophie, Emma, Ava, Isabella, Paige, Chloe, Sadie, Olivia

Joss *(English)* ♀ ♂   RATING: ★★★
Little Goth—Originally short for Jocelyn or Joshua; Joss Stone, singer; Joss Whedon, TV writer/producer
People think of Joss as intelligent, creative, cool, popular, funny
People who like the name Joss also like James, Quinn, Sawyer, Addison, Harper, Julian, Logan, Rory, Jude, Beckett

Josue *(Spanish)* ♂   RATING: ★★★★
Variation of Joshua
People think of Josue as handsome, funny, cool, young, sexy
People who like the name Josue also like Joshua, Alejandro, Joseph, Jonathan, Diego, Javier, Joaquin, Joel, Jacob, Jeremy

Journey *(American)* ♀ ♂   RATING: ★★★★
A trip or experience from one place to another
People think of Journey as creative, pretty, energetic, intelligent, leader
People who like the name Journey also like Jaden, Justice, Jade, Jordan, Hayden, Jada, Jersey, Dakota, Caden, Madison

Jovan *(Slavic)* ♂   RATING: ★★★★
God is gracious
People think of Jovan as handsome, intelligent, funny, creative, popular
People who like the name Jovan also like Jayden, Jadon, Kaden, Joshua, Jonah, Gabriel, Jacob, Justin, Elijah, Jaron

Jovanna *(Slavic)* ♀   RATING: ★★☆
God is gracious
People think of Jovanna as creative, intelligent, funny, pretty, caring
People who like the name Jovanna also like Jadyn, Juliana, Adriana, Johanna, Giovanna, Jacqueline, Jazzelle, Isabella, Jaclyn, Jovianne

Jovia *(Latin)* ♀   RATING: ★★★
Happy
People think of Jovia as ethnic, handsome, intelligent, nerdy, quiet
People who like the name Jovia also like Jola, Janya, Jana, Joella, Carmela, Kaylana, Dove, Camilla, Ada, Dulce

Jovianne *(French)* ♀   RATING: ★★★☆
Happy
People think of Jovianne as pretty, intelligent, funny, young, elegant
People who like the name Jovianne also like Jovanna, Jazzelle, Joelle, Jovita, Janelle, Jeslyn, Jacinda, Jennessa, Josephine, Jazlynn

Jovie *(American)* ♀   RATING: ★★★☆
Joyful
People think of Jovie as pretty, creative, popular, intelligent, sporty
People who like the name Jovie also like Ava, Eva, Zoe, Lacey, Libby, Penelope, Bella, Kate, Lucy, Laine

Jovita *(Latin)* ♀   RATING: ★★
Happy
People think of Jovita as pretty, intelligent, funny, caring, creative
People who like the name Jovita also like Jovanna, Jovianne, Juanita, Jolene, Jalena, Johanna, Jacinda, Jia Li, Jenna, Janika

Joy *(Latin)* ♀   RATING: ★★☆
Happiness
People think of Joy as pretty, funny, caring, intelligent, creative
People who like the name Joy also like Faith, Grace, Hope, Hannah, Emma, Paige, Ava, Chloe, Olivia, Abigail

Joyce *(English)* ♀   RATING: ★★☆
Little Lord—Also perhaps short for rejoice; Joyce DeWitt, actress; James Joyce, author
People think of Joyce as caring, intelligent, pretty, funny, creative
People who like the name Joyce also like Faith, Joy, Jasmine, Hannah, Grace, Isabelle, Jessica, Hailey, Emily, Jillian

Joylyn *(American)* ♀   RATING: ★★★★
Combination of Joy and Lynn
People think of Joylyn as pretty, creative, caring, cool, intelligent
People who like the name Joylyn also like Jadyn, Jazlynn, Kaelyn, Jeslyn, Faith, Hannah, Jaclyn, Grace, Cailyn, Isabella

Juan *(Spanish)* ♂   RATING: ★★★☆
God is gracious—Variation of John; Juan Williams, journalist; Don Juan, legendary romancer; San Juan, city in Puerto Rico
People think of Juan as funny, handsome, cool, intelligent, caring

People who like the name Juan also like José, Javier, Carlos, Miguel, Antonio, Julio, Alejandro, Joshua, Adrian, Diego

Juana (*Spanish*) ♀   RATING: ★★★☆
God is gracious—Variation of Joan
People think of Juana as pretty, funny, cool, sexy, intelligent
People who like the name Juana also like Juanita, Johanna, Josephine, Janika, Jasmin, Jenibelle, Isabel, Janice, Jamila, Jessica

Juandalynn (*Spanish*) ♀   RATING: ★★☆
Combination of Juan and Gwendolynn
People think of Juandalynn as religious, weird, exotic, young, aggressive
People who like the name Juandalynn also like Jazlynn, Jyotika, Juana, Juanita, Jennessa, Jia Li, Jenibelle, Jorjanna, Jazzelle, Jetta

Juanita (*Spanish*) ♀   RATING: ★★★☆
God is gracious
People think of Juanita as caring, pretty, funny, intelligent, creative
People who like the name Juanita also like Isabella, Jacqueline, Adriana, Josephine, Gabriella, Isabel, Daniela, Jessica, Mercedes, Jasmine

Jubal (*Hebrew*) ♂   RATING: ★★★☆
Ram
People think of Jubal as caring, funny, energetic, creative, popular
People who like the name Jubal also like Judah, Joshua, Jacob, Jonas, Adam, Gideon, Justus, Jeremiah, Jaxon, Julius

Jud (*English*) ♂   RATING: ★★★☆
Variation of Judd
People think of Jud as trustworthy, cool, unpopular, boy next door, popular
People who like the name Jud also like Jonah, Jase, Jed, Jeremiah, Jared, Jebediah, Jayden, Jerrick, Joseph, Jake

Juda (*Hebrew*) ♀   RATING: ★★
From Judah
People think of Juda as wild, loser, unpopular, untrustworthy, weird
People who like the name Juda also like Jora, Jadyn, Jael, Jira, Jetta, Jessie, Jara, Jera, Jana, Juana

Judah (*Hebrew*) ♂   RATING: ★★
Praised
People think of Judah as leader, handsome, intelligent, creative, religious
People who like the name Judah also like Josiah, Elijah, Jonah, Jeremiah, Noah, Gabriel, Isaiah, Isaac, Micah, Joshua

Judd (*English*) ♂   RATING: ★★★★
To flow down—Short for Jordan; Judd Nelson, actor
People think of Judd as handsome, funny, intelligent, aggressive, popular

People who like the name Judd also like Ethan, Jackson, Jace, Jacob, Gabriel, Kaden, Jayden, Jonah, Jack, Isaac

Jude (*English*) ♀ ♂   RATING: ★★★
From Judaea—Jude Law, actor
People think of Jude as handsome, intelligent, cool, creative, funny
People who like the name Jude also like Hayden, Jade, Parker, Jaden, Julian, James, Riley, Jordan, Logan, Avery

Judith (*Hebrew*) ♀   RATING: ★★★★
From Judaea
People think of Judith as intelligent, caring, pretty, trustworthy, creative
People who like the name Judith also like Jessica, Julia, Laura, Jacqueline, Grace, Faith, Jillian, Lauren, Rebecca, Joanna

Judson (*English*) ♂   RATING: ★★★★
Son of Judd—Variarion of Jordan; also a surname
People think of Judson as intelligent, funny, caring, energetic, cool
People who like the name Judson also like Jackson, Grayson, Jayden, Emerson, Landon, Holden, Maddox, Jaxon, Jacob, Dawson

Judy (*English*) ♀   RATING: ★★
From Judaea—Short for Judith; Judy Garland, actress/singer; Judy Holliday, actress/singer
People think of Judy as caring, pretty, trustworthy, funny, intelligent
People who like the name Judy also like Jessica, Julia, Julie, Juliet, Judith, Jasmine, Maggie, Fiona, Jennifer, Jackie

Jui (*Sanskrit/East Indian*) ♀   RATING: ★★★
Flower
People think of Jui as pretty, caring, cool, unpopular, loser
People who like the name Jui also like Jaya, Jia Li, Jyotika, Jorah, Jasmine, Jessenia, Juji, Jamuna, Julia, Jora

Juin (*French*) ♀   RATING: ★★☆
Born in June
People think of Juin as artsy, creative, girl next door, quiet, intelligent
People who like the name Juin also like Jolie, Joie, Jana, Juliette, Jackie, Josephine, Jara, Jacqueline, Jordane, Jezebel

Juji (*African*) ♀   RATING: ★★★☆
Heap of love—Possibly short for Julia or Judith
People think of Juji as pretty, funny, popular, exotic, caring
People who like the name Juji also like Jahzara, Jia Li, Aiko, Femi, Ayanna, Johari, Jolie, Kya, Jacinda, Jeslyn

Jules *(French)* ♀ ♂   RATING: ★★★★
Downy—Also an American nickname for Julie, Julia, or Julian; Jules Verne, author
> People think of Jules as creative, intelligent, cool, trustworthy, funny
> People who like the name Jules also like Julian, Jaden, Jordan, Jude, Jade, Madison, Caden, Logan, Hayden, Avery

Julia *(Latin)* ♀   RATING: ★★★☆
Downy—Julia Roberts, actress; Julia Stiles, actress
> People think of Julia as pretty, funny, intelligent, caring, creative
> People who like the name Julia also like Olivia, Ava, Emma, Hannah, Grace, Isabella, Emily, Claire, Natalie, Ella

Julian *(Latin)* ♀ ♂   RATING: ★★★★
Downy
> People think of Julian as handsome, intelligent, funny, creative, cool
> People who like the name Julian also like Jaden, Jordan, Hayden, Logan, Dylan, Aidan, Christian, Caden, Cameron, Evan

Juliana *(Spanish)* ♀   RATING: ★★★☆
Feminine form of Julian
> People think of Juliana as pretty, funny, intelligent, caring, creative
> People who like the name Juliana also like Isabella, Julia, Adriana, Olivia, Hannah, Ava, Grace, Gabriella, Jillian, Emma

Julianna *(English)* ♀   RATING: ★★★☆
Feminine form of Julian
> People think of Julianna as pretty, funny, caring, intelligent, creative
> People who like the name Julianna also like Isabella, Hannah, Emma, Olivia, Julia, Hailey, Gabriella, Grace, Ava, Abigail

Julianne *(French)* ♀   RATING: ★★★★
Feminine form of Julian
> People think of Julianne as pretty, intelligent, funny, caring, creative
> People who like the name Julianne also like Hannah, Grace, Isabella, Julianna, Emma, Jillian, Julia, Isabelle, Gabrielle, Olivia

Julie *(French)* ♀   RATING: ★★★★
Variation of Julia
> People think of Julie as pretty, funny, caring, intelligent, creative
> People who like the name Julie also like Julia, Hannah, Grace, Emily, Emma, Hailey, Faith, Natalie, Isabella, Chloe

Juliet *(English)* ♀   RATING: ★★★
Downy—Character in *Romeo and Juliet* by William Shakespeare
> People think of Juliet as pretty, intelligent, elegant, creative, young

People who like the name Juliet also like Grace, Isabella, Olivia, Hannah, Faith, Charlotte, Ava, Emma, Isabelle, Julia

Juliette *(French)* ♀   RATING: ★★★☆
Downy—Variation of Juliet
> People think of Juliette as pretty, elegant, funny, intelligent, creative
> People who like the name Juliette also like Isabella, Isabelle, Ava, Emma, Olivia, Chloe, Hannah, Ella, Gabrielle, Grace

Julinka *(Hungarian)* ♀   RATING: ★★☆
Short for Julia
> People think of Julinka as loser, caring, ethnic, creative, slow
> People who like the name Julinka also like Joella, Jazzelle, Jazlynn, Jia Li, Joelle, Janika, Janelle, Juniper, Jelena, Julisha

Julio *(Spanish)* ♂   RATING: ★★★★
Variation of Julius
> People think of Julio as aggressive, big, criminal, lazy, loser
> People who like the name Julio also like Antonio, Javier, Juan, Miguel, Diego, Carlos, Joshua, José, Alejandro, Rafael

Julisha *(American)* ♀   RATING: ★★★☆
Combination of Julia and Letitia
> People think of Julisha as pretty, intelligent, sexy, popular, lazy
> People who like the name Julisha also like Jazlynn, Jazzelle, Janelle, Jennessa, Jadyn, Jenaya, Jalena, Jania, Janika, Jamila

Julius *(Latin)* ♂   RATING: ★★★☆
Downy
> People think of Julius as handsome, intelligent, powerful, leader, caring
> People who like the name Julius also like Gabriel, Jacob, Jayden, Alexander, Noah, Tristan, Justin, Elijah, Ethan, Caleb

July *(English)* ♀ ♂   RATING: ★★★☆
Born in July
> People think of July as pretty, intelligent, caring, funny, creative
> People who like the name July also like Madison, Jade, Jordan, Taylor, Brooke, Jaden, Bailey, Riley, Dakota, Dallas

Jumoke *(African)* ♀ ♂   RATING: ★★★☆
Everyone loves the child
> People think of Jumoke as young, intelligent, popular, ethnic, pretty
> People who like the name Jumoke also like Jorryn, Jie, Jela, Akia, Jada, Jiva, Jarah, Lolovivi, Janus, Jamie

Jun *(Chinese)* ♂   RATING: ★★★★
Handsome—Also a unisex name meaning esteemed people
> People think of Jun as handsome, intelligent, creative, caring, cool
> People who like the name Jun also like Jon, Julius, Jayden, Joshua, Jedrek, Jeremiah, Josiah, Jeremy, Long, Jeffrey

June *(Latin)* ♀   RATING: ★★☆
Born in June—The month was named after the Roman goddess Juno
> People think of June as pretty, caring, funny, creative, intelligent
> People who like the name June also like Grace, Faith, Emma, Paige, Ava, April, Hannah, Charlotte, Violet, Abigail

Jung *(German)* ♂   RATING: ★★
Young—Carl Jung, psychiatrist/founder of analytical psychology
> People think of Jung as intelligent, aggressive, big, weird, cool
> People who like the name Jung also like Asher, Jaeger, Braun, Edan, Jonas, Jorn, Silver, Wolfgang, August, Clyde

Junior *(English)* ♂   RATING: ★☆
The young, child
> People think of Junior as funny, cool, handsome, sexy, popular
> People who like the name Junior also like Justin, Jacob, Jack, Jake, Jayden, Jared, Jackson, Joshua, Nathan, Anthony

Juniper *(Latin)* ♀   RATING: ★★★☆
Juniper berry
> People think of Juniper as pretty, creative, artsy, intelligent, exotic
> People who like the name Juniper also like Jasmine, Aurora, Fiona, Ivy, Violet, Iris, Chloe, Hannah, Audrey, Hazel

Junipero *(Spanish)* ♂   RATING: ★★☆
Juniper tree
> People think of Junipero as ethnic, intelligent, aggressive, weird, poor
> People who like the name Junipero also like Diego, Federico, Sebastian, Milagro, Ferdinand, Thomas, Adriano, Fernando, Gavin, Jacob

Junius *(Latin)* ♂   RATING: ★★★☆
Youthful
> People think of Junius as aggressive, cool, leader, creative, young
> People who like the name Junius also like Jonas, Jayden, Julius, Justin, Justus, Joshua, Jonah, Joaquin, Jace, Jeremiah

Juno *(Latin)* ♀♂   RATING: ★★
Goddess of marriage and childbirth—Juno, film title and character
> People think of Juno as intelligent, cool, powerful, aggressive, leader
> People who like the name Juno also like Jade, Jordan, Echo, Jalen, Julian, James, Jazz, Jensen, Mika, Jax

Justice *(English)* ♀♂   RATING: ★★★★
Justice
> People think of Justice as intelligent, popular, leader, funny, creative
> People who like the name Justice also like Jaden, Jade, Jordan, Caden, Dakota, Hayden, Cadence, Madison, Logan, Bailey

Justin *(English)* ♂   RATING: ★★★★
Just, fair—Justin Timberlake, singer
> People think of Justin as handsome, funny, cool, intelligent, caring
> People who like the name Justin also like Jacob, Ethan, Joshua, Jason, Nathan, Matthew, Brandon, Jayden, Nicholas, Jared

Justine *(English)* ♀   RATING: ★★☆
Feminine form of Justin
> People think of Justine as pretty, funny, caring, creative, intelligent
> People who like the name Justine also like Hailey, Faith, Paige, Olivia, Gabrielle, Hannah, Jasmine, Jessica, Abigail, Isabella

Justise *(American)* ♀   RATING: ★★★
Variation of Justice
> People think of Justise as funny, pretty, powerful, leader, exotic
> People who like the name Justise also like Justine, Jadyn, Jazlynn, Josie, Jasmine, Juliette, Jillian, Jasmin, Janelle, Faith

Justus *(Latin)* ♂   RATING: ★★★★
Just, fair
> People think of Justus as intelligent, handsome, caring, trustworthy, leader
> People who like the name Justus also like Gabriel, Jayden, Ethan, Jacob, Isaiah, Kaden, Jadon, Jonah, Elijah, Joshua

Jyoti *(Sanskrit/East Indian)* ♀   RATING: ★★★☆
Light
> People think of Jyoti as intelligent, pretty, popular, trustworthy, funny
> People who like the name Jyoti also like Jyotika, Jaya, Janika, Jia Li, Jahzara, Johari, Jeslyn, Jui, Jadzia, Jamuna

Jyotika *(Sanskrit/East Indian)* ♀   RATING: ★★★
Light, flame
> People think of Jyotika as exotic, funny, intelligent, elegant, sexy
> People who like the name Jyotika also like Jyoti, Jaya, Jia Li, Jahzara, Jamuna, Jui, Joelle, Joella, Janika, Jetta

— 𝕂 —

Kaamil (*Arabic*) ♂   RATING: ★★★
Perfect, complete
> People think of Kaamil as intelligent, funny, pretty, cool, powerful
> People who like the name Kaamil also like Kaden, Kalil, Khalil, Kael, Gabriel, Kadeem, Kamal, Amir, Ethan, Kamran

Kabibe (*African*) ♀   RATING: ★★★
Little lady
> People think of Kabibe as pretty, young, quiet, exotic, popular
> People who like the name Kabibe also like Kabira, Kachina, Kaida, Kamili, Kya, Kacela, Kacy, Kainda, Kailani, Kaia

Kabili (*African*) ♂   RATING: ★★★
Honest, brave—Swahili origin
> People think of Kabili as creative, handsome, intelligent, popular, young
> People who like the name Kabili also like Kaden, Kadin, Kaemon, Kasim, Kadeem, Kaamil, Kimoni, Kaelem, Kareem, Kael

Kabira (*Arabic*) ♀   RATING: ★★
Noble, great
> People think of Kabira as exotic, pretty, winner, creative, quiet
> People who like the name Kabira also like Kaira, Kaida, Kailani, Kabibe, Kacela, Kachina, Kaiya, Kaelyn, Kya, Kacia

Kacela (*American*) ♀   RATING: ★★
Variation of Kacey
> People think of Kacela as pretty, intelligent, artsy, elegant, trendy
> People who like the name Kacela also like Kacia, Kaydence, Kabira, Kaida, Kailani, Kaira, Kachina, Kaelyn, Kacy, Isabella

Kachina (*Native American*) ♀   RATING: ★★★☆
Spirit—Hopi origin; also a toy doll in Native American culture
> People think of Kachina as pretty, creative, funny, exotic, young
> People who like the name Kachina also like Kaya, Kailani, Kaida, Kaelyn, Kaliska, Kaira, Kabira, Soraya, Kaiya, Kacela

Kacia (*Greek*) ♀   RATING: ★★★☆
Acacia tree—Short for Acacia; also a Latin variation of Kacey
> People think of Kacia as intelligent, funny, energetic, caring, sexy
> People who like the name Kacia also like Kaelyn, Kaia, Kacy, Kaira, Kaida, Kaiya, Ava, Kaleigh, Kiara, Chloe

Kacy (*American*) ♀   RATING: ★★★★
Vigilant in war—Variation of Casey
> People think of Kacy as funny, pretty, popular, cool, caring
> People who like the name Kacy also like Kailey, Faith, Hailey, Paige, Lacey, Kaelyn, Isabella, Grace, Chloe, Emma

Kade (*American*) ♀♂   RATING: ★★★★
Stout, sturdy—Variation of Cade
> People think of Kade as handsome, intelligent, popular, funny, caring
> People who like the name Kade also like Caden, Cade, Jaden, Hayden, Jade, Logan, Bailey, Addison, Madison, Riley

Kadeem (*Arabic*) ♂   RATING: ★★
Ancient, former—Variation of Qadeem; Kadeem Hardison, actor
> People think of Kadeem as funny, handsome, young, popular, cool
> People who like the name Kadeem also like Kaden, Kadin, Kareem, Kael, Jabari, Kaelem, Kalil, Keagan, Kaamil, Darius

Kaden (*American*) ♂   RATING: ★★★★☆
Fighter—Variation of Caden; also spelled Kayden or Kaiden
> People think of Kaden as handsome, energetic, intelligent, funny, popular
> People who like the name Kaden also like Aiden, Jayden, Ethan, Caleb, Braden, Keagan, Landon, Gavin, Kaleb, Aden

Kadin (*Arabic*) ♂   RATING: ★★★★
Companion—Pronounced *Ka-DEEN*
> People think of Kadin as energetic, funny, handsome, intelligent, cool
> People who like the name Kadin also like Kaden, Aiden, Jayden, Kaleb, Caleb, Ethan, Braden, Aden, Landon, Keagan

Kael (*Celtic/Gaelic*) ♂   RATING: ★★★★☆
Slender—Variation of Cael
> People think of Kael as handsome, leader, intelligent, energetic, creative
> People who like the name Kael also like Kaden, Aiden, Keagan, Liam, Kail, Tristan, Cole, Ethan, Kane, Gabriel

Kaelem (*American*) ♂   RATING: ★★★☆
Combination of Caleb and Callum; also formed by the letters K, L, and M
> People think of Kaelem as popular, funny, handsome, cool, intelligent
> People who like the name Kaelem also like Kaden, Kael, Kaleb, Keagan, Kellan, Kail, Ethan, Jayden, Aden, Aiden

Kaelin (*Celtic/Gaelic*) ♀♂   RATING: ★★★★
Pure—Variation of Cailin; also combination of Kay and Lynn; also spelled Kaylin
> People think of Kaelin as pretty, creative, intelligent, caring, funny

People who like the name Kaelin also like Caden, Jaden, Aidan, Keegan, Hayden, Riley, Logan, Mackenzie, Madison, Teagan

Kaelyn (*Celtic/Gaelic*) ♀   RATING: ★★★☆
Pure—Variation of Cailin
People think of Kaelyn as pretty, funny, intelligent, creative, popular
People who like the name Kaelyn also like Cailyn, Kailey, Kayla, Kaitlyn, Hailey, Jadyn, Paige, Isabella, Hannah, Emma

Kaemon (*Japanese*) ♂   RATING: ★★★☆
Joyful
People think of Kaemon as handsome, leader, powerful, cool, intelligent
People who like the name Kaemon also like Kaden, Keitaro, Hiroshi, Ryu, Akio, Kael, Keiji, Haruki, Makoto, Aiden

Kaethe (*German*) ♀   RATING: ★★★★
Pure—Short for Katherine
People think of Kaethe as caring, pretty, cool, creative, funny
People who like the name Kaethe also like Kaelyn, Kaida, Kaia, Kailani, Kaira, Kailey, Kachina, Kala, Kaiya, Kaleigh

Kafele (*African*) ♂   RATING: ★★★☆
Worth dying for
People think of Kafele as powerful, intelligent, energetic, handsome, caring
People who like the name Kafele also like Kaden, Kail, Kael, Kami, Kayonga, Kale, Kamran, Kabili, Keiji, Kasim

Kagami (*Japanese*) ♀   RATING: ★☆
Mirror
People think of Kagami as pretty, young, elegant, creative, exotic
People who like the name Kagami also like Kaida, Kaori, Keiko, Kaiya, Kaiyo, Amaya, Inari, Kyoko, Emiko, Hitomi

Kahlilia (*American*) ♀   RATING: ★★☆
Sincere friend—Feminine form of Khalil; also combination of Callie and Lilia
People think of Kahlilia as pretty, exotic, creative, caring, young
People who like the name Kahlilia also like Kailani, Kaelyn, Kaira, Kaia, Kaiya, Kalila, Kaida, Kailey, Kamaria, Kaleigh

Kai (*Hawaiian*) ♀♂   RATING: ★★★★
Ocean—Also Welsh variation of Caius; pronounced *Kye*
People think of Kai as intelligent, cool, creative, handsome, popular
People who like the name Kai also like Caden, Jaden, Hayden, Aidan, Dylan, Riley, Logan, Bailey, Madison, Jade

Kaia (*Scandinavian*) ♀   RATING: ★★★★☆
Pure—Short for Katherine
People think of Kaia as pretty, intelligent, creative, energetic, caring
People who like the name Kaia also like Kaiya, Ava, Kaya, Kaelyn, Chloe, Keira, Kyla, Isabella, Kaira, Kaida

Kaida (*Japanese*) ♀   RATING: ★★★★☆
Little dragon
People think of Kaida as pretty, intelligent, exotic, creative, powerful
People who like the name Kaida also like Kaiya, Amaya, Kaelyn, Kaia, Kailani, Kaira, Keaira, Kaori, Aiko, Sakura

Kaikoura (*Maori*) ♀   RATING: ★★★
New Zealand place name
People think of Kaikoura as exotic, artsy, creative, pretty, intelligent
People who like the name Kaikoura also like Leilani, Kaiya, Kaelyn, Ophelia, Ava, Kaia, Rosaleen, Kala, Danelea, Selene

Kail (*Celtic/Gaelic*) ♀♂   RATING: ★★☆
Slender—Variation of Cael
People think of Kail as intelligent, handsome, caring, cool, leader
People who like the name Kail also like Kael, Kaden, Keagan, Aiden, Kale, Kane, Gabriel, Liam, Conner, Cole

Kailani (*Hawaiian*) ♀   RATING: ★★★
Sea and sky
People think of Kailani as pretty, exotic, creative, sexy, intelligent
People who like the name Kailani also like Leilani, Kaelyn, Ailani, Kamea, Keani, Kaia, Kaiya, Isabella, Kaida, Malia

Kailas (*Sanskrit/East Indian*) ♀♂   RATING: ★★☆
Shiva's mountain residence
People think of Kailas as energetic, leader, funny, intelligent, creative
People who like the name Kailas also like Kaelin, Kai, Kaili, Kalani, Caden, Kyan, Hayden, Kendall, Kade, Kalei

Kailey (*English*) ♀   RATING: ★★★☆
Slender—Variation of Kayley
People think of Kailey as pretty, funny, caring, energetic, intelligent
People who like the name Kailey also like Hailey, Kaelyn, Kaleigh, Kaylee, Paige, Kayla, Kaitlyn, Hannah, Faith, Cailyn

Kaili (*Hawaiian*) ♀♂   RATING: ★★★★☆
A Hawaiian deity
People think of Kaili as pretty, creative, young, energetic, popular
People who like the name Kaili also like Kai, Kalani, Madison, Kalei, Kaelin, Caden, Bailey, Jaden, Kaley, Hayden

Kainda (*African*) ♀ RATING: ★★★☆
Hunter's daughter—From the Tharaka tribe of Kenya
People think of Kainda as pretty, ethnic, creative, trustworthy, funny
People who like the name Kainda also like Kailani, Kaida, Kaira, Kabira, Kaelyn, Kya, Karimah, Kacela, Kaia, Kalea

Kaipo (*Hawaiian*) ♂ RATING: ★★★★
Sweetheart
People think of Kaipo as weird, pretty, handsome, funny, leader
People who like the name Kaipo also like Kanoa, Kale, Keoni, Kael, Lulani, Keon, Kaden, Kelii, Kapono, Kail

Kaira (*Greek*) ♀ RATING: ★★★★
Right or opportune moment—Feminine form of Kairos
People think of Kaira as pretty, intelligent, creative, caring, popular
People who like the name Kaira also like Kaelyn, Keira, Kyla, Kaia, Kara, Kyra, Kiara, Kaiya, Kailey, Kayla

Kairos (*Greek*) ♂ RATING: ★★★★
Right or opportune moment
People think of Kairos as elegant, powerful, exotic, quiet, creative
People who like the name Kairos also like Kyros, Kaden, Aiden, Sirius, Tristan, Calix, Damien, Kael, Ambrose, Kadin

Kaiser (*German*) ♂ RATING: ★★★★
Leader—Also a title of nobility
People think of Kaiser as leader, intelligent, powerful, aggressive, handsome
People who like the name Kaiser also like Kaden, Keagan, Kaleb, Aiden, Gage, Caleb, Drake, Landon, Ethan, Kael

Kaitlin (*Celtic/Gaelic*) ♀ RATING: ★★★☆
Pure
People think of Kaitlin as pretty, funny, creative, caring, intelligent
People who like the name Kaitlin also like Kaitlyn, Caitlyn, Kaelyn, Caitlin, Hannah, Hailey, Kailey, Kayla, Katelyn, Emma

Kaitlyn (*Celtic/Gaelic*) ♀ RATING: ★★★★
Pure
People think of Kaitlyn as pretty, funny, caring, creative, intelligent
People who like the name Kaitlyn also like Caitlin, Hailey, Hannah, Kaelyn, Paige, Katelyn, Abigail, Emma, Kayla, Isabella

Kaiya (*Japanese*) ♀ RATING: ★★★★☆
Forgiveness—Variation of Kaiyo
People think of Kaiya as pretty, creative, caring, intelligent, energetic
People who like the name Kaiya also like Kaia, Kaelyn, Kaida, Kaya, Amaya, Kaira, Kyla, Kya, Jadyn, Kailani

Kaiyo (*Japanese*) ♀ RATING: ★★★☆
Forgiveness
People think of Kaiyo as pretty, exotic, quiet, ethnic, popular
People who like the name Kaiyo also like Kaiya, Kaida, Keiko, Kaori, Kagami, Amaya, Kioko, Aiko, Kimi, Kohana

Kala (*Sanskrit/East Indian*) ♀ RATING: ★★★☆
Art—Pronounced KAH-la
People think of Kala as pretty, funny, intelligent, trustworthy, caring
People who like the name Kala also like Kayla, Kaelyn, Kali, Kara, Kyla, Ava, Hailey, Kailey, Isabella, Ella

Kalani (*Hawaiian*) ♀♂ RATING: ★★★★☆
The heavens
People think of Kalani as pretty, exotic, creative, funny, energetic
People who like the name Kalani also like Kai, Kaili, Nalani, Jaden, Keanu, Jade, Madison, Caden, Kalei, Kaelin

Kalare (*Greek*) ♀ RATING: ★★★
Clear, bright
People think of Kalare as girl next door, exotic, pretty, sexy, artsy
People who like the name Kalare also like Kaelyn, Kaira, Kaida, Kalista, Kailani, Kaia, Kamea, Kalea, Kiara, Kaiya

Kalb (*Hebrew*) ♂ RATING: ★★
Dog—Variation of Caleb
People think of Kalb as powerful, funny, sneaky, cool, weird
People who like the name Kalb also like Kaden, Kaleb, Caleb, Ethan, Jacob, Keagan, Noah, Braden, Kadin, Cole

Kale (*Hawaiian*) ♂ RATING: ★★☆
Man—Variation of Charles
People think of Kale as handsome, caring, funny, energetic, intelligent
People who like the name Kale also like Kaden, Ethan, Kael, Caleb, Cole, Kaleb, Cale, Noah, Keagan, Tristan

Kalea (*Hawaiian*) ♀ RATING: ★★★★☆
Illustrious—Variation of Clare
People think of Kalea as pretty, energetic, creative, funny, intelligent
People who like the name Kalea also like Kaelyn, Kailey, Kyla, Kaiya, Kayla, Kaleigh, Kaia, Kiana, Kaylee, Kailani

Kaleb (*Hebrew*) ♂ RATING: ★★★☆
Dog—Variation of Caleb
People think of Kaleb as handsome, funny, intelligent, energetic, caring
People who like the name Kaleb also like Caleb, Kaden, Ethan, Jacob, Aiden, Noah, Elijah, Jayden, Isaac, Gabriel

Kalei (*Hawaiian*) ♀♂ RATING: ★★★
One who works for the king—Also means lei (flower necklace)
People think of Kalei as pretty, young, caring, funny, creative

People who like the name Kalei also like Kaili, Kai, Caden, Jaden, Kalani, Kaley, Kaelin, Bailey, Madison, Kalin

Kaleigh *(English)* ♀   RATING: ★★★☆
Who is like God?—Variation of Kayley or Chaeli
People think of Kaleigh as pretty, funny, creative, popular, caring
People who like the name Kaleigh also like Kailey, Kaelyn, Kyleigh, Hailey, Hannah, Kaylee, Paige, Kaitlyn, Isabella, Faith

Kaley *(English)* ♀♂   RATING: ★★★☆
Slender—Variation of Kayley
People think of Kaley as pretty, funny, creative, caring, popular
People who like the name Kaley also like Bailey, Madison, Jaden, Hayden, Riley, Caden, Mackenzie, Logan, Caley, Haley

Kali *(Sanskrit/East Indian)* ♀   RATING: ★★★☆
A maiden, a bud
People think of Kali as pretty, funny, creative, intelligent, caring
People who like the name Kali also like Kaelyn, Kira, Hailey, Kalli, Kailey, Kiara, Chloe, Ava, Callie, Emma

Kalil *(Arabic)* ♂   RATING: ★★★★
Friend
People think of Kalil as cool, intelligent, sexy, energetic, handsome
People who like the name Kalil also like Khalil, Kaden, Kadin, Malik, Kaleb, Kael, Kareem, Jayden, Kail, Caleb

Kalila *(Arabic)* ♀   RATING: ★★★★☆
Beloved
People think of Kalila as pretty, creative, intelligent, trustworthy, energetic
People who like the name Kalila also like Kaelyn, Kailani, Kaiya, Isabella, Kyla, Kamilah, Kaia, Kailey, Layla, Kayla

Kalin *(American)* ♀♂   RATING: ★★★★
Combination of Caleb and Colin
People think of Kalin as caring, funny, cool, pretty, intelligent
People who like the name Kalin also like Caden, Jaden, Hayden, Kaelin, Logan, Addison, Keegan, Madison, Brayden, Reese

Kalinda *(Sanskrit/East Indian)* ♀   RATING: ★★★★
The sun
People think of Kalinda as pretty, caring, energetic, intelligent, trustworthy
People who like the name Kalinda also like Kaelyn, Kalista, Kendra, Kiara, Kaleigh, Katarina, Jasmine, Kali, Larissa, Leilani

Kaliska *(Native American)* ♀   RATING: ★★★☆
Coyote chasing deer—Miwok origin
People think of Kaliska as exotic, pretty, creative, energetic, leader

People who like the name Kaliska also like Kalista, Kachina, Kiona, Kailani, Kaya, Keaira, Keira, Kaida, Kiara, Hailey

Kalista *(Greek)* ♀   RATING: ★★★★☆
Most beautiful one—Variation of Calista
People think of Kalista as pretty, intelligent, creative, leader, caring
People who like the name Kalista also like Calista, Kaelyn, Isabella, Callista, Keira, Kailey, Hailey, Ava, Kaydence, Kayla

Kalkin *(Sanskrit/East Indian)* ♂   RATING: ★★
Last incarnation of Vishnu, the Hindu God
People think of Kalkin as powerful, trustworthy, weird, ethnic, creative
People who like the name Kalkin also like Kaden, Kami, Kishan, Ketan, Karan, Karston, Keagan, Kael, Kamal, Gagan

Kalli *(American)* ♀   RATING: ★★★
Beautiful—Variation of Callie
People think of Kalli as pretty, popular, funny, creative, energetic
People who like the name Kalli also like Kali, Callie, Kailey, Kaelyn, Chloe, Hailey, Kayla, Kaleigh, Kaylee, Kara

Kallima *(English)* ♀   RATING: ★★★☆
Butterfly
People think of Kallima as pretty, exotic, sexy, trustworthy, cool
People who like the name Kallima also like Kaira, Kaelyn, Kalista, Kailani, Kamea, Kaiya, Kaya, Kyla, Kaia, Keira

Kalliyan *(Cambodian)* ♀   RATING: ★★★☆
Best
People think of Kalliyan as pretty, intelligent, artsy, creative, popular
People who like the name Kalliyan also like Kaelyn, Kaleigh, Keaira, Kailani, Kaydence, Kamilah, Gabrielle, Kayla, Aaralyn, Kalli

Kalona *(American)* ♀   RATING: ★★
Colony—Amish town in Iowa
People think of Kalona as old-fashioned, religious, sneaky, wild, ethnic
People who like the name Kalona also like Keira, Keaira, Kailani, Kaliska, Jesimae, Kaleigh, Kali, Kiona, Kacia, Kaida

Kaloni *(Hawaiian)* ♀   RATING: ★★
The sky
People think of Kaloni as pretty, creative, caring, cool, funny
People who like the name Kaloni also like Kailani, Leilani, Kamea, Keani, Kaelyn, Kaya, Kaleigh, Kaydence, Keola, Keala

Kalonice *(Greek)* ♀   RATING: ★★★
Beauty's victory
People think of Kalonice as pretty, exotic, intelligent, popular, powerful

People who like the name Kalonice also like Kaira, Kailani, Kaydence, Kalare, Kaloni, Kalista, Kamea, Kacela, Cassandra, Keani

Kaloosh (*Armenian*) ♂   RATING: ★★☆
Pentecost
People think of Kaloosh as weird, loser, nerdy, big, sexy
People who like the name Kaloosh also like Kasim, Kaelem, Kane, Kayonga, Karan, Kaiser, Kareem, Kaden, Kaemon, Kamran

Kalyan (*Sanskrit/East Indian*) ♀♂   RATING: ★★★
Fortunate
People think of Kalyan as intelligent, caring, funny, cool, trustworthy
People who like the name Kalyan also like Jaden, Kaelin, Caden, Hayden, Madison, Logan, Riley, Kai, Keegan, Kiran

Kalyca (*Greek*) ♀   RATING: ★★★☆
Rosebud
People think of Kalyca as pretty, energetic, creative, artsy, caring
People who like the name Kalyca also like Kaelyn, Kalista, Kyra, Kailani, Kaira, Kaydence, Kaida, Kyla, Chloe, Keely

Kamal (*Arabic*) ♂   RATING: ★★★★
Perfection—In Sanskrit, means lotus flower
People think of Kamal as intelligent, handsome, funny, cool, popular
People who like the name Kamal also like Kaden, Jayden, Kamali, Elijah, Jamar, Kalil, Kail, Kamil, Kamran, Kadin

Kamala (*Sanskrit/East Indian*) ♀   RATING: ★★★★
Lotus
People think of Kamala as pretty, intelligent, creative, caring, exotic
People who like the name Kamala also like Kamaria, Kamana, Karma, Kali, Kiana, Kiara, Kamea, Kamilah, Kaia, Keiko

Kamali (*Arabic*) ♂   RATING: ★★★
Perfection
People think of Kamali as caring, exotic, intelligent, pretty, powerful
People who like the name Kamali also like Kaden, Kamal, Jabari, Kalil, Khalil, Kail, Kael, Gabriel, Elijah, Jayden

Kamana (*Sanskrit/East Indian*) ♀   RATING: ★★★
Desire, wish
People think of Kamana as exotic, pretty, caring, young, creative
People who like the name Kamana also like Kamala, Kamaria, Kailani, Kimaya, Kamea, Kalinda, Keaira, Kali, Kya, Kaloni

Kamara (*American*) ♀   RATING: ★★★☆
Combination of Camilla and Tamara
People think of Kamara as pretty, exotic, funny, intelligent, creative

People who like the name Kamara also like Aaliyah, Kaelyn, Kimaya, Amaya, Keira, Kaydence, Samara, Destiny, Jadyn, Kalista

Kamaria (*Persian*) ♀   RATING: ★★★★☆
Moon
People think of Kamaria as pretty, funny, intelligent, caring, creative
People who like the name Kamaria also like Kailani, Kaida, Kaiya, Kaelyn, Kamea, Keaira, Kaya, Kya, Kaira, Kaia

Kame (*African*) ♂   RATING: ★★☆
Desolate, arid—Pronounced KAY-may
People think of Kame as exotic, weird, unpopular, uptight, wild
People who like the name Kame also like Kasim, Kaden, Kamran, Kayonga, Kazi, Kimoni, Kalb, Kane, Kanelo, Kenyi

Kamea (*Hawaiian*) ♀   RATING: ★★★★☆
Precious one—Pronounced Ka-MAY-ah
People think of Kamea as pretty, creative, intelligent, funny, caring
People who like the name Kamea also like Kailani, Kaelyn, Kaya, Keona, Kaia, Keani, Kaiya, Leilani, Kaira, Kalea

Kamella (*Hungarian*) ♀   RATING: ★★★☆
Perfect—Variation of Camilla
People think of Kamella as pretty, funny, intelligent, creative, caring
People who like the name Kamella also like Kaelyn, Isabella, Kamilah, Keira, Kiara, Jasmine, Kaydence, Gabriella, Kyla, Kalista

Kameryn (*American*) ♀♂   RATING: ★★★★
Bent nose—Variation of Cameron
People think of Kameryn as pretty, popular, funny, cool, energetic
People who like the name Kameryn also like Camryn, Cameron, Hayden, Jaden, Madison, Mackenzie, Jordan, Caden, Logan, Keegan

Kami (*Sanskrit/East Indian*) ♂   RATING: ★★★★
Whose desires are fulfilled
People think of Kami as pretty, funny, caring, trustworthy, intelligent
People who like the name Kami also like Kaden, Ethan, Jayden, Kane, Keagan, Kael, Gabriel, Caleb, Ian, Noah

Kamiko (*Japanese*) ♀   RATING: ★★★
Little turtle
People think of Kamiko as pretty, exotic, creative, quiet, funny
People who like the name Kamiko also like Kaida, Sakura, Hitomi, Kimi, Keiko, Kioko, Kaori, Emiko, Kaiya, Sora

Kamil (*Arabic*) ♂   RATING: ★★★★
Perfect
People think of Kamil as intelligent, funny, handsome, sexy, leader

People who like the name Kamil also like Kaden, Kadin, Kalil, Kael, Kamal, Kareem, Kami, Kaleb, Ethan, Jamil

Kamilah (*Arabic*) ♀   RATING: ★★☆
Perfect
> People think of Kamilah as pretty, intelligent, funny, exotic, creative
> People who like the name Kamilah also like Kaelyn, Isabella, Kaya, Adriana, Kyla, Keaira, Hailey, Kalista, Keira, Chloe

Kamili (*African*) ♀   RATING: ★★☆
Perfection—Variation of Kamil
> People think of Kamili as pretty, exotic, creative, intelligent, sexy
> People who like the name Kamili also like Kya, Kamilah, Keeya, Kayin, Kaira, Kailani, Kanoni, Jahzara, Kissa, Kabibe

Kamilia (*Polish*) ♀   RATING: ★★★
Camellia flower
> People think of Kamilia as pretty, popular, caring, artsy, energetic
> People who like the name Kamilia also like Kamilah, Kaleigh, Jadyn, Isabella, Isabelle, Kaydence, Kailey, Kyla, Faith, Gabriella

Kamin (*Japanese*) ♂   RATING: ★★★
Joyful—Variation of Kaemon
> People think of Kamin as funny, powerful, leader, young, intelligent
> People who like the name Kamin also like Kaemon, Keitaro, Haru, Makoto, Haruki, Ryu, Keiji, Hiroshi, Suoh, Goro

Kamran (*Persian*) ♂   RATING: ★★★★
Successful
> People think of Kamran as handsome, cool, sexy, powerful, funny
> People who like the name Kamran also like Kaden, Keagan, Kaleb, Ethan, Jayden, Kadin, Tristan, Caleb, Korbin, Ian

Kana (*Japanese*) ♀♂   RATING: ★★★★
Powerful—In Hebrew, means plant or shoot
> People think of Kana as intelligent, funny, creative, powerful, pretty
> People who like the name Kana also like Kiyoshi, Yuki, Kai, Kumi, Kin, Rin, Kalani, Hiroko, Jade, Hoshi

Kanan (*Arabic*) ♀   RATING: ★★★
Merchant, trader—Variation of Canaan
> People think of Kanan as intelligent, aggressive, funny, popular, creative
> People who like the name Kanan also like Jadyn, Kaelyn, Kaydence, Kailey, Kya, Chloe, Kyla, Canan, Kaya, Keena

Kande (*African*) ♀   RATING: ★★★
Firstborn daughter
> People think of Kande as exotic, creative, funny, pretty, energetic

People who like the name Kande also like Kissa, Kya, Kanoni, Kalista, Keshia, Kaelyn, Kamili, Kaiya, Kamea, Kaida

Kane (*Celtic/Gaelic*) ♂   RATING: ★★★★
Battle—In Japanese, means golden; in Hawaiian, means man; pronounced *KAH-nay*
> People think of Kane as handsome, funny, intelligent, popular, powerful
> People who like the name Kane also like Kaden, Keagan, Aiden, Cole, Kael, Ethan, Tristan, Liam, Jayden, Noah

Kanelo (*African*) ♂   RATING: ★★
Enough—From the Xhosa tribe of South Africa
> People think of Kanelo as weird, ethnic, leader, intelligent, wealthy
> People who like the name Kanelo also like Kame, Kazi, Kasim, Kayonga, Ilori, Makalo, Darian, Kimoni, Kaleb, Kojo

Kanga (*Native American*) ♀♂   RATING: ★★★
A raven
> People think of Kanga as cool, creative, young, powerful, girl next door
> People who like the name Kanga also like Kishi, Mika, Kione, Kiyoshi, Keanu, Kansas, Misu, Kieve, Kalyan, Misae

Kanha (*Sanskrit/East Indian*) ♂   RATING: ★★☆
Name of Lord Krishna
> People think of Kanha as winner, intelligent, aggressive, energetic, sporty
> People who like the name Kanha also like Kalkin, Kaushal, Kishan, Kami, Kartik, Ketan, Karan, Arnav, Jatin, Gaurav

Kaniesa (*American*) ♀   RATING: ★★★
Combination af Candice and Anisa
> People think of Kaniesa as pretty, trustworthy, caring, creative, popular
> People who like the name Kaniesa also like Kiana, Kalista, Kailey, Keyanna, Kya, Kaelyn, Kaydence, Kamaria, Janika, Kiandra

Kanika (*Sanskrit/East Indian*) ♀   RATING: ★★★
An atom, particle
> People think of Kanika as pretty, intelligent, caring, funny, creative
> People who like the name Kanika also like Kara, Kiara, Keaira, Keira, Kaori, Kailani, Kaida, Janika, Kiora, Kaira

Kanoa (*Hawaiian*) ♂   RATING: ★★★☆
Free one
> People think of Kanoa as creative, intelligent, young, cool, exotic
> People who like the name Kanoa also like Keoni, Kale, Kaden, Kapono, Keon, Kaipo, Keiran, Kael, Kail, Kimo

Kanoni (*African*) ♀   RATING: ★★☆
LIttle bird—Ugandan origin
> People think of Kanoni as creative, quiet, ethnic, energetic, exotic

People who like the name Kanoni also like Kailani, Karimah, Karasi, Kamili, Kaia, Keani, Kande, Kya, Kaloni, Kacela

Kansas *(Native American)* ♀♂　　RATING: ★★★☆
People of the south wind—Sioux origin; U.S. state
People think of Kansas as pretty, creative, wild, cool, popular
People who like the name Kansas also like Dakota, Cadence, Kendall, Hayden, Addison, Logan, Dallas, Cameron, Jordan, Caden

Kantana *(Japanese)* ♀　　RATING: ★★★
Sword, blade
People think of Kantana as leader, powerful, quiet, young, trustworthy
People who like the name Kantana also like Kaiya, Sakura, Haruko, Luna, Alexa, Yoko, Aaliyah, Adriana, Fabienne, Hoshiko

Kaori *(Japanese)* ♀　　RATING: ★★☆
Fragrant
People think of Kaori as pretty, intelligent, exotic, young, creative
People who like the name Kaori also like Kaiya, Kaida, Keiko, Sakura, Aiko, Amaya, Kioko, Kaoru, Kagami, Kaiyo

Kaoru *(Japanese)* ♀　　RATING: ★★★★
Fragrant
People think of Kaoru as pretty, energetic, funny, intelligent, popular
People who like the name Kaoru also like Kaori, Kaida, Keiko, Kioko, Kuri, Kagami, Kyoko, Kaiya, Kaiyo, Kohana

Kapila *(Sanskrit/East Indian)* ♀　　RATING: ★★☆
Gentle woman
People think of Kapila as pretty, exotic, caring, young, cool
People who like the name Kapila also like Kanika, Kamana, Kalinda, Kerani, Kavindra, Kali, Ishana, Chandra, Avani, Kirtana

Kapono *(Hawaiian)* ♂　　RATING: ★★★
Righteous
People think of Kapono as big, funny, powerful, exotic, energetic
People who like the name Kapono also like Kanoa, Keon, Keoni, Kale, Kelii, Konala, Kimo, Kaipo, Lulani, Palani

Kara *(Italian)* ♀　　RATING: ★★
Dear—Variation of Cara
People think of Kara as pretty, funny, caring, intelligent, creative
People who like the name Kara also like Kaelyn, Keira, Kayla, Hannah, Emma, Paige, Grace, Faith, Kira, Kiara

Karah *(American)* ♀　　RATING: ★★★★
Dear—Variation of Cara
People think of Karah as pretty, funny, creative, intelligent, caring
People who like the name Karah also like Kara, Kaelyn, Kailey, Paige, Keira, Kaleigh, Kayla, Hannah, Olivia, Faith

Karan *(Sanskrit/East Indian)* ♂　　RATING: ★★☆
Helper, companion
People think of Karan as intelligent, caring, popular, handsome, funny
People who like the name Karan also like Kaden, Kael, Kami, Keiran, Kaleb, Kaemon, Kail, Kane, Lance, Kale

Karasi *(African)* ♀　　RATING: ★★★
Life and wisdom
People think of Karasi as pretty, creative, leader, caring, sexy
People who like the name Karasi also like Kanoni, Kya, Kabira, Kaya, Kamaria, Kamili, Kailani, Kumani, Kari, Karimah

Kare *(Scandinavian)* ♂　　RATING: ★★☆
Curly haired
People think of Kare as intelligent, artsy, young, powerful, caring
People who like the name Kare also like Kane, Kael, Kami, Kail, Kaden, Tristan, Karan, Kaemon, Kelvin, Kamal

Kareem *(Arabic)* ♂　　RATING: ★★★☆
Gracious, generous—Kareem Abdul-Jabar, basketball player
People think of Kareem as handsome, intelligent, funny, caring, cool
People who like the name Kareem also like Kaden, Jamal, Jayden, Kalil, Jabari, Anthony, Jamar, Isaiah, Kamil, Khalil

Karen *(Scandinavian)* ♀　　RATING: ★★☆
Pure—Danish variation of Katherine; Karen Black, actress; Karen Blixen, author; Karen Carpenter, singer
People think of Karen as caring, funny, pretty, intelligent, trustworthy
People who like the name Karen also like Grace, Hannah, Rebecca, Faith, Emily, Claire, Elizabeth, Hailey, Jessica, Laura

Karena *(Scandinavian)* ♀　　RATING: ★★★☆
Pure—Variation of Karen or Carina
People think of Karena as caring, funny, pretty, intelligent, cool
People who like the name Karena also like Karina, Kaelyn, Isabella, Kara, Kiara, Faith, Hannah, Sabrina, Kiana, Gabrielle

Kari *(Scandinavian)* ♀　　RATING: ★★★
Pure—Short for Karen
People think of Kari as caring, pretty, funny, creative, intelligent
People who like the name Kari also like Kara, Faith, Hailey, Kayla, Kaelyn, Hannah, Emma, Paige, Emily, Amber

Karida *(Arabic)* ♀　　RATING: ★★★
Pure, loyal
People think of Karida as young, intelligent, pretty, trustworthy, caring
People who like the name Karida also like Kaya, Kalista, Destiny, Kayla, Kera, Felicia, Felicity, Keena, Larissa, Keyanna

320

Karif *(Arabic)* ♂   RATING: ★★☆
Arrived in autumn
> People think of Karif as handsome, sporty, young, leader, ethnic
> People who like the name Karif also like Keagan, Kael, Kaden, Kareem, Jack, Christopher, Jacob, Keenan, Knox, Clay

Karik *(American)* ♂   RATING: ★★
From Carrick, Scotland—Variation of Carrick
> People think of Karik as criminal, creative, intelligent, caring, funny
> People who like the name Karik also like Kaden, Kaleb, Keagan, Kadin, Kael, Aiden, Korbin, Ryker, Ethan, Kyson

Karim *(Arabic)* ♂   RATING: ★★★★
Generous
> People think of Karim as handsome, intelligent, caring, cool, funny
> People who like the name Karim also like Kareem, Kalil, Kaleb, Kaden, Kael, Kamali, Rashid, Kamil, Keenan, Kaiser

Karimah *(Arabic)* ♀   RATING: ★★★☆
Generous
> People think of Karimah as pretty, intelligent, creative, caring, funny
> People who like the name Karimah also like Kya, Kamea, Kailani, Kamilah, Kamaria, Kanoni, Kabira, Kaya, Kainda, Kimaya

Karin *(Scandinavian)* ♀   RATING: ★★☆
Pure—Swedish variation of Katherine
> People think of Karin as caring, intelligent, pretty, funny, trustworthy
> People who like the name Karin also like Emily, Kara, Hannah, Kaitlyn, Emma, Karina, Karen, Isabelle, Kiara, Kiara

Karina *(Scandinavian)* ♀   RATING: ★★★
Pure—Variation of Karin or Carina
> People think of Karina as pretty, funny, caring, intelligent, cool
> People who like the name Karina also like Isabella, Kaelyn, Olivia, Hannah, Kara, Gabriella, Kayla, Kiara, Sabrina, Kailey

Karinda *(American)* ♀   RATING: ★★★☆
Combination of Karin and Lucinda
> People think of Karinda as funny, intelligent, trustworthy, girl next door, young
> People who like the name Karinda also like Kalista, Keely, Keira, Kara, Kaelyn, Karlyn, Bella, Karena, Karina, Kendra

Karis *(Greek)* ♀   RATING: ★★★★☆
Graceful
> People think of Karis as pretty, creative, funny, caring, energetic
> People who like the name Karis also like Kaelyn, Chloe, Keely, Paige, Keira, Ella, Kayla, Kara, Grace, Ava

Karise *(Latin)* ♀   RATING: ★★★☆
Dearest one—Variation of Karissa
> People think of Karise as pretty, funny, young, elegant, caring
> People who like the name Karise also like Kaelyn, Keira, Karis, Kayla, Karena, Kaira, Hailey, Kari, Isabella, Keely

Karl *(German)* ♂   RATING: ★★★☆
Man—Variation of Charles
> People think of Karl as handsome, funny, intelligent, caring, cool
> People who like the name Karl also like Nathan, Ethan, Jack, Jacob, Justin, Paul, Owen, William, Luke, Nicholas

Karla *(German)* ♀   RATING: ★★★★
Feminine form of Karl
> People think of Karla as pretty, funny, intelligent, caring, cool
> People who like the name Karla also like Kayla, Faith, Grace, Kailey, Lauren, Kara, Carla, Jasmine, Cassandra, Emma

Karli *(American)* ♀   RATING: ★★★★
Feminine form of Karl
> People think of Karli as pretty, funny, caring, creative, cool
> People who like the name Karli also like Kailey, Kaelyn, Kayla, Hailey, Emma, Kaylee, Grace, Carly, Kylee, Keira

Karlyn *(American)* ♀   RATING: ★★★★☆
Feminine form of Karl
> People think of Karlyn as pretty, intelligent, popular, funny, creative
> People who like the name Karlyn also like Kaelyn, Kaydence, Ashlyn, Kailey, Kaitlyn, Cailyn, Grace, Karli, Hannah, Kyla

Karma *(Sanskrit/East Indian)* ♀ RATING: ★★★★
Fate
> People think of Karma as exotic, pretty, intelligent, creative, powerful
> People who like the name Karma also like Kaelyn, Harmony, Kaira, Ava, Eva, Chloe, Kailey, Faith, Autumn, Hazel

Karman *(English)* ♂   RATING: ★★☆
Man—Also a surname
> People think of Karman as intelligent, handsome, cool, funny, trustworthy
> People who like the name Karman also like Kaden, Keagan, Owen, Kane, Jayden, Kadin, Kael, Maddox, Keiran, Kaleb

Karmina *(American)* ♀   RATING: ★★★☆
Song—Variation of Carmina
> People think of Karmina as pretty, creative, funny, popular, caring
> People who like the name Karmina also like Kyla, Samara, Kalista, Kamaria, Kailani, Kayla, Kendra, Kaiya, Kaydence, Kiana

Karmiti *(Native American)* ♀   RATING: ★★☆
Trees
People think of Karmiti as exotic, leader, ethnic, caring, poor
People who like the name Karmiti also like Kaya, Kilenya, Kimimela, Kimama, Koleyna, Dyani, Kineks, Kiona, Kaliska, Kirima

Karna *(African)* ♀   RATING: ★★★
Horn of an animal—South African origin
People think of Karna as caring, trustworthy, leader, sporty, funny
People who like the name Karna also like Kamili, Kissa, Kayin, Kainda, Karimah, Keshia, Kaya, Kamaria, Kiden, Kya

Karsen *(American)* ♀ ♂   RATING: ★★★★
Christian—Variation of Carson
People think of Karsen as intelligent, popular, funny, creative, energetic
People who like the name Karsen also like Hayden, Caden, Keaton, Carson, Parker, Addison, Jaden, Carter, Bailey, Logan

Karsten *(German)* ♀ ♂   RATING: ★★★★☆
Christian
People think of Karsten as handsome, popular, intelligent, energetic, funny
People who like the name Karsten also like Hayden, Karsen, Kyler, Jaden, Caden, Addison, Keaton, Bailey, Parker, Kasen

Karston *(English)* ♂   RATING: ★★★☆
From Karl's town
People think of Karston as handsome, intelligent, quiet, caring, creative
People who like the name Karston also like Kaden, Keagan, Kyson, Landon, Ethan, Carsten, Holden, Grayson, Jayden, Tristan

Kartik *(Sanskrit/East Indian)* ♂   RATING: ★★★
Month name
People think of Kartik as intelligent, handsome, sexy, funny, creative
People who like the name Kartik also like Kaushal, Kami, Ketan, Adarsh, Kanha, Gautam, Kishan, Kalkin, Karan, Devesh

Karuka *(Sanskrit/East Indian)* ♀   RATING: ★★☆
Art of heaven
People think of Karuka as quiet, creative, elegant, exotic, artsy
People who like the name Karuka also like Ketaki, Kusuma, Kanika, Kerani, Keiko, Kavindra, Kirtana, Kali, Kimaya, Guri

Kasen *(Scandinavian)* ♀ ♂   RATING: ★★★★
Pure—Variation of Catherine
People think of Kasen as handsome, intelligent, creative, funny, caring
People who like the name Kasen also like Caden, Hayden, Jaden, Kyler, Keaton, Keegan, Karsen, Mason, Landen, Logan

Kasi *(Sanskrit/East Indian)* ♀   RATING: ★★★★
Shining
People think of Kasi as pretty, caring, intelligent, trustworthy, funny
People who like the name Kasi also like Kacy, Kali, Kailey, Chloe, Kylee, Kyla, Karli, Kyleigh, Kayla, Isabella

Kasia *(Polish)* ♀   RATING: ★★☆
Pure—Short for Katherine; pronounced *KASH-a*
People think of Kasia as pretty, funny, intelligent, caring, energetic
People who like the name Kasia also like Kassia, Kiara, Keira, Kya, Kaelyn, Kyla, Kara, Kaiya, Kaida, Kaira

Kasim *(African)* ♂   RATING: ★★★☆
Controller of anger—Swahili origin
People think of Kasim as funny, handsome, cool, intelligent, powerful
People who like the name Kasim also like Kaden, Kimoni, Kame, Kadin, Ajani, Kayonga, Keagan, Kareem, Kamal, Aiden

Kaspar *(German)* ♂   RATING: ★★★☆
Treasurer—Variation of Caspar
People think of Kaspar as popular, intelligent, cool, funny, weird
People who like the name Kaspar also like Jasper, Kaden, Jacob, Aiden, Oliver, Caleb, Tristan, Seth, Casper, Keagan

Kass *(English)* ♀ ♂   RATING: ★★
She who entangles men—Short for Kassandra
People think of Kass as aggressive, weird, caring, intelligent, quiet
People who like the name Kass also like Hayden, Hunter, Kai, Kennedy, Dylan, Addison, Connor, Jade, Cade, Logan

Kassandra *(Greek)* ♀   RATING: ★★★★
She who entangles men
People think of Kassandra as pretty, funny, caring, intelligent, creative
People who like the name Kassandra also like Cassandra, Isabella, Hailey, Faith, Abigail, Hannah, Samantha, Gabriella, Sabrina, Adriana

Kassia *(American)* ♀   RATING: ★★☆
Cinnamon
People think of Kassia as pretty, caring, funny, creative, young
People who like the name Kassia also like Kaelyn, Keira, Kyla, Kailey, Kasia, Kayla, Katia, Kaleigh, Katarina, Kendra

Kassidy *(Celtic/Gaelic)* ♀ ♂   RATING: ★★★★
Curly haired
People think of Kassidy as pretty, funny, energetic, creative, young
People who like the name Kassidy also like Cassidy, Madison, Bailey, Mackenzie, Hayden, Logan, Jaden, Riley, Addison, Caden

Kat *(English)* ♀ RATING: ★★☆
Pure—Short for Katherine; Kat Deeley, TV host
> People think of Kat as funny, creative, pretty, energetic, cool
> People who like the name Kat also like Bella, Kay, Paige, Kate, Faith, Claire, Layla, Kara, Grace, Kailey

Kata *(Japanese)* ♀ RATING: ★★☆
Worthy
> People think of Kata as pretty, sexy, exotic, caring, energetic
> People who like the name Kata also like Kaida, Kaiya, Kaori, Keiko, Kaiyo, Kagami, Kioko, Kimi, Kuri, Inari

Katalin *(Hungarian)* ♀ RATING: ★★★★
Pure—Variation of Katherine
> People think of Katalin as pretty, sexy, intelligent, popular, caring
> People who like the name Katalin also like Kaitlyn, Kaelyn, Katelyn, Isabella, Hailey, Kaitlin, Caitlyn, Kailey, Hannah, Katarina

Katarina *(Italian)* ♀ RATING: ★★★★
Pure—Variation of Katherine; Katarina Witt, figure skater
> People think of Katarina as pretty, funny, caring, intelligent, creative
> People who like the name Katarina also like Isabella, Hannah, Gabriella, Isabelle, Gabrielle, Bianca, Olivia, Hailey, Faith, Grace

Kate *(English)* ♀ RATING: ★★★☆
Pure—Short for Katherine; Kate Hudson, actress; Kate Moss, model; Kate Winslet, actress
> People think of Kate as pretty, funny, intelligent, caring, creative
> People who like the name Kate also like Emma, Grace, Ava, Olivia, Hannah, Ella, Claire, Emily, Lauren, Isabella

Kateb *(Arabic)* ♂ RATING: ★☆
Writer
> People think of Kateb as weird, nerdy, intelligent, creative, funny
> People who like the name Kateb also like Kaden, Kamali, Kayonga, Kasim, Kalil, Kareem, Karim, Kami, Kamran, Kamil

Kateisha *(American)* ♀ RATING: ★★☆
Combination of Kat and Keisha
> People think of Kateisha as exotic, cool, pretty, young, sexy
> People who like the name Kateisha also like Abigail, Makayla, Jadzia, Jaelyn, Keisha, Jazlynn, Adriana, Jaela, Abbie, Aaralyn

Katelin *(American)* ♀ RATING: ★★★☆
Pure
> People think of Katelin as pretty, creative, funny, intelligent, popular
> People who like the name Katelin also like Katelyn, Kaitlyn, Kaitlin, Caitlyn, Hannah, Hailey, Kaelyn, Caitlin, Kayla, Kailey

Katelyn *(American)* ♀ RATING: ★★★★
Pure—Also spelled Katelynn
> People think of Katelyn as pretty, funny, caring, intelligent, creative
> People who like the name Katelyn also like Kaitlyn, Hannah, Caitlyn, Hailey, Kaelyn, Emma, Kayla, Isabella, Paige, Emily

Katen *(Dutch)* ♀ RATING: ★★☆
Pure—Short for Katherine
> People think of Katen as pretty, popular, creative, funny, cool
> People who like the name Katen also like Kaelyn, Kiley, Keely, Kate, Kyla, Kayla, Kaydence, Emma, Regan, Jadyn

Katerina *(Slavic)* ♀ RATING: ★★★☆
Pure—Variation of Catherine or Katherine
> People think of Katerina as pretty, intelligent, elegant, exotic, young
> People who like the name Katerina also like Isabella, Anya, Eva, Arianna, Emma, Abigail, Elise, Natalie, Adeline, Sabrina

Katet *(American)* ♂ RATING: ★★☆
A group joined by destiny—Created by Stephen King
> People think of Katet as powerful, boy next door, old-fashioned, trustworthy, funny
> People who like the name Katet also like Caine, Karman, Slone, Brooks, Tudor, Kateb, Kale, Karik, Broox, Karim

Katherine *(Greek)* ♀ RATING: ★★★☆
Pure—Also spelled Katharine or Catherine; Katharine McPhee, singer
> People think of Katherine as pretty, intelligent, funny, caring, creative
> People who like the name Katherine also like Elizabeth, Hannah, Grace, Emma, Emily, Abigail, Isabella, Olivia, Ava, Sarah

Kathleen *(Celtic/Gaelic)* ♀ RATING: ★★★★
Pure
> People think of Kathleen as pretty, caring, funny, intelligent, creative
> People who like the name Kathleen also like Hannah, Katherine, Elizabeth, Faith, Grace, Emma, Hailey, Emily, Kathryn, Olivia

Kathryn *(English)* ♀ RATING: ★★★
Pure
> People think of Kathryn as pretty, intelligent, funny, caring, creative
> People who like the name Kathryn also like Hannah, Kaitlyn, Elizabeth, Grace, Abigail, Emma, Isabella, Isabelle, Olivia, Ava

Kathy *(Celtic/Gaelic)* ♀ RATING: ★★☆
Pure—Short for Katherine; also spelled Kathie; Kathie Lee Gifford, TV host
> People think of Kathy as caring, funny, pretty, creative, intelligent
> People who like the name Kathy also like Kate, Katie, Emily, Kathleen, Megan, Jessica, Amanda, Mandy, Maggie, Heather

Katia *(Slavic)* ♀   RATING: ★★★★
Pure—Short for Katherine
> People think of Katia as pretty, intelligent, caring, funny, creative
> People who like the name Katia also like Nadia, Isabella, Hannah, Keira, Emma, Mia, Natalia, Kiara, Kaelyn, Katarina

Katie *(Celtic/Gaelic)* ♀   RATING: ★★★
Pure, virginal—Short for Kathleen or Katherine; Katie Holmes, actress
> People think of Katie as funny, pretty, caring, creative, intelligent
> People who like the name Katie also like Emma, Kate, Emily, Hannah, Hailey, Grace, Jessica, Isabella, Lauren, Chloe

Katima *(American)* ♀   RATING: ★★★
Powerful daughter—Variation of Fatima
> People think of Katima as exotic, powerful, pretty, intelligent, creative
> People who like the name Katima also like Kaya, Katina, Keaira, Kamea, Karena, Kara, Kesia, Keena, Kendra, Kabira

Katina *(Italian)* ♀   RATING: ★★★☆
Pure—Short for Katherine
> People think of Katina as pretty, funny, caring, intelligent, popular
> People who like the name Katina also like Kalista, Katarina, Katrina, Kaelyn, Isabella, Kara, Karina, Keaira, Bianca, Gianna

Kato *(Latin)* ♂   RATING: ★★★★
Good judgment—Kato Kaelin, celebrity
> People think of Kato as intelligent, leader, handsome, young, exotic
> People who like the name Kato also like Kaden, Kael, Kyran, Kevin, Kadin, Kale, Noah, Kane, Keagan, Enzo

Katoka *(Hungarian)* ♀   RATING: ★★
Pure—Short for Katherine
> People think of Katoka as exotic, weird, pretty, powerful, sexy
> People who like the name Katoka also like Kaya, Keiko, Keely, Keira, Kiden, Kohana, Kolina, Kaliska, Kayla, Kiora

Katriel *(Hebrew)* ♀♂   RATING: ★★☆
God is my crown—Masculine in Hebrew; usually feminine in English
> People think of Katriel as intelligent, caring, leader, elegant, funny
> People who like the name Katriel also like Jaden, Azriel, Kaelin, Evan, Kendall, Adriel, Jordan, Elisha, Eden, Aubrey

Katrina *(German)* ♀   RATING: ★★★★
Pure—Variation of Catherine
> People think of Katrina as pretty, funny, caring, intelligent, creative
> People who like the name Katrina also like Hannah, Sabrina, Hailey, Isabella, Olivia, Emily, Natalie, Emma, Grace, Katarina

Katungi *(African)* ♂   RATING: ★★☆
Rich—Ugandan origin
> People think of Katungi as big, old-fashioned, poor, slow, lazy
> People who like the name Katungi also like Kayonga, Kasim, Kame, Kazi, Keagan, Kimoni, Kojo, Kaseko, Kaipo, Kabili

Katy *(Celtic/Gaelic)* ♀   RATING: ★★★☆
Pure, virginal—Short for Katherine or Catherine
> People think of Katy as pretty, funny, caring, creative, intelligent
> People who like the name Katy also like Katie, Kate, Kayla, Kaitlyn, Emma, Kacy, Kaelyn, Hannah, Keira, Paige

Kaula *(African)* ♀   RATING: ★★☆
Buying
> People think of Kaula as pretty, funny, exotic, intelligent, cool
> People who like the name Kaula also like Kayin, Kaydence, Kumani, Kamaria, Kamili, Karasi, Keyah, Keshia, Kia, Koleyna

Kaushal *(Sanskrit/East Indian)* ♂   RATING: ★★★
Clever
> People think of Kaushal as handsome, intelligent, caring, creative, trustworthy
> People who like the name Kaushal also like Ketan, Kami, Karan, Gaurav, Adarsh, Chatura, Kalkin, Kanha, Kartik, Divyesh

Kaveri *(Sanskrit/East Indian)* ♀   RATING: ★★★☆
River
> People think of Kaveri as pretty, popular, young, intelligent, leader
> People who like the name Kaveri also like Keira, Kiara, Kaori, Kailani, Kamala, Kirtana, Komala, Kaydence, Keaira, Kamana

Kavi *(Sanskrit/East Indian)* ♀♂   RATING: ★★
Wise poet
> People think of Kavi as intelligent, pretty, funny, exotic, caring
> People who like the name Kavi also like Kiran, Kyan, Caden, Kai, Hayden, Jaden, Sage, Kasen, Phoenix, Keegan

Kavindra *(Sanskrit/East Indian)* ♀   RATING: ★★
Poet
> People think of Kavindra as creative, exotic, elegant, caring, intelligent
> People who like the name Kavindra also like Kimaya, Kamala, Calandra, Kiandra, Kiara, Kaydence, Kalinda, Kamea, Kirtana, Kaira

Kawena *(Hawaiian)* ♀   RATING: ★★★
Rosy reflection in the sky
> People think of Kawena as creative, pretty, exotic, cool, young
> People who like the name Kawena also like Kailani, Keani, Keala, Kaloni, Keona, Kiele, Kaida, Keaira, Keiki, Konane

324

Kay *(Greek)* ♀
RATING: ★★★☆
Rejoice
People think of Kay as pretty, caring, intelligent, funny, creative
People who like the name Kay also like Kayla, Hailey, Faith, Emma, Paige, Kaylee, Grace, Hannah, Mia, Kate

Kaya *(Scandinavian)* ♀
RATING: ★★★★
Pure—Short for Katherine
People think of Kaya as pretty, creative, funny, intelligent, caring
People who like the name Kaya also like Kaia, Kaiya, Kaelyn, Kyla, Ava, Kayla, Keira, Maya, Kya, Layla

Kayanna *(American)* ♀
RATING: ★★★☆
Combination of Kay and Anna; also a variation of Quiana
People think of Kayanna as pretty, wealthy, popular, stuck-up, sexy
People who like the name Kayanna also like Jaelyn, Alana, Kira, Kaelyn, Jahzara, Kaitlin, Amaya, Caitlyn, Kiersten, Kacia

Kaycee *(American)* ♀ ♂
RATING: ★★★★
From the initals K.C.
People think of Kaycee as pretty, funny, popular, caring, creative
People who like the name Kaycee also like Jaden, Taylor, Riley, Madison, Caden, Bailey, Logan, Mackenzie, Hayden, Jordan

Kaydence *(American)* ♀
RATING: ★★★★
Musical—Variation of Cadence
People think of Kaydence as pretty, energetic, popular, funny, intelligent
People who like the name Kaydence also like Kaelyn, Hailey, Jadyn, Paige, Kailey, Faith, Isabella, Chloe, Cailyn, Abigail

Kayin *(African)* ♀
RATING: ★★☆
Long-awaited child—From the Yoruba tribe of Nigeria
People think of Kayin as intelligent, caring, energetic, funny, creative
People who like the name Kayin also like Kaelyn, Kaya, Kya, Kyra, Kyla, Kaydence, Keira, Keely, Kayla, Kaiya

Kayla *(Celtic/Gaelic)* ♀
RATING: ★★★★
Pure, beloved—Variation of Kay, Katherine, or Michaela
People think of Kayla as pretty, funny, caring, creative, intelligent
People who like the name Kayla also like Kaelyn, Hannah, Hailey, Emma, Kaitlyn, Ava, Isabella, Kaylee, Kailey, Brianna

Kaylana *(American)* ♀
RATING: ★★★
Combination of Kay and Lana
People think of Kaylana as pretty, popular, energetic, funny, exotic
People who like the name Kaylana also like Kaydence, Kaelyn, Kayla, Kyla, Kaylee, Kailey, Gabriella, Makayla, Kiana, Abrianna

Kaylee *(American)* ♀
RATING: ★★★☆
Who is like God?—Variation of Chaeli; also combination of Kay and Lee
People think of Kaylee as pretty, funny, caring, creative, popular
People who like the name Kaylee also like Kailey, Hailey, Kayla, Kaelyn, Emma, Paige, Hannah, Kylee, Kaleigh, Chloe

Kayleen *(American)* ♀
RATING: ★★★☆
Pure lass—Variation of Colleen or Cailean
People think of Kayleen as pretty, funny, caring, creative, young
People who like the name Kayleen also like Kaylee, Kailey, Kaelyn, Hailey, Hannah, Kayla, Kaitlyn, Isabella, Kaydence, Kaleigh

Kayleigh *(American)* ♀
RATING: ★★★★
Who is like God?—Variation of Chaeli
People think of Kayleigh as pretty, intelligent, caring, funny, energetic
People who like the name Kayleigh also like Emma, Ava, Kyleigh, Abigail, Hannah, Olivia, Kaylee, Kaleigh, Chloe, Kailey

Kayley *(American)* ♀
RATING: ★★★★
Who is like God?—Variation of Chaeli
People think of Kayley as funny, pretty, young, intelligent, energetic
People who like the name Kayley also like Emily, Kaleigh, Hailey, Alexia, Brianna, Kailey, Kaylee, Adrianna, Emma, Kayla

Kaylor *(American)* ♀ ♂
RATING: ★★★☆
Variation of Taylor; also combination of Kay and Taylor
People think of Kaylor as energetic, pretty, popular, funny, trustworthy
People who like the name Kaylor also like Jaden, Caden, Kyler, Hayden, Kade, Addison, Kasen, Carson, Bailey, Keaton

Kayo *(American)* ♂
RATING: ★★★
From the initials K.O.
People think of Kayo as big, aggressive, sporty, powerful, wild
People who like the name Kayo also like Kaden, Kail, Kaleb, Kale, Ethan, Kadin, Keagan, Kael, Kyson, Keenan

Kayonga *(African)* ♂
RATING: ★★☆
Ash
People think of Kayonga as intelligent, poor, loser, caring, powerful
People who like the name Kayonga also like Kazi, Kasim, Kame, Kaden, Kale, Kanelo, Kafele, Kadin, Kaseko, Katungi

Kaysar *(Arabic)* ♂
RATING: ★★★★
King
People think of Kaysar as intelligent, leader, handsome, exotic, cool
People who like the name Kaysar also like Kaden, Kaiser, Keagan, Keiran, Karston, Kadin, Kaleb, Keenan, Kayo, Christopher

Kaz *(Polish)* ♂   RATING: ★★★☆
Vain—Short for Cassius
> People think of Kaz as funny, sporty, aggressive, cool, energetic
> People who like the name Kaz also like Maddox, Kaden, Colin, Kael, Conner, Ace, Nash, Cole, Ian, Seth

Kazi *(African)* ♂   RATING: ★★★
Work—Ugandan origin
> People think of Kazi as cool, intelligent, funny, energetic, wild
> People who like the name Kazi also like Kayonga, Keagan, Kaden, Kael, Kadin, Kasim, Kame, Adam, Kanelo, Kimoni

Keagan *(Celtic/Gaelic)* ♂   RATING: ★★★
Fiery; son of Eagan
> People think of Keagan as funny, energetic, handsome, intelligent, popular
> People who like the name Keagan also like Kaden, Aiden, Ethan, Landon, Tristan, Braden, Gavin, Caleb, Noah, Owen

Keahi *(Hawaiian)* ♀♂   RATING: ★★★★
Flames, fire
> People think of Keahi as exotic, powerful, elegant, leader, young
> People who like the name Keahi also like Kai, Keanu, Kalani, Kaili, Keegan, Kalei, Kegan, Lani, Kiyoshi, Kiran

Keaira *(Celtic/Gaelic)* ♀   RATING: ★★★
Little dark one
> People think of Keaira as pretty, creative, sexy, funny, intelligent
> People who like the name Keaira also like Keira, Kiara, Kaelyn, Kira, Kyla, Kara, Ciara, Kayla, Keely, Kera

Keala *(Hawaiian)* ♀   RATING: ★★★★☆
Path
> People think of Keala as pretty, exotic, sexy, popular, intelligent
> People who like the name Keala also like Keani, Kailani, Kaelyn, Kyla, Keaira, Kayla, Kalea, Leilani, Kaleigh, Kamea

Keani *(Hawaiian)* ♀   RATING: ★★★★
The wave, breeze
> People think of Keani as pretty, energetic, funny, intelligent, exotic
> People who like the name Keani also like Kailani, Keala, Leilani, Keona, Kamea, Kaelyn, Kaia, Kaya, Keaira, Keira

Keanu *(Hawaiian)* ♀♂   RATING: ★★☆
Cool mountain breeze—Keanu Reeves, actor
> People think of Keanu as handsome, cool, creative, intelligent, exotic
> People who like the name Keanu also like Kai, Kalani, Keegan, Dylan, Jaden, Kyle, Hayden, Dakota, Caden, Keaton

Keaton *(English)* ♀♂   RATING: ★★★
Hawk's town—Buster Keaton, actor; Diane Keaton, actress; Michael Keaton, actor
> People think of Keaton as handsome, intelligent, funny, popular, cool
> People who like the name Keaton also like Hayden, Caden, Keegan, Logan, Parker, Jaden, Mason, Payton, Addison, Riley

Kedem *(Hebrew)* ♂   RATING: ★★☆
Old, ancient
> People think of Kedem as intelligent, weird, quiet, exotic, loser
> People who like the name Kedem also like Keagan, Kaleb, Caleb, Kael, Eli, Kane, Slade, Kaiser, Ethan, Kaden

Kedma *(Hebrew)* ♀   RATING: ★★
Toward the East
> People think of Kedma as weird, ethnic, pretty, exotic, uptight
> People who like the name Kedma also like Keilah, Cynzia, Keiki, Kyria, Jetta, Kalila, Calixte, Cora, Lilah, Darla

Keefe *(Celtic/Gaelic)* ♂   RATING: ★★★★
Handsome, beloved
> People think of Keefe as handsome, intelligent, funny, weird, cool
> People who like the name Keefe also like Kael, Keiran, Keefer, Keagan, Noah, Aiden, Kellan, Keenan, Kane, Kaden

Keefer *(Celtic/Gaelic)* ♂   RATING: ★★★☆
Handsome, beloved
> People think of Keefer as handsome, intelligent, leader, funny, cool
> People who like the name Keefer also like Kiefer, Keagan, Kaden, Aiden, Liam, Owen, Ethan, Conner, Ian, Landon

Keegan *(Celtic/Gaelic)* ♀♂   RATING: ★★★★
Small and fiery, bright flame—Variation of Kegan; Keegan-Michael Key, actor/comedian
> People think of Keegan as energetic, funny, handsome, intelligent, popular
> People who like the name Keegan also like Logan, Caden, Hayden, Riley, Kegan, Aidan, Teagan, Reagan, Addison, Jaden

Keelan *(Celtic/Gaelic)* ♀♂   RATING: ★★★★
Lean
> People think of Keelan as handsome, funny, intelligent, caring, popular
> People who like the name Keelan also like Keegan, Hayden, Caden, Kaelin, Keaton, Teagan, Logan, Jaden, Kegan, Riley

Keelia *(Celtic/Gaelic)* ♀   RATING: ★★★☆
Beautiful—Variation of Keely
> People think of Keelia as pretty, caring, trustworthy, intelligent, young
> People who like the name Keelia also like Keely, Keaira, Kaelyn, Keira, Kiara, Kiley, Kyla, Kyleigh, Kayla, Keena

Keelin *(Celtic/Gaelic)* ♀♂   RATING: ★★☆
Fair and slender
> People think of Keelin as funny, pretty, intelligent, energetic, creative
> People who like the name Keelin also like Keegan, Keelan, Kaelin, Kegan, Hayden, Teagan, Riley, Caden, Kieran, Brayden

Keelty *(Celtic/Gaelic)* ♀   RATING: ★★★
From the woods
> People think of Keelty as exotic, loser, slow, nerdy, aggressive
> People who like the name Keelty also like Keaira, Keely, Keira, Keita, Kaelyn, Kiley, Keena, Kara, Kera, Kiara

Keely *(Celtic/Gaelic)* ♀   RATING: ★★
Beautiful—Also spelled Keeley; Keely Smith, singer
> People think of Keely as pretty, funny, creative, intelligent, caring
> People who like the name Keely also like Kaelyn, Chloe, Paige, Kiley, Emma, Keira, Hailey, Olivia, Isabella, Hannah

Keen *(Celtic/Gaelic)* ♀♂   RATING: ★★★
Wailing in mourning—From the Irish Caoineadh meaning I lament
> People think of Keen as powerful, cool, creative, trustworthy, funny
> People who like the name Keen also like Keeran, Kieran, Kellen, Kerry, Keir, Kegan, Keegan, Keelin, Keelan, Keaton

Keena *(Celtic/Gaelic)* ♀   RATING: ★★☆
Brave
> People think of Keena as pretty, funny, intelligent, cool, caring
> People who like the name Keena also like Kaelyn, Keely, Keira, Kyla, Keaira, Kara, Kiley, Kera, Kiara, Kenna

Keenan *(Celtic/Gaelic)* ♂   RATING: ★★★★
Little and ancient—Also spelled Kenan or Keenen; Kenan Thompson, comedian/actor; Keenen Ivory Wayans, actor/director; Keenan Wynn, actor
> People think of Keenan as handsome, funny, intelligent, caring, popular
> People who like the name Keenan also like Keagan, Kaden, Aiden, Keiran, Liam, Ethan, Gavin, Tristan, Landon, Cole

Keene *(Celtic/Gaelic)* ♂   RATING: ★★★☆
Ancient—Variation of Cian
> People think of Keene as slow, loser, lazy, poor, slow
> People who like the name Keene also like Liam, Aiden, Tristan, Kane, Kael, Kaden, Cole, Noah, Kellan, Keefer

Keeran *(Celtic/Gaelic)* ♀♂   RATING: ★★★★
Little dark one—Variation of Kieran
> People think of Keeran as handsome, intelligent, aggressive, funny, caring
> People who like the name Keeran also like Kieran, Keegan, Logan, Hayden, Kaelin, Aidan, Kegan, Riley, Keelan, Caden

Keesa *(Russian)* ♀♂   RATING: ★★★
Kitten
> People think of Keesa as pretty, energetic, intelligent, creative, trustworthy
> People who like the name Keesa also like Kassidy, Luca, Keegan, Teagan, Shea, Phoenix, Keanu, Mischa, Logan, Kenzie

Keeya *(African)* ♀   RATING: ★★☆
Garden flower
> People think of Keeya as pretty, creative, young, caring, funny
> People who like the name Keeya also like Kya, Kiara, Kaelyn, Kaiya, Keira, Kia, Kiana, Ayanna, Kaya, Keyanna

Keften *(American)* ♂   RATING: ★★
Town of Kevin
> People think of Keften as unpopular, untrustworthy, weird, lazy, nerdy
> People who like the name Keften also like Dustin, Darrion, Emanuel, Kelvin, Kaden, Ian, Kael, Keenan, Ken, Aiden

Kegan *(Celtic/Gaelic)* ♀♂   RATING: ★★★★
Bright shining flame—Variation of Keegan
> People think of Kegan as funny, handsome, intelligent, young, sporty
> People who like the name Kegan also like Keegan, Caden, Logan, Hayden, Jaden, Riley, Madison, Teagan, Aidan, Addison

Kei *(African)* ♀♂   RATING: ★★★★
Sandy, white—South African origin
> People think of Kei as exotic, intelligent, powerful, creative, pretty
> People who like the name Kei also like Kai, Kyrie, Kyan, Dylan, Hayden, Caden, Keegan, Kalei, Kyle, Kaili

Keiji *(Japanese)* ♂   RATING: ★★★☆
Lead cautiously
> People think of Keiji as intelligent, handsome, sexy, funny, cool
> People who like the name Keiji also like Keitaro, Kaemon, Hiroshi, Akio, Haru, Haruki, Ryu, Suoh, Shino, Makoto

Keiki *(Hawaiian)* ♀   RATING: ★★★
Child
> People think of Keiki as energetic, funny, trendy, wild, artsy
> People who like the name Keiki also like Kailani, Keiko, Keani, Kamea, Keala, Kiele, Kaida, Keona, Kiki, Leilani

Keiko *(Japanese)* ♀   RATING: ★★★★
Blessing
> People think of Keiko as intelligent, pretty, funny, caring, trustworthy
> People who like the name Keiko also like Kaiya, Kaori, Kaida, Aiko, Sakura, Kioko, Kimi, Emiko, Kaiyo, Amaya

Keilah *(Hebrew)* ♀   RATING: ★★★
Citadel
> People think of Keilah as pretty, funny, energetic, intelligent, caring
> People who like the name Keilah also like Kaelyn, Keira, Kyla, Kayla, Hannah, Kyra, Kiana, Kiara, Jadyn, Kailey

Keir *(Celtic/Gaelic)* ♀ ♂   RATING: ★★★★☆
Black
> People think of Keir as intelligent, handsome, caring, sexy, cool
> People who like the name Keir also like Kieran, Kyle, Kai, Hayden, Keegan, Aidan, Kyan, Quinn, Kegan, Logan

Keira *(Celtic/Gaelic)* ♀   RATING: ★★★★☆
Black haired—Also spelled Kiera; Keira Knightley, actress
> People think of Keira as pretty, intelligent, funny, popular, creative
> People who like the name Keira also like Kaelyn, Kiara, Emma, Ava, Kayla, Paige, Olivia, Isabella, Keaira, Grace

Keiran *(Celtic/Gaelic)* ♂   RATING: ★★★★☆
Little and dark
> People think of Keiran as handsome, intelligent, cool, funny, creative
> People who like the name Keiran also like Aiden, Liam, Ethan, Tristan, Keagan, Kaden, Noah, Caleb, Owen, Gavin

Keisha *(American)* ♀   RATING: ★★★★
Her life
> People think of Keisha as pretty, caring, funny, intelligent, sexy
> People who like the name Keisha also like Kayla, Keira, Jasmine, Faith, Kiara, Paige, Hailey, Kendra, Caitlyn, Isabella

Keita *(Celtic/Gaelic)* ♀   RATING: ★★★★
Forest
> People think of Keita as pretty, exotic, intelligent, leader, creative
> People who like the name Keita also like Keira, Keaira, Keely, Kaya, Kiara, Kaelyn, Kira, Kerri, Kara, Kera

Keitaro *(Japanese)* ♂   RATING: ★★
Blessed
> People think of Keitaro as intelligent, funny, handsome, trustworthy, caring
> People who like the name Keitaro also like Kaemon, Keiji, Hiroshi, Haruki, Ryu, Makoto, Akio, Suoh, Haru, Shino

Keith *(Celtic/Gaelic)* ♂   RATING: ★★☆
Warrior descending—Keith Carradine, actor; Keith Richards, musician
> People think of Keith as handsome, intelligent, funny, caring, trustworthy
> People who like the name Keith also like Ethan, Jacob, Nicholas, Ian, Kevin, Nathan, Matthew, Justin, Joshua, Brandon

Keitha *(Celtic/Gaelic)* ♀   RATING: ★★
Female warrior
> People think of Keitha as pretty, intelligent, caring, cool, trustworthy
> People who like the name Keitha also like Kaelyn, Keaira, Keira, Keely, Kiara, Kaida, Keena, Alana, Kara, Kella

Keladry *(American)* ♀ ♂   RATING: ★★★★
Unknown meaning
> People think of Keladry as leader, energetic, powerful, trustworthy, aggressive
> People who like the name Keladry also like Kyrie, Katriel, Kalani, Keanu, Keeran, Killian, Keir, Brooklyn, Kameryn, Kieran

Kelby *(English)* ♀ ♂   RATING: ★★★★
From the ridge farm—Originally a surname
> People think of Kelby as funny, creative, intelligent, popular, caring
> People who like the name Kelby also like Caden, Hayden, Keegan, Logan, Kyler, Kegan, Keaton, Avery, Jaden, Riley

Kelda *(Scandinavian)* ♀   RATING: ★★★☆
A fountain
> People think of Kelda as pretty, caring, trustworthy, funny, intelligent
> People who like the name Kelda also like Keira, Kara, Kaydence, Kaya, Karena, Leila, Aeryn, Katina, Keaira, Kera

Kele *(Native American)* ♂   RATING: ★★★☆
Sparrow hawk—Hopi origin
> People think of Kele as powerful, leader, quiet, cool, young
> People who like the name Kele also like Kaden, Dasan, Keiran, Kail, Kelton, Chayton, Mikasi, Gavin, Keagan, Dyami

Kelii *(Hawaiian)* ♂   RATING: ★★★
Chief
> People think of Kelii as funny, wild, untrustworthy, powerful, intelligent
> People who like the name Kelii also like Kale, Keon, Kanoa, Lulani, Kapono, Keoni, Kaipo, Kane, Konala, Palani

Kelin *(American)* ♀   RATING: ★★★
Slender boy—Variation of Caelan
> People think of Kelin as creative, caring, energetic, trustworthy, cool
> People who like the name Kelin also like Kaelyn, Hannah, Keely, Kayla, Kara, Olivia, Keira, Kacy, Kiden, Kylee

Kelis *(American)* ♀   RATING: ★★★★
Beautiful—Also spelled Kellis, Kellys, or Kelys
> People think of Kelis as pretty, creative, sexy, popular, energetic
> People who like the name Kelis also like Aaliyah, Layla, Kyla, Kaydence, Kailani, Kayla, Keely, Kaelyn, Kya, Mia

Kella *(Celtic/Gaelic)* ♀   RATING: ★★★★☆
Warrior—Variation of Kelly
> People think of Kella as pretty, popular, intelligent, creative, funny
> People who like the name Kella also like Kara, Keira, Kayla, Kyla, Kaelyn, Keaira, Kiara, Kellyn, Isabella, Hannah

Kellan *(Celtic/Gaelic)* ♂   RATING: ★★★★
Powerful
> People think of Kellan as handsome, intelligent, powerful, leader, popular
> People who like the name Kellan also like Kaden, Keagan, Aiden, Keiran, Ethan, Gavin, Tristan, Landon, Caleb, Kael

Kellen *(Celtic/Gaelic)* ♀ ♂   RATING: ★★★★
Powerful
> People think of Kellen as intelligent, handsome, energetic, funny, sporty
> People who like the name Kellen also like Hayden, Logan, Caden, Avery, Addison, Reagan, Aidan, Keegan, Parker, Teagan

Kelley *(Celtic/Gaelic)* ♀ ♂   RATING: ★★★
Bright headed—Variation of Kelly; David E. Kelley, screenwriter
> People think of Kelley as funny, pretty, caring, intelligent, creative
> People who like the name Kelley also like Kyle, Ryan, Hayden, Logan, Riley, Connor, Kelly, Dylan, Kelsey, Madison

Kelli *(American)* ♀   RATING: ★★★★
Bright headed—Variation of Kelly
> People think of Kelli as funny, pretty, caring, intelligent, creative
> People who like the name Kelli also like Hailey, Chloe, Kacy, Leah, Hannah, Isabella, Jessica, Faith, Grace, Lacey

Kellsie *(American)* ♀ ♂   RATING: ★★★
Island of the ships—Variation of Chelsea
> People think of Kellsie as funny, popular, pretty, caring, creative
> People who like the name Kellsie also like Kelsey, Hayden, Madison, Bailey, Mackenzie, Caden, Riley, Jaden, Kirsten, Taylor

Kelly *(Celtic/Gaelic)* ♀ ♂   RATING: ★★★
Bright headed—Also a surname; Kelly Clarkson, singer; Kelly Preston, actress
> People think of Kelly as funny, pretty, caring, intelligent, creative
> People who like the name Kelly also like Ryan, Madison, Riley, James, Ashley, Jordan, Kyle, Kimberly, Taylor, Brooke

Kellyn *(Celtic/Gaelic)* ♀   RATING: ★★★☆
Powerful—Variation of Kellen
> People think of Kellyn as intelligent, creative, pretty, funny, caring

> People who like the name Kellyn also like Kaelyn, Keira, Keely, Kiley, Kyla, Paige, Kaitlyn, Ava, Olivia, Caelan

Kelsea *(Scandinavian)* ♀ ♂   RATING: ★★★☆
Island of the ships
> People think of Kelsea as pretty, funny, energetic, intelligent, young
> People who like the name Kelsea also like Kelsey, Bailey, Madison, Logan, Hayden, Mackenzie, Kassidy, Jordan, Brooke, Riley

Kelsey *(Celtic/Gaelic)* ♀ ♂   RATING: ★★★
Island of the ships—Kelsey Grammer, actor
> People think of Kelsey as funny, pretty, caring, creative, intelligent
> People who like the name Kelsey also like Madison, Bailey, Mackenzie, Riley, Taylor, Logan, Hayden, Brooke, Morgan, Cameron

Kelton *(English)* ♂   RATING: ★★☆
From the calf farm—Originally a surname
> People think of Kelton as handsome, intelligent, caring, creative, cool
> People who like the name Kelton also like Kaden, Keagan, Kenton, Aiden, Kyson, Landon, Kellan, Jayden, Cole, Tristan

Kelvin *(Celtic/Gaelic)* ♂   RATING: ★★★☆
A river in Scotland
> People think of Kelvin as funny, handsome, cool, intelligent, caring
> People who like the name Kelvin also like Kaden, Keagan, Kevin, Jacob, Aiden, Cole, Gavin, Keith, Nicholas, Ethan

Keme *(Native American)* ♀ ♂   RATING: ★★☆
Secret—Algonquin origin
> People think of Keme as sexy, exotic, ethnic, winner, lazy
> People who like the name Keme also like Kelsey, Dante, Kaley, Renny, Kalin, Logan, River, Butch, Corentine, Devan

Kemp *(English)* ♂   RATING: ★★★★
Fighter
> People think of Kemp as handsome, funny, intelligent, popular, caring
> People who like the name Kemp also like Kaden, Landon, Jackson, Keith, Keenan, Kane, Ryker, Tristan, Kenton, Kyson

Ken *(Celtic/Gaelic)* ♂   RATING: ★★☆
Handsome—Ken Howard, actor; Ken Kesey, author; Ken, toy doll
> People think of Ken as handsome, funny, intelligent, cool, aggressive
> People who like the name Ken also like Ian, Keith, Kevin, Scott, Daniel, Cody, Ethan, Eric, David, Colin

Kenadia *(American)* ♀   RATING: ★★★
Chief
> People think of Kenadia as intelligent, pretty, caring, trustworthy, weird

People who like the name Kenadia also like Kendra, Keira, Kaydence, Kyla, Keani, Keaira, Kenisha, Keena, Destiny, Katarina

Kenadie *(Celtic/Gaelic)* ♀ ♂   RATING: ★★☆
Helmeted chief—Variation of Kennedy
People think of Kenadie as pretty, funny, intelligent, energetic, creative
People who like the name Kenadie also like Keegan, Kennedy, Mackenzie, Addison, Logan, Caden, Hayden, Reagan, Kenzie, Kendall

Kenaz *(Hebrew)* ♂   RATING: ★★★
Bright
People think of Kenaz as handsome, intelligent, nerdy, exotic, ethnic
People who like the name Kenaz also like Kaden, Kaleb, Korbin, Keenan, Keiran, Abel, Isaac, Jaron, Koen, Kiril

Kenda *(English)* ♀   RATING: ★★★★
Child of clear, cool water
People think of Kenda as caring, pretty, creative, funny, intelligent
People who like the name Kenda also like Kendra, Keira, Kara, Kyla, Kaydence, Kyra, Kayla, Kenna, Kaelyn, Faith

Kendahl *(American)* ♀ ♂   RATING: ★★★
From the River Kent—Variation of Kendall
People think of Kendahl as funny, energetic, leader, cool, popular
People who like the name Kendahl also like Kendall, Keegan, Hayden, Mackenzie, Addison, Caden, Landen, Madison, Mckenna, Kennedy

Kendaleigha *(American)* ♀   RATING: ★★★
Valley of the storm—Combination of Kendall and Leigh
People think of Kendaleigha as elegant, exotic, cool, quiet, intelligent
People who like the name Kendaleigha also like Kaydence, Keira, Kenisha, Keaira, Kiana, Krisalyn, Keely, Kyleigh, Jazlynn, Kendra

Kendall *(English)* ♀ ♂   RATING: ★★★
Valley of the River Kent
People think of Kendall as pretty, funny, intelligent, popular, caring
People who like the name Kendall also like Madison, Hayden, Addison, Logan, Riley, Mackenzie, Avery, Bailey, Taylor, Caden

Kendi *(African)* ♀ ♂   RATING: ★★★★☆
The loved one
People think of Kendi as pretty, intelligent, creative, trustworthy, funny
People who like the name Kendi also like Keegan, Kenzie, Kai, Kitoko, Kegan, Keanu, Kendall, Kade, Kenley, Bailey

Kendis *(American)* ♀ ♂   RATING: ★★
Pure—Combination of Ken and Candace
People think of Kendis as funny, intelligent, exotic, artsy, caring

People who like the name Kendis also like Kendi, Kendall, Kenley, Kasen, Keelin, Kyler, Kindle, Kelby, Kieran, Kenzie

Kendra *(English)* ♀   RATING: ★★★
Water baby; magical
People think of Kendra as pretty, funny, caring, creative, intelligent
People who like the name Kendra also like Kayla, Hailey, Kaelyn, Hannah, Paige, Ava, Keira, Faith, Isabella, Olivia

Kenelm *(English)* ♂   RATING: ★★☆
Bold helmet
People think of Kenelm as caring, powerful, old-fashioned, handsome, intelligent
People who like the name Kenelm also like Slade, Nicodemus, Kelvin, Hart, Holden, Karston, Flint, Gibson, Gordon, Dixon

Kenisha *(American)* ♀   RATING: ★★★☆
Beautiful, prosperous—Combination of Ken and Keisha
People think of Kenisha as pretty, sexy, funny, intelligent, trustworthy
People who like the name Kenisha also like Keisha, Kiana, Kendra, Kailani, Keshia, Keaira, Kalista, Keyanna, Keira, Kimaya

Kenley *(English)* ♀ ♂   RATING: ★★☆
Royal meadow
People think of Kenley as caring, intelligent, creative, pretty, funny
People who like the name Kenley also like Hayden, Addison, Avery, Caden, Keaton, Bailey, Kendall, Logan, Keegan, Parker

Kenna *(Celtic/Gaelic)* ♀   RATING: ★★★
Beautiful—Feminine form of Kenneth
People think of Kenna as pretty, funny, caring, creative, intelligent
People who like the name Kenna also like Kaelyn, Keira, Emma, Kyla, Ava, Grace, Paige, Kiara, Ella, Isabella

Kennan *(Celtic/Gaelic)* ♂   RATING: ★★☆
Ancient—Variation of Keene
People think of Kennan as intelligent, cool, handsome, funny, creative
People who like the name Kennan also like Keagan, Kaden, Aiden, Keenan, Landon, Kaleb, Kelton, Gavin, Keiran, Liam

Kennedy *(Celtic/Gaelic)* ♀ ♂   RATING: ★★★★
Kennedi
Ugly; helmet head—Originally a medieval surname referring to a head deformity; John F. Kennedy, U.S. president
People think of Kennedy as pretty, funny, intelligent, popular, creative
People who like the name Kennedy also like Hayden, Madison, Addison, Reagan, Riley, Logan, Parker, Avery, Mackenzie, Bailey

Kenneth (Celtic/Gaelic) ♂   RATING: ★★★
Handsome—Kenneth Branagh, actor
People think of Kenneth as handsome, intelligent, funny, caring, cool
People who like the name Kenneth also like Ethan, Jacob, Nicholas, Nathan, Matthew, Benjamin, Justin, Joshua, Andrew, Ian

Kennice (English) ♀   RATING: ★★★☆
Beautiful
People think of Kennice as pretty, funny, intelligent, caring, creative
People who like the name Kennice also like Kaelyn, Kaydence, Kya, Keely, Kara, Kendra, Kenisha, Kelis, Kamea, Kaira

Kennita (American) ♀   RATING: ★★
Combination of Ken and Nita; also a feminine form of Kenneth
People think of Kennita as trustworthy, pretty, creative, powerful, young
People who like the name Kennita also like Kaydence, Kenisha, Kolina, Keona, Kelis, Kimaya, Keely, Keaira, Kamala, Kya

Kenny (Celtic/Gaelic) ♂   RATING: ★★★☆
Handsome—Kenny G., musician
People think of Kenny as funny, handsome, cool, sexy, caring
People who like the name Kenny also like Kevin, Ethan, Jack, Kenneth, Aaron, Jacob, Cody, Keith, Justin, Adam

Kensley (American) ♀♂   RATING: ★★★☆
Combination of Ken and Lesley
People think of Kensley as energetic, funny, pretty, trustworthy, lazy
People who like the name Kensley also like Kenley, Addison, Avery, Bailey, Cadence, Hayden, Ashton, Kenzie, Keegan, Kinsey

Kent (Welsh) ♂   RATING: ★★☆
Bright white—Also a city in England; Clark Kent (aka Superman); comic book, TV, and movie character; Kent State University, Ohio
People think of Kent as handsome, intelligent, funny, trustworthy, caring
People who like the name Kent also like Ethan, Cole, Gavin, Ian, Luke, Nathan, Jacob, Grant, Caleb, Lance

Kentavious (American) ♂   RATING: ★★★
Created name
People think of Kentavious as creative, weird, big, popular, lazy
People who like the name Kentavious also like Kaden, Jabari, Darius, Dajuan, Isaac, Keon, Keith, Kaleb, Jayden, Keagan

Kenton (English) ♂   RATING: ★★★★
From the town of Kent
People think of Kenton as handsome, intelligent, funny, creative, caring

People who like the name Kenton also like Kaden, Landon, Ethan, Kelton, Braden, Kyson, Keagan, Tristan, Aiden, Grayson

Kentucky (Native American) ♀♂   RATING: ★★★
Land of tomorrow—Iroquois origin; U.S. state
People think of Kentucky as weird, unpopular, lazy, old-fashioned, loser
People who like the name Kentucky also like Kansas, Kindle, Kennedy, Texas, Keegan, Dakota, Kourtney, Kimball, Alabama, Kyrie

Kenya (Hebrew) ♀   RATING: ★★★★
Animal horn—Also a country in Africa
People think of Kenya as pretty, caring, funny, intelligent, young
People who like the name Kenya also like Hailey, Faith, Keira, Aaliyah, Eva, Paige, Jadyn, Kara, Hannah, Isabella

Kenyi (African) ♂   RATING: ★★★
Male born after three or more girls
People think of Kenyi as aggressive, young, powerful, sporty, cool
People who like the name Kenyi also like Kasim, Kame, Kimoni, Keoni, Isaiah, Ethan, Simba, Anwar, Kazi, Jabulani

Kenyon (English) ♀♂   RATING: ★★★★
From the mound of Einion
People think of Kenyon as handsome, funny, intelligent, popular, caring
People who like the name Kenyon also like Hayden, Keaton, Kendall, Logan, Caden, Jaden, Landen, Preston, Bailey, Addison

Kenzie (Celtic/Gaelic) ♀♂   RATING: ★★★★
Light skinned
People think of Kenzie as funny, pretty, energetic, cool, popular
People who like the name Kenzie also like Mackenzie, Riley, Madison, Bailey, Keegan, Hayden, Logan, Addison, Taylor, Avery

Keola (Hawaiian) ♀   RATING: ★★★☆
The life
People think of Keola as intelligent, caring, pretty, creative, trendy
People who like the name Keola also like Keona, Keani, Kamea, Kailani, Kaloni, Keala, Kaelyn, Kaya, Kya, Kera

Keon (Hawaiian) ♂   RATING: ★★☆
God is gracious
People think of Keon as handsome, popular, intelligent, funny, cool
People who like the name Keon also like Kaden, Keoni, Kyson, Jayden, Ethan, Keagan, Kian, Kaleb, Kane, Joshua

Keona (Hawaiian) ♀   RATING: ★★★★☆
God's gracious gift
People think of Keona as pretty, creative, caring, funny, exotic

People who like the name Keona also like Kailani, Kaelyn, Kamea, Kiana, Keani, Kayla, Kiara, Keaira, Keira, Keyanna

Keoni (*Hawaiian*) ♂   RATING: ★★★★
God is gracious—Variation of John
People think of Keoni as funny, intelligent, sexy, handsome, creative
People who like the name Keoni also like Keon, Kaden, Kanoa, Ethan, Keagan, Caleb, Jayden, Kale, Aiden, Kaleb

Kera (*Celtic/Gaelic*) ♀   RATING: ★★★☆
Pure—Varaition of Katherine
People think of Kera as pretty, creative, caring, funny, energetic
People who like the name Kera also like Keira, Kaelyn, Kara, Kyla, Kiara, Kayla, Kira, Keaira, Kyra, Kaira

Keran (*Armenian*) ♀ ♂   RATING: ★★★
Wooden post
People think of Keran as leader, artsy, creative, young, exotic
People who like the name Keran also like Kieran, Keegan, Kiran, Kegan, Hayden, Logan, Kendall, Keeran, Teagan, Kasen

Kerani (*Sanskrit/East Indian*) ♀   RATING: ★★★
Sacred bells
People think of Kerani as exotic, creative, artsy, ethnic, intelligent
People who like the name Kerani also like Kimaya, Kanika, Kirtana, Kailani, Keani, Kaydence, Kaori, Kamala, Kavindra, Ketaki

Keren (*Hebrew*) ♀   RATING: ★★★★
Ray, beam; strength, power—Also used in English-speaking countries as a form of Kerenhappuch, name of one of the daughters of the Biblical prophet Job
People think of Keren as pretty, creative, intelligent, caring, funny
People who like the name Keren also like Keira, Kera, Kaya, Kiersten, Kerryn, Kellyn, Kyra, Kara, Karah, Dara

Kermit (*Celtic/Gaelic*) ♂   RATING: ★★★☆
Free man—Variation of Dermot; Kermit the Frog, Muppets character
People think of Kermit as funny, intelligent, handsome, nerdy, weird
People who like the name Kermit also like Keagan, Kevin, Isaac, Ian, Liam, Jack, Keiran, Garrett, Keith, Griffin

Kern (*Celtic/Gaelic*) ♀ ♂   RATING: ★★
Dark-haired child—Jerome Kern, composer
People think of Kern as quiet, intelligent, funny, caring, trustworthy
People who like the name Kern also like Kegan, Keegan, Killian, Keaton, Keeran, Kiran, Kasen, Keir, Rory, Kelby

Kerr (*Celtic/Gaelic*) ♀ ♂   RATING: ★★
A marshland—Deborah Kerr, actress
People think of Kerr as weird, handsome, intelligent, creative, exotic

People who like the name Kerr also like Hayden, Logan, Parker, Riley, Kyle, Keegan, Kieran, Dylan, Keir, Flynn

Kerri (*Celtic/Gaelic*) ♀   RATING: ★★★★
Dark, mysterious
People think of Kerri as caring, funny, pretty, trustworthy, intelligent
People who like the name Kerri also like Kiara, Keira, Kira, Keaira, Kara, Sabrina, Kayla, Hailey, Faith, Kate

Kerry (*Celtic/Gaelic*) ♀ ♂   RATING: ★★★☆
Dark princess
People think of Kerry as funny, caring, intelligent, pretty, creative
People who like the name Kerry also like Kieran, Madison, Riley, Kelly, Ryan, James, Jade, Hayden, Logan, Aidan

Kerryn (*American*) ♀   RATING: ★★☆
Dusky, pure—Combination of Keren and Kerry
People think of Kerryn as intelligent, caring, pretty, funny, leader
People who like the name Kerryn also like Kaelyn, Kiersten, Keira, Kendra, Kaydence, Jillian, Kyla, Jadyn, Gabrielle, Kylee

Kert (*American*) ♂   RATING: ★★★
Simple pleasures
People think of Kert as nerdy, intelligent, unpopular, wild, leader
People who like the name Kert also like Kaden, Edward, Ethan, Keith, Caleb, Jacob, Lance, Kaleb, Cole, Kane

Keshia (*American*) ♀   RATING: ★★★★
Created name—Keshia Knight Pulliam, actress
People think of Keshia as pretty, funny, caring, sexy, cool
People who like the name Keshia also like Keisha, Kaelyn, Keira, Kayla, Kyla, Jasmine, Kailey, Faith, Ciara, Kya

Kesia (*American*) ♀   RATING: ★★★★
Earthbound
People think of Kesia as pretty, intelligent, cool, trustworthy, funny
People who like the name Kesia also like Kaia, Kayla, Kyla, Keaira, Kyra, Kiara, Kaelyn, Keira, Keyanna, Kaida

Kesler (*American*) ♂   RATING: ★★★☆
Independent, energetic
People think of Kesler as energetic, intelligent, cool, popular, trustworthy
People who like the name Kesler also like Kaden, Keagan, Kyson, Maddox, Kelton, Ethan, Braden, Owen, Cole, Conner

Ketaki (*Sanskrit/East Indian*) ♀   RATING: ★★☆
Flower
People think of Ketaki as pretty, intelligent, young, lazy, ethnic
People who like the name Ketaki also like Kusuma, Kerani, Kirtana, Kimaya, Karuka, Kanika, Komala, Kavindra, Kaveri, Kirti

Ketan *(Sanskrit/East Indian)* ♂   RATING: ★★★☆
Home
> People think of Ketan as cool, intelligent, handsome, caring, popular
> People who like the name Ketan also like Kaden, Keagan, Kyson, Kaleb, Kael, Ethan, Landon, Tristan, Kennan, Korbin

Ketill *(Scandinavian)* ♀♂   RATING: ★☆
Helmet, small pot—Nordic name from the Viking period
> People think of Ketill as big, exotic, criminal, ethnic, loser
> People who like the name Ketill also like Kendi, Kirby, Kenadie, Kelby, Kendall, Kory, Kione, Kendis, Kiho, Kizzy

Kevin *(Celtic/Gaelic)* ♂   RATING: ★★★
Handsome, beautiful—Kevin Bacon, actor; Kevin Costner, actor; Kevin Dillon, actor; Kevin Kline, actor
> People think of Kevin as handsome, funny, intelligent, caring, cool
> People who like the name Kevin also like Ethan, Jacob, Matthew, Nathan, Justin, Jason, Andrew, Nicholas, Aaron, Ian

Kevina *(Celtic/Gaelic)* ♀   RATING: ★★★
Handsome, beautiful—Feminine form of Kevin
> People think of Kevina as caring, intelligent, pretty, funny, young
> People who like the name Kevina also like Kiara, Keaira, Keira, Keelia, Kaelyn, Keyanna, Kirra, Faith, Keitha, Kera

Kevine *(Celtic/Gaelic)* ♀   RATING: ★★★
Beautiful—Feminine form of Kevin
> People think of Kevine as powerful, creative, pretty, funny, weird
> People who like the name Kevine also like Keely, Kiara, Kaelyn, Kiley, Keaira, Keira, Kera, Kyrene, Kayla, Kellyn

Kevlyn *(American)* ♀   RATING: ★★★☆
Combination of Kevin and Lyn
> People think of Kevlyn as pretty, funny, intelligent, creative, popular
> People who like the name Kevlyn also like Kiley, Kaelyn, Kaydence, Kylar, Keely, Kiersten, Kailey, Calista, Kiara, Kalista

Kevork *(Armenian)* ♂   RATING: ★★☆
Farmer
> People think of Kevork as exotic, ethnic, stuck-up, artsy, weird
> People who like the name Kevork also like Kamal, Kamali, Kurt, Minowa, Kaden, Kian, Kaloosh, Jericho, Kellan, Keenan

Keyah *(African)* ♀   RATING: ★★★☆
In good health—West African origin
> People think of Keyah as pretty, intelligent, funny, popular, exotic
> People who like the name Keyah also like Kya, Kaia, Kiara, Kaiya, Keyanna, Kia, Kiana, Kaelyn, Ayanna, Kayin

Keyanna *(American)* ♀   RATING: ★★★★☆
Living with grace
> People think of Keyanna as pretty, funny, caring, cool, sexy
> People who like the name Keyanna also like Kaelyn, Kiana, Kiara, Kaydence, Kyla, Keaira, Jadyn, Keira, Adriana, Aaliyah

Kezia *(Hebrew)* ♀   RATING: ★★★★☆
Tree bark—Variation of Ketzia
> People think of Kezia as pretty, caring, intelligent, cool, funny
> People who like the name Kezia also like Keziah, Kaia, Kiana, Keely, Kyla, Kesia, Kiara, Kara, Keaira, Kaiya

Keziah *(Hebrew)* ♀   RATING: ★★
Daughter of Job
> People think of Keziah as pretty, intelligent, funny, caring, creative
> People who like the name Keziah also like Kezia, Kyla, Kaia, Kiana, Kya, Kaya, Kaleigh, Faith, Abigail, Kiara

Khalil *(Arabic)* ♂   RATING: ★★★★
Friend—Khalil Gibran, author/poet
> People think of Khalil as handsome, intelligent, popular, funny, creative
> People who like the name Khalil also like Kalil, Kaden, Kadin, Amir, Malik, Jayden, Keon, Elijah, Kaleb, Keiran

Khalon *(American)* ♂   RATING: ★★★★
Strong warrior
> People think of Khalon as handsome, cool, powerful, aggressive, intelligent
> People who like the name Khalon also like Kaden, Kael, Aiden, Kellan, Keagan, Kyson, Ethan, Jayden, Khalil, Keoni

Khanh *(Vietnamese)* ♀♂   RATING: ★☆
Unknown meaning
> People think of Khanh as funny, intelligent, trustworthy, young, exotic
> People who like the name Khanh also like Kelsey, Kyrie, Keelin, Kizzy, Kei, Kirby, Kelsea, Kolton, Keeran, Keelan

Khoi *(Vietnamese)* ♂   RATING: ★★★☆
Unknown meaning
> People think of Khoi as handsome, exotic, intelligent, funny, weird
> People who like the name Khoi also like Keitaro, Kurt, Kamal, Kimoni, Kobe, Kyran, Kaden, Kane, Kato, Garrick

Khuong *(Vietnamese)* ♀♂   RATING: ★★☆
Unknown meaning
> People think of Khuong as quiet, weird, ethnic, intelligent, trustworthy
> People who like the name Khuong also like Khuyen, Keanu, Kenyon, Kenzie, Kendall, Kione, Kieve, Kyrie, Kindle, Kolton

Khuyen *(Vietnamese)* ♀♂   RATING: ★★☆
Advise
> People think of Khuyen as creative, intelligent, elegant, nerdy, quiet

People who like the name Khuyen also like Khuong, Kavi, Keanu, Kindle, Kione, Kyrie, Keladry, Kerry, Keir, Kieve

Kia *(African)* ♀   RATING: ★★★
Hill—Also a car manufacturer
People think of Kia as pretty, funny, caring, intelligent, creative
People who like the name Kia also like Kya, Mia, Keira, Faith, Mya, Kiana, Kiara, Eva, Kira, Chloe

Kian *(American)* ♂   RATING: ★★★★☆
Hill—Variation of Kia
People think of Kian as intelligent, handsome, cool, popular, energetic
People who like the name Kian also like Kaden, Ethan, Keagan, Liam, Aiden, Landon, Owen, Braden, Tristan, Caleb

Kiana *(American)* ♀   RATING: ★★★
Living with grace—Also spelled Kianna
People think of Kiana as pretty, funny, creative, intelligent, caring
People who like the name Kiana also like Kiara, Keira, Kaelyn, Kyla, Hailey, Hannah, Isabella, Arianna, Kailey, Faith

Kiandra *(English)* ♀   RATING: ★★★★
Water baby; magical—Variation of Kendra
People think of Kiandra as pretty, caring, creative, popular, sexy
People who like the name Kiandra also like Kiara, Kendra, Kiana, Kaydence, Gabriella, Kaelyn, Isabella, Jadyn, Keira, Hailey

Kianga *(African)* ♀   RATING: ★★★☆
Sunshine—Congo origin
People think of Kianga as pretty, exotic, creative, powerful, ethnic
People who like the name Kianga also like Kamili, Karasi, Kumani, Jahzara, Kya, Isabis, Kanoni, Kiden, Kaya, Kande

Kiara *(Celtic/Gaelic)* ♀   RATING: ★★★☆
Small, dark
People think of Kiara as pretty, funny, intelligent, caring, popular
People who like the name Kiara also like Keira, Keaira, Kaelyn, Kira, Ciara, Kiana, Kayla, Kara, Isabella, Kyla

Kiden *(African)* ♀   RATING: ★★★★
Female born after three or more boys
People think of Kiden as pretty, intelligent, caring, elegant, quiet
People who like the name Kiden also like Kya, Kaelyn, Kiara, Jadyn, Kissa, Keira, Kendra, Kiley, Kayin, Paige

Kiefer *(German)* ♂   RATING: ★★★★☆
Pine tree; barrelmaker—Also a surname; Kiefer Sutherland, actor
People think of Kiefer as handsome, intelligent, funny, sexy, cool

People who like the name Kiefer also like Keefer, Ethan, Kaden, Aiden, Gavin, Keagan, Ian, Owen, Liam, Tristan

Kiele *(Hawaiian)* ♀   RATING: ★★★★☆
Fragrant blossom
People think of Kiele as pretty, creative, intelligent, funny, sexy
People who like the name Kiele also like Kailani, Kiley, Keely, Kaelyn, Leilani, Keala, Keani, Keira, Kylie, Malia

Kieran *(Celtic/Gaelic)* ♀ ♂   RATING: ★★★
Little dark one—Also spelled Keiran
People think of Kieran as intelligent, handsome, funny, caring, cool
People who like the name Kieran also like Aidan, Logan, Keegan, Hayden, Riley, Caden, Dylan, Connor, Mackenzie, Ryan

Kiernan *(Celtic/Gaelic)* ♂   RATING: ★★★★☆
Small one from the past
People think of Kiernan as intelligent, handsome, funny, creative, caring
People who like the name Kiernan also like Keiran, Keagan, Aiden, Liam, Tristan, Tiernan, Keenan, Ethan, Braeden, Ian

Kiersten *(Scandinavian)* ♀   RATING: ★★★
Annointed
People think of Kiersten as pretty, funny, caring, intelligent, energetic
People who like the name Kiersten also like Kaelyn, Paige, Abigail, Hannah, Chloe, Olivia, Kaleigh, Isabella, Kailey, Hailey

Kiet *(Thai)* ♂   RATING: ★★★
Honor
People think of Kiet as young, caring, popular, exotic, wealthy
People who like the name Kiet also like Kael, Niran, Kyran, Brandon, Kellan, Keiji, Kenton, Ryu, Kail, Malachi

Kieu *(Vietnamese)* ♀   RATING: ★★★
Unknown meaning
People think of Kieu as caring, young, funny, pretty, trustworthy
People who like the name Kieu also like Keala, Kassia, Kaia, Kay, Kyra, Keelia, Kiersten, Kohana, Kaori, Katie

Kieve *(Welsh)* ♀ ♂   RATING: ★★★
Mythical name
People think of Kieve as exotic, trustworthy, sexy, funny, creative
People who like the name Kieve also like Kyan, Kai, Kyler, Kione, Kieran, Kiran, Keeran, Cade, Kasen, Kegan

Kiho *(African)* ♀ ♂   RATING: ★★☆
Fog
People think of Kiho as exotic, creative, poor, energetic, winner
People who like the name Kiho also like Kione, Kendi, Kishi, Kei, Keanu, Kiyoshi, Kozue, Kanga, Kai, Kory

Kijana *(African)* ♀ ♂   RATING: ★★★☆
Youth—Kiswahili origin
> People think of Kijana as energetic, powerful, leader, sneaky, intelligent
> People who like the name Kijana also like Kalani, Keanu, Kai, Ashanti, Kendi, Kione, Kameryn, Keelan, Mahari, Kieran

Kiki *(Spanish)* ♀   RATING: ★★
Short for names beginning with K
> People think of Kiki as funny, pretty, cool, young, caring
> People who like the name Kiki also like Isabella, Mia, Faith, Ava, Kari, Bella, Grace, Layla, Lily, Olivia

Kilenya *(Native American)* ♀   RATING: ★★★
Coughing fish—Miwok origin
> People think of Kilenya as exotic, old-fashioned, lazy, funny, elegant
> People who like the name Kilenya also like Kiana, Kaya, Kaelyn, Kaliska, Koleyna, Kiona, Kimimela, Kimama, Kiara, Keaira

Kiley *(Celtic/Gaelic)* ♀   RATING: ★★★☆
Good-looking
> People think of Kiley as pretty, funny, creative, popular, intelligent
> People who like the name Kiley also like Kaelyn, Kailey, Hailey, Kylee, Chloe, Keely, Paige, Kayla, Kyla, Kyleigh

Killian *(Celtic/Gaelic)* ♀ ♂   RATING: ★★★☆
Church, monk's cell—Variation of Cillian
> People think of Killian as intelligent, handsome, creative, funny, caring
> People who like the name Killian also like Logan, Keegan, Hayden, Kieran, Aidan, Caden, Riley, Teagan, Addison, Avery

Kim *(English)* ♀ ♂   RATING: ★★★☆
Short for Kimberly or Kimball—Kim Cattrall, actress; Kim Delaney, actress; Kim Novak, actress
> People think of Kim as funny, caring, pretty, creative, intelligent
> People who like the name Kim also like Kimberly, Kelly, Jade, Ashley, Taylor, Jamie, Kyle, James, Ryan, Jordan

Kimama *(Native American)* ♀   RATING: ★☆
Butterfly—Shoshone origin
> People think of Kimama as exotic, quiet, cool, elegant, creative
> People who like the name Kimama also like Kimimela, Kaya, Kachina, Kaliska, Kimaya, Kilenya, Kineks, Keely, Kwanita, Keaira

Kimaya *(Sanskrit/East Indian)* ♀   RATING: ★★★★☆
Divine
> People think of Kimaya as intelligent, caring, pretty, exotic, creative
> People who like the name Kimaya also like Kaelyn, Kaiya, Kya, Kailani, Kaya, Amaya, Kaydence, Kiara, Kamaria, Keona

Kimball *(English)* ♀ ♂   RATING: ★★★
Royal bold
> People think of Kimball as weird, creative, poor, old-fashioned, caring
> People who like the name Kimball also like Kendall, Keaton, Caden, Keegan, Logan, Parker, Kennedy, Kirsten, Kinsey, Bailey

Kimber *(American)* ♀   RATING: ★★★★
Short for Kimberly
> People think of Kimber as funny, intelligent, pretty, sexy, creative
> People who like the name Kimber also like Kaydence, Ava, Faith, Isabella, Olivia, Chloe, Kaelyn, Emma, Bella, Abigail

Kimberly *(English)* ♀ ♂   RATING: ★★☆
From the meadow of the royal fortress—Originally a surname; also spelled Kimberley
> People think of Kimberly as funny, pretty, caring, intelligent, creative
> People who like the name Kimberly also like Madison, Brooke, Taylor, Jordan, Ashley, Courtney, Ryan, Dylan, Holly, Mackenzie

Kimi *(Japanese)* ♀   RATING: ★★★★
She who is without equal
> People think of Kimi as funny, intelligent, creative, caring, pretty
> People who like the name Kimi also like Kaida, Keiko, Kaiya, Kaori, Sakura, Kioko, Chloe, Kuri, Amaya, Emiko

Kimimela *(Native American)* ♀   RATING: ★★★☆
Butterfly—Sioux origin
> People think of Kimimela as exotic, pretty, funny, creative, trustworthy
> People who like the name Kimimela also like Kimama, Kaya, Kachina, Kaelyn, Kaleigh, Kilenya, Kaliska, Koleyna, Kendra, Kiona

Kimmy *(English)* ♀   RATING: ★★
Short for Kimberly
> People think of Kimmy as pretty, funny, trustworthy, intelligent, cool
> People who like the name Kimmy also like Hannah, Emma, Grace, Olivia, Isabella, Kacy, Kimi, Mia, Lacey, Gracie

Kimn *(English)* ♀ ♂   RATING: ★★☆
Ruler—Variation of Kim, Kimberly, or Kimberely
> People think of Kimn as ethnic, weird, wealthy, cool, powerful
> People who like the name Kimn also like Kieve, Kione, Kiyoshi, Kiral, Kishi, Keahi, Ketill, Katriel, Kindle, Kelby

Kimo *(Hawaiian)* ♂   RATING: ★★
Supplanter—Variation of James
> People think of Kimo as handsome, trustworthy, intelligent, popular, sporty
> People who like the name Kimo also like Kanoa, Kale, Keon, Kapono, Ethan, Kaden, Korbin, Chase, Kelii, Keoni

Kimoni *(African)* ♂ RATING: ★★★
Great man—South African origin
> People think of Kimoni as exotic, creative, caring, popular, handsome
> People who like the name Kimoni also like Kasim, Kamal, Ajani, Keoni, Jabari, Khalil, Kame, Hajari, Kazi, Kyson

Kin *(Japanese)* ♀♂ RATING: ★★★☆
Golden—In English, means members of the family
> People think of Kin as intelligent, cool, young, sexy, powerful
> People who like the name Kin also like Kiyoshi, Kana, Kumi, Sanyu, Rin, Mitsu, Hoshi, Yuki, Maro, Ren

Kina *(Hawaiian)* ♀ RATING: ★★☆
China
> People think of Kina as pretty, sexy, intelligent, popular, funny
> People who like the name Kina also like Kailani, Ava, Keely, Kya, Kara, Chloe, Keona, Kira, Kaia, Mia

Kindle *(American)* ♀♂ RATING: ★★☆
Set fire
> People think of Kindle as pretty, wild, funny, creative, powerful
> People who like the name Kindle also like Jaden, Caden, Kendall, Keaton, Hayden, Jade, Addison, Keegan, Kinsey, Riley

Kineks *(Native American)* ♀ RATING: ★☆
Rosebud
> People think of Kineks as weird, big, exotic, criminal, boy next door
> People who like the name Kineks also like Kachina, Kaya, Kimama, Kaliska, Kimimela, Kwanita, Donoma, Kilenya, Koleyna, Kiona

Kineta *(Greek)* ♀ RATING: ★★
Full of energy
> People think of Kineta as energetic, creative, exotic, ethnic, wild
> People who like the name Kineta also like Kisha, Kyra, Kyria, Kendra, Kachina, Kanika, Keiko, Kimaya, Keena, Kenisha

Kinfe *(African)* ♀♂ RATING: ★★★
Wing—Ethiopian origin
> People think of Kinfe as exotic, aggressive, ethnic, wild, leader
> People who like the name Kinfe also like Kione, Kendi, Kizzy, Krishna, Kishi, Kiran, Kendall, Kiyoshi, Keahi, Kalin

King *(American)* ♂ RATING: ★★★
Ruler—King Donovan, actor; *King Kong*, movie and gorilla character; Stephen King, author
> People think of King as powerful, sexy, handsome, leader, aggressive
> People who like the name King also like Kaden, Kaleb, Jackson, Elijah, Justin, Braden, Keagan, Jack, Caleb, Cruz

Kinga *(Hungarian)* ♀ RATING: ★★★
Bravery in war
> People think of Kinga as funny, caring, pretty, intelligent, trustworthy
> People who like the name Kinga also like Sorena, Anya, Virika, Gisela, Isolde, Layla, Sadie

Kingston *(English)* ♂ RATING: ★★★
From the king's town
> People think of Kingston as handsome, powerful, intelligent, wealthy, leader
> People who like the name Kingston also like Jackson, Ethan, Aiden, Gavin, Maddox, Kaden, Gabriel, Tristan, Holden, Jayden

Kinion *(American)* ♂ RATING: ★★★
Stone of Einion—Variation of Kenyon
> People think of Kinion as loser, creative, trustworthy, nerdy, religious
> People who like the name Kinion also like Kyson, Keenan, Kelton, Coen, Kaden, Landon, Kyran, Kynan, Kenton, Tristan

Kinipela *(Hawaiian)* ♀ RATING: ★★★
Wave—Often used as a Hawaiian translation of Jennifer
> People think of Kinipela as pretty, artsy, exotic, weird, ethnic
> People who like the name Kinipela also like Kailani, Keani, Keala, Kawena, Kina, Keola, Kiele, Kamea, Kaloni, Keiki

Kinsey *(English)* ♀♂ RATING: ★★★★
King's victory—Kinsey Millhone, character in Sue Grafton novels
> People think of Kinsey as pretty, funny, intelligent, creative, energetic
> People who like the name Kinsey also like Addison, Hayden, Caden, Kenzie, Parker, Avery, Bailey, Mackenzie, Madison, Jaden

Kioko *(Japanese)* ♀ RATING: ★★★★
Meets world with happiness
> People think of Kioko as funny, caring, creative, exotic, cool
> People who like the name Kioko also like Kaida, Keiko, Kaori, Kaiya, Kohana, Aiko, Kumiko, Kimi, Emiko, Sakura

Kiona *(Native American)* ♀ RATING: ★★★★
Brown hills
> People think of Kiona as pretty, popular, funny, exotic, intelligent
> People who like the name Kiona also like Kaya, Kiana, Kiara, Keira, Kiora, Kailani, Kaliska, Keyanna, Keona, Bianca

Kione *(African)* ♀♂ RATING: ★★☆
Someone who comes from nowhere
> People think of Kione as intelligent, wild, young, handsome, exotic
> People who like the name Kione also like Kiran, Keanu, Kieve, Kieran, Kiyoshi, Kyan, Kumi, Keeran, Kai, Shea

336

Kiora *(Aborigine)* ♀   RATING: ★★☆
Greetings—From the Maori greeting "kia ora," meaning hello and good-bye
> People think of Kiora as pretty, exotic, intelligent, young, artsy
> People who like the name Kiora also like Kiara, Keaira, Keira, Kira, Kaelyn, Kara, Kyla, Fiona, Kiana, Kaira

Kipling *(English)* ♀♂   RATING: ★★★
From Cuppel's people—Rudyard Kipling, author/poet
> People think of Kipling as intelligent, winner, weird, leader, unpopular
> People who like the name Kipling also like Kirby, Keaton, Kendall, Kinsey, Parker, Hayden, Kyler, Keegan, Sawyer, Jameson

Kipp *(English)* ♀♂   RATING: ★★
From the hill
> People think of Kipp as funny, intelligent, trustworthy, creative, leader
> People who like the name Kipp also like Sawyer, Hunter, Parker, Kendall, Logan, Quinn, Caden, Evan, Riley, Corbin

Kira *(Celtic/Gaelic)* ♀   RATING: ★★★★☆
Black—Variation of Ciara or Kyra
> People think of Kira as pretty, creative, intelligent, funny, caring
> People who like the name Kira also like Keira, Kiara, Kara, Ava, Kayla, Kyra, Kyla, Keaira, Kaelyn, Chloe

Kirabo *(African)* ♀♂   RATING: ★★★
Gift from God—Ugandan origin
> People think of Kirabo as ethnic, exotic, intelligent, winner, leader
> People who like the name Kirabo also like Kendi, Kitoko, Kione, Kiho, Kuron, Kei, Yohance, Kiros, Kieve, Krishna

Kiral *(Turkish)* ♀♂   RATING: ★★
Supreme chief—Variation of the surname Kral
> People think of Kiral as sexy, exotic, handsome, winner, big
> People who like the name Kiral also like Kiran, Kieran, Kieve, Kyrie, Kasen, Kegan, Kyan, Kindle, Kai, Kelby

Kiran *(Sanskrit/East Indian)* ♀♂   RATING: ★★★
Ray of light
> People think of Kiran as intelligent, funny, caring, cool, pretty
> People who like the name Kiran also like Kieran, Hayden, Caden, Jaden, Keegan, Logan, Aidan, Kaelin, Kai, Landen

Kirby *(English)* ♀♂   RATING: ★★
From the village with the church
> People think of Kirby as funny, intelligent, creative, cool, caring
> People who like the name Kirby also like Riley, Bailey, Logan, Parker, Kendall, Hayden, Madison, Keegan, Jordan, Jaden

Kiri *(Cambodian)* ♀♂   RATING: ★★★
Mountain—Also a Maori name; Kiri Te Kanawa, opera singer
> People think of Kiri as pretty, caring, intelligent, funny, creative
> People who like the name Kiri also like Kai, Riley, Jade, Hayden, Keegan, Jordan, Logan, Kaili, Drew, Brooke

Kiril *(Greek)* ♂   RATING: ★★★
Lord—Variation of Cyril; also a Russian name
> People think of Kiril as intelligent, caring, weird, artsy, quiet
> People who like the name Kiril also like Kael, Kyros, Keiran, Alexander, Kaden, Tristan, Kenaz, Gabriel, Karan, Keagan

Kirima *(Native American)* ♀   RATING: ★★☆
Hill—Banti Eskimo origin
> People think of Kirima as artsy, intelligent, trendy, funny, exotic
> People who like the name Kirima also like Kaya, Kimama, Kiona, Catori, Kaliska, Kimimela, Kilenya, Halona, Kachina, Cholena

Kirit *(Sanskrit/East Indian)* ♀♂   RATING: ★☆
Shining like the sun
> People think of Kirit as young, creative, caring, funny, intelligent
> People who like the name Kirit also like Kiran, Kavi, Krishna, Kalyan, Deven, Kailas, Kieve, Deva, Kelby, Jiva

Kirk *(Scandinavian)* ♂   RATING: ★★★☆
Owned by the church—Kirk Cameron, actor; Kirk Gibson, baseball player
> People think of Kirk as handsome, funny, intelligent, cool, caring
> People who like the name Kirk also like Ethan, Ian, Kaden, Caleb, Owen, Jacob, Justin, Cody, Nathan, Cole

Kirkan *(Armenian)* ♂   RATING: ★★
Watchful—Variation of Gregory
> People think of Kirkan as wealthy, big, powerful, boy next door, winner
> People who like the name Kirkan also like Keagan, Korbin, Kaden, Kyson, Kenton, Keith, Koen, Kelton, Kent, Tyson

Kiros *(African)* ♀♂   RATING: ★★
Lord—Variation of Cyrus
> People think of Kiros as cool, wealthy, trustworthy, winner, leader
> People who like the name Kiros also like Kitoko, Kendi, Kiyoshi, Keanu, Kijana, Katriel, Kasen, Kai, Kendall, Kione

Kirra *(English)* ♀   RATING: ★★★★
Australian place name
> People think of Kirra as pretty, intelligent, creative, funny, popular
> People who like the name Kirra also like Kiara, Kira, Keira, Keaira, Kera, Kaelyn, Kyla, Chloe, Kiora, Kendra

Kirsi *(Scandinavian)* ♀   RATING: ★★☆
Amaranth blossoms—Finnish origin
> People think of Kirsi as funny, creative, pretty, intelligent, popular
> People who like the name Kirsi also like Kiara, Keaira, Kyra, Keira, Kiana, Kira, Kylee, Klara, Kendra, Brielle

Kirsten *(German)* ♀ ♂   RATING: ★★★★
Christian—Also spelled Kyrsten; Kirsten Dunst, actress
> People think of Kirsten as pretty, funny, caring, intelligent, creative
> People who like the name Kirsten also like Madison, Bailey, Mackenzie, Taylor, Hayden, Brooke, Cameron, Morgan, Riley, Jaden

Kirstie *(Scandinavian)* ♀   RATING: ★★★★
Short for Kristen; also spelled Kirsty—Kirstie Alley, actress
> People think of Kirstie as trendy, popular, winner, lazy, energetic
> People who like the name Kirstie also like Callie, Makenna, Ashlyn, Kaelyn, Lanie, Kylie, Paige, Kaylee, Bianca, Natalie

Kirtana *(Sanskrit/East Indian)* ♀   RATING: ★★★
Prayer song
> People think of Kirtana as pretty, intelligent, exotic, powerful, funny
> People who like the name Kirtana also like Kimaya, Kirti, Kavindra, Kerani, Komali, Kaveri, Komala, Kamala, Laksha, Ketaki

Kirti *(Sanskrit/East Indian)* ♀   RATING: ★★★
Fame
> People think of Kirti as caring, pretty, trustworthy, intelligent, energetic
> People who like the name Kirti also like Kirtana, Komali, Kaveri, Kimaya, Komala, Kerani, Kali, Kamala, Kamana, Ketaki

Kisha *(Slavic)* ♀   RATING: ★★★★
Rainfall
> People think of Kisha as pretty, caring, funny, intelligent, sexy
> People who like the name Kisha also like Kiara, Kayla, Hailey, Kaya, Kaira, Keisha, Kaelyn, Kyla, Kara, Kailey

Kishan *(Sanskrit/East Indian)* ♂   RATING: ★★★☆
Black—Variation of Krishna
> People think of Kishan as aggressive, handsome, intelligent, funny, powerful
> People who like the name Kishan also like Kaden, Kamran, Adit, Ketan, Khalil, Keon, Kami, Kyran, Keagan, Ashwin

Kishi *(Native American)* ♀ ♂   RATING: ★★★☆
Night—In Japanese, means beach or seashore
> People think of Kishi as caring, intelligent, energetic, young, sexy
> People who like the name Kishi also like Kanga, Mika, Kiyoshi, Kai, Keanu, Kiran, Helki, Kione, Keahi, Misae

Kiss *(American)* ♀ ♂   RATING: ★★☆
Expression of caring
> People think of Kiss as sexy, pretty, exotic, stuck-up, popular
> People who like the name Kiss also like Angel, Kai, Love, Jaden, Madison, Justice, Jada, Taylor, Jade, Hayden

Kissa *(African)* ♀   RATING: ★★★
First-born daughter—Kenyan origin
> People think of Kissa as pretty, exotic, sexy, funny, creative
> People who like the name Kissa also like Kya, Kande, Abigail, Kia, Kiana, Layla, Kailey, Kyra, Keely, Kendra

Kistna *(Sanskrit/East Indian)* ♂   RATING: ★★
Black—Variation of Krishna
> People think of Kistna as creative, powerful, cool, exotic, ethnic
> People who like the name Kistna also like Kishan, Charan, Devesh, Ketan, Hastin, Chetan, Adit, Jagat, Chitt, Deepak

Kit *(American)* ♀ ♂   RATING: ★★★☆
Short for Katherine or Christopher—Kit Carson, Old West lawman
> People think of Kit as pretty, creative, young, cool
> People who like the name Kit also like Scout, Julian, Mackenzie, Sam, Carter, Ashley, Jamie, Paxton, Will, Tyler

Kita *(Japanese)* ♀   RATING: ★★★★
North
> People think of Kita as pretty, creative, funny, cool, wild
> People who like the name Kita also like Kaida, Kaya, Kyra, Mia, Keiko, Kimi, Kira, Kaori, Kuri, Kendra

Kitena *(American)* ♀   RATING: ★★☆
Kitten-like
> People think of Kitena as sexy, trustworthy, girl next door, young, intelligent
> People who like the name Kitena also like Isabella, Gabriela, Camelia, Gabrielle, Jacqueline, Katelin, Annabella, Annalise, Dahlia, Caitlyn

Kitoko *(African)* ♀ ♂   RATING: ★★
Beautiful—Congo origin
> People think of Kitoko as quiet, caring, creative, leader, intelligent
> People who like the name Kitoko also like Kendi, Kiyoshi, Kiros, Kumi, Keanu, Kalani, Kione, Kirabo, Kai, Akia

Kitra *(Hebrew)* ♀   RATING: ★★★
Crown
> People think of Kitra as pretty, exotic, intelligent, creative, funny
> People who like the name Kitra also like Kiana, Kiara, Keyanna, Katia, Isabella, Kaelyn, Kaori, Ava, Kaya, Kendra

Kitty (English) ♀   RATING: ★★
Pure—Short for Katherine; also means a baby cat;
Kitty Carlisle, actress/singer
> People think of Kitty as pretty, funny, energetic, intelligent, popular
> People who like the name Kitty also like Belle, Grace, Isabelle, Daisy, Faith, Hailey, Emily, Lily, Bella, Elizabeth

Kiyoshi (Japanese) ♀♂   RATING: ★★★★☆
Bright, shining, clear
> People think of Kiyoshi as intelligent, quiet, caring, cool, young
> People who like the name Kiyoshi also like Kana, Kin, Kumi, Hoshi, Yuki, Mitsu, Seiko, Rin, Hiroko, Sanyu

Kizzy (Hebrew) ♀♂   RATING: ★★★★
From the cassia tree; variation of Kezia
> People think of Kizzy as pretty, funny, energetic, creative, intelligent
> People who like the name Kizzy also like Kai, Keegan, Keanu, Jaden, Hayden, Riley, Caden, Taylor, Toby, Bailey

Klara (Hungarian) ♀   RATING: ★★★★
Illustrious—Variation of Clara
> People think of Klara as creative, intelligent, pretty, elegant, caring
> People who like the name Klara also like Kaydence, Kiara, Kylee, Kayla, Kara, Kiley, Claire, Kyla, Keira, Kaelyn

Klarika (Hungarian) ♀   RATING: ★★★
Illustrious—Short for Clare
> People think of Klarika as creative, pretty, elegant, girl next door, powerful
> People who like the name Klarika also like Klara, Keira, Kanika, Keaira, Mia, Kara, Kaida, Kiara, Kynthia, Kioko

Klaus (German) ♂   RATING: ★★★★
Victory of the people—Originally short for Niklaus; Klaus von Bülow, British aristocrat
> People think of Klaus as intelligent, handsome, caring, creative, leader
> People who like the name Klaus also like Oliver, Luke, Thomas, Damien, Vincent, Patrick, Lucas, Jacob, William, Ethan

Knoton (Native American) ♂   RATING: ★★☆
Wind
> People think of Knoton as big, exotic, caring, religious, ethnic
> People who like the name Knoton also like Kenton, Kynan, Dasan, Landon, Hakan, Kynton, Mikasi, Kyson, Edan, Kelton

Knox (English) ♂   RATING: ★★★★
From the hillock—Originally a surname
> People think of Knox as powerful, handsome, leader, wild, cool
> People who like the name Knox also like Maddox, Holden, Jackson, Kaden, Jett, Owen, Noah, Gavin, Landon, Ethan

Knute (Scandinavian) ♂   RATING: ★★★
Knot—Knute Rockne, football player
> People think of Knute as leader, handsome, winner, trustworthy, powerful
> People who like the name Knute also like Kane, Ike, Kirk, Emery, Seamus, Ethan, Maddox, Colin, Drake, Ian

Kobe (Hebrew) ♂   RATING: ★★★☆
Supplanter—Short for Jacob; also a variation of Coby
> People think of Kobe as sporty, popular, handsome, funny, energetic
> People who like the name Kobe also like Kaden, Kaleb, Ethan, Caleb, Jacob, Noah, Keagan, Aiden, Cody, Gavin

Kochava (Hebrew) ♀   RATING: ★★★
Star
> People think of Kochava as pretty, intelligent, exotic, caring, weird
> People who like the name Kochava also like Kaya, Kya, Kimaya, Kohana, Kiora, Keola, Kesia, Kolina, Keaira, Kailani

Koen (Dutch) ♂   RATING: ★★★☆
Bold, daring—Variation of Cohen; also in Hebrew, means priest
> People think of Koen as handsome, intelligent, leader, caring, energetic
> People who like the name Koen also like Kaden, Coen, Aiden, Keagan, Ethan, Kael, Jayden, Aden, Owen, Landon

Kohana (Japanese) ♀   RATING: ★★
Little flower—Also a Sioux name meaning swift
> People think of Kohana as exotic, creative, caring, young, artsy
> People who like the name Kohana also like Kaida, Sakura, Kaori, Keiko, Kioko, Kaiya, Amaya, Kimi, Kuri, Kaiyo

Kojo (African) ♂   RATING: ★☆
Born on Monday—From the Ashanti tribe of Ghana
> People think of Kojo as handsome, cool, trustworthy, intelligent, funny
> People who like the name Kojo also like Kimoni, Kanelo, Kent, Kame, Kazi, Kasim, Cody, Jasper, Kareem, Anwar

Koko (Japanese) ♀   RATING: ★★
Stork—Also a Native American name meaning night
> People think of Koko as intelligent, funny, wild, leader, creative
> People who like the name Koko also like Keiko, Kimi, Kuri, Kohana, Kaori, Kioko, Kyoko, Kura, Koto, Aiko

Koleyna (Native American) ♀   RATING: ★★
Coughing fish—Miwok origin
> People think of Koleyna as sexy, exotic, weird, ethnic, wild
> People who like the name Koleyna also like Kilenya, Kiona, Kaya, Kimimela, Kachina, Kaliska, Kamaria, Keyanna, Kimama, Kyra

Kolina *(Slavic)* ♀   RATING: ★★☆
Victory of the people—Short for Nikolai
- People think of Kolina as artsy, pretty, exotic, creative, weird
- People who like the name Kolina also like Kyla, Kaelyn, Kamea, Keely, Kiara, Katina, Kaia, Keaira, Kalista, Keira

Kolton *(English)* ♀♂   RATING: ★★★★
Cole's town—Variation of Colton
- People think of Kolton as handsome, cool, sporty, intelligent, popular
- People who like the name Kolton also like Logan, Caden, Hayden, Keaton, Jaden, Kyler, Keegan, Mason, Parker, Madison

Kolya *(Slavic)* ♂   RATING: ★★
Victory of the people—Short for Nikolai
- People think of Kolya as intelligent, caring, creative, funny, ethnic
- People who like the name Kolya also like Kael, Gabriel, Kellan, Kostya, Kail, Isaac, Kaden, Seth, Xander, Keiran

Komala *(Sanskrit/East Indian)* ♀   RATING: ★★★
Tender, delicate
- People think of Komala as sexy, trustworthy, quiet, caring, exotic
- People who like the name Komala also like Komali, Kamala, Kaya, Keaira, Kamana, Kirtana, Kala, Kyla, Kiara, Kya

Komali *(Sanskrit/East Indian)* ♀   RATING: ★★★
Tender, delicate
- People think of Komali as leader, exotic, caring, wealthy, powerful
- People who like the name Komali also like Komala, Kailani, Kamala, Karma, Kirtana, Kamaria, Kya, Kiora, Jaya, Kali

Konala *(Hawaiian)* ♂   RATING: ★★★
World ruler—Variation of Donald
- People think of Konala as creative, sexy, boy next door, funny, popular
- People who like the name Konala also like Kanoa, Keoni, Keon, Kale, Kelii, Kapono, Kaipo, Kimo, Palani, Edan

Konane *(Hawaiian)* ♀   RATING: ★★★
Glow like moonlight
- People think of Konane as quiet, ethnic, exotic, creative, artsy
- People who like the name Konane also like Keani, Kailani, Keala, Kamaria, Keona, Kaloni, Kamea, Keira, Kawena, Keola

Kong *(Chinese)* ♂   RATING: ★★★
Bright—*King Kong*, movie and character
- People think of Kong as big, weird, loser, leader, cool
- People who like the name Kong also like Jared, Benjamin, Kane, Gage, Lance, Kaden, Ethan, Keagan, Jack, Noah

Korbin *(Latin)* ♂   RATING: ★★☆
Raven
- People think of Korbin as handsome, intelligent, popular, creative, energetic
- People who like the name Korbin also like Kaden, Keagan, Ethan, Jayden, Kaleb, Caleb, Gavin, Aiden, Braden, Ian

Kordell *(English)* ♀♂   RATING: ★★★
Rope maker—Variation of Cordell
- People think of Kordell as funny, creative, popular, intelligent, big
- People who like the name Kordell also like Kendall, Kyler, Caden, Jaden, Keaton, Kenley, Kegan, Hayden, Keeran, Keegan

Koren *(Hebrew)* ♂   RATING: ★★★★
Shining, beaming
- People think of Koren as trustworthy, creative, funny, intelligent, caring
- People who like the name Koren also like Kaden, Aiden, Jayden, Isaac, Seth, Korbin, Caleb, Keiran, Kadin, Noah

Korene *(Greek)* ♀   RATING: ★★★
Maiden—Variation of Corinne
- People think of Korene as funny, caring, pretty, intelligent, girl next door
- People who like the name Korene also like Keira, Kori, Isabelle, Kiara, Kyra, Jadyn, Kaira, Kaelyn, Kyria, Kyla

Kori *(American)* ♀   RATING: ★★★☆
Hollow—Variation of Corey; also from the Greek word Kore meaning maiden
- People think of Kori as pretty, funny, intelligent, creative, caring
- People who like the name Kori also like Kaydence, Kaelyn, Kyla, Keely, Paige, Kailey, Hailey, Kiley, Faith, Emma

Korrine *(American)* ♀   RATING: ★★★
Maiden—Variation of Corinne
- People think of Korrine as pretty, caring, girl next door, funny, intelligent
- People who like the name Korrine also like Kaydence, Kaelyn, Keira, Kiana, Kyra, Kiersten, Kayla, Corinne, Kyla, Isabelle

Kort *(American)* ♂   RATING: ★★☆
From Courtenay, France—Short for Courtney
- People think of Kort as cool, sporty, trustworthy, caring, popular
- People who like the name Kort also like Kaden, Keagan, Cort, Korbin, Cole, Kane, Conner, Ian, Caleb, Luke

Kory *(American)* ♀♂   RATING: ★★☆
Hollow—Variation of Corey
- People think of Kory as funny, cool, handsome, caring, intelligent
- People who like the name Kory also like Logan, Riley, Jaden, Kyle, Keegan, Jordan, Kassidy, Dylan, Connor, Mason

Kostya *(Slavic)* ♂ RATING: ★★★☆
Constant—Short for Konstantin
People think of Kostya as exotic, ethnic, intelligent, cool, creative
People who like the name Kostya also like Kolya, Kyros, Kyran, Keiran, Kellan, Kamran, Ketan, Kato, Dmitri, Karan

Kosuke *(Japanese)* ♀ RATING: ★★★☆
Rising sun
People think of Kosuke as trustworthy, intelligent, caring, cool, funny
People who like the name Kosuke also like Kumiko, Kaida, Kaori, Keiko, Kimi, Kioko, Emiko, Sakura, Kaiya, Kuri

Koto *(Japanese)* ♀ RATING: ★★★
Harp-like musical instrument
People think of Koto as pretty, intelligent, ethnic, weird, quiet
People who like the name Koto also like Keiko, Kaori, Kimi, Kioko, Kaida, Kuri, Kumiko, Kyoko, Kosuke, Kaoru

Kourtney *(American)* ♀♂ RATING: ★★★★
From Courtenay, France—Variation of Courtney
People think of Kourtney as pretty, funny, caring, energetic, intelligent
People who like the name Kourtney also like Madison, Taylor, Kassidy, Brooke, Mackenzie, Courtney, Kendall, Jordan, Kirsten, Jaden

Kovit *(Thai)* ♂ RATING: ★★
Expert
People think of Kovit as weird, loser, nerdy, exotic, untrustworthy
People who like the name Kovit also like Korbin, Stian, Kyros, Keiran, Keith, Kenaz, Jovan, Kellan, Heller, Koen

Kozue *(Japanese)* ♀♂ RATING: ★★★
Tree branches
People think of Kozue as quiet, funny, weird, pretty, creative
People who like the name Kozue also like Kiyoshi, Kumi, Kin, Kana, Maemi, Mitsu, Maro, Hoshi, Hiroko, Sanyu

Kreeli *(American)* ♀ RATING: ★★★
Possibly from the surname Creeley
People think of Kreeli as creative, stuck-up, trendy, wild, pretty
People who like the name Kreeli also like Kya, Krisalyn, Kyra, Kyrene, Keely, Kiley, Kalista, Kaydence, Kori, Kylee

Krikor *(Armenian)* ♂ RATING: ★★☆
Watchful—Variation of Gregory
People think of Krikor as weird, powerful, ethnic, sexy, aggressive
People who like the name Krikor also like Kaden, Korbin, Koen, Gabriel, Elijah, Kale, Keagan, Knox, Xander, Soren

Kris *(American)* ♀♂ RATING: ★★★★
Short for names beginning with Kris or Chris—Variation of Chris; Kris Kristofferson, singer/songwriter
People think of Kris as funny, caring, intelligent, cool, trustworthy
People who like the name Kris also like Kyle, Hayden, Ryan, Jordan, Kirsten, Jade, Kyler, Christian, James, Bailey

Krisalyn *(American)* ♀ RATING: ★★★★
Combination of Kris and Lynn
People think of Krisalyn as creative, pretty, intelligent, trustworthy, religious
People who like the name Krisalyn also like Kaelyn, Jadyn, Kaydence, Kaleigh, Kyla, Ashlyn, Cailyn, Keely, Kailey, Kiersten

Krishna *(Sanskrit/East Indian)* ♀♂ RATING: ★★★
Black
People think of Krishna as caring, cool, aggressive, intelligent, funny
People who like the name Krishna also like Keanu, Kai, Kiran, Kavi, Kalani, Kyrie, Keahi, Keeran, Hayden, Jade

Krista *(Scandinavian)* ♀ RATING: ★★★☆
Christian—Also spelled Christa or Crista
People think of Krista as pretty, funny, caring, creative, trustworthy
People who like the name Krista also like Hannah, Grace, Hailey, Emma, Faith, Isabella, Kayla, Olivia, Natalie, Kendra

Kristen *(German)* ♀♂ RATING: ★★★
Christian—Also a male name in Norway as a variation of Kristian; also spelled Krystyn; Kristen Bell, actress; Kristen Kreuk, actress
People think of Kristen as funny, pretty, caring, intelligent, creative
People who like the name Kristen also like Hailey, Hannah, Lauren, Paige, Emily, Kaitlyn, Erin, Samantha, Kayla, Natalie

Kristian *(Scandinavian)* ♀♂ RATING: ★★★
Christian
People think of Kristian as funny, intelligent, creative, caring, cool
People who like the name Kristian also like Christian, Madison, Jaden, Bailey, Caden, Jordan, Tyler, Dakota, Kyler, Hayden

Kristin *(German)* ♀ RATING: ★★★☆
Christian—Kristin Davis, actress; Kristin Scott Thomas, actress
People think of Kristin as pretty, caring, funny, intelligent, creative
People who like the name Kristin also like Lauren, Kristen, Hailey, Emily, Isabella, Hannah, Elizabeth, Grace, Natalie, Kaitlyn

Kristina *(Slavic)* ♀ RATING: ★★★★
Christian
People think of Kristina as pretty, funny, caring, intelligent, creative

People who like the name Kristina also like Isabella, Kaitlyn, Gabriella, Hailey, Elizabeth, Jessica, Lauren, Faith, Samantha, Hannah

Kristine (*Scandinavian*) ♀ RATING: ★★★
Christian
People think of Kristine as pretty, funny, caring, creative, intelligent
People who like the name Kristine also like Kristin, Hannah, Isabella, Lauren, Jacqueline, Hailey, Jessica, Kristen, Emily, Isabelle

Kristjana (*Scandinavian*) ♀ RATING: ★★★☆
Christian
People think of Kristjana as ethnic, exotic, pretty, religious, elegant
People who like the name Kristjana also like Kya, Kaelyn, Kaia, Isabella, Kyla, Keira, Kaira, Kaleigh, Kiersten, Karina

Kristopher (*American*) ♂ RATING: ★★★★
Christ bearer—Variation of Christopher
People think of Kristopher as handsome, funny, intelligent, caring, cool
People who like the name Kristopher also like Christopher, Kaden, Alexander, Jacob, Matthew, Kaleb, Ethan, Nicholas, Gabriel, Benjamin

Kristy (*English*) ♀ RATING: ★★☆
Short for names beginning with Krist; also spelled Kristi
People think of Kristy as pretty, funny, caring, trustworthy, creative
People who like the name Kristy also like Hailey, Hannah, Emily, Isabella, Emma, Faith, Gabriella, Kayla, Isabelle, Jenna

Krisztian (*Hungarian*) ♂ RATING: ★★★
Christian—Variation of Christian
People think of Krisztian as handsome, cool, intelligent, popular, funny
People who like the name Krisztian also like Kaden, Kristopher, Kaleb, Keagan, Joshua, Elijah, Gabriel, Samuel, Tristan, Liam

Krystal (*American*) ♀ RATING: ★★☆
A clear, brilliant glass—Variation of Crystal
People think of Krystal as pretty, funny, caring, creative, intelligent
People who like the name Krystal also like Hailey, Faith, Jasmine, Hannah, Amber, Kayla, Isabella, Gabrielle, Paige, Kaitlyn

Ksena (*Polish*) ♀ RATING: ★★
Guest, host—Variation of Xena
People think of Ksena as pretty, ethnic, funny, sexy, exotic
People who like the name Ksena also like Liana, Kamea, Danae, Kaiya, Keyah, Anaya, Kiersten, Kasia, Ceana, Kyla

Kuma (*Japanese*) ♀ RATING: ★★★☆
Bear
People think of Kuma as funny, intelligent, powerful, trustworthy, aggressive
People who like the name Kuma also like Kaiya, Kaiyo, Kaori, Kimi, Kuri, Kaida, Keiko, Kohana, Mai, Kura

Kumani (*African*) ♀ RATING: ★★★★
Destiny—West African origin
People think of Kumani as exotic, ethnic, creative, pretty, funny
People who like the name Kumani also like Kya, Kailani, Jahzara, Kaiya, Kaya, Kamaria, Keani, Kaia, Keaira, Keiko

Kumi (*Japanese*) ♀ ♂ RATING: ★★★★
Braid
People think of Kumi as trustworthy, caring, intelligent, elegant, energetic
People who like the name Kumi also like Kiyoshi, Kana, Kin, Seiko, Maro, Mitsu, Kozue, Maemi, Hoshi, Hiroko

Kumiko (*Japanese*) ♀ RATING: ★★★★
Braid
People think of Kumiko as pretty, exotic, cool, artsy, intelligent
People who like the name Kumiko also like Kioko, Keiko, Kaori, Emiko, Kaida, Kaiya, Kosuke, Miyoko, Sakura, Amaya

Kuniko (*Japanese*) ♀ RATING: ★★★
Child from the country
People think of Kuniko as ethnic, trendy, intelligent, weird, caring
People who like the name Kuniko also like Kaori, Kaiya, Kumiko, Kioko, Kaida, Keiko, Kyoko, Kohana, Sakura, Kuri

Kuper (*Hebrew*) ♂ RATING: ★★☆
Copper
People think of Kuper as funny, poor, slow, intelligent, nerdy
People who like the name Kuper also like Kaden, Kaleb, Korbin, Ethan, Koen, Caleb, Jackson, Kyson, Keagan, Isaac

Kura (*Japanese*) ♀ RATING: ★★★☆
Treasure house
People think of Kura as creative, exotic, young, funny, leader
People who like the name Kura also like Kuri, Keiko, Kaori, Kohana, Kaiyo, Kimi, Kaida, Kaiya, Kioko, Kagami

Kuri (*Japanese*) ♀ RATING: ★★★☆
Chestnut
People think of Kuri as pretty, exotic, quiet, intelligent, creative
People who like the name Kuri also like Keiko, Kaori, Kura, Kaida, Kimi, Kaiya, Kioko, Kohana, Kaiyo, Kyoko

Kuron (*African*) ♀ ♂ RATING: ★★☆
Thanks
People think of Kuron as trustworthy, powerful, aggressive, nerdy, caring

People who like the name Kuron also like Kione, Kiran, Kijana, Keeran, Kyrie, Kendi, Keran, Kirabo, Kieve, Keelan

Kurt *(American)* ♂   RATING: ★★★★
Courteous—Short for Curtis or Conrad; Kurt Cobain, singer/songwriter
> People think of Kurt as handsome, intelligent, funny, cool, caring
> People who like the name Kurt also like Ethan, Jacob, Isaac, Caleb, Aaron, Joshua, Luke, Matthew, Nicholas, Jack

Kusuma *(Sanskrit/East Indian)* ♀   RATING: ★★☆
Yellow bloom
> People think of Kusuma as pretty, creative, popular, funny, exotic
> People who like the name Kusuma also like Ketaki, Kimaya, Kirtana, Kerani, Kamala, Karuka, Kuri, Keiko, Jaya, Kavindra

Kuval *(Sanskrit/East Indian)* ♂   RATING: ★★☆
Water lily
> People think of Kuval as sneaky, trustworthy, religious, boy next door, ethnic
> People who like the name Kuval also like Nitesh, Kami, Amish, Nirav, Chatura, Arav, Ketan, Manas, Mannan, Dulal

Kwanita *(Native American)* ♀   RATING: ★★★
God is gracious—Variation of Juanita
> People think of Kwanita as sexy, caring, pretty, ethnic, energetic
> People who like the name Kwanita also like Kachina, Kaya, Kiona, Ayasha, Kimama, Kaliska, Kilenya, Halona, Soraya, Gianna

Kya *(American)* ♀   RATING: ★★★
Feminine form of Kai
> People think of Kya as pretty, funny, creative, caring, intelligent
> People who like the name Kya also like Kyla, Kyra, Kaya, Kaia, Kaelyn, Kaiya, Ava, Mia, Keira, Kia

Kyan *(American)* ♀♂   RATING: ★★★★☆
Ancient—Variation of Cian; also possibly a variation of Cyan or Ryan
> People think of Kyan as handsome, energetic, intelligent, creative, popular
> People who like the name Kyan also like Caden, Jaden, Hayden, Kai, Kyler, Logan, Parker, Dylan, Keegan, Ryder

Kyla *(American)* ♀   RATING: ★★★
Narrow—Feminine form of Kyle
> People think of Kyla as pretty, funny, caring, creative, intelligent
> People who like the name Kyla also like Kayla, Kaelyn, Ava, Emma, Keira, Kylee, Hailey, Isabella, Kiley, Grace

Kylar *(American)* ♀   RATING: ★★★★
Church, monk's cell—Variation of Kyler; also a combination of Kyle and Schuyler
> People think of Kylar as energetic, young, funny, intelligent, caring

People who like the name Kylar also like Kyla, Kaelyn, Kylee, Kiley, Kyleigh, Jadyn, Ashlyn, Ava, Keira, Kailey

Kyle *(Celtic/Gaelic)* ♀♂   RATING: ★★★
Narrow—Kyle MacLachlan, actor
> People think of Kyle as handsome, funny, cool, intelligent, caring
> People who like the name Kyle also like Ryan, Dylan, Tyler, Logan, Riley, Evan, Taylor, Connor, Hayden, Madison

Kylee *(English)* ♀   RATING: ★★★★☆
Boomerang—Variation of Kylie
> People think of Kylee as pretty, funny, caring, energetic, creative
> People who like the name Kylee also like Kaylee, Kailey, Kaelyn, Hailey, Kyleigh, Kiley, Kylie, Kyla, Paige, Kayla

Kyleigh *(English)* ♀   RATING: ★★★
Boomerang—Variation of Kylie
> People think of Kyleigh as pretty, funny, caring, energetic, young
> People who like the name Kyleigh also like Kaleigh, Kaelyn, Hailey, Kylee, Kailey, Hannah, Kiley, Paige, Kylie, Jadyn

Kylemore *(Celtic/Gaelic)* ♂   RATING: ★☆
Long narrows of a river, or mountains
> People think of Kylemore as weird, poor, unpopular, loser, creative
> People who like the name Kylemore also like Keiran, Keagan, Kelton, Tristan, Edan, Keenan, Sullivan, Owen, Kael, Callahan

Kylene *(American)* ♀   RATING: ★★★★☆
Narrow—Feminine form of Kyle
> People think of Kylene as pretty, caring, creative, energetic, intelligent
> People who like the name Kylene also like Kyla, Kaelyn, Kyleigh, Kiara, Kylee, Keira, Kaitlyn, Kiley, Kylar, Kyra

Kyler *(German)* ♀♂   RATING: ★★★★
Church, monk's cell—Also a surname; variation of Cillian
> People think of Kyler as handsome, funny, intelligent, popular, creative
> People who like the name Kyler also like Caden, Hayden, Jaden, Riley, Keegan, Logan, Addison, Parker, Tyler, Madison

Kylia *(American)* ♀   RATING: ★★★★
Narrow—Feminine form of Kyle
> People think of Kylia as popular, pretty, sexy, girl next door, funny
> People who like the name Kylia also like Kylie, Kyla, Kaelyn, Kailey, Kyra, Kiara, Hailey, Kayla, Kylee, Kiana

Kylie *(Aborigine)* ♀   RATING: ★★★★
Boomerang—Feminine form of Kyle; Kylie Minogue, singer
> People think of Kylie as pretty, funny, caring, energetic, creative

People who like the name Kylie also like Hailey, Emma, Paige, Chloe, Ava, Hannah, Kailey, Kayla, Kylee, Isabella

Kyna *(English)* ♀   RATING: ★★☆
Royal—Feminine form of Kyne
> People think of Kyna as intelligent, pretty, caring, popular, funny
> People who like the name Kyna also like Kyra, Kyla, Kylee, Keena, Kya, Kaia, Kyria, Kaydence, Keira, Kaelyn

Kynan *(Welsh)* ♂   RATING: ★★☆
Hound
> People think of Kynan as intelligent, handsome, energetic, caring, funny
> People who like the name Kynan also like Kaden, Keagan, Aiden, Tristan, Kael, Ethan, Keenan, Kyson, Jayden, Kaleb

Kyne *(English)* ♂   RATING: ★★★
Royal—Also a word for cattle
> People think of Kyne as handsome, sexy, creative, powerful, popular
> People who like the name Kyne also like Ethan, Kyson, Kane, Kail, Kaden, Keagan, Kael, Jayden, Kaleb, Braden

Kynthia *(Greek)* ♀   RATING: ★★★
From Kynthos—Variation of Cynthia
> People think of Kynthia as exotic, pretty, young, trustworthy, intelligent
> People who like the name Kynthia also like Kyra, Kamaria, Keaira, Kiara, Kyria, Kendra, Kaira, Kyna, Katina, Keira

Kynton *(English)* ♂   RATING: ★★☆
From the royal manor—Variation of Kinton; also a surname
> People think of Kynton as cool, sporty, winner, nerdy, caring
> People who like the name Kynton also like Kaden, Kyson, Jayden, Kenton, Keagan, Kelton, Aiden, Koen, Kyran, Tristan

Kyoko *(Japanese)* ♀   RATING: ★★
Mirror
> People think of Kyoko as pretty, creative, intelligent, exotic, elegant
> People who like the name Kyoko also like Keiko, Kioko, Kaori, Kagami, Kaiya, Kaida, Sakura, Kimi, Aiko, Kuri

Kyra *(Greek)* ♀   RATING: ★★★☆
Lady—Feminine form of Kyros; pronounced *KY-ruh* or *KEE-ruh*; also from the Irish name Ciara meaning black; Kyra Sedgwick, actress
> People think of Kyra as pretty, funny, creative, caring, intelligent
> People who like the name Kyra also like Kyla, Keira, Ava, Kaelyn, Kayla, Kira, Olivia, Kiara, Hailey, Chloe

Kyran *(American)* ♂   RATING: ★★★
From Cyrene, Libya
> People think of Kyran as handsome, sporty, intelligent, funny, leader

People who like the name Kyran also like Kaden, Keagan, Keiran, Aiden, Kyson, Kael, Ethan, Jayden, Tristan, Kaleb

Kyrene *(Greek)* ♀   RATING: ★★★☆
From Cyrene, Libya
> People think of Kyrene as pretty, caring, young, religious, energetic
> People who like the name Kyrene also like Keira, Kaelyn, Kyria, Kiara, Kyra, Kyla, Kara, Keely, Kayla, Kyleigh

Kyria *(Greek)* ♀   RATING: ★★★★
Lady
> People think of Kyria as pretty, caring, funny, creative, young
> People who like the name Kyria also like Kyra, Keira, Kyla, Kiara, Kira, Kaira, Kaelyn, Kylie, Kailey, Keaira

Kyrie *(Greek)* ♀ ♂   RATING: ★★★★☆
The Lord—Pronounced *KEE-ree-ay*
> People think of Kyrie as pretty, funny, intelligent, caring, energetic
> People who like the name Kyrie also like Caden, Jaden, Hayden, Madison, Logan, Jade, Bailey, Taylor, Riley, Brooke

Kyros *(Greek)* ♂   RATING: ★★☆
Lord—Variation of Cyrus
> People think of Kyros as intelligent, powerful, leader, energetic, creative
> People who like the name Kyros also like Kael, Kaden, Kyran, Aiden, Kairos, Kane, Kyson, Keiran, Draco, Sirius

Kyson *(English)* ♂   RATING: ★★★★
Son of Ky—Variation of the surname Kison
> People think of Kyson as cool, handsome, intelligent, young, creative
> People who like the name Kyson also like Kaden, Braden, Jayden, Keagan, Landon, Jackson, Aiden, Ethan, Tyson, Kaleb

——— 🄛 ———

La Cienega *(Spanish)* ♀   RATING: ★★★
The swamp, marshes—Also a street in Los Angeles
> People think of La Cienega as popular, stuck-up, exotic, pretty, sexy
> People who like the name La Cienega also like Anastasia, Ladonna, Lakeisha, Jasmine, Sabrina, Aaliyah, Layla, Mercedes, Labonita, Lacey

Laasya *(Sanskrit/East Indian)* ♀   RATING: ★★★☆
Dance
> People think of Laasya as pretty, exotic, sexy, creative, trendy
> People who like the name Laasya also like Layla, Belle, Lacey, Lana, Lakia, Lalasa, Laina, Leilani, Lahela, Lalita

Laban *(Hebrew)* ♂   RATING: ★☆
White
> People think of Laban as aggressive, powerful, funny, wealthy, lazy
> People who like the name Laban also like Aden, Noah, Samuel, Gabriel, Kaden, Gideon, Galen, Nathan, Jeremiah, Zachariah

Labonita *(Spanish)* ♀   RATING: ★★★
Beautiful one
> People think of Labonita as sexy, pretty, exotic, intelligent, trendy
> People who like the name Labonita also like Layla, Ladonna, Lareina, Larissa, Leala, Lalita, La Cienega, Linette, Lelia, Latanya

Lacey *(English)* ♀   RATING: ★★★
Decorated with lace—Also a surname from the ancient De Laci family, from Lassey, France
> People think of Lacey as pretty, funny, caring, creative, popular
> People who like the name Lacey also like Hailey, Paige, Faith, Hannah, Emma, Grace, Chloe, Olivia, Ava, Lainey

Lachlan *(Celtic/Gaelic)* ♂   RATING: ★★★☆
From the land of lakes
> People think of Lachlan as handsome, intelligent, popular, caring, funny
> People who like the name Lachlan also like Liam, Declan, Noah, Ethan, Tristan, Lucas, Jack, Jackson, Oliver, Aiden

Lacole *(American)* ♀   RATING: ★★★☆
Combination of La and Nicole
> People think of Lacole as pretty, cool, intelligent, funny, creative
> People who like the name Lacole also like Lainey, Layla, Larissa, Cailyn, Abrianna, Laina, Lacey, Lorelei, Jadyn, Lana

Lacy *(English)* ♀   RATING: ★★★☆
Decorated with lace
> People think of Lacy as pretty, funny, caring, creative, young
> People who like the name Lacy also like Lacey, Hannah, Hailey, Paige, Emma, Grace, Lily, Chloe, Olivia, Faith

Lada *(Slavic)* ♀   RATING: ★★
Goddess of love and fertility
> People think of Lada as powerful, creative, young, intelligent, pretty
> People who like the name Lada also like Layla, Lana, Laina, Lola, Lala, Cailyn, Lacey, Eva, Laine, Leyna

Laddie *(English)* ♂   RATING: ★★★
Attendant
> People think of Laddie as energetic, funny, young, weird, lazy
> People who like the name Laddie also like Landers, Jackson, Lance, Oliver, Owen, Asher, Liam, Lawson, Samson, Leland

Ladonna *(Spanish)* ♀   RATING: ★★
The woman
> People think of Ladonna as intelligent, creative, pretty, funny, caring
> People who like the name Ladonna also like Layla, Sabrina, Gabriella, Jasmine, Isabella, Heather, Laina, Lana, Lola, Lainey

Lael *(Hebrew)* ♀   RATING: ★★
Of God
> People think of Lael as pretty, caring, intelligent, creative, religious
> People who like the name Lael also like Liana, Layla, Leah, Samara, Lea, Abigail, Ava, Hannah, Lana, Grace

Lahela *(Hawaiian)* ♀   RATING: ★★★★☆
Ewe—Variation of Rachel
> People think of Lahela as pretty, exotic, funny, creative, caring
> People who like the name Lahela also like Layla, Leilani, Laina, Kailani, Leila, Malia, Kaelyn, Gabriella, Lana, Lola

Laik *(American)* ♂   RATING: ★★★
From near the lake—Variation of Lake
> People think of Laik as exotic, young, untrustworthy, old-fashioned, wild
> People who like the name Laik also like Ian, Asher, Lachlan, Viggo, Aimon, Kael, Aden, Egan, Ciaran, Nathan

Laina *(American)* ♀   RATING: ★★★★☆
Variation of Alaina
> People think of Laina as pretty, intelligent, creative, caring, funny
> People who like the name Laina also like Layla, Lana, Lainey, Ava, Hailey, Lacey, Alaina, Isabella, Grace, Kaelyn

Laine *(English)* ♀   RATING: ★★★★
Dweller in a lane—Originally a surname
> People think of Laine as pretty, funny, intelligent, popular, creative
> People who like the name Laine also like Paige, Ava, Olivia, Claire, Lauren, Lainey, Faith, Chloe, Grace, Hailey

Lainey *(English)* ♀   RATING: ★★★★
Servant of St. Cainneach—Also short for Elaine
> People think of Lainey as pretty, funny, intelligent, popular, girl next door
> People who like the name Lainey also like Hailey, Paige, Lacey, Ava, Olivia, Hannah, Emma, Kaelyn, Lexi, Grace

Laird *(Celtic/Gaelic)* ♂   RATING: ★★★☆
Lord
> People think of Laird as intelligent, handsome, cool, leader, powerful
> People who like the name Laird also like Liam, Owen, Tristan, Lachlan, Finn, Aiden, Baird, Landon, Declan, Ethan

Lajita *(Sanskrit/East Indian)* ♀   RATING: ★★☆
Modesty
> People think of Lajita as ethnic, sexy, exotic, elegant, wealthy

People who like the name Lajita also like Laksha, Laranya, Latika, Lahela, Laasya, Lavanya, Kalinda, Lakia, Lalasa, Avani

Lajos (*Hungarian*) ♂   RATING: ★☆
Famous warrior—Variation of Louis
People think of Lajos as boy next door, cool, handsome, sexy, caring
People who like the name Lajos also like Lamar, Laszlo, Lalo, Latif, Alijah, Lancelot, Leander, Zarek, Lucian, Landis

Lakeisha (*American*) ♀   RATING: ★★
Combination of La and Keisha
People think of Lakeisha as pretty, funny, sexy, cool, ethnic
People who like the name Lakeisha also like Latisha, Aaliyah, Latoya, Keisha, Nakeisha, Faith, Larissa, Latrisha, Kayla, Jasmine

Laken (*American*) ♀♂   RATING: ★★★★
From the lake—Also spelled Lakin
People think of Laken as funny, pretty, cool, creative, caring
People who like the name Laken also like Logan, Caden, Hayden, Landen, Jaden, Parker, Addison, Madison, Bailey, Hunter

Lakia (*Sanskrit/East Indian*) ♀   RATING: ★★★★☆
Born on Thursday
People think of Lakia as pretty, funny, young, sexy, caring
People who like the name Lakia also like Layla, Lalita, Lanica, Lana, Larissa, Lakeisha, Laksha, Kayla, Makayla, Kaya

Lakota (*Native American*) ♀♂   RATING: ★★★☆
Tribe name
People think of Lakota as energetic, pretty, funny, creative, young
People who like the name Lakota also like Dakota, Jade, Dylan, Spencer, Blake, Landen, Logan, Mason, Caden, Connor

Laksha (*Sanskrit/East Indian*) ♀   RATING: ★☆
Aim, object
People think of Laksha as pretty, wild, religious, ethnic, poor
People who like the name Laksha also like Lajita, Lakia, Latisha, Kalinda, Lavanya, Larissa, Latanya, Layla, Nisha, Laasya

Lakshmi (*Sanskrit/East Indian*) ♀   RATING: ★★☆
Prosperity
People think of Lakshmi as intelligent, pretty, religious, slow, caring
People who like the name Lakshmi also like Karma, Asha, Alka, Devaki, Laksha, Alpana, Kamala, Anjali, Kerani, Kapila

Lakyle (*American*) ♀♂   RATING: ★★★☆
Combination of La and Kyle
People think of Lakyle as ethnic, pretty, trustworthy, cool, exotic
People who like the name Lakyle also like Logan, Landen, Hayden, Aidan, Caden, Landry, Laramie, Layne, Camdyn, Lavender

Lala (*Slavic*) ♀   RATING: ★★★
Tulip
People think of Lala as pretty, funny, weird, creative, young
People who like the name Lala also like Layla, Leah, Faith, Sadie, Olivia, Lilly, Lacey, Jadyn, Lola, Ava

Lalaine (*American*) ♀   RATING: ★★★☆
Combination of La and Laine—Lalaine Vergara-Paras, actress
People think of Lalaine as creative, pretty, funny, exotic, sexy
People who like the name Lalaine also like Layla, Lacey, Lainey, Faith, Paige, Sabrina, Anastasia, Isabella, Hailey, Hannah

Lalana (*Sanskrit/East Indian*) ♀   RATING: ★★★
Playing
People think of Lalana as exotic, pretty, funny, young, energetic
People who like the name Lalana also like Layla, Larissa, Chandra, Lilianna, Lakia, Lana, Leala, Lalaine, Lalita, Kala

Lalasa (*Persian*) ♀   RATING: ★☆
Love, friendship
People think of Lalasa as sexy, pretty, funny, quiet, trustworthy
People who like the name Lalasa also like Laasya, Lalita, Lana, Lacey, Lorelei, Labonita, Lalaine, Lainey, Lavanya, Anastasia

Laleh (*Persian*) ♀   RATING: ★★★☆
Tulip
People think of Laleh as pretty, funny, creative, exotic, intelligent
People who like the name Laleh also like Layla, Serenity, Lilah, Sadie, Lilianna, Lacey, Leila, Chloe, Ava, Lainey

Lali (*Greek*) ♀   RATING: ★★★★
Well spoken—Short for Eulalia
People think of Lali as pretty, creative, caring, funny, sexy
People who like the name Lali also like Layla, Lana, Lala, Lorelei, Lacey, Lea, Lalaine, Lalita, Lainey, Lara

Lalita (*Sanskrit/East Indian*) ♀   RATING: ★★★★
Sweet, elegant
People think of Lalita as pretty, exotic, elegant, intelligent, caring
People who like the name Lalita also like Layla, Lorelei, Leilani, Larissa, Leala, Leila, Gabriella, Aurora, Lana, Lara

346

Lalo *(Spanish)* ♂ RATING: ★★
Rich guardian—Short for Eduardo
> People think of Lalo as funny, cool, caring, energetic, popular
> People who like the name Lalo also like Pablo, Ramón, Rafael, Andrés, Rojelio, Federico, Alejandro, Macario, Francisco, Ruben

Lam *(Vietnamese)* ♂ RATING: ★★★
Forest
> People think of Lam as young, funny, weird, trustworthy, caring
> People who like the name Lam also like Lamar, Lamont, Ryu, Landers, Rex, Landis, Larry, Aldon, Adair, Read

Lamar *(Spanish)* ♂ RATING: ★★★★
From the sea
> People think of Lamar as handsome, funny, cool, caring, sexy
> People who like the name Lamar also like Jamal, Lamont, Jamar, Lance, Isaac, Ethan, Xavier, Justin, Jayden, Marcus

Lamis *(Arabic)* ♀ RATING: ★★★☆
Soft
> People think of Lamis as pretty, funny, caring, quiet, popular
> People who like the name Lamis also like Lalita, Lakia, Laina, Leala, Leilani, Lael, Lilith, Lala, Lana, Linette

Lamont *(French)* ♂ RATING: ★★★☆
From the mountain
> People think of Lamont as handsome, funny, intelligent, popular, sexy
> People who like the name Lamont also like Lamar, Landon, Kaden, Jayden, Damien, Lance, Gavin, Tristan, Aden, Jason

Lamya *(Arabic)* ♀ RATING: ★☆
Dark complexion
> People think of Lamya as pretty, caring, sexy, young, intelligent
> People who like the name Lamya also like Layla, Lakia, Amaya, Adriana, Lana, Ebony, Latisha, Leila, Keaira, Lorelei

Lan *(Vietnamese)* ♀ RATING: ★★
Orchid—Also a Chinese name
> People think of Lan as funny, intelligent, young, trustworthy, elegant
> People who like the name Lan also like Leilani, Liana, Lamis, Leyna, Lilah, Lark, Lilith, Lei, Lael, Lexine

Lana *(Slavic)* ♀ RATING: ★★★★
Light—Short for Svetlana; Lana Turner, actress
> People think of Lana as pretty, intelligent, caring, funny, creative
> People who like the name Lana also like Ava, Layla, Alana, Hannah, Emma, Olivia, Paige, Hailey, Isabella, Ella

Lanai *(Hawaiian)* ♀ RATING: ★★★★☆
Terrace, veranda
> People think of Lanai as pretty, exotic, creative, intelligent, cool
> People who like the name Lanai also like Leilani, Kailani, Layla, Isabella, Lorelei, Ailani, Lana, Isabel, Olivia, Malia

Lance *(English)* ♂ RATING: ★★☆
Land—Lance Armstrong, cyclist; Lance Henriksen, actor
> People think of Lance as handsome, intelligent, funny, cool, trustworthy
> People who like the name Lance also like Landon, Ethan, Lucas, Caleb, Luke, Nathan, Ian, Gavin, Jacob, Zachary

Lancelot *(French)* ♂ RATING: ★★★☆
Land—Sir Lancelot, knight of the Round Table in Arthurian legend
> People think of Lancelot as powerful, handsome, intelligent, leader, trustworthy
> People who like the name Lancelot also like Jacob, Landon, Ethan, Gabriel, Nicholas, Benjamin, Aaron, Tristan, Luke, Jack

Landen *(English)* ♀ ♂ RATING: ★★★☆
From the long hill—Variation of Landon
> People think of Landen as handsome, intelligent, funny, popular, creative
> People who like the name Landen also like Hayden, Logan, Caden, Jaden, Madison, Parker, Addison, Riley, Bailey, Payton

Lander *(English)* ♂ RATING: ★★★☆
Of the land
> People think of Lander as caring, handsome, funny, intelligent, creative
> People who like the name Lander also like Landon, Holden, Lawson, Ethan, Kaden, Noah, Cole, Isaac, Jackson, Keagan

Landers *(English)* ♂ RATING: ★★★
Descendent of the countryside dweller
> People think of Landers as leader, intelligent, handsome, trustworthy, sporty
> People who like the name Landers also like Lawson, Landon, Lander, Jackson, Holden, Owen, Braden, Maddox, Harrison, Noah

Landis *(American)* ♂ RATING: ★★☆
Highwayman—Also a German surname
> People think of Landis as intelligent, handsome, cool, funny, aggressive
> People who like the name Landis also like Landon, Kaden, Lawson, Braden, Keagan, Aiden, Gage, Gabriel, Tristan, Liam

Landon *(English)* ♂ RATING: ★★★☆
From the long hill—Michael Landon, actor
> People think of Landon as handsome, popular, intelligent, funny, cool

People who like the name Landon also like Ethan, Aiden, Noah, Gavin, Caleb, Kaden, Tristan, Jackson, Braden, Jayden

Landry *(English)* ♀♂   RATING: ★★☆
Land ruler
> People think of Landry as leader, intelligent, popular, sporty, creative
> People who like the name Landry also like Logan, Avery, Hayden, Landen, Addison, Parker, Riley, Caden, Reagan, Reese

Lane *(English)* ♀♂   RATING: ★★★★
From the lane—Originally a surname
> People think of Lane as handsome, intelligent, funny, popular, caring
> People who like the name Lane also like Logan, Hayden, Caden, Parker, Addison, Mason, Landen, Bailey, Riley, Jaden

Lanelle *(American)* ♀   RATING: ★★☆
Combination of Lana and Elle
> People think of Lanelle as pretty, intelligent, trustworthy, sexy, caring
> People who like the name Lanelle also like Janelle, Larissa, Lacey, Leah, Lauren, Hailey, Isabella, Faith, Chloe, Lorelei

Lang *(Scandinavian)* ♀♂   RATING: ★★
Tall man
> People think of Lang as handsome, funny, energetic, powerful, caring
> People who like the name Lang also like Lane, Lavender, Logan, London, Lee, Layne, Leigh, Lindley, Lyndon, Leighton

Langer *(Scandinavian)* ♂   RATING: ★★☆
Tall man—Variation of Lang
> People think of Langer as slow, sporty, handsome, trendy, lazy
> People who like the name Langer also like Latham, Jayden, Braden, Lamont, Lance, Dane, Maddox, Latimer, Conner, Gage

Langston *(English)* ♂   RATING: ★★★☆
From the tall man's town—Langston Hughes, poet/writer
> People think of Langston as handsome, intelligent, leader, creative, powerful
> People who like the name Langston also like Landon, Gabriel, Holden, Jackson, Braden, Elijah, Ethan, Maddox, Emerson, Noah

Lani *(Hawaiian)* ♀♂   RATING: ★★★
Heaven; chief—Lani Hall, singer
> People think of Lani as pretty, intelligent, caring, funny, exotic
> People who like the name Lani also like Logan, Hayden, Jade, Bailey, Dakota, Jaden, Kai, Riley, Kalani, Madison

Lanica *(American)* ♀   RATING: ★★★
Combination of Lana and Monica
> People think of Lanica as pretty, popular, young, funny, cool
> People who like the name Lanica also like Leilani, Layla, Lana, Lakia, Lilianna, Latisha, Leanna, Leandra, Lareina, Liana

Lanie *(American)* ♀   RATING: ★★★★
Short from Lane or Elaine
> People think of Lanie as pretty, funny, popular, young, creative
> People who like the name Lanie also like Lainey, Layla, Lexi, Hailey, Lauren, Isabella, Lacey, Mia, Ella, Gracie

Lankston *(English)* ♂   RATING: ★★
From the tall man's town
> People think of Lankston as big, funny, intelligent, aggressive, leader
> People who like the name Lankston also like Landon, Lawson, Asher, Braden, Langston, Grayson, Leland, Holden, Braeden, Anson

Lanton *(English)* ♂   RATING: ★★☆
From the long town
> People think of Lanton as lazy, quiet, weird, intelligent, pretty
> People who like the name Lanton also like Landon, Grayson, Braden, Jackson, Maddox, Gage, Jayden, Drake, Darian, Lawson

Lanza *(Italian)* ♀♂   RATING: ★★☆
Lancer—Also a Spanish surname
> People think of Lanza as exotic, big, powerful, nerdy, lazy
> People who like the name Lanza also like Lani, Landen, London, Laramie, Larue, Lisle, Leal, Lave, Lavey, Lavi

Lapis *(Egyptian)* ♀   RATING: ★★★☆
Lapis lazuli, a semiprecious stone
> People think of Lapis as exotic, pretty, artsy, lazy, weird
> People who like the name Lapis also like Isis, Layla, Lotus, Fiona, Lara, Ciara, Lila, Lark, Giselle, Keira

Laqueta *(American)* ♀   RATING: ★★
Created name
> People think of Laqueta as pretty, intelligent, quiet, caring, trustworthy
> People who like the name Laqueta also like Laquinta, Latanya, Latisha, Layla, Latoya, Labonita, Lanica, Latifah, Larissa, Leandra

Laquinta *(American)* ♀   RATING: ★☆
The fifth
> People think of Laquinta as funny, pretty, cool, sexy, caring
> People who like the name Laquinta also like Laqueta, Latisha, Larissa, Latrisha, Layla, Latoya, Latifah, Latanya, Leandra, Lavinia

Lara *(Russian)* ♀ RATING: ★★★
Smile—Short for Larisa
> People think of Lara as pretty, intelligent, funny, caring, creative
> People who like the name Lara also like Lana, Grace, Lauren, Hannah, Emma, Ava, Layla, Faith, Olivia, Chloe

Laraine *(American)* ♀ RATING: ★★★★☆
From Lorraine, France—Variation of Lorraine
> People think of Laraine as pretty, cool, intelligent, creative, caring
> People who like the name Laraine also like Lauren, Larissa, Layla, Hailey, Leah, Lorelei, Lexi, Isabella, Lainey, Claire

Laramie *(French)* ♀ ♂ RATING: ★★
From the leafy grove
> People think of Laramie as pretty, intelligent, funny, young, caring
> People who like the name Laramie also like Logan, Landen, Teagan, Blaine, Caden, Parker, London, Rory, Morgan, Avery

Laranya *(American)* ♀ RATING: ★★★
Combination of Lara and Anya
> People think of Laranya as creative, artsy, pretty, exotic, cool
> People who like the name Laranya also like Leilani, Lavanya, Laura, Lauren, Lavinia, Leighanna, Larissa, Latanya, Layla, Lysandra

Lareina *(Spanish)* ♀ RATING: ★★☆
The queen
> People think of Lareina as pretty, exotic, sexy, caring, intelligent
> People who like the name Lareina also like Adriana, Layla, Gabriella, Leandra, Lilianna, Larissa, Lana, Isabel, Latanya, Laina

Larisa *(Spanish)* ♀ RATING: ★★★★
The smile
> People think of Larisa as pretty, intelligent, caring, trustworthy, funny
> People who like the name Larisa also like Larissa, Faith, Lacey, Hannah, Lauren, Layla, Marisa, Hailey, Paige, Lainey

Larissa *(Greek)* ♀ RATING: ★★★★
Cheerful
> People think of Larissa as pretty, funny, creative, caring, intelligent
> People who like the name Larissa also like Hailey, Isabella, Marissa, Hannah, Olivia, Lacey, Layla, Lauren, Carissa, Paige

Lark *(American)* ♀ RATING: ★★
Songbird—Lark Voorhies, actress
> People think of Lark as pretty, funny, creative, cool, energetic
> People who like the name Lark also like Olivia, Grace, Chloe, Faith, Lorelei, Ivy, Ava, Genevieve, Layla, Paige

Larkin *(English)* ♀ RATING: ★★★☆
From Laurentum, Italy—Also means birdlike or like a lark
> People think of Larkin as pretty, intelligent, creative, funny, caring
> People who like the name Larkin also like Ava, Olivia, Hannah, Scarlett, Lark, Grace, Paige, Abigail, Lilly, Zoey

Larry *(English)* ♂ RATING: ★★☆
From Laurentum, Italy—Also short for Lawrence; Larry David, screenwriter/actor; Larry Hagman, actor
> People think of Larry as funny, handsome, caring, cool, intelligent
> People who like the name Larry also like Justin, David, Jack, Jacob, Andrew, Luke, Anthony, Benjamin, Lawrence, Jake

Lars *(Scandinavian)* ♂ RATING: ★★
From Laurentum, Italy
> People think of Lars as intelligent, handsome, funny, cool, creative
> People who like the name Lars also like Ian, Landon, Gabriel, Luke, Ethan, Lucas, Owen, Liam, Noah, Benjamin

Larue *(French)* ♀ ♂ RATING: ★★
Dweller by the road—Also a surname
> People think of Larue as creative, pretty, trustworthy, funny, intelligent
> People who like the name Larue also like Landen, Logan, Laramie, Lane, Addison, London, Paxton, Landry, Leighton, Caden

Larya *(Slavic)* ♀ RATING: ★★★☆
Short for Larisa
> People think of Larya as pretty, exotic, funny, powerful, religious
> People who like the name Larya also like Layla, Lainey, Larissa, Laranya, Lana, Leah, Lavinia, Laurel, Lacey, Lara

Lassie *(Celtic/Gaelic)* ♀ RATING: ★★★
Young girl, maiden—Lassie, dog from TV and film
> People think of Lassie as creative, caring, intelligent, trustworthy, elegant
> People who like the name Lassie also like Lauren, Lacey, Sabrina, Laura, Lesley, Libby, Lana, Bridget, Lilly, Fiona

Laszlo *(Hungarian)* ♂ RATING: ★☆
Glory rule
> People think of Laszlo as intelligent, trustworthy, funny, powerful, creative
> People who like the name Laszlo also like Lazarus, Jack, Maddox, Gabriel, Leo, Xavier, Nathan, Caleb, Ace, Lucius

Lata *(Sanskrit/East Indian)* ♀ RATING: ★★☆
Creeping vine or branch
> People think of Lata as intelligent, funny, exotic, powerful, popular
> People who like the name Lata also like Jaya, Komali, Komala, Lalana, Lavanya, Gaura, Devi, Jyotika, Laina, Sheela

Latanya *(American)* ♀   RATING: ★★★☆
Combination of La and Tanya
   People think of Latanya as pretty, caring, intelligent, cool, funny
   People who like the name Latanya also like Latoya, Layla, Latisha, Tatiana, Larissa, Lorelei, Sabrina, Lana, Kayla, Leila

Latham *(English)* ♂   RATING: ★★★☆
Dweller at the barns—Originally a surname
   People think of Latham as creative, exotic, intelligent, weird, caring
   People who like the name Latham also like Liam, Landon, Lachlan, Aiden, Reece, Lawson, Lance, Jackson, Tristan, Chase

Lathrop *(English)* ♂   RATING: ★★☆
From the farm on clay soil—Originally a surname
   People think of Lathrop as old-fashioned, lazy, aggressive, leader, powerful
   People who like the name Lathrop also like Latimer, Lazaro, Lazar, Landers, Laszlo, Livingston, Landon, Aiden, Gilbert, Laddie

Latif *(Arabic)* ♂   RATING: ★★★
Elegant, delicate, subtle
   People think of Latif as intelligent, caring, trustworthy, handsome, funny
   People who like the name Latif also like Lamar, Malachi, Lawrence, Laban, Ethan, Liam, Gabriel, Alagan, Lance, Lawson

Latifah *(Arabic)* ♀   RATING: ★★★☆
Elegant, delicate, subtle—Queen Latifah, actress/singer
   People think of Latifah as funny, aggressive, exotic, pretty, sexy
   People who like the name Latifah also like Latisha, Layla, Latoya, Latanya, Latrisha, Aaliyah, Larissa, Leila, Linette, Hannah

Latika *(Sanskrit/East Indian)* ♀   RATING: ★★★
Creeper, vine
   People think of Latika as pretty, cool, creative, sexy, caring
   People who like the name Latika also like Laranya, Latanya, Leah, Layla, Latisha, Laura, Lavanya, Latoya, Lakeisha, Leela

Latimer *(English)* ♂   RATING: ★☆
Interpreter—Originally a surname
   People think of Latimer as loser, trustworthy, funny, creative, old-fashioned
   People who like the name Latimer also like Xavier, Maddox, Reece, Maynard, Lincoln, Justin, Lance, Nathan, Lancelot, Lawson

Latisha *(American)* ♀   RATING: ★★
Joy—Variation of Letitia
   People think of Latisha as pretty, funny, caring, cool, sexy

People who like the name Latisha also like Layla, Larissa, Lakeisha, Latoya, Faith, Lauren, Latanya, Keisha, Latrisha, Laura

Latona *(Latin)* ♀   RATING: ★★★
Goddess name—In Roman mythology, the mother of Apollo and Diana
   People think of Latona as pretty, sexy, trustworthy, funny, energetic
   People who like the name Latona also like Latoya, Latisha, Latrisha, Larissa, Layla, Lorelei, Lana, Lavinia, Lalita, Latanya

Latoya *(American)* ♀   RATING: ★★
Created name—La Toya Jackson, singer
   People think of Latoya as pretty, sexy, funny, intelligent, caring
   People who like the name Latoya also like Latanya, Latisha, Aaliyah, Faith, Jasmine, Leah, Desiree, Paige, Destiny, Hailey

Latrisha *(American)* ♀   RATING: ★★★☆
Combination of La and Tricia
   People think of Latrisha as aggressive, pretty, trustworthy, popular, intelligent
   People who like the name Latrisha also like Latisha, Latoya, Lakeisha, Layla, Latanya, Laura, Larissa, Leandra, Latona, Larisa

Laura *(Latin)* ♀   RATING: ★★★
Laurel—Laura Bush, U.S. first lady; Laura Ingalls Wilder, author; Laura Nyro, singer
   People think of Laura as pretty, funny, caring, intelligent, creative
   People who like the name Laura also like Lauren, Hannah, Emily, Grace, Emma, Sarah, Faith, Hailey, Olivia, Elizabeth

Laurel *(English)* ♀   RATING: ★★★☆
Laurel
   People think of Laurel as pretty, intelligent, creative, funny, caring
   People who like the name Laurel also like Lauren, Olivia, Faith, Hannah, Emma, Paige, Chloe, Abigail, Grace, Isabella

Laurelin *(American)* ♀   RATING: ★★★
Land of the valley of singing gold—Character in *The Lord of the Rings* by J.R.R. Tolkien
   People think of Laurelin as intelligent, old-fashioned, aggressive, weird, popular
   People who like the name Laurelin also like Lilianna, Lauren, Aaralyn, Madeline, Ella, Laurel, Keira, Amelia, Lilah, Claudia

Lauren *(American)* ♀   RATING: ★★★☆
Laurel—Lauren Hutton, model/actress
   People think of Lauren as pretty, funny, caring, intelligent, creative
   People who like the name Lauren also like Hannah, Grace, Olivia, Emma, Emily, Paige, Ava, Hailey, Isabella, Natalie

350

Laurence *(English)* ♀♂   RATING: ★★★☆
Laurel—Variation of Lawrence; also a feminine form in France; Laurence Fishburne, actor; Laurence Olivier, actor
> People think of Laurence as intelligent, handsome, funny, caring, cool
> People who like the name Laurence also like James, Logan, Hayden, Ryan, Cameron, Dylan, Jade, Christian, Jaden, Sean

Laurent *(French)* ♂   RATING: ★★★☆
Crowned with laurel
> People think of Laurent as intelligent, handsome, funny, caring, cool
> People who like the name Laurent also like Liam, Ethan, Oliver, Kaden, Gabriel, Jacques, Lucien, Justin, Landon, Alexander

Laurie *(English)* ♀♂   RATING: ★★☆
Laurel—Short for Laurence or Laura; "Annie Laurie," Irish song
> People think of Laurie as pretty, caring, funny, intelligent, creative
> People who like the name Laurie also like Madison, Hayden, Bailey, Taylor, Lindsey, Tyler, Jade, Jordan, Holly, Logan

Lavada *(American)* ♀   RATING: ★★★☆
Combination of La and Vada
> People think of Lavada as creative, wild, pretty, caring, elegant
> People who like the name Lavada also like Layla, Lavanya, Larissa, Lawanda, Latanya, Latisha, Laura, Latrisha, Latona, Lalita

Lavali *(Sanskrit/East Indian)* ♀   RATING: ★★☆
Poetic meter
> People think of Lavali as pretty, intelligent, exotic, sporty, artsy
> People who like the name Lavali also like Himani, Niyati, Denali, Kirtana, Laura, Lilianna, Lara, Faith, Maya, Laasya

Lavanya *(Sanskrit/East Indian)* ♀   RATING: ★★★★
Grace
> People think of Lavanya as pretty, creative, intelligent, popular, caring
> People who like the name Lavanya also like Laranya, Leilani, Larissa, Layla, Latika, Leah, Lakia, Lacey, Lavinia, Laksha

Lave *(French)* ♀♂   RATING: ★★
Lava
> People think of Lave as exotic, artsy, weird, energetic, old-fashioned
> People who like the name Lave also like Logan, Lane, Landry, Lavi, Lee, Jade, Landen, London, Lani, Layne

Lavender *(English)* ♀   RATING: ★★★☆
A purple flowering plant; also a light purple color
> People think of Lavender as pretty, creative, artsy, quiet, elegant

> People who like the name Lavender also like Jade, Madison, Bailey, Logan, Brooke, Dakota, Liberty, Holly, Sage, Riley

Laverick *(American)* ♀♂   RATING: ★★☆
Wildly independent—Variation of Maverick
> People think of Laverick as wild, young, lazy, funny, powerful
> People who like the name Laverick also like Maverick, Caden, Jade, Oakley, Cadence, Hayden, Brayden, Devon, Jordan, Yeardleigh

Laverne *(American)* ♀   RATING: ★★★☆
The alder tree—Feminine form of Vernon; *Laverne and Shirley*, TV show
> People think of Laverne as funny, intelligent, old-fashioned, elegant, caring
> People who like the name Laverne also like Lauren, Layla, Giselle, Latanya, Lenore, Laurel, Leandra, Laura, Laraine, Leala

Lavey *(American)* ♀♂   RATING: ★★★
Joined—Variation of Levi
> People think of Lavey as exotic, sporty, winner, funny, powerful
> People who like the name Lavey also like Landen, Lavi, Logan, Landry, Lavender, Lane, Caden, Brody, Jaden, Lindley

Lavi *(Hebrew)* ♀♂   RATING: ★★★☆
Lion
> People think of Lavi as trustworthy, energetic, creative, powerful, aggressive
> People who like the name Lavi also like Logan, Lani, Landen, Lavey, Lex, Jordan, Lave, Lee, Layne, Jaden

Lavina *(Latin)* ♀   RATING: ★★★★
Woman of Rome
> People think of Lavina as pretty, caring, intelligent, trustworthy, sexy
> People who like the name Lavina also like Lavinia, Layla, Leah, Leala, Lilianna, Lea, Lauren, Laraine, Larissa, Laina

Lavinia *(Latin)* ♀   RATING: ★★★☆
Woman of Rome—In Roman mythology, daughter of King Latinus
> People think of Lavinia as pretty, elegant, intelligent, funny, sexy
> People who like the name Lavinia also like Olivia, Layla, Larissa, Lavina, Sophia, Laurel, Isabella, Leah, Emma, Ava

Lavonne *(American)* ♀   RATING: ★★★☆
Combination of La and Yvonne—Also spelled Lavonn
> People think of Lavonne as trustworthy, pretty, intelligent, caring, funny
> People who like the name Lavonne also like Linette, Lauren, Latanya, Larissa, Layla, Lanelle, Leighanna, Lynette, Lorraine, Leanna

Lawanda *(American)* ♀   RATING: ★★★☆
Combination of La and Wanda—LaWanda Paige,
actress
- People think of Lawanda as caring, trustworthy, creative, sexy, pretty
- People who like the name Lawanda also like Larissa, Lorelei, Layla, Lauren, Latrisha, Felicity, Linette, Laurel, Latanya, Lilith

Lawrence *(English)* ♂   RATING: ★★★☆
Laurel—*Lawrence of Arabia*, film
- People think of Lawrence as handsome, intelligent, funny, trustworthy, caring
- People who like the name Lawrence also like Lucas, Gabriel, Jacob, Ethan, Nicholas, William, Matthew, Benjamin, Alexander, Landon

Lawrencia *(Latin)* ♀   RATING: ★★★
Laurel—Feminine form of Lawrence
- People think of Lawrencia as pretty, sexy, young, lazy, popular
- People who like the name Lawrencia also like Laura, Lauren, Leandra, Lanelle, Lavinia, Latisha, Laurel, Leanna, Latoya, Laquinta

Lawson *(English)* ♂   RATING: ★★☆
Son of Lawrence
- People think of Lawson as handsome, intelligent, popular, energetic, funny
- People who like the name Lawson also like Jackson, Landon, Dawson, Grayson, Holden, Kaden, Noah, Ethan, Braden, Owen

Laxmi *(Sanskrit/East Indian)* ♀   RATING: ★★☆
Wealth
- People think of Laxmi as weird, exotic, trendy, ethnic, nerdy
- People who like the name Laxmi also like Abrianna, Butterfly, Belle, Ariadne, Gaura, Saba, Adele, Anahid, Abril, Angelie

Layan *(Arabic)* ♀   RATING: ★★★
Soft, gentle
- People think of Layan as pretty, quiet, elegant, caring, intelligent
- People who like the name Layan also like Layla, Amaya, Kyra, Kara, Ciara, Nadia, Liana, Lilianna, Trinity, Leila

Layla *(Arabic)* ♀   RATING: ★★★
Night, black
- People think of Layla as pretty, creative, intelligent, exotic, funny
- People who like the name Layla also like Ava, Ella, Olivia, Isabella, Emma, Grace, Chloe, Paige, Hannah, Lila

Layne *(English)* ♀♂   RATING: ★★★
Dweller by the road
- People think of Layne as funny, creative, intelligent, energetic, caring
- People who like the name Layne also like Logan, Hayden, Landen, Caden, Parker, Lane, Riley, Reese, Jaden, Avery

Layton *(English)* ♂   RATING: ★★★☆
From the town by the canal
- People think of Layton as handsome, intelligent, funny, cool, popular
- People who like the name Layton also like Landon, Kaden, Ethan, Jacob, Aiden, Gavin, Jayden, Holden, Keagan, Tristan

Lazar *(Hungarian)* ♂   RATING: ★★★
God has helped—Variation of Lazarus
- People think of Lazar as weird, popular, energetic, sexy, aggressive
- People who like the name Lazar also like Landon, Jayden, Lamar, Nathan, Liam, Jeremy, Maddox, Kaden, Ethan, Nathaniel

Lazaro *(Spanish)* ♂   RATING: ★★★☆
God has helped
- People think of Lazaro as handsome, funny, intelligent, trustworthy, caring
- People who like the name Lazaro also like Giovanni, Gabriel, Laszlo, Rafael, Antonio, Lucas, Joaquin, Diego, Julio, Nicholas

Lazarus *(Hebrew)* ♂   RATING: ★★★★
God has helped
- People think of Lazarus as powerful, intelligent, handsome, caring, leader
- People who like the name Lazarus also like Gabriel, Elijah, Malachi, Jeremiah, Isaac, Isaiah, Ethan, Josiah, Micah, Ishmael

Le *(Chinese)* ♀♂   RATING: ★★★☆
Joy
- People think of Le as funny, cool, creative, exotic, quiet
- People who like the name Le also like Lee, Logan, Li, Lani, Landen, Landry, Lindsey, London, Lex, Luca

Lea *(Hebrew)* ♀   RATING: ★★★★
Weary—Lea Thompson, actress
- People think of Lea as pretty, funny, intelligent, creative, caring
- People who like the name Lea also like Leah, Mia, Hannah, Paige, Layla, Isabella, Olivia, Ava, Emma, Lauren

Leah *(Hebrew)* ♀   RATING: ★★★
Weary—Leah Remini, actress
- People think of Leah as pretty, funny, caring, intelligent, creative
- People who like the name Leah also like Hannah, Emma, Paige, Olivia, Ava, Grace, Hailey, Chloe, Lauren, Isabella

Leal *(French)* ♀♂   RATING: ★★★☆
Faithful
- People think of Leal as intelligent, creative, caring, pretty, trustworthy
- People who like the name Leal also like London, Landen, Lani, Lolovivi, Lane, Lex, Loyal, Lee, Lynne, Leigh

Leala (*English*) ♀ RATING: ★★★★☆
Faithful
> People think of Leala as pretty, intelligent, funny, popular, caring
> People who like the name Leala also like Layla, Ava, Leila, Lila, Lana, Leah, Leela, Lexi, Liana, Emma

Leander (*Greek*) ♂ RATING: ★★
Lion man
> People think of Leander as intelligent, powerful, handsome, leader, energetic
> People who like the name Leander also like Liam, Lysander, Gabriel, Alexander, Xander, Kaden, Lucas, Aiden, Asher, Lucian

Leandra (*Italian*) ♀ RATING: ★★★☆
Lion man
> People think of Leandra as pretty, intelligent, caring, funny, creative
> People who like the name Leandra also like Layla, Isabella, Lilianna, Lysandra, Olivia, Lana, Gabriella, Kaelyn, Lauren, Larissa

Leane (*American*) ♀ RATING: ★★☆
Combination of Lee and Ann
> People think of Leane as pretty, sexy, intelligent, girl next door, funny
> People who like the name Leane also like Lana, Kaelyn, Layla, Lauren, Kyla, Liana, Leann, Grace, Leanna, Keira

Leann (*English*) ♀ RATING: ★★★☆
Combination of Lee and Ann—Also spelled Leanne or LeAnn; LeAnn Rimes, singer
> People think of Leann as pretty, funny, caring, intelligent, creative
> People who like the name Leann also like Hailey, Lauren, Faith, Leah, Leanna, Emily, Hannah, Emma, Paige, Nicole

Leanna (*English*) ♀ RATING: ★★★☆
Combination of Lee and Anna
> People think of Leanna as pretty, funny, creative, caring, intelligent
> People who like the name Leanna also like Isabella, Hannah, Hailey, Lauren, Leah, Emma, Layla, Arianna, Faith, Lana

Leatrix (*American*) ♀ RATING: ★☆
Combination of Leah and Beatrix
> People think of Leatrix as weird, aggressive, criminal, artsy, nerdy
> People who like the name Leatrix also like Lark, Lanelle, Larissa, Livvy, Lexi, Lillian, Layla, Lysandra, Lidia, Lilah

Leavitt (*English*) ♂ RATING: ★☆
Wolf cub—Originally a surname
> People think of Leavitt as handsome, wild, energetic, young, old
> People who like the name Leavitt also like Jackson, Landon, Lucian, Holden, Brighton, Aiden, Leland, Grady, Lawson, Jagger

Lecea (*American*) ♀ RATING: ★★★☆
Of a noble kind—Short for Alicia
> People think of Lecea as trendy, artsy, lazy, powerful, leader
> People who like the name Lecea also like Layla, Liana, Lana, Leala, Lesa, Leyna, Lael, Leane, Lelia, Lysa

Leda (*Greek*) ♀ RATING: ★★
Lady—In Greek mythology, the mother of Helen of Troy and Clytemnestra
> People think of Leda as pretty, exotic, intelligent, funny, caring
> People who like the name Leda also like Layla, Lara, Eva, Maia, Larissa, Lark, Lilith, Lorelei, Chloe, Lida

Ledell (*English*) ♀ RATING: ★★
From the loud spring—Originally a surname
> People think of Ledell as ethnic, intelligent, caring, leader, trustworthy
> People who like the name Ledell also like Layla, Leane, Lorelei, Lexi, Lareina, Leandra, Lenore, Latanya, Lilly, Laraine

Lee (*English*) ♀ ♂ RATING: ★★☆
Field—Also short for names beginning with Lee; Lee Majors, actor; Lee Marvin, actor; Lee Meriwether, actress; Tommy Lee, musician
> People think of Lee as funny, caring, intelligent, cool, trustworthy
> People who like the name Lee also like Logan, Leigh, Taylor, Riley, James, Ryan, Jordan, Dylan, Bailey, Hayden

Leela (*Sanskrit/East Indian*) ♀ RATING: ★★★★
Sport, play
> People think of Leela as pretty, creative, funny, caring, energetic
> People who like the name Leela also like Layla, Leila, Leala, Lila, Leena, Lana, Leah, Lilah, Mia, Chloe

Leena (*Arabic*) ♀ RATING: ★★☆
Tenderness—Also a variation of Helena
> People think of Leena as pretty, intelligent, caring, trustworthy, creative
> People who like the name Leena also like Lena, Layla, Lana, Lorelei, Leah, Leela, Grace, Lacey, Emma, Olivia

Leeto (*Greek*) ♀ RATING: ★★☆
Hidden—Variation of Leto
> People think of Leeto as weird, artsy, handsome, loser, poor
> People who like the name Leeto also like Anaya, Iris, Luna, Simone, Cailyn, Alake, Giselle, Daisy, Emma, Francesca

Lefty (*American*) ♂ RATING: ★★★
Usually a nickname for people who are left-handed
> People think of Lefty as nerdy, weird, poor, sneaky, loser
> People who like the name Lefty also like Langston, Wade, Laszlo, Kermit, Bob, Lance, Levi, Laird, Landon, Luke

Legrand *(French)* ♂   RATING: ★★☆
The tall or large one
> People think of Legrand as handsome, leader, quiet, intelligent, cool
> People who like the name Legrand also like Burke, Padgett, Brigham, Sinclair, Percy, Dax, Kaden, Davis, Constantine, Chauncey

Lehana *(African)* ♂   RATING: ★★☆
One who refuses—Lesotho origin
> People think of Lehana as pretty, energetic, popular, creative, exotic
> People who like the name Lehana also like Gabriel, Elijah, Jayden, Isaac, Liam, Ethan, Isaiah, Cole, Lachlan, Kaden

Lei *(Chinese)* ♀   RATING: ★★☆
Flower bud
> People think of Lei as pretty, creative, elegant, intelligent, caring
> People who like the name Lei also like Leah, Lana, Leila, Leilani, Lexi, Chloe, Mia, Faith, Layla, Laurel

Leia *(Hebrew)* ♀   RATING: ★★★☆
Weary—Princess Leia, character in *Star Wars*
> People think of Leia as pretty, caring, intelligent, creative, young
> People who like the name Leia also like Leah, Layla, Hannah, Leila, Olivia, Ava, Ella, Keira, Lana, Lara

Leif *(Scandinavian)* ♂   RATING: ★★
Heir—Leif Garrett, actor/singer
> People think of Leif as handsome, intelligent, creative, cool, caring
> People who like the name Leif also like Liam, Noah, Landon, Owen, Tristan, Finn, Jacob, Seth, Lucas, Aiden

Leigh *(English)* ♀♂   RATING: ★★★☆
Field—Janet Leigh, actress; Vivien Leigh, actress
> People think of Leigh as pretty, funny, intelligent, caring, creative
> People who like the name Leigh also like Madison, Hayden, Brooke, Bailey, Morgan, Taylor, Logan, Riley, Mackenzie, Dylan

Leigha *(American)* ♀   RATING: ★★★☆
Variation of Leigh or Leah
> People think of Leigha as pretty, caring, funny, creative, cool
> People who like the name Leigha also like Hannah, Emma, Leah, Grace, Hailey, Ella, Lexi, Paige, Ava, Layla

Leighanna *(English)* ♀   RATING: ★★☆
Combination of Leigh and Anna
> People think of Leighanna as pretty, young, girl next door, caring, funny
> People who like the name Leighanna also like Lilianna, Isabella, Hannah, Layla, Grace, Hailey, Gabriella, Faith, Kaleigh, Chloe

Leighna *(American)* ♀   RATING: ★★★★
Variation of Lena
> People think of Leighna as pretty, sexy, leader, exotic, caring
> People who like the name Leighna also like Leighanna, Lexi, Isabella, Layla, Lauren, Isabelle, Ava, Bella, Lena, Laina

Leighton *(English)* ♀♂   RATING: ★★★
From the town by the meadow
> People think of Leighton as handsome, intelligent, funny, caring, popular
> People who like the name Leighton also like Logan, Hayden, Addison, Landen, Caden, Riley, Madison, Parker, Payton, Avery

Leiko *(Hawaiian)* ♀   RATING: ★★★★
Little flower
> People think of Leiko as pretty, exotic, intelligent, creative, young
> People who like the name Leiko also like Leilani, Layla, Leila, Aiko, Li Mei, Mahina, Lorelei, Keiki, Lahela, Keiko

Leila *(Arabic)* ♀   RATING: ★★★
Night, black—Also spelled Laila or Lyla
> People think of Leila as pretty, intelligent, creative, funny, exotic
> People who like the name Leila also like Layla, Ava, Olivia, Grace, Isabella, Emma, Ella, Chloe, Eva, Mia

Leilani *(Hawaiian)* ♀   RATING: ★★★☆
Heavenly flower
> People think of Leilani as pretty, exotic, creative, caring, intelligent
> People who like the name Leilani also like Kailani, Lorelei, Ailani, Layla, Isabella, Leila, Ava, Chloe, Olivia, Emma

Lel *(Slavic)* ♂   RATING: ★★☆
Taker
> People think of Lel as lazy, funny, leader, elegant, creative
> People who like the name Lel also like Burian, Adli, Adit, Adlai, Barke, Latham, Lerato, Alfred, Luce, Willem

Lela *(Spanish)* ♀   RATING: ★★★
Lofty
> People think of Lela as pretty, creative, caring, funny, intelligent
> People who like the name Lela also like Layla, Lola, Ella, Leila, Ava, Eva, Grace, Leala, Chloe, Bella

Leland *(English)* ♂   RATING: ★★★★
Meadowland—Leland Hayward, playwright
> People think of Leland as handsome, sexy, intelligent, trustworthy, funny
> People who like the name Leland also like Landon, Liam, Aiden, Noah, Elijah, Owen, Ian, Tristan, Kaden, Caleb

L

Lelia *(Latin)* ♀   RATING: ★★★
Unknown meaning—Variation of Laelia
> People think of Lelia as pretty, intelligent, creative, trustworthy, caring
> People who like the name Lelia also like Layla, Lily, Lilly, Bella, Leila, Lilia, Isabella, Ava, Lilianna, Lilah

Lemuel *(Hebrew)* ♂   RATING: ★☆
Devoted to God
> People think of Lemuel as leader, intelligent, handsome, caring, religious
> People who like the name Lemuel also like Gabriel, Jeremiah, Aaron, Nathaniel, Elijah, Jayden, Isaac, Isaiah, Joel, Samuel

Len *(American)* ♀♂   RATING: ★★★☆
Short for Leonard or Helena
> People think of Len as handsome, intelligent, nerdy, cool, creative
> People who like the name Len also like Lee, Jade, Avery, Cameron, Raven, Nolan, Hunter, Leslie, Logan, Blaze

Lena *(Hebrew)* ♀   RATING: ★★☆
Woman of Magdala—Short for Magdalena; Lena Zavaroni, singer
> People think of Lena as pretty, intelligent, caring, creative, funny
> People who like the name Lena also like Ava, Ella, Lana, Emma, Olivia, Isabella, Grace, Eva, Leah, Chloe

Lencho *(African)* ♂   RATING: ★★
Lion
> People think of Lencho as poor, sneaky, creative, criminal, cool
> People who like the name Lencho also like Liam, Leander, Lemuel, Leo, Robert, Sterling, Aaron, Lewis, William, Lionel

Lenci *(Hungarian)* ♀   RATING: ★★☆
Light—Short for Elena
> People think of Lenci as old-fashioned, creative, popular, funny, ethnic
> People who like the name Lenci also like Lena, Lara, Lorelei, Lily, Leyna, Lila, Leilani, Lottie, Lycoris, Lilly

Lenka *(Slavic)* ♀   RATING: ★★
Light—Short for Elena
> People think of Lenka as intelligent, pretty, sexy, funny, elegant
> People who like the name Lenka also like Layla, Lilia, Lara, Lena, Bianca, Sora, Leena, Lexi, Lilith, Leyna

Lennon *(Celtic/Gaelic)* ♀♂   RATING: ★★★★☆
Dear one—John Lennon, singer/songwriter
> People think of Lennon as creative, intelligent, artsy, handsome, cool
> People who like the name Lennon also like Logan, Hayden, Aidan, London, Parker, Avery, Dylan, Riley, Caden, Jude

Lenora *(Spanish)* ♀   RATING: ★★
Light—Variation of Eleanor
> People think of Lenora as pretty, intelligent, caring, funny, creative
> People who like the name Lenora also like Lenore, Layla, Bella, Isabella, Victoria, Faith, Bianca, Fiona, Lorelei, Genevieve

Lenore *(French)* ♀   RATING: ★★★★
Light—Variation of Eleanor
> People think of Lenore as pretty, elegant, intelligent, creative, artsy
> People who like the name Lenore also like Eleanor, Lorelei, Lenora, Claire, Olivia, Genevieve, Phoebe, Chloe, Charlotte, Faith

Leo *(Italian)* ♂   RATING: ★★☆
Lion—Used for children born under this astrological sign
> People think of Leo as handsome, intelligent, cool, caring, funny
> People who like the name Leo also like Noah, Oliver, Jack, Liam, Luke, Lucas, Ethan, Owen, Jacob, Isaac

Leola *(American)* ♀   RATING: ★★
Lioness—Feminine form of Leo
> People think of Leola as pretty, intelligent, caring, creative, funny
> People who like the name Leola also like Liona, Layla, Isabella, Leona, Sienna, Leila, Angelina, Lina, Gianna, Lucia

Leoma *(American)* ♀   RATING: ★★★
Lion—Feminine form of Leo
> People think of Leoma as creative, pretty, ethnic, powerful, leader
> People who like the name Leoma also like Leyna, Leola, Leala, Lelia, Lorelei, Layla, Lareina, Lilac, Linette, Linnea

Leon *(French)* ♂   RATING: ★★
Lion
> People think of Leon as handsome, intelligent, funny, cool, caring
> People who like the name Leon also like Leo, Lucas, Ethan, Liam, Jack, Aiden, Isaac, Joshua, Jacob, Aaron

Leona *(Italian)* ♀   RATING: ★★★☆
Lion—Feminine form of Leon; also a Hebrew name, Leeona, meaning my strength
> People think of Leona as pretty, intelligent, funny, caring, creative
> People who like the name Leona also like Fiona, Layla, Isabelle, Liona, Olivia, Lily, Lana, Ava, Isabella, Lenora

Leonard *(English)* ♂   RATING: ★★
Lion brave—Leonard Bernstein, composer/conductor; Leonard Maltin, movie reviewer; Leonard Nimoy, actor/author/poet
> People think of Leonard as intelligent, handsome, funny, caring, cool
> People who like the name Leonard also like Alexander, Justin, Charles, Leo, Benjamin, Ethan, Edward, Lucas, Gabriel, Jack

Leonardo *(Italian)* ♂   RATING: ★★★☆
Lion brave—Leonardo da Vinci, artist; Leonardo DiCaprio, actor
> People think of Leonardo as handsome, intelligent, cool, sexy, funny
> People who like the name Leonardo also like Leo, Alexander, Gabriel, Lucas, Sebastian, Ethan, Benjamin, Nicholas, Michael, Matthew

Leone *(Italian)* ♂   RATING: ★★★★
Lion—Also Sierra Leone; Tea Leone, actress
> People think of Leone as leader, trustworthy, sexy, funny, pretty
> People who like the name Leone also like Leo, Leonardo, Ethan, Leon, Jacob, Nathan, Lucas, Justin, Liam, Fabian

Leonie *(French)* ♀   RATING: ★★★★
Lioness
> People think of Leonie as pretty, creative, funny, intelligent, caring
> People who like the name Leonie also like Olivia, Leah, Mia, Leona, Layla, Ava, Lana, Naomi, Ella, Phoebe

Leonor *(Spanish)* ♀   RATING: ★★★
Light—Variation of Eleanor
> People think of Leonor as intelligent, creative, pretty, caring, elegant
> People who like the name Leonor also like Hailey, Clara, Lily, Zoe, Cynthia, Gabriella, Simone, Elena, Violet, Iris

Leonora *(Italian)* ♀   RATING: ★★
Light—Variation of Eleanor
> People think of Leonora as pretty, intelligent, elegant, caring, sexy
> People who like the name Leonora also like Lenora, Lilianna, Ophelia, Helena, Leona, Iris, Lana, Lorelei, Amelia, Aurora

Leontyne *(American)* ♀   RATING: ★★★
Lion—Leontyne Price, opera singer
> People think of Leontyne as nerdy, unpopular, loser, criminal, weird
> People who like the name Leontyne also like Leona, Leonie, Lisette, Leola, Libby, Lorraine, Lavinia, Lauren, Leighanna, Leala

Leopold *(English)* ♂   RATING: ★★★☆
People bold
> People think of Leopold as intelligent, handsome, powerful, leader, wealthy
> People who like the name Leopold also like Gabriel, Liam, Leo, Oliver, Jack, Ethan, Benjamin, Nicholas, Sebastian, Caleb

Leora *(Hebrew)* ♀   RATING: ★★☆
Light
> People think of Leora as pretty, elegant, creative, intelligent, energetic
> People who like the name Leora also like Layla, Liana, Liora, Lana, Aurora, Lila, Grace, Leyna, Leona, Lily

Lequoia *(American)* ♀   RATING: ★★★
The sequoia tree—Also a combination of Le and Sequoia
> People think of Lequoia as pretty, exotic, ethnic, aggressive, leader
> People who like the name Lequoia also like Kaya, Kiona, Leilani, Jazlynn, Aleshanee, Sokanon, Larissa, Leona, Layla, Alora

Lerato *(African)* ♂   RATING: ★★★☆
Song of my soul
> People think of Lerato as sexy, creative, caring, intelligent, pretty
> People who like the name Lerato also like Lucian, Leander, Liam, Lysander, Ryu, Drake, Jaser, Korbin, Leo, Dmitri

Leroy *(American)* ♂   RATING: ★★★☆
King
> People think of Leroy as intelligent, handsome, cool, funny, caring
> People who like the name Leroy also like Leo, Aaron, Jack, Lance, Caleb, Oliver, Ethan, Leon, Kaden, Jacob

Les *(English)* ♀♂   RATING: ★★
Short for Lester or Lesley
> People think of Les as handsome, quiet, funny, intelligent, energetic
> People who like the name Les also like Hayden, Riley, Parker, Jesse, Camden, Wesley, Caden, Jaden, Cade, Lex

Lesa *(American)* ♀   RATING: ★★★★
Variation of Lisa
> People think of Lesa as trustworthy, caring, funny, pretty, creative
> People who like the name Lesa also like Liana, Layla, Lana, Leyna, Lexi, Lara, Larissa, Sabrina, Lisa, Lisette

Lesley *(English)* ♀   RATING: ★★☆
Joy—From Lece, a medieval form of Letitia; also a place in Scotland; Lesley-Anne Down, actress; Lesley Ann Warren, actress
> People think of Lesley as pretty, funny, intelligent, caring, trustworthy
> People who like the name Lesley also like Lauren, Hailey, Natalie, Hannah, Faith, Emma, Lacey, Emily, Grace, Samantha

Leslie *(English)* ♀♂   RATING: ★★★☆
Joy—From Lece, a medieval form of Letitia; also a place in Scotland; Leslie Caron, actress; Leslie Howard, actor; Leslie Nielsen, actor
> People think of Leslie as funny, pretty, intelligent, caring, creative
> People who like the name Leslie also like Madison, Taylor, Logan, Hayden, Mackenzie, Riley, Brooke, Bailey, Jordan, Cameron

Lester *(English)* ♂   RATING: ★★★
From Leicester, England
> People think of Lester as handsome, caring, intelligent, cool, trustworthy

People who like the name Lester also like Justin, Jackson, Lucas, Joshua, Landon, Jacob, Benjamin, Gabriel, Isaac, Bradley

Lethia *(Greek)* ♀   RATING: ★★★
Forgetfulness—From the River Lethe
People think of Lethia as creative, funny, caring, sexy, weird
People who like the name Lethia also like Lenore, Leola, Linore, Larissa, Lorelei, Chloe, Phoebe, Laurel, Lavinia, Lily

Leticia *(Spanish)* ♀   RATING: ★★
Joy
People think of Leticia as pretty, funny, caring, intelligent, creative
People who like the name Leticia also like Adriana, Layla, Daniela, Isabella, Jacqueline, Jasmine, Larissa, Latisha, Marissa, Isabel

Letitia *(Latin)* ♀   RATING: ★★★☆
Joy
People think of Letitia as pretty, caring, intelligent, trustworthy, funny
People who like the name Letitia also like Layla, Olivia, Laura, Leah, Lara, Amelia, Liana, Lana, Larissa, Chelsea

Lev *(Hebrew)* ♂   RATING: ★★★☆
Heart
People think of Lev as intelligent, leader, creative, caring, artsy
People who like the name Lev also like Ethan, Gabriel, Isaac, Levi, Noah, Aden, David, Micah, Joshua, Aiden

Levana *(Hebrew)* ♀   RATING: ★★★☆
Moon; white
People think of Levana as pretty, intelligent, elegant, creative, sexy
People who like the name Levana also like Layla, Samara, Liana, Leilani, Leah, Leanna, Livana, Leyna, Lana, Lavinia

Levenia *(Latin)* ♀   RATING: ★★★
Variation of Lavinia
People think of Levenia as sexy, pretty, creative, popular, funny
People who like the name Levenia also like Levana, Leanna, Liana, Lavinia, Linette, Mariah, Lilianna, Serenity, Lavina, Letitia

Leverett *(French)* ♂   RATING: ★★★
Young hare
People think of Leverett as creative, caring, cool, intelligent, big
People who like the name Leverett also like Landon, Holden, Drake, Lucas, Everett, Lucius, Liam, Lawson, Blade, Baxter

Levi *(Hebrew)* ♂   RATING: ★★★★☆
Joined
People think of Levi as handsome, funny, intelligent, cool, caring

People who like the name Levi also like Noah, Ethan, Caleb, Elijah, Isaac, Owen, Jacob, Landon, Aiden, Seth

Levia *(Hebrew)* ♀   RATING: ★★★☆
Joined—Feminine form of Levi
People think of Levia as elegant, weird, pretty, caring, wild
People who like the name Levia also like Liana, Lauren, Leila, Lilly, Lilianna, Lacey, Leah, Natalie, Samara, Leala

Leviticus *(Latin)* ♂   RATING: ★★☆
Referring to the descendants of Levi—Also a book of the Bible
People think of Leviticus as powerful, handsome, leader, aggressive, cool
People who like the name Leviticus also like Levi, Matthew, Maddox, Isaac, Sebastian, Gabriel, Malachi, Ethan, Felix, Tristan

Levy *(Hebrew)* ♂   RATING: ★★★☆
Joined
People think of Levy as caring, handsome, creative, popular, trustworthy
People who like the name Levy also like Levi, Gabriel, Elijah, Zachary, Isaiah, Ethan, Landon, Jacob, Caleb, Isaac

Lew *(English)* ♂   RATING: ★★★
Famed warrior—Short for Lewis
People think of Lew as wild, sporty, sneaky, sexy, powerful
People who like the name Lew also like Aiden, Leander, Isaac, Reece, Lucas, Luke, Levi, Lucian, Rhett, Lewis

Lewa *(African)* ♀   RATING: ★★
Beautiful—Place in Kenya
People think of Lewa as weird, exotic, ethnic, girl next door, sexy
People who like the name Lewa also like Linette, Lily, Layla, Lucinda, Latifah, Maisha, Lara, Leala, Hannah, Iris

Lewis *(English)* ♂   RATING: ★★☆
Famed warrior—Jerry Lewis, actor/comedian; Juliette Lewis, actress
People think of Lewis as handsome, funny, caring, intelligent, cool
People who like the name Lewis also like Ethan, Jack, Jacob, Oliver, Luke, Liam, Nathan, Isaac, Aaron, Lucas

Lex *(English)* ♀♂   RATING: ★★☆
Short for Alexander or Alexis; Lex Barker, actor; Lex Luthor, comic character in Superman series
People think of Lex as cool, handsome, powerful, leader, intelligent
People who like the name Lex also like Logan, Landen, Jaden, Hayden, Riley, Parker, Madison, Dakota, Caden, Jade

Lexi *(Greek)* ♀   RATING: ★★★☆
Short for Alexander or Alexis; also spelled Lexie
People think of Lexi as pretty, popular, funny, sexy, cool
People who like the name Lexi also like Paige, Hailey, Ava, Emma, Lacey, Faith, Chloe, Alexa, Isabella, Hannah

Lexine *(English)* ♀ RATING: ★★
Defender of men—Short for Alexis and Alexandra
People think of Lexine as intelligent, pretty, funny, creative, caring
People who like the name Lexine also like Lexi, Layla, Lara, Leyna, Paige, Leilani, Lana, Lauren, Laraine, Lysandra

Lexis *(American)* ♀ ♂ RATING: ★★★
Defender of men—Short for Alexis
People think of Lexis as handsome, wild, boy next door, winner, old
People who like the name Lexis also like Reagan, Logan, Kyle, Alexis, Brooklyn, Riley, Avery, Ainsley, Sean, Danny

Leyna *(American)* ♀ RATING: ★★★★☆
Light—Short for Elena
People think of Leyna as pretty, caring, creative, intelligent, energetic
People who like the name Leyna also like Layla, Lexi, Lana, Liana, Ava, Lainey, Leilani, Lena, Nadia, Laina

Lezane *(American)* ♂ RATING: ★★☆
Combination of Le and Zane
People think of Lezane as intelligent, weird, leader, pretty, cool
People who like the name Lezane also like Landon, Lorenzo, Jevonte, Lawrence, Dayshaun, Deshawn, Lincoln, Lowell, Lucas, Malachi

Li *(Chinese)* ♀ ♂ RATING: ★★★★
Pretty; powerful—As a female name, means pretty; for a male, powerful
People think of Li as pretty, intelligent, caring, powerful, young
People who like the name Li also like Liberty, Love, Le, Lynn, London, Lee, Lynne, Raine, Lane, Lolovivi

Li Hua *(Chinese)* ♀ RATING: ★★★
Pear blossom—Can also mean pretty and talented
People think of Li Hua as pretty, ethnic, exotic, weird, quiet
People who like the name Li Hua also like Li Mei, Li Ming, Larissa, Ling, Lian, Laquinta, Lark, Leyna, Layla, Laranya

Li Mei *(Chinese)* ♀ RATING: ★★★★☆
Pretty rose
People think of Li Mei as pretty, exotic, intelligent, caring, artsy
People who like the name Li Mei also like Li Ming, Jia Li, Lian, Leilani, Lorelei, Faith, Lily, Lana, Lara, Sakura

Li Ming *(Chinese)* ♀ RATING: ★★★☆
Pretty; bright
People think of Li Ming as pretty, intelligent, lazy, stuck-up, sneaky
People who like the name Li Ming also like Li Mei, Jia Li, Li Hua, Ling, Lian, Aiko, Lavinia, Leilani, Lila, Bianca

Lia *(Italian)* ♀ RATING: ★★★
Weary
People think of Lia as pretty, funny, intelligent, caring, creative
People who like the name Lia also like Ava, Mia, Layla, Leah, Eva, Ella, Olivia, Lana, Liana, Lexi

Liam *(Celtic/Gaelic)* ♂ RATING: ★★☆
Strong-willed warrior—Variation of William; Liam Neeson, actor
People think of Liam as handsome, intelligent, funny, caring, cool
People who like the name Liam also like Ethan, Aiden, Noah, Owen, Tristan, Ian, Caleb, Lucas, Landon, Gavin

Lian *(Chinese)* ♀ RATING: ★★★★☆
Lotus
People think of Lian as pretty, intelligent, caring, creative, funny
People who like the name Lian also like Liana, Lia, Layla, Lina, Iris, Li Mei, Lily, Leila, Sakura, Emma

Liana *(Hebrew)* ♀ RATING: ★★★
My God has answered—Short for Eliana
People think of Liana as pretty, creative, funny, intelligent, caring
People who like the name Liana also like Layla, Hannah, Lana, Jadyn, Ava, Grace, Isabella, Gianna, Alana, Abigail

Liang *(Chinese)* ♂ RATING: ★★★
Good, fine
People think of Liang as young, pretty, winner, cool, trustworthy
People who like the name Liang also like Aden, Leander, Llewellyn, Nathan, Ryu, Draco, Lamont, Makoto, Jasper, Lachlan

Libba *(American)* ♀ RATING: ★★★
God is my oath—Short for Elizabeth
People think of Libba as pretty, popular, artsy, girl next door, young
People who like the name Libba also like Libby, Lana, Larissa, Linette, Leanna, Laurel, Lillian, Lark, Lorelei, Lisette

Libby *(English)* ♀ RATING: ★★★★
God is my oath—Short for Elizabeth; Libby Holman, singer
People think of Libby as pretty, funny, creative, caring, intelligent
People who like the name Libby also like Emma, Olivia, Paige, Hannah, Chloe, Grace, Abigail, Lilly, Faith, Ella

Liberty *(American)* ♀ ♂ RATING: ★★★☆
Freedom—Statue of Liberty
People think of Liberty as pretty, creative, funny, caring, energetic
People who like the name Liberty also like Dakota, Madison, Bailey, Jade, Logan, Hayden, Mackenzie, Jaden, Justice, Riley

358

Libra (Latin) ♀ RATING: ★★★★
The scales, equality—Used for children born under this astrological sign
People think of Libra as sexy, powerful, creative, exotic, cool
People who like the name Libra also like Lira, Lexi, Luna, Lilianna, Lily, Lilly, Libby, Leah, Kendra, Bianca

Licia (Spanish) ♀ RATING: ★★★★
Happy—Short for Felicia
People think of Licia as pretty, trustworthy, caring, intelligent, creative
People who like the name Licia also like Liana, Laura, Lilianna, Larissa, Lana, Lacey, Layla, Lexi, Libby, Leah

Lida (Russian) ♀ RATING: ★★★★
People's favor—Short for Ludmila
People think of Lida as pretty, caring, intelligent, creative, funny
People who like the name Lida also like Layla, Lilith, Liana, Lina, Laurel, Lita, Leyna, Lilianna, Lola, Hannah

Lidia (Polish) ♀ RATING: ★★★
From Lydia, Greece
People think of Lidia as pretty, caring, creative, funny, intelligent
People who like the name Lidia also like Lydia, Olivia, Nadia, Isabella, Amelia, Ella, Isabelle, Fiona, Hannah, Layla

Liesel (German) ♀ RATING: ★★☆
God is my oath—Short for Elizabeth
People think of Liesel as pretty, intelligent, creative, caring, funny
People who like the name Liesel also like Olivia, Ava, Paige, Lorelei, Hannah, Felicity, Audrey, Emma, Lily, Isabella

Lieu (Vietnamese) ♀ RATING: ★★★
Willow tree
People think of Lieu as intelligent, creative, funny, artsy, caring
People who like the name Lieu also like Latanya, Ling, Liesel, Lorelei, Lexi, Lexine, Lian, Li Mei, Satya, Lizeth

Liko (Hawaiian) ♂ RATING: ★★★
Bud
People think of Liko as exotic, sporty, funny, cool, boy next door
People who like the name Liko also like Noah, Ace, Liam, Jason, Leo, Lionel, Milo, Lulani, Kaden, Wade

Lila (Persian) ♀ RATING: ★★★★
Lilac tree
People think of Lila as pretty, creative, intelligent, caring, elegant
People who like the name Lila also like Layla, Ava, Lily, Ella, Grace, Isabella, Olivia, Chloe, Emma, Eva

Lilac (Latin) ♀ RATING: ★★☆
Bluish purple—Also a purple flower or tree
People think of Lilac as pretty, young, quiet, artsy, creative

People who like the name Lilac also like Grace, Violet, Lilly, Faith, Chloe, Lila, Scarlett, Lily, Hope, Layla

Lilah (Persian) ♀ RATING: ★★★★
Lilac tree
People think of Lilah as pretty, elegant, creative, intelligent, caring
People who like the name Lilah also like Layla, Lily, Ava, Lila, Chloe, Emma, Olivia, Hannah, Eva, Isabella

Lilia (English) ♀ RATING: ★★★
Lily
People think of Lilia as pretty, elegant, caring, intelligent, creative
People who like the name Lilia also like Isabella, Ava, Lily, Lila, Olivia, Lilianna, Lilly, Layla, Eva, Ella

Lilianna (English) ♀ RATING: ★★★★
Combination of Lily and Anna; also spelled Liliana
People think of Lilianna as pretty, intelligent, creative, funny, elegant
People who like the name Lilianna also like Isabella, Olivia, Gabriella, Ava, Grace, Layla, Hannah, Hailey, Emma, Lily

Liliha (Hawaiian) ♀ RATING: ★★★☆
Angry disregard
People think of Liliha as exotic, pretty, ethnic, young, artsy
People who like the name Liliha also like Lilia, Lilah, Layla, Lilianna, Leilani, Lila, Lanica, Lexi, Lilith, Lilly

Lilika (Hungarian) ♀ RATING: ★★
Lily
People think of Lilika as creative, pretty, young, elegant, ethnic
People who like the name Lilika also like Lilia, Lilianna, Layla, Leilani, Lila, Aurora, Lilah, Lexi, Lilith, Lorelei

Lilike (Hungarian) ♀ RATING: ★★
Lily
People think of Lilike as weird, pretty, artsy, girl next door, funny
People who like the name Lilike also like Lilika, Laraine, Lilah, Lilka, Lilith, Lorelei, Lilac, Lilly, Lilia, Lavinia

Lilith (Arabic) ♀ RATING: ★★★★☆
Of the night—Dr. Lilith Sternin Crane, character Cheers and Frasier
People think of Lilith as pretty, sexy, intelligent, powerful, exotic
People who like the name Lilith also like Layla, Lorelei, Aurora, Lily, Iris, Fiona, Olivia, Chloe, Charlotte, Ivy

Lilka (Polish) ♀ RATING: ★★
Lily—Short for Lilia
People think of Lilka as pretty, trustworthy, intelligent, powerful, weird
People who like the name Lilka also like Lilith, Lilia, Leyna, Layla, Lilika, Lara, Lila, Lorelei, Lola, Lilah

Lilli *(English)* ♀   RATING: ★★★☆
Lily
People think of Lilli as pretty, caring, funny, intelligent, creative
People who like the name Lilli also like Lilly, Lily, Olivia, Isabella, Emma, Ella, Ava, Eva, Layla, Grace

Lillian *(English)* ♀   RATING: ★★★★
Lily—Also spelled Lilian; Lillian Hellman, playwright
People think of Lillian as pretty, intelligent, caring, creative, funny
People who like the name Lillian also like Olivia, Ava, Grace, Abigail, Emma, Isabella, Hannah, Chloe, Ella, Isabelle

Lilliana *(English)* ♀   RATING: ★★★☆
Combination of Lily and Anna
People think of Lilliana as pretty, intelligent, elegant, creative, caring
People who like the name Lilliana also like Isabella, Lilianna, Olivia, Lillian, Grace, Lilly, Abigail, Ava, Chloe, Hannah

Lilly *(English)* ♀   RATING: ★★★★
Lily
People think of Lilly as pretty, funny, creative, caring, intelligent
People who like the name Lilly also like Emma, Grace, Isabella, Ava, Olivia, Hannah, Lily, Ella, Chloe, Faith

Lilo *(Hawaiian)* ♀ ♂   RATING: ★★★☆
Generous one—*Lilo and Stitch*, movie
People think of Lilo as creative, caring, pretty, funny, young
People who like the name Lilo also like Kai, Skylar, Riley, Logan, Madison, Keanu, Jade, Dylan, Lavender, Dakota

Liluye *(Native American)* ♀   RATING: ★★★☆
Singing hawk while soaring
People think of Liluye as exotic, caring, cool, ethnic, pretty
People who like the name Liluye also like Kaya, Luyu, Layla, Lorelei, Chenoa, Kiona, Sora, Tala, Lila, Catori

Lily *(English)* ♀   RATING: ★★★☆
Lily flower
People think of Lily as pretty, caring, creative, funny, intelligent
People who like the name Lily also like Ava, Emma, Grace, Olivia, Isabella, Ella, Hannah, Chloe, Emily, Isabelle

Limon *(Spanish)* ♀ ♂   RATING: ★★★
Lemon
People think of Limon as weird, slow, loser, unpopular, nerdy
People who like the name Limon also like Logan, Lee, Leighton, Lavender, Landen, Lang, Lex, Lucky, Lani, Layne

Lin *(Latin)* ♀   RATING: ★★☆
Pretty—Short for Linda
People think of Lin as creative, funny, pretty, trustworthy, popular
People who like the name Lin also like Lexi, Lara, Lily, Lauren, Lea, Emma, Lei, Lana, Lia, Leah

Lina *(Italian)* ♀   RATING: ★★★
Short for names ending in Lina
People think of Lina as pretty, funny, intelligent, caring, creative
People who like the name Lina also like Lana, Isabella, Lena, Layla, Liana, Mia, Leah, Gianna, Lucia, Ava

Linaeve *(American)* ♀   RATING: ★★★
Tree of song—Combination of Linnea and Maeve; science/myth fiction name
People think of Linaeve as quiet, pretty, exotic, trendy, leader
People who like the name Linaeve also like Hazel, Layla, Leilani, Lia, Lenora, Li Mei, Lily, Liana, Genevieve, Laurel

Lincoln *(English)* ♂   RATING: ★★
From the lake settlement—Abraham Lincoln, U.S. president
People think of Lincoln as intelligent, handsome, leader, powerful, trustworthy
People who like the name Lincoln also like Jackson, Landon, Noah, Ethan, Owen, Lucas, Jacob, Emerson, Maddox, Elijah

Linda *(Spanish)* ♀   RATING: ★★
Pretty one—Linda Dano, actress; Linda McCartney, photographer; Linda Ronstadt, singer
People think of Linda as pretty, caring, funny, intelligent, trustworthy
People who like the name Linda also like Emily, Laura, Emma, Heather, Lisa, Lauren, Michelle, Nicole, Hannah, Elizabeth

Lindley *(English)* ♀ ♂   RATING: ★★☆
From the lime wood—Originally a surname
People think of Lindley as pretty, popular, intelligent, trendy, caring
People who like the name Lindley also like Logan, Hayden, Landen, Hadley, Addison, Bailey, Avery, Ainsley, Caden, Aubrey

Lindsay *(English)* ♀ ♂   RATING: ★★★
From the lake settlement island—Lindsay Wagner, actress/spokesperson
People think of Lindsay as pretty, funny, caring, intelligent, creative
People who like the name Lindsay also like Madison, Mackenzie, Lindsey, Bailey, Ryan, Jordan, Taylor, Morgan, Logan, Brooke

Lindsey *(English)* ♀ ♂   RATING: ★★★
From the lake settlement island—Also spelled Lynsey
People think of Lindsey as pretty, funny, caring, intelligent, creative

People who like the name Lindsey also like Madison, Brooke, Taylor, Logan, Mackenzie, Jordan, Riley, Hayden, Morgan, Ryan

Lindy *(English)* ♀   RATING: ★★☆
Short for Lindsay or Linda
People think of Lindy as pretty, caring, funny, intelligent, energetic
People who like the name Lindy also like Lauren, Lainey, Emily, Grace, Lexi, Paige, Hannah, Macy, Lorelei, Lana

Linette *(English)* ♀   RATING: ★★★☆
Pretty one—Variation of Lynn
People think of Linette as pretty, intelligent, caring, trustworthy, elegant
People who like the name Linette also like Lynette, Hannah, Isabella, Isabelle, Hailey, Lisette, Giselle, Layla, Olivia, Lauren

Ling *(Chinese)* ♀♂   RATING: ★★★☆
Sound of jade; dawn—As a female name, means sound of jade; as a unisex name, means dawn
People think of Ling as intelligent, pretty, elegant, leader, quiet
People who like the name Ling also like Li Mei, Lila, Layla, Li Ming, Leyna, Lana, Lara, Lauren, Leah, Lexi

Linh *(Vietnamese)* ♀♂   RATING: ★★★★
Unknown meaning
People think of Linh as pretty, caring, funny, intelligent, quiet
People who like the name Linh also like Lani, Lave, Lavey, Lavi, Lolovivi, Lorant, Layne, Landen, Logan, Loki

Linnea *(Scandinavian)* ♀   RATING: ★★★★
Lime tree—Also a flower that Swedish botanist Carl Linnaeus named after himself
People think of Linnea as pretty, intelligent, creative, caring, funny
People who like the name Linnea also like Olivia, Ava, Lynnea, Isabella, Lily, Fiona, Sophia, Charlotte, Genevieve, Lorelei

Linore *(English)* ♀   RATING: ★★★
Light—Variation of Eleanor
People think of Linore as pretty, girl next door, elegant, intelligent, old-fashioned
People who like the name Linore also like Laurel, Lilith, Lenore, Lillian, Linette, Lorelei, Lenora, Lauren, Lydia, Lilia

Linus *(Greek)* ♂   RATING: ★★
Flax colored—Linus Pauling, scientist; Linus Torvalds, creator of Linux; *Peanuts* character
People think of Linus as intelligent, handsome, creative, cool, caring
People who like the name Linus also like Liam, Oliver, Lucas, Isaac, Miles, Oscar, Simon, Felix, Noah, Ian

Liona *(Italian)* ♀   RATING: ★★☆
Lioness
People think of Liona as powerful, pretty, leader, exotic, caring

People who like the name Liona also like Layla, Lina, Leona, Leola, Isabella, Lana, Leandra, Isabelle, Lucia, Luciana

Lionel *(English)* ♂   RATING: ★★
Lion—Lionel Hampton, musician; Lionel Richie, singer; brand of toy trains
People think of Lionel as handsome, sexy, funny, intelligent, caring
People who like the name Lionel also like Ethan, Liam, Aaron, Justin, Leo, Alexander, Isaac, Jacob, Nathan, Nicholas

Liora *(Hebrew)* ♀   RATING: ★★☆
My might
People think of Liora as elegant, intelligent, creative, caring, pretty
People who like the name Liora also like Liana, Layla, Leila, Leora, Lorelei, Kiara, Lilianna, Leah, Liona, Lia

Lira *(Latin)* ♀   RATING: ★★★★
Harp—Also Italian currency
People think of Lira as pretty, exotic, funny, intelligent, energetic
People who like the name Lira also like Lyra, Lorelei, Layla, Lilia, Lilith, Laura, Lilly, Lavinia, Luna, Leah

Lirit *(Hebrew)* ♀   RATING: ★★★★
Musical
People think of Lirit as exotic, intelligent, elegant, caring, quiet
People who like the name Lirit also like Lila, Layla, Liana, Lark, Leila, Lydia, Lena, Lilith, Lorelei, Lana

Lis *(Scandinavian)* ♀   RATING: ★★★☆
God is my oath—Short for Elisabeth
People think of Lis as creative, pretty, funny, artsy, intelligent
People who like the name Lis also like Lara, Lisa, Lisette, Liana, Lise, Lilith, Lorelei, Lilianna, Larissa, Lisbet

Lisa *(English)* ♀   RATING: ★★★☆
God is my oath—Short for Elisabeth; Lisa Kudrow, actress; Lisa Marie Presley, singer/daughter of Elvis Presley
People think of Lisa as funny, pretty, caring, intelligent, trustworthy
People who like the name Lisa also like Hannah, Emily, Lauren, Elizabeth, Natalie, Sarah, Emma, Amber, Rebecca, Hailey

Lisbet *(German)* ♀   RATING: ★★
God is my oath—Short for Elisabeth
People think of Lisbet as pretty, intelligent, funny, cool, exotic
People who like the name Lisbet also like Lisette, Lizbeth, Lauren, Liana, Isabella, Larissa, Lorelei, Layla, Laura, Lilianna

Lise *(German)* ♀   RATING: ★★★☆
God is my oath—Short for Elisabeth
People think of Lise as pretty, trustworthy, creative, sexy, energetic

People who like the name Lise also like Ava, Liana, Grace, Lily, Lisette, Lara, Hannah, Claire, Julia, Elise

Liseli (African) ♀   RATING: ★★★☆
Light—Zambian origin
People think of Liseli as exotic, sexy, popular, pretty, girl next door
People who like the name Liseli also like Liana, Leyna, Lia, Leila, Leilani, Liora, Lorelei, Layla, Lily, Lisette

Lisette (French) ♀   RATING: ★★★★
God is my oath—Short for Elisabeth
People think of Lisette as pretty, intelligent, caring, funny, trustworthy
People who like the name Lisette also like Giselle, Isabelle, Isabella, Charlotte, Gabrielle, Grace, Linette, Jacqueline, Lilianna, Layla

Lisimba (African) ♀   RATING: ★★☆
Lion—Tanzanian origin
People think of Lisimba as funny, exotic, creative, sneaky, wild
People who like the name Lisimba also like Lareina, Liseli, Leandra, Lila, Li Mei, Layla, Lisa, Lana, Leona, Lisette

Lisle (French) ♀ ♂   RATING: ★★
Of the island
People think of Lisle as pretty, creative, artsy, cool, elegant
People who like the name Lisle also like Hayden, Logan, Luca, Lani, Landen, Lavender, London, Leighton, Lyric, Reese

Lissa (American) ♀   RATING: ★★★☆
God is my oath—Short for Melissa or Elizabeth
People think of Lissa as pretty, creative, funny, intelligent, caring
People who like the name Lissa also like Melissa, Michelle, Rebecca, Sarah, Lauren, Maria, Marie, Lainey, Ann, Adriana

Lita (Spanish) ♀   RATING: ★★★★
Short for Carlita—Lita Ford, singer
People think of Lita as pretty, sexy, wild, creative, funny
People who like the name Lita also like Layla, Ava, Lola, Luna, Lila, Grace, Emma, Bianca, Lina, Olivia

Liv (Scandinavian) ♀   RATING: ★★★
Cover, shield; life—Also short for Olivia; Liv Tyler, actress; Liv Ullman, actress
People think of Liv as pretty, creative, intelligent, caring, elegant
People who like the name Liv also like Ava, Olivia, Eva, Ella, Emma, Lily, Lana, Elle, Mia, Isabella

Livana (Hebrew) ♀   RATING: ★★★
White
People think of Livana as pretty, creative, girl next door, lazy, artsy
People who like the name Livana also like Liora, Liana, Layla, Livia, Leyna, Levana, Lilianna, Lila, Lorelei, Lina

Livi (English) ♀   RATING: ★★★
Elf army—Short for Olivia
People think of Livi as pretty, funny, intelligent, creative, young
People who like the name Livi also like Olivia, Layla, Lexi, Liv, Ava, Bella, Livia, Eva, Lana, Emma

Livia (Latin) ♀   RATING: ★★★
Envious—Also short for Olivia
People think of Livia as pretty, intelligent, funny, creative, caring
People who like the name Livia also like Olivia, Lydia, Ava, Isabella, Layla, Mia, Claire, Liv, Abigail, Sophia

Livingston (English) ♂   RATING: ★★
From Lewin's town—Livingston Taylor, musician
People think of Livingston as handsome, intelligent, leader, wealthy, powerful
People who like the name Livingston also like Langston, Lawson, Jackson, Landon, Miles, Radley, Lucas, Wade, Kaden, Anderson

Livvy (English) ♀   RATING: ★★☆
Elf army—Short for Olivia
People think of Livvy as pretty, young, trustworthy, artsy, powerful
People who like the name Livvy also like Olivia, Lily, Elle, Livia, Lainey, Lexi, Ella, Bella, Layla, Libby

Lixue (Chinese) ♀   RATING: ★★☆
Pretty snow
People think of Lixue as pretty, exotic, weird, creative, intelligent
People who like the name Lixue also like Li Mei, Lian, Layla, Lilah, Lara, Liesel, Lia, Mairi, Gemma, Lovette

Liz (English) ♀   RATING: ★★★☆
God is my oath—Short for Elizabeth
People think of Liz as funny, pretty, intelligent, cool, caring
People who like the name Liz also like Isabel, Kate, Faith, Elizabeth, Lauren, Lexi, Laura, Hailey, Claire, Grace

Liza (English) ♀   RATING: ★★☆
God is my oath—Short for Elizabeth; Liza Minnelli, actress/singer
People think of Liza as funny, pretty, creative, caring, cool
People who like the name Liza also like Hannah, Leah, Grace, Isabella, Ella, Lilly, Eliza, Emma, Eva, Olivia

Lizbeth (English) ♀   RATING: ★★★★
God is my oath—Short for Elizabeth
People think of Lizbeth as funny, pretty, intelligent, caring, young
People who like the name Lizbeth also like Isabella, Elizabeth, Lauren, Hannah, Elisabeth, Emma, Larissa, Grace, Gabriella, Olivia

Lizeth (American) ♀   RATING: ★★★☆
God is my oath—Short for Elizabeth
People think of Lizeth as pretty, funny, intelligent, young, sexy

People who like the name Lizeth also like Lisette, Lisbet, Libby, Larissa, Lisa, Layla, Lauren, Leandra, Leilani, Linette

Lizette *(French)* ♀   RATING: ★★★
God is my oath—Short for Elizabeth
People think of Lizette as pretty, intelligent, creative, funny, caring
People who like the name Lizette also like Lisette, Lilianna, Angelina, Linette, Isabelle, Leilani, Suzette, Elise, Bianca, Isabella

Lizina *(American)* ♀   RATING: ★★
God is my oath—Short for Elizabeth
People think of Lizina as caring, religious, artsy, popular, trendy
People who like the name Lizina also like Liana, Lisette, Lesa, Layla, Linette, Jana, Lisa, Leandra, Latisha, Samara

Llewellyn *(Welsh)* ♂   RATING: ★★★☆
Leader
People think of Llewellyn as intelligent, handsome, creative, funny, trustworthy
People who like the name Llewellyn also like Liam, Noah, Lachlan, Ewan, Lysander, Keagan, Ethan, Drake, Leander, Lucas

Lloyd *(Welsh)* ♂   RATING: ★★
Gray—Lloyd Bridges, actor; Lloyd Richards, director
People think of Lloyd as funny, handsome, caring, intelligent, cool
People who like the name Lloyd also like Jacob, Aaron, Lucas, Ethan, Jack, Isaac, Oliver, Nathan, Adam, Owen

Lluvia *(Spanish)* ♀   RATING: ★★★★
Rain—Pronounced *YU-vee-ah*
People think of Lluvia as pretty, exotic, caring, intelligent, elegant
People who like the name Lluvia also like Lareina, Lola, Lelia, Layla, Lupita, Leala, Leilani, Lela, Laurel, Leane

Lluvy *(Spanish)* ♀   RATING: ★★★
Rain
People think of Lluvy as sexy, exotic, cool, wild, girl next door
People who like the name Lluvy also like Lola, Lolita, Lainey, Ivy, Giselle, Ladonna, Chloe, Jadyn, Savannah, La Cienega

Loan *(Vietnamese)* ♀   RATING: ★★★
Unknown meaning
People think of Loan as caring, pretty, intelligent, creative, quiet
People who like the name Loan also like Liv, Liona, Liana, Lyris, Laurel, Lanelle, Larissa, Lana, Lia, Lovey

Lobo *(Spanish)* ♂   RATING: ★★★
Wolf
People think of Lobo as old, lazy, unpopular, loser, weird
People who like the name Lobo also like Alejandro, Ryu, Joaquin, Maddox, Julio, Levi, Luis, Lucas, Luke, Bruce

Loc *(Vietnamese)* ♂   RATING: ★☆
Bud
People think of Loc as caring, ethnic, powerful, creative, sexy
People who like the name Loc also like Andrew, Livingston, Baxter, Jayden, Lowell, Leon, Lance, Aden, Levi, Armand

Lochana *(Sanskrit/East Indian)* ♀   RATING: ★★☆
Illuminating
People think of Lochana as pretty, creative, ethnic, funny, sexy
People who like the name Lochana also like Kerani, Gaura, Ketaki, Kusuma, Jyotika, Kavindra, Kirtana, Kimaya, Laksha, Bhavna

Locke *(English)* ♀♂   RATING: ★★★★
Lock, fastening—Originally a surname
People think of Locke as intelligent, handsome, creative, cool, powerful
People who like the name Locke also like Logan, Bailey, Hayden, London, Dylan, Landen, Sawyer, Ryder, Parker, Caden

Lodovico *(Italian)* ♂   RATING: ★★★
Famous warrior
People think of Lodovico as intelligent, leader, powerful, ethnic, weird
People who like the name Lodovico also like Salvatore, Llewellyn, Lucius, Lucas, Landon, Lucian, Lazzaro, Ryu, Drago, Leonardo

Loe *(Hawaiian)* ♀♂   RATING: ★★
King
People think of Loe as elegant, popular, sexy, exotic, wealthy
People who like the name Loe also like Lani, Kai, Logan, London, Kalei, Lilo, Kaili, Lave, Leighton, Lavi

Logan *(Celtic/Gaelic)* ♀♂   RATING: ★★★☆
From the hollow—Logan Clendening, medical author; Logan Pearsall Smith, author
People think of Logan as handsome, intelligent, funny, popular, cool
People who like the name Logan also like Riley, Hayden, Madison, Dylan, Caden, Connor, Bailey, Taylor, Parker, Mason

Lois *(Greek)* ♀   RATING: ★★
Better—Lois Lane, character in *Superman*
People think of Lois as pretty, intelligent, caring, funny, creative
People who like the name Lois also like Layla, Leah, Erin, Lily, Lydia, Lauren, Emily, Lana, Lucy, Lexi

Lok *(Chinese)* ♂   RATING: ★★★
Joy—Cantonese spelling
People think of Lok as funny, criminal, creative, loser, exotic
People who like the name Lok also like Jadon, Beau, Kaden, Jackson, Leone, Dawson, Dasan, Ace, Wes, Kiefer

Lokesh *(Sanskrit/East Indian)* ♂　　RATING: ★★☆
Lord of the world
  People think of Lokesh as cool, intelligent, caring, handsome, aggressive
  People who like the name Lokesh also like Arnav, Abhay, Adarsh, Rupin, Devesh, Adit, Ashwin, Ravi, Indivar, Jagat

Loki *(Scandinavian)* ♀♂　　RATING: ★★★★
Trickster God
  People think of Loki as intelligent, wild, funny, sneaky, energetic
  People who like the name Loki also like Logan, Raven, Riley, London, Jade, Aidan, Caden, Luca, Jaden, Blake

Lola *(Spanish)* ♀　　RATING: ★★★☆
Sorrows—Short for Dolores; Lola Falana, singer/dancer
  People think of Lola as pretty, sexy, funny, exotic, creative
  People who like the name Lola also like Ava, Layla, Ella, Isabella, Olivia, Bella, Chloe, Lily, Mia, Grace

Lolita *(Spanish)* ♀　　RATING: ★★★☆
Sorrows—Short for Lola; also identified with a young seductress because of the novel *Lolita* by Vladimir Nabokov
  People think of Lolita as sexy, pretty, exotic, elegant, young
  People who like the name Lolita also like Lola, Ava, Carmelita, Lorelei, Natalya, Ophelia, Sofia, Lilith, Catalina, Evangeline

Lolonyo *(African)* ♂　　RATING: ★★★
Love is beautiful
  People think of Lolonyo as exotic, creative, pretty, ethnic, intelligent
  People who like the name Lolonyo also like Jabari, Lemuel, Lulani, Leander, Balthasar, Ajani, Lencho, Kimoni, Ja, Anando

Lolovivi *(African)* ♀♂　　RATING: ★☆
There's always love
  People think of Lolovivi as exotic, caring, weird, creative, stuck-up
  People who like the name Lolovivi also like London, Laramie, Love, Lani, Leal, Jumoke, Li, Kendi, Lucky, Loyal

Loman *(German)* ♂　　RATING: ★☆
From the wood land—Also an American surname; Willy Loman, character in *Death of a Salesman* by Arthur Miller
  People think of Loman as popular, powerful, slow, old, big
  People who like the name Loman also like Liam, Aden, Keagan, Braeden, Merric, Brendan, Lachlan, Kael, Owen, Edan

Lona *(Hungarian)* ♀　　RATING: ★★
Light—Short for Ilona
  People think of Lona as pretty, trustworthy, intelligent, creative, caring

People who like the name Lona also like Layla, Lana, Sophie, Lexi, Mabel, Lila, Lisa, Lia, Lara, Hazel

Lonato *(Italian)* ♂　　RATING: ★★
From Lonato del Garda, Italy
  People think of Lonato as ethnic, unpopular, weird, winner, big
  People who like the name Lonato also like Lachlan, Anoki, Neka, Dasan, Lucian, Apiatan, Ahanu, Ezhno, Landis, Chayton

London *(English)* ♀♂　　RATING: ★★
From the great river—Jack London, author; Julie London, actress
  People think of London as pretty, popular, creative, trendy, funny
  People who like the name London also like Logan, Hayden, Brooklyn, Madison, Parker, Riley, Addison, Bailey, Caden, Landen

Long *(Chinese)* ♂　　RATING: ★★★☆
Dragon
  People think of Long as intelligent, sexy, funny, trustworthy, caring
  People who like the name Long also like Ryu, Drake, Draco, Ace, Liam, Lance, Lowell, Jason, Jabir, Lloyd

Lonna *(Slavic)* ♀　　RATING: ★★☆
Light—Variation of Helen
  People think of Lonna as pretty, creative, caring, intelligent, funny
  People who like the name Lonna also like Lorelei, Lona, Layla, Liana, Lana, Lainey, Lilly, Laurel, Larissa, Lilianna

Lora *(Spanish)* ♀　　RATING: ★★★☆
Laurel
  People think of Lora as pretty, caring, funny, creative, trustworthy
  People who like the name Lora also like Emma, Laura, Lauren, Emily, Lana, Lara, Leah, Hannah, Olivia, Lily

Lorand *(Hungarian)* ♀♂　　RATING: ★★☆
Famous land—Variation of Orlando
  People think of Lorand as intelligent, sexy, exotic, caring, creative
  People who like the name Lorand also like Lorant, Landen, London, Lorin, Lyndon, Lex, Lyle, Landry, Layne, Loren

Lorant *(Hungarian)* ♀♂　　RATING: ★★☆
Famous land—Variation of Orlando
  People think of Lorant as big, cool, old-fashioned, funny, powerful
  People who like the name Lorant also like Lorand, Landen, Logan, Lex, Lorin, London, Lyndon, Layne, Sage, Leighton

Lore *(American)* ♀♂　　RATING: ★★★☆
Crowned with laurel—Variation of Laura, Lorelai, or Lorne; also means history or story
  People think of Lore as intelligent, pretty, leader, creative, cool

People who like the name Lore also like Logan, Sage, Ryan, Brody, London, Landen, Leighton, Lindsey, Jesse, Parker

364

Lorelei (German) ♀ RATING: ★★★★☆
Alluring enchantress—Also spelled Lorelai; Lorelei Lee, character in *Gentlemen Prefer Blondes*, played by Marilyn Monroe
People think of Lorelei as pretty, funny, energetic, creative, intelligent
People who like the name Lorelei also like Chloe, Ava, Isabella, Emma, Abigail, Paige, Hannah, Grace, Olivia, Hailey

Lorelle (American) ♀ RATING: ★★★★
Laurel—Variation of Laurel
People think of Lorelle as pretty, intelligent, caring, funny, wild
People who like the name Lorelle also like Lorelei, Lacey, Laurel, Isabella, Chloe, Layla, Lauren, Hailey, Jasmine, Laraine

Loren (American) ♀♂ RATING: ★★★☆
Laurel—Variation of Lauren
People think of Loren as intelligent, funny, caring, trustworthy, pretty
People who like the name Loren also like Logan, Hayden, Riley, Madison, Caden, Morgan, Jaden, Parker, Taylor, Ryan

Lorena (English) ♀ RATING: ★★☆
Laurel—Variation of Lauren
People think of Lorena as pretty, funny, caring, intelligent, cool
People who like the name Lorena also like Isabella, Olivia, Hailey, Adriana, Bianca, Laura, Lauren, Victoria, Lana, Natalia

Lorene (American) ♀ RATING: ★★★
Laurel—Variation of Lauren
People think of Lorene as trustworthy, intelligent, creative, funny, caring
People who like the name Lorene also like Lauren, Layla, Lilly, Laura, Isabella, Isabelle, Leanna, Lana, Laurel, Lillian

Lorenzo (Italian) ♂ RATING: ★★★☆
Laurel—Variation of Laurence
People think of Lorenzo as handsome, funny, cool, intelligent, caring
People who like the name Lorenzo also like Nicholas, Ethan, Lucas, Gabriel, Isaac, Alexander, Giovanni, Sebastian, Antonio, Benjamin

Loretta (Italian) ♀ RATING: ★★★☆
Laurel—Variation of Lora; Loretta Swit, actress; Loretta Young, actress
People think of Loretta as funny, pretty, trustworthy, intelligent, creative
People who like the name Loretta also like Olivia, Isabella, Bianca, Layla, Lana, Bella, Lorelei, Scarlett, Sophia, Lorena

Lori (American) ♀ RATING: ★★☆
Laurel
People think of Lori as pretty, caring, funny, intelligent, creative
People who like the name Lori also like Paige, Leah, Emma, Faith, Emily, Hailey, Natalie, Lauren, Laura, Samantha

Lorie (American) ♀ RATING: ★★★☆
Laurel
People think of Lorie as caring, pretty, trustworthy, funny, creative
People who like the name Lorie also like Lori, Lauren, Paige, Natalie, Lacey, Lilly, Emily, Keely, Katelyn, Vanessa

Lorimer (English) ♂ RATING: ★★
Harness maker—Originally a surname
People think of Lorimer as stuck-up, nerdy, aggressive, weird, sexy
People who like the name Lorimer also like Lachlan, Josiah, Landon, Aaron, Jeremy, Leander, Lysander, Joshua, Justin, Isaac

Lorin (English) ♀♂ RATING: ★★★★
Laurel—Variation of Lauren
People think of Lorin as intelligent, creative, caring, pretty, trustworthy
People who like the name Lorin also like Logan, Landen, Parker, Madison, Loren, Riley, Hayden, Jordan, Caden, Spencer

Lorinda (Spanish) ♀ RATING: ★★★
Combination of Lora and Linda
People think of Lorinda as pretty, intelligent, caring, trustworthy, creative
People who like the name Lorinda also like Kaelyn, Kendra, Lorelei, Veronica, Kyla, Emma, Jessica, Cailyn, Madeline, Dawn

Loring (English) ♀♂ RATING: ★★★
From Lorraine, France—Originally a surname
People think of Loring as aggressive, ethnic, lazy, loser, energetic
People who like the name Loring also like Logan, Luka, Lavender, Lani, Lynley, Loren, Lyndon, Layne, Lynn, Leighton

Lorna (Celtic/Gaelic) ♀ RATING: ★★★☆
Fox—Feminine form of Lorne; Lorna Luft, singer
People think of Lorna as intelligent, pretty, caring, funny, creative
People who like the name Lorna also like Ava, Bella, Emily, Layla, Chloe, Ella, Emma, Genevieve, Eva, Olivia

Lorne (English) ♀♂ RATING: ★★
Fox—Scottish place name; Lorne Michaels, TV producer/writer
People think of Lorne as intelligent, handsome, funny, trustworthy, leader
People who like the name Lorne also like Hayden, Parker, Quinn, Rowan, Jude, Jade, Jaden, Riley, Reese, Preston

Lorraine *(French)* ♀   RATING: ★★★★
From Lorraine, France
> People think of Lorraine as caring, pretty, intelligent, funny, creative
> People who like the name Lorraine also like Lauren, Elizabeth, Olivia, Emma, Isabelle, Hannah, Jasmine, Isabella, Grace, Emily

Lorretta *(English)* ♀   RATING: ★★★☆
Laurel
> People think of Lorretta as pretty, funny, intelligent, aggressive, powerful
> People who like the name Lorretta also like Isabella, Loretta, Charlotte, Isabelle, Larissa, Heather, Lorraine, Lydia, Hailey, Jacqueline

Lot *(Hebrew)* ♂   RATING: ★☆
Hidden, veiled
> People think of Lot as poor, criminal, religious, unpopular, old-fashioned
> People who like the name Lot also like Levi, Asher, Adam, Jack, Holden, Heath, Jared, Jeremy, Jett, Jonah

Lotta *(Italian)* ♀   RATING: ★★★☆
Free—Short for Carlotta
> People think of Lotta as pretty, funny, exotic, sexy, girl next door
> People who like the name Lotta also like Laurel, Lottie, Emma, Bella, Lily, Laura, Lara, Lauren, Lia, Sofia

Lotte *(German)* ♀   RATING: ★★
Free—Variation of Charlotte
> People think of Lotte as pretty, intelligent, popular, funny, sexy
> People who like the name Lotte also like Lottie, Lorelei, Liesel, Lola, Lilly, Scarlett, Layla, Emma, Leah, Luna

Lottie *(English)* ♀   RATING: ★★★★
Free—Short for Charlotte
> People think of Lottie as pretty, funny, creative, caring, intelligent
> People who like the name Lottie also like Lucy, Lilly, Lily, Layla, Grace, Charlotte, Bella, Emma, Scarlett, Isabella

Lotus *(Greek)* ♀   RATING: ★★★☆
The flower
> People think of Lotus as pretty, exotic, intelligent, artsy, creative
> People who like the name Lotus also like Lola, Lilly, Layla, Chloe, Iris, Faith, Lily, Harmony, Fiona, Luna

Lou *(German)* ♂   RATING: ★★
Famed warrior—Short for Louis or Louise; Lou Gehrig, baseball player; Lou Rawls, singer; Lou Reed, musician
> People think of Lou as funny, caring, cool, creative, leader
> People who like the name Lou also like Lucas, Jacob, Leo, Wade, Ace, Roman, Maddox, Miles, Victor, Henry

Louanna *(English)* ♀   RATING: ★★★☆
Combination of Lou and Anna
> People think of Louanna as intelligent, pretty, funny, caring, creative

People who like the name Louanna also like Layla, Bianca, Lilianna, Luana, Isabella, Lilliana, Larissa, Laurel, Louisa, Lydia

Louie *(English)* ♂   RATING: ★★
Famous warrior—Short for Louis or Louise
> People think of Louie as handsome, funny, caring, cool, intelligent
> People who like the name Louie also like Louis, Jacob, Jack, Oliver, Ethan, Leo, Lucas, Noah, Henry, Lewis

Louis *(German)* ♂   RATING: ★★★☆
Famed warrior—Pronounced *LOO-iss* or *LOO-ee*; Louis Armstrong, trumpeter/singer; Louis Prima, singer
> People think of Louis as handsome, funny, intelligent, cool, caring
> People who like the name Louis also like Lucas, Nicholas, Ethan, Jack, Benjamin, Lewis, William, Luke, Oliver, Alexander

Louisa *(English)* ♀   RATING: ★★★☆
Famous warrior—Louisa May Alcott, author
> People think of Louisa as pretty, intelligent, funny, caring, creative
> People who like the name Louisa also like Olivia, Lucy, Emma, Charlotte, Louise, Amelia, Grace, Sophia, Emily, Hannah

Louise *(English)* ♀   RATING: ★★
Famous warrior—Louise Lasser, actress
> People think of Louise as pretty, caring, funny, intelligent, trustworthy
> People who like the name Louise also like Emma, Louisa, Sophie, Grace, Elizabeth, Emily, Lucy, Hannah, Charlotte, Olivia

Louisiana *(American)* ♀   RATING: ★★★☆
U.S. state, named in honor of Louis XIV of France
> People think of Louisiana as creative, funny, artsy, powerful, pretty
> People who like the name Louisiana also like Georgia, Isabella, Juliet, Layla, Lydia, Charlotte, Emma, Genevieve, Lucy, Lilly

Lourdes *(French)* ♀   RATING: ★★
Vision of the Virgin Mary—Also a French place name
> People think of Lourdes as caring, intelligent, pretty, elegant, creative
> People who like the name Lourdes also like Ava, Isabella, Giselle, Eva, Paige, Olivia, Layla, Ella, Natalia, Lily

Louvain *(English)* ♀ ♂   RATING: ★★★
City in Belgium
> People think of Louvain as funny, loser, nerdy, ethnic, trustworthy
> People who like the name Louvain also like London, Lani, Landen, Lave, Lindley, Lane, Lennon, Leighton, Lyndon, Lee

Love (English) ♀♂   RATING: ★★
Full of love
> People think of Love as sexy, pretty, caring, popular, funny
> People who like the name Love also like Logan, Jade, Hayden, London, Bailey, Liberty, Lucky, Jaden, Rain, Madison

Lovette (English) ♀   RATING: ★☆
Little loved one
> People think of Lovette as pretty, intelligent, exotic, sexy, creative
> People who like the name Lovette also like Layla, Scarlett, Belle, Lily, Linette, Aurora, Serenity, Lynette, Roxanne, Lottie

Lovey (American) ♀   RATING: ★★★
Loved one—Also a term of endearment
> People think of Lovey as pretty, young, popular, caring, sexy
> People who like the name Lovey also like Lovie, Lovette, Lily, Ava, Larissa, Roxanne, Emma, Mia, Lucinda, Layla

Lovie (American) ♀   RATING: ★★★☆
Loved one
> People think of Lovie as pretty, caring, funny, young, creative
> People who like the name Lovie also like Layla, Lovey, Isabella, Isabelle, Bella, Gemma, Callie, Olivia, Gracie, Kali

Lowell (English) ♂   RATING: ★★★☆
Little wolf—Originally a surname
> People think of Lowell as intelligent, creative, handsome, caring, cool
> People who like the name Lowell also like Lucas, Caleb, Maddox, Liam, Ethan, Landon, Jacob, Owen, Jackson, Nathan

Lowri (Welsh) ♀   RATING: ★★★★
Laurel—Variation of Laura
> People think of Lowri as intelligent, creative, funny, pretty, trustworthy
> People who like the name Lowri also like Layla, Arwen, Rhiannon, Lyra, Genevieve, Aurora, Mairwen, Gwyneth, Lorelei, Chloe

Loyal (English) ♀♂   RATING: ★★
Faithful, true
> People think of Loyal as trustworthy, handsome, quiet, creative, intelligent
> People who like the name Loyal also like Love, Liberty, Lyric, London, Justice, Lucky, Logan, Bliss, Ryan, Blair

Luana (Hawaiian) ♀   RATING: ★★
Enjoyment
> People think of Luana as pretty, funny, intelligent, creative, caring
> People who like the name Luana also like Layla, Lorelei, Leah, Grace, Leilani, Leila, Larisa, Lilianna, Liana, Bianca

Luca (Italian) ♀♂   RATING: ★★☆
From Lucania, Italy
> People think of Luca as handsome, intelligent, cool, creative, funny
> People who like the name Luca also like Logan, Luka, Hayden, Dylan, Riley, Aidan, Julian, Caden, Addison, Ryan

Lucas (Greek) ♂   RATING: ★★★
From Lucania, Italy—George Lucas, filmmaker
> People think of Lucas as handsome, intelligent, funny, caring, cool
> People who like the name Lucas also like Ethan, Jacob, Noah, Caleb, Nathan, Nicholas, Zachary, Landon, Owen, Isaac

Luce (Latin) ♂   RATING: ★★
Light—Variation of Lucus or Lucius
> People think of Luce as intelligent, pretty, cool, sexy, popular
> People who like the name Luce also like Lucas, Lucius, Isaac, Luke, Lucian, Calix, Leo, Kaden, Lysander, Edan

Lucia (Italian) ♀   RATING: ★★★
Light—*Lucia di Lammermoor*, Donizetti opera
> People think of Lucia as pretty, intelligent, funny, caring, creative
> People who like the name Lucia also like Isabella, Olivia, Ava, Grace, Luciana, Ella, Eva, Mia, Sophia, Lucy

Lucian (English) ♂   RATING: ★★★★☆
Light
> People think of Lucian as intelligent, powerful, handsome, leader, creative
> People who like the name Lucian also like Lucas, Gabriel, Lucius, Liam, Tristan, Aiden, Lucien, Sebastian, Landon, Gavin

Luciana (Italian) ♀   RATING: ★★★☆
Light
> People think of Luciana as pretty, sexy, creative, elegant, exotic
> People who like the name Luciana also like Isabella, Lucia, Gianna, Natalia, Gabriella, Olivia, Sienna, Ava, Angelina, Lilianna

Lucida (Latin) ♀   RATING: ★★★
Clear
> People think of Lucida as pretty, exotic, cool, artsy, intelligent
> People who like the name Lucida also like Lucinda, Lucia, Lila, Loretta, Scarlett, Lorena, Luciana, Serena, Chloe, Grace

Lucie (French) ♀   RATING: ★★★
Light—Variation of Lucy
> People think of Lucie as pretty, funny, young, caring, creative
> People who like the name Lucie also like Olivia, Lucy, Sophie, Ella, Isabelle, Charlotte, Emma, Lily, Isabella, Lilly

Lucien *(French)* ♂   RATING: ★★★★☆
Light
> People think of Lucien as intelligent, handsome, creative, powerful, leader
> People who like the name Lucien also like Gabriel, Lucian, Lucas, Tristan, Lucius, Aiden, Liam, Alexander, Ethan, Elijah

Lucifer *(Latin)* ♂   RATING: ★★★
Bringer of light
> People think of Lucifer as aggressive, powerful, untrustworthy, criminal, sneaky
> People who like the name Lucifer also like Damien, Alexander, Lucius, Lucien, Hades, Drake, Adrian, Lucas, Aiden, Lucian

Lucille *(French)* ♀   RATING: ★★
Light—Lucille Ball, actress/comedian; B. B. King's guitar
> People think of Lucille as pretty, caring, intelligent, funny, creative
> People who like the name Lucille also like Olivia, Charlotte, Lucy, Grace, Isabelle, Faith, Lillian, Emma, Sophia, Isabella

Lucinda *(Spanish)* ♀   RATING: ★★
Light—Variation of Lucy
> People think of Lucinda as pretty, creative, intelligent, caring, funny
> People who like the name Lucinda also like Olivia, Isabella, Bianca, Ava, Fiona, Audrey, Lucy, Amelia, Victoria, Cassandra

Lucine *(American)* ♀   RATING: ★★★★
Light—Variation of Lucy
> People think of Lucine as pretty, intelligent, creative, young, powerful
> People who like the name Lucine also like Selene, Layla, Leila, Maeve, Lorelei, Lucinda, Fiona, Kali, Giselle, Tatiana

Lucio *(Italian)* ♂   RATING: ★★
Light
> People think of Lucio as funny, powerful, caring, cool, handsome
> People who like the name Lucio also like Gabriel, Lucas, Giovanni, Lucian, Lorenzo, Marco, Vincent, Matteo, Luigi, Paolo

Lucius *(Latin)* ♂   RATING: ★★★★
Light
> People think of Lucius as powerful, handsome, intelligent, leader, creative
> People who like the name Lucius also like Lucian, Lucas, Gabriel, Lucien, Sebastian, Liam, Xavier, Elijah, Alexander, Tristan

Lucky *(American)* ♀♂   RATING: ★★
Fortunate—Usually used as a nickname
> People think of Lucky as funny, cool, energetic, sporty, intelligent

> People who like the name Lucky also like Logan, Madison, London, Hayden, Parker, Dakota, Caden, Jaden, Love, Taylor

Lucrece *(French)* ♀   RATING: ★★☆
Unknown meaning—Variation of Lucretia
> People think of Lucrece as slow, ethnic, nerdy, unpopular, weird
> People who like the name Lucrece also like Lita, Laura, Leila, Lucia, Leora, Lexi, Lily, Lillian, Olivia, Layla

Lucretia *(Latin)* ♀   RATING: ★★★☆
Unknown meaning
> People think of Lucretia as intelligent, pretty, sexy, creative, caring
> People who like the name Lucretia also like Lorelei, Lucinda, Lily, Larissa, Lilith, Amelia, Paige, Lavinia, Fiona, Leila

Lucus *(American)* ♂   RATING: ★★★
From Lucania, Italy—Variation of Lucas
> People think of Lucus as popular, handsome, cool, funny, caring
> People who like the name Lucus also like Jacob, Ethan, Lucas, Caleb, Luke, Aiden, Landon, Nathan, Elijah, Gabriel

Lucy *(English)* ♀   RATING: ★★
Light—*I Love Lucy*, TV show; "Lucy in the Sky with Diamonds," Beatles song; *Peanuts* character
> People think of Lucy as pretty, funny, intelligent, caring, creative
> People who like the name Lucy also like Olivia, Grace, Charlotte, Emma, Lily, Ava, Hannah, Ella, Abigail, Isabella

Ludlow *(English)* ♂   RATING: ★★
From the loud river hill
> People think of Ludlow as cool, caring, artsy, popular, old-fashioned
> People who like the name Ludlow also like Jackson, Lawson, Langston, Leland, Landers, Landon, Harlow, Ian, Nicholas, Everett

Ludmila *(Slavic)* ♀   RATING: ★★★
People's favor
> People think of Ludmila as intelligent, pretty, elegant, creative, caring
> People who like the name Ludmila also like Constance, Ailish, Esmerelda, Andromeda, Margarita, Lenore, Serenity, Persephone, Serendipity, Desiree

Ludwig *(German)* ♂   RATING: ★★★
Famous warrior—Variation of Lewis; Ludwig van Beethoven, composer
> People think of Ludwig as intelligent, leader, creative, powerful, trustworthy
> People who like the name Ludwig also like Wolfgang, Nathan, Luke, Vincent, Leonardo, Adrian, Oscar, Braden, Albert, Donovan

368

Luella *(American)* ♀ RATING: ★★★☆
Combination of Lou and Ella—Luella Parsons, gossip columnist
> People think of Luella as pretty, creative, funny, intelligent, artsy
> People who like the name Luella also like Layla, Ava, Lorelei, Lola, Isabella, Ella, Grace, Bella, Olivia, Leila

Luigi *(Italian)* ♂ RATING: ★☆
Famous warrior—Variation of Louis
> People think of Luigi as funny, handsome, intelligent, cool, popular
> People who like the name Luigi also like Marco, Nicholas, Leo, Lucas, Giovanni, Lucio, Mario, Romeo, Gabriel, Valentino

Luis *(Spanish)* ♂ RATING: ★★
Famous warrior—Variation of Louis
> People think of Luis as funny, handsome, cool, intelligent, sexy
> People who like the name Luis also like Antonio, Alejandro, Isaac, Diego, Justin, Miguel, Ethan, Lucas, Carlos, Adrian

Luka *(Slavic)* ♀♂ RATING: ★★★★☆
From Lucania, Italy—Variation of Luke
> People think of Luka as intelligent, handsome, creative, caring, energetic
> People who like the name Luka also like Luca, Logan, Riley, Jaden, Caden, Hayden, Kai, Dylan, Morgan, Madison

Lukas *(German)* ♂ RATING: ★★★★
From Lucania, Italy—Lukas Haas, actor
> People think of Lukas as handsome, intelligent, cool, funny, popular
> People who like the name Lukas also like Lucas, Ethan, Jacob, Noah, Landon, Luke, Zachary, Aiden, Nathan, Gabriel

Luke *(English)* ♂ RATING: ★★★
From Lucania, Italy—Luke Perry, actor; Luke Skywalker, character in *Star Wars*, named after the writer/director George Lucas; Luke Wilson, actor
> People think of Luke as handsome, funny, intelligent, cool, caring
> People who like the name Luke also like Ethan, Noah, Jacob, Jack, Matthew, Lucas, Benjamin, Caleb, Owen, Nathan

Luken *(American)* ♂ RATING: ★★★☆
From Lucania, Italy—Variation of Luke
> People think of Luken as funny, handsome, caring, creative, trustworthy
> People who like the name Luken also like Kaden, Lucas, Liam, Tristan, Landon, Braeden, Ethan, Reece, Noah, Braden

Lukman *(Arabic)* ♂ RATING: ★★★
Wise, intelligent
> People think of Lukman as weird, nerdy, funny, handsome, popular

> People who like the name Lukman also like Lucas, Andrew, Jeremiah, Adam, Antony, Lincoln, Aaron, Nicholas, Augustus, Jason

Lula *(English)* ♀ RATING: ★★
Famous warrior—Short for Louisa
> People think of Lula as pretty, creative, funny, caring, artsy
> People who like the name Lula also like Layla, Lola, Lila, Ava, Lulu, Bella, Ella, Olivia, Isabella, Eva

Lulani *(Hawaiian)* ♂ RATING: ★★★
Highest heaven
> People think of Lulani as exotic, funny, creative, leader, young
> People who like the name Lulani also like Keoni, Aden, Drake, Kelii, Maddox, Mauli, Kaipo, Kaden, Kanoa, Keagan

Lulu *(English)* ♀ RATING: ★★
Famous warrior—Short for Louise; also an Arabic name meaning pearl
> People think of Lulu as pretty, funny, creative, cool, caring
> People who like the name Lulu also like Layla, Lola, Ava, Lily, Lucy, Ella, Mia, Grace, Elle, Audrey

Lumina *(Slavic)* ♀ RATING: ★★
Sunshine—Romanian origin
> People think of Lumina as elegant, pretty, intelligent, exotic, quiet
> People who like the name Lumina also like Luna, Lila, Layla, Lucia, Celeste, Bella, Lenore, Serena, Lyra, Linette

Luna *(Italian)* ♀ RATING: ★★☆
The moon
> People think of Luna as pretty, creative, intelligent, exotic, artsy
> People who like the name Luna also like Aurora, Ava, Olivia, Layla, Emma, Mia, Eva, Lily, Bella, Isabella

Lundy *(Scandinavian)* ♀♂ RATING: ★★★
Grove—Scottish place names
> People think of Lundy as popular, wealthy, caring, wild, leader
> People who like the name Lundy also like Landen, Leighton, Riley, Lindley, Landry, Logan, Reese, London, Raine, Lynley

Lunet *(Welsh)* ♀ RATING: ★★★
Holy image
> People think of Lunet as religious, pretty, lazy, funny, winner
> People who like the name Lunet also like Seren, Aria, Melangell, Kagami, Tegan, Kimi, Lark, Cashlin, Biana, Season

Lunette *(French)* ♀ RATING: ★★★
Little moon—Also French for spectacles (glasses)
> People think of Lunette as pretty, intelligent, elegant, exotic, caring

People who like the name Lunette also like Linette, Luna, Lynette, Lilly, Juliette, Lucia, Lorelei, Giselle, Layla, Elle

Lupe (Spanish) ♀ RATING: ★★★☆
From the river of the wolf—Short for Guadalupe
People think of Lupe as popular, cool, funny, pretty, caring
People who like the name Lupe also like Lola, Lana, Isabel, Giselle, Mercedes, Lilly, Lupita, Lucy, Lillian, Marisol

Lupita (Spanish) ♀ RATING: ★★★★
From the river of the wolf—Short for Lupe or Guadalupe
People think of Lupita as pretty, funny, caring, creative, intelligent
People who like the name Lupita also like Lola, Lupe, Lilliana, Lluvia, Lucia, Linda, Leela, Lenora, Layla, Leena

Luthando (African) ♂ RATING: ★★★
Love—South African origin
People think of Luthando as handsome, big, intelligent, exotic, powerful
People who like the name Luthando also like Adair, Amando, Luke, Nemesio, Lazzaro, Jovan, Lucio, Jamal, Lucus, Julius

Luther (English) ♂ RATING: ★★★
People army—Luther Vandross, singer
People think of Luther as intelligent, handsome, leader, caring, funny
People who like the name Luther also like Ethan, Isaac, Nicholas, Aiden, Lucas, Jackson, Caleb, Luke, Jacob, Owen

Luyu (Native American) ♀ RATING: ★★★
Wild dove—Miwok origin
People think of Luyu as weird, exotic, young, wild, funny
People who like the name Luyu also like Liluye, Kaya, Miakoda, Ayasha, Kimama, Layla, Dyani, Leila, Leilani, Tallulah

Luz (Spanish) ♀ ♂ RATING: ★☆
Light—Also a unisex Hebrew name, meaning almond tree
People think of Luz as pretty, funny, caring, intelligent, young
People who like the name Luz also like Paz, Sol, Luca, Jade, London, Sage, Logan, Lyle, Liberty, Landen

Ly (Vietnamese) ♀ ♂ RATING: ★★★☆
Reason
People think of Ly as funny, pretty, intelligent, cool, popular
People who like the name Ly also like Logan, London, Rumer, Landen, Lyre, Lyle, Loki, Lyndon, Kione, Layne

Lyall (English) ♂ RATING: ★★★☆
Lion—Variation of Lionel
People think of Lyall as intelligent, handsome, sexy, leader, uptight

People who like the name Lyall also like Liam, Lachlan, Riordan, Kael, Kellan, Keiran, Fynn, Nathaniel, Neil, Cian

Lycoris (Greek) ♀ RATING: ★★★☆
Twilight
People think of Lycoris as intelligent, exotic, creative, pretty, quiet
People who like the name Lycoris also like Lilith, Layla, Dysis, Lorelei, Aradia, Leila, Desdemona, Lucine, Sora, Lyris

Lydia (Greek) ♀ RATING: ★★★
From Lydia, Greece—Lydia Frazier Heston, actress/wife of Charlton Heston
People think of Lydia as pretty, intelligent, funny, caring, creative
People who like the name Lydia also like Olivia, Ava, Emma, Abigail, Grace, Sophia, Natalie, Hannah, Ella, Isabella

Lydie (French) ♀ RATING: ★★★★
From Lydia, Greece
People think of Lydie as pretty, creative, cool, girl next door, energetic
People who like the name Lydie also like Lydia, Sadie, Layla, Ava, Lainey, Elle, Lila, Sophie, Madeline, Paige

Lydon (English) ♀ ♂ RATING: ★★★
Descendent of Lodan—Christopher Lydon, journalist; John Lydon, musician
People think of Lydon as handsome, popular, pretty, creative, ethnic
People who like the name Lydon also like Caden, Hayden, Landen, Jaden, Addison, Baden, Lane, Rowan, Bryce, Cade

Lyle (English) ♀ ♂ RATING: ★★
From the island—Also a surname; Lyle Lovett, singer; Lyle Waggoner, actor/comedian; Lyle, Lyle Crocodile, children's book
People think of Lyle as funny, intelligent, cool, creative, caring
People who like the name Lyle also like Logan, Riley, Jaden, Landen, Hayden, Kyle, Caden, Parker, Dylan, Connor

Lyn (English) ♀ RATING: ★★☆
From the lake—Also short for Lynda
People think of Lyn as caring, pretty, intelligent, funny, creative
People who like the name Lyn also like Lauren, Faith, Grace, Emily, Sarah, Hannah, Eva, Chloe, Lily, Rebecca

Lynda (Spanish) ♀ RATING: ★★★★
Pretty one
People think of Lynda as caring, pretty, funny, intelligent, trustworthy
People who like the name Lynda also like Leah, Lydia, Amanda, Faith, Laura, Emily, Belinda, Lucinda, Victoria, Linda

Lynde *(German)* ♀♂　　　RATING: ★★★☆
Gentle—Also an American surname; Paul Lynde, actor/comedian
> People think of Lynde as intelligent, caring, pretty, energetic, funny
> People who like the name Lynde also like Layne, Landen, Logan, Lyndon, Lane, Leigh, Lindley, Landry, London, Hayden

Lyndon *(English)* ♀♂　　　RATING: ★★★
From the flax hill—Lyndon Baines Johnson, U.S. president
> People think of Lyndon as handsome, cool, caring, creative, intelligent
> People who like the name Lyndon also like Caden, Logan, Hayden, Landen, Parker, Madison, Jaden, Riley, Addison, Preston

Lyndsey *(English)* ♀♂　　　RATING: ★★★
From the lake settlement island
> People think of Lyndsey as funny, pretty, caring, trustworthy, intelligent
> People who like the name Lyndsey also like Lindsey, Madison, Mackenzie, Jordan, Sydney, Taylor, Morgan, Bailey, Lindsay, Hayden

Lynelle *(American)* ♀　　　RATING: ★★★★☆
Variation of Lynn
> People think of Lynelle as pretty, intelligent, funny, trustworthy, caring
> People who like the name Lynelle also like Kaelyn, Layla, Linette, Lynette, Janelle, Lanelle, Isabella, Grace, Jadyn, Rianna

Lyneth *(English)* ♀　　　RATING: ★★
Variation of Lynette
> People think of Lyneth as pretty, intelligent, young, trustworthy, quiet
> People who like the name Lyneth also like Laurel, Lynette, Lorelei, Gwyneth, Layla, Lyn, Lia, Lynnea, Charlotte, Arwen

Lynette *(French)* ♀　　　RATING: ★★★★
Pretty one—Variation of Lynn
> People think of Lynette as pretty, caring, intelligent, funny, creative
> People who like the name Lynette also like Linette, Isabelle, Isabella, Jacqueline, Layla, Hannah, Jasmine, Nadia, Hailey, Cassandra

Lynley *(English)* ♀♂　　　RATING: ★★☆
From the flax meadow
> People think of Lynley as pretty, caring, popular, young, intelligent
> People who like the name Lynley also like Addison, Lindley, Hadley, Hayden, Logan, Landen, Riley, Ainsley, Caden, Aubrey

Lynn *(Celtic/Gaelic)* ♀♂　　　RATING: ★★★☆
From the lake—Lynn Redgrave, actress
> People think of Lynn as funny, caring, pretty, creative, intelligent

People who like the name Lynn also like Logan, Madison, Riley, Hayden, Taylor, Jordan, Bailey, Ryan, Jade, Kyle

Lynna *(English)* ♀　　　RATING: ★★★★
From the lake—Variation of Lynn
> People think of Lynna as caring, pretty, creative, intelligent, artsy
> People who like the name Lynna also like Lana, Jenna, Leilani, Lila, Laurel, Lorelei, Layla, Leighanna, Lara, Larissa

Lynne *(English)* ♀♂　　　RATING: ★★★★☆
From the lake
> People think of Lynne as caring, pretty, funny, intelligent, creative
> People who like the name Lynne also like Lynn, Ryan, Leigh, Tyler, Riley, Logan, Jade, Mackenzie, Hayden, Jocelyn

Lynnea *(Scandinavian)* ♀　　　RATING: ★★★★☆
Flower—Variation of Linnea
> People think of Lynnea as pretty, caring, funny, creative, intelligent
> People who like the name Lynnea also like Linnea, Kaelyn, Lilianna, Layla, Lily, Isabella, Olivia, Lexi, Lilliana, Liana

Lynton *(English)* ♀♂　　　RATING: ★★★
From the hillside town
> People think of Lynton as popular, trustworthy, intelligent, funny, cool
> People who like the name Lynton also like Landen, Keaton, Camdyn, Lyndon, Logan, Payton, London, Hadley, Riley, Parker

Lyra *(Latin)* ♀　　　RATING: ★★★★☆
Lyre, harp
> People think of Lyra as pretty, intelligent, creative, energetic, elegant
> People who like the name Lyra also like Layla, Ava, Ivy, Iris, Aurora, Chloe, Lily, Kiara, Mia, Hazel

Lyre *(English)* ♀♂　　　RATING: ★★
Lyre, harp—From the Greek name Lyris
> People think of Lyre as artsy, funny, quiet, untrustworthy, exotic
> People who like the name Lyre also like Logan, Lyric, Landen, Layne, Lavender, Lynn, Hayden, Jaden, Sage, Cade

Lyric *(English)* ♀♂　　　RATING: ★★★☆
Song words
> People think of Lyric as creative, pretty, artsy, popular, intelligent
> People who like the name Lyric also like Hayden, Logan, Jaden, Avery, London, Jade, Riley, Cadence, Dylan, Caden

Lyris *(Greek)* ♀　　　RATING: ★★
Lyre, harp
> People think of Lyris as pretty, creative, intelligent, young, artsy

People who like the name Lyris also like Lyra, Lilith, Lorelei, Lexi, Lydia, Maris, Jadyn, Laurel, Chloe, Daphne

Lysa (American) ♀   RATING: ★★☆

God is my oath—Short for Elisabeth

People think of Lysa as pretty, intelligent, creative, caring, trustworthy

People who like the name Lysa also like Lana, Larissa, Lexi, Layla, Lauren, Leah, Kailey, Lainey, Lilly, Lorelei

Lysander (Greek) ♂   RATING: ★★

One who is freed

People think of Lysander as handsome, intelligent, powerful, creative, caring

People who like the name Lysander also like Gabriel, Alexander, Noah, Leander, Liam, Xander, Aiden, Tristan, Sebastian, Lucas

Lysandra (Greek) ♀   RATING: ★★☆

One who is freed

People think of Lysandra as pretty, exotic, funny, elegant, sexy

People who like the name Lysandra also like Leandra, Cassandra, Layla, Lilianna, Larissa, Isabella, Gabrielle, Leilani, Bianca, Samara

Mab (Celtic/Gaelic) ♀   RATING: ★★★

Intoxicating—Variation of Maeve; Queen Mab, from *The Faerie Queene*

People think of Mab as funny, powerful, intelligent, popular, exotic

People who like the name Mab also like Maeve, Mabel, Mae, Maggie, Mabyn, Macayle, Meara, Aeryn, Mairead, Madge

Mabel (English) ♀   RATING: ★★★★

Lovable

People think of Mabel as pretty, caring, intelligent, funny, creative

People who like the name Mabel also like Grace, Hannah, Isabella, Olivia, Emma, Hazel, Abigail, Chloe, Bella, Faith

Mabli (Welsh) ♀   RATING: ★★★

Lovable—Variation of Mabel

People think of Mabli as pretty, young, elegant, artsy, exotic

People who like the name Mabli also like Mabel, Madelia, Maha, Maisie, Adamma, Malaika, Mahal, Malia, Maggie, Maeko

Mabon (Welsh) ♂   RATING: ★★☆

Divine son

People think of Mabon as artsy, intelligent, young, old-fashioned, quiet

People who like the name Mabon also like Malone, Maddox, Macon, Ace, Maddock, Maston, Matthias, Marius, Aiden, Malcolm

Mabyn (Welsh) ♀   RATING: ★★★☆

Divine son

People think of Mabyn as weird, powerful, pretty, young, intelligent

People who like the name Mabyn also like Mabel, Maeve, Jadyn, Kaelyn, Ava, Sadie, Macy, Madelyn, Maren, Aeryn

Mac (Celtic/Gaelic) ♂   RATING: ★★☆

Son of—Short for names beginning with Mac or Mc

People think of Mac as cool, funny, handsome, popular, intelligent

People who like the name Mac also like Jack, Max, Owen, Maddox, Noah, Aiden, Liam, Jake, Luke, Finn

Macadrian (American) ♀   RATING: ★★★☆

Combination of Mac and Adrian

People think of Macadrian as pretty, exotic, elegant, cool, creative

People who like the name Macadrian also like Makenna, Caelan, Maegan, Kaelyn, Makaila, Cailyn, Mabel, Macayle, Madeleine, Madelyn

Macarena (Spanish) ♀   RATING: ★★★

Blessed

People think of Macarena as exotic, pretty, popular, young, sexy

People who like the name Macarena also like Magdalena, Lacole, Laina, Mariana, Maceo, Laine, Lolita, Lucinda, Marianela, Lainey

Macaria (Greek) ♀   RATING: ★★★★☆

Happy—In Greek mythology, the daughter of Herakles

People think of Macaria as pretty, funny, caring, exotic, creative

People who like the name Macaria also like Makaila, Malaika, Macayle, Makara, Maya, Makayla, Cassandra, Malia, Alana, Samara

Macario (Spanish) ♂   RATING: ★★★☆

Happy

People think of Macario as intelligent, handsome, energetic, weird, funny

People who like the name Macario also like Mateo, Maddox, Gabriel, Marcello, Marco, Antonio, Diego, Malcolm, Xavier, Malik

Macawi (Native American) ♀   RATING: ★★☆

Female coyote—Sioux origin

People think of Macawi as nerdy, loser, lazy, old, old-fashioned

People who like the name Macawi also like Chaela, Ayasha, Cayla, Kaliska, Tolinka, Analise, Janika, Kayla, Kayanna, Kira

Macayle (American) ♀   RATING: ★★★

Who is like God?—Variation of Michaela; also possibly a variation of the surname McHale

People think of Macayle as pretty, creative, caring, trendy, funny

People who like the name Macayle also like Makayla, Mckayla, Makenna, Kaelyn, Hailey, Maegan, Macy, Abigail, Jadyn, Hannah

372

Mace *(English)* ♂   RATING: ★★★☆
Gift of God—Medieval variation of Matthew
> People think of Mace as powerful, intelligent, handsome, creative, funny
> People who like the name Mace also like Maddox, Kaden, Jace, Caleb, Ian, Gage, Aiden, Chase, Ethan, Gabriel

Maceo *(Spanish)* ♀   RATING: ★★★
Gift of God—Variation of Matteo or Matthew
> People think of Maceo as handsome, creative, funny, exotic, cool
> People who like the name Maceo also like Sadie, Nascha, Macarena, Lupe, Olivia, Naiara, Maia, Aiko, Samara, Jara

Macha *(Native American)* ♀   RATING: ★★★
Aurora—Sioux origin
> People think of Macha as weird, exotic, creative, intelligent, aggressive
> People who like the name Macha also like Mahina, Aurora, Macaria, Mahalia, Mabel, Cassandra, Madeline, Mada, Mabyn, Magnolia

Machiko *(Japanese)* ♀   RATING: ★★★☆
Fortunate one
> People think of Machiko as pretty, creative, exotic, elegant, intelligent
> People who like the name Machiko also like Maeko, Mai, Masako, Miyoko, Sakura, Michiko, Mieko, Keiko, Amaya, Miya

Mackenzie *(Celtic/Gaelic)* ♀♂   RATING: ★★★☆
Son of Kenneth—Also spelled Mckenzie; MacKenzie Phillips, actress
> People think of Mackenzie as pretty, funny, popular, creative, intelligent
> People who like the name Mackenzie also like Madison, Riley, Logan, Bailey, Taylor, Morgan, Hayden, Addison, Cameron, Jordan

Macon *(French)* ♂   RATING: ★★
Mason
> People think of Macon as funny, handsome, creative, intelligent, caring
> People who like the name Macon also like Landon, Aiden, Maddox, Kaden, Braden, Jackson, Noah, Gage, Caleb, Ethan

Macy *(English)* ♀♂   RATING: ★★★☆
From Massy, France—Also a surname; Macy Gray, singer
> People think of Macy as pretty, funny, popular, energetic, creative
> People who like the name Macy also like Olivia, Ava, Paige, Emma, Ella, Grace, Hannah, Isabella, Chloe, Mia

Macyn *(American)* ♀   RATING: ★★★★
Mason—Variation of Mason
> People think of Macyn as pretty, energetic, intelligent, funny, popular

> People who like the name Macyn also like Kaelyn, Jadyn, Madelyn, Cailyn, Macy, Olivia, Makenna, Ashlyn, Kaydence, Makayla

Mada *(Arabic)* ♀   RATING: ★★★☆
Farthest point
> People think of Mada as leader, artsy, creative, exotic, intelligent
> People who like the name Mada also like Mabyn, Mahina, Mahdis, Mai, Macha, Maeve, Maeko, Mardea, Madelia, Mahsa

Madden *(Celtic/Gaelic)* ♀♂   RATING: ★★★☆
Little dog—Joel and Benji Madden, singer/songwriter brothers
> People think of Madden as handsome, popular, funny, sporty, energetic
> People who like the name Madden also like Madison, Mason, Hayden, Caden, Logan, Parker, Mackenzie, Addison, Riley, Jaden

Maddock *(Welsh)* ♂   RATING: ★★
Good
> People think of Maddock as handsome, unpopular, sporty, trustworthy, wild
> People who like the name Maddock also like Maddox, Kaden, Jackson, Gavin, Owen, Aiden, Tristan, Ethan, Ian, Gabriel

Maddox *(English)* ♂   RATING: ★★★★
Son of Madog
> People think of Maddox as handsome, popular, cool, intelligent, powerful
> People who like the name Maddox also like Aiden, Ethan, Landon, Noah, Kaden, Jackson, Caleb, Tristan, Gavin, Gabriel

Maddy *(English)* ♀   RATING: ★★★☆
Woman of Magdala—Short for Madeleine or Madison; also spelled Maddie
> People think of Maddy as funny, pretty, popular, young, creative
> People who like the name Maddy also like Macy, Paige, Maggie, Emma, Madeline, Grace, Hannah, Madeleine, Madelyn, Sadie

Madeleine *(French)* ♀   RATING: ★★★☆
Woman of Magdala—Also spelled Madeline, Madelyne, Maddelyne, Mahdeline, Mahdelyn, or Madeleina; Madeleine L'Engle, author; Princess Madeleine of Sweden
> People think of Madeleine as pretty, intelligent, funny, creative, elegant
> People who like the name Madeleine also like Olivia, Isabella, Hannah, Abigail, Ava, Madelyn, Madeline, Grace, Emma, Isabelle

Madelia *(English)* ♀   RATING: ★★☆
Woman of Magdala—Variation of Madeline
> People think of Madelia as pretty, funny, popular, exotic, intelligent

People who like the name Madelia also like Madeline, Madelyn, Madeleine, Isabella, Amelia, Mabel, Malia, Macy, Isabelle, Maya

Madelina *(Spanish)* ♀   RATING: ★★★
Woman of Magdala
People think of Madelina as pretty, young, exotic, girl next door, wild
People who like the name Madelina also like Gabriella, Isabella, Amelia, Madelyn, Catalina, Madeline, Natalia, Ava, Madeleine, Bella

Madeline *(English)* ♀   RATING: ★★★
Woman of Magdala
People think of Madeline as pretty, intelligent, funny, caring, creative
People who like the name Madeline also like Olivia, Emma, Hannah, Abigail, Isabella, Grace, Ava, Ella, Madelyn, Isabelle

Madelyn *(English)* ♀   RATING: ★★★☆
Woman of Magdala
People think of Madelyn as pretty, funny, intelligent, creative, caring
People who like the name Madelyn also like Olivia, Isabella, Madeline, Hannah, Abigail, Emma, Ava, Grace, Hailey, Paige

Madge *(English)* ♀   RATING: ★★★
Pearl—Short for Margaret
People think of Madge as funny, intelligent, caring, energetic, trustworthy
People who like the name Madge also like Mabel, Maggie, Madeline, Mab, Mae, Maeve, Macy, Olivia, Maisie, Macaria

Madison *(English)* ♀ ♂   RATING: ★★★☆
Son of Matthew—Also spelled Maddison; originally a surname; character in the movie *Splash*; James Madison, U.S. president
People think of Madison as pretty, funny, popular, creative, intelligent
People who like the name Madison also like Mackenzie, Riley, Bailey, Taylor, Hayden, Addison, Logan, Morgan, Mason, Caden

Madlaina *(Rumantsch)* ♀   RATING: ★★☆
Woman of Magdala—Variation of Madeline
People think of Madlaina as pretty, old-fashioned, quiet, weird, trendy
People who like the name Madlaina also like Fiona, Charlotte, Genevieve, Deidra, Hermione, Lorelei, Dahlia, Lydia, Isabella, Jacqueline

Madonna *(Latin)* ♀   RATING: ★★★
My lady—In the Bible, another name for Mary, mother of Jesus Christ; Madonna, singer/actress
People think of Madonna as sexy, popular, pretty, intelligent, powerful
People who like the name Madonna also like Mabel, Jennifer, Madeline, Felicity, Amber, Isabella, Maggie, Michelle, Eva, Melissa

Madra *(Spanish)* ♀   RATING: ★★
Motherly
People think of Madra as caring, weird, exotic, slow, sneaky
People who like the name Madra also like Mae, Mabel, Malia, Madelyn, Marcia, Maya, Martina, Mairead, Natasha, Malin

Madrid *(Spanish)* ♀ ♂   RATING: ★★☆
From Madrid, Spain
People think of Madrid as exotic, ethnic, weird, energetic, funny
People who like the name Madrid also like Cairo, Dylan, Brooke, Dakota, Mercury, Paris, Aquarius, Milan, Pisces, Harley

Madrona *(Welsh)* ♀   RATING: ★★★
Mother Goddess
People think of Madrona as exotic, pretty, winner, sneaky, powerful
People who like the name Madrona also like Adriana, Madeline, Mabel, Maya, Macy, Magdalena, Jemma, Jacqueline, Jane, Jadyn

Mae *(English)* ♀   RATING: ★★☆
Month of May—Also short for names beginning with M; Mae West, actress/pundit
People think of Mae as pretty, caring, creative, intelligent, funny
People who like the name Mae also like Ava, Grace, Emma, Faith, Olivia, Mia, Ella, Paige, Chloe, Hannah

Maegan *(American)* ♀   RATING: ★★☆
Pearl—Variation of Megan
People think of Maegan as pretty, funny, caring, creative, intelligent
People who like the name Maegan also like Paige, Olivia, Meagan, Kaelyn, Hannah, Faith, Hailey, Emily, Emma, Lauren

Maeko *(Japanese)* ♀   RATING: ★★★★
Truthful child—Also spelled Meiko, Mayco, or Mayko
People think of Maeko as pretty, trustworthy, exotic, quiet, intelligent
People who like the name Maeko also like Mai, Sakura, Mieko, Aiko, Machiko, Kaiya, Miyo, Amaya, Kaida, Emiko

Maemi *(Japanese)* ♀ ♂   RATING: ★★★★
Honest child
People think of Maemi as pretty, young, creative, intelligent, exotic
People who like the name Maemi also like Mitsu, Maro, Kiyoshi, Hoshi, Asa, Seiko, Nori, Makani, Kumi, Sanyu

Maeron *(American)* ♀ ♂   RATING: ★★★
Combination of Mae and Ron
People think of Maeron as pretty, young, old-fashioned, wild, aggressive
People who like the name Maeron also like Maeryn, Madison, Aidan, Morrigan, Madden, Jaden, Skye, Farren, Mackenzie, Quinn

373

Maeryn *(American)* ♀ ♂   RATING: ★★☆
Combination of Mae and Taryn
> People think of Maeryn as pretty, caring, elegant, artsy, creative
> People who like the name Maeryn also like Madison, Aidan, Avery, Caden, Hayden, Logan, Mackenzie, Mason, Maeron, Marin

Maeve *(Celtic/Gaelic)* ♀   RATING: ★★★★☆
Intoxicating—Also spelled Maive or Mayve; Maeve Binchy, author; Maeve Quinlan, actress
> People think of Maeve as pretty, intelligent, creative, funny, caring
> People who like the name Maeve also like Fiona, Ava, Mae, Olivia, Genevieve, Ella, Paige, Chloe, Charlotte, Emma

Magali *(French)* ♀   RATING: ★★★☆
Pearl—Provençal variation of Margaret
> People think of Magali as pretty, cool, funny, intelligent, caring
> People who like the name Magali also like Mariana, Leilani, Makayla, Denise, Juliana, Aaliyah, Isabella, Cassandra, Ailani, Anaïs

Magan *(Greek)* ♀ ♂   RATING: ★★★★
Pearl—Short for Margaret
> People think of Magan as pretty, funny, caring, cool, sexy
> People who like the name Magan also like Madison, Morgan, Mackenzie, Bailey, Jaden, Jordan, Mason, Taylor, Ashley, Caden

Magar *(Armenian)* ♂   RATING: ★★
Lucky
> People think of Magar as aggressive, nerdy, loser, old, pretty
> People who like the name Magar also like Macario, Macon, Maddox, Maddock, Malik, Mateo, Sanders, Ismet, Mace, Miles

Magda *(Polish)* ♀   RATING: ★★
Woman of Magdala—Short for Magdalen
> People think of Magda as intelligent, pretty, funny, creative, cool
> People who like the name Magda also like Maeve, Maggie, Genevieve, Daphne, Audrey, Mae, Magdalen, Macy, Magdalena, Madeleine

Magdalen *(English)* ♀   RATING: ★★★★
Woman of Magdala
> People think of Magdalen as exotic, pretty, intelligent, elegant, creative
> People who like the name Magdalen also like Madeline, Olivia, Maggie, Madelyn, Madeleine, Ava, Amelia, Mabel, Isabella, Emma

Magdalena *(Spanish)* ♀   RATING: ★★
Woman of Magdala
> People think of Magdalena as pretty, intelligent, elegant, caring, creative
> People who like the name Magdalena also like Isabella, Gabriella, Madeleine, Madeline, Genevieve, Olivia, Adriana, Sophia, Maggie, Scarlett

Magdalene *(Latin)* ♀   RATING: ★★☆
Woman of Magdala—In the Bible, Mary Magdelene is a follower of Christ
> People think of Magdalene as pretty, intelligent, caring, creative, trustworthy
> People who like the name Magdalene also like Magdalena, Madeleine, Isabella, Olivia, Madeline, Magnolia, Charlotte, Magdalen, Chloe, Ava

Magdalia *(English)* ♀   RATING: ★★★
Woman of Magdala
> People think of Magdalia as ethnic, weird, artsy, exotic, powerful
> People who like the name Magdalia also like Maeve, Genevieve, Maggie, Mckayla, Macayle, Mabel, Maire, Meara, Magdalena, Rhona

Magee *(Celtic/Gaelic)* ♂   RATING: ★★★
Son of Aodh
> People think of Magee as funny, caring, trustworthy, pretty, leader
> People who like the name Magee also like Mac, Maddox, Gabriel, Eli, Grant, Jacob, Finley, Jack, Grady, Jackson

Maggie *(English)* ♀   RATING: ★★★
Pearl—Short for Margaret; Maggie Smith, actress; Grandma Maggie from www.babynames.com
> People think of Maggie as pretty, funny, caring, creative, intelligent
> People who like the name Maggie also like Hannah, Olivia, Grace, Emma, Ava, Ella, Emily, Paige, Abigail, Sophie

Magic *(American)* ♀ ♂   RATING: ★★★☆
Full of Wonder—Earvin "Magic" Johnson, basketball player
> People think of Magic as creative, weird, funny, powerful, popular
> People who like the name Magic also like Mackenzie, Madison, Jade, Madden, Phoenix, Jaden, Maverick, Preston, Mason, Dylan

Magnar *(Polish)* ♂   RATING: ★☆
Northern might
> People think of Magnar as powerful, aggressive, leader, intelligent, cool
> People who like the name Magnar also like Maddox, Malcolm, Maddock, Macario, Mace, Maynard, Malik, Ryu, Manelin, Milek

Magnolia *(French)* ♀   RATING: ★★
Flower name
> People think of Magnolia as pretty, elegant, creative, exotic, caring
> People who like the name Magnolia also like Isabella, Madeleine, Violet, Madeline, Genevieve, Scarlett, Maggie, Faith, Hannah, Ophelia

Magnum *(Latin)* ♂   RATING: ★★★
Big, great—*Magnum P.I.*, TV show
> People think of Magnum as sexy, powerful, intelligent, trustworthy, handsome
> People who like the name Magnum also like Xavier, Maddox, Malone, Malik, Micah, Matthew, Noah, Mikko, Caleb, Gavin

Magnus *(Latin)* ♂   RATING: ★★★☆
Big, great
> People think of Magnus as powerful, intelligent, handsome, leader, sporty
> People who like the name Magnus also like Gabriel, Maddox, Oliver, Liam, Maximus, Samuel, Noah, Miles, Matthias, Atticus

Maha *(Arabic)* ♀   RATING: ★★★☆
Shining
> People think of Maha as pretty, intelligent, funny, caring, exotic
> People who like the name Maha also like Malaika, Mabel, Mia, Maya, Makaila, Maeko, Malia, Mahal, Mandisa, Mali

Mahak *(Arabic)* ♂   RATING: ★★☆
Waning of the moon
> People think of Mahak as pretty, girl next door, intelligent, leader, cool
> People who like the name Mahak also like Manas, Malachi, Maxim, Malik, Gagan, Mattias, Hades, Makoto, Medwin, Tariq

Mahal *(Arabic)* ♀   RATING: ★☆
Love—Filipino origin
> People think of Mahal as exotic, pretty, ethnic, intelligent, creative
> People who like the name Mahal also like Mahala, Maha, Makaila, Malaika, Mabel, Mandy, Maya, Maeko, Jia Li, Mariah

Mahala *(Hebrew)* ♀   RATING: ★★★☆
Sickness
> People think of Mahala as pretty, exotic, creative, weird, intelligent
> People who like the name Mahala also like Mahalia, Makayla, Mahalah, Olivia, Isabella, Makaila, Mahlah, Ava, Hannah, Kaelyn

Mahalah *(Hebrew)* ♀   RATING: ★★★
Sickness
> People think of Mahalah as pretty, caring, ethnic, weird, energetic
> People who like the name Mahalah also like Mahala, Mahalia, Madeleine, Makayla, Malia, Michaela, Malaya, Mabel, Mali, Shakira

Mahalia *(Hebrew)* ♀   RATING: ★★★★☆
Sickness—Mahalia Jackson, singer
> People think of Mahalia as intelligent, pretty, creative, caring, sexy
> People who like the name Mahalia also like Malia, Mahala, Makaila, Makayla, Maya, Aaliyah, Mia, Olivia, Maia, Jasmine

Mahari *(Sanskrit/East Indian)* ♀♂   RATING: ★★
Divine maiden—Variation of Oriya; South Indian origin
> People think of Mahari as pretty, powerful, intelligent, exotic, caring
> People who like the name Mahari also like Mahdi, Makaio, Makani, Mackenzie, Jaden, Morgan, Dakota, Jalen, Kijana, Mason

Mahdi *(Arabic)* ♀♂   RATING: ★★
Rightly guided
> People think of Mahdi as intelligent, handsome, caring, sexy, funny
> People who like the name Mahdi also like Mahari, Makaio, Maemi, Mariatu, Makani, Maik, Morgan, Maeryn, Maro, Jada

Mahdis *(Persian)* ♀   RATING: ★★★☆
Moonlike
> People think of Mahdis as pretty, energetic, young, intelligent, sexy
> People who like the name Mahdis also like Mahsa, Mahina, Maeve, Mabyn, Mai, Mahola, Malia, Magnolia, Maha, Maris

Mahendra *(Sanskrit/East Indian)* ♂   RATING: ★★☆
God Indra
> People think of Mahendra as handsome, intelligent, caring, cool, creative
> People who like the name Mahendra also like Manas, Mandar, Malachi, Omanand, Rohan, Mabon, Myron, Ravi, Manjit, Ram

Mahesa *(Sanskrit/East Indian)* ♀   RATING: ★★★
Lord Shiva
> People think of Mahesa as religious, intelligent, pretty, aggressive, ethnic
> People who like the name Mahesa also like Mallika, Manasa, Maina, Jaya, Malini, Malia, Mahina, Mai, Maeve, Mandara

Mahina *(Hawaiian)* ♀   RATING: ★★
Moon
> People think of Mahina as pretty, exotic, creative, artsy, caring
> People who like the name Mahina also like Malia, Leilani, Malana, Maeve, Kailani, Makana, Maleah, Mahdis, Mai, Mahalia

Mahlah *(Hebrew)* ♀   RATING: ★★★
Sickness
> People think of Mahlah as quiet, pretty, poor, untrustworthy, unpopular
> People who like the name Mahlah also like Mahala, Mali, Mai, Malia, Mahalia, Madeleine, Makaila, Marli, Malaika, Malana

Mahogany *(English)* ♀   RATING: ★★★☆
Dark red wood—Also spelled Mahogony; often used for brunettes or people with dark skin
> People think of Mahogany as pretty, caring, intelligent, cool, sexy

375

People who like the name Mahogany also like Faith, Mercedes, Mallory, Olivia, Jasmine, Harmony, Macy, Paige, Madeline, Makayla

Mahola (*Native American*) ♀   RATING: ★★★
Dance
  People think of Mahola as uptight, weird, ethnic, poor, old
  People who like the name Mahola also like Malia, Maeko, Maha, Mahsa, Mahdis, Moriah, Mahina, Marcena, Maita, Malaika

Mahon (*Celtic/Gaelic*) ♂   RATING: ★★★
Bear cub
  People think of Mahon as poor, ethnic, weird, powerful, old
  People who like the name Mahon also like Liam, Callahan, Merric, Edan, Malcolm, Owen, Kane, Finley, Aden, Dallin

Mahsa (*Persian*) ♀   RATING: ★★★★
Like the moon
  People think of Mahsa as pretty, sexy, funny, elegant, young
  People who like the name Mahsa also like Mahdis, Mahina, Mai, Maeve, Mahola, Malia, Maha, Malana, Mali, Mara

Mai (*Japanese*) ♀   RATING: ★★★★
Brightness
  People think of Mai as pretty, caring, funny, intelligent, young
  People who like the name Mai also like Mia, Mae, Maeko, Paige, Ava, Sakura, Kaiya, Aiko, Amaya, Maya

Maia (*Latin*) ♀   RATING: ★★★★
Great
  People think of Maia as pretty, intelligent, creative, funny, caring
  People who like the name Maia also like Maya, Ava, Mia, Chloe, Eva, Isabella, Olivia, Ella, Paige, Grace

Maida (*Armenian*) ♀   RATING: ★★
Maiden
  People think of Maida as pretty, intelligent, caring, energetic, young
  People who like the name Maida also like Maya, Maia, Malia, Mairwen, Mabel, Madelia, Mira, Maina, Maris, Mahdis

Maija (*Scandinavian*) ♀   RATING: ★★★★
Sea of bitterness—Variation of Mary
  People think of Maija as pretty, creative, caring, energetic, funny
  People who like the name Maija also like Jolie, Anika, Maia, Maya, Mali, Macy, Mia, Miranda, Julia, Maggie

Maik (*English*) ♀♂   RATING: ★★★
Who is like God?—Variation of Mike
  People think of Maik as weird, funny, intelligent, exotic, wild

People who like the name Maik also like Makani, Marek, Makaio, Maemi, Mahdi, Jade, Mason, Makya, Madison, Maeryn

Maili (*Celtic/Gaelic*) ♀   RATING: ★★★☆
Sea of bitterness—Variation of Molly or Mary
  People think of Maili as pretty, caring, funny, intelligent, creative
  People who like the name Maili also like Malia, Ava, Ella, Maya, Mia, Layla, Maille, Maeve, Keaira, Keira

Maille (*French*) ♀   RATING: ★★★★
Coin
  People think of Maille as pretty, popular, caring, sexy, creative
  People who like the name Maille also like Macayle, Madeline, Kaelyn, Makenna, Maisie, Maeve, Fiona, Mae, Makayla, Genevieve

Maimun (*Arabic*) ♀♂   RATING: ★★☆
Lucky
  People think of Maimun as exotic, weird, popular, artsy, old-fashioned
  People who like the name Maimun also like Makaio, Makani, Mahdi, Maemi, Makya, Manning, Maitland, Maro, Matty, Merrick

Maina (*Sanskrit/East Indian*) ♀   RATING: ★★★
Messenger of God
  People think of Maina as pretty, caring, sexy, sporty, quiet
  People who like the name Maina also like Mallika, Maren, Malia, Mahesa, Malana, Mai, Mahina, Marcena, Maya, Mae

Maine (*French*) ♀♂   RATING: ★★★
Mainland—U.S. state
  People think of Maine as intelligent, funny, old-fashioned, caring, sporty
  People who like the name Maine also like Madison, Taylor, Hayden, Riley, Spencer, Mason, Morgan, Cameron, Tyler, Jordan

Maire (*Celtic/Gaelic*) ♀   RATING: ★★★☆
Sea of bitterness—Variation of Mary; pronounced *MOY-ra*
  People think of Maire as pretty, creative, caring, funny, wild
  People who like the name Maire also like Maggie, Maeve, Moira, Keira, Emma, Madeline, Erin, Genevieve, Grace, Mae

Mairead (*Celtic/Gaelic*) ♀   RATING: ★★
Pearl—Variation of Margaret
  People think of Mairead as pretty, creative, intelligent, funny, caring
  People who like the name Mairead also like Maeve, Genevieve, Moira, Maire, Fiona, Maura, Grace, Keaira, Gabrielle, Hazel

Mairi *(Celtic/Gaelic)* ♀ RATING: ★★☆
Sea of bitterness—Scottish variation of Mary; pronounced *MAH-ree*
People think of Mairi as pretty, creative, intelligent, artsy, elegant
People who like the name Mairi also like Mae, Macayle, Maeve, Makayla, Moira, Keira, Kaelyn, Keaira, Kiara, Genevieve

Mairwen *(Welsh)* ♀ RATING: ★★★☆
Blessed Mary
People think of Mairwen as pretty, quiet, religious, caring, trustworthy
People who like the name Mairwen also like Arwen, Morwen, Aelwen, Elwyn, Maeve, Isolde, Rhiannon, Gwendolyn, Lorelei, Gwyneth

Maisha *(African)* ♀ RATING: ★★★★
Life—Kiswahili origin
People think of Maisha as pretty, intelligent, creative, young, winner
People who like the name Maisha also like Malaika, Myeisha, Ayanna, Mai, Maia, Malia, Maya, Mya, Makaila, Mandisa

Maisie *(English)* ♀ RATING: ★★★★☆
Pearl—Short for Margaret
People think of Maisie as pretty, funny, creative, caring, intelligent
People who like the name Maisie also like Macy, Olivia, Ella, Mia, Grace, Maggie, Madeleine, Ava, Chloe, Paige

Maita *(Spanish)* ♀ RATING: ★★★☆
Combination of Maria and Teresa
People think of Maita as pretty, creative, funny, caring, quiet
People who like the name Maita also like Malana, Malaya, Malia, Maha, Malaika, Mai, Mahola, Mahesa, Mahina, Maia

Maitland *(English)* ♀♂ RATING: ★★★☆
From the unproductive lands—Mary Maitland, actress
People think of Maitland as funny, intelligent, creative, pretty, trustworthy
People who like the name Maitland also like Hayden, Mackenzie, Madison, Parker, Mason, Keegan, Jordan, Morgan, Addison, Reagan

Maj *(Scandinavian)* ♀♂ RATING: ★★★
Sea of bitterness—Short for Mary
People think of Maj as exotic, weird, intelligent, unpopular, artsy
People who like the name Maj also like Makani, Makya, Magan, Maemi, Maik, Maitland, Maimun, Haven, Maro, Jorryn

Maja *(Scandinavian)* ♀ RATING: ★★★★☆
Sea of bitterness
People think of Maja as intelligent, pretty, sexy, caring, creative
People who like the name Maja also like Maya, Maia, Mia, Mya, Emma, Mai, Maisha, Layla, Malana, Malia

Majed *(Arabic)* ♂ RATING: ★★★
Glorious, noble
People think of Majed as exotic, handsome, cool, sexy, funny
People who like the name Majed also like Malik, Malachi, Micah, Mansour, Magnar, Makoto, Malo, Maddox, Major, Habib

Major *(Latin)* ♂ RATING: ★★★☆
Better
People think of Major as handsome, sporty, intelligent, funny, powerful
People who like the name Major also like Maddox, Gabriel, Tyson, Miles, Jacob, Ethan, Wade, Jackson, Lincoln, Dillon

Makaila *(American)* ♀ RATING: ★★★★
Who is like God?—Variation of Michaela
People think of Makaila as pretty, creative, intelligent, funny, caring
People who like the name Makaila also like Makayla, Mckayla, Hailey, Jadyn, Kaelyn, Makenna, Adriana, Isabella, Cailyn, Hannah

Makaio *(Hawaiian)* ♀♂ RATING: ★★★★
Gift of God
People think of Makaio as handsome, popular, caring, exotic, intelligent
People who like the name Makaio also like Makani, Kai, Jaden, Caden, Mahari, Maemi, Madison, Mahdi, Dakota, Jesse

Makala *(American)* ♀ RATING: ★★★★
Who is like God?—Variation of Michaela
People think of Makala as pretty, funny, popular, intelligent, creative
People who like the name Makala also like Makayla, Makaila, Mckayla, Hailey, Kayla, Makenna, Hannah, Kailey, Kaelyn, Paige

Makalo *(African)* ♂ RATING: ★★★
Wonder, surprise
People think of Makalo as exotic, intelligent, handsome, creative, funny
People who like the name Makalo also like Malik, Malachi, Milo, Mikaili, Maddox, Makoto, Mariano, Isaac, Mateo, Manelin

Makana *(Hawaiian)* ♀ RATING: ★★☆
Gift
People think of Makana as pretty, intelligent, leader, creative, caring
People who like the name Makana also like Malia, Makala, Makayla, Makenna, Makaila, Kailani, Malana, Leilani, Kaelyn, Hannah

Makani *(Hawaiian)* ♀♂ RATING: ★★★☆
The wind
People think of Makani as exotic, intelligent, cool, young, popular
People who like the name Makani also like Kai, Makaio, Kalani, Nalani, Keanu, Madison, Maemi, Mahari, Lani, Makya

378

Makara *(Sanskrit/East Indian)* ♀   RATING: ★★☆
Born under Capricorn—Also Hebrew meaning blessing
> People think of Makara as popular, pretty, funny, exotic, leader
> People who like the name Makara also like Makayla, Makenna, Malana, Malaya, Macaria, Makaila, Makana, Malia, Macy, Kiara

Makayla *(American)* ♀   RATING: ★★
Who is like God?—Variation of Michaela
> People think of Makayla as pretty, funny, intelligent, young, caring
> People who like the name Makayla also like Hailey, Hannah, Emma, Mckayla, Isabella, Kayla, Paige, Makenna, Kaelyn, Abigail

Makelina *(Hawaiian)* ♀   RATING: ★★☆
Woman of Magdala—Variation of Magdelene
> People think of Makelina as exotic, artsy, ethnic, pretty, sexy
> People who like the name Makelina also like Malia, Makenna, Malana, Maleah, Makayla, Magdalena, Madeleine, Makana, Isabella, Madeline

Makenna *(American)* ♀   RATING: ★★★
Son of Kenneth—Variation of McKenna
> People think of Makenna as pretty, funny, energetic, popular, caring
> People who like the name Makenna also like Makayla, Kaelyn, Emma, Olivia, Hannah, Ava, Isabella, Chloe, Hailey, Paige

Makoto *(Japanese)* ♂   RATING: ★★★★
Sincere, honest
> People think of Makoto as handsome, trustworthy, cool, intelligent, powerful
> People who like the name Makoto also like Haruki, Ryu, Hiroshi, Keitaro, Kaemon, Akio, Matsu, Yukio, Haru, Shino

Makya *(Native American)* ♀ ♂   RATING: ★★
One who hunts eagles
> People think of Makya as pretty, creative, funny, intelligent, trustworthy
> People who like the name Makya also like Madison, Mika, Mackenzie, Jaden, Dakota, Caden, Cadence, Hayden, Jalen, Jordan

Mala *(Sanskrit/East Indian)* ♀   RATING: ★★★☆
Necklace, garland
> People think of Mala as pretty, exotic, sexy, aggressive, creative
> People who like the name Mala also like Maia, Malia, Mali, Mira, Magnolia, Layla, Maya, Mai, Marisa, Mara

Malachi *(Hebrew)* ♂   RATING: ★★☆
My messenger—Malachi McCourt, poet/author
> People think of Malachi as handsome, intelligent, leader, powerful, creative
> People who like the name Malachi also like Elijah, Micah, Isaiah, Gabriel, Noah, Caleb, Isaac, Ethan, Jeremiah, Maddox

Malaika *(African)* ♀   RATING: ★★☆
Angel—Kiswahili origin
> People think of Malaika as pretty, intelligent, energetic, creative, cool
> People who like the name Malaika also like Maisha, Makaila, Jahzara, Ayanna, Makayla, Myeisha, Mandisa, Maha, Layla, Macaria

Malana *(Hawaiian)* ♀   RATING: ★★★★☆
Calming, relaxing
> People think of Malana as pretty, exotic, caring, intelligent, elegant
> People who like the name Malana also like Malia, Makenna, Malaya, Maleah, Makayla, Hannah, Leilani, Layla, Maya, Isabella

Malaya *(English)* ♀   RATING: ★★★★☆
From Malaysia
> People think of Malaya as pretty, popular, exotic, funny, creative
> People who like the name Malaya also like Malia, Malana, Makayla, Layla, Jadyn, Makaila, Maya, Makenna, Ava, Mariah

Malcolm *(Celtic/Gaelic)* ♂   RATING: ★★☆
Follower of St. Columbus—Malcolm McDowell, actor; Malcolm McLaren, musician/producer
> People think of Malcolm as handsome, intelligent, funny, cool, caring
> People who like the name Malcolm also like Ian, Ethan, Jacob, Liam, Owen, Gabriel, Nicholas, Tristan, Aiden, Noah

Maleah *(Hawaiian)* ♀   RATING: ★★★★
Sea of bitterness—Variation of Mary
> People think of Maleah as pretty, funny, intelligent, creative, energetic
> People who like the name Maleah also like Malia, Makenna, Malana, Madelyn, Emma, Leah, Ava, Makayla, Chloe, Olivia

Malha *(Hebrew)* ♀   RATING: ★★
Queen—Also spelled Mallha, Malhia, Mylha, Malyhi, or Malhie
> People think of Malha as ethnic, exotic, caring, lazy, old
> People who like the name Malha also like Mari, Malia, Malina, Mariam, Mai, Maeko, Maleah, Leah, Jahzara, Maha

Mali *(Arabic)* ♀   RATING: ★★★
Full, rich
> People think of Mali as pretty, funny, creative, caring, popular
> People who like the name Mali also like Mia, Malia, Maya, Ava, Layla, Ella, Isabelle, Emma, Macy, Lily

Malia *(Hawaiian)* ♀   RATING: ★★★
Calm, peaceful
> People think of Malia as pretty, funny, creative, exotic, caring
> People who like the name Malia also like Ava, Maya, Isabella, Mia, Ella, Grace, Olivia, Leilani, Kailani, Hannah

Maliha *(Arabic)* ♀   RATING: ★★★
Attractive, beautiful
> People think of Maliha as funny, pretty, sexy, popular, intelligent
> People who like the name Maliha also like Malia, Eva, Isabella, Maleah, Ava, Gabriella, Samira, Maya, Rhianna, Mya

Malik *(Arabic)* ♂   RATING: ★★★★
King
> People think of Malik as handsome, popular, intelligent, funny, powerful
> People who like the name Malik also like Malachi, Maddox, Jayden, Elijah, Ethan, Gabriel, Isaac, Tristan, Xavier, Kaden

Malika *(Arabic)* ♀   RATING: ★★☆
Queen—Also spelled Mallika or Malikah
> People think of Malika as pretty, cool, funny, caring, intelligent
> People who like the name Malika also like Makaila, Malia, Mia, Kyla, Malaika, Maya, Madelyn, Kayla, Makayla, Jasmine

Malin *(Scandinavian)* ♀   RATING: ★★☆
Woman of Magdela—Short for Madelyn
> People think of Malin as pretty, creative, funny, caring, intelligent
> People who like the name Malin also like Maylin, Maren, Mabyn, Chloe, Madelyn, Tatum, Macyn, Jadyn, Lorelei, Maya

Malina *(Scandinavian)* ♀   RATING: ★★★
Woman of Magdala
> People think of Malina as pretty, creative, intelligent, caring, funny
> People who like the name Malina also like Isabella, Malia, Ava, Mya, Olivia, Mia, Madeline, Maya, Nadia, Grace

Malinda *(American)* ♀   RATING: ★★★★
Combination of Malia and Linda
> People think of Malinda as pretty, funny, caring, creative, trustworthy
> People who like the name Malinda also like Madeline, Marissa, Sabrina, Makayla, Malissa, Hailey, Hannah, Melinda, Miranda, Grace

Malini *(Sanskrit/East Indian)* ♀   RATING: ★★★☆
Garlanded
> People think of Malini as pretty, intelligent, creative, exotic, caring
> People who like the name Malini also like Manasa, Mandara, Mythri, Mahesa, Mallika, Malia, Meghana, Marlee, Mrinal, Madeline

Malise *(Celtic/Gaelic)* ♀   RATING: ★★★★
Servant of Jesus
> People think of Malise as powerful, exotic, elegant, young, untrustworthy
> People who like the name Malise also like Keaira, Maeve, Keira, Maura, Kiara, Maisie, Mae, Kira, Kaelyn, Ciara

Malissa *(Greek)* ♀   RATING: ★★☆
Honeybee—Variation of Melissa
> People think of Malissa as pretty, caring, trustworthy, funny, intelligent
> People who like the name Malissa also like Marissa, Hailey, Faith, Melissa, Hannah, Jessica, Lacey, Maegan, Clarissa, Natalie

Malkia *(Hebrew)* ♀   RATING: ★★★
Queen of God
> People think of Malkia as pretty, trustworthy, ethnic, caring, intelligent
> People who like the name Malkia also like Malaika, Maisha, Myeisha, Jadyn, Makayla, Mandisa, Malaya, Maha, Makenna, Jahzara

Mallika *(Sanskrit/East Indian)* ♀   RATING: ★★
Scent of Jasmine
> People think of Mallika as intelligent, exotic, popular, pretty, sexy
> People who like the name Mallika also like Jaya, Maya, Mia, Maina, Malia, Makayla, Mahesa, Malika, Shyla, Monisha

Malloren *(American)* ♀   RATING: ★★☆
Combination of Mallory and Loren
> People think of Malloren as energetic, intelligent, trendy, nerdy, aggressive
> People who like the name Malloren also like Mallory, Jillian, Jeslyn, Chloe, Kaydence, Maris, Karlyn, Mara, Emma, Jenna

Mallory *(French)* ♀   RATING: ★★★
Ill-omened—Also spelled Mallorie or Malory; Mallory Keaton, character on *Family Ties*
> People think of Mallory as pretty, funny, caring, intelligent, creative
> People who like the name Mallory also like Olivia, Hannah, Paige, Grace, Natalie, Emma, Abigail, Claire, Isabella, Hailey

Mallow *(American)* ♀♂   RATING: ★☆
From Malow, Germany—Also a German surname
> People think of Mallow as leader, weird, cool, trustworthy, big
> People who like the name Mallow also like Maeron, Maeryn, Mackenzie, Monroe, Madden, Darby, Paisley, Keegan, Morrigan, Logan

Malo *(Hawaiian)* ♂   RATING: ★★★
Winner
> People think of Malo as pretty, winner, leader, powerful, popular
> People who like the name Malo also like Milo, Mace, Marcel, Miles, Maddox, Nero, Mauli, Marco, Enzo, Troy

Malone *(Celtic/Gaelic)* ♂   RATING: ★★★
Devoted to St. John—Originally a surname; from the phrase "Maol Eoin," meaning servant of St. John
> People think of Malone as funny, pretty, wild, trustworthy, leader

People who like the name Malone also like Maddox, Miles, Macon, Malcolm, Aiden, Keagan, Jack, Mac, Mace, Mckenzie

Malvina *(Celtic/Gaelic)* ♀   RATING: ★★★
Smooth brow
> People think of Malvina as pretty, creative, intelligent, elegant, funny
> People who like the name Malvina also like Makaila, Mabel, Mara, Marisela, Marcena, Jenna, Malise, Jennelle, Maire, Mahogany

Manas *(Sanskrit/East Indian)* ♂   RATING: ★★★
Intelligence
> People think of Manas as intelligent, winner, powerful, cool, funny
> People who like the name Manas also like Mannan, Nirav, Ashwin, Mandar, Adit, Rushil, Savir, Manjit, Alagan, Macario

Manasa *(Sanskrit/East Indian)* ♀   RATING: ★★★
Intelligence—Feminine form of Manas
> People think of Manasa as intelligent, caring, funny, trustworthy, pretty
> People who like the name Manasa also like Mahesa, Mallika, Malini, Mandara, Mythri, Jaya, Monisha, Meghana, Marcella, Mahina

Manda *(English)* ♀   RATING: ★★☆
Lovable—Short for Amanda
> People think of Manda as pretty, creative, trustworthy, funny, caring
> People who like the name Manda also like Mallory, Melody, Mae, Mandy, Maia, Jadyn, Marissa, Madelyn, Mia, Maya

Mandana *(Persian)* ♀   RATING: ★★
Everlasting—A Persian queen; Mandana Jones, actress
> People think of Mandana as pretty, sexy, intelligent, exotic, creative
> People who like the name Mandana also like Marcella, Mandara, Mahala, Madelyn, Mandira, Adalia, Jasmine, Mandelina, Mariam, Mirella

Mandar *(Sanskrit/East Indian)* ♂   RATING: ★★★
Coral tree
> People think of Mandar as intelligent, handsome, powerful, popular, creative
> People who like the name Mandar also like Manas, Manjit, Maddox, Micah, Miles, Malcolm, Rohan, Mohan, Macario, Marcus

Mandara *(Sanskrit/East Indian)* ♀   RATING: ★★
Coral tree—Feminine form of Mandar
> People think of Mandara as exotic, pretty, quiet, creative, ethnic
> People who like the name Mandara also like Mallika, Malini, Makara, Manasa, Mai, Mabel, Isabella, Kalinda, Laranya, Makaila

Mandel *(German)* ♀♂   RATING: ★★
Almond
> People think of Mandel as handsome, caring, intelligent, aggressive, sexy
> People who like the name Mandel also like Mason, Kyler, Madison, Mackenzie, Jade, Logan, Sean, Marek, Willow, Jordan

Mandelina *(American)* ♀   RATING: ★★★☆
Lovable—Variation of Amanda
> People think of Mandelina as exotic, energetic, funny, caring, wild
> People who like the name Mandelina also like Malinda, Madeleine, Madeline, Malia, Makayla, Isabella, Marcella, Maggie, Mabel, Bianca

Mandell *(German)* ♀♂   RATING: ★★☆
Almond
> People think of Mandell as handsome, funny, sexy, aggressive, intelligent
> People who like the name Mandell also like Madden, Madison, Christian, Jaden, Noel, Jordan, Landen, Mason, Myles, Chandler

Mandira *(Sanskrit/East Indian)* ♀   RATING: ★★
Temple, melody
> People think of Mandira as exotic, caring, pretty, ethnic, funny
> People who like the name Mandira also like Chandra, Maeve, Mallika, Cassandra, Mandara, Denali, Isadora, Maylin, Daphne, Miliani

Mandisa *(African)* ♀   RATING: ★★★☆
Sweet—South African origin; also spelled Mandissa, Manndisa, Mandisia, or Mendisia
> People think of Mandisa as sexy, intelligent, pretty, powerful, exotic
> People who like the name Mandisa also like Malaika, Maisha, Maha, Kya, Myeisha, Jahzara, Ayanna, Mandy, Jacinda, Mansa

Mandla *(African)* ♂   RATING: ★★☆
Strength—Zulu origin
> People think of Mandla as sexy, quiet, slow, trendy, old-fashioned
> People who like the name Mandla also like Mac, Marcus, Matthew, Melvin, Monte, Maddock, Mingan, Mahak, Magnum, Maddox

Mandy *(Latin)* ♀   RATING: ★★☆
Lovable—Short for Amanda; Mandy Moore, singer/actress; "Mandy," by Barry Manilow
> People think of Mandy as pretty, caring, funny, creative, intelligent
> People who like the name Mandy also like Faith, Hailey, Hannah, Paige, Emma, Emily, Lacey, Natalie, Megan, Isabella

Manelin *(Persian)* ♂   RATING: ★★
Prince of princes
> People think of Manelin as handsome, exotic, caring, funny, pretty

People who like the name Manelin also like Maddox, Kaden, Malik, Mace, Darius, Kael, Kadin, Malcolm, Emery, Marshall

Manica (*African*) ♀   RATING: ★★☆
Place in Mozambique
People think of Manica as exotic, caring, pretty, intelligent, loser
People who like the name Manica also like Malaika, Aaliyah, Jessica, Makenna, Mansa, Maisha, Malinda, Myeisha, Alicia, Maya

Manjit (*Sanskrit/East Indian*) ♂   RATING: ★☆
Light of the mind
People think of Manjit as sexy, funny, intelligent, caring, quiet
People who like the name Manjit also like Mandar, Gaurav, Deepak, Manas, Ashwin, Dinesh, Ajay, Naresh, Absolom, Llewellyn

Manju (*Sanskrit/East Indian*) ♀   RATING: ★★★
Sweet
People think of Manju as intelligent, caring, pretty, creative, young
People who like the name Manju also like Maha, Mallika, Mandara, Makana, Mandisa, Malaika, Mali, Mythri, Malini, Malia

Mannan (*Arabic*) ♂   RATING: ★★★
Very generous
People think of Mannan as leader, powerful, sexy, intelligent, cool
People who like the name Mannan also like Manas, Maddox, Mattox, Ruhan, Makalo, Seth, Arav, Matthew, Liam, Nirav

Manning (*English*) ♀♂   RATING: ★★★☆
Son of man
People think of Manning as leader, handsome, boy next door, sporty, trustworthy
People who like the name Manning also like Parker, Mason, Madison, Addison, Mackenzie, Hayden, Preston, Caden, Payton, Logan

Manny (*American*) ♂   RATING: ★★★
God is with us—Short for Manuel; also slang for male nanny
People think of Manny as cool, funny, handsome, intelligent, popular
People who like the name Manny also like Ethan, Jacob, Justin, Michael, Xavier, Kaden, Ian, Marco, Manuel, Aaron

Manolo (*Spanish*) ♂   RATING: ★★★
God is with us
People think of Manolo as handsome, young, elegant, exotic, aggressive
People who like the name Manolo also like Mateo, Milo, Fabian, Micah, Marcello, Dominic, Malo, Mario, Marco, Marlon

Manon (*French*) ♀   RATING: ★★
Sea of bitterness—Variation of Mary; also spelled Mannon or Maenon
People think of Manon as intelligent, creative, pretty, funny, elegant
People who like the name Manon also like Jolie, Marguerite, Madeleine, Chloe, Miette, Malin, Juliette, Josephine, Maren, Marie

Manoush (*Persian*) ♀   RATING: ★☆
Sweet
People think of Manoush as religious, ethnic, nerdy, creative, intelligent
People who like the name Manoush also like Mai, Mandisa, Maeve, Mandara, Mahsa, Mahdis, Mairwen, Makaila, Maha, Malaika

Mansa (*African*) ♀   RATING: ★☆
Third-born girl
People think of Mansa as leader, intelligent, pretty, cool, powerful
People who like the name Mansa also like Mardea, Mandisa, Manica, Maha, Malaika, Maisha, Malkia, Myeisha, Mateja, Mahala

Mansour (*Arabic*) ♂   RATING: ★★★
One who triumphs
People think of Mansour as powerful, funny, handsome, intelligent, sexy
People who like the name Mansour also like Micah, Malik, Marlon, Matthew, Ishmael, Isaac, Morpheus, Magnar, Josiah, Malachi

Manton (*English*) ♂   RATING: ★★
From the sandy earth—Originally a surname
People think of Manton as big, caring, funny, intelligent, sexy
People who like the name Manton also like Maddox, Ryker, Jackson, Holden, Trenton, Sebastian, Denton, Marcus, Troy, Grayson

Mantreh (*Persian*) ♀   RATING: ★☆
Divine words
People think of Mantreh as exotic, criminal, intelligent, girl next door, winner
People who like the name Mantreh also like Mabel, Marissa, Maire, Maralah, Manoush, Mali, Masako, Malvina, Maisha, Mandy

Manuel (*Spanish*) ♂   RATING: ★★★☆
God is with us
People think of Manuel as handsome, funny, intelligent, cool, trustworthy
People who like the name Manuel also like Gabriel, Matthew, Emanuel, Michael, Elijah, Nathaniel, Isaac, Anthony, Samuel, Daniel

Manuela (*Hebrew*) ♀   RATING: ★★
God is with us
People think of Manuela as pretty, caring, funny, creative, intelligent

People who like the name Manuela also like Mariana, Makayla, Mckayla, Gabrielle, Mariah, Janelle, Makaila, Mandy, Jadyn, Moriah

Mao *(Japanese)* ♀   RATING: ★★☆
True center—Mao Zedong (Tze-Tung), Chinese political leader
    People think of Mao as powerful, funny, cool, exotic, slow
    People who like the name Mao also like Colette, Toki, Nanami, Twyla, Mabli, Yui, Biana, Umeko, Emiko, Masumi

Mar *(Spanish)* ♀♂   RATING: ★★★☆
The sea
    People think of Mar as intelligent, sexy, creative, cool, funny
    People who like the name Mar also like Marin, Marek, Matias, Kai, Jordan, Luz, Lyndon, Maeryn, Mackenzie, Morgan

Mara *(Hebrew)* ♀   RATING: ★★★☆
Sea of bitterness—Variation of Mary
    People think of Mara as pretty, intelligent, creative, caring, funny
    People who like the name Mara also like Ava, Maya, Olivia, Eva, Emma, Hannah, Ella, Grace, Chloe, Isabella

Maralah *(Hebrew)* ♀   RATING: ★★
From Maralah, Palestine—Also a Biblical place name
    People think of Maralah as pretty, religious, girl next door, loser, big
    People who like the name Maralah also like Minya, Kaya, Ayasha, Mabel, Marcia, Miakoda, Makaila, Mandy, Mariah, Malaika

Marc *(French)* ♂   RATING: ★★★
Warlike—Marc Anthony, singer; Franz Marc, painter
    People think of Marc as handsome, funny, intelligent, cool, caring
    People who like the name Marc also like Matthew, Ethan, Jacob, Michael, Nicholas, Mark, Lucas, Nathan, Luke, Jack

Marcel *(French)* ♂   RATING: ★★★☆
Young warrior—Also a form of hairstyle, created by French hairdresser Marcel Grateau; Marcel Marceau, mime
    People think of Marcel as intelligent, handsome, cool, funny, sexy
    People who like the name Marcel also like Marcus, Ethan, Miles, Tristan, Marcell, Ian, Justin, Xavier, Michael, Jack

Marcelino *(Spanish)* ♂   RATING: ★★★
Young warrior—Variation of Marcel
    People think of Marcelino as handsome, trustworthy, sexy, funny, powerful
    People who like the name Marcelino also like Anthony, Andrés, Diego, Marcus, Gabriel, Alejandro, Antonio, Mateo, Andrew, Christopher

Marcell *(English)* ♂   RATING: ★★★☆
Young warrior
    People think of Marcell as funny, handsome, intelligent, energetic, popular
    People who like the name Marcell also like Marcel, Marcus, Elijah, Matthew, Lucas, Michael, Isaac, Nathan, Nicholas, Marcello

Marcella *(Latin)* ♀   RATING: ★★★☆
Young warrior
    People think of Marcella as pretty, intelligent, caring, funny, creative
    People who like the name Marcella also like Isabella, Olivia, Bella, Sophia, Faith, Scarlett, Hannah, Marissa, Madeleine, Gabriella

Marcello *(Latin)* ♂   RATING: ★★☆
Young warrior—Marcello Mastroianni, actor
    People think of Marcello as handsome, intelligent, sexy, cool, funny
    People who like the name Marcello also like Dominic, Gabriel, Marco, Maddox, Lucas, Matteo, Vincent, Marcellus, Marcus, Giovanni

Marcellus *(Latin)* ♂   RATING: ★★★☆
Young warrior
    People think of Marcellus as handsome, intelligent, powerful, leader, cool
    People who like the name Marcellus also like Marcus, Marcello, Malachi, Xavier, Marcell, Maddox, Marcel, Gabriel, Matthew, Marius

Marcena *(Latin)* ♀   RATING: ★★★
Martial
    People think of Marcena as intelligent, quiet, pretty, trustworthy, funny
    People who like the name Marcena also like Marcella, Marcia, Marissa, Mahina, Mai, Marci, Marlena, Mariana, Maire, Marsha

March *(English)* ♀♂   RATING: ★★★
Month of March; walk in unison—Used for children born in this month; originally from Mars, the Greek God of war
    People think of March as creative, artsy, winner, lazy, trendy
    People who like the name March also like Avery, Madison, Mason, Piper, Lane, Phoenix, Orion, Taylor, Parker, Forest

Marci *(American)* ♀   RATING: ★★★☆
Warlike
    People think of Marci as caring, pretty, trustworthy, funny, creative
    People who like the name Marci also like Emma, Macy, Hailey, Mandy, Olivia, Faith, Jenna, Hannah, Marissa, Eva

Marcia *(Latin)* ♀   RATING: ★★
Warlike—Marcia Brady, character on *The Brady Bunch*; Marcia Cross, actress; Marcia Gay Harden, actress
    People think of Marcia as caring, pretty, intelligent, funny, trustworthy

People who like the name Marcia also like Monica, Mariah, Felicity, Mandy, Julia, Olivia, Emma, Miranda, Alicia, Grace

Marcie *(English)* ♀   RATING: ★★★★
Warlike—Short for Marcia or Marcella
People think of Marcie as pretty, funny, creative, caring, energetic
People who like the name Marcie also like Macy, Olivia, Faith, Emily, Hailey, Paige, Michelle, Hannah, Amelia, Grace

Marco *(Italian)* ♂   RATING: ★★☆
Warlike
People think of Marco as handsome, funny, intelligent, cool, sexy
People who like the name Marco also like Marcus, Anthony, Nicholas, Lucas, Mario, Matthew, Matteo, Michael, Gabriel, Jacob

Marcus *(Latin)* ♂   RATING: ★★☆
Warlike—*Marcus Welby MD*, TV show
People think of Marcus as handsome, funny, cool, intelligent, sexy
People who like the name Marcus also like Lucas, Ethan, Jacob, Matthew, Alexander, Nicholas, Nathan, Gabriel, Isaac, Zachary

Marcy *(American)* ♀   RATING: ★★★☆
Warlike—Feminine form of Marcus
People think of Marcy as pretty, creative, caring, funny, intelligent
People who like the name Marcy also like Macy, Paige, Maggie, Mandy, Natalie, Grace, Faith, Olivia, Molly, Victoria

Mardea *(African)* ♀   RATING: ★★☆
Last—Ghanaian origin
People think of Mardea as creative, leader, elegant, untrustworthy, cool
People who like the name Mardea also like Mansa, Mandisa, Maire, Malaika, Mahola, Mahdis, Mara, Mallika, Mali, Mahalah

Mardi *(French)* ♀   RATING: ★★
Tuesday—Mardi Gras (Fat Tuesday), celebratory carnival
People think of Mardi as pretty, funny, creative, energetic, cool
People who like the name Mardi also like Marlee, Mia, Sophie, Keely, Mara, Marley, Macy, Jessica, Maggie, Mari

Mare *(English)* ♀♂   RATING: ★★★☆
Sea of bitterness—Variation of Mary; Mare Winningham, actress
People think of Mare as creative, exotic, funny, intelligent, energetic
People who like the name Mare also like Marin, Marek, Jade, Morgan, Madison, James, Jaden, Maine, Aidan, Ryder

Maree *(American)* ♀   RATING: ★★★☆
Sea of bitterness
People think of Maree as caring, creative, funny, intelligent, pretty
People who like the name Maree also like Isabella, Marissa, Madeleine, Madeline, Arabella, Paige, Hannah, Abigail, Makayla, Mari

Mareike *(Dutch)* ♀   RATING: ★★★
Sea of bitterness—Variation of Maria
People think of Mareike as creative, pretty, trustworthy, caring, quiet
People who like the name Mareike also like Chloe, Keely, Isabelle, Celeste, Keona, Simone, Abigail, Deirdra, Julianna, Hosanna

Marek *(Polish)* ♀♂   RATING: ★★☆
Warlike
People think of Marek as intelligent, handsome, powerful, leader, aggressive
People who like the name Marek also like Merrick, Caden, Hayden, Jaden, Logan, Mason, Aidan, Parker, Reese, Madison

Maren *(Scandinavian)* ♀   RATING: ★★★★☆
Pearl—Short for Margaret or Mary
People think of Maren as pretty, intelligent, creative, funny, elegant
People who like the name Maren also like Ella, Ava, Chloe, Grace, Olivia, Maya, Maeve, Macy, Claire, Paige

Marenda *(Latin)* ♀   RATING: ★★☆
Admirable—Variation of Miranda
People think of Marenda as elegant, pretty, artsy, intelligent, cool
People who like the name Marenda also like Mariah, Miranda, Marcella, Makayla, Felicity, Emma, Abigail, Marisa, Mckayla, Malinda

Margaret *(English)* ♀   RATING: ★★☆
Pearl—Also spelled Margret; Margaret Mead, anthropologist; Margaret Mitchell, author
People think of Margaret as intelligent, pretty, caring, funny, creative
People who like the name Margaret also like Olivia, Abigail, Charlotte, Elizabeth, Grace, Hannah, Madeline, Maggie, Amelia, Claire

Margarita *(Spanish)* ♀   RATING: ★★★☆
Pearl—Variation of Margaret; also a sweet alcoholic drink
People think of Margarita as pretty, funny, intelligent, caring, cool
People who like the name Margarita also like Mercedes, Margaret, Marguerite, Bianca, Jasmine, Amelia, Madeline, Roxanne, Gabriella, Julia

Margaux *(French)* ♀   RATING: ★★
Pearl—Margaux Hemingway, actress
People think of Margaux as pretty, funny, popular, elegant, intelligent

People who like the name Margaux also like Margot, Ava, Claire, Grace, Sophia, Chloe, Sophie, Olivia, Isabelle, Simone

Marge *(American)* ♀   RATING: ★☆
Pearl—Short for Margaret
  People think of Marge as old-fashioned, pretty, caring, intelligent, quiet
  People who like the name Marge also like Maggie, Kimi, Belinda, Iris, Melissa, Mary, Maxine, Olivia, Jenna, Margaret

Marged *(Welsh)* ♀   RATING: ★☆
Pearl—Variation of Margaret
  People think of Marged as poor, quiet, exotic, loser, lazy
  People who like the name Marged also like Arwen, Mairwen, Morwen, Maeve, Gwyneth, Maren, Aderyn, Telyn, Wren, Isolde

Margie *(English)* ♀   RATING: ★★★☆
Pearl—Short for Margaret
  People think of Margie as pretty, caring, funny, intelligent, creative
  People who like the name Margie also like Maggie, Amber, Madeleine, Audrey, Mabel, Marissa, Emma, Grace, Hannah, Mandy

Margo *(French)* ♀   RATING: ★★★★
Pearl
  People think of Margo as pretty, intelligent, funny, trustworthy, creative
  People who like the name Margo also like Olivia, Maggie, Ava, Chloe, Paige, Sophia, Emma, Macy, Charlotte, Claire

Margot *(French)* ♀   RATING: ★★★☆
Pearl
  People think of Margot as intelligent, pretty, creative, artsy, elegant
  People who like the name Margot also like Ava, Olivia, Madeline, Sadie, Audrey, Scarlett, Paige, Fiona, Margaux, Charlotte

Marguerite *(French)* ♀   RATING: ★★★★
Pearl—Variation of Margaret
  People think of Marguerite as pretty, intelligent, elegant, caring, creative
  People who like the name Marguerite also like Jacqueline, Charlotte, Genevieve, Olivia, Madeline, Isabelle, Sophia, Scarlett, Giselle, Madeleine

Mari *(Hebrew)* ♀   RATING: ★★☆
Sea of bitterness
  People think of Mari as pretty, intelligent, creative, funny, caring
  People who like the name Mari also like Mia, Ava, Olivia, Emma, Chloe, Eva, Hannah, Maya, Isabella, Paige

Maria *(Latin)* ♀   RATING: ★★★
Sea of bitterness—Variation of Mary; Maria Shriver, journalist
  People think of Maria as pretty, funny, caring, intelligent, creative

People who like the name Maria also like Emma, Grace, Isabella, Olivia, Sophia, Mia, Elizabeth, Paige, Hannah, Marie

Mariah *(American)* ♀   RATING: ★★★★
Sea of bitterness—Mariah Carey, singer
  People think of Mariah as pretty, funny, caring, creative, intelligent
  People who like the name Mariah also like Paige, Hannah, Aaliyah, Olivia, Hailey, Faith, Isabella, Savannah, Makayla, Grace

Mariam *(Hebrew)* ♀   RATING: ★★☆
Sea of bitterness
  People think of Mariam as pretty, intelligent, caring, funny, young
  People who like the name Mariam also like Hannah, Miriam, Abigail, Eva, Leah, Mariah, Paige, Isabel, Samantha, Grace

Marian *(English)* ♀   RATING: ★★☆
Sea of bitterness—Medieval variation of Mary
  People think of Marian as pretty, intelligent, caring, funny, trustworthy
  People who like the name Marian also like Olivia, Grace, Hannah, Abigail, Victoria, Emma, Sophia, Audrey, Charlotte, Isabelle

Mariana *(Spanish)* ♀   RATING: ★★★★
Sea of bitterness
  People think of Mariana as pretty, intelligent, funny, caring, creative
  People who like the name Mariana also like Isabella, Adriana, Juliana, Olivia, Hannah, Daniela, Lilianna, Arianna, Gabriella, Gabriela

Marianela *(Spanish)* ♀   RATING: ★★★
Beloved star—Combination of Maria and Estela; Marianela Pereyra, TV host
  People think of Marianela as pretty, funny, creative, young, caring
  People who like the name Marianela also like Mariana, Alegria, Candace, Sophia, Naomi, Sofia, Selena, Dawn, Valencia, Isabel

Mariangely *(American)* ♀   RATING: ★★☆
Maria of the angels
  People think of Mariangely as quiet, pretty, young, intelligent, cool
  People who like the name Mariangely also like Coral, Carissa, Destiny, Clarissa, Adamina, Mirielle, Esmeralda, Evania, Fiona, Soraya

Marianne *(French)* ♀   RATING: ★★★★
Sea of bitterness
  People think of Marianne as pretty, creative, caring, intelligent, funny
  People who like the name Marianne also like Hannah, Natalie, Samantha, Olivia, Grace, Hailey, Lauren, Mariana, Victoria, Madeleine

Mariano *(Italian)* ♂   RATING: ★★★★
Warlike—Variation of Marianus or Marius
> People think of Mariano as handsome, funny, intelligent, sexy, cool
> People who like the name Mariano also like Marco, Matteo, Massimo, Gabriel, Mario, Matthew, Giovanni, Carmine, Marcello, Mateo

Mariatu *(African)* ♀♂   RATING: ★★☆
Sea of bitterness
> People think of Mariatu as ethnic, quiet, intelligent, poor, loser
> People who like the name Mariatu also like Mahdi, Mahari, Muna, Kijana, Maro, Milandu, Myles, Makaio, Makya, Maemi

Maribel *(Spanish)* ♀   RATING: ★★★★
Combination of Maria and Isabel
> People think of Maribel as pretty, caring, funny, intelligent, trustworthy
> People who like the name Maribel also like Isabella, Mirabelle, Mirabel, Isabelle, Mabel, Isabel, Mia, Gabriella, Marisol, Olivia

Maribeth *(American)* ♀   RATING: ★★☆
Combination of Maria and Elizabeth
> People think of Maribeth as funny, pretty, creative, intelligent, caring
> People who like the name Maribeth also like Isabella, Hailey, Grace, Hannah, Madelyn, Lacey, Abigail, Mirabelle, Faith, Lauren

Maricela *(Spanish)* ♀   RATING: ★★★☆
Combination of Maria and Celia
> People think of Maricela as pretty, funny, cool, caring, creative
> People who like the name Maricela also like Marisela, Mariana, Marisol, Isabella, Gabriela, Maribel, Gabriella, Marissa, Ariana, Isabel

Marie *(French)* ♀   RATING: ★★★
Sea of bitterness—Variation of Mary; Marie Antoinette, queen of France; Marie Curie, scientist
> People think of Marie as pretty, intelligent, caring, funny, creative
> People who like the name Marie also like Grace, Emma, Elizabeth, Hannah, Isabella, Faith, Natalie, Paige, Samantha, Olivia

Mariel *(English)* ♀   RATING: ★★★★
Sea of bitterness—Variation of Mary; Mariel Hemingway, actress
> People think of Mariel as pretty, intelligent, funny, caring, creative
> People who like the name Mariel also like Isabella, Jillian, Mia, Isabel, Nadia, Mariana, Ella, Gabrielle, Macy, Madeleine

Marietta *(English)* ♀   RATING: ★★★☆
Sea of bitterness—Variation of Mary; *Naughty Marietta*, operetta by Victor Herbert
> People think of Marietta as intelligent, caring, creative, elegant, pretty

> People who like the name Marietta also like Charlotte, Isabella, Amelia, Mabel, Scarlett, Miranda, Lauren, Hazel, Jasmine, Isabelle

Mariette *(French)* ♀   RATING: ★★★☆
Sea of bitterness—Variation of Mary
> People think of Mariette as pretty, caring, intelligent, funny, trustworthy
> People who like the name Mariette also like Madeline, Jacqueline, Scarlett, Marietta, Jaclyn, Lauren, Jasmine, Madelyn, Isabelle, Paige

Marigold *(English)* ♀   RATING: ★★
Yellow flower
> People think of Marigold as pretty, creative, intelligent, caring, quiet
> People who like the name Marigold also like Mabel, Scarlett, Magnolia, Olivia, Madeleine, Violet, Iris, Macy, Melody, Ivy

Marija *(Slavic)* ♀   RATING: ★★★
Bitter sea
> People think of Marija as pretty, energetic, funny, trustworthy, winner
> People who like the name Marija also like Maria, Constance, Prudence, Maja, Jane, Rosemary, Zuzana, Jolene, Tatiana, Arista

Marijke *(Slavic)* ♀   RATING: ★★★☆
Sea of bitterness—Variation of Mary
> People think of Marijke as intelligent, funny, artsy, pretty, creative
> People who like the name Marijke also like Marika, Mariska, Marlis, Maleah, Marissa, Maire, Marcella, Mira, Maria, Marlie

Marika *(Polish)* ♀   RATING: ★★★☆
Sea of bitterness—Variation of Mary
> People think of Marika as pretty, intelligent, funny, creative, cool
> People who like the name Marika also like Maya, Chloe, Mae, Kara, Mara, Mia, Marisa, Julia, Kyla, Janika

Mariko *(Japanese)* ♀   RATING: ★★
Circle
> People think of Mariko as pretty, intelligent, creative, energetic, artsy
> People who like the name Mariko also like Maeko, Mai, Masako, Sakura, Miyoko, Miyo, Amaya, Nariko, Emiko, Misa

Marilee *(American)* ♀   RATING: ★★☆
Combination of Mary and Lee
> People think of Marilee as funny, trustworthy, pretty, creative, caring
> People who like the name Marilee also like Olivia, Madelyn, Marlee, Madeleine, Emily, Madeline, Emma, Jadyn, Macy, Cailyn

Marilla *(American)* ♀   RATING: ★★★
Combination of Mary and Priscilla
> People think of Marilla as intelligent, leader, trustworthy, creative, pretty

People who like the name Marilla also like Nina, Odette, Vienna, Bethany, Lila, Sienna, Valencia, Kaida, Bianca, Naomi

Marilu *(American)* ♀ RATING: ★★
Combination of Mary and Lu—Marilu Henner, actress/author
People think of Marilu as pretty, caring, funny, sexy, young
People who like the name Marilu also like Marilyn, Marcella, Mallory, Johanna, Marcie, Marli, Marlo, Mariana, Jasmine, Jennie

Marilyn *(American)* ♀ RATING: ★★★★
Combination of Mary and Lynn—Marilyn Manson, musician; Marilyn Monroe, actress
People think of Marilyn as pretty, intelligent, caring, funny, sexy
People who like the name Marilyn also like Isabella, Hailey, Hannah, Paige, Madeline, Faith, Grace, Eva, Audrey, Madelyn

Marin *(Latin)* ♀ ♂ RATING: ★★★★☆
Of the sea
People think of Marin as pretty, creative, intelligent, funny, elegant
People who like the name Marin also like Morgan, Addison, Avery, Mason, Logan, Madison, Parker, Aidan, Riley, Hayden

Marina *(Latin)* ♀ RATING: ★★☆
Of the sea
People think of Marina as pretty, intelligent, funny, caring, creative
People who like the name Marina also like Isabella, Ava, Maya, Olivia, Grace, Emma, Marissa, Hannah, Mia, Paige

Marinel *(Latin)* ♀ ♂ RATING: ★★★
Of the sea
People think of Marinel as creative, intelligent, pretty, young, caring
People who like the name Marinel also like Marin, Morgan, Marek, Makya, Mason, Morrigan, Madden, Madison, Mare, Marlow

Mario *(Italian)* ♂ RATING: ★★
Warlike—Mario Andretti, race car driver; Mario Lopez, actor; Mario Van Peebles, actor/director; Mario, video game character
People think of Mario as funny, handsome, cool, intelligent, popular
People who like the name Mario also like Marco, Gabriel, Marcus, Matthew, Aaron, Jacob, Xavier, David, Mark, Isaac

Marion *(Hebrew)* ♀ ♂ RATING: ★★★☆
Sea of bitterness—Variation of Mary
People think of Marion as intelligent, caring, creative, funny, trustworthy
People who like the name Marion also like Madison, James, Logan, Jordan, Jaden, Morgan, Preston, Taylor, Mason, Parker

Maris *(Latin)* ♀ RATING: ★★★★
Of the sea—From Stella Maris, meaning star of the sea
People think of Maris as pretty, intelligent, creative, funny, caring
People who like the name Maris also like Olivia, Maren, Ava, Paige, Mia, Maeve, Chloe, Audrey, Bella, Ella

Marisa *(Italian)* ♀ RATING: ★★★
Sea of bitterness—Variation of Maria; Marisa Berenson, actress; Marisa Tomei, actress
People think of Marisa as pretty, funny, intelligent, caring, creative
People who like the name Marisa also like Marissa, Hailey, Olivia, Isabella, Hannah, Paige, Mia, Emma, Alyssa, Ava

Marisela *(Spanish)* ♀ RATING: ★★★★
Sea of bitterness—Variation of Maria
People think of Marisela as pretty, intelligent, funny, caring, creative
People who like the name Marisela also like Marisol, Isabella, Marisa, Marissa, Gabriella, Marcella, Bella, Jasmine, Giselle, Mirabel

Mariska *(Hungarian)* ♀ RATING: ★★★★
Sea of bitterness—Variation of Mary; Mariska Hargitay, actress
People think of Mariska as pretty, intelligent, elegant, caring, funny
People who like the name Mariska also like Olivia, Isabella, Emma, Lorelei, Felicity, Paige, Ella, Marisa, Natalie, Marissa

Marisol *(Spanish)* ♀ RATING: ★★★☆
Combination of Maria and Sol—Marisol Nichols, actress
People think of Marisol as pretty, funny, intelligent, caring, cool
People who like the name Marisol also like Isabella, Olivia, Chloe, Hannah, Mia, Bianca, Faith, Marissa, Grace, Marisela

Marissa *(English)* ♀ RATING: ★★★★
Sea of bitterness—Variation of Marisa
People think of Marissa as pretty, funny, caring, intelligent, creative
People who like the name Marissa also like Hannah, Paige, Hailey, Isabella, Alyssa, Olivia, Emma, Natalie, Grace, Chloe

Maritza *(Spanish)* ♀ RATING: ★★★☆
Sea of bitterness—Variation of Maria
People think of Maritza as pretty, funny, caring, intelligent, cool
People who like the name Maritza also like Marissa, Marisol, Isabella, Marisa, Mia, Mercedes, Monica, Miranda, Maya, Mariah

Mariuerla *(Scandinavian)* ♀ RATING: ★★☆
Wagtail bird
People think of Mariuerla as ethnic, exotic, elegant, unpopular, intelligent

People who like the name Mariuerla also like Mardea, Mahola, Marcena, Maire, Manoush, Makaila, Mathilda, Maritza, Masako, Maita

People who like the name Markku also like Marcel, Marius, Marcus, Mario, Marlon, Marc, Max, Marnin, Marvin, Mattox

Marius *(Latin)* ♂ RATING: ★★☆
Warlike
People think of Marius as handsome, intelligent, caring, powerful, creative
People who like the name Marius also like Marcus, Gabriel, Alexander, Matthew, Gavin, Tristan, Matthias, Maddox, Lucius, Miles

Marja *(Scandinavian)* ♀ RATING: ★★
Sea of bitterness—Variation of Maria or Mary
People think of Marja as creative, funny, pretty, wild, caring
People who like the name Marja also like Layla, Ivy, Iris, Emma, Sonja, Josephine, Jacqueline, Lucy, Mara, Dara

Marjean *(American)* ♀ RATING: ★☆
Combination of Mary and Jean
People think of Marjean as creative, funny, sneaky, aggressive, loser
People who like the name Marjean also like Maeve, Maire, Mae, Moira, Malise, Marvene, Macayle, Maisie, Maura, Maegan

Marjorie *(English)* ♀ RATING: ★★
Pearl—Variation of Margaret
People think of Marjorie as caring, pretty, intelligent, trustworthy, funny
People who like the name Marjorie also like Margaret, Paige, Jillian, Jacqueline, Lillian, Sophie, Charlotte, Monica, Mallory, Madeline

Mark *(Latin)* ♂ RATING: ★★★
Warlike—Mark Twain, author; Mark Wahlberg, actor
People think of Mark as handsome, funny, intelligent, caring, cool
People who like the name Mark also like Matthew, Michael, Ethan, Luke, Jacob, David, Nicholas, Joshua, Nathan, Jason

Marka *(African)* ♀♂ RATING: ★★★
A people in Western Africa
People think of Marka as quiet, ethnic, religious, energetic, exotic
People who like the name Marka also like Mahari, Mashaka, Mariatu, Makya, Mika, Madison, Mahdi, Menefer, Muna, Marvel

Marketa *(Persian)* ♀ RATING: ★★★
Pearl—Variation of Margaret
People think of Marketa as weird, energetic, aggressive, wild, creative
People who like the name Marketa also like Makaila, Kya

Markku *(Scandinavian)* ♂ RATING: ★☆
Rebellious—Finnish variation of Mark
People think of Markku as cool, intelligent, creative, handsome, exotic

Marla *(American)* ♀ RATING: ★★
Combination of Maria and Magdalene—Also short for Marlene
People think of Marla as pretty, funny, intelligent, trustworthy, caring
People who like the name Marla also like Macy, Mia, Mara, Marissa, Ava, Chloe, Miranda, Maya, Natalie, Layla

Marlas *(American)* ♀♂ RATING: ★★☆
Combination of Maria and Magdalene
People think of Marlas as religious, trustworthy, caring, nerdy, boy next door
People who like the name Marlas also like Magan, Marin, Marlow, Marek, Marlin, Marion, Maeryn, Myles, Mars, Jayme

Marlee *(American)* ♀ RATING: ★★★★☆
Combination of Mary and Lee—Also short for Marlene; Marlee Matlin, actress
People think of Marlee as pretty, funny, creative, cool, intelligent
People who like the name Marlee also like Ava, Emma, Isabella, Macy, Olivia, Mia, Marley, Hannah, Paige, Grace

Marlena *(German)* ♀ RATING: ★★★☆
Combination of Mary and Magdalena
People think of Marlena as pretty, funny, intelligent, creative, caring
People who like the name Marlena also like Isabella, Marissa, Madeline, Olivia, Sophia, Amelia, Maya, Paige, Mia, Mariana

Marlene *(German)* ♀ RATING: ★★
Combination of Mary and Magdalene—Marlene Dietrich, actress
People think of Marlene as pretty, funny, caring, intelligent, creative
People who like the name Marlene also like Mariah, Hailey, Monica, Michelle, Marlena, Marilyn, Sabrina, Hannah, Marissa, Mallory

Marley *(English)* ♀ RATING: ★★★★
From the boundary field—Originally a surname; Bob Marley, musician
People think of Marley as creative, pretty, funny, popular, cool
People who like the name Marley also like Ava, Olivia, Ella, Macy, Mia, Isabella, Emma, Hannah, Paige, Grace

Marli *(English)* ♀ RATING: ★★☆
Combination of Maria and Magdalene
People think of Marli as pretty, creative, funny, cool, intelligent
People who like the name Marli also like Marlee, Marlie, Mia, Paige, Emma, Jadyn, Macy, Hailey, Ava, Ella

Marlie *(American)* ♀   RATING: ★★★★☆
Combination of Mary and Magdalene
People think of Marlie as pretty, funny, creative, cool, energetic
People who like the name Marlie also like Marley, Marli, Grace, Ava, Marlee, Natalie, Olivia, Macy, Emma, Madelyn

Marlin *(American)* ♀♂   RATING: ★★★
Combination of Maria and Magdalene—Also a fish
People think of Marlin as funny, intelligent, popular, caring, sexy
People who like the name Marlin also like Mason, Morgan, Parker, Taylor, Blake, James, Hadley, Mackenzie, Logan, Hayden

Marlis *(German)* ♀   RATING: ★★★☆
Combination of Maria and Elisabeth
People think of Marlis as pretty, leader, intelligent, creative, trustworthy
People who like the name Marlis also like Mae, Maren, Maeve, Mallory, Marijke, Marika, Maris, Mara, Mary, Maegan

Marlo *(English)* ♀   RATING: ★★
Lake remains—Also a surname; Marlo Thomas, actress
People think of Marlo as pretty, intelligent, funny, creative, energetic
People who like the name Marlo also like Ava, Macy, Mallory, Marlee, Olivia, Marly, Marissa, Mia, Gwyneth, Marli

Marlon *(American)* ♂   RATING: ★★★☆
Little warlike one—Marlon Wayans, actor/comedian
People think of Marlon as funny, handsome, intelligent, cool, caring
People who like the name Marlon also like Ethan, Tristan, Gabriel, Maddox, Noah, Miles, Nathan, Owen, Justin, Isaac

Marlow *(English)* ♀♂   RATING: ★★★★
Lake remains—Also a surname; Christopher Marlowe, poet
People think of Marlow as intelligent, creative, old-fashioned, artsy, elegant
People who like the name Marlow also like Madison, Mason, Bailey, Morgan, Parker, Hayden, Spencer, Logan, Mackenzie, Harper

Marly *(English)* ♀   RATING: ★★★☆
Combination of Maria and Magdalene
People think of Marly as creative, intelligent, energetic, caring, leader
People who like the name Marly also like Macy, Olivia, Ava, Grace, Hannah, Paige, Gracie, Ella, Maddy, Eva

Marnie *(American)* ♀   RATING: ★★★★☆
From the sea—Short for Marna or Marina; Marnie Nixon, singer
People think of Marnie as pretty, intelligent, funny, creative, caring
People who like the name Marnie also like Macy, Paige, Emma, Ava, Hannah, Mia, Chloe, Maggie, Olivia, Grace

Marnin *(Hebrew)* ♂   RATING: ★★
Causing joy
People think of Marnin as intelligent, leader, caring, popular, creative
People who like the name Marnin also like Mattox, Meir, Micol, Maddox, Michal, Maxim, Mendel, Marcel, Makoto, Mio

Marnina *(Hebrew)* ♀   RATING: ★★
Causing joy
People think of Marnina as cool, energetic, pretty, trustworthy, creative
People who like the name Marnina also like Mandy, Makaila, Mari, Mirella, Mariah, Jadyn, Moriah, Mariam, Michelle, Marcella

Maro *(Japanese)* ♀♂   RATING: ★★
Myself
People think of Maro as funny, energetic, leader, trustworthy, handsome
People who like the name Maro also like Maemi, Mitsu, Kiyoshi, Seiko, Natsu, Kumi, Rin, Sanyu, Asa, Kin

Marrim *(English)* ♀♂   RATING: ★★
Unknown meaning—From the video game "Myst"
People think of Marrim as old-fashioned, old, exotic, intelligent, unpopular
People who like the name Marrim also like Marlow, Matty, Maverick, Marek, Maitland, Maro, Mercer, Morgan, Jordan, Jameson

Mars *(Greek)* ♀♂   RATING: ★★★☆
God of War—Also a planet
People think of Mars as aggressive, powerful, leader, sexy, funny
People who like the name Mars also like Phoenix, Orion, Hayden, Mercury, Justice, Madison, Moon, Blair, Artemis, Jade

Marsha *(American)* ♀   RATING: ★★
Warlike—Variation of Marcia
People think of Marsha as pretty, funny, caring, trustworthy, intelligent
People who like the name Marsha also like Megan, Olivia, Mandy, Mariah, Marissa, Melanie, Heather, Macy, Jessica, Madeline

Marshall *(French)* ♂   RATING: ★★★☆
Horse keeper
People think of Marshall as funny, intelligent, handsome, caring, energetic
People who like the name Marshall also like Ethan, Jackson, Owen, Nathan, Matthew, Lucas, Mitchell, Landon, Zachary, Benjamin

Marta *(Slavic)* ♀   RATING: ★★★☆
Lady—Variation of Martha
People think of Marta as pretty, intelligent, creative, funny, caring
People who like the name Marta also like Clara, Lara, Fiona, Mara, Emma, Sophia, Audrey, Charlotte, Julia, Maggie

Martha *(Hebrew)* ♀   RATING: ★★★☆
Lady—Martha Graham, choreographer; Martha
Stewart, TV host/media mogul; Martha Washington,
U.S. first lady
People think of Martha as pretty, caring, intelligent, creative, funny
People who like the name Martha also like Hannah,
Elizabeth, Grace, Margaret, Mary, Lucy, Charlotte, Olivia,
Maggie, Eva

Martin *(Latin)* ♂   RATING: ★★
Servant of Mars, God of war—Dr. Martin Luther King
Jr., civil rights activist; Martin Lawrence, actor/comedian; Martin Scorsese, filmmaker; Martin Sheen, actor
People think of Martin as funny, handsome, intelligent,
caring, trustworthy
People who like the name Martin also like Matthew,
Nathan, Nicholas, Benjamin, Ethan, Jacob, Michael,
Daniel, Jason, Zachary

Martina *(Latin)* ♀   RATING: ★★☆
Servant of Mars, God of war—Feminine form of Martin;
Martina Navratilova, tennis player
People think of Martina as caring, pretty, funny, intelligent, creative
People who like the name Martina also like Olivia, Faith,
Felicity, Grace, Angelina, Victoria, Miranda, Scarlett,
Charlotte, Marissa

Martine *(French)* ♀   RATING: ★★★★☆
Servant of Mars, God of war—Feminine form of Martin
People think of Martine as pretty, intelligent, funny,
sexy, creative
People who like the name Martine also like Claire,
Genevieve, Emma, Olivia, Fiona, Madeleine, Giselle,
Jacqueline, Bella, Maggie

Martinez *(Spanish)* ♂   RATING: ★★★
Descendant of Martin—Also a surname
People think of Martinez as funny, creative, leader, intelligent, caring
People who like the name Martinez also like Marc,
Maurice, Melvin, Moses, Mateusz, Owen, Romeo, Ozzy,
Heath, Marcel

Martirio *(Spanish)* ♂   RATING: ★★
Martyr
People think of Martirio as aggressive, artsy, exotic, religious, stuck-up
People who like the name Martirio also like Mac, Marcus,
Matthew, Melvin, Monte, Maddock, Mingan, Mahak,
Magnus, Maddox

Marty *(English)* ♂   RATING: ★★
Servant of Mars, God of war—Short for Martin; Marty
Ingalls, actor/comedian
People think of Marty as funny, handsome, caring, intelligent, creative
People who like the name Marty also like Martin, Ethan,
Matthew, Justin, Jared, Michael, Adam, Noah, Ian,
William

Marv *(American)* ♂   RATING: ★★☆
Great lord—Short for Marvin, a form of Merfyn
People think of Marv as weird, old-fashioned, boy next
door, intelligent, old
People who like the name Marv also like Marvin, Marcus,
Mac, Neil, Mark, Marco, Mario, Remington, Marc, Marty

Marva *(Hebrew)* ♀   RATING: ★★★
Sage (herb)
People think of Marva as funny, pretty, intelligent, caring, religious
People who like the name Marva also like Mabel,
Jennessa, Marlo, Maggie, Jenny, Marla, Mara, Jocasta,
Marcia, Janet

Marvel *(French)* ♀♂   RATING: ★★★
To wonder, admire—Also a comic book company
People think of Marvel as weird, intelligent, cool, funny,
elegant
People who like the name Marvel also like Maverick,
Jersey, Justice, Hayden, Mason, Preston, Phyre, Matias,
Mayes, Marlow

Marvela *(Spanish)* ♀   RATING: ★★★
To wonder, admire
People think of Marvela as weird, wealthy, popular,
energetic, funny
People who like the name Marvela also like Camille,
Magnolia, Genevieve, Mabel, Marisela, Isabella, Maisha,
Marcie, Michelle, Martine

Marvene *(American)* ♀   RATING: ★☆
Great lady—Feminine form of Marvin
People think of Marvene as nerdy, pretty, poor, lazy,
old-fashioned
People who like the name Marvene also like Malise, Mae,
Maeve, Maire, Marjean, Maisie, Moira, Maegan, Maura,
Maureen

Marvin *(English)* ♂   RATING: ★★★☆
Great lord—Variation of Merfyn
People think of Marvin as handsome, intelligent, funny,
cool, caring
People who like the name Marvin also like Ethan,
Matthew, Adam, Justin, Marcus, Oliver, Jack, Nathan,
Kevin, William

Mary *(Hebrew)* ♀   RATING: ★★★☆
Sea of bitterness—Mother of Jesus Christ; Mary Tyler
Moore, actress; Mary-Louise Parker, actress; Mary
Pickford, actress
People think of Mary as caring, pretty, funny, intelligent,
creative
People who like the name Mary also like Grace,
Elizabeth, Emma, Olivia, Emily, Abigail, Hannah, Anna,
Sarah, Lucy

Maryland *(American)* ♀♂   RATING: ★★★
Mary's land—U.S. state, named for Henrietta Maria
(queen of Charles I of England)
People think of Maryland as intelligent, creative, young,
girl next door, funny

People who like the name Maryland also like Madison, Mackenzie, Meredith, Montana, Manning, Jordan, Cassidy, Minnesota, Evelyn, Dakota

Masako (*Japanese*) ♀ RATING: ★★★☆
Justice
People think of Masako as intelligent, exotic, creative, elegant, caring
People who like the name Masako also like Miyoko, Maeko, Mai, Miyo, Machiko, Sakura, Mariko, Kimi, Nariko, Michiko

Mashaka (*African*) ♀ ♂ RATING: ★☆
Trouble—Tanzanian origin
People think of Mashaka as wild, exotic, creative, aggressive, sneaky
People who like the name Mashaka also like Makya, Myles, Mahari, Musoke, Mika, Marka, Merrill, Mason, Misha, Makaio

Masiela (*Spanish*) ♀ RATING: ★★☆
More sky—From the phrase *más cielo* meaning more sky or more heaven
People think of Masiela as creative, girl next door, cool, exotic, sexy
People who like the name Masiela also like Nadia, Ciara, Heidi, Samara, Analiese, Elani, Gisela, Irisa, Rufina, Ziraili

Masih (*Persian*) ♂ RATING: ★★★
Blessed one; Christ
People think of Masih as handsome, religious, quiet, intelligent, weird
People who like the name Masih also like Micah, Marcus, Elijah, Marc, Mateo, Josiah, Mikel, Michael, Brandon, Manuel

Maso (*Italian*) ♂ RATING: ★★☆
Twin—Short for Tomaso
People think of Maso as big, lazy, boy next door, ethnic, aggressive
People who like the name Maso also like Maurilio, Malcolm, Maurizio, Maston, Mauro, Macon, Mario, Miles, Maddox, Matteo

Mason (*French*) ♀ ♂ RATING: ★★★☆
Stone worker—Mason Williams, composer; *Perry Mason*, TV show
People think of Mason as handsome, intelligent, funny, popular, caring
People who like the name Mason also like Madison, Logan, Hayden, Caden, Riley, Parker, Addison, Morgan, Dylan, Bailey

Massachusetts (*Native American*) ♀ ♂ RATING: ★★☆
Around the big hill—U.S. state from a tribe name
People think of Massachusetts as weird, poor, unpopular, loser, nerdy
People who like the name Massachusetts also like Madison, Minnesota, Texas, Dakota, Cameron, Manning, Kansas, London, Bailey, Willow

Massimo (*Italian*) ♂ RATING: ★★★★
Greatest
People think of Massimo as handsome, powerful, intelligent, popular, sexy
People who like the name Massimo also like Matteo, Maddox, Mateo, Marco, Giovanni, Nico, Sebastian, Lorenzo, Leonardo, Tyson

Maston (*English*) ♂ RATING: ★★★
From the marsh settlement
People think of Maston as handsome, leader, caring, powerful, sporty
People who like the name Maston also like Maddox, Micah, Kaden, Max, Merric, Ian, Michael, Gavin, Mark, Marshall

Masumi (*Japanese*) ♀ RATING: ★★★
Beauty; true purity
People think of Masumi as sexy, exotic, pretty, creative, artsy
People who like the name Masumi also like Sakura, Gen, Misaki, Mai, Nami, Misa, Kimi, Miya, Ryuu, Toki

Matana (*Hebrew*) ♀ RATING: ★★
Gift
People think of Matana as creative, pretty, caring, intelligent, trustworthy
People who like the name Matana also like Mateja, Mireille, Liana, Naomi, Mari, Marnina, Malaika, Moriah, Mirella, Mahola

Matat (*Hebrew*) ♀ RATING: ★★☆
Gift
People think of Matat as exotic, weird, creative, ethnic, intelligent
People who like the name Matat also like Matana, Mari, Moriah, Malha, Maeve, Mandy, Mateja, Malinda, Manju, Malia

Mateja (*Slavic*) ♀ RATING: ★★★★☆
Gift of God—Feminine form of Matthew
People think of Mateja as pretty, intelligent, creative, exotic, young
People who like the name Mateja also like Matana, Makaila, Myeisha, Makayla, Mia, Mireya, Ceana, Malaika, Malia, Olivia

Mateo (*Spanish*) ♂ RATING: ★★★★☆
Gift of God—Variation of Matthew
People think of Mateo as handsome, caring, popular, intelligent, cool
People who like the name Mateo also like Gabriel, Noah, Matteo, Elijah, Ethan, Aiden, Maddox, Caleb, Tristan, Lucas

Materia (*Latin*) ♀ RATING: ★★☆
Of the human world
People think of Materia as pretty, powerful, intelligent, unpopular, lazy
People who like the name Materia also like Julia, Marigold, Marsha, Mabel, Mandy, Marcy, Mariah, Marvene, May, Malkia

Mateusz *(Polish)* ♂   RATING: ★★★
Gift of God—Variation of Matthew
> People think of Mateusz as handsome, popular, young, cool, trustworthy
> People who like the name Mateusz also like Marcus, Marcell, Mike, Marcello, Michael, Marcellus, Matt, Maddox, Matteo, Aiden

Mathilda *(German)* ♀   RATING: ★★★☆
Battle might
> People think of Mathilda as intelligent, pretty, creative, young, funny
> People who like the name Mathilda also like Olivia, Madeleine, Matilda, Charlotte, Hannah, Amelia, Madeline, Chloe, Alice, Isabella

Mathilde *(French)* ♀   RATING: ★★★☆
Battle might
> People think of Mathilde as intelligent, pretty, funny, elegant, powerful
> People who like the name Mathilde also like Mabel, Ophelia, Josephine, Madeleine, Isabelle, Scarlett, Madeline, Hannah, Sophie, Lucy

Mathura *(Sanskrit/East Indian)* ♀   RATING: ★☆
Birthplace of Krishna
> People think of Mathura as quiet, poor, exotic, religious, funny
> People who like the name Mathura also like Mitali, Manju, Mahesa, Monisha, Mythri, Manasa, Malini, Maina, Mallika, Meghana

Matia *(Spanish)* ♀   RATING: ★★★☆
Gift of God—Feminine form of Matthew
> People think of Matia as pretty, creative, intelligent, trustworthy, exotic
> People who like the name Matia also like Maya, Marcella, Adriana, Madelyn, Anya, Marcia, Malaya, Isabella, Reina, Mia

Matias *(Spanish)* ♀♂   RATING: ★★★★
Gift of God—Variation of Matthew
> People think of Matias as handsome, intelligent, cool, funny, popular
> People who like the name Matias also like Madison, Luca, Julian, Aidan, Mason, Logan, Mackenzie, Caden, Hayden, Morgan

Matilda *(English)* ♀   RATING: ★★
Battle might—English queen in the twelfth century
> People think of Matilda as intelligent, pretty, creative, funny, caring
> People who like the name Matilda also like Olivia, Amelia, Grace, Madeline, Charlotte, Ava, Isabella, Ella, Abigail, Phoebe

Matilde *(French)* ♀   RATING: ★★★☆
Battle might
> People think of Matilde as intelligent, pretty, creative, young, cool
> People who like the name Matilde also like Matilda, Mabel, Madeleine, Madeline, Mathilda, Grace, Maisie, Mariah, Mae, Maren

Matsu *(Japanese)* ♂   RATING: ★★
Pine
> People think of Matsu as loser, quiet, nerdy, intelligent, unpopular
> People who like the name Matsu also like Makoto, Akio, Hiroshi, Haruki, Ryu, Haru, Keitaro, Shino, Keiji, Kaemon

Matt *(English)* ♂   RATING: ★★★☆
Gift of God—Short for Matthew; Matt Damon, actor; Matt LeBlanc, actor
> People think of Matt as funny, handsome, cool, intelligent, sexy
> People who like the name Matt also like Matthew, Jacob, Jake, Justin, Luke, Ethan, Nathan, Jack, Ian, Mark

Mattea *(Latin)* ♀   RATING: ★★★☆
Gift of God
> People think of Mattea as big, ethnic, sexy
> People who like the name Mattea also like Ava, Gianna, Audrey, Georgia, Hannah, Isabella, Scarlett, Ella, Elle, Charlotte

Matteo *(Italian)* ♂   RATING: ★★★★
Gift of God—Variation of Matthew
> People think of Matteo as handsome, intelligent, creative, caring, popular
> People who like the name Matteo also like Mateo, Ethan, Noah, Gabriel, Lucas, Aiden, Giovanni, Matthew, Nicholas, Nathaniel

Matteus *(American)* ♂   RATING: ★★★
Gift of God—Variation of Matthew or Mateusz
> People think of Matteus as old-fashioned, creative, trustworthy, handsome, caring
> People who like the name Matteus also like Benjamin, Nathaniel, Adrian, Maddox, Micah, Matthias, Maximos, Elijah, Ethan, Samuel

Matthew *(English)* ♂   RATING: ★★★★
Gift of God—From the Greek form (Matthias) of the Hebrew name Matatiyah of the Biblical apostle; also spelled Mathew; Matthew Broderick, actor; Matthew McConaughey, actor; Matthew Perry, actor
> People think of Matthew as handsome, funny, intelligent, caring, cool
> People who like the name Matthew also like Ethan, Jacob, Nicholas, Joshua, Nathan, Michael, Andrew, Benjamin, Zachary, Noah

Matthias *(Greek)* ♂   RATING: ★☆
Gift of God—Variation of Matthew
> People think of Matthias as handsome, intelligent, leader, powerful, caring
> People who like the name Matthias also like Matthew, Gabriel, Ethan, Nathaniel, Elijah, Noah, Micah, Nicholas, Alexander, Isaac

Mattia *(Rumantsch)* ♂   RATING: ★★★
Gift of God—Variation of Matthew
> People think of Mattia as creative, sexy, intelligent, caring, funny

People who like the name Mattia also like Brennan, Mattias, Sebastian, Matthias, Macon, Mac, Marcel, Carsten, Maddock, Tobias

Mattias (Hebrew) ♂   RATING: ★★★★☆
Gift of God
People think of Mattias as intelligent, handsome, caring, powerful, sporty
People who like the name Mattias also like Matthias, Micah, Gabriel, Ethan, Jonas, Noah, Liam, Tobias, Elijah, Joshua

Mattox (English) ♂   RATING: ★★
Son of Madog—Variation of Maddox
People think of Mattox as cool, powerful, creative, big, sporty
People who like the name Mattox also like Maddox, Landon, Jackson, Noah, Kaden, Jayden, Aiden, Holden, Tristan, Caleb

Matty (English) ♀♂   RATING: ★★★☆
Short for Matilda or Matthew
People think of Matty as funny, energetic, cool, creative, young
People who like the name Matty also like Madison, Jaden, Mason, Hayden, Mackenzie, Bailey, Caden, Morgan, Logan, Riley

Maude (French) ♀   RATING: ★★★
Battle might—Variation of Matilda; *Maude*, TV show
People think of Maude as intelligent, pretty, creative, energetic, caring
People who like the name Maude also like Mabel, Macy, Madeleine, Matilda, Margaret, Maeve, Audrey, Olivia, Grace, Maya

Mauli (Hawaiian) ♂   RATING: ★★★
Dark skinned—Variation of Maurice
People think of Mauli as intelligent, exotic, leader, caring, sporty
People who like the name Mauli also like Lulani, Kale, Keoni, Malo, Malik, Mele, Kaden, Miles, Mikaili, Matthew

Maura (Celtic/Gaelic) ♀   RATING: ★★★★
Sea of bitterness—Variation of Maire or Mary
People think of Maura as pretty, intelligent, funny, creative, caring
People who like the name Maura also like Olivia, Grace, Keira, Paige, Ava, Fiona, Maeve, Ella, Emma, Claire

Maureen (Celtic/Gaelic) ♀   RATING: ★★★☆
Sea of bitterness—Variation of Maire or Mary; Maureen McCormick, actress; Maureen Stapleton, actress
People think of Maureen as pretty, intelligent, funny, caring, creative
People who like the name Maureen also like Fiona, Maggie, Erin, Faith, Hannah, Olivia, Felicity, Keira, Abigail, Maura

Maurice (French) ♂   RATING: ★★
Dark skinned
People think of Maurice as handsome, funny, cool, caring, intelligent

People who like the name Maurice also like Marcus, Xavier, Matthew, Isaac, Jacob, Nathan, Michael, Gabriel, Tyson, Kevin

Mauricio (Spanish) ♂   RATING: ★★★
Dark; Moor
People think of Mauricio as handsome, intelligent, sexy, cool, trustworthy
People who like the name Mauricio also like Adrian, Leonardo, Alejandro, Enrique, Maximo, Giovanni, Sebastian, Gabriel, Mateo, Jayden

Maurilio (Italian) ♂   RATING: ★☆
Moor
People think of Maurilio as sporty, sexy, energetic, trustworthy, powerful
People who like the name Maurilio also like Marco, Mariano, Massimo, Maurizio, Mario, Matteo, Michelangelo, Mattox, Maddox, Mauro

Maurizio (Italian) ♂   RATING: ★★★
Dark akinned—Variation of Maurice
People think of Maurizio as handsome, intelligent, popular, cool, energetic
People who like the name Maurizio also like Massimo, Matteo, Marco, Mariano, Gabriel, Michelangelo, Leonardo, Giovanni, Nicholas, Sebastian

Mauro (Italian) ♂   RATING: ★★★★
Dark skinned
People think of Mauro as handsome, intelligent, cool, caring, funny
People who like the name Mauro also like Mateo, Maurizio, Gabriel, Adrian, Valentino, Marlon, Matteo, Lucas, Mariano, Paulo

Maurus (Rumantsch) ♂   RATING: ★★☆
Dark skinned
People think of Maurus as cool, aggressive, caring, creative, powerful
People who like the name Maurus also like Malachi, Gideon, Gabriel, Jonas, Darius, Ephraim, Jeremiah, Morton, Bryson, Mattias

Mauve (American) ♀   RATING: ★★
Purplish color
People think of Mauve as creative, artsy, weird, funny, old-fashioned
People who like the name Mauve also like Maggie, Maeve, Maisie, Jazlynn, Jeslyn, Jadyn, Macy, Mirabelle, Genevieve, Jaclyn

Mave (Celtic/Gaelic) ♀   RATING: ★★★★
Intoxicating—Variation of Maeve
People think of Mave as pretty, intelligent, sexy, quiet, elegant
People who like the name Mave also like Maeve, Mae, Chloe, Maegan, Paige, Genevieve, Fiona, Breanna, Claire, Meara

Maverick *(American)*　♀♂　　RATING: ★★★★
Wildly independent
- People think of Maverick as handsome, cool, intelligent, energetic, leader
- People who like the name Maverick also like Mason, Madison, Logan, Hayden, Riley, Mackenzie, Parker, Caden, Jaden, Hunter

Mavis *(English)*　♀　　RATING: ★★★
Song thrush—Mavis Beacon, typing tutor; Mavis Staples, singer
- People think of Mavis as funny, pretty, intelligent, popular, energetic
- People who like the name Mavis also like Mabel, Maeve, Hazel, Madeleine, Daphne, Margo, Megan, Grace, Genevieve, Scarlett

Max *(Latin)*　♂　　RATING: ★★☆
Greatest—Short for Maximillian or Maxwell; Max Crumm, singer
- People think of Max as handsome, funny, cool, intelligent, popular
- People who like the name Max also like Jack, Ethan, Noah, Jacob, Owen, Jake, Benjamin, Luke, Oliver, Jackson

Maxim *(Russian)*　♂　　RATING: ★★★☆
Greatest—Also a proverbial saying; also a men's magazine
- People think of Maxim as handsome, intelligent, sexy, cool, powerful
- People who like the name Maxim also like Gabriel, Max, Alexander, Maddox, Oliver, Jacob, Maxwell, Noah, Jackson, Sebastian

Maxima *(Latin)*　♀　　RATING: ★★★☆
Greatest—Feminine form of Maxim
- People think of Maxima as intelligent, powerful, trustworthy, exotic, creative
- People who like the name Maxima also like Mariah, Melania, Minerva, Mckayla, Marcena, Mabel, Marcella, Jenna, Maya, Michaela

Maxime *(French)*　♀　　RATING: ★★
Greatest—Variation of Maxima
- People think of Maxime as intelligent, funny, sexy, weird, creative
- People who like the name Maxime also like Madeleine, Margaux, Maxine, Maya, Giselle, Genevieve, Charlotte, Beatrice, Miette, Mariana

Maximilian *(Latin)*　♂　　RATING: ★★★
Greatest—Maximilian Schell, actor
- People think of Maximilian as intelligent, handsome, powerful, leader, cool
- People who like the name Maximilian also like Maxwell, Alexander, Benjamin, Maximus, Ethan, Sebastian, Zachary, Nicholas, Oliver, Maddox

Maximo *(Spanish)*　♂　　RATING: ★★☆
The greatest; top
- People think of Maximo as powerful, intelligent, old-fashioned, funny, energetic
- People who like the name Maximo also like Michael, Gabriel, Isaiah, Diego, Sebastian, Maxim, Joshua, Maximilian, Nicholas, Maxton

Maximos *(Greek)*　♂　　RATING: ★★
Greatest
- People think of Maximos as powerful, handsome, intelligent, leader, aggressive
- People who like the name Maximos also like Maximus, Matthew, Maximilian, Marcus, Mateo, Maxwell, Maxim, Miles, Noah, Liam

Maximus *(Latin)*　♂　　RATING: ★★
Greatest
- People think of Maximus as powerful, leader, handsome, intelligent, aggressive
- People who like the name Maximus also like Maximilian, Maddox, Alexander, Sebastian, Gabriel, Ethan, Owen, Marcus, Jack, Noah

Maxine *(French)*　♀　　RATING: ★★☆
Greatest—Maxine Andrews, of the Andrews Sisters singing group
- People think of Maxine as pretty, funny, intelligent, caring, trustworthy
- People who like the name Maxine also like Olivia, Hannah, Grace, Emma, Bianca, Mia, Paige, Natalie, Hailey, Ava

Maxton *(English)*　♂　　RATING: ★★★
From Maccus's town—Originally a surname
- People think of Maxton as energetic, intelligent, sporty, winner, handsome
- People who like the name Maxton also like Maddox, Jackson, Max, Maxwell, Maxim, Braxton, Holden, Jacob, Micah, Miles

Maxwell *(English)*　♂　　RATING: ★★★☆
From Maccus's spring—Also a surname; Maxwell, singer; Maxwell House, brand of coffee
- People think of Maxwell as handsome, intelligent, funny, cool, caring
- People who like the name Maxwell also like Jackson, Ethan, Alexander, Owen, Oliver, Noah, Jack, Matthew, Benjamin, Max

May *(English)*　♀　　RATING: ★★★☆
Goddess Maia—The month of May, named for the Greek goddess of spring
- People think of May as pretty, caring, funny, creative, young
- People who like the name May also like Grace, Mia, Lily, Ella, Faith, Olivia, Mae, Hannah, Maya, Emma

Maya *(English)*　♀　　RATING: ★★★☆
Variation of May or Maia
- People think of Maya as pretty, intelligent, creative, funny, caring
- People who like the name Maya also like Mia, Ava, Olivia, Isabella, Emma, Ella, Hannah, Chloe, Grace, Eva

393

Mayda (Armenian) ♀   RATING: ★★
Maiden
> People think of Mayda as funny, elegant, artsy, caring, young
> People who like the name Mayda also like Mia, Marly, Hannah, Maya, Cailyn, Rianna, Mckayla, Mea, Maren, Marie

Mayer (German) ♂   RATING: ★★☆
Steward—Also an American surname of various origins
> People think of Mayer as handsome, funny, exotic, cool, creative
> People who like the name Mayer also like Maddox, Fynn, Elias, Walker, Miles, Kaden, Major, Marcus, Jack, Emerson

Mayes (English) ♀♂   RATING: ★★
Servant; child of Matthew—Originally a surname
> People think of Mayes as caring, quiet, old-fashioned, artsy, boy next door
> People who like the name Mayes also like Mason, Sawyer, Logan, Hayden, Morgan, Caden, Marek, Reese, Lane, Rylie

Maylin (Chinese) ♀   RATING: ★★★★
Beautiful jade—Variation of Mei Lin
> People think of Maylin as pretty, intelligent, funny, creative, caring
> People who like the name Maylin also like Madelyn, Faith, Paige, Maya, Chloe, Isabella, Hannah, Jadyn, Bella, Cailyn

Maynard (English) ♂   RATING: ★☆
Brave strength
> People think of Maynard as intelligent, creative, powerful, funny, trustworthy
> People who like the name Maynard also like Xavier, Maddox, Gabriel, Malcolm, Matthew, Miles, Tyson, Marius, Marshall, Jackson

Mayten (American) ♀   RATING: ★★☆
Born on the tenth of May
> People think of Mayten as funny, unpopular, pretty, loser, creative
> People who like the name Mayten also like Maylin, Ella, Regan, Macayle, Macy, Cailyn, Mckayla, Marissa, Rianna, Jadyn

McIntyre (Celtic/Gaelic) ♂   RATING: ★★☆
Son of the carpenter—Joey McIntyre, singer
> People think of Mcintyre as sexy, unpopular, popular, cool, old-fashioned
> People who like the name Mcintyre also like Maxwell, Mac, Marius, Miles, Luke, Maddox, Marcus, Marty, Merric, Max

Mckale (American) ♀♂   RATING: ★★★★
Who is like God?—Variation of Michael
> People think of Mckale as intelligent, handsome, powerful, caring, weird

People who like the name Mckale also like Mckenna, Logan, Mackenzie, Madison, Jaden, Caden, Hayden, Mason, Riley, Reagan

Mckayla (American) ♀   RATING: ★★★☆
Who is like God?—Variation of Michaela
> People think of Mckayla as pretty, funny, energetic, young, popular
> People who like the name Mckayla also like Makayla, Hailey, Hannah, Paige, Isabella, Kaelyn, Kayla, Abigail, Faith, Savannah

Mckenna (Celtic/Gaelic) ♀♂   RATING: ★★★★
Son of Kenneth
> People think of Mckenna as pretty, funny, energetic, creative, intelligent
> People who like the name Mckenna also like Mackenzie, Madison, Riley, Logan, Addison, Bailey, Caden, Morgan, Hayden, Reagan

Mckenzie (Celtic/Gaelic) ♂   RATING: ★★★★
Son of Kenneth—Also a surname
> People think of Mckenzie as pretty, funny, popular, caring, cool
> People who like the name Mckenzie also like Aiden, Ethan, Landon, Jackson, Jacob, Kaden, Caleb, Matthew, Noah, Nicholas

Mckile (American) ♂   RATING: ★★☆
Combination of Mac and Kyle
> People think of Mckile as religious, boy next door, sporty, funny, intelligent
> People who like the name Mckile also like Kaden, Keagan, Tristan, Aiden, Kael, Mac, Jackson, Braeden, Liam, Maddox

Mea (Italian) ♀   RATING: ★★★
Mine
> People think of Mea as pretty, caring, sexy, exotic, young
> People who like the name Mea also like Mia, Isabella, Mya, Maya, Ella, Gianna, Ava, Olivia, Emma, Bella

Mead (English) ♀♂   RATING: ★★★
From the meadow—Originally a surname
> People think of Mead as caring, young, creative, powerful, funny
> People who like the name Mead also like Madison, Sawyer, Logan, Morgan, Marin, Myles, Parker, Taylor, Tyler, Greer

Meadow (American) ♀   RATING: ★★☆
Field of grass or vegetation
> People think of Meadow as pretty, creative, caring, artsy, funny
> People who like the name Meadow also like Paige, Isabella, Grace, Hannah, Faith, Olivia, Autumn, Summer, Savannah, Harmony

Meagan (American) ♀   RATING: ★★★★
Pearl—Variation of Megan
> People think of Meagan as pretty, funny, creative, caring, intelligent

People who like the name Meagan also like Megan, Hannah, Hailey, Emily, Natalie, Emma, Maegan, Lauren, Paige, Olivia

Meaghan *(American)* ♀   RATING: ★★★★
Pearl—Variation of Megan
People think of Meaghan as funny, pretty, intelligent, creative, caring
People who like the name Meaghan also like Maegan, Meagan, Paige, Megan, Emma, Hannah, Kaelyn, Meghan, Grace, Caitlyn

Meara *(Celtic/Gaelic)* ♀   RATING: ★★☆
Mirthful—Anne Meara, actress
People think of Meara as pretty, intelligent, caring, funny, energetic
People who like the name Meara also like Keira, Maeve, Moira, Aeryn, Maura, Olivia, Kaelyn, Keaira, Meriel, Erin

Meda *(Greek)* ♀   RATING: ★★★
Cunning—Variation of Medea
People think of Meda as intelligent, caring, pretty, exotic, sexy
People who like the name Meda also like Kaya, Cocheta, Ayasha, Ayita, Luyu, Miakoda, Neena, Talli, Donoma, Kaliska

Medea *(Greek)* ♀   RATING: ★★★★☆
Cunning—In Greek mythology, wife of Jason of the Argonauts
People think of Medea as powerful, intelligent, exotic, creative, aggressive
People who like the name Medea also like Aurora, Aradia, Athena, Isis, Layla, Maeve, Arwen, Kali, Chandra, Aria

Media *(Greek)* ♀   RATING: ★★☆
Communication
People think of Media as weird, intelligent, caring, creative, funny
People who like the name Media also like Maya, Melanie, Melissa, Magdalen, Melba, Megara, Melaney, Monica, Marla, Mariana

Medina *(Hebrew)* ♀   RATING: ★★★☆
City, state
People think of Medina as caring, funny, intelligent, trustworthy, creative
People who like the name Medina also like Makayla, Samira, Amal, Saleema, Geneva, Freya, Mariana, Genevieve, Keely, Amelie

Medusa *(Greek)* ♀   RATING: ★★★
Cunning—In Greek mythology, a woman with hair of live snakes
People think of Medusa as weird, sneaky, exotic, aggressive, criminal
People who like the name Medusa also like Medea, Pandora, Melody, Minerva, Aurora, Desdemona, Megara, Marla, Maya, Magdalen

Medwin *(German)* ♂   RATING: ★☆
Powerful friend
People think of Medwin as intelligent, nerdy, creative, caring, quiet
People who like the name Medwin also like Marlon, Malik, Malcolm, Marshall, Maddox, Maynard, Ethan, Marcus, Milo, Matthias

Meena *(Sanskrit/East Indian)* ♀   RATING: ★★★☆
Gem
People think of Meena as pretty, funny, caring, intelligent, elegant
People who like the name Meena also like Maya, Olivia, Layla, Mia, Sadie, Kyra, Ava, Nadia, Bella, Neena

Meg *(English)* ♀   RATING: ★★★★
Pearl—Short for Megan or Margaret; Meg Ryan, actress
People think of Meg as pretty, funny, caring, intelligent, creative
People who like the name Meg also like Ava, Olivia, Ella, Megan, Maggie, Molly, Emma, Grace, Mia, Audrey

Megan *(Welsh)* ♀   RATING: ★★★
Pearl
People think of Megan as funny, pretty, caring, creative, intelligent
People who like the name Megan also like Hannah, Emily, Olivia, Paige, Grace, Lauren, Emma, Abigail, Hailey, Chloe

Megara *(Greek)* ♀   RATING: ★★★☆
Grudge—Variation of Megaera
People think of Megara as exotic, aggressive, intelligent, weird, energetic
People who like the name Megara also like Cassandra, Odette, Jasmine, Melody, Giselle, Scarlett, Gabriella, Iris, Aurora, Genevieve

Meghan *(American)* ♀   RATING: ★★★☆
Pearl—Variation of Megan
People think of Meghan as pretty, funny, caring, intelligent, creative
People who like the name Meghan also like Hannah, Paige, Emma, Samantha, Natalie, Olivia, Megan, Hailey, Emily, Lauren

Meghana *(Sanskrit/East Indian)* ♀   RATING: ★★
Cloud
People think of Meghana as pretty, intelligent, caring, young, artsy
People who like the name Meghana also like Malini, Mallika, Maegan, Manasa, Mythri, Mitali, Mandara, Miranda, Melody, Bhavna

Meghdad *(Persian)* ♂   RATING: ★★☆
Heavenly justice
People think of Meghdad as ethnic, funny, weird, big, intelligent
People who like the name Meghdad also like Faris, Darius, Yazid, Bijan, Asher, Adish, Lulani, Oma, Manelin, Merric

396

Mei (*Chinese*) ♀   RATING: ★★☆
Plum
> People think of Mei as intelligent, pretty, caring, creative, elegant
> People who like the name Mei also like Mia, Mai, Ella, Mya, Isabella, Maya, Grace, Mea, Paige, Ava

Meiling (*Chinese*) ♀   RATING: ★★★☆
Beautiful, delicate
> People think of Meiling as pretty, exotic, intelligent, elegant, caring
> People who like the name Meiling also like Sakura, Li Mei, Mulan, Jia Li, Aiko, Emiko, Samantha, Ling, Hoshiko, Mai

Meir (*Hebrew*) ♂   RATING: ★★★☆
One who shines
> People think of Meir as powerful, creative, leader, popular, funny
> People who like the name Meir also like Gabriel, Micah, Elijah, Maddox, Seth, Malik, Benjamin, Noah, Asher, Marnin

Meira (*Hebrew*) ♀   RATING: ★★★★☆
Shining
> People think of Meira as intelligent, creative, energetic, funny, girl next door
> People who like the name Meira also like Olivia, Mia, Maya, Keira, Meara, Mira, Hannah, Layla, Kiara, Gabrielle

Mekelle (*American*) ♀   RATING: ★★★
Who is like God?—Varition of Michaela
> People think of Mekelle as exotic, pretty, religious, cool, trustworthy
> People who like the name Mekelle also like Jadyn, Mckayla, Makaila, Makenna, Cailyn, Hannah, Makayla, Kaelyn, Natalie, Abigail

Mel (*American*) ♀♂   RATING: ★★★☆
Short for Melanie or Melvin—Mel Blanc, voice of Bugs Bunny and Daffy Duck; Mel Brooks, actor/director; Mel Gibson, actor
> People think of Mel as funny, pretty, sexy, cool, intelligent
> People who like the name Mel also like Nolan, Madison, Caley, Mason, Connor, Jade, Quinn, Skye, Morgan, Brody

Melaney (*Greek*) ♀   RATING: ★★★★
Black
> People think of Melaney as pretty, funny, intelligent, popular, caring
> People who like the name Melaney also like Hailey, Faith, Madelyn, Macy, Emma, Melody, Grace, Natalie, Isabella, Emily

Melangell (*Welsh*) ♀   RATING: ★☆
Dear angel
> People think of Melangell as pretty, caring, old, intelligent, weird
> People who like the name Melangell also like Morwen, Kara, Keaira, Morgana, Kaya, Melania, Kyla, Jane, Mirabelle, Gwennan

Melania (*Greek*) ♀   RATING: ★★★★
Black
> People think of Melania as exotic, pretty, elegant, sexy, intelligent
> People who like the name Melania also like Ava, Isabella, Melanie, Melina, Adriana, Layla, Olivia, Giselle, Sienna, Mia

Melanie (*Greek*) ♀   RATING: ★★★★
Black—Melanie Griffith, actress
> People think of Melanie as pretty, funny, caring, intelligent, creative
> People who like the name Melanie also like Natalie, Hannah, Emily, Olivia, Paige, Hailey, Abigail, Emma, Chloe, Isabella

Melanion (*Greek*) ♂   RATING: ★★
Black—In Greek mythology, the husband of Atalanta
> People think of Melanion as powerful, exotic, funny, loser, trustworthy
> People who like the name Melanion also like Lysander, Demetrius, Dashiell, Maximus, Wyatt, Calix, Merric, Sirius, Matthias, Demitrius

Melantha (*Greek*) ♀   RATING: ★★
Combination of Mel and –antha
> People think of Melantha as exotic, aggressive, caring, stuck-up, leader
> People who like the name Melantha also like Melora, Cassandra, Melinda, Maura, Melanie, Fiona, Melanthe, Medea, Myrtle, Maya

Melanthe (*Greek*) ♀   RATING: ★★★☆
Combination of Mel and –anthe
> People think of Melanthe as pretty, exotic, artsy, intelligent, ethnic
> People who like the name Melanthe also like Melantha, Xanthe, Melora, Melanie, Melinda, Megara, Millicent, Mona, Monica, Myrtle

Melba (*English*) ♀   RATING: ★★★
From Melbourne, Australia—Also a type of toast; Melba Moore, singer/actress
> People think of Melba as pretty, caring, funny, intelligent, leader
> People who like the name Melba also like Melanie, Melissa, Maya, Melora, Mimis, Marjorie, Jasmine, Melody, Mindy, Micheline

Melchior (*Hebrew*) ♂   RATING: ★★★
God is my light
> People think of Melchior as intelligent, powerful, cool, handsome, creative
> People who like the name Melchior also like Malachi, Aiden, Morpheus, Alistair, Milek, Maddox, Maxim, Matthias, Hiroshi, Constantine

Mele (*Hawaiian*) ♂   RATING: ★★★☆
Song
> People think of Mele as cool, intelligent, exotic, slow, popular
> People who like the name Mele also like Noah, Isaac, Owen, Elijah, Cole, Mauli, Aiden, Caleb, Maddox, Mikaili

Meli *(Greek)* ♀ RATING: ★★★☆
Short for Melissa, Melina, or Melinda
> People think of Meli as funny, pretty, intelligent, trustworthy, energetic
> People who like the name Meli also like Topanga, Kiona, Mari, Kaya, Shania, Lexi, Miakoda, Mia, Sahkyo, Tazanna

Melia *(English)* ♀ RATING: ★★☆
Work—Also a Greek mythological name meaning ash tree
> People think of Melia as pretty, intelligent, exotic, caring, funny
> People who like the name Melia also like Malia, Maya, Mia, Olivia, Isabella, Madelyn, Emma, Layla, Grace, Ella

Melina *(Greek)* ♀ RATING: ★★★★
Honey—Melina Kanakaredes, actress
> People think of Melina as pretty, funny, creative, caring, intelligent
> People who like the name Melina also like Ava, Isabella, Olivia, Mia, Chloe, Adriana, Ella, Emma, Grace, Angelina

Melinda *(American)* ♀ RATING: ★★☆
Black, beautiful—Combination of Mel and Linda; Melinda Doolittle, singer
> People think of Melinda as pretty, caring, funny, intelligent, trustworthy
> People who like the name Melinda also like Melissa, Miranda, Hannah, Melanie, Marissa, Melody, Hailey, Isabella, Olivia, Natalie

Meliora *(Latin)* ♀ RATING: ★★☆
Better—Used in Cornwall, UK
> People think of Meliora as artsy, pretty, funny, intelligent, elegant
> People who like the name Meliora also like Marisela, Melinda, Melora, Miyoko, Michaela, Mahalia, Arwen, Melania, Oriana, Carmelita

Melisande *(French)* ♀ RATING: ★★
Labor strength—Medieval variation of Millicent
> People think of Melisande as pretty, creative, intelligent, artsy, elegant
> People who like the name Melisande also like Giselle, Genevieve, Josephine, Isabelle, Miette, Madeleine, Maeve, Lorelei, Mia, Aurora

Melissa *(Greek)* ♀ RATING: ★★★
Bee—Melissa Etheridge, singer/songwriter; Melissa Gilbert, actress; Melissa Joan Hart, actress; Melissa Leo, actress
> People think of Melissa as pretty, funny, caring, intelligent, creative
> People who like the name Melissa also like Jessica, Emily, Hannah, Rebecca, Natalie, Emma, Lauren, Olivia, Hailey, Samantha

Melissan *(American)* ♀ RATING: ★★☆
Labor strength—Variation of Millicent
> People think of Melissan as lazy, old-fashioned, aggressive, weird, girl next door

People who like the name Melissan also like Melissa, Melisande, Maren, Mae, Melanie, Marian, Mairwen, Mariana, Keira, Mara

Melita *(Italian)* ♀ RATING: ★★
Bee—Variation of Melissa
> People think of Melita as pretty, funny, creative, popular, intelligent
> People who like the name Melita also like Angelina, Isabella, Mercedes, Gianna, Miranda, Madeline, Mariah, Matilda, Sienna, Mea

Melodie *(French)* ♀ RATING: ★★★★
Song, melody
> People think of Melodie as pretty, creative, funny, intelligent, caring
> People who like the name Melodie also like Melody, Paige, Isabella, Isabelle, Hannah, Faith, Chloe, Hailey, Mia, Melanie

Melody *(English)* ♀ RATING: ★★★★
Melody
> People think of Melody as pretty, creative, funny, caring, intelligent
> People who like the name Melody also like Harmony, Faith, Paige, Hailey, Isabella, Grace, Chloe, Hannah, Emma, Olivia

Melor *(Russian)* ♂ RATING: ★★
Communist name, acronym from the first letters of Marx, Engels, Lenin, October, and Revolution
> People think of Melor as ethnic, aggressive, untrustworthy, uptight, young
> People who like the name Melor also like Frey, Boden, Mahon, Kiefer, Curran, Lucius, Antoine, Olin, Hansel, Drake

Melora *(Russian)* ♀ RATING: ★★★★
From the first letters of Marx, Engels, Lenin, October, and Revolution—Feminine form of Melor
> People think of Melora as intelligent, creative, elegant, exotic, artsy
> People who like the name Melora also like Melanie, Ophelia, Melody, Cordelia, Aurora, Maya, Genevieve, Chloe, Nadia, Gabrielle

Melosa *(Spanish)* ♀ RATING: ★★★
Sweet
> People think of Melosa as exotic, ethnic, pretty, energetic, creative
> People who like the name Melosa also like Senona, Aurora, Isabel, Mercedes, Audrey, Calista, Mora, Melody, Emberlynn, Bella

Melva *(Celtic/Gaelic)* ♀ RATING: ★★★
Gentle lady—Feminine form of Melvin
> People think of Melva as caring, creative, funny, intelligent, elegant
> People who like the name Melva also like Maura, Mckayla, Maire, Moira, Meagan, Makayla, Malise, Maisie, Megan, Maggie

398

Melvin *(English)* ♂ RATING: ★★★
Gentle lord—Melvin Belli, attorney; Melvin Douglas, actor
> People think of Melvin as funny, handsome, popular, caring, cool
> People who like the name Melvin also like Jason, Matthew, Maxwell, Kevin, Justin, Jackson, Marvin, Oliver, Adam, Marshall

Melvina *(Celtic/Gaelic)* ♀ RATING: ★★★☆
Gentle lady—Feminine form of Melvin
> People think of Melvina as pretty, old-fashioned, intelligent, caring, old
> People who like the name Melvina also like Maire, Mckayla, Moira, Melva, Macayle, Maura, Mairi, Maisie, Mairead, Meg

Melvyn *(Celtic/Gaelic)* ♂ RATING: ★☆
Gentle lord
> People think of Melvyn as nerdy, weird, funny, trustworthy, intelligent
> People who like the name Melvyn also like Ethan, Owen, Malcolm, Glenn, Duncan, Keagan, Alan, Colin, Melvin, Galvin

Memphis *(Greek)* ♀♂ RATING: ★★
Established, beautiful—Variation of the Egyptian Mennefer
> People think of Memphis as handsome, cool, funny, intelligent, energetic
> People who like the name Memphis also like Parker, Madison, Logan, Dakota, Caden, Mason, Hayden, Riley, Ryder, Phoenix

Mena *(Sanskrit/East Indian)* ♀ RATING: ★★★☆
Woman, mother-goddess—Mena Suvari, actress
> People think of Mena as funny, exotic, caring, sexy, pretty
> People who like the name Mena also like Mia, Mina, Ava, Ella, Sophia, Bianca, Meena, Fiona, Kyra, Olivia

Mendel *(German)* ♂ RATING: ★★★
Little man
> People think of Mendel as intelligent, quiet, creative, caring, leader
> People who like the name Mendel also like Samuel, Daniel, Gabriel, Benjamin, Malachi, Isaac, Michael, Adam, Meir, Josiah

Mendie *(German)* ♀♂ RATING: ★★★
Little man—Originally short for Mendel
> People think of Mendie as funny, girl next door, unpopular, intelligent, lazy
> People who like the name Mendie also like Morgan, Mischa, Abby, Jaden, Meredith, Hayden, Mason, Justice, Jordan, Kenley

Menefer *(Egyptian)* ♀♂ RATING: ★★☆
Established, beautiful—Original name of Memphis, Egypt
> People think of Menefer as intelligent, artsy, exotic, pretty, energetic

> People who like the name Menefer also like Morgan, Makya, Myles, Marlas, Meris, Mischa, Makaio, Magan, Memphis, Montana

Menora *(Hebrew)* ♀ RATING: ★★★
Candelabra
> People think of Menora as quiet, wealthy, exotic, wild, religious
> People who like the name Menora also like Lorelei, Melissa, Magnolia, Mariah, Meadow, Helena, Mara, Aurora, Heather, Mirabelle

Mercedes *(Spanish)* ♀ RATING: ★★★★
Merciful—Also a brand of cars; Mercedes Ruehl, actress
> People think of Mercedes as pretty, funny, sexy, intelligent, popular
> People who like the name Mercedes also like Faith, Paige, Olivia, Isabella, Hailey, Chloe, Savannah, Hannah, Ava, Destiny

Mercer *(English)* ♀♂ RATING: ★★★
Merchant—Mercer Mayer, author; Johnny Mercer, songwriter; Mabel Mercer, jazz singer
> People think of Mercer as powerful, sexy, winner, trendy, wild
> People who like the name Mercer also like Parker, Mason, Sawyer, Hayden, Spencer, Logan, Riley, Landen, Paxton, Reagan

Mercia *(English)* ♀ RATING: ★★
Mercy—Variation of Mercedes or Marsha; also an ancient British kingdom
> People think of Mercia as caring, pretty, elegant, exotic, religious
> People who like the name Mercia also like Mariah, Morrisa, Mckayla, Myra, Melody, Ciara, Moira, Marietta, Macy, Mia

Mercury *(Latin)* ♀♂ RATING: ★★★☆
God of trade—Also a planet
> People think of Mercury as cool, creative, intelligent, aggressive, leader
> People who like the name Mercury also like Madison, Sage, Logan, Phoenix, James, Justice, Dakota, Paxton, Taylor, Blair

Mercy *(English)* ♀ RATING: ★★
Compassion
> People think of Mercy as pretty, caring, intelligent, creative, religious
> People who like the name Mercy also like Faith, Grace, Hope, Olivia, Melody, Emma, Chloe, Bianca, Macy, Scarlett

Meredith *(Welsh)* ♀♂ RATING: ★★
Lord—The meaning of Mere is unknown, but –dith means lord; Meredith Baxter, actress; Meredith Wilson, composer
> People think of Meredith as pretty, intelligent, funny, caring, creative

People who like the name Meredith also like Madison, Morgan, Addison, Hayden, Logan, Mackenzie, Avery, Taylor, Riley, Ryan

Mererid *(Welsh)* ♀　　RATING: ★★☆
Pearl—Variation of Margaret
　People think of Mererid as nerdy, pretty, loser, weird, creative
　People who like the name Mererid also like Brigid, Minjonet, Malise, Faye, Faylinn, Alaska, Brynja, Hester, Branwen, Hyacinth

Meria *(American)* ♀　　RATING: ★★☆
Sea of bitterness—Variation of Maria
　People think of Meria as creative, wild, sexy, exotic, cool
　People who like the name Meria also like Miniya, Ivy, Iris, Isabel, Myeisha, Maha, Nicole, Cassandra, Kate, Hailey

Meridian *(American)* ♀♂　　RATING: ★★★★
Middle, center
　People think of Meridian as intelligent, artsy, young, powerful, wild
　People who like the name Meridian also like Madison, Morgan, Mason, Hayden, Mackenzie, Payton, Reese, Jocelyn, Jade, Mischa

Meriel *(Celtic/Gaelic)* ♀　　RATING: ★★★★
Sea bright—Variation of Muriel
　People think of Meriel as pretty, intelligent, creative, funny, cool
　People who like the name Meriel also like Kaelyn, Meara, Maeve, Aeryn, Genevieve, Kara, Brea, Moira, Caelan, Maisie

Merinda *(Spanish)* ♀　　RATING: ★★★☆
Combination of Mer and -inda
　People think of Merinda as pretty, caring, intelligent, funny, creative
　People who like the name Merinda also like Miranda, Marisa, Marissa, Melinda, Malinda, Jillian, Melissa, Clarissa, Isabella, Fiona

Meris *(Latin)* ♀♂　　RATING: ★★★☆
Of the sea
　People think of Meris as pretty, creative, popular, caring, funny
　People who like the name Meris also like Morgan, Aidan, Marin, Parker, Mason, Merrick, Caden, Dorian, Meredith, Madison

Merle *(English)* ♀♂　　RATING: ★★★☆
Blackbird—Merle Haggard, singer/songwriter; Merle Oberon, actress
　People think of Merle as caring, funny, intelligent, popular, creative
　People who like the name Merle also like Meryl, Morgan, Raven, Mika, Kyle, Drew, Marlin, Montana, Marvel, Sydney

Merlin *(Latin)* ♂　　RATING: ★★★☆
Variation of Myrddin—Also magician/wizard of Arthurian legend
　People think of Merlin as intelligent, caring, handsome, cool, powerful
　People who like the name Merlin also like Felix, Drake, Noah, Elijah, Aiden, Isaac, Xavier, Tristan, Ian, Ethan

Merric *(Celtic/Gaelic)* ♂　　RATING: ★★☆
Fame rule
　People think of Merric as handsome, leader, powerful, sexy, cool
　People who like the name Merric also like Aiden, Tristan, Liam, Keagan, Braeden, Owen, Gavin, Cole, Conner, Kaden

Merrick *(English)* ♀♂　　RATING: ★★☆
Fame rule
　People think of Merrick as handsome, intelligent, leader, powerful, cool
　People who like the name Merrick also like Hayden, Logan, Mason, Parker, Landen, Morgan, Caden, Madison, Jaden, Marek

Merridy *(American)* ♀　　RATING: ★★★
Happy song—Combination of Merry and Melody; also possibly short for Meredith
　People think of Merridy as artsy, creative, elegant, wealthy, trendy
　People who like the name Merridy also like Dani, Keira, Melina, Aira, Cora, Erin, Kiersten, Caroline, Gwen, Mia

Merrill *(English)* ♀♂　　RATING: ★★★☆
From the pleasant hill
　People think of Merrill as intelligent, trustworthy, creative, cool, artsy
　People who like the name Merrill also like Hayden, Logan, Morgan, Mason, Meredith, Madison, Reese, Parker, Cameron, James

Merritt *(English)* ♀♂　　RATING: ★★★☆
From the boundary gate
　People think of Merritt as intelligent, funny, creative, caring, cool
　People who like the name Merritt also like Mason, Parker, Hayden, Addison, Avery, Riley, Logan, Bennett, Meredith, Madison

Merry *(English)* ♀　　RATING: ★★
Cheerful, happy—Also short for names beginning with Mer
　People think of Merry as pretty, caring, funny, intelligent, leader
　People who like the name Merry also like Molly, Melody, Maggie, Sophie, Amy, Mabel, Arwen, Marissa, Autumn, Felicity

Mertice *(American)* ♀　　RATING: ★★
Lord—Variation of Meredith
　People think of Mertice as unpopular, girl next door, old, old-fashioned, lazy

People who like the name Mertice also like Devorah, Calista, Arianna, Angelique, Sadah, Katelyn, Cyrah, Manoush, Nichole, Corinne

Merton *(English)* ♀♂   RATING: ★☆
From the lake town
People think of Merton as weird, loser, nerdy, unpopular, quiet
People who like the name Merton also like Mason, Connor, Morgan, Merrick, Tanner, Paxton, Taylor, Jordan, Raven, Reilly

Merv *(American)* ♂   RATING: ★☆
Great lord—Short for Mervin; Merv Griffin, TV producer
People think of Merv as trustworthy, intelligent, caring, leader, powerful
People who like the name Merv also like Mac, Malcolm, Mervin, Merric, Liam, Finn, Owen, Braeden, Paddy, Ewan

Mervin *(Welsh)* ♂   RATING: ★☆
Great lord—Mervin LeRoy, director
People think of Mervin as leader, funny, popular, handsome, caring
People who like the name Mervin also like Liam, Jason, Ian, Lucas, Paul, Kevin, Justin, Marvin, Patrick, Brian

Mervyn *(Welsh)* ♂   RATING: ★☆
Great lord
People think of Mervyn as intelligent, handsome, leader, creative, popular
People who like the name Mervyn also like Ronan, Merric, Liam, Edan, Paddy, Nolen, Malcolm, Owen, Tristan, Devlin

Meryl *(English)* ♀♂   RATING: ★★★☆
Combination of Mary and Louise—Meryl Streep, actress
People think of Meryl as funny, intelligent, pretty, creative, cool
People who like the name Meryl also like Meredith, Madison, Merrill, Quinn, Maeryn, Morgan, Marin, Evelyn, Aubrey, Jordan

Meryle *(American)* ♀♂   RATING: ★★☆
Combination of Mary and Louise—Variation of Meryl
People think of Meryle as old-fashioned, old, unpopular, nerdy, weird
People who like the name Meryle also like Merrill, Meryl, Mayes, Lyndon, Myles, Jermaine, Merrick, Jordan, Montana, Meredith

Messina *(Italian)* ♀♂   RATING: ★★★
Place in Italy—Loggins & Messina, musical group
People think of Messina as pretty, funny, sexy, trustworthy, powerful
People who like the name Messina also like Madison, Morgan, Mackenzie, Jocelyn, Ariel, Mckenna, Bailey, Mckale, Jordan, Blair

Meta *(German)* ♀   RATING: ★★★
Pearl—Short for Margareta
People think of Meta as trustworthy, artsy, intelligent, caring, creative
People who like the name Meta also like Anika, Mia, Elsa, Annika, Josephine, Lorelei, Anya, Milla, Aliana, Margot

Metcalf *(English)* ♀♂   RATING: ★★
Herdsman—Laurie Metcalf, actress
People think of Metcalf as pretty, funny, intelligent, cool, caring
People who like the name Metcalf also like Devon, Ashling, Alexis, Addison, Beverly, Joe, Keir, Kenley, Kieran, Lyndsey

Metea *(Greek)* ♀   RATING: ★★★
Gentle
People think of Metea as exotic, pretty, elegant, quiet, religious
People who like the name Metea also like Maya, Ava, Paige, Layla, Monica, Madelyn, Kyra, Melina, Mia, Medea

Metta *(Scandinavian)* ♀   RATING: ★★★
Pearl—Short for Margaretta
People think of Metta as intelligent, popular, artsy, old-fashioned, powerful
People who like the name Metta also like Thora, Kaya, Margaret, Miette, Mira, Caroline, Lena, Melisande, Elsa, Matilda

Meyshia *(American)* ♀   RATING: ★★★
Who is like God?—Variation of Mischa
People think of Meyshia as religious, pretty, quiet, sexy, creative
People who like the name Meyshia also like Myeisha, Maya, Makaila, Mya, Mia, Mariah, Mateja, Mercedes, Makayla, Maisha

Mhina *(African)* ♀♂   RATING: ★★★
Delightful
People think of Mhina as exotic, ethnic, pretty, creative, popular
People who like the name Mhina also like Mika, Mahdi, Musoke, Madison, Akia, Misae, Mischa, Maemi, Morgan, Makya

Mia *(Scandinavian)* ♀   RATING: ★★★☆
Sea of bitterness—Short for Maria
People think of Mia as pretty, funny, intelligent, caring, popular
People who like the name Mia also like Ava, Olivia, Emma, Ella, Isabella, Chloe, Mya, Maya, Grace, Paige

Miach *(Celtic/Gaelic)* ♀♂   RATING: ★★★
Honorable, proud
People think of Miach as energetic, handsome, popular, cool, creative
People who like the name Miach also like Addison, Rory, Brayden, Aidan, Logan, Cael, Mackenzie, Avery, Caden, Connor

Miakoda *(American)* ♀　　RATING: ★★★★
Created for a series of science fiction books by Jane Fancher
　People think of Miakoda as exotic, creative, powerful, intelligent, cool
　People who like the name Miakoda also like Kaya, Layla, Kachina, Ayasha, Mia, Dyani, Hateya, Kiona, Cocheta, Leilani

Micaella *(American)* ♀　　RATING: ★★★★
Who is like God?—Variation of Michaela
　People think of Micaella as pretty, creative, intelligent, caring, trustworthy
　People who like the name Micaella also like Michaela, Mckayla, Makayla, Makaila, Isabella, Mikayla, Makenna, Olivia, Breanna, Jadyn

Micah *(Hebrew)* ♂　　RATING: ★★★
Who is like God?
　People think of Micah as intelligent, handsome, funny, caring, creative
　People who like the name Micah also like Noah, Elijah, Caleb, Ethan, Isaac, Isaiah, Gabriel, Ian, Aiden, Jacob

Michael *(Hebrew)* ♂　　RATING: ★★★★
Who is like God?—In the Bible, an archangel; Michael Douglas, actor; Michael J. Fox, actor; Michael Jordan, basketball player
　People think of Michael as handsome, funny, intelligent, caring, cool
　People who like the name Michael also like Matthew, Nicholas, Andrew, Ethan, Nathan, Jacob, Daniel, Joshua, Christopher, Benjamin

Michaela *(English)* ♀　　RATING: ★★★★
Who is like God?—Feminine form of Michael; pronounced *Mi-KAY-la*
　People think of Michaela as pretty, funny, creative, intelligent, caring
　People who like the name Michaela also like Olivia, Isabella, Hannah, Abigail, Makayla, Emma, Grace, Paige, Chloe, Gabrielle

Michal *(Hebrew)* ♂　　RATING: ★★☆
Who is like God?
　People think of Michal as caring, intelligent, creative, funny, cool
　People who like the name Michal also like Micah, Michael, Nathaniel, Zachary, Maddox, Jackson, Josiah, Aaron, Jadon, Noah

Micheal *(Celtic/Gaelic)* ♂　　RATING: ★★★☆
Who is like God?—Variation of Michael; pronounced *Me-HAWL*
　People think of Micheal as handsome, funny, caring, cool, intelligent
　People who like the name Micheal also like Matthew, Jacob, Nicholas, Michael, Nathan, Christopher, Alexander, Andrew, Joshua, Justin

Michel *(French)* ♂　　RATING: ★★☆
Who is like God?—Pronounced *Mee-SHELL*
　People think of Michel as intelligent, handsome, cool, funny, caring
　People who like the name Michel also like Michael, Christopher, William, Bradley, Gabriel, Nathan, Seth, Daniel, Micheal, Benjamin

Michelangelo *(Italian)* ♂　　RATING: ★★★★
Archangel Michael—Michelangelo Buonarroti, artist/architect/inventor
　People think of Michelangelo as artsy, creative, handsome, intelligent, elegant
　People who like the name Michelangelo also like Gabriel, Michael, Leonardo, Angelo, Marco, David, Matthew, Giovanni, Nicholas, Sebastian

Michele *(French)* ♀　　RATING: ★★★☆
Who is like God?—Feminine form of Michel
　People think of Michele as pretty, caring, funny, intelligent, creative
　People who like the name Michele also like Mia, Emily, Olivia, Lauren, Paige, Melissa, Michelle, Isabella, Elizabeth, Grace

Micheline *(French)* ♀　　RATING: ★★★★
Who is like God?—Feminine form of Michel
　People think of Micheline as pretty, caring, funny, intelligent, cool
　People who like the name Micheline also like Michelle, Mallory, Isabella, Isabelle, Michaela, Madeleine, Jacqueline, Janelle, Giselle, Janette

Michelle *(French)* ♀　　RATING: ★★★
Who is like God?—Michelle Pfeiffer, actress; Michelle Yeoh, actress; Sarah Michelle Gellar, actress
　People think of Michelle as pretty, funny, caring, intelligent, creative
　People who like the name Michelle also like Nicole, Hannah, Emily, Elizabeth, Natalie, Isabella, Emma, Grace, Faith, Chloe

Michi *(Japanese)* ♀　　RATING: ★★
Righteous way
　People think of Michi as pretty, creative, intelligent, funny, young
　People who like the name Michi also like Mai, Mieko, Miya, Midori, Masako, Aiko, Mina, Machiko, Michiko, Miyo

Michigan *(Native American)* ♀♂　　RATING: ★★★
Great lake—U.S. state
　People think of Michigan as artsy, aggressive, funny, sporty, handsome
　People who like the name Michigan also like Morgan, Madison, Logan, Minnesota, Montana, Riley, Mason, Ryan, Dakota, Reese

Michiko *(Japanese)* ♀　　RATING: ★★★★
Beauty, wisdom
　People think of Michiko as pretty, young, intelligent, funny, trustworthy

People who like the name Michiko also like Mai, Aiko, Miyoko, Sakura, Miyo, Keiko, Amaya, Mieko, Suki, Masako

Michon (*French*) ♀ ♂   RATING: ★★
Who is like God?—Variation of Michel
People think of Michon as funny, trustworthy, pretty, weird, intelligent
People who like the name Michon also like Mason, Riley, Jaden, Miracle, Mischa, Milan, Landen, Kasen, Tayte, Reagan

Mick (*English*) ♂   RATING: ★★★☆
Who is like God?—Short for Michael; Mick Jagger, singer/songwriter
People think of Mick as cool, handsome, popular, funny, leader
People who like the name Mick also like Jack, Jackson, Mark, Miles, Mitch, Jake, Tyson, Max, Matthew, Cole

Mickey (*American*) ♀ ♂   RATING: ★★★☆
Who is like God?—Short for Michael; Mickey Mouse, cartoon character
People think of Mickey as funny, caring, cool, popular, creative
People who like the name Mickey also like Madison, Taylor, Mackenzie, Bailey, Mason, Dylan, Parker, Morgan, Sean, Jesse

Micol (*American*) ♂   RATING: ★★
Who is like God?—Variation of Michael
People think of Micol as creative, intelligent, pretty, cool, caring
People who like the name Micol also like Micah, Maddox, Michal, Isaac, Marnin, Jadon, Mattox, Griffin, Ronan, Malik

Midori (*Japanese*) ♀   RATING: ★★★☆
Green—Midori Ito, figure skater
People think of Midori as pretty, funny, creative, young, intelligent
People who like the name Midori also like Sakura, Amaya, Aiko, Mai, Kaida, Ayame, Emiko, Miyoko, Mieko, Miya

Mieko (*Japanese*) ♀   RATING: ★★★★
Already prosperous
People think of Mieko as pretty, exotic, intelligent, caring, energetic
People who like the name Mieko also like Maeko, Miya, Miyoko, Mai, Aiko, Kaiya, Miyo, Michiko, Midori, Amaya

Miette (*French*) ♀   RATING: ★★★★☆
Pearl—Short for Marguerite
People think of Miette as pretty, elegant, young, artsy, creative
People who like the name Miette also like Giselle, Isabella, Minjonet, Madeleine, Adeline, Mirabelle, Camille, Isabelle, Ava, Melisande

Mignon (*French*) ♀   RATING: ★★★★
Delicate, graceful—Also filet mignon, a prime cut of beef
People think of Mignon as pretty, intelligent, funny, caring, creative
People who like the name Mignon also like Miette, Isabelle, Madeleine, Giselle, Jolie, Sophie, Simone, Adeline, Melisande, Marcella

Miguel (*Spanish*) ♂   RATING: ★★★☆
Who is like God?
People think of Miguel as handsome, funny, cool, intelligent, popular
People who like the name Miguel also like Ethan, Diego, Gabriel, Antonio, Javier, Joshua, Carlos, Xavier, Jacob, Isaac

Mihaly (*Hungarian*) ♂   RATING: ★★☆
Who is like God?
People think of Mihaly as powerful, caring, popular, handsome, stuck-up
People who like the name Mihaly also like Nathaniel, Malachi, Mykelti, Mikko, Jayden, Matthew, Jeremy, Mikaili, Michael, Ethan

Mika (*Native American*) ♀ ♂   RATING: ★★★☆
Raccoon—Osage origin
People think of Mika as pretty, intelligent, creative, funny, young
People who like the name Mika also like Madison, Dakota, Jade, Hayden, Jaden, Morgan, Bailey, Mackenzie, Mason, Aidan

Mikaia (*American*) ♀ ♂   RATING: ★★★★
Who is like God?—Variation of Micah
People think of Mikaia as pretty, leader, creative, funny, exotic
People who like the name Mikaia also like Madison, Jaden, Caden, Mackenzie, Mika, Morgan, Mckenna, Cadence, Hayden, Sage

Mikaili (*African*) ♂   RATING: ★★★☆
Who is like God?
People think of Mikaili as intelligent, pretty, creative, popular, leader
People who like the name Mikaili also like Caleb, Jayden, Kaden, Maddox, Micah, Aiden, Malachi, Malik, Isaiah, Tristan

Mikasi (*Native American*) ♂   RATING: ★★★☆
Coyote
People think of Mikasi as exotic, wild, ethnic, creative, intelligent
People who like the name Mikasi also like Aiden, Mingan, Dyami, Kele, Gavin, Mikaili, Chayton, Landon, Drake, Ezhno

Mikayla (*American*) ♀   RATING: ★★★★
Who is like God?—Variation of Michaela
People think of Mikayla as pretty, funny, creative, caring, intelligent

People who like the name Mikayla also like Isabella, Makayla, Hannah, Savannah, Emma, Hailey, Paige, Olivia, Kayla, Mckayla

Mike *(English)* ♂ RATING: ★★☆
Who is like God?—Short for Michael; Mike Douglas, talk show host
People think of Mike as funny, cool, handsome, caring, sexy
People who like the name Mike also like Matthew, Michael, Jacob, David, Justin, Jake, Mark, Jason, Jack, Aaron

Mikel *(American)* ♂ RATING: ★★★★
Who is like God?—Variation of Michael
People think of Mikel as handsome, funny, caring, energetic, popular
People who like the name Mikel also like Jayden, Kaden, Matthew, Micah, Michael, Nathan, Aiden, Isaiah, Noah, Owen

Mikhail *(Russian)* ♂ RATING: ★★★★
Who is like God?—Variation of Michael; Mikhail Baryshnikov, ballet dancer; Mikhail Gorbachev, Soviet leader
People think of Mikhail as handsome, intelligent, trustworthy, leader, creative
People who like the name Mikhail also like Jayden, Gabriel, Aiden, Nicholai, Caleb, Tristan, Ian, Liam, Kaden, Micah

Miki *(Japanese)* ♀ RATING: ★★★★
Flower stalk
People think of Miki as funny, pretty, caring, creative, cool
People who like the name Miki also like Mai, Mieko, Kaori, Sakura, Kaiya, Miya, Kimi, Mina, Misa, Michi

Mikiesha *(American)* ♀ RATING: ★★☆
Her life—Combination of Michaela and Kiesha
People think of Mikiesha as funny, wild, sneaky, pretty, leader
People who like the name Mikiesha also like Serenity, Chantel, Anastasia, Bebe, Aphrodite, Gabrielle, Brandi, Brittney, Lakeisha, Jazziell

Mikkel *(German)* ♀♂ RATING: ★★☆
Who is like God?—Variation of Michael
People think of Mikkel as cool, intelligent, young, leader, weird
People who like the name Mikkel also like Jaden, Caden, Logan, Parker, Taylor, Connor, Dylan, Preston, Riley, Alexis

Mikko *(Scandinavian)* ♂ RATING: ★★★★
Who is like God?
People think of Mikko as funny, cool, creative, caring, winner
People who like the name Mikko also like Mateo, Milo, Aiden, Matthew, Micah, Ian, Isaac, Maxim, Jason, Manuel

Mila *(Slavic)* ♀ RATING: ★★★★
People's favor—Short for Ludmila; Mila Kunis, actress
People think of Mila as pretty, exotic, creative, intelligent, popular
People who like the name Mila also like Ava, Mia, Ella, Isabella, Eva, Charlotte, Bella, Nadia, Mira, Amelia

Milad *(Persian)* ♂ RATING: ★★★
Birth
People think of Milad as intelligent, cool, funny, handsome, young
People who like the name Milad also like Malcolm, Matthias, Mendel, Marius, Maximus, Darrius, Zarek, Makoto, Maxwell, Manelin

Milagra *(Spanish)* ♀ RATING: ★★★
Miracle
People think of Milagra as exotic, elegant, pretty, cool, young
People who like the name Milagra also like Milagros, Melodie, Sierra, Meriel, Ciara, Chloe, Celeste, Cassandra, Blythe, Felicity

Milagro *(Spanish)* ♂ RATING: ★☆
Miracle
People think of Milagro as creative, exotic, caring, trustworthy, intelligent
People who like the name Milagro also like Mateo, Joaquin, Benjamin, Max, Sebastian, Macario, Nicholas, Miles, Malik, Fernando

Milagros *(Spanish)* ♀ RATING: ★★★☆
Miracles—From the Virgin Mary; short for Senora de los Milagros (Woman of Miracles)
People think of Milagros as pretty, intelligent, caring, elegant, quiet
People who like the name Milagros also like Marisol, Adriana, Esperanza, Mariana, Maya, Jasmine, Marilyn, Maritza, Johanna, Melody

Milan *(Latin)* ♀♂ RATING: ★★☆
From the middle of the plain—Also a city in Italy
People think of Milan as intelligent, popular, sexy, funny, pretty
People who like the name Milan also like Madison, Mason, Jaden, Hayden, Bailey, Reese, London, Riley, Mackenzie, Luca

Miland *(Latin)* ♂ RATING: ★★☆
From the middle of the plain
People think of Miland as handsome, exotic, cool, sexy, powerful
People who like the name Miland also like Tristan, Miles, Marshall, Mortimer, Milton, Merric, Raghnall, Valin, Mikasi, Chase

Milandu *(African)* ♀♂ RATING: ★★☆
A case to answer—Botswana origin
People think of Milandu as big, powerful, exotic, funny, creative
People who like the name Milandu also like Mariatu, Muna, Menefer, Mashaka, Musoke, Kendi, Jermaine, Marka, Themba, Teshi

404

Mildred *(English)* ♀　　RATING: ★★★
Mild strength—Mildred Dresselhaus, physicist
　People think of Mildred as intelligent, caring, old-fashioned, trustworthy, pretty
　People who like the name Mildred also like Mabel, Fiona, Matilda, Emily, Hazel, Ruby, Amelia, Penelope, Maggie, Melissa

Milek *(Polish)* ♂　　RATING: ★★★
Victorious people
　People think of Milek as handsome, energetic, old, loser, ethnic
　People who like the name Milek also like Miles, Maddox, Gabriel, Micah, Caleb, Malik, Jeremiah, Xander, Xavier, Darian

Milena *(Russian)* ♀　　RATING: ★★★☆
People's love
　People think of Milena as pretty, intelligent, exotic, creative, caring
　People who like the name Milena also like Isabella, Amelia, Bella, Ariana, Marina, Emma, Olivia, Chloe, Arianna, Lara

Miles *(Latin)* ♂　　RATING: ★★★
Soldier—Probably originally short for Michael; Miles Davis, jazz musician; Miles Standish, pilgrim/settler
　People think of Miles as handsome, intelligent, funny, caring, cool
　People who like the name Miles also like Noah, Owen, Ethan, Ian, Jackson, Oliver, Jacob, Aiden, Lucas, Isaac

Miley *(American)* ♀　　RATING: ★★★★★
Smiley—From the nickname "Smiley" given to Miley Cyrus, singer/actress
　People think of Miley as pretty, funny, cool, popular, creative
　People who like the name Miley also like Emma, Emily, Mia, Hannah, Chloe, Lily, Grace, Paige, Keely, Olivia

Mili *(Hebrew)* ♀　　RATING: ★★☆
Who is for me?
　People think of Mili as pretty, creative, funny, elegant, popular
　People who like the name Mili also like Mia, Millie, Maya, Emma, Lilly, Eva, Mea, Layla, Mya, Macy

Miliani *(Hawaiian)* ♀　　RATING: ★★☆
Gentle caress—Variation of Mililani
　People think of Miliani as pretty, exotic, young, caring, artsy
　People who like the name Miliani also like Leilani, Malia, Kailani, Ailani, Maya, Giselle, Isabella, Aolani, Malana, Nadia

Milica *(Slavic)* ♀　　RATING: ★★★★
Work—Variation of Emilia
　People think of Milica as funny, pretty, intelligent, caring, creative
　People who like the name Milica also like Melissa, Mira, Mariana, Megan, Miranda, Maggie, Maylin, Mckayla, Myra, Madelyn

Milla *(German)* ♀　　RATING: ★★★★
Industrious—Also short for Camilla; Milla Jovovich, model/actress
　People think of Milla as pretty, elegant, intelligent, exotic, creative
　People who like the name Milla also like Ella, Ava, Mia, Scarlett, Grace, Isabella, Bella, Olivia, Emma, Audrey

Miller *(English)* ♀♂　　RATING: ★★★★
Mill worker—Arthur Miller, playwright; Dennis Miller, comedian
　People think of Miller as intelligent, cool, caring, funny, popular
　People who like the name Miller also like Parker, Mason, Logan, Bailey, Addison, Sawyer, Madison, Reese, Morgan, Hayden

Millicent *(English)* ♀　　RATING: ★★★☆
Mild strength
　People think of Millicent as intelligent, pretty, funny, caring, creative
　People who like the name Millicent also like Penelope, Hannah, Maisie, Ophelia, Amelia, Olivia, Josephine, Madeleine, Claire, Eleanor

Millie *(English)* ♀　　RATING: ★★★★
Mild strength—Short for Mildred or Millicent
　People think of Millie as pretty, funny, intelligent, caring, creative
　People who like the name Millie also like Grace, Amelia, Mia, Ella, Ellie, Olivia, Molly, Lucy, Ava, Emma

Mills *(English)* ♀♂　　RATING: ★★★☆
Near the mills
　People think of Mills as intelligent, funny, handsome, energetic, creative
　People who like the name Mills also like Jesse, Jaden, Mason, Spencer, Madison, Parker, Jude, Myles, Miller, Aidan

Milly *(English)* ♀　　RATING: ★★☆
Short for Mildred or Millicent
　People think of Milly as funny, pretty, caring, popular, intelligent
　People who like the name Milly also like Molly, Emily, Grace, Lucy, Ella, Amelia, Lilly, Olivia, Daisy, Paige

Milne *(English)* ♀♂　　RATING: ★★☆
From the mill—A. A. Milne, author
　People think of Milne as weird, unpopular, popular, sexy, intelligent
　People who like the name Milne also like Murphy, Teagan, Dallas, Piper, Joey, Darcy, Milan, Monroe, Loyal, Demi

Milo *(English)* ♂　　RATING: ★★★★
Soldier—Variation of Miles
　People think of Milo as intelligent, handsome, funny, cool, creative
　People who like the name Milo also like Oliver, Miles, Noah, Owen, Sebastian, Jack, Caleb, Ethan, Liam, Maddox

Milt (English) ♂   RATING: ★★
From the mill town—Short for Milton
> People think of Milt as old, nerdy, poor, old-fashioned, unpopular
> People who like the name Milt also like Milton, Maddox, Chase, Cody, Mac, Edison, Morton, Chip, Cole, Micah

Milton (English) ♂   RATING: ★☆
From the mill town—Milton Berle, comedian
> People think of Milton as intelligent, handsome, funny, trustworthy, caring
> People who like the name Milton also like Jacob, Oliver, Miles, Malcolm, Lucas, Nicholas, Mitchell, Victor, Owen, Maddox

Mimi (French) ♀   RATING: ★★★☆
Short for names beginning with M
> People think of Mimi as pretty, funny, creative, intelligent, popular
> People who like the name Mimi also like Mia, Layla, Chloe, Eva, Belle, Mya, Paige, Lily, Bianca, Lexi

Mimir (Scandinavian) ♀♂   RATING: ★☆
God of prophecy
> People think of Mimir as weird, big, unpopular, old-fashioned, nerdy
> People who like the name Mimir also like Morgan, Raven, Loki, Phoenix, Morrigan, Moon, Murray, Mckenna, Wynn, Mercury

Mimis (Greek) ♀   RATING: ★★☆
Goddess of harvest
> People think of Mimis as weird, sexy, old-fashioned, sneaky, funny
> People who like the name Mimis also like Melody, Medea, Melinda, Melissa, Minerva, Melanie, Maya, Melora, Melantha, Melina

Mina (English) ♀   RATING: ★★☆
Strong-willed warrior—Short for Wilhelmina; also a Persian name meaning blue glass or gem; also a Japanese name meaning south
> People think of Mina as pretty, creative, intelligent, funny, elegant
> People who like the name Mina also like Mia, Ella, Ava, Miya, Nadia, Amaya, Mai, Misa, Olivia, Paige

Minda (American) ♀   RATING: ★★★☆
Combination of Mel and Linda, or short for Melinda
> People think of Minda as energetic, intelligent, trustworthy, pretty, creative
> People who like the name Minda also like Layla, Maren, Marissa, Mercedes, Macy, Madeleine, Ava, Marla, Lara, Mckayla

Mindy (American) ♀   RATING: ★★★☆
Combination of Mel and Linda, or short for Melinda
> People think of Mindy as pretty, funny, caring, intelligent, creative
> People who like the name Mindy also like Mandy, Faith, Hailey, Hannah, Molly, Natalie, Olivia, Melissa, Melody, Paige

Minerva (Latin) ♀   RATING: ★★★☆
Goddess of wisdom
> People think of Minerva as intelligent, leader, pretty, powerful, elegant
> People who like the name Minerva also like Aurora, Hermione, Miranda, Fiona, Athena, Penelope, Genevieve, Ivy, Ophelia, Maeve

Ming (Chinese) ♀♂   RATING: ★★★
Bright
> People think of Ming as intelligent, pretty, funny, caring, popular
> People who like the name Ming also like Christian, Channing, Banks, Cyd, Arden, Cai, Brody, Jordan, Carlin, Jules

Ming Yue (Chinese) ♀♂   RATING: ★★★☆
Bright moon
> People think of Ming Yue as pretty, quiet, funny, artsy, young
> People who like the name Ming Yue also like Kiyoshi, Yuki, Musoke, Yue, London, Mika, Yi Min, Phoenix, Maverick, Maemi

Mingan (Native American) ♂   RATING: ★★★☆
Gray wolf—Algonquin origin
> People think of Mingan as leader, intelligent, powerful, wild, handsome
> People who like the name Mingan also like Mikasi, Faolan, Dyami, Hakan, Chayton, Paytah, Tokala, Tuari, Tocho, Ulric

Minh (Vietnamese) ♂   RATING: ★☆
Bright, clever
> People think of Minh as intelligent, creative, quiet, caring, trustworthy
> People who like the name Minh also like Micah, Fionn, Miguel, Daire, Björn, José, Heath, Marcel, Theodore, Idris

Miniya (Arabic) ♀   RATING: ★★★☆
Wish, desire
> People think of Miniya as pretty, creative, intelligent, artsy, exotic
> People who like the name Miniya also like Myeisha, Meria, Malkia, Jahzara, Kya, Miliani, Malaika, Miyanda, Mara, Miyoko

Minjonet (French) ♀   RATING: ★★★★
Combination of Min and Jonet
> People think of Minjonet as elegant, pretty, stuck-up, artsy, ethnic
> People who like the name Minjonet also like Miette, Madeleine, Mirabelle, Melisande, Giselle, Meadow, Scarlett, Linette, Genevieve, Mallory

Minna (German) ♀   RATING: ★★★☆
Strong-willed warrior—Short for Wilhelmina or Minnie
> People think of Minna as creative, caring, intelligent, pretty, funny
> People who like the name Minna also like Mia, Milla, Olivia, Maya, Leila, Mina, Grace, Maren, Bella, Megan

406

Minnesota (*Native American*) ♀♂   RATING: ★★★☆
Sky-colored water—Sioux origin; U.S. state
> People think of Minnesota as pretty, caring, intelligent, young, old-fashioned
>
> People who like the name Minnesota also like Madison, Montana, Dakota, Tennessee, Parker, Hayden, Missouri, London, Mason, Morgan

Minnie (*English*) ♀   RATING: ★★★☆
Sea of bitterness—Vairation of Mary; Minnie Mouse, cartoon character; Minnie Pearl, comedian
> People think of Minnie as pretty, intelligent, caring, funny, creative
>
> People who like the name Minnie also like Daisy, Molly, Maggie, Macy, Bella, Hazel, Meg, Scarlett, Megan, Maddy

Minor (*American*) ♀♂   RATING: ★☆
Junior, younger
> People think of Minor as funny, aggressive, cool, caring, intelligent
>
> People who like the name Minor also like Caden, Skye, Logan, Morgan, Sage, Jordan, Jaden, Hayden, Skylar, Rylan

Minowa (*Japanese*) ♂   RATING: ★★☆
Unknown meaning
> People think of Minowa as artsy, weird, elegant, unpopular, old-fashioned
>
> People who like the name Minowa also like Avonaco, Maddox, Micol, Hinto, Inoke, Asher, Airell, Makoto, Odakota, Quana

Minty (*English*) ♀   RATING: ★★★☆
Short for Aminta or Araminta—Originating in the play *The Confederacy* by John Vanbrugh
> People think of Minty as exotic, aggressive, funny, wild, lazy
>
> People who like the name Minty also like Olivia, Maisie, Melanie, Ivy, Penelope, Meg, Mabyn, Miranda, Sophie, Mimi

Minya (*Arabic*) ♀   RATING: ★★☆
Wish, desire
> People think of Minya as exotic, pretty, sexy, intelligent, trendy
>
> People who like the name Minya also like Kaya, Maya, Kiona, Myra, Topanga, Mckayla, Winona, Chloe, Desiree, Maralah

Minze (*German*) ♂   RATING: ★★☆
Mint
> People think of Minze as weird, exotic, creative, artsy, cool
>
> People who like the name Minze also like Slade, Micah, Michael, Ryker, Mohawk, Monte, Manny, Rhys, Kaden, Jett

Mio (*Spanish*) ♂   RATING: ★★★☆
Mine
> People think of Mio as young, funny, exotic, intelligent, cool
>
> People who like the name Mio also like Tristan, Micah, Mikko, Mateo, Xavier, Rafael, Gabriel, Malo, Milo, Max

Mira (*Latin*) ♀   RATING: ★★★☆
Look, admirable—Short for Miranda; Mira Sorvino, actress
> People think of Mira as pretty, intelligent, creative, caring, elegant
>
> People who like the name Mira also like Mia, Ava, Maya, Chloe, Olivia, Ella, Eva, Myra, Emma, Bella

Mirabel (*English*) ♀   RATING: ★★★★
Wondrous
> People think of Mirabel as pretty, intelligent, creative, exotic, trustworthy
>
> People who like the name Mirabel also like Mirabelle, Isabella, Isabel, Maribel, Olivia, Mia, Bella, Isabelle, Lily, Madeleine

Mirabelle (*French*) ♀   RATING: ★★☆
Wondrous
> People think of Mirabelle as pretty, elegant, creative, artsy, intelligent
>
> People who like the name Mirabelle also like Isabella, Isabelle, Olivia, Annabelle, Madeleine, Grace, Hannah, Gabriella, Abigail, Faith

Miracle (*American*) ♀♂   RATING: ★★★☆
Divine act
> People think of Miracle as pretty, intelligent, caring, funny, creative
>
> People who like the name Miracle also like Madison, Mackenzie, Taylor, Jaden, Justice, Jordan, Liberty, Bailey, Sydney, Jade

Mirage (*French*) ♀♂   RATING: ★★★★
Illusion, fantasy
> People think of Mirage as exotic, pretty, intelligent, sexy, powerful
>
> People who like the name Mirage also like Maverick, Ember, Miracle, Hayden, Jade, Madison, Jaden, Justice, Logan, Phoenix

Mirah (*Arabic*) ♀   RATING: ★★★☆
Glad
> People think of Mirah as pretty, popular, quiet, elegant, caring
>
> People who like the name Mirah also like Mira, Maya, Chloe, Olivia, Myra, Nadia, Mia, Sophie, Kyra, Josie

Miranda (*Latin*) ♀   RATING: ★★★
Admirable—Also spelled Maranda, Myranda, and Meranda; character in *The Tempest* by William Shakespeare; Miranda Lambert, singer; Miranda Richardson, actress
> People think of Miranda as pretty, funny, creative, intelligent, caring
>
> People who like the name Miranda also like Isabella, Hannah, Olivia, Paige, Samantha, Natalie, Grace, Abigail, Hailey, Faith

Mirari (*Portuguese*) ♀   RATING: ★★★☆
Miracle
> People think of Mirari as exotic, creative, popular, sexy, young

People who like the name Mirari also like Leilani, Ava, Malia, Kailani, Malaika, Kya, Mckayla, Aitana, Adia, Mireya

Mircea *(Slavic)* ♀ RATING: ★★
Peace
People think of Mircea as powerful, intelligent, popular, aggressive, nerdy
People who like the name Mircea also like Maida, Mirella, Mercia, Malia, Miranda, Leyna, Mariah, Makaila, Maylin, Makenna

Mireille *(French)* ♀ RATING: ★★
Admirable
People think of Mireille as pretty, caring, intelligent, creative, cool
People who like the name Mireille also like Mirella, Mirabelle, Mireya, Giselle, Grace, Gabrielle, Hannah, Liana, Ava, Arielle

Mirella *(Italian)* ♀ RATING: ★★★★
Admirable
People think of Mirella as pretty, intelligent, funny, creative, caring
People who like the name Mirella also like Mireille, Mireya, Mirabelle, Marcella, Moriah, Isabella, Giselle, Arianna, Miranda, Gabrielle

Mireya *(French)* ♀ RATING: ★★★★☆
Admirable
People think of Mireya as pretty, intelligent, caring, funny, creative
People who like the name Mireya also like Mirella, Liana, Grace, Mireille, Jadyn, Isabella, Mia, Samara, Makayla, Moriah

Miri *(Hebrew)* ♀ RATING: ★★★☆
Sea of bitterness—Short for Miriam
People think of Miri as pretty, intelligent, trustworthy, creative, caring
People who like the name Miri also like Mari, Mira, Mia, Miriam, Isabella, Maya, Kyra, Macy, Miya, Mina

Miriam *(Hebrew)* ♀ RATING: ★★★☆
Sea of bitterness
People think of Miriam as pretty, intelligent, caring, funny, creative
People who like the name Miriam also like Hannah, Grace, Abigail, Olivia, Eva, Naomi, Amelia, Madeline, Sophia, Chloe

Mirielle *(French)* ♀ RATING: ★★★★
Sea bright—Variation of Muriel
People think of Mirielle as pretty, elegant, creative, cool, funny
People who like the name Mirielle also like Isabelle, Mirabelle, Giselle, Madeleine, Claire, Mireille, Belle, Chloe, Brielle, Jolie

Mirit *(Hebrew)* ♀ RATING: ★★★
Sea of bitterness—Variation of Miriam
People think of Mirit as weird, energetic, exotic, caring, cool

People who like the name Mirit also like Jillian, Mercedes, Mallory, Miriam, Giselle, Maisie, Miri, Ivy, Melisande, Rhiannon

Miroslav *(Slavic)* ♂ RATING: ★☆
Peace, glory
People think of Miroslav as intelligent, handsome, funny, sexy, trustworthy
People who like the name Miroslav also like Michael, Titus, Oliver, David, Tristan, William, Jack, Matthew, Maxim, Gabriel

Mirra *(Italian)* ♀ RATING: ★★★☆
Myrrh—Also a surname
People think of Mirra as creative, intelligent, funny, energetic, pretty
People who like the name Mirra also like Mira, Grace, Olivia, Myra, Mia, Maya, Chloe, Bella, Meara, Mirabelle

Misa *(Japanese)* ♀ RATING: ★★★☆
Beautiful bloom
People think of Misa as pretty, creative, caring, elegant, artsy
People who like the name Misa also like Miya, Mai, Mina, Amaya, Miyo, Aiko, Kaori, Michiko, Kaida, Midori

Misae *(Native American)* ♀♂ RATING: ★★★☆
White sun—Osage origin
People think of Misae as exotic, creative, energetic, sporty, trustworthy
People who like the name Misae also like Mika, Misu, Nida, Makya, Kishi, Morgan, Mahari, Dakota, Misha, Maeryn

Misaki *(Japanese)* ♀ RATING: ★★★
Beautiful bloom
People think of Misaki as exotic, caring, elegant, pretty, uptight
People who like the name Misaki also like Nami, Kaida, Suki, Sakura, Hana, Misa, Amarante, Masumi, Mai, Yoko

Mischa *(Russian)* ♀♂ RATING: ★★★★
Who is like God?—Variation of Michael; Mischa Barton, actress
People think of Mischa as pretty, popular, sexy, intelligent, creative
People who like the name Mischa also like Madison, Hayden, Bailey, Riley, Dylan, Mackenzie, Morgan, Aidan, Parker, Logan

Misha *(Russian)* ♀♂ RATING: ★★★★
Who is like God?—Variation of Michael
People think of Misha as pretty, intelligent, funny, creative, caring
People who like the name Misha also like Mischa, Madison, Sasha, Hayden, Mika, Riley, Morgan, Logan, Ryan, Piper

Mississippi *(Native American)* ♀♂ RATING: ★★★
Father of waters—Ojibwa origin; U.S. state
People think of Mississippi as weird, loser, nerdy, aggressive, old-fashioned

408

People who like the name Mississippi also like Missouri, Montana, Minnesota, Murphy, Mischa, Madison, Moon, Mason, Zephyr, Misu

Missouri *(Native American)* ♀♂　　　RATING: ★★★
Village of large canoes—U.S. state
People think of Missouri as poor, unpopular, quiet, criminal, girl next door
People who like the name Missouri also like Mississippi, Minnesota, Mackenzie, Montana, Kansas, Memphis, Michigan, Nebraska, Maverick, Dakota

Missy *(American)* ♀　　　RATING: ★★★☆
Bee—Short for Melissa; also a nickname for a young lady
People think of Missy as pretty, funny, popular, caring, creative
People who like the name Missy also like Mandy, Molly, Misty, Faith, Maggie, Hailey, Macy, Megan, Monica, Emma

Mist *(American)* ♀　　　RATING: ★★☆
Particles of water
People think of Mist as cool, handsome, exotic, wild, leader
People who like the name Mist also like Savanna, Phoebe, Luna, Gracie, Serena, Mystery, Ivy, Savannah, Callista, Sapphire

Mistico *(Italian)* ♀　　　RATING: ★★
Mystic
People think of Mistico as intelligent, creative, elegant, exotic, quiet
People who like the name Mistico also like Donatella, Angelina, Cira, Aurora, Mita, Melita, Miliani, Misty, Pia, Aria

Misty *(American)* ♀　　　RATING: ★★★☆
Covered with mist, dew—"Misty," classic song
People think of Misty as pretty, funny, caring, trustworthy, intelligent
People who like the name Misty also like Hailey, Faith, Paige, Destiny, Jasmine, Chloe, Sabrina, Melody, Molly, Amber

Mita *(Sanskrit/East Indian)* ♀　　　RATING: ★★★☆
Fixed, grounded
People think of Mita as caring, funny, trustworthy, intelligent, pretty
People who like the name Mita also like Stella, Sienna, Mira, Mea, Lina, Gemma, Mabel, Misa, Mia, Jaya

Mitali *(Sanskrit/East Indian)* ♀　　　RATING: ★★★☆
Friendship
People think of Mitali as pretty, intelligent, wild, ethnic, quiet
People who like the name Mitali also like Avani, Eshana, Denali, Monisha, Mythri, Malini, Niyati, Kimaya, Ishana, Meghana

Mitch *(American)* ♂　　　RATING: ★★★★
Who is like God?—Short for Mitchell
People think of Mitch as funny, cool, handsome, sexy, intelligent
People who like the name Mitch also like Mitchell, Ethan, Jack, Jacob, Nathan, Jake, Lucas, Matthew, Nicholas, Seth

Mitchell *(American)* ♂　　　RATING: ★★★★
Who is like God?—Variation of Michael; also a surname
People think of Mitchell as handsome, funny, cool, intelligent, popular
People who like the name Mitchell also like Ethan, Matthew, Nathan, Jacob, Nicholas, Jackson, Zachary, Owen, Noah, Caleb

Mitsu *(Japanese)* ♀♂　　　RATING: ★★
Light; honey, nectar
People think of Mitsu as creative, intelligent, pretty, trustworthy, energetic
People who like the name Mitsu also like Kiyoshi, Seiko, Hoshi, Natsu, Maemi, Maro, Sanyu, Rin, Kana, Kumi

Mitsuko *(Japanese)* ♀　　　RATING: ★★★
Child of light
People think of Mitsuko as cool, intelligent, pretty, exotic, criminal
People who like the name Mitsuko also like Mai, Ai, Nami, Sakura, Miya, Maeko, Misa, Miu, Misaki, Amber

Miu *(Japanese)* ♀　　　RATING: ★★★
Beautiful feather
People think of Miu as pretty, quiet, funny, stuck-up, elegant
People who like the name Miu also like Miya, Mitsuko, Xia, Sakura, Mai, Kalista, Misa, Nami, Misaki, Maeko

Miya *(Japanese)* ♀　　　RATING: ★★★
Sacred house
People think of Miya as pretty, intelligent, creative, caring, funny
People who like the name Miya also like Mia, Mya, Amaya, Maya, Mai, Kaiya, Mina, Misa, Faith, Miyoko

Miyanda *(African)* ♀　　　RATING: ★★
Unknown meaning—Zambian origin
People think of Miyanda as exotic, quiet, artsy, unpopular, aggressive
People who like the name Miyanda also like Malaika, Myeisha, Maisha, Jahzara, Kya, Ayanna, Mardea, Miniya, Mansa, Mckayla

Miyo *(Japanese)* ♀　　　RATING: ★★★☆
Beautiful child
People think of Miyo as exotic, quiet, intelligent, creative, artsy
People who like the name Miyo also like Miyoko, Aiko, Maeko, Mai, Miya, Emiko, Amaya, Kaori, Sakura, Masako

Miyoko *(Japanese)* ♀　　　RATING: ★★
Beautiful child
People think of Miyoko as pretty, exotic, creative, caring, intelligent

People who like the name Miyoko also like Miyo, Emiko, Nariko, Kaida, Amaya, Aiko, Sakura, Miya, Keiko, Kaori

Mizell *(English)* ♀♂   RATING: ★★★
Wood cutter—Originally a surname
People think of Mizell as religious, ethnic, funny, old-fashioned, loser
People who like the name Mizell also like Madison, Misha, Morgan, Matias, Kirsten, Kameryn, Madden, Landen, Emlyn, Mckenna

Mizu *(Japanese)* ♂   RATING: ★★☆
Water
People think of Mizu as nerdy
People who like the name Mizu also like Ryu, Daisuke, Haru, Aki, Damian, Horus, Shino, Makoto, Yamir, Itachi

Mliss *(Cambodian)* ♀   RATING: ★☆
Flower—Pronounced *M-LEES*; also short for Melissa
People think of Mliss as loser, nerdy, sexy, exotic, wild
People who like the name Mliss also like Maeve, Mya, Mia, Melodie, Desiree, Mairwen, Darlene, Candice, Morwen, Diana

Mo *(American)* ♀♂   RATING: ★★★
Dark skinned—Short for Morris, Maureen, or names beginning with Mo
People think of Mo as popular, cool, pretty, energetic, creative
People who like the name Mo also like Riley, Moon, Mason, Murray, Mercury, Sam, Mckenna, Morgan, Marion, Madison

Moana *(Hawaiian)* ♀   RATING: ★★★★
Ocean
People think of Moana as cool, pretty, caring, creative, intelligent
People who like the name Moana also like Moanna, Kailani, Leilani, Chloe, Malia, Keala, Samara, Giselle, Malana, Aurora

Moanna *(Hawaiian)* ♀   RATING: ★★★☆
Ocean
People think of Moanna as exotic, creative, funny, pretty, leader
People who like the name Moanna also like Moana, Makayla, Juliette, Johanna, Macy, Marcella, Bella, Makana, Keona, Maya

Modesta *(Latin)* ♀   RATING: ★★
Modest
People think of Modesta as elegant, pretty, caring, quiet, leader
People who like the name Modesta also like Melody, Misty, Mirabelle, Morrisa, Mariah, Mindy, Moira, Fiona, Mckayla, Maribeth

Modesto *(Italian)* ♂   RATING: ★★☆
Modest
People think of Modesto as stuck-up, handsome, leader, old-fashioned, funny

People who like the name Modesto also like Michelangelo, Marshall, Mario, Marco, Marcus, Matteo, Gabriel, Mariano, Leone, Thomas

Modesty *(American)* ♀   RATING: ★★★
Without conceit
People think of Modesty as sexy, intelligent, pretty, caring, young
People who like the name Modesty also like Melody, Bridget, Faith, Grace, Harmony, Molly, Serenity, Chloe, Destiny, Nicolette

Moe *(American)* ♀♂   RATING: ★★★
Dark skinned—Short for Morris, Maureen, or names beginning with Mo; Moe Howard, comedian
People think of Moe as weird, loser, lazy, slow, criminal
People who like the name Moe also like Morgan, Cameron, Monroe, Blake, Blair, Bailey, Holly, Murphy, Colby, Logan

Moesha *(American)* ♀   RATING: ★★
Born of (a god)—Variation of Moeshe or Moses; *Moesha*, TV show
People think of Moesha as popular, funny, cool, ethnic, creative
People who like the name Moesha also like Monique, Aaliyah, Mandy, Melanie, Maya, Mariah, Monica, Mya, Mia, Phoebe

Moeshe *(Hebrew)* ♂   RATING: ★★☆
Born of (a god)—Variation of Moses; pronounced *MOY-sha*
People think of Moeshe as nerdy, powerful, intelligent, ethnic, weird
People who like the name Moeshe also like Micah, Moshe, Morpheus, Michelangelo, Morathi, Morty, Jens, Mattias, Moses, Tristan

Mohammed *(Arabic)* ♂   RATING: ★★★
Praised
People think of Mohammed as religious, leader, popular, intelligent, handsome
People who like the name Mohammed also like Michael, Miguel, Henry, Mitch, Moses, Chester, Marvin, Abraham, Joshua, Michelangelo

Mohan *(Sanskrit/East Indian)* ♂   RATING: ★★★☆
Attractive
People think of Mohan as cool, popular, handsome, funny, intelligent
People who like the name Mohan also like Myron, Joshua, Ravi, Micah, Liam, Mandar, Mitchell, Ethan, Manas, Noah

Mohawk *(Native American)* ♂   RATING: ★★★
Tribe name—Also a hairstyle associated with the tribe: shaved head on both sides with a line of hair down the middle of the scalp
People think of Mohawk as wild, weird, ethnic, nerdy, funny
People who like the name Mohawk also like Miles, Tyson, Tucker, Mitch, Jett, Micah, Blade, Sebastian, Maddock, Marshall

Mohsen *(Arabic)* ♂   RATING: ★★☆
Benefactor
> People think of Mohsen as loser, unpopular, nerdy, weird, religious
> People who like the name Mohsen also like Moeshe, Mohan, Monty, Molimo, Morris, Malik, Moises, Morse, Mort, Myron

Moira *(Celtic/Gaelic)* ♀   RATING: ★★★☆
Sea of bitterness—Variation of Mary
> People think of Moira as intelligent, pretty, creative, funny, caring
> People who like the name Moira also like Fiona, Olivia, Maura, Genevieve, Audrey, Maeve, Chloe, Paige, Keira, Emma

Moises *(French)* ♂   RATING: ★★★☆
Born of (a God)
> People think of Moises as handsome, funny, intelligent, cool, creative
> People who like the name Moises also like Isaac, Elijah, Ian, Ismael, Gavin, Micah, Adrian, Joshua, Isaiah, Moses

Moke *(Hawaiian)* ♀♂   RATING: ★★☆
Born of (a God)—Variation of Moses
> People think of Moke as weird, unpopular, slow, loser, ethnic
> People who like the name Moke also like Maik, Makani, More, Montana, Keanu, Mika, Moral, Nikita, Monahan, Monet

Molimo *(Native American)* ♂   RATING: ★★☆
Unkown menaing—Miwok origin
> People think of Molimo as loser, poor, lazy, aggressive, quiet
> People who like the name Molimo also like Malo, Mingan, Tokala, Mohawk, Mikasi, Dmitri, Dasan, Yanisin, Moses, Devlin

Molly *(English)* ♀   RATING: ★★★
Sea of bitterness—Variation of Mary
> People think of Molly as pretty, funny, caring, intelligent, creative
> People who like the name Molly also like Grace, Olivia, Emma, Hannah, Emily, Ella, Ava, Chloe, Paige, Abigail

Mona *(Arabic)* ♀   RATING: ★★★★
Desires, wishes—*Mona Lisa*, portrait by Leonardo da Vinci
> People think of Mona as creative, pretty, intelligent, caring, funny
> People who like the name Mona also like Olivia, Mia, Nora, Molly, Isabella, Layla, Maya, Monica, Nadia, Bella

Monahan *(Celtic/Gaelic)* ♀♂   RATING: ★★
Descendant of the little monk—Also a surname
> People think of Monahan as loser, trustworthy, religious, intelligent, caring
> People who like the name Monahan also like Mckenna, Mackenzie, Madden, Monroe, Sean, Morrigan, Brayden, Logan, Murphy, Sloane

Monet *(French)* ♀♂   RATING: ★★
To be heard—Also a surname; short for Simon; Claude Monet, artist
> People think of Monet as pretty, intelligent, creative, funny, caring
> People who like the name Monet also like Morgan, Madison, Caden, Mason, Bailey, Addison, Monroe, Jaden, Piper, Reese

Monica *(Latin)* ♀   RATING: ★★
Adviser—Assumed to be from the Latin verb *monere*, which means to advise
> People think of Monica as pretty, funny, caring, intelligent, creative
> People who like the name Monica also like Olivia, Emma, Natalie, Veronica, Hannah, Melissa, Rebecca, Grace, Paige, Isabella

Monifa *(Arabic)* ♀   RATING: ★☆
Eminent, exalted
> People think of Monifa as pretty, intelligent, caring, funny, energetic
> People who like the name Monifa also like Monisha, Malaika, Mirabelle, Kamilah, Nailah, Nakia, Kya, Isis, Morwen, Jendayi

Monique *(French)* ♀   RATING: ★★☆
Adviser—Variation of Monica
> People think of Monique as pretty, funny, intelligent, caring, cool
> People who like the name Monique also like Dominique, Olivia, Monica, Isabella, Jasmine, Bianca, Chloe, Hailey, Paige, Michelle

Monisha *(Sanskrit/East Indian)* ♀   RATING: ★★★★
Intellectual
> People think of Monisha as pretty, popular, creative, young, caring
> People who like the name Monisha also like Keisha, Melanie, Marissa, Monica, Jazzelle, Monita, Mallika, Mia, Monifa, Latanya

Monissa *(American)* ♀   RATING: ★★☆
Combination of Monica and Vanessa
> People think of Monissa as sexy, exotic, pretty, powerful, caring
> People who like the name Monissa also like Marissa, Malinda, Fiona, Maggie, Makayla, Monisha, Monica, Mckayla, Malissa, Makaila

Monita *(Sanskrit/East Indian)* ♀   RATING: ★★★
Honored, respected—Also short for Mona
> People think of Monita as young, pretty, caring, intelligent, creative
> People who like the name Monita also like Monisha, Mercedes, Lola, Melanie, Maribel, Minjonet, Larissa, Mia, Moriah, Mythri

Monroe *(Celtic/Gaelic)* ♀♂   RATING: ★★★★
From the hill—Also a surname
> People think of Monroe as leader, creative, intelligent, handsome, funny

People who like the name Monroe also like Logan, Mason, Parker, Madison, Hayden, Riley, Morgan, Bailey, Addison, Mackenzie

Montague (*English*) ♂   RATING: ★★
From the pointed hill—Also a surname from a French place name; Montague family in *Romeo and Juliet* by William Shakespeare
People think of Montague as aggressive, powerful, trustworthy, popular, intelligent
People who like the name Montague also like Mortimer, Maddox, Marshall, Jacob, Owen, Isaac, Landon, Donovan, Miles, Jackson

Montana (*Latin*) ♀ ♂   RATING: ★★☆
Mountain—U.S. state; Joe Montana, football player
People think of Montana as pretty, creative, popular, funny, intelligent
People who like the name Montana also like Dakota, Madison, Morgan, Riley, Mackenzie, Bailey, Mason, Taylor, Hayden, Parker

Monte (*English*) ♂   RATING: ★★
Short for names beginning with Mont; Monte Carlo, city in Monaco
People think of Monte as handsome, powerful, intelligent, funny, leader
People who like the name Monte also like Maddox, Montgomery, Monty, Xavier, Vincent, Oscar, Tristan, Maxwell, Oliver, Travis

Montego (*Spanish*) ♂   RATING: ★★★
Mountainous—Montego Bay, Jamaica
People think of Montego as powerful, energetic, religious, weird, wild
People who like the name Montego also like Diego, Noah, Montgomery, Moses, Andrew, Theodore, Manuel, Xavier, Benjamin, Emanuel

Montenegro (*Spanish*) ♂   RATING: ★★
Black mountain—Also a European country
People think of Montenegro as big, powerful, ethnic, intelligent, artsy
People who like the name Montenegro also like Orlando, Anthony, Montego, Montgomery, Zachary, Moses, Manny, Angelo, Ace, Juan

Montgomery (*English*) ♂   RATING: ★★★☆
From the hill of the powerful man—Montgomery Clift, actor; Elizabeth Montgomery, actress; Robert Montgomery, actor
People think of Montgomery as handsome, intelligent, cool, wealthy, leader
People who like the name Montgomery also like Jackson, Maddox, Noah, Gabriel, Matthew, Oliver, Tristan, Nicholas, Walker, Landon

Montsho (*American*) ♀   RATING: ★★☆
Black—From a South African surname
People think of Montsho as weird, stuck-up, aggressive, funny, religious

People who like the name Montsho also like Miyanda, Mansa, Malaika, Maisha, Manica, Miniya, Mutia, Maha, Monita, Kamili

Monty (*English*) ♂   RATING: ★★★☆
Short for names beginning with Mont—Monty Hall, game show host; Monty Python, comedy group
People think of Monty as handsome, funny, caring, cool, intelligent
People who like the name Monty also like Oliver, Jack, Milo, Isaac, Montgomery, Jasper, Leo, Max, Marcus, Harry

Moon (*American*) ♀ ♂   RATING: ★★★
From the moon—Soleil Moon Frye, actress
People think of Moon as creative, artsy, exotic, powerful, cool
People who like the name Moon also like Rain, Phoenix, Skye, Madison, Dakota, Jaden, Piper, Sky, Willow, Raven

Moon-unit (*American*) ♀ ♂   RATING: ★★★☆
One that orbits the moon—Created by singer Frank Zappa for his daughter
People think of Moon-unit as weird, loser, unpopular, nerdy, exotic
People who like the name Moon-unit also like Logan, Madison, Preston, Jaden, Hayden, Parker, Myles, Caden, Moon, Kendall

Mora (*Spanish*) ♀   RATING: ★★★★
Blackberry
People think of Mora as pretty, intelligent, exotic, artsy, creative
People who like the name Mora also like Maya, Eva, Nora, Mia, Ava, Nadia, Mya, Myra, Bella, Isabella

Morag (*Celtic/Gaelic*) ♀   RATING: ★★★
Great—Also a Hebrew name meaning threshing sledge; also a place in the Gaza Strip
People think of Morag as creative, intelligent, funny, pretty, caring
People who like the name Morag also like Maeve, Morna, Moira, Aeryn, Maire, Meara, Muriel, Keira, Michaela, Genevieve

Moral (*American*) ♀ ♂   RATING: ★★☆
Lovely thoughts
People think of Moral as loser, artsy, intelligent, stuck-up, uptight
People who like the name Moral also like Hayden, Morrigan, Morgan, Monroe, Montana, Blair, Madison, Moon, Monet, Mirage

Morathi (*American*) ♂   RATING: ★☆
Created for the science fiction game Warhammer Fantasy
People think of Morathi as big, boy next door, ethnic, intelligent, weird
People who like the name Morathi also like Morpheus, Ajani, Malik, Malachi, Moses, Dmitri, Phomello, Maddock, Josiah, Muhammad

412

More (English) ♀ ♂ RATING: ★☆
Great
> People think of More as weird, wild, intelligent, pretty, cool
> People who like the name More also like Monroe, Myles, Moon, Morgan, Mason, Madison, Morrigan, Monet, Maverick, Moral

Morela (Portuguese) ♀ RATING: ★★★
Brunette
> People think of Morela as pretty, sexy, exotic, popular, elegant
> People who like the name Morela also like Mercedes, Mira, Miranda, Mabel, Marissa, Madeleine, May, Maya, Moira, Mora

Morey (Celtic/Gaelic) ♀ ♂ RATING: ★★
Proud—Also short for Morris; Morey Amsterdam, actor/comedian
> People think of Morey as big, old-fashioned, lazy, loser, girl next door
> People who like the name Morey also like Morley, Morgan, Madison, Parker, Jaden, Mason, Reagan, Riley, Monroe, Blaine

Morgan (Welsh) ♀ ♂ RATING: ★★★☆
Great circle
> People think of Morgan as pretty, funny, intelligent, creative, caring
> People who like the name Morgan also like Madison, Logan, Mackenzie, Riley, Taylor, Bailey, Hayden, Mason, Dylan, Jordan

Morgana (Welsh) ♀ RATING: ★★★☆
Great circle
> People think of Morgana as pretty, creative, intelligent, funny, popular
> People who like the name Morgana also like Rhiannon, Arwen, Aurora, Scarlett, Isabella, Genevieve, Bianca, Charlotte, Kyla, Gwendolyn

Moriah (Hebrew) ♀ RATING: ★★★★
God is my teacher
> People think of Moriah as pretty, funny, creative, caring, intelligent
> People who like the name Moriah also like Mariah, Hannah, Makayla, Jadyn, Isabella, Isabelle, Sophia, Gabrielle, Faith, Grace

Moriko (Japanese) ♀ RATING: ★★★
Forest child
> People think of Moriko as wild, artsy, funny, creative, intelligent
> People who like the name Moriko also like Devi, Giza, Reiko, Sola, Guadalupe, Mai, Mitsuko, Ayame, Hana, Silvana

Morley (English) ♀ ♂ RATING: ★★★☆
From the moor field—Morley Safer, commentator
> People think of Morley as funny, trustworthy, creative, handsome, cool

> People who like the name Morley also like Caden, Riley, Hayden, Jaden, Madison, Morgan, Hadley, Oakley, Parker, Mason

Morna (Celtic/Gaelic) ♀ RATING: ★★★
High-spirited—Variation of Muirne
> People think of Morna as caring, creative, funny, intelligent, popular
> People who like the name Morna also like Myrna, Maeve, Moira, Meara, Kaelyn, Alana, Genevieve, Maura, Morag, Riona

Morpheus (Greek) ♂ RATING: ★☆
God of dreams—Character in *The Matrix*
> People think of Morpheus as powerful, intelligent, exotic, creative, weird
> People who like the name Morpheus also like Drake, Aiden, Isaac, Sirius, Michael, Lucian, Ryu, Gabriel, Lysander, Anakin

Morrie (American) ♂ RATING: ★★
Dark skinned—Short for Morris
> People think of Morrie as loser, intelligent, caring, nerdy, old
> People who like the name Morrie also like Jackson, Oliver, Dillon, Mitch, Mitchell, Marty, Jack, Montgomery, Morris, Owen

Morrigan (Celtic/Gaelic) ♀ ♂ RATING: ★★★★☆
War goddess
> People think of Morrigan as pretty, powerful, intelligent, aggressive, energetic
> People who like the name Morrigan also like Morgan, Teagan, Madison, Aidan, Logan, Riley, Reagan, Keegan, Brayden, Connor

Morris (Latin) ♂ RATING: ★★
Dark skinned—Morris Chestnut, actor; Morris Day, singer
> People think of Morris as handsome, funny, intelligent, caring, trustworthy
> People who like the name Morris also like Maddox, Owen, Jared, Seth, Nathan, Nicholas, Ethan, Oliver, Aiden, Caleb

Morrisa (American) ♀ RATING: ★★★☆
Dark skinned—Feminine form of Morris
> People think of Morrisa as funny, intelligent, caring, young, pretty
> People who like the name Morrisa also like Marissa, Mariah, Marisa, Kiara, Melissa, Sabrina, Larissa, Heather, Maura, Alissa

Morrison (English) ♀ ♂ RATING: ★★★☆
Son of Morris
> People think of Morrison as intelligent, artsy, cool, young, powerful
> People who like the name Morrison also like Mason, Parker, Madison, Bailey, Hayden, Sawyer, Addison, Carter, Morgan, Taylor

Morse *(English)* ♂   RATING: ★★☆
Dark skinned—Also a surname from Maurice or Morris; Morse code, named after Samuel F. B. Morse, inventor of the telegraph
  People think of Morse as intelligent, handsome, creative, cool, funny
  People who like the name Morse also like Montgomery, Miles, Holt, Morton, Drake, Marcus, Moses, Radley, Montague, Edison

Mort *(English)* ♂   RATING: ★☆
From the Moor town—Short for Morton
  People think of Mort as nerdy, weird, lazy, funny, loser
  People who like the name Mort also like Mortimer, Morton, Moses, Maddox, Monte, Montgomery, Milton, Marshall, Chester, Mac

Mortimer *(English)* ♂   RATING: ★☆
From the still pond—Mortimer Snerd, radio character
  People think of Mortimer as nerdy, intelligent, weird, loser, unpopular
  People who like the name Mortimer also like Montague, Jacob, Marshall, Matthew, Milton, Zachary, Malcolm, Isaac, Montgomery, Michael

Morton *(English)* ♂   RATING: ★★★
From the Moor town—Morton Downey, Irish tenor; Gary Morton, comedian
  People think of Morton as intelligent, old, caring, trustworthy, handsome
  People who like the name Morton also like Milton, Fletcher, Wade, Owen, Jackson, Holden, Miles, Dawson, Melvin, Clayton

Morty *(French)* ♂   RATING: ★☆
From the still pond—Short for Mortimer
  People think of Morty as funny, weird, old, loser, intelligent
  People who like the name Morty also like Marty, Montgomery, Monty, Marlon, Montague, Milton, Drake, Morse, Tristan, Mortimer

Morwen *(Welsh)* ♀   RATING: ★★★☆
Maiden—Also spelled Morwynn
  People think of Morwen as weird, nerdy, unpopular, artsy, intelligent
  People who like the name Morwen also like Arwen, Mairwen, Rhiannon, Morgana, Gwendolyn, Morwenna, Rhoswen, Aeryn, Aurora, Aelwen

Morwenna *(Welsh)* ♀   RATING: ★☆
Maiden—Cornish origin
  People think of Morwenna as funny, creative, caring, pretty, weird
  People who like the name Morwenna also like Morwen, Morgana, Mairwen, Rhiannon, Arwen, Maeve, Aelwen, Gwendolyn, Cordelia, Isolde

Moseph *(American)* ♂   RATING: ★★☆
Combination of Moses and Joseph
  People think of Moseph as weird, artsy, creative, caring, nerdy

People who like the name Moseph also like Raphael, Manuel, Gustav, Mateo, Magnum, Nash, Maurus, Malone, Cedric, Josh

Moses *(Egyptian)* ♂   RATING: ★★★☆
Born of (a God)—Probably from the same origin as Ramesses or Ramses
  People think of Moses as caring, leader, powerful, handsome, religious
  People who like the name Moses also like Noah, Isaac, Isaiah, Elijah, Gabriel, Jonah, Matthew, Ian, Jacob, Joshua

Moshe *(Hebrew)* ♂   RATING: ★★
Drawn out of the water—Variation of Moses; Moshe Dayan, Israeli military leader
  People think of Moshe as handsome, religious, young, intelligent, caring
  People who like the name Moshe also like Elijah, Moeshe, Micah, Ethan, Moses, Wade, Joshua, Montgomery, Kale, Morris

Moss *(English)* ♂   RATING: ★☆
Born of (a God)—Originally from Moses; also a surname meaning dweller by the peat bog; Moss Hart, playwright; Margaret, Susan, Kate, Jennifer, and Mallory Moss, creators of BabyNames.com
  People think of Moss as trustworthy, leader, creative, funny, handsome
  People who like the name Moss also like Maddox, Marlon, Isaac, Mace, Noah, Holden, Oliver, Micah, Maxwell, Kaden

Mostyn *(Welsh)* ♀ ♂   RATING: ★★★
From the mossy town
  People think of Mostyn as handsome, creative, trustworthy, intelligent, cool
  People who like the name Mostyn also like Morrigan, Morley, Madison, Morgan, Aidan, Hayden, Monroe, Brogan, Merritt, Jorryn

Moya *(Spanish)* ♀   RATING: ★★★★
From Moya, Spain—Also short for Maire; variation of Mary
  People think of Moya as pretty, funny, creative, intelligent, caring
  People who like the name Moya also like Mirabelle, Mia, Mirabel, Isabella, Stella, Maya, Miranda, Tori, Monique, Miriam

Mrinal *(Sanskrit/East Indian)* ♀   RATING: ★☆
Lotus stalk
  People think of Mrinal as religious, creative, weird, intelligent, energetic
  People who like the name Mrinal also like Malini, Deepnita, Manasa, Mythri, Monita, Monisha, Parvani, Mallika, Ishana, Meghana

Mugisa *(African)* ♀ ♂   RATING: ★★
Blessing—Ugandan origin
  People think of Mugisa as intelligent, exotic, creative, slow, funny

People who like the name Mugisa also like Mhina, Musoke, Katriel, Vasha, Misae, Nuru, Kendi, Kione, Nyoka, Kijana

Muhammad *(Arabic)* ♂ RATING: ★★★☆
Praised
People think of Muhammad as religious, powerful, popular, intelligent, leader
People who like the name Muhammad also like Jason, Moses, Micah, Faris, Matthew, Michael, Charles, Andrew, Joseph, Malik

Mulan *(Chinese)* ♀ RATING: ★★★★
Wood orchid—*Mulan*, animated film
People think of Mulan as pretty, exotic, leader, creative, intelligent
People who like the name Mulan also like Sakura, Jasmine, Mia, Maya, Belle, Kaida, Arwen, Sabrina, Layla, Emma

Muna *(Arabic)* ♀♂ RATING: ★☆
Desires, wishes
People think of Muna as funny, pretty, sexy, cool, creative
People who like the name Muna also like Mariatu, Mahari, Jensen, Jada, Makaio, Ashanti, Mahdi, Kendi, Maemi, Menefer

Muncel *(Slavic)* ♀♂ RATING: ★★
Romanian place name—Also an American surname
People think of Muncel as sneaky, slow, old-fashioned, pretty, old
People who like the name Muncel also like Matty, Jules, Marion, Connor, Jersey, Jensen, Jie, Marek, Mckenna, Morgan

Munin *(Scandinavian)* ♀♂ RATING: ★★☆
Memory
People think of Munin as weird, quiet, pretty, exotic, artsy
People who like the name Munin also like Morgan, Kasen, Mimir, Luka, Myles, Corbin, Mason, Mischa, Montana, Rune

Muniya *(Arabic)* ♀ RATING: ★☆
Wish, desire
People think of Muniya as exotic, pretty, religious, quiet, loser
People who like the name Muniya also like Monisha, Kanoni, Mahina, Eshana, Manasa, Mallika, Kya, Mari, Mythri, Mili

Mura *(Japanese)* ♀ RATING: ★★☆
Village
People think of Mura as exotic, ethnic, loser, pretty, big
People who like the name Mura also like Miya, Mina, Miyoko, Midori, Mai, Mieko, Miyo, Masako, Nozomi, Inari

Murgatroyd *(English)* ♀ RATING: ★★☆
From Margaret's clearing—Originally a Yorkshire surname
People think of Murgatroyd as weird, nerdy, old, unpopular, loser

People who like the name Murgatroyd also like Blithe, Bethwyn, Bianca, Violet, Ella, Beatrix, Nola, Blythe, Bernadette, Chloe

Muriel *(Celtic/Gaelic)* ♀ RATING: ★★★
Sea bright—Muriel Siebert, first woman to own a seat on the New York Stock Exchange; Muriel Spark, novelist/critic/poet
People think of Muriel as intelligent, pretty, funny, caring, elegant
People who like the name Muriel also like Abigail, Hazel, Mae, Moira, Jillian, Sophia, Gwendolyn, Alana, Genevieve, Gabrielle

Murphy *(Celtic/Gaelic)* ♀♂ RATING: ★★
Sea warrior—Also a surname
People think of Murphy as funny, intelligent, energetic, cool, handsome
People who like the name Murphy also like Parker, Madison, Logan, Riley, Mackenzie, Bailey, Mason, Brody, Morgan, Connor

Murray *(English)* ♀♂ RATING: ★★
From the sea town—Also a surname
People think of Murray as caring, intelligent, creative, funny, cool
People who like the name Murray also like Morgan, Madison, Mason, Bailey, Logan, Taylor, Riley, Murphy, Jordan, Parker

Murron *(Celtic/Gaelic)* ♀♂ RATING: ★☆
Sea white
People think of Murron as pretty, intelligent, popular, elegant, creative
People who like the name Murron also like Morrigan, Monroe, Murphy, Maeron, Mckenna, Maeryn, Monahan, Aidan, Mason, Cameron

Musetta *(French)* ♀ RATING: ★★★☆
Little muse
People think of Musetta as artsy, nerdy, exotic, young, intelligent
People who like the name Musetta also like Miette, Mirabelle, Odette, Belle, Mariette, Giselle, Maeve, Cosette, Aurora, Genevieve

Musoke *(African)* ♀♂ RATING: ★★☆
Rainbow—Ugandan origin
People think of Musoke as powerful, quiet, ethnic, trustworthy, funny
People who like the name Musoke also like Ming Yue, Mahari, Kione, Teshi, Hayden, Mhina, Moon, Phoenix, Madison, Mahdi

Mutia *(Arabic)* ♀ RATING: ★★☆
Liberal, generous
People think of Mutia as exotic, sexy, lazy, wild, pretty
People who like the name Mutia also like Myeisha, Mandisa, Miniya, Maisha, Mansa, Malaika, Miyanda, Kumani, Kissa, Jamila

Muunokhoi *(Mongolian)* ♂ RATING: ★★☆
Vicious dog
> People think of Muunokhoi as exotic, handsome, aggressive, criminal, wild
> People who like the name Muunokhoi also like Abdukrahman, Zahar, Enapay, Carolos, Abdulrahman, Valerian, Pallaton, Upendo, Zbigniew, Bartholemew

Mya *(American)* ♀ RATING: ★★★☆
Mine—Pronounced *MY-ah* or *MEE-yah*
> People think of Mya as pretty, funny, intelligent, popular, energetic
> People who like the name Mya also like Mia, Ava, Maya, Olivia, Isabella, Paige, Ella, Eva, Emma, Faith

Myee *(Aborigine)* ♀ RATING: ★★★
Native born
> People think of Myee as pretty, exotic, powerful, sexy, leader
> People who like the name Myee also like Maia, Kiora, Amara, Mieko, Maria, Aleta, Jolie, Mariah, Arianna, Naja

Myeisha *(American)* ♀ RATING: ★★★★
Combination of My and Eisha
> People think of Myeisha as pretty, funny, popular, sexy, trustworthy
> People who like the name Myeisha also like Maisha, Mya, Malaika, Mia, Makaila, Ayanna, Jahzara, Makayla, Kya, Samara

Mykelti *(American)* ♂ RATING: ★★★
Who is like God?—Created by actor Mykelti Williamson from his first name and middle initial, Michael T.
> People think of Mykelti as caring, pretty, popular, intelligent, trustworthy
> People who like the name Mykelti also like Jayden, Josiah, Isaiah, Mikaili, Micah, Malachi, Daemyn, Elijah, Mihaly, Kaden

Myla *(English)* ♀ RATING: ★★★★
Merciful—Myla Goldberg, author
> People think of Myla as pretty, caring, cool, wild, lazy
> People who like the name Myla also like Ava, Mya, Gracie, Olivia, Alexa, Shayla, Kaydence, Jadyn, Makenna, Kaelyn

Myles *(Latin)* ♀♂ RATING: ★★★★
Soldier
> People think of Myles as handsome, intelligent, funny, caring, energetic
> People who like the name Myles also like Mason, Logan, Parker, Dylan, Hayden, Caden, Madison, Preston, Evan, Taylor

Myra *(English)* ♀ RATING: ★★★
Admirable—Created by Fulke Greville, poet, derived from Myrna or Mary
> People think of Myra as pretty, caring, intelligent, funny, creative
> People who like the name Myra also like Mya, Ava, Paige, Maya, Mia, Olivia, Hailey, Layla, Chloe, Mira

Myrilla *(American)* ♀ RATING: ★★★☆
Myrtle—Variation of Myrtilla
> People think of Myrilla as pretty, old-fashioned, weird, quiet, powerful
> People who like the name Myrilla also like Makayla, Mya, Myeisha, Olivia, Ava, Grace, Mirabelle, Amelia, Maya, Maeve

Myrna *(Celtic/Gaelic)* ♀ RATING: ★★★★
High-spirited—Variation of Muirne
> People think of Myrna as caring, trustworthy, funny, intelligent, pretty
> People who like the name Myrna also like Maura, Moira, Maisie, Meagan, Lana, Morna, Mae, Maeve, Muriel, Riona

Myron *(Greek)* ♂ RATING: ★★
Myrrh, an ancient spice
> People think of Myron as funny, intelligent, handsome, caring, cool
> People who like the name Myron also like Kaden, Miles, Caleb, Ethan, Noah, Owen, Nathan, Ian, Lucas, Landon

Myrrh *(Greek)* ♀ RATING: ★★★
Ancient Egyptian spice used in incense and perfumes
> People think of Myrrh as elegant, pretty, wild, creative, quiet
> People who like the name Myrrh also like Isis, Chione, Kiara, Sanura, Monifa, Kamilah, Malise, Ciara, Giselle, Maeve

Myrtle *(English)* ♀ RATING: ★☆
Myrtle bush
> People think of Myrtle as old-fashioned, funny, caring, trustworthy, loser
> People who like the name Myrtle also like Matilda, Mabel, Maggie, Hazel, Melanie, Melissa, Melody, Sophie, Laurel, Millicent

Mystery *(English)* ♀ RATING: ★★
Unexplained
> People think of Mystery as exotic, creative, intelligent, sexy, pretty
> People who like the name Mystery also like Faith, Destiny, Paige, Harmony, Trinity, Melody, Sapphire, Scarlett, Summer, Hope

Mythri *(Sanskrit/East Indian)* ♀ RATING: ★★★☆
Friendship
> People think of Mythri as young, pretty, quiet, religious, sexy
> People who like the name Mythri also like Malini, Mallika, Morwen, Monita, Lilith, Manasa, Denali, Mabyn, Midori, Leila

Naara *(Japanese)* ♀ RATING: ★★★
Deer
> People think of Naara as nerdy, lazy, big, loser, winner
> People who like the name Naara also like Desiree, Angie, Gin, Mai, Toki, Anahid, Navya, Miu, Angela, Hana

415

Naava *(Hebrew)* ♀   RATING: ★★★★
Beautiful
> People think of Naava as pretty, intelligent, cool, funny, quiet
> People who like the name Naava also like Naomi, Nadia, Naeva, Jadyn, Rachel, Kyla, Ava, Zoe, Grace, Faith

Nabila *(Arabic)* ♀   RATING: ★★
Noble, excellent
> People think of Nabila as pretty, caring, intelligent, funny, exotic
> People who like the name Nabila also like Nailah, Layla, Nadalia, Nadia, Naida, Samira, Ella, Hazel, Ivy, Adia

Nadalia *(Portuguese)* ♀   RATING: ★★★☆
Born on Christmas day—Variation of Natalie
> People think of Nadalia as pretty, exotic, caring, sexy, elegant
> People who like the name Nadalia also like Nadia, Natalia, Adriana, Sabrina, Naomi, Isabella, Ava, Nadine, Fiona, Gabrielle

Nadda *(Arabic)* ♀   RATING: ★★★
Dew
> People think of Nadda as intelligent, popular, ethnic, pretty, funny
> People who like the name Nadda also like Nadia, Nabila, Nichole, Samara, Aaliyah, Rachael, Abia, Olivia, Noura, Maegan

Nadia *(Slavic)* ♀   RATING: ★★★★
Hope—Nadia Comeneci, gymnast
> People think of Nadia as pretty, funny, intelligent, creative, caring
> People who like the name Nadia also like Olivia, Isabella, Natalie, Paige, Ava, Natalia, Hannah, Naomi, Sophia, Chloe

Nadie *(English)* ♀   RATING: ★★
Hope—Short for Nadia; also means no one in Spanish
> People think of Nadie as pretty, caring, intelligent, quiet, trustworthy
> People who like the name Nadie also like Nadia, Natalie, Sadie, Lacey, Gabrielle, Mia, Faith, Natasha, Lexi, Hailey

Nadine *(French)* ♀   RATING: ★★★
Hope—Variation of Nadia
> People think of Nadine as pretty, funny, intelligent, caring, trustworthy
> People who like the name Nadine also like Nadia, Natalie, Paige, Hannah, Naomi, Isabelle, Faith, Olivia, Hailey, Sabrina

Naeva *(French)* ♀   RATING: ★★★★
Ingenue
> People think of Naeva as exotic, pretty, elegant, artsy, young
> People who like the name Naeva also like Nadia, Nevaeh, Naida, Layla, Adeline, Giselle, Naomi, Ava, Nieve, Fiona

Naflah *(Arabic)* ♀   RATING: ★★☆
Overabundance
> People think of Naflah as nerdy, loser, weird, uptight, trendy
> People who like the name Naflah also like Tangia, Nasya, Tyronica, Neona, Misa, Neorah, Nailah, Tanaya, Naomi, Devorah

Nafuna *(African)* ♀   RATING: ★★★
Delivered feet-first—Ugandan origin
> People think of Nafuna as unpopular, weird, old, old-fashioned, slow
> People who like the name Nafuna also like Latifah, Naeva, Iris, Nuala, Latoya, Jazzelle, Miyoko, Ophelia, Marissa, Posy

Naiara *(Spanish)* ♀   RATING: ★★★★☆
City in the Basque country
> People think of Naiara as pretty, exotic, funny, young, energetic
> People who like the name Naiara also like Nailah, Nayana, Naiya, Amaya, Abrianna, Aaralyn, Gabriella, Kiara, Kaelyn, Nadia

Naida *(Arabic)* ♀   RATING: ★★★★
Water nymph
> People think of Naida as pretty, intelligent, young, exotic, creative
> People who like the name Naida also like Nadia, Naiya, Naeva, Chloe, Iris, Isabella, Aurora, Amaya, Jasmine, Natalia

Naif *(Arabic)* ♂   RATING: ★★★
Excess, surplus
> People think of Naif as young, ethnic, wealthy, religious, funny
> People who like the name Naif also like Noah, Nash, Neal, Nayef, Nazario, Nishan, Mattias, Noam, Arif, Liam

Nailah *(Arabic)* ♀   RATING: ★★★★☆
Successful
> People think of Nailah as pretty, intelligent, funny, creative, caring
> People who like the name Nailah also like Nyla, Nadia, Naiya, Layla, Nala, Aaliyah, Amaya, Gabrielle, Kamilah, Ava

Naima *(Arabic)* ♀   RATING: ★★★★
Delight, contentedness
> People think of Naima as pretty, intelligent, exotic, creative, cool
> People who like the name Naima also like Aaliyah, Naomi, Nadia, Eva, Lorelei, Layla, Samara, Chloe, Olivia, Emma

Nairi *(Armenian)* ♀♂   RATING: ★★★☆
Land of canyons; river—Also an ancient people of Armenia
> People think of Nairi as elegant, artsy, intelligent, pretty, creative
> People who like the name Nairi also like Nalani, Raven, Naveen, Jade, Jaden, Raine, Arien, Madison, Hayden, Quinn

416

Naiser *(African)* ♀♂ RATING: ★★★
Founder of clans
People think of Naiser as handsome, powerful, popular, sexy, cool
People who like the name Naiser also like Addison, Devon, Jordan, Jermaine, Rafferty, Ashton, Avery, Lavender, James, Lani

Naiya *(Arabic)* ♀ RATING: ★★★★☆
Reed, pipe
People think of Naiya as pretty, exotic, intelligent, creative, caring
People who like the name Naiya also like Nadia, Nailah, Layla, Naida, Amaya, Isabella, Naomi, Ava, Chloe, Olivia

Naja *(Arabic)* ♀ RATING: ★★★★
Rescue, escape—Also a name in Greenland meaning a boy's little sister
People think of Naja as pretty, intelligent, creative, exotic, leader
People who like the name Naja also like Nadia, Nailah, Nala, Naiya, Samara, Ayanna, Aaliyah, Hailey, Naomi, Jadyn

Najila *(Arabic)* ♀ RATING: ★★
Name of a plant—Also spelled Najela and Najeela
People think of Najila as pretty, caring, leader, popular, energetic
People who like the name Najila also like Nailah, Nayana, Naida, Kailani, Naja, Niesha, Nimeesha, Nadia, Nenet, Penelope

Najwa *(Arabic)* ♀ RATING: ★★★
Passionate
People think of Najwa as intelligent, caring, exotic, trustworthy, pretty
People who like the name Najwa also like Layla, Nabila, Nakia, Najila, Nailah, Sahara, Naja, Aurora, Cala, Iris

Najya *(Arabic)* ♀ RATING: ★★★
Liberated, free
People think of Najya as pretty, young, energetic, caring, intelligent
People who like the name Najya also like Naja, Nayana, Nadia, Naiya, Nasya, Nuria, Najila, Anaya, Nyla, Rayya

Nakeisha *(American)* ♀ RATING: ★★★☆
Combination of Na and Keisha
People think of Nakeisha as pretty, funny, popular, sexy, trustworthy
People who like the name Nakeisha also like Aaliyah, Savannah, Keisha, Lakeisha, Naomi, Nadia, Keira, Nerissa, Jasmine, Tatiana

Nakia *(Egyptian)* ♀ RATING: ★★★☆
Pure, faithful—Properly transliterated Naqiyah
People think of Nakia as pretty, intelligent, caring, funny, sexy
People who like the name Nakia also like Isis, Nadia, Kiara, Eva, Nailah, Samara, Tiana, Arianna, Naomi, Breanna

Nakisha *(American)* ♀ RATING: ★★★
Combination of Na and Keisha
People think of Nakisha as pretty, energetic, funny, leader, creative
People who like the name Nakisha also like Amelia, Hannah, Rhianna, Tamira, Ava, Emma, Ashlee, Shayla, Rhian, Brea

Nala *(African)* ♀ RATING: ★★★★☆
Luck; gift—Zulu and Swahili origin; character in *The Lion King*
People think of Nala as pretty, intelligent, exotic, caring, young
People who like the name Nala also like Nadia, Layla, Naomi, Olivia, Paige, Mia, Ava, Grace, Hannah, Isabella

Nalani *(Hawaiian)* ♀♂ RATING: ★★☆
Heavens
People think of Nalani as pretty, funny, creative, exotic, intelligent
People who like the name Nalani also like Kalani, Kai, Jaden, Lani, Cadence, Kaili, Jada, Ryan, Avery, Keanu

Nalanie *(Hawaiian)* ♀ RATING: ★★★★☆
Heavens
People think of Nalanie as pretty, exotic, funny, sexy, trendy
People who like the name Nalanie also like Leilani, Nadia, Gabrielle, Natalie, Natalia, Isabella, Noelani, Kailani, Sabrina, Naomi

Nalin *(Sanskrit/East Indian)* ♂ RATING: ★★★★
Lotus flower
People think of Nalin as exotic, creative, sexy, intelligent, elegant
People who like the name Nalin also like Caleb, Noah, Trenton, Nathan, Nathaniel, Xavier, Isaac, Elijah, Oliver, Jace

Nalini *(Sanskrit/East Indian)* ♀ RATING: ★★★★
Lotus, lily
People think of Nalini as pretty, exotic, funny, intelligent, religious
People who like the name Nalini also like Ariana, Aaliyah, Kailani, Kaelyn, Avani, Nayana, Satya, Nalanie, Asha, Naiya

Nalo *(African)* ♀♂ RATING: ★★★
Lovable
People think of Nalo as caring, elegant, creative, sexy, exotic
People who like the name Nalo also like Dante, Phoenix, Neo, Addison, Nolan, Parker, Remy, Dylan, Jaden, Rylie

Nam *(Vietnamese)* ♂ RATING: ★☆
South; manly—Also short for Vietnam
People think of Nam as cool, funny, popular, caring, intelligent
People who like the name Nam also like Remington, Niran, Leon, Nate, Luke, Blade, Nalin, Nathan, Ryu, Bade

418

Nami *(Japanese)* ♀   RATING: ★★★★
Wave
> People think of Nami as pretty, creative, intelligent, young, exotic
> People who like the name Nami also like Sakura, Amaya, Kaida, Ayame, Suki, Emiko, Miya, Nariko, Mai, Aiko

Namir *(Arabic)* ♀♂   RATING: ★★★★
Leopard, panther
> People think of Namir as intelligent, exotic, aggressive, creative, trustworthy
> People who like the name Namir also like Jade, Nalani, Caden, Nida, James, Jaden, Jordan, Winter, Nayan, Riley

Nan *(English)* ♀   RATING: ★☆
Grace—Short for Anne or Nancy
> People think of Nan as old-fashioned, pretty, funny, intelligent, quiet
> People who like the name Nan also like Olivia, Lucy, Ava, Felicity, Ruby, Tess, Jill, Fiona, Cara, Tatum

Nanami *(Japanese)* ♀   RATING: ★★★
Seven seas
> People think of Nanami as creative, intelligent, energetic, exotic
> People who like the name Nanami also like Nani, Umeko, Naava, Shiva, Colette, Nariko, Vonda, Vandana, Mabli, Inaya

Nancy *(English)* ♀   RATING: ★★★
Grace—Variation of Anne; Nancy Cartwright, voice of Bart Simpson (*The Simpsons*) and Chuckie Finster (*Rugrats*); Nancy Reagan, U.S. first lady; Nancy Sinatra, actress/singer
> People think of Nancy as caring, funny, pretty, intelligent, trustworthy
> People who like the name Nancy also like Hannah, Olivia, Samantha, Jessica, Rebecca, Natalie, Grace, Elizabeth, Emily, Melissa

Nanda *(Sanskrit/East Indian)* ♀   RATING: ★★★☆
Full of joy; achiever
> People think of Nanda as pretty, caring, intelligent, exotic, trendy
> People who like the name Nanda also like Nisha, Natesa, Isis, Devi, Neema, Kalinda, Nara, Nina, Shyla, Mina

Nanette *(French)* ♀   RATING: ★★★☆
Grace—Variation of Anne; Nanette Fabray, actress; *No No Nanette*, musical
> People think of Nanette as pretty, intelligent, caring, trustworthy, creative
> People who like the name Nanette also like Nadia, Isabella, Scarlett, Daphne, Madeleine, Jacqueline, Charlotte, Belle, Olivia, Sophie

Nani *(Greek)* ♀   RATING: ★★★☆
Grace—Variation of Anne; also means beautiful in Japanese and Hawaiian
> People think of Nani as pretty, funny, sexy, intelligent, quiet

People who like the name Nani also like Nadia, Isabella, Paige, Naomi, Natasha, Ava, Eva, Bianca, Sophie, Lara

Nanne *(Scandinavian)* ♂   RATING: ★★
Grace—Variation of Anne
> People think of Nanne as weird, nerdy, aggressive, elegant, unpopular
> People who like the name Nanne also like Gage, Lucas, Nikkos, Wendell, Isaac, Matteo, Bo, Werner, Noah, Valentin

Nansen *(Scandinavian)* ♂   RATING: ★☆
Son of Nan—Also a Norwegian surname; Fritjof Nansen, scientist/humanitarian
> People think of Nansen as caring, cool, creative, intelligent, sporty
> People who like the name Nansen also like Noah, Nash, Landon, Nelson, Radley, Ace, Taran, Nolen, Brant, Wade

Nantai *(Native American)* ♂   RATING: ★★
Chief
> People think of Nantai as big, weird, aggressive, powerful, leader
> People who like the name Nantai also like Neka, Dyami, Nodin, Ahanu, Niran, Yuma, Mikasi, Nibaw, Dasan, Mingan

Naolin *(American)* ♀♂   RATING: ★★★☆
Created for online gaming
> People think of Naolin as leader, creative, pretty, powerful, exotic
> People who like the name Naolin also like Nolan, Landen, Nalani, Evelyn, Torrin, Kyan, Ezra, Lennon, Hayden, Reese

Naomh *(Celtic/Gaelic)* ♀   RATING: ★★☆
Holy
> People think of Naomh as intelligent, pretty, elegant, creative, energetic
> People who like the name Naomh also like Paige, Maeve, Ruby, Phalen, Ryann, Shauna, Naomi, Regan, Chloe, Larissa

Naomi *(Hebrew)* ♀   RATING: ★★★★
Beautiful, gentle—Also a Japanese name meaning honest and beauty; Naomi Campbell, model; Naomi Judd, singer; Naomi Watts, actress
> People think of Naomi as pretty, caring, intelligent, funny, creative
> People who like the name Naomi also like Olivia, Hannah, Chloe, Natalie, Nadia, Abigail, Paige, Ava, Isabella, Faith

Naphtali *(Hebrew)* ♀♂   RATING: ★★★
My wrestling—One of the twelve tribes of Israel; traditionally a male name but also used for females
> People think of Naphtali as exotic, leader, artsy, powerful, sexy
> People who like the name Naphtali also like Walidah, Ava, Arabella, Ariella, Aeryn, Isabelle, Bianca, Wafa, Asher, Alina

Napoleon (French) ♂ — RATING: ★★★
From Naples, Italy—Napoleon Bonaparte, politician;
Napoleon Dynamite, movie character
People think of Napoleon as nerdy, intelligent, funny,
powerful, weird
People who like the name Napoleon also like Nicholas,
Xavier, Lucas, Noah, Matthew, Zachary, Tyson, Jack,
Oliver, Alexander

Napua (Hawaiian) ♀ — RATING: ★☆
The flowers
People think of Napua as pretty, intelligent, creative,
caring, quiet
People who like the name Napua also like Keona,
Noelani, Nohealani, Kaloni, Keani, Malia, Kawena, Kailani,
Leilani, Keala

Nara (Native American) ♀ — RATING: ★★★★
Place name
People think of Nara as pretty, intelligent, creative,
funny, trustworthy
People who like the name Nara also like Nadia, Zoe,
Zara, Nora, Kaya, Mara, Paige, Nina, Lana, Cara

Naranbaatar (Mongolian) ♂ — RATING: ★★☆
Sun hero
People think of Naranbaatar as sexy, powerful, hand-
some, exotic, cool
People who like the name Naranbaatar also like Crevan,
Tilden, Abdukrahman, Csongor, Abdulrahman, Ceron,
Holt, Falk, Caleb, Ace

Narcisse (French) ♀ — RATING: ★★★
Narcissus; daffodil
People think of Narcisse as pretty, creative, artsy, ener-
getic, criminal
People who like the name Narcisse also like Genevieve,
Nicolette, Giselle, Jasmine, Bianca, Gwendolyn, Sabrina,
Belle, Anastasia, Juliette

Nardo (Spanish) ♂ — RATING: ★★☆
Bear brave—Short for Bernardo
People think of Nardo as nerdy, weird, loser, unpopular,
stuck-up
People who like the name Nardo also like Nathaniel,
Noah, Nelson, Nero, Navarro, Neville, Napoleon, Niles,
Neron, Nathan

Naresh (Sanskrit/East Indian) ♂ — RATING: ★☆
King
People think of Naresh as intelligent, aggressive, winner,
religious, popular
People who like the name Naresh also like Nathaniel,
Nitesh, Nathan, Darshan, Nigel, Ashwin, Neville, Dinesh,
Isaiah, Ethan

Narges (Persian) ♀ — RATING: ★★★
Narcissus; jonquil
People think of Narges as pretty, cool, trustworthy,
elegant, leader
People who like the name Narges also like Jasmine,
Suna, Nysa, Nyx, Seda, Nixie, Narcisse, Sanam, Sareh,
Neva

Nariko (Japanese) ♀ — RATING: ★★
Thunder
People think of Nariko as exotic, intelligent, creative,
cool, wild
People who like the name Nariko also like Kaida,
Amaya, Miyoko, Sakura, Emiko, Suki, Keiko, Kaori,
Nozomi, Miyo

Narissara (Thai) ♀ — RATING: ★★☆
Smart woman
People think of Narissara as intelligent, exotic, creative,
pretty, powerful
People who like the name Narissara also like Kailani,
Nerissa, Naiya, Naomi, Nadia, Arissa, Aaliyah, Cytheria,
Cadelaria, Naava

Nascha (Native American) ♀ — RATING: ★★★☆
Owl—Navajo origin
People think of Nascha as pretty, exotic, caring, trendy,
ethnic
People who like the name Nascha also like Soraya,
Neena, Layla, Ayasha, Dyani, Satinka, Sora, Kachina,
Kaya, Kwanita

Nash (American) ♂ — RATING: ★★★★
Dweller by the ash tree—Graham Nash, musician;
Ogden Nash, poet
People think of Nash as handsome, cool, intelligent,
leader, popular
People who like the name Nash also like Noah, Kaden,
Maddox, Owen, Ethan, Jackson, Nathan, Luke, Landon,
Gage

Nasha (Persian) ♀♂ — RATING: ★★★☆
Judge
People think of Nasha as pretty, funny, intelligent, cool,
sexy
People who like the name Nasha also like Nolan, Dana,
Ezra, Raine, Kirsten, Taylor, Cassidy, Madison, Sasha,
Sean

Nasia (Greek) ♀ — RATING: ★★
Immortal—Short for Athanasia
People think of Nasia as pretty, intelligent, elegant,
young, sexy
People who like the name Nasia also like Nasya, Nessa,
Nayana, Ava, Naomi, Jadyn, Nydia, Victoria, Kyla, Naja

Nasira (Arabic) ♀ — RATING: ★★★
Friend, helpmate
People think of Nasira as pretty, intelligent, exotic,
funny, leader
People who like the name Nasira also like Nyla, Nailah,
Nia, Nayana, Leila, Nola, Simone, Nerissa, Mia, Nuria

Nasnan (Native American) ♀ — RATING: ★☆
Surrounded by song—British Columbian tribe name
People think of Nasnan as ethnic, weird, quiet, creative,
young
People who like the name Nasnan also like Kaya, Nituna,
Takoda, Neena, Ayasha, Olathe, Etenia, Liluye, Natane,
Layla

Nasser *(Arabic)* ♂   RATING: ★☆
Triumph; help
People think of Nasser as handsome, funny, caring, cool, creative
People who like the name Nasser also like Nash, Jamal, Malik, Nicholas, Amir, Khalil, Jayden, Micah, Kaden, Rashid

Nastaran *(Persian)* ♀   RATING: ★★★
Wild rose
People think of Nastaran as sexy, exotic, pretty, ethnic, intelligent
People who like the name Nastaran also like Sherene, Norah, Sona, Kallima, Nickan, Jasmine, Nicole, Nicolette, Nixie, Norina

Nasya *(Russian)* ♀   RATING: ★★★★
Immortal—Short for Afanasya
People think of Nasya as pretty, creative, funny, caring, intelligent
People who like the name Nasya also like Nadia, Samara, Nailah, Nyla, Natasha, Nia, Kyla, Nasia, Jadyn, Nakia

Nat *(English)* ♀ ♂   RATING: ★★★☆
Short for of Natalie, Nathan, or Nathaniel—Nat King Cole, singer
People think of Nat as cool, funny, popular, handsome, leader
People who like the name Nat also like Ryan, James, Sean, Madison, Evan, Jaden, Will, Addison, Cade, Rider

Natala *(American)* ♀   RATING: ★★★☆
Born on Christmas day—Variation of Natalia
People think of Natala as pretty, cool, popular, sexy, caring
People who like the name Natala also like Nadia, Natalya, Natalie, Natalia, Naomi, Isabella, Natasha, Nora, Abigail, Kailey

Natale *(Italian)* ♀   RATING: ★★★☆
Christmas; birthday
People think of Natale as pretty, intelligent, caring, funny, creative
People who like the name Natale also like Natalia, Isabella, Gabrielle, Natalie, Vanessa, Gwen, Viola, Dawn, Marla, Celeste

Natalia *(Italian)* ♀   RATING: ★★★★
Born on Christmas day
People think of Natalia as pretty, intelligent, funny, caring, creative
People who like the name Natalia also like Isabella, Olivia, Nadia, Natalie, Ava, Sophia, Gabriella, Paige, Emma, Gianna

Natalie *(French)* ♀   RATING: ★★★
Born on Christmas day—Natalie Cole, singer; Natalie Maines, singer; Natalie Wood, actress
People think of Natalie as pretty, funny, caring, intelligent, creative

People who like the name Natalie also like Olivia, Hannah, Emma, Emily, Paige, Hailey, Isabella, Grace, Abigail, Ava

Natalya *(Slavic)* ♀   RATING: ★★★☆
Born on Christmas day
People think of Natalya as pretty, intelligent, sexy, caring, creative
People who like the name Natalya also like Natalia, Nadia, Natalie, Isabella, Olivia, Paige, Hailey, Natasha, Hannah, Gabriella

Natane *(Native American)* ♀   RATING: ★★★☆
Female child—Arapaho origin
People think of Natane as pretty, exotic, intelligent, creative, elegant
People who like the name Natane also like Neena, Miakoda, Kaya, Soraya, Kaliska, Dyani, Hateya, Kiona, Cocheta, Chumani

Natania *(Hebrew)* ♀ ♂   RATING: ★★☆
He gave
People think of Natania as pretty, intelligent, caring, funny, creative
People who like the name Natania also like Jaden, Katriel, Teagan, Dakota, Taryn, Morgan, Taylor, Nalani, Madison, Caden

Nataniela *(Hebrew)* ♀   RATING: ★★☆
Gift of God—Feminine form of Natan or Nathan
People think of Nataniela as intelligent, funny, quiet, exotic, cool
People who like the name Nataniela also like Liana, Abigail, Danya, Tahlia, Tatiana, Adonia, Dominique, Adrianna, Isabella, Jemima

Natara *(American)* ♀   RATING: ★★☆
Combination of Natalie and Tara
People think of Natara as funny, pretty, caring, intelligent, powerful
People who like the name Natara also like Naomi, Nara, Ophelia, Samara, Kiara, Leila, Nadia, Nora, Dara, Chloe

Natasha *(Russian)* ♀   RATING: ★★☆
Born on Christmas day—Variation of Natalia
People think of Natasha as pretty, funny, caring, intelligent, sexy
People who like the name Natasha also like Natalie, Olivia, Isabella, Nadia, Hannah, Samantha, Natalia, Emma, Paige, Hailey

Nate *(English)* ♂   RATING: ★★☆
Short for Nathan or Nathaniel
People think of Nate as handsome, cool, funny, popular, intelligent
People who like the name Nate also like Nathan, Ethan, Noah, Seth, Nathaniel, Jacob, Caleb, Luke, Nicholas, Owen

Natesa *(Sanskrit/East Indian)* ♀   RATING: ★★★☆
Dance lord
People think of Natesa as caring, trendy, intelligent, exotic, trustworthy

People who like the name Natesa also like Nerissa, Giselle, Nadia, Nanda, Natasha, Nayana, Mahesa, Nisha, Opal, Gianna

Nathalie (French) ♀   RATING: ★★★★
Born on Christmas day
People think of Nathalie as pretty, funny, intelligent, caring, trustworthy
People who like the name Nathalie also like Natalie, Olivia, Paige, Hannah, Madeleine, Lauren, Hailey, Chloe, Natalia, Emily

Nathan (Hebrew) ♂   RATING: ★★★☆
He gave—Nathan Fillion, actor; Nathan Lane, singer/actor
People think of Nathan as handsome, funny, intelligent, caring, cool
People who like the name Nathan also like Ethan, Noah, Jacob, Nicholas, Matthew, Zachary, Caleb, Joshua, Aiden, Lucas

Nathaniel (Hebrew) ♂   RATING: ★★★
Gift of God—Nathaniel Hawthorne, author
People think of Nathaniel as handsome, intelligent, funny, caring, creative
People who like the name Nathaniel also like Ethan, Nathan, Noah, Nicholas, Gabriel, Jacob, Caleb, Zachary, Benjamin, Elijah

Natine (African) ♀♂   RATING: ★★☆
Of the Natine tribe
People think of Natine as exotic, energetic, pretty, intelligent, creative
People who like the name Natine also like Kieran, Paxton, Nolan, Rider, Naveen, Spencer, Reese, Ryder, Christian, Cade

Natividad (Spanish) ♀♂   RATING: ★★★
Of the nativity
People think of Natividad as pretty, religious, caring, trustworthy, funny
People who like the name Natividad also like Natine, Natsu, Christian, Neo, Addison, Neely, Carmen, Reda, Billy, Jules

Natsu (Japanese) ♀♂   RATING: ★★★
Born in summer
People think of Natsu as exotic, intelligent, elegant, sexy, wild
People who like the name Natsu also like Mitsu, Sanyu, Kiyoshi, Maro, Seiko, Hoshi, Nori, Yuki, Ren, Hiroko

Nature (American) ♀♂   RATING: ★★
Elements of the natural world
People think of Nature as quiet, artsy, pretty, intelligent, loser
People who like the name Nature also like Rain, Shea, Mackenzie, Nova, Liberty, Taylor, Riley, Phoenix, Justice, Piper

Navarro (Spanish) ♂   RATING: ★★★☆
From Navarre, Spain
People think of Navarro as handsome, creative, powerful, leader, aggressive
People who like the name Navarro also like Noah, Nathaniel, Joaquin, Nazario, Tristan, Nicholas, Ace, Maddox, Xavier, Macario

Naveen (Sanskrit/East Indian) ♀♂   RATING: ★★★★
New—Naveen Andrews, actor
People think of Naveen as intelligent, cool, trustworthy, sexy, powerful
People who like the name Naveen also like Jaden, Riley, Caden, Nolan, Aidan, Logan, Hayden, Reagan, Rylan, Rory

Navid (Persian) ♂   RATING: ★★★☆
Reward; judgment
People think of Navid as handsome, cool, intelligent, energetic, popular
People who like the name Navid also like Noah, Nathan, Neal, Nathaniel, Nicholas, Nalin, David, Jeremiah, Nash, Nevan

Navya (Sanskrit/East Indian) ♀   RATING: ★★★
Young
People think of Navya as pretty, young, caring, funny, intelligent
People who like the name Navya also like Nayana, Neema, Nitya, Nerissa, Fiona, Nessa, Nitara, Nora, Nasya, Nisha

Nay (Persian) ♀   RATING: ★★★☆
Flute
People think of Nay as intelligent, pretty, funny, creative, sexy
People who like the name Nay also like Naida, Tammy, Taya, Olivia, Amal, Amina, Faith, Tale, Taini, Natalia

Nayan (Sanskrit/East Indian) ♀♂   RATING: ★★★
Eye
People think of Nayan as handsome, intelligent, funny, energetic, cool
People who like the name Nayan also like Hayden, Kiran, Luca, Jaden, Caden, Riley, Nova, Raven, Namir, Naveen

Nayana (Sanskrit/East Indian) ♀   RATING: ★★☆
Eye
People think of Nayana as pretty, creative, energetic, funny, intelligent
People who like the name Nayana also like Nadia, Naiara, Navya, Gianna, Nala, Natasha, Naiya, Nisha, Mia, Maya

Nayati (Sanskrit/East Indian) ♂   RATING: ★★☆
Leader
People think of Nayati as handsome, aggressive, intelligent, funny, trustworthy
People who like the name Nayati also like Nishan, Nirav, Darshan, Savir, Angelito, Sanjiv, Ashwin, Shyam, Jagat, Darius

Nayef (Arabic) ♂   RATING: ★☆
Excess, surplus
> People think of Nayef as intelligent, funny, cool, pretty, powerful
> People who like the name Nayef also like Niran, Naif, Nishan, Neal, Nazario, Ayman, Nathan, Nen, Nardo, Nathaniel

Nazario (Italian) ♂   RATING: ★★★
From Nazareth, Israel
> People think of Nazario as aggressive, intelligent, funny, sporty, handsome
> People who like the name Nazario also like Navarro, Noah, Nathaniel, Elijah, Nicholas, Jayden, Nevan, Nishan, Nico, Nelson

Neal (Celtic/Gaelic) ♂   RATING: ★★☆
Champion; passionate
> People think of Neal as caring, intelligent, handsome, funny, trustworthy
> People who like the name Neal also like Nicholas, Neil, Owen, Ian, Nathan, Seth, Noah, Ethan, Aiden, Jacob

Nebraska (Native American) ♀♂   RATING: ★★★
Flat water—Otoe origin; U.S. state
> People think of Nebraska as weird, loser, aggressive, nerdy, old
> People who like the name Nebraska also like Dakota, Madison, Phoenix, Hayden, Nevada, Riley, Mackenzie, Taylor, Parker, Rory

Neci (Slavic) ♀   RATING: ★★
Fiery—Short for Ignacia
> People think of Neci as young, funny, popular, intelligent, leader
> People who like the name Neci also like Chloe, Necia, Mia, Nadia, Penelope, Olivia, Bella, Kaelyn, Ava, Emma

Necia (Spanish) ♀   RATING: ★★★★☆
Fiery—Short for Ignacia
> People think of Necia as intelligent, creative, energetic, pretty, trendy
> People who like the name Necia also like Ava, Neci, Sabrina, Aurora, Bianca, Nadia, Natalia, Olivia, Kaelyn, Mia

Nedaa (Arabic) ♀   RATING: ★★☆
Call to prayer
> People think of Nedaa as funny, pretty, popular, cool, intelligent
> People who like the name Nedaa also like Nyla, Nimeesha, Nuria, Abia, Alima, Nura, Nasya, Kaya, Nysa, Najila

Nedra (American) ♀   RATING: ★★★★
Created name—Possibly feminine form of Ned; also Arden backward
> People think of Nedra as pretty, caring, intelligent, funny, creative
> People who like the name Nedra also like Kendra, Mira, Genevieve, Giselle, Cordelia, Fiona, Lucinda, Deidra, Bianca, Nora

Neely (American) ♀♂   RATING: ★★
Champion; passionate—Short for Neil
> People think of Neely as pretty, funny, intelligent, creative, artsy
> People who like the name Neely also like Riley, Parker, Logan, Madison, Taylor, Reagan, Quinn, Reese, Addison, Hayden

Neema (Persian) ♀   RATING: ★★★☆
Young
> People think of Neema as caring, pretty, funny, intelligent, creative
> People who like the name Neema also like Navya, Neena, Nayana, Nisha, Kaya, Naomi, Nanda, Nitya, Naiya, Camille

Neena (Sanskrit/East Indian) ♀   RATING: ★★☆
Stylish, elegant
> People think of Neena as pretty, caring, funny, cool, trustworthy
> People who like the name Neena also like Kaya, Zoe, Chloe, Layla, Nadia, Nina, Olivia, Sabrina, Sadie, Sophie

Nefret (Egyptian) ♀   RATING: ★★★
Beautiful
> People think of Nefret as leader, handsome, exotic, creative, elegant
> People who like the name Nefret also like Anastasia, Cassandra, Bronwen, Chandra, Asha, Nixie, Serenity, Amber, Faye, Danica

Negeen (Persian) ♀   RATING: ★★★
Gem
> People think of Negeen as funny, exotic, pretty, creative, energetic
> People who like the name Negeen also like Dara, Sareh, Natara, Naida, Neena, Parmida, Zenda, Pilar, Niesha, Brianna

Neha (Sanskrit/East Indian) ♀   RATING: ★★★☆
Love, affection
> People think of Neha as caring, intelligent, pretty, trustworthy, creative
> People who like the name Neha also like Niyati, Avani, Navya, Amara, Makara, Naava, Nayana, Amithi, Nisha, Nilima

Nehemiah (Hebrew) ♂   RATING: ★★★★☆
God has comforted
> People think of Nehemiah as handsome, intelligent, caring, powerful, religious
> People who like the name Nehemiah also like Isaiah, Elijah, Jeremiah, Nathaniel, Noah, Zachariah, Micah, Isaac, Malachi, Gabriel

Neil (Celtic/Gaelic) ♂   RATING: ★★★☆
Champion; passionate—Neil Patrick Harris, actor; Neil Young, singer/musician
> People think of Neil as handsome, funny, intelligent, caring, cool
> People who like the name Neil also like Ian, Nathan, Owen, Seth, Noah, Nicholas, Neal, Ethan, Jacob, Nathaniel

Neith *(Egyptian)* ♀ RATING: ★★★
Ancient Egyptian mother goddess
> People think of Neith as exotic, weird, intelligent, powerful, trustworthy
> People who like the name Neith also like Nailah, Isis, Nile, Monifa, Nakia, Nilima, Lapis, Sagira, Nerissa, Fiona

Neka *(Native American)* ♂ RATING: ★★
Wild goose
> People think of Neka as wild, creative, intelligent, lazy, sexy
> People who like the name Neka also like Noah, Nodin, Aiden, Nantai, Kaden, Leo, Jared, Isaiah, Nathan, Nelson

Nelia *(English)* ♀ RATING: ★★★★
Horn—Short for Cornelia
> People think of Nelia as caring, pretty, creative, funny, intelligent
> People who like the name Nelia also like Nadia, Paige, Shayla, Kyla, Nia, Keira, Genevieve, Keely, Fiona, Lana

Nell *(English)* ♀ RATING: ★★★☆
Light—Variation of Helen or Eleanor
> People think of Nell as intelligent, funny, pretty, creative, caring
> People who like the name Nell also like Mia, Grace, Tess, Eva, Olivia, Chloe, Lily, Ava, Violet, Eleanor

Nella *(American)* ♀ RATING: ★★★
Short for names ending in Nella
> People think of Nella as pretty, sexy, elegant, creative, popular
> People who like the name Nella also like Sienna, Ava, Sierra, Nyla, Nia, Nell, Nala, Jillian, Neva, Hanna

Nellie *(English)* ♀ RATING: ★★☆
Light—Variation of Helen or Eleanor; Nellie Bly, journalist/author
> People think of Nellie as pretty, caring, funny, trustworthy, creative
> People who like the name Nellie also like Olivia, Grace, Paige, Mia, Natalie, Victoria, Claire, Sophie, Sophia, Ava

Nellis *(American)* ♀ RATING: ★★☆
Horn—Variation of Cornelius; also a Dutch surname
> People think of Nellis as quiet, loser, lazy, old-fashioned, untrustworthy
> People who like the name Nellis also like Penelope, Nerys, Scarlett, Eleanor, Maris, Maren, Melanie, Ophelia, Iris, Natalia

Nelly *(English)* ♀ RATING: ★★★
Light—Variation of Helen or Eleanor; Nelly Furtado, singer; Nelly, musician
> People think of Nelly as pretty, cool, sexy, creative, funny
> People who like the name Nelly also like Natalie, Paige, Natasha, Sabrina, Emily, Sophia, Mia, Nadia, Nicole, Olivia

Nelson *(English)* ♂ RATING: ★★
Son of Neil or Nell—Originally a surname; Nelson Riddle, conductor/arranger
> People think of Nelson as intelligent, handsome, funny, caring, cool
> People who like the name Nelson also like Nicholas, Noah, Jackson, Lucas, Nathan, Oliver, Jacob, Owen, Ethan, Samuel

Nemesio *(Spanish)* ♂ RATING: ★★★
Vengeance
> People think of Nemesio as powerful, ethnic, aggressive, sneaky, popular
> People who like the name Nemesio also like Nero, Navarro, Javier, Nathaniel, Neron, Nicholas, Nazario, Noah, Nico, Nigel

Nen *(Egyptian)* ♂ RATING: ★☆
Ancient waters
> People think of Nen as ethnic, exotic, handsome, cool, powerful
> People who like the name Nen also like Nero, Adish, Nalin, Nate, Nayef, Ryu, Naif, Nitesh, Niran, Raanan

Nenet *(Egyptian)* ♀ RATING: ★★★
Goddess of the deep
> People think of Nenet as exotic, powerful, pretty, elegant, intelligent
> People who like the name Nenet also like Isis, Kali, Layla, Devi, Nadia, Aurora, Freya, Chandra, Aradia, Maeve

Neo *(American)* ♀ ♂ RATING: ★★☆
New—Character in *The Matrix*
> People think of Neo as cool, intelligent, handsome, powerful, creative
> People who like the name Neo also like Dylan, Jaden, Logan, Skye, Riley, Reese, Phoenix, Jordan, Nova, Tyler

Neola *(American)* ♀ RATING: ★★★
New—Created in the eighteenth century
> People think of Neola as creative, exotic, intelligent, pretty, artsy
> People who like the name Neola also like Neona, Nola, Olive, Nara, Persephone, Melody, Ophelia, Kiara, Chloe, Nysa

Neona *(American)* ♀ RATING: ★★★★
New
> People think of Neona as pretty, sexy, exotic, trustworthy, caring
> People who like the name Neona also like Evangeline, Sakura, Sofia, Luna, Nadia, Selena, Selene, Naiya, Naomi, Neola

Neorah *(Hebrew)* ♀ RATING: ★★
Light
> People think of Neorah as exotic, quiet, religious, trustworthy, elegant
> People who like the name Neorah also like Liana, Nuria, Samara, Naava, Nasya, Nora, Dara, Sephora, Neona, Liora

424

Nergui *(Mongolian)* ♀♂　　RATING: ★★☆
No name—Used when parents couldn't decide on a name
> People think of Nergui as loser, pretty, lazy, poor, weird
> People who like the name Nergui also like Blaise, Keaton, Bliss, Dyre, Elisha, Kieran, Keesa, Rune, Arden, Azra

Nerice *(American)* ♀　　RATING: ★★★
Nymph—Vairation of Nerissa
> People think of Nerice as intelligent, exotic, ethnic, winner, trustworthy
> People who like the name Nerice also like Krisalyn, Nerissa, Giselle, Lorelei, Cordelia, Telyn, Felicity, Nixie, Fiona, Calista

Nerina *(Greek)* ♀　　RATING: ★★
Sea nymph
> People think of Nerina as exotic, creative, intelligent, artsy, caring
> People who like the name Nerina also like Nerissa, Naiya, Nixie, Lana, Nia, Faye, Mara, Maren, Sabrina, Kara

Nerissa *(Greek)* ♀　　RATING: ★★☆
Nymph
> People think of Nerissa as pretty, intelligent, caring, funny, creative
> People who like the name Nerissa also like Marissa, Olivia, Larissa, Gabrielle, Tessa, Clarissa, Sabrina, Aurora, Bianca, Isabella

Nerita *(Spanish)* ♀　　RATING: ★★☆
Sea snail
> People think of Nerita as pretty, sexy, quiet, nerdy, exotic
> People who like the name Nerita also like Nerissa, Nara, Blanca, Kaya, Latanya, Nerina, Francesca, Sophie, Dara, Rosamund

Nero *(Latin)* ♂　　RATING: ★★
Powerful—Ancient Roman emperor
> People think of Nero as powerful, handsome, leader, intelligent, aggressive
> People who like the name Nero also like Noah, Nico, Oliver, Gavin, Kaden, Nicholas, Xavier, Liam, Drake, Kael

Neron *(Spanish)* ♂　　RATING: ★★☆
Sea
> People think of Neron as sexy, aggressive, caring, energetic, funny
> People who like the name Neron also like Soren, Jayden, Niran, Damien, Gabriel, Aran, Owen, Xander, Noah, Jovan

Nerys *(Welsh)* ♀　　RATING: ★★★☆
Lady
> People think of Nerys as intelligent, pretty, trustworthy, caring, exotic
> People who like the name Nerys also like Isolde, Aeryn, Rhiannon, Bronwyn, Gwyneth, Arwen, Hazel, Gwendolyn, Kellyn, Carys

Nessa *(Latin)* ♀　　RATING: ★★☆
Lamb—Short for Agnes or Vanessa
> People think of Nessa as pretty, funny, creative, cool, caring
> People who like the name Nessa also like Olivia, Faith, Vanessa, Grace, Nadia, Sadie, Tessa, Paige, Victoria, Serena

Nestor *(Greek)* ♂　　RATING: ★★★☆
Traveller
> People think of Nestor as cool, intelligent, funny, handsome, energetic
> People who like the name Nestor also like Nathan, Jacob, Lucas, Caleb, Jared, Xavier, Brandon, Aaron, Oscar, Blade

Neva *(Spanish)* ♀　　RATING: ★★★★
Snow—Also a river in Russia
> People think of Neva as intelligent, caring, pretty, creative, elegant
> People who like the name Neva also like Eva, Ava, Isabella, Maya, Grace, Isabelle, Layla, Nadia, Nora, Ella

Nevada *(Spanish)* ♀♂　　RATING: ★★★★☆
Covered in snow—U.S. state
> People think of Nevada as intelligent, cool, creative, sexy, pretty
> People who like the name Nevada also like Dakota, Parker, Logan, Madison, Taylor, Jade, Mackenzie, Phoenix, Reese, Hayden

Nevaeh *(American)* ♀　　RATING: ★★☆
Heaven—From heaven spelled backward; also spelled Neveah or Neviah
> People think of Nevaeh as pretty, intelligent, creative, caring, popular
> People who like the name Nevaeh also like Ava, Aaliyah, Jadyn, Savannah, Isabella, Hailey, Paige, Faith, Grace, Olivia

Nevan *(Celtic/Gaelic)* ♂　　RATING: ★★☆
Little saint
> People think of Nevan as caring, creative, handsome, funny, quiet
> People who like the name Nevan also like Tristan, Aiden, Noah, Owen, Liam, Nathan, Keagan, Ian, Kaden, Aden

Neve *(Latin)* ♀　　RATING: ★★★★
Snowy—Neve Campbell, actress
> People think of Neve as pretty, creative, intelligent, caring, funny
> People who like the name Neve also like Grace, Ava, Ella, Emma, Eva, Mia, Olivia, Paige, Hannah, Erin

Neville *(French)* ♂　　RATING: ★★★
New town—Aaron Neville, singer
> People think of Neville as caring, handsome, intelligent, trustworthy, funny
> People who like the name Neville also like Noah, Nicholas, William, Nigel, Oliver, Isaac, Owen, Wyatt, Ethan, Jack

Nevin *(Celtic/Gaelic)* ♀♂   RATING: ★★
Saint
> People think of Nevin as cool, funny, caring, intelligent, popular
> People who like the name Nevin also like Caden, Parker, Hayden, Nolan, Logan, Ryan, Jaden, Landen, Devin, Reese

Nevina *(Celtic/Gaelic)* ♀   RATING: ★★★☆
Saint
> People think of Nevina as pretty, sexy, caring, quiet, exotic
> People who like the name Nevina also like Davina, Fiona, Kera, Nelia, Keaira, Maisie, Danelea, Keira, Kaelyn, Hazel

Nevio *(Italian)* ♂   RATING: ★★★
Mole
> People think of Nevio as winner, weird, creative, intelligent, popular
> People who like the name Nevio also like Napoleon, Noah, Nico, Nelson, Niles, Nardo, Niran, Nazario, Nero, Navarro

Newlyn *(Celtic/Gaelic)* ♀♂   RATING: ★★☆
From the church of St. Newelina
> People think of Newlyn as quiet, sporty, poor, unpopular, loser
> People who like the name Newlyn also like Nolan, Logan, Rowan, Reagan, Ryan, Teagan, Parker, Keegan, Reilly, Rory

Newman *(English)* ♂   RATING: ★★★
The new man—Paul Newman, actor
> People think of Newman as big, sexy, uptight, young, old
> People who like the name Newman also like Nathan, Nicholas, Lance, Justin, Weston, Holden, Dalton, Reece, Jackson, Tyson

Newton *(English)* ♂   RATING: ★★★☆
From the new town—Sir Isaac Newton, physicist; Fig Newtons, brand snack food
> People think of Newton as nerdy, popular, loser, leader, creative
> People who like the name Newton also like Nicholas, Jackson, Nelson, Nathan, Dalton, Oliver, Reece, Dawson, Miles, Tristan

Nguyet *(Vietnamese)* ♀   RATING: ★★☆
Moon
> People think of Nguyet as pretty, intelligent, caring, ethnic, young
> People who like the name Nguyet also like Isis, Mahina, Neona, Latona, Charisma, Evangeline, Margot, Kira, Justise, Lark

Nhi *(Vietnamese)* ♀   RATING: ★★★★
Little one
> People think of Nhi as creative, quiet, pretty, young, cool
> People who like the name Nhi also like Sen, Tuyen, Kira, Hoshiko, Isis, Keiko, Sagira, Kaida, Ayame, Keaira

Nhu *(Vietnamese)* ♀   RATING: ★★☆
Alike
> People think of Nhu as quiet, pretty, funny, creative, trustworthy
> People who like the name Nhu also like Phoebe, Natalie, Nhi, Nichole, Kat, Layla, Sophie, Erica, Lea, Liza

Nhung *(Vietnamese)* ♀   RATING: ★★★
Velvet
> People think of Nhung as intelligent, poor, leader, creative, sporty
> People who like the name Nhung also like Hitomi, Gin, Beyoncé, Stasia, Tatiana, Kiara, Amber, Huyen, Nixie, Ayame

Nia *(Welsh)* ♀   RATING: ★★☆
Bright—Variation of Niamh; also short for names ending in Nia; also Swahili meaning purpose; Nia Long, actress; Nia Peeples, actress; Nia Vardalos, writer/actress
> People think of Nia as pretty, intelligent, funny, creative, young
> People who like the name Nia also like Mia, Nadia, Ava, Olivia, Mya, Gabrielle, Keira, Chloe, Tia, Ella

Niabi *(Native American)* ♀♂   RATING: ★★★
Fawn—Osage origin
> People think of Niabi as creative, cool, intelligent, trustworthy, pretty
> People who like the name Niabi also like Nida, Mika, Nalani, Taregan, Misae, Talasi, Helki, Makya, Kione, Namir

Niall *(Celtic/Gaelic)* ♀♂   RATING: ★★
Champion
> People think of Niall as handsome, intelligent, funny, sexy, trustworthy
> People who like the name Niall also like Aidan, Cameron, Rory, Connor, Dylan, Ryan, Kyle, Morgan, Sean, Quinn

Niamh *(Celtic/Gaelic)* ♀   RATING: ★★★★
Bright—Pronounced *NEE-ov* and *NEEV*
> People think of Niamh as pretty, funny, caring, intelligent, creative
> People who like the name Niamh also like Ava, Neve, Aoife, Erin, Grace, Olivia, Eva, Mia, Naomi, Nia

Nibal *(Arabic)* ♀♂   RATING: ★☆
Arrows
> People think of Nibal as religious, pretty, exotic, ethnic, quiet
> People who like the name Nibal also like Nayan, Janus, Nolan, Naveen, Jordan, Winter, Lyre, Jameson, Niel, Ren

Nibaw *(Native American)* ♂   RATING: ★★
Standing tall—Ojibwa origin
> People think of Nibaw as exotic, quiet, weird, popular, powerful
> People who like the name Nibaw also like Nantai, Neka, Nodin, Mingan, Ahanu, Yaholo, Mikasi, Yuma, Kele, Nevio

Niccele *(American)* ♀   RATING: ★★☆
Victory of the people—Variation of Nicole
   People think of Niccele as elegant, poor, trendy, pretty, trustworthy
   People who like the name Niccele also like Desdemona, Gizela, Graziella, Deliz, Delfina, Sherise, Magali, Dalila, Jolie, Gianna

Nichelle *(American)* ♀   RATING: ★★★★
Combination of Nicole and Michelle—Nichelle Nichols, actress
   People think of Nichelle as pretty, caring, funny, creative, trustworthy
   People who like the name Nichelle also like Paige, Naomi, Nicolette, Gabrielle, Natalie, Olivia, Nadia, Hannah, Nichole, Chloe

Nichola *(English)* ♂   RATING: ★★★☆
Victory of the people
   People think of Nichola as pretty, funny, caring, trustworthy, popular
   People who like the name Nichola also like Nicholas, Nicholai, Tristan, Lucas, Gabriel, Jack, Matthew, Nicolas, Ethan, Nathan

Nicholai *(Slavic)* ♂   RATING: ★★★★
Victory of the people
   People think of Nicholai as handsome, intelligent, powerful, cool, leader
   People who like the name Nicholai also like Nicholas, Nathaniel, Noah, Tristan, Nathan, Sebastian, Ethan, Aiden, Gabriel, Lucas

Nicholas *(Greek)* ♂   RATING: ★★★☆
Victory of the people—Russian czar
   People think of Nicholas as handsome, funny, intelligent, caring, cool
   People who like the name Nicholas also like Nathan, Ethan, Matthew, Jacob, Zachary, Noah, Alexander, Benjamin, Joshua, Lucas

Nichole *(American)* ♀   RATING: ★★★
Victory of the people
   People think of Nichole as pretty, funny, caring, creative, intelligent
   People who like the name Nichole also like Natalie, Nicole, Samantha, Hannah, Paige, Hailey, Olivia, Emily, Isabella, Abigail

Nick *(Greek)* ♂   RATING: ★★★☆
Victory of the people—Short for Nicholas; Nick Nolte, actor
   People think of Nick as funny, handsome, cool, popular, sexy
   People who like the name Nick also like Nathan, Nicholas, Jake, Jacob, Jack, Ethan, Matthew, Aaron, Justin, Luke

Nickan *(American)* ♀   RATING: ★★☆
Victory—Variation of Nicholas
   People think of Nickan as weird, slow, artsy, poor, old-fashioned

   People who like the name Nickan also like Skyla, Kiley, Chloe, Jillian, Nyla, Rhian, Nerissa, Layla, Nora, Halle

Nicki *(English)* ♀   RATING: ★★★
Victory of the people—Short for Nicole
   People think of Nicki as pretty, funny, caring, creative, cool
   People who like the name Nicki also like Nikki, Natalie, Paige, Nicole, Faith, Hailey, Nichole, Amber, Lauren, Olivia

Nicky *(English)* ♀ ♂   RATING: ★★★☆
Victory of the people—Short for Nicholas or Nicole
   People think of Nicky as funny, popular, caring, pretty, sexy
   People who like the name Nicky also like Taylor, Jamie, Riley, Jade, James, Logan, Brooklyn, Brooke, Kimberly, Madison

Nico *(Italian)* ♂   RATING: ★★★★
Short for Nicholas or Nicodemus
   People think of Nico as cool, handsome, funny, popular, intelligent
   People who like the name Nico also like Noah, Nicholas, Ethan, Aiden, Gabriel, Caleb, Owen, Kaden, Leo, Sebastian

Nicodemus *(Greek)* ♂   RATING: ★★
Victory of the people—Also a Biblical figure
   People think of Nicodemus as powerful, intelligent, leader, trustworthy, caring
   People who like the name Nicodemus also like Nathaniel, Nicholas, Noah, Elijah, Gabriel, Gage, Alexander, Maximus, Caleb, Benjamin

Nicola *(English)* ♀ ♂   RATING: ★★★
Victory of the people
   People think of Nicola as pretty, funny, caring, intelligent, creative
   People who like the name Nicola also like Hayden, Taylor, Riley, Mackenzie, Madison, Ryan, Parker, Morgan, James, Logan

Nicolao *(Portuguese)* ♂   RATING: ★★☆
Victory of the people
   People think of Nicolao as unpopular, uptight, handsome, criminal, leader
   People who like the name Nicolao also like Emory, Ivan, Xander, Nicolas, Landis, Maddox, Keagan, Jadon, Jamar, Scott

Nicolas *(English)* ♂   RATING: ★★★★
Victory of the people—Variation of Nicholas; Nicolas Cage, actor
   People think of Nicolas as funny, handsome, intelligent, cool, caring
   People who like the name Nicolas also like Nicholas, Ethan, Jacob, Nathan, Zachary, Gabriel, Noah, Nathaniel, Benjamin, Alexander

Nicole *(French)* ♀   RATING: ★★★
Victory of the people—Also spelled Nicolle, Nickole, or Nichole; Nicole Kidman, actress
  People think of Nicole as pretty, funny, caring, intelligent, creative
  People who like the name Nicole also like Natalie, Samantha, Paige, Olivia, Emily, Emma, Hannah, Lauren, Hailey, Faith

Nicolette *(French)* ♀   RATING: ★★☆
Victory of the people—Variation of Nicole; also spelled Nicollette; Nicolette Sheridan, actress
  People think of Nicolette as pretty, intelligent, funny, popular, caring
  People who like the name Nicolette also like Isabella, Paige, Olivia, Chloe, Hailey, Isabelle, Faith, Victoria, Gabrielle, Hannah

Nida *(Native American)* ♀ ♂   RATING: ★★★★
Giant—Omaha origin
  People think of Nida as pretty, intelligent, caring, trustworthy, funny
  People who like the name Nida also like Mika, Nox, Niabi, Dakota, Jada, Connor, Morgan, Robin, Misae, Nori

Niel *(Scandinavian)* ♀ ♂   RATING: ★★★☆
Champion—Variation of Neil
  People think of Niel as intelligent, handsome, creative, cool, funny
  People who like the name Niel also like Ryan, Mason, Kyle, Morgan, Hayden, Jaden, Reese, Logan, Noel, Jude

Niesha *(American)* ♀   RATING: ★★
Pure
  People think of Niesha as pretty, trustworthy, cool, popular, funny
  People who like the name Niesha also like Aaliyah, Nadia, Hailey, Faith, Nisha, Natasha, Nerissa, Nailah, Nadine, Phoebe

Nieve *(Spanish)* ♀   RATING: ★★
Snow, snowy
  People think of Nieve as pretty, elegant, creative, quiet, intelligent
  People who like the name Nieve also like Chloe, Paige, Ella, Ava, Grace, Eva, Phoebe, Olivia, Gabrielle, Neve

Nigel *(English)* ♂   RATING: ★★
Champion—Variation of Neil; Nigel Hawthorne, actor; Nigel Lythgoe, TV producer
  People think of Nigel as intelligent, handsome, funny, caring, sexy
  People who like the name Nigel also like Nathaniel, Noah, Nicholas, Ethan, Caleb, Nathan, Gabriel, Simon, Seth, Aiden

Night *(American)* ♀ ♂   RATING: ★★★☆
Evening—M. Night Shyamalan, filmmaker
  People think of Night as powerful, exotic, intelligent, creative, wild
  People who like the name Night also like Skye, Hayden, Piper, Sage, Phoenix, Rain, Raine, Haven, Shadow, Parker

Nijole *(Slavic)* ♀   RATING: ★★★
Victory of the people—Variation of Nicole
  People think of Nijole as weird, lazy, intelligent, powerful, poor
  People who like the name Nijole also like Nicole, Luna, Melody, Nola, Celeste, Neena, Demeter, Camilla, Prema, Gabrielle

Nika *(Slavic)* ♀   RATING: ★★☆
Bringing victory—Short for Veronika
  People think of Nika as pretty, intelligent, creative, funny, energetic
  People who like the name Nika also like Nadia, Scarlett, Ava, Nora, Olivia, Sofia, Eva, Mia, Nina, Grace

Nike *(Greek)* ♀ ♂   RATING: ★★★☆
Victorious—In Greek mythology, the goddess of victory; also a brand of athletic wear
  People think of Nike as winner, powerful, intelligent, cool, energetic
  People who like the name Nike also like Logan, Madison, Riley, Jade, Cameron, Morgan, Ivory, Paley, Shane, Willow

Nikita *(Slavic)* ♀ ♂   RATING: ★★★★
Victory of the people—Short for Nikolai
  People think of Nikita as pretty, funny, intelligent, caring, creative
  People who like the name Nikita also like Madison, Jade, Dakota, Hayden, Riley, Jordan, Brooke, Jaden, Alexis, Bailey

Nikki *(American)* ♀   RATING: ★★
Victory of the people—Short for Nicole
  People think of Nikki as funny, pretty, cool, caring, creative
  People who like the name Nikki also like Nicole, Paige, Natalie, Samantha, Faith, Chloe, Nicki, Victoria, Vanessa, Leah

Nikkol *(American)* ♀   RATING: ★★★☆
Victory of the people—Variation of Nicole
  People think of Nikkol as creative, artsy, pretty, caring, loser
  People who like the name Nikkol also like Hailey, Olivia, Mia, Mya, Victoria, Kaelyn, Makaila, Nicole, Makayla, Violet

Nikkos *(Greek)* ♂   RATING: ★★
Victory of the people—Short for Nikolas
  People think of Nikkos as intelligent, funny, handsome, caring, trustworthy
  People who like the name Nikkos also like Nicholas, Tristan, Christos, Maximus, Noah, Ian, Nathan, Nicholai, Kaden, Jason

Nile *(English)* ♀   RATING: ★★★☆
From the River Nile
  People think of Nile as intelligent, popular, creative, funny, young
  People who like the name Nile also like Chloe, Scarlett, Olivia, Natalie, Paige, Mia, Nadia, Sophie, Fiona, Isis

428

Niles *(English)* ♂　　RATING: ★★
Son of Neil
> People think of Niles as intelligent, nerdy, funny, wealthy, caring
> People who like the name Niles also like Noah, Owen, Miles, Ian, Nicholas, Jacob, Braden, Kaden, Holden, Reece

Nili *(Hebrew)* ♀♂　　RATING: ★★
The everlasting of Israel will not lie—From the Hebrew words "netzach yisrael lo yishaker"
> People think of Nili as pretty, creative, popular, caring, exotic
> People who like the name Nili also like Lindsay, Nori, London, Nikita, Noel, Reagan, Sawyer, Nolan, Nova, Lavender

Nilima *(Sanskrit/East Indian)* ♀　　RATING: ★★★
Blueness
> People think of Nilima as pretty, sexy, religious, funny, creative
> People who like the name Nilima also like Nayana, Nisha, Kimaya, Eshana, Navya, Nola, Ninarika, Laksha, Niyati, Pallavi

Niloufer *(Persian)* ♀　　RATING: ★★☆
Water lily
> People think of Niloufer as weird, exotic, loser, poor, ethnic
> People who like the name Niloufer also like Berdine, Nydia, Janette, Phyllis, Posy, Simone, Isis, Senna, Larissa, Hosanna

Nils *(Scandinavian)* ♂　　RATING: ★★★
Victory of the people—Variation of Nicholas
> People think of Nils as intelligent, handsome, funny, weird, creative
> People who like the name Nils also like Caleb, Asher, Nelson, Olin, Soren, Thatcher, Giles, Ian, Noah, Cole

Nimeesha *(African)* ♀　　RATING: ★★★★
Princess
> People think of Nimeesha as pretty, intelligent, funny, creative, energetic
> People who like the name Nimeesha also like Jahzara, Myeisha, Ayanna, Niesha, Nerissa, Nicole, Jamila, Kenisha, Malaika, Nala

Nimrod *(Hebrew)* ♂　　RATING: ★★★
Rebellion—In the Bible, a Mesopotamian king
> People think of Nimrod as loser, nerdy, weird, unpopular, slow
> People who like the name Nimrod also like Nathan, Nicholas, Conner, Noah, Aiden, Andrew, Reece, Nolen, Jacob, Jared

Nina *(Spanish)* ♀　　RATING: ★★★☆
Little girl
> People think of Nina as pretty, funny, intelligent, caring, creative
> People who like the name Nina also like Olivia, Mia, Ava, Paige, Eva, Emma, Ella, Naomi, Nadia, Hannah

Ninarika *(Sanskrit/East Indian)* ♀　　RATING: ★★★★
Misty
> People think of Ninarika as ethnic, pretty, exotic, wild, sexy
> People who like the name Ninarika also like Nayana, Eshana, Parvani, Nisha, Samiya, Ishana, Navya, Denali, Niyati, Nilima

Ninon *(French)* ♀　　RATING: ★☆
Grace—Variation of Anne
> People think of Ninon as exotic, funny, popular, elegant, pretty
> People who like the name Ninon also like Miette, Veronique, Lisette, Melisande, Leona, Nadine, Camille, Étoile, Adeline, Linette

Nira *(Hebrew)* ♀　　RATING: ★★☆
Loom
> People think of Nira as pretty, sexy, intelligent, funny, exotic
> People who like the name Nira also like Nadia, Nola, Lana, Naomi, Nyla, Nara, Nora, Paige, Phoebe, Penelope

Niran *(Hebrew)* ♂　　RATING: ★★★
Ploughed field
> People think of Niran as exotic, leader, winner, caring, weird
> People who like the name Niran also like Nathan, Lucian, Sebastian, Kaden, Rohan, Seth, Keiran, Jayden, Caleb, Xander

Nirav *(Sanskrit/East Indian)* ♂　　RATING: ★☆
Quiet
> People think of Nirav as quiet, intelligent, caring, trustworthy, creative
> People who like the name Nirav also like Arnav, Arav, Rushil, Niran, Rohak, Ashwin, Nitesh, Rohan, Suvan, Manas

Nisha *(Sanskrit/East Indian)* ♀　　RATING: ★★★★
Night—Feminine form of Nishi
> People think of Nisha as pretty, intelligent, funny, caring, sexy
> People who like the name Nisha also like Nadia, Tatiana, Faith, Niesha, Layla, Nayana, Chandra, Nerissa, Hailey, Mia

Nishan *(Sanskrit/East Indian)* ♂　　RATING: ★★★
Flag, sign
> People think of Nishan as intelligent, funny, handsome, popular, caring
> People who like the name Nishan also like Nathan, Nevan, Nathaniel, Nicholas, Niran, Nick, Nehemiah, Nitish, Neal, Noah

Nishi *(Sanskrit/East Indian)* ♀　　RATING: ★★
Night
> People think of Nishi as young, pretty, energetic, quiet, creative
> People who like the name Nishi also like Nariko, Kaori, Miyoko, Nozomi, Kohana, Inari, Kagami, Kaida, Keiko, Miyo

Nita *(Spanish)* ♀ RATING: ★★★★
Gift of God—Short for Juanita or Anita; also Indian meaning guided or led
> People think of Nita as caring, intelligent, pretty, funny, trustworthy
> People who like the name Nita also like Nina, Cara, Nadia, Grace, Olivia, Faith, Emma, Mia, Nora, Isabella

Nitara *(Sanskrit/East Indian)* ♀ RATING: ★★★
Having deep roots
> People think of Nitara as exotic, creative, leader, ethnic, loser
> People who like the name Nitara also like Nisha, Amara, Nayana, Natalia, Sitara, Fiona, Naiya, Iliana, Ophelia, Amaya

Nitesh *(Sanskrit/East Indian)* ♂ RATING: ★★★☆
Follower of the correct way
> People think of Nitesh as intelligent, handsome, cool, trustworthy, caring
> People who like the name Nitesh also like Nitish, Niran, Ashwin, Naresh, Nirav, Amish, Atish, Savir, Nalin, Kuval

Nitish *(Sanskrit/East Indian)* ♂ RATING: ★★★
Follower of the correct way—Lord Krishna
> People think of Nitish as intelligent, trustworthy, creative, caring, popular
> People who like the name Nitish also like Nitesh, Ashwin, Nishan, Adit, Adarsh, Amrit, Naresh, Nirav, Ajay, Amish

Nitsa *(Greek)* ♀ RATING: ★★★
Light—Short for Eleni or Elena
> People think of Nitsa as caring, trustworthy, intelligent, pretty, energetic
> People who like the name Nitsa also like Nora, Hypatia, Iola, Lexi, Miranda, Oriana, Tessa, Mariana, Dasha, Elani

Nituna *(Native American)* ♀ RATING: ★★★
My daughter
> People think of Nituna as pretty, girl next door, quiet, creative, young
> People who like the name Nituna also like Neena, Nasnan, Kaliska, Sora, Hateya, Kachina, Kiona, Ayasha, Kaya, Olathe

Nitya *(Sanskrit/East Indian)* ♀ RATING: ★★★
Eternal
> People think of Nitya as energetic, caring, cool, intelligent, trustworthy
> People who like the name Nitya also like Navya, Nisha, Niyati, Samiya, Kamana, Neema, Nayana, Nanda, Saniya, Kalinda

Nitza *(Hebrew)* ♀ RATING: ★★★
Bud from a flower
> People think of Nitza as intelligent, pretty, trustworthy, creative, cool
> People who like the name Nitza also like Nika, Nysa, Nizana, Katrina, Melanie, Nikki, Layla, Nara, Thora, Nola

Nixie *(German)* ♀ RATING: ★★★★
Water sprite
> People think of Nixie as pretty, energetic, exotic, creative, artsy
> People who like the name Nixie also like Nyx, Aurora, Ivy, Layla, Paige, Iris, Scarlett, Lexi, Lorelei, Nerissa

Nixon *(English)* ♂ RATING: ★★★
Son of Nicholas—Richard M. Nixon, U.S. president
> People think of Nixon as powerful, intelligent, handsome, leader, caring
> People who like the name Nixon also like Lincoln, Maddox, Tyson, Jonah, Zander, Dustin, Noah, Emerson, Ethan, Calvin

Niyati *(Sanskrit/East Indian)* ♀ RATING: ★★★
Fate
> People think of Niyati as intelligent, energetic, pretty, elegant, exotic
> People who like the name Niyati also like Nisha, Mahina, Avani, Nayana, Shyla, Parvani, Sitara, Kalinda, Samiya, Chandra

Nizana *(Hebrew)* ♀ RATING: ★★
Flower bud
> People think of Nizana as exotic, pretty, funny, creative, quiet
> People who like the name Nizana also like Nasya, Natasha, Novia, Nadia, Viola, Samara, Magnolia, Nysa, Giselle, Layla

Noah *(Hebrew)* ♂ RATING: ★★★☆
Rest, peace—In the Bible, known for gathering animals and creating an ark for refuge from the big flood; Noah Wylie, actor
> People think of Noah as handsome, caring, intelligent, funny, trustworthy
> People who like the name Noah also like Ethan, Caleb, Elijah, Jacob, Aiden, Owen, Nathan, Gabriel, Isaac, Nicholas

Noam *(Hebrew)* ♂ RATING: ★★
Pleasantness—Noam Chomsky, author/activist
> People think of Noam as intelligent, caring, creative, artsy, religious
> People who like the name Noam also like Noah, Liam, Elijah, Jonah, Micah, Benjamin, Gabriel, Ethan, Caleb, Nathan

Nodin *(Native American)* ♂ RATING: ★★★
Windy day
> People think of Nodin as pretty, loser, powerful, wild, nerdy
> People who like the name Nodin also like Noah, Neka, Nantai, Nolen, Nalin, Nye, Chayton, Nevan, Nathan, Nelson

Noe *(French)* ♀ ♂ RATING: ★★★☆
Rest, peace—Variation of Noah; pronounced *NO-eh*
> People think of Noe as intelligent, caring, cool, artsy, handsome

People who like the name Noe also like Noel, Nolan, Rain, Logan, Piper, Jaden, Reagan, Teagan, Jordan, Remy

Noel *(French)* ♀♂   RATING: ★★☆
Born on Christmas day—Noel Coward, playwright
> People think of Noel as caring, intelligent, pretty, creative, funny
> People who like the name Noel also like Madison, Riley, Hayden, Logan, Parker, Bailey, Taylor, Noelle, Morgan, Ryan

Noelani *(Hawaiian)* ♀   RATING: ★★
Heavenly mist; dew
> People think of Noelani as pretty, creative, caring, funny, intelligent
> People who like the name Noelani also like Leilani, Kailani, Ailani, Nohealani, Malia, Isabella, Olivia, Nalanie, Celeste, Gabrielle

Noelle *(French)* ♀♂   RATING: ★★★★☆
Born on Christmas day
> People think of Noelle as pretty, creative, intelligent, caring, funny
> People who like the name Noelle also like Madison, Hayden, Riley, Parker, Ryan, Addison, Bailey, Mackenzie, Avery, Caden

Nohealani *(Hawaiian)* ♀   RATING: ★★★★☆
Beauty from heaven
> People think of Nohealani as pretty, exotic, caring, intelligent, creative
> People who like the name Nohealani also like Noelani, Kailani, Leilani, Nalanie, Malia, Ailani, Miliani, Nevaeh, Nadia, Isabella

Nola *(Celtic/Gaelic)* ♀   RATING: ★★★★
Fair shoulder—Short for Finola
> People think of Nola as pretty, intelligent, creative, caring, elegant
> People who like the name Nola also like Ava, Olivia, Nora, Isabella, Grace, Ella, Chloe, Sophia, Natalie, Emma

Nolan *(Celtic/Gaelic)* ♀♂   RATING: ★★★
Descendent of the famous one—Nolan Ryan, baseball player
> People think of Nolan as intelligent, handsome, funny, caring, popular
> People who like the name Nolan also like Logan, Parker, Hayden, Riley, Caden, Evan, Mason, Addison, Connor, Avery

Noland *(Celtic/Gaelic)* ♀♂   RATING: ★★☆
Descendent of the famous one
> People think of Noland as intelligent, religious, creative, powerful, old
> People who like the name Noland also like Nolan, Logan, Parker, Payton, Riley, Hayden, Reagan, Tyler, Connor, Teagan

Nolcha *(Native American)* ♀   RATING: ★★☆
Sun
> People think of Nolcha as powerful, weird, old-fashioned, nerdy, old
> People who like the name Nolcha also like Istas, Kaya, Cocheta, Kimama, Miakoda, Nascha, Natane, Sora, Neena, Nasnan

Nolen *(Celtic/Gaelic)* ♂   RATING: ★★★★
Descendent of the famous one
> People think of Nolen as caring, cool, boy next door, weird, leader
> People who like the name Nolen also like Aiden, Owen, Noah, Cole, Landon, Gavin, Liam, Tristan, Ian, Nathan

Noleta *(American)* ♀   RATING: ★★★
Fair shoulder—Variation of Nola
> People think of Noleta as trendy, religious, pretty, trustworthy, funny
> People who like the name Noleta also like Marcella, Perdita, Lucinda, Felicia, Lilianna, Marlena, Cordelia, Lucretia, Cecilia, Lavinia

Noma *(Arabic)* ♀   RATING: ★★★
Resembling someone
> People think of Noma as pretty, ethnic, quiet, exotic, loser
> People who like the name Noma also like Keola, Kiele, Noelani, Olina, Kina, Nora, Kinipela, Malia, Cordelia, Camille

Nona *(Latin)* ♀   RATING: ★★★☆
The ninth
> People think of Nona as pretty, funny, caring, intelligent, trustworthy
> People who like the name Nona also like Grace, Ava, Fiona, Sadie, Gabriella, Cordelia, Maeve, Sofia, Ella, Emily

Nonnie *(Latin)* ♀♂   RATING: ★★★
Ninth—Short for Nona
> People think of Nonnie as trustworthy, intelligent, caring, funny, pretty
> People who like the name Nonnie also like Jordan, Jacey, Rowan, Jesse, Rory, Nolan, Riley, Raven, Rafferty, Hayden

Nora *(English)* ♀   RATING: ★★☆
Honor—Short for Honora or Eleanora; Nora Roberts, author
> People think of Nora as pretty, intelligent, caring, funny, creative
> People who like the name Nora also like Ava, Olivia, Grace, Emma, Ella, Claire, Hannah, Eva, Audrey, Paige

Norah *(English)* ♀   RATING: ★★★★
Honor—Short for Honora or Eleanora; Norah Jones, singer/songwriter
> People think of Norah as pretty, intelligent, caring, elegant, creative
> People who like the name Norah also like Hannah, Olivia, Paige, Emma, Grace, Ella, Ava, Audrey, Sophia, Claire

Noralie (*American*) ♀   RATING: ★★☆
Combination of Nora and Coralie
> People think of Noralie as pretty, caring, intelligent, winner, creative
> People who like the name Noralie also like Nola, Nora, Norah, Naiya, Nala, Adrienne, Natalya, Nyla, Naomi, Belle

Norbert (*German*) ♂   RATING: ★★★
Bright north
> People think of Norbert as funny, intelligent, caring, trustworthy, creative
> People who like the name Norbert also like Nathaniel, Sebastian, Ethan, Sidney, Lars, Dominick, Thomas, William, Florian, Adrian

Noreen (*Celtic/Gaelic*) ♀   RATING: ★★
Honor—Variation of Nora
> People think of Noreen as caring, pretty, creative, funny, intelligent
> People who like the name Noreen also like Hannah, Fiona, Paige, Maureen, Lana, Nora, Norah, Natalie, Phoebe, Naomi

Nori (*Japanese*) ♀♂   RATING: ★★★
Belief
> People think of Nori as pretty, creative, funny, intelligent, caring
> People who like the name Nori also like Rin, Maemi, Sanyu, Natsu, Rory, Parker, Jade, Morgan, Kiyoshi, Asa

Norina (*English*) ♀   RATING: ★★★
Honor—Variation of Noreen
> People think of Norina as pretty, intelligent, funny, exotic, elegant
> People who like the name Norina also like Nora, Noreen, Ivy, Iris, Nadine, Nyla, Norah, Dawn, Hannah, Lilah

Norm (*American*) ♂   RATING: ★★★
Man from the north—Short for Norman; Norm MacDonald, actor/comedian
> People think of Norm as old, weird, lazy, quiet, nerdy
> People who like the name Norm also like Nate, Nick, Norman, Jared, Noah, Neil, Nicholas, Jake, Benjamin, Jack

Norma (*English*) ♀   RATING: ★☆
From the north—Norma Shearer, actress; *Norma*, opera by Bellini
> People think of Norma as pretty, caring, intelligent, funny, trustworthy
> People who like the name Norma also like Norah, Nancy, Nora, Shirley, Naomi, Nicole, Mariah, Cordelia, Natalie, Cecilia

Norman (*English*) ♂   RATING: ★★★☆
Man from the north—Originally the Scandinavians who invaded and conquered Normandy; Norman Mailer, author
> People think of Norman as funny, handsome, intelligent, trustworthy, caring
> People who like the name Norman also like Nathan, Nicholas, Justin, Ethan, Oliver, Jack, Noah, Jacob, Jason, Benjamin

Normandie (*French*) ♀♂   RATING: ★★☆
Land of the northern folk—Variation of Normandy
> People think of Normandie as artsy, caring, elegant, creative, pretty
> People who like the name Normandie also like Merrick, Coty, Sydney, Dylan, Logan, London, Ember, Addison, Mackenzie, Dior

Normandy (*French*) ♀   RATING: ★★★☆
Land of the northern folk—Also a French province
> People think of Normandy as pretty, weird, girl next door, intelligent, unpopular
> People who like the name Normandy also like Paige, Chloe, Faith, Grace, Hope, Mallory, Eva, Harmony, Eve, Emma

Norris (*English*) ♀♂   RATING: ★★★
From the north—Chuck Norris, actor
> People think of Norris as handsome, funny, intelligent, weird, trustworthy
> People who like the name Norris also like Logan, Riley, Spencer, Parker, Hayden, Nolan, Carter, Taylor, Quincy, Connor

Norton (*English*) ♂   RATING: ★★★
From the town in the north—Peter Norton, software mogul (creator of Norton AntiVirus)
> People think of Norton as nerdy, intelligent, cool, handsome, old-fashioned
> People who like the name Norton also like Jack, Jackson, Lucas, Dalton, Nelson, Nathan, Dawson, Nicholas, Ian, Marshall

Norwood (*English*) ♂   RATING: ★★☆
North woods
> People think of Norwood as handsome, intelligent, winner, funny, creative
> People who like the name Norwood also like Nicholas, Rhett, Thatcher, Niles, Landon, Everett, Weston, Brooks, Felton, Harlow

Noura (*Arabic*) ♀   RATING: ★★
Light
> People think of Noura as pretty, funny, cool, intelligent, caring
> People who like the name Noura also like Inara, Layla, Nora, Kiara, Gabrielle, Farah, Chloe, Leyna, Olivia, Samara

Nouvel (*French*) ♀♂   RATING: ★★★
New
> People think of Nouvel as pretty, popular, intelligent, sexy, exotic
> People who like the name Nouvel also like Shiloh, Caden, Remy, Jade, Rory, Ashton, Morgan, Reese, Piper, Avery

Nova (*Latin*) ♀♂   RATING: ★★☆
New
> People think of Nova as creative, intelligent, pretty, caring, powerful

People who like the name Nova also like Reese, Riley, Avery, Phoenix, Raven, Parker, Hayden, Luca, Willow, Jade

Novak (*German*) ♂   RATING: ★★★
Newcomer—Kim Novak, actress
> People think of Novak as funny, energetic, cool, sporty, exotic
> People who like the name Novak also like Deacon, Noah, Nash, Neal, Landon, Blade, Braden, Bryson, Reece, Colton

November (*American*) ♀♂   RATING: ★★★☆
Born in November—Originally meant ninth month on the ancient Roman calendar
> People think of November as pretty, creative, intelligent, weird, artsy
> People who like the name November also like October, December, Phoenix, Morgan, Jade, September, Reese, Raine, Riley, Nevada

Novia (*Spanish*) ♀   RATING: ★★
Girlfriend
> People think of Novia as popular, funny, cool, trustworthy, pretty
> People who like the name Novia also like Nadia, Opal, Destiny, Nyla, Penelope, Nala, Adriana, Nia, Ivy, Mia

Nowles (*English*) ♀♂   RATING: ★★
Dweller at the hilltop
> People think of Nowles as weird, girl next door, nerdy, loser, artsy
> People who like the name Nowles also like Jade, Parker, Noel, Nolan, Hayden, Jordan, Landen, Nova, Winter, Reese

Nox (*Latin*) ♀♂   RATING: ★★★★☆
Night
> People think of Nox as powerful, intelligent, aggressive, exotic, cool
> People who like the name Nox also like Caden, Phoenix, London, Jaden, Raven, Aidan, Logan, Jade, Jordan, Raine

Nozomi (*Japanese*) ♀   RATING: ★★★☆
Hope
> People think of Nozomi as intelligent, creative, caring, cool, elegant
> People who like the name Nozomi also like Kohana, Nariko, Emiko, Miyoko, Suki, Kaori, Ayame, Amaya, Keiko, Sakura

Nu (*Vietnamese*) ♀   RATING: ★☆
Girl
> People think of Nu as pretty, intelligent, funny, cool, quiet
> People who like the name Nu also like Vera, Normandy, Savannah, Femi, Melody, Orenda, Emma, Nola, Sari, Flower

Nuala (*Celtic/Gaelic*) ♀   RATING: ★★★★☆
Fair Shoulder—Short form of the name Fionnuala.
> People think of Nuala as pretty, intelligent, funny, popular, creative
> People who like the name Nuala also like Fiona, Maeve, Genevieve, Lana, Nia, Nola, Sabrina, Keira, Penelope, Ciara

Nubia (*English*) ♀   RATING: ★★★★
From Nubia, Africa—A region believed to have existed since 3800 BC, located in southern Egypt and northern Sudan
> People think of Nubia as pretty, intelligent, exotic, funny, caring
> People who like the name Nubia also like Isis, Leilani, Nile, Nakia, Ailani, Eva, Tahirah, Nailah, Giselle, Ciara

Nuhad (*Arabic*) ♀♂   RATING: ★☆
Brave
> People think of Nuhad as ethnic, religious, pretty, slow, funny
> People who like the name Nuhad also like Nuri, Nayan, Naolin, Neely, Nyoka, Nox, Noel, Norris, Isra, Nova

Nuncio (*Italian*) ♂   RATING: ★★★
Messenger—Variation of Anuncio
> People think of Nuncio as leader, handsome, loser, cool, lazy
> People who like the name Nuncio also like Lucian, Nyack, Niran, Navarro, Newton, Nash, Navid, Napoleon, Neal, Nicholas

Nura (*Arabic*) ♀   RATING: ★★★☆
Light
> People think of Nura as exotic, pretty, funny, trustworthy, caring
> People who like the name Nura also like Noura, Nyla, Nola, Nadia, Inara, Isis, Nia, Fiona, Nara, Neena

Nuri (*Hebrew*) ♀♂   RATING: ★★★☆
My fire—Also Arabic meaning bright and luminous
> People think of Nuri as creative, funny, energetic, caring, intelligent
> People who like the name Nuri also like Nori, Morgan, Nox, Nalani, Logan, Nida, Noelle, Nayan, Jade, Nova

Nuria (*Arabic*) ♀   RATING: ★★
Luminous, bright
> People think of Nuria as pretty, intelligent, caring, funny, elegant
> People who like the name Nuria also like Liana, Nadia, Nora, Nyla, Samara, Nia, Freya, Sophia, Enya, Eva

Nuru (*African*) ♀♂   RATING: ★★★
Light—Swahili origin
> People think of Nuru as intelligent, ethnic, religious, pretty, quiet
> People who like the name Nuru also like Nori, Nida, Nuri, Bliss, Nyoka, Jazz, Isra, Natsu, Nalo, Rune

Nusa *(Hungarian)* ♀ RATING: ★★★
Grace
> People think of Nusa as stuck-up, lazy, trustworthy, artsy, funny
> People who like the name Nusa also like Nadia, Zora, Lily, Vega, Olivia, Rowena, Zada, Enya, Ruth, Nina

Nyack *(African)* ♂ RATING: ★☆
Won't give up
> People think of Nyack as exotic, nerdy, caring, ethnic, loser
> People who like the name Nyack also like Ajani, Aiden, Neal, Raimi, Yaro, Niran, Aaron, Akio, Nero, Nitesh

Nyako *(African)* ♀♂ RATING: ★★★
Girl
> People think of Nyako as caring, energetic, exotic, intelligent, pretty
> People who like the name Nyako also like Nyoka, Kione, Liberty, Natsu, Luca, Luka, Jensen, Ember, Nuri, Nalani

Nydia *(Latin)* ♀ RATING: ★★★★
A safe place, nest
> People think of Nydia as pretty, caring, trustworthy, funny, elegant
> People who like the name Nydia also like Nadia, Olivia, Naomi, Nora, Bianca, Natasha, Giselle, Bella, Natalia, Natalie

Nye *(Welsh)* ♂ RATING: ★★★☆
Golden—Short for Aneirin; Nye Bevan, politician; Bill Nye, The Science Guy
> People think of Nye as intelligent, funny, caring, popular, weird
> People who like the name Nye also like Kaden, Noah, Liam, Cole, Leo, Isaac, Drake, Owen, Aden, Nash

Nyeki *(African)* ♀ RATING: ★★☆
Second wife
> People think of Nyeki as ethnic, quiet, creative, sneaky, trustworthy
> People who like the name Nyeki also like Nydia, Nyx, Nyla, Keshia, Nasira, Joanna, Nitara, Destiny, Catalina, Naomi

Nyla *(American)* ♀ RATING: ★★★★☆
Combination of N and Isla
> People think of Nyla as pretty, intelligent, funny, caring, energetic
> People who like the name Nyla also like Nadia, Layla, Kyla, Paige, Chloe, Ava, Nailah, Ella, Olivia, Natalie

Nyoka *(English)* ♀♂ RATING: ★★★★
Also Swahili meaning snake; character in *Nyoka the Junglegirl* by Edgar Rice Burroughs
> People think of Nyoka as exotic, sexy, intelligent, creative, leader
> People who like the name Nyoka also like Kione, Nalani, Blake, Phoenix, Ember, Lyric, Nyako, Ezra, Blaine, James

Nysa *(Greek)* ♀ RATING: ★★★★
Lame—Also spelled Nissa or Nyssa
> People think of Nysa as intelligent, cool, pretty, young, exotic
> People who like the name Nysa also like Nyla, Nadia, Mia, Ava, Zoe, Olivia, Amaya, Nala, Layla, Chloe

Nyx *(Greek)* ♀ RATING: ★★★☆
Night—In Greek mythology, the daughter of Chaos and a primordial goddess of the night
> People think of Nyx as exotic, intelligent, creative, pretty, powerful
> People who like the name Nyx also like Nixie, Ivy, Arwen, Iris, Ava, Desdemona, Aeryn, Faye, Gypsy, Fiona

─────── 🅾 ───────

Oakes *(English)* ♀♂ RATING: ★☆
Dweller by the oak tree
> People think of Oakes as intelligent, nerdy, quiet, weird, lazy
> People who like the name Oakes also like Parker, Oakley, Caden, Jaden, Bailey, Landen, Ryder, Quinn, Raine, Phoenix

Oakley *(English)* ♀♂ RATING: ★★★★
From the oak tree field—Also a surname; Annie Oakley, sharpshooter
> People think of Oakley as popular, funny, cool, handsome, intelligent
> People who like the name Oakley also like Parker, Hayden, Bailey, Riley, Logan, Caden, Madison, Addison, Mason, Ryder

Obedience *(English)* ♀♂ RATING: ★★☆
Obedience
> People think of Obedience as uptight, quiet, loser, unpopular, stuck-up
> People who like the name Obedience also like Justice, Madison, Cassidy, Shadow, Mackenzie, Blair, Paris, Sydney, Dakota, Jade

Obelia *(Greek)* ♀ RATING: ★★★
Needle
> People think of Obelia as weird, old, unpopular, quiet, big
> People who like the name Obelia also like Ophelia, Odessa, Ivy, Odette, Olivia, Adalia, Fiona, Nadia, Selena, Pandora

Oberon *(German)* ♀♂ RATING: ★★★☆
Noble bear—Variation of Auberon; king of the fairies *A Midsummer Night's Dream* by William Shakespeare
> People think of Oberon as powerful, handsome, leader, big, wild
> People who like the name Oberon also like Phoenix, Orion, Parker, Riley, Jaden, Evan, Hayden, Caden, Dylan, Zane

433

Obert (French) ♂   RATING: ★★☆
Noble bright—Variation of Aubert
> People think of Obert as lazy, big, old-fashioned, intelligent, stuck-up
> People who like the name Obert also like Quade, Edgar, Xavier, Trevor, Corbett, Monte, Newton, Korbin, Larry, Owen

Ocean (Greek) ♀♂   RATING: ★★
Sea
> People think of Ocean as creative, pretty, intelligent, young, caring
> People who like the name Ocean also like Rain, Skye, Madison, River, Willow, Jade, Phoenix, Hayden, Logan, Dakota

Oceana (Greek) ♀   RATING: ★★★★
From the sea
> People think of Oceana as pretty, creative, young, sexy, exotic
> People who like the name Oceana also like Aurora, Jasmine, Faith, Savannah, Anastasia, Paige, Iris, Chloe, Gabrielle, Hailey

Octavia (Latin) ♀   RATING: ★★★★
Eighth
> People think of Octavia as pretty, intelligent, funny, creative, leader
> People who like the name Octavia also like Olivia, Ophelia, Isabella, Paige, Aurora, Genevieve, Nadia, Odessa, Scarlett, Violet

Octavian (Latin) ♂   RATING: ★★★
Eighth—Ancient ruler of Rome, aka Augustus
> People think of Octavian as artsy, creative, elegant, wealthy, trendy
> People who like the name Octavian also like Xavier, Conrad, Cale, Brier, Duka, Max, Tristan, Deo, Brandon, Duke

Octavio (Latin) ♂   RATING: ★★
Eighth—Octavio Paz, author
> People think of Octavio as funny, handsome, popular, intelligent, cool
> People who like the name Octavio also like Xavier, Oliver, Fabian, Gabriel, Diego, Victor, Orlando, Matthew, Adrian, Oscar

Octavious (Latin) ♂   RATING: ★★★☆
Eighth
> People think of Octavious as intelligent, aggressive, powerful, cool, trustworthy
> People who like the name Octavious also like Xavier, Nicholas, Nathaniel, Octavius, Marcus, Sebastian, Patrick, Brandon, Maximus, Ian

Octavius (Greek) ♂   RATING: ★★★☆
Eighth
> People think of Octavius as handsome, powerful, intelligent, cool, leader
> People who like the name Octavius also like Xavier, Gabriel, Oliver, Darius, Jacob, Nicholas, Xander, Isaac, Nathaniel, Zachary

October (American) ♀♂   RATING: ★★★
Born in October—Originally meant eighth month in the ancient Roman calendar
> People think of October as creative, pretty, intelligent, exotic, artsy
> People who like the name October also like Rain, Bailey, Phoenix, Madison, Riley, Hayden, Reagan, Sage, Jaden, Piper

Odakota (Native American) ♂   RATING: ★★★
Friend—Sioux origin
> People think of Odakota as weird, intelligent, big, lazy, criminal
> People who like the name Odakota also like Chayton, Aiden, Kaden, Drake, Ohanzee, Jacob, Jared, Noah, Isaiah, Mingan

Oded (Hebrew) ♂   RATING: ★★★
To encourage—Oded Fehr, actor
> People think of Oded as handsome, intelligent, religious, sexy, caring
> People who like the name Oded also like Reece, Owen, Dillon, Tobias, Elias, Gabriel, Silas, Samuel, Kevin, Milton

Odeda (Hebrew) ♀   RATING: ★★☆
To encourage
> People think of Odeda as intelligent, poor, stuck-up, exotic, caring
> People who like the name Odeda also like Beth, Ebony, Abigail, Octavia, Ophelia, Serenity, Jaclyn, Olivia, Titania, Odette

Odele (German) ♀   RATING: ★★★
Wealth—Variation of Odile
> People think of Odele as intelligent, pretty, cool, wealthy, young
> People who like the name Odele also like Odette, Olivia, Stella, Phoebe, Paige, Abigail, Charlotte, Odessa, Sophie, Opal

Odelia (Hebrew) ♀   RATING: ★★★★
I will thank God—Also an English variation of Odile
> People think of Odelia as pretty, old-fashioned, ethnic, leader, intelligent
> People who like the name Odelia also like Ophelia, Olivia, Hannah, Isabella, Odessa, Abigail, Amelia, Natalie, Sabrina, Isabelle

Odell (English) ♀♂   RATING: ★★
From the woad hill
> People think of Odell as intelligent, cool, caring, funny, trustworthy
> People who like the name Odell also like Oakley, Parker, Jaden, Madison, Blaine, Jalen, Hayden, Preston, Blair, Bailey

Odessa (Greek) ♀   RATING: ★★★★
Long journey—From odyssey
> People think of Odessa as intelligent, pretty, creative, caring, exotic
> People who like the name Odessa also like Olivia, Paige, Isabella, Ophelia, Aurora, Faith, Scarlett, Penelope, Nadia, Bianca

Odetta (French) ♀　　　RATING: ★★★
Wealth
People think of Odetta as pretty, intelligent, elegant, artsy, creative
People who like the name Odetta also like Odessa, Odette, Camille, Charlotte, Olivia, Paige, Magnolia, Giselle, Adeline, Macy

Odette (French) ♀　　　RATING: ★★★
Wealth—The swan in *Swan Lake* by Tchaikovsky
People think of Odette as pretty, elegant, intelligent, caring, creative
People who like the name Odette also like Olivia, Aurora, Paige, Giselle, Charlotte, Scarlett, Nadia, Faith, Belle, Isabella

Odgerel (Mongolian) ♀　　　RATING: ★★
Starlight
People think of Odgerel as exotic, powerful, young, slow, poor
People who like the name Odgerel also like Xalvadora, Uzuri, Yepa, Parvati, Wakanda, Zenevieva, Umaymah, Qacha, Okalani, Obelia

Odin (Scandinavian) ♀ ♂　　　RATING: ★★★★
Divine creative inspiration
People think of Odin as powerful, intelligent, handsome, leader, cool
People who like the name Odin also like Logan, Jaden, Hayden, Quinn, Caden, Orion, Landen, Riley, Phoenix, Mason

Odina (Scandinavian) ♀　　　RATING: ★★★
Divine creative inspiration—Feminine form of Odin
People think of Odina as creative, artsy, sexy, powerful, intelligent
People who like the name Odina also like Fiona, Olivia, Raina, Felicia, Cleo, Gwendolyn, Mae, Vanna, Gaia, Kyra

Odysseus (Greek) ♂　　　RATING: ★★★☆
Guide, traveler
People think of Odysseus as powerful, aggressive, leader, intelligent, handsome
People who like the name Odysseus also like Alexander, Oliver, Gabriel, Sirius, Isaac, Jacob, Aiden, Lysander, Jack, Vincent

Ofira (Hebrew) ♀　　　RATING: ★★★☆
Gold
People think of Ofira as pretty, exotic, caring, leader, trustworthy
People who like the name Ofira also like Oriana, Olivia, Samara, Iris, Rae, Rea, Ophelia, Orli, Nerina, Odette

Ogden (English) ♂　　　RATING: ★★★☆
From the oak valley—Ogden Nash, poet
People think of Ogden as intelligent, weird, powerful, old-fashioned, nerdy
People who like the name Ogden also like Everett, Reece, Owen, Drake, Noah, Keagan, Weston, Oliver, Nash, Silas

Ohanzee (Native American) ♂　　　RATING: ★★★☆
Shadow—Sioux origin
People think of Ohanzee as ethnic, quiet, weird, energetic, cool
People who like the name Ohanzee also like Dyami, Chayton, Mikasi, Ezhno, Odakota, Tokala, Viho, Tavarius, Quana, Yuma

Ohio (Native American) ♀ ♂　　　RATING: ★★★
Large river—U.S. state
People think of Ohio as loser, unpopular, weird, creative, lazy
People who like the name Ohio also like Paris, Dakota, Utah, Bailey, October, London, Payton, Quincy, Ocean, Parker

Oihane (Spanish) ♀　　　RATING: ★★☆
From the forest—Basque origin
People think of Oihane as exotic, wild, quiet, poor, caring
People who like the name Oihane also like Zaila, Anastacia, Abrianna, Faylinn, Jara, Kacia, Fallon, La Cienega, Alana, Alyssa

Oistin (Celtic/Gaelic) ♂　　　RATING: ★☆
Venerable—Variation of Austin
People think of Oistin as loser, weird, nerdy, unpopular, old
People who like the name Oistin also like Rhys, Taran, Kaden, Jake, Saeran, Tobias, Dominic, Lance, Pryce, Matthew

Ojal (Sanskrit/East Indian) ♀　　　RATING: ★★★
Vision
People think of Ojal as exotic, sexy, ethnic, cool, trustworthy
People who like the name Ojal also like Opal, Nanda, Nisha, Shyla, Laksha, Manasa, Navya, Anjali, Nilima, Keira

Ojas (Sanskrit/East Indian) ♂　　　RATING: ★★☆
Strong one
People think of Ojas as big, old, old-fashioned, poor, weird
People who like the name Ojas also like Arav, Arnav, Ruhan, Ashwin, Savir, Rupin, Abhay, Devesh, Lokesh, Kanha

Okal (African) ♀ ♂　　　RATING: ★★
To cross
People think of Okal as weird, ethnic, poor, loser, nerdy
People who like the name Okal also like Rain, Parker, Sailor, Jade, Talen, Lindsey, Ocean, Storm, Tyler, Lavender

Okalani (Hawaiian) ♀　　　RATING: ★★★☆
Heaven
People think of Okalani as pretty, cool, winner, intelligent, popular
People who like the name Okalani also like Leilani, Kailani, Ulani, Noelani, Ailani, Miliani, Gabriella, Alohilani, Nohealani, Isis

436

Okapi *(African)* ♀♂   RATING: ★★★
Animal with long neck—Also a type of giraffe
> People think of Okapi as exotic, wild, ethnic, pretty, sexy
> People who like the name Okapi also like Topaz, Ashanti, Tyler, Phoenix, Cameron, Andrea, Musoke, Myles, Lavender, Jade

Oke *(Hawaiian)* ♀♂   RATING: ★☆
Deer lover—Variation of Oscar
> People think of Oke as young, caring, popular, funny, intelligent
> People who like the name Oke also like Kai, Kalani, Keanu, Nalani, Bailey, Mackenzie, Lani, Lilo, Quinn, Kaili

Oki *(Japanese)* ♀   RATING: ★★★☆
Ocean centered
> People think of Oki as pretty, creative, leader, popular, powerful
> People who like the name Oki also like Sakura, Suki, Kioko, Keiko, Kuri, Nariko, Miyoko, Kaida, Emiko, Maeko

Oklahoma *(Native American)* ♀♂   RATING: ★★☆
Red people—Choctaw origin; U.S. state
> People think of Oklahoma as weird, loser, poor, old-fashioned, cool
> People who like the name Oklahoma also like Tennessee, Minnesota, October, Montana, Nevada, Reagan, Nebraska, Texas, Illinois, Reese

Okoth *(African)* ♀♂   RATING: ★★☆
Born when it was raining—Kenyan origin
> People think of Okoth as exotic, big, intelligent, leader, weird
> People who like the name Okoth also like Moon, Lani, Nox, Xola, Kiyoshi, Kindle, Keanu, Nalani, Hunter, Jesse

Oksana *(Slavic)* ♀   RATING: ★★
Praise be to God—Oksana Baiul, Olympic figure skater
> People think of Oksana as pretty, funny, caring, intelligent, creative
> People who like the name Oksana also like Nadia, Hannah, Olivia, Natalie, Danika, Gabrielle, Faith, Grace, Natalya, Elizabeth

Oktyabrina *(Russian)* ♀   RATING: ★★★
October Revolution—Also commemorates the Revolution of 1917, celebrated in October
> People think of Oktyabrina as exotic, intelligent, trustworthy, poor, lazy
> People who like the name Oktyabrina also like Desdemona, Penelope, Bianca, Hyacinth, Ophelia, Bernadette, Persephone, Mistico, Olencia, Patience

Olaf *(Scandinavian)* ♂   RATING: ★☆
Ancestor's heir—A king and patron saint of Norway
> People think of Olaf as handsome, intelligent, criminal, old, big
> People who like the name Olaf also like Felix, Balthasar, Fox, Oliver, David, Lars, Owen, Bartholomew, Tristan, Bradley

Olathe *(Native American)* ♀   RATING: ★☆
Lovely, beautiful
> People think of Olathe as pretty, exotic, powerful, caring, old-fashioned
> People who like the name Olathe also like Kaya, Ayasha, Kwanita, Donoma, Kachina, Kiona, Nasnan, Nituna, Orenda, Olisa

Ole *(Scandinavian)* ♂   RATING: ★★★
Ancestor's heir—Variation of Olaf
> People think of Ole as old, old-fashioned, big, caring, leader
> People who like the name Ole also like Oliver, Jerome, Desmond, Wyatt, Owen, Lincoln, Oscar, Curtis, August, Brian

Oleg *(Slavic)* ♂   RATING: ★★★☆
Holy—Oleg Cassini, designer
> People think of Oleg as handsome, creative, funny, winner, powerful
> People who like the name Oleg also like Trevor, Isaac, Oliver, Xander, Justin, Jason, Jayden, Lucas, Merric, Desmond

Olencia *(American)* ♀   RATING: ★★
Combination of Olivia and Valencia
> People think of Olencia as slow, cool, elegant, artsy, exotic
> People who like the name Olencia also like Ophelia, Persephone, Penelope, Nicolette, Opal, Odessa, Paige, Olivia, Oriana, Bella

Olesia *(Polish)* ♀   RATING: ★★★★
Holy—Short for Olga
> People think of Olesia as pretty, funny, creative, cool, exotic
> People who like the name Olesia also like Olivia, Emma, Cassandra, Felicity, Ophelia, Paige, Jasmine, Gabriella, Gabrielle, Scarlett

Olga *(Slavic)* ♀   RATING: ★★★
Holy—Feminine form of Oleg; Olga Korbut, gymnast
> People think of Olga as pretty, funny, intelligent, creative, caring
> People who like the name Olga also like Olivia, Ophelia, Paige, Ingrid, Nadia, Isabella, Fiona, Hope, Grace, Bella

Oliana *(American)* ♀   RATING: ★★★☆
Combination of Olivia and Liana
> People think of Oliana as pretty, funny, leader, intelligent, popular
> People who like the name Oliana also like Olivia, Bianca, Gabriella, Lorelei, Patience, Rianna, Isabella, Larissa, Oriana, Scarlett

Olicia *(American)* ♀   RATING: ★★☆
Of noble kin—Variation of Alicia
> People think of Olicia as pretty, trustworthy, funny, cool, creative
> People who like the name Olicia also like Destiny, Iliana, Anya, Tyra, Grace, Naomi, Oliana, Olivia, Laurel, Ava

Olin *(Scandinavian)* ♂ RATING: ★★★★
Ancestor's heir—Variation of Olaf; Ken Olin, actor
People think of Olin as intelligent, caring, creative, handsome, quiet
People who like the name Olin also like Owen, Oliver, Kaden, Noah, Ian, Landon, Maddox, Xavier, Wade, Miles

Olina *(Scandinavian)* ♀ RATING: ★★★☆
Ancestor's heir—Feminine form of Olaf
People think of Olina as intelligent, pretty, leader, trustworthy, creative
People who like the name Olina also like Olivia, Malia, Kaya, Opal, Olive, Bella, Kyla, Noelani, Leilani, Olesia

Olinda *(American)* ♀ RATING: ★★★
Combination of Olivia and Yolanda
People think of Olinda as exotic, pretty, elegant, energetic, artsy
People who like the name Olinda also like Bella, Lauren, Marissa, Bianca, Laurel, Maggie, Olive, Bridget, Olivia, Felicity

Olisa *(American)* ♀ RATING: ★★
Combination of Olivia and Elisa
People think of Olisa as young, funny, intelligent, creative, cool
People who like the name Olisa also like Olivia, Grace, Isabella, Kaya, Macy, Paige, Felicity, Samara, Tehya, Soraya

Olive *(English)* ♀ RATING: ★★
Fruit of the olive tree—Olive Oyl, character on *Popeye*
People think of Olive as creative, intelligent, pretty, artsy, funny
People who like the name Olive also like Olivia, Violet, Scarlett, Ivy, Eva, Hazel, Ava, Ophelia, Grace, Emma

Oliver *(English)* ♂ RATING: ★★☆
Elf army—Oliver Platt, actor; Oliver Reed, actor; Oliver Stone, filmmaker; *Oliver Twist* by Charles Dickens
People think of Oliver as handsome, intelligent, funny, caring, cool
People who like the name Oliver also like Owen, Noah, Ethan, Jack, Benjamin, Jacob, Nicholas, Lucas, Alexander, Sebastian

Olivia *(English)* ♀ RATING: ★★☆
Elf army—Feminine form of Oliver; Olivia D'Abo, actress; Olivia de Haviland, actress
People think of Olivia as pretty, funny, intelligent, caring, creative
People who like the name Olivia also like Ava, Emma, Isabella, Grace, Hannah, Ella, Sophia, Abigail, Paige, Chloe

Ollie *(English)* ♂ RATING: ★★
Elf army—Short for Oliver
People think of Ollie as funny, energetic, handsome, caring, cool
People who like the name Ollie also like Oliver, Ethan, Owen, Jack, Luke, Jake, Noah, Max, Oscar, Nathan

Olson *(Scandinavian)* ♂ RATING: ★★☆
Son of Olaf—Also spelled Olsen; Mary-Kate and Ashley Olsen, twin actresses
People think of Olson as popular, boy next door, leader, funny, lazy
People who like the name Olson also like Owen, Gavin, Oliver, Weston, Ian, Caleb, Holden, Jadon, Korbin, Grayson

Olwen *(Welsh)* ♀ RATING: ★★★☆
White track
People think of Olwen as intelligent, pretty, creative, trustworthy, quiet
People who like the name Olwen also like Arwen, Gwendolyn, Olivia, Lorelei, Gwyneth, Rhiannon, Laurel, Genevieve, Chloe, Charlotte

Olympe *(French)* ♀ RATING: ★☆
Olympian
People think of Olympe as weird, stuck-up, wild, creative, untrustworthy
People who like the name Olympe also like Genevieve, Lauren, Olivia, Maeve, Belle, Magnolia, Pierrette, Ophelia, Giselle, Heloise

Olympia *(Greek)* ♀ RATING: ★★
Mountain of the Gods—Olympia Dukakis, actress
People think of Olympia as pretty, powerful, intelligent, elegant, creative
People who like the name Olympia also like Olivia, Ophelia, Anastasia, Isabella, Phoebe, Felicity, Chloe, Paige, Grace, Opal

Oma *(Arabic)* ♂ RATING: ★★★
Giver of life
People think of Oma as trustworthy, caring, funny, intelligent, quiet
People who like the name Oma also like Noah, Omar, Faris, Maddox, Oliver, Grayson, Lawson, Caleb, Ignatius, Garrick

Omana *(Sanskrit/East Indian)* ♀ RATING: ★☆
Help, kindness
People think of Omana as religious, creative, young, trustworthy, elegant
People who like the name Omana also like Kerani, Eshana, Kamala, Malini, Ona, Sienna, Samara, Nayana, Opal, Nisha

Omanand *(Sanskrit/East Indian)* ♂ RATING: ★☆
Joy of Om
People think of Omanand as aggressive, ethnic, weird, nerdy, powerful
People who like the name Omanand also like Mahendra, Manas, Pravin, Hajari, Ravi, Rohan, Rishi, Manjit, Rupin, Ram

Omar *(Arabic)* ♂ RATING: ★★★
Long lived—Omar Sharif, actor; Sidney Omarr, astrologer/columnist
People think of Omar as handsome, funny, intelligent, cool, popular

People who like the name Omar also like Isaac, Adam, Xavier, Nathan, Oscar, Adrian, Noah, Oliver, Ethan, Ian

Omega (Greek) ♀♂   RATING: ★★★
Last—The final letter of the Greek alphabet
People think of Omega as intelligent, creative, energetic, funny, weird
People who like the name Omega also like Phoenix, Orion, Shadow, Hunter, Echo, October, Ezra, Raven, Jade, Storm

On (Chinese) ♂   RATING: ★★★
Peace
People think of On as weird, unpopular, loser, old, untrustworthy
People who like the name On also like Sanjay, Chi, William, Tokala, Ulric, Jack, Zander, Draco, Angelo, Elvin

Ona (Slavic) ♀   RATING: ★★★★
Grace—Variation of Anna; also a West African name meaning fire
People think of Ona as creative, intelligent, quiet, cool, caring
People who like the name Ona also like Ava, Olivia, Emma, Eva, Genevieve, Grace, Ella, Aurora, Nadia, Lana

Onaedo (African) ♀   RATING: ★★
Gold—Ibo origin
People think of Onaedo as criminal, artsy, unpopular, nerdy, loser
People who like the name Onaedo also like Oriana, Juji, Isolde, Esme, Keiko, Hazina, Olathe, Lapis, Julisha, Miyoko

Onan (Hebrew) ♂   RATING: ★★
Strength, power
People think of Onan as sexy, nerdy, weird, powerful, creative
People who like the name Onan also like Kaden, Aiden, Elijah, Ian, Olin, Keagan, Mace, Drake, Alden, Jackson

Onaona (Hawaiian) ♀   RATING: ★★☆
Sweet smell
People think of Onaona as exotic, lazy, weird, ethnic, pretty
People who like the name Onaona also like Okalani, Keola, Leilani, Oliana, Oprah, Alohilani, Kailani, Kaloni, Kiele, Miliani

Onawa (Native American) ♀   RATING: ★☆
Awake
People think of Onawa as pretty, intelligent, ethnic, creative, caring
People who like the name Onawa also like Kaya, Kiona, Minya, Halona, Neena, Nasnan, Nituna, Ayasha, Ayita, Oneida

Ondrea (Slavic) ♀♂   RATING: ★★★☆
Manly, womanly—Variation of Andrea
People think of Ondrea as creative, intelligent, pretty, leader, popular

People who like the name Ondrea also like Jaden, Riley, Rory, Sydney, Jocelyn, Hayden, Oakley, Morgan, Rylee, Payton

Oneida (Native American) ♀   RATING: ★☆
Eagerly awaited—Also a tribe
People think of Oneida as exotic, pretty, trustworthy, funny, intelligent
People who like the name Oneida also like Orenda, Sora, Neena, Ayasha, Kaya, Olathe, Olesia, Cocheta, Zitkalasa, Miakoda

Onella (Hungarian) ♀   RATING: ★★★
Torch light
People think of Onella as popular, exotic, creative, poor, girl next door
People who like the name Onella also like Penelope, Olina, Sophie, Olivia, Maggie, Rosaleen, Helena, Victoria, Dawn, Lily

Oni (Native American) ♀   RATING: ★★★☆
Born on holy ground
People think of Oni as pretty, cool, funny, intelligent, exotic
People who like the name Oni also like Kaya, Sora, Kiona, Luyu, Dyani, Hateya, Ayasha, Cocheta, Olisa, Chenoa

Onofre (Spanish) ♂   RATING: ★☆
Peace warrior—Variation of Humphrey
People think of Onofre as cool, weird, ethnic, powerful, lazy
People who like the name Onofre also like Joaquin, Absolom, Israel, Enrique, Diego, Alijah, Navarro, Esteban, Ezekiel, Alejandro

Onslow (Arabic) ♂   RATING: ★★☆
Hill of the passionate one
People think of Onslow as big, unpopular, exotic, slow, poor
People who like the name Onslow also like Elias, Ethan, Leland, Darwin, Jonah, Phineas, Ishmael, Favian, Gideon, Fox

Ontibile (African) ♀   RATING: ★☆
God is watching over me—Botswana origin
People think of Ontibile as pretty, trustworthy, exotic, caring, wild
People who like the name Ontibile also like Fedora, Calista, Masako, Elpida, Mandira, Euridice, Gianna, Serena, Lavinia, Saskia

Oona (Celtic/Gaelic) ♀   RATING: ★★★☆
One
People think of Oona as intelligent, pretty, funny, creative, artsy
People who like the name Oona also like Una, Mae, Fiona, Ava, Maeve, Layla, Genevieve, Mabel, Ella, Olivia

Opa (Native American) ♀   RATING: ★★★
Owl—Choctaw origin
People think of Opa as winner, lazy, weird, creative, young

People who like the name Opa also like Olathe, Olive, Orenda, Rebecca, Koleyna, Satinka, Natane, Neena, Velvet, Nituna

Opal *(Sanskrit/East Indian)* ♀   RATING: ★★
Precious gem
> People think of Opal as pretty, intelligent, elegant, creative, caring
> People who like the name Opal also like Violet, Olivia, Faith, Pearl, Paige, Grace, Iris, Hazel, Summer, Scarlett

Ophelia *(Greek)* ♀   RATING: ★★★
Helper—Character in William Shakespeare's *Hamlet*
> People think of Ophelia as pretty, elegant, intelligent, creative, caring
> People who like the name Ophelia also like Olivia, Isabella, Scarlett, Sophia, Genevieve, Ava, Violet, Amelia, Charlotte, Aurora

Ophira *(Hebrew)* ♀   RATING: ★★★
Gold
> People think of Ophira as exotic, quiet, ethnic, artsy, pretty
> People who like the name Ophira also like Ophelia, Iris, Persephone, Genevieve, Penelope, Ivy, Scarlett, Olivia, Aurora, Pandora

Ophrah *(Hebrew)* ♀   RATING: ★☆
Young deer
> People think of Ophrah as powerful, wealthy, old, ethnic, caring
> People who like the name Ophrah also like Violet, Ophelia, Josephine, Oprah, Olivia, Sarah, Samantha, Sandra, Daphne, Zoe

Oprah *(Hebrew)* ♀   RATING: ★★
Gazelle—Misspelling of Orpah; Oprah Winfrey, talk show host (Winfrey says her name was originally Orpah on her birth certificate, but was constantly mispronounced by her family; they legally changed her name to Oprah when she was a year old)
> People think of Oprah as powerful, wealthy, caring, leader, intelligent
> People who like the name Oprah also like Faith, Elizabeth, Naomi, Lilly, Harmony, Melody, Roxanne, Sophie, Isabella, Ophelia

Ora *(Spanish)* ♀   RATING: ★★★☆
Gold
> People think of Ora as pretty, intelligent, caring, funny, trustworthy
> People who like the name Ora also like Olivia, Ava, Ivy, Kara, Iris, Dara, Mia, Zoe, Lacey, Opal

Orabella *(Italian)* ♀   RATING: ★★★
Beautiful gold
> People think of Orabella as pretty, weird, sexy, popular, intelligent
> People who like the name Orabella also like Isabella, Gabriella, Olivia, Bella, Giovanna, Ophelia, Bianca, Luna, Octavia, Arabella

Oracle *(Greek)* ♀ ♂   RATING: ★★★
Prophecy
> People think of Oracle as intelligent, creative, religious, powerful, funny
> People who like the name Oracle also like Phoenix, Raine, Hayden, Jade, Raven, Sydney, Riley, Lavender, London, Madison

Oral *(Latin)* ♂   RATING: ★★★
Speaker, word—Oral Roberts, evangelist
> People think of Oral as exotic, weird, boy next door, sexy, wild
> People who like the name Oral also like Gabriel, Roderick, Jacob, Alexander, Darius, Braeden, Jason, Conner, Augustus, Stephen

Oralee *(American)* ♀   RATING: ★★★
Golden—Variation of Aurelie
> People think of Oralee as pretty, weird, trustworthy, young, quiet
> People who like the name Oralee also like Felicity, Olivia, Larissa, Hannah, Claire, Layla, Emberlynn, Gabrielle, Giselle, Madeline

Oran *(Celtic/Gaelic)* ♀ ♂   RATING: ★★★★☆
Green
> People think of Oran as creative, energetic, intelligent, funny, handsome
> People who like the name Oran also like Logan, Caden, Aidan, Rory, Nolan, Riley, Quinn, Reagan, Hayden, Rowan

Orane *(French)* ♀ ♂   RATING: ★★★
Rising—Variation of Auriane
> People think of Orane as funny, exotic, sexy, cool, energetic
> People who like the name Orane also like Oran, Caden, Teagan, Terran, Paxton, Zephyr, Kellen, Orien, Phoenix, Ryan

Orde *(English)* ♂   RATING: ★★☆
Point, sword—Originally a surname
> People think of Orde as nerdy, loser, sneaky, slow, religious
> People who like the name Orde also like Hayes, Jayden, Ronan, Jett, Elias, Kaden, Orsen, Orsin, Orson, Garrick

Ordell *(English)* ♀ ♂   RATING: ★☆
Little knife
> People think of Ordell as lazy, weird, big, loser, aggressive
> People who like the name Ordell also like Landen, Parker, Logan, Jaden, Carson, James, Beverly, Taylor, Preston, Connor

Orea *(Latin)* ♀   RATING: ★★
Variation of Aurea
> People think of Orea as intelligent, funny, pretty, artsy, energetic
> People who like the name Orea also like Sofia, Olivia, Chloe, Oria, Nora, Phoebe, Kaya, Sophie, Tess, Ava

440

Orella *(Italian)* ♀ RATING: ★★★
Golden—Variation of Aurelia or Aurelius
People think of Orella as pretty, cool, energetic, sexy, powerful
People who like the name Orella also like Sienna, Isabella, Gemma, Stella, Natalia, Arabella, Gianna, Bella, Scarlett, Vera

Oren *(Hebrew)* ♂ RATING: ★★
Jerusalem pine
People think of Oren as handsome, intelligent, leader, creative, trustworthy
People who like the name Oren also like Owen, Noah, Ethan, Oliver, Kaden, Caleb, Nathan, Gabriel, Tristan, Xander

Orenda *(Native American)* ♀ RATING: ★★★★
Great spirit—Iroquois origin; also a term for God
People think of Orenda as exotic, intelligent, creative, elegant, loser
People who like the name Orenda also like Kaya, Kendra, Odessa, Tana, Winona, Wakanda, Vera, Satinka, Sora, Neena

Orestes *(Greek)* ♂ RATING: ★☆
Mountain dweller—In Greek mythology, the son of Agamemnon
People think of Orestes as handsome, leader, creative, powerful, intelligent
People who like the name Orestes also like Lysander, Thaddeus, Xavier, Cadmus, Bishop, Leander, Sirius, Tristan, Fox, Drake

Oria *(Latin)* ♀ RATING: ★★★☆
Variation of Aurea
People think of Oria as pretty, exotic, weird, quiet, ethnic
People who like the name Oria also like Oriana, Chloe, Layla, Kaelyn, Luna, Aurora, Giselle, Olivia, Hazel, Ophelia

Oriana *(Latin)* ♀ RATING: ★★☆
Golden
People think of Oriana as pretty, intelligent, caring, funny, creative
People who like the name Oriana also like Olivia, Isabella, Kiara, Kaelyn, Layla, Aurora, Paige, Adriana, Fiona, Ava

Oriel *(French)* ♀♂ RATING: ★★★☆
Gold
People think of Oriel as pretty, intelligent, sexy, creative, trustworthy
People who like the name Oriel also like Teagan, Jade, Raven, Orion, Parker, Rowan, Shae, Rory, Skye, Piper

Orien *(Latin)* ♀♂ RATING: ★★☆
The Orient; the East
People think of Orien as young, creative, intelligent, ethnic, caring
People who like the name Orien also like Caden, Jaden, Orion, Hayden, Logan, Riley, Dylan, Parker, Landen, Aidan

Orinda *(Hebrew)* ♀ RATING: ★★☆
Pine trees
People think of Orinda as pretty, caring, creative, energetic, elegant
People who like the name Orinda also like Olivia, Larissa, Olina, Opal, Odelia, Odessa, Lavinia, Martina, Isabella, Keisha

Oringo *(African)* ♂ RATING: ★★☆
He who likes the hunt—Ugandan origin; also a place in Uganda
People think of Oringo as exotic, sneaky, big, weird, loser
People who like the name Oringo also like Pancho, Othello, Ringo, Omar, Owen, Pablo, Taffy, Paco, Pedro, Oscar

Oriole *(Latin)* ♀♂ RATING: ★★★
Golden—Also a bird; also a baseball team
People think of Oriole as artsy, elegant, intelligent, creative, quiet
People who like the name Oriole also like Parker, Hayden, Brooklyn, Jordan, Sage, London, Raven, Paris, River, Willow

Orion *(Greek)* ♀♂ RATING: ★★☆
Dweller on the mountain—In Greek mythology, a hunter; also a constellation
People think of Orion as handsome, intelligent, powerful, leader, trustworthy
People who like the name Orion also like Hayden, Caden, Logan, Riley, Phoenix, Parker, Piper, Quinn, Dylan, Jaden

Orlando *(Italian)* ♂ RATING: ★★★★
Famous land—Also a city in Florida; Orlando Bloom, actor; Orlando Jones, actor/comedian
People think of Orlando as handsome, sexy, funny, popular, cool
People who like the name Orlando also like Elijah, Ethan, Oliver, Gabriel, Nathan, Tristan, Noah, Nicholas, Benjamin, William

Orleans *(French)* ♀♂ RATING: ★★★
Golden—Also a city in France; also New Orleans, city in Louisiana
People think of Orleans as sexy, funny, creative, cool, handsome
People who like the name Orleans also like Madison, Piper, Spencer, Parker, London, Sydney, Riley, Sasha, Hayden, Shadow

Orli *(Hebrew)* ♀ RATING: ★★★☆
You are my light
People think of Orli as weird, artsy, pretty, leader, intelligent
People who like the name Orli also like Olivia, Keira, Zoe, Oralee, Lily, Naomi, Liana, Sophia, Belle, Emma

Orly *(Hebrew)* ♀♂ RATING: ★★★☆
You are my light
People think of Orly as intelligent, creative, funny, popular, cool

People who like the name Orly also like Dylan, Jaden, Hayden, Logan, Oakley, Piper, Riley, Caden, Tyler, Taylor

Orma *(African)* ♀   RATING: ★☆
Free men—A Kenyan tribe
People think of Orma as old-fashioned, religious, nerdy, unpopular, old
People who like the name Orma also like Kiki, Penelope, Lupe, Delilah, Daria, Lana, Lena, Olivia, Stella, Gypsy

Ormand *(English)* ♂   RATING: ★★☆
Descendent of the red one—Variation of Ormond, an Irish surname
People think of Ormand as handsome, old, loser, weird, creative
People who like the name Ormand also like Zachary, Caleb, Lucian, Owen, Tristan, Isaac, Matthew, Seth, Anton, Ian

Ormanda *(Celtic/Gaelic)* ♀   RATING: ★☆
Descendent of the red one—Feminine form of Ormand
People think of Ormanda as nerdy, loser, sexy, unpopular, weird
People who like the name Ormanda also like Nerina, Cordelia, Richelle, Mariska, Josephine, Kaydence, Roxanne, Samantha, Vevina, Portia

Orn *(Scandinavian)* ♂   RATING: ★★☆
Eagle
People think of Orn as sexy, handsome, exotic, loser, big
People who like the name Orn also like Anakin, Nero, Ace, Troy, Axel, Fox, Orlando, Hiroshi, Ivan, Jett

Ornella *(Italian)* ♀   RATING: ★★★☆
Flowering ash tree—Ornella Muti, actress
People think of Ornella as pretty, funny, intelligent, exotic, caring
People who like the name Ornella also like Isabella, Gemma, Natalia, Orella, Fiorella, Luciana, Camila, Italia, Terra, Arianna

Ornice *(American)* ♀   RATING: ★☆
Combination of Ornella and Janice
People think of Ornice as nerdy, unpopular, weird, girl next door, poor
People who like the name Ornice also like Aurora, Onaona, Serena, Orpah, Amaranta, Oprah, Precious, Cecilia, Flower, Cordelia

Oro *(Spanish)* ♂   RATING: ★☆
Gold
People think of Oro as handsome, intelligent, powerful, sexy, cool
People who like the name Oro also like Xavier, Irving, Aden, Dominic, Merlin, Nathaniel, Ajax, Brandon, Montego, Roscoe

Orpah *(Hebrew)* ♀   RATING: ★★☆
Fawn
People think of Orpah as old-fashioned, old, weird, creative, powerful

People who like the name Orpah also like Lily, Evangeline, Genevieve, Maisie, Sephora, Miriam, Fleur, Delphine, Cecily, Renée

Orrick *(English)* ♂   RATING: ★★
Sword ruler—Originally a surname
People think of Orrick as unpopular, big, weird, artsy, old-fashioned
People who like the name Orrick also like Ethan, Orrin, Oliver, Owen, Warrick, Zander, Tristan, Xander, Gavin, Holden

Orrin *(Celtic/Gaelic)* ♂   RATING: ★★
Green—Variation of Odhran; Orrin Hatch, U.S. senator
People think of Orrin as handsome, intelligent, caring, funny, trustworthy
People who like the name Orrin also like Owen, Liam, Aiden, Kaden, Oren, Conner, Tristan, Landon, Gavin, Keagan

Orsen *(English)* ♂   RATING: ★★
Bear cub—Variation of Orson
People think of Orsen as quiet, old-fashioned, old, handsome, religious
People who like the name Orsen also like Ethan, Oscar, Owen, Orson, Seth, Wade, Xavier, Nathaniel, Alexander, Maddox

Orsin *(English)* ♂   RATING: ★★
Bear cub—Variation of Orson
People think of Orsin as funny, nerdy, old-fashioned, weird, intelligent
People who like the name Orsin also like Orson, Orsen, Jayden, Kaden, Owen, Oren, Rainer, Korbin, Dillon, Edison

Orsina *(Italian)* ♀   RATING: ★★
Bear
People think of Orsina as exotic, pretty, religious, girl next door, lazy
People who like the name Orsina also like Luciana, Seren, Milena, Bella, Orabella, Lilia, Jalena, Dawn, Coral, Shayna

Orson *(English)* ♂   RATING: ★★★☆
Bear cub—Orson Bean, actor; Orson Scott Card, author; Orson Welles, actor/director
People think of Orson as intelligent, handsome, cool, aggressive, sexy
People who like the name Orson also like Owen, Noah, Oscar, Oliver, Tristan, Ethan, Landon, Samuel, Ian, Jackson

Orville *(French)* ♂   RATING: ★☆
Golden city—Orville Redenbacher, popcorn manufacturer; Orville Wright, airplane pioneer
People think of Orville as old-fashioned, handsome, lazy, intelligent, creative
People who like the name Orville also like Owen, Isaac, Oliver, Marshall, Wade, Theodore, Bradley, Nicholas, Mortimer, Beau

Orya *(Russian)* ♀ RATING: ★★☆
Peace—Short for Irina
People think of Orya as intelligent, weird, funny, creative, old-fashioned
People who like the name Orya also like Kayla, Iliana, Judith, Ianna, Kaitlyn, Kaelyn, Sophia, Isis, Oliana, Maddy

Osama *(Arabic)* ♂ RATING: ★★☆
Lion-like—Variation of Usama; Osama bin Laden, leader of terrorist organization Al-Qaeda
People think of Osama as criminal, untrustworthy, aggressive, unpopular, religious
People who like the name Osama also like Miles, Jacob, Jeremiah, Brandon, Drake, Oliver, Monty, Owen, Seth, Omar

Osanna *(Greek)* ♀ RATING: ★★★
Praise
People think of Osanna as pretty, quiet, intelligent, creative, caring
People who like the name Osanna also like Olivia, Ophelia, Opal, Olive, Giselle, Gianna, Magnolia, Lydia, Odessa, Isabella

Osborn *(English)* ♂ RATING: ★★★
God bear
People think of Osborn as aggressive, big, energetic, cool, boy next door
People who like the name Osborn also like Oscar, Orsen, Odysseus, Orson, Owen, Ambrose, Ozzie, Aiden, Gavin, Osbourne

Osbourne *(English)* ♂ RATING: ★★☆
God bear—Originally a surname; Ozzy Osbourne, singer
People think of Osbourne as intelligent, popular, trustworthy, creative, cool
People who like the name Osbourne also like Owen, Oliver, Warner, Everett, Drake, Gabriel, Dalton, Foster, Sebastian, Ethan

Oscar *(Celtic/Gaelic)* ♂ RATING: ★★★★
Deer lover—Oscar Hammerstein II, lyricist; Oscar Wilde; author; Oscar the Grouch, character on *Sesame Street*
People think of Oscar as handsome, funny, intelligent, cool, caring
People who like the name Oscar also like Oliver, Noah, Owen, Isaac, Jack, Jacob, Ethan, Samuel, Sebastian, Lucas

Osgood *(English)* ♂ RATING: ★☆
God Goth—Also a German tribe
People think of Osgood as old, powerful, weird, loser, quiet
People who like the name Osgood also like Bowen, Sherwood, Fletcher, Keagan, Oliver, Oscar, Radley, Wheeler, Demetrius, Dalton

Osias *(Hebrew)* ♂ RATING: ★★★☆
Salvation
People think of Osias as handsome, powerful, leader, intelligent, aggressive
People who like the name Osias also like Elijah, Gabriel, Noah, Elias, Oliver, Owen, Xander, Jayden, Jeremiah, Liam

Osma *(American)* ♀ RATING: ★☆
Variation of Ozma, created by L. Frank Baum for *The Wizard of Oz* book series
People think of Osma as exotic, funny, powerful, creative, cool
People who like the name Osma also like Samantha, Winifred, Meaghan, Susan, Purity, Kyla, Lilith, Brighid, Marcy, Martina

Osman *(Arabic)* ♂ RATING: ★★
Tender youth
People think of Osman as intelligent, handsome, funny, winner, cool
People who like the name Osman also like Noah, Nasser, Darren, Abram, Niles, Isaiah, Owen, Raymond, Soren, Darnell

Osmond *(English)* ♂ RATING: ★★★
God protector—The Osmonds, singing family
People think of Osmond as intelligent, creative, powerful, funny, religious
People who like the name Osmond also like Lawson, Troy, Sullivan, Nicholas, Noah, Sidney, Felton, Ian, William, Chase

Osric *(English)* ♂ RATING: ★☆
God ruler
People think of Osric as leader, loser, cool, aggressive, trustworthy
People who like the name Osric also like Oliver, Tristan, Finn, Wyatt, Dalton, Merric, Elden, Lawson, Oscar, Anthony

Ossie *(English)* ♂ RATING: ★★★
Short for names beginning with Os; Ossie Davis, actor/musician (from the mispronunciation of his initials, R.C.)
People think of Ossie as weird, popular, unpopular, funny, trustworthy
People who like the name Ossie also like Elliot, Reece, Maddox, Ian, Landon, Otto, Noah, Keagan, Owen, Ozzie

Oswald *(English)* ♂ RATING: ★☆
God rule—Lee Harvey Oswald, assassin of U.S. President John Kennedy
People think of Oswald as nerdy, intelligent, handsome, funny, caring
People who like the name Oswald also like Oliver, Owen, Oscar, Wade, Lucas, Maxwell, Ian, Vincent, Charles, Edmund

Othello *(Italian)* ♂ RATING: ★★★☆
Prosperous—Play and character by William Shakespeare
People think of Othello as creative, intelligent, powerful, leader, aggressive

People who like the name Othello also like Oliver, Lysander, Owen, Noah, Jacob, Xavier, Orlando, Tristan, Caleb, Lancelot

Otieno (*African*) ♂ RATING: ★★☆
Born at night—Kenyan origin
People think of Otieno as sexy, intelligent, trustworthy, sneaky, funny
People who like the name Otieno also like Liam, Xavier, Oliver, Othello, Jayden, Demetrius, Saber, Sirius, Reuben, Saeran

Otis (*English*) ♂ RATING: ★★
Wealth—Otis Redding, singer/songwriter; *Milo and Otis*, film
People think of Otis as handsome, intelligent, caring, funny, creative
People who like the name Otis also like Oliver, Oscar, Owen, Felix, Miles, Noah, Isaac, Seth, Wade, Ethan

Ottavia (*Rumantsch*) ♀ RATING: ★★☆
Eighth
People think of Ottavia as exotic, ethnic, pretty, young, intelligent
People who like the name Ottavia also like Octavia, Imogene, Odessa, Lucia, Odetta, Olivia, Cyrah, Tevy, Ashlyn, Ballari

Otto (*German*) ♂ RATING: ★★★☆
Wealth—Otto Preminger, director/actor
People think of Otto as intelligent, handsome, cool, creative, popular
People who like the name Otto also like Oliver, Owen, Isaac, Oscar, Leo, Noah, Ian, Kaden, Aiden, Sebastian

Otylia (*Polish*) ♀ RATING: ★★★☆
Wealth—Variation of Odile
People think of Otylia as pretty, elegant, creative, caring, exotic
People who like the name Otylia also like Opal, Ophelia, Hazel, Electra, Hypatia, Giselle, Ebony, Genevieve, Oriana, Cecilia

Ouida (*French*) ♀ RATING: ★★★
Famous warrior—Nickname of Louise de la Ramee, author
People think of Ouida as exotic, funny, old-fashioned, creative, religious
People who like the name Ouida also like Giselle, Cecile, Étoile, Elle, Isolde, Miette, Selene, Fifi, Geraldine, Lucille

Ova (*Latin*) ♀ RATING: ★★
Egg
People think of Ova as weird, unpopular, loser, nerdy, poor
People who like the name Ova also like Caroline, Princess, Ava, Emma, Erin, Estelle, Pearl, Eva, Opal, Maggie

Overton (*English*) ♀♂ RATING: ★★
From the riverbank town
People think of Overton as wealthy, intelligent, elegant, funny, caring

People who like the name Overton also like Logan, London, Hayden, Oakley, Hadley, Pierce, Riley, Keegan, Merrick, Reegan

Ovid (*Latin*) ♂ RATING: ★★★
Sheep—Roman poet
People think of Ovid as weird, religious, old, nerdy, winner
People who like the name Ovid also like Byron, Harlow, Oren, Reece, Reuel, Ogden, Adair, Wycliff, Palani, Celestine

Ovidio (*Spanish*) ♂ RATING: ★☆
Sheep herder—Variation of Ovid
People think of Ovidio as loser, aggressive, intelligent, sporty, old-fashioned
People who like the name Ovidio also like Esteban, Kael, Hidalgo, Tejano, Constantine, Damien, Brandon, Azizi, Cordero, Pablo

Owen (*Welsh*) ♂ RATING: ★★★★
Desire born—Owen Hargreaves, soccer player; Owen Wilson, actor; Clive Owen, actor
People think of Owen as handsome, intelligent, funny, caring, popular
People who like the name Owen also like Ethan, Noah, Aiden, Ian, Gavin, Jacob, Nathan, Liam, Caleb, Oliver

Owena (*Welsh*) ♀ RATING: ★★☆
Desire born—Feminine form of Owen
People think of Owena as pretty, big, nerdy, poor, wealthy
People who like the name Owena also like Ivy, Gwen, Olwen, Laurel, Jennifer, Bianca, Bella, Grace, Heather, Rowena

Ownah (*Celtic/Gaelic*) ♀ RATING: ★★☆
Unity—Variation of Una
People think of Ownah as exotic, weird, ethnic, cool, wild
People who like the name Ownah also like Riona, Maille, Mairi, Rona, Finna, Lesley, Rosina, Maeve, Maire, Hazel

Oya (*African*) ♀♂ RATING: ★☆
Wind warrior goddess—Yoruban origin
People think of Oya as exotic, weird, elegant, wild, caring
People who like the name Oya also like Kieran, Mika, Ezra, Nida, Makya, Flynn, Naolin, Niabi, Ennis, Taregan

Oz (*Hebrew*) ♀♂ RATING: ★★★☆
Strength, courage—Also short for names beginning with Os, like Oswald
People think of Oz as funny, intelligent, cool, leader, creative
People who like the name Oz also like Logan, Phoenix, Riley, Parker, Taylor, Dylan, Orion, Kai, Hayden, Connor

444

Ozzie *(English)* ♂   RATING: ★★★
Short for names beginning with Os—Also spelled Ossie or Ozzy; Ozzie Nelson, actor; Ozzy Osbourne, musician
> People think of Ozzie as cool, wild, energetic, weird, funny
> People who like the name Ozzie also like Ozzy, Oscar, Kaden, Aiden, Nathan, Ian, Aden, Ollie, Tristan, Oliver

Pabla *(Spanish)* ♀   RATING: ★★★
Small—Variation of Paula
> People think of Pabla as lazy, pretty, leader, poor, artsy
> People who like the name Pabla also like Paige, Palma, Purity, Paloma, Posy, Pearl, Perdita, Pebbles, Pilar, Paprika

Pablo *(Spanish)* ♂   RATING: ★★★☆
Small—Variation of Paul
> People think of Pablo as handsome, cool, funny, caring, intelligent
> People who like the name Pablo also like Samuel, Diego, Noah, Pedro, Carlos, Caleb, Jacob, Paco, Lucas, Xavier

Paco *(Spanish)* ♂   RATING: ★★★
Free—Short for Francisco; Paco de Lucía, flamenco guitarist; Paco Rabanne, designer
> People think of Paco as cool, funny, energetic, popular, intelligent
> People who like the name Paco also like Pablo, Pedro, Pancho, Felix, Diego, Juan, Francisco, Julio, Ruben, Miguel

Paddington *(English)* ♂   RATING: ★★☆
The estate of Padda—Also a street in London; Paddington Bear, children's character by Michael Bond
> People think of Paddington as old-fashioned, caring, nerdy, unpopular, intelligent
> People who like the name Paddington also like Henry, Oscar

Paddy *(Celtic/Gaelic)* ♂   RATING: ★★★☆
Noble—Short for Patrick; Paddy Chayefsky, author
> People think of Paddy as funny, sexy, intelligent, cool, caring
> People who like the name Paddy also like Liam, Patrick, Tristan, Seamus, Sullivan, Aiden, Trevor, Cole, Malcolm, Ian

Padgett *(English)* ♂   RATING: ★★★
Attendant
> People think of Padgett as powerful, popular, weird, boy next door, sexy
> People who like the name Padgett also like Reece, Isaac, Owen, Percy, Pascal, Percival, Tyson, Braden, Elijah, Gage

Padma *(Sanskrit/East Indian)* ♀   RATING: ★★★☆
Lotus—Padma Lakshmi, actress/model
> People think of Padma as pretty, intelligent, elegant, exotic, caring
> People who like the name Padma also like Paige, Penelope, Parvati, Violet, Aurora, Ophelia, Persephone, Jasmine, Phoebe, Nadia

Page *(English)* ♀♂   RATING: ★★★
Attendant—Variation of Paige; Jimmy Page, musician
> People think of Page as pretty, funny, creative, popular, intelligent
> People who like the name Page also like Madison, Bailey, Taylor, Hayden, Logan, Jaden, Parker, Caden, Mackenzie, Payton

Pahana *(Native American)* ♀♂   RATING: ★★★
Lost white brother—Hopi origin
> People think of Pahana as exotic, weird, lazy, slow, old
> People who like the name Pahana also like Pillan, Mika, Makya, Pyralis, Kanga, Payton, Phoenix, Misae, Nida, Taregan

Paige *(English)* ♀   RATING: ★★★
Assistant—Paige Davis, actress/singer; Paige O'Hara, singer/voiceover artist; Paige Turco, actress
> People think of Paige as pretty, funny, popular, caring, creative
> People who like the name Paige also like Olivia, Hannah, Emma, Hailey, Grace, Chloe, Faith, Ava, Isabella, Abigail

Paisley *(Celtic/Gaelic)* ♀♂   RATING: ★★★★
Church—Also a Scottish place name; also a design pattern; Paisley Park, music studio owned by Prince
> People think of Paisley as pretty, creative, caring, artsy, funny
> People who like the name Paisley also like Parker, Payton, Bailey, Madison, Hayden, Addison, Riley, Logan, Presley, Peyton

Paiva *(Portuguese)* ♀   RATING: ★★★
Name of a tributary of the Douro river
> People think of Paiva as intelligent, pretty, exotic, funny, elegant
> People who like the name Paiva also like Padma, Paige, Paloma, Posy, Svea, Ivy, Nixie, Palesa, Pippa, Petra

Paki *(African)* ♀   RATING: ★★★
Witness—Xhosa origin
> People think of Paki as ethnic, aggressive, poor, pretty, criminal
> People who like the name Paki also like Paige, Penelope, Pearl, Patience, Pilar, Pakuna, Pamela, Palila, Isis, Perdita

Pakuna *(Native American)* ♀   RATING: ★★☆
Deer jumping downhill—Miwok origin
> People think of Pakuna as exotic, aggressive, pretty, energetic, loser
> People who like the name Pakuna also like Topanga, Kachina, Kaya, Wakanda, Peta, Zaltana, Takoda, Kailani, Winona, Kaliska

Palani *(Hawaiian)* ♂   RATING: ★★☆
Free man—Variation of Frank
> People think of Palani as wild, exotic, popular, poor, cool
> People who like the name Palani also like Keoni, Gabriel, Tristan, Kaipo, Anthony, Beau, Jayden, Aiden, Kelii, Keon

Palesa *(African)* ♀   RATING: ★★
Rose—South African origin
> People think of Palesa as pretty, exotic, young, caring, sexy
> People who like the name Palesa also like Pearl, Paiva, Penelope, Paloma, Padma, Pamela, Patience, Sapphire, Ilyssa, Paprika

Paley *(English)* ♀♂   RATING: ★★☆
From the pale field
> People think of Paley as intelligent, weird, girl next door, young, cool
> People who like the name Paley also like Parker, Paisley, Payton, Riley, Caden, Hadley, Jaden, Piper, Paxton, Madison

Palila *(Hawaiian)* ♀   RATING: ★★
Bird
> People think of Palila as exotic, pretty, caring, creative, elegant
> People who like the name Palila also like Kailani, Penelope, Malia, Leilani, Aurora, Calandra, Pearl, Yasmin, Belle, Kaloni

Pallas *(Greek)* ♀♂   RATING: ★★★☆
Youth
> People think of Pallas as pretty, intelligent, creative, artsy, girl next door
> People who like the name Pallas also like Phoenix, Parker, London, Payton, Quinn, Zephyr, Paxton, Willow, Oakley, Peyton

Pallaton *(Native American)* ♂   RATING: ★☆
Fighter
> People think of Pallaton as powerful, big, exotic, young, handsome
> People who like the name Pallaton also like Hakan, Paytah, Shilah, Ranger, Caleb, Mingan, Chayton, Tokala, Wyatt, Kaden

Pallavi *(Sanskrit/East Indian)* ♀   RATING: ★★★★
New leaves
> People think of Pallavi as intelligent, creative, pretty, caring, popular
> People who like the name Pallavi also like Padma, Parvati, Parvani, Panchali, Premala, Priti, Prema, Paiva, Divya, Pandora

Palma *(Spanish)* ♀   RATING: ★★★
Palm
> People think of Palma as pretty, intelligent, funny, cool, girl next door
> People who like the name Palma also like Paloma, Pilar, Pandora, Portia, Paige, Petra, Lenora, Sabina, Pabla, Prema

Palmer *(English)* ♂   RATING: ★★☆
Holy land pilgrim—Also a surname
> People think of Palmer as funny, intelligent, leader, trustworthy, handsome
> People who like the name Palmer also like Noah, Jackson, Ethan, Owen, Walker, Lucas, Nathan, Zachary, Wade, Tristan

Paloma *(Spanish)* ♀   RATING: ★★★☆
A dove—Paloma Picasso, jewelry designer
> People think of Paloma as pretty, creative, intelligent, caring, exotic
> People who like the name Paloma also like Olivia, Penelope, Eva, Phoebe, Isabella, Paige, Aurora, Grace, Marisol, Pilar

Palti *(Hebrew)* ♂   RATING: ★★
My deliverance
> People think of Palti as creative, trustworthy, sneaky, cool, intelligent
> People who like the name Palti also like Pelham, Penda, Pascal, Palmer, Brandon, Pryce, Pirro, Zakiya, Platt, Jacob

Pam *(English)* ♀   RATING: ★★★
All honey—Short for Pamela
> People think of Pam as caring, intelligent, funny, pretty, creative
> People who like the name Pam also like Pamela, Paige, Pearl, Rachel, Faith, Emma, Samantha, Daisy, Penny, Tammy

Pamela *(English)* ♀   RATING: ★★★☆
All honey—Invented by Sir Philip Sidney for a poem in the 1580s; also used by Samuel Richardson for his novel *Pamela* in the 1740s
> People think of Pamela as pretty, caring, funny, intelligent, trustworthy
> People who like the name Pamela also like Paige, Samantha, Sabrina, Natalie, Olivia, Sarah, Rebecca, Hannah, Vanessa, Rachel

Pamelia *(English)* ♀   RATING: ★★★
All honey—Combination of Pamela and Amelia
> People think of Pamelia as pretty, powerful, sexy, exotic, popular
> People who like the name Pamelia also like Pamela, Vanessa, Pandora, Victoria, Penelope, Rachael, Paige, Tiffany, Pearl, Samantha

Panchali *(Sanskrit/East Indian)* ♀   RATING: ★★★
Princess
> People think of Panchali as elegant, pretty, sexy, wild, ethnic
> People who like the name Panchali also like Padma, Pallavi, Parvani, Parvati, Prema, Pamela, Premala, Parisa, Priti, Kamana

Pancho *(Spanish)* ♂   RATING: ★☆
Free—Short for Francisco; Pancho Villa, Mexican revolutionary
> People think of Pancho as big, funny, weird, cool, sexy

People who like the name Pancho also like Pablo, Paco, Diego, Carlos, Julio, Eduardo, Francisco, Lucas, Enrique, Pedro

Pandora (*Greek*) ♀ RATING: ★★★★
All gifts—In Greek mythology, the woman who opened a box in which there were all the evils of the world
People think of Pandora as creative, intelligent, pretty, elegant, artsy
People who like the name Pandora also like Persephone, Aurora, Penelope, Scarlett, Phoebe, Ophelia, Paige, Patience, Cassandra, Ivy

Paniz (*Persian*) ♀ RATING: ★★★☆
Candy
People think of Paniz as pretty, exotic, weird, caring, creative
People who like the name Paniz also like Paloma, Pamela, Pamelia, Parvani, Pia, Pearl, Portia, Pebbles, Pandora, Peggy

Pansy (*American*) ♀ RATING: ★★★
Violet flower—Also means someone who is easily tricked or conned; also derogatory for homosexual
People think of Pansy as pretty, slow, trendy, unpopular, loser
People who like the name Pansy also like Amanda, Hazel, Kaylee, Summer, Raeanne, Chameli, Brenna, Hilde, Keely, Francine

Panthea (*Greek*) ♀ RATING: ★★★
All goddess
People think of Panthea as exotic, pretty, creative, sexy, trustworthy
People who like the name Panthea also like Pandora, Ophelia, Persephone, Penelope, Desdemona, Aurora, Psyche, Iris, Phaedra, Paprika

Panya (*Slavic*) ♀ RATING: ★★☆
Crown—Short for Stephania; also Hindi meaning to be praised
People think of Panya as funny, leader, energetic, lazy, young
People who like the name Panya also like Penelope, Patience, Pandora, Paige, Ivy, Nara, Padma, Faith, Parmida, Pilar

Panyin (*African*) ♀ RATING: ★★★
Older twin—Fante/Ghanaian origin; also Native American with the same meaning
People think of Panyin as pretty, intelligent, sneaky, creative, caring
People who like the name Panyin also like Rachel, Rachael, Pearl, Padma, Patience, Pippa, Palesa, Penelope, Kiara, Paprika

Paola (*Italian*) ♀ RATING: ★★★★
Small—Variation of Paula
People think of Paola as pretty, intelligent, funny, caring, cool
People who like the name Paola also like Olivia, Isabella, Paloma, Bianca, Natalia, Nicole, Paige, Fiona, Sofia, Natalie

Paolo (*Italian*) ♂ RATING: ★★★★
Small—Variation of Paul
People think of Paolo as handsome, intelligent, cool, funny, caring
People who like the name Paolo also like Gabriel, Jacob, Sebastian, Marco, Owen, Ethan, Lucas, Noah, Oliver, Diego

Papina (*Native American*) ♀ RATING: ★☆
Ivy
People think of Papina as artsy, unpopular, pretty, aggressive, quiet
People who like the name Papina also like Penelope, Pepper, Phoebe, Paiva, Wakanda, Paloma, Aurora, Sora, Patience, Sienna

Paprika (*English*) ♀ RATING: ★☆
Spice—A reddish spice, sometimes used as a name for redheads
People think of Paprika as energetic, exotic, funny, weird, girl next door
People who like the name Paprika also like Paige, Scarlett, Penelope, Faith, Sapphire, Pearl, Patience, Pippa, Penny, Pamela

Paquita (*Spanish*) ♀ RATING: ★★☆
Free—Feminine form of Paco
People think of Paquita as sexy, funny, popular, pretty, girl next door
People who like the name Paquita also like Chiquita, Lenora, Belita, Lola, Adelina, Princess, Alegria, Atalaya, Shaquana, Ventura

Paras (*Sanskrit/East Indian*) ♀ ♂ RATING: ★★★★
Touchstone
People think of Paras as powerful, intelligent, trustworthy, exotic, ethnic
People who like the name Paras also like Paris, Pavan, Phoenix, Parker, Payton, Brooklyn, Pyralis, Kiran, Tate, Porsche

Parees (*Sanskrit/East Indian*) ♂ RATING: ★★
Touchstone
People think of Parees as handsome, funny, cool, big, wealthy
People who like the name Parees also like Joel, Nevan, Arav, Jag, Brandon, Amrit, Savir, Liam, Rupin, Nayati

Paresh (*Sanskrit/East Indian*) ♂ RATING: ★★☆
Supreme spirit
People think of Paresh as caring, funny, trustworthy, cool, exotic
People who like the name Paresh also like Keiran, Korbin, Rohan, Edan, Cyrus, Neron, Bryson, Tristan, Reuel, Llewellyn

Paris (*Greek*) ♀ ♂ RATING: ★★★
From Paris, France—In Greek mythology, Helen of Troy's lover; also Greek mythological name possibly meaning wallet; Paris Hilton, celebrity
People think of Paris as popular, pretty, sexy, trendy, cool

People who like the name Paris also like Madison, Taylor, Parker, London, Hayden, Bailey, Riley, Brooklyn, Ryan, Mackenzie

Parisa *(Persian)* ♀   RATING: ★★★★
Like a fairy
People think of Parisa as pretty, caring, intelligent, funny, young
People who like the name Parisa also like Parmida, Mia, Francesca, Olivia, Kiara, Selena, Portia, Emma, Paige, Aurora

Park *(Chinese)* ♀ ♂   RATING: ★★
Cypress tree—Also a Korean surname
People think of Park as creative, handsome, popular, energetic, funny
People who like the name Park also like Parker, Paris, Phoenix, Page, Mason, Paisley, Madison, Peyton, Preston, Pierce

Parker *(English)* ♀ ♂   RATING: ★★★★
Park keeper—Parker Posey, actress; Parker Stevenson, actor
People think of Parker as intelligent, handsome, funny, cool, popular
People who like the name Parker also like Logan, Hayden, Riley, Preston, Payton, Madison, Addison, Taylor, Carter, Mason

Parkin *(English)* ♀ ♂   RATING: ★★★
Rock—Short for Peter; also a surname
People think of Parkin as popular, intelligent, leader, creative, sporty
People who like the name Parkin also like Parker, Logan, Payton, Rory, Landen, Paxton, Torrin, Caden, Reagan, Teagan

Parlan *(Celtic/Gaelic)* ♀ ♂   RATING: ★★☆
Son of the plough—Variation of Bartholomew
People think of Parlan as intelligent, exotic, artsy, unpopular, weird
People who like the name Parlan also like Parkin, Teagan, Hadley, Paisley, Nolan, Riley, Reagan, Torrin, Logan, Shay

Parley *(English)* ♀ ♂   RATING: ★★★
Trader
People think of Parley as caring, handsome, exotic, funny, sexy
People who like the name Parley also like Parker, Paisley, Payton, Hadley, Hayden, Riley, Madison, Oakley, Presley, Teagan

Parmida *(Persian)* ♀   RATING: ★★★★
Princess—Daughter of King Karoush Hakhamaneshi, one of the wives of King Darius
People think of Parmida as pretty, elegant, young, popular, funny
People who like the name Parmida also like Parisa, Padma, Patience, Perdita, Persephone, Penelope, Prema, Panthea, Grace, Serafina

Parrish *(English)* ♀ ♂   RATING: ★★★☆
Noble; from Paris—Originally a surname
People think of Parrish as funny, caring, energetic, trustworthy, cool
People who like the name Parrish also like Parker, Paxton, Payton, Peyton, Pierce, Keaton, Caden, Paisley, Parson, Nolan

Parry *(Welsh)* ♀ ♂   RATING: ★★
Son of Harry—Also a surname
People think of Parry as creative, cool, funny, quiet, handsome
People who like the name Parry also like Parker, Mason, Teagan, Logan, Harper, Piper, Reese, Phoenix, Poppy, Hunter

Parson *(English)* ♀ ♂   RATING: ★★☆
Minister, clergy
People think of Parson as handsome, intelligent, leader, religious, boy next door
People who like the name Parson also like Parker, Payton, Preston, Taylor, Paxton, Jaden, Peyton, Addison, Riley, Logan

Parvani *(Sanskrit/East Indian)* ♀   RATING: ★★★
Full moon
People think of Parvani as pretty, cool, sexy, exotic, nerdy
People who like the name Parvani also like Padma, Panchali, Niyati, Parvati, Pallavi, Ninarika, Eshana, Paige, Penelope, Phoebe

Parvati *(Sanskrit/East Indian)* ♀   RATING: ★★★☆
Daughter of the mountain
People think of Parvati as exotic, pretty, popular, sexy, funny
People who like the name Parvati also like Padma, Opal, Phoebe, Penelope, Patience, Paige, Hermione, Pallavi, Violet, Ophelia

Pascal *(French)* ♂   RATING: ★★
Easter
People think of Pascal as intelligent, handsome, creative, caring, cool
People who like the name Pascal also like Oliver, Tristan, Noah, Owen, Simon, Gabriel, Nathan, Victor, Adrian, Jacob

Pascale *(French)* ♀   RATING: ★★★★
Easter—Feminine form of Pascal
People think of Pascale as pretty, intelligent, caring, creative, funny
People who like the name Pascale also like Paige, Penelope, Giselle, Olivia, Phoebe, Madeleine, Genevieve, Mallory, Chloe, Veronica

Pascha *(Russian)* ♀ ♂   RATING: ★★★
Small—Short for Pavel
People think of Pascha as creative, intelligent, exotic, artsy, elegant
People who like the name Pascha also like Pasha, Mischa, Paisley, Poppy, Taylor, Payton, Peyton, Ryder, Sasha, Spencer

448

Pascual (*Spanish*) ♂   RATING: ★★☆
Easter
> People think of Pascual as funny, handsome, caring, trustworthy, sneaky
> People who like the name Pascual also like Raúl, Iago, Rafael, Julio, Maximo, Sebastian, Hidalgo, Diego, Adelio, Pablo

Pasha (*Russian*) ♀♂   RATING: ★★★☆
Small—Short for Pavel
> People think of Pasha as winner, sexy, intelligent, cool, creative
> People who like the name Pasha also like Parker, Sasha, Piper, Paris, Phoenix, Sage, Paisley, Pascha, Pierce, Luca

Passion (*American*) ♀   RATING: ★★★
Strong desire
> People think of Passion as sexy, pretty, caring, exotic, cool
> People who like the name Passion also like Precious, Patience, Faith, Hailey, Sadie, Bethany, Christina, Hope, Rhianna, Destiny

Pat (*English*) ♀♂   RATING: ★★
Noble—Short for Patrick or Patricia; Pat Benatar, singer/musician
> People think of Pat as funny, cool, popular, caring, handsome
> People who like the name Pat also like Sam, Phoenix, Presley, Jamie, Parker, Jade, Jordan, Puma, Logan, Fred

Patch (*American*) ♂   RATING: ★★
Noble—Short for Patrick; Patch Adams, medical doctor
> People think of Patch as weird, quiet, caring, young, nerdy
> People who like the name Patch also like Seth, Noah, Owen, Wade, Jackson, Xander, Finn, Tyson, Ethan, Isaac

Patia (*Greek*) ♀   RATING: ★★★
Most high—Short for Hypatia
> People think of Patia as intelligent, elegant, popular, big, creative
> People who like the name Patia also like Penelope, Petra, Pia, Phaedra, Rhea, Sofia, Pandora, Mia, Mina, Paige

Patience (*English*) ♀   RATING: ★★★☆
Patience
> People think of Patience as pretty, caring, intelligent, creative, energetic
> People who like the name Patience also like Faith, Paige, Serenity, Olivia, Hannah, Hailey, Trinity, Scarlett, Grace, Hope

Patrice (*French*) ♀   RATING: ★★★☆
Noble
> People think of Patrice as intelligent, pretty, funny, caring, creative
> People who like the name Patrice also like Paige, Olivia, Patience, Phoebe, Hannah, Lauren, Natalie, Victoria, Hailey, Samantha

Patricia (*English*) ♀   RATING: ★★
Noble—Patricia Heaton, actress; Patricia Neal, actress
> People think of Patricia as pretty, intelligent, caring, funny, trustworthy
> People who like the name Patricia also like Samantha, Victoria, Rebecca, Natalie, Paige, Elizabeth, Nicole, Olivia, Vanessa, Hannah

Patrick (*English*) ♂   RATING: ★★★★
Noble—Patrick Duffy, actor; Patrick Stewart, actor; Patrick Swayze, actor
> People think of Patrick as handsome, funny, intelligent, cool, caring
> People who like the name Patrick also like Nicholas, Matthew, Ethan, Nathan, Jacob, Owen, Alexander, Benjamin, Aiden, Noah

Patsy (*English*) ♀♂   RATING: ★★★☆
Noble—Short for Patricia; Patsy Cline, singer
> People think of Patsy as funny, intelligent, caring, creative, old-fashioned
> People who like the name Patsy also like Paris, Patty, Piper, Parker, Holly, Poppy, Taylor, Phoenix, Ryan, Madison

Patty (*English*) ♀♂   RATING: ★☆
Noble—Short for Patrick or Patricia; also spelled Patti; Patty Hearst, heiress; Patti Page, singer; Peppermint Patty, *Peanuts* character
> People think of Patty as pretty, funny, caring, intelligent, cool
> People who like the name Patty also like Patsy, Kim, Holly, James, Paris, Kelly, Kimberly, Toby, Payton, Vicky

Paul (*Latin*) ♂   RATING: ★★☆
Small—Disciple of Christ; Paul McCartney, singer/songwriter; Paul Newman, actor; Paul Rudd, actor; Paul Walker, actor
> People think of Paul as handsome, funny, intelligent, caring, cool
> People who like the name Paul also like Matthew, David, Nicholas, Ethan, Jack, Michael, Benjamin, Nathan, Jacob, Samuel

Paula (*Latin*) ♀   RATING: ★★★☆
Small—Paula Abdul, choreographer/singer; Paula Poundstone, comedian
> People think of Paula as pretty, caring, funny, intelligent, creative
> People who like the name Paula also like Paige, Samantha, Faith, Sarah, Natalie, Rebecca, Pamela, Nicole, Patricia, Grace

Paulette (*French*) ♀   RATING: ★★
Small—Paulette Goddard, actress
> People think of Paulette as pretty, caring, intelligent, creative, funny
> People who like the name Paulette also like Paige, Olivia, Nicolette, Patricia, Paulina, Penelope, Victoria, Jacqueline, Lauren, Phoebe

Paulina (*Spanish*) ♀　　　　　RATING: ★★
Small—Short for Paula; Paulina Porizkova, model/
actress
> People think of Paulina as funny, pretty, intelligent, car-
> ing, creative
> People who like the name Paulina also like Isabella,
> Olivia, Paula, Sabrina, Paige, Natalia, Hannah, Emma,
> Jasmine, Bianca

Pauline (*French*) ♀　　　　　RATING: ★★★★
Small—Short for Paula
> People think of Pauline as funny, pretty, caring, trust-
> worthy, intelligent
> People who like the name Pauline also like Paige,
> Nicole, Sarah, Isabelle, Hailey, Faith, Olivia, Heather,
> Madeleine, Madeline

Paulo (*Portuguese*) ♂　　　　　RATING: ★★★☆
Small—Variation of Paul
> People think of Paulo as handsome, funny, intelligent,
> sexy, caring
> People who like the name Paulo also like Pablo, Pedro,
> Paolo, Rafael, Thomas, Adrian, Milo, Gabriel, Nicholas,
> Lorenzo

Paulos (*Portuguese*) ♂　　　　　RATING: ★★★
Small—Variation of Paul
> People think of Paulos as caring, young, funny, hand-
> some, slow
> People who like the name Paulos also like Henri, Felix,
> Phillip, Xander, Gunther, Rex, Abel, Jacob, Tomas,
> Francis

Pavan (*Sanskrit/East Indian*) ♀♂　　　　　RATING: ★★★★
Breeze
> People think of Pavan as funny, cool, popular, exotic,
> winner
> People who like the name Pavan also like Payton,
> Parker, Piper, Paxton, Caden, Preston, Jaden, Phoenix,
> Page, Perrin

Pavel (*Russian*) ♂　　　　　RATING: ★★★★
Small—Variation of Paul
> People think of Pavel as intelligent, handsome, cool,
> sexy, funny
> People who like the name Pavel also like Seth, Nathan,
> Elijah, Lucas, Jack, Basil, Nicholai, Holden, Nicholas,
> Vincent

Pax (*Latin*) ♀♂　　　　　RATING: ★★★☆
Peace—Adopted son of Angelina Jolie and Brad Pitt
> People think of Pax as leader, intelligent, weird, creative,
> artsy
> People who like the name Pax also like Paxton, Phoenix,
> Parker, Riley, Logan, Dakota, Hayden, Payton, Jaden,
> Pierce

Paxton (*English*) ♀♂　　　　　RATING: ★★★★
From Pacca's town—Paxton Whitehead, actor
> People think of Paxton as intelligent, funny, popular,
> energetic, creative

> People who like the name Paxton also like Payton,
> Parker, Hayden, Preston, Caden, Logan, Riley, Addison,
> Mason, Jaden

Paytah (*Native American*) ♂　　　　　RATING: ★☆
Fire—Sioux origin
> People think of Paytah as funny, wild, quiet, leader, poor
> People who like the name Paytah also like Aiden,
> Hakan, Kaden, Mingan, Pallaton, Mikasi, Dasan, Quentin,
> Koen, Isaac

Payton (*English*) ♀♂　　　　　RATING: ★★★★
From Pacca's town—Walter Payton, football player
> People think of Payton as pretty, popular, funny, caring,
> creative
> People who like the name Payton also like Parker,
> Hayden, Madison, Riley, Logan, Caden, Peyton, Taylor,
> Preston, Bailey

Paz (*Spanish*) ♀♂　　　　　RATING: ★★★☆
Peace—La Paz, capital city of Bolivia
> People think of Paz as exotic, creative, intelligent, funny,
> cool
> People who like the name Paz also like Phoenix, Paxton,
> Luz, Ezra, Paisley, Piper, Quinn, Rain, Devon, Payton

Pearl (*English*) ♀　　　　　RATING: ★★★★
Pearl—Pearl Buck, author/adoption advocate
> People think of Pearl as pretty, elegant, intelligent, cre-
> ative, caring
> People who like the name Pearl also like Paige, Violet,
> Faith, Grace, Olivia, Scarlett, Ruby, Isabella, Phoebe,
> Opal

Pearlie (*English*) ♀　　　　　RATING: ★★★
Pearl—*Pearlie Victorious*, Broadway play
> People think of Pearlie as pretty, girl next door, elegant,
> funny, weird
> People who like the name Pearlie also like Pearl, Pearly,
> Patience, Victoria, Paige, Penelope, Polly, Pamelia,
> Pebbles, Prema

Pearly (*English*) ♀　　　　　RATING: ★★★☆
Pearl
> People think of Pearly as stuck-up, old, old-fashioned,
> untrustworthy, girl next door
> People who like the name Pearly also like Pearl, Pamela,
> Pamelia, Pearlie, Phoebe, Rebecca, Patience, Pebbles,
> Penelope, Petra

Pebbles (*American*) ♀　　　　　RATING: ★★★
Small rocks—Character on *The Flintstones*; Pebbles
(aka Perri Reid), singer
> People think of Pebbles as pretty, funny, young, caring,
> energetic
> People who like the name Pebbles also like Penelope,
> Phoebe, Pearl, Daisy, Precious, Patience, Paige, Princess,
> Pepper, Faith

Pedro (*Spanish*) ♂　　　　　RATING: ★★★☆
Rock—Varaition of Peter; Pedro Almodovar, filmmaker
> People think of Pedro as funny, handsome, cool, intel-
> ligent, popular

People who like the name Pedro also like Pablo, Diego, Anthony, Isaac, Xavier, Carlos, Alejandro, Antonio, Gabriel, Jacob

Peers *(English)* ♂ RATING: ★★☆
Rock—Variation of Peter
People think of Peers as intelligent, loser, weird, cool, funny
People who like the name Peers also like Liam, Palmer, Maddox, Roman, Ronan, Everett, Patrick, Jace, Reece, Jackson

Pegeen *(Celtic/Gaelic)* ♀ RATING: ★★★
Pearl—Short for Margaret
People think of Pegeen as creative, energetic, trustworthy, lazy, loser
People who like the name Pegeen also like Skyla, Keely, Peggy, Meara, Rosaleen, Phiala, Kyleigh, Briana, Aeryn, Mckayla

Peggy *(English)* ♀ RATING: ★★
Pearl—Short for Margaret; Peggy Fleming, figure skater; Peggy Lee, singer; Peggy Noonan, author/columnist
People think of Peggy as caring, funny, pretty, trustworthy, intelligent
People who like the name Peggy also like Polly, Maisie, Maggie, Victoria, Paige, Erin, Olivia, Penelope, Genevieve, Mae

Peigi *(Celtic/Gaelic)* ♀ RATING: ★★☆
Pearl—Short for Margaret
People think of Peigi as pretty, poor, artsy, weird, energetic
People who like the name Peigi also like Rhona, Maeve, Kaelyn, Bridget, Hazel, Malise, Genevieve, Maire, Mairi, Mairead

Pekelo *(Hawaiian)* ♂ RATING: ★★☆
Stone
People think of Pekelo as funny, caring, lazy, creative, boy next door
People who like the name Pekelo also like Palani, Lulani, Kelii, Kale, Mauli, Kaipo, Kapono, Akamu, Analu, Kanoa

Pelagia *(Greek)* ♀ RATING: ★☆
Sea
People think of Pelagia as pretty, intelligent, religious, sexy, trustworthy
People who like the name Pelagia also like Penelope, Genevieve, Pandora, Parmida, Persephone, Petra, Paloma, Panthea, Perdita, Melody

Pelham *(English)* ♂ RATING: ★★☆
From Peola's village
People think of Pelham as weird, creative, nerdy, slow, loser
People who like the name Pelham also like Palmer, Rhys, Platt, Penn, Penda, Price, Valin, Kynan, Tristan, Garren

Pello *(Greek)* ♂ RATING: ★☆
Stone
People think of Pello as weird, nerdy, unpopular, handsome, ethnic
People who like the name Pello also like Mateo, Emilio, Miles, Michelangelo, Apollo, Massimo, Seth, Tristan, Asher, Marius

Pelton *(English)* ♂ RATING: ★★☆
From the town of Peola's Barrow
People think of Pelton as unpopular, funny, lazy, slow, weird
People who like the name Pelton also like Tristan, Dalton, Trenton, Tyson, Holden, Kaden, Vance, Noah, Troy, Weston

Pembroke *(English)* ♀ ♂ RATING: ★★★
From Pembroke, Wales
People think of Pembroke as weird, uptight, energetic, nerdy, young
People who like the name Pembroke also like Parker, Pierce, Riley, Keegan, Sawyer, Paxton, Phoenix, Jordan, Tyler, Morgan

Penda *(English)* ♂ RATING: ★★☆
Unknown meaning—King of Mercia (England)
People think of Penda as weird, old-fashioned, exotic, nerdy, ethnic
People who like the name Penda also like Maddox, Palmer, Justin, Hayes, Fox, Mattox, Roman, Aaron, Pryce, Javana

Penelope *(Greek)* ♀ RATING: ★★☆
With a web over her face—Penelope Cruz, actress; Penelope Ann Miller, actress; Penelope Pitstop, cartoon character
People think of Penelope as pretty, intelligent, funny, caring, creative
People who like the name Penelope also like Phoebe, Olivia, Chloe, Paige, Isabella, Scarlett, Sophia, Ava, Charlotte, Abigail

Penha *(African)* ♀ ♂ RATING: ★★☆
Beloved—Swahili origin
People think of Penha as pretty, unpopular, ethnic, nerdy, quiet
People who like the name Penha also like Paris, Pierce, Park, Pembroke, Parker, Poppy, Paisley, Page, Preston, Phoenix

Penn *(English)* ♂ RATING: ★★★☆
Lives by the hill—Penn Jillette, comedian; Sean Penn, actor
People think of Penn as creative, weird, cool, lazy, poor
People who like the name Penn also like Finn, Jack, Finley, Owen, Holden, Oliver, Tristan, Cole, Ethan, Gabriel

Penney *(English)* ♀ RATING: ★★
With a web over her face—Short for Penelope
People think of Penney as pretty, caring, girl next door, lazy, funny

People who like the name Penney also like Penelope, Paige, Penny, Kailey, Hailey, Faith, Rachael, Phoebe, Polly, Kacy

Pennie (English) ♀   RATING: ★★★☆
With a web over her face—Short for Penelope
People think of Pennie as pretty, funny, caring, creative, wild
People who like the name Pennie also like Paige, Penelope, Phoebe, Penney, Rachael, Rachel, Penny, Kacy, Pearl, Sophie

Pennsylvania (English) ♀♂   RATING: ★★★
Penn's woodland—U.S. state, named for Sir William Penn
People think of Pennsylvania as nerdy, old-fashioned, poor, weird, unpopular
People who like the name Pennsylvania also like Paris, Payton, September, Page, Parker, Park, Phoenix, Poppy, Paxton, Willow

Penny (English) ♀   RATING: ★★★
With a web over her face—Short for Penelope; also a coin in U.S. currency; Penny Marshall, actress/director
People think of Penny as funny, pretty, creative, trustworthy, caring
People who like the name Penny also like Paige, Olivia, Penelope, Lucy, Sarah, Hannah, Emma, Grace, Natalie, Phoebe

Peony (Greek) ♀   RATING: ★★★
Flower
People think of Peony as pretty, exotic, elegant, artsy, funny
People who like the name Peony also like Phoebe, Penelope, Scarlett, Ophelia, Ella, Ava, Paige, Iris, Isabella, Sabrina

Pepin (French) ♂   RATING: ★★
Determined
People think of Pepin as nerdy, caring, creative, young, funny
People who like the name Pepin also like Seth, Aden, Oliver, Slade, Theodore, David, Isaac, Liam, Xavier, Zander

Pepper (American) ♀   RATING: ★★
Hot spice
People think of Pepper as pretty, popular, creative, energetic, intelligent
People who like the name Pepper also like Paige, Phoebe, Olivia, Penelope, Scarlett, Chloe, Savannah, Summer, Faith, Grace

Percival (French) ♂   RATING: ★★★
Pierce valley
People think of Percival as intelligent, nerdy, stuck-up, quiet, old-fashioned
People who like the name Percival also like Nathaniel, Nicholas, Pascal, Ian, Zachary, Gabriel, Lancelot, Oliver, Theodore, Jacob

Percy (French) ♂   RATING: ★★★
Pierce valley—Short for Percival; Percy Sledge, singer
People think of Percy as intelligent, nerdy, stuck-up, uptight, old-fashioned
People who like the name Percy also like Oliver, Ethan, Nicholas, Noah, Theodore, Benjamin, Nathan, Wade, Isaac, Zachary

Perdita (Latin) ♀   RATING: ★☆
Lost—Character in *A Winter's Tale* by William Shakespeare
People think of Perdita as pretty, funny, intelligent, elegant, wild
People who like the name Perdita also like Paige, Penelope, Ophelia, Olivia, Iris, Aurora, Pippa, Petula, Cordelia, Ivy

Perdy (English) ♀   RATING: ★☆
Lost—Short for Perdita
People think of Perdy as nerdy, old, weird, poor, winner
People who like the name Perdy also like Pippa, Bella, Cordelia, Scarlett, Portia, Paprika, Pearl, Princess, Perdita, Grace

Peregrine (Latin) ♀♂   RATING: ★★★★
Wanderer—Also peregrine falcon
People think of Peregrine as intelligent, handsome, funny, energetic, creative
People who like the name Peregrine also like Piper, Phoenix, Parker, Willow, Rowan, Hayden, Dylan, Perrin, Quinn, Evelyn

Peri (Greek) ♀   RATING: ★★★★
Dweller by the pear tree—Feminine form of Perry; Peri Gilpin, actress
People think of Peri as pretty, energetic, funny, caring, young
People who like the name Peri also like Paige, Phoebe, Ava, Penelope, Pepper, Sophie, Emma, Sara, Phaedra, Chloe

Perlita (Italian) ♀   RATING: ★★☆
Little pearl
People think of Perlita as pretty, intelligent, caring, cool, popular
People who like the name Perlita also like Ava, Aria, Graziella, Aida, Lucia, Gabriella, Adrina, Bianca, Lola, Camilla

Perpetua (Spanish) ♀   RATING: ★★☆
Everlasting
People think of Perpetua as creative, pretty, exotic, weird, religious
People who like the name Perpetua also like Lareina, Delfina, Juliet, Matilda, Aitana, Daniela, Adriana, Floramaria, Melita, Estrella

Perrin (English) ♀♂   RATING: ★★
Rock—Variation of Peter; also spelled Perryn
People think of Perrin as intelligent, handsome, caring, trustworthy, leader

People who like the name Perrin also like Parker, Piper, Hayden, Caden, Quinn, Avery, Harper, Reese, Preston, Sawyer

Perry (English) ♂   RATING: ★★★☆
Dweller by the pear tree
People think of Perry as funny, intelligent, cool, caring, handsome
People who like the name Perry also like Owen, Noah, Oliver, Jacob, Ethan, Jack, Nathan, Zachary, Caleb, Lucas

Persephone (Greek) ♀   RATING: ★★★★
Bringer of destruction—In Greek mythology, the daughter of Demeter
People think of Persephone as pretty, intelligent, elegant, creative, exotic
People who like the name Persephone also like Penelope, Ophelia, Phoebe, Pandora, Scarlett, Genevieve, Chloe, Aurora, Paige, Iris

Perth (English) ♂   RATING: ★★☆
Thorny bush—Also a county in Scotland; also a city in Australia
People think of Perth as weird, nerdy, uptight, old, loser
People who like the name Perth also like Kaden, Oliver, Owen, Caleb, Jack, Deacon, Justin, Keagan, Landon, Liam

Peta (Native American) ♀   RATING: ★★★☆
Golden eagle—Blackfoot origin; also a feminine form of Peter; also an acronym for People for the Ethical Treatment of Animals
People think of Peta as creative, pretty, caring, intelligent, cool
People who like the name Peta also like Phoebe, Paige, Stella, Kaya, Penelope, Hannah, Tallulah, Layla, Scarlett, Kayla

Pete (English) ♂   RATING: ★★★☆
Rock—Pete Sampras, tennis player; Pete Townshend, musician; Pete Wentz, musician
People think of Pete as funny, sexy, handsome, popular, cool
People who like the name Pete also like Jack, Peter, Justin, Seth, Patrick, Paul, Michael, Luke, Jason, Ethan

Peter (Greek) ♂   RATING: ★★☆
Rock—Apostle of Christ; Peter Gabriel, singer/songwriter; Peter Sellers, actor/comedian; Peter Pan, children's storybook character
People think of Peter as handsome, funny, intelligent, caring, cool
People who like the name Peter also like Matthew, Nicholas, Jacob, William, Samuel, Benjamin, Patrick, Nathan, Ethan, Jack

Petit (French) ♀♂   RATING: ★★
Small
People think of Petit as pretty, young, quiet, nerdy, slow
People who like the name Petit also like Pasha, Demi, Holly, Paris, Paisley, Puma, Parlan, Coy, Parley, Prosper

Petra (Greek) ♀   RATING: ★★★☆
Rock
People think of Petra as intelligent, pretty, creative, funny, exotic
People who like the name Petra also like Phoebe, Olivia, Penelope, Isabella, Stella, Scarlett, Paige, Zoe, Violet, Chloe

Petronella (English) ♀   RATING: ★☆
Rock—Variation of Petra
People think of Petronella as intelligent, pretty, creative, popular, caring
People who like the name Petronella also like Penelope, Anastasia, Blossom, Serenity, Scarlett, Aurora, Isadora, Petunia, Patience, Serena

Petula (English) ♀   RATING: ★☆
Combination of Petal and Tulip—Petula Clark, singer
People think of Petula as intelligent, pretty, exotic, trustworthy, young
People who like the name Petula also like Posy, Perdita, Petunia, Ruby, Paige, Lucinda, Ivy, Ophelia, Patience, Stella

Petunia (English) ♀   RATING: ★★★
Flower
People think of Petunia as old-fashioned, funny, elegant, caring, sexy
People who like the name Petunia also like Pearl, Paige, Phoebe, Fiona, Olivia, Penelope, Patience, Violet, Hailey, Heather

Peyton (English) ♀♂   RATING: ★★★
From Pacca's town—Peyton Manning, football player; *Peyton Place*, soap opera.
People think of Peyton as popular, pretty, intelligent, funny, creative
People who like the name Peyton also like Hayden, Riley, Parker, Payton, Madison, Logan, Addison, Caden, Bailey, Taylor

Phaedra (Greek) ♀   RATING: ★★☆
Glowing
People think of Phaedra as pretty, intelligent, caring, creative, exotic
People who like the name Phaedra also like Persephone, Aurora, Phoebe, Ophelia, Fiona, Olivia, Penelope, Ivy, Pandora, Genevieve

Phailin (Thai) ♀   RATING: ★★
Sapphire
People think of Phailin as pretty, exotic, cool, intelligent, ethnic
People who like the name Phailin also like Tailynn, Rianna, Keaira, Keira, Phoebe, Olivia, Fallon, Phaedra, Kaelyn, Chloe

Phalen (Latin) ♀   RATING: ★★★
Peaceful
People think of Phalen as intelligent, cool, funny, exotic, elegant

People who like the name Phalen also like Paige, Lexi, Maren, Jadyn, Fiona, Sadie, Lainey, Ashlyn, Phailin, Phoebe

Pharell *(American)* ♂   RATING: ★★★☆
Descendant of the valorous man—Variation of Farrell; Pharrell Williams, singer/rapper
People think of Pharell as creative, sexy, popular, cool, trendy
People who like the name Pharell also like Isaac, Xavier, Maddox, Noah, Gabriel, Jayden, Jared, Kaden, Quentin, Lucas

Phenyo *(African)* ♀   RATING: ★★☆
Victory—Botswana origin
People think of Phenyo as weird, loser, ethnic, funny, nerdy
People who like the name Phenyo also like Penelope, Paulina, Penny, Pearl, Phailin, Patience, Pilar, Ophelia, Petra, Phylicia

Pherenike *(Greek)* ♀   RATING: ★★☆
Victorious one
People think of Pherenike as sporty, elegant, winner, powerful, creative
People who like the name Pherenike also like Delphine, Dara, Cosette, Cicily, Cherry, Charleigh, Celestyn, Cara, Cady, Aretha

Phiala *(Celtic/Gaelic)* ♀   RATING: ★★
Irish saint
People think of Phiala as intelligent, pretty, exotic, caring, old
People who like the name Phiala also like Maeve, Keaira, Kaelyn, Meara, Keira, Kera, Genevieve, Skyla, Kiara, Rhona

Phil *(Greek)* ♂   RATING: ★★
Lover of horses—Short for Philip; Phil Caveretta, baseball player; Phil Hartman, actor/comedian; "Dr. Phil" McGraw, talk show host
People think of Phil as funny, handsome, caring, intelligent, cool
People who like the name Phil also like Jake, Jason, Seth, Justin, Scott, Benjamin, David, Ian, Adam, Patrick

Phila *(Greek)* ♀   RATING: ★★☆
Love
People think of Phila as girl next door, energetic, caring, intelligent, weird
People who like the name Phila also like Philana, Phoebe, Posy, Philantha, Patia, Phylicia, Pomona, Pascale, Phaedra, Piera

Philana *(Greek)* ♀   RATING: ★★☆
Lover of horses—Feminine form of Philip
People think of Philana as cool, pretty, artsy, exotic, sexy
People who like the name Philana also like Philena, Penelope, Phoebe, Ophelia, Philomena, Philantha, Maeve, Larissa, Peony, Posy

Philander *(Greek)* ♂   RATING: ★★☆
Lover of man
People think of Philander as loser, unpopular, nerdy, untrustworthy, handsome
People who like the name Philander also like Leander, Dmitri, Elias, Lysander, Sirius, Cicero, Socrates, Thaddeus, Constantine, Raphael

Philantha *(Greek)* ♀   RATING: ★★
Lover of flowers
People think of Philantha as pretty, intelligent, creative, quiet, exotic
People who like the name Philantha also like Philana, Penelope, Paulette, Petronella, Portia, Leighanna, Phila, Pierrette, Philena, Psyche

Philena *(Greek)* ♀   RATING: ★★
Lover of mankind
People think of Philena as old-fashioned, stuck-up, aggressive, big, trendy
People who like the name Philena also like Philana, Lily, Patience, Philomena, Penelope, Mercedes, Philantha, Perdita, Pippa, Fiona

Philip *(Greek)* ♂   RATING: ★★★☆
Lover of horses—Philip K. Dick, author; Philip Roth, author
People think of Philip as handsome, intelligent, funny, caring, trustworthy
People who like the name Philip also like Nathan, Ethan, Nicholas, Zachary, Benjamin, Matthew, Alexander, William, Noah, Andrew

Philippa *(Greek)* ♀   RATING: ★★
Lover of horses—Feminine form of Philip
People think of Philippa as pretty, intelligent, caring, funny, sexy
People who like the name Philippa also like Olivia, Penelope, Charlotte, Paige, Hannah, Chloe, Grace, Scarlett, Stella, Phoebe

Phillip *(Greek)* ♂   RATING: ★★★★
Lover of horses
People think of Phillip as funny, handsome, intelligent, caring, cool
People who like the name Phillip also like Nicholas, Ethan, William, Benjamin, Patrick, Matthew, Zachary, Nathan, Jacob, Daniel

Phillipa *(Greek)* ♀   RATING: ★★★☆
Lover of horses—Feminine form of Phillip
People think of Phillipa as intelligent, pretty, popular, caring, creative
People who like the name Phillipa also like Paige, Olivia, Philippa, Chloe, Eleanor, Lauren, Maisie, Elizabeth, Amelia, Jasmine

Philomena *(Greek)* ♀   RATING: ★★★★
Strong friend
People think of Philomena as pretty, funny, trustworthy, intelligent, popular

453

454

People who like the name Philomena also like Penelope, Phoebe, Evangeline, Persephone, Pandora, Genevieve, Ophelia, Patience, Felicity, Aurora

Philyra *(Greek)* ♀   RATING: ★★★☆
Love of music
People think of Philyra as pretty, creative, exotic, artsy, cool
People who like the name Philyra also like Phaedra, Ophelia, Psyche, Dysis, Calliope, Penelope, Phylicia, Qamra, Phyliss, Amaya

Phineas *(Hebrew)* ♂   RATING: ★★
Nubian
People think of Phineas as intelligent, creative, handsome, leader, funny
People who like the name Phineas also like Noah, Oliver, Nathaniel, Xavier, Liam, Tristan, Sebastian, Holden, Isaac, Owen

Phinnaeus *(Hebrew)* ♂   RATING: ★★★
Nubian—Phinnaeus Moder, son of actress Julia Roberts
People think of Phinnaeus as creative, energetic, popular, artsy, handsome
People who like the name Phinnaeus also like Finn, Noah, Tristan, Oliver, Jack, Owen, Sebastian, Gavin, Griffin, Cole

Phoebe *(Greek)* ♀   RATING: ★★★
Bright, shining—Also spelled Pheobe; Phoebe Buffay, character on *Friends*; Phoebe Cates, actress
People think of Phoebe as pretty, funny, creative, caring, intelligent
People who like the name Phoebe also like Paige, Chloe, Olivia, Hannah, Emma, Faith, Grace, Zoe, Abigail, Ava

Phoenix *(Greek)* ♀♂   RATING: ★★★★☆
Bloodred—Joaquin Phoenix, actor; River Phoenix, actor
People think of Phoenix as intelligent, creative, powerful, exotic, energetic
People who like the name Phoenix also like Parker, Logan, Dakota, Hayden, Riley, Madison, Piper, Jade, Caden, Dylan

Phomello *(African)* ♂   RATING: ★★☆
Succeed—South African origin
People think of Phomello as weird, sexy, trustworthy, poor, old-fashioned
People who like the name Phomello also like Maddox, Deacon, Pedro, Mace, Morathi, Galvin, Joel, Maddock, Minowa, Jayden

Phong *(Vietnamese)* ♂   RATING: ★★★
Wind
People think of Phong as intelligent, weird, funny, cool, lazy
People who like the name Phong also like Micah, Soren, Deacon, Jonas, Jonah, Gage, Ethan, Gordon, Jerold, Balthasar

Phuc *(Vietnamese)* ♂   RATING: ★★★
Blessing
People think of Phuc as funny, sexy, loser, quiet, poor
People who like the name Phuc also like Gabriel, Trent, Lance, Trevor, Alexander, Jayden, Xander, Van, Landon, Isaiah

Phuoc *(Vietnamese)* ♂   RATING: ★★☆
Blessing—Variation of Phuc
People think of Phuoc as loser, weird, ethnic, nerdy, quiet
People who like the name Phuoc also like Colt, Cole, Waylon, Dermot, Demetrius, Deiter, Davis, Titus, Dalton, Constantine

Phuong *(Vietnamese)* ♀   RATING: ★☆
Phoenix
People think of Phuong as trustworthy, intelligent, funny, creative, cool
People who like the name Phuong also like Phailin, Penelope, Petunia, Paloma, Pascale, Perdita, Philana, Purity, Peri, Maisie

Phylicia *(American)* ♀   RATING: ★★★★
Combination of Phyllis and Felicia—Phylicia Allen Rashad, actress
People think of Phylicia as pretty, intelligent, funny, caring, cool
People who like the name Phylicia also like Phoebe, Paige, Penelope, Phaedra, Olivia, Precious, Vanessa, Sabrina, Lydia, Pandora

Phyliss *(Greek)* ♀   RATING: ★★★
Green leaves
People think of Phyliss as old-fashioned, old, nerdy, weird, caring
People who like the name Phyliss also like Penelope, Grace, Giselle, Portia, Paula, Philyra, Phoebe, Phylicia, Estelle, Ophelia

Phyllis *(Greek)* ♀   RATING: ★★★
Green leaves—Phyllis Diller, comedian
People think of Phyllis as caring, pretty, funny, intelligent, old-fashioned
People who like the name Phyllis also like Olivia, Penelope, Paige, Phoebe, Charlotte, Mallory, Victoria, Tamara, Felicity, Phylicia

Phyre *(American)* ♀♂   RATING: ★★★☆
Fire
People think of Phyre as exotic, powerful, leader, creative, wild
People who like the name Phyre also like Phoenix, Parker, Caden, Paxton, Piper, Hunter, Raven, Camdyn, Payton, Riley

Pia *(Italian)* ♀   RATING: ★★★☆
Pious—Pia Lindstrom, newscaster; Pia Zadora, singer
People think of Pia as pretty, funny, creative, intelligent, cool
People who like the name Pia also like Paige, Ella, Mia, Grace, Ava, Chloe, Phoebe, Penelope, Zoe, Tia

Picabo *(American)* ♀   RATING: ★★★
From the children's game peek-a-boo; also a town in Idaho; Picabo Street, Olympic skier
> People think of Picabo as energetic, unpopular, loser, poor, intelligent
> People who like the name Picabo also like Paige, Penelope, Zoe, Olivia, Phoebe, Isabella, Belle, Genevieve, Pebbles, Sadie

Pier *(English)* ♀ ♂   RATING: ★★★
Rock—Short for Peter
> People think of Pier as cool, creative, energetic, caring, aggressive
> People who like the name Pier also like Pierce, Parker, Porter, Preston, Piper, Parrish, Paris, Presley, Piperel, Poppy

Piera *(Italian)* ♀   RATING: ★★★☆
Rock—Variation of Petra
> People think of Piera as exotic, intelligent, creative, funny, pretty
> People who like the name Piera also like Paige, Phoebe, Elle, Paulette, Penelope, Genevieve, Brielle, Pierrette, Madeleine, Gianna

Pierce *(English)* ♀ ♂   RATING: ★★★
Rock—Variation of Peter; Pierce Brosnan, actor
> People think of Pierce as handsome, intelligent, sexy, popular, powerful
> People who like the name Pierce also like Parker, Hayden, Preston, Logan, Riley, Mason, Payton, Caden, Avery, Madison

Pierina *(Italian)* ♀   RATING: ★★☆
Made of stone
> People think of Pierina as pretty, young, sexy, aggressive, powerful
> People who like the name Pierina also like Adrienne, Velia, Allegra, Morgana, Constance, Jessica, Maria, Marisa, Josephina, Lia

Pierre *(French)* ♂   RATING: ★★☆
Rock—Variation of Peter; Pierre Bouvier, musician; Pierre Cardin, designer; Pierre Trudeau, former Canadian prime minister
> People think of Pierre as handsome, funny, cool, sexy, intelligent
> People who like the name Pierre also like Oliver, Gabriel, Nicholas, Noah, Adrian, Nathan, Matthew, Ethan, Jack, Caleb

Pierrette *(French)* ♀   RATING: ★★★
Rock—Feminine form of Pierre
> People think of Pierrette as pretty, girl next door, old-fashioned, creative, exotic
> People who like the name Pierrette also like Paulette, Paige, Pleasance, Pascale, Piera, Pauline, Belle, Juliette, Cosette, Genevieve

Pieta *(Latin)* ♀   RATING: ★★☆
Piety, religiousness—Also a representation of the Virgin Mary lamenting the death of Jesus
> People think of Pieta as religious, exotic, elegant, creative, sexy
> People who like the name Pieta also like Phoebe, Chloe, Paige, Lilah, Fallon, Madeleine, Imogen, Ophelia, Abigail, Peta

Pilar *(Spanish)* ♀   RATING: ★★
Pillar (of strength)
> People think of Pilar as pretty, intelligent, caring, funny, creative
> People who like the name Pilar also like Olivia, Penelope, Isabella, Nadia, Paloma, Sophia, Paige, Phoebe, Mia, Bianca

Pilialoha *(Hawaiian)* ♀   RATING: ★★★
Beloved
> People think of Pilialoha as exotic, pretty, weird, artsy, girl next door
> People who like the name Pilialoha also like Miliani, Kawena, Malia, Keala, Kinipela, Kaloni, Ulani, Keani, Alohilani, Nohealani

Pillan *(Native American)* ♀ ♂   RATING: ★★☆
God of stormy weather
> People think of Pillan as caring, leader, sexy, intelligent, young
> People who like the name Pillan also like Pyralis, Pavan, Nida, Mika, Pahana, Shea, Makya, Perrin, Phoenix, Misae

Pilot *(American)* ♀ ♂   RATING: ★★★
Ship or plane operator
> People think of Pilot as intelligent, handsome, trendy, aggressive, sneaky
> People who like the name Pilot also like Parker, Caden, Ryder, Piper, Addison, Avery, London, Skylar, Seven, Kyle

Ping *(Chinese)* ♀ ♂   RATING: ★★★☆
Duckweed—Mandarin origin
> People think of Ping as creative, funny, nerdy, ethnic, pretty
> People who like the name Ping also like Page, Paris, Parker, Phoenix, Piper, Perrin, Preston, Presley, Poppy, Paxton

Pink *(American)* ♀   RATING: ★★
Light red color; healthy—Pink, singer
> People think of Pink as pretty, sexy, cool, funny, popular
> People who like the name Pink also like Paige, Princess, Purity, Grace, Rebecca, Patience, Sugar, Ivy, Violet, Melody

Piper *(English)* ♀ ♂   RATING: ★★☆
Flute player—Piper Laurie, actress; Piper Perabo, actress
> People think of Piper as pretty, creative, intelligent, funny, energetic
> People who like the name Piper also like Parker, Riley, Logan, Madison, Hayden, Reese, Bailey, Peyton, Taylor, Payton

456

Piperel (English) ♀♂　　　RATING: ★★★
Pepper
> People think of Piperel as weird, funny, wealthy, sneaky, criminal
> People who like the name Piperel also like Phoenix, Piper, Pier, Hadley, Pierce, Hayden, Perrin, Paris, Willow, Monet

Pippa (English) ♀　　　RATING: ★★★★
Lover of horses—Short for Phillipa
> People think of Pippa as pretty, funny, creative, energetic, young
> People who like the name Pippa also like Paige, Olivia, Phoebe, Lucy, Penelope, Ava, Grace, Emma, Bella, Lily

Piri (Hungarian) ♀　　　RATING: ★★☆
Old, ancient
> People think of Piri as stuck-up, unpopular, lazy, pretty, powerful
> People who like the name Piri also like Maren, Millicent, Aderyn, Gemma, Kiersten, Lyris, Olivia, Ramona, Aelwen, Eleanor

Pirro (Italian) ♂　　　RATING: ★★★
Rock—Variation of Peter; also an American surname
> People think of Pirro as weird, caring, nerdy, aggressive, loser
> People who like the name Pirro also like Rohan, Ryker, Kaden, Korbin, Gavin, Noah, Constantine, Ben, Landon, Nathaniel

Pisces (Latin) ♀♂　　　RATING: ★★★☆
The fish—Used for children born under this astrological sign
> People think of Pisces as creative, pretty, intelligent, funny, leader
> People who like the name Pisces also like Phoenix, Paris, Parker, Payton, Piper, Blake, Bailey, Paxton, Sydney, Pierce

Placido (Spanish) ♂　　　RATING: ★★★
Calm, quiet—Placido Domingo, opera singer
> People think of Placido as exotic, quiet, handsome, intelligent, lazy
> People who like the name Placido also like Nathan, Angelo, Nathaniel, Raymond, Tommy, Benjamin, Gino, Mariano, Leo, Thomas

Plato (Greek) ♂　　　RATING: ★★★
Strong shoulders—Greek philosopher
> People think of Plato as powerful, intelligent, funny, winner, young
> People who like the name Plato also like Wyatt, Theodore, Gabriel, Wade, Hercules, Jacob, Socrates, Aristotle, Mateo, Odysseus

Platt (English) ♂　　　RATING: ★★☆
Dweller by the footbridge—Oliver Platt, actor
> People think of Platt as slow, quiet, loser, old-fashioned, energetic
> People who like the name Platt also like Garren, Penda, Pryce, Lanton, Mattox, Maddox, Taran, Jamison, Jett, Fox

Pleasance (French) ♀　　　RATING: ★★☆
Agreeable
> People think of Pleasance as unpopular, nerdy, quiet, weird, trustworthy
> People who like the name Pleasance also like Paige, Precious, Purity, Patience, Trinity, Serenity, Aurora, Eternity, Harmony, Chloe

Pluto (Latin) ♀♂　　　RATING: ★★★
Roman god of the underworld—In mythology, the brother of Zeus and Neptune; also a former planet demoted to a dwarf planet; Pluto, Disney character
> People think of Pluto as weird, funny, artsy, popular, unpopular
> People who like the name Pluto also like Dante, Desi, Des, Loki, Odin, Lucky, Zo, Jerry, Alta, Jude

Polly (English) ♀　　　RATING: ★★★
Great sorrow—Variation of Molly; also a nickname for Paula; Polly Bergen, actress; Polly Holliday, actress
> People think of Polly as pretty, funny, intelligent, caring, creative
> People who like the name Polly also like Paige, Grace, Olivia, Sophie, Lucy, Molly, Phoebe, Faith, Hannah, Ella

Pollyanna (English) ♀　　　RATING: ★★★
Combination of Polly and Anna; also a person with an overly optimistic view on life; *Pollyanna*, book and film
> People think of Pollyanna as pretty, funny, creative, trustworthy, popular
> People who like the name Pollyanna also like Chloe, Morgana, Ruby, Paprika, Sephora, Summer, Kiana, Felicity, Scarlett, Abrianna

Pomona (Latin) ♀　　　RATING: ★★★
Fruit tree—Goddess of fruit
> People think of Pomona as old-fashioned, caring, loser, poor, nerdy
> People who like the name Pomona also like Pandora, Psyche, Phoebe, Phaedra, Patience, Ophelia, Persephone, Penelope, Posy, Padma

Ponce (Spanish) ♂　　　RATING: ★☆
Ocean—Also a surname; Juan Ponce de León, conquistador
> People think of Ponce as sexy, old-fashioned, lazy, creative, intelligent
> People who like the name Ponce also like Esteban, Pancho, Joaquin, Feo, Landon, Ajay, Randall, Hidalgo, Julio, Theodore

Pooh (American) ♂　　　RATING: ★★★
Little one—Often used for pets or stuffed animals, or as a pet name for humans; from Winnie the Pooh, storybook character named after a bear in the Winnipeg zoo named Winnipeg Pooh
> People think of Pooh as loser, nerdy, weird, lazy, slow
> People who like the name Pooh also like Caleb, Ethan, Christopher, Ian, Nathan, Nicholas, Andrew, Aaron, Jacob, Byron

Pooky (American) ♀♂   RATING: ★★★
Cute person—Also a term of endearment
People think of Pooky as funny, weird, young, wild, pretty
People who like the name Pooky also like Piper, Peyton, Taylor, Phoenix, Parker, Cadence, Morgan, Page, Hunter, Paris

Popo (Native American) ♀♂   RATING: ★★☆
Tall rye grass—Crow origin; also means a kiss in Korean and excrement in Spanish; also urban slang for police officer
People think of Popo as weird, funny, loser, creative, poor
People who like the name Popo also like Mika, Riley, Pooky, Jax, Caden, Wiley, Zo, Cam, Aidan, Toby

Poppy (Latin) ♀♂   RATING: ★★
From the flower—Poppy Montgomery, actress
People think of Poppy as pretty, creative, funny, caring, intelligent
People who like the name Poppy also like Piper, Bailey, Parker, Madison, Holly, James, Willow, Riley, Charlie, Quinn

Porfirio (Italian) ♂   RATING: ★★★
Purple
People think of Porfirio as intelligent, handsome, funny, powerful, creative
People who like the name Porfirio also like Tristan, Drake, Maddox, Giovanni, Etienne, Gabriel, Morpheus, Amadeus, Lucian, Agostino

Porsche (German) ♀♂   RATING: ★★★☆
Offering—Brand of a car manufacturer
People think of Porsche as pretty, sexy, popular, funny, cool
People who like the name Porsche also like Taylor, Parker, Preston, Logan, Phoenix, Paris, Madison, Jordan, Dakota, Presley

Porter (English) ♀♂   RATING: ★★★★
Doorkeeper—Cole Porter, composer
People think of Porter as funny, intelligent, sporty, trustworthy, cool
People who like the name Porter also like Parker, Preston, Hayden, Logan, Addison, Payton, Carter, Sawyer, Mason, Taylor

Portia (Latin) ♀   RATING: ★★★★
Roman clan name—Portia di Rossi, actress; character in *The Merchant of Venice* by William Shakespeare
People think of Portia as pretty, intelligent, funny, sexy, popular
People who like the name Portia also like Olivia, Paige, Ava, Bianca, Chloe, Isabella, Phoebe, Bella, Mia, Nadia

Posh (English) ♀♂   RATING: ★★
Elegant—Originally an acronym for Port Out, Starboard Home, the best part of a traveling ship for high-class people; Posh Spice, stage name for Victoria Beckham
People think of Posh as old-fashioned, popular, aggressive, girl next door, sexy
People who like the name Posh also like Aubrey, Page, Sage, Oracle, Lyle, Phoenix, James, Logan, Brayden, Jade

Posy (English) ♀   RATING: ★☆
Small flower
People think of Posy as pretty, artsy, nerdy, creative, popular
People who like the name Posy also like Paige, Fiona, Ava, Phoebe, Violet, Scarlett, Penelope, Sadie, Ophelia, Ella

Potter (English) ♂   RATING: ★★★☆
Pot maker—Also a surname; Harry Potter, character in novels by J. K. Rowling
People think of Potter as funny, trustworthy, intelligent, wild, leader
People who like the name Potter also like Noah, Owen, Trevor, Zachary, Jackson, Tyson, Nathan, Oliver, Gavin, William

Pouria (Persian) ♂   RATING: ★★☆
Hero
People think of Pouria as powerful, creative, sexy, handsome, cool
People who like the name Pouria also like Xerxes, Bijan, Zarek, Adish, Bardia, Kyran, Darius, Siyavash, Darrius, Cyrus

Powa (Native American) ♂   RATING: ★★☆
Wealthy
People think of Powa as big, aggressive, sneaky, sexy, exotic
People who like the name Powa also like Brandon, Jacob, Seth, Ezhno, Chi, William, Ryu, Bradley, Wyatt, Shaman

Powell (Welsh) ♂   RATING: ★★★
Son of Howell—William Powell, actor
People think of Powell as handsome, intelligent, trustworthy, cool, powerful
People who like the name Powell also like Cole, Collin, Nico, Owen, Hudson, Nicholas, Vincent, Lance, Liam, Samuel

Prairie (American) ♀♂   RATING: ★★★
Flatland
People think of Prairie as weird, old-fashioned, quiet, creative, artsy
People who like the name Prairie also like Parker, Bailey, Madison, Jaden, Willow, Phoenix, Riley, Piper, Caden, Winter

458

Pranet *(Sanskrit/East Indian)* ♂ RATING: ★★☆
Leader
> People think of Pranet as creative, nerdy, funny, weird, cool
> People who like the name Pranet also like Pravar, Prem, Abhay, Devesh, Lokesh, Dhaval, Nalin, Kuval, Nitesh, Nirav

Pravar *(Sanskrit/East Indian)* ♂ RATING: ★★☆
Chief
> People think of Pravar as aggressive, cool, loser, caring, leader
> People who like the name Pravar also like Pranet, Pravin, Amish, Ojas, Arav, Adit, Arnav, Adarsh, Prem, Indra

Pravat *(Thai)* ♂ RATING: ★★☆
History
> People think of Pravat as handsome, intelligent, creative, untrustworthy, young
> People who like the name Pravat also like Xavier, Kaden, Fox, Lucas, Chi, Wyatt, Chance, Xander, Gavin, Jake

Pravin *(Sanskrit/East Indian)* ♂ RATING: ★★★
Expert
> People think of Pravin as intelligent, trustworthy, handsome, caring, energetic
> People who like the name Pravin also like Xavier, Seth, Rohan, Tyson, Aden, Nalin, Kaden, Xander, Ravi, Wade

Precious *(American)* ♀ RATING: ★★★☆
Precious one
> People think of Precious as pretty, funny, popular, caring, young
> People who like the name Precious also like Patience, Faith, Destiny, Princess, Paige, Trinity, Aaliyah, Serenity, Hope, Eternity

Prem *(Sanskrit/East Indian)* ♂ RATING: ★☆
Love, affection
> People think of Prem as cool, nerdy, young, weird, caring
> People who like the name Prem also like Rohan, Ashwin, Sanjay, Nalin, Gagan, Pravin, Ravi, Adit, Valin, Arnav

Prema *(Sanskrit/East Indian)* ♀ RATING: ★★★
Love, affection
> People think of Prema as pretty, ethnic, slow, exotic, creative
> People who like the name Prema also like Paige, Padma, Premala, Parmida, Pia, Posy, Pilar, Pippa, Portia, Penelope

Premala *(Sanskrit/East Indian)* ♀ RATING: ★★☆
Loving
> People think of Premala as elegant, creative, ethnic, caring, weird
> People who like the name Premala also like Prema, Pallavi, Parvani, Parvati, Padma, Pia, Posy, Panchali, Priti, Palesa

Prentice *(English)* ♀♂ RATING: ★★
Apprentice—Originally a surname
> People think of Prentice as popular, handsome, caring, funny, intelligent
> People who like the name Prentice also like Preston, Parker, Caden, Paxton, Payton, Pierce, Spencer, Hayden, Riley, Quinn

Presencia *(Spanish)* ♀ RATING: ★★
Presence
> People think of Presencia as leader, exotic, powerful, popular, energetic
> People who like the name Presencia also like Perdita, Raina, Savanna, Isabella, Petunia, Parmida, Lola, Pelagia, Premala, Parisa

Presley *(English)* ♀♂ RATING: ★★★★☆
From the priest's field—Also a surname; Elvis Presley, singer/actor
> People think of Presley as pretty, funny, intelligent, popular, creative
> People who like the name Presley also like Preston, Parker, Payton, Hayden, Logan, Reese, Addison, Taylor, Riley, Madison

Presta *(Spanish)* ♀ RATING: ★★
Hurry, quick
> People think of Presta as exotic, weird, funny, sexy, aggressive
> People who like the name Presta also like Hope, Pauline, Natalie, Pearl, Isabel, Pamela, Pearly, Priscilla, Justine, Paulette

Preston *(English)* ♀♂ RATING: ★★★
From the priest's town
> People think of Preston as handsome, intelligent, funny, popular, cool
> People who like the name Preston also like Parker, Hayden, Logan, Payton, Madison, Riley, Mason, Taylor, Caden, Spencer

Prewitt *(English)* ♂ RATING: ★☆
Brave, valorous
> People think of Prewitt as funny, young, powerful, aggressive, trustworthy
> People who like the name Prewitt also like Jackson, Emerson, Owen, Reece, Mitchell, Ian, Holden, Jayden, Kaden, Caleb

Price *(English)* ♂ RATING: ★★
Son of Rhys—British pronunciation of the Welsh phrase *Ap Rhys*
> People think of Price as creative, cool, powerful, intelligent, caring
> People who like the name Price also like Owen, Pryce, Jayden, Landon, Kaden, Noah, Tucker, Ian, Walker, Oliver

Primavera *(Spanish)* ♀ RATING: ★★☆
Springtime
> People think of Primavera as funny, weird, exotic, lazy, caring

People who like the name Primavera also like Pebbles, Magnolia, Phoebe, Vera, Pleasance, Paloma, Pearl, Lola, Parvati, Princess

Primo *(Italian)* ♂   RATING: ★★★
Firstborn
People think of Primo as cool, handsome, creative, popular, energetic
People who like the name Primo also like Gabriel, Giovanni, Landon, Emilio, Victor, Salvatore, Gage, Roman, Dominic, Draco

Prince *(Latin)* ♂   RATING: ★★★☆
Royal son—Prince, musician; Prince Jackson, son of Michael Jackson
People think of Prince as powerful, handsome, popular, funny, leader
People who like the name Prince also like Nathan, Tyson, Jacob, Isaiah, Alexander, Lucas, Xavier, Isaac, Victor, Justin

Princess *(English)* ♀   RATING: ★★★☆
Royal daughter
People think of Princess as pretty, popular, funny, sexy, caring
People who like the name Princess also like Precious, Destiny, Faith, Paige, Jasmine, Nicole, Aaliyah, Sabrina, Patience, Jessica

Prisca *(Latin)* ♀   RATING: ★☆
Ancient
People think of Prisca as intelligent, pretty, funny, energetic, caring
People who like the name Prisca also like Posy, Ophelia, Pippa, Penelope, Cordelia, Perdita, Bianca, Hazel, Felicity, Scarlett

Priscilla *(Latin)* ♀   RATING: ★★☆
Ancient—Priscilla Presley, actress
People think of Priscilla as pretty, funny, intelligent, caring, creative
People who like the name Priscilla also like Isabella, Victoria, Sabrina, Olivia, Samantha, Vanessa, Emma, Paige, Abigail, Rebecca

Pritam *(Sanskrit/East Indian)* ♂   RATING: ★★☆
Lover
People think of Pritam as cool, sexy, intelligent, creative, handsome
People who like the name Pritam also like Adarsh, Arnav, Gaurav, Chetan, Adit, Arav, Rupin, Amrit, Prem, Ashwin

Priti *(Sanskrit/East Indian)* ♀   RATING: ★★★☆
Love
People think of Priti as pretty, caring, creative, intelligent, cool
People who like the name Priti also like Padma, Pallavi, Patience, Prema, Panchali, Tanuja, Parvati, Serenity, Parvani, Premala

Priya *(Sanskrit/East Indian)* ♀   RATING: ★★★☆
Beloved
People think of Priya as pretty, intelligent, creative, caring, young
People who like the name Priya also like Anaya, Isabella, Anya, Padma, Pallavi, Freya, Suki, Adia, Rhian, Amara

Priyanka *(Sanskrit/East Indian)* ♀   RATING: ★★★
Kind
People think of Priyanka as pretty, intelligent, funny, creative, caring
People who like the name Priyanka also like Deepnita, Priya, Priti, Pallavi, Denali, Ishana, Premala, Devi, Mrinal, Shreya

Probert *(English)* ♂   RATING: ★★☆
Son of Robert
People think of Probert as nerdy, loser, weird, old-fashioned, sexy
People who like the name Probert also like Vinny, Wood, Vashon, Satchel, Tameron, Terrel, Trory, Tavarius, Woods, Tavorian

Prosper *(Latin)* ♀♂   RATING: ★★
Fortune
People think of Prosper as caring, intelligent, energetic, trustworthy, leader
People who like the name Prosper also like Ezra, Sawyer, Pierce, Piper, Parker, Hayden, Willow, Oakley, Phoenix, Tanner

Prudence *(English)* ♀   RATING: ★★★☆
Cautious; intelligent
People think of Prudence as intelligent, caring, pretty, creative, trustworthy
People who like the name Prudence also like Phoebe, Paige, Faith, Penelope, Patience, Scarlett, Chloe, Felicity, Prue, Hailey

Prue *(English)* ♀   RATING: ★★
Short for Prudence or Prunella
People think of Prue as pretty, intelligent, creative, caring, powerful
People who like the name Prue also like Phoebe, Paige, Prudence, Faith, Chloe, Mia, Scarlett, Hailey, Ava, Olivia

Prunella *(Latin)* ♀   RATING: ★★☆
Little plum
People think of Prunella as weird, old-fashioned, pretty, uptight, unpopular
People who like the name Prunella also like Priscilla, Fiona, Cordelia, Portia, Ophelia, Prudence, Cleo, Purity, Paloma, Octavia

Pryce *(English)* ♂   RATING: ★★☆
Son of Rhys—Variation of Price
People think of Pryce as intelligent, powerful, young, popular, wealthy
People who like the name Pryce also like Kaden, Jayden, Caleb, Ian, Seth, Tristan, Ethan, Owen, Cole, Gavin

Psalm *(Hebrew)* ♀♂ RATING: ★★★
Song
> People think of Psalm as religious, intelligent, creative, caring, quiet
> People who like the name Psalm also like Phoenix, Eden, Paris, Sage, Brooklyn, Rylie, Landen, Paisley, Skye, James

Psyche *(Greek)* ♀ RATING: ★★★☆
The soul—Pronounced *SY-kee*
> People think of Psyche as pretty, creative, artsy, intelligent, elegant
> People who like the name Psyche also like Pandora, Persephone, Penelope, Ophelia, Phoebe, Chloe, Paige, Aurora, Phaedra, Ivy

Pules *(Native American)* ♀ RATING: ★★
Pidgeon—Algonquin origin
> People think of Pules as loser, old-fashioned, weird, nerdy, girl next door
> People who like the name Pules also like Sora, Pabla, Patience, Olisa, Psyche, Peta, Pakuna, Penney, Pearl, Phenyo

Puma *(Latin)* ♀♂ RATING: ★★★☆
Mountain lion—Also a brand of athletic wear
> People think of Puma as aggressive, exotic, intelligent, energetic, wild
> People who like the name Puma also like Phoenix, Paris, Parker, Piper, Logan, James, Porsche, Bailey, Poppy, Payton

Purity *(English)* ♀ RATING: ★★★☆
Unsullied, clean
> People think of Purity as pretty, trustworthy, religious, girl next door, young
> People who like the name Purity also like Patience, Paige, Faith, Serenity, Harmony, Precious, Destiny, Lacey, Felicity, Hope

Pyotr *(Russian)* ♂ RATING: ★★☆
Rock—Variation of Peter; Pyotr Ilych Tchaikovsky, composer
> People think of Pyotr as handsome, exotic, trustworthy, powerful, artsy
> People who like the name Pyotr also like Christopher, Ethan, Tokala, Jacob, Sebastian, Benjamin, Jason, Johnathan, Peter, Alexander

Pyralis *(Greek)* ♀♂ RATING: ★☆
Of fire
> People think of Pyralis as exotic, weird, powerful, aggressive, intelligent
> People who like the name Pyralis also like Phoenix, Hayden, Pavan, Caden, Parker, Artemis, Payton, Riley, Perrin, Lyric

— 🅠 —

Qabil *(Arabic)* ♂ RATING: ★★★
Able
> People think of Qabil as ethnic, criminal, loser, weird, lazy
> People who like the name Qabil also like Wade, Xander, Faris, David, Rhys, Qamar, Malik, Kaleb, Cedric, Shadi

Qacha *(Mongolian)* ♀ RATING: ★★
Flank
> People think of Qacha as weird, big, old, unpopular, criminal
> People who like the name Qacha also like Quasar, Qwara, Umaymah, Uzuri, Xalvadora, Xochitl, Safara, Xolani, Tanginika, Aderyn

Qadan *(Mongolian)* ♀♂ RATING: ★★☆
Cliff
> People think of Qadan as popular, loser, weird, unpopular, girl next door
> People who like the name Qadan also like Addison, Rylan, Quennell, Caden, Mason, Quillan, Oran, Jocelyn, Lyndon, Ainsley

Qadr *(Arabic)* ♀ RATING: ★★
Power, Fate
> People think of Qadr as quiet, weird, unpopular, exotic, ethnic
> People who like the name Qadr also like Quintessa, Qismah, Devorit, Dena, Quiana, Ulan, Didina, Ura, Kilenya, Dustine

Qamar *(Arabic)* ♂ RATING: ★★★☆
Moon
> People think of Qamar as handsome, intelligent, popular, caring, trustworthy
> People who like the name Qamar also like Xadrian, Quentin, Uriah, Demitrius, Nicholas, Aiden, Kamali, Quade, Xavier, Taariq

Qamra *(Greek)* ♀ RATING: ★★★☆
Moon
> People think of Qamra as pretty, young, exotic, artsy, sexy
> People who like the name Qamra also like Penelope, Calandra, Dysis, Neona, Xylia, Zabrina, Selena, Kiara, Quiana, Qwara

Qays *(Arabic)* ♂ RATING: ★★☆
Firm
> People think of Qays as funny, handsome, weird, cool, exotic
> People who like the name Qays also like Adish, Quade, Quana, Quentin, Xanto, Xarles, Kael, Xavier, Rida, Nayef

Qi *(Chinese)* ♀ RATING: ★☆
Fine jade—Mandarin origin; can also mean outstanding, distinguished, special, and pretty
> People think of Qi as unpopular, weird, pretty, nerdy, untrustworthy

People who like the name Qi also like Zi, Destiny, Xia, Qiana, Hailey, Kyla, Amaya, Paige, Xaria, Quynh

Qiana *(Arabic)* ♀   RATING: ★★★☆
Singers
People think of Qiana as pretty, creative, caring, funny, popular
People who like the name Qiana also like Jadyn, Tiana, Olivia, Kiana, Kaelyn, Rianna, Iliana, Cailyn, Hannah, Trinity

Qiao *(Chinese)* ♀ ♂   RATING: ★★★☆
Pretty; handsome
People think of Qiao as pretty, elegant, ethnic, exotic, caring
People who like the name Qiao also like Rong, Qing Yuan, Yue Yan, Quennell, Quillan, Wing, Quincy, Val, Xenophon, Xola

Qimat *(Arabic)* ♀ ♂   RATING: ★★★
Valuable
People think of Qimat as ethnic, cool, wild, powerful, leader
People who like the name Qimat also like Quennell, Pavan, Quillan, Quincy, Quinlan, Connor, Tacey, Ash, Meryl, Wynn

Qing *(Chinese)* ♀   RATING: ★★★
Aqua colored
People think of Qing as exotic, pretty, intelligent, creative, funny
People who like the name Qing also like Xiao Hong, Xin Qian, Coralie, Queenie, Ulan, Xylia, Qi, Colette, Ulani, Xanthe

Qing Yuan *(Chinese)* ♀ ♂   RATING: ★★★
Deep water; clear spring—Mandarin origin
People think of Qing Yuan as weird, ethnic, exotic, sexy, nerdy
People who like the name Qing Yuan also like Xing Xing, Dakota, Yuki, Yue, Ming Yue, Unique, Quennell, Dallas, Tao, Quincy

Qismah *(Arabic)* ♀   RATING: ★★☆
Destiny, fate
People think of Qismah as exotic, intelligent, funny, weird, artsy
People who like the name Qismah also like Sahirah, Paloma, Selena, Chloe, Saniya, Qwara, Amadahy, Qiana, Kalinda, Qadr

Quade *(Celtic/Gaelic)* ♂   RATING: ★★☆
Descendent of Uad
People think of Quade as caring, handsome, funny, intelligent, creative
People who like the name Quade also like Kaden, Xander, Ethan, Keagan, Xavier, Noah, Wade, Quentin, Isaac, Braden

Quana *(Native American)* ♂   RATING: ★★★☆
Aromatic—Comanche origin
People think of Quana as caring, creative, sexy, funny, pretty

People who like the name Quana also like Tristan, Quade, Quentin, Anakin, Kaden, Dmitri, Dasan, Javier, Dash, Mace

Quanda *(American)* ♀   RATING: ★★★
Variation of Wanda—also phonetic spelling of Q&A
People think of Quanda as ethnic, intelligent, funny, sexy, loser
People who like the name Quanda also like Quintessa, Shantell, Quintana, Ilyssa, Paige, Quinta, Mabel, Sabrina, Raina, Roxanne

Quang *(Vietnamese)* ♂   RATING: ★★★
Clear
People think of Quang as intelligent, weird, sneaky, creative, nerdy
People who like the name Quang also like Quana, Randolph, Ryu, Adam, Albert, Habib, Taariq, Upendo, Rocky, Dumi

Quant *(Dutch)* ♀ ♂   RATING: ★★☆
Rogue—Also a surname; Mary Quant, designer
People think of Quant as weird, intelligent, unpopular, sneaky, criminal
People who like the name Quant also like Madison, Rider, Quennell, Ryder, Sean, Lorin, Piper, Quillan, Willow, Shadow

Quasar *(English)* ♀   RATING: ★★★
Meteorite
People think of Quasar as nerdy, weird, old-fashioned, loser, lazy
People who like the name Quasar also like Quintessa, Quiana, Qwara, Qiana, Xanthe, Querida, Mabel, Pandora, Qamra, Quinta

Quasim *(Arabic)* ♂   RATING: ★★★
Just, fair
People think of Quasim as exotic, handsome, young, weird, powerful
People who like the name Quasim also like Demetrius, Xavier, Sanders, Mateo, Kamali, Lysander, Xander, Samuel, Galen, David

Queenie *(English)* ♀   RATING: ★★★
Queen
People think of Queenie as pretty, caring, funny, intelligent, cool
People who like the name Queenie also like Olivia, Sabrina, Victoria, Isabella, Isabelle, Faith, Paige, Savannah, Hazel, Scarlett

Quenby *(Scandinavian)* ♀ ♂   RATING: ★★★
From the queen's manor
People think of Quenby as artsy, old-fashioned, elegant, creative, exotic
People who like the name Quenby also like Quinn, Quincy, Hadley, Dakota, Jaden, Paxton, Quillan, Hayden, Keegan, Teagan

Quennell (*English*) ♀♂   RATING: ★★
Woman battle—Originally a surname
> People think of Quennell as unpopular, trustworthy, funny, creative, uptight
> People who like the name Quennell also like Raven, Qwin, Riley, Quillan, Madison, Quincy, Unique, Quinlan, Cadence, Caden

Quentin (*Latin*) ♂   RATING: ★★★★
Fifth—Quentin Tarantino, filmmaker
> People think of Quentin as handsome, funny, intelligent, caring, cool
> People who like the name Quentin also like Ethan, Owen, Tristan, Noah, Zachary, Ian, Xavier, Gavin, Nicholas, Isaac

Querida (*Spanish*) ♀   RATING: ★★★☆
Beloved
> People think of Querida as exotic, pretty, quiet, young, slow
> People who like the name Querida also like Giselle, Aurora, Quintessa, Zoe, Nadia, Scarlett, Amber, Isis, Veronica, Qamra

Questa (*Latin*) ♀   RATING: ★★★
Seeking
> People think of Questa as weird, artsy, big, exotic, loser
> People who like the name Questa also like Olivia, Qamra, Felicity, Xaria, Hannah, Evangeline, Amanda, Saniya, Emma, Aida

Quiana (*American*) ♀   RATING: ★★☆
Singers—Also a soft, synthetic material popular in the 1970s
> People think of Quiana as pretty, popular, funny, caring, cool
> People who like the name Quiana also like Qiana, Cailyn, Kaelyn, Olivia, Jadyn, Kailey, Claire, Nadia, Dawn, Vanessa

Quilla (*English*) ♀   RATING: ★★★
A quill
> People think of Quilla as wild, pretty, powerful, funny, trustworthy
> People who like the name Quilla also like Scarlett, Amelia, Adeline, Felicia, Paige, Sabrina, Bella, Fiona, Olivia, Audrey

Quillan (*Celtic/Gaelic*) ♀♂   RATING: ★★★☆
Cub
> People think of Quillan as intelligent, leader, funny, handsome, cool
> People who like the name Quillan also like Quinlan, Quinn, Riley, Caden, Teagan, Aidan, Hadley, Reagan, Keegan, Quin

Quin (*Celtic/Gaelic*) ♀♂   RATING: ★★★☆
Descendent of Conn
> People think of Quin as funny, cool, intelligent, creative, energetic
> People who like the name Quin also like Quinn, Logan, Parker, Riley, Hayden, Reese, Taylor, Caden, Payton, Addison

Quincy (*French*) ♀♂   RATING: ★★☆
From Quincy, France—Quincy Jones, musician/producer
> People think of Quincy as intelligent, popular, funny, cool, handsome
> People who like the name Quincy also like Quinn, Parker, Hayden, Bailey, Logan, Mason, Preston, Payton, Caden, Taylor

Quinlan (*Celtic/Gaelic*) ♀♂   RATING: ★★★★
Descendent of the handsome man
> People think of Quinlan as intelligent, caring, funny, handsome, popular
> People who like the name Quinlan also like Quinn, Hayden, Teagan, Riley, Aidan, Logan, Parker, Caden, Reagan, Addison

Quinn (*Celtic/Gaelic*) ♀♂   RATING: ★★★
Descendent of Conn—Also a surname
> People think of Quinn as intelligent, funny, creative, caring, energetic
> People who like the name Quinn also like Logan, Hayden, Riley, Parker, Aidan, Avery, Addison, Caden, Reese, Reagan

Quinta (*Latin*) ♀   RATING: ★★☆
Fifth
> People think of Quinta as weird, pretty, intelligent, unpopular, ethnic
> People who like the name Quinta also like Quintessa, Quintana, Victoria, Marissa, Sabrina, Samantha, Audrey, Hope, Quanda, Isabella

Quintana (*Spanish*) ♀   RATING: ★☆
From the country house—Also a surname
> People think of Quintana as sexy, exotic, pretty, intelligent, young
> People who like the name Quintana also like Quintessa, Faith, Felicity, Quinta, Alana, Jasmine, Yasmin, Marissa, Jennessa, Anastasia

Quintessa (*Latin*) ♀   RATING: ★★★
Fifth—Variation of Quintessence
> People think of Quintessa as creative, pretty, intelligent, sexy, young
> People who like the name Quintessa also like Scarlett, Faith, Paige, Vanessa, Veronica, Odessa, Olivia, Zabrina, Penelope, Victoria

Quintin (*Latin*) ♂   RATING: ★★★☆
Fifth
> People think of Quintin as handsome, funny, intelligent, cool, popular
> People who like the name Quintin also like Ethan, Kaden, Gavin, Aiden, Caleb, Landon, Owen, Tristan, Zachary, Noah

Quinto (*Spanish*) ♂   RATING: ★★★
Fifth
> People think of Quinto as intelligent, powerful, old-fashioned, aggressive, lazy

People who like the name Quinto also like Alejandro, Xavier, Quito, Urbano, Desiderio, Alijah, Esteban, Qamar, Raúl, Manny

Quito *(Spanish)* ♂   RATING: ★★★
Fifth—Also the capital city of Ecuador
People think of Quito as weird, criminal, old-fashioned, aggressive, uptight
People who like the name Quito also like Xavier, Xander, Quade, Quentin, Lysander, Brandon, Gage, Julio, Micah, Roland

Quynh *(Vietnamese)* ♀   RATING: ★☆
Night-blooming flower
People think of Quynh as intelligent, pretty, caring, creative, elegant
People who like the name Quynh also like Amaya, Qamra, Qi, Fiona, Kaida, Sakura, Nyx, Xantara, Isis, Augusta

Qwara *(African)* ♀   RATING: ★★★
Ethiopian tribe name
People think of Qwara as exotic, ethnic, poor, energetic, loser
People who like the name Qwara also like Qamra, Zara, Hailey, Opal, Cassandra, Ciara, Faith, Kiara, Quintessa, Kendra

Qwin *(Celtic/Gaelic)* ♀ ♂   RATING: ★★★
Variation of Quinn
People think of Qwin as creative, intelligent, pretty, artsy, young
People who like the name Qwin also like Quinn, Logan, Quin, Taylor, Jaden, Riley, Hayden, Madison, Caden, Parker

Raanan *(Hebrew)* ♂   RATING: ★★
Fresh, green, flourishing
People think of Raanan as exotic, handsome, creative, religious, cool
People who like the name Raanan also like Kaden, Aiden, Elijah, Aden, Benjamin, Reuben, Reece, Gabriel, Caleb, Rohan

Rabia *(Arabic)* ♀ ♂   RATING: ★★★☆
Spring
People think of Rabia as pretty, funny, intelligent, weird, caring
People who like the name Rabia also like Rain, Raine, Raven, Rafiki, Ryder, Paris, Nida, Jada, Reese, Nikita

Race *(English)* ♂   RATING: ★★★
Running competition
People think of Race as weird, sporty, popular, energetic, winner
People who like the name Race also like Reece, Wade, Landon, Tristan, Jace, Noah, Ryker, Jett, Tyson, Rhett

Rach *(American)* ♀   RATING: ★★
Ewe—Short for Rachel
People think of Rach as pretty, funny, creative, caring, wild
People who like the name Rach also like Rae, Rachel, Rebecca, Paige, Rachael, Renée, Rane, Raina, Reba, Hailey

Rachael *(Hebrew)* ♀   RATING: ★★★☆
Ewe—Also spelled Raechel or Racheal; Rachael Leigh Cook, actress; Rachael Ray, celebrity chef
People think of Rachael as pretty, funny, caring, creative, intelligent
People who like the name Rachael also like Hannah, Rebecca, Paige, Abigail, Samantha, Hailey, Natalie, Olivia, Sarah, Lauren

Rachana *(Sanskrit/East Indian)* ♀   RATING: ★★★
Creation
People think of Rachana as ethnic, exotic, funny, creative, caring
People who like the name Rachana also like Raina, Rachael, Raeanne, Rhiannon, Anastasia, Hannah, Gabriella, Rachel, Faith, Aaralyn

Rachel *(Hebrew)* ♀   RATING: ★★★★
Ewe—Rachel Bilson, actress; Rachel Green, character on *Friends*; Rachel Ward, actress
People think of Rachel as pretty, funny, caring, intelligent, creative
People who like the name Rachel also like Hannah, Olivia, Emma, Rebecca, Abigail, Natalie, Paige, Sarah, Emily, Grace

Rachelle *(French)* ♀   RATING: ★★★☆
Ewe
People think of Rachelle as pretty, funny, caring, trustworthy, intelligent
People who like the name Rachelle also like Paige, Hailey, Hannah, Isabella, Rachael, Isabelle, Rachel, Olivia, Gabrielle, Gabriella

Rachna *(Sanskrit/East Indian)* ♀   RATING: ★★★
Creation
People think of Rachna as exotic, pretty, stuck-up, caring, sexy
People who like the name Rachna also like Rachana, Raina, Rachael, Ramya, Rupali, Rachel, Radha, Raeanne, Nisha, Rania

Racquel *(French)* ♀   RATING: ★★★☆
Ewe—Variation of Rachel or Raquel
People think of Racquel as girl next door, stuck-up, exotic, cool, wealthy
People who like the name Racquel also like Felicity, Gabriella, Monique, Giselle, Brie, Hannah, Jazlynn, Kylie, Lark, Makenna

Rad *(English)* ♂   RATING: ★★★☆
Short for Radley
People think of Rad as funny, energetic, creative, exotic, cool

People who like the name Rad also like Wade, Radley, Brock, Xander, Sebastian, Braden, Trey, Walker, Blade, Kaden

Radha *(Sanskrit/East Indian)* ♀   RATING: ★★★★
Prosperity—Radha Mitchell, actress
People think of Radha as exotic, pretty, funny, creative, caring
People who like the name Radha also like Ramona, Bianca, Raina, Rachana, Opal, Ava, Raisa, Rebecca, Isis, Iris

Radley *(English)* ♂   RATING: ★★★★
From the red field—Originally a surname
People think of Radley as intelligent, handsome, funny, leader, popular
People who like the name Radley also like Reece, Kaden, Tristan, Braden, Ethan, Owen, Holden, Maddox, Keagan, Noah

Radwan *(Persian)* ♂   RATING: ★★☆
Keeper of a vineyard
People think of Radwan as funny, aggressive, handsome, sexy, intelligent
People who like the name Radwan also like Radley, Ryu, Raanan, Rafael, Faolan, Remington, Reece, Zander, Aden, Rohan

Rae *(English)* ♀   RATING: ★★★☆
Short for Rachel or Raymond—Rae Dawn Chong, actress
People think of Rae as pretty, creative, funny, intelligent, caring
People who like the name Rae also like Paige, Ava, Faith, Olivia, Chloe, Emma, Grace, Abigail, Isabella, Mae

Raeanne *(American)* ♀   RATING: ★★★★☆
Combination of Rae and Anne
People think of Raeanne as pretty, popular, intelligent, caring, creative
People who like the name Raeanne also like Kaelyn, Paige, Rianna, Olivia, Faith, Hailey, Grace, Isabella, Hannah, Savannah

Raed *(Arabic)* ♂   RATING: ★★☆
Pioneer
People think of Raed as handsome, sexy, caring, cool, religious
People who like the name Raed also like Nathaniel, Niles, Radley, Dallan, Ramses, Dyson, Cedric, Giles, Reece

Raewyn *(Welsh)* ♀   RATING: ★★★
Combination of Rae and Wynn—Primarily popular in Australia
People think of Raewyn as pretty, caring, artsy, creative, trustworthy
People who like the name Raewyn also like Rebecca, Arwen, Wren, Regan, Kaelyn, Olivia, Raisa, Ava, Abigail, Iliana

Rafael *(Spanish)* ♂   RATING: ★★★☆
God has healed
People think of Rafael as handsome, funny, intelligent, cool, sexy
People who like the name Rafael also like Gabriel, Xavier, Nathaniel, Jacob, Benjamin, Sebastian, Nicholas, Ethan, Isaac, Adrian

Rafe *(English)* ♂   RATING: ★★★☆
Wolf counsel—Variation of Ralph; originally pronounced *Ralf*
People think of Rafe as handsome, cool, leader, sexy, trustworthy
People who like the name Rafe also like Tristan, Noah, Ethan, Owen, Gabriel, Liam, Jack, Landon, Reece, Holden

Rafer *(German)* ♂   RATING: ★★★
Unknown meaning—Also an American surname; Rafer Johnson, Olympic athlete
People think of Rafer as weird, funny, aggressive, powerful, criminal
People who like the name Rafer also like Tristan, Liam, Braeden, Riordan, Keiran, Aiden, Cole, Bowen, Sloan, Mac

Raffaello *(Italian)* ♂   RATING: ★★★
God has healed—Variation of Raphael
People think of Raffaello as handsome, wealthy, funny, popular, artsy
People who like the name Raffaello also like Angelo, Draco, Gabriel, Giovanni, Michelangelo, Rafael, Emilio, Nathaniel, Matteo, Raphael

Rafferty *(Celtic/Gaelic)* ♀ ♂   RATING: ★★★☆
Abundance
People think of Rafferty as handsome, popular, creative, intelligent, cool
People who like the name Rafferty also like Logan, Rory, Riley, Rowan, Reagan, Ryder, Addison, Parker, Hayden, Sawyer

Rafi *(Arabic)* ♂   RATING: ★★
Exalted
People think of Rafi as creative, handsome, intelligent, funny, winner
People who like the name Rafi also like Jonah, Noah, Adam, Oliver, Ethan, Levi, Rafael, Isaac, Caleb, Micah

Rafiki *(African)* ♀ ♂   RATING: ★☆
Friend—Variation of Rafiq; Kiswahili origin
People think of Rafiki as exotic, wild, intelligent, energetic, funny
People who like the name Rafiki also like Raven, Rain, Payton, Dakota, Dante, Rabia, Ryan, Riley, Rylie, Quincy

Raghnall *(Celtic/Gaelic)* ♂   RATING: ★★★
Advice rule—From the Norse Ragnvaldr
People think of Raghnall as unpopular, aggressive, powerful, weird, lazy
People who like the name Raghnall also like Aiden, Tiergan, Riordan, Winfred, Arthur, Sloan, Tristan, Rafer, Nevan, Nolen

Raheem *(Arabic)* ♂ RATING: ★★★☆
Compassionate
   People think of Raheem as handsome, funny, popular, powerful, cool
   People who like the name Raheem also like Dayshaun, Jamar, Jamal, Jeremiah, Elijah, Deshawn, Isaiah, Jamil, Rashid, Jabari

Rahiq *(Arabic)* ♀ RATING: ★★☆
Best wine
   People think of Rahiq as handsome, intelligent, exotic, ethnic, creative
   People who like the name Rahiq also like Raisa, Raina, Ramya, Rasha, Ramla, Raja, Rochelle, Rach, Raeanne, Rachael

Raimi *(Arabic)* ♂ RATING: ★★★☆
Fond
   People think of Raimi as creative, popular, funny, pretty, powerful
   People who like the name Raimi also like Gavin, Gabriel, Jayden, Reece, Caleb, Landon, Lucas, Owen, Elijah, Xavier

Rain *(American)* ♀♂ RATING: ★★☆
Abundant blessings from above—Also spelled Rainn or Rayne; Rainn Wilson, actor
   People think of Rain as creative, pretty, intelligent, exotic, caring
   People who like the name Rain also like Raine, Riley, Caden, Jaden, Sage, Reese, Madison, River, Hayden, Raven

Raina *(Slavic)* ♀ RATING: ★★★★
Queen
   People think of Raina as pretty, intelligent, creative, caring, funny
   People who like the name Raina also like Paige, Ava, Olivia, Isabella, Rianna, Reina, Hannah, Jadyn, Abigail, Gabriella

Raine *(French)* ♀♂ RATING: ★★★
Queen
   People think of Raine as pretty, intelligent, creative, caring, funny
   People who like the name Raine also like Rain, Riley, Hayden, Caden, Reese, Logan, Jaden, Skye, Ryder, Jade

Rainer *(English)* ♂ RATING: ★★★☆
Army counsel—Pronounced *RYE-ner*; Rainer Maria Rilke, poet
   People think of Rainer as intelligent, handsome, creative, funny, energetic
   People who like the name Rainer also like Jackson, Reece, Kaden, Aiden, Gabriel, Radley, Noah, Oliver, Nathan, Ethan

Raisa *(Hebrew)* ♀ RATING: ★★
Rose—Also Russian of unknown meaning, and Arabic meaning princess; Raisa Gorbachev, wife of Russian politician
   People think of Raisa as pretty, intelligent, funny, creative, sexy

People who like the name Raisa also like Raina, Ava, Paige, Scarlett, Reina, Rachel, Olivia, Samara, Eva, Renée

Raisie *(Hebrew)* ♀ RATING: ★★★
Short for Raisa
   People think of Raisie as artsy, exotic, creative, pretty, wild
   People who like the name Raisie also like Maisie, Raisa, Shaylee, Aeryn, Rianne, Kiara, Kaelyn, Shayla, Kayla, Rosa

Raja *(Sanskrit/East Indian)* ♀ RATING: ★★
King—Also an Indian ruler
   People think of Raja as exotic, intelligent, popular, powerful, leader
   People who like the name Raja also like Raina, Aurora, Iris, Zoey, Sitara, Kiara, Olivia, Enya, Isabella, Nadia

Rajan *(Sanskrit/East Indian)* ♂ RATING: ★★★
King
   People think of Rajan as intelligent, handsome, winner, young, creative
   People who like the name Rajan also like Ruhan, Taariq, Raheem, Rohan, Mohan, Raman, Ruben, Beau, Rashid, Ryu

Raleigh *(English)* ♀♂ RATING: ★★★
From the red or rye field—City in North Carolina
   People think of Raleigh as creative, intelligent, pretty, funny, cool
   People who like the name Raleigh also like Riley, Reagan, Hayden, Addison, Madison, Parker, Reese, Jaden, Bailey, Logan

Ralph *(English)* ♂ RATING: ★☆
Wolf counsel—Pronounced *Ralf* or *Rafe*; Ralph Cramden, character on *The Honeymooners*; Ralph Waldo Emerson, writer/poet; Ralph Vaughan Williams, composer
   People think of Ralph as handsome, funny, intelligent, caring, trustworthy
   People who like the name Ralph also like Isaac, Oliver, Patrick, Benjamin, Alexander, Aaron, Nathan, Jacob, David, Victor

Ralston *(English)* ♂ RATING: ★★★
From Ralph's town
   People think of Ralston as handsome, trustworthy, leader, old-fashioned, popular
   People who like the name Ralston also like Holden, Braden, Reece, Wade, Jackson, Landon, Radley, Lawson, Ethan, Jayden

Ram *(Sanskrit/East Indian)* ♂ RATING: ★★★
Godlike
   People think of Ram as aggressive, intelligent, powerful, leader, religious
   People who like the name Ram also like Rohan, Ramses, Ravi, Samson, Owen, Aiden, Adam, Rex, Ryu, William

466

Raman *(Sanskrit/East Indian)* ♂ RATING: ★★★
Merriment; amour
People think of Raman as intelligent, caring, cool, energetic, young
People who like the name Raman also like Ramón, Nalin, Vadin, Ravi, Samuel, Fabian, Simon, Nash, Roman, Titus

Ramira *(Spanish)* ♀ RATING: ★★★
Wise; famous
People think of Ramira as popular, pretty, caring, exotic, sexy
People who like the name Ramira also like Reia, Renée, Riona, Sabrina, Selena, Rosaline, Gabriela, Kayla, Tatiana, Trinity

Ramiro *(Spanish)* ♂ RATING: ★★★★
Supreme judge—From Saint Ramirus
People think of Ramiro as handsome, funny, caring, cool, intelligent
People who like the name Ramiro also like Ramón, Javier, Xavier, Romeo, Gabriel, Sergio, Aaron, Isaac, Diego, Damien

Ramla *(Swahili)* ♀ RATING: ★★☆
Prophet
People think of Ramla as pretty, caring, funny, creative, quiet
People who like the name Ramla also like Raisa, Regina, Rachel, Ramona, Rachana, Ramya, Serafina, Rebecca, Rachael, Raisie

Ramón *(Spanish)* ♂ RATING: ★★★★
Counsel protection—Also spelled Ramone; variation of Raymond
People think of Ramón as handsome, funny, cool, caring, sexy
People who like the name Ramón also like Xavier, Ricardo, Diego, Ruben, Isaac, Jacob, Carlos, Nicholas, Adrian, Rafael

Ramona *(Spanish)* ♀ RATING: ★★★★
Counsel protection—Feminine form of Ramón; children's book character by Beverly Cleary
People think of Ramona as pretty, funny, creative, caring, intelligent
People who like the name Ramona also like Olivia, Rebecca, Ava, Violet, Amelia, Faith, Penelope, Fiona, Paige, Sabrina

Ramses *(Egyptian)* ♂ RATING: ★★★☆
Son of Ra—A series of Egyptian Pharoahs
People think of Ramses as handsome, powerful, intelligent, aggressive, popular
People who like the name Ramses also like Xavier, Gabriel, Xander, Nathaniel, Rhett, Isaac, Aiden, Elijah, Tristan, Lucas

Ramya *(Sanskrit/East Indian)* ♀ RATING: ★★★★
Pleasing, delightful
People think of Ramya as pretty, young, intelligent, cool, caring

People who like the name Ramya also like Raina, Amaya, Raisa, Anaya, Isis, Regina, Reina, Saniya, Samiya, Rania

Ranae *(American)* ♀ RATING: ★★☆
Resurrected—Variation of Renée
People think of Ranae as pretty, caring, popular, funny, sexy
People who like the name Ranae also like Renée, Paige, Raeanne, Jadyn, Faith, Rae, Kaelyn, Raina, Natalie, Zoe

Rance *(English)* ♂ RATING: ★★★
Shield
People think of Rance as funny, aggressive, sexy, cool, trustworthy
People who like the name Rance also like Reece, Jace, Tristan, Ryker, Seth, Noah, Radley, Royce, Tyson, Landon

Randa *(American)* ♀ RATING: ★★★
Admirable—Short for Miranda
People think of Randa as pretty, caring, funny, popular, energetic
People who like the name Randa also like Paige, Rae, Reyna, Destiny, Jasmine, Rena, Rhianna, Camila, Skyla, Abigail

Randall *(English)* ♂ RATING: ★★★☆
Shield wolf—Variation of Randolph
People think of Randall as handsome, funny, intelligent, caring, cool
People who like the name Randall also like Ethan, Nicholas, Benjamin, Jacob, Nathan, Aaron, Lucas, Nathaniel, Samuel, Isaac

Randi *(English)* ♀♂ RATING: ★★★★
Short for Miranda or Randall
People think of Randi as funny, pretty, caring, creative, intelligent
People who like the name Randi also like Riley, Reese, Morgan, Madison, Mackenzie, Taylor, Ryan, Bailey, Jaden, Dakota

Randilyn *(American)* ♀ RATING: ★★★☆
Combination of Randi and Lynn
People think of Randilyn as pretty, leader, girl next door, quiet, sexy
People who like the name Randilyn also like Kaelyn, Faith, Hailey, Ashlyn, Cailyn, Jadyn, Rosalyn, Madelyn, Paige, Kaitlyn

Randolph *(English)* ♂ RATING: ★★
Shield wolf
People think of Randolph as funny, intelligent, caring, trustworthy, leader
People who like the name Randolph also like Thomas, Nicholas, Rudolph, Raymond, Todd, Gregory, Anthony, Luke, Patrick, Bradley

Randy *(English)* ♀♂ RATING: ★★☆
Short for Randall or Miranda
People think of Randy as handsome, funny, caring, intelligent, cool

People who like the name Randy also like Ryan, Taylor, Riley, Logan, Kyle, Jordan, Evan, Tyler, Dylan, Madison

Rane (*English*) ♀   RATING: ★★★★
Queen—Variation of Raine
People think of Rane as pretty, intelligent, powerful, elegant, creative
People who like the name Rane also like Paige, Rae, Faith, Raina, Ryann, Olivia, Eva, Serenity, Hailey, Jadyn

Ranee (*Sanskrit/East Indian*) ♀   RATING: ★★★★
Queen
People think of Ranee as pretty, creative, popular, funny, intelligent
People who like the name Ranee also like Renée, Paige, Rebecca, Ranae, Chloe, Rachael, Faith, Hailey, Hannah, Rae

Ranger (*English*) ♂   RATING: ★★
Forest protector—Originally a surname
People think of Ranger as aggressive, powerful, handsome, sporty, leader
People who like the name Ranger also like Reece, Noah, Tristan, Lucas, Remington, Owen, Ian, Wade, Jackson, Tyson

Rangle (*American*) ♂   RATING: ★★☆
Cowboy
People think of Rangle as energetic, funny, weird, sporty, aggressive
People who like the name Rangle also like Rhett, Buck, Landon, Radley, Ray, Nash, Colt, Rocky, Woody, William

Rangsey (*Cambodian*) ♂   RATING: ★★★
Seven colors
People think of Rangsey as pretty, lazy, intelligent, elegant, powerful
People who like the name Rangsey also like Brinley, Rhett, Bradley, Wyman, Radley, Bonner, Chayton, Altan, Reeves, Bowen

Rania (*Arabic*) ♀   RATING: ★★★★
To gaze
People think of Rania as pretty, intelligent, elegant, creative, funny
People who like the name Rania also like Raina, Reina, Reia, Reyna, Isabella, Giselle, Tatiana, Layla, Ramya, Gabrielle

Ranit (*Hebrew*) ♀   RATING: ★★★
She is singing
People think of Ranit as exotic, artsy, weird, pretty, funny
People who like the name Ranit also like Rachel, Rachana, Rayya, Lael, Fawn, Reba, Jael, Rebecca, Rena, Amber

Ranjana (*Sanskrit/East Indian*) ♀   RATING: ★★★
Entertaining
People think of Ranjana as intelligent, pretty, funny, unpopular, popular

People who like the name Ranjana also like Rekha, Raja, Rachana, Ramya, Jyotika, Rasha, Radha, Priyanka, Regina, Rahiq

Ranjeet (*Sanskrit/East Indian*) ♂   RATING: ★★☆
Victorious in battle
People think of Ranjeet as ethnic, exotic, caring, handsome, trustworthy
People who like the name Ranjeet also like Rida, Raghnall, Rendor, Waylon, Dermot, Demetrius, Deiter, Davis, Titus, Dalton

Ranjit (*Sanskrit/East Indian*) ♂   RATING: ★★★
Victorious in battle
People think of Ranjit as funny, powerful, intelligent, aggressive, caring
People who like the name Ranjit also like Ajay, Alagan, Nirav, Ashwin, Arnav, Sanjiv, Manas, Dulal, Prem, Nitish

Raphael (*Hebrew*) ♂   RATING: ★★
God has healed—Raphael, Renaissance artist
People think of Raphael as handsome, intelligent, cool, creative, caring
People who like the name Raphael also like Gabriel, Elijah, Nathaniel, Michael, Sebastian, Isaac, Zachary, Oliver, Nathan, Ethan

Raphaela (*Italian*) ♀   RATING: ★★
God has healed—Feminine form of Raphael
People think of Raphaela as pretty, sexy, intelligent, creative, powerful
People who like the name Raphaela also like Sophia, Isabella, Rebecca, Gabriella, Ava, Naomi, Sofia, Olivia, Bianca, Sarah

Rapoto (*Rumantsch*) ♂   RATING: ★★☆
Counsel; bold
People think of Rapoto as poor, old-fashioned, weird, sneaky, funny
People who like the name Rapoto also like Mattia, Egil, Fadey, Clyde, Dermot, Pascal, Demetrius, Deiter, Davis, Jedidiah

Raquel (*Spanish*) ♀   RATING: ★★☆
Ewe—Variation of Rachel; Raquel Welch, actress
People think of Raquel as pretty, funny, intelligent, sexy, caring
People who like the name Raquel also like Isabella, Olivia, Paige, Adriana, Victoria, Veronica, Rachel, Hannah, Vanessa, Gabriella

Rasha (*Arabic*) ♀   RATING: ★★★☆
Young gazelle
People think of Rasha as pretty, intelligent, exotic, funny, popular
People who like the name Rasha also like Raina, Raisa, Rayya, Reina, Rasia, Layla, Shaina, Rania, Adriana, Rhian

Rashid (*Arabic*) ♂   RATING: ★★★☆
Rightly guided
People think of Rashid as intelligent, handsome, cool, funny, powerful

468

People who like the name Rashid also like Amir, Jamal, Raheem, Tristan, Elijah, Isaiah, Jamil, Nathan, Malik, Nasser

Rashida *(Arabic)* ♀   RATING: ★★
Rightly guided—Feminine form of Rashid
People think of Rashida as pretty, intelligent, caring, sexy, funny
People who like the name Rashida also like Regina, Aaliyah, Rianna, Reina, Ratana, Rozalia, Raina, Raisa, Rhea, Rena

Rasia *(Polish)* ♀   RATING: ★★★☆
Well spoken—Variation of Euphrasia
People think of Rasia as exotic, pretty, sexy, creative, intelligent
People who like the name Rasia also like Raisa, Rasha, Raina, Reina, Grace, Zofia, Rayya, Rianna, Rhian, Destiny

Ratana *(Thai)* ♀   RATING: ★★★☆
Crystal
People think of Ratana as creative, funny, cool, weird, loser
People who like the name Ratana also like Raina, Rasha, Tatiana, Tiana, Nadia, Rianna, Shyla, Ilyssa, Layla, Rosalyn

Raúl *(Spanish)* ♂   RATING: ★★★☆
Wolf counsel—Variation of Ralph; Raúl Julia, actor
People think of Raúl as handsome, funny, sexy, intelligent, caring
People who like the name Raúl also like Rafael, Diego, Xavier, Anthony, Carlos, Joaquin, Lucas, Antonio, Victor, Alejandro

Raven *(English)* ♀♂   RATING: ★★★☆
Blackbird—Raven-Symone, actress/singer; *The Raven*, poem by Edgar Allan Poe
People think of Raven as pretty, intelligent, creative, cool, funny
People who like the name Raven also like Riley, Hayden, Jaden, Jade, Caden, Madison, Logan, Bailey, Taylor, Dakota

Ravi *(Sanskrit/East Indian)* ♂   RATING: ★★
Sun—Ravi Shankar, musician
People think of Ravi as intelligent, handsome, caring, cool, funny
People who like the name Ravi also like Rohan, Gavin, Noah, Tristan, Aiden, Liam, Ryu, Kaden, Sebastian, Miles

Ray *(English)* ♂   RATING: ★★
Short for names beginning with Ray—Ray Bradbury, author; Ray Charles, singer/musician; Ray Liotta, actor; Ray Romano, actor/comedian
People think of Ray as funny, cool, handsome, caring, intelligent
People who like the name Ray also like Nathan, Justin, Raymond, Aaron, Ethan, Cole, Reece, Michael, Noah, Alexander

Raymond *(English)* ♂   RATING: ★★★☆
Counsel protection—Raymond Burr, actor
People think of Raymond as handsome, funny, intelligent, caring, cool
People who like the name Raymond also like Nathan, Nicholas, Benjamin, Samuel, Matthew, Jacob, Ethan, Justin, Andrew, Gabriel

Rayya *(Arabic)* ♀   RATING: ★★★★
Fragrant breeze
People think of Rayya as pretty, creative, intelligent, exotic, funny
People who like the name Rayya also like Raina, Rianna, Reya, Layla, Jadyn, Rea, Kayla, Rhea, Gabriella, Isabella

Razi *(Hebrew)* ♀   RATING: ★★★★
My secret
People think of Razi as cool, exotic, funny, creative, trustworthy
People who like the name Razi also like Raina, Rebecca, Sadie, Renée, Harmony, Jadyn, Shaylee, Roxy, Dara, Ebony

Raziya *(Arabic)* ♀   RATING: ★★★
Agreeable, good-natured
People think of Raziya as pretty, exotic, intelligent, sexy, trustworthy
People who like the name Raziya also like Rianna, Tatiana, Tanaya, Saniya, Raina, Jazlynn, Adriana, Trinity, Raeanne, Ramya

Rea *(English)* ♀   RATING: ★★★☆
Flowing—Variation of Rhea
People think of Rea as funny, pretty, creative, sexy, elegant
People who like the name Rea also like Rhea, Rae, Paige, Rianna, Mia, Renée, Olivia, Ava, Rhian, Grace

Read *(English)* ♂   RATING: ★★★
Red haired
People think of Read as funny, intelligent, cool, handsome, trendy
People who like the name Read also like Reece, Noah, Wade, Owen, Radley, Aiden, Isaac, Landon, Fynn, Jayden

Reagan *(Celtic/Gaelic)* ♀♂   RATING: ★★★★☆
Little king—Ronald Reagan, U.S. president
People think of Reagan as pretty, intelligent, funny, popular, energetic
People who like the name Reagan also like Riley, Logan, Madison, Hayden, Bailey, Addison, Reese, Taylor, Parker, Mackenzie

Reba *(American)* ♀   RATING: ★★★☆
Snare—Short for Rebecca; Reba McEntire, singer/actress
People think of Reba as funny, caring, pretty, intelligent, popular
People who like the name Reba also like Rebecca, Renée, Paige, Savannah, Trinity, Sara, Isabella, Faith, Samantha, Scarlett

Rebecca *(Hebrew)* ♀   RATING: ★★★★
Snare—In the Bible, the wife of Isaac; Rebecca De Mornay, actress; Rebecca Welles, author; *Rebecca of Sunnybrook Farm*, children's novel by Kate Douglas Wiggin
> People think of Rebecca as pretty, funny, caring, intelligent, creative
> People who like the name Rebecca also like Hannah, Rachel, Samantha, Abigail, Emily, Olivia, Emma, Sarah, Elizabeth, Natalie

Rebekah *(Hebrew)* ♀   RATING: ★★★☆
Snare—Older variation of Rebecca
> People think of Rebekah as pretty, caring, funny, intelligent, creative
> People who like the name Rebekah also like Hannah, Abigail, Rebecca, Elizabeth, Grace, Faith, Rachel, Paige, Natalie, Olivia

Rebekka *(Hebrew)* ♀   RATING: ★★★☆
Snare—Variation of Rebecca; also spelled Rebekkah
> People think of Rebekka as pretty, intelligent, funny, energetic, trustworthy
> People who like the name Rebekka also like Hannah, Rebecca, Abigail, Rebekah, Rachael, Olivia, Rachel, Isabella, Paige, Samantha

Red *(English)* ♀ ♂   RATING: ★★★
Red haired—Mostly used as a nickname for people with reddish hair; Red Buttons, comedian; Red Skelton, comedian
> People think of Red as cool, funny, wild, powerful, energetic
> People who like the name Red also like Riley, Logan, Reese, Rain, Ryan, Sage, Rylie, River, Cameron, Reed

Reda *(Arabic)* ♀ ♂   RATING: ★★★
Favored by God
> People think of Reda as intelligent, caring, trustworthy, funny, creative
> People who like the name Reda also like Riley, Raven, Rabia, Ryder, Rune, Reid, Remi, Ren, Nida, Nowles

Redell *(American)* ♀ ♂   RATING: ★★★
Wolf counsel—Also a surname, probably of German origin
> People think of Redell as funny, intelligent, weird, trustworthy, sneaky
> People who like the name Redell also like Caden, Jaden, Reagan, Talen, Jalen, Rylie, Reilly, Rollin, Dakota, Cadence

Redford *(English)* ♂   RATING: ★★★
From the red ford—Robert Redford, actor/filmmaker
> People think of Redford as powerful, aggressive, intelligent, handsome, leader
> People who like the name Redford also like Jackson, Walker, Rhett, Lincoln, Wade, Sebastian, Remington, Wyatt, Seth, Radley

Reece *(English)* ♂   RATING: ★★★★
Running—Variation of Rhys
> People think of Reece as handsome, popular, funny, energetic, caring
> People who like the name Reece also like Ethan, Noah, Kaden, Owen, Aiden, Caleb, Cole, Jackson, Landon, Jacob

Reed *(English)* ♀ ♂   RATING: ★★★☆
A reed; red haired
> People think of Reed as intelligent, funny, handsome, cool, trustworthy
> People who like the name Reed also like Reese, Parker, Riley, Logan, Caden, Reagan, Hayden, Ryder, Addison, Mason

Reegan *(American)* ♀ ♂   RATING: ★★★☆
Little king
> People think of Reegan as popular, intelligent, funny, energetic, leader
> People who like the name Reegan also like Reagan, Riley, Reese, Caden, Jaden, Hayden, Logan, Madison, Payton, Bailey

Reem *(Arabic)* ♀   RATING: ★★★
Gazelle
> People think of Reem as creative, popular, trustworthy, energetic, ethnic
> People who like the name Reem also like Rose, Rebecca, Ryann, Colette, Ella, Ranit, Vega, Roberta, Wren, Rosetta

Reese *(Welsh)* ♀ ♂   RATING: ★★★★☆
Running—Variation of Rhys; Reese Witherspoon, actress
> People think of Reese as funny, popular, pretty, energetic, intelligent
> People who like the name Reese also like Riley, Hayden, Madison, Parker, Addison, Bailey, Logan, Avery, Taylor, Reagan

Reeves *(English)* ♂   RATING: ★★★
Servant; child of the steward—Originally a surname
> People think of Reeves as intelligent, trustworthy, popular, cool, handsome
> People who like the name Reeves also like Reece, Ethan, Landon, Holden, Cole, Grayson, Jack, Jacob, Noah, Jackson

Regan *(Celtic/Gaelic)* ♀   RATING: ★★★★
Queen—Character in *King Lear* by William Shakespeare; character in *The Exorcist*, film and novel
> People think of Regan as pretty, intelligent, funny, popular, creative
> People who like the name Regan also like Olivia, Paige, Ava, Emma, Grace, Hannah, Chloe, Hailey, Isabella, Abigail

Reggie *(English)* ♀ ♂   RATING: ★★
Short for Reginald or Regina—Reggie Jackson, baseball player
> People think of Reggie as cool, handsome, funny, popular, intelligent

People who like the name Reggie also like Ryan, Logan, Hayden, Riley, Cameron, Taylor, Caden, Parker, Madison, Bailey

Regina *(Latin)* ♀ RATING: ★★★★
Queen
People think of Regina as pretty, intelligent, trust-worthy, funny, caring
People who like the name Regina also like Natalie, Sabrina, Olivia, Isabella, Vanessa, Samantha, Isabelle, Paige, Roxanne, Rebecca

Reginald *(English)* ♂ RATING: ★★
Counsel; bold
People think of Reginald as handsome, intelligent, funny, sexy, caring
People who like the name Reginald also like Xavier, Richard, Raymond, Nathan, Maddox, Aaron, Reece, Isaac, Lucas, Landon

Regis *(Latin)* ♂ RATING: ★★★
Ruler, kingly—Regis Philbin, TV host/actor
People think of Regis as funny, leader, intelligent, caring, cool
People who like the name Regis also like Nathan, Benjamin, Anthony, Gavin, Ethan, Dominic, Zachary, Nicholas, Reuben, Joaquin

Rehan *(Armenian)* ♀ RATING: ★★☆
Sweet basil
People think of Rehan as handsome, intelligent, caring, popular, cool
People who like the name Rehan also like Rhian, Jadyn, Kaelyn, Reia, Rianna, Ryann, Raina, Reina, Rhiannon, Regan

Reia *(Spanish)* ♀ RATING: ★★☆
Queen
People think of Reia as pretty, exotic, creative, elegant, intelligent
People who like the name Reia also like Reina, Rhea, Raina, Rianna, Reya, Rea, Mia, Ella, Reyna, Ava

Reid *(English)* ♀♂ RATING: ★★★
Red headed
People think of Reid as intelligent, handsome, funny, sporty, popular
People who like the name Reid also like Reese, Riley, Logan, Parker, Hayden, Reed, Ryan, Mason, Caden, Reagan

Reidar *(Scandinavian)* ♂ RATING: ★☆
Home army
People think of Reidar as powerful, intelligent, aggressive, leader, cool
People who like the name Reidar also like Rohan, Gabriel, Reece, Soren, Rhys, Kael, Liam, Roman, Rainer, Ronan

Reiko *(Japanese)* ♀ RATING: ★★★
Gratitude—Reiko Aylesworth, actress
People think of Reiko as intelligent, pretty, energetic, creative, funny

People who like the name Reiko also like Inari, Aneko, Emiko, Maeko, Kaida, Nariko, Amaya, Kamiko, Hitomi, Nozomi

Reilly *(Celtic/Gaelic)* ♀♂ RATING: ★★★
Descendant of Roghallach—John C. Reilly, actor
People think of Reilly as funny, pretty, intelligent, caring, cool
People who like the name Reilly also like Riley, Reagan, Logan, Bailey, Madison, Mackenzie, Hayden, Reese, Taylor, Parker

Reina *(Spanish)* ♀ RATING: ★★☆
Queen—Also spelled Rayna
People think of Reina as pretty, intelligent, caring, funny, cool
People who like the name Reina also like Raina, Reyna, Olivia, Isabella, Rianna, Reia, Sophia, Gianna, Gabriella, Paige

Rekha *(Sanskrit/East Indian)* ♀ RATING: ★★★☆
A line, mark
People think of Rekha as creative, pretty, trustworthy, intelligent, popular
People who like the name Rekha also like Rachana, Reia, Reina, Manasa, Rehan, Ranjana, Rena, Radha, Rashida, Ramya

Remedy *(American)* ♀♂ RATING: ★★★☆
Cure
People think of Remedy as creative, intelligent, elegant, pretty, trustworthy
People who like the name Remedy also like Parker, Hayden, Jaden, Rain, Raven, Madison, Raleigh, Remy, Raine, Taylor

Remi *(French)* ♀♂ RATING: ★★★★
Oarsman; remedy—Variation of Remy
People think of Remi as cool, funny, intelligent, creative, popular
People who like the name Remi also like Riley, Remy, Reese, Logan, Caden, Ryan, Ryder, Rory, Madison, Hayden

Remington *(English)* ♂ RATING: ★★★★
From the ridge town—Remington Steele, TV show
People think of Remington as handsome, leader, intelligent, cool, energetic
People who like the name Remington also like Jackson, Noah, Aiden, Kaden, Maddox, Landon, Grayson, Ethan, Dawson, Tyson

Remy *(French)* ♀♂ RATING: ★★★★
Oarsman; remedy—From Remigius meaning oarsman or Remedius meaning remedy
People think of Remy as creative, funny, sexy, intelligent, cool
People who like the name Remy also like Riley, Reese, Remi, Ryder, Logan, Rory, Ryan, Hayden, Piper, Jaden

Ren *(Japanese)* ♀♂ RATING: ★★★☆
Lotus—*Ren and Stimpy*, TV show
People think of Ren as intelligent, cool, creative, funny, trustworthy
People who like the name Ren also like Rin, Reese, Riley, Ryan, Logan, Raven, Quinn, Rain, Raine, Rowan

Rena *(Hebrew)* ♀ RATING: ★★★★
Joy
People think of Rena as pretty, caring, funny, intelligent, trustworthy
People who like the name Rena also like Raina, Olivia, Eva, Mia, Renée, Reina, Rebecca, Rachel, Paige, Rianna

Renata *(Italian)* ♀ RATING: ★★★★
Reborn
People think of Renata as pretty, intelligent, funny, creative, elegant
People who like the name Renata also like Raina, Isabella, Reina, Natalia, Victoria, Lorelei, Renée, Rebecca, Sophia, Nadia

Renate *(French)* ♀♂ RATING: ★★
Reborn—Renate Tibaldi, opera singer
People think of Renate as creative, trustworthy, intelligent, funny, pretty
People who like the name Renate also like Raven, Renny, River, Reagan, Remy, Ryan, Rylie, Reid, Rey, Rory

Rendor *(Hungarian)* ♂ RATING: ★★★
Police officer
People think of Rendor as exotic, unpopular, big, sneaky, untrustworthy
People who like the name Rendor also like Quade, Aiden, Rhett, Reece, Nestor, Roderick, Leander, Luke, Lukas, Rafer

René *(French)* ♂ RATING: ★★★★
Reborn—René Auberjonois, actor; René Descartes, philosopher/writer
People think of René as funny, intelligent, creative, cool, caring
People who like the name René also like Gabriel, Aaron, Ethan, Noah, David, Jacob, Elijah, Jason, Nathan, Nathaniel

Renée *(French)* ♀ RATING: ★★☆
Reborn—Renée Estevez; Renée Zellweger, actress
People think of Renée as pretty, caring, funny, intelligent, creative
People who like the name Renée also like Paige, Olivia, Natalie, Faith, Grace, Emma, Hailey, Chloe, Hannah, Victoria

Renny *(Celtic/Gaelic)* ♀♂ RATING: ★★★★
Son of Reynald
People think of Renny as intelligent, funny, creative, energetic, trustworthy
People who like the name Renny also like Riley, Rylie, Rory, Logan, Reilly, Ryan, Reese, Mackenzie, Rylee, Nolan

Reth *(African)* ♂ RATING: ★★★
King
People think of Reth as wealthy, aggressive, poor, sexy, energetic
People who like the name Reth also like Wade, Noah, Read, Reece, Justin, Jadon, Radley, Xander, Ralston, Roderick

Reuben *(Hebrew)* ♂ RATING: ★★★★
Behold, a son—Also a sandwich
People think of Reuben as intelligent, handsome, caring, creative, trustworthy
People who like the name Reuben also like Isaac, Ethan, Samuel, Seth, Elijah, Caleb, Noah, Gabriel, Nathan, Benjamin

Reuel *(Hebrew)* ♂ RATING: ★★★☆
Friend of God
People think of Reuel as trustworthy, intelligent, powerful, religious, winner
People who like the name Reuel also like Reuben, Ravi, Gabriel, Ethan, Raphael, Isaiah, Rohan, Elijah, Isaac, Ryu

Revelin *(English)* ♂ RATING: ★★
Pride, rebellion—Originally a surname
People think of Revelin as intelligent, powerful, leader, creative, handsome
People who like the name Revelin also like Devlin, Aiden, Liam, Riordan, Galvin, Kaden, Kail, Aden, Braeden, Kane

Rex *(Latin)* ♂ RATING: ★★
King—Rex Harrison, actor; Rex Reed, journalist
People think of Rex as handsome, leader, cool, intelligent, powerful
People who like the name Rex also like Jacob, Ethan, Noah, Maddox, Owen, Oliver, Jack, Max, Nathan, Isaac

Rey *(Spanish)* ♀♂ RATING: ★★★☆
King
People think of Rey as cool, popular, funny, intelligent, caring
People who like the name Rey also like Ryan, Remy, Reese, Rain, Jade, Landen, Remi, Riley, Shay, Bailey

Reya *(Spanish)* ♀ RATING: ★★★★☆
Queen
People think of Reya as pretty, intelligent, funny, creative, caring
People who like the name Reya also like Reyna, Reina, Reia, Rianna, Ella, Ava, Raina, Olivia, Maya, Rhea

Reyna *(Spanish)* ♀ RATING: ★★★★☆
Queen
People think of Reyna as pretty, intelligent, sexy, funny, caring
People who like the name Reyna also like Raina, Reina, Rianna, Reya, Isabella, Olivia, Adriana, Mia, Savannah, Gabriella

471

472

Reynard *(French)* ♂ RATING: ★★☆
Counsel brave—Also a fox
People think of Reynard as popular, handsome, funny, caring, leader
People who like the name Reynard also like Marcel, Wyatt, André, Pascal, Rupert, Yves, Percival, Laurent, Ansel, Jacques

Reynold *(English)* ♂ RATING: ★★★
Counsel; bold—Variation of Reginald
People think of Reynold as sexy, funny, intelligent, creative, cool
People who like the name Reynold also like Tyson, Nathan, Richard, Benjamin, William, David, Russell, Wade, Aaron, Luke

Reza *(Arabic)* ♂ RATING: ★★★★
Consent, agreement—Also a variation of Theresa
People think of Reza as funny, intelligent, caring, handsome, creative
People who like the name Reza also like Aiden, Idris, Reuben, Gabriel, Cedric, Noah, Redford, Reece, Ravi, Kaden

Rhaxma *(Greek)* ♀ RATING: ★☆
Unknown meaning
People think of Rhaxma as exotic, weird, aggressive, lazy, sneaky
People who like the name Rhaxma also like Juji, Benecia, Rae, Fiona, Lucy, Olivia, Ronni, Dulcinea, Emiko, Renée

Rhea *(Greek)* ♀ RATING: ★★★☆
Flowing—Rhea Perlman, actress
People think of Rhea as pretty, caring, funny, creative, intelligent
People who like the name Rhea also like Paige, Rianna, Rea, Renée, Ava, Mia, Rae, Olivia, Chloe, Maya

Rhett *(American)* ♂ RATING: ★★☆
Created name—Rhett Butler, character from *Gone With the Wind* by Margaret Mitchell
People think of Rhett as handsome, intelligent, sexy, powerful, leader
People who like the name Rhett also like Noah, Seth, Ethan, Braden, Wyatt, Tristan, Landon, Gavin, Reece, Owen

Rhian *(Welsh)* ♀ RATING: ★★★★
Great queen—Short for Rhiannon
People think of Rhian as pretty, funny, intelligent, creative, energetic
People who like the name Rhian also like Rhiannon, Rianna, Kaelyn, Ryann, Paige, Rianne, Olivia, Keira, Zoe, Regan

Rhianna *(Welsh)* ♀ RATING: ★★★★☆
Great queen—Variation of Rhiannon
People think of Rhianna as pretty, intelligent, funny, popular, caring
People who like the name Rhianna also like Rhiannon, Paige, Rianna, Hailey, Olivia, Isabella, Hannah, Abigail, Kaelyn, Ava

Rhiannon *(Welsh)* ♀ RATING: ★★★☆
Great queen—Pronounced *hree-ANN-on*; song by Fleetwood Mac
People think of Rhiannon as pretty, intelligent, creative, funny, caring
People who like the name Rhiannon also like Paige, Olivia, Rianna, Chloe, Hannah, Isabella, Rhian, Grace, Kaelyn, Savannah

Rhianu *(Welsh)* ♀ RATING: ★★☆
Fair maiden
People think of Rhianu as quiet, unpopular, old-fashioned, ethnic, aggressive
People who like the name Rhianu also like Abrianna, Rhiannon, Rhianna, Petula, Carys, Liana, Ruana, Shamara, Kiara, Adalia

Rhoda *(Greek)* ♀ RATING: ★☆
Rose
People think of Rhoda as caring, trustworthy, pretty, intelligent, funny
People who like the name Rhoda also like Roxanne, Hailey, Paige, Rebecca, Lillian, Sabrina, Lilly, Hannah, Lauren, Mariah

Rhodes *(Greek)* ♀♂ RATING: ★★★☆
Roses
People think of Rhodes as intelligent, quiet, lazy, weird, artsy
People who like the name Rhodes also like Riley, Ryder, Logan, Caden, Parker, Rider, Reese, Hayden, Reagan, Reed

Rhody *(American)* ♀♂ RATING: ★★☆
Rose—Short for Rhoda or Rhodes
People think of Rhody as pretty, young, trendy, girl next door, intelligent
People who like the name Rhody also like Quinn, Brayden, Ren, Tarin, Blair, Blaine, Dakota, Breckin, Tanner, Hayden

Rhona *(Celtic/Gaelic)* ♀ RATING: ★★
From the rough island
People think of Rhona as funny, caring, pretty, trustworthy, intelligent
People who like the name Rhona also like Riona, Maeve, Keira, Lana, Alana, Mae, Fiona, Rianne, Sabrina, Kaelyn

Rhonda *(English)* ♀ RATING: ★★★☆
Probably from the Rhondda River—Rhonda Fleming, actress; "Help Me, Rhonda" song by The Beach Boys
People think of Rhonda as caring, intelligent, funny, trustworthy, pretty
People who like the name Rhonda also like Rebecca, Renée, Paula, Roxanne, Veronica, Victoria, Sabrina, Wendy, Faith, Stephanie

Rhoslyn *(Welsh)* ♀♂ RATING: ★★★★
Rose soft—Variation of Rosalind; also a Welsh place name meaning moor pool; Rhoslyn Jones, opera singer
People think of Rhoslyn as pretty, intelligent, creative, elegant, caring

People who like the name Rhoslyn also like Riley, Reese, Hayden, Jocelyn, Taylor, Piper, Madison, Jaden, Logan, Reagan

Rhoswen *(Welsh)* ♀　　　　RATING: ★★★★
Fair, blessed rose
People think of Rhoswen as pretty, elegant, creative, quiet, caring
People who like the name Rhoswen also like Kaelyn, Aeryn, Maeve, Riona, Rhiannon, Genevieve, Fiona, Rosaleen, Arwen, Rhian

Rhys *(Welsh)* ♂　　　　RATING: ★★☆
Running
People think of Rhys as intelligent, handsome, cool, funny, popular
People who like the name Rhys also like Ethan, Reece, Liam, Oliver, Tristan, Owen, Noah, Jack, Caleb, Cole

Rianna *(American)* ♀　　　　RATING: ★★★★☆
Variation of Rhianna
People think of Rianna as pretty, funny, intelligent, caring, young
People who like the name Rianna also like Paige, Rhiannon, Isabella, Olivia, Kaelyn, Hailey, Faith, Arianna, Hannah, Emma

Rianne *(American)* ♀　　　　RATING: ★★★
Variation of Rhian
People think of Rianne as funny, pretty, intelligent, young, energetic
People who like the name Rianne also like Rianna, Kaelyn, Ryann, Paige, Rhiannon, Rhian, Hailey, Hannah, Shayla, Gabrielle

Ricardo *(Spanish)* ♂　　　　RATING: ★★☆
Brave ruler—Variation of Richard; Ricardo Montalban, actor
People think of Ricardo as handsome, funny, cool, intelligent, popular
People who like the name Ricardo also like Antonio, Carlos, Diego, Nicholas, Xavier, Rafael, Gabriel, Ramón, Adrian, Alejandro

Ricci *(Italian)* ♀♂　　　　RATING: ★★★☆
Curly haired—Christina Ricci, actress
People think of Ricci as young, pretty, intelligent, creative, caring
People who like the name Ricci also like Rory, Kai, Rider, Ariel, Jess, Devon, Angel, Blaine, Remi, Bailey

Rich *(English)* ♂　　　　RATING: ★★★
Brave ruler—Short for Richard
People think of Rich as funny, handsome, sexy, intelligent, trustworthy
People who like the name Rich also like Jack, Nicholas, Andrew, David, Aaron, Jacob, Nathan, Justin, Richard, Joshua

Richard *(English)* ♂　　　　RATING: ★★☆
Brave ruler—Richard Avedon, photographer; Richard Branson, business mogul; Richard Burton, actor; Richard Gere, actor; Richard Simmons, workout guru
People think of Richard as handsome, funny, intelligent, caring, trustworthy
People who like the name Richard also like Matthew, William, Alexander, Jacob, Nicholas, Michael, Daniel, Christopher, David, Nathan

Richelle *(American)* ♀　　　　RATING: ★★★★
Combination of Richard and Rachelle
People think of Richelle as pretty, funny, creative, caring, trustworthy
People who like the name Richelle also like Rochelle, Rachelle, Rachael, Paige, Hailey, Gabrielle, Sabrina, Isabella, Isabelle, Faith

Richmond *(English)* ♂　　　　RATING: ★★★
The protector king—Also a borough in London, England, and a city in Virginia
People think of Richmond as handsome, intelligent, funny, winner, trustworthy
People who like the name Richmond also like Royce, Clayton, Rockwell, Reth, Truman, Emil, Fineen, Zeus, Hamish, Ryker

Rick *(English)* ♂　　　　RATING: ★★★☆
Brave ruler—Short for Richard; Rick Dees, radio DJ; Rick Springfield, singer
People think of Rick as handsome, funny, cool, intelligent, caring
People who like the name Rick also like Adam, Nathan, Eric, Justin, Luke, Jack, Aaron, Jake, Nicholas, Ethan

Ricky *(American)* ♂　　　　RATING: ★★
Brave ruler—Short for Richard; Ricky Martin, singer/actor; Ricky Ricardo, character on *I Love Lucy*
People think of Ricky as funny, handsome, cool, popular, intelligent
People who like the name Ricky also like Jacob, Nathan, Matthew, Seth, Ethan, Michael, Jake, Andrew, Aaron, Jason

Rico *(Spanish)* ♂　　　　RATING: ★★
Brave ruler—Short for Ricardo
People think of Rico as funny, cool, sexy, popular, handsome
People who like the name Rico also like Romeo, Antonio, Ricardo, Xavier, Jayden, Jacob, Anthony, Aaron, Gabriel, Ethan

Rida *(Arabic)* ♂　　　　RATING: ★★★
Consent, agreement
People think of Rida as intelligent, pretty, caring, sexy, popular
People who like the name Rida also like Brandon, Blade, Tyson, Jasper, Robert, Byron, Reynold, Ralph, Wheaton, Noah

473

Rider *(English)* ♀♂ RATING: ★★★★
Knight, mounted warrior
People think of Rider as popular, handsome, creative, sporty, powerful
People who like the name Rider also like Ryder, Riley, Parker, Hayden, Caden, Logan, Reese, Bailey, Taylor, Madison

Riel *(Spanish)* ♂ RATING: ★★★☆
Short for Gabriel
People think of Riel as intelligent, funny, creative, quiet, aggressive
People who like the name Riel also like Gabriel, Elijah, Ryker, Asher, Oliver, Samuel, Noah, Rafael, Aran, Rhys

Rigg *(English)* ♀♂ RATING: ★★☆
Dweller by the ridge—Diana Rigg, actress
People think of Rigg as handsome, loser, criminal, aggressive, quiet
People who like the name Rigg also like Ryder, Rider, Rain, Sawyer, James, Riley, Landen, Piper, Tyler, Rollin

Rihanna *(Arabic)* ♀ RATING: ★★★★
Sweet basil—Rihanna, singer
People think of Rihanna as pretty, popular, sexy, cool, creative
People who like the name Rihanna also like Rhianna, Aaliyah, Rianna, Brianna, Olivia, Kayla, Paige, Ciara, Arianna, Savannah

Riku *(Japanese)* ♂ RATING: ★★★☆
Land, continent
People think of Riku as cool, handsome, leader, popular, sexy
People who like the name Riku also like Ryu, Akio, Haruki, Hiroshi, Jason, Keitaro, Rhett, Haru, Derek, Jayden

Riley *(Celtic/Gaelic)* ♀♂ RATING: ★★★★
Descendant of Roghallach
People think of Riley as funny, popular, energetic, intelligent, creative
People who like the name Riley also like Madison, Bailey, Logan, Hayden, Taylor, Ryan, Mackenzie, Caden, Dylan, Addison

Rimona *(Hebrew)* ♀ RATING: ★★
Pomegranate
People think of Rimona as pretty, loser, nerdy, old-fashioned, winner
People who like the name Rimona also like Rebecca, Sabrina, Raisa, Sharona, Sophie, Sarina, Riona, Naomi, Regina, Rianna

Rin *(Japanese)* ♀♂ RATING: ★★
Companion
People think of Rin as intelligent, pretty, caring, young, energetic
People who like the name Rin also like Ren, Yuki, Seiko, Kana, Sanyu, Kiyoshi, Nori, Asa, Hoshi, Rain

Ringo *(Japanese)* ♂ RATING: ★★★★
Apple—Ringo Starr, drummer
People think of Ringo as cool, funny, weird, artsy, young
People who like the name Ringo also like Ryu, Haruki, Jiro, Makoto, Hiroshi, Keitaro, Yasuo, Akio, Romeo, Yukio

Rini *(American)* ♀ RATING: ★★★☆
Short for names ending in -rina
People think of Rini as creative, caring, trustworthy, young, pretty
People who like the name Rini also like Sakura, Kaida, Suki, Aiko, Amaya, Kimi, Keiko, Kaori, Mina, Kohana

Rio *(Spanish)* ♀♂ RATING: ★★
River
People think of Rio as cool, creative, intelligent, sexy, funny
People who like the name Rio also like Kai, Riley, River, Raven, Logan, Addison, Bailey, Madison, Remi, Teagan

Riona *(Celtic/Gaelic)* ♀ RATING: ★★★★
Queenlike
People think of Riona as pretty, intelligent, exotic, girl next door, caring
People who like the name Riona also like Fiona, Alana, Keaira, Sabrina, Keira, Kaelyn, Rhona, Maeve, Kiara, Rhoswen

Riordan *(Celtic/Gaelic)* ♂ RATING: ★★★★
Royal poet—Rick Riordan, author
People think of Riordan as handsome, intelligent, creative, leader, powerful
People who like the name Riordan also like Tristan, Liam, Aiden, Tiernan, Keiran, Declan, Keagan, Braeden, Ronan, Owen

Risa *(Italian)* ♀ RATING: ★★★★
Short for Marisa—Also Japanese meaning gossamer of the village
People think of Risa as pretty, funny, creative, intelligent, energetic
People who like the name Risa also like Raina, Rianna, Sienna, Paige, Samara, Mia, Eva, Olivia, Grace, Reina

Rishi *(Sanskrit/East Indian)* ♂ RATING: ★★★
Sage
People think of Rishi as intelligent, cool, handsome, funny, caring
People who like the name Rishi also like Ravi, Lokesh, Rohan, Ram, Finley, Naresh, Chatura, Rupin, Gaurav, Gyan

Rita *(Spanish)* ♀ RATING: ★★★
Pearl—Short for Margarita; Rita Coolidge, singer; Rita Hayworth, actress; Rita Moreno, actress
People think of Rita as pretty, caring, intelligent, funny, creative
People who like the name Rita also like Rebecca, Victoria, Samantha, Renée, Sabrina, Olivia, Jessica, Faith, Grace, Amanda

Riva (*Hebrew*) ♀   RATING: ★★
Maiden
> People think of Riva as artsy, pretty, caring, young, intelligent
> People who like the name Riva also like Rianna, Samara, Roxanne, Ruth, Vega, Rena, Eva, Ivy, Layla, Paige

River (*English*) ♀♂   RATING: ★★★★☆
Flowing body of water—River Phoenix, actor
> People think of River as creative, cool, intelligent, caring, handsome
> People who like the name River also like Riley, Rain, Ryder, Parker, Logan, Hayden, Reese, Phoenix, Ryan, Raine

Rivera (*Spanish*) ♀♂   RATING: ★★★
Lives near the river—Chita Rivera, actress/dancer; Geraldo Rivera, journalist
> People think of Rivera as pretty, young, caring, creative, intelligent
> People who like the name Rivera also like Raleigh, Reilly, Caden, Payton, Dante, Carter, Jaden, Julian, Rowan, Quinn

Rivka (*Hebrew*) ♀   RATING: ★★
Snare—Variation of Rebecca; in the Bible, the wife of Isaac
> People think of Rivka as pretty, intelligent, funny, exotic, creative
> People who like the name Rivka also like Raisa, Isis, Liana, Aurora, Samara, Maya, Eva, Naomi, Eve, Wren

Rizzo (*Italian*) ♀♂   RATING: ★★★
Curly haired—Character in *Grease*; Ratso Rizzo, character in *Midnight Cowboy*
> People think of Rizzo as cool, leader, energetic, funny, creative
> People who like the name Rizzo also like Luca, Domani, Piper, Ryder, Saxon, Reese, Zasha, Madison, Phoenix, Peyton

Roald (*English*) ♂   RATING: ★★☆
Counsel rule—Variation of Ronald; Roald Dahl, author
> People think of Roald as intelligent, creative, wealthy, leader, funny
> People who like the name Roald also like Tristan, Liam, Wyatt, Owen, Dalton, Fletcher, Garrison, Ean, Marlon, Noah

Roana (*Spanish*) ♀   RATING: ★★★
Reddish-brown skin
> People think of Roana as pretty, creative, funny, exotic, caring
> People who like the name Roana also like Rianna, Reina, Rianne, Rhian, Sienna, Raina, Rhea, Paige, Trinity, Rehan

Rob (*English*) ♂   RATING: ★★☆
Bright fame—Short for Robert; Rob Lowe, actor; Rob Reiner, actor/director; Rob Zombie, musician
> People think of Rob as funny, intelligent, handsome, cool, caring

> People who like the name Rob also like Jacob, Nathan, Patrick, Jason, Adam, Joshua, Scott, Nicholas, Nick, Luke

Robbin (*English*) ♀♂   RATING: ★★★☆
Bright fame—Variation of Robert
> People think of Robbin as pretty, caring, funny, intelligent, energetic
> People who like the name Robbin also like Ryan, Taylor, Madison, Robin, Jordan, Riley, Reese, Hayden, Parker, Raven

Robert (*English*) ♂   RATING: ★★☆
Bright fame—Robert Kennedy, U.S. attorney general; Robert Frost, writer/poet; Robert Redford, actor/director
> People think of Robert as funny, handsome, intelligent, caring, cool
> People who like the name Robert also like William, Daniel, Michael, Ethan, Nicholas, Andrew, Matthew, Christopher, David, Jacob

Roberta (*English*) ♀   RATING: ★★★
Bright fame—Feminine form of Robert
> People think of Roberta as pretty, funny, intelligent, caring, creative
> People who like the name Roberta also like Rebecca, Scarlett, Ruby, Victoria, Laurel, Roxanne, Rosalie, Bianca, Audrey, Olivia

Roberto (*Italian*) ♂   RATING: ★★★☆
Bright fame—Variation of Robert
> People think of Roberto as handsome, cool, funny, sexy, intelligent
> People who like the name Roberto also like Robert, Orlando, Ruben, Joseph, Romeo, David, Marco, Ramón, Julio, Antonio

Robin (*English*) ♀♂   RATING: ★★★☆
Bright fame—Variation of Robert; Robin Gibb, musician; Robin Hood, legendary thief; Robin Williams, actor
> People think of Robin as funny, caring, intelligent, creative, pretty
> People who like the name Robin also like Ryan, Morgan, Jordan, Madison, Reese, Riley, Logan, Taylor, Jade, Holly

Robinson (*English*) ♂   RATING: ★★★
Son of Robin—Also a surname; *Robinson Crusoe*, novel by Daniel Defoe
> People think of Robinson as intelligent, sexy, leader, cool, funny
> People who like the name Robinson also like Landon, Jacob, Owen, Edison, Aiden, Jefferson, Hudson, Benson, Jackson, Liam

Robyn (*English*) ♀♂   RATING: ★★★★
Bright fame—Variation of Robert
> People think of Robyn as pretty, funny, caring, intelligent, creative
> People who like the name Robyn also like Riley, Ryan, Sydney, Taylor, Madison, Logan, Brooke, Morgan, Robin, Reese

476

Rocco *(Italian)* ♂ RATING: ★★★★☆
Rest—Also short for Rockne
> People think of Rocco as handsome, cool, funny, leader, intelligent
> People who like the name Rocco also like Noah, Oliver, Roman, Maddox, Ethan, Leo, Nico, Gabriel, Tristan, Aiden

Roch *(French)* ♀ RATING: ★★☆
Rest—Variation of Rocco
> People think of Roch as powerful, leader, caring, intelligent, popular
> People who like the name Roch also like Genevieve, Skyla, Zora, Eve, Roxie, Lourdes, Chloe, Roxy, Reba, Roxanne

Rochelle *(French)* ♀ RATING: ★★★
Rest—Feminine form of Roch
> People think of Rochelle as pretty, funny, caring, intelligent, trustworthy
> People who like the name Rochelle also like Sabrina, Renée, Rebecca, Paige, Rachelle, Samantha, Gabrielle, Jasmine, Hailey, Isabella

Rocio *(Spanish)* ♀ RATING: ★★
Dew
> People think of Rocio as pretty, funny, cool, intelligent, sexy
> People who like the name Rocio also like Olivia, Isabella, Hazel, Marisol, Giselle, Melinda, Miranda, Phoebe, Serenity, Deanna

Rock *(English)* ♂ RATING: ★★★
Rock—Rock Hudson, actor; Rock (aka Rahman) Harper, chef
> People think of Rock as aggressive, powerful, leader, popular, cool
> People who like the name Rock also like Jackson, Miles, Lincoln, Wade, Jake, Brock, Samuel, Cole, Noah, Zachary

Rockwell *(English)* ♂ RATING: ★★
From the rock well—Norman Rockwell, painter
> People think of Rockwell as handsome, old-fashioned, intelligent, sexy, cool
> People who like the name Rockwell also like Maxwell, Tucker, Nicholas, Gabriel, Oliver, Wyatt, Tyson, Russell, Ethan, Remington

Rocky *(English)* ♂ RATING: ★★
Rocky—Rocky Graziano, boxer; *Rocky & Bullwinkle*, TV show; *Rocky*, series of movies
> People think of Rocky as handsome, cool, funny, popular, aggressive
> People who like the name Rocky also like Oliver, Jacob, Samuel, Ethan, Tyson, Cole, Joshua, Brock, Jack, Noah

Rod *(English)* ♂ RATING: ★★★
Short for Roderick or Rodney
> People think of Rod as funny, cool, handsome, caring, sexy
> People who like the name Rod also like Adam, Brock, Brandon, Jake, Noah, Jacob, Cole, Jason, Isaac, Reece

Rodd *(English)* ♂ RATING: ★☆
Short for Roderick or Rodney
> People think of Rodd as nerdy, old, uptight, caring, weird
> People who like the name Rodd also like Brent, Ian, Brandon, Denton, Anson, Jackson, Wade, Winston, Nathan, Blade

Roddy *(English)* ♂ RATING: ★★★
Short for Roderick or Rodney—Roddy McDowall, actor
> People think of Roddy as funny, caring, weird, lazy, loser
> People who like the name Roddy also like Jasper, Radley, Roden, Landon, Randall, Jack, Liam, Aiden, Jake, Ranger

Roden *(English)* ♂ RATING: ★★
From the swift river—Also an English place name
> People think of Roden as handsome, intelligent, trustworthy, energetic, powerful
> People who like the name Roden also like Ronan, Kaden, Reece, Radley, Keagan, Jayden, Rohan, Aiden, Noah, Braden

Roderick *(English)* ♂ RATING: ★★★☆
Famous ruler
> People think of Roderick as handsome, funny, intelligent, trustworthy, caring
> People who like the name Roderick also like Tristan, Ethan, Tyson, Kaden, Landon, Broderick, Nathan, Xander, Ian, Walker

Rodney *(English)* ♂ RATING: ★★★★
From the island in the swift river—Rodney Dangerfield, comedian
> People think of Rodney as handsome, intelligent, funny, caring, trustworthy
> People who like the name Rodney also like Nathan, Owen, Scott, Nicholas, David, Justin, Jason, Travis, Seth, Joshua

Rodrigo *(Spanish)* ♂ RATING: ★★★☆
Famous ruler—Variation of Roderick
> People think of Rodrigo as handsome, intelligent, cool, funny, young
> People who like the name Rodrigo also like Victor, Leonardo, Vincent, Ramiro, Eduardo, Ricardo, Robert, Fabian, Nicholas, Diego

Rogene *(American)* ♀♂ RATING: ★★★
Famous spear—Feminine form of Roger; Rogene White, actor
> People think of Rogene as intelligent, caring, trustworthy, pretty, aggressive
> People who like the name Rogene also like Remy, Rey, Rylee, Jocelin, Riley, Elie, Rhodes, Renate, Talon, Reese

Roger *(English)* ♂ RATING: ★★
Famous spear—Roger Daltrey, singer/musician; Roger Ebert, movie critic/author; Roger Moore, actor
> People think of Roger as handsome, intelligent, funny, caring, cool

People who like the name Roger also like Nathan, Nicholas, Jason, Peter, David, Nathaniel, Seth, Lucas, Michael, Simon

Rohak *(Arabic)* ♂   RATING: ★★☆
Unknown meaning
People think of Rohak as poor, unpopular, lazy, weird, wild
People who like the name Rohak also like Rohan, Rushil, Nirav, Ruhan, Ashwin, Adit, Ryker, Raanan, Raimi, Taran

Rohan *(Sanskrit/East Indian)* ♂   RATING: ★★★★
Ascending
People think of Rohan as handsome, intelligent, cool, funny, popular
People who like the name Rohan also like Ethan, Owen, Ronan, Tristan, Kaden, Seth, Noah, Aiden, Aden, Jacob

Roho *(African)* ♂   RATING: ★★☆
Soul—Kiswahili origin
People think of Roho as funny, weird, loser, ethnic, sporty
People who like the name Roho also like Joel, Ade, Jack, Leon, Lucas, Luke, Raanan, Wells, Jake, Ryker

Roja *(Spanish)* ♀   RATING: ★★★
Red
People think of Roja as exotic, intelligent, pretty, creative, leader
People who like the name Roja also like Reba, Ruby, Razi, Rosa, Amaya, Rebecca, Rhea, Rowa, Rasha, Ryann

Rojelio *(Spanish)* ♂   RATING: ★★★
Request
People think of Rojelio as handsome, funny, caring, powerful, ethnic
People who like the name Rojelio also like Rafael, Ricardo, Antonio, Alejandro, Andrés, Raúl, Carlos, Alberto, Javier, Ruben

Roland *(English)* ♂   RATING: ★★
Famous land
People think of Roland as handsome, intelligent, leader, funny, powerful
People who like the name Roland also like Gabriel, Owen, Nathan, Oliver, Tyson, Ethan, Noah, Tristan, Gavin, Lucas

Rolando *(Spanish)* ♂   RATING: ★☆
Famous land—Variation of Roland
People think of Rolando as funny, cool, handsome, caring, popular
People who like the name Rolando also like Carlos, Ricardo, Antonio, Rafael, Ruben, Adrian, Leonardo, Orlando, Vincent, Fernando

Rolf *(Scandinavian)* ♂   RATING: ★☆
Famous wolf—Also a German variation of Rudolf
People think of Rolf as intelligent, handsome, caring, creative, trustworthy
People who like the name Rolf also like Ulric, Warrick, Drake, Noah, Sloan, Erik, Rhett, Rutherford, Warren, Simon

Rollin *(English)* ♀♂   RATING: ★★★
Wolf counsel—Variation of Rawlin
People think of Rollin as cool, popular, sexy, creative, funny
People who like the name Rollin also like Ryder, Riley, Landen, Jaden, Logan, Parker, Rory, Hayden, Caden, Nolan

Rollins *(English)* ♂   RATING: ★★☆
Son of Rolf
People think of Rollins as leader, intelligent, handsome, cool, sneaky
People who like the name Rollins also like Reeves, Remington, Jackson, Radley, Jonas, Ross, Rutherford, Rockwell, Harrison, Randall

Rollo *(English)* ♂   RATING: ★★
Famous wolf
People think of Rollo as cool, funny, creative, intelligent, handsome
People who like the name Rollo also like Jacob, Aaron, Ace, Romeo, Jake, Laszlo, Rex, Jeremiah, Lachlan, Leo

Roma *(Italian)* ♀   RATING: ★★★★
From Rome, Italy—Roma Downey, actress
People think of Roma as pretty, intelligent, cool, funny, creative
People who like the name Roma also like Ava, Isabella, Natalia, Olivia, Sienna, Bella, Eva, Audrey, Mia, Ivy

Romaine *(French)* ♀   RATING: ★★★☆
From Rome, Italy—Also a type of lettuce
People think of Romaine as caring, handsome, creative, intelligent, funny
People who like the name Romaine also like Victoria, Maeve, Jenaya, Ryann, Patience, India, Renée, Gabrielle, Olivia, Giselle

Roman *(English)* ♂   RATING: ★★☆
From Rome, Italy—Roman Polanski, filmmaker
People think of Roman as handsome, powerful, leader, intelligent, cool
People who like the name Roman also like Noah, Ethan, Gabriel, Tristan, Gavin, Jackson, Elijah, Owen, Lucas, Jacob

Rome *(Italian)* ♀♂   RATING: ★★★☆
From Rome, Italy
People think of Rome as powerful, handsome, leader, intelligent, popular
People who like the name Rome also like Riley, London, Ryder, Ryan, Jordan, Caden, Phoenix, Sage, Jaden, Rowan

Romeo *(Italian)* ♂   RATING: ★★☆
From Rome, Italy—Character in *Romeo and Juliet* by William Shakespeare; Lil' Romeo, rapper
People think of Romeo as handsome, sexy, popular, cool, intelligent
People who like the name Romeo also like Elijah, Noah, Ethan, Jacob, Nathan, Lucas, Xavier, Aaron, Jayden, Roman

478

Romney (Welsh) ♂   RATING: ★★
From the broad river—Mitt Romney, politician
> People think of Romney as creative, sexy, intelligent, caring, pretty
> People who like the name Romney also like Ethan, Reece, Liam, Ronan, Rhys, Troy, Riordan, Jacob, Ranger, Tristan

Romy (German) ♀♂   RATING: ★★☆
The herb rosemary—Also a feminine form of Roman
> People think of Romy as pretty, funny, intelligent, creative, young
> People who like the name Romy also like Reese, Madison, Remy, Rory, Bailey, Logan, Ryan, Parker, Caden, Riley

Ron (English) ♂   RATING: ★★★☆
Counsel rule—Short for Ronald; Ron Howard, actor/filmmaker
> People think of Ron as funny, handsome, cool, caring, intelligent
> People who like the name Ron also like William, Nicholas, Adam, Jack, Brian, Aaron, Daniel, Luke, Cody, Michael

Rona (Hebrew) ♀   RATING: ★★★★
Song
> People think of Rona as pretty, funny, creative, caring, intelligent
> People who like the name Rona also like Keira, Fiona, Kara, Riona, Rhona, Mae, Kiara, Keaira, Erin, Kellyn

Ronald (English) ♂   RATING: ★☆
Counsel rule—Ronald Klink, politician; Ronald McDonald, clown mascot
> People think of Ronald as funny, handsome, caring, intelligent, cool
> People who like the name Ronald also like William, Robert, Jacob, Christopher, Daniel, Nicholas, Aaron, Gabriel, Scott, Matthew

Ronalee (American) ♀   RATING: ★★★
Combination of Rona and Lee
> People think of Ronalee as caring, girl next door, trustworthy, pretty, old-fashioned
> People who like the name Ronalee also like Rianna, Rianne, Shirley, Sabrina, Janelle, Leanna, Rebecca, Sophia, Belle, Nichole

Ronan (Celtic/Gaelic) ♂   RATING: ★★☆
Little seal
> People think of Ronan as intelligent, handsome, powerful, cool, creative
> People who like the name Ronan also like Liam, Owen, Ethan, Tristan, Aiden, Noah, Ian, Declan, Gavin, Keiran

Ronat (Celtic/Gaelic) ♀   RATING: ★★☆
Seal
> People think of Ronat as big, aggressive, weird, caring, religious
> People who like the name Ronat also like Maeve, Rona, Rhona, Maura, Riona, Rosaleen, Maili, Moira, Aislin, Cecily

Ronda (English) ♀   RATING: ★★★☆
Variation of Rhonda
> People think of Ronda as caring, intelligent, funny, pretty, trustworthy
> People who like the name Ronda also like Sarah, Rebecca, Veronica, Rachel, June, Kendra, Laura, Victoria, Roxanne, Julie

Rong (Chinese) ♀♂   RATING: ★★☆
Martial—Mandarin origin; unisex name, used mostly for males
> People think of Rong as weird, creative, intelligent, caring, powerful
> People who like the name Rong also like Rhoslyn, Reilly, Ryo, Li, Le, Robin, Rider, Redell, Riley, Rhodes

Ronia (Scandinavian) ♀   RATING: ★★★★
Character in *Ronia the Robber's Daughter* by Astrid Lindgren
> People think of Ronia as pretty, intelligent, energetic, sexy, caring
> People who like the name Ronia also like Rianna, Liana, Samara, Kaelyn, Seanna, Rebekka, Gianna, Reyna, Aliana, Roxanne

Ronli (Hebrew) ♀   RATING: ★★★
Joy is mine
> People think of Ronli as pretty, intelligent, creative, young, energetic
> People who like the name Ronli also like Mia, Rena, Ronni, Rini, Rianna, Tahlia, Shayna, Kiana, Drea, Enya

Ronna (American) ♀   RATING: ★★★☆
Bringing victory—Short for Veronica
> People think of Ronna as pretty, intelligent, trustworthy, funny, energetic
> People who like the name Ronna also like Cara, Grace, Maura, Cora, Rianne, Sierra, Rhiannon, Jenna, Kenna, Gwen

Ronni (English) ♀   RATING: ★★★☆
Bringing victory—Short for Veronica
> People think of Ronni as caring, intelligent, pretty, funny, creative
> People who like the name Ronni also like Rena, Renée, Callie, Rebecca, Rachel, Sara, Ryann, Jadyn, Roxanne, Jessica

Ronnie (English) ♀♂   RATING: ★★★☆
Short for Ronald or Veronica
> People think of Ronnie as funny, handsome, caring, intelligent, cool
> People who like the name Ronnie also like Ryan, Jordan, Hayden, Madison, Taylor, Brooke, Reese, Jesse, Jade, Ronny

Ronny (English) ♀♂   RATING: ★★
Short for Ronald or Veronica
> People think of Ronny as funny, caring, intelligent, cool, handsome
> People who like the name Ronny also like Ryan, Ronnie, Riley, Reese, Rylie, Rory, Caden, Rowan, Hayden, Sean

Roosevelt *(Dutch)* ♂   RATING: ★★★
From the rose field—Also an American surname;
Eleanor Roosevelt, first lady/activist; Franklin D.
Roosevelt, U.S. president; Theodore Roosevelt, U.S.
president
> People think of Roosevelt as intelligent, trustworthy,
> handsome, leader, powerful
> People who like the name Roosevelt also like Russell,
> Aaron, Roman, Benjamin, Jackson, Adam, Alexander,
> Jacob, Thomas, Nathaniel

Rory *(Celtic/Gaelic)* ♀ ♂   RATING: ★★★
Red king—Also short for Roderick
> People think of Rory as intelligent, funny, caring, cool,
> creative
> People who like the name Rory also like Riley, Logan,
> Hayden, Ryan, Reese, Reagan, Aidan, Parker, Madison,
> Connor

Ros *(English)* ♀   RATING: ★★★
Rose—Short for names beginning with Ros, most
often Rosalind
> People think of Ros as creative, caring, funny, artsy,
> leader
> People who like the name Ros also like Ryann, Roxanne,
> Rosalyn, Rosa, Charlotte, Rosie, Sofia, Erica, Rossa,
> Stella

Rosa *(Latin)* ♀   RATING: ★★★☆
Rose—Rosa Parks, civil rights activist
> People think of Rosa as pretty, caring, funny, intelligent,
> trustworthy
> People who like the name Rosa also like Rose, Olivia,
> Grace, Isabella, Eva, Ruby, Ella, Amelia, Ava, Faith

Rosalba *(Latin)* ♀   RATING: ★★★☆
White rose
> People think of Rosalba as pretty, trustworthy, exotic,
> caring, funny
> People who like the name Rosalba also like Rosalia,
> Rosaleen, Rosa, Rosalyn, Regina, Reina, Rosina,
> Serafina, Roxanne, Aurora

Rosaleen *(Celtic/Gaelic)* ♀   RATING: ★★★★
Little rose
> People think of Rosaleen as pretty, caring, trustworthy,
> quiet, funny
> People who like the name Rosaleen also like Rosalyn,
> Fiona, Sabrina, Kaelyn, Paige, Isabella, Maeve, Kayla,
> Keira, Abigail

Rosalia *(Latin)* ♀   RATING: ★★★☆
Rose
> People think of Rosalia as pretty, caring, funny, intel-
> ligent, exotic
> People who like the name Rosalia also like Isabella,
> Rosalyn, Rosalie, Natalia, Gabriella, Rosa, Victoria,
> Olivia, Lorelei, Sophia

Rosalie *(French)* ♀   RATING: ★★★★
Rose—Variation of Rosalia
> People think of Rosalie as pretty, elegant, intelligent,
> creative, caring

> People who like the name Rosalie also like Isabella,
> Olivia, Grace, Isabelle, Rosalyn, Hannah, Paige, Natalie,
> Eva, Abigail

Rosalind *(English)* ♀   RATING: ★★☆
Pretty rose—Characters in *As You Like It* and *Romeo
and Juliet* by William Shakespeare
> People think of Rosalind as pretty, intelligent, caring,
> creative, funny
> People who like the name Rosalind also like Rosalyn,
> Scarlett, Isabella, Aurora, Victoria, Olivia, Sophia, Paige,
> Rosaline, Grace

Rosaline *(Spanish)* ♀   RATING: ★★☆
Little rose
> People think of Rosaline as pretty, intelligent, elegant,
> artsy, creative
> People who like the name Rosaline also like Rosalyn,
> Isabella, Scarlett, Olivia, Isabelle, Rosalind, Emma, Eva,
> Victoria, Natalie

Rosalyn *(Spanish)* ♀   RATING: ★★☆
Little rose—Also spelled Rosalynn; Rosalynn Carter,
first lady
> People think of Rosalyn as pretty, caring, elegant, intel-
> ligent, creative
> People who like the name Rosalyn also like Isabella,
> Olivia, Paige, Isabelle, Hannah, Hailey, Faith, Gabrielle,
> Emma, Grace

Rosamund *(English)* ♀   RATING: ★☆
Horse protection
> People think of Rosamund as pretty, intelligent, artsy,
> caring, creative
> People who like the name Rosamund also like Matilda,
> Iris, Rhiannon, Violet, Ivy, Ophelia, Moira, Charlotte,
> Grace, Emma

Rosario *(Spanish)* ♀   RATING: ★★★☆
Rosary—Rosario Dawson, actress
> People think of Rosario as funny, caring, creative,
> pretty, intelligent
> People who like the name Rosario also like Olivia,
> Isabella, Mia, Sofia, Victoria, Isabel, Cecilia, Esperanza,
> Angelica, Hannah

Roscoe *(Scandinavian)* ♂   RATING: ★★★☆
From the deer forest
> People think of Roscoe as handsome, trustworthy, intel-
> ligent, powerful, creative
> People who like the name Roscoe also like Oliver,
> Benjamin, Noah, Sebastian, Lucas, Elijah, Aiden,
> Jackson, Xavier, Ethan

Rose *(English)* ♀   RATING: ★★★★
Rose—Rose Kennedy, mother of U.S. president John F.
Kennedy
> People think of Rose as pretty, caring, creative, funny,
> intelligent
> People who like the name Rose also like Grace, Olivia,
> Elizabeth, Lily, Emma, Paige, Hannah, Ava, Faith, Isabella

Roseanne *(English)* ♀   RATING: ★★★
Gracious rose—Combination of Rose and Anne;
Roseanne Barr, actress/comedian
> People think of Roseanne as funny, pretty, creative,
> intelligent, caring
> People who like the name Roseanne also like Rose,
> Rosemarie, Roxanne, Rebecca, Samantha, Jessica,
> Rosalie, Rachel, Rosemary, Vanessa

Rosemarie *(French)* ♀   RATING: ★★★★
The herb rosemary—Also a combination of Rose and
Marie
> People think of Rosemarie as pretty, intelligent, caring,
> funny, creative
> People who like the name Rosemarie also like Isabella,
> Rose, Samantha, Paige, Hailey, Victoria, Rosemary,
> Scarlett, Isabelle, Elizabeth

Rosemary *(English)* ♀   RATING: ★★★☆
Herb
> People think of Rosemary as pretty, intelligent, caring,
> creative, trustworthy
> People who like the name Rosemary also like Rose,
> Olivia, Scarlett, Grace, Faith, Violet, Sabrina, Samantha,
> Hannah, Victoria

Rosetta *(Italian)* ♀   RATING: ★★★☆
Little rose—Rosetta Stone, an ancient Egyptian
artifact
> People think of Rosetta as pretty, trustworthy, intel-
> ligent, sexy, funny
> People who like the name Rosetta also like Angelina,
> Loretta, Rose, Isabella, Bianca, Gabriella, Arianna,
> Sienna, Kayla, Rosalie

Roshaun *(American)* ♂   RATING: ★★
Combination of Roland and Shaun
> People think of Roshaun as intelligent, handsome, lead-
> er, sexy, powerful
> People who like the name Roshaun also like André,
> Tyrell, Robert, Raheem, Dayshaun, Jamar, Jeremiah,
> Aiden, Terrel, Jevonte

Rosie *(English)* ♀   RATING: ★★★☆
Rose flower—Short for Rose; Rosie O'Donnell, comedian; Rosie Perez, actress
> People think of Rosie as pretty, funny, caring, creative,
> intelligent
> People who like the name Rosie also like Rose, Sophie,
> Lilly, Ruby, Grace, Paige, Phoebe, Lucy, Daisy, Olivia

Rosina *(Italian)* ♀   RATING: ★★☆
Rose—Variation of Rosa
> People think of Rosina as caring, funny, creative, pretty,
> intelligent
> People who like the name Rosina also like Rosaleen,
> Sabrina, Isabella, Rose, Rosie, Rianne, Aeryn, Rosalia,
> Lana, Rianna

Rosine *(German)* ♀   RATING: ★★★
Rose—Variation of Rosa
> People think of Rosine as religious, wild, big, trust-
> worthy, funny

People who like the name Rosine also like Kaya, Lorelei,
Rosina, Sora, Rozene, Rosaline, Layla, Ophelia, Tallulah,
Kiona

Ross *(Celtic/Gaelic)* ♂   RATING: ★★★
Headland—Also a region of Scotland; Ross Geller,
character on *Friends*; Ross Porter, sportscaster
> People think of Ross as handsome, funny, intelligent,
> cool, caring
> People who like the name Ross also like Ethan, Owen,
> Tristan, Noah, Jack, Ian, Benjamin, Seth, Scott, Aiden

Rossa *(Italian)* ♀   RATING: ★★★
Red—Also a feminine form of Ross
> People think of Rossa as pretty, quiet, poor, exotic,
> young
> People who like the name Rossa also like Rosa,
> Rosemarie, Sabrina, Roxanne, Rosina, Rebecca,
> Penelope, Renée, Tessa, Faith

Rousseau *(French)* ♀ ♂   RATING: ★★☆
Red haired—Pronounced *ROO-so*; Jean-Jacques
Rousseau, philosopher
> People think of Rousseau as creative, girl next door,
> energetic, funny, wild
> People who like the name Rousseau also like Dante,
> Harper, Willow, Theron, Oakley, Kennedy, London,
> Connor, Jordan, Indiana

Rowa *(Arabic)* ♀   RATING: ★★
Lovely vision
> People think of Rowa as sexy, weird, powerful, intel-
> ligent, ethnic
> People who like the name Rowa also like Rhea, Layla,
> Freya, Sephora, Olivia, Zoey, Rena, Keira, Jena, Serena

Rowan *(English)* ♀ ♂   RATING: ★★★★☆
Rowan tree—Rowan Atkinson, comedian/actor
> People think of Rowan as intelligent, creative, pretty,
> caring, funny
> People who like the name Rowan also like Riley, Logan,
> Hayden, Reese, Reagan, Ryder, Aidan, Avery, Addison,
> Parker

Rowanne *(American)* ♀   RATING: ★★★☆
Combination of Rowan and Anne
> People think of Rowanne as pretty, artsy, creative, cool,
> caring
> People who like the name Rowanne also like Rianna,
> Paige, Kendra, Olivia, Rianne, Gabrielle, Rhian, Renée,
> Victoria, Sienna

Rowdy *(American)* ♀ ♂   RATING: ★☆
Loud, spirited—Rowdy Gaines, swimmer
> People think of Rowdy as wild, energetic, aggressive,
> funny, powerful
> People who like the name Rowdy also like Riley, Rory,
> Dakota, Paxton, Hayden, Logan, Rider, Caden, Spencer,
> Parker

Rowena *(English)* ♀ RATING: ★★★★
Fame joy
People think of Rowena as caring, intelligent, pretty, trustworthy, creative
People who like the name Rowena also like Fiona, Olivia, Keira, Maeve, Genevieve, Rhiannon, Lana, Arwen, Paige, Aurora

Roxanne *(English)* ♀ RATING: ★★★☆
Dawn—From a Persian name; Alexander the Great's first wife; character in *Cyrano de Bergerac* by Edmond Rostand; song by The Police
People think of Roxanne as pretty, funny, sexy, intelligent, caring
People who like the name Roxanne also like Faith, Paige, Sabrina, Scarlett, Veronica, Samantha, Sophia, Olivia, Isabella, Victoria

Roxie *(American)* ♀ RATING: ★★★☆
Dawn—Short for Roxanne; Roxie Hart, character in *Chicago*
People think of Roxie as pretty, sexy, cool, wild, energetic
People who like the name Roxie also like Roxy, Roxanne, Paige, Isabella, Lexi, Scarlett, Sophie, Chloe, Faith, Hailey

Roxy *(American)* ♀ RATING: ★★★★
Dawn—Short for Roxanne
People think of Roxy as pretty, sexy, popular, wild, cool
People who like the name Roxy also like Paige, Roxanne, Roxie, Faith, Chloe, Ruby, Hannah, Bella, Olivia, Sadie

Roy *(Celtic/Gaelic)* ♂ RATING: ★★
Red—Also a French surname meaning king; Roy Campanella, baseball player; Roy Orbison, singer; Roy Rogers, singer/actor
People think of Roy as handsome, funny, intelligent, cool, powerful
People who like the name Roy also like Jason, Justin, Robert, Owen, Seth, Nathan, Nicholas, Daniel, Russell, Adam

Royal *(English)* ♀♂ RATING: ★★★☆
Of the king
People think of Royal as powerful, handsome, intelligent, leader, wealthy
People who like the name Royal also like Ryder, Riley, Jaden, Raven, Parker, Logan, Jordan, Madison, Rain, Raine

Royce *(English)* ♂ RATING: ★★★★
Of a famous kin—Originally a surname from Rohese
People think of Royce as cool, handsome, intelligent, trustworthy, leader
People who like the name Royce also like Reece, Landon, Ethan, Tyson, Kaden, Cole, Tristan, Seth, Owen, Jackson

Roz *(English)* ♀ RATING: ★★★☆
Rose—Short for names beginning with Ros, most often Rosalind
People think of Roz as leader, caring, funny, creative, intelligent
People who like the name Roz also like Sadie, Nora, Persephone, Zoe, Evie, Bernadette, Penelope, Phoebe, Genevieve, Lei

Roza *(Polish)* ♀ RATING: ★★★
Rose
People think of Roza as pretty, sexy, trustworthy, young, leader
People who like the name Roza also like Rosina, Mia, Ewa, Olesia, Gizela, Rosa, Seda, Zofia, Isabella, Rosine

Rozalia *(Hungarian)* ♀ RATING: ★★★
Rose
People think of Rozalia as pretty, creative, exotic, old-fashioned, sexy
People who like the name Rozalia also like Trinity, Renée, Rebecca, Natalia, Sapphire, Nadia, Stella, Paige, Olivia, Rianna

Rozene *(English)* ♀ RATING: ★★
Rose
People think of Rozene as sexy, pretty, loser, trustworthy, popular
People who like the name Rozene also like Rosine, Roxanne, Tazanna, Kaya, Ayasha, Rhiannon, Orenda, Tiva, Topanga, Wakanda

Ruana *(Persian)* ♀ RATING: ★★★
Soul
People think of Ruana as exotic, cool, creative, old-fashioned, artsy
People who like the name Ruana also like Rianna, Raina, Rhiannon, Layla, Samara, Samira, Rhian, Tiana, Rea, Rosaleen

Rubaina *(Sanskrit/East Indian)* ♀ RATING: ★☆
Bright
People think of Rubaina as pretty, weird, powerful, intelligent, sexy
People who like the name Rubaina also like Rachana, Raina, Ishana, Selena, Rhiannon, Eshana, Shyla, Serafina, Mandira, Rania

Ruben *(Spanish)* ♂ RATING: ★★★☆
Behold, a son—Ruben Studdard, singer
People think of Ruben as funny, handsome, cool, caring, intelligent
People who like the name Ruben also like Reuben, Isaac, Jacob, Samuel, Gabriel, Ethan, Nathan, Noah, Oliver, Adrian

Ruby *(English)* ♀ RATING: ★★☆
Red gemstone
People think of Ruby as pretty, funny, caring, intelligent, creative
People who like the name Ruby also like Scarlett, Olivia, Ava, Grace, Lily, Violet, Ella, Charlotte, Lucy, Isabella

482

Ruchira *(Sanskrit/East Indian)* ♀   RATING: ★★☆
Bright, brilliant
People think of Ruchira as girl next door, sexy, intelligent, young, popular
People who like the name Ruchira also like Rayya, Raina, Reina, Rania, Rubaina, Rupali, Tanika, Nayana, Rasha, Rini

Rudolph *(English)* ♂   RATING: ★★★
Famous wolf—Rudolph Valentino, actor; "Rudolph the Red-Nosed Reindeer," Christmas song
People think of Rudolph as intelligent, creative, trustworthy, funny, caring
People who like the name Rudolph also like Randolph, Victor, Noah, Ethan, Jared, Oliver, Zachary, Peter, Felix, Vincent

Rudy *(American)* ♂   RATING: ★★
Famous wolf—Short for Rudolph; Rudy Giuliani, politician
People think of Rudy as funny, handsome, cool, caring, sexy
People who like the name Rudy also like Noah, Nathan, Jack, Ethan, Lucas, Oliver, Owen, Reece, Cody, Zachary

Rue *(English)* ♀   RATING: ★★★★
Herb—Also short for Ruth; Rue McClanahan, actress
People think of Rue as pretty, artsy, creative, intelligent, caring
People who like the name Rue also like Rae, Ava, Phoebe, Scarlett, Ruby, Iris, Wren, Sophie, Rhea, Grace

Rufina *(Italian)* ♀   RATING: ★☆
Red haired
People think of Rufina as popular, pretty, sexy, exotic, cool
People who like the name Rufina also like Camilla, Sienna, Cascata, Fiorella, Gianna, Luciana, Melita, Natalia, Ruby, Lucia

Rufus *(Latin)* ♂   RATING: ★☆
Red haired
People think of Rufus as handsome, intelligent, energetic, funny, cool
People who like the name Rufus also like Jasper, Oscar, Rupert, Oliver, Felix, Jack, Jacob, Seth, Max, Rocco

Ruggiero *(Italian)* ♂   RATING: ★★☆
Famous spear—Variation of Roger
People think of Ruggiero as weird, aggressive, big, leader, winner
People who like the name Ruggiero also like Baldasarre, Ryu, Adam, Anthony, Brian, Raanan, Leone, Raffaello, Ralston, Lorenzo

Ruhan *(Arabic)* ♂   RATING: ★★
Spiritual
People think of Ruhan as ethnic, aggressive, young, caring, powerful
People who like the name Ruhan also like Rohan, Rohak, Ashwin, Nirav, Raanan, Rushil, Amish, Raimi, Nitesh, Sanjay

Rui *(Spanish)* ♂   RATING: ★★★
Famous ruler—Short for Rodrigo
People think of Rui as handsome, caring, energetic, young, trustworthy
People who like the name Rui also like Raghnall, Vashon, Radley, Radwan, Rick, Russell, Rafael, Arkadiy, Daire, Randall

Rujula *(Arabic)* ♂   RATING: ★★
Masculinity
People think of Rujula as ethnic, exotic, energetic, aggressive, intelligent
People who like the name Rujula also like Javana, Tovi, Indra, Kynan, Espen, Toviel, Price, Dumi, Pelham, Ravi

Rumer *(English)* ♀♂   RATING: ★★
Fame; Rome pilgrim—Also a surname; Rumer Godden, author; Rumer Willis, daughter of Bruce Willis and Demi Moore
People think of Rumer as pretty, intelligent, creative, popular, exotic
People who like the name Rumer also like Ryder, Riley, Rowan, Parker, London, Piper, River, Reese, Logan, Scout

Rumor *(American)* ♀♂   RATING: ★★
Falsity
People think of Rumor as creative, untrustworthy, wild, criminal, artsy
People who like the name Rumor also like Riley, Ryder, Ryan, Piper, Hayden, Rumer, Jordan, Reese, Parker, Rylee

Rune *(German)* ♀♂   RATING: ★★
A secret
People think of Rune as intelligent, powerful, creative, exotic, quiet
People who like the name Rune also like Ryder, Logan, Riley, Rowan, Raven, Rain, Sage, Piper, Rory, Hayden

Rupali *(Sanskrit/East Indian)* ♀   RATING: ★★★☆
Most beautiful
People think of Rupali as pretty, trustworthy, intelligent, creative, caring
People who like the name Rupali also like Rachna, Meena, Rachana, Ramya, Chandra, Indira, Tarika, Divya, Jaya, Keely

Rupert *(French)* ♂   RATING: ★★
Bright fame—Rupert Everett, actor; Rupert Holmes, musician; Rupert Murdoch, media mogul
People think of Rupert as handsome, intelligent, caring, popular, funny
People who like the name Rupert also like William, Jacob, Jack, Elijah, Oliver, Benjamin, Daniel, Caleb, Seth, Noah

Rupin *(Sanskrit/East Indian)* ♂   RATING: ★★☆
Handsome
People think of Rupin as sexy, nerdy, intelligent, ethnic, boy next door
People who like the name Rupin also like Lokesh, Rushil, Devesh, Nirav, Manas, Arnav, Adit, Rishi, Nitesh, Suvan

Rushil *(Sanskrit/East Indian)* ♂   RATING: ★★★☆
Charming
> People think of Rushil as funny, intelligent, handsome, cool, popular
> People who like the name Rushil also like Adit, Rohak, Nirav, Ashwin, Ruhan, Savir, Rohan, Arnav, Manas, Amish

Russ *(English)* ♂   RATING: ★★★☆
Red—Short for Russell; Russ Feingold, politician
> People think of Russ as handsome, funny, popular, trustworthy, caring
> People who like the name Russ also like Russell, Justin, Jack, Wade, Jacob, Nicholas, Zach, Lucas, Jake, Nathan

Russell *(English)* ♂   RATING: ★★★★
Red—Also spelled Russel; Russell Crowe, actor; Russell Simmons, music producer
> People think of Russell as handsome, funny, intelligent, caring, cool
> People who like the name Russell also like Ethan, Nicholas, Nathan, Owen, Matthew, Noah, Justin, Benjamin, Jacob, Oliver

Russo *(Italian)* ♂   RATING: ★★
Red haired—Rene Russo, actress
> People think of Russo as sexy, loser, lazy, weird, big
> People who like the name Russo also like Russell, Russ, Rainer, Liam, Malcolm, Roman, Demetrius, Reece, Wheeler, Jefferson

Russom *(English)* ♂   RATING: ★☆
Red—Originally a surname
> People think of Russom as weird, poor, unpopular, lazy, criminal
> People who like the name Russom also like Bradley, Brandon, Blade, Lachlan, Rhys, Race, Jacob, Javier, Rainer, Adam

Rusti *(American)* ♀♂   RATING: ★★★
Redheaded
> People think of Rusti as cool, wild, pretty, funny, weird
> People who like the name Rusti also like Rusty, Ryder, Reese, Raine, Riley, Madison, Rylie, Reilly, Remi, Rory

Rusty *(American)* ♀♂   RATING: ★★★☆
Redheaded—Also a nickname for a red-haired person
> People think of Rusty as caring, handsome, funny, sporty, cool
> People who like the name Rusty also like Ryan, Parker, Taylor, Riley, Madison, Logan, Dakota, Toby, Tyler, Tanner

Ruth *(Hebrew)* ♀   RATING: ★★
Friendship—Ruth Buzzi, comedian; "Dr. Ruth" Westheimer, sex therapist; "Babe" Ruth, baseball player
> People think of Ruth as caring, pretty, intelligent, trustworthy, funny
> People who like the name Ruth also like Grace, Hannah, Abigail, Olivia, Elizabeth, Emma, Sarah, Rebecca, Sophia, Rachel

Rutherford *(English)* ♂   RATING: ★★★
From the cattle ford—Rutherford B. Hayes, U.S. president
> People think of Rutherford as nerdy, old-fashioned, uptight, old, loser
> People who like the name Rutherford also like Remington, Radley, Russell, Livingston, Ryker, Weston, Anderson, Nicholas, Jackson, Tristan

Ryan *(Celtic/Gaelic)* ♀♂   RATING: ★★★☆
King—Ryan O'Neal, actor; Ryan Seacrest, TV host
> People think of Ryan as funny, handsome, intelligent, cool, caring
> People who like the name Ryan also like Riley, Tyler, Dylan, Logan, Taylor, Madison, Hayden, Evan, Kyle, Cameron

Ryann *(American)* ♀   RATING: ★★★
Combination of Ryan and Anne
> People think of Ryann as pretty, funny, intelligent, caring, popular
> People who like the name Ryann also like Paige, Kaelyn, Emma, Olivia, Ava, Isabella, Regan, Hailey, Hannah, Ella

Ryder *(English)* ♀♂   RATING: ★★★
Knight, mounted warrior
> People think of Ryder as handsome, popular, cool, leader, powerful
> People who like the name Ryder also like Riley, Hayden, Parker, Logan, Caden, Reese, Ryan, Bailey, Madison, Dylan

Ryker *(American)* ♂   RATING: ★★☆
Becoming rich—Also a surname
> People think of Ryker as handsome, intelligent, powerful, leader, sporty
> People who like the name Ryker also like Kaden, Reece, Aiden, Jackson, Tristan, Ethan, Landon, Gavin, Maddox, Gage

Rylan *(English)* ♀♂   RATING: ★★★★☆
From the rye land
> People think of Rylan as handsome, popular, intelligent, funny, cool
> People who like the name Rylan also like Riley, Caden, Hayden, Logan, Ryan, Ryder, Reagan, Jaden, Rylie, Reese

Ryland *(English)* ♀♂   RATING: ★★★★
From the rye land
> People think of Ryland as handsome, intelligent, popular, creative, cool
> People who like the name Ryland also like Rylan, Riley, Ryder, Caden, Hayden, Parker, Logan, Rylee, Addison, Reagan

Rylee *(Celtic/Gaelic)* ♀♂   RATING: ★★★☆
Descendant of Roghallach
> People think of Rylee as pretty, funny, energetic, popular, intelligent
> People who like the name Rylee also like Riley, Rylie, Madison, Bailey, Hayden, Caden, Reagan, Logan, Taylor, Rylan

Rylie *(Celtic/Gaelic)* ♀♂   RATING: ★★★★
Descendant of Roghallach
> People think of Rylie as pretty, funny, popular, energetic, caring
> People who like the name Rylie also like Riley, Rylee, Reese, Logan, Hayden, Madison, Bailey, Caden, Reagan, Ryan

Ryo *(Japanese)* ♀♂   RATING: ★★★☆
Excellent
> People think of Ryo as intelligent, creative, handsome, exotic, cool
> People who like the name Ryo also like Aidan, Logan, Jade, Ryan, Raven, Rylie, Rain, River, Rin, Kai

Ryu *(Japanese)* ♂   RATING: ★★★★
Dragon
> People think of Ryu as powerful, leader, handsome, cool, aggressive
> People who like the name Ryu also like Suoh, Hiroshi, Akio, Haru, Haruki, Drake, Xander, Kaden, Keitaro, Xavier

Ryuu *(Japanese)* ♀   RATING: ★★★
Dragon
> People think of Ryuu as intelligent, wild, creative, exotic, powerful
> People who like the name Ryuu also like Kohana, Reiko, Kaida, Sakura, Radha, Inari, Hisano, Tama, Yoshiko, Haruko

—— ⬛ˢ ——

Saba *(Arabic)* ♀   RATING: ★★★☆
Submit
> People think of Saba as funny, intelligent, pretty, young, exotic
> People who like the name Saba also like Sabina, Sada, Sabrina, Sachi, Sabine, Sapphire, Layla, Sera, Victoria, Sabah

Sabah *(Arabic)* ♀   RATING: ★★★
Morning
> People think of Sabah as sexy, funny, pretty, caring, trustworthy
> People who like the name Sabah also like Samara, Sachi, Sabrina, Nadia, Sahara, Sadah, Serenity, Hannah, Sari, Saba

Sabella *(American)* ♀   RATING: ★★★☆
Consecrated to God—Variation of Isabella
> People think of Sabella as pretty, elegant, exotic, intelligent, sexy
> People who like the name Sabella also like Isabella, Sadie, Sabrina, Samantha, Sabina, Savannah, Ava, Scarlett, Hannah, Serenity

Saber *(French)* ♂   RATING: ★★★★
Sword
> People think of Saber as powerful, aggressive, exotic, cool, handsome

> People who like the name Saber also like Kaden, Aiden, Seth, Tristan, Tyson, Maddox, Drake, Blade, Slade, Sirius

Sabin *(French)* ♂   RATING: ★★☆
Sabine man—The Sabines were an ancient Italian tribe
> People think of Sabin as handsome, intelligent, caring, cool, creative
> People who like the name Sabin also like Saber, Kaden, Ethan, Liam, Noah, Maddox, Gabriel, Nicholas, Slade, Chase

Sabina *(Latin)* ♀   RATING: ★★★★
Sabine woman
> People think of Sabina as pretty, creative, intelligent, caring, funny
> People who like the name Sabina also like Sabrina, Sophia, Sabine, Isabella, Samantha, Samara, Nadia, Amelia, Sophie, Sienna

Sabine *(French)* ♀   RATING: ★★☆
Variation of Sabina
> People think of Sabine as pretty, creative, intelligent, elegant, exotic
> People who like the name Sabine also like Ava, Sabina, Isabella, Scarlett, Olivia, Sophie, Sabrina, Ella, Sadie, Gabrielle

Sabra *(Hebrew)* ♀   RATING: ★★
Cactus fruit
> People think of Sabra as pretty, intelligent, caring, creative, funny
> People who like the name Sabra also like Samara, Sabina, Sabrina, Sophia, Sofia, Sahara, Sierra, Sabine, Serenity, Chloe

Sabriel *(English)* ♀♂   RATING: ★★★★
Combination of S and Gabriel—Character in the Abhorsen trilogy by Garth Nix
> People think of Sabriel as intelligent, creative, powerful, pretty, exotic
> People who like the name Sabriel also like Jaden, Caden, Cadence, Aidan, Reese, Quinn, Skye, Jade, Skylar, Teagan

Sabrina *(Celtic/Gaelic)* ♀   RATING: ★★★
From the river Severn—*Sabrina, the Teenage Witch*, comic/TV character
> People think of Sabrina as pretty, funny, intelligent, caring, creative
> People who like the name Sabrina also like Samantha, Olivia, Isabella, Sophia, Paige, Hannah, Savannah, Sadie, Hailey, Abigail

Sachet *(Sanskrit/East Indian)* ♀♂   RATING: ★★★
Pure existence, thought—Also means perfumed in French
> People think of Sachet as intelligent, pretty, creative, cool, sexy
> People who like the name Sachet also like Sage, Sanjeet, Sasha, Sawyer, Paris, Ryder, Haley, Logan, Skylar, Pavan

Sachi *(Japanese)* ♀   RATING: ★★
Girl child of bliss
- People think of Sachi as pretty, intelligent, creative, young, funny
- People who like the name Sachi also like Sada, Sakura, Suki, Aiko, Amaya, Keiko, Kaida, Kioko, Emiko, Inari

Sada *(Japanese)* ♀   RATING: ★★★★
Pure one—Also mean good fortune in Arabic; Sada Thompson, actress
- People think of Sada as intelligent, pretty, exotic, trust-worthy, creative
- People who like the name Sada also like Sachi, Sakura, Suki, Amaya, Sadie, Kaida, Kaiya, Kaori, Kohana, Ayame

Sadah *(Arabic)* ♀   RATING: ★★
Most fortunate
- People think of Sadah as lazy, young, intelligent, energetic, cool
- People who like the name Sadah also like Samara, Sada, Layla, Sabah, Sachi, Sadie, Selena, Savannah, Serena, Sabrina

Saddam *(Arabic)* ♂   RATING: ★★☆
Brave—Rare name; Saddam Hussein, former leader of Iraq
- People think of Saddam as criminal, aggressive, untrust-worthy, unpopular, loser
- People who like the name Saddam also like Seth, Saber, Elijah, Gage, Cole, Jacob, Gaylord, Damien, Thomas, William

Sadie *(English)* ♀   RATING: ★★★☆
Princess—Variation of Sarah
- People think of Sadie as pretty, funny, creative, caring, intelligent
- People who like the name Sadie also like Ava, Olivia, Sophie, Chloe, Paige, Emma, Hannah, Ella, Grace, Isabella

Sadiki *(African)* ♀ ♂   RATING: ★★★☆
Faithful—Ugandan origin
- People think of Sadiki as exotic, young, quiet, creative, funny
- People who like the name Sadiki also like Saidi, Logan, Jade, Seiko, Dante, Sarki, Dakota, Reese, Phoenix, Sabriel

Saeed *(Arabic)* ♂   RATING: ★★☆
Fortunate, auspicious
- People think of Saeed as intelligent, caring, cool, hand-some, sexy
- People who like the name Saeed also like Malik, Caleb, Jabari, Fabian, Seth, Idris, Ethan, Nathan, Nathaniel, Nicholas

Saeran *(Celtic/Gaelic)* ♂   RATING: ★★
Noble
- People think of Saeran as powerful, intelligent, creative, exotic, leader
- People who like the name Saeran also like Keiran, Tristan, Liam, Keagan, Aiden, Kael, Tiernan, Gabriel, Lachlan, Braeden

Safa *(Arabic)* ♀   RATING: ★★★
Pure
- People think of Safa as pretty, intelligent, ethnic, funny, caring
- People who like the name Safa also like Sumayah, Sahara, Sabah, Sana, Sona, Inaya, Jinan, Tabitha, Inara, Noura

Safara *(African)* ♀   RATING: ★★★☆
Fire—Wolof origin
- People think of Safara as exotic, pretty, powerful, creative, intelligent
- People who like the name Safara also like Sahara, Sadie, Sapphire, Samara, Samira, Sabrina, Selena, Sierra, Serafina, Nala

Safari *(Swahili)* ♀ ♂   RATING: ★★★
Journey, expedition—From Arabic word *safar* meaning journey
- People think of Safari as exotic, pretty, funny, creative, caring
- People who like the name Safari also like Sydney, River, Phoenix, Storm, Diamond, Jada, Shae, Brooklyn, Paris, Brooke

Saffron *(English)* ♀   RATING: ★★★★☆
Yellow flower—Also a spice from the saffron flower
- People think of Saffron as pretty, creative, artsy, intelligent, exotic
- People who like the name Saffron also like Scarlett, Sapphire, Olivia, Sadie, Ava, Summer, Chloe, Paige, Phoebe, Sienna

Sage *(English)* ♀ ♂   RATING: ★★★★☆
Herb; prophet
- People think of Sage as intelligent, creative, pretty, funny, caring
- People who like the name Sage also like Riley, Hayden, Bailey, Caden, Jade, Madison, Logan, Jaden, Parker, Reese

Sagira *(Arabic)* ♀   RATING: ★★
Little one
- People think of Sagira as exotic, pretty, popular, quiet, elegant
- People who like the name Sagira also like Sanura, Sahirah, Sakura, Saniya, Tahirah, Sahara, Isis, Sachi, Sada, Genevieve

Sagittarius *(Latin)* ♀   RATING: ★★★☆
The archer—Used for children born under this astro-logical sign
- People think of Sagittarius as funny, pretty, sexy, energetic, cool
- People who like the name Sagittarius also like Sapphire, Saffron, Serenity, Sadie, Sabrina, Faith, Virginia, Lana, Samantha, Alana

Sahara *(Arabic)* ♀   RATING: ★★★★
Dawn—Also a variation of Sarah; also a desert in Northern Africa
- People think of Sahara as pretty, exotic, creative, intelligent, caring

People who like the name Sahara also like Savannah, Sienna, Samara, Sierra, Faith, Sadie, Serenity, Sabrina, Hannah, Paige

Sahirah *(Arabic)* ♀　　　RATING: ★★★★
Wakeful
People think of Sahirah as pretty, sexy, intelligent, exotic, elegant
People who like the name Sahirah also like Sahara, Samara, Tahirah, Saniya, Samira, Samiya, Sarai, Sanaa, Soraya, Sagira

Sahkyo *(Native American)* ♀　　　RATING: ★★★
Mink—Navajo origin
People think of Sahkyo as funny, creative, wild, exotic, artsy
People who like the name Sahkyo also like Sokanon, Sora, Soraya, Sada, Salali, Summer, Tallulah, Snana, Sabina, Shania

Saidi *(Arabic)* ♀ ♂　　　RATING: ★★★☆
Fortunate, auspicious—Variation of Saeed
People think of Saidi as funny, intelligent, popular, creative, girl next door
People who like the name Saidi also like Jaden, Sage, Hayden, Taylor, Caden, Aidan, Skylar, Bailey, Mackenzie, Riley

Sailor *(American)* ♀ ♂　　　RATING: ★★★☆
Boat man
People think of Sailor as pretty, popular, creative, trendy, cool
People who like the name Sailor also like Sawyer, Parker, Ryder, Scout, Caden, Bailey, Madison, Addison, Piper, Sage

Saima *(Arabic)* ♀　　　RATING: ★★★☆
Fasting woman
People think of Saima as pretty, trustworthy, young, intelligent, funny
People who like the name Saima also like Samara, Samira, Sada, Sabrina, Layla, Sadie, Lara, Sana, Semira, Lilith

Sakina *(Arabic)* ♀　　　RATING: ★★★★
Calm, comfort; presence of God
People think of Sakina as pretty, caring, intelligent, trustworthy, creative
People who like the name Sakina also like Saniya, Samira, Samara, Sahara, Sabrina, Samiya, Sahirah, Selina, Sakura, Sadie

Saku *(Japanese)* ♀ ♂　　　RATING: ★★★★
Remembrance of the Lord—Variation of Zachary
People think of Saku as exotic, intelligent, religious, funny, elegant
People who like the name Saku also like Seiko, Sanyu, Hoshi, Kiyoshi, Yuki, Rin, Nori, Mitsu, Kana, Natsu

Sakura *(Japanese)* ♀　　　RATING: ★★★☆
Cherry blossom
People think of Sakura as pretty, caring, intelligent, young, creative

People who like the name Sakura also like Suki, Amaya, Kaida, Aiko, Kaori, Keiko, Ayame, Mai, Emiko, Kaiya

Sal *(English)* ♀ ♂　　　RATING: ★★★
Short for Sally or Salvatore
People think of Sal as funny, handsome, sexy, cool, aggressive
People who like the name Sal also like Parker, Sage, Riley, Toby, Tyler, Ryan, Spencer, Jaden, Reese, Page

Salali *(Native American)* ♀　　　RATING: ★☆
Squirrel—Cherokee origin; also a place in Mozambique
People think of Salali as exotic, pretty, wild, trustworthy, funny
People who like the name Salali also like Sora, Tala, Shania, Soraya, Sokanon, Takoda, Sahkyo, Kiona, Shada, Ayasha

Salama *(Arabic)* ♀　　　RATING: ★☆
Peace, security—Can also mean lightning in Finnish
People think of Salama as funny, lazy, exotic, sneaky, pretty
People who like the name Salama also like Sanura, Sahirah, Selena, Samara, Sanaa, Sagira, Sahara, Sakina, Tahirah, Saniya

Saleema *(Arabic)* ♀　　　RATING: ★★★
Healthy, protected
People think of Saleema as caring, pretty, creative, funny, intelligent
People who like the name Saleema also like Samara, Samira, Sahara, Sabrina, Selena, Selima, Layla, Seanna, Saniya, Sabina

Salene *(American)* ♀　　　RATING: ★★★☆
Heaven—Variation of Celine
People think of Salene as pretty, sexy, exotic, intelligent, creative
People who like the name Salene also like Selene, Selena, Sabrina, Paige, Samara, Samantha, Sadie, Sarina, Serena, Scarlett

Salim *(Arabic)* ♂　　　RATING: ★★★★
Healthy, complete
People think of Salim as handsome, intelligent, caring, funny, leader
People who like the name Salim also like Nicholas, Alexander, Sebastian, Damien, Maddox, Anthony, Yaser, Chad, Oliver, Malik

Sally *(English)* ♀　　　RATING: ★★
Short for Sarah—Sally Field, actress; Sally Ride, astronaut; Sally Struthers, actress
People think of Sally as pretty, funny, caring, intelligent, creative
People who like the name Sally also like Samantha, Sarah, Sadie, Scarlett, Grace, Lucy, Sophie, Emily, Paige, Rachel

Salma *(Arabic)* ♀　　　RATING: ★★★★
Beautiful woman—Salma Hayek, actress
People think of Salma as sexy, pretty, caring, cool, intelligent

People who like the name Salma also like Sofia, Sophia, Sadie, Selena, Samantha, Olivia, Samara, Eva, Savannah, Mia

Salome (Hebrew) ♀ RATING: ★★★★
Welcome, peace—From the Hebrew word shalom
People think of Salome as pretty, intelligent, exotic, creative, caring
People who like the name Salome also like Olivia, Naomi, Samara, Eva, Sabrina, Sofia, Savannah, Scarlett, Charlotte, Zoe

Salus (Latin) ♂ RATING: ★★★
Healthy
People think of Salus as exotic, aggressive, powerful, sexy, nerdy
People who like the name Salus also like Sirius, Gabriel, Lucas, Tobias, Saeran, Garren, Sabin, Darwin, Adam, Todd

Salvador (Spanish) ♂ RATING: ★★
Savior—Salvador Dalí, artist
People think of Salvador as funny, intelligent, handsome, cool, creative
People who like the name Salvador also like Xavier, Victor, Diego, Jacob, Pablo, Samuel, Sebastian, Lucas, Carlos, Oliver

Salvatore (Italian) ♂ RATING: ★★★★
Savior
People think of Salvatore as handsome, intelligent, funny, popular, cool
People who like the name Salvatore also like Vincent, Giovanni, Nicholas, Carmine, Michael, Gabriel, Tristan, Dominic, Valentino, Nathaniel

Sam (English) ♀♂ RATING: ★★★
Short for Samuel or Samantha—Sam Neill, actor; Sam Raimi, actor/director; Sam Waterston, actor
People think of Sam as funny, cool, intelligent, handsome, popular
People who like the name Sam also like Ryan, Taylor, James, Riley, Logan, Tyler, Madison, Charlie, Evan, Bailey

Samah (Arabic) ♀ RATING: ★★★
Bounty, generosity
People think of Samah as caring, intelligent, funny, creative, trustworthy
People who like the name Samah also like Samara, Sarai, Samira, Samiya, Samantha, Saima, Scarlett, Semira, Shakira, Sabah

Saman (Persian) ♀♂ RATING: ★★★☆
Jasmine
People think of Saman as caring, intelligent, funny, trustworthy, handsome
People who like the name Saman also like Julian, Rider, Sawyer, James, Parker, Teagan, Storm, Skye, Spencer, Dante

Samantha (American) ♀ RATING: ★★★
Combination of Samuel and Anthea—There is a misconception that Samantha is an Old English or Hebrew name, but it was first recorded in the Southern United States just after 1800
People think of Samantha as pretty, funny, caring, creative, intelligent
People who like the name Samantha also like Hannah, Olivia, Emma, Abigail, Emily, Paige, Isabella, Natalie, Sabrina, Grace

Samara (Arabic) ♀ RATING: ★★★☆
Result, reward
People think of Samara as pretty, creative, funny, intelligent, caring
People who like the name Samara also like Samantha, Hannah, Olivia, Isabella, Ava, Paige, Savannah, Sabrina, Samira, Sophia

Sameya (Arabic) ♀ RATING: ★★★
Exalted, sublime
People think of Sameya as exotic, pretty, popular, young, intelligent
People who like the name Sameya also like Sanaa, Samiya, Tanaya, Ava, Kaiya, Eliza, Jennessa, Mai, Naomi, Viola

Samira (Arabic) ♀ RATING: ★★★★
Entertaining companion
People think of Samira as pretty, creative, intelligent, funny, caring
People who like the name Samira also like Samara, Samiya, Sahara, Saniya, Semira, Layla, Serenity, Sienna, Amaya, Nadia

Samiya (Sanskrit/East Indian) ♀ RATING: ★★★★
High, elevated
People think of Samiya as pretty, intelligent, funny, exotic, caring
People who like the name Samiya also like Samara, Saniya, Samira, Amaya, Sanaa, Anaya, Sarai, Serenity, Soraya, Sarina

Sammy (English) ♀♂ RATING: ★★★
Short for Samuel or Samantha—Sammy Davis Jr., singer/actor
People think of Sammy as funny, cool, caring, popular, young
People who like the name Sammy also like Sam, Taylor, Riley, Jordan, Madison, Jaden, Bailey, Tyler, Logan, Ryan

Samson (Hebrew) ♂ RATING: ★★
Sun; service—Originally from Shimshon
People think of Samson as intelligent, handsome, powerful, leader, caring
People who like the name Samson also like Samuel, Noah, Jackson, Ethan, Oliver, Isaac, Zachary, Elijah, Sebastian, Seth

488

Samuel *(Hebrew)* ♂   RATING: ★★★
His name is God—Samuel Goldwyn, film producer;
Samuel L. Jackson, actor
> People think of Samuel as handsome, intelligent, funny,
> caring, cool
> People who like the name Samuel also like Benjamin,
> Jacob, Noah, Ethan, Gabriel, Joshua, Matthew, Nathan,
> Zachary, Nicholas

Samuru *(Japanese)* ♂   RATING: ★★★
His name is God—Variation of Samuel
> People think of Samuru as powerful, ethnic, sneaky,
> exotic, leader
> People who like the name Samuru also like Ryu, Haru,
> Shino, Hiroshi, Suoh, Keitaro, Haruki, Makoto, Kaemon,
> Yasuo

Sana *(Arabic)* ♀   RATING: ★★★☆
Brightness, radiance
> People think of Sana as pretty, intelligent, funny, trust-
> worthy, young
> People who like the name Sana also like Sanaa, Sadie,
> Samara, Lana, Sara, Savanna, Serena, Samantha, Sari,
> Layla

Sanaa *(Arabic)* ♀   RATING: ★★★★
Brightness, radiance—Sanaa Lathan, actress
> People think of Sanaa as pretty, intelligent, sexy, cre-
> ative, exotic
> People who like the name Sanaa also like Samara,
> Saniya, Sarai, Samiya, Aaliyah, Anaya, Sana, Amaya,
> Ayanna, Layla

Sanam *(Arabic)* ♀   RATING: ★★★☆
Beloved, mistress
> People think of Sanam as pretty, trendy, cool, funny,
> creative
> People who like the name Sanam also like Serena,
> Saura, Sera, Serenity, Samara, Samira, Seda, Saniya,
> Satya, Sana

Sancha *(Spanish)* ♀   RATING: ★★★
Holy
> People think of Sancha as pretty, exotic, ethnic, cool,
> caring
> People who like the name Sancha also like Samara,
> Saniya, Salma, Sara, Selena, Savanna, Sandra, Shaina,
> Seanna, Sabina

Sancho *(Spanish)* ♂   RATING: ★★★
Holy
> People think of Sancho as religious, funny, nerdy, loser,
> cool
> People who like the name Sancho also like Javier,
> Carlos, Pedro, Samuel, Nicholas, Sebastian, Santos,
> Salvador, Enrique, Aden

Sanders *(English)* ♂   RATING: ★★★☆
Son of Alexander—From the Greek name Alexander
> People think of Sanders as creative, intelligent, power-
> ful, funny, handsome
> People who like the name Sanders also like Tristan,
> Ethan, Owen, Walker, Miles, Isaac, Oliver, Holden, Noah,
> Jackson

Sandra *(English)* ♀   RATING: ★★☆
Short for Alexandra—Sandra Bullock, actress; Sandra
Dee, actress
> People think of Sandra as caring, funny, pretty, intel-
> ligent, creative
> People who like the name Sandra also like Samantha,
> Sabrina, Vanessa, Sarah, Victoria, Hannah, Abigail,
> Laura, Rebecca, Sophia

Sandro *(Italian)* ♂   RATING: ★★★☆
Short for Alessandro
> People think of Sandro as handsome, cool, funny, intel-
> ligent, trustworthy
> People who like the name Sandro also like Fabian,
> Salvatore, Gabriel, Matteo, Mario, Valentino, Vittorio,
> Giancarlo, Carmine, Dino

Sandy *(English)* ♀♂   RATING: ★★☆
Short for Alexander or Sandra
> People think of Sandy as pretty, funny, caring, trust-
> worthy, intelligent
> People who like the name Sandy also like Tyler, Taylor,
> Madison, Jade, Holly, Hayden, Sean, Morgan, Sam, Sasha

Sanford *(English)* ♂   RATING: ★★★
From the sandy ford—Also a surname; Sanford
Meisner, acting coach
> People think of Sanford as intelligent, trustworthy,
> handsome, sexy, funny
> People who like the name Sanford also like Jacob,
> Tristan, Noah, Tyson, Ethan, Lucas, Samson, Walker,
> Russell, Timothy

Sani *(Native American)* ♂   RATING: ★★
The old one—Navajo origin
> People think of Sani as pretty, ethnic, intelligent, power-
> ful, religious
> People who like the name Sani also like Ryu, Tokala,
> Xavier, Ethan, Seth, Xander, Sebastian, Stone, Damian,
> Jayden

Saniya *(Arabic)* ♀   RATING: ★★★★☆
High, exalted
> People think of Saniya as pretty, intelligent, caring,
> popular, sexy
> People who like the name Saniya also like Samiya,
> Sanaa, Samara, Samira, Amaya, Anaya, Sarai, Seanna,
> Shania, Soraya

Sanja *(German)* ♀   RATING: ★★★☆
Wisdom
> People think of Sanja as pretty, creative, intelligent,
> sexy, caring
> People who like the name Sanja also like Sofia,
> Sara, Sonja, Sophia, Samara, Sarah, Emma, Seanna,
> Samantha, Sandra

Sanjay (*Sanskrit/East Indian*) ♂ RATING: ★★★★
Victory in battle; victory over judging self—Variation of Sanjaya
People think of Sanjay as intelligent, handsome, caring, popular, young
People who like the name Sanjay also like Seth, Sanjiv, Ajay, Ashwin, Rohan, Tristan, Savir, Ethan, Sebastian, Dominic

Sanjaya (*Sanskrit/East Indian*) ♂ RATING: ★★★
Victory in battle; victory over judging self; Sanjaya Malakar, singer
People think of Sanjaya as unpopular, loser
People who like the name Sanjaya also like Jackson

Sanjeet (*Sanskrit/East Indian*) ♀♂ RATING: ★★★
Invincible
People think of Sanjeet as ethnic, intelligent, unpopular, untrustworthy, funny
People who like the name Sanjeet also like Sachet, Sadiki, Seven, Jiva, Sasha, Sol, Sevilen, Arya, Sovann, Shae

Sanjiv (*Sanskrit/East Indian*) ♂ RATING: ★☆
To live together
People think of Sanjiv as intelligent, energetic, sexy, funny, leader
People who like the name Sanjiv also like Sanjay, Ashwin, Savir, Amish, Alagan, Adit, Adarsh, Sunesh, Tarun, Ajay

Sanne (*German*) ♀ RATING: ★★★☆
Lily—Short for Susanna
People think of Sanne as quiet, intelligent, creative, trustworthy, pretty
People who like the name Sanne also like Scarlett, Samantha, Sabrina, Sadie, Selene, Serena, Saniya, Sapphire, Samara, Salene

Santa (*Italian*) ♀♂ RATING: ★★★
Saint, holy—Santa Claus, Christmas icon
People think of Santa as big, popular, caring, funny, trustworthy
People who like the name Santa also like Sam, Taylor, Sasha, Sandy, Logan, Scout, Spencer, Satin, Santana, Sawyer

Santana (*Spanish*) ♀♂ RATING: ★★★☆
Holy—Band named after lead guitarist Carlos Santana
People think of Santana as creative, funny, sexy, caring, cool
People who like the name Santana also like Dakota, Madison, Jordan, Riley, Bailey, Skylar, Jade, Jaden, Brooklyn, Taylor

Santino (*Italian*) ♂ RATING: ★★★☆
Little saint—Santino Rice, designer
People think of Santino as handsome, popular, intelligent, powerful, cool
People who like the name Santino also like Sebastian, Vincent, Leo, Dominic, Jacob, Lorenzo, Nicholas, Salvatore, Nico, Angelo

Santo (*Spanish*) ♂ RATING: ★★★☆
Holy
People think of Santo as intelligent, cool, religious, popular, trustworthy
People who like the name Santo also like Santos, Damien, Nicholas, Pablo, Paco, Giovanni, Antonio, Salvador, Sancho, Mateo

Santos (*Spanish*) ♂ RATING: ★★★★
Holy
People think of Santos as funny, cool, sexy, popular, handsome
People who like the name Santos also like Xavier, Anthony, Nicholas, Jacob, Carlos, Sirius, Drake, Samuel, Adrian, Silas

Santuzza (*Italian*) ♀ RATING: ★★☆
Variation of Santa
People think of Santuzza as aggressive, weird, creative, girl next door, poor
People who like the name Santuzza also like Delfina, Obelia, Vita, Bibiana, Bianca, Sarafina, Saveria, Fiorenza, Gratiana, Lina

Sanura (*Arabic*) ♀ RATING: ★★
Kitten
People think of Sanura as pretty, creative, exotic, sexy, caring
People who like the name Sanura also like Sagira, Sakura, Selene, Sahirah, Saniya, Selena, Layla, Sora, Sauda, Scarlett

Sanyu (*Japanese*) ♀♂ RATING: ★★★☆
Happiness
People think of Sanyu as energetic, leader, creative, popular, funny
People who like the name Sanyu also like Seiko, Saku, Rin, Kiyoshi, Natsu, Yuki, Mitsu, Nori, Hoshi, Kin

Saoirse (*Celtic/Gaelic*) ♀ RATING: ★★★★
Freedom—Pronounced *SEER-sha*
People think of Saoirse as intelligent, creative, pretty, exotic, trustworthy
People who like the name Saoirse also like Fiona, Aoife, Genevieve, Maeve, Sabrina, Keaira, Siobhan, Aurora, Rhiannon, Sorcha

Sapphire (*English*) ♀ RATING: ★★★★☆
Gemstone
People think of Sapphire as pretty, creative, exotic, young, intelligent
People who like the name Sapphire also like Scarlett, Serenity, Sabrina, Savannah, Summer, Jasmine, Faith, Paige, Destiny, Trinity

Sara (*Hebrew*) ♀ RATING: ★★★☆
Princess—Sara Lee, snack manufacturer; Sara Helena Lumholdt, singer; Sara Paxton, actress
People think of Sara as pretty, funny, caring, intelligent, creative
People who like the name Sara also like Sarah, Samantha, Emma, Hannah, Olivia, Paige, Emily, Grace, Abigail, Isabella

490

Sarafina *(Italian)* ♀   RATING: ★★★★☆
Seraphim
> People think of Sarafina as pretty, caring, young, intelligent, creative
> People who like the name Sarafina also like Isabella, Sabrina, Serafina, Sophia, Sarina, Olivia, Scarlett, Angelina, Stella, Viviana

Sarah *(Hebrew)* ♀   RATING: ★★★
Princess—Sarah Bernhardt, actress; Sarah Jessica Parker, actress; Sarah Vaughn, singer
> People think of Sarah as pretty, funny, caring, intelligent, creative
> People who like the name Sarah also like Hannah, Emma, Emily, Grace, Samantha, Abigail, Olivia, Elizabeth, Paige, Lauren

Sarai *(Hebrew)* ♀   RATING: ★★★☆
My princess—In the Bible, the wife of Abraham
> People think of Sarai as pretty, funny, caring, intelligent, creative
> People who like the name Sarai also like Samara, Sari, Sadie, Sarah, Serenity, Sarina, Scarlett, Sanaa, Sabrina, Sara

Saraid *(Celtic/Gaelic)* ♀   RATING: ★★★
Excellent, fine
> People think of Saraid as quiet, popular, unpopular, elegant, leader
> People who like the name Saraid also like Kiara, Sabrina, Juliet, Keira, Cathleen, Caelan, Sarah, Danelea, Kylie, Emma

Sarama *(Arabic)* ♀   RATING: ★★
Harshness, bravery
> People think of Sarama as powerful, exotic, leader, pretty, intelligent
> People who like the name Sarama also like Semira, Selena, Sahara, Samara, Saniya, Safara, Amber, Samira, Raina, Serena

Saran *(African)* ♀   RATING: ★★★
Joy—Guinea and Cote D'Ivoire origin; also a Hindi name meaning refuge or sanctuary
> People think of Saran as pretty, funny, intelligent, creative, caring
> People who like the name Saran also like Jadyn, Samara, Grace, Sarai, Shayla, Sara, Sophia, Samantha, Semira, Hannah

Sareh *(Persian)* ♀   RATING: ★★★☆
Pure
> People think of Sareh as sexy, pretty, exotic, funny, intelligent
> People who like the name Sareh also like Sarai, Sadie, Samara, Sera, Cara, Shayla, Samiya, Saniya, Sari, Alyssa

Sargent *(English)* ♂   RATING: ★☆
Sergeant; servant; officer—Sargent Shriver, founder of the Peace Corps
> People think of Sargent as aggressive, leader, big, weird, powerful
> People who like the name Sargent also like Slade, Sebastian, Maddox, Ranger, Saber, Tyson, Sidney, Seth, Samson, Stone

Sari *(Hebrew)* ♀   RATING: ★★★
Princess—Variation of Sarah; also a Hindi form of clothing
> People think of Sari as pretty, intelligent, creative, caring, funny
> People who like the name Sari also like Sadie, Sarai, Samara, Ava, Chloe, Olivia, Sarah, Sabrina, Layla, Paige

Sariah *(American)* ♀   RATING: ★★★★
Princess—Combination of Sarah and Mariah
> People think of Sariah as pretty, trendy, lazy, powerful, winner
> People who like the name Sariah also like Emma, Hannah, Olivia, Lydia, Isabella, Kyla, Sari, Claire, Veronica, Aaralyn

Sarika *(Sanskrit/East Indian)* ♀   RATING: ★★★
A bird known for its lovely song; also a Hungarian variation of Sara
> People think of Sarika as pretty, caring, funny, trustworthy, exotic
> People who like the name Sarika also like Samara, Samiya, Sarina, Aaliyah, Kayla, Makaila, Shyla, Shanti, Rebecca, Mia

Sarina *(Hebrew)* ♀   RATING: ★★★★
Princess; one who laughs—Variation of Sara
> People think of Sarina as pretty, funny, caring, creative, energetic
> People who like the name Sarina also like Sabrina, Serena, Sofia, Olivia, Savannah, Sadie, Samara, Selena, Sienna, Paige

Sarki *(African)* ♀ ♂   RATING: ★☆
Chief
> People think of Sarki as powerful, leader, pretty, handsome, sexy
> People who like the name Sarki also like Sanyu, Sasha, Shadow, Saxen, Seiko, Selas, Sadiki, Sabriel, Sawyer, Shay

Sarmad *(Persian)* ♂   RATING: ★★☆
Eternal, everlasting
> People think of Sarmad as ethnic, funny, powerful, handsome, trustworthy
> People who like the name Sarmad also like Kyran, Sirius, Savir, Sanjay, Shyam, Siyavash, Darius, Darrius, Asho, Suvan

Saroja *(Sanskrit/East Indian)* ♀   RATING: ★★★
Lotus
> People think of Saroja as pretty, exotic, intelligent, artsy, sexy
> People who like the name Saroja also like Samiya, Sarika, Savita, Shreya, Somatra, Satya, Bhavna, Sheela, Shalin, Shila

Sasha *(Russian)* ♀ ♂ RATING: ★★★
Short for Alexander—Sasha, reggaeton DJ; Sasha Krivtsov, musician
   People think of Sasha as pretty, intelligent, funny, sexy, creative
   People who like the name Sasha also like Madison, Taylor, Logan, Bailey, Ryan, Hayden, Riley, Sydney, Morgan, Dylan

Sashi *(Sanskrit/East Indian)* ♀ RATING: ★★★
Moon
   People think of Sashi as pretty, exotic, creative, funny, energetic
   People who like the name Sashi also like Sarina, Sarai, Mia, Amara, Chloe, Lila, Shanti, Stella, Ruby, Opal

Sasilvia *(American)* ♀ RATING: ★☆
Variation of Sylvia
   People think of Sasilvia as pretty, intelligent, weird, religious, cool
   People who like the name Sasilvia also like Samantha, Sabina, Sabrina, Selena, Sanura, Samara, Seanna, Lysandra, Salene, Leola

Saskia *(Slavic)* ♀ RATING: ★★★★
Protector of mankind
   People think of Saskia as pretty, intelligent, creative, funny, caring
   People who like the name Saskia also like Samara, Layla, Sophia, Scarlett, Charlotte, Sofia, Hannah, Freya, Maya, Olivia

Sasson *(Hebrew)* ♀ ♂ RATING: ★★★
Joy
   People think of Sasson as funny, leader, artsy, sneaky, creative
   People who like the name Sasson also like Sasha, Sawyer, Sage, Reese, Storm, Saxon, Sam, Jaden, Shane, Skye

Satchel *(American)* ♂ RATING: ★★★
Bag—Leroy Robert "Satchel" Paige, baseball player (before playing baseball player, Paige was a porter at a train station, where he got his nickname)
   People think of Satchel as funny, creative, intelligent, popular, caring
   People who like the name Satchel also like Seth, Maddox, Zachary, Miles, Finn, Jacob, Oliver, Holden, Ethan, Jackson

Satin *(English)* ♀ ♂ RATING: ★★★
Smooth, shiny cloth
   People think of Satin as untrustworthy, aggressive, criminal, loser, weird
   People who like the name Satin also like Sage, Taylor, Storm, Jade, Sasha, Madison, Bailey, Brooke, Shadow, Skye

Satinka *(American)* ♀ RATING: ★☆
Combination of Satin and Katinka
   People think of Satinka as powerful, exotic, sexy, quiet, cool

People who like the name Satinka also like Shania, Soraya, Sabrina, Sora, Sokanon, Talli, Satu, Miakoda, Sarai, Kachina

Satu *(Scandinavian)* ♀ RATING: ★★★☆
Fairy tale—Finnish variation of Saga, which is of Japanese origin
   People think of Satu as exotic, intelligent, pretty, creative, funny
   People who like the name Satu also like Sakura, Sada, Sabrina, Sebille, Kiara, Selena, Amaya, Faylinn, Suki, Seda

Saturday *(American)* ♀ ♂ RATING: ★★★
Born on Saturday—From Saturn, the Roman God of agriculture
   People think of Saturday as loser, weird, nerdy, lazy, poor
   People who like the name Saturday also like Sasha, Sunday, Spencer, September, Wednesday, Sawyer, Sydney, Tyler, Logan, Storm

Saturn *(Latin)* ♂ RATING: ★★☆
Roman God of agriculture—Also a planet
   People think of Saturn as aggressive, artsy, intelligent, boy next door, big
   People who like the name Saturn also like Gideon, Lucian

Satya *(Sanskrit/East Indian)* ♀ RATING: ★★★☆
Truth
   People think of Satya as intelligent, exotic, trustworthy, quiet, funny
   People who like the name Satya also like Saniya, Samara, Kaya, Sienna, Serena, Sachi, Amara, Anaya, Shyla, Sophia

Sauda *(Arabic)* ♀ RATING: ★★
Black; love
   People think of Sauda as exotic, sexy, pretty, intelligent, aggressive
   People who like the name Sauda also like Layla, Sanura, Sanaa, Amaya, Kali, Sari, Ebony, Sahirah, Sera, Kiara

Saul *(Hebrew)* ♂ RATING: ★★
Borrowed—In the Old Testament, the king of Israel and father of Jonathan; also in the New Testament, St. Paul's original name; Saul Bellow, writer; Saul Stokes, musician; Saul Williams, poet
   People think of Saul as funny, handsome, cool, intelligent, sexy
   People who like the name Saul also like Isaac, Seth, Samuel, Noah, Ethan, Jacob, Elijah, Solomon, Lucas, Isaiah

Saura *(Arabic)* ♀ RATING: ★★★☆
Wealth
   People think of Saura as pretty, artsy, exotic, wealthy, funny
   People who like the name Saura also like Serenity, Sana, Samara, Chloe, Shanti, Savannah, Sephora, Layla, Scarlett, Victoria

Savanna (*Spanish*) ♀   RATING: ★★★★
Open plain
> People think of Savanna as pretty, funny, caring, popular, creative
> People who like the name Savanna also like Savannah, Hailey, Olivia, Sierra, Hannah, Emma, Samantha, Isabella, Sabrina, Paige

Savannah (*Spanish*) ♀   RATING: ★★★★
Open plain—Also a city in Georgia
> People think of Savannah as pretty, funny, creative, caring, intelligent
> People who like the name Savannah also like Hannah, Paige, Isabella, Olivia, Emma, Hailey, Ava, Abigail, Grace, Samantha

Savarna (*Sanskrit/East Indian*) ♀   RATING: ★★★
Like God—Wife of the sun god
> People think of Savarna as exotic, pretty, funny, elegant, religious
> People who like the name Savarna also like Shanti, Samiya, Kalinda, Scarlett, Sitara, Savita, Gita, Savannah, Satya, Kanika

Savea (*Scandinavian*) ♀   RATING: ★★☆
The Swedish nation
> People think of Savea as pretty, exotic, aggressive, big, intelligent
> People who like the name Savea also like Ava, Savannah, Sienna, Samara, Sophia, Sadie, Soraya, Svea, Layla, Saniya

Saveria (*Italian*) ♀   RATING: ★★★
New house—Variation of Xavier
> People think of Saveria as exotic, intelligent, creative, pretty, energetic
> People who like the name Saveria also like Sienna, Sierra, Samira, Scarlett, Savannah, Savea, Sahara, Samara, Sarafina, Cianna

Savir (*Sanskrit/East Indian*) ♂   RATING: ★★★
Patient
> People think of Savir as aggressive, powerful, funny, leader, cool
> People who like the name Savir also like Arnav, Sunesh, Adit, Sanjay, Sebastian, Ashwin, Tariq, Tarak, Kaden, Amish

Savita (*Sanskrit/East Indian*) ♀   RATING: ★★★
Best in the universe
> People think of Savita as pretty, funny, intelligent, energetic, leader
> People who like the name Savita also like Samiya, Sevita, Sarina, Samira, Saniya, Lilianna, Sitara, Samara, Sona, Savannah

Savvy (*American*) ♀   RATING: ★★★☆
Smart—Also short for Savannah
> People think of Savvy as creative, intelligent, cool, exotic, pretty
> People who like the name Savvy also like Ava, Mia, Scarlett, Belle, Seanna, Sienna, Samara, Savanna, Paige, Sapphire

Sawyer (*English*) ♀♂   RATING: ★★★
Woodcutter
> People think of Sawyer as handsome, popular, funny, intelligent, cool
> People who like the name Sawyer also like Parker, Hayden, Logan, Spencer, Riley, Mason, Addison, Ryder, Taylor, Carter

Saxen (*Celtic/Gaelic*) ♀♂   RATING: ★★★☆
Swordsman
> People think of Saxen as handsome, powerful, wild, aggressive, cool
> People who like the name Saxen also like Riley, Sawyer, Caden, Teagan, Rylan, Quinn, Logan, Skye, Hayden, Reagan

Saxon (*English*) ♀♂   RATING: ★★★★
Germanic tribe
> People think of Saxon as intelligent, cool, handsome, powerful, popular
> People who like the name Saxon also like Logan, Taylor, Bailey, Mason, Hayden, Riley, Addison, Jaden, Parker, Tanner

Saxton (*English*) ♀♂   RATING: ★★★
From the village of the Saxons
> People think of Saxton as cool, popular, funny, young, aggressive
> People who like the name Saxton also like Paxton, Sawyer, Parker, Hayden, Jaden, Payton, Preston, Sydney, Caden, Spencer

Scarlett (*English*) ♀   RATING: ★★★★
Red—Also spelled Scarlet; Scarlett Johansson, actress; Scarlett O'Hara, character in *Gone With the Wind*
> People think of Scarlett as pretty, sexy, elegant, intelligent, popular
> People who like the name Scarlett also like Olivia, Isabella, Charlotte, Ava, Savannah, Paige, Sophia, Grace, Violet, Chloe

Schuyler (*Dutch*) ♀♂   RATING: ★★☆
Scholar—Pronounced *SKY-ler*; Schuyler Fisk, actress
> People think of Schuyler as creative, intelligent, funny, caring, pretty
> People who like the name Schuyler also like Parker, Hayden, Spencer, Sawyer, Riley, Logan, Skylar, Reagan, Mackenzie, Peyton

Scorpio (*Latin*) ♀♂   RATING: ★☆
The scorpion—Used for children born under this astrological sign
> People think of Scorpio as intelligent, exotic, handsome, energetic, aggressive
> People who like the name Scorpio also like Jade, Shadow, Phoenix, Storm, Brooke, Ryan, Skye, Sean, Page, Dakota

Scot (*English*) ♂   RATING: ★★★☆
Of Scottish origin—Variation of Scott
> People think of Scot as funny, creative, handsome, leader, boy next door

People who like the name Scot also like Scott, Daniel, Benjamin, Isaac, Luke, Nathan, Troy, Adam, Joshua, Seth

Scott *(English)* ♂   RATING: ★★★
Of Scottish origin—Also short for Prescott; Scott Baio, actor; Scott Wolf, actor
People think of Scott as funny, handsome, caring, intelligent, cool
People who like the name Scott also like Ethan, Nathan, Matthew, Jacob, Seth, Nicholas, Joshua, Michael, Benjamin, Jason

Scout *(American)* ♀♂   RATING: ★★★☆
First explorer—Scout Willis, daughter of Demi Moore and Bruce Willis
People think of Scout as energetic, creative, leader, funny, cool
People who like the name Scout also like Parker, Sawyer, Ryder, Riley, Hayden, Reese, Avery, Logan, Piper, Caden

Seamus *(Celtic/Gaelic)* ♂   RATING: ★★
Supplanter—Variation of James; pronounced *SHAY-muhs*
People think of Seamus as handsome, intelligent, funny, cool, popular
People who like the name Seamus also like Liam, Tristan, Noah, Aiden, Owen, Oliver, Caleb, Jack, Sebastian, Isaac

Sean *(Celtic/Gaelic)* ♀♂   RATING: ★★★
God is gracious—Variation of John; pronounced *SHAWN* or *SHAAN* (Irish); Sean Astin, actor; Sean Lennon, singer; Sean Penn, actor
People think of Sean as handsome, funny, intelligent, cool, caring
People who like the name Sean also like Ryan, Riley, Logan, Dylan, Shane, Taylor, Evan, Aidan, Tyler, Madison

Seanna *(American)* ♀   RATING: ★★★★
God is gracious—Feminine form of Sean
People think of Seanna as pretty, funny, popular, creative, caring
People who like the name Seanna also like Sienna, Savannah, Sabrina, Paige, Sadie, Hannah, Isabella, Samantha, Hailey, Sierra

Season *(Latin)* ♀   RATING: ★★
Sowing, planting
People think of Season as pretty, intelligent, funny, creative, trendy
People who like the name Season also like Paige, Faith, Grace, Serenity, Summer, Lily, Lacey, Samantha, Serena, Amber

Seath *(Celtic/Gaelic)* ♀♂   RATING: ★★★
Wolfish—Also a Scottish surname
People think of Seath as intelligent, handsome, leader, cool, wild
People who like the name Seath also like Caden, Sean, Sage, Bailey, Shae, Riley, Hayden, Shane, Logan, Blake

Sebastian *(Greek)* ♂   RATING: ★★★
Venerable—Sebastian Bach, musician; Sebastian LeFebvre, musician; Sebastian, lobster character in Disney's *The Little Mermaid*
People think of Sebastian as handsome, intelligent, popular, cool, creative
People who like the name Sebastian also like Ethan, Gabriel, Noah, Tristan, Oliver, Elijah, Alexander, Zachary, Lucas, Jacob

Sebastien *(French)* ♂   RATING: ★★☆
Venerable—Variation of Sebastian
People think of Sebastien as handsome, intelligent, funny, sexy, cool
People who like the name Sebastien also like Sebastian, Tristan, Oliver, Ethan, Jacob, Noah, Gabriel, Caleb, Elijah, Seth

Sebille *(English)* ♀   RATING: ★★★★
Variation of Sybil; also a French surname; from the Legend of King Arthur
People think of Sebille as slow, young, weird, pretty, unpopular
People who like the name Sebille also like Shaylee, Samara, Sephora, Faylinn, Seda, Aurora, Aeryn, Emma, Sabrina, Cordelia

Secia *(Spanish)* ♀   RATING: ★★★
Short for Cecilia
People think of Secia as cool, pretty, exotic, caring, elegant
People who like the name Secia also like Sela, Samara, Samiya, Sophia, Sadie, Scarlett, Selena, Selina, Sarina, Seanna

Seda *(Armenian)* ♀   RATING: ★★★★☆
Spirit of the forest—Jon Seda, actor
People think of Seda as creative, pretty, elegant, intelligent, exotic
People who like the name Seda also like Serena, Selena, Sienna, Sera, Ava, Sebille, Sada, Rhian, Sora, Fiona

Seeley *(English)* ♀♂   RATING: ★★★
Very happy—From a surname derived from the Old English word *Selig*, and the same origin as silly
People think of Seeley as funny, intelligent, pretty, creative, energetic
People who like the name Seeley also like Jada, Riley, Morgan, Sage, Rory, Quinlan, Shay, Cooper, Skye, Mason

Seema *(Arabic)* ♀   RATING: ★★
Forehead, face
People think of Seema as caring, pretty, intelligent, funny, trustworthy
People who like the name Seema also like Savanna, Seanna, Sara, Sarah, Selena, Salma, Selina, Selma, Saniya, Semira

Sef *(German)* ♂   RATING: ★★★
Short for Joseph
People think of Sef as poor, criminal, lazy, wild, intelligent

493

494

People who like the name Sef also like Seth, Samuel, Gabriel, Cyrus, Xander, Cole, Owen, Isaac, Beck, Holden

Seghen *(African)* ♀♂   RATING: ★★★
Ostrich—Eritrean origin
People think of Seghen as cool, pretty, intelligent, exotic, ethnic
People who like the name Seghen also like Shae, Sawyer, Tanner, Parker, Rowan, Shannon, Rylan, Brayden, Corbin, Caden

Seifer *(German)* ♂   RATING: ★★★★
Victory peace—Variation of Siegfried
People think of Seifer as aggressive, handsome, leader, powerful, intelligent
People who like the name Seifer also like Seth, Sebastian, Aiden, Tristan, Sirius, Titus, Gabriel, Xavier, Sidney, Xander

Seiko *(Japanese)* ♀♂   RATING: ★★★★
Force, truth
People think of Seiko as leader, powerful, intelligent, cool, exotic
People who like the name Seiko also like Sanyu, Saku, Yuki, Rin, Kiyoshi, Mitsu, Hoshi, Hiroko, Kana, Maro

Sela *(Hebrew)* ♀   RATING: ★★☆
Rock—Sela Ward, actress
People think of Sela as pretty, intelligent, creative, funny, caring
People who like the name Sela also like Ava, Samara, Sadie, Chloe, Samantha, Selah, Sienna, Sofia, Isabella, Olivia

Selah *(Hebrew)* ♀   RATING: ★★☆
Rock
People think of Selah as pretty, intelligent, creative, elegant, caring
People who like the name Selah also like Hannah, Ava, Sadie, Olivia, Naomi, Samara, Sarah, Sophia, Ella, Abigail

Selam *(African)* ♀   RATING: ★★★
Peace—Eritrean origin
People think of Selam as creative, intelligent, funny, pretty, caring
People who like the name Selam also like Saran, Selima, Seanna, Ryann, Isabis, Sanaa, Mora, Olivia, Selena, Sophie

Selas *(African)* ♀♂   RATING: ★★★
Trinity
People think of Selas as pretty, funny, girl next door, ethnic, quiet
People who like the name Selas also like Seiko, Riley, Sawyer, Shane, Seath, Sean, Logan, Hayden, Shae, Caden

Selena *(Spanish)* ♀   RATING: ★★★★
Moon—Variation of Selene; Selena Quintanilla-Pérez, singer
People think of Selena as pretty, funny, caring, creative, intelligent

People who like the name Selena also like Sabrina, Serena, Isabella, Faith, Savannah, Samantha, Olivia, Selene, Jasmine, Hannah

Selene *(Greek)* ♀   RATING: ★★☆
Moon
People think of Selene as pretty, intelligent, creative, elegant, sexy
People who like the name Selene also like Selena, Serena, Sabrina, Paige, Faith, Salene, Isabelle, Gabrielle, Olivia, Samantha

Selia *(English)* ♀   RATING: ★★☆
Heaven—Variation of Celia
People think of Selia as creative, pretty, energetic, intelligent, cool
People who like the name Selia also like Sabrina, Seanna, Keira, Skyla, Lana, Shayla, Serena, Sophia, Scarlett, Selena

Selima *(Hebrew)* ♀   RATING: ★★★
Brings comfort, peace
People think of Selima as pretty, sneaky, funny, caring, weird
People who like the name Selima also like Shaina, Seanna, Samara, Samantha, Selah, Sarah, Saleema, Selena, Ruth, Selina

Selina *(English)* ♀   RATING: ★★☆
Moon—Variation of Selena
People think of Selina as pretty, funny, caring, trustworthy, intelligent
People who like the name Selina also like Selena, Sabrina, Selene, Serena, Olivia, Sophia, Savannah, Jasmine, Isabella, Samantha

Selma *(English)* ♀   RATING: ★★
God's helmet—Variation of Anselm; Selma Blair, actress
People think of Selma as pretty, sexy, funny, intelligent, exotic
People who like the name Selma also like Stella, Samantha, Hannah, Olivia, Sienna, Scarlett, Bianca, Bella, Eva, Nadia

Sema *(Turkish)* ♀   RATING: ★★★
Sky
People think of Sema as funny, pretty, creative, young, artsy
People who like the name Sema also like Sebille, Samara, Sela, Sanura, Sofia, Sephora, Seda, Selah, Serenity, Lana

Semah *(Arabic)* ♀   RATING: ★☆
Forehead, face
People think of Semah as creative, winner, nerdy, loser, ethnic
People who like the name Semah also like Samara, Samira, Saran, Semira, Sumayah, Selia, Selima, Sanura, Selah, Sebille

Semira *(Arabic)* ♀
Nighttime companion
RATING: ★★★★
   People think of Semira as exotic, funny, pretty, caring, sexy
   People who like the name Semira also like Samara, Samira, Samiya, Saniya, Sarai, Sanaa, Amaya, Anaya, Soraya, Serenity

Sen *(Vietnamese)* ♀
Lotus flower
RATING: ★★★☆
   People think of Sen as pretty, intelligent, creative, sexy, cool
   People who like the name Sen also like Layla, Iris, Serenity, Violet, Sakura, Selene, Sienna, Serena, Sapphire, Kiara

Senalda *(Spanish)* ♀
Victory power
RATING: ★★☆
   People think of Senalda as exotic, weird, sexy, uptight, elegant
   People who like the name Senalda also like Lola, Veronica, Mercedes, Reina, Lenora, Amanda, Bianca, Teresa, Sabrina, Samantha

Sence *(Spanish)* ♀
Holy—Pronounced *SEN-SAY*
RATING: ★★☆
   People think of Sence as pretty, sexy, intelligent, untrustworthy, trustworthy
   People who like the name Sence also like Savanna, Sofia, Eloise, Idalia, Lela, Sima, Ariana, Bianca, Adrina, Shila

Senna *(English)* ♀
Senna plant
RATING: ★★★★☆
   People think of Senna as pretty, exotic, sexy, intelligent, funny
   People who like the name Senna also like Sienna, Sierra, Sofia, Samara, Lexi, Inara, Cianna, Amanda, Paige, Sera

Senona *(Spanish)* ♀
Lively
RATING: ★★☆
   People think of Senona as energetic, religious, creative, exotic, pretty
   People who like the name Senona also like Samara, Seanna, Sarai, Raina, Savannah, Selene, Sarina, Sierra, Serafina, Scarlett

Senta *(German)* ♀
Holy—Variation of Santa
RATING: ★★
   People think of Senta as creative, caring, funny, energetic, leader
   People who like the name Senta also like Satya, Sora, Saskia, Sela, Satu, Sandra, Savannah, Samara, Saniya, Selia

Seoras *(Celtic/Gaelic)* ♂
Farmer—Variation of George
RATING: ★★★
   People think of Seoras as cool, funny, quiet, big, trustworthy
   People who like the name Seoras also like Ewan, Faolan, Sloan, Aiden, Seamus, Tristan, Slade, Darren, Edan, Devlin

Sephora *(Hebrew)* ♀
Bird—From the old Hebrew names Tzipporah or Zipporah; also a brand of cosmetics
RATING: ★★★★
   People think of Sephora as exotic, pretty, intelligent, elegant, sexy
   People who like the name Sephora also like Scarlett, Sophia, Aurora, Sapphire, Bella, Sadie, Sabrina, Olivia, Sienna, Samara

September *(American)* ♀ ♂
Born in September—Originally the seventh month in the ancient Roman calendar
RATING: ★★★☆
   People think of September as pretty, creative, funny, popular, artsy
   People who like the name September also like Sage, Jade, Parker, December, Madison, Addison, Skye, Storm, Dakota, Winter

Sequoia *(Native American)* ♀ ♂
Giant redwood tree—Cherokee origin
RATING: ★★
   People think of Sequoia as creative, intelligent, caring, pretty, funny
   People who like the name Sequoia also like Dakota, Logan, Sage, Madison, Hayden, Phoenix, Taylor, Sydney, Sawyer, Sasha

Sera *(American)* ♀
Seraphim—Short for Seraphina
RATING: ★★★☆
   People think of Sera as pretty, intelligent, caring, sexy, creative
   People who like the name Sera also like Serafina, Sarah, Sara, Emma, Chloe, Sadie, Samara, Sofia, Serena, Kara

Serafina *(Latin)* ♀
Seraphim, angel
RATING: ★★★★☆
   People think of Serafina as pretty, intelligent, elegant, creative, caring
   People who like the name Serafina also like Olivia, Scarlett, Sofia, Sera, Serena, Isabella, Sabrina, Chloe, Serenity, Samantha

Seren *(Welsh)* ♀
Star
RATING: ★★★☆
   People think of Seren as pretty, intelligent, creative, elegant, caring
   People who like the name Seren also like Ava, Chloe, Scarlett, Bronwyn, Isabel, Olivia, Anya, Amelia, Serenity, Aislinn

Serena *(Latin)* ♀
Serene, calm—Serena Williams, tennis player
RATING: ★★★
   People think of Serena as pretty, funny, intelligent, caring, creative
   People who like the name Serena also like Sabrina, Isabella, Olivia, Selena, Sophia, Hannah, Samantha, Paige, Sienna, Faith

Serendipity *(American)* ♀
Fateful meeting
RATING: ★★★☆
   People think of Serendipity as artsy, creative, pretty, elegant, caring

People who like the name Serendipity also like Serenity, Trinity, Sophie, Sabrina, Sadie, Scarlett, Harmony, Savannah, Isabella, Destiny

Serenity *(English)* ♀   RATING: ★★★☆
Peaceful disposition
> People think of Serenity as pretty, intelligent, caring, creative, elegant
> People who like the name Serenity also like Trinity, Faith, Savannah, Paige, Harmony, Destiny, Hailey, Scarlett, Sadie, Chloe

Sereno *(Spanish)* ♂   RATING: ★★☆
Calm, serene
> People think of Sereno as winner, handsome, cool, wild, intelligent
> People who like the name Sereno also like Sirius, Soren, Santos, Lucian, Jovan, Sergio, Seth, Spiro, Korbin, Serge

Serge *(English)* ♂   RATING: ★★
Servant—Short for Sergei
> People think of Serge as handsome, sexy, intelligent, powerful, leader
> People who like the name Serge also like Nathan, Seth, Simon, Vincent, Samuel, Nathaniel, Benjamin, Scott, Trent, Kaden

Sergei *(Russian)* ♂   RATING: ★★★
Servant
> People think of Sergei as handsome, intelligent, sexy, popular, caring
> People who like the name Sergei also like Ian, Nicholas, Tristan, Sebastian, Landon, Maddox, Oliver, Seth, Ronan, Eric

Sergio *(Italian)* ♂   RATING: ★★★☆
Servant
> People think of Sergio as funny, handsome, cool, sexy, caring
> People who like the name Sergio also like Sebastian, Diego, Victor, Xavier, Gabriel, Romeo, Fabian, Jacob, Anthony, Vincent

Serwa *(Arabic)* ♀   RATING: ★★☆
Rich, wealthy
> People think of Serwa as ethnic, quiet, weird, exotic, old-fashioned
> People who like the name Serwa also like Sera, Soraya, Sarah, Selina, Sevda, Seda, Samiya, Serena, Sahirah, Selena

Sesen *(African)* ♀   RATING: ★★
To wish for more—Eritrean origin
> People think of Sesen as exotic, weird, pretty, intelligent, ethnic
> People who like the name Sesen also like Serenity, Shayla, Samira, Selena, Seanna, Semira, Seda, Shasa, Sora, Serena

Seth *(Hebrew)* ♂   RATING: ★★★
Appointed—Seth Green, actor; Seth Thomas, clock maker
> People think of Seth as handsome, funny, intelligent, cool, caring
> People who like the name Seth also like Ethan, Noah, Caleb, Jacob, Nathan, Owen, Aiden, Zachary, Elijah, Ian

Sevan *(Armenian)* ♀   RATING: ★★★
Life-giving sweet water
> People think of Sevan as pretty, leader, sneaky, creative, weird
> People who like the name Sevan also like Sapphire, Sadie, Saffron, Symber, Simone, Shyla, Suri, Zoey, Daphne, Dominique

Sevda *(Turkish)* ♀   RATING: ★★★
Passion, love
> People think of Sevda as funny, intelligent, sexy, exotic, cool
> People who like the name Sevda also like Samira, Raisa, Seda, Serena, Samiya, Sareh, Sokanon, Soraya, Sanne, Sera

Seven *(American)* ♀♂   RATING: ★★
The number seven
> People think of Seven as cool, creative, intelligent, funny, popular
> People who like the name Seven also like Sage, Hayden, Parker, Caden, Logan, Jaden, Skye, Riley, Sawyer, Skylar

Severin *(French)* ♀♂   RATING: ★★★★
Severe
> People think of Severin as intelligent, creative, handsome, funny, cool
> People who like the name Severin also like Sawyer, Sage, Pierce, Phoenix, Seven, Aidan, Sasha, Quinn, Raven, Skye

Severino *(Latin)* ♂   RATING: ★★
Severe
> People think of Severino as young, ethnic, weird, powerful, aggressive
> People who like the name Severino also like Sebastian, Vincent, Gabriel, Lucian, Fabian, Alejandro, Landon, Santo, Slone, Jagger

Sevgi *(Turkish)* ♀   RATING: ★★★
Love
> People think of Sevgi as pretty, caring, ethnic, poor, intelligent
> People who like the name Sevgi also like Sari, Sareh, Serenity, Sanam, Satinka, Soraya, Sofia, Selena, Selene, Sandra

Sevilen *(Turkish)* ♀♂   RATING: ★★
Loved
> People think of Sevilen as exotic, poor, caring, elegant, wealthy
> People who like the name Sevilen also like Skylar, Severin, Sheridan, Seven, Sage, Sovann, Solaris, Seiko, Selas, Schuyler

Sevita *(Sanskrit/East Indian)* ♀ RATING: ★★★
Cherished
People think of Sevita as exotic, ethnic, cool, popular, old-fashioned
People who like the name Sevita also like Samara, Saniya, Samira, Serenity, Samiya, Shyla, Sundari, Seanna, Sonia, Serafina

Seyah *(Arabic)* ♀♂ RATING: ★★☆
Borough in Riyadh, Saudi Arabia
People think of Seyah as exotic, pretty, ethnic, funny, cool
People who like the name Seyah also like Shae, Saxton, Sawyer, Seghen, Saxen, Shane, Rylan, Sasson, Sevilen, Lane

Seymour *(French)* ♂ RATING: ★★★
From the village of St. Maur
People think of Seymour as intelligent, handsome, creative, old-fashioned, funny
People who like the name Seymour also like Oliver, Trevor, Owen, Marshall, Oscar, Sidney, Nicholas, Sebastian, Isaac, Jacob

Sezja *(Russian)* ♀ RATING: ★★★
Protector—Variation of Sasha; also a pet name for Alexandra
People think of Sezja as pretty, creative, trustworthy, elegant, weird
People who like the name Sezja also like Stasia, Leyna, Anielka, Raisa, Sela, Lida, Sahara, Lilka, Semira, Sierra

Shaan *(Sanskrit/East Indian)* ♂ RATING: ★★★
Pride—Urdu/Hindustani origin
People think of Shaan as cool, young, caring, ethnic, artsy
People who like the name Shaan also like Amish, Sanjay, Savir, Stefan, Damian, Sabin, Alagan, Saber, Lucas, Elkan

Shada *(Native American)* ♀ RATING: ★★★☆
Pelican—Also a Persian female name meaning glad or cheerful
People think of Shada as pretty, caring, cool, intelligent, sneaky
People who like the name Shada also like Shaylee, Shayla, Shyla, Shania, Tatum, Soraya, Sora, Zoe, Shayna, Skyla

Shadan *(Persian)* ♀ RATING: ★★★
Cheerful, prosperous
People think of Shadan as powerful, exotic, sexy, cool, popular
People who like the name Shadan also like Sadie, Zoey, Shaylee, Jadyn, Kaelyn, Seanna, Regan, Kaleigh, Shyla, Shaina

Shadi *(Arabic)* ♂ RATING: ★★
Singer
People think of Shadi as intelligent, sexy, funny, caring, cool
People who like the name Shadi also like David, Seth, Jayden, Gabriel, Aden, Malik, Tristan, Elijah, Isaac, Noah

Shadow *(English)* ♀♂ RATING: ★★★★☆
Shade from sun
People think of Shadow as powerful, intelligent, cool, sneaky, creative
People who like the name Shadow also like Storm, Raven, Phoenix, Skye, Jade, Sage, Bailey, Jaden, Riley, Taylor

Shae *(Celtic/Gaelic)* ♀♂ RATING: ★★★★☆
Hawk
People think of Shae as pretty, funny, creative, popular, intelligent
People who like the name Shae also like Shay, Jaden, Caden, Riley, Hayden, Logan, Bailey, Reagan, Skye, Sage

Shaina *(American)* ♀ RATING: ★★★
God is gracious—Feminine form of Shane
People think of Shaina as pretty, funny, caring, creative, intelligent
People who like the name Shaina also like Shayna, Shayla, Sadie, Hannah, Paige, Hailey, Savannah, Grace, Shaylee, Samantha

Shakila *(Arabic)* ♀ RATING: ★★★★☆
Beautiful
People think of Shakila as pretty, intelligent, creative, funny, caring
People who like the name Shakila also like Shakina, Samara, Shakira, Samiya, Shayla, Saniya, Shaina, Tiana, Grace, Ayanna

Shakina *(African)* ♀ RATING: ★★★★
Beautiful one
People think of Shakina as pretty, caring, sexy, creative, funny
People who like the name Shakina also like Shakila, Samara, Ayanna, Shaina, Shakira, Jahzara, Semira, Tiana, Shanti, Samiya

Shakir *(Arabic)* ♂ RATING: ★★
Thankful
People think of Shakir as handsome, young, cool, popular, sporty
People who like the name Shakir also like Jabari, Malik, Sebastian, Isaiah, Simeon, Jamar, Anthony, Ajani, Savir, Jamal

Shakira *(Arabic)* ♀ RATING: ★★★☆
Thankful—Feminine form of Shakir; Shakira, singer
People think of Shakira as pretty, sexy, popular, exotic, cool
People who like the name Shakira also like Aaliyah, Sabrina, Isabella, Faith, Destiny, Jasmine, Savannah, Samara, Sapphire, Victoria

Shakirah *(Arabic)* ♀ RATING: ★★★☆
Thankful—Variation of Shakira
People think of Shakirah as creative, popular, pretty, exotic, cool
People who like the name Shakirah also like Savannah, Samara, Selena, Sahara, Scarlett, Shanti, Mariah, Sapphire, Nevaeh, Naomi

Shakti *(Sanskrit/East Indian)* ♀ RATING: ★★★
Ability, strength
People think of Shakti as exotic, pretty, sexy, powerful, weird
People who like the name Shakti also like Shanti, Shyla, Samiya, Samara, Shaina, Niyati, Sitara, Sarai, Shayla, Isis

Shalin *(Sanskrit/East Indian)* ♀ RATING: ★★☆
Cotton plant
People think of Shalin as creative, intelligent, funny, young, trustworthy
People who like the name Shalin also like Cailyn, Jadyn, Shaylee, Savannah, Ashlyn, Shayla, Paige, Shaina, Hailey, Trinity

Shalom *(Hebrew)* ♀ ♂ RATING: ★★★★
Peace—Shalom Harlow, fashion model
People think of Shalom as creative, intelligent, trustworthy, artsy, funny
People who like the name Shalom also like Shiloh, Spencer, Shane, Riley, Hayden, Saxon, Reagan, Sloane, Sydney, Dakota

Shalon *(American)* ♀ RATING: ★★★
Flat clearing—Variation of Sharon
People think of Shalon as pretty, funny, intelligent, energetic, caring
People who like the name Shalon also like Rianne, Simone, Shaina, Shakila, Nevaeh, Shandi, Eman, Kaelyn, Kaydence, Selene

Shaman *(Sanskrit/East Indian)* ♂ RATING: ★★☆
Holy man; Buddhist monk
People think of Shaman as religious, popular, aggressive, powerful, stuck-up
People who like the name Shaman also like Seth, Shakir, Isaiah, Gabriel, Savir, Sidney, Solomon, Angelo, Tokala, Sterling

Shamara *(Arabic)* ♀ RATING: ★★★★
Fennel
People think of Shamara as pretty, intelligent, caring, funny, sexy
People who like the name Shamara also like Samara, Shamira, Shakira, Sahara, Serenity, Selena, Samira, Sabrina, Trinity, Aaliyah

Shamira *(Hebrew)* ♀ RATING: ★★
Protector
People think of Shamira as pretty, caring, intelligent, cool, creative
People who like the name Shamira also like Samara, Shaina, Shamara, Sabrina, Samira, Shakira, Samiya, Shayla, Selena, Shakila

Shamus *(Celtic/Gaelic)* ♂ RATING: ★★★★
Supplanter—Variation of James; pronounced *Shay-muhs*
People think of Shamus as handsome, intelligent, creative, caring, leader
People who like the name Shamus also like Seamus, Aiden, Liam, Keagan, Cole, Tristan, Lucas, Xavier, Zachary, Gavin

Shan *(Chinese)* ♀ ♂ RATING: ★★
Coral—Mandarin origin
People think of Shan as funny, intelligent, sexy, pretty, creative
People who like the name Shan also like Shay, Shane, Shae, Sage, Sasha, Sawyer, Skylar, Shiloh, Sky, Skye

Shana *(American)* ♀ RATING: ★★★
God is gracious—Feminine form of Shane
People think of Shana as pretty, funny, caring, creative, intelligent
People who like the name Shana also like Samantha, Shayna, Shaina, Paige, Sarah, Isabella, Hailey, Shayla, Hannah, Savannah

Shanae *(English)* ♀ RATING: ★★★☆
God is gracious—Variation of Shana
People think of Shanae as pretty, funny, caring, popular, sexy
People who like the name Shanae also like Samara, Shayla, Shayna, Seanna, Shaina, Shaylee, Shana, Savannah, Rianna, Jadyn

Shandi *(American)* ♀ RATING: ★★★★
Combination of Shana and Sandy
People think of Shandi as pretty, creative, funny, caring, intelligent
People who like the name Shandi also like Shaylee, Samara, Shayla, Zoe, Natalie, Sabrina, Mia, Shaina, Paige, Zoey

Shandra *(American)* ♀ RATING: ★★★★
Variation of Sandra or Chandra
People think of Shandra as creative, pretty, caring, funny, cool
People who like the name Shandra also like Sabrina, Rebecca, Cassandra, Abrianna, Kaelyn, Shayla, Larissa, Shayna, Gabriella, Rachael

Shane *(Celtic/Gaelic)* ♀ ♂ RATING: ★★★☆
God is gracious—Variation of John or Sean
People think of Shane as handsome, funny, intelligent, cool, caring
People who like the name Shane also like Ryan, Logan, Riley, Taylor, Sean, Dylan, Tyler, Hayden, Evan, Madison

Shani *(Hebrew)* ♀ RATING: ★★★★
Scarlet, crimson—Also a feminine form of Shane
People think of Shani as pretty, funny, caring, intelligent, creative
People who like the name Shani also like Shaylee, Shayla, Mia, Keely, Shayna, Paige, Jadyn, Seanna, Shaina, Sienna

Shania *(Native American)* ♀ RATING: ★★★★
I'm on my way—Ojibway origin; Shania Twain, singer
People think of Shania as pretty, funny, intelligent, caring, popular
People who like the name Shania also like Shayla, Savannah, Sabrina, Shaina, Hailey, Aaliyah, Samantha, Scarlett, Hannah, Samara

Shanna *(American)* ♀   RATING: ★★★★
Variation of Shannon or Shana
People think of Shanna as pretty, funny, caring, intelligent, trustworthy
People who like the name Shanna also like Olivia, Savannah, Sabrina, Samantha, Shayla, Emma, Hannah, Shana, Isabella, Natalie

Shannan *(Celtic/Gaelic)* ♀♂   RATING: ★★★
Old—Variation of Shannon
People think of Shannan as pretty, funny, caring, intelligent, creative
People who like the name Shannan also like Shannon, Shannen, Shane, Ryan, Riley, Sean, Mackenzie, Taylor, Hayden, Shay

Shannen *(American)* ♀♂   RATING: ★★★★
Old—Variation of Shannon; Shannen Doherty, actress
People think of Shannen as pretty, funny, cool, creative, popular
People who like the name Shannen also like Shannon, Shane, Sean, Ryan, Logan, Shannan, Riley, Morgan, Hayden, Taylor

Shannon *(Celtic/Gaelic)* ♀♂   RATING: ★★★
Old—Also spelled Shanon; also a river in Ireland
People think of Shannon as funny, pretty, intelligent, caring, creative
People who like the name Shannon also like Ryan, Madison, Riley, Taylor, Mackenzie, Morgan, Sean, Logan, Tyler, Bailey

Shanta *(Sanskrit/East Indian)* ♀   RATING: ★★★★
Serenity, calm
People think of Shanta as caring, intelligent, pretty, sexy, creative
People who like the name Shanta also like Shanti, Serenity, Renée, Samantha, Shakira, Samara, Shyla, Shaina, Sophia, Raina

Shantell *(American)* ♀   RATING: ★★☆
Variation of Chantal
People think of Shantell as funny, pretty, sexy, caring, popular
People who like the name Shantell also like Paige, Sabrina, Chantel, Isabella, Faith, Hailey, Mariah, Jasmine, Savannah, Samantha

Shanti *(Sanskrit/East Indian)* ♀   RATING: ★★★★
Peace, calm
People think of Shanti as pretty, exotic, creative, caring, intelligent
People who like the name Shanti also like Serenity, Aaliyah, Trinity, Shyla, Sabrina, Chloe, Sapphire, Selena, Jasmine, Jadyn

Shanton *(French)* ♀   RATING: ★★
We sing
People think of Shanton as intelligent, young, sexy, popular, trendy
People who like the name Shanton also like Sienna, Laurel, Natalie, Kiley, Jadyn, Shayla, Lauren, Shayna, Skyla, Jeslyn

Shaquana *(American)* ♀   RATING: ★★★
Combination of Shaquille and Anna
People think of Shaquana as pretty, funny, popular, sexy, caring
People who like the name Shaquana also like Honey, Sapphire, Selena, Jenaya, Shakila, Shamira, Jazzelle, Sabrina, Serenity, Ebony

Shaquille *(American)* ♂   RATING: ★★★
Handsome—Variation of Shakil; Shaquille O'Neal, basketball player
People think of Shaquille as funny, sexy, popular, handsome, sporty
People who like the name Shaquille also like Sebastian, Jacob, Shawn, Isaiah, Pharell, Nathaniel, Trevor, Tyson, Jayden, Jackson

Shari *(Hebrew)* ♀   RATING: ★★★☆
Flat clearing—Short for Sharon; also a variation of Cheri; Shari Lewis, puppeteer/children's show host
People think of Shari as pretty, funny, caring, creative, intelligent
People who like the name Shari also like Sara, Sarah, Sabrina, Savannah, Lacey, Sheri, Hope, Sofia, Samara, Shaylee

Sharis *(American)* ♀   RATING: ★★★
Flat clearing—Variation of Sharon
People think of Sharis as pretty, funny, intelligent, creative, caring
People who like the name Sharis also like Shaina, Sarah, Sofia, Shaylee, Seanna, Shyla, Samara, Sophie, Shayla, Hailey

Sharla *(American)* ♀   RATING: ★★
Variation of Charlotte
People think of Sharla as pretty, caring, funny, creative, intelligent
People who like the name Sharla also like Shayla, Shaylee, Skyla, Serenity, Sabrina, Tessa, Kiara, Serena, Chloe, Charlotte

Sharlene *(American)* ♀   RATING: ★★★☆
Free—Variation of Charlene
People think of Sharlene as pretty, intelligent, funny, sexy, creative
People who like the name Sharlene also like Scarlett, Belle, Paige, Serenity, Sadie, Jasmine, Samantha, Sienna, Isabelle, Sabrina

Sharne *(American)* ♀   RATING: ★★★☆
God is gracious—Variation of Shana
People think of Sharne as funny, trustworthy, pretty, intelligent, exotic
People who like the name Sharne also like Shanae, Shayla, Samara, Layla, Shaylee, Ava, Sarah, Phoebe, Shaina, Shayna

Sharon *(Hebrew)* ♀   RATING: ★★★☆
Flat clearing—Sharon Osbourne, music promoter/wife of Ozzy Osbourne; Sharon Stone, actress
People think of Sharon as caring, pretty, funny, intelligent, creative

500

People who like the name Sharon also like Sarah, Samantha, Rebecca, Rachel, Elizabeth, Sabrina, Sara, Rachael, Lauren, Jennifer

Sharona *(Hebrew)* ♀ RATING: ★★★☆
Flat clearing—"My Sharona," song by The Knack
People think of Sharona as pretty, funny, creative, energetic, intelligent
People who like the name Sharona also like Sabrina, Scarlett, Fiona, Shaina, Stella, Felicity, Roxanne, Shayla, Abigail, Amelia

Sharvani *(Sanskrit/East Indian)* ♀ RATING: ★★
Name of the goddess Parvati
People think of Sharvani as sexy, funny, trustworthy, young, loser
People who like the name Sharvani also like Shyla, Sarai, Samara, Shanti, Shayna, Samiya, Shayla, Shaylee, Soraya, Raina

Shasa *(African)* ♀ RATING: ★★
Precious water
People think of Shasa as intelligent, pretty, caring, creative, powerful
People who like the name Shasa also like Samara, Sophie, Savanna, Kaida, Kara, Isabella, Rhian, Sophia, Sera, Natasha

Shasta *(Sanskrit/East Indian)* ♀ ♂ RATING: ★★
Praised, commended—Also a brand of soda pop
People think of Shasta as creative, trustworthy, pretty, caring, funny
People who like the name Shasta also like Sage, Skylar, Dakota, Jade, Taylor, Sasha, Hayden, Parker, Logan, Shae

Shateque *(American)* ♀ RATING: ★★☆
Combination of Sha and Tique
People think of Shateque as popular, ethnic, exotic, intelligent, cool
People who like the name Shateque also like Kyria, Shaina, Selena, Sofia, Shanti, Saniya, Jasmine, Zelda, Tasanee, Carolina

Shaun *(English)* ♂ RATING: ★★★★
God is gracious—Variation of Sean; Shaun Cassidy, TV producer
People think of Shaun as handsome, funny, caring, intelligent, cool
People who like the name Shaun also like Tristan, Nathan, Matthew, Shawn, Ethan, Seth, Ian, Aiden, Jacob, Zachary

Shauna *(Celtic/Gaelic)* ♀ RATING: ★★★☆
God is gracious—Feminine form of Shaun
People think of Shauna as pretty, funny, caring, intelligent, creative
People who like the name Shauna also like Paige, Sabrina, Sarah, Hailey, Grace, Samantha, Faith, Rebecca, Seanna, Shayla

Shaunna *(Celtic/Gaelic)* ♀ RATING: ★★★☆
God is gracious—Feminine form of Shaun
People think of Shaunna as funny, pretty, caring, intelligent, trustworthy
People who like the name Shaunna also like Erin, Sabrina, Shayla, Faith, Shaylee, Paige, Sarah, Grace, Emma, Shauna

Shaw *(English)* ♂ RATING: ★★
Dweller by the wood—Originally a surname; George Bernard Shaw, playwright
People think of Shaw as powerful, unpopular, sporty, intelligent, sneaky
People who like the name Shaw also like Walker, Slade, Seth, Gage, Jackson, Owen, Graham, Ian, Holden, Noah

Shawdi *(Persian)* ♀ RATING: ★★★
Joy
People think of Shawdi as pretty, intelligent, creative, funny, energetic
People who like the name Shawdi also like Shaina, Samiya, Scarlett, Samara, Shayla, Shaylee, Sadie, Sofia, Seanna, Skyla

Shawn *(American)* ♂ RATING: ★★★
God is gracious—Variation of Sean
People think of Shawn as handsome, funny, caring, cool, intelligent
People who like the name Shawn also like Matthew, Ethan, Nathan, Aiden, Nicholas, Aaron, Zachary, Michael, Seth, Jacob

Shawna *(American)* ♀ RATING: ★★☆
God is gracious—Feminine form of Shawn
People think of Shawna as funny, pretty, caring, creative, trustworthy
People who like the name Shawna also like Paige, Samantha, Savannah, Olivia, Hannah, Shayla, Sarah, Natalie, Sabrina, Faith

Shay *(Celtic/Gaelic)* ♀ ♂ RATING: ★★★
Hawk
People think of Shay as pretty, funny, popular, cool, young
People who like the name Shay also like Shae, Riley, Shea, Caden, Jaden, Logan, Hayden, Taylor, Reese, Reagan

Shayla *(American)* ♀ RATING: ★★★★
Combination of Shay and Layla
People think of Shayla as pretty, funny, caring, creative, intelligent
People who like the name Shayla also like Shaylee, Kayla, Paige, Kaelyn, Ava, Shayna, Isabella, Hailey, Skyla, Layla

Shaylee *(American)* ♀ RATING: ★★★
Combination of Shay and Lee
People think of Shaylee as pretty, funny, creative, caring, intelligent
People who like the name Shaylee also like Shayla, Kaelyn, Hailey, Paige, Sabrina, Sadie, Skyla, Ashlyn, Hannah, Savannah

Shayna (American) ♀   RATING: ★★★★
God is gracious—Feminine form of Shane; also of
Yiddish origin meaning beautiful
> People think of Shayna as pretty, funny, caring, intel-
> ligent, creative
> People who like the name Shayna also like Shayla,
> Shaina, Shaylee, Paige, Jadyn, Hailey, Samantha,
> Hannah, Olivia, Layla

Shayne (American) ♀ ♂   RATING: ★★★
God is gracious—Variation of Shane
> People think of Shayne as aggressive, funny, caring,
> popular, intelligent
> People who like the name Shayne also like Shane,
> Jaden, Riley, Logan, Ryan, Caden, Hayden, Taylor,
> Jordan, Bailey

Shea (Celtic/Gaelic) ♀ ♂   RATING: ★★★★☆
Hawk
> People think of Shea as intelligent, funny, pretty, caring,
> creative
> People who like the name Shea also like Riley, Shay,
> Logan, Shae, Reese, Aidan, Reagan, Teagan, Ryan,
> Caden

Sheadon (American) ♂   RATING: ★★★☆
Combination of Shea and Don
> People think of Sheadon as popular, sporty, energetic,
> handsome, creative
> People who like the name Sheadon also like Kaden,
> Tristan, Jayden, Braeden, Landon, Braden, Noah,
> Sebastian, Sheldon, Slade

Sheba (Arabic) ♀   RATING: ★★★★
Kingdom in Arabia—Also short for Bathsheba
> People think of Sheba as exotic, pretty, powerful, funny,
> popular
> People who like the name Sheba also like Aurora,
> Sahara, Layla, Violet, Celeste, Sadie, Isis, Jasmine,
> Sabrina, Samantha

Sheehan (Celtic/Gaelic) ♀   RATING: ★★
Descendent of the peaceful one
> People think of Sheehan as caring, creative, artsy, intel-
> ligent, leader
> People who like the name Sheehan also like Sabrina,
> Kaelyn, Maeve, Bridget, Shaylee, Shayla, Skyla, Meara,
> Keira, Breanna

Sheela (Sanskrit/East Indian) ♀   RATING: ★★★☆
Modesty; good character
> People think of Sheela as funny, pretty, intelligent, car-
> ing, cool
> People who like the name Sheela also like Sophia,
> Selena, Sitara, Shyla, Roxanne, Sherri, Sheena, Amanda,
> Sierra, Sabrina

Sheena (Celtic/Gaelic) ♀   RATING: ★★★★
God is gracious—Variation of Jean; Sheena Easton,
singer
> People think of Sheena as pretty, caring, funny, intel-
> ligent, creative

People who like the name Sheena also like Sabrina,
Shayla, Seanna, Fiona, Hailey, Kiara, Alana, Lana, Trinity,
Megan

Sheera (Hebrew) ♀   RATING: ★★★
Poetry
> People think of Sheera as pretty, energetic, funny,
> powerful, leader
> People who like the name Sheera also like Samara,
> Sheena, Scarlett, Shira, Sephora, Sitara, Selena, Sierra,
> Sophia, Shamira

Sheila (Celtic/Gaelic) ♀   RATING: ★★
Blind—Variation of Celia
> People think of Sheila as caring, pretty, funny, intel-
> ligent, creative
> People who like the name Sheila also like Sabrina, Faith,
> Sarah, Fiona, Breanna, Jessica, Jennifer, Shayla, Rachel,
> Julia

Shel (English) ♀ ♂   RATING: ★★★
Short for Michelle, Shelley, or Sheldon—Shel
Silverstein, author
> People think of Shel as quiet, pretty, intelligent, cool,
> creative
> People who like the name Shel also like Shayne, Shay,
> Shae, Sage, Sawyer, Julian, Storm, Shields, Skye, Shiloh

Shelagh (Celtic/Gaelic) ♀   RATING: ★☆
Blind—Variation of Celia
> People think of Shelagh as pretty, funny, leader, cre-
> ative, popular
> People who like the name Shelagh also like Rosaleen,
> Bridget, Sabrina, Erin, Genevieve, Maeve, Ryann, Peigi,
> Rhona, Ciara

Shelby (English) ♀ ♂   RATING: ★★☆
From the town in the hollow
> People think of Shelby as pretty, funny, caring, creative,
> energetic
> People who like the name Shelby also like Madison,
> Riley, Taylor, Bailey, Sydney, Logan, Mackenzie, Parker,
> Hayden, Morgan

Sheldon (English) ♂   RATING: ★★☆
Town in the valley—Sheldon Harnick, lyricist/songwrit-
er; Sheldon Leonard, TV producer/director
> People think of Sheldon as handsome, funny, intelligent,
> cool, creative
> People who like the name Sheldon also like Ethan,
> Landon, Tristan, Kaden, Nathan, Aiden, Jackson, Owen,
> Sebastian, Jacob

Shell (American) ♀   RATING: ★★☆
Animal covering
> People think of Shell as funny, sexy, pretty, intelligent,
> popular
> People who like the name Shell also like Lilly, Emily,
> Sofia, Amy, Tammy, Cassie, Ellie, Apple, Emma, Cady

Shelley *(English)* ♀♂ RATING: ★★☆
From the sloping field—Also a surname; Shelley Long, actress; Shelley Winters, actress; Mary Shelley, author
People think of Shelley as funny, pretty, creative, caring, trustworthy
People who like the name Shelley also like Shannon, Shelby, Shelly, Madison, Sydney, Skylar, Jordan, Jaden, Cassidy, Kimberly

Shelly *(English)* ♀♂ RATING: ★★☆
From the sloping field
People think of Shelly as pretty, funny, caring, intelligent, trustworthy
People who like the name Shelly also like Shelby, Taylor, Sydney, Ryan, Shannon, Madison, Riley, Sean, Lindsey, Mackenzie

Sheng *(Chinese)* ♂ RATING: ★★★
Victory
People think of Sheng as intelligent, caring, weird, young, pretty
People who like the name Sheng also like Ethan, Seth, Suoh, Sloan, Lance, Stash, Shino, Nicholas, Jett, Marco

Shepry *(American)* ♀ RATING: ★★
Friendly, honest mediator
People think of Shepry as pretty, artsy, creative, quiet, nerdy
People who like the name Shepry also like Shaylee, Sora, Soraya, Shayla, Sonora, Summer, Sherene, Sophia, Sophie, Sofia

Sherene *(Persian)* ♀ RATING: ★★★☆
Sweet, pleasant
People think of Sherene as pretty, intelligent, caring, creative, sexy
People who like the name Sherene also like Sarina, Samara, Soraya, Serenity, Simone, Syrita, Shiri, Sabrina, Charisse, Shayla

Sheri *(American)* ♀ RATING: ★★★★
Darling—Variation of Cherie
People think of Sheri as pretty, caring, funny, intelligent, trustworthy
People who like the name Sheri also like Sarah, Paige, Sara, Sadie, Sophie, Faith, Rebecca, Sabrina, Summer, Samantha

Sheridan *(Celtic/Gaelic)* ♀♂ RATING: ★★★★
Unknown meaning—Possibly related to a word meaning to seek
People think of Sheridan as intelligent, funny, pretty, creative, popular
People who like the name Sheridan also like Madison, Mackenzie, Logan, Hayden, Reagan, Riley, Aidan, Morgan, Parker, Sydney

Sherine *(Persian)* ♀ RATING: ★★★☆
Sweet, pleasant
People think of Sherine as pretty, caring, funny, creative, intelligent

People who like the name Sherine also like Shaina, Sabrina, Selena, Stella, Sherene, Tiana, Shayla, Keisha, Jenna, Lilah

Sherise *(American)* ♀ RATING: ★★★★
Grace, beauty, kindness—Variation of Charisse
People think of Sherise as pretty, intelligent, caring, funny, sexy
People who like the name Sherise also like Jasmine, Trinity, Olivia, Charisse, Hailey, Grace, Sierra, Chloe, Faith, Serenity

Sherlock *(English)* ♂ RATING: ★★★
Fair haired—Sherlock Holmes, fictional detective
People think of Sherlock as intelligent, creative, energetic, handsome, leader
People who like the name Sherlock also like Graham, Oliver, Sidney, Sirius, Jacob, Gabriel, Jackson, Tyson, Victor, Wade

Sherman *(English)* ♂ RATING: ★★★☆
Cloth cutter—Sherman Hemsley, actor
People think of Sherman as funny, intelligent, handsome, cool, caring
People who like the name Sherman also like Justin, Scott, Dalton, Sheldon, Wade, Gordon, Sebastian, Jackson, William, Oliver

Sherri *(American)* ♀ RATING: ★★★★
Darling—Variation of Cherie
People think of Sherri as caring, intelligent, funny, pretty, trustworthy
People who like the name Sherri also like Samantha, Sabrina, Sarah, Sara, Shaina, Stephanie, Summer, Amanda, Rebecca, Renée

Sherrill *(American)* ♀ RATING: ★★★
Variation of Cheryl
People think of Sherrill as pretty, funny, intelligent, trustworthy, girl next door
People who like the name Sherrill also like Ronalee, Katalin, Shaylee, Simone, Noreen, Marla, Clarissa, Gianna, Mariel, Sahara

Sherry *(American)* ♀ RATING: ★★
Darling—Variation of Cherie; also spelled Sherrie; also a fortified wine
People think of Sherry as caring, pretty, funny, intelligent, trustworthy
People who like the name Sherry also like Sarah, Faith, Rebecca, Victoria, Jessica, Stephanie, Rose, Renée, Elizabeth, Hailey

Sherwood *(English)* ♂ RATING: ★★
From the shire wood—Sherwood Schwartz, TV producer; Sherwood Forest, legendary home of Robin Hood
People think of Sherwood as caring, creative, old-fashioned, weird, cool
People who like the name Sherwood also like Owen, Sloan, Scott, Lucas, Conner, Lawson, Findlay, Fletcher, Hanley, Jackson

Sheryl (*English*) ♀   RATING: ★★★☆
Variation of Cheryl—Sheryl Crow, singer
People think of Sheryl as pretty, caring, funny, sexy, trustworthy
People who like the name Sheryl also like Victoria, Vanessa, Faith, Sophie, Hailey, Stacey, Stephanie, Paige, Olivia, Hannah

Shiela (*Celtic/Gaelic*) ♀   RATING: ★★
Heaven—Variation of Celia
People think of Shiela as pretty, caring, intelligent, funny, energetic
People who like the name Shiela also like Sabrina, Shaylee, Sarah, Caitlin, Samantha, Shayla, Hailey, Natalie, Stephanie, Sheila

Shields (*English*) ♀ ♂   RATING: ★★★☆
Of the shallows—Also a surname; Brooke Shields, model/actress
People think of Shields as cool, intelligent, quiet, creative, powerful
People who like the name Shields also like Sawyer, Parker, Shane, Jaden, Sutton, Sage, Shiloh, Hadley, Saxen, Skylar

Shila (*Sanskrit/East Indian*) ♀   RATING: ★★★★
Rock
People think of Shila as pretty, caring, trustworthy, funny, creative
People who like the name Shila also like Shyla, Shayla, Skyla, Hailey, Paige, Ava, Cailyn, Jadyn, Hannah, Isabel

Shilah (*Native American*) ♂   RATING: ★★★☆
Brother—Navajo origin
People think of Shilah as pretty, caring, creative, trustworthy, funny
People who like the name Shilah also like Maddox, Tristan, Kaden, Sebastian, Noah, Isaac, Slade, Elijah, Micah, Jayden

Shiloah (*American*) ♀ ♂   RATING: ★★★☆
His gift
People think of Shiloah as exotic, popular, trendy, creative, funny
People who like the name Shiloah also like Shiloh, Logan, Spencer, Skylar, Skye, Sheridan, Caden, Hayden, Payton, Sydney

Shiloh (*Hebrew*) ♀ ♂   RATING: ★★★★
His gift—Battle of Shiloh, 1862; a song by the same name followed
People think of Shiloh as pretty, intelligent, caring, creative, cool
People who like the name Shiloh also like Riley, Bailey, Logan, Caden, Hayden, Madison, Dakota, Parker, Taylor, Reese

Shima (*Native American*) ♀   RATING: ★★★★
Mother—Navajo origin
People think of Shima as pretty, leader, young, popular, trustworthy

People who like the name Shima also like Shania, Soraya, Ayasha, Sachi, Snana, Topanga, Sora, Shayla, Sokanon, Sabrina

Shing (*Chinese*) ♂   RATING: ★☆
Victory—Cantonese variation of Cheng
People think of Shing as ethnic, cool, loser, aggressive, quiet
People who like the name Shing also like Seifer, Keiji, Shino, Vincent, Axel, Seth, Ephraim, Koren, Severino, Sheldon

Shino (*Japanese*) ♂   RATING: ★★★☆
Stem of bamboo
People think of Shino as intelligent, quiet, weird, cool, trustworthy
People who like the name Shino also like Hiroshi, Ryu, Suoh, Keitaro, Kaemon, Samuru, Makoto, Keiji, Akio, Haru

Shira (*Hebrew*) ♀   RATING: ★★★
Poetry
People think of Shira as pretty, creative, caring, intelligent, funny
People who like the name Shira also like Samara, Sofia, Hannah, Shayna, Kyra, Liana, Sienna, Sierra, Eva, Soraya

Shiri (*Hebrew*) ♀   RATING: ★★★★☆
My song
People think of Shiri as pretty, exotic, creative, caring, intelligent
People who like the name Shiri also like Samara, Shira, Soraya, Naomi, Selena, Sari, Sofia, Shayna, Talia, Shyla

Shirin (*Persian*) ♀   RATING: ★★★★
Sweet—A Persian queen
People think of Shirin as pretty, creative, caring, intelligent, funny
People who like the name Shirin also like Samara, Sarah, Sofia, Shayla, Shayna, Sian, Shira, Sarai, Shiri, Serena

Shirina (*American*) ♀   RATING: ★★★☆
Love song
People think of Shirina as pretty, weird, caring, quiet, funny
People who like the name Shirina also like Samara, Sabrina, Selena, Shakina, Seanna, Samiya, Sharvani, Shayla, Sherene, Shania

Shirley (*English*) ♀   RATING: ★★★☆
Bright meadow—Shirley Temple Black, former child star/U.S. ambassador to Ghana; *Laverne & Shirley*, TV show
People think of Shirley as funny, caring, pretty, trustworthy, creative
People who like the name Shirley also like Sabrina, Sarah, Emily, Scarlett, Sophie, Isabella, Nicole, Nancy, Sofia, Bianca

Shirlyn (*English*) ♀   RATING: ★★★
Bright meadow
People think of Shirlyn as pretty, caring, intelligent, trustworthy, young

503

People who like the name Shirlyn also like Summer, Shirley, Stella, Skyla, Rosalie, Natalie, Erin, Faith, Aeryn, Rhiannon

Shiva *(Persian)* ♀   RATING: ★★★☆
Beauty
People think of Shiva as exotic, powerful, pretty, intelligent, sexy
People who like the name Shiva also like Sitara, Mia, Serenity, Shira, Genevieve, Scarlett, Seanna, Layla, Suri, Sabrina

Shlomo *(Hebrew)* ♂   RATING: ★☆
His peace
People think of Shlomo as nerdy, weird, lazy, loser, intelligent
People who like the name Shlomo also like Ethan, Seth, Sebastian, Sheldon, Sinjin, Silas, Levi, Stu, Theodore, Zander

Shmuel *(Hebrew)* ♂   RATING: ★★☆
His name is God
People think of Shmuel as religious, ethnic, intelligent, caring, trustworthy
People who like the name Shmuel also like Airell, Emil, Lance, Nate, Asher, Amadeus, Adam, Baruch, Chael, Sebastian

Shmuley *(Hebrew)* ♂   RATING: ★★
His name is God—Short for Shmuel; Rabbi Shmuley Boteach, counselor/author
People think of Shmuley as weird, unpopular, poor, slow, lazy
People who like the name Shmuley also like Noah, Charles, Paul, Zebulon, Zedekiah, Benjamin, Zeke, Clyde, Dermot, Pascal

Shona *(Hebrew)* ♀   RATING: ★★★☆
Feminine form of John
People think of Shona as funny, pretty, caring, creative, intelligent
People who like the name Shona also like Hannah, Selena, Emma, Shayla, Sabrina, Summer, Rebecca, Sienna, Serena, Hailey

Shoney *(Celtic/Gaelic)* ♀♂   RATING: ★★★☆
Sea God
People think of Shoney as funny, pretty, old-fashioned, intelligent, weird
People who like the name Shoney also like Sloane, Teagan, Skye, Shae, Rory, Shea, Riley, Shannon, Hadley, Sheridan

Shoshana *(Hebrew)* ♀   RATING: ★★★★
Lily—Shoshana Bean, actress/singer
People think of Shoshana as pretty, intelligent, creative, artsy, caring
People who like the name Shoshana also like Shoshanah, Sofia, Charlotte, Sephora, Savannah, Isabella, Sabrina, Hannah, Sophia, Samara

Shoshanah *(Hebrew)* ♀   RATING: ★★
Lily
People think of Shoshanah as pretty, creative, caring, trustworthy, funny
People who like the name Shoshanah also like Shoshana, Hannah, Sarah, Savannah, Samara, Sephora, Sabrina, Scarlett, Tatiana, Emma

Shoushan *(Armenian)* ♀   RATING: ★★☆
Lily
People think of Shoushan as exotic, ethnic, weird, artsy, creative
People who like the name Shoushan also like Suri, Tiana, Tatiana, Shoshana, Shoshanah, Sirvat, Siran, Samara, Imogene, Sundari

Shouta *(Japanese)* ♂   RATING: ★★☆
Soaring, big
People think of Shouta as poor, old-fashioned, intelligent, unpopular, boy next door
People who like the name Shouta also like Aki, Luke, Mizu, Washi, Yasuo, Kaemon, Itachi, Kamin, Ryu, Tsubasa

Shreya *(Sanskrit/East Indian)* ♀   RATING: ★★★
Favorable
People think of Shreya as pretty, intelligent, creative, energetic, young
People who like the name Shreya also like Samiya, Ishana, Kanika, Sashi, Shanti, Avani, Niyati, Shila, Sitara, Mitali

Shu Fang *(Chinese)* ♀   RATING: ★☆
Kind, gentle; warm, pretty; fragrant
People think of Shu Fang as unpopular, powerful, pretty, creative, ethnic
People who like the name Shu Fang also like Suki, Sienna, Sarah, Sora, Abigail, Kioko, Kosuke, Sada, Koko, Ayame

Shuang *(Chinese)* ♀♂   RATING: ★☆
Bright, clear—Mandarin origin; also means open-hearted
People think of Shuang as ethnic, intelligent, weird, artsy, cool
People who like the name Shuang also like Shiloah, Zhi, Skye, Sheridan, Li, Sasha, Camdyn, Shiloh, Sovann, Yue Yan

Shubha *(Hebrew)* ♂   RATING: ★★☆
Auspicious
People think of Shubha as exotic, winner, funny, religious, weird
People who like the name Shubha also like Skipper, Oswald, Stew, Sherlock, Simeon, Mitch, Nate, Shakir, Shino, Silver

Shui *(Chinese)* ♀♂   RATING: ★★☆
Water
People think of Shui as creative, caring, cool, weird, intelligent
People who like the name Shui also like Caden, Sky, Infinity, Jade, Angel, Hiroko, Sean, Kin, Shadow, Ali

Shulamit (Hebrew) ♀   RATING: ★★☆
Peaceful
- People think of Shulamit as intelligent, religious, caring, winner, pretty
- People who like the name Shulamit also like Delilah, Aulani, Amaris, Tabitha, Lahela, Devorit, Galia, Isis, Mea, Ulan

Shyam (Sanskrit/East Indian) ♂   RATING: ★★★☆
Dark
- People think of Shyam as intelligent, trustworthy, popular, exotic, handsome
- People who like the name Shyam also like Seth, Savir, Sanjay, Soren, Stian, Keiran, Rohan, Silvain, Saeran, Suoh

Shyla (Sanskrit/East Indian) ♀   RATING: ★★☆
Goddess
- People think of Shyla as pretty, funny, creative, caring, popular
- People who like the name Shyla also like Shayla, Skyla, Shaylee, Layla, Sienna, Ava, Sadie, Paige, Sierra, Savannah

Sian (Welsh) ♀   RATING: ★★★★
God's gracious gift—Pronounced 'sharn
- People think of Sian as pretty, funny, caring, intelligent, creative
- People who like the name Sian also like Sienna, Samara, Seanna, Paige, Grace, Olivia, Sofia, Chloe, Keira, Rhian

Sibley (English) ♀ ♂   RATING: ★★
Brother; sister
- People think of Sibley as intelligent, elegant, loser, stuck-up, old-fashioned
- People who like the name Sibley also like Hayden, Hadley, Addison, Spencer, Riley, Taylor, Sydney, Peyton, Jaden, Jordan

Sibyl (Latin) ♀   RATING: ★★★
Seer
- People think of Sibyl as weird, old-fashioned, intelligent, elegant, pretty
- People who like the name Sibyl also like Sadie, Olivia, Paige, Sofia, Hailey, Scarlett, Sybil, Hannah, Sophia, Celeste

Sid (English) ♂   RATING: ★★★☆
Short for Sidney—Sid Caesar, comedian/TV host; Sid Vicious, musician
- People think of Sid as funny, sexy, energetic, cool, weird
- People who like the name Sid also like Seth, Wade, Miles, Sidney, Ian, Scott, Trent, Ethan, Damien, Maddox

Sidney (French) ♂   RATING: ★★★☆
Variation of St. Denys—Sidney Omarr, astrologer/columnist; Sidney Poitier, actor
- People think of Sidney as funny, intelligent, creative, caring, popular
- People who like the name Sidney also like Ethan, Noah, Owen, Gavin, Aiden, Jackson, Jacob, Tristan, Nicholas, Landon

Sidone (American) ♀   RATING: ★★
It is heard—Combination of Sidney and Simone
- People think of Sidone as energetic, artsy, sneaky, unpopular, creative
- People who like the name Sidone also like Sidonie, Sienna, Shantell, Sissy, Samara, Sarai, Samantha, Scarlett, Selena, Siran

Sidonia (Latin) ♀   RATING: ★★★
To ensnare
- People think of Sidonia as pretty, creative, intelligent, exotic, energetic
- People who like the name Sidonia also like Scarlett, Olivia, Ophelia, Sophia, Sofia, Samantha, Skyla, Ivy, Aurora, Penelope

Sidonie (French) ♀   RATING: ★★★★
From Sidon, Lebanon
- People think of Sidonie as pretty, intelligent, funny, exotic, creative
- People who like the name Sidonie also like Simone, Sabrina, Sadie, Sienna, Samantha, Scarlett, Sophia, Charlotte, Sofia, Renée

Sidra (Latin) ♀   RATING: ★★
Star born
- People think of Sidra as funny, intelligent, pretty, creative, exotic
- People who like the name Sidra also like Samara, Scarlett, Sofia, Chloe, Ava, Olivia, Isadora, Sadie, Grace, Nadia

Sienna (Italian) ♀   RATING: ★★★
Reddish brown
- People think of Sienna as pretty, creative, popular, intelligent, exotic
- People who like the name Sienna also like Sierra, Ava, Isabella, Olivia, Savannah, Paige, Ella, Sophia, Emma, Chloe

Sierra (Spanish) ♀   RATING: ★★★
Mountain
- People think of Sierra as pretty, funny, creative, intelligent, caring
- People who like the name Sierra also like Sienna, Savannah, Paige, Olivia, Ava, Isabella, Chloe, Hailey, Hannah, Emma

Sigfried (German) ♂   RATING: ★★☆
Victory, peace
- People think of Sigfried as stuck-up, uptight, ethnic, energetic, old
- People who like the name Sigfried also like Giovanni, Mauro, Iago, Miguel, Ea, Pascual, Giuseppe, Jeremiah, Milton, Saul

Signa (Scandinavian) ♀   RATING: ★★☆
Signal, sign
- People think of Signa as artsy, cool, caring, pretty, funny
- People who like the name Signa also like Sonja, Sofia, Freja, Sophie, Sidra, Nadia, Sierra, Kate, Svea, Violet

Sigourney *(Scandinavian)* ♀♂   RATING: ★★☆
The conqueror—Sigourney Weaver, actress
> People think of Sigourney as creative, intelligent, pretty, funny, cool
> People who like the name Sigourney also like Skye, Hayden, Reese, Mackenzie, Sydney, Parker, Riley, Jordan, Reagan, Sheridan

Sika *(African)* ♀   RATING: ★★★
Money
> People think of Sika as pretty, funny, intelligent, sexy, powerful
> People who like the name Sika also like Sapphire, Samara, Samira, Sora, Suki, Shakila, Nina, Shyla, Sonya, Sabrina

Silas *(Latin)* ♂   RATING: ★★★★☆
Man of the forest
> People think of Silas as handsome, intelligent, creative, leader, trustworthy
> People who like the name Silas also like Noah, Ethan, Owen, Gabriel, Liam, Elijah, Isaac, Gavin, Caleb, Oliver

Síle *(Celtic/Gaelic)* ♀   RATING: ★★☆
Blind—Variation of Cecile
> People think of Síle as creative, intelligent, powerful, pretty, elegant
> People who like the name Síle also like Suri, Saoirse, Sanne, Fiona, Harmony, Soraya, Rane, Sabrina, Serenity, Isabelle

Sileas *(Celtic/Gaelic)* ♀   RATING: ★★
Heaven—Variation of Celia
> People think of Sileas as intelligent, quiet, exotic, creative, powerful
> People who like the name Sileas also like Skyla, Sinéad, Maeve, Saoirse, Shayla, Phiala, Sheehan, Moira, Siobhan, Eavan

Silence *(American)* ♀♂   RATING: ★★☆
No sound
> People think of Silence as quiet, pretty, artsy, sexy, creative
> People who like the name Silence also like Addison, Shadow, Diamond, Blaise, Sage, Paris, Eden, Lyric, London, Aspen

Sileny *(Slavic)* ♀   RATING: ★★★★
Moonlight, silence
> People think of Sileny as pretty, quiet, elegant, artsy, intelligent
> People who like the name Sileny also like Selena, Serena, Scarlett, Selene, Aysel, Stella, Shayla, Chandra, Sora, Shirley

Silvain *(French)* ♂   RATING: ★★★
Forest
> People think of Silvain as intelligent, funny, wild, big, creative
> People who like the name Silvain also like Sebastian, Lucien, Miles, Seth, Lucas, Sinclair, Sirius, Alain, Sylvain, Sullivan

Silvana *(Latin)* ♀   RATING: ★★★★
Forest
> People think of Silvana as pretty, intelligent, funny, creative, sexy
> People who like the name Silvana also like Sofia, Sylvana, Sienna, Olivia, Isabella, Tiana, Sophia, Selena, Keira, Lilianna

Silver *(English)* ♂   RATING: ★★★★
A metal element—Also the color
> People think of Silver as cool, funny, creative, sexy, trustworthy
> People who like the name Silver also like Sirius, Xavier, Drake, Tristan, Sebastian, Slade, Seth, Xander, Chase, Reece

Silvia *(Latin)* ♀   RATING: ★★★★
Of the forest
> People think of Silvia as pretty, intelligent, caring, creative, funny
> People who like the name Silvia also like Sophia, Olivia, Sabrina, Sofia, Eva, Victoria, Scarlett, Sophie, Sylvia, Samantha

Silvine *(French)* ♀   RATING: ★★☆
Forest
> People think of Silvine as pretty, untrustworthy, poor, lazy, girl next door
> People who like the name Silvine also like Devi, Brianna, Vera, Portia, Rhian, Sarina, Breanna, Sabine, Gia, Giza

Sima *(Hebrew)* ♀   RATING: ★★★☆
Treasure—Also an Indian (Sanskrit) name meaning border
> People think of Sima as pretty, funny, exotic, intelligent, creative
> People who like the name Sima also like Samara, Sela, Sofia, Saniya, Sarai, Sari, Selah, Shaina, Savanna, Shira

Simba *(African)* ♂   RATING: ★★★☆
Lion—Kiswahili origin; character in *The Lion King*
> People think of Simba as energetic, leader, cool, powerful, caring
> People who like the name Simba also like Ethan, Oliver, Sebastian, Seth, Lucas, Tristan, Jayden, Cole, Cody, Jacob

Simbala *(Sanskrit/East Indian)* ♀   RATING: ★★☆
Pond
> People think of Simbala as exotic, sexy, powerful, creative, weird
> People who like the name Simbala also like Shyla, Samiya, Sohalia, Sevita, Opal, Sharvani, Svara, Parvani, Sitara, Vyomini

Simeon *(Greek)* ♂   RATING: ★★★☆
To be heard—Variation of Simon
> People think of Simeon as handsome, funny, caring, creative, trustworthy
> People who like the name Simeon also like Samuel, Gabriel, Simon, Seth, Elijah, Micah, Isaiah, Noah, Isaac, Gideon

Simon (Hebrew) ♂   RATING: ★★☆
To be heard—Simon Cowell, music producer/judge on
American Idol
  People think of Simon as intelligent, handsome, caring,
funny, trustworthy
  People who like the name Simon also like Samuel,
Noah, Oliver, Ethan, Benjamin, Isaac, Jacob, Owen,
Sebastian, Seth

Simone (French) ♀   RATING: ★★★★
To be heard—Simone Signoret, actress; Nina Simone,
singer
  People think of Simone as pretty, intelligent, funny, cre-
ative, caring
  People who like the name Simone also like Olivia, Paige,
Chloe, Sophia, Sophie, Isabella, Ava, Scarlett, Sofia,
Phoebe

Sinclair (English) ♂   RATING: ★★★★
From St. Clair, France—Originally a surname
  People think of Sinclair as intelligent, creative, popular,
powerful, funny
  People who like the name Sinclair also like Kaden,
Sebastian, Emerson, Xavier, Tristan, Sidney, Samuel,
Aiden, Lucas, Noah

Sine (Celtic/Gaelic) ♀   RATING: ★★
God is gracious—Variation of Jane
  People think of Sine as intelligent, religious, funny, lazy,
caring
  People who like the name Sine also like Sinéad, Saoirse,
Tieve, Keira, Moira, Sheena, Sileas, Brea, Aoife, Fiona

Sinéad (Celtic/Gaelic) ♀   RATING: ★★★★
God is gracious—Variation of Janet; pronounced *Shi-
NAYD*; Sinéad O'Connor, singer
  People think of Sinéad as pretty, funny, caring, popular,
intelligent
  People who like the name Sinéad also like Siobhan,
Maeve, Fiona, Sabrina, Sadie, Keira, Paige, Phoebe, Erin,
Grace

Sinjin (English) ♂   RATING: ★★★★
St. John
  People think of Sinjin as handsome, intelligent, creative,
cool, powerful
  People who like the name Sinjin also like Aiden, Tristan,
Seth, Sirius, Aden, Deacon, Tiernan, Wyatt, Sidney,
Samuel

Siobhan (Celtic/Gaelic) ♀   RATING: ★★★☆
God is gracious—Variation of Joan; pronounced *Shih-
VON* or *Shih-WAN*
  People think of Siobhan as pretty, intelligent, funny,
creative, caring
  People who like the name Siobhan also like Fiona, Keira,
Sophia, Hannah, Olivia, Sabrina, Chloe, Abigail, Erin,
Rhiannon

Siofra (Celtic/Gaelic) ♀   RATING: ★★★
Elf
  People think of Siofra as pretty, intelligent, creative,
funny, artsy

People who like the name Siofra also like Keaira, Kiara,
Seren, Saoirse, Laurel, Erin, Fiona, Gemma, Iliana, Lily

Siran (Armenian) ♀   RATING: ★★
Sweet love—Short for Siranoush
  People think of Siran as pretty, exotic, sexy, creative,
elegant
  People who like the name Siran also like Samara, Sian,
Rianna, Sierra, Shayla, Sienna, Sadie, Maya, Selene,
Paige

Sirius (Greek) ♂   RATING: ★★★★☆
Dog star—Brightest star named after the Greek God
Osirus
  People think of Sirius as handsome, intelligent, popular,
powerful, cool
  People who like the name Sirius also like Tristan,
Seth, Xander, Sebastian, Xavier, Oliver, Damien, Cyrus,
Alexander, Drake

Sirvat (Armenian) ♀   RATING: ★★☆
Rose of love—Variation of Sirvart
  People think of Sirvat as funny, big, ethnic, artsy,
aggressive
  People who like the name Sirvat also like Siran, Shaylee,
Shoshanah, Rosaline, Shepry, Solange, Tazanna,
Rosalyn, Sidra, Sora

Sissy (American) ♀   RATING: ★☆
Short for Cecilia—Also a nickname for sister; also
slang for a cowardly person; Sissy Spacek, actress
  People think of Sissy as pretty, funny, young, cool, wild
  People who like the name Sissy also like Sabrina, Grace,
Shayla, Bridget, Sadie, Sophie, Chelsea, Scarlett, Stella,
Paige

Sitara (Sanskrit/East Indian) ♀   RATING: ★★
Starlight
  People think of Sitara as pretty, exotic, creative, intel-
ligent, cool
  People who like the name Sitara also like Samara, Shyla,
Sakura, Selena, Sora, Kiara, Chandra, Layla, Serenity,
Giselle

Siusan (Celtic/Gaelic) ♀   RATING: ★★☆
Lily—Variation of Susan
  People think of Siusan as quiet, artsy, pretty, lazy, leader
  People who like the name Siusan also like Shayla,
Seanna, Sabrina, Sorcha, Shaylee, Sissy, Erin, Sheila,
Rhoswen, Brianna

Sivan (Hebrew) ♀ ♂   RATING: ★★★★
Third month in the Jewish calendar
  People think of Sivan as intelligent, pretty, caring, popu-
lar, sexy
  People who like the name Sivan also like Jaden, Sovann,
Shae, Skylar, Shane, Syshe, Skye, Shalom, Saxen, Seiko

Siyamak (Persian) ♂   RATING: ★★★
Solitary
  People think of Siyamak as intelligent, exotic, powerful,
handsome, aggressive

People who like the name Siyamak also like Sullivan, Siyavash, Adish, Seth, Sirius, Drake, Donovan, Xerxes, Keiran, Soren

Siyanda *(African)* ♀   RATING: ★★★
We are growing—Zulu origin
People think of Siyanda as intelligent, energetic, pretty, leader, creative
People who like the name Siyanda also like Sitara, Semira, Samara, Shakina, Tiana, Soraya, Sherene, Sumayah, Savannah, Serenity

Siyavash *(Persian)* ♂   RATING: ★☆
Black bull
People think of Siyavash as aggressive, exotic, intelligent, wild, funny
People who like the name Siyavash also like Faris, Siyamak, Kyran, Darrius, Kaden, Saeran, Slade, Ryker, Sebastian, Aiden

Skah *(Native American)* ♂   RATING: ★★★
White—Navajo origin
People think of Skah as uptight, big, young, trustworthy, unpopular
People who like the name Skah also like Dasan, Kele, Sani, Shilah, Noah, Dyami, Soren, Shaw, Sirius, Suoh

Skip *(American)* ♂   RATING: ★★★
Short for Skipper
People think of Skip as funny, handsome, caring, energetic, boy next door
People who like the name Skip also like Seth, Jacob, Lance, Ian, Scott, Lucas, Noah, Simon, Owen, Tucker

Skipper *(English)* ♂   RATING: ★★★☆
Ship captain or master—Often a nickname for a wealthy man who owns a yacht
People think of Skipper as loser, funny, nerdy, young, sporty
People who like the name Skipper also like Scott, Tristan, Jack, Jacob, Wade, Seth, Oliver, Skip, Finn, Thomas

Skule *(Scandinavian)* ♀♂   RATING: ★★★
Hide
People think of Skule as weird, untrustworthy, young, wild, quiet
People who like the name Skule also like Skylar, Sully, Shea, Shiloh, Seath, Sovann, Shiloah, Saxon, Shelley, Kieve

Sky *(American)* ♀♂   RATING: ★★★☆
Sky—Also spelled Skyy
People think of Sky as pretty, cool, intelligent, creative, popular
People who like the name Sky also like Skye, Skylar, Jade, Rain, Jaden, Taylor, Riley, Sage, Hayden, Bailey

Skye *(Celtic/Gaelic)* ♀♂   RATING: ★★★★
From the Isle of Skye—Also short for Skylar; also a variation of Sky
People think of Skye as pretty, creative, funny, caring, intelligent

People who like the name Skye also like Riley, Skylar, Madison, Logan, Taylor, Dakota, Jade, Bailey, Hayden, Jaden

Skyla *(American)* ♀   RATING: ★★★★
Scholar—Variation of Schuyler
People think of Skyla as pretty, funny, intelligent, popular, young
People who like the name Skyla also like Shayla, Shaylee, Kaelyn, Paige, Kyla, Savannah, Hailey, Isabella, Jadyn, Hannah

Skylar *(American)* ♀♂   RATING: ★★★
Scholar—Variation of Schuyler; also spelled Skyler
People think of Skylar as pretty, funny, creative, intelligent, popular
People who like the name Skylar also like Madison, Riley, Hayden, Logan, Taylor, Jaden, Caden, Parker, Mackenzie, Bailey

Slade *(English)* ♂   RATING: ★★★★
Dweller in the valley
People think of Slade as handsome, intelligent, powerful, leader, cool
People who like the name Slade also like Kaden, Seth, Maddox, Tristan, Sloan, Aiden, Landon, Gage, Reece, Ethan

Sloan *(Celtic/Gaelic)* ♂   RATING: ★★
Warrior
People think of Sloan as cool, intelligent, creative, sexy, powerful
People who like the name Sloan also like Tristan, Aiden, Owen, Cole, Gavin, Ethan, Keagan, Seth, Noah, Kaden

Sloane *(Celtic/Gaelic)* ♀♂   RATING: ★★★★
Warrior
People think of Sloane as pretty, cool, intelligent, popular, sexy
People who like the name Sloane also like Avery, Riley, Logan, Parker, Hayden, Reagan, Sawyer, Teagan, Quinn, Addison

Slone *(Celtic/Gaelic)* ♂   RATING: ★★
Warrior
People think of Slone as trustworthy, pretty, energetic, caring, creative
People who like the name Slone also like Sloan, Cole, Tristan, Kaden, Aiden, Jackson, Owen, Gavin, Slade, Seth

Smith *(English)* ♂   RATING: ★★
Blacksmith—Also a surname
People think of Smith as funny, cool, intelligent, sexy, caring
People who like the name Smith also like Jackson, Tucker, Noah, Owen, Jack, Ethan, William, Oliver, Walker, Grayson

Snana *(Native American)* ♀   RATING: ★★☆
Jingles like bells—Sioux origin
People think of Snana as nerdy, weird, energetic, stuck-up, loser

People who like the name Snana also like Sokanon, Soraya, Sora, Winona, Shima, Sahkyo, Soyala, Shania, Yamka, Tiva

Snow *(English)* ♀ RATING: ★★★☆
Frozen rain—Phoebe Snow, singer
People think of Snow as cool, pretty, creative, intelligent, young
People who like the name Snow also like Summer, Scarlett, Ivy, Faith, Sapphire, Violet, Melody, Harmony, Serenity, Rose

Snowy *(English)* ♀ ♂ RATING: ★★★
Filled with frozen rain
People think of Snowy as pretty, funny, caring, cool, creative
People who like the name Snowy also like Shadow, Shannon, Stormy, Holly, Star, Sunny, Storm, Sage, Cassidy, Piper

Socorro *(Spanish)* ♀ RATING: ★★★☆
Help, succour
People think of Socorro as intelligent, caring, cool, weird, funny
People who like the name Socorro also like Savannah, Aimee, Serena, Sophia, Zofia, Lauren, Livi, Naomi, Paige, Penelope

Socrates *(Greek)* ♂ RATING: ★★★☆
Whole rule—Socrates, ancient Greek philosopher/writer
People think of Socrates as intelligent, leader, powerful, cool, trustworthy
People who like the name Socrates also like Aristotle, Oliver, Sirius, Sebastian, Constantine, Griffin, Xavier, Atticus, Lysander, Noah

Sofia *(Spanish)* ♀ RATING: ★★★★
Wisdom—Sofia Coppola, filmmaker
People think of Sofia as pretty, intelligent, creative, elegant, funny
People who like the name Sofia also like Sophia, Olivia, Isabella, Ava, Sophie, Chloe, Mia, Emma, Ella, Eva

Sohalia *(Sanskrit/East Indian)* ♀ RATING: ★★★☆
Moon glow
People think of Sohalia as pretty, intelligent, exotic, old-fashioned, energetic
People who like the name Sohalia also like Sitara, Chandra, Soraya, Kaya, Selena, Sauda, Shyla, Kamaria, Anika, Satya

Sokanon *(Native American)* ♀ RATING: ★★★
Rain—Algonquin origin
People think of Sokanon as exotic, ethnic, pretty, old-fashioned, powerful
People who like the name Sokanon also like Sora, Soraya, Snana, Sahkyo, Shania, Satinka, Takoda, Salali, Soyala, Tallulah

Sol *(Spanish)* ♀ ♂ RATING: ★★
Sun—Also short for Solomon, Soledad, or Solange
People think of Sol as intelligent, funny, popular, handsome, cool
People who like the name Sol also like Sean, Sawyer, Kai, Tate, Skye, Luca, Sasha, Logan, Phoenix, London

Sola *(Spanish)* ♀ RATING: ★★★
She who is alone
People think of Sola as uptight, exotic
People who like the name Sola also like Seda, Devi, Sylvana, Seren, Giza, Seema, Guadalupe, Sela, Zaila, Toril

Solada *(Thai)* ♀ RATING: ★★
Listener
People think of Solada as exotic, trustworthy, creative, quiet, artsy
People who like the name Solada also like Sofia, Solana, Samara, Sophie, Selena, Soraya, Saffron, Sidonie, Sahara, Samira

Solana *(Latin)* ♀ RATING: ★★☆
Wind from the east—Also a Spanish name meaning sunshine
People think of Solana as exotic, pretty, caring, sexy, energetic
People who like the name Solana also like Serena, Sofia, Selena, Soraya, Samara, Sienna, Olivia, Lucia, Sarina, Scarlett

Solange *(French)* ♀ RATING: ★★
Solemn
People think of Solange as pretty, sexy, intelligent, creative, elegant
People who like the name Solange also like Giselle, Samara, Simone, Soleil, Aaliyah, Sabrina, Sofia, Selene, Stella, Tatiana

Solaris *(Latin)* ♀ ♂ RATING: ★★
Of the sun
People think of Solaris as powerful, pretty, intelligent, exotic, popular
People who like the name Solaris also like Skye, Raine, Skylar, Sydney, Sage, Hayden, Phoenix, Willow, Ryder, Reese

Soledad *(Spanish)* ♀ RATING: ★☆
Solitude—Title of the Virgin Mary; Soledad O'Brien, journalist
People think of Soledad as funny, pretty, caring, intelligent, cool
People who like the name Soledad also like Sofia, Pilar, Marisol, Isabel, Sophia, Samara, Phoebe, Savannah, Sarah, Selena

Soleil *(French)* ♀ RATING: ★★☆
Sun—Soleil Moon Frye, actress
People think of Soleil as pretty, creative, artsy, exotic, intelligent
People who like the name Soleil also like Sienna, Scarlett, Giselle, Sadie, Chloe, Ava, Sofia, Savannah, Sophie, Aurora

510

Solomon *(Hebrew)* ♂ RATING: ★★★★
Peace
People think of Solomon as intelligent, handsome, powerful, caring, leader
People who like the name Solomon also like Samuel, Noah, Isaac, Simon, Seth, Elijah, Isaiah, Gabriel, Benjamin, Owen

Solstice *(English)* ♀ RATING: ★★★
Time of year when the sun is at its greatest distance from the celestial equator
People think of Solstice as artsy, pretty, exotic, intelligent, creative
People who like the name Solstice also like Sienna, Sierra, Sapphire, Sadie, Celeste, Trinity, Serenity, Autumn, Scarlett, Chloe

Somatra *(Sanskrit/East Indian)* ♀ RATING: ★★☆
Greater than the moon
People think of Somatra as sexy, pretty, intelligent, elegant, sneaky
People who like the name Somatra also like Sohalia, Sarina, Sitara, Chandra, Selena, Sofia, Cassandra, Selina, Suzette, Tatiana

Sona *(Sanskrit/East Indian)* ♀ RATING: ★★★★
Gold
People think of Sona as pretty, intelligent, exotic, caring, creative
People who like the name Sona also like Sora, Sofia, Sera, Sana, Samara, Soraya, Shayla, Samiya, Sienna, Sada

Sondra *(American)* ♀ RATING: ★★★☆
Variation of Sandra—Also short for Alexandra or Cassandra
People think of Sondra as creative, caring, funny, pretty, intelligent
People who like the name Sondra also like Sonya, Sophia, Sandra, Sofia, Sophie, Giselle, Bianca, Serena, Sabrina, Monica

Sonel *(Hebrew)* ♀ RATING: ★★
Lily—Variation of Susan
People think of Sonel as intelligent, sexy, funny, caring, powerful
People who like the name Sonel also like Sora, Sephora, Sanne, Sona, Soraya, Sophia, Sofia, Sonja, Serena, Samara

Sonia *(Slavic)* ♀ RATING: ★★★★
Wisdom—Variation of Sophia
People think of Sonia as pretty, funny, intelligent, caring, creative
People who like the name Sonia also like Sophia, Sofia, Olivia, Hannah, Nadia, Sonya, Sabrina, Paige, Grace, Sophie

Sonja *(Scandinavian)* ♀ RATING: ★★★★
Wisdom—Variation of Sophia; Sonja Henie, figure skater
People think of Sonja as intelligent, pretty, funny, creative, caring

People who like the name Sonja also like Sophia, Nadia, Sophie, Sofia, Olivia, Sonya, Samantha, Hailey, Sonia, Sarah

Sonnagh *(Celtic/Gaelic)* ♀ ♂ RATING: ★☆
A mound, rampart
People think of Sonnagh as artsy, exotic, ethnic, pretty, loser
People who like the name Sonnagh also like Sean, Murphy, Cameron, Shoney, Reilly, Sheridan, Reagan, Shea, Connor, Shannon

Sonny *(American)* ♂ RATING: ★★★★
Our son—Nickname for a male child; Sonny Bono, singer/actor/politician
People think of Sonny as handsome, funny, cool, popular, intelligent
People who like the name Sonny also like Ethan, Seth, Nathan, Jack, Caleb, Jake, Adam, Oliver, Wade, Scott

Sonora *(Spanish)* ♀ RATING: ★★
Pleasant sounding
People think of Sonora as pretty, exotic, creative, caring, young
People who like the name Sonora also like Olivia, Sofia, Sophia, Sienna, Sadie, Samara, Serena, Sophie, Nora, Sierra

Sonya *(Russian)* ♀ RATING: ★★★☆
Wisdom—Variation of Sophia
People think of Sonya as pretty, funny, caring, creative, intelligent
People who like the name Sonya also like Sophia, Olivia, Sophie, Sofia, Sabrina, Sonia, Ava, Eva, Victoria, Nadia

Sophia *(Greek)* ♀ RATING: ★★★
Wisdom—Sophia Loren, actress
People think of Sophia as pretty, intelligent, elegant, caring, creative
People who like the name Sophia also like Olivia, Isabella, Ava, Sophie, Emma, Grace, Ella, Hannah, Abigail, Chloe

Sophie *(French)* ♀ RATING: ★★★
Wisdom—Also spelled Sofie
People think of Sophie as pretty, funny, intelligent, caring, creative
People who like the name Sophie also like Sophia, Olivia, Chloe, Emma, Ava, Hannah, Isabella, Grace, Sadie, Ella

Sora *(Japanese)* ♀ RATING: ★★★★☆
Sky
People think of Sora as caring, trustworthy, funny, young, energetic
People who like the name Sora also like Sakura, Sophia, Kaya, Sophie, Ava, Sadie, Soraya, Amaya, Scarlett, Sofia

Soraya *(Persian)* ♀ RATING: ★★★★
Princess—Variation of Sarah; also a constellation
People think of Soraya as pretty, exotic, intelligent, creative, funny

People who like the name Soraya also like Samara, Amaya, Kaya, Sabrina, Isabella, Sarai, Sienna, Serenity, Sadie, Kailani

Sorcha *(Celtic/Gaelic)* ♀   RATING: ★★
Bright, radiant
People think of Sorcha as pretty, intelligent, creative, caring, energetic
People who like the name Sorcha also like Aeryn, Genevieve, Fiona, Rhiannon, Ava, Keira, Sabrina, Aurora, Saoirse, Kaelyn

Soren *(Scandinavian)* ♂   RATING: ★★★★☆
Severe
People think of Soren as intelligent, handsome, creative, powerful, cool
People who like the name Soren also like Tristan, Noah, Seth, Aiden, Liam, Owen, Sebastian, Gabriel, Ethan, Kaden

Sorena *(Scandinavian)* ♀   RATING: ★★★☆
Feminine form of Soren
People think of Sorena as pretty, funny, quiet, intelligent, creative
People who like the name Sorena also like Sienna, Serena, Jasmine, Sierra, Sorina, Sapphire, Sephora, Sofia, Tabitha, Gabrielle

Sorina *(American)* ♀   RATING: ★★★☆
Peaceful, serene—Variation of Serena
People think of Sorina as pretty, sexy, intelligent, elegant, caring
People who like the name Sorina also like Sophia, Serena, Sarina, Sabrina, Sofia, Samara, Selena, Samantha, Olivia, Sienna

Sorley *(English)* ♂   RATING: ★★★
Summer traveler; Viking—Originally a surname
People think of Sorley as powerful, aggressive, energetic, wealthy, intelligent
People who like the name Sorley also like Silas, Tristan, Miles, Holden, Hanley, Jackson, Drake, Maddox, Chase, Slade

Soto *(Spanish)* ♂   RATING: ★★☆
Forest grove
People think of Soto as sexy, intelligent, creative, artsy, cool
People who like the name Soto also like Brian, Isaac, Charlton, Basil, Michelangelo, Miles, Adam, Caleb, Johnathan, David

Southern *(American)* ♀ ♂   RATING: ★★★
From the south
People think of Southern as powerful, elegant, trustworthy, popular, weird
People who like the name Southern also like Sawyer, Sydney, Liberty, Jordan, Sheridan, Storm, Skye, London, Sky, Madison

Sovann *(Cambodian)* ♀ ♂   RATING: ★★★☆
Gold—Pronounced SO-van
People think of Sovann as exotic, elegant, creative, sexy, artsy
People who like the name Sovann also like Skylar, Sawyer, Sage, Logan, Sivan, Talen, Terran, Lyndon, Landen, Tanner

Soyala *(Native American)* ♀   RATING: ★★★☆
Winter solstice—Hopi origin
People think of Soyala as creative, ethnic, artsy, elegant, exotic
People who like the name Soyala also like Soraya, Sokanon, Sora, Kaya, Snana, Serenity, Samira, Satya, Skyla, Neena

Spence *(English)* ♂   RATING: ★★★★
Butler—Short for Spencer; also a surname
People think of Spence as handsome, intelligent, leader, sporty, popular
People who like the name Spence also like Seth, Reece, Tristan, Caleb, Noah, Owen, Aiden, Ethan, Jacob, Cole

Spencer *(English)* ♀ ♂   RATING: ★★★☆
Butler, steward—Spencer Tracy, actor
People think of Spencer as funny, cool, handsome, intelligent, popular
People who like the name Spencer also like Parker, Logan, Hayden, Riley, Taylor, Preston, Madison, Tyler, Connor, Caden

Speranza *(Italian)* ♀   RATING: ★★★
Hope
People think of Speranza as exotic, pretty, weird, ethnic, girl next door
People who like the name Speranza also like Isabella, Serena, Scarlett, Sienna, Serafina, Mia, Ophelia, Ivy, Isis, Penelope

Spike *(American)* ♂   RATING: ★☆
Long, heavy nail—Spike Jones, musician; Spike Lee, filmmaker
People think of Spike as cool, aggressive, criminal, powerful, sexy
People who like the name Spike also like Seth, Drake, Blade, Ethan, Aaron, Wade, Nathan, Lucas, Kaden, Jack

Spiro *(Greek)* ♂   RATING: ★★★☆
Basket—Short for Spyridon; Spiro Agnew, U.S. vice president
People think of Spiro as powerful, intelligent, cool, handsome, aggressive
People who like the name Spiro also like Seth, Sirius, Cyrus, Ethan, Xander, Aiden, Constantine, Nicholas, Sebastian, Soren

Sprague *(English)* ♂   RATING: ★★★
Alert, lively—Originally a surname
People think of Sprague as energetic, funny, winner, trustworthy, weird
People who like the name Sprague also like Colt, Slade, Sinclair, Step, Keith, Sterling, Deiter, Lucas, Marshall, Sidney

511

512

Spyridon (*Greek*) ♂   RATING: ★★☆
Basket
> People think of Spyridon as intelligent, trustworthy, creative, leader, winner
> People who like the name Spyridon also like Sirius, Sidney, Silas, Nicodemus, Thaddeus, Sterling, Socrates, Jamison, Slade, Leander

Squire (*English*) ♀ ♂   RATING: ★★☆
Knight's aide
> People think of Squire as nerdy, weird, stuck-up, sneaky, loser
> People who like the name Squire also like Cade, Zephyr, Devon, Cary, Caley, Cael, Ari, Angel, Ali, Brayden

Stacey (*Greek*) ♀   RATING: ★★☆
Resurrection—Originally short for Anastasia; also an English surname
> People think of Stacey as pretty, funny, caring, trustworthy, intelligent
> People who like the name Stacey also like Paige, Samantha, Sarah, Rebecca, Stephanie, Natalie, Hailey, Faith, Lauren, Jessica

Stacia (*English*) ♀   RATING: ★★☆
Resurrection—Short for Anastasia
> People think of Stacia as pretty, funny, intelligent, caring, creative
> People who like the name Stacia also like Olivia, Paige, Sophie, Sienna, Sofia, Shaylee, Stasia, Scarlett, Hailey, Grace

Stacie (*English*) ♀   RATING: ★★★☆
Resurrection—Short for Anastasia
> People think of Stacie as funny, caring, pretty, creative, trustworthy
> People who like the name Stacie also like Paige, Faith, Hailey, Natalie, Samantha, Lacey, Sophie, Grace, Hannah, Sarah

Stacy (*English*) ♀ ♂   RATING: ★★☆
Resurrection—Originally short for Anastasia; also a surname
> People think of Stacy as funny, pretty, caring, creative, intelligent
> People who like the name Stacy also like Taylor, Madison, Ryan, Sydney, Morgan, Ashley, Kimberly, Bailey, Brooke, Jade

Stan (*English*) ♂   RATING: ★★
Short for Stanley—Stan Laurel, comedian/actor
> People think of Stan as funny, intelligent, trustworthy, lazy, energetic
> People who like the name Stan also like Seth, Scott, Stanley, Simon, Owen, Justin, Brian, Nicholas, David, Todd

Stanislaus (*Slavic*) ♂   RATING: ★★★
Becoming glorious
> People think of Stanislaus as intelligent, trustworthy, handsome, weird, caring
> People who like the name Stanislaus also like Tristan, Sheldon, Stephen, Sebastian, Stanley, Curtis, Russell, Alastair, Miles, Jackson

Stanislav (*Slavic*) ♂   RATING: ★★★☆
Becoming glorious
> People think of Stanislav as intelligent, handsome, sexy, caring, cool
> People who like the name Stanislav also like Vladimir, Gabriel, Matthew, Scott, Seth, Lucas, Zachary, Silvain, Xavier, Dominic

Stanislaw (*Polish*) ♂   RATING: ★★★
Becoming glorious—Stanislaw Lem, author
> People think of Stanislaw as handsome, trustworthy, aggressive, intelligent, funny
> People who like the name Stanislaw also like Simon, Jackson, Alexander, Maximilian, Xander, Gregory, Silvain, Sloan, Stavros, Stewart

Stanley (*English*) ♂   RATING: ★★
From the stony field
> People think of Stanley as handsome, intelligent, cool, funny, caring
> People who like the name Stanley also like Jacob, Thomas, Travis, Nicholas, Samuel, Scott, David, Jason, Nathan, Isaac

Stanton (*English*) ♂   RATING: ★★★☆
From the stony town—Originally a surname
> People think of Stanton as intelligent, handsome, funny, leader, powerful
> People who like the name Stanton also like Tristan, Seth, Landon, Tucker, Kaden, Holden, Jackson, Sebastian, Reece, Lucas

Star (*American*) ♀ ♂   RATING: ★★★★
Star—Also spelled Starr; Star Jones, talk show host/attorney; Ringo Starr, musician
> People think of Star as pretty, funny, popular, cool, sexy
> People who like the name Star also like Sky, Skye, Jade, Storm, Rain, Madison, Bailey, Dakota, Logan, Jaden

Starbuck (*English*) ♀ ♂   RATING: ★★☆
From the river where stakes were got—Also a surname; also a nickname; character in *Moby Dick* by Herman Melville
> People think of Starbuck as weird, loser, nerdy, aggressive, intelligent
> People who like the name Starbuck also like Storm, Morgan, Sydney, Mackenzie, Raven, Jade, Phoenix, Toby, Taylor, Dylan

Stash (*American*) ♂   RATING: ★☆
Sun's rays
> People think of Stash as creative, sporty, wild, cool, sexy
> People who like the name Stash also like Kaden, Slade, Sloan, Tristan, Stone, Jayden, Aiden, Brendon, Jackson, Keiran

Stasia (*Russian*) ♀   RATING: ★★★★☆
Resurrection—Short for Anastasia
> People think of Stasia as creative, intelligent, pretty, caring, energetic
> People who like the name Stasia also like Anastasia, Paige, Olivia, Scarlett, Trinity, Bella, Isabella, Anya, Sabrina, Serenity

Stavros (*Greek*) ♂   RATING: ★★★☆
Cross
> People think of Stavros as handsome, powerful, wealthy, popular, exotic
> People who like the name Stavros also like Sebastian, Tristan, Maddox, Xander, Lucas, Peter, Sven, William, Noah, Emerson

Stedman (*English*) ♂   RATING: ★★☆
From the farmstead—Stedman Graham, entrepreneur
> People think of Stedman as big, slow, powerful, intelligent, quiet
> People who like the name Stedman also like Sullivan, Holden, Sloan, Reece, Drake, Sinclair, Topher, Dalton, Beau, Sidney

Stefan (*German*) ♂   RATING: ★★★★
Crown
> People think of Stefan as handsome, sexy, cool, funny, intelligent
> People who like the name Stefan also like Tristan, Jacob, Ethan, Nathan, Seth, Sebastian, Gabriel, Nicholas, Zachary, Aiden

Stefanie (*German*) ♀   RATING: ★★★☆
Crown
> People think of Stefanie as pretty, funny, intelligent, caring, creative
> People who like the name Stefanie also like Stephanie, Samantha, Sabrina, Sarah, Natalie, Rebecca, Faith, Paige, Victoria, Sophie

Stefanos (*Greek*) ♂   RATING: ★★☆
Crown
> People think of Stefanos as handsome, creative, popular, sexy, intelligent
> People who like the name Stefanos also like Nicholas, Andreas, André, Sebastian, Jacob, Marcus, Jason, Erik, Stefan, Adrian

Steffi (*German*) ♀   RATING: ★★
Short for Stephanie—Steffi Graf, tennis player
> People think of Steffi as pretty, funny, popular, young, caring
> People who like the name Steffi also like Isabella, Sophie, Sophia, Sofia, Olivia, Summer, Stella, Zoey, Sadie, Steffie

Steffie (*English*) ♀   RATING: ★★★☆
Short for Stephanie
> People think of Steffie as funny, pretty, young, caring, cool
> People who like the name Steffie also like Paige, Steffi, Stephanie, Jasmine, Sophie, Shantell, Larissa, Emma, Nicole, Amber

Stella (*Latin*) ♀   RATING: ★★☆
Star—Stella McCartney, designer
> People think of Stella as pretty, intelligent, creative, elegant, funny
> People who like the name Stella also like Ava, Olivia, Isabella, Sophia, Ella, Sophie, Scarlett, Grace, Chloe, Bella

Step (*American*) ♂   RATING: ★★☆
Short for Stephen
> People think of Step as nerdy, weird, loser, young, criminal
> People who like the name Step also like Seth, Simon, Aden, Cole, Spike, Tyson, Gage, Vince, Ryker, Stew

Stephan (*Greek*) ♂   RATING: ★★☆
Crown
> People think of Stephan as handsome, funny, intelligent, caring, cool
> People who like the name Stephan also like Ethan, Nicholas, Alexander, Zachary, Nathan, Jacob, Seth, Ian, Samuel, Tristan

Stephanie (*French*) ♀   RATING: ★★★
Crown—Feminine form of Stephen
> People think of Stephanie as pretty, funny, caring, intelligent, creative
> People who like the name Stephanie also like Samantha, Natalie, Paige, Emily, Olivia, Rebecca, Jessica, Hannah, Sarah, Victoria

Stephen (*Greek*) ♂   RATING: ★★★
Crown—Stephen Hawking, scientist; Stephen King, author
> People think of Stephen as handsome, funny, intelligent, caring, cool
> People who like the name Stephen also like Nicholas, Matthew, Michael, Nathan, Ethan, Andrew, Jacob, Zachary, Thomas, William

Sterling (*English*) ♂   RATING: ★★★★
Starling—Originally a surname
> People think of Sterling as handsome, intelligent, funny, energetic, creative
> People who like the name Sterling also like Noah, Kaden, Aiden, Tristan, Jackson, Sebastian, Keagan, Ethan, Jayden, Emerson

Stesha (*Slavic*) ♂   RATING: ★★★
Crown—Short for Stephen
> People think of Stesha as intelligent, weird, pretty, trustworthy, funny
> People who like the name Stesha also like Asher, Sirius, Kaemon, Mikhail, Silas, Liam, Slade, Sebastien, Kaden, Aiden

Steve (*English*) ♂   RATING: ★★
Short for Stephen—Steve Jobs, CEO of Apple computers
> People think of Steve as funny, handsome, intelligent, cool, caring

People who like the name Steve also like Steven, Justin, Jason, Nicholas, Eric, Jack, David, Matthew, Brian, Andrew

514

Steven *(Greek)* ♂　　　　　　RATING: ★★★☆
Crown—Steven Seagal, actor; Steven Sondheim, composer; Steven Spielberg, filmmaker
People think of Steven as funny, handsome, intelligent, caring, cool
People who like the name Steven also like Nathan, Matthew, Nicholas, Michael, Jacob, William, Andrew, Scott, Justin, Jason

Stevie *(English)* ♀♂　　　　RATING: ★★
Short for Stephen or Stephanie—Stevie Nicks, singer; Stevie Wonder, singer/songwriter
People think of Stevie as pretty, funny, popular, caring, cool
People who like the name Stevie also like Taylor, Hayden, Sean, Riley, Logan, Morgan, Skye, Dylan, Tyler, Payton

Stew *(English)* ♂　　　　　　RATING: ★★☆
Steward of the estate or castle—Short for Stewart
People think of Stew as loser, nerdy, unpopular, cool, funny
People who like the name Stew also like Seth, Stewart, Simon, Adam, Stu, Stuart, Scott, Jacob, Ethan, Aaron

Stewart *(Celtic/Gaelic)* ♂　　RATING: ★★★☆
Steward of the estate or castle—James Stewart, actor; Martha Stewart, TV host/media mogul
People think of Stewart as intelligent, handsome, funny, caring, popular
People who like the name Stewart also like Stuart, Ethan, Seth, Owen, Tristan, Ian, Nicholas, Jacob, Samuel, Nathan

Stian *(Scandinavian)* ♂　　　RATING: ★★★☆
Wanderer
People think of Stian as sexy, intelligent, cool, handsome, creative
People who like the name Stian also like Soren, Seth, Slade, Kaden, Lucian, Sebastian, Halden, Korbin, Maddox, Rohan

Stillman *(English)* ♂　　　　RATING: ★☆
Fisherman—Originally a surname
People think of Stillman as big, quiet, caring, uptight, cool
People who like the name Stillman also like Trenton, Maddox, Jackson, Galen, Holden, Walker, Drake, Clayton, Wade, Sidney

Stockton *(English)* ♂　　　　RATING: ★★★
From the monastery town—Originally a surname
People think of Stockton as sporty, intelligent, wealthy, powerful, energetic
People who like the name Stockton also like Jackson, Tristan, Landon, Weston, Tucker, Griffin, Holden, Wade, Sullivan, Wyatt

Stone *(American)* ♂　　　　　RATING: ★★★☆
Rock—Stone Phillips, TV host
People think of Stone as handsome, powerful, cool, energetic, leader
People who like the name Stone also like Seth, Kaden, Gage, Jackson, Noah, Landon, Cole, Zachary, Tristan, Chase

Storm *(American)* ♀♂　　　　RATING: ★★★★☆
Forceful, turbulent weather
People think of Storm as powerful, energetic, cool, wild, aggressive
People who like the name Storm also like Skye, Rain, Sage, Riley, Jaden, Madison, Ryder, Caden, Logan, Shadow

Stormy *(American)* ♀♂　　　RATING: ★★
Impetuous nature
People think of Stormy as creative, pretty, energetic, funny, wild
People who like the name Stormy also like Bailey, Riley, Hayden, Skye, Storm, Sage, Dakota, Skylar, Caden, Taylor

Strom *(German)* ♂　　　　　　RATING: ★★
Stream, flow—Strom Thurmond, U.S. senator
People think of Strom as powerful, weird, old-fashioned, trustworthy, wealthy
People who like the name Strom also like Seth, Landon, Xavier, Xander, Samuel, Stone, Miles, Soren, Lance, Noah

Stu *(English)* ♂　　　　　　　RATING: ★★★
Steward of the estate or castle—Short for Stuart
People think of Stu as old-fashioned, loser, nerdy, old, intelligent
People who like the name Stu also like Seth, Simon, Stuart, Russell, Stew, Stewart, Scott, Ethan, Jacob, Sidney

Stuart *(Celtic/Gaelic)* ♂　　RATING: ★★
Steward of the estate or castle—Also a Scottish surname; character in *Stuart Little*
People think of Stuart as intelligent, funny, handsome, caring, cool
People who like the name Stuart also like Owen, Scott, Nicholas, Ian, Ethan, Nathan, Zachary, Andrew, Samuel, Benjamin

Studs *(American)* ♂　　　　　RATING: ★★
Knobby nail head—Louis "Studs" Terkel, author/historian
People think of Studs as big, criminal, loser, aggressive, lazy
People who like the name Studs also like Spike, Woody, Step, Xakery, Silvain, Colt, Stanley, Jack, Stew, Scott

Suave *(American)* ♀♂　　　　RATING: ★★★
Smooth
People think of Suave as weird, exotic, wild, young, funny
People who like the name Suave also like Sasha, Shay, Sage, Stormy, Santana, Seyah, Saturday, Landen, Sunday, Shannon

Suchi *(Sanskrit/East Indian)* ♀   RATING: ★☆
Radiant glow
> People think of Suchi as intelligent, unpopular, creative, young, pretty
> People who like the name Suchi also like Sitara, Sunila, Saura, Denali, Sumana, Samara, Tamanna, Sachi, Shyla, Sohalia

Suchin *(Thai)* ♀   RATING: ★☆
Beautiful thought
> People think of Suchin as popular, creative, pretty, cool, ethnic
> People who like the name Suchin also like Shiri, Sokanon, Suki, Suri, Emiko, Sachi, Solange, Sunee, Sitara, Soraya

Sue *(English)* ♀   RATING: ★★★☆
Lily—Short for Susan; Sue Grafton, author
> People think of Sue as caring, pretty, funny, intelligent, creative
> People who like the name Sue also like Iris, Emma, Sarah, Sophie, Hailey, Victoria, Lilly, Susan, Nicole, Sophia

Suelita *(Spanish)* ♂   RATING: ★☆
Little lily—Short for Susan
> People think of Suelita as ethnic, pretty, quiet, religious, weird
> People who like the name Suelita also like Angelo, Rhys, Stavros, Diego, Stephan, Malcolm, Slade, Daniel, Samuel, Seamus

Sugar *(American)* ♀   RATING: ★★★☆
Sweet crystal spice—Also a nickname for someone who is sweet
> People think of Sugar as pretty, sexy, girl next door, funny, cool
> People who like the name Sugar also like Summer, Scarlett, Princess, Faith, Grace, Honey, Melody, Snow, Emma, Zoey

Sukey *(English)* ♀   RATING: ★★★☆
Lily—Short for Susan
> People think of Sukey as funny, creative, trustworthy, pretty, artsy
> People who like the name Sukey also like Suki, Rini, Sada, Amaya, Sakura, Mina, Sachi, Nariko, Miya, Michi

Suki *(Japanese)* ♀   RATING: ★★★★
Beloved
> People think of Suki as pretty, creative, intelligent, caring, funny
> People who like the name Suki also like Sakura, Aiko, Amaya, Kaida, Keiko, Emiko, Sachi, Sada, Sadie, Mai

Sullivan *(Celtic/Gaelic)* ♂   RATING: ★★★★
Dark-eyed—Sullivan Ballou, politician; Ed Sullivan, TV host; Susan Sullivan, actress
> People think of Sullivan as intelligent, popular, handsome, leader, funny
> People who like the name Sullivan also like Owen, Liam, Tristan, Jackson, Noah, Ethan, Ian, Keagan, Landon, Harrison

Sully *(English)* ♀♂   RATING: ★★★★
From the south field—Variation of the surname Sudeley; also short for Sullivan
> People think of Sully as intelligent, cool, popular, handsome, powerful
> People who like the name Sully also like Bailey, Sawyer, Logan, Riley, Aidan, Ryan, Shane, Taylor, Sage, Piper

Sulwyn *(Welsh)* ♀   RATING: ★★★
Sun blessed, fair—Pronounced *seel-win*
> People think of Sulwyn as elegant, intelligent, girl next door, funny, poor
> People who like the name Sulwyn also like Mairwen, Aelwen, Olwen, Rhiannon, Shayla, Caelan, Bronwyn, Gwendolyn, Rianna, Morwen

Sumana *(Sanskrit/East Indian)* ♀   RATING: ★★★
Flower
> People think of Sumana as exotic, pretty, elegant, cool, creative
> People who like the name Sumana also like Sitara, Sundari, Shyla, Ishana, Sunila, Suchi, Shanti, Samara, Sumitra, Sienna

Sumayah *(Arabic)* ♀   RATING: ★★
Unknown meaning—The first martyr in Islam
> People think of Sumayah as pretty, intelligent, exotic, creative, elegant
> People who like the name Sumayah also like Samara, Soraya, Samiya, Samira, Sarai, Sahara, Shaylee, Jahzara, Sahirah, Savannah

Sumitra *(Sanskrit/East Indian)* ♀   RATING: ★★
Good friend
> People think of Sumitra as pretty, powerful, young, cool, funny
> People who like the name Sumitra also like Sundari, Sitara, Sunila, Sumana, Sanaa, Sumayah, Sakina, Saniya, Svara, Sevita

Summer *(English)* ♀   RATING: ★★★★
Warm season—Summer Bartholomew, model/actress; Summer Sanders, TV host
> People think of Summer as pretty, popular, funny, creative, energetic
> People who like the name Summer also like Paige, Scarlett, Savannah, Olivia, Faith, Chloe, Autumn, Hannah, Ava, Grace

Suna *(Turkish)* ♀   RATING: ★★★
Duck
> People think of Suna as exotic, creative, pretty, sexy, caring
> People who like the name Suna also like Sienna, Luna, Sofia, Sephora, Stella, Violet, Sadie, Sophia, Sora, Lara

Sundari *(Sanskrit/East Indian)* ♀   RATING: ★★★☆
Beautiful
> People think of Sundari as exotic, funny, pretty, sexy, intelligent
> People who like the name Sundari also like Sienna, Sadie, Shyla, Renée, Sitara, Soleil, Tatiana, Samara, Chandra, Ophelia

Sunday (American) ♀♂   RATING: ★★★☆
Born on Sunday
  People think of Sunday as intelligent, caring, pretty, creative, artsy
  People who like the name Sunday also like Piper, Storm, Madison, Riley, Wednesday, Phoenix, Sydney, Taylor, Sky, Skye

Sundown (American) ♀♂   RATING: ★★☆
Dusk, sunset
  People think of Sundown as exotic, poor, artsy, creative, loser
  People who like the name Sundown also like Sawyer, Sydney, Storm, Madison, Shadow, Jaden, Stormy, Winter, Forest, Sunday

Sunee (Thai) ♀   RATING: ★★
Good thing
  People think of Sunee as pretty, popular, creative, young, artsy
  People who like the name Sunee also like Sadie, Simone, Isabelle, Sophie, Belle, Faith, Scarlett, Hope, Sierra, Tasanee

Sunesh (Sanskrit/East Indian) ♂   RATING: ★★☆
Good
  People think of Sunesh as energetic, sexy, popular, young, winner
  People who like the name Sunesh also like Suvan, Savir, Arnav, Adit, Sanjay, Ashwin, Amish, Ajay, Sanjiv, Abhay

Sunila (Sanskrit/East Indian) ♀   RATING: ★★★☆
Very blue; sapphire blue
  People think of Sunila as exotic, pretty, cool, funny, young
  People who like the name Sunila also like Saniya, Sumitra, Sona, Samara, Shayna, Svara, Soraya, Shyla, Sitara, Suchi

Sunny (English) ♀♂   RATING: ★★★☆
Bright; of the sun—Sunny Bak, photographer
  People think of Sunny as funny, pretty, creative, energetic, young
  People who like the name Sunny also like Jade, Piper, Reese, Madison, Parker, Logan, Raven, Hayden, Dakota, Sydney

Sunshine (English) ♀   RATING: ★★★☆
Rays of sunlight
  People think of Sunshine as pretty, creative, funny, artsy, caring
  People who like the name Sunshine also like Jasmine, Summer, Scarlett, Chloe, Lily, April, Princess, Charlotte, Emily, Sadie

Suoh (Japanese) ♂   RATING: ★★★★
Dragon
  People think of Suoh as handsome, powerful, leader, wealthy, trustworthy
  People who like the name Suoh also like Ryu, Keitaro, Hiroshi, Shino, Haruki, Haru, Kaemon, Yukio, Yasuo, Akio

Suri (Persian) ♀   RATING: ★★☆
Red rose—Also spelled Souri; Suri Cruise, daughter of Tom Cruise and Katie Holmes
  People think of Suri as pretty, exotic, elegant, creative, intelligent
  People who like the name Suri also like Ava, Paige, Chloe, Sienna, Sadie, Hailey, Sari, Sophie, Layla, Sierra

Suruchi (Sanskrit/East Indian) ♀   RATING: ★★☆
Great delight, happiness
  People think of Suruchi as young, pretty, exotic, caring, ethnic
  People who like the name Suruchi also like Shreya, Syrita, Shanti, Kamana, Somatra, Tarika, Bhavna, Sheela, Niyati, Svetlana

Susan (Hebrew) ♀   RATING: ★★☆
Lily—Susan B. Anthony, feminist/suffragette; Susan Sarandon, actress; Susan Sontag, author
  People think of Susan as caring, intelligent, pretty, funny, trustworthy
  People who like the name Susan also like Sarah, Samantha, Rebecca, Hannah, Rachel, Grace, Elizabeth, Abigail, Paige, Sophia

Susane (French) ♀   RATING: ★★★☆
Lily
  People think of Susane as caring, funny, pretty, quiet, winner
  People who like the name Susane also like Samantha, Violet, Isabelle, Nicole, Paige, Charlotte, Valerie, Denise, Madeleine, Suzanne

Susanna (Hebrew) ♀   RATING: ★★☆
Lily—William Shakespeare's daughter
  People think of Susanna as pretty, intelligent, funny, caring, creative
  People who like the name Susanna also like Samantha, Olivia, Sarah, Emily, Natalie, Rebecca, Hannah, Emma, Sophia, Sabrina

Susannah (Hebrew) ♀   RATING: ★★★
Lily
  People think of Susannah as pretty, creative, intelligent, caring, funny
  People who like the name Susannah also like Hannah, Samantha, Olivia, Savannah, Charlotte, Sophia, Abigail, Emma, Sarah, Isabelle

Sushi (Japanese) ♀   RATING: ★★☆
Raw fish
  People think of Sushi as weird, quiet, ethnic, unpopular, old-fashioned
  People who like the name Sushi also like Halo, Karma, Shiva, Chakra

Susie (English) ♀   RATING: ★★
Short for Susan—Susie Wynne, figure skater
  People think of Susie as pretty, caring, funny, trustworthy, young
  People who like the name Susie also like Sophie, Rebecca, Charlotte, Emma, Scarlett, Olivia, Eva, Lily, Samantha, Grace

Sutton *(English)* ♀♂   RATING: ★★
From the south town
> People think of Sutton as cool, weird, popular, wealthy, intelligent
> People who like the name Sutton also like Parker, Addison, Sawyer, Hayden, Preston, Madison, Avery, Ryder, Logan, Riley

Suvan *(Sanskrit/East Indian)* ♂   RATING: ★★★
The sun
> People think of Suvan as intelligent, exotic, wealthy, pretty, handsome
> People who like the name Suvan also like Sunesh, Arnav, Nirav, Taran, Sanjay, Savir, Nalin, Shaun, Tanav, Garren

Suzanne *(French)* ♀   RATING: ★★☆
Lily—Variation of Susan; Suzanne Pleshette, actress; Suzanne Sommers, actress
> People think of Suzanne as funny, caring, creative, pretty, intelligent
> People who like the name Suzanne also like Olivia, Samantha, Victoria, Sarah, Natalie, Elizabeth, Sabrina, Hailey, Grace, Sophie

Suzette *(French)* ♀   RATING: ★★★★
Variation of Susan
> People think of Suzette as pretty, intelligent, funny, creative, caring
> People who like the name Suzette also like Samantha, Sabrina, Scarlett, Sadie, Isabelle, Violet, Olivia, Isabella, Paige, Elizabeth

Suzuki *(Japanese)* ♀   RATING: ★★★☆
Bell tree—Also a brand of car
> People think of Suzuki as pretty, sexy, exotic, cool, girl next door
> People who like the name Suzuki also like Suki, Sakura, Sachi, Kaori, Sada, Kumiko, Kioko, Inari, Masako, Kimi

Suzy *(English)* ♀   RATING: ★★★☆
Short for Susan or Suzanne
> People think of Suzy as pretty, funny, intelligent, popular, creative
> People who like the name Suzy also like Paige, Grace, Sophie, Emma, Josie, Laura, Zoey, Sadie, Scarlett, Isabella

Svana *(Scandinavian)* ♀   RATING: ★★★
Swanlike
> People think of Svana as exotic, pretty, old-fashioned, elegant, cool
> People who like the name Svana also like Svara, Jadyn, Savanna, Gabrielle, Shayla, Eva, Sophia, Samantha, Tatum, Nadia

Svara *(Sanskrit/East Indian)* ♀   RATING: ★★★☆
Breathing
> People think of Svara as pretty, popular, ethnic, young, quiet
> People who like the name Svara also like Svana, Shyla, Samara, Ziarre, Shaylee, Tatiana, Sienna, Samira, Ava, Saniya

Svea *(Scandinavian)* ♀   RATING: ★★★
Sweden—The Swedish word for Sweden
> People think of Svea as pretty, creative, energetic, exotic, caring
> People who like the name Svea also like Linnea, Savea, Sophia, Stella, Ava, Sierra, Kera, Sofia, Leah, Sienna

Svein *(Scandinavian)* ♂   RATING: ★★☆
Boy, young man
> People think of Svein as weird, intelligent, ethnic, loser, funny
> People who like the name Svein also like Soren, Sven, Seth, Stian, Björn, Savir, Serge, Slade, Nero, Shaun

Sven *(Scandinavian)* ♂   RATING: ★★
Boy, young man
> People think of Sven as handsome, sexy, intelligent, young, cool
> People who like the name Sven also like Seth, Noah, Tristan, Xavier, Oliver, William, Owen, Ian, Jack, Holden

Sveta *(Slavic)* ♀   RATING: ★★★☆
Light
> People think of Sveta as funny, pretty, popular, young, exotic
> People who like the name Sveta also like Svetlana, Sonja, Cecilia, Lorelei, Sonya, Tatiana, Sofia, Dasha, Delia, Sissy

Svetlana *(Slavic)* ♀   RATING: ★★
Light
> People think of Svetlana as pretty, exotic, sexy, funny, creative
> People who like the name Svetlana also like Isabella, Nadia, Tatiana, Scarlett, Anastasia, Ava, Violet, Giselle, Adriana, Savannah

Swaantje *(Dutch)* ♀   RATING: ★★☆
Swanlike
> People think of Swaantje as weird, exotic, nerdy, boy next door, ethnic
> People who like the name Swaantje also like Sirvat, Lizeth, Philyra, Destiny, Selena, Gianna, Shaquana, Sissy, Evangeline, Vevina

Swain *(English)* ♂   RATING: ★★★
Boy, servant—Originally a surname
> People think of Swain as creative, lazy, religious, intelligent, young
> People who like the name Swain also like Holden, Noah, Kaden, Isaac, Weston, Owen, Jayden, Maddox, Slade, Garrett

Swann *(English)* ♀♂   RATING: ★★★
Swan—Variation of Swain; originally a surname
> People think of Swann as pretty, intelligent, caring, quiet, exotic
> People who like the name Swann also like Sydney, Skylar, Brooke, Lindsey, Taylor, Paris, Phoenix, Lani, Winter, Skye

517

Syaoran *(Chinese)* ♂   RATING: ★★★★
Little wolf
> People think of Syaoran as handsome, intelligent, trustworthy, powerful, leader
> People who like the name Syaoran also like Aiden, Suoh, Sheng, Long, Suelita, Slade, Sprague, Faolan, Ryu, Simba

Sybil *(Greek)* ♀   RATING: ★★
Prophetess—Sybil Andrews, artist; Sybil Danning, actress
> People think of Sybil as intelligent, creative, pretty, caring, trustworthy
> People who like the name Sybil also like Chloe, Phoebe, Sibyl, Sophia, Sophie, Sofia, Olivia, Sadie, Penelope, Scarlett

Sydnee *(French)* ♀♂   RATING: ★★★★
Variation of St. Denys
> People think of Sydnee as pretty, intelligent, funny, popular, creative
> People who like the name Sydnee also like Sydney, Skylar, Madison, Mackenzie, Bailey, Taylor, Parker, Jaden, Hayden, Riley

Sydney *(French)* ♀♂   RATING: ★★★★
Variation of St. Denys—Sydney Pollack, filmmaker
> People think of Sydney as funny, pretty, creative, intelligent, caring
> People who like the name Sydney also like Madison, Riley, Taylor, Logan, Morgan, Mackenzie, Bailey, Hayden, Addison, Parker

Sylvain *(French)* ♂   RATING: ★★★
Of the forest—Sylvain Sylvain, musician
> People think of Sylvain as intelligent, handsome, caring, funny, trustworthy
> People who like the name Sylvain also like Kaden, Silvain, Seth, Gabriel, Sebastian, Keagan, Jayden, Torrance, Joshua, Zachary

Sylvana *(Latin)* ♀   RATING: ★★
Of the forest
> People think of Sylvana as pretty, exotic, creative, artsy, intelligent
> People who like the name Sylvana also like Silvana, Sienna, Cassandra, Sofia, Bianca, Liana, Savannah, Silvia, Sophia, Ava

Sylvester *(English)* ♂   RATING: ★★★☆
From the forest—Sylvester Stallone, actor; Sylvester, Looney Tunes character
> People think of Sylvester as handsome, cool, intelligent, caring, funny
> People who like the name Sylvester also like Sebastian, Oliver, Vincent, Xavier, Victor, Alexander, Zachary, Felix, Oscar, Isaac

Sylvia *(Latin)* ♀   RATING: ★★☆
Forest—Sylvia Plath, writer
> People think of Sylvia as pretty, intelligent, caring, creative, funny

People who like the name Sylvia also like Sophia, Olivia, Sophie, Hannah, Sabrina, Ava, Samantha, Lydia, Sofia, Stella

Sylvie *(French)* ♀   RATING: ★★★★
Forest—Variation of Sylvia
> People think of Sylvie as pretty, intelligent, creative, caring, funny
> People who like the name Sylvie also like Sophie, Sadie, Madeleine, Ava, Stella, Paige, Olivia, Scarlett, Isabelle, Amelie

Symber *(American)* ♀   RATING: ★★☆
Combination of Simone and Kimber
> People think of Symber as artsy, weird, pretty, creative, lazy
> People who like the name Symber also like Skyla, Olivia, Simone, Eva, Cambree, Kendra, Zoey, Brie, Krisalyn, Keely

Symona *(American)* ♀   RATING: ★★★
To be heard—Variation of Simone
> People think of Symona as pretty, exotic, quiet, aggressive, creative
> People who like the name Symona also like Olivia, Simone, Serena, Sabrina, Samantha, Syrita, Selena, Summer, Sienna, Sierra

Synclair *(English)* ♂   RATING: ★★
From St. Clair, France—Originally a surname
> People think of Synclair as pretty, energetic, sexy, powerful, intelligent
> People who like the name Synclair also like Sebastian, Sinclair, Tristan, Owen, Aiden, Jackson, Oliver, Graham, Ian, Zachary

Synnove *(Scandinavian)* ♀   RATING: ★★
Sun gift
> People think of Synnove as creative, caring, exotic, intelligent, funny
> People who like the name Synnove also like Fiona, Astrid, Genevieve, Rianna, Sophia, Lily, Evangeline, Isis, Ava, Freja

Syrita *(American)* ♀   RATING: ★★★★
Sun—Feminine form of Cyrus
> People think of Syrita as intelligent, pretty, cool, funny, caring
> People who like the name Syrita also like Soraya, Samara, Isabella, Sarina, Sabrina, Seanna, Saniya, Sadie, Serena, Sarai

Syshe *(Hebrew)* ♀♂   RATING: ★★★
Street
> People think of Syshe as funny, sexy, intelligent, untrustworthy, energetic
> People who like the name Syshe also like Sasha, Hayden, Skye, Shea, Jaden, Elan, Cadence, Shane, Cade, Brynn

Taariq (*Arabic*) ♂   RATING: ★★★
Morning star
> People think of Taariq as intelligent, cool, handsome, leader, funny
> People who like the name Taariq also like Tristan, Tyson, Tariq, Tyrell, Tareq, Damian, Kaden, Jayden, Jabari, Taran

Tab (*American*) ♂   RATING: ★★★
Created name—Tab Hunter (aka Arthur Andrew Kehn), actor
> People think of Tab as funny, cool, wild, sexy, intelligent
> People who like the name Tab also like Tad, Mac, Aiden, Tucker, Miles, Slade, Tyson, Zander, Owen, Holden

Taban (*Arabic*) ♂   RATING: ★★
Resplendent; shining
> People think of Taban as intelligent, creative, trustworthy, quiet, exotic
> People who like the name Taban also like Tristan, Kaden, Tiergan, Trey, Tobias, Owen, Taran, Braeden, Ethan, Reece

Taber (*Hungarian*) ♂   RATING: ★★★☆
Camp
> People think of Taber as handsome, funny, leader, cool, powerful
> People who like the name Taber also like Tristan, Kaden, Aiden, Tucker, Caleb, Jacob, Vance, Wyatt, Jayden, Trevor

Tabitha (*Hebrew*) ♀   RATING: ★★☆
A gazelle—Tabitha Soren, MTV reporter; character on *Bewitched*
> People think of Tabitha as pretty, funny, creative, caring, trustworthy
> People who like the name Tabitha also like Samantha, Paige, Olivia, Sabrina, Hannah, Abigail, Isabella, Grace, Faith, Hailey

Tablita (*Native American*) ♀   RATING: ★☆
Tiara—Hopi origin
> People think of Tablita as pretty, poor, energetic, funny, weird
> People who like the name Tablita also like Macha, Sora, Kaya, Tallulah, Tazanna, Ayasha, Taini, Dyani, Sabrina, Fala

Tacey (*English*) ♀♂   RATING: ★★★★
Fruitful—Short for Eustacia
> People think of Tacey as pretty, trustworthy, funny, sexy, energetic
> People who like the name Tacey also like Teagan, Taylor, Taryn, Riley, Hayden, Hadley, Caden, Jaden, Payton, Avery

Tacita (*Latin*) ♀   RATING: ★★★
Silent
> People think of Tacita as quiet, pretty, intelligent, creative, caring
> People who like the name Tacita also like Tahlia, Tanaya, Tabitha, Tadita, Tavita, Tameka, Tana, Tiana, Sabina, Keisha

Tacy (*English*) ♀♂   RATING: ★★★☆
Fruitful—Short for Eustacia; also a surname
> People think of Tacy as pretty, funny, weird, young, trustworthy
> People who like the name Tacy also like Tacey, Riley, Dakota, Tanner, Jaden, Toby, Taylor, Cadence, Taryn, Parker

Tad (*American*) ♂   RATING: ★★
Praise—Short for Thaddaeus
> People think of Tad as handsome, funny, caring, intelligent, cool
> People who like the name Tad also like Tristan, Ethan, Kaden, Todd, Aiden, Tyson, Cole, Noah, Owen, Benjamin

Tadelesh (*African*) ♂   RATING: ★★
Lucky
> People think of Tadelesh as exotic, sexy, intelligent, powerful, winner
> People who like the name Tadelesh also like Tyrell, Tahmores, Taariq, Makalo, Tyson, Tadeo, Tokala, Tavon, Aloysius, Macario

Tadeo (*Spanish*) ♂   RATING: ★★★
Praise—Variation of Thaddeus
> People think of Tadeo as handsome, creative, weird, caring, trustworthy
> People who like the name Tadeo also like Diego, Carlos, Tobias, Samuel, Tristan, Xavier, Elijah, Macario, Pedro, Pablo

Tadhg (*Celtic/Gaelic*) ♂   RATING: ★★★☆
Poet, philosopher
> People think of Tadhg as handsome, creative, caring, popular, cool
> People who like the name Tadhg also like Liam, Owen, Tristan, Declan, Teague, Riordan, Tiergan, Finn, Cillian, Callum

Tadita (*Native American*) ♀   RATING: ★★★
Runner—Omaha origin
> People think of Tadita as energetic, funny, trustworthy, pretty, creative
> People who like the name Tadita also like Tacita, Tallulah, Tanisha, Tahlia, Topanga, Tala, Tabitha, Kaya, Kiona, Taini

Taffy (*Welsh*) ♂   RATING: ★★★
Short for Dafydd; also a soft candy
> People think of Taffy as funny, trustworthy, sexy, weird, cool
> People who like the name Taffy also like Tristan, Teddy, Rhett, Tyson, Tucker, Slade, Taran, Landon, Seth, Jasper

520

Tahirah (*Arabic*) ♀   RATING: ★★★★
Pure
> People think of Tahirah as creative, intelligent, pretty, funny, young
> People who like the name Tahirah also like Tahlia, Tatiana, Tiana, Tanaya, Sahirah, Tariana, Nailah, Saniya, Samara, Jahzara

Tahlia (*Hebrew*) ♀   RATING: ★★★
Morning dew
> People think of Tahlia as pretty, funny, caring, intelligent, creative
> People who like the name Tahlia also like Talia, Olivia, Ava, Tabitha, Tatiana, Hannah, Tiana, Chloe, Thalia, Paige

Tahmores (*Persian*) ♂   RATING: ★☆
Sturdy fox, weasel
> People think of Tahmores as trustworthy, handsome, intelligent, creative, aggressive
> People who like the name Tahmores also like Tyson, Tadelesh, Lucian, Taliesin, Tyrell, Taariq, Tavorian, Tokala, Adish, Tameron

Tai (*Chinese*) ♀ ♂   RATING: ★★☆
Person from Thailand—Tai Babilonia, figure skater
> People think of Tai as funny, intelligent, cool, energetic, popular
> People who like the name Tai also like Kai, Taylor, Hayden, Madison, Ty, Jade, Tyler, Logan, Riley, Parker

Tai Yang (*Chinese*) ♂   RATING: ★★★
Sun
> People think of Tai Yang as loser, ethnic, funny, nerdy, wild
> People who like the name Tai Yang also like Tadeo, Terence, Tarun, Valentino, Yukio, Kael, Yardan, Ryu, Tocho, Taban

Taifa (*Arabic*) ♀ ♂   RATING: ★★☆
Nation, tribe, princedom
> People think of Taifa as ethnic, exotic, quiet, aggressive, girl next door
> People who like the name Taifa also like Teshi, Tene, Taima, Tully, Themba, Taregan, Tiassale, Dakota, Rabia, Tallys

Tailynn (*American*) ♀   RATING: ★★☆
Combination of Tai and Lynn
> People think of Tailynn as pretty, caring, energetic, sexy, intelligent
> People who like the name Tailynn also like Kaelyn, Cailyn, Paige, Jadyn, Talia, Hailey, Hannah, Tahlia, Isabella, Gabriella

Taima (*Native American*) ♀ ♂   RATING: ★★★☆
Thunder crash
> People think of Taima as exotic, pretty, intelligent, popular, creative
> People who like the name Taima also like Dakota, Caden, Taylor, Teagan, Talen, Riley, Tacey, Raven, Jaden, Tyler

Taini (*Native American*) ♀   RATING: ★★
Returning moon—Omaha origin
> People think of Taini as caring, exotic, young, funny, cool
> People who like the name Taini also like Tala, Tehya, Kaya, Tahlia, Takoda, Talli, Amaya, Topanga, Tiana, Sora

Taipa (*Native American*) ♀   RATING: ★★★
Wingspan—Miwok origin
> People think of Taipa as creative, exotic, pretty, cool, intelligent
> People who like the name Taipa also like Taini, Tala, Takoda, Tehya, Tallulah, Tablita, Tadita, Tawana, Amayeta, Talulah

Tait (*Polish*) ♀ ♂   RATING: ★★☆
Cheerful
> People think of Tait as funny, creative, intelligent, energetic, trustworthy
> People who like the name Tait also like Tate, Teagan, Tanner, Riley, Caden, Payton, Parker, Sage, Logan, Reese

Taite (*English*) ♀ ♂   RATING: ★★★☆
Cheerful
> People think of Taite as funny, sporty, pretty, energetic, young
> People who like the name Taite also like Tate, Teagan, Caden, Riley, Tanner, Logan, Parker, Taylor, Reagan, Hayden

Taja (*American*) ♀   RATING: ★★★☆
Short for Anastasia
> People think of Taja as pretty, creative, popular, intelligent, sexy
> People who like the name Taja also like Talia, Tahlia, Tanaya, Tiana, Trinity, Tatiana, Takala, Tahirah, Tailynn, Tia

Takala (*Native American*) ♀   RATING: ★★
Corn tassel
> People think of Takala as exotic, weird, ethnic, wild, creative
> People who like the name Takala also like Taja, Tameka, Tahlia, Tanaya, Tanginika, Tariana, Tahirah, Talia, Tamira, Tatiana

Takoda (*Native American*) ♀   RATING: ★★★★
Friend to everyone—Sioux origin
> People think of Takoda as caring, powerful, funny, intelligent, energetic
> People who like the name Takoda also like Kaya, Topanga, Tala, Tallulah, Tehya, Hailey, Soraya, Trinity, Ayasha, Tatum

Tal (*Hebrew*) ♀ ♂   RATING: ★★★★
Morning dew—Sometimes short for Tallie or Talia
> People think of Tal as creative, funny, handsome, exotic, caring
> People who like the name Tal also like Taylor, Tyler, Evan, Tate, Paxton, Ryan, Ty, Dylan, Hayden, Cade

Tala *(Native American)* ♀ RATING: ★★★★
Wolf
People think of Tala as intelligent, pretty, wild, creative, energetic
People who like the name Tala also like Talia, Amaya, Kaya, Kaida, Layla, Kali, Tara, Tahlia, Takoda, Ella

Talaith *(Welsh)* ♀ RATING: ★★☆
Crown
People think of Talaith as exotic, elegant, caring, weird, lazy
People who like the name Talaith also like Hafwen, Tahlia, Synnove, Thisbe, Biana, Anchoret, Apple, Keola, Seren, Raewyn

Talasi *(Native American)* ♀ ♂ RATING: ★★★
Cornflower
People think of Talasi as energetic, exotic, old-fashioned, creative, weird
People who like the name Talasi also like Mika, Nida, Taregan, Niabi, Dakota, Misae, Kishi, Helki, Quinn, Taima

Talbot *(English)* ♂ RATING: ★★
Valley bold
People think of Talbot as intelligent, trustworthy, old-fashioned, funny, nerdy
People who like the name Talbot also like Tristan, Walker, Noah, Wade, Gabriel, Quentin, Holden, Ian, Sidney, Lucas

Tale *(Egyptian)* ♀ RATING: ★★★☆
Green
People think of Tale as exotic, young, wild, weird, artsy
People who like the name Tale also like Taya, Tala, Tamara, Sadie, Tabitha, Tahirah, Teela, Nailah, Eve, Naeva

Talen *(American)* ♀ ♂ RATING: ★★★★★
Variation of Talon
People think of Talen as handsome, popular, sporty, leader, cool
People who like the name Talen also like Caden, Jaden, Hayden, Teagan, Parker, Tanner, Riley, Logan, Landen, Madison

Talia *(Hebrew)* ♀ RATING: ★★★
Morning dew—Talia Shire, actress
People think of Talia as pretty, funny, creative, caring, intelligent
People who like the name Talia also like Ava, Olivia, Isabella, Grace, Paige, Chloe, Tahlia, Eva, Ella, Mia

Taliesin *(Welsh)* ♂ RATING: ★★
Radiant brow—Mythical poet in Welsh lore
People think of Taliesin as creative, cool, intelligent, powerful, popular
People who like the name Taliesin also like Tristan, Gareth, Rhys, Kael, Gavin, Asher, Aiden, Alexander, Braeden, Liam

Taline *(Armenian)* ♀ RATING: ★★★☆
A town in Armenia
People think of Taline as cool, pretty, intelligent, young, funny

People who like the name Taline also like Summer, Vivian, Sophie, Talia, Sadie, Selene, Talleen, Tanith, Pearl, Tiana

Talisa *(American)* ♀ RATING: ★★☆
Combination of Talia and Lisa
People think of Talisa as pretty, funny, intelligent, caring, trustworthy
People who like the name Talisa also like Talia, Talisha, Tatiana, Samara, Tahlia, Jadyn, Tiana, Tanaya, Tyra, Elise

Talisha *(American)* ♀ RATING: ★★★★
Combination of Talitha and Alisha
People think of Talisha as pretty, funny, sexy, caring, popular
People who like the name Talisha also like Tahlia, Talisa, Aaliyah, Tiana, Tatiana, Jasmine, Talia, Tanisha, Tameka, Danika

Talitha *(Hebrew)* ♀ RATING: ★★★★
Maiden; child
People think of Talitha as pretty, creative, intelligent, funny, caring
People who like the name Talitha also like Tahlia, Tabitha, Tatiana, Chloe, Isabelle, Talia, Gabrielle, Grace, Talisha, Zoe

Talleen *(Armenian)* ♀ RATING: ★★☆
Variation of Taline
People think of Talleen as exotic, aggressive, unpopular, pretty, untrustworthy
People who like the name Talleen also like Marissa, Summer, Sabrina, Tiana, Calista, Tamira, Tanika, Makayla, Shanti, Scarlett

Talli *(Native American)* ♀ RATING: ★★★★
Town—Creek origin; short for Tallulah
People think of Talli as intelligent, funny, pretty, cool, caring
People who like the name Talli also like Ella, Tia, Talia, Sadie, Tahlia, Layla, Keely, Tala, Callie, Mia

Tallis *(English)* ♀ ♂ RATING: ★★★☆
Forehead
People think of Tallis as intelligent, energetic, creative, funny, pretty
People who like the name Tallis also like Talen, Sage, Teagan, Tarin, Tallys, Torrin, Willow, Landen, Connor, Rowan

Tallulah *(Native American)* ♀ RATING: ★★★★
Town—Creek origin; Tallulah Bankhead, actress; Tallulah River and Tallulah Falls, Georgia
People think of Tallulah as pretty, creative, artsy, exotic, intelligent
People who like the name Tallulah also like Olivia, Scarlett, Ava, Ella, Lola, Isabella, Tabitha, Eva, Lily, Grace

Tallys *(English)* ♀ ♂ RATING: ★★
Forehead—Variation of Tallis
People think of Tallys as artsy, funny, weird, popular, pretty

People who like the name Tallys also like Teagan, Taryn, Tallis, Talon, Taylor, Tayten, Piper, Tierney, Tarin, Morgan

Talmai *(Hebrew)* ♂　　　　RATING: ★★
Mound, hill
People think of Talmai as loser, weird, wild, funny, unpopular
People who like the name Talmai also like Tameron, Tarun, Tremain, Talbot, Taliesin, Tuari, Thian, Mohan, Trory, Vachel

Talon *(English)* ♀♂　　　　RATING: ★★☆
Bird claw
People think of Talon as handsome, popular, leader, cool, intelligent
People who like the name Talon also like Caden, Talen, Hayden, Riley, Jaden, Tanner, Parker, Taylor, Logan, Bailey

Talor *(Hebrew)* ♀　　　　RATING: ★★★☆
Morning dew
People think of Talor as pretty, funny, cool, popular, young
People who like the name Talor also like Hailey, Paige, Faith, Sadie, Olivia, Kailey, Abigail, Isabella, Chloe, Grace

Talulah *(Native American)* ♀　　　　RATING: ★★★★
Leaping water—Choctaw origin
People think of Talulah as pretty, artsy, creative, cool, intelligent
People who like the name Talulah also like Tallulah, Scarlett, Paige, Olivia, Grace, Lola, Chloe, Ella, Ava, Penelope

Tam *(Hebrew)* ♂　　　　RATING: ★★★★
Innocent, honest, naive
People think of Tam as funny, intelligent, caring, creative, young
People who like the name Tam also like Nathan, Owen, Jared, Todd, Miles, Nate, Micah, Tucker, Trent, Taran

Tama *(Japanese)* ♀　　　　RATING: ★★★☆
Jewel—Tama Janowitz, novelist
People think of Tama as pretty, funny, energetic, intelligent, creative
People who like the name Tama also like Sakura, Kaori, Suki, Ayame, Amaya, Kaida, Kohana, Inari, Mina, Keiko

Tamah *(Hebrew)* ♀　　　　RATING: ★★
Innocent, honest, naive
People think of Tamah as pretty, trustworthy, young, caring, creative
People who like the name Tamah also like Tanaya, Tamara, Tahlia, Samara, Tiana, Trinity, Talor, Tamia, Talisa, Tamar

Tamal *(Sanskrit/East Indian)* ♀　　　　RATING: ★★★☆
Dark tree
People think of Tamal as powerful, exotic, leader, popular, winner
People who like the name Tamal also like Tamanna, Tarika, Ebony, Delilah, Iris, Tarala, Tanuja, Cassandra, Alanna, Kali

Tamanna *(Sanskrit/East Indian)* ♀　　　　RATING: ★★★☆
Desire
People think of Tamanna as pretty, intelligent, cool, creative, sexy
People who like the name Tamanna also like Tarika, Tanaya, Tanika, Tarala, Triveni, Tanuja, Tessa, Kamana, Tvisha, Tarannum

Tamar *(Hebrew)* ♀　　　　RATING: ★★★☆
Palm tree
People think of Tamar as pretty, caring, intelligent, creative, funny
People who like the name Tamar also like Tamara, Samara, Talia, Tatiana, Hannah, Tara, Chloe, Giselle, Maya, Tahlia

Tamara *(Russian)* ♀　　　　RATING: ★★★★
Palm tree
People think of Tamara as pretty, funny, intelligent, creative, caring
People who like the name Tamara also like Paige, Samantha, Faith, Hannah, Gabrielle, Hailey, Tabitha, Victoria, Olivia, Sabrina

Tamarr *(American)* ♀　　　　RATING: ★★
Variation of Tamar
People think of Tamarr as ethnic, sexy, artsy, loser, sneaky
People who like the name Tamarr also like Abrianna, Sahara, Kacy, Alayna, Serenity, Garnet, Tyra, Vera, Samara, Roxie

Tamary *(American)* ♀♂　　　　RATING: ★★★
Palm tree
People think of Tamary as pretty, exotic, creative, trustworthy, intelligent
People who like the name Tamary also like Taryn, Tayten, Holly, Brooklyn, Caden, Jaden, Cadence, Skye, Paris, Parker

Tamas *(Hungarian)* ♂　　　　RATING: ★★★
Twin—Variation of Thomas
People think of Tamas as big, trustworthy, slow, quiet, intelligent
People who like the name Tamas also like Tristan, Tyson, Kael, Dane, Kaden, Conner, Edan, Marcus, Nicholas, Eamon

Tamasha *(American)* ♀　　　　RATING: ★☆
Combination of Tamar and Asha
People think of Tamasha as creative, intelligent, funny, pretty, ethnic
People who like the name Tamasha also like Tamira, Talisha, Tasha, Tanisha, Tamitha, Tamara, Taya, Kassandra, Tanika, Tariana

Tamasine *(English)* ♀　　　　RATING: ★★★
Twin
People think of Tamasine as wild, pretty, artsy, exotic, creative
People who like the name Tamasine also like Kimi, Toshi, Haruko, Kaida, Yoshi, Aiko, Sakura, Rini, Miyoko, Amaya

Tamatha *(American)* ♀   RATING: ★★
Combination of Tamar and Tabatha
> People think of Tamatha as caring, pretty, religious, intelligent, creative
>
> People who like the name Tamatha also like Tamara, Taya, Bianca, Tammy, Trista, Oliana, Talisha, Tabitha, Talitha, Isabella

Tamber *(American)* ♀   RATING: ★★★☆
Music pitch—Variation of the musical term timbre; pronounced *TAM-ber*; also spelled Tambre
> People think of Tamber as creative, pretty, funny, trustworthy, intelligent
>
> People who like the name Tamber also like Summer, Tabitha, Jadyn, Tessa, Chloe, Rhiannon, Zoe, Olivia, Lorelei, Nadia

Tameka *(American)* ♀   RATING: ★★★★
Variation of Tamika
> People think of Tameka as pretty, funny, intelligent, caring, sexy
>
> People who like the name Tameka also like Tamika, Tahlia, Tatiana, Tanika, Tiana, Talisha, Aaliyah, Trinity, Layla, Tamara

Tamera *(English)* ♀   RATING: ★★★★
Variation of Tamara—Tamera Mowry, actress
> People think of Tamera as pretty, funny, caring, intelligent, creative
>
> People who like the name Tamera also like Tamara, Paige, Hannah, Samara, Hailey, Faith, Tabitha, Destiny, Olivia, Gabrielle

Tameron *(American)* ♂   RATING: ★★★★
Combination of Tam and Cameron
> People think of Tameron as leader, popular, handsome, trendy, young
>
> People who like the name Tameron also like Kaden, Tristan, Jayden, Tyson, Aiden, Landon, Maddox, Noah, Jackson, Caleb

Tamesis *(English)* ♀♂   RATING: ★★★☆
Dark one—The river Thames
> People think of Tamesis as powerful, creative, exotic, elegant, aggressive
>
> People who like the name Tamesis also like Tynan, Talen, Nox, Teagan, Darcy, Taima, Seath, Shoney, Theron, Kerry

Tamia *(Latin)* ♀   RATING: ★★★★
Chipmunk—Variation of Tammy or Tamara
> People think of Tamia as pretty, intelligent, funny, young, cool
>
> People who like the name Tamia also like Aaliyah, Tiana, Mia, Tamara, Tatiana, Tia, Tiara, Tanaya, Tyra, Trinity

Tamika *(American)* ♀   RATING: ★★★☆
Combination of Tamar and –ika
> People think of Tamika as pretty, funny, caring, sexy, intelligent
>
> People who like the name Tamika also like Tatiana, Tameka, Tahlia, Trinity, Tanika, Aaliyah, Tabitha, Destiny, Kayla, Tyra

Tamira *(American)* ♀   RATING: ★★☆
A spice; palm tree—Variation of Tamara
> People think of Tamira as pretty, funny, creative, trustworthy, young
>
> People who like the name Tamira also like Tamara, Tatiana, Tessa, Tamika, Tiara, Aaliyah, Talisha, Talia, Tiana, Sabrina

Tamitha *(American)* ♀   RATING: ★★☆
Combination of Tamar and Tabitha
> People think of Tamitha as creative, caring, young, leader, trustworthy
>
> People who like the name Tamitha also like Tamira, Tabitha, Larissa, Sarah, Tameka, Tana, Talisha, Malissa, Marissa, Kera

Tamma *(American)* ♀   RATING: ★★
Variation of Tammy
> People think of Tamma as pretty, funny, creative, cool, sexy
>
> People who like the name Tamma also like Tamara, Sabrina, Jemma, Tammy, Emma, Shaina, Jana, Kara, Tara, Dara

Tammy *(English)* ♀   RATING: ★★★☆
Short for Tamsin or Tamara—Tammy Faye Bakker, evangelist/author; Tammy Wynette, singer
> People think of Tammy as funny, pretty, caring, trustworthy, intelligent
>
> People who like the name Tammy also like Samantha, Hannah, Amber, Rebecca, Paige, Emily, Sabrina, Emma, Rachel, Jasmine

Tamra *(American)* ♀   RATING: ★★★★
Variation of Tamara
> People think of Tamra as funny, pretty, caring, trustworthy, creative
>
> People who like the name Tamra also like Paige, Tamara, Hailey, Sophie, Isabella, Isabelle, Hannah, Natalie, Tessa, Faith

Tamsyn *(English)* ♀   RATING: ★★★☆
A twin
> People think of Tamsyn as sexy, funny, intelligent, cool, popular
>
> People who like the name Tamsyn also like Ashleigh, Pippa, Aaliyah, Christina, Layla, Megan, Pearlie, Tatum, Tanaya, Paprika

Tamyra *(American)* ♀   RATING: ★★★☆
Combination of Tamar and Myra—Tamyra Gray, singer/actress
> People think of Tamyra as pretty, popular, funny, cool, caring
>
> People who like the name Tamyra also like Tamara, Paige, Trinity, Savannah, Tiana, Victoria, Keira, Tatiana, Tyra, Jadyn

Tan *(Vietnamese)* ♂   RATING: ★★★☆
New
> People think of Tan as aggressive, funny, young, intelligent, nerdy

People who like the name Tan also like Thomas, Arne, Quade, Shaun, Stephen, Taffy, Marshall, Levi, Ralph, Terence

Tana *(American)* ♀ RATING: ★★★★
Short for Montana
People think of Tana as funny, caring, pretty, intelligent, trustworthy
People who like the name Tana also like Tiana, Tatiana, Tessa, Paige, Tegan, Nadia, Emma, Talia, Layla, Sabrina

Tanav *(Sanskrit/East Indian)* ♂ RATING: ★★★
Flute
People think of Tanav as quiet, cool, ethnic, sporty, weird
People who like the name Tanav also like Tanay, Tarak, Viral, Varen, Suvan, Rohak, Rushil, Tariq, Savir, Arnav

Tanay *(Sanskrit/East Indian)* ♂ RATING: ★★★
From the family
People think of Tanay as intelligent, funny, weird, cool, caring
People who like the name Tanay also like Tanav, Tarak, Rohak, Rushil, Savir, Amish, Arav, Arnav, Tyson, Taran

Tanaya *(Sanskrit/East Indian)* ♀ RATING: ★★★★
Daughter
People think of Tanaya as aggressive, caring, big, cool, pretty
People who like the name Tanaya also like Tahlia, Tiana, Tatiana, Talia, Anaya, Tahirah, Tania, Tarika, Ayanna, Tiara

Tandice *(American)* ♀ RATING: ★★☆
Combination of Tania and Candice
People think of Tandice as popular, energetic, creative, leader, weird
People who like the name Tandice also like Chloe, Summer, Tahlia, Tatum, Natalie, Felicity, Sienna, Mercedes, Tamber, Jasmine

Tanessa *(American)* ♀ RATING: ★★★
Combination of Tania and Vanessa
People think of Tanessa as sporty, creative
People who like the name Tanessa also like Tynice, Tessa, Tanaya, Tiana, Trinity, Tariana, Tahlia, Tailynn, Eva, Jamila

Tangia *(American)* ♀ RATING: ★★★
The angel
People think of Tangia as sexy, funny, creative, cool, energetic
People who like the name Tangia also like Tanaya, Topanga, Tarika, Tyronica, Tatiana, Tiana, Nerissa, Raisa, Tessa, Tanginika

Tanginika *(American)* ♀ RATING: ★★☆
Lake goddess
People think of Tanginika as ethnic, weird, exotic, pretty, wild
People who like the name Tanginika also like Tatiana, Tameka, Tana, Tarika, Tamika, Violet, Tanika, Takala, Tania, Tanisha

Tania *(Russian)* ♀ RATING: ★★★★
Fairy queen—Originally short for Tatiana
People think of Tania as pretty, funny, intelligent, caring, creative
People who like the name Tania also like Tatiana, Nadia, Talia, Tahlia, Vanessa, Sofia, Tiana, Sabrina, Tanaya, Emma

Taniel *(Armenian)* ♂ RATING: ★★★
Variation of Daniel
People think of Taniel as sexy, intelligent, creative, caring, trustworthy
People who like the name Taniel also like Tristan, Taran, Keagan, Seth, Sebastian, Kaden, Xavier, Owen, Tameron, Darian

Tanika *(Sanskrit/East Indian)* ♀ RATING: ★★
Rope
People think of Tanika as pretty, caring, creative, funny, sexy
People who like the name Tanika also like Tamika, Tarika, Tameka, Tanisha, Tiana, Tanaya, Tyra, Talia, Tamanna, Tahlia

Tanis *(Greek)* ♀ RATING: ★★★☆
Serpent
People think of Tanis as intelligent, pretty, funny, creative, trustworthy
People who like the name Tanis also like Tatiana, Hailey, Iris, Thais, Justine, Sabina, Sienna, Thea, Veronica, Cassandra

Tanisha *(American)* ♀ RATING: ★★★★
Variation of Tania
People think of Tanisha as pretty, funny, caring, intelligent, sexy
People who like the name Tanisha also like Tiana, Talisha, Tanika, Faith, Tamara, Tahlia, Tamika, Gabriella, Tameka, Kayla

Tanith *(Greek)* ♀ RATING: ★★☆
Goddess of love—Tanith Belbin, figure skater
People think of Tanith as pretty, intelligent, exotic, creative, artsy
People who like the name Tanith also like Chloe, Talia, Tatum, Leah, Kaelyn, Zoey, Phoebe, Olivia, Tessa, Felicity

Tannar *(English)* ♀♂ RATING: ★★☆
Leather worker
People think of Tannar as cool, handsome, funny, young, intelligent
People who like the name Tannar also like Tanner, Caden, Taylor, Parker, Logan, Tyler, Hayden, Payton, Jaden, Teagan

Tanner *(German)* ♀♂ RATING: ★★☆
Leather worker
People think of Tanner as funny, handsome, cool, sporty, intelligent
People who like the name Tanner also like Parker, Taylor, Logan, Hayden, Caden, Riley, Tyler, Mason, Preston, Connor

Tannis *(Greek)* ♀   RATING: ★★★☆
Variation of Tanith
    People think of Tannis as pretty, intelligent, creative,
    caring, trustworthy
    People who like the name Tannis also like Chloe, Tessa,
    Tanith, Tegan, Summer, Emma, Paige, Tess, Giselle, Keira

Tansy *(Native American)* ♀   RATING: ★★★★
Flower—Hopi origin
    People think of Tansy as pretty, energetic, funny, caring,
    sexy
    People who like the name Tansy also like Sadie, Tessa,
    Tabitha, Tatiana, Tahlia, Talia, Ivy, Olivia, Madeleine, Layla

Tanuja *(Sanskrit/East Indian)* ♀   RATING: ★★★
Daughter
    People think of Tanuja as pretty, intelligent, caring,
    trustworthy, creative
    People who like the name Tanuja also like Tarika,
    Tanaya, Tanika, Tamanna, Tarala, Tarannum, Tvisha,
    Triveni, Toral, Tamal

Tanwen *(Welsh)* ♀   RATING: ★★★
White fire
    People think of Tanwen as creative, intelligent, wild,
    weird, young
    People who like the name Tanwen also like Sorcha,
    Kenda, Halle, Celeste, Juliet, Kendra, Athena, Rhiannon,
    Ildri, Maren

Tanya *(Russian)* ♀   RATING: ★★★★
Fairy queen
    People think of Tanya as pretty, funny, caring, intelli-
    gent, trustworthy
    People who like the name Tanya also like Sabrina, Paige,
    Olivia, Hannah, Rebecca, Vanessa, Hailey, Nadia, Sarah,
    Natalie

Tao *(Chinese)* ♀ ♂   RATING: ★★★★
Peach, long life—Also a female Japanese name
    People think of Tao as creative, handsome, caring,
    funny, ethnic
    People who like the name Tao also like Kai, Taylor,
    Connor, Teagan, Devon, Logan, Dakota, Hayden, Aidan,
    Skye

Tappen *(Welsh)* ♀ ♂   RATING: ★★☆
Top of the hanging rock
    People think of Tappen as handsome, sexy, exotic, wild,
    powerful
    People who like the name Tappen also like Teagan,
    Tanner, Taylor, Logan, Lyndon, Tayten, Monroe, Piper,
    Tarin, London

Tara *(Celtic/Gaelic)* ♀   RATING: ★★★
Tower; hillside—Tara Lipinski, figure skater; Tara Reid,
actress
    People think of Tara as pretty, funny, caring, intelligent,
    creative
    People who like the name Tara also like Paige, Hannah,
    Hailey, Emma, Grace, Olivia, Ava, Erin, Chloe, Keira

Tarachand *(Sanskrit/East Indian)* ♀ ♂   RATING: ★★★
Star
    People think of Tarachand as exotic, weird, ethnic,
    aggressive, loser
    People who like the name Tarachand also like Tene,
    Deven, Topaz, Tallis, Taima, Tallys, Tayten, Deva, Daruka,
    Virendra

Tarak *(Sanskrit/East Indian)* ♂   RATING: ★★
Protector
    People think of Tarak as handsome, intelligent, power-
    ful, exotic, energetic
    People who like the name Tarak also like Tristan, Gavin,
    Taran, Kaden, Maddox, Tariq, Ian, Gabriel, Jayden, Caleb

Tarala *(Sanskrit/East Indian)* ♀   RATING: ★★★
Honeybee
    People think of Tarala as pretty, caring, funny, girl next
    door, intelligent
    People who like the name Tarala also like Tarika,
    Tamanna, Tanaya, Tanika, Tarannum, Tanuja, Tamara,
    Tamal, Tvisha, Triveni

Taran *(Celtic/Gaelic)* ♂   RATING: ★★★☆
Thunder—Also Persian meaning white rose or field
    People think of Taran as intelligent, caring, cool, funny,
    creative
    People who like the name Taran also like Tristan, Kaden,
    Keagan, Aiden, Noah, Ethan, Gavin, Braden, Jayden,
    Landon

Tarana *(African)* ♀   RATING: ★★☆
Born during the day—From the Hausa tribe of Nigeria
    People think of Tarana as exotic, quiet, pretty, powerful,
    popular
    People who like the name Tarana also like Tariana,
    Tanisha, Tanika, Tazara, Trista, Tabitha, Deandra, Tanaya,
    Gabriella, Tamara

Tarangini *(Sanskrit/East Indian)* ♀   RATING: ★★☆
River
    People think of Tarangini as pretty, exotic, creative,
    funny, sexy
    People who like the name Tarangini also like Tarika,
    Tanika, Tarala, Devica, Triveni, Trishna, Teja, Tarannum,
    Tanuja, Tamanna

Tarannum *(Sanskrit/East Indian)* ♀   RATING: ★★☆
Melody
    People think of Tarannum as sexy, weird, poor, wealthy,
    unpopular
    People who like the name Tarannum also like Tarika,
    Tanika, Tanuja, Tamanna, Tarala, Triveni, Tanaya, Tvisha,
    Toral, Tamal

Taregan *(Native American)* ♀ ♂   RATING: ★★☆
Crane—Algonquin origin
    People think of Taregan as weird, exotic, quiet, unpopu-
    lar, old-fashioned
    People who like the name Taregan also like Teagan,
    Mika, Tanner, Dakota, Logan, Talen, Payton, Torrin,
    Theron, Taryn

Tareq (*Arabic*) ♂ RATING: ★★★☆
Path
People think of Tareq as leader, sexy, intelligent, religious, caring
People who like the name Tareq also like Tariq, Tristan, Tyson, Taariq, Malik, Kaden, Trey, Taurean, Kyson, Maddox

Tariana (*American*) ♀ RATING: ★★★
Combination of Tara and Ariana—Also possibly a variation of the Welsh word *tarian* meaning shield
People think of Tariana as pretty, popular, cool, trendy, elegant
People who like the name Tariana also like Tatiana, Tiana, Talia, Tahlia, Tailynn, Trinity, Rianna, Abrianna, Paige, Tanaya

Tarika (*Sanskrit/East Indian*) ♀ RATING: ★★
Star
People think of Tarika as exotic, pretty, wild, energetic, powerful
People who like the name Tarika also like Tanaya, Tanika, Tiana, Tanuja, Tamanna, Tanisha, Tarala, Tahirah, Talia, Tiara

Tarin (*American*) ♀♂ RATING: ★★★★
Of the earth—Variation of Terran or Taran
People think of Tarin as creative, funny, caring, cool, pretty
People who like the name Tarin also like Taryn, Caden, Teagan, Riley, Jaden, Hayden, Torrin, Talen, Aidan, Payton

Tariq (*Sanskrit/East Indian*) ♂ RATING: ★★★☆
Morning star
People think of Tariq as handsome, intelligent, funny, caring, cool
People who like the name Tariq also like Tristan, Tareq, Taariq, Tarak, Jayden, Tavon, Malik, Jabari, Tyson, Amir

Tarisai (*African*) ♀ RATING: ★★
Look, behold—Zimbabwe origin
People think of Tarisai as pretty, sexy, exotic, caring, unpopular
People who like the name Tarisai also like Terehasa, Tanisha, Tazara, Tarana, Tasanee, Tarika, Tanaya, Trinity, Butterfly, Tatiana

Tarmon (*Celtic/Gaelic*) ♂ RATING: ★★☆
Church land—Irish place name; also a surname
People think of Tarmon as handsome, trustworthy, boy next door, young, trendy
People who like the name Tarmon also like Tristan, Tremain, Tiergan, Eamon, Aiden, Tiernan, Taran, Keagan, Torrance, Braeden

Taru (*Sanskrit/East Indian*) ♂ RATING: ★★★
Small plant
People think of Taru as powerful, weird, quiet, pretty, caring
People who like the name Taru also like Tarak, Fai, Taran, Haru, Haruki, Gage, Taliesin, Troy, Tokala, Caleb

Tarun (*Sanskrit/East Indian*) ♂ RATING: ★★★☆
Young male
People think of Tarun as intelligent, young, exotic, handsome, sexy
People who like the name Tarun also like Taran, Tristan, Tarak, Varun, Tavon, Ethan, Conner, Seth, Reece, Trent

Taryn (*American*) ♀♂ RATING: ★★★
Combination of Tara and Erin; also a variation of Taran or Terran
People think of Taryn as pretty, funny, caring, creative, intelligent
People who like the name Taryn also like Hayden, Riley, Teagan, Taylor, Madison, Caden, Addison, Logan, Aidan, Jaden

Tas (*Hungarian*) ♂ RATING: ★★★
Mythological name
People think of Tas as exotic, aggressive, powerful, funny, cool
People who like the name Tas also like Isaiah, Troy, Tyson, Kaleb, Caleb, Caesar, Darian, Theo, Levi, Anthony

Tasanee (*Thai*) ♀ RATING: ★★★☆
Beautiful view
People think of Tasanee as pretty, exotic, popular, funny, intelligent
People who like the name Tasanee also like Tahirah, Tiana, Tegan, Tahlia, Tansy, Tanaya, Keyanna, Sunee, Tessa, Tarika

Tasha (*English*) ♀ RATING: ★★★★
Born on Christmas day—Short for Natasha
People think of Tasha as pretty, funny, caring, creative, intelligent
People who like the name Tasha also like Tessa, Olivia, Paige, Hailey, Hannah, Sadie, Samantha, Tiffany, Vanessa, Natalie

Tasmine (*American*) ♀ RATING: ★★★☆
Combination of Tamsin and Jasmine
People think of Tasmine as pretty, intelligent, exotic, funny, caring
People who like the name Tasmine also like Paige, Jasmine, Tabitha, Tegan, Phoebe, Scarlett, Natalia, Tiana, Tameka, Olivia

Tasnim (*Arabic*) ♀ RATING: ★★★
Paradise fountain
People think of Tasnim as pretty, funny, intelligent, young, creative
People who like the name Tasnim also like Tara, Josephine, Serenity, Scarlett, Bianca, Talor, Rosaleen, Eve, Tatiana, Kiley

Tassos (*Greek*) ♂ RATING: ★★★
Resurrection—Short for Anastasios
People think of Tassos as handsome, creative, trustworthy, caring, funny
People who like the name Tassos also like Tristan, Matthias, Miles, Telly, Luke, Jayden, Tertius, Xenos, Sanders, Thanos

Tasya *(Slavic)* ♀   RATING: ★★★
Short for Anastasia
> People think of Tasya as pretty, exotic, funny, popular, trustworthy
> People who like the name Tasya also like Talia, Tatiana, Trinity, Thalia, Tiana, Nadia, Olivia, Tessa, Raina, Telyn

Tate *(English)* ♀ ♂   RATING: ★★★
Cheerful—Tate Donovan, actor
> People think of Tate as intelligent, handsome, popular, funny, caring
> People who like the name Tate also like Parker, Tanner, Logan, Taylor, Avery, Hayden, Reese, Riley, Caden, Addison

Tatiana *(Russian)* ♀   RATING: ★★★
Fairy queen
> People think of Tatiana as pretty, funny, intelligent, creative, caring
> People who like the name Tatiana also like Isabella, Nadia, Tiana, Olivia, Ava, Natalia, Adriana, Aaliyah, Gabriella, Anastasia

Tatum *(English)* ♀   RATING: ★★☆
Cheerful, full of spirit—Tatum O'Neal, actress
> People think of Tatum as pretty, funny, popular, energetic, creative
> People who like the name Tatum also like Paige, Ava, Olivia, Chloe, Sadie, Ella, Grace, Emma, Isabella, Tegan

Taurean *(American)* ♂   RATING: ★★
Born under the sign of taurus
> People think of Taurean as funny, handsome, cool, sexy, aggressive
> People who like the name Taurean also like Tristan, Taran, Tyson, Jayden, Torrance, Kaden, Maddox, Noah, Tyrell, Trey

Tauret *(Egyptian)* ♀   RATING: ★★☆
Goddess of pregnant women—Also spelled Taweret
> People think of Tauret as exotic, aggressive, artsy, weird, criminal
> People who like the name Tauret also like Isis, Tana, Tahirah, Kali, Deirdre, Tanith, Sanura, Tale, Nenet, Lorelei

Taurus *(Latin)* ♀ ♂   RATING: ★★★☆
The bull—Used for children born under this astrological sign
> People think of Taurus as aggressive, powerful, big, cool, sporty
> People who like the name Taurus also like Taylor, James, Ireland, Jade, Aquarius, Sydney, Cameron, Raven, Shane, Jordan

Tausiq *(Arabic)* ♂   RATING: ★★☆
Reinforcement
> People think of Tausiq as ethnic, aggressive, slow, powerful, criminal
> People who like the name Tausiq also like Tariq, Taurean, Thaman, Tareq, Tavon, Marcus, Vance, Jabari, Tavorian, Tanav

Tavaril *(English)* ♀   RATING: ★★
Character in the *Lord of the Rings* trilogy by J.R.R. Tolkein; in the novels, it means nymph of the forest
> People think of Tavaril as old, lazy, energetic, old-fashioned, poor
> People who like the name Tavaril also like Danika, Julia, Hailey, Callie, Edie, Kaitlyn, Cindy, Erika, Jana, Lacey

Tavarius *(American)* ♂   RATING: ★★★
Combination of Tavis and Darius
> People think of Tavarius as handsome, intelligent, aggressive, sexy, cool
> People who like the name Tavarius also like Jayden, Tameron, Tavorian, Isaiah, Darius, Tristan, Terrel, Tyrell, Taurean, Romeo

Tave *(American)* ♂   RATING: ★★★
Short for Gustave
> People think of Tave as powerful, sporty, popular, winner, cool
> People who like the name Tave also like Kaden, Taran, Reece, Chase, Chance, Tristan, Trenton, Levi, Jace, Drake

Tavi *(English)* ♀   RATING: ★★
Eighth—Short for Octavia
> People think of Tavi as creative, intelligent, artsy, funny, energetic
> People who like the name Tavi also like Talia, Tessa, Tegan, Olivia, Trinity, Tiana, Zoe, Aurora, Natalie, Thalia

Tavia *(English)* ♀   RATING: ★★☆
Eighth—Short for Octavia
> People think of Tavia as funny, pretty, intelligent, creative, sexy
> People who like the name Tavia also like Olivia, Talia, Tatiana, Ava, Tahlia, Tiana, Tessa, Eva, Tabitha, Bella

Tavis *(Celtic/Gaelic)* ♂   RATING: ★★★
Variation of Thomas—Tavis Smiley, journalist/author
> People think of Tavis as leader, caring, cool, creative, young
> People who like the name Tavis also like Aiden, Grayson, Lucas, Liam, Noah, Tristan, Taran, Aden, Everett, Keagan

Tavita *(Spanish)* ♀   RATING: ★★☆
Eighth—Short for Octavia; also possibly a Samoan name
> People think of Tavita as funny, creative, sexy, exotic, lazy
> People who like the name Tavita also like Tavia, Terena, Tanisha, Tacita, Tarika, Maggie, Tiara, Fiona, Tasha, Trista

Tavon *(American)* ♂   RATING: ★★☆
Combination of Tavis and Avon
> People think of Tavon as handsome, popular, aggressive, sexy, cool
> People who like the name Tavon also like Tristan, Kaden, Aiden, Jayden, Tyson, Trey, Tameron, Gavin, Xavier, Trent

528

Tavorian *(American)* ♂ RATING: ★★★
Combination of Tavis and Dorian
People think of Tavorian as loser, sexy, powerful, old, handsome
People who like the name Tavorian also like Tavarius, Taurean, Tyson, Tavon, Tyreak, Isaiah, Tyrone, André, Tameron, Tony

Tawana *(Persian)* ♀ RATING: ★★★★
Able, robust
People think of Tawana as pretty, aggressive, exotic, intelligent, sexy
People who like the name Tawana also like Tamara, Tanisha, Taini, Teresa, Selena, Tala, Tameka, Tallulah, Shania, Kaya

Tawny *(English)* ♀ RATING: ★★★☆
Golden brown—Tawny Kitaen, actress
People think of Tawny as pretty, funny, creative, caring, cool
People who like the name Tawny also like Trinity, Paige, Faith, Hailey, Tori, Olivia, Tessa, Bianca, Isabella, Savannah

Taya *(American)* ♀ RATING: ★★★★
Variation of Tea or Taylor
People think of Taya as pretty, creative, intelligent, energetic, funny
People who like the name Taya also like Ava, Olivia, Paige, Layla, Talia, Tiana, Tehya, Mya, Kyla, Ella

Taye *(African)* ♂ RATING: ★★☆
He has been seen—Ethiopian origin; pronounced *TAY-yeh*; also an American name, pronounced *TAY*; Taye Diggs, actor
People think of Taye as cool, handsome, intelligent, caring, sporty
People who like the name Taye also like Kaden, Tristan, Trey, Cole, Jayden, Braden, Micah, Tyson, Jackson, Gabriel

Taylor *(English)* ♀♂ RATING: ★★★☆
Tailor
People think of Taylor as funny, pretty, popular, cool, intelligent
People who like the name Taylor also like Madison, Tyler, Riley, Logan, Bailey, Hayden, Mackenzie, Dylan, Ryan, Jordan

Tayte *(English)* ♀♂ RATING: ★★★★
Cheerful
People think of Tayte as funny, popular, energetic, handsome, intelligent
People who like the name Tayte also like Tate, Taylor, Teagan, Caden, Payton, Hayden, Jaden, Tayten, Tanner, Tyler

Tayten *(American)* ♀♂ RATING: ★★★★
Combination of Tayte and -en
People think of Tayten as funny, handsome, creative, young, sporty

People who like the name Tayten also like Caden, Teagan, Payton, Jaden, Talen, Hayden, Riley, Tate, Taylor, Tanner

Tazanna *(Native American)* ♀ RATING: ★★★★
Princess
People think of Tazanna as pretty, young, exotic, leader, popular
People who like the name Tazanna also like Tatiana, Tiana, Sabrina, Soraya, Sadie, Tana, Tazara, Tanaya, Tala, Talli

Tazara *(Arabic)* ♀ RATING: ★★★☆
Elegance, grace
People think of Tazara as exotic, pretty, funny, powerful, young
People who like the name Tazara also like Tatiana, Tazanna, Tahlia, Tiana, Talia, Jahzara, Trinity, Lana, Tariana, Larissa

Tea *(Spanish)* ♀ RATING: ★★★★
Gift of God—Short for Dorotea or Dorothea; pronounced *Taya*; Tea Leone, actress
People think of Tea as pretty, funny, energetic, exotic, creative
People who like the name Tea also like Tia, Ava, Layla, Ella, Paige, Olivia, Mia, Sienna, Emma, Sophia

Teagan *(Celtic/Gaelic)* ♀♂ RATING: ★★★★
Little poet—Variation of Teague or Tegan
People think of Teagan as pretty, creative, funny, intelligent, energetic
People who like the name Teagan also like Riley, Hayden, Logan, Reagan, Caden, Addison, Keegan, Taylor, Parker, Aidan

Teague *(Celtic/Gaelic)* ♂ RATING: ★★★★
A poet
People think of Teague as intelligent, caring, popular, creative, trustworthy
People who like the name Teague also like Tristan, Liam, Keagan, Owen, Noah, Aiden, Cole, Declan, Ian, Ethan

Teal *(American)* ♀♂ RATING: ★★★☆
Greenish blue color—Also a breed of duck
People think of Teal as creative, intelligent, artsy, pretty, funny
People who like the name Teal also like Ryder, Teagan, Tyler, Taylor, Caden, Sage, Parker, Hayden, Madison, Jade

Ted *(English)* ♂ RATING: ★★
Short for Edward or Theodore—Ted Danson, actor
People think of Ted as funny, handsome, caring, cool, sexy
People who like the name Ted also like Adam, Jack, Jacob, William, Matthew, David, Owen, Ethan, Benjamin, Trevor

Teddington *(English)* ♂ RATING: ★★★
From the town of Tedda's people
People think of Teddington as nerdy, old-fashioned, stuck-up, quiet, loser

People who like the name Teddington also like Baxter, Nicholas, Teddy, Oliver, Jacob, Ethan, Todd, Jackson, Trevor, Adam

Teddy *(English)* ♂   RATING: ★★
Short for Edward or Theodore—Teddy Roosevelt, U.S. president; teddy bear, children's toy named after Roosevelt
People think of Teddy as funny, caring, handsome, popular, trustworthy
People who like the name Teddy also like Jacob, Noah, Jack, Benjamin, Oliver, Gabriel, Theodore, Zachary, Nathan, Owen

Tedros *(African)* ♂   RATING: ★☆
Gift of God—Ethiopian origin; variation of Theodore
People think of Tedros as intelligent, energetic, wealthy, elegant, ethnic
People who like the name Tedros also like Theodore, Tobias, Jeremiah, Othello, Shaun, Theo, Jonathan, Manuel, Noah, Seth

Teela *(American)* ♀   RATING: ★★★★
Combination of Tea and Leela
People think of Teela as pretty, creative, funny, intelligent, exotic
People who like the name Teela also like Tiana, Talia, Tahlia, Hailey, Tessa, Olivia, Tamara, Sadie, Thalia, Tana

Teenie *(American)* ♀♂   RATING: ★★★
Small one—Originally a nickname for a small person
People think of Teenie as unpopular, loser, weird, young, poor
People who like the name Teenie also like Taylor, Hayden, Payton, Tate, Riley, Teagan, Tyler, Reilly, Devan, Morgan

Tefo *(African)* ♂   RATING: ★★
Payment—Used in Lesotho and Botswana
People think of Tefo as criminal, weird, loser, quiet, old-fashioned
People who like the name Tefo also like Makalo, Pedro, Lincoln, Troy, Jonathan, Milo, Tadeo, Tadelesh, Tyson, Alaric

Tegan *(Welsh)* ♀   RATING: ★★★
Pretty, fair
People think of Tegan as pretty, funny, intelligent, caring, creative
People who like the name Tegan also like Paige, Ava, Regan, Olivia, Chloe, Isabella, Tatum, Sadie, Grace, Hailey

Tegeen *(American)* ♀   RATING: ★★
Combination of Tea and Pegeen
People think of Tegeen as weird, creative, popular, exotic, girl next door
People who like the name Tegeen also like Tegan, Shaylee, Zoe, Paige, Zoey, Regan, Sophie, Isabelle, Sadie, Olivia

Tehya *(American)* ♀   RATING: ★★★★☆
Variation of Taya—Also a person from Tehran
People think of Tehya as pretty, energetic, caring, creative, funny
People who like the name Tehya also like Taya, Kaya, Tiana, Takoda, Tala, Tahlia, Tanaya, Tegan, Talia, Tatiana

Teige *(Celtic/Gaelic)* ♂   RATING: ★★★
A poet—Pronounced *tyge* (as in tiger); also a variation of the Irish name Tadg
People think of Teige as quiet, intelligent, artsy, exotic, big
People who like the name Teige also like Aiden, Teague, Kaden, Taran, Trey, Wyatt, Tristan, Keagan, Maddox, Holden

Teigra *(Rumantsch)* ♀   RATING: ★★
Tigress
People think of Teigra as exotic, powerful, wild, aggressive, sexy
People who like the name Teigra also like Tala, Tarika, Scarlett, Calista, Thalia, Giselle, Keira, Penelope, Tasha, Tyra

Teja *(Sanskrit/East Indian)* ♀   RATING: ★★★
Radiant—Variation of Deja
People think of Teja as pretty, funny, intelligent, young, cool
People who like the name Teja also like Eva, Mia, Triveni, Tanuja, Renée, Tahlia, Destiny, Sophia, Tia, Sofia

Tejana *(Spanish)* ♀   RATING: ★★★
Texan female
People think of Tejana as exotic, wild, lazy, poor, young
People who like the name Tejana also like Tehya, Tiana, Tatiana, Tahlia, Thalia, Mercedes, Tahirah, Tia, Tiara, Taja

Tejano *(Spanish)* ♂   RATING: ★★
Texan male—Also a form of Mexican-American music
People think of Tejano as weird, slow, poor, ethnic, funny
People who like the name Tejano also like Kaden, Lorenzo, Ricardo, Tristan, Xavier, Carlos, Ajani, Macario, Alijah, Zeshawn

Tekla *(Italian)* ♀   RATING: ★★★☆
Glory of God—Variation of Thekla
People think of Tekla as intelligent, caring, pretty, funny, leader
People who like the name Tekla also like Tasha, Penelope, Tasmine, Tameka, Isabella, Tatiana, Telma, Tiana, Tamara, Tazara

Tekli *(Polish)* ♀   RATING: ★★☆
Glory of God—Variation of Thekla
People think of Tekli as ethnic, religious, quiet, young, pretty
People who like the name Tekli also like Tara, Natalia, Roza, Tolla, Tariana, Tamia, Elsie, Makayla, Myrrh, Elise

Telema *(Spanish)* ♀   RATING: ★★☆
Will—Variation of Thelma
> People think of Telema as old-fashioned, old, poor, eth-
> nic, unpopular
> People who like the name Telema also like Telma,
> Terentia, Chika, Tanya, Metea, Thais, Tegan, Tetsu, Tamia,
> Nysa

Telemachus *(Greek)* ♂   RATING: ★☆
Decisive battle—In Greek mythology, the son of
Odysseus and Penelope; pronounced *Teh-LEM-a-kiss*
> People think of Telemachus as powerful, leader, aggres-
> sive, weird, loser
> People who like the name Telemachus also like Sirius,
> Lysander, Constantine, Liam, Socrates, Amadeus, Jacob,
> Thaddeus, Morpheus, Odysseus

Teleri *(Welsh)* ♀   RATING: ★★★
Your Eleri—Also a Welsh river
> People think of Teleri as funny, pretty, creative, popular,
> trustworthy
> People who like the name Teleri also like Rhiannon,
> Morgana, Lillian, Hazel, Guenevere, Genevieve, Laurel,
> Chloe, Arwen, Tess

Telissa *(American)* ♀   RATING: ★★★
Variation of Melissa
> People think of Telissa as young, pretty, cool, popular,
> lazy
> People who like the name Telissa also like Tamyra,
> Clarissa, Kyla, Cailyn, Tamara, Theresa, Velma, Madelyn,
> Melodie, Meagan

Telly *(Greek)* ♂   RATING: ★★
Best—Short for Aristotelis or Aristotle; Telly Sevalas,
actor
> People think of Telly as funny, young, caring, lazy, wild
> People who like the name Telly also like Miles, Tristan,
> Cole, Max, Isaac, Isaiah, Jacob, Taran, Tyson, Dax

Telma *(Italian)* ♀   RATING: ★★☆
Variation of Thelma
> People think of Telma as pretty, intelligent, funny,
> elegant, quiet
> People who like the name Telma also like Velma,
> Tatiana, Vanessa, Deborah, Layla, Nora, Thalia, Tasha,
> Natalia, Melanie

Telyn *(Welsh)* ♀   RATING: ★★★
Harp
> People think of Telyn as artsy, intelligent, pretty, cre-
> ative, exotic
> People who like the name Telyn also like Tailynn, Tegan,
> Ava, Sadie, Talia, Paige, Kaelyn, Tana, Olivia, Tatum

Temima *(Hebrew)* ♀   RATING: ★★☆
Whole, perfect
> People think of Temima as quiet, exotic, funny, untrust-
> worthy, intelligent
> People who like the name Temima also like Temira,
> Tegan, Rena, Selima, Talitha, Tori, Tamara, Tahlia,
> Katherine, Destiny

Temira *(Hebrew)* ♀   RATING: ★★☆
Tall
> People think of Temira as funny, pretty, sexy, intelligent,
> energetic
> People who like the name Temira also like Trinity,
> Trista, Tabitha, Tatiana, Tamira, Tamara, Tegan, Tahlia,
> Samantha, Tierra

Temperance *(English)* ♀   RATING: ★★★★
Moderation, self-control
> People think of Temperance as intelligent, pretty, trust-
> worthy, powerful, leader
> People who like the name Temperance also like Sophia,
> Isabella, Ava, Abigail, Trinity, Emma, Pearl, Patience,
> Chloe, Lilly

Tempest *(English)* ♀ ♂   RATING: ★★
Stormy—Also spelled Tempestt; Tempestt Bledsoe,
actress
> People think of Tempest as wild, powerful, cool, intel-
> ligent, pretty
> People who like the name Tempest also like Jade,
> Raven, Jaden, Riley, Teagan, Piper, Willow, Parker,
> Madison, Phoenix

Temple *(English)* ♀ ♂   RATING: ★★★☆
A sanctuary
> People think of Temple as religious, cool, pretty, cre-
> ative, sexy
> People who like the name Temple also like Piper, Storm,
> Reese, Shiloh, Tempest, Teagan, Shadow, Jade, Parker,
> Winter

Templeton *(English)* ♂   RATING: ★☆
Town of sanctuary
> People think of Templeton as intelligent, sexy, nerdy,
> energetic, powerful
> People who like the name Templeton also like Jackson,
> Tristan, Alexander, Holden, Tucker, Dalton, Winslow,
> Miles, Weston, Isaac

Temujin *(Mongolian)* ♂   RATING: ★★☆
Of iron; blacksmith—Original name of Genghis Khan,
conqueror
> People think of Temujin as aggressive, powerful, leader,
> intelligent, big
> People who like the name Temujin also like Coen,
> Ciaran, Keiran, Chi, Galvin, Yukio, Caine, Paddy, Radley,
> Donovan

Tenauri *(American)* ♂   RATING: ★★☆
Created name
> People think of Tenauri as intelligent, handsome, funny,
> trustworthy, artsy
> People who like the name Tenauri also like Holden,
> Malachi, Tyson, Yeriel, Nate, Palani, Alexei, Zedekiah,
> Tariq, Drake

Tendai *(African)* ♀   RATING: ★★★☆
Be thankful to God—Zimbabwe origin
> People think of Tendai as pretty, cool, ethnic, intelligent,
> religious

People who like the name Tendai also like Terehasa, Talisa, Thea, Samara, Tarana, Gianna, Ziraili, Keona, Makaila, Jana

Tender *(American)* ♀　　　RATING: ★★☆
Sensitive, soft
People think of Tender as poor, quiet, boy next door, ethnic, wild
People who like the name Tender also like Grace, Serena, Patience, Gabrielle, Jewel, Isabella, Destiny, Serenity, Trinity, Precious

Tene *(African)* ♀ ♂　　　RATING: ★★★
Love—From the Euroba dialect; pronounced *TEN-ay*
People think of Tene as pretty, creative, funny, intelligent, caring
People who like the name Tene also like Tate, Teshi, Tayten, Jordan, Tyree, Tarachand, Parker, Talen, Trace, Teva

Teneil *(American)* ♀ ♂　　　RATING: ★★
Variation of Tenniel
People think of Teneil as pretty, funny, sexy, caring, popular
People who like the name Teneil also like Tarin, Tanner, Tayte, Tayten, Teagan, Tempest, Tyler, Taryn, Trace, Bailey

Tenen *(African)* ♂　　　RATING: ★★☆
Born on Monday
People think of Tenen as big, sexy, old, quiet, leader
People who like the name Tenen also like Tristan, Maddox, Jackson, Taye, Jayden, Braden, Cole, Jett, Lawson, Kaden

Teness *(American)* ♀　　　RATING: ★★☆
Short for Tennessee—Also a combination of Tess and Vanessa
People think of Teness as big, elegant, artsy, trustworthy, untrustworthy
People who like the name Teness also like Terena, Tamma, Tiana, Tatiana, Tegan, Natasha, Tess, Carly, Keely, Tazanna

Tennessee *(Native American)* ♀ ♂　RATING: ★★★★
Gathering place—Cherokee origin; also spelled Tenesea; Tennessee Williams, playwright
People think of Tennessee as popular, cool, funny, pretty, creative
People who like the name Tennessee also like Taylor, Reese, Parker, Memphis, Madison, Mackenzie, Bailey, Brooklyn, Liberty, Phoenix

Tennis *(English)* ♂　　　RATING: ★★☆
Game played with ball and rackets—From the French word *tenez* meaning hold or receive; also a variation of Dennis
People think of Tennis as nerdy, stuck-up, sporty, loser, weird
People who like the name Tennis also like Trent, Abie, Aaron, Alexander, Alexavier, Adam, Theo, Tim, Adrian, Timothy

Tennyson *(English)* ♂　　　RATING: ★★★
Son of Dennis—Variation of Dennison; Alfred Lord Tennyson, poet
People think of Tennyson as intelligent, creative, artsy, handsome, cool
People who like the name Tennyson also like Tristan, Emerson, Noah, Grayson, Holden, Braden, Micah, Walker, Caleb, Aiden

Teo *(Italian)* ♂　　　RATING: ★★★☆
Divine gift—Short for Teodoro or Theodore
People think of Teo as handsome, funny, intelligent, popular, creative
People who like the name Teo also like Theo, Tyson, Isaac, Trey, Samuel, Lucas, Ethan, Elliot, Simon, Adrian

Teofila *(Italian)* ♀　　　RATING: ★★☆
House of God
People think of Teofila as exotic, cool, weird, powerful, trendy
People who like the name Teofila also like Aria, Domenica, Tekla, Donatella, Adrina, Terra, Angelina, Camila, Bambi, Gabriella

Terah *(American)* ♀　　　RATING: ★★★
Variation of Terra or Tara
People think of Terah as pretty, creative, intelligent, caring, trustworthy
People who like the name Terah also like Terra, Samara, Olivia, Faith, Paige, Zoey, Kara, Gabrielle, Trinity, Victoria

Teranika *(American)* ♀　　　RATING: ★★★☆
Combination of Terra and Nika
People think of Teranika as sexy, girl next door, creative, sporty, stuck-up
People who like the name Teranika also like Genevieve, Bridget, Malise, Isla, Trista, Keira, Saoirse, Meara, Bidelia, Ryann

Terehasa *(African)* ♀　　　RATING: ★★★
Blessed—Ethiopian origin
People think of Terehasa as pretty, ethnic, young, old-fashioned, trendy
People who like the name Terehasa also like Tendai, Tarisai, Tanisha, Tonya, Tarana, Terena, Thandiwe, Taya, Tarala, Tahirah

Terena *(English)* ♀　　　RATING: ★★
Unknown meaning—Feminine form of Terence
People think of Terena as pretty, popular, funny, young, caring
People who like the name Terena also like Tessa, Taya, Talia, Trista, Tatiana, Larissa, Tavia, Tavita, Tyra, Selena

Terence *(Latin)* ♂　　　RATING: ★★★☆
Unknown meaning
People think of Terence as handsome, cool, intelligent, funny, caring
People who like the name Terence also like Tristan, Nathan, Ethan, Terrence, Tyson, Trent, Seth, Timothy, Lucas, Aiden

Terentia *(Latin)* ♀   RATING: ★★☆
Unknown meaning—Feminine form of Terence
People think of Terentia as intelligent, exotic, funny, weird, leader
People who like the name Terentia also like Tanisha, Terena, Tamika, Tamira, Jovita, Tacita, Tavita, Malia, Marcia, Thalia

Teresa *(Spanish)* ♀   RATING: ★★★☆
Harvester—Variation of Theresa; St. Teresa of Avila, Spanish mystic nun
People think of Teresa as pretty, caring, trustworthy, funny, intelligent
People who like the name Teresa also like Elizabeth, Samantha, Vanessa, Olivia, Natalie, Grace, Isabella, Victoria, Jessica, Sophia

Terpsichore *(Latin)* ♀   RATING: ★★☆
To delight in dance—In Greek mythology, the muse of dance
People think of Terpsichore as old-fashioned, exotic, ethnic, poor, criminal
People who like the name Terpsichore also like Gabrielle, Amber, Angelique, Abbie, Olivia, Ambrosine, Atira, Athalia, Victoria, Violet

Terra *(Italian)* ♀   RATING: ★★★
Earth
People think of Terra as pretty, caring, funny, intelligent, creative
People who like the name Terra also like Tara, Tessa, Sienna, Isabella, Samantha, Trinity, Natalia, Paige, Hailey, Emma

Terran *(American)* ♀♂   RATING: ★★★
Of the earth
People think of Terran as funny, creative, cool, energetic, trustworthy
People who like the name Terran also like Caden, Teagan, Taryn, Jaden, Talen, Tarin, Aidan, Logan, Torrin, Hayden

Terrel *(English)* ♂   RATING: ★★☆
Stubborn—Also a surname; also spelled Tirrell or Tyrrell
People think of Terrel as handsome, funny, cool, sexy, caring
People who like the name Terrel also like Tyrell, Terence, Tyson, Tristan, Trey, Terrence, Tavon, Justin, Jayden, Nathan

Terrell *(English)* ♂   RATING: ★★★★
Stubborn
People think of Terrell as aggressive, handsome, loser, lazy, energetic
People who like the name Terrell also like Terrence, Anthony, Jason, Aaron, Owen, Ethan, Calvin, Shawn, Alexander, Christopher

Terrence *(English)* ♂   RATING: ★★★☆
Unknown meaning—Variation of Terence; Terrence Howard, actor
People think of Terrence as handsome, funny, intelligent, caring, sexy
People who like the name Terrence also like Tristan, Ethan, Zachary, Nicholas, Jacob, Trevor, Samuel, Vincent, Tyson, Seth

Terrene *(American)* ♀   RATING: ★★☆
Unknown meaning—Feminine form of Terence
People think of Terrene as aggressive, funny, creative, caring, cool
People who like the name Terrene also like Shaylee, Rhiannon, Felicity, Victoria, Tegan, Shayla, Scarlett, Skyla, Tailynn, Terena

Terri *(English)* ♀   RATING: ★★
Unknown meaning—Short for Theresa; also spelled Teri; Teri Garr, actress; Teri Hatcher, actress
People think of Terri as funny, caring, pretty, trustworthy, intelligent
People who like the name Terri also like Natalie, Samantha, Sarah, Stephanie, Rebecca, Amber, Renée, Nicole, Paige, Tori

Terrian *(American)* ♀♂   RATING: ★★★☆
Combination of Terence and Darian
People think of Terrian as funny, creative, popular, powerful, leader
People who like the name Terrian also like Terran, Talen, Jaden, Torrin, Caden, Taryn, Tayten, Tevin, Taylor, Teagan

Terrica *(American)* ♀   RATING: ★★
Combination of Teresa and Erica
People think of Terrica as pretty, funny, popular, cool, creative
People who like the name Terrica also like Tiara, Tailynn, Thalia, Tiana, Trinity, Tessa, Paige, Serenity, Tariana, Kiana

Terris *(English)* ♀♂   RATING: ★★
Son of Thierry—Originally a surname
People think of Terris as funny, intelligent, popular, caring, trustworthy
People who like the name Terris also like Teagan, Taylor, Tate, Riley, Ryder, Ryan, Tanner, Jaden, Kyler, Rylan

Terrwyn *(Welsh)* ♀   RATING: ★★☆
Fair, brave
People think of Terrwyn as girl next door, old-fashioned, trendy, trustworthy, intelligent
People who like the name Terrwyn also like Aelwen, Arwen, Kiara, Aurora, Bronwyn, Amelie, Kaya, Aislinn, Gwendolyn, Kyra

Terry *(English)* ♀♂   RATING: ★★★☆
Short for Terence or Theresa—Terry Gilliam, actor/writer
People think of Terry as funny, cool, caring, intelligent, trustworthy

People who like the name Terry also like Taylor, Sam, Sean, Jade, Tyler, Ryan, Kelly, Logan, Jamie, Jesse

Terryal (*American*) ♀♂   RATING: ★★
Combination of Terry and Ariel
People think of Terryal as pretty, exotic, funny, sexy, cool
People who like the name Terryal also like Taylor, Tyler, Brooke, Carmen, Lindsey, Landen, Tierney, Winter, Hunter, Jordan

Tertia (*Latin*) ♀   RATING: ★★☆
Third
People think of Tertia as elegant, pretty, old-fashioned, trustworthy, intelligent
People who like the name Tertia also like Tessa, Kalista, Pelagia, Dara, Thea, Bianca, Theresa, Gabriella, Melody, Thalia

Tertius (*Latin*) ♂   RATING: ★★☆
Third
People think of Tertius as intelligent, handsome, sexy, aggressive, weird
People who like the name Tertius also like Theodore, Thaddeus, Cicero, Troy, Titus, Othello, Kairos, Timothy, Orestes, Vincent

Teryl (*American*) ♀   RATING: ★★★
Combination of Terrell and Beryl
People think of Teryl as funny, creative, intelligent, pretty, trustworthy
People who like the name Teryl also like Tierra, Laurel, Olivia, Terah, Luna, Talia, Terrene, Cordelia, Telyn, Trista

Teshi (*African*) ♀♂   RATING: ★★★
Cheerful, full of laughter—Ghanaian origin
People think of Teshi as funny, big, energetic, weird, popular
People who like the name Teshi also like Tate, Tene, Tayte, Musoke, Diara, Teagan, Tyree, Vian, Akia, Mahari

Tesla (*Slavic*) ♀   RATING: ★★★
From Thessaly, Greece—Nikola Tesla, inventor/electrical engineer
People think of Tesla as funny, girl next door, exotic
People who like the name Tesla also like Trinity, Bianca, Tia, Zahra, Jaclyn, Eleanor, Vienna, Helena, Trista, Zoie

Tess (*English*) ♀   RATING: ★★★
Harvester—Short for Theresa
People think of Tess as pretty, funny, intelligent, energetic, creative
People who like the name Tess also like Tessa, Olivia, Grace, Emma, Paige, Ella, Ava, Chloe, Isabella, Hannah

Tessa (*English*) ♀   RATING: ★★★
Harvester—Variation of Theresa
People think of Tessa as pretty, funny, creative, intelligent, caring
People who like the name Tessa also like Emma, Olivia, Paige, Grace, Ava, Hannah, Isabella, Ella, Chloe, Hailey

Tessica (*American*) ♀   RATING: ★★★
Combination of Tess and Jessica
People think of Tessica as creative, caring, pretty, elegant, sexy
People who like the name Tessica also like Tessa, Bella, Paige, Tiana, Fiona, Sabrina, Lauren, Larissa, Isabella, Gabrielle

Tetsu (*Japanese*) ♀   RATING: ★★★
Iron
People think of Tetsu as creative, exotic, powerful, leader, intelligent
People who like the name Tetsu also like Kaori, Kaida, Kimi, Amaya, Nariko, Keiko, Emiko, Yoshiko, Suki, Tama

Teva (*Hebrew*) ♀♂   RATING: ★★★☆
Nature
People think of Teva as intelligent, creative, trustworthy, energetic, pretty
People who like the name Teva also like Landen, Morgan, Riley, Jaden, Hayden, Teagan, Talen, Reese, Logan, Caden

Tevin (*American*) ♀♂   RATING: ★★☆
Combination of Terence and Kevin—Tevin Campbell, singer.
People think of Tevin as handsome, funny, intelligent, cool, young
People who like the name Tevin also like Teagan, Jaden, Tanner, Caden, Talen, Taylor, Skylar, Logan, Tyler, Riley

Tevy (*Cambodian*) ♀   RATING: ★★★☆
Angel
People think of Tevy as exotic, creative, pretty, cool, weird
People who like the name Tevy also like Bella, Tatum, Tegan, Thea, Tia, Zoe, Chloe, Tuyen, Grace, Zoey

Tex (*American*) ♀♂   RATING: ★★
From Texas—A common nickname for men from Texas; Tex Ritter, singer; Tex Williams, musician
People think of Tex as handsome, popular, wild, leader, cool
People who like the name Tex also like Logan, Taylor, Tate, Hunter, Carter, Sawyer, Madison, Parker, Tyler, Hayden

Texas (*Native American*) ♀♂   RATING: ★★★☆
Friends—U.S. state
People think of Texas as leader, powerful, sporty, popular, cool
People who like the name Texas also like Dakota, Madison, Dallas, Taylor, Parker, Hayden, Jaden, Sydney, Jordan, Preston

Thackary (*English*) ♀♂   RATING: ★★★☆
Dweller by the nook where the reeds for thatching grew
People think of Thackary as intelligent, creative, nerdy, old-fashioned, artsy
People who like the name Thackary also like Parker, Taylor, Logan, Riley, Hayden, Caden, Addison, Jaden, Sawyer, Rowan

Thad (*Greek*) ♂ RATING: ★★
Praise—Short for Thaddaeus
People think of Thad as handsome, intelligent, popular, trustworthy, creative
People who like the name Thad also like Seth, Ethan, Kaden, Ian, Wade, Noah, Tristan, Aiden, Caleb, Cole

Thaddeus (*Greek*) ♂ RATING: ★★
Praise—Also spelled Thaddaeus or Thadeus
People think of Thaddeus as handsome, intelligent, funny, caring, leader
People who like the name Thaddeus also like Noah, Ethan, Tristan, Nathaniel, Owen, Seth, Isaac, Xander, Sebastian, Caleb

Thadine (*American*) ♀ RATING: ★★☆
Feminine form of Thaddeus
People think of Thadine as pretty, quiet, creative, winner, loser
People who like the name Thadine also like Tonya, Dara, Talitha, Tyra, Salome, Theodora, Julia, Tamar, Diana, Thora

Thady (*Greek*) ♀♂ RATING: ★★☆
Praise—Short for Thaddeus
People think of Thady as trustworthy, caring, poor, weird, religious
People who like the name Thady also like Brody, Rylee, Skye, Toby, Kaley, Magan, Skylar, Teagan, Reagan, Blaine

Thai (*Vietnamese*) ♂ RATING: ★★★☆
From Thailand
People think of Thai as energetic, funny, trustworthy, handsome, exotic
People who like the name Thai also like Tristan, Trey, Jayden, Ethan, Kaden, Tyson, Lucas, Cole, Elijah, Ian

Thais (*Greek*) ♀ RATING: ★★★★☆
The bond—Pronounced *TAY-iss*; *Thais*, novel by Anatole France and opera by Massenet
People think of Thais as pretty, funny, intelligent, creative, sexy
People who like the name Thais also like Thalia, Karis, Genevieve, Dysis, Rhian, Zoe, Tiana, Lia, Maya, Rhea

Thalassa (*Greek*) ♀ RATING: ★★
The sea
People think of Thalassa as pretty, intelligent, artsy, elegant, creative
People who like the name Thalassa also like Thalia, Cassandra, Larissa, Rhea, Scarlett, Titania, Tatiana, Tessa, Summer, Anastasia

Thalia (*Greek*) ♀ RATING: ★★☆
Festive—In Greek mythology, one of the nine muses
People think of Thalia as pretty, funny, intelligent, creative, caring
People who like the name Thalia also like Talia, Tahlia, Isabella, Olivia, Natalia, Chloe, Tatiana, Adriana, Ava, Gabrielle

Thaman (*Arabic*) ♂ RATING: ★★☆
Price, worth
People think of Thaman as old, caring, loser, weird, trustworthy
People who like the name Thaman also like Taran, Tristan, Tarak, Hastin, Jayden, Kyson, Valin, Varun, Kellan, Ciaran

Thandiwe (*African*) ♀ RATING: ★★★☆
Beloved—Zimbabwe origin; pronounced *TAN-dee*; Thandiwe (Thandie) Newton, actress
People think of Thandiwe as pretty, sexy, young, ethnic, intelligent
People who like the name Thandiwe also like Tanaya, Tehya, Tiaret, Terehasa, Maisha, Kaya, Kalinda, Kate, Tansy, Tirzah

Thane (*English*) ♀♂ RATING: ★★☆
Warrior; landowner—In Anglo-Saxon England, a man who held land because he provided military service to his lord
People think of Thane as handsome, intelligent, caring, leader, trustworthy
People who like the name Thane also like Caden, Jaden, Parker, Hayden, Teagan, Tanner, Tate, Logan, Riley, Sawyer

Thanh (*Vietnamese*) ♂ RATING: ★★★☆
Brilliant
People think of Thanh as intelligent, caring, cool, funny, pretty
People who like the name Thanh also like Declan, Titus, Soren, Tobias, Alexander, Adrian, Donovan, Hugh, Samson, Tristan

Thanos (*Greek*) ♂ RATING: ★★★☆
Death
People think of Thanos as aggressive, powerful, intelligent, sexy, handsome
People who like the name Thanos also like Aiden, Tristan, Titus, Xander, Theodore, Sloan, Thad, Alexander, Trenton, Keagan

Thao (*Vietnamese*) ♀ RATING: ★★★☆
Respectful of parents
People think of Thao as intelligent, pretty, trustworthy, creative, caring
People who like the name Thao also like Thea, Isabella, Tanika, Scarlett, Olivia, Emily, Toki, Tansy, Tanaya, Vera

Thatcher (*English*) ♂ RATING: ★★☆
Roof maker—Originally a surname; Margaret Thatcher, British prime minister
People think of Thatcher as intelligent, handsome, powerful, leader, cool
People who like the name Thatcher also like Jackson, Tristan, Holden, Tucker, Ethan, Noah, Owen, Walker, Grayson, Oliver

Thea (*Greek*) ♀ RATING: ★★☆
Gift of God—Short for Dorothea
People think of Thea as pretty, intelligent, creative, funny, caring

People who like the name Thea also like Ava, Olivia, Ella, Sophia, Mia, Isabella, Tessa, Hannah, Paige, Zoe

Thelma *(Greek)* ♀　　　　　RATING: ★☆
Will—Possibly a combination of Theodora and Alma; *Thelma & Louise*, film; character in *Thelma* by Marie Corelli
People think of Thelma as funny, caring, pretty, creative, intelligent
People who like the name Thelma also like Stella, Nichole, Phoebe, Sophie, Pamela, Zoe, Ruby, Matilda, Penelope, Mabel

Thelred *(English)* ♀♂　　　　RATING: ★★
Noble counsel—Variation of Ethelred
People think of Thelred as nerdy, artsy, weird, ethnic, old-fashioned
People who like the name Thelred also like Yohance, Rylan, Janus, Ketill, Merrick, Brody, Skylar, Marek, Vaughn, Phyre

Thema *(African)* ♀　　　　　RATING: ★★★
Queen—Egyptian origin
People think of Thema as wealthy, funny, trendy, popular, aggressive
People who like the name Thema also like Mandisa, Mutia, Miniya, Meria, Tana, Tiana, Shamara, Malkia, Ivy, Tarika

Themba *(African)* ♀♂　　　　RATING: ★★☆
Trust, hope, faith—Nguni origin
People think of Themba as intelligent, creative, handsome, cool, weird
People who like the name Themba also like Tiassale, Teshi, Shane, Tene, Tallys, Tynan, Scorpio, Taima, Mariatu, Pembroke

Theo *(Greek)* ♂　　　　　RATING: ★★☆
Divine gift—Short for Theodore or Theodorus; Theo Huxtable, character on *The Cosby Show*; Theo van Gogh, brother of artist Vincent van Gogh
People think of Theo as handsome, intelligent, funny, cool, caring
People who like the name Theo also like Noah, Ethan, Oliver, Tristan, Leo, Seth, Isaac, Jack, Sebastian, Caleb

Theodora *(Greek)* ♀　　　　RATING: ★★★☆
Divine gift—Feminine form of Theodore
People think of Theodora as pretty, intelligent, caring, creative, funny
People who like the name Theodora also like Scarlett, Olivia, Penelope, Victoria, Isadora, Violet, Iris, Genevieve, Tabitha, Anastasia

Theodore *(Greek)* ♂　　　　RATING: ★★☆
Divine gift—Theodore Roosevelt, U.S. president
People think of Theodore as intelligent, handsome, caring, funny, leader
People who like the name Theodore also like Zachary, Oliver, Benjamin, Alexander, Gabriel, Ethan, Jacob, Samuel, Nathaniel, William

Theola *(American)* ♀　　　　RATING: ★★
Combination of Thea and Ola
People think of Theola as weird, pretty, trustworthy, funny, elegant
People who like the name Theola also like Theone, Thalia, Theodora, Thisbe, Thera, Thea, Tanith, Thyra, Theophilia, Thetis

Theone *(Greek)* ♀　　　　　RATING: ★★★
Gift from God
People think of Theone as powerful, caring, creative, leader, intelligent
People who like the name Theone also like Thea, Theola, Thalia, Tiana, Thera, Theodora, Ophelia, Theophilia, Giselle, Genevieve

Theophilia *(Greek)* ♀　　　　RATING: ★★★
Friendship of God
People think of Theophilia as exotic, pretty, elegant, unpopular, trustworthy
People who like the name Theophilia also like Thalia, Persephone, Theodora, Ophelia, Pandora, Vanessa, Penelope, Genevieve, Zoe, Celeste

Theophilus *(Greek)* ♂　　　　RATING: ★★★☆
Loving God
People think of Theophilus as intelligent, leader, creative, handsome, funny
People who like the name Theophilus also like Alexander, Theodore, Gabriel, Zander, Timothy, Thaddeus, Benjamin, Morpheus, Noah, Zachariah

Theoris *(Greek)* ♂　　　　　RATING: ★☆
God
People think of Theoris as nerdy, ethnic, exotic, leader, creative
People who like the name Theoris also like Xander, Tristan, Xavier, Thaddeus, Timothy, Vincent, Tarmon, Eamon, Quentin, Thomas

Thera *(Greek)* ♀　　　　　RATING: ★★★
Short for Theresa
People think of Thera as intelligent, creative, caring, pretty, energetic
People who like the name Thera also like Thalia, Thea, Samara, Amara, Nadia, Zoe, Theone, Tessa, Theresa, Xylia

Theresa *(Greek)* ♀　　　　RATING: ★★★☆
Harvester—Theresa Brewer, singer
People think of Theresa as pretty, caring, funny, intelligent, trustworthy
People who like the name Theresa also like Elizabeth, Samantha, Natalie, Victoria, Sarah, Rachel, Paige, Gabrielle, Rebecca, Hannah

Therese *(French)* ♀　　　　RATING: ★★★★
Harvester—Variation of Theresa
People think of Therese as pretty, intelligent, caring, trustworthy, funny
People who like the name Therese also like Isabelle, Theresa, Gabrielle, Charlotte, Victoria, Belle, Madeleine, Claire, Abigail, Nadine

535

Theresia *(Greek)* ♀   RATING: ★★
Harvester—Variation of Theresa
People think of Theresia as pretty, creative, intelligent, caring, young
People who like the name Theresia also like Tessa, Theresa, Cassandra, Therese, Zoe, Olivia, Lily, Tess, Hailey, Katarina

Theron *(Greek)* ♀ ♂   RATING: ★★★★☆
Hunter—Charlize Theron, actress
People think of Theron as handsome, intelligent, caring, funny, cool
People who like the name Theron also like Jaden, Talen, Caden, Teagan, Hayden, Reese, Mason, Sawyer, Avery, Morgan

Thessaly *(Greek)* ♀ ♂   RATING: ★★★
A region in Greece
People think of Thessaly as elegant, powerful, wealthy, old-fashioned, exotic
People who like the name Thessaly also like Holland, Greer, Hadley, Oakley, Vian, Bricen, Briar, Vaughn, Matias, Rafferty

Theta *(Greek)* ♀   RATING: ★★★
Eighth letter of the Greek alphabet
People think of Theta as energetic, powerful, weird, untrustworthy, trustworthy
People who like the name Theta also like Thea, Thalia, Ophelia, Thyra, Tiana, Zoe, Rini, Melody, Xylia, Sephora

Thetis *(Greek)* ♀   RATING: ★★★
Disposer
People think of Thetis as intelligent, powerful, caring, trustworthy, creative
People who like the name Thetis also like Penelope, Xanthe, Ophelia, Thea, Thisbe, Sybil, Psyche, Isis, Philyra, Thalia

Thi *(Vietnamese)* ♀   RATING: ★★★
Single female
People think of Thi as pretty, sexy, young, cool, ethnic
People who like the name Thi also like Tia, Kiara, Sienna, Sierra, Grace, Tea, Savannah, Molly, Neva, Destiny

Thian *(Vietnamese)* ♂   RATING: ★★★
Smooth
People think of Thian as funny, cool, creative, artsy, popular
People who like the name Thian also like Tristan, Kaden, Trent, Liam, Jayden, Wade, Travis, Trey, Maddox, Nash

Thijs *(Dutch)* ♂   RATING: ★★☆
Gift of God—Short for Matthijs; pronounced *TICE*
People think of Thijs as handsome, intelligent, powerful, weird, creative
People who like the name Thijs also like Nicholas, Aiden, Liam, Ciaran, Gavin, Cruz, Tristan, Taye, Brennan, Davis

Thimba *(Swahili)* ♂   RATING: ★☆
Lion hunter
People think of Thimba as exotic, young, powerful, wild, leader
People who like the name Thimba also like Tokala, Taariq, Todd, Thanos, Tyrell, Tadelesh, Tadhg, Tristan, Branden, Taffy

Thina *(Greek)* ♀   RATING: ★★☆
Short for Athina
People think of Thina as weird, leader, pretty, ethnic, wild
People who like the name Thina also like Thalia, Thea, Tiana, Tessa, Theresa, Kaya, Thora, Thyra, Vanessa, Veronica

Thisbe *(Greek)* ♀   RATING: ★★★☆
Lover
People think of Thisbe as artsy, pretty, exotic, weird, big
People who like the name Thisbe also like Thalia, Penelope, Zoe, Xanthe, Phoebe, Tanith, Topanga, Dysis, Daphne, Tallulah

Thom *(Greek)* ♂   RATING: ★★
Twin—Short for Thomas
People think of Thom as intelligent, creative, aggressive, wealthy, cool
People who like the name Thom also like Thomas, Jacob, Liam, Todd, Theo, Tristan, Lucas, Nathan, Seth, Trey

Thomae *(Greek)* ♀   RATING: ★★
Twin—Feminine form of Thomas
People think of Thomae as creative, intelligent, trustworthy, ethnic, wild
People who like the name Thomae also like Therese, Toral, Thina, Thora, Thelma, Tvisha, Teja, Theodora, Tolla, Devorah

Thomas *(Greek)* ♂   RATING: ★★★
A twin—Apostle of Christ; Thomas Edison, inventor
People think of Thomas as handsome, funny, intelligent, caring, cool
People who like the name Thomas also like William, Nicholas, Jacob, Matthew, Benjamin, Ethan, Nathan, Samuel, Zachary, Alexander

Thor *(Scandinavian)* ♂   RATING: ★★★☆
Norse god of thunder
People think of Thor as powerful, aggressive, handsome, leader, intelligent
People who like the name Thor also like Tristan, Xavier, Noah, Gabriel, Ian, Drake, Tyson, Oliver, Troy, Seth

Thora *(Scandinavian)* ♀   RATING: ★★★★
Thunder—Feminine form of Thor; Thora Birch, actress
People think of Thora as powerful, intelligent, creative, leader, energetic
People who like the name Thora also like Scarlett, Olivia, Fiona, Victoria, Nora, Stella, Ivy, Violet, Sofia, Astrid

Thorne (*English*) ♂   RATING: ★★★☆
From the thorn bush—Also a surname
> People think of Thorne as powerful, funny, intelligent, handsome, energetic
> People who like the name Thorne also like Tristan, Holden, Aiden, Xander, Kaden, Tucker, Cole, Seth, Gage, Reece

Thornton (*English*) ♂   RATING: ★★
From the thorny town—Thornton Wilder, author/playwright
> People think of Thornton as nerdy, old-fashioned, loser, weird, unpopular
> People who like the name Thornton also like Tristan, Lucas, Jackson, Walker, Nicholas, Sebastian, Dawson, Dalton, Miles, Thatcher

Thu (*Vietnamese*) ♀ ♂   RATING: ★★★☆
Autumn
> People think of Thu as intelligent, weird, trustworthy, creative, pretty
> People who like the name Thu also like Yuki, Teshi, Emlyn, Mika, Orly, Kieran, James, Aidan, Kiyoshi, Dylan

Thuong (*Vietnamese*) ♀ ♂   RATING: ★★☆
Love tenderly
> People think of Thuong as nerdy, weird, loser, unpopular, exotic
> People who like the name Thuong also like Torrin, Tiassale, Trace, Haven, Kalin, Kenyon, Tarin, Jersey, Rollin, Lavender

Thuraya (*Arabic*) ♀   RATING: ★★★
Stars and the planets
> People think of Thuraya as creative, intelligent, trustworthy, religious, caring
> People who like the name Thuraya also like Soraya, Olivia, Tanaya, Noura, Tahirah, Tien, Thalassa, Jena, Thalia, Tahlia

Thurman (*English*) ♂   RATING: ★★★
Servant of Thor—Also a surname; Uma Thurman, actress
> People think of Thurman as intelligent, handsome, aggressive, caring, leader
> People who like the name Thurman also like Tyson, Tucker, Maxwell, Nicholas, Jackson, Christopher, Andrew, Jason, Tristan, William

Thurston (*Scandinavian*) ♂   RATING: ★★★☆
Thor's stone—Thurston Howell III, character on *Gilligan's Island*; Thurston Moore, musician
> People think of Thurston as creative, intelligent, cool, leader, old-fashioned
> People who like the name Thurston also like Trenton, Tristan, Wade, Trent, Trevor, Gavin, Holden, Aden, Sebastian, Kaden

Thuy (*Vietnamese*) ♀   RATING: ★★★☆
Water
> People think of Thuy as caring, funny, pretty, young, energetic
> People who like the name Thuy also like Tama, Tallulah, Shasa, Tana, Tarika, Tulia, Talulah, Toni, Trisha, Kaida

Thuyet (*Vietnamese*) ♂   RATING: ★★☆
Theory
> People think of Thuyet as weird, old-fashioned, nerdy, aggressive, lazy
> People who like the name Thuyet also like Whitby, Demetrius, Rangsey, Xander, Broderick, Livingston, Bowen, Bastien, Diallo, Forrester

Thwaite (*English*) ♂   RATING: ★★
From the meadow
> People think of Thwaite as weird, stuck-up, nerdy, poor, old-fashioned
> People who like the name Thwaite also like Tybalt, Dane, Soren, Malcolm, Latham, Titus, Ismet, Ingo, Ryu, Pablo

Thy (*Vietnamese*) ♀   RATING: ★★★
Poetry
> People think of Thy as trustworthy, poor, popular, weird, young
> People who like the name Thy also like Trinity, Claire, Uzuri, Grace, Serenity, Zoe, Lila, India, Chloe, Hero

Thyra (*Scandinavian*) ♀   RATING: ★★
Goddess
> People think of Thyra as intelligent, pretty, caring, trustworthy, creative
> People who like the name Thyra also like Tyra, Tatiana, Tanith, Tiana, Chloe, Tabitha, Thea, Thalia, Kyra, Patience

Tia (*Spanish*) ♀   RATING: ★★★☆
Aunt—Also short for names containing –tia or similar syllable; Tia Mowry, actress
> People think of Tia as pretty, funny, intelligent, caring, popular
> People who like the name Tia also like Mia, Paige, Tiana, Ella, Ava, Olivia, Chloe, Grace, Mya, Savannah

Tiana (*American*) ♀   RATING: ★★★
Fairy queen—Short for Tatiana
> People think of Tiana as pretty, funny, popular, caring, intelligent
> People who like the name Tiana also like Tatiana, Tia, Tiara, Isabella, Adriana, Jadyn, Talia, Mia, Hailey, Paige

Tiara (*Latin*) ♀   RATING: ★★☆
Crown
> People think of Tiara as pretty, funny, popular, sexy, intelligent
> People who like the name Tiara also like Tiana, Tia, Trinity, Paige, Tatiana, Ciara, Faith, Mia, Kiara, Destiny

Tiaret (*African*) ♀   RATING: ★★★☆
Lioness
> People think of Tiaret as exotic, pretty, wild, sexy, powerful
> People who like the name Tiaret also like Tala, Serena, Tyra, Kiara, Scarlett, Tanith, Toril, Kara, Keira, Kari

538

Tibor *(Hungarian)* ♂ RATING: ★★★☆
From the Tiber river
People think of Tibor as intelligent, handsome, criminal, caring, funny
People who like the name Tibor also like Tristan, Tobias, Taban, Keagan, Theo, Trey, Colton, Chase, Todd, Tucker

Tiburon *(Spanish)* ♂ RATING: ★☆
Shark—Possibly also a variation of Tiberinus
People think of Tiburon as powerful, leader, aggressive, cool, wild
People who like the name Tiburon also like Liam, Sebastian, Ryu, Pablo, Tyrell, Tokala, Lucas, Byron, Taran, Ranger

Tien *(Vietnamese)* ♀ RATING: ★★
Fairy
People think of Tien as intelligent, pretty, trustworthy, caring, artsy
People who like the name Tien also like Tana, Ivy, Vera, Tatiana, Fiona, Zoe, Chloe, Trinity, Sapphire, Kiara

Tiergan *(Celtic/Gaelic)* ♂ RATING: ★★★☆
Strong willed
People think of Tiergan as leader, energetic, powerful, intelligent, handsome
People who like the name Tiergan also like Tiernan, Keagan, Tristan, Liam, Aiden, Kael, Braeden, Devlin, Keiran, Merric

Tiernan *(Celtic/Gaelic)* ♂ RATING: ★★★★
Little lord, chief—Variation of Tigernan
People think of Tiernan as handsome, intelligent, caring, creative, popular
People who like the name Tiernan also like Tristan, Liam, Keagan, Keiran, Tiergan, Kiernan, Owen, Aiden, Ethan, Braeden

Tierney *(Celtic/Gaelic)* ♀♂ RATING: ★★☆
Lord—Variation of Tigernach; pronounced *TEER-nee*
People think of Tierney as pretty, funny, creative, intelligent, popular
People who like the name Tierney also like Teagan, Riley, Quinn, Hayden, Aidan, Taryn, Reagan, Parker, Addison, Logan

Tierra *(Spanish)* ♀ RATING: ★★★★
Land—Possibly also a variation of Tiara
People think of Tierra as pretty, funny, intelligent, young, sexy
People who like the name Tierra also like Tiara, Sierra, Tiana, Trinity, Tatiana, Sienna, Serenity, Keira, Tia, Olivia

Tieve *(Celtic/Gaelic)* ♀ RATING: ★★★
Hillside
People think of Tieve as quiet, exotic, intelligent, ethnic, religious
People who like the name Tieve also like Maeve, Riona, Meara, Mave, Saoirse, Sheehan, Genevieve, Phiala, Rhona, Keira

Tiffany *(English)* ♀ RATING: ★★☆
Appearance of God—Medieval English variation of Theophania; also spelled Tiffani or Tiffanie; Tiffany, singer; Tiffani Thiessen, actress.
People think of Tiffany as pretty, funny, caring, intelligent, trustworthy
People who like the name Tiffany also like Samantha, Paige, Victoria, Natalie, Emily, Hailey, Vanessa, Hannah, Olivia, Faith

Tiger *(American)* ♀♂ RATING: ★★★☆
Powerful cat; tiger—Tiger Woods, golfer
People think of Tiger as energetic, aggressive, exotic, powerful, leader
People who like the name Tiger also like Phoenix, Raven, Dakota, Jade, Jaden, Riley, Blake, Piper, Willow, Madison

Tilden *(English)* ♂ RATING: ★★☆
From Tila's valley—Originally a surname
People think of Tilden as big, nerdy, handsome, sporty, funny
People who like the name Tilden also like Kaden, Tristan, Holden, Jayden, Tyson, Aden, Aiden, Jack, Miles, Landon

Tillie *(English)* ♀ RATING: ★★☆
Battle strength—Short for Matilda; Tillie Olsen, poet/author
People think of Tillie as pretty, funny, creative, popular, intelligent
People who like the name Tillie also like Paige, Sadie, Grace, Lilly, Tilly, Olivia, Sophie, Ella, Millie, Ava

Tilly *(English)* ♀ RATING: ★☆
Battle strength—Short for Matilda
People think of Tilly as pretty, funny, creative, young, caring
People who like the name Tilly also like Lilly, Sophie, Paige, Molly, Mia, Sadie, Lily, Ella, Daisy, Grace

Tim *(Greek)* ♂ RATING: ★★★☆
To honor God—Short for Timothy; Tim Allen, actor; Tim Burton, director; Tim Conway, actor/comedian
People think of Tim as funny, cool, handsome, intelligent, caring
People who like the name Tim also like Timothy, Justin, Benjamin, Matthew, Adam, Jason, Ethan, Jake, Michael, Scott

Timber *(American)* ♀♂ RATING: ★★★
Wood, strong
People think of Timber as pretty, caring, funny, trustworthy, powerful
People who like the name Timber also like Riley, Parker, Tyler, Mason, Ryder, Tanner, Skylar, Trace, Bailey, Sawyer

Timberly *(American)* ♀ RATING: ★★★☆
Combination of Timber and Kimberly—Character on *Hey, Arnold!*
People think of Timberly as pretty, energetic, intelligent, trustworthy, popular

People who like the name Timberly also like Paige, Natalie, Emily, Lainey, Trinity, Hannah, Kaelyn, Zoey, Vanessa, Lacey

Timothy *(Greek)* ♂   RATING: ★★★
To honor God—Timothy Hutton, actor
People think of Timothy as funny, handsome, intelligent, caring, trustworthy
People who like the name Timothy also like Nicholas, Matthew, Benjamin, Zachary, Joshua, Thomas, Samuel, Nathan, Ethan, Alexander

Tina *(English)* ♀   RATING: ★★☆
Short for names ending in –tina—Tina Louise, actress; Tina Turner, singer
People think of Tina as funny, pretty, caring, intelligent, creative
People who like the name Tina also like Sabrina, Samantha, Tiffany, Rebecca, Jessica, Amber, Paige, Faith, Sophia, Hailey

Ting *(Chinese)* ♀   RATING: ★★★
Slim, graceful—Mandarin origin
People think of Ting as pretty, elegant, intelligent, creative, quiet
People who like the name Ting also like Grace, Isabelle, Bella, Natasha, Elle, Tamah, Opal, Tia, Tiana, Bice

Tino *(Italian)* ♂   RATING: ★★★★
Little (or junior)—Short for names ending in –tino
People think of Tino as funny, cool, handsome, intelligent, sexy
People who like the name Tino also like Nico, Tony, Benjamin, Trey, Anthony, Leo, Ethan, Troy, Emilio, Isaac

Tiombe *(African)* ♀   RATING: ★☆
Shy—West African origin
People think of Tiombe as quiet, ethnic, young, exotic, intelligent
People who like the name Tiombe also like Keeya, Mansa, Topanga, Tuyet, Tahirah, Ayanna, Tiponya, Maha, Thisbe, Tivona

Tiona *(American)* ♀   RATING: ★★★★
Fairy queen
People think of Tiona as pretty, cool, funny, creative, caring
People who like the name Tiona also like Tiana, Tiara, Trinity, Tariana, Tatiana, Tyra, Rianna, Tia, Tori, Olivia

Tip *(American)* ♀♂   RATING: ★☆
Nickname
People think of Tip as funny, sexy, poor, wild, handsome
People who like the name Tip also like Toby, Logan, Ty, Remi, Liberty, Taylor, Elie, Tiger, Shane, Teagan

Tiponya *(Native American)* ♀   RATING: ★★☆
Great horned owl—Miwok origin
People think of Tiponya as intelligent, uptight, artsy, powerful, old-fashioned
People who like the name Tiponya also like Thisbe, Tallulah, Winona, Topanga, Thora, Dea, Tiva, Orenda, Wakanda, Peta

Tirza *(Hebrew)* ♀   RATING: ★★
Pleasing
People think of Tirza as caring, pretty, creative, funny, intelligent
People who like the name Tirza also like Tirzah, Lana, Olivia, Trinity, Tahlia, Ruth, Tyra, Sari, Lorelei, Shaina

Tirzah *(Hebrew)* ♀   RATING: ★★★★☆
Pleasing
People think of Tirzah as pretty, caring, creative, intelligent, trustworthy
People who like the name Tirzah also like Tirza, Naomi, Tahlia, Talia, Keira, Tanaya, Lana, Nadia, Kara, Tegan

Tisha *(American)* ♀   RATING: ★★★☆
Joy—Short for Letitia
People think of Tisha as pretty, funny, caring, intelligent, sexy
People who like the name Tisha also like Trisha, Victoria, Amber, Mia, Tiara, Paige, Tamara, Tasha, Lacey, Tori

Titania *(Greek)* ♀   RATING: ★★★★
Land of giants—Character in *A Midsummer Night's Dream* by William Shakespeare
People think of Titania as powerful, pretty, sexy, intelligent, leader
People who like the name Titania also like Tatiana, Scarlett, Tiana, Ophelia, Vanessa, Nadia, Trinity, Isabella, Tabitha, Aurora

Titus *(Greek)* ♂   RATING: ★★
Giant—*Titus Andronicus* by William Shakespeare
People think of Titus as handsome, powerful, intelligent, leader, trustworthy
People who like the name Titus also like Tobias, Ethan, Noah, Gabriel, Seth, Elijah, Caleb, Jacob, Benjamin, Ian

Tiva *(Native American)* ♀   RATING: ★★★
Dance—Hopi origin
People think of Tiva as exotic, elegant, sexy, energetic, artsy
People who like the name Tiva also like Tehya, Ayita, Sora, Tala, Kaya, Layla, Topanga, Tazanna, Ayasha, Soraya

Tivona *(Hebrew)* ♀   RATING: ★★
Nature lover
People think of Tivona as creative, intelligent, caring, exotic, pretty
People who like the name Tivona also like Ophelia, Penelope, Thalia, Olivia, Naomi, Tabitha, Samara, Topanga, Ivy, Takoda

Tiya *(American)* ♀   RATING: ★★★
Variation of Tia or Tea
People think of Tiya as popular, pretty, funny, young, trustworthy
People who like the name Tiya also like Tanaya, Tori, Kira, Tyra, Lara, Tala, Taya, Trinity, Tanika, Iris

540

Toan (*Vietnamese*) ♀♂   RATING: ★★★
Safe, secure
People think of Toan as trustworthy, caring, creative, weird, sexy
People who like the name Toan also like Tynan, Tracen, Tacey, Taregan, Kyan, Naolin, Teagan, Torrin, Tyne, Kasen

Tobiah (*Hebrew*) ♂   RATING: ★★☆
God is good
People think of Tobiah as handsome, powerful, intelligent
People who like the name Tobiah also like Landon, Daniel, Patrick, Tobias, Thomas, Malachi, Micah, Dean, Calvin, Finley

Tobias (*Hebrew*) ♂   RATING: ★★★★
God is good
People think of Tobias as intelligent, handsome, caring, creative, funny
People who like the name Tobias also like Noah, Gabriel, Elijah, Tristan, Jacob, Isaac, Caleb, Ethan, Nathaniel, Samuel

Tobit (*Hebrew*) ♀   RATING: ★☆
Good
People think of Tobit as caring, quiet, trustworthy, unpopular, powerful
People who like the name Tobit also like Tatum, Faith, Felicity, Celeste, Sofia, Olivia, Erelah, Greta, Joan, Rimona

Toby (*English*) ♀♂   RATING: ★★☆
God is good—Short for Tobiah or Tobias
People think of Toby as funny, handsome, caring, cool, intelligent
People who like the name Toby also like Riley, Taylor, Logan, Bailey, Tyler, Parker, Hayden, Ryan, Jaden, Evan

Tocho (*Native American*) ♂   RATING: ★☆
Mountain lion—Hopi origin
People think of Tocho as exotic, wild, ethnic, lazy, powerful
People who like the name Tocho also like Mingan, Tokala, Sani, Tuari, Yaholo, Mikasi, Yuma, Ahanu, Ezhno, Hakan

Todd (*English*) ♂   RATING: ★★☆
Fox—Also spelled Tod
People think of Todd as handsome, funny, intelligent, trustworthy, caring
People who like the name Todd also like Nathan, Scott, Seth, Nicholas, Ethan, Zachary, Trevor, Jacob, Matthew, Ian

Tokala (*Native American*) ♂   RATING: ★★★☆
Fox—Dakota origin
People think of Tokala as intelligent, exotic, wild, leader, pretty
People who like the name Tokala also like Ryu, Hakan, Todd, Aiden, Sani, Tuari, Gabriel, Taran, Tyson, Isaac

Toki (*Japanese*) ♀   RATING: ★☆
Time of Opportunity
People think of Toki as exotic, cool, creative, artsy, pretty
People who like the name Toki also like Nariko, Yori, Sakura, Miyo, Keiko, Kaori, Miya, Suki, Inari, Kimi

Tokori (*Native American*) ♀♂   RATING: ★★☆
Owl—Hopi origin
People think of Tokori as handsome, creative, intelligent, leader, trustworthy
People who like the name Tokori also like Tai, Jariah, Jade, Camryn, Toby, Camdyn, Alex, Kieran, Madison, Kegan

Tolinka (*Native American*) ♀   RATING: ★☆
Coyote's ear—Miwok origin; originally Tolikna, but Americanized to Tolinka
People think of Tolinka as exotic, ethnic, weird, quiet, poor
People who like the name Tolinka also like Takoda, Topanga, Tala, Kaliska, Tivona, Shania, Salali, Tiva, Tallulah, Sokanon

Tolla (*Spanish*) ♀   RATING: ★★
Marsh—Catalan origin; possibly also a surname
People think of Tolla as weird, loser, wild, religious, unpopular
People who like the name Tolla also like Tillie, Talisa, Thalia, Tyronica, Tendai, Tamah, Olivia, Posy, Theodora, Teela

Tom (*Greek*) ♂   RATING: ★★☆
Short for Thomas—Also Hebrew meaning innocence or purity; Tom Cruise, actor; Tom Hanks, actor; Tom Petty, singer/songwriter
People think of Tom as funny, handsome, cool, intelligent, popular
People who like the name Tom also like Jack, Thomas, Luke, Jake, Adam, Matthew, Nathan, Samuel, Daniel, Jacob

Tomai (*Greek*) ♀♂   RATING: ★★★
Variation of Thomas—Also a surname
People think of Tomai as lazy, poor, artsy, creative, energetic
People who like the name Tomai also like Thady, Tamesis, Theron, Bell, Teagan, Tayte, Scorpio, Tracen, Hayden, Pierce

Tomas (*Scandinavian*) ♂   RATING: ★★★
Variation of Thomas
People think of Tomas as funny, handsome, intelligent, cool, caring
People who like the name Tomas also like Thomas, Samuel, Nicholas, Lucas, Noah, Matthew, Gabriel, Jacob, Daniel, Joshua

Tomi (*Japanese*) ♀♂   RATING: ★★★★
Rich
People think of Tomi as funny, intelligent, popular, trustworthy, pretty

People who like the name Tomi also like Nori, Rin, Asa, Yuki, Kiyoshi, Natsu, Ren, Kana, Maro, Hoshi

Tommy (English) ♂ RATING: ★★★
A twin—Short for Thomas; Tommy Hilfiger, designer; *Tommy*, rock opera by The Who
People think of Tommy as funny, cool, handsome, popular, sexy
People who like the name Tommy also like Matthew, Thomas, Ethan, Adam, Nathan, Tristan, Travis, Jacob, Patrick, Jack

Tomoko (Japanese) ♀ RATING: ★★★☆
Intelligent
People think of Tomoko as intelligent, pretty, caring, artsy, creative
People who like the name Tomoko also like Emiko, Miyoko, Yoshiko, Nariko, Keiko, Kaida, Yoko, Kaori, Kumiko, Sakura

Tomoyo (Japanese) ♀ RATING: ★★★★
Intelligent—Variation of Tomoko
People think of Tomoyo as intelligent, pretty, artsy, creative, caring
People who like the name Tomoyo also like Sakura, Miyoko, Yoshiko, Yoko, Nariko, Amaya, Tomoko, Emiko, Yoshino, Miyo

Toni (English) ♀ RATING: ★★☆
Short for Antonia—Toni Collette, actress; Toni Morrison, author
People think of Toni as funny, pretty, caring, trustworthy, intelligent
People who like the name Toni also like Tori, Paige, Hailey, Zoe, Tiffany, Faith, Emma, Samantha, Trinity, Nicole

Tony (English) ♂ RATING: ★★☆
Short for Antony—Also the award for outstanding U.S. theater productions; Tony Bennett, singer; Tony Shalhoub, actor
People think of Tony as funny, handsome, cool, intelligent, popular
People who like the name Tony also like Jason, Travis, Nathan, Justin, Matthew, Troy, Scott, Anthony, William, Timothy

Tonya (American) ♀ RATING: ★★★★
Short for Antonia; also a variation of Tanya
People think of Tonya as pretty, funny, caring, trustworthy, creative
People who like the name Tonya also like Faith, Hailey, Tiffany, Natalie, Samantha, Sarah, Sabrina, Rebecca, Hannah, Paige

Topanga (Native American) ♀ RATING: ★★★☆
A place above; where the mountain meets the sea—Topanga Canyon, California place name
People think of Topanga as pretty, intelligent, exotic, creative, artsy
People who like the name Topanga also like Phoebe, Trinity, Paige, Belle, Sabrina, Tabitha, Lorelei, Savannah, Serenity, Isabella

Topaz (Latin) ♀♂ RATING: ★★★★
Golden gem
People think of Topaz as pretty, trendy, cool, young, creative
People who like the name Topaz also like Jade, Taylor, Madison, Dakota, Sage, Teagan, Rain, Paris, Skye, Hayden

Topher (American) ♂ RATING: ★★★★
Christ bearer—Short for Christopher; Topher Grace, actor
People think of Topher as cool, intelligent, sporty, creative, leader
People who like the name Topher also like Tristan, Owen, Noah, Ethan, Jackson, Ian, Oliver, Gavin, Landon, Aiden

Topper (English) ♀♂ RATING: ★★★
One who attached the wool to the distaff for spinning—Originally a surname; Topper Headon, drummer
People think of Topper as funny, popular, caring, artsy, cool
People who like the name Topper also like Taylor, Parker, Tyler, Tanner, Piper, Tate, Rory, Logan, Jordan, Preston

Toral (Sanskrit/East Indian) ♀ RATING: ★★★
Folk heroine
People think of Toral as powerful, pretty, loser, cool, caring
People who like the name Toral also like Tessa, Tamanna, Samara, Jadyn, Tanaya, Tarala, Kaelyn, Summer, Tanuja, Kailey

Torgny (Scandinavian) ♂ RATING: ★★☆
Thor's roar
People think of Torgny as intelligent, loser, unpopular, funny, energetic
People who like the name Torgny also like Tristan, Timothy, Tarak, Trey, Taban, Cole, Glen, Langston, Thurman, Cargan

Tori (English) ♀ RATING: ★★★
Short for Victoria—Tori Spelling, actress
People think of Tori as pretty, funny, intelligent, caring, creative
People who like the name Tori also like Paige, Victoria, Hailey, Chloe, Olivia, Emma, Isabella, Hannah, Faith, Tessa

Torie (American) ♀ RATING: ★★★
Short for Victoria
People think of Torie as pretty, funny, intelligent, energetic, popular
People who like the name Torie also like Tori, Hailey, Paige, Victoria, Zoey, Hannah, Samantha, Sophie, Tessa, Hope

Toril (Scandinavian) ♀ RATING: ★★★☆
Thor's battle—Variation of Thorhild
People think of Toril as pretty, cool, intelligent, old, creative

541

People who like the name Toril also like Thora, Tansy, Kiara, Tyra, Kaida, Maura, Scarlett, Sonja, Tanika, Freja

Torn *(American)* ♂ RATING: ★★☆
Torn—Rip Torn, actor
People think of Torn as weird, loser, poor, girl next door, aggressive
People who like the name Torn also like Maddox, Jace, Slade, Taran, Walker, Darian, Sebastian, Griffin, Thorne, Kaden

Torolf *(Scandinavian)* ♂ RATING: ★★
Thor's wolf
People think of Torolf as weird, aggressive, powerful, handsome, exotic
People who like the name Torolf also like Rudolph, Ulric, Revelin, Wolfgang, Markku, Canute, Marcel, Xerxes, Zev, Faolan

Torrance *(English)* ♂ RATING: ★★
Variation of Terence
People think of Torrance as funny, cool, popular, sexy, handsome
People who like the name Torrance also like Tristan, Ethan, Aiden, Landon, Tyson, Trey, Gabriel, Kaden, Wyatt, Trenton

Torrin *(Celtic/Gaelic)* ♀♂ RATING: ★★★★
From the hills
People think of Torrin as leader, handsome, funny, intelligent, young
People who like the name Torrin also like Teagan, Logan, Reagan, Hayden, Tarin, Taryn, Caden, Riley, Jaden, Aidan

Torsten *(Scandinavian)* ♂ RATING: ★★★★
Stone of Thor
People think of Torsten as handsome, intelligent, creative, leader, energetic
People who like the name Torsten also like Tristan, Tiergan, Holden, Carsten, Thurston, Reece, Soren, Landon, Ryker, Tyson

Torvald *(Scandinavian)* ♂ RATING: ★★
Thor's rule
People think of Torvald as handsome, sexy, aggressive, unpopular, exotic
People who like the name Torvald also like Elijah, Xander, Thurston, Gunther, Brennan, Carsten, Vaughan, Gavan, Nathan, Nathaniel

Tory *(English)* ♀♂ RATING: ★★★
Short for Victoria
People think of Tory as funny, energetic, creative, intelligent, cool
People who like the name Tory also like Taylor, Tyler, Riley, Bailey, Ryan, Jaden, Hayden, Madison, Sydney, Logan

Tosca *(Italian)* ♀ RATING: ★★★☆
From Tuscany, Italy—Floria Tosca, character in *Tosca* by Puccini
People think of Tosca as exotic, pretty, intelligent, elegant, creative
People who like the name Tosca also like Bianca, Bella, Ruby, Scarlett, Emma, Francesca, Genevieve, Olivia, Roxy, Grace

Toshi *(Japanese)* ♀ RATING: ★★★☆
Year of plenty
People think of Toshi as energetic, funny, cool, intelligent, caring
People who like the name Toshi also like Yoshi, Haruko, Sakura, Kaida, Nariko, Nami, Emiko, Aiko, Yoshiko, Keiko

Totie *(English)* ♀ RATING: ★☆
Variation of Charlotte—Totie Fields, comedian
People think of Totie as weird, pretty, funny, nerdy, sneaky
People who like the name Totie also like Grace, Mckayla, Terena, Pippa, Tatum, Tessa, Callie, Ella, Vivi, Zinnia

Touré *(African)* ♂ RATING: ★★
Family of Soussou or Maninka
People think of Toure as aggressive, handsome, funny, weird, trendy
People who like the name Toure also like Oliver, Saber, Taye, Maddox, Pryce, Taariq, Terrel, Tadeo, Taban, Trey

Tova *(Hebrew)* ♀ RATING: ★★★★
Good—Tova Borgnine, cosmetic designer
People think of Tova as creative, caring, elegant, intelligent, artsy
People who like the name Tova also like Tovah, Olivia, Abigail, Stella, Hazel, Belle, Zoe, Talia, Tabitha, Samara

Tovah *(Hebrew)* ♀ RATING: ★★★☆
Good—Tovah Felsuh, actress
People think of Tovah as pretty, caring, popular, energetic, cool
People who like the name Tovah also like Tova, Ziva, Tessa, Olivia, Grace, Tori, Lily, Sephora, Sadie, Ivy

Tove *(Scandinavian)* ♂ RATING: ★★☆
Short for Torvald
People think of Tove as intelligent, pretty, winner, energetic, caring
People who like the name Tove also like Dane, Edwin, Owen, Clement, Birch, Jim, Keiji, Roosevelt, Tam, Van

Tovi *(Hebrew)* ♂ RATING: ★★★☆
My goodness
People think of Tovi as exotic, intelligent, funny, creative, powerful
People who like the name Tovi also like Taran, Walker, Rhys, Toviel, Jett, Tyson, Tristan, Levi, Zev, Gabriel

Toviel *(Hebrew)* ♂ RATING: ★☆
My God is goodness
People think of Toviel as powerful, young, ethnic, cool, caring

People who like the name Toviel also like Tobias, Gabriel, Tovi, Pryce, Elias, Isaiah, Mattox, Zedekiah, Taran, Josiah

Townsend (*English*)　♂　　　RATING: ★★★
From the end of the town—Pete Townsend, musician
People think of Townsend as popular, intelligent, cool, old-fashioned, nerdy
People who like the name Townsend also like Tristan, Tucker, William, Thornton, Jackson, Walker, Anderson, Weston, Landon, Warren

Toyah (*English*)　♀　　　RATING: ★★
Toy—Toyah Willcox, singer
People think of Toyah as funny, pretty, cool, intelligent, young
People who like the name Toyah also like Tanaya, Aaliyah, Talia, Tanika, Tessa, Trinity, Tanuja, Tehya, Torie, Tirza

Trace (*English*)　♀♂　　　RATING: ★★★★
From Tracy, France—Variation of Tracy
People think of Trace as funny, handsome, cool, caring, intelligent
People who like the name Trace also like Taylor, Logan, Hayden, Tanner, Caden, Parker, Mason, Riley, Tyler, Reese

Tracen (*American*)　♀♂　　　RATING: ★★★
From Tracy, France—Variation of Tracy
People think of Tracen as quiet, cool, creative, pretty, caring
People who like the name Tracen also like Teagan, Caden, Hayden, Tanner, Landen, Parker, Logan, Taylor, Mason, Jaden

Tracey (*English*)　♀♂　　　RATING: ★★★☆
From Tracy, France—Variation of Tracy; also spelled Tracie
People think of Tracey as lazy, funny, caring, pretty, trustworthy
People who like the name Tracey also like Taylor, Madison, Tyler, Kimberly, Ryan, Shannon, Brooke, Ashley, Tracy, Morgan

Traci (*English*)　♀　　　RATING: ★★★
From Tracy, France—Variation of Tracy; Traci Lords, actress
People think of Traci as caring, funny, pretty, trustworthy, intelligent
People who like the name Traci also like Samantha, Vanessa, Tiffany, Paige, Sabrina, Nicole, Lauren, Hailey, Faith, Rebecca

Tracy (*English*)　♀♂　　　RATING: ★★★☆
From Tracy, France—Also an Irish surname meaning descendent of the fierce one
People think of Tracy as funny, caring, intelligent, pretty, trustworthy
People who like the name Tracy also like Taylor, Ryan, Kimberly, Brooke, Ashley, Madison, Holly, Shannon, Lindsey, Morgan

Trang (*Vietnamese*)　♀　　　RATING: ★★★★
Serious, intelligent
People think of Trang as intelligent, pretty, caring, creative, cool
People who like the name Trang also like Tonya, Bella, Tress, Emily, Celeste, Tristana, Bethany, Tanaya, Tierra, Tirzah

Tranquilla (*Spanish*)　♀　　　RATING: ★★
Calm, tranquil
People think of Tranquilla as loser, weird, nerdy, intelligent, slow
People who like the name Tranquilla also like Jasmine, Bianca, Samantha, Evangeline, Violet, Zabrina, Grace, Summer, India, Tameka

Trapper (*American*)　♀♂　　　RATING: ★★★
Trapper—Trapper John, character on *M*A*S*H*
People think of Trapper as creative, cool, trustworthy, weird, funny
People who like the name Trapper also like Parker, Spencer, Tanner, Hunter, Hayden, Sawyer, Tyler, Paxton, River, Ryder

Travis (*English*)　♂　　　RATING: ★★☆
From the crossing or tollgate—Also a surname; Travis Tritt, singer; Randy Travis, singer
People think of Travis as handsome, funny, intelligent, cool, caring
People who like the name Travis also like Trevor, Ethan, Jacob, Tristan, Nathan, Zachary, Justin, Lucas, Nicholas, Trent

Trella (*Spanish*)　♀　　　RATING: ★★
Star—Short for Estrella
People think of Trella as pretty, creative, artsy, religious, trustworthy
People who like the name Trella also like Mercedes, Tegan, Teresa, Kayla, Sabrina, Tahlia, Regan, Tabitha, Ella, Cordelia

Tremain (*Celtic/Gaelic*)　♂　　　RATING: ★★
From the town of the stone—Cornish place name; also an English surname
People think of Tremain as funny, sporty, young, handsome, powerful
People who like the name Tremain also like Tristan, Torrance, Jayden, Trenton, Keiran, Liam, Trevor, Teague, Tarmon, Tiernan

Trent (*English*)　♂　　　RATING: ★★★
Thirty—Also a surname meaning from the river Trent or liable to flood
People think of Trent as handsome, funny, intelligent, cool, caring
People who like the name Trent also like Tristan, Trevor, Ethan, Seth, Caleb, Noah, Landon, Travis, Trey, Jacob

Trenton (*English*)　♂　　　RATING: ★★★★☆
From the town by the river Trent—Also a town in New Jersey
People think of Trenton as handsome, intelligent, funny, popular, cool

People who like the name Trenton also like Tristan, Ethan, Landon, Trevor, Kaden, Trent, Gavin, Caleb, Aiden, Noah

Tress (English) ♀ 　　　RATING: ★★★
Long hair—Tress MacNeille, voiceover artist
People think of Tress as funny, creative, artsy, energetic, elegant
People who like the name Tress also like Trista, Keira, Scarlett, Tessa, Victoria, Rianna, Mia, Serenity, Lana, Grace

Treva (English) ♀ 　　　RATING: ★★★☆
Prudent—Feminine form of Trevor
People think of Treva as caring, intelligent, funny, trustworthy, pretty
People who like the name Treva also like Twyla, Scarlett, Tyra, Thalia, Trista, Rhian, Olivia, Tavia, Tessa, Terena

Trevelian (Celtic/Gaelic) ♂ 　　　RATING: ★★★
From the homestead of Elian—Cornish place name; also an English surname
People think of Trevelian as aggressive, powerful, handsome, caring, sexy
People who like the name Trevelian also like Tristan, Saeran, Gareth, Taran, Aiden, Merric, Gavin, Soren, Levi, Jayden

Trevet (English) ♂ 　　　RATING: ★★☆
Tripod—Originally a surname
People think of Trevet as weird, nerdy, aggressive, criminal, handsome
People who like the name Trevet also like Tristan, Owen, Tiergan, Trey, Gavin, Aiden, Trent, Dawson, Micah, Gage

Trevor (Celtic/Gaelic) ♂ 　　　RATING: ★★★
Prudent
People think of Trevor as handsome, funny, intelligent, cool, caring
People who like the name Trevor also like Ethan, Tristan, Zachary, Nathan, Aiden, Travis, Caleb, Jacob, Nicholas, Noah

Trey (Italian) ♂ 　　　RATING: ★★★
Three
People think of Trey as handsome, cool, funny, popular, intelligent
People who like the name Trey also like Tristan, Ethan, Aiden, Landon, Trevor, Kaden, Trent, Caleb, Noah, Seth

Triage (French) ♀♂ 　　　RATING: ★★
Process of managing injured people—Pronounced TREE-azhe
People think of Triage as creative, unpopular, quiet, exotic, nerdy
People who like the name Triage also like Parker, Blaise, Riley, Sydney, Paris, Coty, Madison, Jax, Sawyer, Connor

Trianna (American) ♀ 　　　RATING: ★★★
Noble, gracious—Combination of Tricia and Anna
People think of Trianna as pretty, popular, trendy, sexy, sneaky

People who like the name Trianna also like Suri, Carly, Kailey, Thalia, Rihanna, Kayla, Tiana, Ayla, Kirsi, Athalia

Tricia (Latin) ♀ 　　　RATING: ★★★☆
Noble—Short for Patricia
People think of Tricia as caring, funny, pretty, intelligent, trustworthy
People who like the name Tricia also like Samantha, Paige, Rebecca, Olivia, Vanessa, Rachel, Chloe, Trisha, Hailey, Hannah

Trilby (English) ♀♂ 　　　RATING: ★★
From Thorolf's farm—Also a surname; also a type of hat; Trilby O'Ferrall, character in *Trilby* by George du Maurier
People think of Trilby as pretty, creative, young, funny, trustworthy
People who like the name Trilby also like Shelby, Hayden, Madison, Taryn, Taylor, Teagan, Riley, Piper, Quinn, Logan

Trina (English) ♀ 　　　RATING: ★★☆
Short for Katrina
People think of Trina as pretty, intelligent, caring, funny, creative
People who like the name Trina also like Sabrina, Tessa, Paige, Samantha, Trista, Faith, Trinity, Savannah, Sophia, Olivia

Trinh (Vietnamese) ♀ 　　　RATING: ★★
Pure
People think of Trinh as pretty, creative, trustworthy, exotic, quiet
People who like the name Trinh also like Layla, Trina, Tansy, Tonya, Tuyen, Thyra, Talia, Tiara, Tabitha, Tehya

Trini (Spanish) ♀ 　　　RATING: ★★★☆
Holy trinity—Short for Trinidad; Trini Lopez, musician
People think of Trini as caring, aggressive, intelligent, trustworthy, funny
People who like the name Trini also like Grace, Trinity, Tara, Ivy, Paige, Tia, Naomi, Gabriella, Faith, Zoey

Trinidad (Spanish) ♀ 　　　RATING: ★★☆
Holy trinity—Also a country in the Caribbean
People think of Trinidad as exotic, ethnic, intelligent, pretty, funny
People who like the name Trinidad also like Allegra, Antonia, Isabella, Octavia, Clara, Helena, Devorah, Mahlah, Rae, Kamala

Trinity (English) ♀ 　　　RATING: ★★★★
Holy trinity
People think of Trinity as pretty, intelligent, funny, creative, caring
People who like the name Trinity also like Faith, Serenity, Paige, Destiny, Hailey, Savannah, Chloe, Hannah, Olivia, Ava

Trish (English) ♀ 　　　RATING: ★★★☆
Noble—Short for Patricia
People think of Trish as funny, pretty, creative, trustworthy, intelligent

People who like the name Trish also like Samantha, Trisha, Faith, Jessica, Hailey, Amber, Paige, Savannah, Sabrina, Rebecca

Trisha *(English)* ♀　　　　　RATING: ★★☆
Noble—Short for Patricia; also a Hindi name meaning desire or thirst
People think of Trisha as funny, pretty, caring, intelligent, trustworthy
People who like the name Trisha also like Hailey, Samantha, Natalie, Paige, Tiffany, Rebecca, Olivia, Grace, Hannah, Faith

Trishna *(Sanskrit/East Indian)* ♀　　　　　RATING: ★★☆
Thirst, desire
People think of Trishna as popular, pretty, ethnic, aggressive, cool
People who like the name Trishna also like Tarika, Triveni, Tamanna, Tanika, Denali, Tvisha, Tarala, Tarannum, Teja, Tanuja

Triska *(Slavic)* ♀　　　　　RATING: ★★★
Sliver—Czech place name; also a surname
People think of Triska as pretty, intelligent, exotic, artsy, cool
People who like the name Triska also like Trina, Tien, Trinity, Keira, Stella, Terah, Kera, Celeste, Kiara, Calista

Trista *(American)* ♀　　　　　RATING: ★★★★
Tumult—Feminine form of Tristan
People think of Trista as pretty, funny, caring, intelligent, creative
People who like the name Trista also like Paige, Chloe, Hailey, Olivia, Emma, Isabella, Faith, Tara, Natalie, Tessa

Tristan *(Celtic/Gaelic)* ♂　　　　　RATING: ★★★☆
Tumult—Probably also from the French word *triste* meaning sad, from the doomed romance of Tristan and Isolde; also spelled Tristen or Tristin; *Tristan und Isolde*, opera by Wagner
People think of Tristan as handsome, intelligent, caring, popular, leader
People who like the name Tristan also like Aiden, Ethan, Noah, Landon, Caleb, Gabriel, Kaden, Gavin, Owen, Jacob

Tristana *(Spanish)* ♀　　　　　RATING: ★★☆
Tumult—Feminine form of Tristan
People think of Tristana as pretty, elegant, caring, exotic, sexy
People who like the name Tristana also like Trista, Olivia, Natalia, Paige, Ava, Isabella, Trinity, Tierra, Tatiana, Tiana

Tristessa *(Italian)* ♀　　　　　RATING: ★★★
Sadness—From the French word *tristesse* meaning sadness; also a combination of Trista and Vanessa
People think of Tristessa as pretty, intelligent, exotic, artsy, creative
People who like the name Tristessa also like Tristana, Theodora, Isadora, Bianca, Oriana, Rhiannon, Cordelia, Cassandra, Tessa, Bethany

Tristram *(English)* ♂　　　　　RATING: ★★★★
Combination of Tristan and Bertram—Character in *Tristram Shandy* by Laurence Sterne
People think of Tristram as handsome, intelligent, weird, funny, energetic
People who like the name Tristram also like Tristan, Ethan, Gavin, Dominic, Patrick, Isaac, Gage, Gavan, Anthony, Owen

Triveni *(Sanskrit/East Indian)* ♀　　　　　RATING: ★★★
Where three sacred rivers meet
People think of Triveni as caring, intelligent, cool, religious, young
People who like the name Triveni also like Tamanna, Tanaya, Tanika, Tarika, Tvisha, Tanuja, Tarannum, Tarala, Denali

Trixie *(English)* ♀　　　　　RATING: ★★
Bringer of joy—Short for Beatrix
People think of Trixie as pretty, popular, intelligent, sexy, energetic
People who like the name Trixie also like Scarlett, Sadie, Trinity, Lexi, Paige, Roxy, Faith, Tabitha, Sabrina, Sophie

Trory *(Celtic/Gaelic)* ♂　　　　　RATING: ★★
Unknown meaning—Probably from a village in Ireland
People think of Trory as weird, unpopular, criminal, nerdy, wild
People who like the name Trory also like Caleb, Trey, Reece, Nathan, Tristan, Lucas, Gabe, Thatcher, Travis, Trenton

Troy *(Celtic/Gaelic)* ♂　　　　　RATING: ★★☆
Water; footsoldier—Troy Donahue, actor
People think of Troy as handsome, intelligent, funny, cool, popular
People who like the name Troy also like Tristan, Ethan, Cole, Trey, Trevor, Caleb, Aiden, Tyson, Zachary, Jacob

Troya *(Celtic/Gaelic)* ♀　　　　　RATING: ★★☆
Water; footsoldier—Feminine form of Troy
People think of Troya as cool, young, funny, creative, aggressive
People who like the name Troya also like Emma, Zora, Fiona, Maya, Anna, Ailis, Camille, Faylinn, Caelan, Kacia

Truda *(Polish)* ♀　　　　　RATING: ★★☆
Spear strength—Short for Gertruda
People think of Truda as wild, leader, powerful, funny, weird
People who like the name Truda also like Trista, Talulah, Tamira, Marigold, Myrtle, Terena, Tarika, Tameka, Rowena, Tamika

Trude *(German)* ♀　　　　　RATING: ★☆
Spear strength—Short for Gertrude
People think of Trude as weird, old, big, old-fashioned, unpopular
People who like the name Trude also like Naomi, Tallulah, Talulah, Trinity, Tawny, Nickan, Teryl, Tynice, Lira, Terah

Trudy (*English*) ♀ 　 RATING: ★★
Spear strength—Short for Gertrude
> People think of Trudy as pretty, caring, trustworthy, intelligent, creative
> People who like the name Trudy also like Olivia, Samantha, Grace, Sophie, Maggie, Vanessa, Emma, Phoebe, Daisy, Sabrina

Trula (*German*) ♀ 　 RATING: ★★
True
> People think of Trula as caring, trustworthy, intelligent, elegant, religious
> People who like the name Trula also like Tanisha, Tyra, Tanith, Tavita, Terena, Trina, Tiana, Tamira, Tarika, Trista

Truly (*English*) ♀ 　 RATING: ★★★☆
Honestly—Truly Scrumptious, character in *Chitty Chitty Bang Bang*
> People think of Truly as pretty, trustworthy, creative, young, intelligent
> People who like the name Truly also like Scarlett, Bella, Harmony, Hope, Sabrina, Sophie, Trinity, Faith, Felicity, Lucy

Truman (*English*) ♂ 　 RATING: ★★★☆
Faithful man—Also a surname; Truman Capote, author; Harry S. Truman, U.S. president
> People think of Truman as handsome, trustworthy, intelligent, leader, old-fashioned
> People who like the name Truman also like Noah, Holden, Oliver, Tristan, Jackson, Walker, Lucas, Griffin, Liam, Tucker

Trumble (*English*) ♂ 　 RATING: ★★☆
Strong bold—Originally a surname
> People think of Trumble as aggressive, winner, big, energetic, funny
> People who like the name Trumble also like Conner, Tucker, Tristan, Rockwell, Brice, Reece, Radley, Thaddeus, Rhett, Ranger

Trung (*Vietnamese*) ♀♂ 　 RATING: ★★★
Medium
> People think of Trung as loser, sexy, weird, handsome, powerful
> People who like the name Trung also like Linh, Kiral, Nyoka, Orly, Zayn, Loki, Kieve, Thu, Limon, Kumi

Truong (*Vietnamese*) ♂ 　 RATING: ★★
School, field
> People think of Truong as cool, funny, weird, quiet, boy next door
> People who like the name Truong also like Titus, Altan, Kyros, Sereno, Dacian, Emil, Soren, Magar, Dragan, Damek

Trusha (*American*) ♀ 　 RATING: ★★☆
Noble—Variation of Trisha
> People think of Trusha as weird, winner, intelligent, sneaky, popular
> People who like the name Trusha also like Tulia, Triveni, Tessica, Trista, Tristana, Talisha, Taline, Makaila, Rea, Reina

Trygg (*Scandinavian*) ♂ 　 RATING: ★★★
True
> People think of Trygg as big, intelligent, cool, caring, aggressive
> People who like the name Trygg also like Liam, Tristan, Tucker, Cole, Silas, Trey, Alden, Tyson, Trenton, Jack

Tryna (*English*) ♀ 　 RATING: ★★★
Variation of Trina
> People think of Tryna as popular, pretty, intelligent, trustworthy, creative
> People who like the name Tryna also like Tiana, Paige, Tessa, Trinity, Kyra, Tiffany, Kera, Phylicia, Thalia, Faith

Trynt (*English*) ♂ 　 RATING: ★★★
Thirty—Variation of Trent
> People think of Trynt as leader, handsome, nerdy, lazy, weird
> People who like the name Trynt also like Tristan, Trent, Trenton, Trey, Aiden, Braden, Seth, Ethan, Gavin, Kaden

Tryphena (*Greek*) ♀ 　 RATING: ★★★
Delicate
> People think of Tryphena as exotic, creative, pretty, sexy, wild
> People who like the name Tryphena also like Thalia, Thisbe, Tanith, Rhea, Iris, Melody, Thea, Thetis, Tanaya, Kalista

Tsubasa (*Japanese*) ♂ 　 RATING: ★★★
Wings
> People think of Tsubasa as handsome, funny, pretty, leader, creative
> People who like the name Tsubasa also like Keitaro, Kaemon, Kamin, Itachi, Ryu, Daiki, Adish, Shouta, Aaron, Luke

Tu (*Vietnamese*) ♂ 　 RATING: ★☆
Bright, sharp—Also means you in Spanish
> People think of Tu as young, intelligent, creative, funny, sneaky
> People who like the name Tu also like Gabriel, Grayson, Tyson, Harrison, Joshua, Saeran, Nathan, Bradley, Julio, Kato

Tuan (*Vietnamese*) ♂ 　 RATING: ★★★☆
Chivalrous lord, gentlemanly
> People think of Tuan as handsome, cool, funny, caring, intelligent
> People who like the name Tuan also like Tristan, Tameron, Tyson, Trey, Tareq, Trent, Troy, Xander, Theodore, Tudor

Tuari (*Native American*) ♂ 　 RATING: ★★★☆
Young eagle
> People think of Tuari as exotic, trustworthy, leader, intelligent, handsome
> People who like the name Tuari also like Tokala, Tocho, Dasan, Mingan, Chayton, Hakan, Kaden, Tristan, Ezhno, Tyson

Tucker (*English*) ♂　　　　　RATING: ★★★★
Tucker of cloth
　People think of Tucker as handsome, funny, energetic,
　intelligent, popular
　People who like the name Tucker also like Tristan,
　Ethan, Noah, Owen, Jackson, Landon, Aiden, Walker,
　Trevor, Conner

Tudor (*Welsh*) ♂　　　　　RATING: ★☆
People king—Also the surname of English royalty;
Elizabeth I; Henry VIII
　People think of Tudor as intelligent, handsome, caring,
　creative, powerful
　People who like the name Tudor also like Tristan, Lucas,
　Theodore, Cole, Nicholas, Ian, Liam, Ethan, Walker,
　Lucian

Tuesday (*American*) ♀ ♂　　　　　RATING: ★★
Born on Tuesday—Tuesday Weld (born Susan Ker
Weld), actress; she called herself "Tu-tu" (for "Sue-
Sue") when she was young and the nickname then
got elongated to Tuesday
　People think of Tuesday as pretty, funny, popular, cool,
　energetic
　People who like the name Tuesday also like Wednesday,
　Parker, Piper, Taylor, Quinn, Riley, Madison, Phoenix,
　Sage, Tyler

Tulia (*Swahili*) ♀　　　　　RATING: ★★★☆
Calm, quiet
　People think of Tulia as pretty, funny, quiet, elegant,
　intelligent
　People who like the name Tulia also like Talia, Tatiana,
　Tiana, Raina, Keira, Aurora, Jasmine, Tahlia, Trinity,
　Thalia

Tully (*Celtic/Gaelic*) ♀ ♂　　　　　RATING: ★★
From the little hill
　People think of Tully as funny, creative, intelligent, car-
　ing, cool
　People who like the name Tully also like Riley, Teagan,
　Brody, Quinn, Torrin, Logan, Blair, Harper, Reilly, Rowan

Tumo (*African*) ♂　　　　　RATING: ★★
Fame
　People think of Tumo as funny, big, sporty, leader,
　caring
　People who like the name Tumo also like Tenen, Makalo,
　Phomello, Oliver, Tedros, Keefer, Tadelesh, Baruch,
　Desiderio, Brice

Tunder (*Hungarian*) ♀　　　　　RATING: ★★
Fairy
　People think of Tunder as weird, pretty, ethnic, girl next
　door, loser
　People who like the name Tunder also like Aimee,
　Gabriella, Calla, Gabrielle, Tatiana, Channah, Freya,
　Annabelle, Ella, Cheri

Tupac (*Aztec/Nahuatl*) ♂　　　　　RATING: ★★★★
Warrior; messenger—Túpac Amaru II, an Incan revolu-
tionary; Tupac Shakur, singer/rapper
　People think of Tupac as powerful, leader, popular, intel-
　ligent, aggressive
　People who like the name Tupac also like Tristan,
　Tyrone, Tyson, Trey, Terence, Isaiah, Malachi, Travis,
　Quentin, Xavier

Turi (*Scandinavian*) ♂　　　　　RATING: ★★★
Of Thor
　People think of Turi as funny, big, exotic, weird,
　intelligent
　People who like the name Turi also like Tristan, Tadeo,
　Diego, Tuari, Taban, Maddox, Theo, Vito, Alvaro, Valin

Turner (*English*) ♂　　　　　RATING: ★★☆
Lathe worker—Also a surname; Ted Turner, media
mogul; Tina Turner, singer
　People think of Turner as funny, intelligent, handsome,
　cool, popular
　People who like the name Turner also like Tucker,
　Tristan, Jackson, Ethan, Walker, Kaden, Landon, Trevor,
　Tyson, Owen

Tut (*Egyptian*) ♂　　　　　RATING: ★★★
Image—Nickname for King Tutankhamen of Egypt
　People think of Tut as big, aggressive, leader, exotic,
　powerful
　People who like the name Tut also like Tristan, Marcel,
　Gordon, Trey, Anakin, Marshall, Thomas, Zander, Xander,
　Mace

Tuvya (*Hebrew*) ♂　　　　　RATING: ★☆
God's goodness
　People think of Tuvya as religious, weird, stuck-up,
　nerdy, exotic
　People who like the name Tuvya also like Tymon, Tarak,
　Tadelesh, Tobias, Gavril, Asher, Alijah, Gabriel, Trey,
　Toviel

Tuwa (*Native American*) ♀　　　　　RATING: ★★☆
Earth—Hopi origin
　People think of Tuwa as ethnic, quiet, creative, loser,
　energetic
　People who like the name Tuwa also like Tehya, Tiva,
　Topanga, Sora, Neena, Tallulah, Ayasha, Taini, Cocheta,
　Talulah

Tuyen (*Vietnamese*) ♀　　　　　RATING: ★★★☆
Angel
　People think of Tuyen as intelligent, caring, quiet,
　young, elegant
　People who like the name Tuyen also like Tevy, Tuyet,
　Tatiana, Trinh, Tehya, Vevina, Thea, Melangell, Tangia,
　Tansy

Tuyet (*Vietnamese*) ♀　　　　　RATING: ★★★☆
Snow
　People think of Tuyet as pretty, quiet, intelligent, ethnic,
　young

People who like the name Tuyet also like Tuyen, Kumani, Tehya, Tallulah, Kya, Topanga, Delilah, Tanaya, Thalia, Melody

Tvisha (*Sanskrit/East Indian*) ♀ RATING: ★★★
Bright
> People think of Tvisha as intelligent, powerful, energetic, exotic, winner
> People who like the name Tvisha also like Tanika, Tarika, Tamanna, Tanuja, Triveni, Tanaya, Tarannum, Tarala, Tanisha, Trishna

Twila (*American*) ♀ ♂ RATING: ★★★☆
Twilight
> People think of Twila as creative, trustworthy, caring, intelligent, pretty
> People who like the name Twila also like Morgan, Willow, Teagan, Holly, Skylar, Taryn, Tate, Kendall, Taylor, Tyler

Twyla (*American*) ♀ RATING: ★★★★
Twilight—Twyla Tharp, dancer/choreographer
> People think of Twyla as pretty, intelligent, trustworthy, caring, funny
> People who like the name Twyla also like Tabitha, Tessa, Tatum, Olivia, Shayla, Scarlett, Vivian, Hannah, Veronica, Paige

Ty (*American*) ♀ ♂ RATING: ★★★★
Short for Tyrone or Tyler—Ty Cobb, baseball player
> People think of Ty as handsome, funny, cool, popular, intelligent
> People who like the name Ty also like Tyler, Taylor, Riley, Hayden, Caden, Parker, Bailey, Dylan, Reese, Logan

Tyanne (*American*) ♀ RATING: ★★★☆
Combination of Ty and Anne
> People think of Tyanne as pretty, leader, funny, intelligent, cool
> People who like the name Tyanne also like Tiana, Trinity, Tessa, Tyra, Tailynn, Talia, Trista, Paige, Rianne, Tanaya

Tybalt (*English*) ♂ RATING: ★★★☆
People bold—Variation of Theobald; pronounced *TIB-bult*; character in *Romeo and Juliet* by William Shakespeare
> People think of Tybalt as handsome, cool, powerful, leader, aggressive
> People who like the name Tybalt also like Xavier, Xander, Gabriel, Oliver, Lysander, Tobias, Aiden, Tristan, Owen, Tyson

Tyler (*English*) ♀ ♂ RATING: ★★★☆
Tile maker—Tyler Hilton, singer/actor; Tyler Perry, author/actor
> People think of Tyler as funny, handsome, cool, intelligent, popular
> People who like the name Tyler also like Taylor, Ryan, Riley, Dylan, Logan, Madison, Hayden, Bailey, Connor, Jordan

Tyme (*English*) ♀ ♂ RATING: ★★★
Thyme herb
> People think of Tyme as creative, weird, artsy, pretty, trendy
> People who like the name Tyme also like Sage, Teagan, Skye, Logan, Taylor, Skylar, Tyler, Madison, Tyne, Reese

Tymon (*English*) ♂ RATING: ★★★☆
Honor, praise—Variation of Timon
> People think of Tymon as handsome, caring, sexy, cool, intelligent
> People who like the name Tymon also like Tyson, Tristan, Torrance, Thaddeus, Jayden, Tyrell, Micah, Trenton, Nathan, Kaden

Tynan (*Celtic/Gaelic*) ♀ ♂ RATING: ★★
Dark
> People think of Tynan as intelligent, handsome, creative, cool, powerful
> People who like the name Tynan also like Teagan, Torrin, Aidan, Logan, Skye, Riley, Tyler, Tarin, Caden, Taryn

Tyne (*English*) ♀ ♂ RATING: ★★★★☆
A river—Also a nickname for names ending in –tine
> People think of Tyne as intelligent, young, funny, creative, wild
> People who like the name Tyne also like Talen, Teagan, Madison, Thane, Taylor, Logan, Torrin, Tynan, Parker, Tyler

Tynice (*American*) ♀ RATING: ★★★
Combination of Ty and Bernice—Pronounced *TY-neese*
> People think of Tynice as pretty, young, sexy, funny, girl next door
> People who like the name Tynice also like Trinity, Tanaya, Tyronica, Tyanne, Tyra, Tahlia, Tiana, Tariana, Taja, Tierra

Tyra (*Scandinavian*) ♀ RATING: ★★★
God of battle—Also a Celtic name meaning land; Tyra Banks, model/TV host
> People think of Tyra as pretty, funny, popular, intelligent, cool
> People who like the name Tyra also like Paige, Trinity, Victoria, Nadia, Hailey, Tara, Faith, Olivia, Kayla, Tiana

Tyreak (*American*) ♂ RATING: ★★★☆
Combination of Tyrone and Dominique
> People think of Tyreak as sexy, handsome, young, caring, powerful
> People who like the name Tyreak also like Tyson, Tyrone, Tyrell, Jayden, Tristan, Terrel, Terence, Taurean, Tavon, Tameron

Tyree (*Celtic/Gaelic*) ♀ ♂ RATING: ★★☆
Island off Scotland
> People think of Tyree as popular, caring, funny, creative, intelligent
> People who like the name Tyree also like Tyrique, Jaden, Terran, Riley, Teagan, Ryan, Taylor, Jade, Caden, Aidan

Tyrell (*English*) ♂　　RATING: ★★★☆
Stubborn—Variation of Terrell
- People think of Tyrell as handsome, funny, popular, sexy, cool
- People who like the name Tyrell also like Tyrone, Tyson, Tristan, Kaden, Trey, Xavier, Jayden, Ethan, Terrel, Nathan

Tyrese (*American*) ♂　　RATING: ★★★☆
Combination of Ty and Reese—Tyrese Gibson, actor/singer
- People think of Tyrese as handsome, popular, sexy, intelligent, cool
- People who like the name Tyrese also like Tyrone, Tyrell, Tristan, Tyson, Travis, Terrence, Jayden, Damian, Kaden, André

Tyrique (*American*) ♀♂　　RATING: ★★★★
Combination of Tyrone and Dominique
- People think of Tyrique as handsome, popular, young, sexy, intelligent
- People who like the name Tyrique also like Tyree, Jaden, Tyler, Jade, Cadence, Jordan, Dakota, Hayden, Dante, Madison

Tyrone (*Celtic/Gaelic*) ♂　　RATING: ★★★☆
From the land of Eoghan—Tyrone Power, actor
- People think of Tyrone as handsome, funny, cool, sexy, intelligent
- People who like the name Tyrone also like Tyson, Tyrell, Tristan, Ethan, Troy, Caleb, Xavier, Nathan, Jayden, Jacob

Tyronica (*American*) ♀　　RATING: ★★★☆
Combination of Tyrone and Veronica
- People think of Tyronica as pretty, criminal, sneaky, intelligent, leader
- People who like the name Tyronica also like Tyra, Tiana, Isis, Veronica, Trinity, Jazlynn, Tynice, Roxanne, Vanessa, Tessa

Tyson (*English*) ♂　　RATING: ★★★★
Firebrand; son of Denis—Also spelled Tycen; Tyson Beckford, fashion model; Mike Tyson, boxer
- People think of Tyson as handsome, funny, cool, sporty, popular
- People who like the name Tyson also like Tristan, Ethan, Kaden, Jackson, Landon, Aiden, Zachary, Caleb, Trevor, Braden

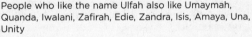

Uday (*Arabic*) ♂　　RATING: ★★
One who runs fast—Uday Hussein, son of Saddam Hussein
- People think of Uday as powerful, sporty, wealthy, intelligent, cool
- People who like the name Uday also like Umed, Gaurav, Ashwin, Vinay, Manas, Atish, Tarun, Nitesh, Adit, Rohak

Udell (*English*) ♂　　RATING: ★☆
From the yew valley—Originally a surname
- People think of Udell as nerdy, aggressive, religious, sexy, winner
- People who like the name Udell also like Xadrian, Xander, Samuel, Faolan, Jared, Kaden, Xavier, Orlando, Adair, Marcus

Ugo (*Italian*) ♂　　RATING: ★★★
Mind, spirit—Variation of Hugo; Ugo Tognazzi, actor
- People think of Ugo as weird, nerdy, loser, big, wild
- People who like the name Ugo also like Xavier, Wade, Aaron, Samuel, Ulric, Hugo, Nicholas, Isaac, Jacob, Xander

Ula (*American*) ♀　　RATING: ★★★☆
Jewel of the sea
- People think of Ula as pretty, exotic, funny, intelligent, artsy
- People who like the name Ula also like Una, Lana, Paige, Sabrina, Maeve, Iris, Olivia, Ava, Kara, Skyla

Ulani (*Hawaiian*) ♀　　RATING: ★★★☆
Cheerful
- People think of Ulani as exotic, pretty, creative, cool, sexy
- People who like the name Ulani also like Leilani, Ailani, Kailani, Olivia, Okalani, Noelani, Gabrielle, Miliani, Nadia, Faith

Ulema (*Arabic*) ♂　　RATING: ★☆
Scholars
- People think of Ulema as big, unpopular, slow, sexy, exotic
- People who like the name Ulema also like Xavier, Quentin, Ulysses, Xander, Edwin, Julio, Lehana, Rex, Tristan, Caleb

Ulf (*German*) ♀♂　　RATING: ★☆
Wolf
- People think of Ulf as weird, aggressive, funny, old-fashioned, old
- People who like the name Ulf also like Dylan, Page, Ryder, Riley, Reese, Jude, Kizzy, Demi, Quinn, Rain

Ulfah (*Arabic*) ♀　　RATING: ★☆
Affection, intimacy
- People think of Ulfah as loser, old, nerdy, lazy, pretty
- People who like the name Ulfah also like Umaymah, Quanda, Iwalani, Zafirah, Edie, Zandra, Isis, Amaya, Una, Unity

Ull (*German*) ♀♂　　RATING: ★★☆
Wolf power—Short for Ulric; also a Norse god of skiers
- People think of Ull as loser, big, nerdy, lazy, powerful
- People who like the name Ull also like Ulf, Xola, Blaze, Rune, Kiyoshi, Aquarius, Liberty, Angel, Merle, Mitsu

Ulla (*Scandinavian*) ♀　　RATING: ★☆
Short for Ulrike
- People think of Ulla as pretty, creative, exotic, powerful, intelligent

People who like the name Ulla also like Scarlett, Genna, Winifred, Una, Ula, Sheena, Maisie, Shawna, Lana, Mae

Ulmer (*English*) ♂ RATING: ★★☆
Famous wolf
People think of Ulmer as lazy, weird, untrustworthy, quiet, nerdy
People who like the name Ulmer also like Ulric, Quentin, Xavier, Wilmer, Tavon, Albert, Keagan, Wolfgang, Arthur, Felix

Ulric (*English*) ♂ RATING: ★☆
Wolf ruler
People think of Ulric as powerful, intelligent, leader, creative, quiet
People who like the name Ulric also like Xavier, Liam, William, Isaac, Tobias, Xander, Owen, Ian, Zander, Drake

Ulysses (*Latin*) ♂ RATING: ★★
Wounded in the thigh—Variation of Odysseus; Ulysses S. Grant, U.S. president
People think of Ulysses as intelligent, handsome, cool, leader, popular
People who like the name Ulysses also like Xavier, Gabriel, Elijah, Victor, Matthew, Isaiah, Zachary, Nicholas, Benjamin, Aaron

Uma (*Sanskrit/East Indian/Israeli*) ♀ RATING: ★☆
Tranquility; nation—Used for children born on Israeli Independence Day; also a Sanskrit name meaning tranquility; Uma Thurman, actress
People think of Uma as pretty, exotic, creative, intelligent, sexy
People who like the name Uma also like Olivia, Paige, Fiona, Ava, Abigail, Layla, Sofia, Giselle, Sadie, Nadia

Umay (*Turkish*) ♀ RATING: ★☆
Hope
People think of Umay as exotic, cool, pretty, artsy, nerdy
People who like the name Umay also like Faith, Opal, Ulani, Hannah, Alexa, Scarlett, Emma, Caitlyn, Hope, Elizabeth

Umaymah (*Arabic*) ♀ RATING: ★★☆
Young mother
People think of Umaymah as aggressive, poor, stuck-up, religious, pretty
People who like the name Umaymah also like Xantara, Qwara, Xalvadora, Xochitl, Quasar, Fatima, Zaltana, Ujana, Nozomi, Qi

Umberto (*Italian*) ♂ RATING: ★★★
Bright warrior
People think of Umberto as funny, handsome, sexy, powerful, intelligent
People who like the name Umberto also like Ulysses, Zachary, Giovanni, Salvatore, Xavier, Giancarlo, Gabriel, Justin, Lazzaro, Dominic

Umed (*Sanskrit/East Indian*) ♂ RATING: ★☆
Hope
People think of Umed as popular, handsome, ethnic, trustworthy, intelligent
People who like the name Umed also like Uday, Suvan, Kuval, Vatsa, Manas, Viral, Xhaiden, Xylon, Vadin, Upton

Umeko (*Japanese*) ♀ RATING: ★★★☆
Plum blossom child
People think of Umeko as creative, ethnic, intelligent, exotic, quiet
People who like the name Umeko also like Sakura, Nariko, Suki, Kohana, Kaida, Mai, Amaya, Emiko, Kaori, Keiko

Umika (*Sanskrit/East Indian*) ♀ RATING: ★★★
Goddess
People think of Umika as exotic, pretty, ethnic, creative, caring
People who like the name Umika also like Kaida, Shyla, Opal, Umeko, Zelda, Giselle, Jasmine, Sabrina, Ciara, Jacqueline

Ummi (*Sanskrit/East Indian*) ♀ RATING: ★★☆
My mother
People think of Ummi as weird, poor, unpopular, loser, ethnic
People who like the name Ummi also like Savannah, Kaiya, Rianna, Regan, Amani, Una, Queenie, Viviana, Eve, Ivy

Umut (*Turkish*) ♀ ♂ RATING: ★☆
Hope
People think of Umut as unpopular, untrustworthy, nerdy, old, old-fashioned
People who like the name Umut also like

Una (*Celtic/Gaelic*) ♀ RATING: ★★★☆
Unity
People think of Una as pretty, creative, intelligent, caring, funny
People who like the name Una also like Fiona, Ava, Keira, Olivia, Sabrina, Ivy, Oona, Scarlett, Nadia, Aurora

Unique (*American*) ♀ ♂ RATING: ★★★☆
Unlike others
People think of Unique as pretty, funny, sexy, creative, popular
People who like the name Unique also like Jaden, Whitney, Jade, Madison, Payton, Jordan, Taylor, Logan, Ocean, Riley

Unity (*American*) ♀ RATING: ★★★☆
Oneness
People think of Unity as pretty, powerful, sexy, creative, intelligent
People who like the name Unity also like Trinity, Faith, Serenity, Harmony, Victoria, Paige, Destiny, Grace, Hailey, Olivia

Unna *(German)* ♀　　RATING: ★★★
Woman
> People think of Unna as pretty, slow, lazy, girl next door, sexy
> People who like the name Unna also like Una, Paige, Hannah, Hailey, Olivia, Maggie, Zoey, Scarlett, Luna, Aurora

Uorsin *(Rumantsch)* ♂　　RATING: ★★☆
Bear
> People think of Uorsin as leader, aggressive, big, nerdy, poor
> People who like the name Uorsin also like Uba, Upendo, Xenos, Xadrian, Urbano, Quana, Xerxes, Quentin, Uday, Upton

Upendo *(African)* ♂　　RATING: ★★☆
Love—Tamzanian origin
> People think of Upendo as ethnic, quiet, caring, funny, weird
> People who like the name Upendo also like Uba, Zikomo, Raúl, Jayden, Zesiro, Saeran, Tokala, Quentin, Zev, Fisseha

Upton *(Egyptian)* ♂　　RATING: ★★☆
High village—Upton Sinclair, author
> People think of Upton as stuck-up, uptight, wealthy, poor, unpopular
> People who like the name Upton also like Wade, Xavier, Quentin, Vance, Dalton, Tyson, Gabriel, Noah, Ian, Isaac

Ura *(Sanskrit/East Indian)* ♀　　RATING: ★☆
The heart
> People think of Ura as weird, slow, poor, sexy, exotic
> People who like the name Ura also like Amara, Kasi, Komala, Kalinda, Manda, Tanaya, Karma, Kamana, Anila, Minjonet

Urania *(Greek)* ♀　　RATING: ★★★☆
Heavenly
> People think of Urania as intelligent, creative, caring, pretty, weird
> People who like the name Urania also like Qiana, Faith, Olivia, Victoria, Qamra, Quiana, Vanessa, Paige, Salene, Quintessa

Urbain *(French)* ♀♂　　RATING: ★☆
From the city
> People think of Urbain as exotic, quiet, big, trustworthy, cool
> People who like the name Urbain also like Blaise, Talen, Urban, Spencer, Quinn, Mason, Parker, Payton, Quincy, Tyler

Urban *(Latin)* ♀♂　　RATING: ★★★☆
From the city—Keith Urban, singer
> People think of Urban as artsy, cool, sexy, handsome, winner
> People who like the name Urban also like Payton, Parker, Hayden, Jaden, Mason, Addison, Preston, Taylor, Paris, Paxton

Urbana *(Italian)* ♀　　RATING: ★★☆
From the city
> People think of Urbana as intelligent, funny, elegant, girl next door, creative
> People who like the name Urbana also like Bianca, Questa, Fern, Jennifer, Aisling, Lilac, Oriana, Dawn, Amy, Bella

Urbano *(Spanish)* ♂　　RATING: ★☆
From the city
> People think of Urbano as loser, aggressive, young, big, wealthy
> People who like the name Urbano also like Fernando, Orlando, Joaquin, Alejandro, Heath, Luis, Salvatore, Ulric, Manny, Andrés

Uri *(Hebrew)* ♀♂　　RATING: ★☆
My light, flame, fire—Uri Geller, psychic/author
> People think of Uri as creative, intelligent, weird, ethnic, cool
> People who like the name Uri also like Caden, Jaden, Parker, Quinn, Payton, Brody, Madison, Connor, Willow, Blake

Uriah *(Hebrew)* ♂　　RATING: ★★★☆
God is my light—Uriah Heap, character in *David Copperfield* by Charles Dickens
> People think of Uriah as intelligent, handsome, energetic, creative, religious
> People who like the name Uriah also like Isaiah, Elijah, Noah, Gabriel, Ethan, Isaac, Jeremiah, Caleb, Micah, Josiah

Urian *(Welsh)* ♂　　RATING: ★☆
City born
> People think of Urian as nerdy, weird, big, loser, intelligent
> People who like the name Urian also like Uriah, Uriel, Noah, Kaden, Tristan, Landon, Galen, Jayden, Holden, Caleb

Uriel *(Hebrew)* ♂　　RATING: ★★★★
God is my light
> People think of Uriel as handsome, intelligent, funny, sexy, caring
> People who like the name Uriel also like Gabriel, Noah, Uriah, Ethan, Tristan, Isaiah, Nathaniel, Isaac, Elijah, Micah

Urit *(Hebrew)* ♀　　RATING: ★★☆
Light
> People think of Urit as weird, handsome, ethnic, old-fashioned, intelligent
> People who like the name Urit also like Ruth, Lara, Leah, Wendy, Jenna, Zara, Talisa, Ursula, Dolly, Erica

Urja *(Sanskrit/East Indian)* ♀　　RATING: ★★
Energy
> People think of Urja as ethnic, exotic, powerful, sneaky, energetic
> People who like the name Urja also like Ura, Ummi, Urmi

552

Urmi *(Sanskrit/East Indian)* ♀   RATING: ★★
Wave
> People think of Urmi as exotic, pretty, sexy, young, poor
> People who like the name Urmi also like Blythe, Breena, Viva

Ursa *(Latin)* ♀   RATING: ★☆
Bear
> People think of Ursa as creative, exotic, powerful, weird, artsy
> People who like the name Ursa also like Zelda, Olivia, Mia, Penelope, Delilah, Ava, Nicole, Ursula, Veronica, Emily

Ursula *(Scandinavian)* ♀   RATING: ★★
Female bear—Also spelled Ursala; character in Disney's *The Little Mermaid*
> People think of Ursula as pretty, intelligent, funny, creative, caring
> People who like the name Ursula also like Olivia, Paige, Violet, Hannah, Victoria, Phoebe, Vanessa, Isabella, Iris, Ophelia

Urvi *(Sanskrit/East Indian)* ♀   RATING: ★★★
The earth
> People think of Urvi as intelligent, pretty, trustworthy, funny, creative
> People who like the name Urvi also like Tanuja, Priti, Sumana, Sunila, Tanika, Svara, Avani, Uzuri, Opal, Roxanne

Usher *(American)* ♂   RATING: ★★★
People escort—Usher Raymond IV, singer
> People think of Usher as sexy, popular, cool, handsome, intelligent
> People who like the name Usher also like Xavier, Warren, Nick, Tyrone, Victor, Scott, Jared, Justin, Jason, Derrick

Usoa *(Basque)* ♀   RATING: ★☆
Dove
> People think of Usoa as pretty, creative, ethnic, wild, weird
> People who like the name Usoa also like Ujana, Zabrina, Zafirah, Nyla, Pearl, Selene, Sienna, Velika, Dara, Anila

Usra *(Sanskrit/East Indian)* ♀   RATING: ★★
Dawn
> People think of Usra as weird, nerdy, loser, exotic, ethnic
> People who like the name Usra also like Neena, Gypsy, Jasmine, Aisha, Umika, Uttara, Opal, Sarina, Femi, Ivy

Uta *(Japanese)* ♀   RATING: ★★★
Song
> People think of Uta as creative, exotic, sexy, weird, wild
> People who like the name Uta also like Nariko, Yoko, Keiko, Tama, Sakura, Kohana, Suki, Rini, Sada, Kaori

Utah *(Native American)* ♀ ♂   RATING: ★★★
People of the mountain—Ute origin; U.S. state
> People think of Utah as trendy, powerful, funny, girl next door, popular

People who like the name Utah also like Parker, Dakota, London, Sawyer, Paxton, Riley, Payton, Carter, Jordan, Connor

Uttara *(Sanskrit/East Indian)* ♀   RATING: ★☆
Royal daughter; star
> People think of Uttara as sexy, pretty, young, elegant, trustworthy
> People who like the name Uttara also like Eshana, Daphne, Kalinda, Ophelia, Jasmine, Shyla, Iris, Keira, Opal, Ishana

Uyen *(Vietnamese)* ♀   RATING: ★★★☆
Unknown meaning
> People think of Uyen as caring, pretty, funny, intelligent, creative
> People who like the name Uyen also like Lara, Erin, Violet, Tessa, Mai, Wren, Ellie, Nichole, Grace, Phoebe

Uzuri *(African)* ♀   RATING: ★★★☆
Beauty
> People think of Uzuri as exotic, ethnic, pretty, creative, quiet
> People who like the name Uzuri also like Nadia, Zuri, Genevieve, Bianca, Gabrielle, Giselle, Yasmin, Mia, Maya, Tiana

Vachel *(French)* ♂   RATING: ★☆
Cowherd
> People think of Vachel as weird, unpopular, nerdy, poor, loser
> People who like the name Vachel also like Valin, Vadin, Victor, Isaac, Sullivan, Abel, Vladimir, Zach, Seth, Faolan

Vadin *(Sanskrit/East Indian)* ♂   RATING: ★★★
Unknown meaning
> People think of Vadin as powerful, quiet, popular, sexy, intelligent
> People who like the name Vadin also like Kaden, Tristan, Xander, Xavier, Valin, Aiden, Noah, Ethan, Ian, Seth

Vahe *(Armenian)* ♂   RATING: ★★
Best
> People think of Vahe as caring, intelligent, leader, aggressive, winner
> People who like the name Vahe also like Vadin, Valin, Vartan, Zaccheus, Valdemar, Chael, Deron, Illias, Vidar, Isaac

Vail *(English)* ♀ ♂   RATING: ★★★☆
Dweller in the valley—Also a surname; also a town in Colorado
> People think of Vail as creative, cool, young, exotic, caring
> People who like the name Vail also like Parker, Sage, Caden, Addison, Reese, Riley, Ryder, Landen, Oakley, Dakota

Val *(English)* ♀♂   RATING: ★★★
Short for Valentine or Valerie—Val Kilmer, actor
  People think of Val as funny, popular, creative, intelligent, cool
  People who like the name Val also like Wesley, Logan, Parker, Connor, Riley, Payton, Jade, Ryan, Sean, Quinn

Vala *(English)* ♀   RATING: ★★☆
Chosen
  People think of Vala as pretty, intelligent, exotic, energetic, sexy
  People who like the name Vala also like Nadia, Tala, Ava, Rachel, Valerie, Paige, Vera, Hailey, Vivian, Calista

Valdemar *(Scandinavian)* ♂   RATING: ★★★☆
Famous rule—Variation of Waldemar
  People think of Valdemar as leader, weird, powerful, aggressive, old-fashioned
  People who like the name Valdemar also like Xavier, Vladimir, Thomas, Isaac, Tristan, Oliver, Miles, Vincent, Alexander, Gabriel

Valencia *(Spanish)* ♀   RATING: ★★★★
Strength, health—Also a Spanish place name; also a type of orange
  People think of Valencia as pretty, funny, intelligent, sexy, creative
  People who like the name Valencia also like Victoria, Olivia, Isabella, Vanessa, Natalia, Veronica, Nadia, Paige, Violet, Genevieve

Valentin *(Rumantsch)* ♂   RATING: ★★★
Strength, health
  People think of Valentin as handsome, caring, creative, young, intelligent
  People who like the name Valentin also like Gabriel, Fabian, Valentino, Noah, Tristan, Xavier, Roman, William, Maddox, Nicholas

Valentina *(Latin)* ♀   RATING: ★★★☆
Strength, health
  People think of Valentina as pretty, intelligent, funny, popular, caring
  People who like the name Valentina also like Isabella, Victoria, Olivia, Bella, Vanessa, Bianca, Sofia, Valeria, Sabrina, Scarlett

Valentine *(English)* ♀♂   RATING: ★★
Strength, health—St. Valentine; Valentine's Day
  People think of Valentine as intelligent, caring, creative, sexy, pretty
  People who like the name Valentine also like Raven, Jade, Madison, Hayden, Willow, Bailey, Riley, James, Jaden, Winter

Valentino *(Italian)* ♂   RATING: ★★
Strength, health
  People think of Valentino as handsome, sexy, popular, powerful, intelligent
  People who like the name Valentino also like Gabriel, Vincent, Noah, Nicholas, Romeo, Alexander, Victor, Leo, Zachary, Giovanni

Valeria *(Italian)* ♀   RATING: ★★☆
Strength
  People think of Valeria as pretty, intelligent, funny, cool, creative
  People who like the name Valeria also like Isabella, Valerie, Vanessa, Natalia, Victoria, Viviana, Veronica, Olivia, Valentina, Sabrina

Valerian *(English)* ♂   RATING: ★★★
Strength—Also an herb
  People think of Valerian as handsome, energetic, cool, intelligent, leader
  People who like the name Valerian also like Adrian, Nicholas, Gideon, Tristan, Vincent, Victor, Lucian, Xavier, Warrick, Michael

Valerie *(French)* ♀   RATING: ★★☆
Strength—Also spelled Valarie, Vallari, or Vallerie; Valerie Bertinelli, actress; Valerie Harper, actress; Valerie Perrine, actress
  People think of Valerie as pretty, caring, funny, intelligent, creative
  People who like the name Valerie also like Victoria, Natalie, Vanessa, Hannah, Veronica, Paige, Olivia, Samantha, Hailey, Isabelle

Valeska *(Slavic)* ♀   RATING: ★★★★
Short for names beginning with Val or Vlad
  People think of Valeska as pretty, intelligent, energetic, creative, trustworthy
  People who like the name Valeska also like Valencia, Sienna, Fiona, Nadia, Valerie, Sephora, Samara, Gabrielle, Jasmine, Sapphire

Valiant *(English)* ♀♂   RATING: ★★
Brave—Prince Valiant, comic character
  People think of Valiant as winner, powerful, intelligent, trustworthy, leader
  People who like the name Valiant also like Riley, Phoenix, Willow, Dante, Sage, Shadow, Hayden, Rain, Bailey, Madison

Valin *(Sanskrit/East Indian)* ♂   RATING: ★★
Monkey king
  People think of Valin as handsome, powerful, intelligent, cool, creative
  People who like the name Valin also like Tristan, Xander, Galen, Kaden, Xavier, Vadin, Damien, Zander, Vance, Holden

Valkyrie *(Scandinavian)* ♀   RATING: ★★★★☆
Chooser of the slain—In Norse mythology, those that swooped down on the battlefield and carried away the souls of the fallen
  People think of Valkyrie as powerful, leader, aggressive, pretty, exotic
  People who like the name Valkyrie also like Aurora, Pandora, Scarlett, Paige, Naomi, Sephora, Adrienne, Victoria, Genevieve, Selene

553

Vallerie *(English)* ♀ RATING: ★★☆
Strength
People think of Vallerie as pretty, intelligent, funny, popular, creative
People who like the name Vallerie also like Valerie, Victoria, Vanessa, Faith, Samantha, Natalie, Paige, Hailey, Rachel, Sabrina

Valley *(American)* ♀ RATING: ★★★
Between the mountains
People think of Valley as pretty, old-fashioned, nerdy, unpopular, artsy
People who like the name Valley also like Scarlett, Anastasia, Autumn, Mia, Aurora, Velvet, Victoria, Summer, Violet, Paige

Valmai *(English)* ♀ RATING: ★★★
Possibly from the male Welsh name Gwalchmai meaning hawk of May
People think of Valmai as funny, creative, quiet, weird, pretty
People who like the name Valmai also like Arwen, Aelwen, Maeve, Mairwen, Rhiannon, Morwen, Morgana, Gwendolyn, Sian, Rianna

Valonia *(American)* ♀ RATING: ★★☆
Combination of Val– and –onia
People think of Valonia as weird, ethnic, exotic, artsy, sneaky
People who like the name Valonia also like Valora, Jasmine, Elana, Ava, Sabrina, Violet, Iliana, Aurora, Scarlett, Lalaine

Valora *(American)* ♀ RATING: ★★★☆
Bravery—Variation of valor
People think of Valora as pretty, aggressive, energetic, intelligent, big
People who like the name Valora also like Vanessa, Kiara, Cassandra, Scarlett, Olivia, Victoria, Violet, Aurora, Vera, Sabrina

Valterra *(American)* ♀ RATING: ★★★
Feminine form of Valter
People think of Valterra as old-fashioned, weird, popular, pretty, creative
People who like the name Valterra also like Valencia, Zabrina, Rachel, Valora, Andra, Venecia, Scarlett, Amy, Keaira, Renée

Valtina *(American)* ♀ RATING: ★★
Combination of Valerie and Tina; also short for Valentina
People think of Valtina as stuck-up, weird, big, poor, old-fashioned
People who like the name Valtina also like Valentina, Veronica, Amanda, Valencia, Valeria, Victoria, Sabrina, Kaitlyn, Valora, Anastasia

Vaman *(Sanskrit/East Indian)* ♂ RATING: ★★
Lord Vishnu
People think of Vaman as loser, weird, nerdy, aggressive, poor

People who like the name Vaman also like Vatsa, Varen, Valin, Vijay, Vadin, Viral, Varun, Amish, Van, Vinay

Van *(American)* ♂ RATING: ★★★☆
From the family of—Also short for names beginning or ending with Van; Van Cliburn, concert pianist; Van Johnson, actor; Van Morrison, musician
People think of Van as funny, handsome, intelligent, cool, popular
People who like the name Van also like Isaac, Vance, Xavier, Gavin, Walker, Jacob, Oliver, Owen, Ian, Ethan

Vance *(English)* ♂ RATING: ★★★★
From the marsh—Originally a surname
People think of Vance as handsome, funny, intelligent, popular, creative
People who like the name Vance also like Ethan, Zachary, Seth, Tristan, Owen, Ian, Chase, Gavin, Nathan, Landon

Vandana *(Sanskrit/East Indian)* ♀ RATING: ★☆
Worship
People think of Vandana as intelligent, pretty, exotic, cool, funny
People who like the name Vandana also like Victoria, Zabrina, Liana, Shaina, Kacy, Unity, Trinity, Venecia, Amanda, Angelina

Vanessa *(English)* ♀ RATING: ★★★★☆
Combination of Van and Esther—Created by the poet Jonathan Swift for his friend Esther Van Homrigh
People think of Vanessa as pretty, funny, caring, intelligent, creative
People who like the name Vanessa also like Victoria, Samantha, Veronica, Olivia, Natalie, Isabella, Paige, Hannah, Hailey, Emma

Vangie *(Greek)* ♀ RATING: ★★★
Messenger of good news—Short for Evangeline
People think of Vangie as leader, pretty, intelligent, criminal, funny
People who like the name Vangie also like Vanessa, Amelia, Zoey, Megan, Olivia, Sofia, Brea, Veronica, Yoshi, Victoria

Vanida *(Sanskrit/East Indian)* ♀ RATING: ★★★
Wife, beloved woman—Also used in Thailand
People think of Vanida as sexy, exotic, pretty, aggressive, lazy
People who like the name Vanida also like Sachi, Winona, Vanessa, Danika, Violet, Amalie, Zaria, Shayla, Tiana, Sabrina

Vanig *(Armenian)* ♀ RATING: ★☆
Maiden of Van, a small town in Armenia
People think of Vanig as powerful, aggressive, wealthy, funny, leader
People who like the name Vanig also like Aadi, Sari, Maxine, Nanette, Odessa, Sadie, Samantha, Selia, Tamara, Tea

Vanna *(Cambodian)* ♀   RATING: ★★
Golden colored—Also a nickname for Vanessa or
Giovanna; Vanna White, TV personality
   People think of Vanna as sexy, pretty, young, exotic,
   creative
   People who like the name Vanna also like Ava, Vanessa,
   Sadie, Bianca, Lana, Mia, Veronica, Isabella, Nadia, Paige

Vanya *(Slavic)* ♀ ♂   RATING: ★★★★
Variation of Ivan
   People think of Vanya as creative, intelligent, cool,
   funny, pretty
   People who like the name Vanya also like Jaden, Riley,
   Madison, Peyton, Skylar, Caden, Piper, Kaelin, Paris,
   Parker

Varali *(Sanskrit/East Indian)* ♀   RATING: ★★★
Moon
   People think of Varali as exotic, pretty, artsy, loser, wild
   People who like the name Varali also like Vyomini,
   Varana, Tala, Sitara, Valora, Venya, Varsha, Vanessa,
   Kaida, Aiko

Varana *(Sanskrit/East Indian)* ♀   RATING: ★★☆
Selecting, choosing
   People think of Varana as creative, unpopular, aggres-
   sive, young, funny
   People who like the name Varana also like Vinaya,
   Venya, Varali, Vianca, Vyomini, Summer, Yasmin,
   Serenity, Vanessa, Varsha

Varden *(English)* ♂   RATING: ★★☆
From Verdun, France—Originally a surname
   People think of Varden as old, aggressive, untrust-
   worthy, powerful, lazy
   People who like the name Varden also like Kaden,
   Xavier, Xander, Tyson, Tristan, Trenton, Damien, Vance,
   Jayden, Landon

Varen *(Sanskrit/East Indian)* ♂   RATING: ★★
Gifts
   People think of Varen as creative, intelligent, trust-
   worthy, aggressive, ethnic
   People who like the name Varen also like Kaden, Soren,
   Weston, Valin, Vincent, Aiden, Jayden, Kyran, Landon,
   Warren

Varian *(French)* ♂   RATING: ★★★☆
Variable
   People think of Varian as handsome, creative, intelli-
   gent, trustworthy, powerful
   People who like the name Varian also like Xadrian,
   Kaden, Xavier, Jayden, Maddox, Slade, Noah, Holden,
   Seth, Aiden

Varick *(German)* ♂   RATING: ★★★★
Honorable defender
   People think of Varick as leader, handsome, aggressive,
   intelligent, cool
   People who like the name Varick also like Zander,
   Vance, Warrick, Xander, Tristan, Gideon, Keagan, Caleb,
   Kaden, Lucas

Variel *(Spanish)* ♀   RATING: ★★☆
Changeable, different—Also a surname
   People think of Variel as creative, pretty, elegant, intel-
   ligent, quiet
   People who like the name Variel also like Violet, Raina,
   Tatiana, Daphne, Aria, Karina, Larissa, Ruby, Valeria,
   Vega

Varius *(Latin)* ♂   RATING: ★★☆
Different, diverse
   People think of Varius as leader, energetic, intelligent,
   weird, artsy
   People who like the name Varius also like Varun, Varick,
   Calum, Korbin, Calix, Whittaker, Owen, Julius, Valentino,
   Valin

Varro *(Latin)* ♂   RATING: ★★
Durable, strong—Originally a surname
   People think of Varro as exotic, ethnic, big, poor,
   criminal
   People who like the name Varro also like Valin, Aurelio,
   Luis, Silas, Orlando, Ace, Paul, Nico, Nero, Miles

Varsha *(Sanskrit/East Indian)* ♀   RATING: ★☆
Rain
   People think of Varsha as intelligent, pretty, creative,
   quiet, caring
   People who like the name Varsha also like Opal, Varana,
   Varali, Serenity, Victoria, Sephora, Paige, Jillian, Renée,
   Shaina

Vartan *(Armenian)* ♂   RATING: ★★★☆
Rose
   People think of Vartan as uptight, criminal, aggressive,
   leader, sneaky
   People who like the name Vartan also like Tristan,
   Varen, Kaden, Walker, Xander, Lucian, Weston, Korbin,
   Vahe, Beau

Vartouhi *(Armenian)* ♀   RATING: ★★★
Rose maiden
   People think of Vartouhi as pretty, sexy, poor, trendy,
   stuck-up
   People who like the name Vartouhi also like Wakanda,
   Zenevieva, Yessica, Xalvadora, Shoshanah, Parvati,
   Veronique, Rozene, Yanichel, Zitkalasa

Varun *(Sanskrit/East Indian)* ♂   RATING: ★☆
God
   People think of Varun as intelligent, popular, young,
   cool, caring
   People who like the name Varun also like Ashwin, Vinay,
   Tarun, Vatsa, Varen, Sanjay, Damien, Caleb, Valin, Victor

Varuna *(Sanskrit/East Indian)* ♂   RATING: ★★☆
God
   People think of Varuna as religious, quiet, old-fashioned,
   trustworthy, pretty
   People who like the name Varuna also like Ronan,
   Penda, Valin, Vinay, Aram, Victor, Veradis, Vance, Adam,
   Owen

Varvara *(Slavic)* ♀   RATING: ★★★
Variation of Barbara
> People think of Varvara as creative, aggressive, wild, trustworthy, winner
> People who like the name Varvara also like Sophia, Zoe, Zoey, Aurora, Hannah, Millicent, Nora, Venus, Anastasia, Thera

Vasant *(Sanskrit/East Indian)* ♀♂   RATING: ★★★
Spring season
> People think of Vasant as sporty, leader, trustworthy, intelligent, trendy
> People who like the name Vasant also like Virendra, Evelyn, Tallys, Jiva, Veda, Pavan, Tarin, Harper, Taryn, Tate

Vasanta *(Sanskrit/East Indian)* ♀   RATING: ★★
Spring
> People think of Vasanta as aggressive, exotic, sexy, trustworthy, funny
> People who like the name Vasanta also like Vasanti, Somatra, Sitara, Kylee, Varana, Kya, Jeanine, Savita, Cordelia, Calista

Vasanti *(Sanskrit/East Indian)* ♀   RATING: ★★★
From springtime
> People think of Vasanti as exotic, intelligent, creative, artsy, ethnic
> People who like the name Vasanti also like Sitara, Samara, Vinaya, Victoria, Shanti, Elisabeth, Alexandria, Lorelei, Samantha, Melanie

Vaschel *(French)* ♂   RATING: ★★☆
Variation of Vachel
> People think of Vaschel as intelligent, handsome, powerful, elegant, lazy
> People who like the name Vaschel also like Dalton, Tristan, Ephraim, Tyson, Rhys, Cody, Brennan, Jeremiah, Edan, Raphael

Vasha *(Russian)* ♀♂   RATING: ★★★
Short for names such as Vladimir
> People think of Vasha as intelligent, sexy, pretty, leader, creative
> People who like the name Vasha also like Sasha, Skye, Taylor, Madison, Piper, Keanu, Topaz, Shae, Phoenix, Liberty

Vashon *(American)* ♂   RATING: ★★★
God is gracious, merciful
> People think of Vashon as intelligent, handsome, exotic, wealthy, sexy
> People who like the name Vashon also like Jayden, Deshawn, Isaiah, Braden, Dayshaun, Darian, Jacob, Josiah, Zeshawn, Zachary

Vasilis *(Greek)* ♂   RATING: ★★★☆
Kingly
> People think of Vasilis as intelligent, funny, popular, weird, powerful
> People who like the name Vasilis also like Jack, Drake, Andrew, Keagan, Beau, Theodore, Vasska, Lysander, Vincent, Jasper

Vasska *(Slavic)* ♂   RATING: ★★★
Royal, kingly—Short for Vasily
> People think of Vasska as intelligent, exotic, sneaky, powerful, leader
> People who like the name Vasska also like Vasilis, Varick, Varian, Vartan, Asher, Donovan, Titus, Dane, Faris, Vidor

Vasudha *(Sanskrit/East Indian)* ♀   RATING: ★★☆
Earth
> People think of Vasudha as quiet, caring, pretty, intelligent, trustworthy
> People who like the name Vasudha also like Kanika, Shreya, Vyomini, Suruchi, Virika, Kapila, Vinanti, Visala, Varali, Himani

Vasundhara *(Sanskrit/East Indian)* ♀   RATING: ★★☆
Earth
> People think of Vasundhara as cool, unpopular, poor, exotic, ethnic
> People who like the name Vasundhara also like Varali, Vasudha, Varana, Vyomini, Visala, Vinanti, Vala, Zamora, Zsa Zsa, Vanida

Vatsa *(Sanskrit/East Indian)* ♂   RATING: ★★
Son
> People think of Vatsa as big, powerful, creative, ethnic, funny
> People who like the name Vatsa also like Varen, Varun, Vaman, Viral, Vadin, Arav, Arnav, Ashwin, Vijay, Nalin

Vatusia *(African)* ♀   RATING: ★★★
They leave us behind
> People think of Vatusia as exotic, weird, unpopular, ethnic, uptight
> People who like the name Vatusia also like Vyomini, Cecilia, Titania, Vianca, Zivanka, Kaydence, Beryl, Violet, Derica, Zelda

Vaughan *(English)* ♂   RATING: ★★★★
Small
> People think of Vaughan as handsome, intelligent, funny, creative, caring
> People who like the name Vaughan also like Tristan, Ethan, Noah, Xavier, Seth, Nathan, Zachary, Walker, Wyatt, Wade

Vaughn *(English)* ♀♂   RATING: ★★☆
Small
> People think of Vaughn as intelligent, handsome, caring, cool, funny
> People who like the name Vaughn also like Parker, Hayden, Logan, Quinn, Preston, Riley, Addison, Avery, Taylor, Aidan

Vea *(Spanish)* ♀   RATING: ★★
Seen
> People think of Vea as pretty, exotic, elegant, funny, trustworthy
> People who like the name Vea also like Vera, Vivian, Chloe, Zoe, Ava, Layla, Aurora, Kara, Kera, Tia

Veanna *(American)* ♀   RATING: ★★★☆
Combination of V and Anna
> People think of Veanna as pretty, exotic, caring, elegant, trendy
> People who like the name Veanna also like Vienna, Veronica, Isabella, Paige, Layla, Sienna, Olivia, Nadia, Viviana, Eva

Veata *(Cambodian)* ♀   RATING: ★★★
Wind—Pronounced *Vee-AY-ta*
> People think of Veata as pretty, exotic, artsy, intelligent, cool
> People who like the name Veata also like Zoey, Winona, Dara, Channary, Zora, Rhian, Olivia, Penelope, Jane, Gabriella

Veda *(Sanskrit/East Indian)* ♀ ♂   RATING: ★★★★
Eternal knowledge
> People think of Veda as intelligent, pretty, creative, artsy, caring
> People who like the name Veda also like Parker, Addison, Willow, Hayden, Riley, Reese, Logan, Jordan, Dylan, Sage

Vega *(Arabic)* ♀   RATING: ★★☆
Stooping eagle—The brightest star in the Lyra constellation
> People think of Vega as energetic, powerful, creative, cool, intelligent
> People who like the name Vega also like Aurora, Ivy, Ava, Wren, Violet, Vera, Olivia, Phoebe, Emma, Scarlett

Velia *(Italian)* ♀   RATING: ★★★
Hidden, veiled
> People think of Velia as elegant, intelligent, pretty, wild, exotic
> People who like the name Velia also like Adrina, Anya, Dawn, Aria, Viola, Gianna, Sienna, Adrienne, Harriet, Aida

Velika *(Slavic)* ♀   RATING: ★★★
Great
> People think of Velika as artsy, caring, ethnic, creative, intelligent
> People who like the name Velika also like Vera, Kara, Veronica, Vanessa, Kera, Zabrina, Kayla, Kyla, Vita, Vianca

Velma *(Greek)* ♀   RATING: ★★★
Strong-willed warrior—Short for Wilhelmina
> People think of Velma as caring, intelligent, pretty, trustworthy, funny
> People who like the name Velma also like Veronica, Victoria, Vanessa, Vivian, Melanie, Olivia, Penelope, Stacey, Sabrina, Sarah

Velvet *(American)* ♀   RATING: ★★★
Soft fabric
> People think of Velvet as caring, pretty, elegant, intelligent, artsy
> People who like the name Velvet also like Violet, Paige, Scarlett, Victoria, Daisy, Sapphire, Sabrina, Vanessa, Veronica, Autumn

Venda *(African)* ♀   RATING: ★★☆
Of the Bantu people—South African origin
> People think of Venda as powerful, trustworthy, pretty, popular, funny
> People who like the name Venda also like Victoria, Darla, Zora, Summer, Tiana, Velvet, Regina, Shamara, Talisa, Viola

Venecia *(Latin)* ♀   RATING: ★★★☆
From Venice, Italy
> People think of Venecia as intelligent, sexy, pretty, energetic, funny
> People who like the name Venecia also like Bella, Sienna, Victoria, Vienna, Valencia, Valentina, Aurora, Sofia, Celeste, Trinity

Venedict *(American)* ♂   RATING: ★★
Variation of Benedict
> People think of Venedict as big, intelligent, creative, young, energetic
> People who like the name Venedict also like Diedrick, Deacon, Tristan, Keiran, Woods, Calix, Calhoun, Kael, Vladimir, Owen

Venetia *(Latin)* ♀   RATING: ★★
Woman of Venice
> People think of Venetia as intelligent, pretty, trustworthy, elegant, popular
> People who like the name Venetia also like Vanessa, Aurora, Sophia, Phoebe, Charlotte, Ophelia, Selena, Tessa, Fiona, Eva

Venice *(Italian)* ♀   RATING: ★★☆
English name of an Italian city
> People think of Venice as exotic, intelligent, artsy, pretty, creative
> People who like the name Venice also like Vienna, Victoria, Isabella, Olivia, Sienna, Scarlett, Vanessa, Natalia, Mia, Violet

Ventana *(Spanish)* ♀   RATING: ★★
Window
> People think of Ventana as exotic, pretty, caring, wild, young
> People who like the name Ventana also like Valencia, Selene, Tatiana, Tiana, Serena, Kiara, Vienna, Iliana, Bridget, Tierra

Ventura *(Spanish)* ♀   RATING: ★★★
Good fortune—Originally short for *buenaventura*, meaning "have a good trip" or "God be with you"
> People think of Ventura as creative, exotic, lazy, wild, funny
> People who like the name Ventura also like Valencia, Pandora, Kendra, Kaya, Keaira, Velvet, Selene, Veronica, Rhian, Venecia

Venus *(Greek)* ♀   RATING: ★★★★
Goddess of love—The second closest planet to the sun; Venus Williams, tennis player
> People think of Venus as pretty, sexy, creative, exotic, powerful

People who like the name Venus also like Vanessa, Aurora, Paige, Summer, Phoebe, Victoria, Serenity, Veronica, Cassandra, Trinity

Venya *(Sanskrit/East Indian)* ♀   RATING: ★★
Lovable

People think of Venya as pretty, caring, creative, aggressive, powerful

People who like the name Venya also like Paige, Gianna, Kiara, Sienna, Tiana, Thalia, Saniya, Sephora, Shyla, Summer

Vera *(Russian)* ♀   RATING: ★★
Faith

People think of Vera as intelligent, pretty, caring, creative, elegant

People who like the name Vera also like Ava, Violet, Olivia, Sophia, Eva, Stella, Iris, Vivian, Sadie, Scarlett

Veradis *(Thai)* ♂   RATING: ★★★
Unknown meaning

People think of Veradis as quiet, exotic, poor, artsy, intelligent

People who like the name Veradis also like Tristan, Rohan, Salvatore, Saeran, Andrew, Keiran, Varuna, Sebastian, Jayden, Xylon

Veradisia *(American)* ♀   RATING: ★★★
Feminine form of Veradis

People think of Veradisia as elegant, loser, cool, creative, sneaky

People who like the name Veradisia also like Veronique, Aaralyn, Olivia, Anastasia, Adeline, India, Ophelia, Scarlett, Adelaide, Naeva

Verda *(Spanish)* ♀   RATING: ★☆
Truth

People think of Verda as loser, aggressive, old, exotic, weird

People who like the name Verda also like Vera, Olivia, Veronica, Adeline, Isabella, Penelope, Phoebe, Calla, Bella, Emily

Verdad *(Spanish)* ♀   RATING: ★☆
Truth

People think of Verdad as loser, poor, old, lazy, unpopular

People who like the name Verdad also like Teresa, Tiara, Tatiana, Shanae, Tegan, Layla, Nora, Verda, Leilani, Vianca

Verdi *(Italian)* ♀   RATING: ★★★☆
Green—Giuseppe Verdi, composer

People think of Verdi as exotic, girl next door, intelligent, wild, trustworthy

People who like the name Verdi also like Sienna, Terra, Iris, Roma, Layla, Isabella, Nadia, Gianna, Vera, Gemma

Verena *(German)* ♀   RATING: ★★★★
Feminine form of names beginning with Ver

People think of Verena as intelligent, pretty, caring, trustworthy, creative

People who like the name Verena also like Veronica, Vera, Sienna, Serena, Summer, Sapphire, Victoria, Vienna, Sierra, Aurora

Verina *(English)* ♀   RATING: ★★★
Truth

People think of Verina as pretty, trustworthy, intelligent, funny, artsy

People who like the name Verina also like Genevieve, Nadine, Serena, Victoria, Rozalia, Elena, Arianna, Jacqueline, Rowena, Regina

Verity *(Latin)* ♀   RATING: ★★★★
Truth

People think of Verity as intelligent, pretty, caring, funny, elegant

People who like the name Verity also like Scarlett, Faith, Grace, Felicity, Violet, Paige, Victoria, Olivia, Sadie, Phoebe

Verlee *(American)* ♀♂   RATING: ★★
Combination of Vernon and Lee

People think of Verlee as funny, trustworthy, intelligent, elegant, old-fashioned

People who like the name Verlee also like Eden, Reese, Avery, Mischa, Whitney, Baylee, Willow, Winter, Hayden, Shannon

Vermont *(French)* ♀♂   RATING: ★★★
Green mountain—U.S. state

People think of Vermont as unpopular, uptight, untrustworthy, funny, trendy

People who like the name Vermont also like Wisconsin, Sydney, Morgan, Ryder, Valentine, Michigan, Raven, Reese, Nebraska, Payton

Vern *(American)* ♂   RATING: ★★★☆
Alder tree—Short for Vernon

People think of Vern as creative, cool, sexy, trustworthy, old-fashioned

People who like the name Vern also like Victor, Vance, Miles, Owen, Seth, Patrick, Mitch, Wade, Wayne, Samuel

Verna *(American)* ♀   RATING: ★★★☆
Feminine form of Verne

People think of Verna as caring, trustworthy, funny, intelligent, creative

People who like the name Verna also like Sofia, Kara, Olivia, Eleanor, Samantha, Veronica, Kayla, Ophelia, Irene, Nancy

Vernados *(Greek)* ♂   RATING: ★☆
Variation of Bernard

People think of Vernados as ethnic, big, old-fashioned, loser, boy next door

People who like the name Vernados also like Thanos, Alexander, Arthur, Alejandro, Zero, Valin, Raghnall, Theodore, Branden, Thad

Verne *(English)* ♂   RATING: ★★★
Dweller among the ferns—Originally a surname

People think of Verne as intelligent, funny, creative, unpopular, caring

People who like the name Verne also like Darius, Seth, Wade, Leo, Damian, Noah, Vance, Jonas, Wendell, Gabriel

Vernon *(English)* ♂　　　RATING: ★★
Alder tree—Originally a surname
People think of Vernon as handsome, funny, intelligent, trustworthy, aggressive
People who like the name Vernon also like Isaac, Gabriel, Jacob, Victor, Warren, Ethan, Nathan, Trevor, William, Dillon

Verona *(Italian)* ♀　　　RATING: ★★★
Truth—Also someone from Verona, Italy
People think of Verona as funny, caring, intelligent, aggressive, creative
People who like the name Verona also like Viola, Isabella, Ophelia, Scarlett, Aurora, Vera, Isolde, Gabrielle, Lorelei, Ava

Veronica *(Greek)* ♀　　　RATING: ★★★
Bringing victory—From the Greek phrase *bere nike*; often mistaken for a variation of Verona
People think of Veronica as pretty, funny, intelligent, caring, creative
People who like the name Veronica also like Victoria, Vanessa, Olivia, Isabella, Samantha, Paige, Natalie, Hannah, Sabrina, Faith

Veronique *(French)* ♀　　　RATING: ★★★★
Bringing victory—Variation of Veronica
People think of Veronique as pretty, cool, intelligent, sexy, creative
People who like the name Veronique also like Veronica, Vanessa, Victoria, Isabelle, Giselle, Monique, Jacqueline, Nicolette, Isabella, Madeleine

Verrill *(French)* ♂　　　RATING: ★★☆
Faithful
People think of Verrill as old, old-fashioned, loser, weird, religious
People who like the name Verrill also like André, Jacques, Dashiell, Marcel, Andrew, Reynard, Augustin, Donovan, Percival, Laurent

Veruca *(Latin)* ♀　　　RATING: ★★★
Wart—Variation of Verruca; Veruca Salt, character in *Charlie and the Chocolate Factory* by Roald Dahl
People think of Veruca as stuck-up, aggressive, powerful, wealthy, pretty
People who like the name Veruca also like Violet, Veronica, Victoria, Amelia, Sophia, Scarlett, Zoe, Paige, Zoey, Kendra

Vesna *(Slavic)* ♀　　　RATING: ★☆
Messenger—Goddess of the spring
People think of Vesna as intelligent, pretty, sexy, trustworthy, popular
People who like the name Vesna also like Isis, Paige, Tatiana, Belle, Bella, Gabrielle, Danica, Bianca, Odessa, Zora

Vesta *(Latin)* ♀　　　RATING: ★★★
Goddess of the hearth
People think of Vesta as trustworthy, creative, exotic, intelligent, pretty
People who like the name Vesta also like Bella, Celeste, Violet, Olivia, Wren, Veronica, Emma, Vega, Bianca, Iris

Veta *(Spanish)* ♀　　　RATING: ★★★☆
Intelligent
People think of Veta as intelligent, creative, pretty, caring, trustworthy
People who like the name Veta also like Violet, Isabella, Sofia, Ava, Vera, Lily, Daphne, Vita, Gwendolyn, Eve

Vevay *(American)* ♀♂　　　RATING: ★★★
A place in Indiana, named after Vevey, Switzerland
People think of Vevay as trustworthy, exotic, weird, trendy, girl next door
People who like the name Vevay also like Shea, Terran, Torrin, Connor, Tierney, Naveen, Taryn, Nolan, Mckale, Riley

Vevina *(Celtic/Gaelic)* ♀　　　RATING: ★★★☆
Sweet lady
People think of Vevina as intelligent, pretty, trustworthy, elegant, artsy
People who like the name Vevina also like Fiona, Rosaleen, Kara, Genevieve, Kaelyn, Keaira, Davina, Kiara, Vivian, Veronica

Vi *(American)* ♀　　　RATING: ★★
Violet—Short for Violet
People think of Vi as pretty, elegant, intelligent, creative, energetic
People who like the name Vi also like Chloe, Violet, Zoe, Vera, Elle, Lily, Lucy, Isabelle, Faith, Ava

Vian *(English)* ♀♂　　　RATING: ★★★★
Full of life—Short for Vivian
People think of Vian as caring, creative, pretty, cool, intelligent
People who like the name Vian also like Aidan, Reese, Cade, Caden, Logan, Riley, Jaden, Kasen, Mason, Kaelin

Vianca *(American)* ♀　　　RATING: ★★
Fair skinned, white—Variation of Bianca
People think of Vianca as pretty, energetic, sexy, cool, funny
People who like the name Vianca also like Vanessa, Bianca, Veronica, Victoria, Vienna, Viviana, Isabella, Rachel, Hailey, Rianna

Vic *(English)* ♀♂　　　RATING: ★★★
Short for Victor—Vic Damone, singer
People think of Vic as funny, cool, intelligent, sexy, young
People who like the name Vic also like Aidan, Vicki, Parker, Landen, Logan, Will, Kyle, Riley, Randy, Quinn

Vice *(Latin)* ♀♂　　　RATING: ★★☆
Change—Also a moral depravity
People think of Vice as unpopular, aggressive, weird, ethnic, untrustworthy

People who like the name Vice also like Puma, Jade, Myles, Bailey, Hayden, Nova, Brody, Dylan, Kaycee, Pier

Vicki *(English)* ♀♂　　　　　　　RATING: ★★★☆

Short for Victoria—Vicki Carr, singer

People think of Vicki as caring, pretty, funny, trustworthy, intelligent

People who like the name Vicki also like Vicky, Taylor, Madison, Holly, Morgan, Jade, Ryan, Kimberly, Tyler, Sasha

Vicky *(English)* ♀♂　　　　　　　RATING: ★★★☆

Short for Victoria

People think of Vicky as funny, pretty, intelligent, caring, cool

People who like the name Vicky also like Vicki, Taylor, Ryan, Holly, Kimberly, Brooke, Madison, Jamie, Shannon, Kelly

Victor *(Latin)* ♂　　　　　　　　RATING: ★★☆

Winner, conqueror—Victor Hugo, author

People think of Victor as handsome, intelligent, funny, cool, sexy

People who like the name Victor also like Vincent, Nicholas, Gabriel, Zachary, Alexander, Ethan, Nathan, Xavier, Nathaniel, Jacob

Victoria *(Latin)* ♀　　　　　　　RATING: ★★★

Winner, conqueror—Also a Canadian city; Victoria Principal, actress; Queen Victoria, queen of England

People think of Victoria as pretty, funny, intelligent, caring, creative

People who like the name Victoria also like Olivia, Isabella, Veronica, Abigail, Emma, Paige, Samantha, Grace, Hannah, Elizabeth

Victorin *(Rumantsch)* ♂　　　　　RATING: ★★☆

Winner, conqueror

People think of Victorin as powerful, winner, wealthy, stuck-up, nerdy

People who like the name Victorin also like Ulysses, Isaac, Jonah, Sebastian, Korbin, Baxter, Dexter, Jack, Clinton, Gwyn

Vida *(Latin)* ♀　　　　　　　　　RATING: ★★★★

Life

People think of Vida as pretty, caring, popular, intelligent, creative

People who like the name Vida also like Eva, Ava, Vivian, Celeste, Ella, Mia, Sofia, Vega, Emma, Ivy

Vidal *(Spanish)* ♂　　　　　　　RATING: ★★★☆

Vital—Vidal Sassoon, hair stylist/entrepreneur; Gore Vidal, author

People think of Vidal as handsome, sexy, exotic, trustworthy, funny

People who like the name Vidal also like Diego, Xavier, Salvador, Javier, Sebastian, Victor, Ramón, Xander, Tristan, Miles

Vidar *(Scandinavian)* ♂　　　　　RATING: ★★★

Forest battler

People think of Vidar as powerful, weird, slow, aggressive, loser

People who like the name Vidar also like Soren, Stian, Lucius, Saeran, Darrius, Sef, Gareth, Zaccheus, Geir, Reidar

Vidor *(Hungarian)* ♂　　　　　　RATING: ★☆

Happy

People think of Vidor as old-fashioned, nerdy, criminal, creative, weird

People who like the name Vidor also like Korbin, Vasska, Asher, Vasilis, Adish, Holden, Xander, Zorion, Dragan, Damek

Vienna *(Latin)* ♀　　　　　　　　RATING: ★★★★☆

From wine country—Also a city in Austria; also a city in Virginia

People think of Vienna as pretty, elegant, creative, intelligent, exotic

People who like the name Vienna also like Sienna, Isabella, Ava, Victoria, Olivia, Scarlett, Violet, Paige, Emma, Sierra

Viet *(Vietnamese)* ♂　　　　　　RATING: ★☆

Of Vietnamese descent

People think of Viet as young, cool, intelligent, ethnic, funny

People who like the name Viet also like Jacob, William, Harry, Gomer, Mattox, Ferrol, Franklin, Garron, Griffin, Harlow

Viggo *(Scandinavian)* ♂　　　　　RATING: ★★★★

Battle, warlike—Viggo Mortensen, actor

People think of Viggo as handsome, intelligent, artsy, leader, energetic

People who like the name Viggo also like Xander, Seth, Tristan, Noah, Ethan, Wyatt, William, Gavin, Ian, Gabriel

Viho *(Native American)* ♂　　　　RATING: ★★☆

Chief—Probably Cheyenne origin

People think of Viho as sexy, slow, ethnic, powerful, old

People who like the name Viho also like Dasan, Ahanu, Ohanzee, Yuma, Nantai, Kele, Mingan, Ezhno, Dyami, Yaholo

Vijay *(Sanskrit/East Indian)* ♂　　RATING: ★★★☆

Victorious

People think of Vijay as intelligent, caring, cool, handsome, trustworthy

People who like the name Vijay also like Gabriel, Ajay, Tristan, Sanjay, Ashwin, Victor, Maddox, Vaman, Vincent, Oliver

Vila *(Hungarian)* ♂　　　　　　　RATING: ★★★

Strong-willed warrior—Variation of William

People think of Vila as exotic, weird, wealthy, artsy, boy next door

People who like the name Vila also like Rex, Kaden, Luke, Liam, Vance, Kiefer, Heller, Oliver, Raffaello, Tam

Vilina *(Sanskrit/East Indian)* ♀   RATING: ★★★
Dedicated
> People think of Vilina as caring, pretty, trustworthy, energetic, creative
> People who like the name Vilina also like Viveka, Fiona, Natasha, Virika, Nadia, Grace, Venya, Rianna, Viola, Serena

Ville *(French)* ♀   RATING: ★★★☆
Town
> People think of Ville as sexy, handsome, creative, popular, cool
> People who like the name Ville also like Celeste, Princess, Marlee, Vivian, Emma, Helena, Olivia, Sophia, Virginia, Sunshine

Villette *(French)* ♀   RATING: ★★☆
Small village
> People think of Villette as exotic, artsy, trendy, popular, energetic
> People who like the name Villette also like Scarlett, Violet, Yvette, Daphne, Paige, Lisette, Victoria, Sephora, Ophelia, Cassandra

Vilmos *(Hungarian)* ♂   RATING: ★★
Strong-willed warrior—Variation of William
> People think of Vilmos as weird, aggressive, sneaky, powerful, ethnic
> People who like the name Vilmos also like Tristan, Demitrius, Hagen, Dmitri, Troy, Raghnall, Damien, Vince, Wyndham, Arthur

Vin *(English)* ♂   RATING: ★★★☆
Victorious—Short for Vincent
> People think of Vin as handsome, intelligent, popular, leader, powerful
> People who like the name Vin also like Vince, Ethan, Vance, Aiden, Van, Owen, Cole, Ian, Noah, Seth

Vina *(Spanish)* ♀   RATING: ★★★★
From the vineyard
> People think of Vina as funny, pretty, intelligent, cool, caring
> People who like the name Vina also like Layla, Vera, Mia, Heather, Viviana, Dawn, Patience, Ivy, Lara, Lauren

Vinanti *(Sanskrit/East Indian)* ♀   RATING: ★★☆
Request
> People think of Vinanti as pretty, cool, ethnic, energetic, funny
> People who like the name Vinanti also like Natalia, Jasmine, Patience, Anya, Renée, Calista, Diana, Vinaya, Nicolette, Viveka

Vinata *(Sanskrit/East Indian)* ♀   RATING: ★★☆
Humble
> People think of Vinata as ethnic, pretty, funny, aggressive, artsy
> People who like the name Vinata also like Vinanti, Cassandra, Rimona, Vivian, Michaela, Visala, Savannah, Shaylee, Nevaeh, Vyomini

Vinay *(Sanskrit/East Indian)* ♂   RATING: ★★★☆
Modest
> People think of Vinay as handsome, cool, sexy, intelligent, creative
> People who like the name Vinay also like Varun, Ashwin, Varuna, Sanjay, Sanjiv, Suvan, Mattox, Thomas, Tarun, Conner

Vinaya *(Sanskrit/East Indian)* ♀   RATING: ★★★
Modest
> People think of Vinaya as exotic, intelligent, leader, popular, funny
> People who like the name Vinaya also like Varana, Veronica, Kaya, Venya, Rhian, Shakila, Karina, Malaya, Katelyn, Adriana

Vince *(English)* ♂   RATING: ★★☆
Victorious—Short for Vincent; Vince Vaughn, actor
> People think of Vince as handsome, funny, intelligent, popular, cool
> People who like the name Vince also like Vincent, Nathan, Ethan, Jacob, Seth, Zachary, Ian, Owen, Aiden, Caleb

Vincent *(Latin)* ♂   RATING: ★★☆
Victorious—Vincent D'Onofrio, actor; Vincent Price, actor; Vincent van Gogh, artist
> People think of Vincent as handsome, intelligent, funny, cool, caring
> People who like the name Vincent also like Ethan, Nicholas, Zachary, Victor, Gabriel, Alexander, Nathan, Jacob, Matthew, Aiden

Vine *(English)* ♀ ♂   RATING: ★★
Vineyard worker
> People think of Vine as weird, intelligent, pretty, exotic, nerdy
> People who like the name Vine also like James, Raven, Phoenix, Taylor, Winter, Jade, Hayden, Blake, Topaz, Blair

Vinita *(Sanskrit/East Indian)* ♀   RATING: ★★☆
Knowledge
> People think of Vinita as intelligent, pretty, trustworthy, funny, creative
> People who like the name Vinita also like Vienna, Victoria, Trista, Callie, Vinanti, Veronica, Tori, Sashi, Sienna, Tyanne

Vinnie *(English)* ♂   RATING: ★★★☆
Victorious—Short for Vincent
> People think of Vinnie as handsome, funny, powerful, cool, popular
> People who like the name Vinnie also like Orlando, Warren, Daniel, Vincent, Stephen, Trey, Tyson, Matthew, Tommy, Vance

Vinny *(English)* ♂   RATING: ★★★☆
Victorious—Short for Vincent
> People think of Vinny as handsome, funny, cool, intelligent, sexy

People who like the name Vinny also like Nathan, Vince, Ian, Vincent, Wade, Anthony, Ethan, Kaden, Jeremy, Vinnie

Vinson (English) ♂   RATING: ★★★☆
Son of Vincent
People think of Vinson as weird, handsome, ethnic, nerdy, funny
People who like the name Vinson also like Vincent, Tristan, Gabriel, Ethan, Tyson, Jackson, Dawson, William, Ian, Aiden

Viola (Italian) ♀   RATING: ★★
Violet—Also a musical stringed instrument
People think of Viola as pretty, creative, intelligent, elegant, caring
People who like the name Viola also like Violet, Olivia, Isabella, Ava, Emma, Scarlett, Ophelia, Sophia, Layla, Fiona

Violet (French) ♀   RATING: ★★★★
Purple/blue flower
People think of Violet as pretty, intelligent, creative, caring, elegant
People who like the name Violet also like Olivia, Scarlett, Ava, Charlotte, Chloe, Grace, Lily, Victoria, Paige, Isabella

Viral (Sanskrit/East Indian) ♂   RATING: ★★
Precious—In English, means continuously duplicating; also a biological or computer virus
People think of Viral as ethnic, aggressive, weird, criminal, powerful
People who like the name Viral also like Varen, Vatsa, Arav, Arnav, Ashwin, Tanav, Manas, Valin, Suvan, Savir

Virendra (Sanskrit/East Indian) ♀ ♂   RATING: ★★★
Brave noble person
People think of Virendra as intelligent, sexy, weird, unpopular, ethnic
People who like the name Virendra also like Rhoslyn, Pavan, Arya, Vanya, Willow, Tarachand, Jiva, Kalyan, Vasant, Deva

Virgil (Latin) ♂   RATING: ★★★★
Unknown meaning—Virgil, classical Roman poet
People think of Virgil as intelligent, handsome, trustworthy, funny, cool
People who like the name Virgil also like Xavier, Vincent, Seth, William, Oliver, Owen, Felix, Nicholas, Lucas, Xander

Virginia (Latin) ♀   RATING: ★★★☆
Virginal, pure—Virginia Apgar, scientist; Virginia Madsen, actress; Virginia Woolf, author/critic
People think of Virginia as pretty, intelligent, caring, funny, trustworthy
People who like the name Virginia also like Victoria, Olivia, Elizabeth, Abigail, Hannah, Veronica, Samantha, Emma, Charlotte, Paige

Virgo (Latin) ♀ ♂   RATING: ★★
The virgin—Used for children born under this astrological sign
People think of Virgo as intelligent, creative, powerful, caring, exotic
People who like the name Virgo also like Raven, Paris, Valentine, Reese, Sydney, Jade, Rain, Willow, Taylor, Winter

Virika (Sanskrit/East Indian) ♀   RATING: ★★☆
Brave one
People think of Virika as weird, caring, wild, pretty, energetic
People who like the name Virika also like Vilina, Venya, Vinaya, Vyomini, Zafirah, Varana, Viveka, Laranya, Tanika, Avani

Virote (Thai) ♂   RATING: ★★☆
Power
People think of Virote as powerful, exotic, leader, intelligent, nerdy
People who like the name Virote also like Tadelesh, Arnau, Eitan, Tokala, Dhiren, Gideon, Fearghus, Brandon, Bandele, Eldon

Visala (Sanskrit/East Indian) ♀   RATING: ★★☆
Celestial
People think of Visala as uptight, popular, unpopular, powerful, pretty
People who like the name Visala also like Victoria, Natasha, Chloe, Callia, Ella, Felicity, Violet, Lauren, Jaya, Zoe

Vita (Italian) ♀   RATING: ★★
Life
People think of Vita as intelligent, creative, energetic, sexy, cool
People who like the name Vita also like Ava, Isabella, Bella, Stella, Ella, Scarlett, Eva, Victoria, Paige, Summer

Vitalia (Italian) ♀   RATING: ★★★
Full of life
People think of Vitalia as pretty, energetic, exotic, sexy, intelligent
People who like the name Vitalia also like Viviana, Adrina, Zalika, Isabella, Gabriella, Gianna, Zoe, Belle, Aislin, Katarina

Vitalis (Latin) ♂   RATING: ★★★
Alive
People think of Vitalis as intelligent, sexy, creative, leader, young
People who like the name Vitalis also like Soren, Zander, Korbin, Kyros, Thaddeus, Zero, Zeno, Mateo, Sanders, Calix

Vito (Italian) ♂   RATING: ★★
Life
People think of Vito as powerful, intelligent, handsome, popular, funny
People who like the name Vito also like Vincent, Nico, Salvatore, Thomas, Nicholas, Victor, Angelo, Gino, Vittorio, Vince

Vittorio *(Italian)* ♂   RATING: ★★★☆
Winner, conqueror
> People think of Vittorio as intelligent, funny, caring, handsome, powerful
>
> People who like the name Vittorio also like Vincent, Gabriel, Salvatore, Tristan, Vito, Valentino, Giovanni, Angelo, Anthony, Leonardo

Viturin *(Rumantsch)* ♂   RATING: ★★
Winner, conqueror
> People think of Viturin as winner, aggressive, weird, powerful, leader
>
> People who like the name Viturin also like Yorick, Demitrius, Alastair, Holden, Olin, Werner, Wycliff, Torsten, Israel, Patrick

Viva *(Latin)* ♀   RATING: ★★★
Full of life
> People think of Viva as energetic, leader, intelligent, creative, funny
>
> People who like the name Viva also like Ella, Vita, Aria, Gabriella, Aida, Mira, Bella, Neve, Dahlia, Cara

Viveca *(German)* ♀   RATING: ★★★☆
War
> People think of Viveca as pretty, popular, exotic, powerful, artsy
>
> People who like the name Viveca also like Vivian, Olivia, Paige, Sophia, Victoria, Isabella, Zoe, Chloe, Nadia, Violet

Vivek *(Sanskrit/East Indian)* ♂   RATING: ★★★☆
Wisdom, knowledge
> People think of Vivek as intelligent, handsome, winner, funny, powerful
>
> People who like the name Vivek also like Varen, Ethan, Ashwin, Maddox, Xander, Aiden, Vijay, Isaac, Ramses, Caleb

Viveka *(Sanskrit/East Indian)* ♀   RATING: ★★★
Wisdom, knowledge
> People think of Viveka as pretty, exotic, caring, funny, winner
>
> People who like the name Viveka also like Lorelei, Veronica, Shyla, Viveca, Ophelia, Vivian, Freya, Vilina, Paige, Nayana

Vivi *(Latin)* ♀   RATING: ★★
Alive
> People think of Vivi as pretty, funny, young, elegant, creative
>
> People who like the name Vivi also like Bella, Vivian, Viviana, Ava, Vivienne, Violet, Ella, Olivia, Sadie, Sofia

Vivian *(Latin)* ♀   RATING: ★★★★
Alive—Vivian Vance, actress
> People think of Vivian as pretty, intelligent, funny, caring, creative
>
> People who like the name Vivian also like Olivia, Victoria, Sophia, Isabella, Paige, Ava, Grace, Veronica, Violet, Hannah

Viviana *(Italian)* ♀   RATING: ★★★★
Alive
> People think of Viviana as pretty, intelligent, caring, funny, sexy
>
> People who like the name Viviana also like Isabella, Olivia, Victoria, Ava, Natalia, Vanessa, Gianna, Gabriella, Angelina, Vivian

Vivica *(American)* ♀   RATING: ★★★
War—Variation of Viveca; Vivica A. Fox, actress
> People think of Vivica as powerful, pretty, creative, cool, young
>
> People who like the name Vivica also like Adriana, Imani, Desdemona, Harmony, Leilani, Portia, Hazel, Lia, Querida, Samara

Vivien *(French)* ♀   RATING: ★★★★
Alive—Vivien Leigh, actress
> People think of Vivien as pretty, intelligent, elegant, caring, funny
>
> People who like the name Vivien also like Vivian, Olivia, Victoria, Vivienne, Paige, Violet, Isabelle, Sophia, Ava, Scarlett

Vivienne *(French)* ♀   RATING: ★★★☆
Alive
> People think of Vivienne as pretty, intelligent, elegant, sexy, creative
>
> People who like the name Vivienne also like Olivia, Victoria, Vivian, Violet, Isabelle, Genevieve, Ava, Grace, Gabrielle, Audrey

Vlad *(Slavic)* ♂   RATING: ★★★☆
Prince
> People think of Vlad as intelligent, powerful, aggressive, handsome, leader
>
> People who like the name Vlad also like Vladimir, Alexander, Lucas, Victor, Damien, Tristan, Xavier, Felix, Gabriel, Vincent

Vladimir *(Slavic)* ♂   RATING: ★★
Great ruler
> People think of Vladimir as intelligent, handsome, powerful, leader, sexy
>
> People who like the name Vladimir also like Xavier, Vincent, Victor, Xander, Isaac, Gabriel, Nathaniel, Oliver, Zachary, Dmitri

Vlora *(American)* ♀   RATING: ★★
A city in Albania
> People think of Vlora as intelligent, pretty, sexy, ethnic, elegant
>
> People who like the name Vlora also like Viola, Kiara, Valora, Gwyneth, Shayla, Roxanne, Tegan, Mckayla, Sanne, Kayla

Von *(American)* ♀ ♂   RATING: ★★★★
Probably a variation of Vaughn
> People think of Von as handsome, powerful, intelligent, aggressive, cool
>
> People who like the name Von also like Vaughn, Logan, Toby, Bailey, Carter, Parker, Taylor, Addison, Riley, Sean

564

Vonda *(German)* ♀   RATING: ★★★☆
Of Saxony—Variation of Wanda; Vonda Shepard, singer/songwriter
> People think of Vonda as trustworthy, pretty, funny, caring, creative
> People who like the name Vonda also like Ivy, Zoe, Layla, Rhiannon, Enya, Sheena, Bella, Ava, Felicity, Gwendolyn

Vondila *(American)* ♀   RATING: ★★☆
Variation of Vonda
> People think of Vondila as aggressive, lazy, nerdy, unpopular, loser
> People who like the name Vondila also like Vinaya, Dolores, Rhian, Shasa, Dawn, Zenobia, Deirdra, Sarama, Vianca, Deidra

Vondra *(American)* ♀   RATING: ★★★
Combination of Vonda and Sandra
> People think of Vondra as ethnic, pretty, funny, popular, weird
> People who like the name Vondra also like Valora, Nixie, Lydia, Villette, Zora, Delphine, Kendra, Larissa, Lena, Theodora

Vova *(Russian)* ♀   RATING: ★★★
Famous rule
> People think of Vova as cool, weird, ethnic, wild, intelligent
> People who like the name Vova also like Dara, Vyomini, Victoria, Xaria, Sada, Avril, Dulcina, Kuri, Kyria, Isabella

Vox *(Latin)* ♀ ♂   RATING: ★★☆
Voice—Bono Vox, singer
> People think of Vox as weird, criminal, intelligent, creative, aggressive
> People who like the name Vox also like Jax, Charlie, Tate, Aren, Perrin, Willow, Raven, Caden, Hayden, Paxton

Vui *(Vietnamese)* ♀   RATING: ★★☆
Cheerful
> People think of Vui as nerdy, exotic, ethnic, weird, loser
> People who like the name Vui also like Vera, Zi, Zeki, Layla, Mai, Vega, Hue, Zuri, Nhi, Jamila

Vyomini *(Sanskrit/East Indian)* ♀   RATING: ★★★
Divine
> People think of Vyomini as exotic, weird, poor, ethnic, young
> People who like the name Vyomini also like Varali, Varana, Vinaya, Virika, Venya, Victoria, Meena, Mythri, Zenevieva, Viveka

Vyra *(American)* ♀   RATING: ★★★
Truth
> People think of Vyra as exotic, creative, sexy, young, wild
> People who like the name Vyra also like Kaida, Sapphire, Athena, Viveca, Vera, Aira, Lanelle, Vivian, Celeste, Rhiannon

Wade *(English)* ♂   RATING: ★★★☆
Traveler
> People think of Wade as handsome, cool, funny, caring, intelligent
> People who like the name Wade also like Ethan, Wyatt, Walker, Owen, Zachary, Aiden, Landon, Cole, Ian, Noah

Wafa *(Arabic)* ♀ ♂   RATING: ★★★★
Faithful
> People think of Wafa as loser, nerdy, funny, sexy, weird
> People who like the name Wafa also like Aidan, Wynne, Aiken, Layne, Aspen, Blaise, Ash, Ari, Nalani, Logan

Waggoner *(English)* ♂   RATING: ★★☆
Wagon maker
> People think of Waggoner as weird, old-fashioned, funny, unpopular, old
> People who like the name Waggoner also like Warner, Lucas, Jasper, Landon, Jacob, Wendell, Nate, Lawson, Rhett, Nathaniel

Waite *(English)* ♂   RATING: ★★☆
Watchman, guard—Originally a surname
> People think of Waite as quiet, big, lazy, leader, cool
> People who like the name Waite also like Wade, Wyatt, Walker, Kaden, Landon, Noah, Jace, Reece, Maddox, Aden

Wakanda *(Native American)* ♀   RATING: ★★★☆
Possesses magical powers—Sioux origin
> People think of Wakanda as powerful, creative, exotic, ethnic, intelligent
> People who like the name Wakanda also like Kaya, Waneta, Wyanet, Rhian, Orenda, Topanga, Yepa, Zaltana, Sora, Tala

Walda *(German)* ♀   RATING: ★☆
Ruler
> People think of Walda as old, big, unpopular, nerdy, weird
> People who like the name Walda also like Macy, Wilma, Penelope, Teryl, Freida, Marisol, Pearl, Violet, Yana, Jaclyn

Waldemar *(German)* ♂   RATING: ★☆
Famous ruler
> People think of Waldemar as cool, intelligent, funny, creative, handsome
> People who like the name Waldemar also like Jeremy, Warren, Tristan, Valdemar, Rutherford, Livingston, Anderson, Xavier, Brinley, Edison

Walden *(English)* ♂   RATING: ★★
From the valley of the Britons—Also a surname; Walden Pond, place in Massachusetts made famous by the writings of poet Henry David Thoreau
> People think of Walden as intelligent, stuck-up, loser, old-fashioned, funny

People who like the name Walden also like Walker, Noah, Wade, Holden, Jackson, Sebastian, Xavier, Tristan, Ethan, Owen

Waldo (*English*) ♂   RATING: ★★★
God's power—Variation of Oswald; *Where's Waldo*, children's book; Ralph Waldo Emerson, author/poet
People think of Waldo as nerdy, funny, weird, intelligent, loser
People who like the name Waldo also like Jacob, Oliver, Isaac, Benjamin, Jeremiah, Thomas, Jack, Nathan, Wilbur, Edgar

Waldron (*German*) ♂   RATING: ★☆
Mighty raven
People think of Waldron as weird, nerdy, sexy, trustworthy, leader
People who like the name Waldron also like Wyatt, Noah, Wade, Xander, Remington, Wendell, Xadrian, Grayson, William, Radley

Walidah (*Arabic*) ♀   RATING: ★★☆
Young girl, daughter
People think of Walidah as elegant, creative, winner, leader, intelligent
People who like the name Walidah also like Zaviera, Wyanet, Yessica, Zaltana, Zudora, Yovela, Waneta, Xantara, Zivanka, Yanichel

Walker (*English*) ♂   RATING: ★★☆
Fuller of cloth—Originally a surname
People think of Walker as handsome, intelligent, funny, cool, leader
People who like the name Walker also like Jackson, Ethan, Landon, Wyatt, Noah, Wade, Zachary, Owen, Cole, Holden

Wallace (*English*) ♀♂   RATING: ★★★
Foreigner, stranger—Also a surname, applied to the Welsh
People think of Wallace as leader, handsome, intelligent, powerful, caring
People who like the name Wallace also like Logan, Parker, Wesley, Bailey, Hayden, Riley, Mackenzie, Taylor, Madison, Addison

Wallis (*English*) ♀♂   RATING: ★★★☆
Variation of Wallace
People think of Wallis as intelligent, funny, old-fashioned, pretty, energetic
People who like the name Wallis also like Parker, Ryder, Wallace, Harper, Wynn, Raven, Sawyer, Nolan, Willow, Riley

Wally (*English*) ♂   RATING: ★☆
Short for Walter or Wallace—Also British slang for an idiot
People think of Wally as funny, intelligent, popular, nerdy, handsome
People who like the name Wally also like Wade, Walter, Jason, Troy, Ian, Jack, Watson, Owen, Walt, Tristan

Walt (*American*) ♂   RATING: ★★★☆
Army ruler—Short for Walter; Walt Disney, animator; Walt Whitman, writer
People think of Walt as intelligent, caring, handsome, creative, energetic
People who like the name Walt also like Seth, Wade, Luke, Trent, Walker, Owen, Jacob, Walter, Tyson, Nathan

Walter (*English*) ♂   RATING: ★★★
Army ruler—Walter Matthau, actor; Walter Pidgeon, actor
People think of Walter as intelligent, funny, caring, handsome, cool
People who like the name Walter also like William, Benjamin, Thomas, Ethan, Zachary, Jacob, Nicholas, Oliver, Vincent, Gabriel

Walworth (*English*) ♂   RATING: ★★
From the homestead of the Britons—Originally a surname
People think of Walworth as old-fashioned, old, loser, uptight, unpopular
People who like the name Walworth also like Langston, Wentworth, Alton, Warwick, Radley, Warrick, Jeffrey, Adair, Willoughby, Aiden

Wan (*Chinese*) ♀   RATING: ★☆
Gentle, gracious—Mandarin origin
People think of Wan as ethnic, weird, poor, young, unpopular
People who like the name Wan also like Amy, Xiu Juan, Winona, Raeanne, Whisper, Zita, Angelina, Wendy, Wanda, Hannah

Wanda (*Polish*) ♀   RATING: ★★★
A slender, young tree
People think of Wanda as caring, funny, creative, intelligent, pretty
People who like the name Wanda also like Victoria, Vanessa, Faith, Hannah, Hailey, Felicity, Rebecca, Paige, Zoey, Wendy

Wandella (*American*) ♀   RATING: ★★☆
Combination of Wanda and Ella
People think of Wandella as weird, untrustworthy, lazy, big, poor
People who like the name Wandella also like Whisper, Wanda, Ivy, Aurora, Mabel, Wind, Heather, Eve, Fiona, Isabel

Waneta (*Native American*) ♀   RATING: ★☆
Shape-shifter—Also a variation of Juanita
People think of Waneta as exotic, ethnic, pretty, old, wealthy
People who like the name Waneta also like Wakanda, Tala, Topanga, Winona, Fala, Zaltana, Taini, Talulah, Orenda, Elu

Ward (*English*) ♂   RATING: ★★
Guardian
People think of Ward as trustworthy, funny, intelligent, handsome, leader

People who like the name Ward also like Walker, Wade, Landon, Owen, Zachary, Tristan, Wyatt, Noah, Reece, Nathan

Wardah *(Arabic)* ♀ RATING: ★★★☆
Rose
> People think of Wardah as intelligent, cool, pretty, ethnic, young
> People who like the name Wardah also like Sada, Naida, Zabrina, Rhian, Wakanda, Seda, Raisa, Sahara, Opal, Amaya

Warner *(English)* ♂ RATING: ★★★☆
Army guard—Originally a surname
> People think of Warner as handsome, intelligent, young, leader, powerful
> People who like the name Warner also like Walker, Warren, Jackson, Ethan, Wyatt, Landon, Holden, Noah, Wade, Nathan

Warren *(English)* ♂ RATING: ★★☆
Guard—Warren Zevon, musician
> People think of Warren as handsome, intelligent, trustworthy, caring, funny
> People who like the name Warren also like Nathan, Ethan, Owen, Zachary, Tristan, William, Nicholas, Noah, Landon, Seth

Warrick *(English)* ♂ RATING: ★★★
From the town by the river—Originally a surname
> People think of Warrick as loser, untrustworthy, nerdy, handsome, weird
> People who like the name Warrick also like Ethan, Walker, Wyatt, Nathan, Xavier, Owen, Tristan, Noah, Xander, Lucas

Warwick *(English)* ♂ RATING: ★★★☆
From the town by the weir—Originally a surname; Dionne Warwick, singer
> People think of Warwick as intelligent, handsome, energetic, funny, leader
> People who like the name Warwick also like Warrick, Xander, Aiden, Tristan, William, Wyatt, Liam, Walker, Owen, Cole

Wasaki *(African)* ♂ RATING: ★★★
The enemy—Kenyan origin
> People think of Wasaki as aggressive, weird, powerful, nerdy, loser
> People who like the name Wasaki also like Ryu, Alaric, Antonio, Tokala, Warren, Warrick, Alastair, Javier, Bastien, Armand

Waseem *(Arabic)* ♂ RATING: ★☆
Handsome
> People think of Waseem as handsome, funny, popular, young, sexy
> People who like the name Waseem also like Zakiya, Rashid, Wes, Jadon, Nathan, Jabir, Raheem, Warren, Ethan, Jamal

Waseemah *(Arabic)* ♀ RATING: ★☆
Beautiful
> People think of Waseemah as young, exotic, weird, religious, winner
> People who like the name Waseemah also like Jessenia, Yessica, Inara, Naida, Saleema, Alyssa, Zalika, Laraine, Pamela, Gabrielle

Washi *(Japanese)* ♂ RATING: ★★☆
Eagle
> People think of Washi as exotic, weird, artsy, ethnic, cool
> People who like the name Washi also like Ryu, Ringo, Kaemon, Suoh, Haru, Haruki, Keitaro, Keiji, Yasuo, Shino

Washington *(English)* ♂ RATING: ★★
From the town of Wassa's people—English place name; also a surname; also U.S. capital district and U.S. state; George Washington, U.S. president
> People think of Washington as weird, wild, cool, intelligent, old-fashioned
> People who like the name Washington also like William, Wade, Nicholas, Walker, Lucas, Nathan, Ian, Wilson, Emerson, Isaac

Watson *(English)* ♂ RATING: ★★★☆
Son of Walter
> People think of Watson as intelligent, quiet, cool, creative, caring
> People who like the name Watson also like Jackson, Owen, Wyatt, Ethan, Wade, Landon, Noah, Isaac, Nathan, Tyson

Watt *(English)* ♂ RATING: ★★
Army ruler—Short for Walter
> People think of Watt as nerdy, weird, handsome, religious, loser
> People who like the name Watt also like Watson, Zachary, Conner, Kale, Emory, Wade, Wyatt, Eli, Ian, Isaiah

Wattan *(Japanese)* ♀ RATING: ★★
From the homeland
> People think of Wattan as big, exotic, nerdy, funny, weird
> People who like the name Wattan also like Sada, Sakura, Kaiyo, Kohana, Mai, Kaori, Machiko, Yori, Michi, Kuma

Wauna *(Native American)* ♀ RATING: ★★☆
Singing snow goose—Miwok origin
> People think of Wauna as exotic, powerful, creative, sneaky, poor
> People who like the name Wauna also like Wakanda, Yepa, Tawana, Zaltana, Kachina, Winona, Tiponya, Sokanon, Karis, Thora

Waverly *(English)* ♀ ♂ RATING: ★★★★
From the brushwood field—Also a surname; also a place in England
> People think of Waverly as pretty, intelligent, creative, artsy, caring

People who like the name Waverly also like Riley, Willow, Hayden, Parker, Avery, Madison, Addison, Wesley, Reagan, Sawyer

Wayde *(English)* ♂   RATING: ★★★☆
Variation of Wade
People think of Wayde as sexy, handsome, loser, energetic, young
People who like the name Wayde also like Wade, Walker, Kaden, Wyatt, Ethan, Jackson, Tristan, Jayden, Caleb, Zachary

Wayland *(English)* ♂   RATING: ★★★☆
Unknown meaning
People think of Wayland as handsome, intelligent, funny, leader, old-fashioned
People who like the name Wayland also like Waylon, Wyatt, Landon, Walker, Weston, Wade, Jacob, Holden, Kaden, Jayden

Waylon *(English)* ♂   RATING: ★★
Land by the road—Also spelled Weylin; Waylon Jennings, singer/songwriter
People think of Waylon as cool, handsome, popular, creative, wild
People who like the name Waylon also like Wyatt, Walker, Ethan, Braden, Wade, Elijah, Weston, Owen, Jackson, Tristan

Wayne *(English)* ♂   RATING: ★★★☆
Wagon driver—Originally a surname; Wayne Brady, TV host/comedian; Wayne Newton, singer
People think of Wayne as funny, handsome, caring, intelligent, cool
People who like the name Wayne also like William, Nathan, Justin, Jason, Zachary, Wade, Nicholas, Scott, Warren, David

Webb *(English)* ♂   RATING: ★☆
Weaver
People think of Webb as intelligent, funny, handsome, cool, leader
People who like the name Webb also like Wade, William, Weston, Noah, Owen, Dalton, Jack, Walker, Jacob, Warrick

Webster *(English)* ♂   RATING: ★★★☆
Weaver—Daniel Webster, U.S. statesman/lawyer; brand of U.S. dictionary
People think of Webster as intelligent, nerdy, creative, cool, weird
People who like the name Webster also like Jackson, Wade, Nathan, Tucker, Zachary, William, Nicholas, Noah, Walker, Ethan

Wednesday *(American)* ♀♂   RATING: ★★★☆
Born on Wednesday—Wednesday Addams, character on *The Addams Family*
People think of Wednesday as weird, creative, intelligent, pretty, young
People who like the name Wednesday also like Madison, Willow, Logan, Riley, Piper, Taylor, Tuesday, Raven, Jade, Cadence

Wei *(Chinese)* ♀♂   RATING: ★★★☆
Valuable; brillliant—Mandarin origin
People think of Wei as intelligent, caring, funny, quiet, pretty
People who like the name Wei also like Whitney, James, Kai, Li, Nalani, Jaden, Yi Min, Alexis, Yue Yan, Winter

Welcome *(American)* ♀   RATING: ★★☆
Welcome guest
People think of Welcome as weird, nerdy, loser, poor, unpopular
People who like the name Welcome also like Whisper, Paprika, Zoe, Sophie, Serenity, Sapphire, Mystery, Gabriella, Scarlett, Velvet

Weldon *(English)* ♂   RATING: ★★★
From the hill with a well—Originally a surname
People think of Weldon as handsome, funny, leader, trustworthy, intelligent
People who like the name Weldon also like Wade, Weston, Trenton, Walker, Landon, Wyatt, Waylon, Noah, Tristan, Braden

Wells *(English)* ♂   RATING: ★★★☆
From the well—Originally a surname; David Wells, baseball player
People think of Wells as intelligent, funny, powerful, energetic, caring
People who like the name Wells also like Noah, Walker, Holden, Cole, Jack, Owen, Graham, William, Andrew, Liam

Wen *(Chinese)* ♀♂   RATING: ★★★
Culture, writing
People think of Wen as intelligent, trustworthy, caring, young, girl next door
People who like the name Wen also like December, Devon, Daylin, Carmen, Wednesday, Lavender, Zephyr, Zion, Corbin, Mars

Wenda *(German)* ♀   RATING: ★★☆
Variation of Wanda
People think of Wenda as pretty, sexy, trustworthy, quiet, funny
People who like the name Wenda also like Olivia, Faith, Scarlett, Victoria, Bridget, Vanessa, Alana, Felicity, Opal, Ivy

Wendell *(German)* ♂   RATING: ★★★☆
Wanderer, seeker—Also spelled Wendall or Wendahl
People think of Wendell as intelligent, funny, handsome, trustworthy, caring
People who like the name Wendell also like Wade, Nicholas, Warren, William, Oliver, Sebastian, Wyatt, Ethan, Lucas, Jacob

Wendy *(English)* ♀   RATING: ★★★☆
Wendi
Friend—From the phrase "friendy-wendy," created by J. M. Barrie in *Peter Pan*
People think of Wendy as funny, pretty, caring, intelligent, creative

People who like the name Wendy also like Samantha, Olivia, Paige, Rebecca, Grace, Emily, Faith, Victoria, Hannah, Sarah

Wentworth (English) ♂   RATING: ★★★☆
Village of the white people—Wentworth Miller, actor
People think of Wentworth as handsome, intelligent, sexy, trustworthy, cool
People who like the name Wentworth also like Tristan, Owen, Jacob, Zachary, Ethan, Wade, Caleb, Xavier, Noah, Joshua

Werner (German) ♂   RATING: ★★★☆
Army guard
People think of Werner as intelligent, handsome, creative, caring, trustworthy
People who like the name Werner also like Wyatt, Jackson, Weston, Landon, Warner, Jayden, Nathan, Noah, Walker, Owen

Wes (English) ♂   RATING: ★★★☆
From the west field—Short for Wesley
People think of Wes as funny, handsome, cool, sexy, intelligent
People who like the name Wes also like Wade, Ethan, Owen, Seth, Ian, Jacob, Luke, Walker, Wyatt, Aiden

Wesley (English) ♀♂   RATING: ★★★★
From the west field—Originally a surname; Wesley Snipes, actor
People think of Wesley as handsome, intelligent, funny, caring, cool
People who like the name Wesley also like Logan, Hayden, Taylor, Tyler, Riley, Parker, Ryan, Madison, Evan, Connor

West (English) ♂   RATING: ★★★
From the west
People think of West as funny, handsome, leader, popular, intelligent
People who like the name West also like Liam, Weston, Gabriel, Alexander, William, Sebastian, Owen, Elias, Jonah, Leo

Westbrook (English) ♂   RATING: ★★★
From the west brook
People think of Westbrook as leader, cool, old-fashioned, funny, trustworthy
People who like the name Westbrook also like Wyatt, Weston, Walker, Gabriel, Tristan, Reece, Everett, Remington, Broderick, Rhett

Weston (English) ♂   RATING: ★★☆
From the west town
People think of Weston as handsome, intelligent, funny, popular, cool
People who like the name Weston also like Landon, Owen, Ethan, Jackson, Tristan, Wyatt, Kaden, Walker, Noah, Gavin

Wheatley (English) ♂   RATING: ★★★
From the wheat field—Originally a surname
People think of Wheatley as funny, intelligent, exotic, energetic, creative

People who like the name Wheatley also like Weston, Winston, Ian, Wheaton, Brighton, Lucas, Landon, Tristan, Jackson, Liam

Wheaton (English) ♂   RATING: ★★☆
From the wheat town—Originally a surname; Wil Wheaton, actor
People think of Wheaton as nerdy, old-fashioned, loser, poor, boy next door
People who like the name Wheaton also like Weston, Wade, Grayson, Tucker, Noah, Tristan, Landon, Sloan, Ian, Tyson

Wheeler (English) ♂   RATING: ★★★
Wheel maker—Originally a surname
People think of Wheeler as trustworthy, energetic, quiet, lazy, cool
People who like the name Wheeler also like Wyatt, Owen, Nathan, Miles, Thatcher, Holden, Tucker, Keagan, Landon, Drake

Whisper (American) ♀   RATING: ★★★★
Soft voice
People think of Whisper as pretty, quiet, intelligent, creative, caring
People who like the name Whisper also like Paige, Faith, Trinity, Harmony, Sadie, Melody, Victoria, Iris, Olivia, Violet

Whistler (English) ♂   RATING: ★☆
Piper—Also a surname; James McNeill Whistler, artist
People think of Whistler as sporty, wild, handsome, sexy, caring
People who like the name Whistler also like Drake, Xander, Tucker, Ranger, Aiden, Brandon, Jasper, Montgomery, Oliver, Wade

Whitby (English) ♂   RATING: ★★☆
From the white village—Originally a surname
People think of Whitby as stuck-up, old-fashioned, wealthy, weird, unpopular
People who like the name Whitby also like Warren, Wendell, Nicholas, Wade, Bradley, Noah, Cole, Wyatt, Weston, Brighton

Whitcomb (English) ♂   RATING: ★★☆
From the white valley—Originally a surname
People think of Whitcomb as powerful, intelligent, nerdy, leader, weird
People who like the name Whitcomb also like Wilford, Nicholas, Whittaker, Weston, Bradley, Jack, Bradford, Willem, William, Whitby

Whitfield (English) ♂   RATING: ★★★
From the white field—Originally a surname
People think of Whitfield as sexy, intelligent, powerful, stuck-up, creative
People who like the name Whitfield also like Wade, Whittaker, Warrick, Jackson, Willem, Broderick, William, Wyatt, Weston, Whitcomb

Whitley *(English)* ♀♂   RATING: ★★★☆
From the white field—Originally a surname
People think of Whitley as pretty, intelligent, caring, funny, popular
People who like the name Whitley also like Whitney, Hayden, Parker, Bailey, Madison, Reagan, Addison, Reese, Mackenzie, Riley

Whitney *(English)* ♀♂   RATING: ★★☆
From the white island—Also a surname; Whitney Houston, singer; Eli Whitney, inventor
People think of Whitney as pretty, funny, caring, intelligent, creative
People who like the name Whitney also like Taylor, Madison, Logan, Bailey, Riley, Mackenzie, Hayden, Morgan, Parker, Sydney

Whittaker *(English)* ♂   RATING: ★★★
From the white or wheat field—Originally a surname
People think of Whittaker as old, trustworthy, powerful, intelligent, weird
People who like the name Whittaker also like Tristan, Walker, Miles, William, Landon, Samuel, Wade, Liam, Nicholas, Owen

Wiebke *(Dutch)* ♀   RATING: ★★☆
War
People think of Wiebke as elegant, intelligent, sneaky, lazy, weird
People who like the name Wiebke also like Kylar, Ailis, Xylia, Acacia, Aislin, Kaelyn, Dawn, Nevina, Maegan, Coral

Wilbur *(English)* ♂   RATING: ★☆
Will fortress
People think of Wilbur as funny, handsome, young, intelligent, cool
People who like the name Wilbur also like Oliver, Wade, Noah, Isaac, Jacob, Baxter, Thomas, Seamus, Teddy, Nathan

Wilda *(German)* ♀   RATING: ★★★
Untamed
People think of Wilda as funny, trustworthy, caring, wild, intelligent
People who like the name Wilda also like Cecilia, Jennifer, Pamela, Zoey, Lucy, Melanie, Zara, Kendra, Patience, Tatiana

Wiley *(English)* ♀♂   RATING: ★★☆
From the tricky river—Originally a surname; Noah Wiley, actor
People think of Wiley as funny, wild, intelligent, energetic, creative
People who like the name Wiley also like Riley, Caden, Hayden, Parker, Bailey, Ryder, Logan, Taylor, Reese, Jaden

Wilford *(English)* ♂   RATING: ★★★
From the ford by the willows—Originally a surname; Wilford Brimley, actor
People think of Wilford as nerdy, trustworthy, big, creative, caring

People who like the name Wilford also like Benjamin, Nicholas, William, Wade, Andrew, Jack, Whittaker, Whitcomb, Jacob, Wyatt

Wilfred *(English)* ♂   RATING: ★★★
Will peace
People think of Wilfred as funny, handsome, intelligent, caring, quiet
People who like the name Wilfred also like William, Warren, Nathan, Wade, Warrick, Wilson, Jack, Jeremy, Xavier, Oliver

Wilhelm *(German)* ♂   RATING: ★★★
Strong-willed warrior
People think of Wilhelm as handsome, intelligent, powerful, leader, old-fashioned
People who like the name Wilhelm also like Nicholas, Damien, Samuel, Wade, Clarence, Jackson, David, Jacob, Maximilian, Wendell

Wilhelmina *(German)* ♀   RATING: ★☆
Strong-willed warrior—Feminine form of Wilhelm
People think of Wilhelmina as pretty, intelligent, elegant, old-fashioned, creative
People who like the name Wilhelmina also like Amelia, Beatrice, Cecelia, Olivia, Violet, Bella, Rebecca, Evangeline, Phoebe, Chloe

Wilkinson *(English)* ♂   RATING: ★★★
Son of Wilkin
People think of Wilkinson as intelligent, wealthy, cool, powerful, funny
People who like the name Wilkinson also like Weston, Harrison, Wentworth, Warren, Winston, Whitby, Cole, Whittaker, Wheaton, Montgomery

Will *(English)* ♀♂   RATING: ★★★
Strong-willed warrior—Short for William; Will Ferrell, comedian/actor; Will Smith, actor/rapper
People think of Will as handsome, intelligent, funny, caring, cool
People who like the name Will also like Ryan, Logan, Evan, James, Taylor, Tyler, Parker, Connor, Kyle, Hayden

Willa *(American)* ♀   RATING: ★★
Feminine form of Will—Willa Cather, author
People think of Willa as pretty, creative, artsy, intelligent, funny
People who like the name Willa also like Ava, Ella, Olivia, Stella, Bella, Isabella, Chloe, Eva, Grace, Sophie

Willamena *(American)* ♀   RATING: ★★★
Feminine form of William; variation of Wilhelmina
People think of Willamena as old, old-fashioned, funny, weird, unpopular
People who like the name Willamena also like Vivian, Bianca, Penelope, Maggie, Aurora, Astrid, Claudia, Wilhelmina, Adelaide, Willa

Willard *(English)* ♂   RATING: ★★★☆
Will brave—Willard Scott, TV personality
People think of Willard as caring, intelligent, trustworthy, funny, weird

People who like the name Willard also like William, Oliver, Wade, Alexander, Benjamin, Elliott, Tristan, Adam, Noah, Willis

Willem (*Dutch*) ♂ RATING: ★★★★
Strong-willed warrior—Variation of William; Willem Dafoe, actor
People think of Willem as intelligent, handsome, funny, powerful, caring
People who like the name Willem also like Liam, Owen, Tristan, William, Ian, Aiden, Noah, Caleb, Jackson, Jacob

Willene (*American*) ♀ RATING: ★★★
Feminine form of William
People think of Willene as pretty, intelligent, popular, winner, trustworthy
People who like the name Willene also like Veronica, Viviana, Isabella, Wilma, Zoey, Gelsey, Megara, Ryann, Raeanne, Violet

William (*English*) ♂ RATING: ★★★
Strong-willed warrior—Prince William of England; William Shatner, actor
People think of William as handsome, intelligent, funny, caring, trustworthy
People who like the name William also like Benjamin, Ethan, Matthew, Jacob, Nicholas, Noah, Alexander, Zachary, Jack, Thomas

Willis (*English*) ♂ RATING: ★★★☆
Descendant or servant of Will—Character on *Diff'rent Strokes*
People think of Willis as cool, intelligent, handsome, popular, trustworthy
People who like the name Willis also like Wilson, William, Walker, Jackson, Wade, Xavier, Ethan, Noah, Wyatt, Warren

Willoughby (*English*) ♂ RATING: ★★★☆
From the farm by the willows—Originally a surname
People think of Willoughby as creative, caring, intelligent, quiet, powerful
People who like the name Willoughby also like William, Jackson, Aiden, Gabriel, Miles, Jasper, Landon, Drake, Wade, Ian

Willow (*English*) ♀♂ RATING: ★★☆
Willow—Willow Rosenberg, character on *Buffy the Vampire Slayer*
People think of Willow as pretty, creative, intelligent, artsy, caring
People who like the name Willow also like Piper, Logan, Riley, Parker, Bailey, Sage, Hayden, Madison, Taylor, Quinn

Wilma (*American*) ♀ RATING: ★☆
Short for Wilhelmina—Wilma Flintstone, character on *The Flintstones*; Wilma Rudolph, Olympic runner
People think of Wilma as funny, caring, intelligent, pretty, trustworthy
People who like the name Wilma also like Olivia, Matilda, Sophie, Georgia, Penelope, Violet, Faith, Sabrina, Lucy, Mabel

Wilmer (*English*) ♂ RATING: ★☆
Will famous—Wilmer Valderrama, actor
People think of Wilmer as funny, handsome, cool, exotic, popular
People who like the name Wilmer also like Nathan, Wade, Adam, Oliver, Alexander, William, Benjamin, Jacob, Quentin, Nicholas

Wilmet (*English*) ♀♂ RATING: ★★
Variation of William
People think of Wilmet as loser, nerdy, old, unpopular, uptight
People who like the name Wilmet also like Shannon, Parker, Ryan, London, Willow, Connor, Flynn, Paris, Tempest, Rhoslyn

Wilona (*American*) ♀ RATING: ★★★
Combination of Will and Leona
People think of Wilona as pretty, old-fashioned, loser, girl next door, funny
People who like the name Wilona also like Vivian, Scarlett, Felicity, Olivia, Winifred, Violet, Lorelei, Rhiannon, Sabrina, Emily

Wilson (*English*) ♂ RATING: ★★☆
Son of William—Woodrow Wilson, U.S. president
People think of Wilson as intelligent, funny, cool, trustworthy, caring
People who like the name Wilson also like Ethan, William, Walker, Jackson, Lucas, Nicholas, Noah, Jacob, Owen, Landon

Wilton (*English*) ♂ RATING: ★★★
From the farm by the spring or by willows—Originally a surname
People think of Wilton as funny, unpopular, caring, intelligent, popular
People who like the name Wilton also like Wilson, Weston, Trenton, Landon, Wyatt, Tristan, Holden, Nicholas, Tyson, Winston

Winchell (*English*) ♂ RATING: ★★
From the corner—Also a surname; Walter Winchell, newspaper/radio reporter
People think of Winchell as weird, old-fashioned, nerdy, poor, old
People who like the name Winchell also like Wendell, Jack, Willis, Wade, Nicholas, Wilkinson, Wolfgang, Jake, Whittaker, Ryker

Wind (*American*) ♀ RATING: ★★
Moving air
People think of Wind as artsy, wild, exotic, creative, powerful
People who like the name Wind also like Scarlett, Whisper, Grace, Faith, Summer, Heaven, Ivy, Renée, Paige, Bianca

Winda (*Swahili*) ♀ RATING: ★★☆
Hunter
People think of Winda as exotic, aggressive, weird, intelligent, funny

People who like the name Winda also like Charlotte, Chloe, Kara, Layla, Lucinda, Miranda, Jane, Sine, Veronica, Genevieve

Winfield *(English)* ♂   RATING: ★★★
From Wina's field—Originally a surname
> People think of Winfield as nerdy, intelligent, loser, old-fashioned, wealthy
> People who like the name Winfield also like William, Wyatt, Jackson, Aiden, Thomas, Wade, Joseph, Nicholas, Noah, Weston

Winfred *(English)* ♂   RATING: ★★☆
Peace friend
> People think of Winfred as funny, old, old-fashioned, handsome, nerdy
> People who like the name Winfred also like Tristan, Sloan, Mahon, Neal, Arthur, Alistair, Aiden, Raghnall, Cole, Conner

Wing *(Chinese)* ♀♂   RATING: ★★★☆
Glory—Cantonese variation of Rong
> People think of Wing as creative, caring, intelligent, funny, pretty
> People who like the name Wing also like Raven, Neo, Rain, Shadow, Moon, Willow, Reese, Devon, James, Paris

Winifred *(English)* ♀   RATING: ★★★
Peace friend
> People think of Winifred as pretty, funny, intelligent, caring, old-fashioned
> People who like the name Winifred also like Scarlett, Olivia, Penelope, Violet, Ophelia, Genevieve, Fiona, Maggie, Sabrina, Faith

Winka *(Scandinavian)* ♀♂   RATING: ★☆
People of Chile—Also a Danish surname used as a first name; Winka Dubbeldam, architect
> People think of Winka as weird, poor, pretty, funny, sneaky
> People who like the name Winka also like Darby, Cassidy, Ryan, Ember, Sasha, Thane, Nicola, Hollace, Kenyon, Hollis

Winola *(American)* ♀   RATING: ★★★
Combination of Winifred and Ola
> People think of Winola as intelligent, poor, leader, quiet, creative
> People who like the name Winola also like Wren, Genevieve, Winona, Giovanna, Tatiana, Felicity, Gwendolyn, Persephone, Lara, Scarlett

Winona *(Native American)* ♀   RATING: ★★
Firstborn—Lakota origin; Winona Ryder, actress
> People think of Winona as pretty, intelligent, creative, funny, energetic
> People who like the name Winona also like Paige, Olivia, Fiona, Faith, Phoebe, Gwyneth, Emma, Tabitha, Violet, Savannah

Winslow *(English)* ♂   RATING: ★★
From Wina's burial mound—Originally a surname
> People think of Winslow as old-fashioned, intelligent, nerdy, wealthy, quiet
> People who like the name Winslow also like Wade, Winston, Walker, Holden, Reece, Weston, Nicholas, Lucas, Jackson, Owen

Winston *(English)* ♂   RATING: ★★
From Wina's town—Winston Churchill, British prime minister
> People think of Winston as intelligent, handsome, cool, trustworthy, funny
> People who like the name Winston also like Tristan, Wyatt, Owen, Weston, William, Wade, Walker, Nathan, Jackson, Landon

Winter *(American)* ♀♂   RATING: ★★★☆
The season
> People think of Winter as pretty, intelligent, creative, trustworthy, energetic
> People who like the name Winter also like Willow, Sage, Hayden, Phoenix, Rain, Piper, River, Parker, Raine, Riley

Winthrop *(English)* ♂   RATING: ★★☆
From Wymund's farm—Originally a surname
> People think of Winthrop as funny, creative, young, intelligent, sporty
> People who like the name Winthrop also like Winston, Tristan, Oliver, William, Nicholas, Wade, Weldon, Owen, Weston, Matthew

Wirt *(English)* ♂   RATING: ★★
Worthy
> People think of Wirt as weird, loser, nerdy, lazy, old-fashioned
> People who like the name Wirt also like Brone, Brigham, Landers, Ward, Wheeler, Waylon, Alden, Beck, Wheaton, Beacher

Wisconsin *(French)* ♀♂   RATING: ★★★
Gathering of waters—Variation of a Native American word; U.S. state
> People think of Wisconsin as weird, nerdy, loser, old, old-fashioned
> People who like the name Wisconsin also like Vermont, Reagan, Michigan, Nebraska, Wyoming, Montana, Kentucky, Remy, Tennessee, Nevada

Wolcott *(English)* ♂   RATING: ★★☆
From the foreigner's cottage—Originally a surname
> People think of Wolcott as nerdy, unpopular, cool, funny, loser
> People who like the name Wolcott also like Wyatt, Brock, Warrick, Brandon, Troy, Reece, Drake, Conner, Woodward, Fisher

Wolfe *(English)* ♂   RATING: ★★★★
The wolf
> People think of Wolfe as wild, aggressive, powerful, intelligent, handsome

People who like the name Wolfe also like Tristan, Wyatt, Wade, Walker, Jackson, Ethan, Zachary, Aiden, Drake, Kaden

Wolfgang (English)   ♂   RATING: ★★★☆
Wolf way—Wolfgang Amadeus Mozart, composer; Wolfgang Puck, chef
People think of Wolfgang as intelligent, powerful, handsome, aggressive, leader
People who like the name Wolfgang also like Oliver, Vincent, Wolfe, Nathan, Owen, Nicholas, Quentin, Drake, Wade, Xavier

Wood (American)   ♂   RATING: ★★★
From the woods—Short for Woodrow or Woody; Wood Harris, actor
People think of Wood as big, aggressive, lazy, weird, exotic
People who like the name Wood also like Warren, Wade, Xander, Holden, Brennan, Wyatt, Clayton, Samuel, William, Maddox

Woodrow (English)   ♂   RATING: ★★★
From the lane in the woods—Also a surname; Woodrow Wilson, U.S. president
People think of Woodrow as leader, old-fashioned, caring, intelligent, powerful
People who like the name Woodrow also like Wade, Jacob, Justin, Nicholas, Graham, Miles, Isaac, Joshua, Benjamin, Everett

Woods (American)   ♂   RATING: ★★★
Of the woods
People think of Woods as sporty, weird, big, aggressive, old
People who like the name Woods also like Walker, Sloan, Jackson, Holden, Landon, Brooks, Fletcher, Nash, Lucas, Owen

Woodward (English)   ♂   RATING: ★★☆
Forester, wood-keeper—Originally a surname
People think of Woodward as wealthy, sexy, nerdy, old-fashioned, weird
People who like the name Woodward also like Woodrow, Miles, Victor, Warrick, Joshua, Holden, Wyatt, Justin, Sloan, Nicholas

Woody (American)   ♂   RATING: ★☆
From the lane in the woods—Originally short for Woodrow; Woody Allen, actor/director; Woody Harrelson, actor; Woody Woodpecker, cartoon character
People think of Woody as funny, handsome, young, sexy, caring
People who like the name Woody also like Jackson, Nathan, Leo, Benjamin, Jacob, Felix, Nicholas, Noah, Owen, Walker

Worth (American)   ♂   RATING: ★★☆
Wealth, riches
People think of Worth as intelligent, powerful, wealthy, elegant, unpopular

People who like the name Worth also like Silas, Adam, Jack, Abraham, Jared, Nicholas, Taran, Ice, Cody, Jayden

Wray (Scandinavian)   ♂   RATING: ★★★
From the corner—Fay Wray, actress; Link Wray, musician
People think of Wray as wild, intelligent, trustworthy, quiet, young
People who like the name Wray also like Braden, Weston, Brendan, Wade, Lucas, Walker, Wyatt, Rhett, Xander, Xavier

Wren (English)   ♀   RATING: ★★★★
Small bird
People think of Wren as creative, pretty, intelligent, artsy, energetic
People who like the name Wren also like Olivia, Ava, Scarlett, Grace, Sadie, Paige, Emma, Chloe, Phoebe, Ella

Wright (English)   ♂   RATING: ★★★★
Carpenter, worker—Originally a surname; David Wright, baseball player
People think of Wright as creative, leader, popular, powerful, intelligent
People who like the name Wright also like Weston, Wade, Warren, Owen, Trenton, Vance, William, Holden, Lawson, Liam

Wyanet (Native American)   ♀   RATING: ★★★
Beautiful
People think of Wyanet as pretty, popular, intelligent, aggressive, wild
People who like the name Wyanet also like Kaya, Wakanda, Tehya, Chenoa, Zoey, Isabella, Kalista, Wren, Ayasha, Kwanita

Wyatt (English)   ♂   RATING: ★★★
Son of Guy—Originally a surname; Wyatt Earp, U.S. lawman in the Old West
People think of Wyatt as handsome, intelligent, funny, cool, energetic
People who like the name Wyatt also like Ethan, Noah, Owen, Caleb, Aiden, Tristan, Gavin, Landon, Zachary, Cole

Wycliff (English)   ♂   RATING: ★★☆
From the cliff by the bend—Originally a surname
People think of Wycliff as old-fashioned, nerdy, lazy, loser, girl next door
People who like the name Wycliff also like Weston, Graham, Woodrow, Nicholas, Heath, Felton, Jason, Wyatt, Brooks, Warrick

Wylie (English)   ♀♂   RATING: ★★
From the tricky river
People think of Wylie as intelligent, energetic, funny, trustworthy, handsome
People who like the name Wylie also like Riley, Caden, Parker, Bailey, Taylor, Wiley, Rylie, Preston, Logan, Tanner

Wyman *(English)* ♂   RATING: ★★★
Battle protector—Originally a surname; Jane Wyman, actress
> People think of Wyman as aggressive, cool, funny, intelligent, old-fashioned
> People who like the name Wyman also like Tristan, Winston, Walker, Gibson, Holden, Wyatt, Langston, Lawson, Warrick, Reece

Wyndham *(English)* ♂   RATING: ★★★
From Wymond's homestead—Originally a surname
> People think of Wyndham as wealthy, poor, old-fashioned, intelligent, boy next door
> People who like the name Wyndham also like Walker, Weston, Finley, Wade, Nathan, Ian, Wyatt, Holden, Rhett, Landon

Wynn *(Welsh)* ♀ ♂   RATING: ★★☆
Fair, white, blessed
> People think of Wynn as intelligent, pretty, creative, funny, quiet
> People who like the name Wynn also like Quinn, Riley, Parker, Logan, Sydney, Aidan, Reese, Piper, Hayden, Morgan

Wynne *(Welsh)* ♀ ♂   RATING: ★★
Fair, white, blessed
> People think of Wynne as caring, creative, funny, intelligent, elegant
> People who like the name Wynne also like Reese, Quinn, Logan, Hayden, Wynn, Aidan, Willow, Parker, Nolan, Rory

Wynona *(Native American)* ♀   RATING: ★★★
Firstborn—Lakota origin; variation of Winona; also spelled Wynonna; Wynonna Judd, singer
> People think of Wynona as pretty, caring, cool, popular, young
> People who like the name Wynona also like Winona, Scarlett, Sabrina, Veronica, Fiona, Olivia, Penelope, Vivian, Jasmine, Naomi

Wyome *(Native American)* ♀ ♂   RATING: ★★☆
Plain
> People think of Wyome as caring, pretty, creative, quiet, funny
> People who like the name Wyome also like Payton, Riley, Wesley, Madison, Parker, Whitley, Mackenzie, Noel, Kegan, Demi

Wyoming *(Native American)* ♀ ♂   RATING: ★★★
Mountains, valleys—Algonquin origin; U.S. state
> People think of Wyoming as nerdy, weird, lazy, popular, poor
> People who like the name Wyoming also like Winter, Dakota, Bailey, Riley, Caden, Phoenix, Payton, Madison, Cadence, Utah

— **X** —

Xadrian *(American)* ♂   RATING: ★★
Combination of X and Adrian
> People think of Xadrian as sexy, exotic, handsome, cool, leader
> People who like the name Xadrian also like Xavier, Xander, Kaden, Adrian, Gabriel, Aiden, Tristan, Isaac, Maddox, Nathaniel

Xakery *(American)* ♂   RATING: ★★★
Variation of Zachary
> People think of Xakery as loser, criminal, untrustworthy, exotic, unpopular
> People who like the name Xakery also like Xavier, Xander, Zachary, Kaden, Seth, Tristan, Aiden, Xhaiden, Zachariah, Nathan

Xalvadora *(Spanish)* ♀   RATING: ★★
Savior
> People think of Xalvadora as weird, exotic, sneaky, creative, unpopular
> People who like the name Xalvadora also like Xaria, Anastasia, Xantara, Xiomara, Vanessa, Olivia, Xaviera, Victoria, Zabrina, Isadora

Xander *(Greek)* ♂   RATING: ★★★
Defender of men—Short for Alexander
> People think of Xander as handsome, intelligent, funny, energetic, cool
> People who like the name Xander also like Xavier, Zander, Tristan, Ethan, Noah, Zachary, Aiden, Caleb, Gavin, Alexander

Xandy *(American)* ♀ ♂   RATING: ★★
Defender of men—Short for Alexander
> People think of Xandy as sexy, exotic, cool, creative, funny
> People who like the name Xandy also like Paris, Parker, Quin, Holly, Piper, Raven, Reese, Ryan, Cade, Qwin

Xannon *(American)* ♀ ♂   RATING: ★★
Ancient god—Variation of Shannon
> People think of Xannon as weird, creative, stuck-up, powerful, popular
> People who like the name Xannon also like Caden, Riley, Jaden, Hayden, Logan, Cadence, Raine, Zane, Raven, Talen

Xantara *(American)* ♀   RATING: ★★
Protector of the earth
> People think of Xantara as exotic, pretty, sexy, leader, creative
> People who like the name Xantara also like Xylia, Xaria, Xiomara, Xia, Xalvadora, Zabrina, Kaida, Zafirah, Zara, Xena

Xanthe *(Greek)* ♀   RATING: ★★★☆
Golden
> People think of Xanthe as intelligent, pretty, exotic, creative, funny

People who like the name Xanthe also like Olivia, Isis, Genevieve, Paige, Celeste, Giselle, Gabrielle, Penelope, Faith, Mia

Xanthus *(Greek)* ♂   RATING: ★★★
Golden
> People think of Xanthus as intelligent, aggressive, handsome, creative, weird
> People who like the name Xanthus also like Xander, Xavier, Thaddeus, Lysander, Xylon, Zander, Julius, Xenon, Theo, Tristan

Xanti *(Portuguese)* ♂   RATING: ★★★
Short for Xantiago—Variation of St. James
> People think of Xanti as exotic, aggressive, energetic, weird, nerdy
> People who like the name Xanti also like Xavier, Xander, Xadrian, Xylon, Micah, Valentino, Fabian, Quade, Wade, Jared

Xanto *(Italian)* ♂   RATING: ★☆
Golden—Variation of Xanthus
> People think of Xanto as trustworthy, handsome, exotic, powerful, intelligent
> People who like the name Xanto also like Xavier, Xander, Paolo, Thomas, Xanthus, Quade, Michelangelo, Marco, Xenon, Quentin

Xaria *(American)* ♀   RATING: ★★★★
Variation of Zaria
> People think of Xaria as pretty, exotic, energetic, powerful, caring
> People who like the name Xaria also like Zaria, Zara, Olivia, Zoe, Victoria, Jadyn, Xylia, Paige, Xia, Eva

Xarles *(French)* ♂   RATING: ★★★
Man—Variation of Charles
> People think of Xarles as leader, elegant, sneaky, aggressive, winner
> People who like the name Xarles also like Xander, Xylon, Xavier, Xakery, Calix, Kaelem, Lucien, Kael, Rupert, Trevor

Xavier *(Spanish)* ♂   RATING: ★★★
The new house—Often a second name used with Francis in honor of St. Francis Xavier, Catholic missionary
> People think of Xavier as handsome, intelligent, funny, cool, popular
> People who like the name Xavier also like Xander, Gabriel, Zachary, Elijah, Ethan, Noah, Aiden, Tristan, Isaac, Alexander

Xaviera *(Spanish)* ♀   RATING: ★★★☆
The new house—Feminine form of Xavier
> People think of Xaviera as exotic, aggressive, leader, wild, creative
> People who like the name Xaviera also like Xaria, Olivia, Isabella, Adriana, Xaviere, Abigail, Xylia, Hannah, Cassandra, Abrianna

Xaviere *(French)* ♀   RATING: ★★★☆
The new house—Feminine form of Xavier
> People think of Xaviere as aggressive, popular, young, intelligent, creative
> People who like the name Xaviere also like Xaviera, Olivia, Jadyn, Xaria, Hailey, Brielle, Yvette, Isabelle, Sadie, Naomi

Xena *(Greek)* ♀   RATING: ★★★☆
Hospitable—*Xena, Warrior Princess*, TV show
> People think of Xena as exotic, powerful, pretty, aggressive, intelligent
> People who like the name Xena also like Victoria, Paige, Vanessa, Serenity, Zoey, Layla, Veronica, Sabrina, Abigail, Samantha

Xenia *(Greek)* ♀   RATING: ★★★☆
Hospitable
> People think of Xenia as intelligent, creative, pretty, energetic, sexy
> People who like the name Xenia also like Xena, Bianca, Xylia, Zoe, Xaria, Chloe, Olivia, Xanthe, Cassandra, Zandra

Xenon *(Greek)* ♂   RATING: ★☆
Guest, host
> People think of Xenon as creative, powerful, intelligent, energetic, leader
> People who like the name Xenon also like Xavier, Xander, Vance, Kaden, Xylon, Zander, Xadrian, Aiden, Gabriel, Walker

Xenophon *(Greek)* ♀ ♂   RATING: ★★★
Strange voice
> People think of Xenophon as weird, intelligent, exotic, nerdy, artsy
> People who like the name Xenophon also like Zephyr, Pyralis, Artemis, Theron, Morgan, Kieran, Xing Xing, Willow, Keir, Zale

Xenos *(Greek)* ♂   RATING: ★★★
Guest, host
> People think of Xenos as powerful, intelligent, exotic, weird, trustworthy
> People who like the name Xenos also like Xander, Zeno, Xanthus, Braeden, Demetrius, Zero, Drake, Nero, Titus, Cyrus

Xerxes *(Persian)* ♂   RATING: ★★★☆
King, ruler
> People think of Xerxes as powerful, leader, exotic, aggressive, handsome
> People who like the name Xerxes also like Xavier, Xander, Ulric, Gabriel, Xadrian, Xylon, Ulysses, Felix, Adrian, Aaron

Xexilia *(Spanish)* ♀   RATING: ★★★
Blind of self-beauty—Basque variation of Cecilia
> People think of Xexilia as wild, energetic, sexy, ethnic, young
> People who like the name Xexilia also like Xiomara, Adriana, Xylia, Xalvadora, Xaviera, Xaria, Abrianna, Aaliyah, Anastasia, Jacinta

Xhaiden *(American)* ♂ RATING: ★★★☆
Variation of Aiden (created by parent Brian N. Godfrey)
People think of Xhaiden as powerful, exotic, intelligent, leader, creative
People who like the name Xhaiden also like Xander, Xadrian, Xavier, Kaden, Aiden, Jayden, Tristan, Xakery, Aden, Jadon

Xhosa *(African)* ♀ RATING: ★★★
South African origin
People think of Xhosa as exotic, aggressive, pretty, leader, intelligent
People who like the name Xhosa also like Xinavane, Xolani, Xalvadora, Xanthe, Xia, Xiang, Kaida, Angelique, Xiu Juan, Xaria

Xi-wang *(Chinese)* ♀♂ RATING: ★★★
Hope
People think of Xi-wang as nerdy, loser, unpopular, uptight, weird
People who like the name Xi-wang also like Xing, Yi Min, Xing Xing, Xuan, Li, Qing Yuan, Kai, Xiao Chen, James, Kameryn

Xia *(Chinese)* ♀ RATING: ★★★★
Glow of the sunrise—Mandarin origin
People think of Xia as pretty, intelligent, energetic, exotic, creative
People who like the name Xia also like Xaria, Xiomara, Xylia, Paige, Mia, Chloe, Olivia, Zia, Xena, Nadia

Xia He *(Chinese)* ♀ RATING: ★★☆
Summer lotus
People think of Xia He as exotic, poor, intelligent, ethnic, loser
People who like the name Xia He also like Xaria, Zafirah, Xanthe, Qamra, Xia, Xiu Juan, Xiomara, Qi, Zoe, Xochitl

Xiang *(Chinese)* ♀ RATING: ★☆
Fragrant—Mandarin origin
People think of Xiang as quiet, intelligent, lazy, ethnic, funny
People who like the name Xiang also like Xia, Xylia, Xantara, Xolani, Xenia, Anya, Xaria, Xiao Hong, Xiu, Xiomara

Xiao Chen *(Chinese)* ♀♂ RATING: ★★★
Early morning—Mandarin origin
People think of Xiao Chen as intelligent, caring, exotic, pretty, ethnic
People who like the name Xiao Chen also like Cadence, Xi-wang, Kameryn, Bailey, Yuki, Mckenna, Jaden, Joey, Kione, Kiyoshi

Xiao Hong *(Chinese)* ♀ RATING: ★☆
Morning rainbow
People think of Xiao Hong as poor, intelligent, nerdy, exotic, loser
People who like the name Xiao Hong also like Xiang, Xochitl, Qi, Xolani, Xylia, Xia, Jia Li, Xiu Juan, Xin Qian, Xenia

Xin Qian *(Chinese)* ♀ RATING: ★★☆
Happy, beautiful—Mandarin origin
People think of Xin Qian as intelligent, creative, energetic, cool, ethnic
People who like the name Xin Qian also like Jia Li, Xiu Juan, Xiu, Xiomara, Xia, Keona, Aiko, Xiao Hong, Xexilia, Kioko

Xing *(Chinese)* ♀♂ RATING: ★☆
Star
People think of Xing as exotic, creative, wild, pretty, intelligent
People who like the name Xing also like Caden, Xing Xing, Aidan, Sage, Yuki, Xannon, Cade, Xandy, Rain, Kimberly

Xing Xing *(Chinese)* ♀♂ RATING: ★★★
Twin stars
People think of Xing Xing as pretty, creative, young, exotic, caring
People who like the name Xing Xing also like Taylor, Xing, Qing Yuan, Aidan, Unique, Ming Yue, Xenophon, Madison, Kana, Xola

Xiomara *(Spanish)* ♀ RATING: ★★★★
Ready for battle
People think of Xiomara as intelligent, pretty, funny, sexy, exotic
People who like the name Xiomara also like Xaria, Xia, Xylia, Vanessa, Xochitl, Genevieve, Yasmin, Aaliyah, Samara, Jahzara

Xiu *(Chinese)* ♀ RATING: ★★★
Elegant, beautiful—Mandarin origin
People think of Xiu as creative, intelligent, caring, trustworthy, funny
People who like the name Xiu also like Xia, Xuxa, Xaria, Kyla, Qi, Zoey, Jia Li, Zi, Xue, Keira

Xiu Juan *(Chinese)* ♀ RATING: ★★☆
Elegant, graceful—Mandarin origin
People think of Xiu Juan as lazy, nerdy, weird, loser, girl next door
People who like the name Xiu Juan also like Xia, Xin Qian, Xiu, Xalvadora, Wan, Xantara, Jia Li, Xiomara, Yan, Xochitl

Xóchitl *(Aztec/Nahuatl)* ♀ RATING: ★★★☆
Flower—Xóchitl Escobedo, tennis pro
People think of Xóchitl as pretty, funny, intelligent, creative, exotic
People who like the name Xóchitl also like Xiomara, Xia, Xylia, Maya, Fiona, Jasmine, Kiona, Isis, Bianca, Victoria

Xola *(African)* ♀♂ RATING: ★★
Stay on peace—From the Xhosa tribe of South Africa
People think of Xola as exotic, creative, ethnic, elegant, pretty
People who like the name Xola also like Zane, Jade, Jaden, Phoenix, Ember, Madison, James, Parker, Raine, Willow

Xolani *(African)* ♀   RATING: ★★
Please forgive
> People think of Xolani as exotic, intelligent, creative, young, caring
> People who like the name Xolani also like Xaria, Xiomara, Xylia, Jahzara, Xia, Zara, Xenia, Aaliyah, Uzuri, Summer

Xuan *(Vietnamese)* ♀ ♂   RATING: ★★★
Spring
> People think of Xuan as intelligent, funny, caring, religious, quiet
> People who like the name Xuan also like Quillan, Xi-wang, Kyle, Jade, Zane, Kindle, Cameron, Quenby, Quincy, Xenophon

Xue *(Chinese)* ♀   RATING: ★☆
Snow—Mandarin origin
> People think of Xue as creative, intelligent, elegant, girl next door, funny
> People who like the name Xue also like Xylia, Xia, Penelope, Mia, Kyla, Melody, Violet, Layla, Chloe, Zoey

Xue Fang *(Chinese)* ♀   RATING: ★☆
Fragrant snow—Mandarin origin
> People think of Xue Fang as loser, nerdy, funny, aggressive, criminal
> People who like the name Xue Fang also like Sada, Mina, Kaori, Katarina, Xue, Keira, Kya, Kenda, Kyla, Xylia

Xuxa *(Portuguese)* ♀   RATING: ★★
Queen—Pronounced *SHOO-sha*; Xuxa, singer/TV host
> People think of Xuxa as funny, sexy, caring, young, creative
> People who like the name Xuxa also like Xylia, Xiomara, Xaria, Penelope, Xia, Xiu, Ella, Layla, Zoey, Giselle

Xylander *(Greek)* ♂   RATING: ★★★
Forest man
> People think of Xylander as exotic, wild, aggressive, intelligent, old-fashioned
> People who like the name Xylander also like Xylon, Xavier, Vincent, Braeden, Lysander, Maximilian, Victor, Theodore, Oliver, Tyson

Xylia *(Greek)* ♀   RATING: ★★
From the forest—Variation of Sylvia
> People think of Xylia as pretty, exotic, intelligent, creative, quiet
> People who like the name Xylia also like Xaria, Olivia, Xia, Layla, Paige, Ella, Zoey, Abigail, Penelope, Chloe

Xylon *(Greek)* ♂   RATING: ★★★
From the forest
> People think of Xylon as wild, exotic, energetic, intelligent, handsome
> People who like the name Xylon also like Xavier, Xander, Xadrian, Kaden, Zachary, Seth, Tristan, Oliver, Alexander, Zander

Yaakov *(Hebrew)* ♂   RATING: ★☆
Supplanter—Variation of Jacob
> People think of Yaakov as aggressive, old-fashioned, loser, intelligent, cool
> People who like the name Yaakov also like Aaron, Adam, Brian, Yuri, Zachary, Cole, Joshua, Nathan, Nicholas, Ian

Yachi *(Japanese)* ♀   RATING: ★★★
Eight thousand
> People think of Yachi as young, cool, aggressive, artsy, powerful
> People who like the name Yachi also like Yoshiko, Mai, Kuri, Tama, Kaori, Yoshi, Sada, Mina, Kura, Keiko

Yadid *(Hebrew)* ♂   RATING: ★★☆
Beloved
> People think of Yadid as old-fashioned, old, nerdy, quiet, caring
> People who like the name Yadid also like Yair, Yamir, Yaholo, Jared, Nathan, Nathaniel, Yakov, Noah, Yeshaya, Yardan

Yaeger *(German)* ♂   RATING: ★★★
Chase, hunt
> People think of Yaeger as aggressive, big, sexy, sporty, funny
> People who like the name Yaeger also like Caleb, Xavier, Tyson, Jayden, Kiefer, Damien, Anakin, Grayson, Lincoln, Damian

Yael *(Hebrew)* ♀   RATING: ★★★★
Mountain goat
> People think of Yael as intelligent, funny, pretty, caring, elegant
> People who like the name Yael also like Lael, Liana, Maya, Abigail, Hannah, Isabella, Layla, Leah, Jadyn, Nadia

Yagil *(Hebrew)* ♂   RATING: ★☆
He will rejoice—Pronounced *Ya-geel*
> People think of Yagil as loser, poor, old-fashioned, old, nerdy
> People who like the name Yagil also like Yakov, Yadid, Yaholo, Yair, Yahto, Yamir, Yanni, Yaakov, Yasuo, Yuval

Yagmur *(Turkish)* ♀ ♂   RATING: ★★
Rain
> People think of Yagmur as loser, nerdy, sporty, untrustworthy, poor
> People who like the name Yagmur also like Alick, Yue, Yale, Yuki, Yue Yan, Yule, Yu Jie, Adiel, Yancy, Yank

Yaholo *(Native American)* ♂   RATING: ★☆
One who yells—Seminole origin
> People think of Yaholo as weird, unpopular, stuck-up, loser, old
> People who like the name Yaholo also like Yuma, Yahto, Sani, Tocho, Yanisin, Tokala, Yadid, Yukio, Nantai, Mingan

Yahto *(Native American)* ♂ RATING: ★★★
Blue
> People think of Yahto as ethnic, weird, aggressive, wild, popular
> People who like the name Yahto also like Yuma, Yaholo, Yuri, Yamir, Yair, Yanni, Hakan, Quana, Yukio, Adrian

Yair *(Hebrew)* ♂ RATING: ★★★☆
He will enlighten—Pronounced *Ya-EER*
> People think of Yair as handsome, intelligent, sexy, young, caring
> People who like the name Yair also like Yamir, Joseph, Gabriel, Noah, Yeshaya, Yanni, Yeriel, Nathan, Xadrian, Ethan

Yakov *(Slavic)* ♂ RATING: ★☆
Supplanter—Variation of Jacob
> People think of Yakov as poor, nerdy, old-fashioned, ethnic, old
> People who like the name Yakov also like Aaron, Yagil, Jacob, Vladimir, Isaac, Michael, Justin, Kaleb, Nathaniel, Yadid

Yale *(English)* ♀♂ RATING: ★★★
Dweller at the fertile upland—Also a variation of Yael or Jael
> People think of Yale as intelligent, pretty, sexy, young, creative
> People who like the name Yale also like Parker, Logan, Hayden, Reese, Caden, Taylor, Jaden, Riley, Sawyer, Madison

Yalitza *(Spanish)* ♀ RATING: ★★★☆
Unknown meaning
> People think of Yalitza as pretty, intelligent, funny, exotic, caring
> People who like the name Yalitza also like Aurora, Yanichel, Ziarre, Amaya, Adalira, Jazzelle, Adalia, Yelena, Jahzara, Leilani

Yama *(Japanese)* ♂ RATING: ★☆
Mountain—Also a female Hebrew name meaning lake
> People think of Yama as cool, handsome, exotic, big, intelligent
> People who like the name Yama also like Ryu, Hiroshi, Kaemon, Shino, Makoto, Yasuo, Keitaro, Yukio, Haruki, Suoh

Yamal *(Sanskrit/East Indian)* ♂ RATING: ★★☆
One of a twin
> People think of Yamal as popular, winner, caring, young, weird
> People who like the name Yamal also like Yamir, Xavier, Zamir, Caleb, Aden, Elijah, Ian, Gabriel, Landon, Zesiro

Yamha *(Arabic)* ♀ RATING: ★★
Dove
> People think of Yamha as pretty, quiet, loser, poor, young
> People who like the name Yamha also like Akilah, Ilyssa, Valtina, Zaria, Maija, Danika, Yamin, Zariel, Ivette, Janelle

Yamilet *(Spanish)* ♀ RATING: ★★★
Beautiful, elegant—Variation of Jamilah
> People think of Yamilet as funny, pretty, intelligent, sexy, cool
> People who like the name Yamilet also like Yael, Ilyssa, Adora, Elin, Judy, Reyna, Shaylee, Elisa, Larisa, Inaya

Yamin *(Hebrew)* ♀ RATING: ★★
Right hand—Elliot Yamin, singer
> People think of Yamin as exotic, intelligent, ethnic, caring, trustworthy
> People who like the name Yamin also like Phoebe, Penelope, Vanessa, Jacqueline, Nadia, Sabrina, Sienna, Janelle, Amber, Stella

Yamir *(Sanskrit/East Indian)* ♂ RATING: ★★★
Moon
> People think of Yamir as intelligent, handsome, funny, sneaky, aggressive
> People who like the name Yamir also like Zamir, Yair, Nathan, Nathaniel, Ethan, Gabriel, Jayden, Sebastian, Yamal, David

Yamka *(Native American)* ♀ RATING: ★★☆
Budding flower—Hopi origin
> People think of Yamka as pretty, ethnic, religious, quiet, intelligent
> People who like the name Yamka also like Winona, Kaya, Ayasha, Tallulah, Snana, Tehya, Topanga, Wakanda, Taini, Nadia

Yan *(Chinese)* ♀ RATING: ★★★☆
Pretty colors; swallow bird
> People think of Yan as intelligent, funny, pretty, elegant, popular
> People who like the name Yan also like Sakura, Kimi, Kaida, Kioko, Sabrina, Suki, Mai, Raina, Zoey, Keiko

Yana *(Hebrew)* ♀ RATING: ★★★★
He answers
> People think of Yana as pretty, intelligent, funny, caring, creative
> People who like the name Yana also like Hannah, Gabrielle, Abigail, Talia, Samara, Liana, Zara, Grace, Zaria, Vanessa

Yancy *(American)* ♀♂ RATING: ★★★
Possibly a variation of Yankee, a colloquial term for Northerners during the Civil War—Character in "The Popular Girl" by F. Scott Fitzgerald; Yancy Butler, actress
> People think of Yancy as funny, caring, cool, intelligent, creative
> People who like the name Yancy also like Tanner, Riley, Taylor, Dakota, Jordan, Spencer, Quinn, Madison, Connor, Bailey

Yanichel *(Hebrew)* ♀ RATING: ★★★
Gift of God
> People think of Yanichel as pretty, creative, caring, funny, intelligent

People who like the name Yanichel also like Yovela, Yalitza, Abigail, Yana, Yoninah, Veronique, Zelda, Zaria, Yamin, Zandra

Yanisin *(Native American)* ♂ RATING: ★★
Ashamed—Navajo origin
People think of Yanisin as weird, young, unpopular, creative, sporty
People who like the name Yanisin also like Yaholo, Sani, Yuma, Shilah, Tocho, Nodin, Tyson, Molimo, Ahanu, Ezhno

Yank *(Native American)* ♀♂ RATING: ★★☆
U.S. Northerner—Short for Yankee, a colloquial term for Northerners during the Civil War
People think of Yank as weird, aggressive, unpopular, exotic, nerdy
People who like the name Yank also like Yancy, Mika, Taregan, Pahana, Pillan, Misae, Sequoia, Misu, Tal, Taima

Yanka *(Slavic)* ♀ RATING: ★★☆
Feminine form of John
People think of Yanka as exotic, poor, weird, pretty, old-fashioned
People who like the name Yanka also like Yvette, Yana, Liana, Yessica, Shayna, Zaria, Hannah, Xia, Sabrina, Talia

Yanni *(Greek)* ♂ RATING: ★★★★
God is gracious—Variation of John; Yanni, pianist
People think of Yanni as energetic, creative, funny, young, cool
People who like the name Yanni also like Yannis, Elijah, Joshua, Nathaniel, Yeriel, Zachary, Nathan, Jacob, Noah, Jeremiah

Yannis *(Greek)* ♂ RATING: ★★★☆
God is gracious—Variation of John
People think of Yannis as sexy, intelligent, creative, cool, quiet
People who like the name Yannis also like Yanni, Joel, Jayden, Yeriel, Noah, Joshua, Raphael, Johnathan, Jeremiah, Ian

Yaphet *(Hebrew)* ♂ RATING: ★★★
Enlarged—Yaphet Kotto, actor
People think of Yaphet as weird, nerdy, ethnic, loser, boy next door
People who like the name Yaphet also like Yaholo, Nathaniel, Yadid, Uriah, Yair, Uriel, Josiah, Yeshaya, Yanni, Garrett

Yardan *(Hebrew)* ♂ RATING: ★☆
To flow down—Also the river Jordan
People think of Yardan as aggressive, loser, intelligent, ethnic, leader
People who like the name Yardan also like Kadin, Galen, Yves, Yamir, Nasser, Yadid, Valin, Qamar, Yair, Yorick

Yardley *(English)* ♀♂ RATING: ★★★
From the wood where spars were got
People think of Yardley as intelligent, pretty, weird, funny, sporty

People who like the name Yardley also like Parker, Oakley, Hadley, Sawyer, Hayden, Landen, Riley, London, Waverly, Caden

Yaro *(African)* ♂ RATING: ★★★
Son
People think of Yaro as intelligent, young, funny, caring, trustworthy
People who like the name Yaro also like Ajani, Aaron, Nyack, Noah, Ethan, Taran, Zaccheus, Neron, Zamir, Troy

Yaron *(Hebrew)* ♂ RATING: ★★★
He will sing
People think of Yaron as handsome, intelligent, creative, trustworthy, energetic
People who like the name Yaron also like Zachary, Nathan, Noah, Yair, Xander, Ethan, Damian, Ace, Dillon, Weston

Yaser *(Arabic)* ♂ RATING: ★★★
Easy, smooth—Also spelled Yasser; Yasser Arafat, Palestinian leader
People think of Yaser as intelligent, sexy, funny, popular, caring
People who like the name Yaser also like Zahi, Malik, Yamir, Khalil, Jamal, Salim, Jabir, Amir, Nasser, Jacob

Yasma *(Spanish)* ♀ RATING: ★★★
Jasmine—Also a place name: city in Azerbaijan
People think of Yasma as exotic, quiet, pretty, cool, ethnic
People who like the name Yasma also like Yasmin, Jasmine, Yelena, Bella, Keira, Zahra, Zoey, Saffron, Ebony, Vanessa

Yasmin *(Persian)* ♀ RATING: ★★☆
Jasmine—Also spelled Yasmine; Yasmine Bleeth, actress
People think of Yasmin as pretty, funny, popular, intelligent, cool
People who like the name Yasmin also like Jasmine, Olivia, Isabella, Paige, Hannah, Zoe, Faith, Scarlett, Hailey, Gabrielle

Yasu *(Japanese)* ♀♂ RATING: ★★★
Calm
People think of Yasu as artsy, creative, funny, ethnic, religious
People who like the name Yasu also like Flynn, Hoshi, Natsu, Tempest, Peregrine, Rowan, Seiko, Zephyr, Jude, Niall

Yasuo *(Japanese)* ♂ RATING: ★★★
Peaceful one
People think of Yasuo as intelligent, caring, trustworthy, artsy, quiet
People who like the name Yasuo also like Ryu, Suoh, Keitaro, Yukio, Kaemon, Makoto, Haruki, Hiroshi, Yama, Akio

Yates *(English)* ♀♂   RATING: ★☆
Dweller by a gate
- People think of Yates as trustworthy, funny, sexy, intelligent, cool
- People who like the name Yates also like Jaden, Sawyer, Tate, Logan, Parker, Hayden, Caden, Tanner, Tyler, Paisley

Yatima *(African)* ♀   RATING: ★☆
Orphan—Kiswahili origin
- People think of Yatima as poor, weird, young, exotic, old
- People who like the name Yatima also like Jahzara, Yelena, Wakanda, Zelda, Layla, Yalitza, Yasmin, Yanichel, Jezebel, Zariel

Yatin *(Sanskrit/East Indian)* ♂   RATING: ★★☆
Religious devotion
- People think of Yatin as intelligent, religious, handsome, quiet, ethnic
- People who like the name Yatin also like Amish, Tanav, Chitt, Tanay, Yamal, Zayit, Yamir, Yuval, Davu, Clyde

Yauvani *(Sanskrit/East Indian)* ♀   RATING: ★★☆
Full of youth
- People think of Yauvani as popular, exotic, powerful, ethnic, young
- People who like the name Yauvani also like Tanaya, Vianca, Dhyana, Yovela, Ailani, Kailani, Tarika, Drea, Dyani, Vyomini

Yaxha *(Spanish)* ♀♂   RATING: ★★★
Green water—Mayan origin; also an archaeological site in Guatemala
- People think of Yaxha as exotic, creative, sneaky, funny, sporty
- People who like the name Yaxha also like Wednesday, Zane, Blair, Yale, Blaine, Yue, Baylee, Payton, Yardley, Yuki

Yazid *(Arabic)* ♂   RATING: ★☆
Impious
- People think of Yazid as exotic, ethnic, cool, powerful, aggressive
- People who like the name Yazid also like Yamir, Yaser, Karif, Dario, Jabir, Mariano, Qabil, Zarek, Alem, Nayef

Ye *(Chinese)* ♂   RATING: ★★★
Light
- People think of Ye as exotic, sexy, intelligent, aggressive, wealthy
- People who like the name Ye also like Anakin, Vin, Vance, Xylon, Alexander, Zan, Noah, Kaden, Yuma, Tristan

Yeardleigh *(English)* ♀♂   RATING: ★★★
Variation of Yardley
- People think of Yeardleigh as old, intelligent, nerdy, uptight, old-fashioned
- People who like the name Yeardleigh also like Waverly, Piper, Willow, Taylor, Landen, Teagan, Yardley, Cadence, Caden, Avery

Yeardley *(English)* ♀♂   RATING: ★★☆
Variation of Yardley
- People think of Yeardley as old-fashioned, nerdy, loser, old, lazy
- People who like the name Yeardley also like Hadley, Waverly, Willow, Caden, Madison, Riley, Bailey, Oakley, Quinn, Parker

Yehuda *(Hebrew)* ♂   RATING: ★☆
Praise, exalt
- People think of Yehuda as handsome, intelligent, trustworthy, religious, sneaky
- People who like the name Yehuda also like Yanni, Yaron, David, Joshua, Nathan, Yair, Israel, Yaholo, Nathaniel, Jeremiah

Yehudah *(Hebrew)* ♂   RATING: ★★☆
Praise, exalt
- People think of Yehudah as leader, religious, ethnic, untrustworthy, trustworthy
- People who like the name Yehudah also like Yeriel, Willoughby, Jared, Zachary, Kesler, Alejandro, Farrell, Yaholo, Lucas, Neville

Yehudi *(Hebrew)* ♂   RATING: ★★
Praise, exalt—Yehudi Menuhin, violinist
- People think of Yehudi as nerdy, weird, unpopular, exotic, ethnic
- People who like the name Yehudi also like Nansen, Yamir, Napoleon, Nelson, Yehuda, Ye, Niran, Naif, Yuma, Nathan

Yelena *(Portuguese)* ♀   RATING: ★★★★
Variation of Helen
- People think of Yelena as pretty, intelligent, funny, exotic, creative
- People who like the name Yelena also like Yasmin, Isabella, Gabrielle, Faith, Felicity, Nadia, Paige, Grace, Alena, Tiana

Yenge *(African)* ♀♂   RATING: ★★
Wife—South African origin
- People think of Yenge as exotic, ethnic, old-fashioned, wild, criminal
- People who like the name Yenge also like Talen, Tappen, Tannar, Tanner, River, Taylor, Yancy, Yale, Nevin, Dayton

Yepa *(Native American)* ♀   RATING: ★★★☆
Winter princess
- People think of Yepa as funny, elegant, powerful, cool, wild
- People who like the name Yepa also like Tala, Kaya, Wakanda, Kachina, Winona, Soraya, Salali, Taini, Ayita, Kaliska

Yered *(Hebrew)* ♂   RATING: ★★☆
Descendant
- People think of Yered as weird, ethnic, religious, cool, powerful
- People who like the name Yered also like Fabian, Zach, Marlon, Damien, Ulric, Yeriel, Nathan, Nicholas, Alexander, Yuri

579

Yeriel *(Hebrew)* ♂ — RATING: ★★★
God has taught me
> People think of Yeriel as exotic, religious, pretty, old, sexy
> People who like the name Yeriel also like Yanni, Yair, Xadrian, Uriel, Yannis, Yestin, Zedekiah, Nathaniel, Yeshaya, Uriah

Yerodin *(African)* ♂ — RATING: ★★☆
Studious—Congo origin
> People think of Yerodin as young, intelligent, artsy, weird, elegant
> People who like the name Yerodin also like Yeshaya, Asher, Yaron, Dyami, Björn, Zaccheus, Akio, Nathan, Yadid, Bijan

Yeshaya *(Hebrew)* ♂ — RATING: ★☆
God is salvation
> People think of Yeshaya as ethnic, pretty, popular, young, handsome
> People who like the name Yeshaya also like Yair, Zakiya, Asher, Micah, Josiah, Jeremiah, Yanni, Yannis, Yeriel, Tobias

Yessica *(Spanish)* ♀ — RATING: ★★
God beholds—Variation of Jessica
> People think of Yessica as pretty, funny, cool, sexy, popular
> People who like the name Yessica also like Yasmin, Hannah, Lauren, Vanessa, Gabrielle, Faith, Olivia, Samantha, Yvette, Isabella

Yestin *(Welsh)* ♂ — RATING: ★☆
Just—Variation of Justin; pronounced *yess-tin*
> People think of Yestin as creative, intelligent, handsome, sexy, funny
> People who like the name Yestin also like Xadrian, Yves, Tristan, Yeriel, Maddox, Xavier, Ethan, Isaac, Quentin, Walker

Yetta *(American)* ♀ — RATING: ★★★
Short for Henrietta
> People think of Yetta as exotic, ethnic, creative, intelligent, big
> People who like the name Yetta also like Bella, Dara, Eve, Felicity, Natasha, Cara, Maggie, Laura, Mara, Marissa

Yettie *(American)* ♀ — RATING: ★☆
Short for Henrietta
> People think of Yettie as nerdy, creative, criminal, loser, unpopular
> People who like the name Yettie also like Kailey, Vanessa, Kaitlyn, Yessica, Yvette, Yvonne, Vivian, Bella, Sabrina, Sonia

Yetty *(American)* ♀ — RATING: ★☆
Short for Henrietta
> People think of Yetty as unpopular, weird, lazy, slow, big
> People who like the name Yetty also like Yoshiko, Yvonne, Maureen, Matilda, Morela, Mahala, Mabel, Makayla, Zabrina, Persephone

Yeva *(Slavic)* ♀ — RATING: ★★★☆
Varition of Eve
> People think of Yeva as pretty, exotic, cool, young, sexy
> People who like the name Yeva also like Kaya, Isabel, Layla, Eva, Danika, Kyla, Tiva, Kayla, Lucy, Maya

Yi *(Chinese)* ♀ — RATING: ★★★☆
Happy—Mandarin origin
> People think of Yi as funny, caring, pretty, unpopular, quiet
> People who like the name Yi also like Mia, Yoshiko, Zi, Zoey, Yvette, Zia, Xylia, Faye, Mai, Belle

Yi Min *(Chinese)* ♀♂ — RATING: ★★★
Smart—Mandarin origin
> People think of Yi Min as intelligent, quiet, creative, pretty, ethnic
> People who like the name Yi Min also like Yu Jie, Ming Yue, Yue Yan, Yuki, Tao, Li, Zhi, Yue, Wei, Kai

Yi Ze *(Chinese)* ♀ — RATING: ★★★
Happy, shiny as a pearl—Mandarin origin
> People think of Yi Ze as funny, pretty, trustworthy, caring, ethnic
> People who like the name Yi Ze also like Jia Li, Wan, Li Hua, Xiu Juan, Selene, Yoshino, Zi, Xiu, Tama, Yi

Yitro *(Hebrew)* ♂ — RATING: ★★
Plenty
> People think of Yitro as intelligent, nerdy, weird, ethnic, uptight
> People who like the name Yitro also like Yves, Yestin, Yannis, Newton, Johnathan, Yuma, Norman, Yasuo, Warrick, Nash

Yitta *(Hebrew)* ♀ — RATING: ★☆
Light
> People think of Yitta as funny, aggressive, wealthy, leader, religious
> People who like the name Yitta also like Yoninah, Sophia, Bella, Yovela, Sofia, Isabella, Laura, Yeva, Cailyn, Yihana

Yo *(Japanese)* ♀ — RATING: ★☆
Positive—Also Spanish meaning I; also slang to get someone's attention
> People think of Yo as weird, wild, creative, exotic, lazy
> People who like the name Yo also like Kimi, Toshi, Yoshi, Kohana, Kaiya, Keiko, Yoshiko, Yori, Haruko, Sada

Yogi *(Sanskrit/East Indian)* ♀♂ — RATING: ★★★☆
Of the yoga practice—Yogi Berra, baseball player/manager
> People think of Yogi as funny, cool, energetic, sporty, intelligent
> People who like the name Yogi also like Logan, Dakota, Taylor, Sean, Tanner, Hunter, Parker, Lilo, Myles, Jax

Yohance *(African)* ♀♂ — RATING: ★☆
God's gift—From the Hausa tribe of West Africa
> People think of Yohance as intelligent, creative, handsome, energetic, powerful

People who like the name Yohance also like Jesse, Kirabo, Zene, Azriel, Jensen, Jude, Reese, Piper, Rain, Natania

Yoko (*Japanese*) ♀　　RATING: ★★
Positive child—Yoko Ono, artist/musician
People think of Yoko as intelligent, weird, creative, quiet, caring
People who like the name Yoko also like Sakura, Suki, Keiko, Yoshiko, Aiko, Kaori, Yoshi, Nariko, Mai, Kaida

Yoland (*French*) ♀　　RATING: ★★★
Violet flower—Variation of Yolanda
People think of Yoland as caring, artsy, trustworthy, funny, sexy
People who like the name Yoland also like Giselle, Camille, Gigi, Violet, Olivia, Margaux, Blanche, Martine, Yolanda, Madeleine

Yolanda (*Spanish*) ♀　　RATING: ★★★
Violet flower
People think of Yolanda as pretty, caring, funny, intelligent, creative
People who like the name Yolanda also like Victoria, Vanessa, Veronica, Grace, Faith, Olivia, Sabrina, Isabella, Hailey, Summer

Yonah (*Hebrew*) ♀♂　　RATING: ★★
Dove
People think of Yonah as creative, cool, old-fashioned, trustworthy, energetic
People who like the name Yonah also like Jaden, Julian, Shae, Evan, Jude, Kyler, Mackenzie, Tate, Ezra, Austin

Yoninah (*Hebrew*) ♀　　RATING: ★★★
Little dove
People think of Yoninah as pretty, exotic, cool, big, funny
People who like the name Yoninah also like Yana, Yanichel, Yovela, Yelena, Moriah, Zoey, Zulema, Samara, Tahlia, Yamin

Yori (*Japanese*) ♀　　RATING: ★★
Reliable
People think of Yori as exotic, cool, intelligent, quiet, popular
People who like the name Yori also like Amaya, Suki, Sakura, Kaiya, Yoshe, Kaida, Mai, Toki, Keiko, Ayame

Yorick (*Scandinavian*) ♂　　RATING: ★★★
Farmer—Variation of George
People think of Yorick as old-fashioned, poor, lazy, trustworthy, powerful
People who like the name Yorick also like Zachary, Xavier, Owen, Xander, Tristan, Ulric, Wade, Oliver, Warren, Landon

York (*English*) ♂　　RATING: ★★
From the town of Eburos—Also an English place name.
People think of York as intelligent, boy next door, weird, creative, handsome

People who like the name York also like Xavier, Xander, Matthew, Luke, Oliver, Owen, Ian, Miles, Wade, Gavin

Yoruba (*African*) ♀　　RATING: ★★☆
People in Nigeria—Nigerian origin
People think of Yoruba as exotic, creative, leader, trustworthy, quiet
People who like the name Yoruba also like Sidonie, Lawanda, Misty, Sienna, Lavanya, Larissa, Maggie, Margarita, Marta, Sapphire

Yosef (*Hebrew*) ♂　　RATING: ★★★☆
God will add—Variation of Joseph
People think of Yosef as handsome, intelligent, sexy, funny, religious
People who like the name Yosef also like Gabriel, Joel, Zach, Nathaniel, Elijah, Isaac, Joseph, Ethan, Noah, Nathan

Yosefu (*Hebrew*) ♂　　RATING: ★☆
God will add
People think of Yosefu as ethnic, handsome, religious, exotic, funny
People who like the name Yosefu also like Yosef, Yaser, Yamir, Nathaniel, Nen, Norwood, Yestin, Zachary, Nyack, Moises

Yoshe (*Japanese*) ♀　　RATING: ★★
Beauty
People think of Yoshe as exotic, pretty, weird, cool, funny
People who like the name Yoshe also like Yori, Sakura, Suki, Kaida, Kohana, Yoshi, Yoshiko, Nariko, Nozomi, Michiko

Yoshi (*Japanese*) ♀　　RATING: ★★★★
Good, respectful
People think of Yoshi as cool, funny, creative, young, intelligent
People who like the name Yoshi also like Sakura, Suki, Kaida, Toshi, Yoshiko, Yoko, Nariko, Haruko, Yoshino, Ayame

Yoshiko (*Japanese*) ♀　　RATING: ★☆
Good child
People think of Yoshiko as pretty, funny, trustworthy, intelligent, caring
People who like the name Yoshiko also like Sakura, Miyoko, Keiko, Yoko, Nariko, Kaori, Nozomi, Emiko, Tomoko, Kohana

Yoshino (*Japanese*) ♀　　RATING: ★☆
Respectful, good
People think of Yoshino as exotic, quiet, weird, ethnic, nerdy
People who like the name Yoshino also like Yoshiko, Yoshi, Kaori, Yoko, Tomoko, Miyoko, Suki, Kohana, Sakura, Keiko

Yovela (*Hebrew*) ♀　　RATING: ★☆
Jubilee
People think of Yovela as ethnic, exotic, pretty, wealthy, loser

People who like the name Yovela also like Yanichel, Yana, Zoey, Yessica, Xantara, Atara, Olivia, Aviva, Zipporah, Zenevieva

Yu Jie *(Chinese)* ♀♂   RATING: ★★★
Pure, beautiful jade—Mandarin origin
People think of Yu Jie as exotic, artsy, weird, religious, ethnic
People who like the name Yu Jie also like Yue Yan, Yue, Yi Min, Yuki, Ming Yue, Willow, Jaden, Noelle, Kimberly, Whitney

Yue *(Chinese)* ♀♂   RATING: ★★★★
Moon—Commonly used for females
People think of Yue as elegant, pretty, intelligent, caring, creative
People who like the name Yue also like Yuki, Yue Yan, Yu Jie, Kana, Dylan, Kai, Ming Yue, Lilo, Shea, Blake

Yue Yan *(Chinese)* ♀♂   RATING: ★★★
Happy, beautiful—Mandarin origin
People think of Yue Yan as pretty, intelligent, caring, funny, young
People who like the name Yue Yan also like Yu Jie, Yue, Yi Min, Ming Yue, Yuki, Jensen, Kana, Li, Shuang, Wei

Yui *(Japanese)* ♀   RATING: ★★★
Elegant cloth
People think of Yui as pretty, exotic, sexy, quiet, artsy
People who like the name Yui also like Yoshiko, Colette, Toki, Yoshino, Yalitza, Twyla, Kohana, Cynna, Biana, Umeko

Yuki *(Japanese)* ♀♂   RATING: ★★★★☆
Snow; lucky
People think of Yuki as intelligent, pretty, young, popular, cool
People who like the name Yuki also like Rin, Seiko, Kana, Kiyoshi, Sanyu, Saku, Mitsu, Ren, Hoshi, Natsu

Yukiko *(Japanese)* ♂   RATING: ★★★☆
Happiness, snow
People think of Yukiko as powerful, aggressive, sexy, wild, funny
People who like the name Yukiko also like Ryu, Hiroshi, Makoto, Suoh, Yasuo, Haruki, Jiro, Keitaro, Yama, Akio

Yul *(Russian)* ♂   RATING: ★★★
Variation of Julius; Yul Brynner, actor
People think of Yul as intelligent, leader, sporty, winner, exotic
People who like the name Yul also like Yukio, Yadid, Yuval, Yves, Yaholo, Ea, Nigel, Yeshaya, Yuri, Yasuo

Yule *(English)* ♀♂   RATING: ★☆
Of Christmastime
People think of Yule as pretty, winner, popular, nerdy, funny
People who like the name Yule also like Winter, Cassidy, Talon, Tempest, Noel, Taylor, Drew, Jaden, Connor, Dakota

Yuma *(Native American)* ♂   RATING: ★★★
Son of the chief—Quechan origin
People think of Yuma as intelligent, exotic, wild, handsome, cool
People who like the name Yuma also like Yaholo, Yahto, Tokala, Dasan, Xavier, Yuri, Ethan, Dyami, Yanni, Drake

Yuri *(Russian)* ♂   RATING: ★★★☆
Farmer—Variation of George; Yuri Gagarin, cosmonaut
People think of Yuri as intelligent, aggressive, cool, handsome, trustworthy
People who like the name Yuri also like Xavier, Ian, Aiden, Ethan, Andrew, Alexander, Jacob, Noah, Gabriel, Sebastian

Yuuna *(Japanese)* ♀   RATING: ★★★
Sun plant
People think of Yuuna as quiet, pretty, creative, intelligent, funny
People who like the name Yuuna also like Yihana, Ciel, Yachi, Milla, Yi, Yasmin, Yvette, Alexia, Yael, Yvonne

Yuuta *(Japanese)* ♂   RATING: ★★☆
Elegant; big
People think of Yuuta as pretty, cool, young, slow, poor
People who like the name Yuuta also like Yagil, Yadid, Yuri, Yuval, Yair, Yves, Yered, Yvon, Yaholo, Yeriel

Yuval *(Hebrew)* ♂   RATING: ★☆
Brook
People think of Yuval as intelligent, creative, handsome, caring, artsy
People who like the name Yuval also like Yves, Yukio, Yeriel, Yardan, Nathan, Nicholas, Yadid, Yul, Yasuo, Yaholo

Yves *(French)* ♂   RATING: ★★
Yew—Yves Montand, actor; Yves Saint Laurent, designer
People think of Yves as intelligent, sexy, handsome, caring, funny
People who like the name Yves also like Etienne, Seth, Tristan, Lucien, Oliver, Ian, Tyson, Ethan, Noah, Ronan

Yvette *(French)* ♀   RATING: ★★
Yew—Feminine form of Yves; Yvette Mimieux, actress
People think of Yvette as pretty, funny, intelligent, creative, caring
People who like the name Yvette also like Yvonne, Victoria, Vanessa, Paige, Olivia, Faith, Giselle, Zoe, Veronica, Isabella

Yvon *(French)* ♂   RATING: ★★★
Variation of Yves
People think of Yvon as creative, weird, caring, intelligent, leader
People who like the name Yvon also like Yves, Tyson, Yuri, William, Xavier, Nicholas, Jason, Laurent, Joel, Frederick

Yvonne (French) ♀   RATING: ★★☆
Yew—Feminine form of Yves
> People think of Yvonne as pretty, caring, intelligent, funny, creative
> People who like the name Yvonne also like Yvette, Olivia, Victoria, Paige, Veronica, Vanessa, Isabella, Isabelle, Faith, Sabrina

Zabel (Spanish) ♀   RATING: ★★★
God is my oath—Short for Isabel
> People think of Zabel as elegant, pretty, exotic, cool, intelligent
> People who like the name Zabel also like Isabella, Ava, Mai, Izzy, Hazel, Bianca, Janelle, Cassandra, Gabriella, Mia

Zabrina (American) ♀   RATING: ★★★
Latin name of the river Severn in England—Also spelled Zabrinah, Zabreena, or Zabryna
> People think of Zabrina as pretty, funny, popular, wild, creative
> People who like the name Zabrina also like Sabrina, Zoey, Isabella, Paige, Zoe, Victoria, Faith, Zara, Gabrielle, Vanessa

Zaccheus (Hebrew) ♂   RATING: ★★★
Pure, clear, bright
> People think of Zaccheus as leader, intelligent, handsome, cool, young
> People who like the name Zaccheus also like Zachariah, Zachary, Isaac, Noah, Isaiah, Elijah, Gabriel, Xavier, Caleb, Jonah

Zach (English) ♂   RATING: ★★★
Short for Zachary—Also spelled Zac; Zach Braff, actor; Zac Efron, actor/singer
> People think of Zach as funny, cool, handsome, popular, young
> People who like the name Zach also like Zachary, Ethan, Jacob, Noah, Nathan, Caleb, Matthew, Zack, Seth, Aiden

Zacharee (Hebrew) ♀♂   RATING: ★★★☆
God has remembered—Feminine form of Zachary; also spelled Zacharie
> People think of Zacharee as handsome, funny, exotic, intelligent, creative
> People who like the name Zacharee also like Jaden, Caden, Riley, Madison, Logan, Taylor, Hayden, Bailey, Jordan, Addison

Zachariah (Hebrew) ♂   RATING: ★★★★☆
God has remembered
> People think of Zachariah as handsome, intelligent, funny, caring, leader
> People who like the name Zachariah also like Elijah, Zachary, Isaiah, Isaac, Noah, Gabriel, Jeremiah, Nathaniel, Caleb, Ethan

Zachary (Hebrew) ♂   RATING: ★★★☆
God has remembered—Zachary Taylor, U.S. president
> People think of Zachary as handsome, funny, intelligent, cool, caring
> People who like the name Zachary also like Ethan, Jacob, Nicholas, Noah, Nathan, Joshua, Matthew, Caleb, Benjamin, Alexander

Zaci (American) ♂   RATING: ★★★
Short for Zachary
> People think of Zaci as aggressive, loser, lazy, young, funny
> People who like the name Zaci also like Zachariah, Zachary, Seth, Zach, Zander, Kaden, Isaac, Xavier, Zarek, Braden

Zack (Hebrew) ♂   RATING: ★★★☆
Short for Zachary
> People think of Zack as funny, cool, handsome, popular, young
> People who like the name Zack also like Zachary, Jacob, Ethan, Zach, Jake, Jack, Nathan, Luke, Lucas, Ian

Zad (Persian) ♂   RATING: ★★★
Son
> People think of Zad as loser, nerdy, unpopular, weird, poor
> People who like the name Zad also like Waylon, Dermot, Demetrius, Deiter, Davis, Titus, Dalton, Constantine, Draco, Cleavant

Zada (Persian) ♀   RATING: ★☆
Offspring
> People think of Zada as pretty, creative, exotic, intelligent, sexy
> People who like the name Zada also like Zoe, Zaida, Zoey, Sadie, Ava, Zara, Olivia, Faith, Bella, Zaria

Zafirah (Arabic) ♀   RATING: ★☆
Triumphant, successful
> People think of Zafirah as pretty, intelligent, cool, powerful, creative
> People who like the name Zafirah also like Zaina, Zabrina, Zaida, Zarina, Zaria, Zahra, Zahina, Violet, Aaliyah, Zada

Zagiri (Armenian) ♀   RATING: ★★★
Flower
> People think of Zagiri as exotic, ethnic, young, loser, wild
> People who like the name Zagiri also like Zafirah, Zada, Zabrina, Zariel, Zaida, Zola, Zaila, Ziazan, Zahra, Layla

Zahar (Arabic) ♂   RATING: ★★★☆
Shine, sparkle, bloom
> People think of Zahar as exotic, wealthy, artsy, powerful, poor
> People who like the name Zahar also like Zakiya, Zachary, Zamir, Noah, Zachariah, Zahi, Jamal, Ethan, Nathaniel, Adam

583

Zahara *(Arabic)* ♀   RATING: ★★★☆

584

Flower; most exquisite—Zahara Marley Jolie-Pitt, daughter of Angelina Jolie and Brad Pitt

People think of Zahara as exotic, pretty, creative, intelligent, powerful

People who like the name Zahara also like Ava, Sahara, Zahra, Chloe, Zara, Aaliyah, Paige, Ella, Cailyn, Savannah

Zahavah *(Hebrew)* ♀   RATING: ★☆

Golden one—Variation of Zahava

People think of Zahavah as exotic, intelligent, leader, ethnic, pretty

People who like the name Zahavah also like Zabrina, Zara, Zaria, Zada, Isabella, Zafirah, Gabrielle, Zaina, Zariel, Zandeleigh

Zahi *(Arabic)* ♂   RATING: ★★

Glowing, fair

People think of Zahi as pretty, sexy, intelligent, elegant, creative

People who like the name Zahi also like Zahar, Zamir, Zander, Yaser, Zachariah, Zaide, Aden, Zakiya, Zeke, Zaccheus

Zahina *(Arabic)* ♀   RATING: ★★★☆

Intelligent

People think of Zahina as pretty, leader, exotic, intelligent, powerful

People who like the name Zahina also like Zaina, Zafirah, Aaliyah, Zabrina, Zaila, Zaria, Zada, Zahra, Zara, Zaida

Zahra *(Arabic)* ♀   RATING: ★★★☆

Bright, fair

People think of Zahra as pretty, intelligent, caring, funny, exotic

People who like the name Zahra also like Zara, Ava, Zoe, Zoey, Zada, Olivia, Sienna, Zaria, Layla, Yasmin

Zahrah *(Arabic)* ♀   RATING: ★★★

Flower, blossom—Often confused with Zahra

People think of Zahrah as pretty, exotic, popular, religious, intelligent

People who like the name Zahrah also like Layla, Jahzara, Ziarre, Aaliyah, Zaria, Abrianna, Ava, Olivia, Nadia, Sahirah

Zahur *(Arabic)* ♂   RATING: ★☆

Eminent

People think of Zahur as old, lazy, nerdy, loser, old-fashioned

People who like the name Zahur also like Zamir, Zahi, Zarek, Zared, Zakiya, Zareh, Zachariah, Zavad, Keiran, Xander

Zaida *(Arabic)* ♀   RATING: ★★★★

Increasing, surplus

People think of Zaida as pretty, funny, exotic, caring, creative

People who like the name Zaida also like Zada, Zaina, Zaila, Zoe, Nadia, Ava, Sadie, Olivia, Zaria, Zabrina

Zaide *(Arabic)* ♂   RATING: ★★★☆

Increasing, surplus

People think of Zaide as handsome, intelligent, sexy, leader, weird

People who like the name Zaide also like Kaden, Jayden, Zander, Zachary, Xavier, Xander, Maddox, Elijah, Isaac, Gabriel

Zaidin *(English)* ♂   RATING: ★★★☆

Combination of Z and Aiden; also spelled Zaiden or Zaden

People think of Zaidin as intelligent, handsome, leader, funny, energetic

People who like the name Zaidin also like Xander, Aiden, Tristan, Zander, Kaden, Jayden, Holden, Jadon, Xavier, Tobias

Zaila *(Arabic)* ♀   RATING: ★★★☆

Might, power

People think of Zaila as exotic, aggressive, creative, pretty, sexy

People who like the name Zaila also like Zaida, Zaina, Zada, Zaria, Ava, Zoe, Zoey, Layla, Savannah, Abigail

Zain *(Arabic)* ♂   RATING: ★★★☆

Handsome

People think of Zain as handsome, intelligent, powerful, leader, cool

People who like the name Zain also like Kaden, Gage, Xander, Isaiah, Noah, Xavier, Kadin, Maddox, Elijah, Ethan

Zaina *(Arabic)* ♀   RATING: ★★★★

Beautiful

People think of Zaina as pretty, intelligent, caring, young, popular

People who like the name Zaina also like Zaida, Zaria, Zada, Zabrina, Zaila, Zafirah, Zoey, Kyla, Zaynah, Paige

Zaire *(African)* ♀ ♂   RATING: ★★

From Zaire

People think of Zaire as intelligent, young, funny, creative, exotic

People who like the name Zaire also like Jaden, Zane, Logan, Reese, Talen, Bailey, Addison, Jordan, Sage, Cadence

Zajac *(Polish)* ♀ ♂   RATING: ★★☆

Rabbit—Also a surname

People think of Zajac as exotic, sexy, unpopular, weird, aggressive

People who like the name Zajac also like Keegan, Marek, Loki, Blake, Jameson, Jess, Vaughn, Piper, Santana, Preston

Zakiya *(Hebrew)* ♂   RATING: ★★★★

Pure, clear, bright

People think of Zakiya as intelligent, pretty, popular, funny, caring

People who like the name Zakiya also like Zamir, Zachariah, Zahar, Elijah, Isaiah, Gabriel, Jabari, Zavad, Zaide, Zachary

Zakuro (*Japanese*) ♀   RATING: ★★★☆
Pomegranate
> People think of Zakuro as pretty, cool, intelligent, popular, exotic
> People who like the name Zakuro also like Sakura, Kaori, Hitomi, Ayame, Haruko, Nozomi, Keiko, Kaida, Hoshiko, Kuri

Zale (*Polish*) ♀♂   RATING: ★★☆
Unknown meaning—Also a surname
> People think of Zale as leader, young, artsy, creative, energetic
> People who like the name Zale also like Zane, Jaden, Riley, Zephyr, Quinn, Oakley, Paxton, Hayden, Parker, Hadley

Zalika (*Arabic*) ♀   RATING: ★★★★
Wondrously beautiful
> People think of Zalika as pretty, exotic, sexy, creative, young
> People who like the name Zalika also like Zaria, Tahirah, Zafirah, Kamilah, Aaliyah, Kanika, Nailah, Zelda, Zaina, Zada

Zalman (*Hebrew*) ♂   RATING: ★★★
Peaceful—Variation of Solomon
> People think of Zalman as exotic, energetic, sexy, funny, powerful
> People who like the name Zalman also like Zaccheus, Ezekiel, Zamir, Noah, Zan, Zev, Zedekiah, Tyson, Zubin, Elijah

Zaltana (*Native American*) ♀   RATING: ★★★
High mountain
> People think of Zaltana as weird, creative, powerful, young, exotic
> People who like the name Zaltana also like Zamora, Topanga, Tala, Zabrina, Wakanda, Kaya, Kiona, Zafirah, Kaliska, Zahavah

Zamir (*Hebrew*) ♂   RATING: ★★
Songbird
> People think of Zamir as handsome, powerful, intelligent, ethnic, cool
> People who like the name Zamir also like Yamir, Zakiya, Damir, Caleb, Elijah, Isaiah, Amir, Jamar, Zander, Xavier

Zamora (*Spanish*) ♀   RATING: ★★★☆
Person from Zamora, Spain
> People think of Zamora as pretty, sexy, intelligent, funny, powerful
> People who like the name Zamora also like Zabrina, Zara, Zaria, Amora, Zoey, Zandra, Zariel, Zoe, Zola, Odessa

Zan (*Slavic*) ♂   RATING: ★★
Variation of John
> People think of Zan as intelligent, funny, energetic, popular, weird
> People who like the name Zan also like Zander, Xander, Zev, Zachary, Zach, Gabriel, Kaden, Xavier, Zack, Zachariah

Zandeleigh (*American*) ♀   RATING: ★★★
Combination of Zander and Leigh
> People think of Zandeleigh as unpopular, exotic, weird, loser, pretty
> People who like the name Zandeleigh also like Isabella, Zara, Abigail, Zada, Kaleigh, Hannah, Zahavah, Zandra, Zamora, Zoey

Zander (*Greek*) ♂   RATING: ★★★★☆
Defender of men—Variation of Alexander
> People think of Zander as handsome, intelligent, energetic, funny, powerful
> People who like the name Zander also like Xander, Xavier, Zachary, Ethan, Aiden, Tristan, Kaden, Gavin, Caleb, Landon

Zandra (*Greek*) ♀   RATING: ★★☆
Short for Alexandra—Zandra Rhodes, designer
> People think of Zandra as pretty, funny, intelligent, creative, cool
> People who like the name Zandra also like Zoe, Vanessa, Zabrina, Olivia, Zaria, Faith, Zara, Isabella, Hannah, Zoey

Zane (*American*) ♀♂   RATING: ★★★★
Beloved—Also a surname; also possibly a variation of John
> People think of Zane as handsome, intelligent, funny, cool, popular
> People who like the name Zane also like Parker, Caden, Logan, Hayden, Jaden, Riley, Bailey, Avery, Addison, Evan

Zanna (*Latin*) ♀   RATING: ★★★★
Lily—Short for Susanna
> People think of Zanna as pretty, creative, caring, exotic, funny
> People who like the name Zanna also like Zara, Zaria, Olivia, Zada, Zoe, Zoey, Jasmine, Aurora, Eva, Emma

Zanta (*Spanish*) ♀   RATING: ★★★★
Golden—Variation of Xanthe
> People think of Zanta as pretty, intelligent, cool, old-fashioned, energetic
> People who like the name Zanta also like Zara, Zuri, Zabrina, Zanna, Zariel, Zaria, Zaina, Zafirah, Zamora, Zanthe

Zanthe (*Greek*) ♀   RATING: ★★★
Golden—Variation of Xanthe
> People think of Zanthe as pretty, intelligent, exotic, creative, artsy
> People who like the name Zanthe also like Zoe, Xanthe, Olivia, Zandra, Violet, Sophie, Zara, Zaria, Amelia, Xylia

Zara (*English*) ♀   RATING: ★★★★
Princess—Variation of Sarah; also a chain of clothing stores
> People think of Zara as pretty, funny, creative, intelligent, popular
> People who like the name Zara also like Zoe, Ava, Zaria, Isabella, Ella, Eva, Grace, Paige, Olivia, Zoey

586

Zareb (*African*) ♂   RATING: ★☆
Guardian
People think of Zareb as intelligent, powerful, religious, popular, creative
People who like the name Zareb also like Zared, Zavad, Zamir, Zander, Zarek, Zack, Zaide, Adam, Yamir, Zesiro

Zared (*Hebrew*) ♂   RATING: ★★★★
Trap
People think of Zared as handsome, cool, popular, funny, intelligent
People who like the name Zared also like Zarek, Zander, Kaden, Zachariah, Drake, Zachary, Jayden, Ethan, Jared, Deacon

Zareh (*Armenian*) ♂   RATING: ★★★☆
Tears
People think of Zareh as creative, cool, artsy, leader, intelligent
People who like the name Zareh also like Zaccheus, Zarek, Zachariah, Zamir, Gabriel, Zander, Lachlan, Zorion, Lucian, Wyatt

Zarek (*Persian*) ♂   RATING: ★★
May God protect the king
People think of Zarek as wild, powerful, creative, intelligent, handsome
People who like the name Zarek also like Zander, Jayden, Xander, Zachary, Tristan, Nathan, Kaden, Caleb, Aiden, Zachariah

Zaria (*American*) ♀   RATING: ★★★★☆
Princess—Variation of Sarah
People think of Zaria as pretty, intelligent, funny, caring, creative
People who like the name Zaria also like Zara, Zoe, Zariel, Xaria, Isabella, Olivia, Gabrielle, Zoey, Zada, Grace

Zariel (*American*) ♀   RATING: ★★★★
Combination of Zara and Ariel
People think of Zariel as pretty, intelligent, funny, energetic, exotic
People who like the name Zariel also like Zaria, Zara, Zelda, Zabrina, Arabella, Arianna, Gabrielle, Cailyn, Brielle, Zoey

Zarifa (*Arabic*) ♀   RATING: ★★★
Moves with grace
People think of Zarifa as funny, intelligent, creative, elegant, pretty
People who like the name Zarifa also like Zafirah, Kara, Zarina, Kisha, Veronica, Katia, Samara, Kaya, Zara, Zora

Zarina (*Arabic*) ♀   RATING: ★★
Golden
People think of Zarina as pretty, intelligent, caring, funny, creative
People who like the name Zarina also like Zara, Zoe, Zabrina, Zoey, Zada, Faith, Zariel, Zaria, Vanessa, Zafirah

Zarita (*Spanish*) ♀   RATING: ★★★★
Princess—Variation of Sarah
People think of Zarita as pretty, exotic, quiet, cool, wild
People who like the name Zarita also like Zaria, Zabrina, Zara, Zamora, Jahzara, Felicia, Esperanza, Amora, Victoria, Jamila

Zarola (*American*) ♀   RATING: ★★★
Combination of Zara and Carola
People think of Zarola as powerful, weird, energetic, intelligent, ethnic
People who like the name Zarola also like Neena, Ayanna, Nysa, Clover, Shamara, Sahara, Natara, Layla, Sari, Bimala

Zasha (*Russian*) ♀♂   RATING: ★★
Defender of men—Variation of Sasha
People think of Zasha as pretty, sexy, energetic, exotic, trendy
People who like the name Zasha also like Sasha, Ryan, Zane, Bailey, Aidan, Jade, Zephyr, Piper, Zion, Mischa

Zavad (*Hebrew*) ♂   RATING: ★★☆
Gift
People think of Zavad as unpopular, weird, nerdy, exotic, quiet
People who like the name Zavad also like Zakiya, Zachary, Zachariah, Zarek, Zander, Zamir, Zaide, Zedekiah, Zeke, Zayit

Zaviera (*Spanish*) ♀   RATING: ★★
The new house—Variation of Xaviera
People think of Zaviera as pretty, cool, exotic, wild, weird
People who like the name Zaviera also like Samara, Zenevieva, Kaydence, Sahara, Zoey, Zora, Samiya, Ivy, Zaynah, Rianna

Zayit (*Hebrew*) ♂   RATING: ★★☆
Olive—Pronounced *zah-yeet*
People think of Zayit as ethnic, old-fashioned, loser, poor, untrustworthy
People who like the name Zayit also like Zavad, Zakiya, Zarek, Zared, Zachariah, Zamir, Aron, Zahur, Abner, Zalman

Zayn (*Arabic*) ♀♂   RATING: ★★★★
Beautiful
People think of Zayn as intelligent, cool, pretty, exotic, powerful
People who like the name Zayn also like Zane, Caden, Payton, Riley, Parker, Skylar, Madison, Bailey, Mackenzie, Taylor

Zaynah (*Arabic*) ♀   RATING: ★★★★
Beautiful
People think of Zaynah as pretty, intelligent, popular, caring, trustworthy
People who like the name Zaynah also like Zaria, Zaina, Zara, Amaya, Zuri, Samara, Kaelyn, Mia, Trinity, Kyla

Zaza *(Hebrew)* ♀   RATING: ★★★
Movement
> People think of Zaza as exotic, aggressive, funny, intelligent, wild
> People who like the name Zaza also like Zoe, Zara, Zazu, Zora, Olivia, Zoey, Zaria, Emily, Leila, Zelda

Zazu *(Hebrew)* ♀   RATING: ★★★☆
Movement—Variation of Zaza; Zazu Pitts, actress
> People think of Zazu as exotic, wild, creative, slow, funny
> People who like the name Zazu also like Zaza, Zipporah, Zuri, Leila, Scarlett, Zoe, Zara, Ella, Zelda, Emily

Zbigniew *(Polish)* ♂   RATING: ★★★
To get rid of anger
> People think of Zbigniew as weird, handsome, intelligent, cool, wild
> People who like the name Zbigniew also like Zero, Tristan, Zev, Adam, Liam, Zan, Reuben, Zedekiah, Zikomo, Abdukrahman

Zea *(Latin)* ♀   RATING: ★★★☆
Wheat
> People think of Zea as pretty, creative, funny, energetic, intelligent
> People who like the name Zea also like Zoe, Zia, Mia, Zara, Ava, Zelia, Zada, Zaria, Ella, Olivia

Zeal *(English)* ♀ ♂   RATING: ★★
With passion
> People think of Zeal as lazy, energetic, leader, religious, stuck-up
> People who like the name Zeal also like Zane, Zayn, Zasha, Blaine, Ziven, Avery, Paxton, Zene, Devon, Phoenix

Zealand *(Scandinavian)* ♀ ♂   RATING: ★★★
From the sea land—Originally an area of the Netherlands; New Zealand, country in Southwestern Pacific
> People think of Zealand as exotic, aggressive
> People who like the name Zealand also like Jaden, Dakota, Carter, Zaire, Carson, Lani, Cadence, Lindsey, Madison, Eden

Zeb *(English)* ♂   RATING: ★★★★
Short for Zebedee or Zebulon
> People think of Zeb as handsome, funny, cool, intelligent, creative
> People who like the name Zeb also like Zach, Isaac, Zeke, Zachary, Seth, Zander, Levi, Zack, Nathan, Kaden

Zebedeo *(Spanish)* ♂   RATING: ★★★
Gift of God—Variation of Zebedee or Zebediah
> People think of Zebedeo as ethnic, religious, old, old-fashioned, exotic
> People who like the name Zebedeo also like Zikomo, Kaipo, Zander, Zachariah, Lulani, Zachary, Zulu, Zoltan, Zelig, Zoltin

Zebulon *(Hebrew)* ♂   RATING: ★☆
Exalted, honored
> People think of Zebulon as caring, handsome, cool, funny, leader
> People who like the name Zebulon also like Zander, Zeb, Isaiah, Zachariah, Zachary, Zedekiah, Oliver, Xavier, Gideon, Gabriel

Zed *(English)* ♂   RATING: ★★★☆
God is righteousness—Short for Zedekiah
> People think of Zed as aggressive, caring, boy next door, lazy, unpopular
> People who like the name Zed also like Zachary, Zeb, Zach, Seth, Noah, Zeke, Zack, Zander, Ian, Xander

Zedekiah *(Hebrew)* ♂   RATING: ★★★★
God is righteousness
> People think of Zedekiah as powerful, religious, energetic, trustworthy, funny
> People who like the name Zedekiah also like Zachariah, Elijah, Ezekiel, Isaiah, Jedidiah, Isaac, Jeremiah, Noah, Micah, Nathaniel

Zeke *(Hebrew)* ♂   RATING: ★★★★
God will strengthen—Short for Ezekiel
> People think of Zeke as handsome, cool, funny, intelligent, powerful
> People who like the name Zeke also like Ethan, Seth, Elijah, Gabriel, Caleb, Xavier, Zachary, Isaac, Xander, Kaden

Zeki *(Turkish)* ♀   RATING: ★★
Clever
> People think of Zeki as exotic, handsome, intelligent, creative, energetic
> People who like the name Zeki also like Zora, Serenity, Zafirah, Zoey, Prue, Amber, Astrid, Adora, Pippa, Zita

Zelda *(German)* ♀   RATING: ★★★★
Woman warrior—Short for Griselda; "The Legend of Zelda," video game
> People think of Zelda as pretty, powerful, intelligent, elegant, leader
> People who like the name Zelda also like Fiona, Olivia, Zoe, Zoey, Chloe, Penelope, Phoebe, Zara, Veronica, Iris

Zelia *(Greek)* ♀   RATING: ★★★☆
Zeal
> People think of Zelia as pretty, creative, energetic, exotic, intelligent
> People who like the name Zelia also like Zia, Zelda, Zoe, Zandra, Sofia, Olivia, Penelope, Vanessa, Zoey, Zaria

Zelig *(German)* ♂   RATING: ★★★
The blessed one—Yiddish origin; also spelled Selig; *Zelig*, film by Woody Allen; Bud Selig, baseball commissioner
> People think of Zelig as quiet, powerful, funny, intelligent, creative
> People who like the name Zelig also like Zander, Zavad, Xander, Xylon, Zaccheus, Zorion, Zeno, Keagan, Zubin, Zamir

Zena *(Greek)* ♀   RATING: ★★★☆
Hospitable
> People think of Zena as pretty, funny, intelligent, caring, cool
> People who like the name Zena also like Zoe, Olivia, Zoey, Xena, Sabrina, Vanessa, Mia, Zelda, Hailey, Jasmine

Zenas *(Greek)* ♀♂   RATING: ★★★
Gift of Zeus
> People think of Zenas as exotic, intelligent, creative, cool, sexy
> People who like the name Zenas also like Zephyr, Zane, Zenon, Jordan, Evan, Raven, Lilo, Arien, Skylar, Caden

Zenda *(Persian)* ♀   RATING: ★★
Soul, life—Place name in *The Prisoner of Zenda* by Anthony Hope
> People think of Zenda as pretty, exotic, young, elegant, creative
> People who like the name Zenda also like Zelia, Fiona, Zoe, Vera, Zofia, Zuri, Zada, Olivia, Zora, Zara

Zéné *(African)* ♀♂   RATING: ★★
Beautiful—Also the Hungarian word for music; also a city in the Central African Republic
> People think of Zene as exotic, pretty, intelligent, creative, artsy
> People who like the name Zene also like Zane, Zo, Zaire, Kai, Logan, Willow, Zayn, Myles, Morgan, Jaden

Zenevieva *(Slavic)* ♀   RATING: ★★★☆
Woman of the people—Variation of Genevieve
> People think of Zenevieva as exotic, pretty, sexy, young, lazy
> People who like the name Zenevieva also like Scarlett, Zelda, Isadora, Zoey, Victoria, Olivia, Vanessa, Raina, Zaviera, Zelia

Zenia *(Greek)* ♀   RATING: ★★☆
Hospitable—Variation of Xenia
> People think of Zenia as pretty, intelligent, caring, creative, funny
> People who like the name Zenia also like Zoe, Zelia, Zuri, Zaria, Bella, Zara, Zinnia, Venus, Zena, Paige

Zenith *(English)* ♀♂   RATING: ★★★
The very top—Also a brand of electronics
> People think of Zenith as exotic, energetic, leader, intelligent, creative
> People who like the name Zenith also like Phoenix, Zephyr, Zane, Willow, Orion, Nova, Hayden, Riley, Evelyn, Zenon

Zeno *(Greek)* ♂   RATING: ★★★
Guest, host
> People think of Zeno as intelligent, popular, leader, sporty, caring
> People who like the name Zeno also like Zander, Vincent, Oliver, Xander, Thomas, Aiden, Alexander, Wyatt, Zeus, Sirius

Zenobia *(Greek)* ♀   RATING: ★☆
Life of Zeus
> People think of Zenobia as intelligent, pretty, exotic, powerful, caring
> People who like the name Zenobia also like Melody, Thalia, Violet, Cassandra, Anastasia, Zuri, Mia, Zara, Viviana, Adriana

Zenon *(Greek)* ♀♂   RATING: ★★★☆
Guest, host
> People think of Zenon as cool, energetic, handsome, powerful, trustworthy
> People who like the name Zenon also like Zephyr, Rory, Haven, Jade, Caden, Zane, Taylor, Phoenix, Julian, Willow

Zentavious *(American)* ♂   RATING: ★★★
Combination of Zeno and Octavius
> People think of Zentavious as exotic, sexy, aggressive, intelligent, quiet
> People who like the name Zentavious also like Zorion, Zedekiah, Xhaiden, Zeshawn, Kaden, Xakery, Xadrian, Zakiya, Xavier, Zachariah

Zephan *(Celtic/Gaelic)* ♀♂   RATING: ★★★★
Irish saint
> People think of Zephan as cool, intelligent, handsome, creative, popular
> People who like the name Zephan also like Teagan, Zephyr, Rory, Skye, Logan, Aidan, Riley, Caden, Saxen, Reagan

Zephyr *(Greek)* ♀♂   RATING: ★★
West wind
> People think of Zephyr as creative, intelligent, wild, energetic, artsy
> People who like the name Zephyr also like Phoenix, Hayden, Riley, Caden, Orion, Quinn, Willow, Piper, Dylan, Sage

Zephyra *(Greek)* ♀   RATING: ★★★
Strong wind
> People think of Zephyra as powerful, exotic, pretty, intelligent, elegant
> People who like the name Zephyra also like Sephora, Evangeline, Zafirah, Alexia, Ailis, Adalia, Asia, Zola, Cheyenne, Sarafina

Zerlina *(Italian)* ♀   RATING: ★★
Character in *Don Giovanni* by Wolfgang Mozart
> People think of Zerlina as pretty, exotic, funny, leader, creative
> People who like the name Zerlina also like Zofia, Florence, Zola, Victoria, Isadora, Katarina, Zoey, Zelda, Zelia, Gemma

Zero *(Greek)* ♂   RATING: ★★★
Nothing, empty—Zero Mostel, actor
> People think of Zero as loser, unpopular, nerdy, quiet, weird
> People who like the name Zero also like Zander, Drake, Xavier, Damien, Sirius, Walker, Vincent, Sebastian, Axel, Blade

Zeroun *(Armenian)* ♂   RATING: ★★★
Respected, wise
> People think of Zeroun as intelligent, powerful, exotic, quiet, handsome
> People who like the name Zeroun also like Zero, Zamir, Arthur, Zaccheus, Zakiya, Zelig, Zeno, Zevi, Vernados, Valentino

Zeshawn *(American)* ♂   RATING: ★☆
Combination of Ze- and Shawn
> People think of Zeshawn as funny, cool, young, criminal, wild
> People who like the name Zeshawn also like Deshawn, Zachariah, Zakiya, Alijah, Jayden, Zamir, Josiah, Isaiah, Vashon, Dayshaun

Zesireo/Zesiro *(African)* ♂   RATING: ★★★
Firstborn of twins—Ugandan origin
> People think of Zesiro as handsome, ethnic, exotic, wild, energetic
> People who like the name Zesiro also like Zev, Zakiya, Zaide, Zander, Zikomo, Zamir, Zevi, Upendo, Zareb, Brandon

Zeus *(Greek)* ♂   RATING: ★☆
God—Supreme god of the Olympians; in Roman mythology, Jupiter
> People think of Zeus as powerful, intelligent, aggressive, leader, big
> People who like the name Zeus also like Xavier, Zachary, Oliver, Ethan, Zeke, Zander, Xander, Maddox, Gabriel, Tyson

Zev *(Hebrew)* ♂   RATING: ★★★★
Wolf
> People think of Zev as intelligent, handsome, leader, cool, funny
> People who like the name Zev also like Zevi, Zander, Zachary, Gabriel, Zeb, Zan, Xander, Zach, Alexander, Zeke

Zevi *(Hebrew)* ♂   RATING: ★★★
My wolf
> People think of Zevi as exotic, nerdy, trustworthy, pretty, funny
> People who like the name Zevi also like Zev, Zander, Zaide, Zachary, Gabriel, Valin, Zan, Rhett, Xavier, Xander

Zhen *(Chinese)* ♀   RATING: ★★★☆
Precious—Mandarin origin
> People think of Zhen as intelligent, exotic, artsy, creative, pretty
> People who like the name Zhen also like Zara, Mia, Zoey, Zuri, Sienna, Zi, Grace, Zoe, Zaina, Layla

Zhenga *(African)* ♀   RATING: ★☆
African queen—South African origin
> People think of Zhenga as pretty, exotic, weird, powerful, aggressive
> People who like the name Zhenga also like Ziarre, Zafirah, Zuleika, Zenobia, Zipporah, Lareina, Dominique, Xylia, Riona, Jahzara

Zhenya *(Russian)* ♀   RATING: ★★★
Well born—Short for Eugenia
> People think of Zhenya as pretty, trustworthy, caring, intelligent, exotic
> People who like the name Zhenya also like Chahna, Cara, Mareike, Anya, Hana, Samara, Zerlina, Isis, Zaynah, Semira

Zhi *(Chinese)* ♀♂   RATING: ★★★☆
Wisdom, healing—Mandarin origin
> People think of Zhi as intelligent, exotic, handsome, creative, ethnic
> People who like the name Zhi also like Zayn, Li, Taylor, Ziya, Shuang, Logan, Zasha, Kai, Ziv, Zene

Zi *(Chinese)* ♀   RATING: ★★★
Graceful, beautiful—Mandarin origin; usually paired with a second name as an adjective
> People think of Zi as intelligent, pretty, energetic, exotic, loser
> People who like the name Zi also like Zoe, Zoey, Jia Li, Zia, Ava, Xia, Olivia, Aiko, Hope, Zara

Zia *(Latin)* ♀   RATING: ★★★★
Wheat, grain
> People think of Zia as intelligent, creative, exotic, pretty, cool
> People who like the name Zia also like Zoe, Mia, Ava, Olivia, Zea, Bella, Zara, Zaria, Phoebe, Zoey

Ziarre *(American)* ♀   RATING: ★★★☆
Unknown meaning—Possibly Native American meaning goddess of the sky; possibly a variation of Zarah
> People think of Ziarre as exotic, pretty, creative, caring, intelligent
> People who like the name Ziarre also like Zaria, Aurora, Xaria, Zara, Zuri, Isis, Zabrina, Rhiannon, Samara, Zoe

Ziazan *(Armenian)* ♀   RATING: ★☆
Rainbow
> People think of Ziazan as exotic, artsy, weird, pretty, intelligent
> People who like the name Ziazan also like Zabrina, Ryann, Zinnia, Olivia, Ava, Iris, Zafirah, Zariel, Zofia, Zia

Zihna *(Native American)* ♀   RATING: ★★
Spins—Hopi origin
> People think of Zihna as weird, ethnic, exotic, pretty, energetic
> People who like the name Zihna also like Kaya, Zonta, Tallulah, Kiona, Zelia, Tehya, Ziarre, Kimama, Zarina, Zia

Zikomo *(African)* ♂   RATING: ★★☆
Thank you—Ngoni origin
> People think of Zikomo as creative, caring, funny, intelligent, weird
> People who like the name Zikomo also like Zeke, Zakiya, Zavad, Zesiro, Zev, Zahar, Kaden, Xavier, Zoltin, Tokala

Zilya *(Russian)* ♀♂   RATING: ★★
Kingly—Variation of Vasily
> People think of Zilya as pretty, intelligent, powerful, creative, slow

People who like the name Zilya also like Alexis, Mason, Sasha, Payton, Jordan, London, Morgan, Hayden, Jaden, Zasha

Zinna (*Latin*) ♀   RATING: ★★★☆
Rayed flower
People think of Zinna as intelligent, energetic, quiet, elegant, creative
People who like the name Zinna also like Zinnia, Zoe, Zola, Olivia, Penelope, Zaida, Zuri, Zofia, Ziarre, Zia

Zinnia (*Latin*) ♀   RATING: ★★★★
Flower
People think of Zinnia as creative, intelligent, pretty, young, energetic
People who like the name Zinnia also like Zoe, Violet, Zola, Olivia, Scarlett, Francesca, Aurora, Zuri, Iris, Hazel

Zion (*Hebrew*) ♀ ♂   RATING: ★★★★☆
Israel
People think of Zion as intelligent, creative, powerful, leader, handsome
People who like the name Zion also like Jaden, Eden, Zane, Ezra, Phoenix, Caden, James, Jade, Ryan, Logan

Zipporah (*Hebrew*) ♀   RATING: ★★★☆
Bird—In the Bible, the wife of Moses; also spelled Zippora, Ziporah, Zipora, or Tzipora
People think of Zipporah as pretty, exotic, intelligent, caring, creative
People who like the name Zipporah also like Ivy, Sophia, Ava, Zoe, Sephora, Genevieve, Giselle, Mara, Sadie, Iris

Zita (*Spanish*) ♀   RATING: ★★★☆
The seeker
People think of Zita as creative, intelligent, funny, pretty, caring
People who like the name Zita also like Zora, Zoey, Zara, Scarlett, Zoe, Zia, Penelope, Zuri, Violet, Zamora

Zitkala-Sa (*Native American*) ♀   RATING: ★☆
Red bird—Sioux origin
People think of Zitkala-Sa as exotic, ethnic, sexy, wild, energetic
People who like the name Zitkala-Sa also like Kiona, Sora, Shada, Kaya, Oneida, Wakanda, Peta, Zaltana, Liluye, Sokanon

Zitomira (*Slavic*) ♀   RATING: ★★
To live famously
People think of Zitomira as old, ethnic, wealthy, powerful, young
People who like the name Zitomira also like Zarifa, Zivanka, Sonia, Zaviera, Zenevieva, Zafirah, Yoninah, Johanna, Novia, Tendai

Ziv (*Hebrew*) ♀ ♂   RATING: ★★★
Brilliance, brightness
People think of Ziv as handsome, energetic, intelligent, popular, exotic
People who like the name Ziv also like Zayn, Zane, Zion, Zene, Zephyr, Ezra, London, Zody, Zhi, Ziven

Ziva (*Hebrew*) ♀   RATING: ★★
Brilliance, brightness
People think of Ziva as exotic, intelligent, pretty, energetic, aggressive
People who like the name Ziva also like Zara, Zoe, Olivia, Zaria, Zola, Zora, Isabella, Ava, Lucy, Ella

Zivanka (*Slavic*) ♀   RATING: ★☆
Alive
People think of Zivanka as ethnic, loser, creative, cool, pretty
People who like the name Zivanka also like Zabrina, Zenevieva, Stasia, Zola, Zora, Isis, Kara, Zea, Lulu, Zudora

Ziven (*Polish*) ♀ ♂   RATING: ★★★
Vigorous, alive
People think of Ziven as creative, exotic, energetic, young, funny
People who like the name Ziven also like Caden, Phoenix, Winter, Raven, Zane, Piper, Zephyr, Ember, Storm, Talen

Ziya (*Arabic*) ♀ ♂   RATING: ★★★★
Light
People think of Ziya as powerful, pretty, intelligent, cool, exotic
People who like the name Ziya also like Zayn, Kai, Shea, Zane, Nida, Zion, Zephyr, Kendall, Riley, Zilya

Zlata (*Slavic*) ♀   RATING: ★★
Golden
People think of Zlata as exotic, weird, creative, ethnic, stuck-up
People who like the name Zlata also like Zocha, Zorana, Gwyneth, Zhen, Zea, Lynette, Reba, Zi, Zara, Grace

Zlhna (*Native American*) ♀   RATING: ★☆
Spinning—Hopi origin
People think of Zlhna as weird, aggressive, exotic, uptight, cool
People who like the name Zlhna also like Sora, Oni, Sokanon, Hateya, Talli, Kaya, Tallulah, Kiona, Kaliska, Chenoa

Zo (*African*) ♀ ♂   RATING: ★★★
Person of medicine—Liberian origin
People think of Zo as leader, exotic, creative, cool, intelligent
People who like the name Zo also like Zane, Zene, Jade, Piper, Satin, Zasha, Addison, Rory, Riley, Kai

Zoan (*African*) ♀ ♂   RATING: ★★★
Departure
People think of Zoan as exotic, powerful, weird, sexy, unpopular
People who like the name Zoan also like Zody, Zane, Zo, Zasha, Torrin, Sydney, Zene, Zephyr, Zhi, Ziya

Zocha (*Polish*) ♀   RATING: ★★★
Wisdom
People think of Zocha as intelligent, aggressive, funny, leader, artsy

People who like the name Zocha also like Zofia, Zalika, Zarina, Zola, Zosia, Zahina, Zafirah, Genevieve, Lorelei, Celeste

Zody *(American)* ♀♂   RATING: ★★★☆
Combination of Zoe and Cody
People think of Zody as weird, loser, funny, nerdy, young
People who like the name Zody also like Brody, Logan, Parker, Riley, Zane, Phoenix, Payton, Mason, Dakota, Madison

Zoe *(Greek)* ♀   RATING: ★★★
Life—Also spelled Zoë
People think of Zoe as pretty, funny, creative, intelligent, energetic
People who like the name Zoe also like Chloe, Olivia, Paige, Emma, Ava, Hannah, Isabella, Abigail, Grace, Sophia

Zoey *(Greek)* ♀   RATING: ★★★
Life
People think of Zoey as pretty, funny, popular, creative, caring
People who like the name Zoey also like Chloe, Paige, Olivia, Emma, Isabella, Hannah, Zoe, Hailey, Faith, Abigail

Zofia *(Polish)* ♀   RATING: ★★★★
Wisdom—Variation of Sophia
People think of Zofia as intelligent, creative, funny, pretty, exotic
People who like the name Zofia also like Zoey, Zoe, Sophia, Sofia, Zara, Isabella, Zabrina, Bella, Olivia, Ava

Zohar *(Hebrew)* ♂   RATING: ★★★
Light, brilliance
People think of Zohar as poor, powerful, unpopular, untrustworthy, funny
People who like the name Zohar also like Ashwin, Rohak, Nalin, Alagan, Zamir, Nirav, Savir, Zander, Zahi, Zeke

Zohartze *(Spanish)* ♀   RATING: ★★☆
Virgin—Basque origin
People think of Zohartze as unpopular, exotic, stuck-up, sexy, weird
People who like the name Zohartze also like Gemma, Mariska, Brandee, Maggie, Canika, Sephora, Simone, Elizabeth, Dorinda, Kaylana

Zoheret *(Hebrew)* ♀   RATING: ★★★
She shines
People think of Zoheret as exotic, ethnic, aggressive, creative, caring
People who like the name Zoheret also like Yoninah, Ziarre, Zoey, Yael, Yovela, Gabrielle, Samara, Zipporah, Dominique, Nicolette

Zoie *(Greek)* ♀   RATING: ★★★★
Life
People think of Zoie as funny, creative, pretty, energetic, popular

People who like the name Zoie also like Zoe, Zoey, Olivia, Isabella, Chloe, Hailey, Paige, Jadyn, Emma, Ava

Zola *(Latin)* ♀   RATING: ★★
Earth
People think of Zola as pretty, intelligent, creative, exotic, powerful
People who like the name Zola also like Zoe, Zora, Zoey, Grace, Layla, Zara, Olivia, Ava, Zuri, Penelope

Zoltan *(Hungarian)* ♂   RATING: ★★★☆
Life
People think of Zoltan as powerful, creative, funny, intelligent, popular
People who like the name Zoltan also like Xavier, Sebastian, Gabriel, Ethan, Zachary, Zander, Zachariah, Xander, Wyatt, Zoltin

Zoltin *(Hungarian)* ♂   RATING: ★★☆
Life
People think of Zoltin as loser, nerdy, weird, slow, poor
People who like the name Zoltin also like Zoltan, Zander, Zachary, Zavad, Zeke, Xander, Xavier, Holden, Zachariah, Gabriel

Zona *(Latin)* ♀   RATING: ★★★☆
Sash
People think of Zona as caring, intelligent, trustworthy, creative, funny
People who like the name Zona also like Zola, Zaria, Zoe, Kyla, Bella, Daphne, Kara, Dawn, Flora, Fiana

Zonta *(Native American)* ♀   RATING: ★★★
Honest, trustrworthy—Sioux origin
People think of Zonta as pretty, caring, trustworthy, intelligent, girl next door
People who like the name Zonta also like Kaya, Kimama, Chenoa, Orenda, Wyanet, Zihna, Sokanon, Hateya, Tallulah, Zoey

Zora *(Slavic)* ♀   RATING: ★★★★
Dawn—Zora Neale Hurston, author
People think of Zora as pretty, exotic, creative, intelligent, artsy
People who like the name Zora also like Zara, Zoe, Aurora, Zoey, Chloe, Nadia, Violet, Zola, Maya, Isabella

Zorana *(Slavic)* ♀   RATING: ★★★☆
Dawn
People think of Zorana as caring, funny, pretty, young, creative
People who like the name Zorana also like Zora, Zara, Zariel, Zorina, Dessa, Zarina, Zada, Zia, Zaria, Samira

Zorina *(Slavic)* ♀   RATING: ★★★
Golden—Vera Zorina, dancer
People think of Zorina as trustworthy, energetic, funny, sexy, poor
People who like the name Zorina also like Nadia, Zaria, Zora, Zarina, Sienna, Samara, Gianna, Zoe, Isabella, Zara

Zorion (*Portuguese*) ♂   RATING: ★★★☆
Happy
> People think of Zorion as wild, funny, exotic, aggressive, weird
> People who like the name Zorion also like Aiden, Zander, Xavier, Xander, Kaden, Zachary, Zamir, Zachariah, Calix, Xadrian

Zosia (*Polish*) ♀   RATING: ★★★☆
Wisdom—Pronounced *Zo-she-a*
> People think of Zosia as pretty, caring, religious, funny, intelligent
> People who like the name Zosia also like Zofia, Zoe, Zuri, Zoey, Ava, Olesia, Zola, Zora, Zaria, Charlotte

Zoya (*Greek*) ♀   RATING: ★★★☆
Life
> People think of Zoya as pretty, creative, intelligent, caring, funny
> People who like the name Zoya also like Zoe, Zoey, Zara, Emma, Ava, Sophie, Zola, Zaria, Zoie, Zora

Zsa Zsa (*Hungarian*) ♀   RATING: ★★★
Lily—Variation of Susan; also spelled Zsazsa; Zsa Zsa Gabor, actress
> People think of Zsa Zsa as exotic, pretty, sexy, wild, elegant
> People who like the name Zsa Zsa also like Natalie, Zoey, Olivia, Ivy, Lola, Heidi, Penelope, Ophelia, Victoria, Roxanne

Zsoka (*Hungarian*) ♀   RATING: ★★☆
God is my oath
> People think of Zsoka as exotic, funny, unpopular, ethnic, poor
> People who like the name Zsoka also like Devorah, Calista, Arianna, Angelique, Sadah, Katelyn, Cyrah, Manoush, Nichole, Corinne

Zubaida (*Arabic*) ♀   RATING: ★★★
Essence, flower—Also spelled Zubeda or Zubaidah
> People think of Zubaida as caring, pretty, exotic, cool, funny
> People who like the name Zubaida also like Zelda, Ziarre, Waneta, Lula, Zenobia, Tauret, Zitkalasa, Violet, Lilka, Zorana

Zubeda (*Arabic*) ♀   RATING: ★★★
Essence, flower
> People think of Zubeda as pretty, caring, winner, trustworthy, creative
> People who like the name Zubeda also like Tatiana, Venice, Virginia, Kamaria, Venus, Delia, Deanna, Melodie, Beryl, Inocencia

Zubin (*Hebrew*) ♂   RATING: ★★★☆
To honor—Zubin Mehta, conductor
> People think of Zubin as funny, intelligent, handsome, creative, energetic
> People who like the name Zubin also like Zalman, Zedekiah, Zaccheus, Zander, Zach, Xander, Caleb, Zachary, Zarek, Noah

Zudora (*Arabic*) ♀   RATING: ★★☆
Laborer
> People think of Zudora as exotic, sexy, intelligent, religious, cool
> People who like the name Zudora also like Zabrina, Zamora, Zoey, Zuzana, Zipporah, Venus, Sonia, Melody, Zaida, Ziarre

Zula (*African*) ♀   RATING: ★★
Brilliant, ahead—Also a town in Eritrea
> People think of Zula as pretty, exotic, powerful, popular, elegant
> People who like the name Zula also like Zuri, Zoe, Zora, Zia, Zola, Zofia, Nala, Belle, Emma, Zaila

Zuleika (*Arabic*) ♀   RATING: ★★★☆
Brilliant, lovely
> People think of Zuleika as pretty, intelligent, sexy, creative, funny
> People who like the name Zuleika also like Isis, Zafirah, Celeste, Giselle, Zaria, Veronique, Adrienne, Aaliyah, Chloe, Zulema

Zulema (*Hebrew*) ♀   RATING: ★★★☆
Peace
> People think of Zulema as funny, pretty, cool, sexy, intelligent
> People who like the name Zulema also like Bianca, Samara, Zoe, Sofia, Zelda, Zita, Yasmin, Genevieve, Zoey, Kara

Zulimar (*Spanish*) ♀♂   RATING: ★★☆
Blue ocean
> People think of Zulimar as handsome, energetic, winner, boy next door, religious
> People who like the name Zulimar also like Audi, Armani

Zulu (*African*) ♂   RATING: ★★★
Heaven—Also a tribe in South Africa
> People think of Zulu as exotic, ethnic, lazy, weird, religious
> People who like the name Zulu also like Aaron, Jayden, Zeb, Dmitri, Zeno, Matthew, Noah, Aden, Ian, Joseph

Zuna (*African*) ♀   RATING: ★★★
To be sweet—South African origin
> People think of Zuna as pretty, funny, trustworthy, creative, caring
> People who like the name Zuna also like Zuri, Zora, Zoey, Zia, Zola, Nala, Zoya, Zoe, Zaria, Zula

Zuri (*Swahili*) ♀   RATING: ★★★★
Beautiful
> People think of Zuri as pretty, intelligent, creative, caring, funny
> People who like the name Zuri also like Zoe, Zoey, Isabella, Olivia, Zaria, Zara, Zola, Samara, Maya, Bella

Zuriel (*Hebrew*) ♀♂   RATING: ★★★☆
The Lord is my rock
> People think of Zuriel as intelligent, powerful, leader, creative, religious

People who like the name Zuriel also like Azriel, Zion, Jaden, Zephyr, Sabriel, Addison, Shiloh, Elisha, Katriel, Hayden

Zurina (*Spanish*) ♀　　　RATING: ★★★
White
People think of Zurina as exotic, weird, elegant, unpopular, creative
People who like the name Zurina also like Zaria, Zara, Zora, Zita, Clarissa, Chloe, Zorina, Reia, Freya, Mara

Zuwena (*Swahili*) ♀　　　RATING: ★★★
Good
People think of Zuwena as pretty, exotic, young, cool, quiet
People who like the name Zuwena also like Zuri, Hazina, Zulema, Zula, Latifah, Uzuri, Ayanna, Leona, Harsha, Zaina

Zuzana (*Slavic*) ♀　　　RATING: ★★★☆
Lily—Variation of Susanna
People think of Zuzana as pretty, creative, intelligent, elegant, energetic
People who like the name Zuzana also like Zelda, Zofia, Tatiana, Zudora, Zinnia, Jane, Zulema, Zora, Zipporah, Mathilda

Zuzela (*Polish*) ♀　　　RATING: ★★★
City in Poland—Also the wife of Native American Sioux Chief Sitting Bull
People think of Zuzela as exotic, young, weird, powerful, religious
People who like the name Zuzela also like Topanga, Satinka, Zaltana, Tallulah, Winona, Talulah, Orenda, Kilenya, Peta, Miakoda

Zweena (*African*) ♀　　　RATING: ★★★
Beautiful—Moroccan origin; variation of Zeena
People think of Zweena as exotic, sexy, powerful, leader, weird
People who like the name Zweena also like Jamila, Inara, Zaina, Shakina, Ayanna, Mea, Senna, Jia Li, Zuri, Aaliyah

Zwi (*Hebrew*) ♀♂　　　RATING: ★★★
Gazelle—Pronounced *zvee*
People think of Zwi as weird, loser, sexy, nerdy, untrustworthy
People who like the name Zwi also like Zayn, Zo, Sasha, Pooky, Bliss, James, Zane, Evelyn, Addison, Ziv

Zyta (*Polish*) ♀　　　RATING: ★★★☆
Harvester—Short for Teresita
People think of Zyta as exotic, intelligent, weird, energetic, pretty
People who like the name Zyta also like Zytka, Zoe, Chloe, Paige, Zia, Zofia, Isabella, Cianna, Zora, Zoey

Zytka (*Polish*) ♀　　　RATING: ★★★
Rose flower
People think of Zytka as loser, nerdy, poor, weird, exotic
People who like the name Zytka also like Zyta, Zoe, Zoey, Zuri, Zofia, Zora, Elle, Abigail, Isabella, Ivy

Been There, Done That!

T̲H̲E̲ great thing about having more than one million visitors a month to our website is that we can compile a lot of stories from people who have gone through the naming process—just like you. Here are some additional quotes and stories from our members that you may find informative and amusing.

After the Fact

As much as I love thinking about baby names and despite our 10,000 baby name conversations during my pregnancy, my husband and I had not decided on a name for our daughter when we left for the hospital. I wasn't worried. Everyone said I'd see her and automatically her name would come to me. Whatever! What came to me was "I have no clue . . . She doesn't look like any name in particular to me!" We wanted to decide quickly, so we could make the important phone calls. We threw some names out to the hospital staff in the room and everyone had a different opinion. So in the end (it only took about twenty minutes) we went with the first name that we had both liked simultaneously. As it turns out, Sydney Rebecca fit her just perfectly.

—Jill P., Honolulu, Hawaii

When I was born my parents didn't name me until I was 2 months old. I was the sixth child, the fourth daughter, and my parents gave all their children names that began with the letter *C*. Obviously, that made naming me tough. My dad really wanted to name me Candice, and my mom wanted to name me Carley. Finally when I was 2 months old my mom gave in and went with Candice even though she hated the nickname Candy. In our church when a baby is born the father stands up in church and gives the baby a blessing and officially names them. A few weeks after deciding on Candice, the day of my blessing arrived. It was announced that my father was now going to bless his baby and name her Candice. He stood up to do the blessing and named me Carly Ann!

596

They had to go back and change my birth certificate and everything.

—Carly C., Havelock, North Carolina

———— 🐤 ————

We didn't know if we were having a boy or a girl. Either way I had names picked out—it was going to be Isaac or Stella. But my husband never really said much about them. I always *thought* we had agreed on the names. I even went as far as buying the letters to each of the names to put in the nursery—the letters for Stella were out and ready to go because I just *knew* I was having a girl. *Surprise!* I gave birth to a baby boy. My husband and I both got on our cell phones to call our parents right away. While I was being stitched up, I heard my husband say to his parents, "I know what his name is. I just can't tell you yet because Jessie doesn't know." At this point I was really excited and nervous to hear what my child's name was going to be. My husband proceeded to tell me that he thought the baby's name should be Henry in honor of my grandma (her last name). I immediately fell in love with it, and he looked *just* like a Henry, so Henry it was!

—Jessica P., Salt Lake City, Utah

———— 🐤 ————

My parents were told they were having a boy so they only had a boy's name picked out—along with a blue nursery and a bunch of blue clothes. Well, *surprise*, I was a girl and they had no idea what to name me. The soap opera *General Hospital* was playing in the hospital room and my mom heard the name Laura. She said, "Yeah, that works. Laura it is." Alrighty then! My advice to parents: Be

prepared! Thankfully, I like my name, but I wonder sometimes if they had had time to prepare—what would my name have been?

—Laura C., Michigan City, Indiana

———— 🐤 ————

All three times my sister-in-law had a baby she went into the hospital planning to use one name and came home with a baby named something completely different. With my two nephews, they were both going to be Carter; one came home Riley, and the other Jayden. My niece was going to be Loxley, and came home Nadia.

—Annette L., Lapeer, Michigan

Unusual and Created Names

My husband is convinced he made up Kodan's name. We were discussing names one day while riding in the car. I kept pushing Kaden because I loved that name and he thought about it for a minute and said, "Well, how about Kodan instead?" We went home and looked online but couldn't find it on any website or in any name book. Satisfied that no one else would have his son's name, that's the name he wanted! Later on we found out it was a form of martial art.

—Jennifer I., Glendale, Arizona

———— 🐤 ————

My actual name is Shmuel, which is the Hebrew word for the prophet Samuel. Shmuley is to Shmuel as Debbie is to Deborah. I know that outside Orthodox Jewish circles it is a highly uncommon name, but within Orthodox circles it is not. It is a name that I love because

I love the story of the birth of the prophet Samuel of a woman who felt ignored by her husband and diminished as a woman because she didn't have children. Of course she was wrong; I have never believed that a woman's femininity depended on being a mother. Hannah not only had her child but also devoted him selflessly to G-d's service. I have tried to devote my life to the same.

—Rabbi Shmuley Boteach,
leader, author, and star of TLC
Network's *Shalom in the Home*

Unlike others combining their first names for a new baby name, we combined our middle names. Joseph and Louise = Jolize. I figured because there was an actress named Charlize, people would be familiar with the sound of the *z* at the end of it.

—Tanya F., British Columbia, Canada

One of my closest friends named her daughter Winter Jeska. The middle name was created using letters from all of the women in her family . . . her mother, mother-in-law, sister, sister-in-law, and herself.

—Michelle M., Villa Rica, Georgia

My cousin named his boys Cru and Tra. The joke in the family was that they couldn't spell anything longer than three letters.

—Noel H., Fairbanks, Alaska

What Not to Choose

I would never use a name of an ex or someone I had a crush on even if we never went out.

—Kimberly H., Grand Blanc, Michigan

My significant other and I want to avoid family names. We don't want to cause any friction by choosing to honor only a select few family members. Plus, we think duplicating names in our family would just create unnecessary confusion. Also, he has a very common last name, so we are trying to avoid extremely popular or common first names. No sense in giving our child a name as unindividual as John Doe. Our kids will be unique; they will get unique names.

—Laura A., Raleigh, North Carolina

I would never consider a name of an ex, a pet, or even a person that I know or knew. I don't want my children's names to remind me of anyone else.

—Stacie B., Colts Neck, New Jersey

I'd never use the names of an over-publicized celebrity such as Paris or Madonna or people in the news such as murderers and such.

—Melissa M., Sioux Falls, South Dakota

I once ran into a woman named Lasagna—I would never consider food as a name for my child, not even Apple or Coco!

—Samantha R., Jacksonville, Florida

Being a teacher, naming our kids is always a tricky thing for us. I keep telling my husband that the longer I teach, the fewer names we'll have to choose from. There are always a few kids each year that ruin a name or two for me!

—Kristen K., Goshen, Indiana

I am a recruiter for the tech industry and would receive many résumés from India and Indian-Americans. I once received a résumé from a woman named Vajaya (rhymes with Mariah), which is apparently a fairly common Indian female name. I wonder if she realized what it sounded like in English and if she ever considered changing it?

—Jessica B., Los Angeles, California

I saw a birth announcement for a little boy named Lucifer and all I could think of was "that poor child!"

—Kelli J., Florence, Montana

In elementary school, I knew three sisters named April, May, and . . . Lovey! What the heck? It used to annoy me to no end that Lovey's name wasn't June!

—Liana D., Hanover, New Hampshire

Words of Advice

My mother asked if she could name my son because my grandmother named me and I was the first grandchild. She felt that we should start a tradition of grandmothers naming their first grandchild and that I should allow her to name him. She was upset when I told her no!

—Shakira K., Worcester, Massachusetts

When I was pregnant with my daughter, we tried not to tell too many people what her name would be because I didn't want other people's comments to sway me in a different direction. Finally I told everyone the first name would be Mirabella, and from that point on I was told it was way too long. After she was born and everyone found out her full name was Mirabella Lorraine, I was told that I was cruel for giving a child a name that long . . . she'd never learn to spell it! Well, she's a smart kid now and I'm sure she'll be fine.

—Kara G., Kenosha, Wisconsin

When we told people we were naming her Opal, most of them just said, "Oh . . ." We got a few "Oooh, that's different" comments. My parents, though, rallied against Opal for nearly eight months. Every time my mother heard a girl's name, she would say something like, "That would be cute on a little girl." It drove me up the wall, and eventually I ignored her every time she made a comment like that. Fast-forward to the night Opal was born, at four hours old Mum said, "Opal is really starting to grow on me."

—Michelle W., Victoria, Australia

Playground Taunts

I was named after my great-grandmother Annetta. However, in the late '70s, there was only *one* Annette . . . the most famous Mickey Mouse Club member and teen queen, Annette Funicello. No matter what she did, I heard about it: jokes about beach movies, jokes about the Mickey Mouse Club . . . heck, even jokes about peanut butter (because she did commercials). Luckily, it's gotten to the point where most people I talk to haven't heard of her, or don't remember her, so the jokes have dwindled off. Now I'm more apt to hear "Annette Funicello? Who's that?"

—Annette L., Lapeer, Michigan

Chantel is a pretty foolproof name, you'd think, but since kindergarten people would call me "Show and Tell." Even through high school, they'd think they were being clever, when really, I had heard it years before.

—Chantel M., Bloomington, Indiana

From the moment I entered elementary school until the day I graduated college, I always got a comment from *someone* about my name, Mary. When teachers would call out my name during first day of class role call, nine out of ten times they'd make some "funny" joke. As a matter of fact, even today when someone heard my name they started singing, "Mary Mary, Quite Contrary." There are songs and nursery rhymes with the name Mary in them and the Biblical references and the term "Merry Christmas," too! I can go on and on about the teasing potential of the name Mary. However, now I've learned to tease right back. When people will ask, "Mary Mary, quite contrary, how does your garden grow?" I will surprise them with the answer, "Fertilizer."

—Mary B., Britt, Iowa

People use to call me Nosila (Alison backwards) and it really bothered me. And because they knew I hated it, they called Nosila all the time!

—Alison A., New South Wales, Australia

My name is Elizabeth, which I think is a beautiful name. When I was in third grade my teacher called me "Lizardbreath" because she read it in a comic. Of course, all of the third-graders thought that was hilarious, and I was completely embarrassed. I live in a small town and went to a very small school, and consequently I heard Lizardbreath for years until I graduated.

—Elizabeth M., Linton, Indiana

600

I got teased on a daily basis at school because of my name, Aquila. In high school everyone called me Tequila. Since I got so much grief in school because of my name, I promised myself I would not make my child go through that and I would pick an easy name to say and spell.

—Aquila L., Leeds, Alabama

The Crystal Ball

We asked our members to look into the future and predict the top names of 2018. Here are some of their name forecasts:

I am going to say we will move away from the Celtic craze and start to see more Swedish/Scandinavian names popping up, for example: Linnea, Annika, Magnus.

—Courtney W., Ashburn, Virginia

For the UK, I think name trends will go back to the '70s style we had, as these are likely to be grandparents by then: Sarah, Sharon, Lesley, Janet, Joanne, Paul, David, Peter, Alan, Stephen.

—Victoria S., Manchester, England

I think names from our moms' moms' generation will be back: Shirley, Bonnie, Barbara, Barry, George, Franklin. Also, names from TV shows/movies that children around ages 5–10 now watch!

—Melina D., Lexington, Tennessee

I think we are definitely moving to more classic names. I think the current trend of Biblical and Gaelic names for boys will fade away to more of the Victorian-sounding, softer names. There will be less hard vowel and consonant sounds and more soft sounds. For boys I think we'll see: Henry, Theo, Bennett, Emmett, Carter, Max, Edward, George, Jasper, and Charles. For girls the same trend will follow: Abigail, Lydia, Charlotte, Grace, Victoria, Caroline, Lucy, Claire, Amelia, Lily.

—Alison B., San Jose, California

For the U.S., I predict there will be more Latino names on the top lists, like José, Juan, and Maria. Also based upon population influx, I might also think there will be some traditional Asian names (mainly Chinese and Vietnamese) and a nice mix of (traditional) African names.

—Cindy L., Chicago, Illinois

16

Your Final Decision

WE hope that we have provided enough information in this book to help you make the best decision possible in naming your baby. It is one of the most important decisions you'll make during this time—the gift that keeps on giving!

We can't guarantee that your child will be popular or successful if you choose a certain name; however, we have given you a detailed roadmap for your naming process. We hope you will learn from the stories we presented from our visitors—after all, experience is the best teacher!

If you need further support or just want to join other parents who are going through the same decision process as you, please visit us online at www.BabyNames.com. Our community of parents, grandparents, siblings, and hopeful parents can help guide you in this exciting time.

Here is a list of additional sources that may also be helpful to you:

- **U.S. Social Security Office**
  www.ssa.gov/OACT/babynames
  A great source of the most popular names in the United States, from the year 1880 to the present.

- **Wikipedia**
  www.wikipedia.org
  User-generated articles regarding historical figures and some historical name information.

- **Ancestry.com**
  www.ancestry.com
  Tool to map your family history, including access to public records such as marriage, birth, and immigration documents.

- **Behind the Name**
  www.behindthename.com
  An extensive source of given names, surnames, and their etymologies.

Whatever name you choose, we know it will be the perfect one for you and your baby! Congratulations and Mazel Tov from all of us at BabyNames.com.

Endnotes

1. "Interview with Ashley Parker Angel," AOL Music. Available at http://music.aol.com/artists/aim-celebrity-interview/ashley-parker-angel-page-1 (accessed July 24, 2007).

2. "Magic Baby: Moxie Crimefighter," CBSNews.com, June 4, 2005. Available at www.cbsnews.com/stories/2005/06/04/entertainment/main699675.shtml (accessed July 24, 2007).

3. "Paltrow Gives Birth to Baby Girl," WENN/imdb.com, May 17, 2004, www.imdb.com/news/wenn/2004-05-17 (accessed July 24, 2007).

4. Scott Cohen, "I Was the Villain Because I Dared to Say Flower Power Sucked," Circus Raves, no. 123, December 1975.

5. Eric Williams, "A Boy Named ESPN," *The Huffington Post*, March 2, 2007. Available at www.huffingtonpost.com/eric-williams/a-boy-named-espn_b_42505.html (accessed July 24, 2007).

6. "Boomer Esiason," Wikipedia.org. Available at http://en.wikipedia.org/wiki/Boomer_Esiason (accessed July 24, 2007).

7. Cindy Pearlman, "Rainn Reigns," *The Chicago Sun-Times*, March 25, 2007.

Acknowledgments

THE biggest thanks to my business partners and ("ha, you can't fire us") family: mama Peggy Moss aka "Grandma Maggie," baby sis Mallory Moss Rustin, big sis Kate Moss Glinsmann, and big sis Sue Moss. BabyNames.com couldn't have been as wildly popular without you!

To Meg Leder of Perigee, the best editor I could ask for! Thanks for being extremely positive and supportive throughout the whole process. To Jessica Faust at Bookends, who gave me unwavering inspiration to create this book. To Dr. Meredith Cane and Dr. Cleveland Kent Evans, the name experts and true wizards behind the curtain. To John Bresnik, for his mad programming skills, allowing us to make the data into something interesting! Huge hugs and cookies to Greg Domeno and Jay Smith of Cyberverse Online, for their long-term technical dedication to the BabyNames.com website.

To our members who shared their naming stories with us: Brooke C. of Denver, Colorado; Chassidy R. of Montgomery, Alabama; Deserae W. of Lacey, Washington; Jennifer I. of Glendale, Arizona; Jennifer W. of Tifton, Georgia; Jessica M. of Pittsburgh, Pennsylvania; Jessica O. of Plymouth, Michigan; Jill P. of Honolulu, Hawaii; Julia K. of Ann Arbor, Michigan; Kara G. of Kenosha, Wisconsin; Kelly J. of Owatonna, Minnesota; Kimberly H. of Grand Blanc, Michigan; Laura S. of Chicago, Illinois; Linnéa H. of Washington, DC; Michelle W. of Victoria, Australia; Shakira K. of Worcester, Massachusetts; and Tanessa S. of Federal Way, Washington.

And last, but never least, our ongoing appreciation to the millions of people who visit BabyNames.com each month—your support, feedback, and loyalty are priceless to us.

About the Authors

BABYNAMES.COM is owned and operated by the four Moss sisters and their mother, Peggy. Many times we are asked what names *we* chose for our own children—so here are the stories:

Peggy "Grandma Maggie" Moss

Peggy Moss is a four-time mother and four-time grandmother and brings her vast experience in parenting and early childhood to the site in many ways. She writes the weekly parenting advice column, *Ask Grandma Maggie*, as well as running her own teen advice site, *Ask-Anything.com*. Prior to BabyNames.com, Peggy worked in a preschool for emotionally disturbed children and ran her own successful daycare center in Chicago for many years. Peggy loves to be close to her children and their families and currently lives in Denver, Colorado.

What I named my children

Susan Lee (f)—My grandfather had a sister named Susan, and I always loved that name. Susan sounds like a lovely given name to me, and I liked the nicknames Susie for a child and Sue as an adult. Somehow I felt as if the second name had to always be one syllable.

Catherine Jo (f)—My paternal grandmother was named Catherine and was called Kate. My husband's paternal grandmother was called Jo for Josephine. My middle name is Catherine, so it was a traditional family name. Both of the great-grandmothers whose names we used were still alive when Kate was born. The name seemed to fit her somehow.

Jennifer Ann (f)—My maternal grandmother had died before I was born but she had one sister, my Aunt Jennie, who represented that part of the family. I named Jennifer after her and sticking with the one-syllable middle name, used my husband's maternal grandmother, Anna, as the model for it. I was named for my maternal grandmother and since I don't believe it's prudent to name a child after a parent, I went to that grandmother's only sister. This was in a time before the name Jennifer became so popular. Three years later I was told that 90 percent of the girl babies in our hospital were named Jennifer.

Mallory Beth (f)—I heard the name Mallory on television when I was up one night with my daughter, Jennifer, who was still an infant. It was the name of the daughter of Shari Lewis, famous for her kids' show and puppet named

608

Lambchop. I thought if I ever had another child (I did), and it was a girl (it was), then I would name her Mallory. Beth was always a favorite name of mine so I selected that for the middle name as it sounded nice with the euphonious first and last name.

Jennifer Moss

Jennifer Moss founded BabyNames.com back in 1996 as a community site to share her lifelong passion for names and naming. With more than twenty years in technology as a programmer and database architect, Jennifer's expertise helped grow BabyNames.com to one of the most visited parenting sites online. Jennifer served as Director of Technology at SDN Online and Withoutabox.com and served as an Internet strategy consultant to a number of successful new media companies. Jennifer received her undergraduate degree from Northwestern University and currently lives in Los Angeles with her daughter, Miranda.

What I named my children

Miranda Margaret (f)—When my husband and I were dating, I found out that his mother's maiden name was Miranda. I knew right then and there that if we ever got married and had a girl, that would be her name . . . and so it was! I thought the name was unique and mysterious and also loved that it was a Shakespearean name *(The Tempest)*. I wanted to honor my mother, as well, so we used her name, Margaret, as Miranda's middle name. I am a fan of alliterative names, and my daughter's initials are MMM.

Kate Moss Glinsmann

Kate has worked in the field of early childhood education for more than twenty-five years, including fifteen years teaching preschool children with disabilities and eleven years teaching kindergarten. She currently is an English language teacher for grades K–6. She received her undergraduate degree from the University of Iowa with a teaching certificate in early childhood and early childhood special education. Recently Kate received her master's degree in Elementary Education from Viterbo University and an English Language Learners endorsement from William Penn University. Kate currently resides in Iowa and has two adult sons.

What I named my children

Dwight "Ike" Donald (m)—Dwight is his dad's first name, and Donald is my dad (his paternal grandfather), which I used because my dad had no sons. We nicknamed him "Ike" because I loved that name, and I knew it would be unique. It was also his father's nickname. His father was named Dwight Douglas after U.S. President Dwight D. Eisenhower and General Douglas MacArthur.

Peter Austin (m)—Peter was named after his paternal great-grandfather and his great-great-grandfather. Peter also happened to be my grandmother's maiden name! Austin is his paternal grandmother's maiden name.

Mallory Moss Rustin, RN, CNS, ND, PMH-NP

Dr. Mallory Moss Rustin is a nurse practitioner based out of Denver, Colorado. She obtained her bachelor's in psychology from UCLA and her RN, master's, and nursing doctorate from the University of Colorado Health Sciences Center in Denver. Mallory's work includes psychiatry-based

nursing and training at Denver Health Medical Center and University of Colorado Hospital. She currently is a clinical content specialist for one of the largest medical publishing companies in the world. She currently resides in Denver, Colorado, with her husband, Kenny, and daughter, Veronica.

What I named my children

Veronica Lee (f)—We had a very difficult time choosing our daughter's name because our last name was long and of Russian descent. At first we considered alliterative names, but then decided that since her name was difficult to pronounce and exotic, we should just pick a name we both loved and not worry about what came next. Neither of us knew a Veronica growing up and both of us associated her with beautiful and strong women (and characters), including Veronica Lake, Veronica Hammel, and Veronica Lodge. It was easy to pick Veronica's middle name of Lee: Her father and I each had a sister with the middle name of Lee and the exact same spelling!

Sue Moss

Sue Moss worked for fifteen years as a proofreader, editor, and newsletter publisher before returning to college in her mid-thirties. Attending Northwestern University as an adult student, she majored in communication studies and minored in journalism, while working for various technology-based startups in the Chicago area during the late 1990s. In 2000, she relocated to southern California and worked as a content analyst/user researcher for Scient Corp., where she provided market research, usability testing, and content management for Scient's Fortune 500 clients. Sue's scope of work for BabyNames .com includes market and user research, content development, press relations, and management of the BabyNames.com message boards. Sue currently lives in Santa Monica, California, and enjoys being the "favorite auntie" to her four nieces and nephews.